W9-DDF-459

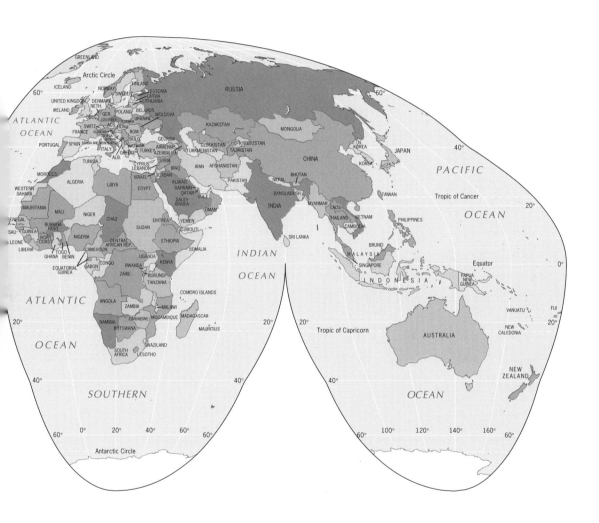

GLOBAL MARKETING MANAGEMENT

GLOBAL MARKETING MANAGEMENT

MASAAKI KOTABE
The University of Texas at Austin

KRISTIAAN HELSEN
Hong Kong University of Science and Technology

JOHN WILEY & SONS, INC.
New York   Chichester   Weinheim   Brisbane   Singapore   Toronto

Acquisitions Editor	Ellen Ford
Marketing Manager	Carlise Paulson
Sr. Production Editor	Jeanine Furino
Cover Designer	Harry Nolan
Cover Photo	William Whitehurst/The Stock Market
Photo Editor	Hilary Newman
Illustration Editor	Anna Melhorn

This book was set in Janson by Digitype and printed and bound by Quebecor. The cover was printed by Phoenix Color Corporation.

This book is printed on acid-free paper. ∞

The paper in this book was manufactured by a mill whose forest management programs include sustained yield harvesting of its timberlands. Sustained yield harvesting principles ensure that the numbers of trees cut each year does not exceed the amount of new growth.

Library of Congress Cataloging in Publication Data:

Kotabe, Masaaki.
    Global marketing management / Masaaki Kotabe, Kristiaan Helsen.
      p. cm.
    Includes index.
    ISBN 0-471-59288-9 (alk. paper)
    1. Export marketing—Management. 2. International business enterprises—Management. I. Helsen, Kristiaan. II. Title.
HF1416.K68 1998
658.8'48—dc21   97-30942
                                                               CIP

Printed in the United States of America
10 9 8 7 6 5 4 3 2 1

ABOUT THE AUTHORS

Masaaki Kotabe is a professor of marketing and international business and Ambassador Edward Clark Centennial Fellow in Business at the University of Texas at Austin. He is also director of research at the Center for International Business Education and Research. Further, he is currently the vice president of the Academy of International Business. He received his Ph.D. in Marketing and International Business at Michigan State University. Dr. Kotabe teaches international marketing, global sourcing strategy (R&D, manufacturing, and marketing interfaces), and Japanese business practices at the undergraduate and MBA levels and theories of international business at the Ph.D. level. He has lectured widely at various business schools around the world, including Germany, Finland, Mexico, Brazil, Japan, Indonesia, and Turkey. For his research, he has worked closely with leading companies such as AT&T, NEC, Philips, Sony, and Ito-Yokado (parent of 7-Eleven stores).

Dr. Kotabe has written many scholarly publications, including books and journal articles. His books include *Global Sourcing Strategy: R&D, Manufacturing, Marketing Interfaces* (1992), *Japanese Distribution System* (with Michael R. Czinkota, 1993), *Anticompetitive Practices in Japan* (with Kent W. Wheiler, 1996), *MERCOSUR and Beyond* (1997), and *Marketing Management* (with Michael R. Czinkota and David Mercer, 1997). He is on the editorial boards of the *Journal of Internal Business Studies*, the *Journal of International Marketing*, the *Journal of World Business*, the *Latin American Economic Abstracts*, and the *International Executive*.

In 1994, the *Journal of International Business Studies* ranked Dr. Kotabe the sixth most productive contributor in international business research in the world in the past 25 years. He is an elected member of the New York Academy of Sciences.

Kristiaan Helsen has been an associate professor of marketing at the Hong Kong University of Science and Technology (HKUST) since 1995. Prior to joining HKUST, he was on the faculty of the University of Chicago for five years. He regularly visits Nijenrode University (Netherlands). Dr. Helsen received his Ph.D. in Marketing at the Wharton School of the University of Pennsylvania.

His research areas include promotional strategy, competitive strategy, and hazard rate modeling. His articles have appeared in journals such as *Marketing Science, Journal of Marketing, Journal of Marketing Research*, and *European Journal of Operations Research*, among others. Dr. Helsen is on the editorial boards of the *International Journal of Research in Marketing* and the *Journal of Marketing*.

PREFACE

Markets have become truly global. If you stand still in your domestic market, you will likely be trampled by competitors from around the world. As one globe-trotting executive put it, "If you don't act right now, somebody else will always do it for you at your expense . . . and quickly." This book is designed to portray this competitive urgency and present how executives should design and execute marketing strategies to optimize their market performance on a global basis.

Marketing in the global arena is a very dynamic discipline. Today, there are many international or global marketing management books vying for their respective niche in the market. It is a mature market. As you will learn in our book, in a mature market, firms tend to focus closely—or maybe, too closely—on immediate product features for sources of differentiation and may inadvertently ignore the fundamental changes that may be re-shaping the industry. Often, those fundamental changes come from outside the industry. The same logic applies to the textbook market. Whether existing textbooks are titled international marketing or global marketing, they continue to be bound by the traditional bilateral (inter-national) view of competition. While any new textbook has to embrace the traditional coverage of existing textbooks, we intend to emphasize the multilateral (global) nature of marketing throughout our book.

We have seen textbooks just replacing the word, "international," with "global." Such a change amounts to a repackaging of an existing product we often see in a mature product market, and it does not necessarily make a textbook globally oriented. We need some paradigm shift to accomplish the task of adding truly global dimensions and realities to a textbook. You might ask, "What fundamental changes are needed for a paradigm shift?" and then, "Why do we need fundamental changes to begin with?"

Our answer is straightforward. Our ultimate objective is to help you prepare for the 21st Century and become an effective manager overseeing global marketing activities in an increasingly competitive environment. You may or may not choose marketing for your career. If you pursue a marketing career, what you will learn in our book will not only have direct relevance but also help you understand how you, as a marketing manager, can affect other business functions for effective corporate performance on a global basis. If you choose other functional areas of business for your career, then our book will help you understand how you will work effectively with marketing people for the same corporate goal.

We believe that our pedagogical orientation not only embraces the existing stock of useful marketing knowledge and methods but also sets itself apart from the competition in a number of fundamental ways, as follows:

Global Orientation

As we indicated at the outset, the term, "global," epitomizes the competitive pressure and market opportunities from around the world and the firm's need to optimize its market performance on a global basis. Whether a company operates domestically or across national boundaries, it can no longer avoid the competitive pressure and market opportunities. For optimal market performance, the firm should also be ready and willing to take advantage of resources on a global basis.

Let us take a look at a hypothetical U.S. company exporting finished products to Western Europe and Japan. Traditionally, this export phenomenon has been treated as a bilateral business transaction between a U.S. company and foreign customers. However, in reality, to the executives of the U.S. company, this export transaction may be nothing more than the last phase of the company's activities they manage. Indeed, this company procures certain components from Japan and Mexico, other components from Malaysia, and also from its domestic sources in the United States, and assembles a finished product in its Singapore plant for export to Western Europe and Japan as well as back to the United States. Indeed, a Japanese supplier of critical components is a joint venture majority-owned by this American company, while a Mexican supplier has a licensing agreement with the U.S. company which provides most of technical knowhow. A domestic supplier in the United States is in fact a subsidiary of a German company. In other words, this particular export transaction by the U.S. company involves a joint venture, a licensing agreement, subsidiary operation, local assembly, and R&D, *all managed* directly or indirectly by the U.S. company. Also think about how these arrangements could affect the company's decisions over product policy, pricing, promotion, and distribution channels.

Many existing textbooks have focused on each of these value-adding activities *as if* they could be investigated independently. Obviously, in reality, they are not independent of each other, and cannot be. We emphasize this multilateral realism by examining these value-adding activities as holistically as possible.

Interdisciplinary Perspective

To complement our global orientation, we will offer an interdisciplinary perspective in all relevant chapters. We are of the strong belief that you cannot become seasoned marketing practitioners without your understanding of how other functional areas interface with marketing.[1] The reverse is also true for non-marketing managers. Some of the exemplary areas in which such a broad understanding of the interface issues is needed are product innovation, designing for manufacturability, product/components standardization, and product positioning. In particular, Japanese competition has made us aware of the importance of these issues, and leading-edge business schools are increasingly adopting such an integrated approach to business education.[2] Our book strongly reflects this state-of-the-art orientation.

Proactive Orientation

Market orientation is a fundamental philosophy of marketing. It is an organizational culture that puts the customers' interest first in order to develop a long-term profitable enterprise.[3] In essence, market orientation symbolizes the *market-driven* firm which is willing to constantly update its strategies using signals from the market-

---

[1]John A. Bermingham, "Executive Insight: Roles of R&D and Manufacturing in Global Marketing Management," *Journal of International Marketing*, 4 (4), 1996, 75–84.

[2]"The Restructured Wharton MBA: Inventing a New Paradigm," *Almanac/The Wharton School*, April 2, 1991, 1–4.

[3]Rohit Deshpande, John U. Farley and Frederick E. Webster, Jr., "Corporate Culture, Customer Orientation and Innovativeness in Japanese Firms: A Quadrad Analysis," *Journal of Marketing*, 57, January 1993, 23–27.

place. Thus, marketing managers take market cues from the *expressed* needs and wants of customers. Consequently, the dominant orientation is that of a firm *reacting* to forces in the marketplace in order to differentiate itself from its competitors. This reactive "outside-in" perspective is reflected in the typical marketing manager's reliance on marketing intelligence, forecasting, and market research.

While not denying this traditional market orientation, we also believe that marketing managers should adopt an "inside-out" perspective and capabilities to shape or drive markets.[4] This aspect of the link between strategic planning and marketing implementation has not been sufficiently treated in existing textbooks.[5] For example, recent trends in technology licensing indicate that technology licensing is increasingly used as a conscious, proactive component of a firm's global product strategy. We believe that it is important for marketers to influence those actions of the firm which are some distance away from the customer in the value chain, because such actions have considerable influence on the size of the market and customer choice in intermediate and end product markets.[6]

Cultural Sensitivity

A book could not be written devoid of its authors' background, expertise, and experiences. Our book represents an amalgam of our truly diverse background, expertise, and experiences across the North and South Americas, Asia, and Western and Eastern Europe. Given our upbringings and work experiences in Japan and Western Europe, respectively, as well as our educational background in the United States, we have always been sensitive not only to cultural differences and diversities but also to similarities.

Realistically speaking, there are more similarities than differences across many countries. In many cases, most of us tend to focus too much on cultural differences rather than similarities; or else, completely ignore differences or similarities. If you look only at cultural differences, you will be led to believe that country markets are uniquely different thus requiring marketing strategy adaptations. If, on the other hand, you do not care about, or care to know about, cultural differences, you may be extending a culture-blind, ethnocentric view of the world. Either way, you may not benefit from the economies of scale and scope accruing from exploiting cultural similarities—and differences.

Over the years, two fundamental counteracting forces have shaped the nature of marketing in the international arena. The same counteracting forces have been revisited by many authors in such terms as "standardization vs. adaptation" (1960s), "globalization vs. localization" (1970s), "global integration vs. local responsiveness" (1980s), and most recently, "scale vs. sensitivity" (1990s).[7] Terms have changed, but

---

[4]Frederick E. Webster, Jr., "The Changing Role of Marketing in the Corporation," *Journal of Marketing*, 56, October 1993, 1–17.

[5]George S. Day and Robin Wensley, "Assessing Advantage: A Framework for Diagnosing Competitive Superiority," *Journal of Marketing*, 52, April 1988, 1–20.

[6]Masaaki Kotabe, Arvind Sahay, and Preet S. Aulakh, "Emerging Roles of Technology Licensing in Development of Global Product Strategy: A Conceptual Framework and Research Propositions," *Journal of Marketing*, 60, January 1996, 73–88.

[7]Martin Sorrell, Group Chief Executive, WPP Group, "Globalization: Scale versus Sensitivity," A speech, Joint Conference of the Korean Marketing Association and the American Marketing Association, May 14–17, 1995.

the quintessence of the strategic dilemma that multinational firms face today has not changed and will probably remain unchanged for years to come. However, they are no longer an either/or issue. Forward-looking, proactive firms have the ability and willingness to accomplish both tasks simultaneously. As we explain later in the text, Honda, for example, developed its Accord car to satisfy the universal customer needs for reliability, drivability, and comfort, but marketed it as a family sedan in Japan, as a commuter car in the United States, and as an inexpensive sports car in Germany, thereby addressing cultural differences in the way people of different nationalities perceive and drive what is essentially the same car.

With our emphasis on global and proactive orientations, however, we will share with you how to hone your expertise to be both culturally sensitive and able to see through the clouds how to benefit from cultural similarities and differences.

Research Orientation

We strongly believe that theory is useful to the extent it helps practices. And there are many useful theories in international marketing practices. Some of these practical theories are a logical extension of generic marketing theories you may have encountered in a marketing course. Others are, however, very much unique to the international environment.

Many people believe—rather erroneously—that international or global marketing is just a logical extension of domestic marketing, and that if you have taken a generic marketing course, you would not need to learn anything international. The international arena is just like a Pandora's box. Once you move into the international arena, there are many more facts, concepts, and frameworks you need to learn than you ever thought of in order to become a seasoned marketing manager working globally. To assist you in acquiring this new knowledge, various theories provide you with the conceptual tools which enable you to abstract, analyze, understand, predict phenomena, and formulate effective decisions. Theories also provide you with an effective means to convey your logic to your peers and bosses with a strong convincing power.

We also apply those theories in our own extensive international work, advising corporate executives, helping them design effective global strategies, and teaching our students at various business schools around the world. Our role as educators is to convey sometimes complex theories in everyday languages. Our effort is reflected well in our textbook. This leads to our next orientation.

Practical Orientation

Not only is this book designed to be user-friendly, but also it emphasizes practice. We believe in experiential learning and practical applications. Rote learning of facts, concepts, and theories is not sufficient. A good marketing manager should be able to put these to practice. We use many examples and anecdotes as well as our own observations and experiences to vividly portray practical applications. This book also contains real-life advanced cases so that you can further apply your newly acquired knowledge to practice and experience for yourself what it takes to be an effective marketing manager internationally.

Therefore, this book has been written primarily for upper-level undergraduate and MBA students who wish to learn practical applications of marketing and related logic and subsequently work internationally. Although we survey foundation materials in our book, we expect that students have completed a basic marketing course.

Instructor Support Materials

To accomplish our stated goals and orientations, we have made a major effort to provide the instructor and the student with practical theories and their explanations using examples, anecdotes, and cases to maximize the student's learning experience. Some of the specific teaching features are:

- **The Global Perspectives** which are inserts in every chapter to bring concrete examples from the global marketing environment into the classroom. They are designed to highlight some of the hottest global topics that students should be aware of and may actually act upon in their career. The instructor can use these inserts to exemplify theory or use them as mini-cases for class discussion.

- **Cases** that are designed to challenge students with real and current business problems and issues. They require in-depth analysis and discussion of various topics covered in the chapters and help students experience how the knowledge they have gained can be applied in real life situations.

- **Videoboxes** provide contemporary, yet fundamental, business problems and issues facing the international marketing managers today. These Videoboxes and video clips may be used effectively as lively "short cases" for class discussions.

- **Maps** which provide economic geography of the world. Students should be knowledgeable about where various economic resources are available and how they shape the nature of trade and investment and thus the nature of global competition. Global marketing could not be appreciated devoid of understanding of economic geography.

- **Review Questions** which help students test themselves with, and summarize, the facts, concepts, and theories and other chapter materials in their own words. We strongly believe that by doing so, students will gain the active working knowledge, rather than passive knowledge by rote learning.

- **Discussion Questions** which help students apply the specific knowledge they learned in each chapter to actual business situations. They are designed to serve as mini-cases. Most of the issues presented in these questions are acute problems facing multinational marketing mangers and have been adopted from recent issues of leading business newspapers and magazines.

- **Information Sources for Global Marketing Management** are added at the end of the book as an appendix. This comprehensive list of sources includes not only published information compiled by various international agencies, governments, and corporations, but also various useful Web sites for accessing international business information on the Internet. A brief description is also provided about the types of information available from each information source.

- **The Instructor's Manual** that is designed provide major assistance to the instructor while allowing flexibility in the course scheduling and teaching emphasis. The materials in the manual include the following:

  a) **Teaching Plans:** Alternative teaching plans and syllabi are included to accommodate the instructor's preferred course structure and teaching schedules. Alternative teaching schedules are developed for the course to be taught in a semester format, on a quarter basis or as an executive seminar.

  b) **Discussion Guidelines:** For each chapter, specific teaching objectives and guidelines are developed to help stimulate classroom discussion.

c) **Exercises Using Various Web Sites on the Internet:** The explosion of information available on the Internet has changed a milieu for intelligence gathering for business decision making for ever. Students need to be well versed in this new information technology. We strongly believe that actual hands-on use of Web site materials on the Internet for solving business problems will provide students with a systematic opportunity to learn how to find and how to use available information for competitive advantage.

d) **Test Bank:** A test bank consists of short essay questions and multiple choice questions. This test bank is also computerized and available to adopters on IBM compatible computer diskettes.

e) **Power Point Slides:** Available on the Web to assist the instructor in preparing presentation materials.

f) **Video Materials:** As indicated earlier, videos provide for students' visualization of critical issues discussed in the cases as well as in the text itself.

Finally, we are delighted to share our teaching experience with you through this book. Our teaching experience is an amalgam of our own learning and knowledge gained through our continued discussion with our colleagues, our students, and our executive friends. We would also like to learn from you, the instructor and the students, who use our book. Not only do we wish that you can learn from our book but we also believe that there are many more things that we can learn from you. We welcome your sincere comments and questions. Our contact addresses are as follows:

Masaaki Kotabe
Ph. (512) 471-5452
e-mail: mike.kotabe@mail.utexas.edu

Kristiaan Helsen
Ph. (852) 2358-7720

◆ ◆ ◆ ◆ ◆ ◆   **ACKNOWLEDGEMENTS**

This book would not have ever materialized without guidance, assistance, and encouragement of many of our mentors, colleagues, students, and executives we have worked with and learned from over the years. We are truly indebted to each one of them. We also thank the many reviewers for their constructive comments and suggestions which helped us improve our argument and clarity and raise the quality of our book.

Preet S. Aulakh
Michigan State University

John R. Brooks
Houston Baptist University

Wendy Bryce
Western Washington University

Peggy Cunningham
Queen's University, Kingston, Ontario

K. C. Dhawan
Concordia University, Montreal, Quebec

P. Everett Ferguson
Iona College

James W. Gentry
University of Nebraska-Lincoln

Braxton Hinchly
University of Massachusetts-Lowell

Alfred C. Holden
Fordham University

Ann T. Kuzma
Mankato State University

D. Maheswaran
New York University

Martin Meyers
University of Wisconsin-Stevens Point

Chip Miller
Pacific Lutheran University

Sukgoo Pak
University of Nebraska-Omaha

Thomas Ponzurick
West Virginia University

C. P. Rao
Old Dominion University

Sunanda Sangwan
Aston University, Birmingham, UK

T. N. Somasundaram
University of San Diego

Scott Swan
College of William and Mary

Peter K. Tat
The University of Memphis

Hildy Teegen
George Washington University

Kathy Frazier Winsted
Pace University, Pleasantville

At the University of Texas at Austin, the first co-author would like to extend thanks to his colleagues. Robert T. Green has built a strong network of foreign business schools that have permitted the first co-author to visit and keep sensitized with local developments around the world. Kate Gillespie has kept him informed of regional marketing issues, particularly, in emerging markets. Tomasz Lenartowicz has provided "insider" insights into Latin American issues. Special thanks also go to several of the first co-author's past and current doctoral students. Aldor Lanctot (now with Dell Computer) and Arvind Sahay (now with London Business School) helped us with ever-changing technology and competitive issues in global marketing. Preet Aulakh (now with Michigan State University) provided intellectual insight, in particular, in the area of transaction cost argument and distribution channel management. Brad McBride (now with Instituto Tecnológico Autónomo de México) offered his expertise in managing in developing countries. Jaishanker Ganesh (now with University of Central Florida) provided a critical review of marketing standardization/adaptation debate. We are also happy to recognize that now they are on their own, practicing and conducting research in the same areas, from which we expect to learn more in the future. Maneesh Chandra and Thomas Burnham, two doctoral students at Texas, also kept us informed of many interesting developments and topics in global marketing, which are reflected throughout our book.

Fundação Getúlio Vargas (FGV), São Paulo, Brazil, has served as an occasional intellectual home to the first co-author. Particularly, Maria Cecilia Coutinho de Arruda, Wilton de Oliveira Bussab, and Alain Stempfer of FGV deserve our special word of appreciation for our maintaining and honing a truly global perspective during the course of writing this textbook. The first co-author also benefited from his association with Xavier Martin, Myles Shaver, and Tish Robinson, and Ya-Ru Chen at New York University and Junzo Ishii at Kobe University, Japan.

The second co-author would like to extend his thanks to MBA students at the University of Chicago, Nijenrode University, Hong Kong University of Science and Technology, and MIM students at Thammassat University (Bangkok). Particularly Joe Giblin and Vincent Chan (Baxter) for assisting with two of the case studies and Wiebeke Vuursteen (now with Nestlé), Edmund Wong and Philip Cheung (now with IBM) for their help with some of the exhibits, and Jimmy Erni for clerical assistance. A word of gratitude for their feedback and encouragement is given to two colleagues who spent their sabbatical at HKUST: Jerry Albaum (University of Oregon) and Al Shocker (University of Minnesota).

We would also like to thank some of the day-to-day "warriors" in the global marketing arena for sharing their insights and experiences with us, in particular:

Doug Barrie (Wrigley Company), Mark Boersma (Blistex), Keith Alm (formerly Sara Lee), F.J. Thompson (Heineken), Monika Sturm (Siemens Hong Kong), Bill Hicks and Jim Austin (Baxter Healthcare), and Olivia Kan (PepsiCo China).

We also thank MBA and undergraduate students at New York University for experimentally using the manuscript version of our textbook in their classes in the Spring 1997 semester. Marcelo F. Perez (now with G. E. Capital) is also acknowledged for helping us with updating ever-changing statistics presented in this book. Their enthusiasm, acceptance, and suggestions allowed us to improve on the book's currentness and readability.

A very special word of appreciation goes to the staff of John Wiley & Sons, Inc., particularly Ellen M. Ford for her continued enthusiasm and support throughout the course of this project.

Finally and most importantly, we are deeply grateful to you, the professors, students, and professionals for using this book. We stand by our book, and sincerely hope that our book adds to your knowledge and expertise. We would also like to continuously improve our product in the future.

As we indicated in the **Preface,** we would like to hear from as you are our valued customers. Thank you!

MASAAKI KOTABE
The University of Texas at Austin

KRISTIAAN HELSEN
Hong Kong University of Science and Technology

CONTENTS

PART FOUR: GLOBAL MARKETING STRATEGY DEVELOPMENT

PART FIVE: MANAGING GLOBAL OPERATIONS

GLOBALIZATION IMPERATIVE

1

HAPTER OVERVIEW

1. WHY GLOBAL MARKETING IS IMPERATIVE 絶対に必要の.
2. GLOBALIZATION OF MARKETS AND COMPETITION
3. EVOLUTION OF GLOBAL MARKETING
  发展.

Marketing products and services around the world, transcending national and political boundaries, is a fascinating phenomenon. The phenomenon, however, is not entirely new. Products have been traded across borders throughout recorded civilization, extending back beyond the Silk Road that once connected East with West from Xian to Rome. What is relatively new about the phenomenon, emerging with large U.S. companies in the 1950s and 1960s and with European and Japanese companies in the 1970s and 1980s, is the large number of companies with interrelated production and sales operations located around the world. The emergence of competitive European and Japanese companies has given the notion of global competition a touch of extra urgency and significance that you see almost daily in print media such as *New York Times, Business Week*, and *Fortune*, as well as TV media such as ABC, CBS, NBC, and CNN.

In this chapter, we will introduce you to the complex and constantly evolving realities of global marketing. The objective is to make you think beyond exporting and importing. As you will learn shortly, despite wide media attention to them, exporting and importing are a relatively small portion of what constitutes international business. We are not saying, however, that exporting and importing are not important. Total world trade volume amounts to more than $4 trillion today. The United States alone exports $400 billion in goods. According to the U.S. Department of Commerce estimate, for every $1 billion in U.S. exports, about 20,000 jobs are created.[1] In other words, U.S. exports support 8 million jobs.

---

[1]Stefan H. Robock, "The Export Myopia of U.S. Multinationals," *Columbia Journal of World Business*, 28 (Summer 1993), pp. 24–32.

◆ ◆ ◆ ◆ ◆ ◆ WHY GLOBAL MARKETING IS IMPERATIVE

We frequently hear the terms such as global markets, global competition, global technology, and global competitiveness. Ten or so years ago, we heard similar words with *international* or *multinational* instead of *global* attached to them. What has happened since the 1980s? Are these terms just fashionable concepts of the time without some deep meanings? Or has something inherently changed in our society?

We believe something profound has indeed happened in our view of competition around the world. About twenty years ago, the world's greatest automobile manufacturers were General Motors, Ford, and Chrysler. Today, companies like Toyota, Honda, and BMW, among others, stand out as competitive nameplates in the automobile market. Similarly, *computer* was almost synonymous with IBM, which dominated the computer business around the world. Today, the computer market is crowded with Toshiba, NEC, Fujitsu, Siemens, and so on. Color TVs were invented in the United States, but today it is almost impossible to find a color TV made by U.S. companies. Instead, foreign brands such as Sony, Panasonic, and Magnavox are in most homes in the United States. Indeed, Zenith is the only remaining U.S. manufacturer that makes TVs at home. Nike is a U.S. company with a truly all-American shoe brand, but its shoes are all made in foreign countries and exported to the United States. Burger King is another American institution managed across the Atlantic Ocean by Grand Met of Britain.

An examination of the top 100 largest companies in the world vividly illustrates the profound changes in competitive milieu that we have seen in the past twenty years (see Exhibit 1-1). Of the top 100 largest industrial companies in the world, 64 were from the United States in 1970; in 1980 the number declined to 45 companies. The latest figure had come down to 24 in 1997. The number of Japanese companies in the top 100 has increased from 8 in 1970 to 29 in 1997, almost a fourfold increase. A similar increase has also been observed with French companies, from three in 1970 to 13 in 1997. The relative decline in the number of U.S. companies in the top 100 largest industrial companies is reflected equally in the banking, insurance, and other services sectors as well. In a nutshell, U.S. dominance of the postwar era in international commerce has been under ever-increasing pressure from abroad.

The changes observed in the past twenty-five years simply reflect that companies from other parts of the world have grown in size relative to those of the United States. In other words, today's environment is characterized by much more competition from around the world than in the past. As a result, many U.S. executives are feeling much more competitive urgency in product development, materials procurement, manufacturing, and marketing around the world. The same competitive pressure equally applies to executives of foreign companies. For example, due to cost pressures in its home country, Hoechst, a German chemicals giant, with its annual revenues larger than those of Dow Chemical and Union Carbide combined, is de-Germanizing its operations by reducing its German work force to only 30 percent of its worldwide total in 1997, down from 70 percent three years earlier and beefing up its U.S. operations from less than 6 percent of its annual revenues to 40 percent by the year 2000.[2] As one globe-trotting executive put it to describe such competitive

---

[2]Greg Steinmetz and Matt Marshall, "How a Chemicals Giant Goes About Becoming a Lot Less German," *Wall Street Journal* (February 18, 1997), pp. A1, A18.

EXHIBIT 1-1
CHANGE IN THE WORLD'S 100 LARGEST COMPANIES
AND THEIR NATIONALITIES

Country	1970	1980	1990	1997*
Japan	8	8	16	29
United States	64	45	33	24
Germany	8	13	12	13
France	3	12	10	13
Switzerland	2	3	3	5
Netherlands**	4	5	3	4
Britain**	9	7	8	4
Italy**	3	4	4	4
South Korea	0	0	2	4
Mexico	0	1	1	1
Venezuela	0	1	1	1
Spain	0	0	2	0
Sweden	0	0	2	0
Belgium	0	1	1	0
Brazil	0	1	1	0
Austria	0	0	1	0
Finland	0	0	1	0
South Africa	0	0	1	0
Canada	0	2	0	0
Australia	1	0	0	0
Total	102	103	102	102

Source: Fortune, various issues up to August 4, 1997.

*Fortune 500 criteria changed to include services firms (including retailing and trading)

**Includes joint nationality of firms (joint nationality has been counted for both the countries), so the total may exceed 100.

pressure, "If you don't do it right now, somebody else will always do it for you at your expense . . . and soon."

It is not only this competitive force that is shaping global business today. Particularly in the past several years, many political and economic events have affected the nature of global competition. The demise of the Soviet Union, the establishment of the European Union and the North American Free Trade Agreement, deregulation, and privatization of state-owned industries around the world have also changed the market environments around the world. Furthermore, the emerging markets of Eastern Europe and the rapidly growing markets of Southeast Asia also add promises to international businesses.

The fluid nature of global markets and competition makes the study of global marketing not only interesting but also challenging and rewarding. The term *global* epitomizes both the competitive pressure and the expanding market opportunities around the world. It does not mean, however, that all companies have to operate globally like IBM, Sony, Phillips, or ABB (Asea Brown Boveri). Whether a company operates domestically or across national boundaries, it can no longer avoid competitive pressure from around the world. Competitive pressure can also come from com-

Many globe-trotting companies have presence even in the farthest corners of the world. Keep in mind an adage, "If you don't do it right now, somebody else will . . . at your expense."

petitors at home. When Weyerhaeuser, a forest products company headquartered in Seattle, Washington, began exporting newspaper rolls to Japan, it had to meet the exacting quality standard that Japanese newspaper publishers demanded—and it did. As a result, this Seattle company now boasts the best newspaper rolls and outperforms other domestic companies in the U.S. market as well. Therefore, even purely domestic companies that have never sold anything abroad cannot be shielded from international competitive pressure. The point is that when we come across the term *global*, we should be made aware of both this intense competitive pressure and expanding market opportunities on a global basis.

◆ ◆ ◆ ◆ ◆ ◆ GLOBALIZATION OF MARKETS AND COMPETITION

When a country's per capita income is less than $5,000, much of the income is spent on food and other necessity items, and very little disposable income remains. However, once per capita income reaches $10,000 or so, the disposable portion of income increases dramatically because the part of the income spent on necessities does not rise nearly as fast as income increases. As a result, people around the world with per capita income of $10,000 and above have considerable purchasing power. With this level of purchasing power, people, *irrespective of their nationality*, tend to enjoy similar educational levels, academic and cultural backgrounds, lifestyles, and access to information. As these cultural and social dimensions begin to resemble each other in many countries, people's desire for material positions, ways of spending leisure time, and aspirations for the future become increasingly similar.[3] Even the deeply rooted food cultures have begun to converge.[4] Therefore, we see young people jogging (American contemporary culture), wearing Nike shoes (an American product made in China), listening to Ace of Base (a Danish rock group recording in Germany) or Madonna (an American pop singer) on a Sony Walkman (a Japanese product) in San Francisco, Amsterdam, Sidney, Tokyo, and São Paulo. Similarly, Yuppies (young urban professionals) in Paris, Hong Kong, Osaka, and Chicago share a common lifestyle, driving a BMW (a German car) to the office, using a Toshiba notebook computer (a Japanese product) at work, signing important documents with an exquisite Parker Pen (made by an ex-British, currently U.S.-headquartered company), and having a quick bite for lunch at McDonald's (an American fast-food restaurant). In the evenings, these people spend their spare time browsing around various Web sites on the Internet to do some "virtual" window shopping. The convergence of consumer needs in many parts of the world translates into tremendous business opportunities for companies willing to risk venturing abroad.

The United States, which enjoys one of the highest per-capita income level in the world, has long been the most important single market for both foreign and domestic companies. As a result of its insatiable demand for foreign products, the United States has been running a trade deficit since 1973—for more than twenty years. As shown in Exhibit 1-2, the U.S. trade deficit has followed a cyclical pattern since 1973. It gradually grew until the early 1980s, then suddenly increased to a record level of more than $160 billion in 1987. This dramatic increase was followed by an equally rapid decrease in trade deficit over the next four years, which has again

EXHIBIT 1-2
U.S. BALANCE OF GOODS, SERVICES, AND INCOME OVER 20-YEAR PERIOD

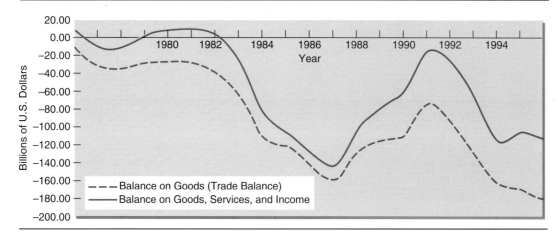

[3]Ohmae, Kenichi "The Triad World View," *Journal of Business Strategy*, 7 (Spring 1987), pp. 8–19.

[4]Alistair K. W. Marshall, "Accounting for East Asian Food Cultures: The Challenges Facing International Food Marketers," *Marketing Theory and Practice: Toward the 21st Century*, Joint Conference of the Korean Marketing Association and the American Marketing Association, May 14–17, 1995, 203–214.

worsened since then. However, despite a significant depreciation in the value of the dollar, the overall balance of goods and balance of goods, services, and income has not improved much (more on this in Chapter 2). In the popular press, the trade deficits have often been portrayed as a declining competitiveness of the United States. This assumes—rather erroneously—that U.S. companies engaged only in exports and imports and that international trade takes place between independent buyers and sellers across national boundaries. In order to appreciate the complexities of global competition, the nature of international trade and international business have to be clarified first, followed by a discussion of *who* manages international trade.

International Trade *versus* International Business

Here we have to understand the distinction between international trade and international business. Indeed, **international trade** consists of exports and imports, say, between the United States and the rest of the world. If U.S. imports exceed U.S. exports, then the nation would register a trade deficit. If the opposite were the case, then the United States would register a trade surplus. On the other hand, **international business** is a broader concept and includes international trade and foreign production. U.S. companies typically market their products in three ways. First, they can export their products from the United States, which is recorded as a U.S. export. Second, they can invest in their foreign production on their own and manufacture those products abroad for sale there. This transaction does not show up as a U.S. export, however. And third, they can contract out manufacturing in whole or part to a company in a foreign country, either by way of licensing or joint venture agreement. Of course, not all companies engage in all three forms of international transaction. Nonetheless, foreign manufacture on their own or on a contractual basis is a viable alternative means to exporting products abroad. Although it is not widely known, foreign production constitutes a much larger portion of international business than international trade.

The extensive international penetration of U.S. and other companies has been referred to as **global reach**.[5] Since the mid-1960s U.S.-owned subsidiaries located around the world have produced and sold three times the value of all U.S. exports. This 3 : 1 ratio of foreign manufacture to international trade has remained largely unchanged, and it becomes much more conspicuous if we look at U.S. business with the twelve-nation European Union, where U.S.-owned subsidiaries sold more than six times the total U. S. exports in 1990. Similarly, European-owned subsidiaries operating in the United States sold five times as much as U.S. imports from Europe.[6] This suggests that experienced companies tend to manufacture overseas much more than they export. On the other hand, Japanese companies have not expanded their foreign manufacturing activities until recently. According to one estimate, more than 90 percent of all the cases of Japanese foreign direct investment have taken place since 1985.[7] Despite their relative inexperi-

---

[5]Richard J. Barnet and R. E. Muller, *Global Reach: The Power of the Multinational Corporations* (New York: Simon and Schuster, 1974).

[6]Dennis J. Encarnation, "Transforming Trade and Investment, American, European, and Japanese Multinationals Across the Triad," a paper presented at the Academy of International Business Annual Meetings, November 22, 1992.

[7]Masaaki Kotabe, "The Promotional Roles of the State Government and Japanese Manufacturing Direct Investment in the United States," *Journal of Business Research*, 27 (June 1993), pp. 131–46.

A Global Reach: Executives increasingly use a global map to visualize their strategy.

ence in international expansion, Japanese subsidiaries registered two-and-a-half times as much foreign sales as all Japanese exports worldwide in 1990.[8]

Who Manages International Trade?

As just discussed, international trade and foreign production are increasingly managed on a global basis. Furthermore, international trade and foreign production are also intertwined in a complex manner. Think about Honda Motors, a Japanese automobile manufacturer. Honda initially exported its Accords and Civics to the United States in the 1970s. By mid-1980s the Japanese company began manufacturing those cars in Marysville, Ohio, in the United States. Now the company exports U.S.-made Accord models to Japan and elsewhere and boasts that it is the largest exporter of U.S.-made automobiles in the United States. Similarly, Texas Instruments has a large semiconductor manufacturing plant in Japan, marketing its semiconductor chips not only in Japan but also exporting them from Japan to the United States and elsewhere. In addition to traditional exporting from their home base, those companies manufacture their products in various foreign countries both for local sale and for further exporting to the rest of the world, including their respective home countries. In other words, multinational companies are increasingly managing the international trade flow within themselves. This phenomenon is called **intra-firm trade**.

Intra-firm trade makes trade statistics more complex to interpret, since part of the international flow of products and components is taking place between affiliated companies within the same corporate system, transcending national boundaries. A survey by United Nations Center on Transnational Corporations reported data on intra-firm trade for the United States, Japan, and Britain.[9] For the United States,

---

[8]Encarnation.

[9]United Nations Center on Transnational Corporations, *Transnational Corporations in World Development: Trends and Perspectives*, New York: United Nations, 1988.

about 30 percent of U.S. exports are attributed to U.S. parent companies transferring products and components to their affiliates overseas, and about 40 percent of U.S. imports are accounted for by foreign affiliates exporting to their U.S. parent companies. For both Japan and Britain, intra-firm transactions account for approximately 30 percent of their total trade flows (exports and imports combined), respectively. These intra-firm trade ratios have been fairly stable over time.[10]

◆ ◆ ◆ ◆ ◆ ◆ EVOLUTION OF GLOBAL MARKETING

What is Marketing?

Marketing is essentially a creative corporate activity involving the planning and execution of the conception, pricing, promotion, and distribution of ideas, products, and services in an exchange that not only *satisfies* customers' current needs but also *anticipates* and *creates* their future needs at a profit.[11] Marketing is not only much broader than selling, it also encompasses the entire company's orientation toward customer satisfaction in a competitive environment. In other words, marketing strategy requires close attention to both customers and competitors. Quite often marketers have focused excessively on satisfying customer needs while ignoring competitors. In the process, competitors have outmaneuvered them in the marketplace with better, less-expensive products. In many cases, U.S. companies have won the battle of discovering and filling customer needs initially, only to be defeated in the competitive war by losing the markets they pioneered.[12]

It is increasingly difficult for companies to avoid the impact of competition from around the world and the convergence of the world's markets. As a result, an increasing number of companies are drawn into marketing activities outside their home country. However, as previously indicated, different companies approach marketing around the world very differently. For example, Michael Dell established Dell Computer because he saw a burgeoning market potential for IBM-compatible personal computers in the United States. After his immediate success at home, he realized a future growth potential would exist in foreign markets. Then his company began exporting Dell PCs to Europe and Japan. In a way this was a predictable pattern of foreign expansion. On the other hand, not all companies go through this predictable pattern. Think about a notebook-size Macintosh computer called the PowerBook 100 that Apple Computer introduced in 1991. In 1989, Apple enlisted Sony, the Japanese consumer electronics giant, to design and manufacture this notebook com-

---

[10]Organization for Economic Cooperation and Development, *Intra-Firm Trade*, Paris, OECD, 1993.

[11]This definition is modified from the American Marketing Association's definition of marketing, and is strongly influenced by Drucker's conception of two entrepreneurial functions—marketing and innovation—that constitute business. Recent thinking about marketing also suggests the task of the marketer is not only to satisfy the current needs and wants of customers, but also to innovate on products and services, anticipating and even creating their future needs and wants. See Peter F. Drucker, *The Practice of Management* (New York: Harper & Brothers, 1954), pp. 37–39; and also Frederick E. Webster, Jr., "The Changing Role of Marketing in the Corporation," *Journal of Marketing*, 56 (October 1992), pp. 1–16.

[12]Steven P. Schnaars, *Marketing Strategy* (New York: Free Press), 1991, pp. 13–15.

puter for both the U.S. and Japanese markets.[13] Sony has world-class expertise in miniaturization and has been a supplier of disk drives, monitors, and power supplies to Apple for various Macintosh models. In an industry, such as personal computers, where technology changes quickly and the existing product becomes obsolete in a short period of time, a window of business opportunity is naturally limited. Therefore, Apple's motivation was to introduce the notebook computer on the markets around the world as soon as it could before competition picked up.

Companies generally develop different marketing strategies depending on the degree of experience and the nature of operations in international markets. Companies tend to evolve over time, accumulating international business experience and learning the advantages and disadvantages associated with complexities of manufacturing and marketing around the world.[14] As a result, many researchers have adopted an evolutionary perspective of internationalization of the company just like the evolution of the species over time. In the following pages we will formally define and explain five stages characterizing the evolution of global marketing. Of course, not all companies go through the complete evolution from a purely domestic marketing stage to a purely global marketing stage. An actual evolution depends also on the economic, cultural, political, and legal environments of various country markets in which the company operates, as well as on the nature of the company's offerings. A key point here is that many companies are constantly under competitive pressure to move forward both *reactively* (responding to the changes in the market and competitive environments) and *proactively* (anticipating the change). Remember, "If you don't do it . . . , somebody else will. . . ."

Therefore, knowing the dynamics of the evolutionary development of international marketing involvement is important for two reasons. First, it helps in the understanding of how companies learn and acquire international experience and how they use it for gaining competitive advantage over time. This may help an executive to be better prepared for the likely change needed in the company's marketing strategy. Second, with this knowledge, a company may be able to compete more effectively by predicting its competitors' likely marketing strategy in advance.

Domestic Marketing

As shown in Exhibit 1-3, there are five identifiable stages in the evolution of marketing across national boundaries.[15] The first stage is **domestic marketing**. Before entry into international markets, many companies focus solely on their domestic market. Their marketing strategy is developed based on information about domestic customer needs and wants, industry trends, economic, technological, and political environments at home. When those companies consider competition, they essentially look at domestic competition. Today, it is highly conceivable that domestic competition is made up of

[13]"Apple's Japanese Ally," *Fortune* (November 4, 1991), pp. 151–52.

[14]William H. Davidson, *Experience Effects in International Investment and Technology Transfer* (Ann Arbor, Mich.: UMI Research Press, 1980).

[15]This section draws from Balaj S. Chakravarthy and Howard V. Perlmutter, "Strategic Planning for A Global Business," *Columbia Journal of World Business* (Summer 1985), pp. 3–10; Susan P. Douglas and C. Samuel Craig, "Evolution of Global Marketing Strategy: Scale, Scope and Synergy," *Columbia Journal of World Business* 24 (Fall 1989), pp. 47–59.

EXHIBIT 1-3
EVOLUTION OF GLOBAL MARKETING

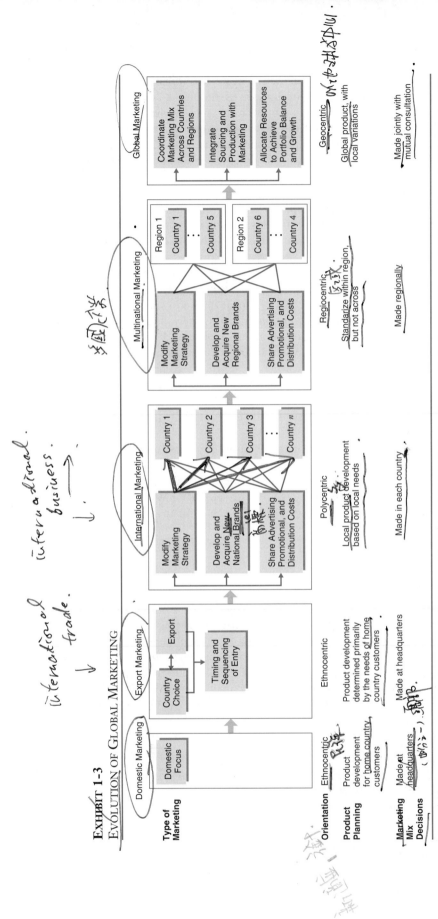

Source: Adapted from Susan P. Douglas and C. Samuel Craig, "Evolution of Global Marketing Strategy: Scale, Scope and Synergy," *Columbia Journal of World Business,* 24 (Fall 1985), p. 50; and Balai S. Chakravarthy and Howard V. Perlmutter, "Strategic Planning for a Global Business," *Columbia Journal of World Business,* 20 (Summer 1985), p. 6.

both domestic competitors and foreign competitors marketing their products in the home market. Domestic marketers tend to be *ethnocentric* and pay little attention to changes taking place in the global marketplace, such as changing lifestyles and market segments, emerging competition, and better products that have yet to arrive in their domestic market. *Ethnocentrism* is defined here as a predisposition of a firm to be predominantly concerned with its viability worldwide and legitimacy only in its home country[16]—that is, where all strategic actions of a company are tailored to domestic responses under similar situations. As a result, they may be vulnerable to the sudden changes forced on them from foreign competition. U.S. automobile and consumer electronics manufacturers suffered from this ethnocentrism in the 1960s and 1970s as a result of their neglect of imminent competition from Japanese low-cost manufacturers.

Export Marketing

The second stage is export marketing. Usually, initial export marketing begins with unsolicited orders from foreign customers. When a company receives an order from abroad, it may reluctantly fill it initially, but it gradually learns the benefit of marketing overseas. In general, in the early stage of export marketing involvement, the internationalization process is a consequence of incremental adjustments to the changing conditions of the company and its environment, rather than a result of its deliberate strategy. Such a pattern is due to the consequence of greater uncertainty in international business, higher costs of information, and the lack of technical knowledge about international marketing activities.

Some companies progress to a more involved stage of internationalization, once three internal conditions are satisfied. First, the management of the company obtains favorable expectations of the attractiveness of exporting based on experience. Second, the company has access to key resources necessary for undertaking additional export-related tasks. Such availability of physical, financial, and managerial resources is closely associated with firm size. Particularly, small companies may have few trained managers, and little time for long-term planning as they are preoccupied with day-to-day operational problems, and consequently find it difficult to become involved in exporting. Third, management is willing to commit adequate resources to export activities.[17] The company's long-term commitment to export marketing depends on how successful management is in overcoming various barriers encountered in international marketing activities. An experienced export marketer has to deal with difficulties in maintaining and expanding export involvement. These difficulties include import/export restrictions, cost and availability of shipping, exchange rate fluctuations, collection of money, and development of distribution channels, among others. Overall, favorable experience appears to be a key component in moving companies along the internationalization continuum. To a large degree an appropriate measure of favorableness for many companies consists of profits. An increase in profits due to a certain activity is likely to increase the company's interest in such activity.[18]

---

[16]Chakravarthy and Perlmutter, pp. 3–10.

[17]S. Tamer Cavusgil, "On the Internationalization Process of Firms," *European Research*, 8 (November 1980), pp. 273–79.

[18]Masaaki Kotabe and Michael R. Czinkota, "State Government Promotion of Manufacturing Exports: A Gap Analysis," *Journal of International Business Studies*, 23 (Fourth Quarter 1992), pp. 637–58.

External pressures also prod companies into export marketing activities. Saturated domestic market may make it difficult for a company to maintain sales volume in an increasingly competitive domestic market; it will become much more serious when foreign competitors begin marketing products in the domestic market. Export marketers begin paying attention to technological and other changes in the global marketplace that domestic marketers tend to ignore. However, export marketers still tend to take an *ethnocentric* approach to foreign markets as being an extension of their domestic market and export products developed primarily for home country customers with limited adaptation to foreign customers' needs.

International Marketing

Once export marketing becomes an integral part of the company's marketing activity, it will begin to seek new directions for growth and expansion. We call this stage **international marketing.** A unique feature of international marketing is its *polycentric* orientation with emphasis on product and promotional adaptation in foreign markets, whenever necessary.[19] Polycentric orientation refers to a predisposition of a firm to the existence of significant local cultural differences across markets, necessitating the operation in each country being viewed independently (i.e., all strategic decisions are thus tailored to suit the cultures of the concerned country). As the company's market share in a number of countries reaches a certain point, it becomes important for the company to defend its position through local competition. Because of local competitors' proximity to, and familiarity of, local customers, they tend to have an inherent "insider" advantage over foreign competition. To strengthen its competitive position, the international marketer begins to adapt products and promotion, if necessary, to meet the needs and wants of local customers in two alternative ways. First, the company may allocate a certain portion of its manufacturing capacity to its export business. Second, because of transportation costs, tariffs, and other regulations, and availability of human and capital resources in the foreign markets, the company may even begin manufacturing locally. BMW has been exporting its cars to the United States for many years. Recently the German company decided to build a manufacturing plant in South Carolina in order to be more adaptive to the changing customer needs in this important market and to take advantage of rather inexpensive resources as a result of the dollar depreciation against the German mark.

If international marketing is taken to the extreme, a company may establish an independent foreign subsidiary in each and every foreign market and have each of the subsidiaries operate independently of each other without any measurable headquarters control. This special case of international marketing is known as **multi-domestic marketing.** Product development, manufacturing, and marketing are all executed by each subsidiary for its own local market. As a result, different product lines, product positioning, and pricing may be observed across those subsidiaries. Few economies of scale benefits can be obtained. However, multi-domestic marketing is useful when customer needs are so different across different national markets that no common product or promotional strategy can be developed. For example,

---

[19]Warren J. Keegan, "Multinational Product Planning: Strategic Alternatives," *Journal of Marketing*, 33 (January 1969), pp. 58–62.

Philips and Unilever have historically been multidomestic in orientation, although they are now coordinating certain functions.

Multinational Marketing

Now the company markets its products in many countries around the world. Management of the company comes to realize the benefit of economies of scale in product development, manufacturing, and marketing by consolidating some of its activities on a regional basis. This *regiocentric* approach suggests that product planning may be standardized within a region (e.g., a group of contiguous and similar countries), such as Western Europe, but not across regions. Products may be manufactured regionally as well. Similarly, advertising, promotional, and distribution costs may also be shared by subsidiaries in the region. In order for the company to develop its regional image in the marketplace, it may develop and acquire new regional brands to beef up its regional operations. General Motors has a regional subsidiary, Opel (headquartered in Germany), to market both GM and Opel cars with a strong European distinction.

Global Marketing

The international (country-by-country) or multinational (region-by-region) orientation, while enabling the consolidation of operations within countries or regions, will tend to result in market fragmentation worldwide, nonetheless. Operational fragmentation leads to higher costs. As many Japanese companies entered the world markets as low-cost manufacturers of reliable products in the 1970s, well-established U.S. and European multinational companies were made acutely aware of the vulnerability of being high-cost manufacturers. Levitt,[20] an arduous globalization proponent, argues:

> Gone are accustomed differences in national or regional preference. Gone are the days when a company could sell last year's models—or lesser versions of advanced products—in the less developed world . . . . The multinational and the global corporation are not the same thing. The multinational corporation operates in a number of countries, and adjusts its products and practices in each—at high relative costs. The global corporation operates with resolute constancy—at low relative cost—as if the entire world (or major regions of it) were a single entity; it sells the same things in the same way everywhere.

Global marketing refers to marketing activities by companies that emphasize (1) reduction of cost inefficiencies and duplication of efforts among their national and regional subsidiaries, (2) opportunities for the transfer of products, brands, and other ideas across subsidiaries, (3) emergence of global customers, and (4) improved linkages among national marketing infrastructures leading to the development of a global marketing infrastructure.[21] Although Levitt's view is somewhat extreme, many researchers agree that global marketing does not necessarily mean standardization of products, promotion, pricing, and distribution worldwide, but rather it is a company's proactive willingness to adopt a global perspective instead of country-by-country or region-by-region perspective in developing a marketing strategy. Al-

---

[20]Theodore Levitt, "The Globalization of Markets," *Harvard Business Review*, 61 (May–June) 1983, pp. 92–102.

[21]Susan P. Douglas and C. Samuel Craig, 1989.

Rolex watches are one example of global marketing at work. The same promotional message and the same product transcend across different cultures.

◆ ◆

*G*LOBAL PERSPECTIVE 1-1

GLOBALIZING THE BUSINESS TERMS BEFORE GLOBALIZING THE FIRM

International was the first word that William Hudson, president and CEO of AMP Inc., Harrisburg, Pennsylvania, told his corporate colleagues to cut from their business vocabularies. Why? The term creates a "Chinese wall" that divides a globalizing company into "domestic" and "international" sides, he explained to A. T. Kearney Inc. officers meeting in Chicago. "It's almost as if you

don't jump over that wall" to work or team together, he said.

Another banished word: *subsidiary*. It conveys "a parent/child relationship," said Mr. Hudson. Headquarters tends to lord its power over foreign and domestic operations and "make them feel like inferior souls." Revising the business lexicon is not easy, Mr. Hudson readily admitted. "Every now and then [one of the words] shows up on a . . . slide when somebody makes a presentation. And I've got to put up my hand and say: 'Erase that word.'"

Source: *Industry Week* (June 7, 1993), pp. 51–53.

though not all companies adopt global marketing, an increasing number of companies are proactively trying to find commonality in their marketing strategy among national subsidiaries (See Global Perspective 1-1). For example, Black & Decker, a U.S. hand tool manufacturer, adopted a global perspective by standardizing and streamlining components such as motors and rotors while maintaining a wide range of product lines, and created a universal image for its products. In this case, it was not standardization of products *per se* but rather the company's effort at standardizing key components and product design for manufacturability to achieve global leadership in cost and value.[22]

So far we focused on complex realities of international trade and investment that have characterized our global economy in the past twenty years. Some vital statistics have been provided. The more statistics we see, the more befuddled we become by the sheer complexities of our global economy. It even seems as though there were not a modicum of orderliness in our global economy, it being just like a jungle. Naturally, we wish the world had been much simpler. In reality, it is becoming ever more complex. Luckily enough, however, economists and business researchers have tried over the years to explain the ever increasing complexities of the global economy in simpler terms. A simplified yet logical view of the world is called a **theory**. Indeed, there are many different ways—theories—of looking at international trade and investment taking place in the world. For those of you interested in understanding some orderliness in the complex world of international trade and investment, we encourage you to read the appendix to this chapter. Some theoretical understanding will not only help you appreciate the competitive world in which we live, but also help you make better strategy decisions for a company you may join shortly or a company you may own.

SUMMARY ◆

World trade has grown from $200 billion to more than $4 trillion in the past two decades. Although world trade volume is significant in and of itself, international business is much more than trade statistics show. Companies from Western Europe, the United States, and Japan collectively produce probably more than three times as much in their foreign markets as they export. And about a third of their exports and imports are transacted on an intra-firm basis between their parent companies and their affiliated companies abroad or between the affiliated companies themselves.

What this all means is that it is almost impossible for domestic company executives to consider their domestic markets and domestic competition alone. If they fail to look beyond their national boundaries, they may unknowingly lose marketing opportunities to competitors that do. Worse yet, foreign competitors will encroach on their hard-earned market position at home so fast that it may be too late for them to respond. International markets are so intertwined that separating international from domestic business may be a futile mental exercise.

Historically, international expansion has always been a strategy consideration after domestic marketing, and has therefore been reactionary to such things as a decline in domestic sales and increased

---

[22]Alvin P. Lehnerd, "Revitalizing the Manufacture and Design for Mature Global Products," in Bruce R. Guile and Harvey Brooks, eds., *Technology and Global Industry* (Washington, D.C.: National Academy Press, 1987), pp. 49–64.

domestic competition. Global marketing is a proactive response to the intertwined nature of business opportunities and competition that know no political boundaries. However, global marketing does not necessarily mean that companies should market the same product in the same way around the world as world markets are converging. To the extent feasible, they probably should. Nonetheless, global marketing is a company's willingness to adopt a global perspective instead of country-by-country or region-by-region perspective in developing a marketing strategy for growth and profit.

REVIEW QUESTIONS ◆

1. Discuss the reasons why international business is much more complex today than it was twenty years ago.

2. What is the nature of global competition?

3. Does international trade accurately reflect the nature of global competition?

4. Why are consumption patterns similar across industrialized countries despite cultural differences?

5. How is global marketing different from international marketing?

6. Why do you think a company should or should not market the same product in the same way around the world?

7. What is proactive standardization?

DISCUSSION QUESTIONS ◆ ◆ ◆ ◆ ◆ ◆ ◆ ◆ ◆ ◆ ◆ ◆ ◆ ◆ ◆ ◆ ◆ ◆ ◆

1. The United States and Japan, the two largest economies in the world, are also the largest importers and exporters of goods and services. However, imports and exports put together comprise only 20 to 30 percent of their GNPs. This percentage has not changed much over the last three decades for both of these countries. Does this imply that the corporations and the media may be overemphasizing globalization? Discuss why you agree or do not agree with the last statement.

2. Merchandise trade today accounts for less than 2 percent of all the foreign exchange transactions around the world. Can one deduce that merchandise plays an insignificant role in today's economies? Why or why not?

3. A major cereal manufacturer produces and markets standardized breakfast cereals to countries around the world. Minor modifications in attributes such as sweetness of the product are made to cater to local needs. However, the core products and brands are standardized. The company entered the Chinese market a few years back and was extremely satisfied with the results. The company's sales continue to grow at a rate of around 50 percent a year in China. Encouraged by its marketing success in China and other Asian countries, and based on the market reforms taking place, the company started operations in India by manufacturing and marketing its products.

Initial response to the product was extremely encouraging, and within one year the company was thinking in terms of rapidly expanding its production capacity. However, after a year, sales tapered off and started to fall. Detailed consumer research seemed to suggest that while the upper-middle social class, especially families where both spouses were working, to whom this product was targeted, adopted the cereals as an alternative meal (i.e., breakfast) for a short time, they eventually returned to the traditional Indian breakfast. The CEOs of some other firms in the food industry in India are quoted as saying that non-Indian snack products and restaurant business are the areas where multinational companies (MNCs) can hope for success. Trying to replace a full meal with a non-Indian product has less of a chance of succeeding. You are a senior executive in the international division of this food MNC with experience of operating in various countries in a product management function. The CEO plans to send you to India on a fact-finding mission to determine answers to these specific questions. What, in your opinion, would be the answers to these questions:

a. Was entering the market with a standardized product a mistake?

b. Was it a problem of the product or the way it was positioned?

c. Given the advantages to be gained through

leveraging of brand equity and product knowledge on a global basis , and the disadvantages of differing local tastes, what would be your strategy for entering new markets.

4. Globalization involves the organization-wide development of a global perspective. This global perspective requires globally thinking managers. Although the benefits of globalization have received widespread atten-
tion, the difficulties in developing managers who think globally has received scant attention. Some senior managers consider this to be a significant stumbling block in the globalization efforts of companies. Do you agree with the concerns of these managers? Would the lack of truly globally thinking managers cause problems for implementing a global strategy? Under what conditions would the effects of this problem vary?

FURTHER READINGS ✦ ✦ ✦ ✦ ✦ ✦ ✦ ✦ ✦ ✦ ✦ ✦ ✦ ✦ ✦ ✦ ✦ ✦ ✦

Bartlett, Christopher A,. and Sumantra Ghoshal. "What Is a Global Manager?" *Harvard Business Review* (September-October, 1992): 124–132.

_____ and _____. "Tap Your Subsidiaries for Global Reach." *Harvard Business Review* (November-December, 1986): 87–94.

Czinkota, Michael R., Ilkka A. Ronkainen, and John J. Tarrant. *The Global Marketing Imperative*. Lincolnwood, Ill.: NTC Business Books, 1995.

Douglas, Susan P., and C. Samuel Craig. *Global Marketing Strategy*. New York: McGraw Hill, 1995.

Emmerji, Louis. "Globalization, Regionalization and World Trade." *Columbia Journal of World Business*, 27 (Summer 1992): 6–13.

Fleenor, Debra. "The Coming and Going of the Global Corporation." *Columbia Journal of World Business*, 28 (Winter 1993): 6–16.

Kashani, Kamran. *Managing Global Marketing: Cases and Text:* Boston: PWS-Kent Pub., 1992.

Yip, George S. "Global Strategy. . . In a World of Nations?" *Sloan Management Review* (Fall 1989): 29–41.

✦ ✦ ✦ ✦ ✦ ✦ ✦ ✦ ✦ ✦ ✦ **APPENDIX** ✦ ✦ ✦ ✦ ✦ ✦ ✦ ✦ ✦ ✦ ✦

Theories are a simplification of the complex realities one way or another. A few important theories will be explained here. Each of the theories provides a number of fundamental principles, with which you can not only appreciate why international trade and investment occur but also prepare for the next impending change you will probably see in a not-so-distant future. These theories are arranged chronologically so that you can better understand what aspect of the ever-increasing complexities of international business each theory was designed to explain.

Comparative Advantage Theory.
At the aggregate level, countries trade with each other for fundamentally the same reasons that individuals exchange products and services for mutual benefit. By doing so, we all benefit collectively. Comparative advantage theory is an arithmetic demonstration made by the English economist, David Ricardo, almost 180 years ago that a country can gain from engaging in trade even if it has an *absolute* advantage or disadvantage. In other words, even if the United States is more efficient in the production of everything than China, both countries will benefit from trade
between them by specializing in what each country can produce *relatively* more efficiently.

Let us demonstrate comparative advantage theory in its simplest form: the world is made up of two countries (the United States and China) and two products (personal computers and desks). We assume that there is only one PC model and only one type of desk. We further assume that labor is the only input to produce both products. Transportation costs are also assumed to be zero. The production conditions and consumption pattern in the two countries before and after trade are presented in Exhibit 1-4. As shown, U.S. labor is assumed to be more productive absolutely in the production of both personal computers (PC) and desks than Chinese labor.

Intuitively, you might argue that since the United States is more productive in both products, U.S. companies will export both PCs and desks to China, and Chinese companies cannot compete with U.S. companies in either product category. Furthermore, you might argue that as China cannot sell anything to the United States, China cannot pay for imports from the United States. Therefore, these two countries cannot engage in trade.

EXHIBIT 1-4
COMPARATIVE ADVANTAGE AT WORK

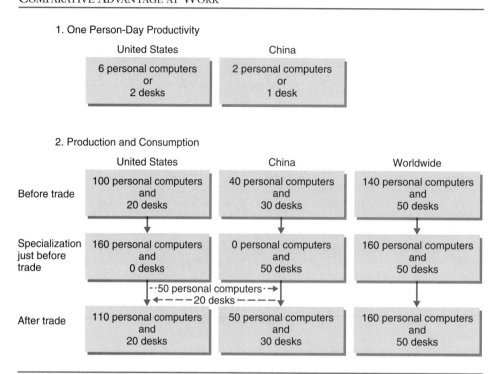

1. One Person-Day Productivity

United States	China
6 personal computers or 2 desks	2 personal computers or 1 desk

2. Production and Consumption

	United States	China	Worldwide
Before trade	100 personal computers and 20 desks	40 personal computers and 30 desks	140 personal computers and 50 desks
Specialization just before trade	160 personal computers and 0 desks	0 personal computers and 50 desks	160 personal computers and 50 desks
	··50 personal computers ·→ ←− − −20 desks − − −→		
After trade	110 personal computers and 20 desks	50 personal computers and 30 desks	160 personal computers and 50 desks

This is essentially the **absolute advantage** argument. Is this argument true? The answer is no.

If you closely look at labor productivity of the two industries, you see that the United States can produce PCs more efficiently than desks compared to the situation in China. The United States has a three to one advantage in PCs, but only a two to one advantage in desks over China. In other words, the United States can produce three PCs instead of a desk (or as few as one-third of a desk per PC), while China can produce two PCs for a desk (or as many as a half desk per PC). Relatively speaking, the United States is comparatively more efficient in making PCs (at a rate of three PCs per desk) than China (at a rate of two PCs per desk). However, China is comparatively more efficient in making desks (at a rate of half a desk per PC) than the United States (at a rate of one third of a desk per PC). Therefore, we say that the United States has a **comparative advantage** in making PCs, while China has a comparative advantage in making desks.

Comparative advantage theory suggests that the United States should specialize in production of PCs, while China should specialize in production of desks. As shown in Exhibit 1-4, the United States produced and consumed 100 PCs and 20 desks, and China produced and consumed 40 PCs and 30 desks. As a whole, the world (the United States and China combined) produced and

consumed 140 PCs and 50 desks. Now as a result of specialization, the United States concentrates all its labor resources on PC production, while China allocates all labor resources to desk production. The United States can produce 60 more PCs by giving up on 20 desks it used to produce (at a rate of three PCs per desk), resulting in a total production of 160 PCs and no desks. Similarly, China can produce 20 more desks by moving its labor from PC production to desk production (at a rate of half a desk per PC), with a total production of 50 desks and no PCs. Now the world as a whole produces 160 PCs and 50 desks.

Before trade occurs, U.S. consumers are willing to exchange as many as three PCs for each desk, while Chinese consumers are willing to exchange as few as two PCs for each desk, given their labor productivity, respectively. Therefore, the price of a desk acceptable to both U.S. and Chinese consumers should be somewhere between two and three PCs. Let us assume that the mutually acceptable price, or **commodity terms of trade** (a price of one good in terms of another), is 2.5 PCs per desk. Now let the United States and China engage in trade at the commodity terms of trade of 2.5 PCs per desk. To simplify our argument, further assume that the United States and China consume the same number of desks after trade as they did before trade, that is, 20 desks and 30 desks, respectively.

In other words, the United States has to import 20 desks from China in exchange for 50 PCs (20 desks × price of a desk in terms of PCs), which are exported to China from the United States. As a result of trade, the United States consumes 110 PCs and 20 desks, while China consumes 50 PCs and 30 desks. Given the same amount of labor resources, both countries respectively consume 10 more PCs while consuming the same number of desks. Obviously, specialization and trade have benefited both countries.

In reality, we rarely exchange one product for another. We use foreign exchange instead. Let us assume that the price of a desk is $900 in the United States and 2,000 yuan in China. Based on the labor productivity in the two countries, the price of a PC should be $300 (at a rate of a third of a desk per PC) in the United States and 1,000 yuan (at a rate of half a desk per PC) in China. As we indicated earlier, U.S. consumers are willing to exchange as many as three PCs for each desk worth $900 in the United States. Three PCs in China are worth 3,000 yuan. Therefore, U.S. consumers are willing to pay as much as 3,000 yuan to import a $900 desk from China. Similarly, Chinese consumers are willing to import a minimum of two PCs (worth 2,000 yuan in China) for each desk they produce (worth $900 in the United States). Therefore, the mutually acceptable exchange rate should be:

$$2{,}000 \text{ yuan} \leq \$900 \leq 3{,}000 \text{ yuan},$$

$$\text{or } 2.22 \text{ yuan} \leq \$1 \leq 3.33 \text{ yuan}.$$

An actual exchange rate will be affected also by consumer demands and money supply situations in the two countries. Nonetheless, it is clear that exchange rates are primarily determined by international trade.

From this simple exercise, we can make a few general statements or **principles of international trade.**

Principle 1: Countries benefit from international trade.
Principle 2: International trade increases worldwide production by specialization.
Principle 3: Exchange rates are determined primarily by traded goods.

By now you might have wondered why U.S. workers are more productive than Chinese workers. So far we have assumed that labor is the only input in economic production. In reality, we do not produce anything with manual labor alone. We use machinery, computers, and other capital equipment (capital for short) to help us produce efficiently. In other words, our implicit assumption was that the United States has more abundant capital relative to labor than China does. Naturally, the more capital we have relative to our labor stock, the less expensive a unit of capital should be relative to a unit of labor. The less expensive a unit of capital relative to a unit of labor,

the more capital we tend to use and specialize in industry that requires a large amount of capital. In other words, the capital–labor endowment ratio affects what type of industry a country tends to specialize in. In general, a capital-abundant country (e.g., the United States) tends to specialize in capital-intensive industry and export capital-intensive products (personal computers), and import labor-intensive products (desks). Conversely, a labor-abundant country (China) tends to specialize in labor-intensive industry and export labor-intensive products (desks), and import capital-intensive products (personal computers). This refined argument is known as **factor endowment theory** of comparative advantage.

The factor endowment theory can be generalized a bit further. For example, the United States is not only capital-abundant but also abundant with a highly educated (i.e., skilled) labor force. Therefore, it is easy to predict that the United States has comparative advantage in skill-intensive industries such as computers and biotechnology and exports a lot of computers and genetically engineered ethical drugs around the world, and imports manual labor-intensive products such as textiles and shoes from labor-abundant countries such as China and Brazil. Global Perspective 1-2 clearly shows that labor productivity alone shows a very erroneous impression of industry competitiveness.

Now you might have begun wondering how comparative advantage arguments will help businesspeople in the real world. Suppose that you work as a strategic planner for Nike. Shoe manufacturing is extremely labor-intensive, while shoe designing is becoming increasingly hi-tech (i.e., skill-intensive). The United States is a relatively skill-abundant and labor-scarce country. Therefore, the country has a comparative advantage in skill-intensive operations but has a comparative disadvantage in labor-intensive operations. There are two ways to use your knowledge of comparative advantage arguments. First, it is easy to predict where competition comes from. Companies from countries like China and Brazil will have a comparative advantage in shoe manufacturing over Nike in the United States. Second, you can advise Nike to establish shoe manufacturing plants in labor-abundant countries instead of in the labor-scarce United States. As we said earlier, shoe designing has become increasingly hi-tech, involving computer-aided designing and development of light, shock-absorbent material, which requires an extremely high level of expertise. Therefore, based on the comparative advantage argument, you suggest that product designing and development be done in the United States, where required expertise is relatively abundant. Indeed, that is what Nike does as a result of global competitive pressure, and has exploited various countries' comparative advantage to its advantage (no pun intended). Nike has product designing and development and special material development conducted in the United States and has manufacturing operations in labor-abundant countries like China and Brazil.

◆ ◆

*G*LOBAL PERSPECTIVE 1-2

It is correct to say, "The best way to improve living standards is to encourage investment in *sophisticated* industries like computers and aerospace." Is it correct to say, "The best way to improve living standards is to encourage investment in industries that provide *high value added per worker*"? The real high-value industries in the United States are extremely capital-intensive sectors like cigarettes and oil refining. High-tech sectors that everyone imagines are the keys to the future, like aircraft and elec-

tronics, are only average in their value added per worker, but are extremely *skill-intensive* industries. Look at these statistics:

Value Added Per Worker	*Thousands*
Cigarettes	$823
Petroleum refining	$270
Automobile	$112
Tires and inner tubes	$101
Aerospace	$86
Electronics	$74
All manufacturing	$73

Adapted from Paul Krugman, "Competitiveness: Does it Matter?" *Fortune* (March 7, 1994), pp. 109–15.

The comparative advantage theory is useful in explaining *inter-industry* trade, say computers and desks, between countries that have very different factor endowments. It suggests efficient allocation of limited resources across national boundaries by specialization and trade, but hardly explains business competition, because computer manufacturers and desk manufacturers do not compete directly. Further, it fails to explain the expansion of trade among the industrialized countries with similar factor endowments. Trade among the twenty or so industrialized countries now constitutes almost 60 percent of world trade, and much of it is intra-industry in nature. In other words, similar products are differentiated either physically or only in the customers' minds and traded across countries. Thus, BMW exports its sports cars to Japan, while Honda exports its competing models to Germany. BMW and Honda compete directly within the same automobile industry. This type of intra-industry competition cannot be explained by comparative advantage theory.

International Product Cycle Theory When business practitioners think of competition, they usually refer to intra-industry competition. Why and how does competition tend to evolve over time and across national boundaries in the same industry? Then, how does a company develop its marketing strategy in the presence of competitors at home and abroad? **International product cycle theory** addresses all these questions.

Several speculations have been made.[23] *First*, a large

domestic market such as the United States makes it possible for U.S companies to enjoy **economies of scale** in mass production and mass marketing, enabling them to become lower-cost producers than their competition in foreign countries. Therefore, those low-cost producers can market their products in foreign markets and still remain profitable. In addition, an **economies of scope** argument augments an economies of scale argument. Companies from a small country can still enjoy economies of scale in production and marketing by extending their business scope beyond their national boundary. For example, Nestlé, a Swiss food company, can enjoy economies of scale by considering European, U.S., and Japanese markets together as its primary market. *Second*, technological innovation can provide an innovative company a competitive advantage, or **technological gap,** over its competitors both at home and abroad. Until competitors learn about and imitate the innovation, the original innovator company enjoys a temporary **monopoly power** around the world. Therefore, it is technological innovators that tend to market new products abroad. *Third*, it is generally the per-capita income level that determines consumers' **preference similarity,** or consumption patterns, irrespective of nationality. Preference similarity explains why intra-industry trade has grown tremendously among the industrialized countries with similar income levels.

Combining these forces with the earlier comparative advantage theory, international product cycle theory was developed in the 1960s and 1970s to explain a realistic,

---

[23]Mordechai E. Kreinin, *International Economics: A Policy Approach*, 5th ed. (New York: Harcourt Brace Jovanovich, 1987), pp. 276–78.

dynamic change in international competition over time and place.[24] This comprehensive theory describes the relationship between trade and investment over the product life cycle.

One of the key underlying assumptions in the international product cycle theory is that "Necessity is the mother of invention." In the United States, where personal incomes and labor costs were the highest in the world particularly in the 1960s and 1970s, consumers desired products that would save their labor and time and satisfy materialistic needs. Historically, U.S. companies developed and introduced many products that were labor- and time-saving or responded to high-income consumer needs, including dishwashers, microwave ovens, automatic washers and dryers, and so on. Similarly, companies in Western Europe tend to innovate on material- and capital-saving products and processes to meet their local consumers' needs and lifestyle orientation. Small and no-frill automobiles and recyclable products are such examples. Japanese companies stress products that conserve not only material and capital but also space to address their local consumers' acute concern about space limitation. Therefore, Japanese companies excel in developing and marketing small energy-efficient products of all kinds.[25]

International product cycle theory suggests that new products are developed primarily to address the needs of the local consumers, only to be demanded by foreign consumers who have similar needs with a similar purchasing power. As the nature of new products and their manufacturing processes becomes widely disseminated over time, the products eventually become mass-produced standard products around the world. At that point, the products' cost competitiveness becomes a determinant of success and failure in global competition. Your knowledge of comparative advantage theory helps your company identify where strong low-cost competitors tend to appear and how the company should plan production locations.

As presented in Exhibit 1-5, the pattern of evolution of the production and marketing process explained in the international product cycle consists of four stages: introduction, growth, maturity, and decline. Let us explain the international product cycle from a U.S. point of view. It is to be reminded, however, that different kinds of product innovations also occur in countries (mostly developed) other than the United States. If so, a similar evolutionary pattern of development will begin from those other industrialized countries.

In the *introductory stage*, a U.S. company innovates on a new product to meet domestic consumers' needs in the U.S. market. A few other U.S. companies may introduce the same product. At this stage, competition is mostly domestic among U.S. companies. Some of those companies may begin exporting the product to a few European countries and Japan where they can find willing buyers similar to U.S. consumers. Product standards are not likely to be established yet. As a result, competing product models or specifications may exist on the market. Prices tend to be high. In the *growth stage*, product standards emerge and mass production becomes feasible. Lower prices spawn price competition. U.S. companies increase exports to Europe and Japan as those foreign markets expand. However, European and Japanese companies also begin producing the product in their own local markets and even begin exporting it to the United States. In the *maturity stage*, many U.S. and foreign companies vie for market share in the international markets. They try to lower prices and differentiate their products to outbid their competition. U.S. companies that have carved out market share in Europe and Japan by exporting decide to make a direct investment in production in those markets to protect their market position there. U.S. and foreign companies also begin to export to developing countries, because more consumers in those developing countries can afford the product as its price falls. Then, in the *decline stage*, companies in the developing countries also begin producing the product and marketing it in the rest of the world. U.S., European, and Japanese companies may also begin locating their manufacturing plants in those developing countries to take advantage of inexpensive labor. The United States eventually begins to import what was once a U.S. innovation.

The international product cycle argument holds true as long as we can assume that innovator companies are not informed about conditions in foreign markets, whether in other industrialized countries or in the developing world. As we amply indicated in Chapter 1, such an assumption has become very iffy. Nor can it be safely assumed that U.S. companies are exposed to a very different home environment from European and Japanese companies. Indeed, the differences among the industrialized countries are reduced to trivial dimensions. Seeking to exploit global scale economies, an increasing number of companies are likely to establish

---

[24]See, for example, Raymond Vernon, "International Investment and International Trade in the Product Cycle," *Quarterly Journal of Economics*, 80 (May 1966), pp. 190–207; "The Location of Economic Activity," *Economic Analysis and the Multinational Enterprise*, John H. Dunning, ed. (London: George Allen and Unwin, 1974), pp. 89–114; and "The Product Cycle Hypothesis in a New International Environment," *Oxford Bulletin of Economics and Statistics*, 41 (November 1979), pp. 255-67.

[25]Vernon, 1979.

EXHIBIT 1-5
INTERNATIONAL PRODUCT CYCLE

	Introduction	Growth	Maturity	Decline
Demand Structure	-Nature of demand not well understood -Consumers willing to pay premium price for a new product	-Price competition begins -Product standard emerging	-Competition based on price and product differentiation	-Mostly price competition
Production	-Short runs, rapidly changing techniques -Dependent on skilled labor	-Mass production	-Long runs with stable techniques -Capital intensive	-Long runs with stable techniques -Lowest cost production needed either by capital intensive production or by massive use of inexpensive labor
Innovator Company Marketing Strategy	-Sales mostly to home-country (e.g., U.S.) consumers -Some exported to other developed countries (e.g., Europe and Japan)	-Increased exports to the other developed countries (e.g., Europe and Japan)	-Innovator company (e.g., U.S.) begins production in Europe and Japan to protect its foreign market from local competition	-Innovator company (U.S.) may begin production in developing countries
International Competition	-A few competitors at home (e.g., U.S.)	-Competitors in developed countries (e.g., Europe and Japan) begin production for their domestic markets -They also begin exporting to the United States	-European and Japanese companies increase exports to the United States -They begin exporting to developing countries	-European and Japanese competitors may begin production in developing countries -Competitors from developing countries also begin exporting to the world

Source: Expanded on Louis T. Wells, Jr., "International Trade: The Product Life Cycle Approach," in Reed Moyer, ed., *International Business: Issues and Concepts* (New York: John Wiley, 1984), pp. 5–22.

various plants in both developed countries and developing countries, and to crosshaul between plants for the manufacture of final products. As an explanation of international business behavior, international product cycle theory has limited explanatory power. It does describe the initial international expansion (exporting followed by direct investment) of many companies, but the mature globetrotting companies of today have succeeded in developing a number of other strategies for surviving in global competition.

Internalization/Transaction Cost Theory
Now that many companies have established plants in various countries, they have to manage their corporate activities across national boundaries. Those companies are conventionally called *multinational companies*. It is inherently

much more complex and difficult to manage corporate activities and market products across national boundaries, rather than from a domestic base. Then why do those multinational companies invest in foreign manufacturing and marketing operations instead of just exporting from their home base? International product cycle theory explains that companies invest abroad reactively once their foreign market positions are threatened by local competitors. Thus, the primary objective of foreign direct investment for the exporting companies is to keep their market positions from being eroded. Are there any proactive reasons for companies to invest overseas?

To address this issue, a new strand of theory has been developed. It is known as **internalization** or **transaction cost theory**. Any company has some proprietary expertise that makes it different from its competitors. Without such expertise no company can sustain its competitive advantage. Such expertise may be reflected in a new product, unique product design, efficient production technique, or even brand image itself. As in the international product cycle argument, a company's expertise may eventually become common knowledge as a result of competitors copying it or reverse-engineering its product. Therefore, it is sometimes to an innovator company's advantage to keep its expertise to itself as long as possible in order to maximize the economic value of the expertise. A company's unique expertise is just like any information. Once information is let out, it becomes a "public good"—and free.

In other words, the multinational company can be considered an organization that uses its internal market to produce and distribute products in an efficient manner in situations where the true value of its expertise cannot be assessed in ordinary external business transactions. Generating expertise or knowledge requires the company to invest in research and development. In most circumstances, it is necessary for the company to overcome this appropriability problem by the creation of a monopolistic internal market (i.e., internalization) when the knowledge advantage can be developed and explored in an optimal manner on a global basis.[26] The motive to internalize knowledge is generally strong when the company needs to invest in business assets (e.g., manufacturing and marketing infrastructure) that have few alternative uses, uses those assets frequently, and faces uncertainty in negotiating, monitoring, and enforcing a contract. Such a situation suggests a high level of transaction costs due to specific assets and contractual uncertainty involved.[27]

The company's expertise can be channeled through three routes to garner competitive advantage: appropriability regime, dominant design, and manufacturing/marketing ability.[28] **Appropriability regime** refers to aspects of the commercial environment that govern a company's ability to retain its technological advantage. It depends on the efficacy of legal mechanisms of protection, such as patents, copyrights, and trade secrets. However, in today's highly competitive market, legal means of protecting proprietary technology have become ineffective as new product innovations are relatively easily reverse-engineered, improved upon, and invented around by competitors without violating patents and other proprietary protections bestowed on them. It is widely recognized that the most effective ways of securing maximum returns from a new product innovation are through lead time and moving fast down the experience curve (i.e., quickly resorting to mass production).[29] Obviously, the value of owning technology has lessened drastically in recent years as the inventor company's temporary monopoly over its technology has shortened.

Dominant design is a narrow class of product designs that begins to emerge as a "standard" design. A company that has won a dominant design status has an absolute competitive advantage over its competition. In an early stage of product development, many competing product designs exist. After considerable trial and error in the marketplace, a product standard tends to emerge. A good case example is Sony's Betamax format and Matsushita's VHS format for VCRs. The Betamax format was technologically superior with better picture quality than the VHS format, but could not play as long to record movies as the VHS. Although the Sony system was introduced slightly earlier than the Matsushita system, the tape's capability to record movies turned out to be fatal to Sony as the VHS tape was increasingly used for rental home movies and home recording of movies. Thus, the VHS has emerged as the worldwide standard for videocassette recording.

Was it simply the act of the "invisible hand" in the marketplace? The answer is clearly no. Matsushita actively licensed its VHS technology to Sanyo, Sharp, and Toshiba for production and supplied VHS-format videocassette recorders to RCA, Magnavox, and GTE Sylvania for resale under their respective brand names.[30] When Philips introduced a cassette tape recorder, a similar active licensing strategy had been employed for a quick adoption as a dominant standard around the world. Despite various government hurdles to stall the Japanese domination of emerging

[26]Alan M. Rugman, ed., New Theories of the Multinational Enterprise (London: Croom Helm, 1982).

[27]Oliver E. Williamson, "The Economics of Organization: The Transaction Cost Approach," *American Journal of Sociology*, 87 (1981), pp. 548–77.

[28]David J. Teece, "Capturing Value from Technological Innovation: Integration, Strategic Partnering, and Licensing Decisions," in Bruce R. Guile and Harvey Brooks, eds., *Technology and Global Industry: Companies and Nations in the World Economy* (Washington, D.C.: National Academy Press), pp. 65–95.

[29]Richard C. Levin, Alvin K. Klevorick, Richard R. Nelson, and Sidney G. Winter, "Appropriating the Returns from Industrial Research and Development," *Brookings Papers on Economic Activity*, 3 (1987), pp. 783–831.

[30]Richard S. Rosenbloom and Michael A. Cusumano, "Technological Pioneering and Competitive Advantage: The Birth of VCR Industry," *California Management Review*, 29 (Summer 1987), pp. 51–76.

HDTV technology, Sony is currently trying to make its format a standard by working its way into Hollywood movie studios. It is clear that a wide adoption of a new product around the world, whether autonomous or deliberated, seems to guarantee it a dominant design status.

Manufacturing and marketing ability is in almost all cases required for successful commercialization of a product innovation. The issue here is to what extent this ability is specialized to the development and commercialization of a new product. Indeed, many successful companies have highly committed their productive assets to closely related areas without diversifying into unrelated businesses. This commitment is crucial. Take semiconductor production for example. A director at SEMATECH (a U.S. government-industry semiconductor manufacturing technology consortium established in Austin, Texas, to regain U.S. competitive edge in semiconductor manufacturing equipment from Japanese competition) admits that despite and because of a rapid technological turnover, any serious company wishing to compete on a state-of-the-art computer chip with the Japanese will have to invest a minimum of a billion dollars in a semiconductor manufacturing equipment and facility. General Motors has invested more than $5 billion for its Saturn project to compete with the Japanese in small car production and marketing. A massive retooling is also necessary for any significant upgrade in both industries. Furthermore, the software side of the manufacturing ability may be even more difficult to match, as it involves such specialized operational aspects as JIT (just-in-time) manufacturing management, quality control, and components sourcing relationships. Irrespective of nationality, those multinational companies that are successful in global markets tend to excel not only in product innovative ability but also in manufacturing and marketing competencies.[31] It is clear that innovative companies committed to manufacturing and marketing excellence will likely remain strong competitors in industry.

These three sources of competitive advantage are not independent of each other. Given the relative ease of learning about competitors' proprietary knowledge without violating patents and other legal protections, many companies resort to mass production and mass marketing to drive down the cost along the experience curve. To do so requires enormous investment in manufacturing capacity. As a result, the efficacy of appropriability regime is highly dependent on investment in manufacturing and marketing ability. Similarly, a wide acceptance of a product is most likely necessary for the product to become a dominant design in the world for a next generation of the product. Thus, mass production and marketing on a global scale is likely to be a necessary, if not sufficient, condition for a company to attain a dominant design status for its product.

It is apparent that patents, copyrights, and trade secrets are not necessarily optimal means of garnering competitive advantage unless they are strongly backed by strengths in innovative manufacturing and marketing on a global basis. Likewise, companies strong in manufacturing without innovative products also suffer from competitive disadvantage. In other words, it takes such an enormous investment to develop new products and to penetrate new markets that few companies can go it alone anymore. Thus, to compete with integrated global competitors, an increasing number of companies have entered into strategic alliances so as to complement their competitive weaknesses with their partner's competitive strengths.

SUMMARY ✦

Three theories that cast some insight into the workings of international business have been reviewed. These theories are not independent of each other. Rather, they supplement each other. Comparative advantage theory is useful when we think broadly about the nature of industrial development and international trade around the world. International product cycle theory helps explain why and how a company initially extends its market horizons abroad and how foreign competitors shape global competition over time and place. Internalization or transaction cost theory provides some answers to how to manage multinational operations in a very competitive world.

There are other theories to supplement our understanding of international business. However, they are beyond the scope of this textbook and are probably unnecessary. Now you can appreciate how international business has expanded in scope over time. With understanding of these theories, we hope you can better understand the rest of the book.

---

[31]Masaaki Kotabe, "Corporate Product Policy and Innovative Behavior of European and Japanese Multinationals: An Empirical Investigation," *Journal of Marketing*, 54 (April 1990), pp. 19–33.

GLOBAL ECONOMIC ENVIRONMENT

2

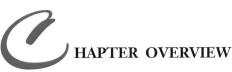

HAPTER OVERVIEW

1. INTERTWINED WORLD ECONOMY
2. ECONOMIC ENVIRONMENT WITHIN A NATION
3. ROLE OF THE GENERAL AGREEMENT ON TARIFFS AND TRADE (GATT) AND THE WORLD TRADE ORGANIZATION (WTO)
4. U.S. POSITION IN FOREIGN DIRECT INVESTMENT AND TRADE
5. INFORMATION TECHNOLOGY AND THE CHANGING NATURE OF COMPETITION
6. REGIONAL ECONOMIC ARRANGEMENTS
7. MULTINATIONAL CORPORATIONS

In no other time in economic history have countries been more economically interdependent than they are today. Although the second half of the twentieth century has seen the highest ever sustained growth rates in Gross Domestic Product (GDP) and Gross National Product (GNP) in the history of mankind, the growth in international flows in goods and services (called *international trade*) has consistently surpassed the growth rate of the world economy. Simultaneously, the growth in international financial flows—which includes foreign direct investment, portfolio investment, and trading in currencies—has achieved a life of its own. The annual trade in goods and services approached $10 trillion in 1997. Daily international financial flows now exceed $1 trillion. The barriers to international trade and financial flows keep getting lower. As a consequence, even a firm that is operating in only one domestic market is not immune to the influence of economic activities external to that market. The net result of these factors has been the increased interdependence of countries and economies, increased competitiveness, and the concomitant need for firms to keep a constant watch on the international economic environment.

◆ ◆ ◆ ◆ ◆ ◆ INTERTWINED WORLD ECONOMY

Despite the relative insularity of the U.S. economy, it too is getting increasingly integrated into the world economy. The dollar value of international trade in goods and services in 1995 for the United States (exports = $700 billion; imports = $810 billion) was $1.5 trillion.[1] Most of the trade in goods was with a few major trading partners, as shown in Exhibit 2-1.

Over the next two decades, however, the markets that hold the greatest potential for dramatic increases in U.S. exports are not the traditional trading partners in Europe and Japan, which now account for the overwhelming bulk of the international trade of the United States. Rather, the greatest commercial opportunities are to be found in ten **Big Emerging Markets** (BEMs): the Chinese Economic Area (CEA: including China, Hong Kong region, and Taiwan), India, South Korea, Mexico, Brazil, Argentina, South Africa, Poland, Turkey, and the Association of Southeast Asian Nations (ASEAN: including Indonesia, Brunei, Malaysia, Singapore, Thailand, the Philippines and Vietnam). Already, there are signs that in the future the biggest trade headache for the United States may not be Japan but China.[2] China's trade surplus with the United States in 1995 was $39 billion; with current trends it will surpass Japan's $59 billion surplus with the United States, which is on its way down. The World Economic Forum's global competitiveness report in 1995 placed Singapore and Hong Kong among the world's top four economies, along with the United

EXHIBIT 2-1
TOP TEN COUNTRIES WITH WHICH
THE U.S. TRADED MERCHANDISE
IN 1995

Country	Total Trade[1] (in US $billion)
Canada	271.16
Japan	187.78
Mexico	107.99
German	59.22
United Kingdom	55.71
Korea, Republic of	49.58
China	57.30
Taiwan	48.26
Singapore	33.88
France	31.49

[1]The values given are for Imports and Exports added together and represent 70.7 percent of U.S. imports, and 63.2 percent of U.S. exports in goods.

Source: U.S. Census Bureau, *Foreign Trade* (March 25, 1996).

---

[1]"U.S. Current Account Transactions," *International Economic Trends* (November 1995), pp. 28–29.

[2]"The New Trade Superpower," *Business Week* (October 16, 1995), pp. 56–57.

"The repairs will take awhile. We need a part from Mexico, a part from Brazil and one from Taiwan."

Even a simple "domestic" job involves inputs from various countries in an intertwined world.

States and Japan. Taiwan was ranked eighteenth and South Korea twenty-fourth, ahead of Spain, Portugal, and Italy.[3]

The importance of international trade and investment cannot be overemphasized for any country—including the United States—though the degree of importance varies by country. For the United States, international trade in goods and services has risen from 10 percent of the GNP in 1970 to about 23 percent in 1995.[4] For Germany, trade forms about 48 percent of the GNP, for Holland about 60 percent (not counting re-exports) and for Japan about 15 percent. Put another way, the U.S. exports and imports goods and services to the tune of $4,400 per year per person, while the comparable figure for Germany is $8,750. Developing countries like India and China tend to have lower percentages, but as they lower trade barriers and join the world economy, their percentages have also started rising. For instance, India's total international trade (exports and imports of goods and services) has risen from $15 billion in 1991 to $60 billion in 1995. This still amounts to only $66 per person per year of international trade. One implication of these figures is that the higher the per capita trade the more closely intertwined is that country's economy with the rest of the world. Intertwining of economies by the process of specialization due to international trade leads to job creation in both the exporting country and the importing country. In Washington state in the United States, one in five jobs depends on international trade.[5]

---

[3]"Now Asia's Tiger Economies are Joining the First World," *Asian Bulletin* (April 1995), pp. 2–3.

[4]"Stocktaking: Implementing the National Export Strategy," *Business America* (October 1995), pp. 28–65.

[5]"Deal is Near for Major Rail Link in NorthWest," *Wall Street Journal* (April 2, 1996), p. A2.

However, beyond the simple figure of trade as a rising percentage of a nation's GDP lies the more interesting question of what rising trade does to the economy of a nation. A nation that is a successful trader—i.e., it makes goods and services that other nations buy and it buys goods and services from other nations—displays a natural inclination to be competitive in the world market. The threat of a possible foreign competitor is a powerful incentive for firms and nations to invest in technology and markets in order to remain competitive. Also, apart from trade flows, foreign direct investment, portfolio investment, and daily financial flows in the international money markets profoundly influence the economies of countries that may be seemingly completely separate.

Foreign Direct Investment

Foreign direct investment—which means investment in manufacturing and service facilities in a foreign country—is another facet of the increasing integration of national economies. It can be thought of as an alternative to exports. As firms invest in manufacturing and distribution facilities outside their home countries to expand into new markets around the world, they have added to the stock of foreign direct investment. The increase in foreign direct investment is also promoted by efforts by many national governments to woo multinationals and by the leverage that the governments of large potential markets such as China and India have in granting access to multinationals. Sometimes trade friction can also promote foreign direct investment. Investment in the United States by Japanese companies is, to an extent, a function of the trade imbalances between the two nations and by the consequent pressure applied by the U.S. government on Japan to do something to reduce the bilateral trade deficit. Toyota Motors of Japan had a total investment of $3.9 billion in the United States and it makes more cars in the United States than it imports from Japan[6]—significantly, this reduces its vulnerability to retaliation by the United States under the Super 301 laws of the **Omnibus Trade and Competitiveness Act of 1988.**

Portfolio Investment

An additional facet to the rising integration of economies has to do with **portfolio investment** (or **indirect investment**) in foreign countries and with money flows in the international financial markets. Portfolio investment refers to investments in foreign countries that are withdrawable at short notice, such as investment in foreign stocks and bonds. In the international financial markets, the borders between nations have, for all practical purposes, disappeared.[7] The enormous quantities of money that get traded on a daily basis have assumed a life of their own. When trading in foreign currencies began, it was as an adjunct transaction to an international trade transaction in goods and services—banks and firms bought and sold currencies to complete the export or import transaction or to hedge the exposure to fluctuations in the ex-

---

[6]"The Japanese are Back—But This Time There's a Difference," *Business Week* (October 31, 1994), pp. 58–59.

[7]Kenichi Ohmae, *The Borderless World* (New York: Harper Collins Books, 1990).

change rates in the currencies of interest in the trade transaction. However, in today's international financial markets, traders trade currencies most of the time without an underlying trade transaction. They trade on the accounts of the banks and financial institutions they work for, mostly on the basis of daily news on inflation rates, interest rates, political events, stock and bond market movements, commodity supplies and demand, and so on. As mentioned earlier, the weekly volume of international trade in currencies exceeds the annual value of the trade in goods and services.

The effect of this proverbial tail wagging the dog is that all nations with even *partially* convertible currencies are exposed to the fluctuations in the currency markets. A rise in the value of the local currency due to these daily flows vis-à-vis other currencies makes exports more expensive (at least in the short run) and can add to the trade deficit or reduce the trade surplus. A rising currency value will also deter foreign investment in the country and will encourage outflow of investment.[8] It may also encourage a decrease in the interest rates in the country if the central bank of that country wants to maintain the currency exchange rate and a decrease in the interest rate would spur local investment. An interesting example is the Mexican meltdown in early 1995 and the massive devaluation of the peso, which was exacerbated by the withdrawal of money by foreign investors. The British sterling pound's turmoil before and after leaving the exchange rate mechanism of Europe is also an instance of the influence of these short-term movements of money.[9] These influences were far more powerful than an investment by a Japanese or German car maker.

Another example is provided by India, which was a largely protected market until 1991. Liberalization is on the way, and while the highest tariff rates have come down from 300 percent to 50 percent, the average tariff rate of 25 percent is still high when compared to tariffs in developed nations.[10] The Indian rupee has changed from being a nonconvertible currency to being convertible on the current account—that is, it is still only partially convertible. Despite these remaining barriers, the international money markets have started having an effect. The crash of the Mexican peso in December 1994 reverberated in India as well, because portfolio investors started viewing all emerging markets with a jaundiced eye. The Indian rupee was under pressure through much of 1995, falling from Rs 31.37/US$ to Rs. 38/US$ before recovering as investors regained confidence. The central bank had to sell dollars and buy rupees to shore up the value of the rupee. This led to a credit crunch, causing a slowdown in export growth.[11] There were adverse effects on the Indian stock markets as well. The point is that, at least in the short run, these daily international flows of money have dealt a blow to the notion of economic independence and nationalism.

Having made the case for increased global economic integration, it is also a fact that the United States continues to be relatively more insulated from the global economy than other nations. In a $6.5 trillion economy, a trade deficit of $150 billion is just 2.3 percent of the GDP. Foreigners owned only 6 percent of the stocks and 14 percent of the bonds in 1993, and despite a surge in overseas investing by Americans, more than 95 percent of the stocks and 97 percent of the bonds owned by

---

[8]"Hot Money," *Business Week* (March 20, 1995), pp. 46–50.

[9]"Multinationals: A Survey," *Economist* (March 27, 1993).

[10]"U.S. Trade Office Urges More Liberalization," *India Abroad* (April 12, 1996), p. 24.

[11]"Coping With a Crash," *Business World* (February 8–21, 1995), pp. 52–59.

Americans were still U.S. stocks and bonds in 1993.[12] About 90 percent of what Americans consume is produced in America—which implies that in the absence of a chain reaction from abroad, the United States is relatively more insulated from external shocks than Germany and China.

The dominant feature of the global economy, however, is that the *share of world output* from the developing nations is rising in a sustained manner, and it has been estimated to overtake the share of the current rich industrial nations before the year 2000 for the first time since about 1830, when China and India accounted for about 60 percent of the manufactured output of the world. If output is measured on the basis of purchasing power parities, then the share of developing nations (including the republics of the former Soviet Union) has been estimated to be 44 percent in 1993. The share of the world manufacturing output produced by the twenty or so countries that are today known as the rich industrial economies moved from about 30 percent in 1830 to almost 80 percent by 1913.[13] As late as 1830, China accounted for 30 percent of the world's manufactured output.

◆ ◆ ◆ ◆ ◆ ◆ ECONOMIC ENVIRONMENT WITHIN A NATION

Although the world economy is getting increasingly integrated, significant differences among the economies of individual nations are likely to persist for some time. These differences manifest themselves in the type of economic systems that are found in different countries. One way to visualize these differences is to look at the method of resource allocation and control and the type of property ownership in an economy. The method of resource allocation and control refers to where the national economy lies in the continuum between a **market economy** and a **command economy**. In a pure market economy the supply and demand of goods and services determine the price; the role of the government is minimal. In the command economy the government determines the supply and the prices and, therefore, the demand. The type of property ownership refers to whether ownership of productive resources in the economy is in private or public hands. Various economic environments are summarized in Exhibit 2-2.

Countries such as the U.S. fall at the **market-private** end of the table, while North Korea and Cuba would be at the **command-public** end of Exhibit 2-2. Most countries in the world would fall in the mixed-mixed box, where resource allocation is a mix of market forces and government-mandated dictates and ownership is partly private and partly public. An interesting sidelight to this discussion is that Western democratic societies have tended to gravitate toward the market-private mode of economics and totalitarian societies toward the command-public mode of economic operation.

This categorization is not without its shortcomings. Japan is very much a democratic society, and on paper its economy uses a market-private mode of operation. However, no economist or observer would say the American economy and the Japanese one operate on the same principles and assumptions. The U.S. government has much less direct control over industry and the economy. Pressure and lobbying

---

[12]"Global Mythmaking," *Newsweek* (May 8, 1995), p. 55.

[13]Paul Bairoch, "International Industrialization Levels from 1750 to 1980," *Journal of European Economic History*, 11 (1982), pp. 36–54.

EXHIBIT 2-2
INTERRELATIONSHIPS BETWEEN CONTROL OF ECONOMIC ACTIVITY AND
OWNERSHIP OF PRODUCTIVE RESOURCES

Ownership Control	Private	Mixed	Public
Market	Market-Private	Market-Mixed	Market-Public
Mixed	Market-Private	Market-Mixed	Market-Public
Command	Command-Private	Command-Mixed	Command-Public

Source: John D. Daniels and Lee H. Radebaugh, *International Business: Environment and Operations*, 7th ed. (Figure 4.1, page 120). © 1995 by Addison-Wesley Publishing Company, Inc. Reprinted by permission of Addison-Wesley Longman, Inc.

groups purporting to represent the people's views are often instrumental in determining economic policy. Firms are not only privately owned, but laws such as the Robinson–Patman Act and the Sherman Act prevent companies from colluding with each other, and the "markets" are thought to be the answer to all economic questions.

The Japanese economy, on the other hand, is characterized by *keiretsus*—groups of firms bound together by strong, informal ties and interlocking ownership. Not only do firms in Japan cooperate openly and thus appear to collude with one another, but also the government, through the Ministry of International Trade and Industry and the Ministry of Finance, has historically been more active in the development and implementation of an industrial policy. The very concept of an *industrial policy* raises furious debates in the United States. Therefore, it was folly for the Democrats under Bill Clinton even to talk about devising a national economic plan—as columnist George Will pointed out during the 1992 presidential campaign.[14] Despite differences, the U.S. and Japanese economies are more similar to one another than they are to the Chinese economy, which has moved from a command-public to the command-mixed mode.

Regardless of the mode of operation of a local economy, if there is one subject on which there is unanimity even among governments of different political hues, that subject is the importance of a telecommunications infrastructure to the economic growth of a nation. Emerging nations realize that they cannot develop their own economies and compete in the world markets without an efficient communications system (See Exhibit 2-3). There appears to be a highly positive relationship between the number of telephone lines per hundred people and the GDP of a nation. Realizing the importance of telecommunications, nation after nation is opening up its telecommunications markets. The developed nations are giving up telecommunications monopolies to increase efficiencies and the developing nations are privatizing their telecommunications operations and are welcoming foreign telecommunications firms. The opening of telecommunications markets is a major determinant of the flow of economic activity, even in developed countries. The opening of German telecommunications markets from 1998, for example, is expected to lead to major investments inflows.

---

[14]James Fallows, *Looking at the Sun* (New York: Pantheon Books, 1994).

EXHIBIT 2-3
TELECOMMUNICATIONS HOTSPOTS

	Main phone lines* per 100 people	Forecast for 2000 (lines/100)	Projected main lines to be added	Investment reqrmt ($ billions)**	Compound average growth rate (%)
ASIA					
China	0.98	3.50	35.5	$53.3	19.3
Thailand	3.10	9.35	4.4	6.6	16.7
India	1.10	2.50	15.2	21.5	12.9
EASTERN EUROPE					
Hungary	12.54	23.80	1.1	1.6	7.8
Poland	10.28	16.62	2.7	4.0	6.7
Russia	15.28	24.50	15.5	23.3	6.7
LATIN AMERICA					
Chile	8.92	19.71	1.8	2.8	12.3
Brazil	6.83	9.49	6.8	10.2	6.4
Mexico	7.54	12.49	6.3	9.4	8.5
UNITED STATES					
U.S.	54.69	65.92	37.2	55.8	2.9

*a main line connects a subscriber to a central switch

**all figures are in U.S. dollars

Source: "The Last Frontier," *Business Week*, (September 18, 1995), pp. 98–114. Reprinted from the September 18, 1995, issue of *Business Week* by special permission, copyright (c) 1995 by The McGraw-Hill Companies, Inc.

◆ ◆ ◆ ◆ ◆ ◆ ROLE OF THE GENERAL AGREEMENT ON TARIFFS AND TRADE (GATT) AND THE WORLD TRADE ORGANIZATION

General Agreements on Tariffs and Trade

In the aftermath of World War II, the then-big powers negotiated the setting up of an **International Trade Organization** (ITO), with the objective of ensuring free trade among nations through negotiated lowering of trade barriers. ITO would have been an international organization operating under the umbrella of the United Nations with statutory powers to enforce agreements. However, when the U.S. government announced, in 1950, that it would not seek congressional approval for the Havana Charter, ITO was effectively dead. Instead, to keep the momentum of increasing trade through the lowering of trade barriers alive, the signatories to ITO agreed to operate under the informal aegis of the **General Agreements on Tariffs and Trade** (GATT). GATT provided a forum for multilateral discussion among countries to reduce trade barriers. Nations met periodically to review the status of world trade and to negotiate mutually agreeable reductions in trade barriers.

The main operating principle of GATT was the concept of **Most Favored Nation** (MFN) status. The MFN status meant that any country that was a member state to a GATT agreement and that extended a reduction in tariff to another nation would have to automatically extend the same benefit to all members of GATT. However, there was no enforcement mechanism, and over time many countries negotiated bilateral agreements, especially for agricultural products, steel, textiles and automobiles. As Global

◆ ◆

GLOBAL PERSPECTIVE 2-1

TRADE BARRIERS, HYPOCRISY, AND THE UNITED STATES

The United States thinks of itself as a leading exponent of free trade and frequently brings actions against other nations as unfair trade partners. Section 301 of the Omnibus Trade and Competitiveness Act empowers the federal government to investigate and retaliate against specific foreign trade barriers judged to be unfair by the United States and to impose up to 100 percent tariffs on exports to the United States from guilty nations unless they satisfy U.S. criteria for fairness. But critics say that the United States is sometimes hypocritical in such actions, because it is as guilty of the very acts of which it is accusing other nations. A Japanese government study alleges that the United States engages in unfair trade practices in ten of the twelve policy areas looked at in the study. This Japanese study suggests that the U.S. quotas on imports has high tariffs and abuses anti-dumping measures.

The United States launched a Section 301 investigation of Japanese citrus quotas. "The removal of Japan's unfair trade barriers could cut the prices of oranges for Japanese consumers by up to a third, according to the U.S. trade representative." Coincidentally, the United States had a 40 percent tariff on Brazilian orange juice imports when the investigation was initiated. The United States used Section 301 against Korea for its beef import quotas, even though the U.S. has beef import quotas that cost U.S. consumers up $870 million in higher prices.

Sources: Abstracted from James Bovard, "A U.S. History of Trade Hypocrisy," *Wall Street Journal* (March 8, 1994), p. A10; "The Great Trade Violator?" *World Press Review* (August 1994), p. 41; Robert S. Greenberger, "Washington Will Boycott WTO Panel," *Wall Street Journal* (February 21, 1997), p. A2; and Michael R. Czinkota and Masaaki Kotabe, "A Marketing Perspective of the U.S. International Trade Commission's Antidumping Actions: An Empirical Inquiry," *Journal of World Business*, 32 (Spring 1997).

Another case was brought against Brazil, Korea, and Taiwan for trade barriers on footwear, even though the United States, at the time of the bringing of the case, had tariffs as high as 67 percent on footwear imports. Many Section 301 complaints have involved agricultural export subsidies, including European Union poultry export subsidies, EU wheat and wheat export subsidies, and Taiwan rice export subsidies. However, in recent years, the United States has provided export subsidies of 111 percent for poultry, 78 percent for wheat flour, 94 percent for wheat, and more than 100 percent for rice.

So, is the United States as guilty as the rest or not? Examining 310 cases filed with the U.S. International Trade Commission (ITC), one recent study has shown unequivocally that the ITC tends to support with an antidumping charge not only those fragmented industries with a declining market, but also more concentrated industries with a stable or even growing market. This finding indicates that for large U.S. firms, antidumping regulations may even be useful as a strategic competitive tool. In other words, like any other country, the U.S. tries to protect what it perceives to be its trade interests—and some of these interests are often driven by local political considerations. The advent of the World Trade Organization (WTO) and the establishment of procedures for hearing and adjudicating complaints will hopefully lead to a reduction in unilateral actions by all countries—including the United States. This means that local political interests will be less able to determine trade policies—which, in a sense, is an infringement of national sovereignty. Infringement of national sovereignty has long been a reason for opposition against lowering trade barriers and forming organizations like WTO in the United States.

At the time of writing this book, the United States is contemplating a boycott of a WTO's panel requested by the European Union to review the legality of certain U.S. trade sanctions against Cuba.

Perspective 2-1 shows, the United States also frequently violated the GATT principles and resorted to unilateral trade sanctions against foreign trading partners.

Although GATT was successful in lowering trade barriers to a substantial extent during its existence from 1948 to 1994, some major shortcomings limited its potential and effectiveness. The initial rounds of GATT concentrated only on the lowering of tariff barriers. As trade in services expanded faster than the trade in goods and

GATT concentrated on merchandise trade, more and more international trade came to be outside the purview of GATT. Second, GATT tended to concentrate mostly on tariffs, and many nations used nontariff barriers to get around the spirit of GATT when they could not increase tariffs. Finally, as developed nations moved from manufacturing-based economies to services- and knowledge-based economies, they felt the need to bring intellectual property within the purview of international agreement, because that was where the competitive advantage lay for firms in the developed nations.

World Trade Organization

The seventh and last round of GATT talks—called the **Uruguay Round**—lasted from 1986 to 1993 and was successful in bringing many agricultural products and textiles under the purview of GATT. It also included provisions for trade in intellectual property for the first time and provided for many services. Most important, perhaps, it set up an international body called the **World Trade Organization** (WTO), which took effect on January 1, 1995. WTO has statutory powers to adjudicate trade disputes among nations. The agreement provides for setting up a permanent international organization (i.e., the World Trade Organization or WTO) headed by a director-general to oversee the smooth functioning of the multilateral trade accords agreed upon under the Uruguay Round. The WTO is the new legal and institutional foundation for a multilateral trading system. It provides the contractual obligations determining how governments frame and implement domestic trade legislation and regulations. Moreover, it is the platform on which trade relations among countries evolve through collective debate, negotiation, and adjudication.

One of the objectives of the developed nations in the Uruguay Round was to get developing nations (primarily Brazil, China, and India) to agree to accept intellectual property rights for product patents in pharmaceuticals, chemicals, and food products. By and large, developing nations have tended not to grant product patents for pharmaceuticals, chemicals, and food products—only process patents have been granted. Thus, many international pharmaceutical firms have complained that the drugs that they produce at a great cost get reproduced at a lower cost by a different process in developing nations like India and China. The justification that the developing nations have given is that if they did not do so, life-saving drugs would be priced out of reach of all but the very rich. As a result of the Uruguay Round, developing nations have agreed to phase in product patents in these areas by the year 2005.[15] Partly as a *quid pro quo* to this agreement, the developed nations have given concessions in other areas, such as the agreement to phase out over ten years beginning 1995 the Multi-Fibre Agreement, which restricted textile exports from the developing countries.[16] Developing country exporters will still face one old problem—add value and the tariff goes up—that is, manufactured goods face a higher tariff than agricultural goods. Exhibit 2-4 gives an idea of the scope of the Uruguay Round of GATT that is manifested through WTO.

---

[15]"A Little Giving, A Little Taking," *Business World* (January 25–February 7, 1995), pp. 46–49.

[16]"The Uruguay Round: Winners and Winners," *World Bank Policy Research Bulletin*, vol. 6, no. 1 (January–February), pp. 2–3.

Exhibit 2-4

A Summary of the Final Act of the Uruguay Round of GATT

- Introduction
- Agreement Establishing the WTO (World Trade Organization)
- General Agreement on Tariffs and Trade 1994
- Uruguay Round Protocol GATT 1994
- Agreement on Agriculture
- Agreement on Sanitary and Phytosanitary Measures
- Decision on Measures Concerning the Possible Negative Effects of the Reform Program on Least-Developed and Net Food-Importing Developing Countries
- Agreement on Textiles and Clothing
- Agreement on Technical Barriers to Trade
- Agreement on Trade-Related Investment Measures
- Agreement on Implementation of Article VI (Anti-Dumping)
- Agreement on Implementation of Article VII (Customs Valuation)
- Agreement on Preshipment Inspection
- Agreement on Rules of Origin
- Agreement on Import Licensing Procedures
- Agreement on Subsidies and Countervailing Measures
- Agreement on Safeguards
- General Agreement on Trade in Services
- Agreement on Trade-Related Aspects of Intellectual Property Rights, Including Trade in Counterfeit Goods
- Understanding on Rules and Procedures Governing the Settlement of Disputes
- Decision of Achieving Greater Coherence in Global Economic Policy-Making

Source: World Trade Organization (http://www.unic.org/wto/ursum-wpf.html), 1996.

Incidentally, the WTO is not simply an extension of GATT. The GATT was a multilateral agreement with no institutional foundations. The WTO is a permanent institution with its own secretariat. The GATT was applied on a provisional basis in strict legal terms. WTO commitments are full and permanent and legally binding under international law. Although GATT was restricted to trade in merchandise goods, WTO includes trade in services and trade-related aspects of intellectual property. It is to be noted that GATT lives on within WTO. The Uruguay Round resulting in GATT, 1994, is an integral part of WTO.

Finally, the WTO dispute settlement mechanism is faster, more automatic, and therefore much less susceptible to blockages than the old GATT system. Once a country indicates to WTO that it has a complaint about the trade practices of another country, an automatic schedule kicks in. The two countries have three months for mutual "consultations" to iron out their differences. If the disputants cannot come to a mutually satisfactory settlement, then the dispute is referred to the Dispute Settlement Mechanism of WTO, under which a decision has to be rendered within six months of the setting up of the panel to resolve the dispute. The decision of the panel is legally binding. Global Perspective 2-2 provides as an example a banana import dispute against the European Union brought by the United States and four Latin American banana-producing countries.

Financial Services in WTO/GATT. Key developed powers and emerging and ex-communist economies, brushing aside a U.S. refusal to join them in a wide-ranging pact opening up global trade in financial services, agreed to a pact that went into

◆ ◆

$\mathcal{G}$LOBAL PERSPECTIVE 2-2

WTO DISPUTE PANEL WORKS DESPITE BLOCKS

In April 1996, the European Union (EU) blocked immediate creation of a dispute panel in the World Trade Organization (WTO) over its controversial banana-import regime. The panel had been requested by the United States and four Latin American banana-producer countries—Guatemala, Honduras, Ecuador, and Mexico. EU told the WTO Dispute Settlement Body (DSB) that consultations to try to find a solution had not yet been exhausted and could not yet agree on formation of a panel, the sources said. But under DSB rules, the EU was not able to block a decision at the following meeting of the body, which took place on May 8, and a panel—which had six months to make its findings known—was automatically created.

Source: clari.biz.world_trade, April 24, 1996.

The five countries argued that the EU banana import regime introduced in July 1993 violated WTO open trade rules because it discriminates in favor of producers from the African, Caribbean, and Pacific (ACP) countries. Two panels set up under the WTO's predecessor, the General Agreement on Tariffs and Trade (GATT), found against Brussels. But under GATT's looser rules, the EU was able to block adoption of the findings by the old trade watchdog. Under the WTO, the EU could appeal against a finding that went against it, but if it lost it would then be ordered to either bring the banana regime into line with the rules or pay compensation to the five. Although not a producer, the United States joined the dispute with the four Latin American states because it argued the EU banana-trade licensing system discriminated against firms outside the Union, including major U.S. companies.

effect in July 1996. The accord, signed in July 1995, was approved by twenty-nine members of the World Trade Organization (WTO), the new global commerce watchdog. Some of its provisions were applied in many countries immediately. But the deal—covering the booming multibillion-dollar trade in banking, insurance, and securities—involves a total of forty-three countries, as the European Union, its main promoter, speaks in the WTO for all its fifteen member states. Additionally, under most-favored-nation (MFN) rules, it will be extended to about fifty more current and pending WTO members with commitments in the sector—ironically, including the United States, which argues the pact does not go far enough.[17]

Among major backers of the deal apart from the EU were Japan, Canada, and Australia from the established economies; India, Malaysia, South Korea, Indonesia, and Singapore in Asia; and Brazil, Chile, and Venezuela in Latin America. For the average person using banks, buying insurance, and selling shares, a WTO spokesman said, "it will mean more providers to choose from, which means more competition, and that should mean a better deal for consumers." For the finance industry in industrialized countries, it will bring guaranteed access—although at varying levels—to the fiercely protected domestic markets of the emerging and transition economies, including Poland and Hungary.

India, for example, has pledged to allow up to 49 percent of foreign equity in stockbroker firms and permit opening of eight instead of five foreign banks or branches a year. Cash-dispensing machines will no longer be counted as branches. Brazil will allow a wider foreign role in the privatization of state-owned banks, while South Korea will raise the limit on foreign investment in domestic companies from

[17]"Financial Services Trade Pact Agreed: U.S. Stands Aside," *Reuters* (July 28, 1995).

10 to 15 percent. The accord officially runs to the end of 1997, when in principle sig-natories can pull out or seek renegotiation. But trade officials say the most likely sce-nario is that it will be extended and improved for a further period. It is the first major deal under the WTO to absorb of the old GATT, and the first big international trade accord since World War II that left out the United States. Washington, under pres-sure from Congress and parts of the U.S. financial service industry, argued that opening offers from developing countries were not enough to justify it throwing wide its domestic market to all other WTO members.

But the EU, which says its companies in the sector will now have access to 90 percent of all world financial business because it already has a bilateral deal with the United States, insisted the package was a good interim deal that could be improved later. Today's achievement should be considered as a key step forward, but by no means the end of the process. In 1997 the review would be an opportunity for fur-ther liberalization. The twenty-nine WTO members who joined the accord were those that improved on offers made in the GATT's seven-year Uruguay Round ne-gotiations. The U.S. government says it will continue talking about a full global pact it could join. But trade diplomats say they doubt this will come for some time—per-haps not before the year 2000, when all WTO service accords are up for review.

U.S. POSITION IN FOREIGN DIRECT INVESTMENT AND TRADE

◆ ◆ ◆ ◆ ◆ ◆ ◆

Foreign direct investment refers to the investment by firms in one nation to create pro-ductive facilities in another nation. In 1993, U.S. firms invested $50 billion over-seas—four times as much as Japanese firms and nearly twice as much as British firms.[18] Cumulative U.S.-owned assets abroad valued at historical cost exceeded $1.5 trillion in 1995. Inflows of foreign direct investment from the developed nations into the developing countries was estimated to be around $100 billion in 1995, with 60 percent of that investment going to Asia.[19] The United States has always been in the forefront of investing in other countries in the twentieth century—much like Britain was in the nineteenth century. In attracting $26 billion of foreign investment in 1995, China was the favorite developing country destination. India appears to be on track to become the next favorite foreign direct investment destination if its eco-nomic liberalization process continues.

U.S. Direct Investment Overseas

The United States has been a significant investor overseas since 1945. The first wave of major investment was part of the Marshall Plan in the 1950s to revitalize the Eu-ropean industries that had been devastated by World War II. The Marshall Plan was not entirely an altruistic gesture. The exigencies of the Cold War required that Western Europe be an economically and militarily strong region. The destruction

---

[18]"Foreign Investment By Multinationals Rebounds, Benefiting China, UN Says," *Wall Street Journal* (August 31, 1994), A2, A5.

[19]Paul Krugman, "Does Third World Growth Hurt First World Prosperity," *Harvard Business Review*, 72 (July–August 1994), pp. 113–121.

EXHIBIT 2-5
U.S. DIRECT INVESTMENT ABROAD
($BILLIONS)

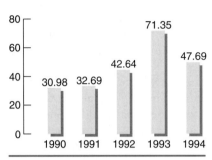

Source: Survey of Current Business, IMF
Papers, Various Issues up to 1996

caused by the Second World War meant that left to their own resources, the countries of Western Europe would have taken a long time to recover and may have proven to be tempting targets for a communist takeover—a prospect that was to be avoided all costs. Also, a vibrant Europe would be an attractive market for American goods and services.

Direct investment abroad continued to grow over the years, with a spurt in the early 1980s. The rise in foreign direct investment was partly due to the massive appreciation of the dollar in the early 1980s. In the late 1980s, the dollar depreciated in value by as much as 50 percent compared to its peak in 1985. The depreciation of the dollar was responsible for a fall in foreign direct investment outflow from the United States and a rise in foreign direct investment inflow into the United States. Exhibit 2-5 shows the direct investment abroad from the United States on a yearly basis. Most of U.S. investment abroad has been concentrated in Europe in general and in Britain in particular. In the 1990s, however, U.S. direct investment has started flowing in increasing amounts into Asian countries, especially into the countries that have been classified as the emerging markets.

Foreign Direct Investment in the United States

Foreign direct investment in the United States, on the other hand, has historically remained at more modest levels in the twentieth century before commencing a sharp climb in the 1980s. Exhibit 2-6 shows foreign direct investment in the United States from 1980 through 1995. Part of the reason for the surge in foreign investment in the United States in the late 1980s (which peaked at $72 billion in 1988) was the fall in the value of the dollar, which made it attractive for investors with stronger currencies such as the Japanese yen and the German mark to buy U.S. assets at bargain-basement prices (this was the same period in which the United States ran its largest trade deficits). For example, in 1989 Japanese firms purchased Rockefeller Center and MCA. Exhibit 2-7 shows the cumulative stock of foreign direct investment from the ten largest investors. Firms based in Britain and the Netherlands have traditionally been the largest investors in the United States, though in recent years, Japanese firms have overtaken them to hold the first spot.

EXHIBIT 2-6
FOREIGN DIRECT INVESTMENT OUTLAYS IN THE UNITED STATES, 1980–1995

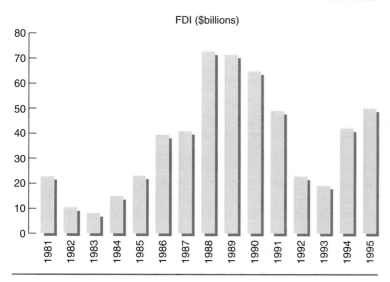

FDI ($billions)

Source: U.S. Department of Commerce, 1996

Balance of Payments Position

As far as the balance of payments position is concerned, the United States has run a persistent deficit on the current account since the first oil shock in 1973. The deficit on the merchandise trade account seems to keep rising with time—and the media exacerbates matters by focusing only on the merchandise trade account—when the fact

EXHIBIT 2-7
FOREIGN DIRECT INVESTMENT STOCK IN THE UNITED STATES, 1986–1994
FOR SIX LARGEST COUNTRIES[20]
($ BILLIONS AT YEAR END—HISTORICAL VALUE)

	1986	1987	1988	1989	1990	1991	1992	1993	1994
Japan	23.4	34.4	51.1	67.3	83.5	95.1	99.6	99.2	103.1
United Kingdom	51.4	75.5	95.7	105.5	108.8	100.4	90.4	102.3	113.5
Netherlands	42.9	46.6	48.1	56.3	64.3	63.1	69.2	72.2	70.6
Canada	18.3	24.7	26.6	30.4	29.5	36.8	37.8	40.1	43.2
Germany	17.4	21.9	25.3	29.0	27.3	28.6	29.2	34.8	39.6
France	7.4	10.1	13.2	16.8	19.6	24.2	23.8	n.a.	n.a.
Switzerland	12.1	13.8	14.4	18.8	17.5	19.2	19.6	19.6	25.3

Source: Statistical Abstracts of the United States (Washington, D.C.: Bureau of Statistics, Treasury Department, various issues up to 1996).

---

[20]See also, Robert Grosse and Len J. Trevino, "Foreign Direct Investment in the United States: An Analysis by Country of Origin," *Journal of International Business Studies,* 27 (1) (1996), pp. 139–55.

is that the United States has been running a persistent surplus on the services trade account during the same period. The fact that by a historical quirk of convention merchandise trade data are accumulated by the U.S. Department of Commerce on a monthly basis, while the services trade data are available only on a quarterly basis, also tends to highlight the merchandise trade deficit.

In the context of trade deficits, there is increasing concern that the *conventional measures* of the deficit may not be an accurate reflection of a country's transactions with the rest of the world. For example, when a wholly owned subsidiary of Texas Instruments in Japan sells microprocessors to a firm in Malaysia, should it show up as an export from Japan to Malaysia or as American export to Malaysia? Under current accounting rules, this transaction shows as a Japanese export to Malaysia. America's National Academy of Sciences (NAS) has suggested measuring trade entirely on the basis of ownership. It defines exports as the sum of three numbers: cross-border sales to foreigners; net sales to foreigners by subsidiaries abroad; and sales by American firms to American subsidiaries of foreign firms. The NAS's approach would result in the United States showing a whopping trade surplus of $164 billion for 1991.[21] If only the net sales by foreign subsidiaries were included, the U.S. would have a surplus of $24 billion on the trade in goods and services against the deficit of $28 billion shown by the conventional trade accepting method. As multinationals spread throughout the world and a substantial proportion of international trade consists of intra-firm transfer, this question will assume increasing importance in the future. Exhibits 2-8 through 2-10 present the data for trade in goods and services together,

EXHIBIT 2-8
U.S. INTERNATIONAL TRADE IN GOODS & SERVICES (BILLION DOLLARS) 1981–1995

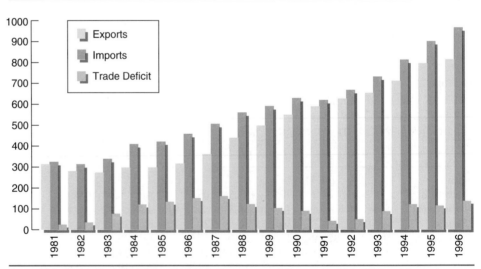

Source: U.S. Foreign Trade Highlights 1995, U.S. Department of Commerce, ITA, 1995 and *Economist Intelligence Unit Country Report*, New York, 1st Quarter, 1997.

[21]"Grossly Distorted Picture," *Economist* (February 5, 1994), p. 71; and William G. Shepherd and Dexter Hutchins, "There's No Trade Deficit, Sam!" *Financial World* (February 23, 1988), pp. 28–32.

EXHIBIT 2-9

U.S. INTERNATIONAL TRADE IN GOODS (BILLION DOLLARS) 1981–1995

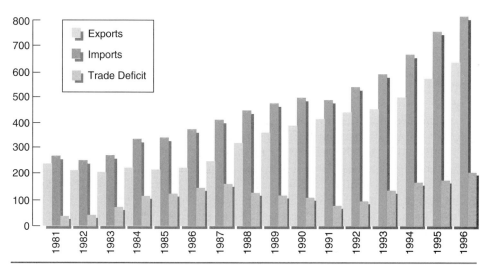

Source: U.S. Foreign Trade Highlights 1995, U.S. Department of Commerce, ITA, 1995 and *Economist Intelligence Unit Country Report*, New York, 1st Quarter, 1997.

goods separately, and services separately respectively, based on the current conventional method of accounting for international trade transactions. Note that while the trade deficit remains substantial, it has declined substantially as a percentage of the sum of imports and exports and as a percentage of the U.S. GDP since peaking in 1987.

EXHIBIT 2-10

U.S. INTERNATIONAL TRADE IN SERVICES (BILLION DOLLARS) 1981–1995

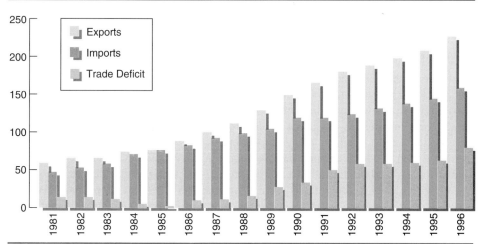

Source: U.S. Foreign Trade Highlights 1995, U.S. Department of Commerce, ITA, 1995 and *Economist Intelligence Unit Country Report*, New York, 1st Quarter, 1997.

◆ ◆ ◆ ◆ ◆ ◆ INFORMATION TECHNOLOGY AND THE CHANGING NATURE OF COMPETITION

As the nature of value-adding activities in developed nations shifts more and more to information creation, manipulation, and analysis, the developed nations have started taking an increased interest in Trade Related Intellectual Property measures (TRIPs). Imagine a farmer in the nineteenth century headed into the twentieth century. The intrinsic value of food will not go away in the new century, but as food becomes cheaper and cheaper to produce, the share of the economy devoted to agriculture will shrink (in the United States agriculture contributes less than 3 percent to the GDP) and so will the margins for the farmer. It would be advisable to move into manufacturing, or at least into food processing, to maintain margins.

An analogous situation faces a content maker for **information-related products** such as software, music, movies, newspapers, magazines, and education in the late-twentieth century headed into the twenty-first century. Until now, content has always been manifested physically—first in people who knew how to do things; then in books, sheet music, records, newspapers, loose-leaf binders, and catalogs; and most recently in tapes, discs, and other electronic media. At first, information could not be "copied": it could only be reimplemented or transferred. People could build new machines or devices that were copies of or improvements on the original; people could tell each other things and share wisdom or techniques to act upon. (Reimplementation was cumbersome and re-use did not take away from the original, but the process of building a new implementation—a new machine or a trained apprentice—took considerable time and physical resources.)

Later, with symbols, paper, and printing presses, people could copy knowledge, and it could be distributed in "fixed" media; performances could be transcribed and recreated from musical scores or scripts. Machines could be mass-produced. With such mechanical and electronic media, intellectual value could easily be reproduced, and the need (or demand from creators) to protect intellectual property arose. New laws enabled owners and creators to control the production and distribution of copies of their works. Although reproduction was easy, it was still mostly a manufacturing process, not something an individual could do easily. It took time and money. Physical implementation contributed a substantial portion of the cost.

Value of Intellectual Property in Information Age

However, with the advent of the Information Age, firms are faced with a new situation; not only is it easy for individuals to make duplicates of many works or to re-use their content in new works, but the physical manifestation of content is almost irrelevant. Over the Internet, any piece of **electronically represented intellectual property** can be almost instantly copied anywhere in the world. Since more and more of value creation in the developed nations is coming from the development and sale of such information-based intellectual property, it is no surprise that developed nations are highly interested in putting strong international intellectual property laws in place. The U.S. insistence on the inclusion of provisions relating to intellectual property in GATT and WTO is a direct consequence. Technology-based protection of electronic information through hardware, software, or a combination thereof in the form of encryption and digital signatures has been suggested as the means of circumventing the problem of unauthorized copying.[22]

Controlling copies (once created by the author or by a third party), however, becomes a complex challenge. A firm can either control something very tightly, limiting distribution to a small, trusted group, or it can rest assured that eventually its product will find its way to a large nonpaying audience—if anyone cares to have it in the first place. But creators of content on the Internet still face the eternal problem: the value of their work generally will not receive recognition without wide distribution. Only by attracting broad attention can an artist or creator hope to attract high payment for copies. Thus, on the Internet, the creators give first performances or books (or whatever) away widely in hopes of recouping with subsequent works. But that breadth of distribution lessens the creator's control of who gets copies and what they do with them. In principle, it should be possible to control and charge for such widely disseminated works, but it will become more and more difficult. People want to pay only for what is perceived as scarce—a personal performance or a custom application, or some tangible manifestation that cannot easily be reproduced (by nature or by fiat; that is why the art world has numbered lithographs, for example).

The trick may be to control not the copies of the firm's information product but instead a relationship with the customers—subscriptions or membership. And that is often what the customers want, because they see it as an assurance of a continuing supply of reliable, timely content. Thus, the role of marketing may be expected to assume increasing importance. A firm can, of course, charge a small amount for mass copies. Metering schemes will allow vendors to charge—in fractions of a penny, if desired—according to usage or users rather than copies. However, it will not much change the overall approaching-zero trend of content pricing. At best, it will make it much easier to charge those low prices.

There are other hurdles for content creators with the emergence of electronic commerce. One is the rise of a truly efficient market for information. Content used to be **unfungible**: it was difficult to replace one item with another. But most information is not unique, though its creators like to believe so. There are now *specs* for content such as stock prices, search criteria, movie ratings, and classifications. In the world of software, for instance, it is becoming easier to define and create products equivalent to a standard. Unknown vendors who can guarantee functionality will squeeze the prices of the market leaders. Of course the leaders (such as Microsoft) can use almost-free content to sell ancillary products or upgrades, because they *are* the leaders and because they have reinvested in loyal distribution channels. The content is advertising for the dealers who resell, as well as for the vendors who create. This transformation in the form of value creation and ease of dissemination implies a jump in economic integration as nations become part of an international electronic commerce network. Not only money but also products and services will flow faster.

The other consequence of fungible content, information products, and electronic networks is an additional assault on the power of national governments to regulate international commerce (See Global Perspective 2-3). Ford uses a product design process whereby designers at Dearborn, Michigan, pass on their day's work in an

---

[22]Ravi Kalaktota and Andrew B. Whinston, *Frontiers of Electronic Commerce* (Reading, Mass.: Addison Wesley, 1996). See Chapter 15.

◆ ◆

$\mathcal{G}$LOBAL PERSPECTIVE 2-3

THE REAL TRUTH ABOUT THE ECONOMY

Because the economies of the developed nations are becoming information intensive—are becoming knowledge economies—the data regarding these economies are coming under increasing scrutiny. The methods of collating data relating to economies were developed in a time when today's developed economies were primarily producers of agricultural and manufactured goods—when the service and information sector of the economy was very small.

For example, business investment in equipment, after adjusting for depreciation, is fully 30 percent higher than the government statistics because the data captures only a fraction of the money that firms spend on software, employee skill upgrades, and telecommunication equipment. Estimates of inflation may also be overstated because they

Adapted from "The Real Truth About the Economy," *Business Week* (November 7, 1994), p. 110.

do not take into account the productivity gains that firms have brought about over the last decade.

From a trade perspective this has two implications. Wrong inflation estimates misstate the value of the dollar in the international money markets because markets take into account the rate of inflation. Additionally, the government no longer classifies exports and imports by whether they are for final sales or for assembly purposes. So it is not clear whether semiconductor chips shipped to South Korea will be plugged into a VCR for sale in Eugene, Oregon, or in Pusan, Korea. This makes it much more difficult to trace net imports and exports.

Furthermore, trade statistics shape the economic climate in which policy decisions are made. In the debate over the 1988 Omnibus Trade Law, which provided U.S. firms with a weapon to defend themselves against foreign competition, the then-available data suggested a trade deficit of $171 billion. Later revisions and the inclusion of trade in services reduced the deficit to $151 billion.

electronic form to an office in Japan, who then pass the baton along to designers in Britain, who pass it back to Dearborn the next day. When the information represented in the design crosses borders, how do the governments of the United States, Japan, and Britain treat this information? How will such exchanges be regulated? Less-open societies like China and Singapore, recognizing the power of electronic networks, are already attempting to regulate the infrastructure of and access to the electronic network.

◆ ◆ ◆ ◆ ◆ ◆ REGIONAL ECONOMIC ARRANGEMENTS

An evolving trend in international economic activity is the formation of multinational trading blocs. These blocs take the form of a group of contiguous countries that decide to have common trading policies for the rest of the world in terms of tariffs and market access but have preferential treatment for one another. Organizational form varies among market regions, but the universal reason for the formation of such groups is to ensure the economic growth and benefit of the participating countries. Regional cooperative agreements have proliferated after the end of World War II. Among the more well-known ones existing today are the European Union and the North American Free Trade Agreement. Some of the lesser-known ones include the MERCOSUR (Southern Cone Free Trade Area) and the Andean Group in South America, the Gulf Cooperation Council in West Asia (GCC), the South Asian Agreement for Regional Cooperation in South Asia (SAARC) and the Association of

South East Asian Nations (ASEAN). The existence and growing influence of these multinational groupings implies that nations need to become part of such groups to remain globally competitive. To an extent, the regional groupings reflect the countervailing force to the increasing integration of the global economy—it is an effort by governments to control the pace of the integration.

Market groups take many forms, depending on the degree of cooperation and inter-relationships, which lead to different levels of integration among the participating countries. There are five levels of formal cooperation among member countries of these regional groupings, ranging from free trade area to the ultimate level of integration—which is political union.

Before the formation of a regional group of nations for freer trade, some governments agree to participate jointly in projects that create economic infrastructure (such as dams, pipelines, roads) and that decrease the levels of barriers from a level of little or no trade to substantial trade. Each country may make a commitment to financing part of the project, such as India and Nepal did for a hydroelectric dam on the Gandak River. Alternatively, they may share expertise on rural development and poverty alleviation programs, may lower trade barriers in selected goods such as in SAARC, which comprises India, Pakistan, Sri Lanka, Bangladesh, Nepal, Maldives, and Bhutan. This type of loose cooperation is considered a precursor to a more formal trade agreement.

Free Trade Area

A **Free Trade Area** has a higher level of integration than a loosely formed regional cooperation and is a formal agreement among two or more countries to reduce or eliminate customs duties and nontariff trade barriers among partner countries. However, member countries are free to maintain individual tariff schedules for countries that do not belong to the free trade group. The North American Free Trade Agreement (NAFTA) is the free trade agreement among Canada, the United States, and Mexico. It provides for elimination of all tariffs on industrial products traded between Canada, Mexico, and the United States within a period of ten years from the date of implementation of the NAFTA agreement—January 1, 1994. NAFTA was preceded by the free trade agreement between Canada and the United States, which went into effect in 1989. The United States has a free trade area agreement with Israel as well.

Another well-known free trade group was the European Free Trade Area (EFTA) comprising Finland, Sweden, Norway, Iceland, Austria, Liechtenstein, and Switzerland; however, five of these recently joined the European Union. Of these nations, Austria, Sweden, and Finland are members of the European Union, and Switzerland has applied to become a member. It appears that the EFTA will gradually merge into the European Union (which we discuss later). MERCOSUR is a free trade area consisting of Brazil, Argentina, Uruguay, and Paraguay, with an automatic schedule for the lowering of internal trade barriers and the ultimate goal of the creation of a customs union.[23] Chile has recently agreed to join MERCOSUR.

---

[23]Maria Cecilia Coutinho de Arruda and Masaaki Kotabe, "MERCOSUR: An Emergent Market in South America," in Masaaki Kotabe, *MERCOSUR and Beyond: The Imminent Emergence of the South American Markets* (Austin, Tex.: The University of Texas at Austin, 1997).

◆ ◆

GLOBAL PERSPECTIVE 2-4

NAFTA PROMISING FREER TRADE MAY END UP LESS FREE

"Whenever the rules do not favor the United States, there is a tendency to bend them," decried Raymond Chrétien, Canada's ambassador to the United States, implying that U.S. politics, particularly in an election year, tends to turn protectionistic. Despite $1 billion in trade each and every day between Canada and the United States, the United States has caused many trade disputes with Canada involving softwood lumber, wheat, dairy products, poultry, and Pacific salmon over the years.

The most recent example involves the U.S. decision to effectively reduce tomato imports from Mexico. Under NAFTA, tomatoes from Mexico are subject to quarterly seasonal quotas. Thus, Mexican growers can make up a temporary slowdown in exports during the remaining part of the quarter. During 1995, there was a 129 percent surge in the volume of tomato exports from Mexico, lead-

Sources: "Dealing with Uncle Sam: Our Ambassador Learns 'Realism'," *Canada Newscan* (May 10, 1996), p. 4; "U.S., Mexico Hope to Solve NAFTA Tomato Dispute," *Austin American Statesman* (January 21, 1996), p. H4.

ing to the U.S. changing the quota rules from a seasonal quota to a weekly quota. Under this unilateral action, if the quota for the week is missed then it is lost for the year—effectively reducing the actual level of exports from the stated quota levels.

The immediate cause for the unilateral action by the United States appears to the deleterious effect that the rise in the tomato exports is having on the tomato growers in Florida. Under pressure from the Florida tomato growers, the U.S. administration has proposed the weekly quota. Under the spirit and letter of NAFTA, the proposal goes against the free trade principle and indeed leads to *less* free trade. However, also under the provisions of NAFTA, Mexico has to first go through a consultative process that can last ninety days. If the dispute cannot be resolved by consultation, then the dispute resolution mechanism (patterned after GATT rules) kicks into effect—but this can take another nine months. In effect, by the time the seasonal quota is reinstated in December 1996, the U.S. presidential election should be over. Once the presidential elections are over, there will be less pressure on Washington to accede to the tomato growers of Florida.

A free trade area is not necessarily free of trade barriers, even among its member countries. Although it is a treaty by which to attempt to develop freer trade among the member countries, trade disputes and restrictions frequently occur, nonetheless (see Global Perspective 2-4). Furthermore, a free trade area can be circumvented by nonmember countries that can export to the nation in a free trade area that has the lowest external tariff, and then transport the goods to the destination country in the free trade area without paying the higher tariff applicable if it had gone directly to the destination country.

Customs Union

The inherent weakness of the free trade area concept may lead to its gradual disappearance in the future—though it may continue to be an attractive stepping stone to a higher level of integration. When members of a free trade area add common external tariffs to the provisions of the free trade agreement then the free trade area becomes a **customs union**.

Therefore, members of a customs union not only have reduced or eliminated tariffs among themselves, but also they have a common external tariff of countries that are not members of the customs union. This prevents nonmember countries from exporting to member countries that have low external tariffs with the goal of sending the exports to a country that has a higher external tariff through the first country that has a low external tariff. The ASEAN is a good example of a currently functional customs union with the goal of a common market. The Treaty of Rome of 1958, which formed the European Economic Community, created a customs union between West Germany, France, Italy, Belgium, Netherlands, and Luxembourg.

Common Market

As cooperation increases among the countries of a customs union, they can form a **common market**. A common market eliminates all tariffs and barriers to trade among members of the common market, adopts a common set of external tariffs on nonmembers, *and* removes all restrictions on the flow of capital and labor among member nations. The 1958 Treaty of Rome that created the European Economic Community had the ultimate goal of the creation of a common market—a goal that was substantially achieved by the early 1990s in Western Europe. German banks can now open branches in Italy, and Portuguese workers can live and work in Luxembourg.

Monetary Union

The **Maastricht Treaty**, which succeeded the Treaty of Rome and called for the creation of a union (and hence the change in name to European Union), has the goal of creating a **monetary union** and ultimately a political union, where the member countries switch over to a common currency and a common central bank. A monetary union represents the fifth level of integration among politically independent countries. In strict technical terms, a monetary union does not require the existence of a common market or a customs union, a free trade area or a regional cooperation for development. However, it is the logical next step to a common market, because it requires the next higher level of cooperation among member nations.

As per the Maastricht Treaty, those European Union member countries will qualify for switching to the common currency to be called the ECU—short for European Currency Unit—that:

- keep their federal budget deficits under 3 percent
- have been a member of the European Monetary System for at least two years before the beginning of the monetary union
- have maintained low levels of inflation (defined differently for different countries in the European countries)

The monetary union also requires member states to bring down public debt as a percentage of GDP to under 60 percent. The current timetable gives a two-year window beginning January 1, 1999, for EU countries to join the monetary union. Given that countries like Belgium have public debts in excess of 100 percent of the GDP, it is unlikely that the single currency will include all countries in the beginning. Issues such as the design of a European currency and the powers of a central bank need to be worked out.

Political Union

The culmination of the process of integration is the creation of a **political union**, which can be another name for a *nation* when such a union truly achieves the levels of integration described here on a voluntary basis. The ultimate stated goal of the

◆ ◆

GLOBAL PERSPECTIVE 2-5

CROSSING NATIONAL BORDERS IS EASIER THAN EVER IN THE EUROPEAN UNION

It is easy to caricature the European Union: fifteen countries squabbling over subsidies, 18,000 Brussels bureaucrats quarreling over perks, and 567 Strasbourg parliamentarians moaning over their relative lack of power. Whatever the latent truth of this caricature, it is also true that no country wants to leave the EU; and plenty are queuing to join, attracted by its economic mass and its implicit promise of security. Monet's dream of modernizing and uniting Western Europe and then drawing in Eastern Europe is alive and well.

The three main institutions of the EU are the Commission, the Council of Ministers, and the European Parliament. The Commission is a body of permanent civil servants and government appointees that administers EU business and proposes and drafts legislation. The Council of Ministers attended by the appropriate government

ministers from the member countries is the EU's legislature and it deliberates in secret. The European Parliament—the only body that is directly elected by the EU citizens—has few of the powers of a national parliament like that of the U.S. Congress or the German Bundestag. This structure, designed for the initial six members, is now creaking with fifteen members, and will need to be changed to accommodate new members.

The single market has moved forward in many areas. From January 1, 1993, Spanish drivers who needed to fill out seventy forms to cross a border can now truck oranges to Holland unhindered by customs officers and border police; German banks can open branches in Italy; Greek students can attend Danish universities by right, and labor can move across borders in the EU. The Schegen Agreement eliminated the need for passports among all EU countries except Britain. The next step is the monetary union, although it is unlikely that all EU members will be able to join it simultaneously. A political union is still distant, due to strong nationalism in many EU nations.

Source: "Survey of the European Union," *Economist* (October 22, 1994).

Maastricht Treaty is a political union. Currently, France and Britain remain the principal opponents of ceding any part of the sovereignty of the nation-state to any envisaged political union.[24] Even the leading proponents of European integration—Germany and France—have reservations about a common defense and foreign policy (See Global Perspective 2-5).

Sometimes, countries come together in a loose political union for historical reasons, as in the British Commonwealth comprising nations that were part of the British Empire. Members received preferential tariffs in the early days, but when Britain joined the European Union this preferential treatment was lost. The group exists as a forum for discussion and common historical ties.

◆ ◆ ◆ ◆ ◆ ◆   ## MULTINATIONAL CORPORATIONS

In the early 1970s Howard Perlmutter, a professor at the Wharton School in Philadelphia, predicted that by 1985 around 80 percent of the noncommunist world's productive assets would be controlled by just 200–300 companies. Researchers at the United Nations reckon that there are now at least 36,000 multinationals controlling some 180,000 affiliates. Within that number, power is indeed concentrated; the United Na-

---

[24]"Survey of the European Union," *Economist* (October 22, 1994).

tions reported that the largest 100 multinationals, excluding those in banking or finance, accounted for $3.1 trillion of worldwide assets in 1990. That gives the top 100 roughly a 16 percent share of the world's productive assets.[25] The top 100 multinationals probably account for about 40–50 percent for all cross-border assets but are far from achieving the dominance that was predicted. However, the forces of economies of scale, lowering trade and investment barriers, need to be close to markets, internalization of operations within the boundaries of one firm and the diffusion of technology will continue to increase the size and influence of multinationals.

The sovereignty of nations will perhaps continue to weaken due to multinationals and the increasing integration of economies, but the threat to sovereignty may not assume the proportions alluded to by some researchers.[26] Multinationals have yet to solve the problem of size. Current trends indicate that beyond a certain size firms tend to become complacent and slow and they falter against competition. They are no longer able to remain focused on their businesses and lack the drive, motivation, and a can-do attitude that permeates smaller firms. Those firms that do focus on their core businesses shed unrelated businesses. General Motors is planning to sell off EDS and Hughes Electronics, reducing its annual revenue from $167 billion to $120 billion. Thus, the nation-state, while considerably weaker than its nineteenth century counterpart, is likely to remain alive and well.

International firms are more international than before. In 1970, of the 7,000 multinationals identified by the United Nations, more than half were from two countries: the United States and Britain. In 1995, less than half of the 36,000 multinationals identified by the United Nations were from four countries: the United States, Japan, Germany, and Switzerland. Britain was seventh. Currency movements, capital surpluses, faster growth rates, and falling trade and investment barriers have all helped multinationals from other countries join the cross-border fray. In today's world it is not unusual for a startup firm to be multinational at its inception.[27] It is now easier than ever for small firms to be in international business through exports and imports. A survey of almost 750 companies by Arthur Andersen & Co. and National Small Business United, a trade group, found that 20 percent of companies with fewer than 500 employees exported product and services in 1994.[28] That is up from 11 percent in 1992, the first year that the survey was conducted. Having a steady market abroad helps to partially offset a domestic downturn as well.

SUMMARY ◆

The world economy is getting increasingly intertwined, and virtually no country that has a steadily rising standard of living is independent of the economic events in the rest of the world. It is almost as if participation in the international economy is a *sine quo non* of economic growth and prosperity—a country has to participate in the world economy in order to grow and prosper—but participation is not without its risks. Events outside one country can have detrimental effect on the economic health of

---

[25]"Multinationals: A Survey," *Economist* (March 27, 1993).

[26]Raymond Vernon, *Sovereignty At Bay* (New York: Basic Books, 1971).

[27]Benjamin M. Oviatt and Patricia P. McDougall, "Toward a Theory of International New Ventures," *Journal of International Business Studies*, 25(1) (1994), pp. 45–64.

[28]"It's a Small (Business) World," *Business Week* (April 17, 1995), pp. 96–101.

that country. The Mexican meltdown of December 1994, with a precipitous depreciation of its peso, is an example of a situation where withdrawal of funds by portfolio investors caused a severe economic crisis. In effect, participating in the international economy imposes its own discipline on a nation, independent of the policies of the government of that nation. This is not to suggest that countries should stay outside the international economic system because of the risks. Those countries that have elected to stay outside the international economic system—autarkies like Burma and North Korea—continue to fall farther behind the rest of the world in terms of living standards and prosperity.

Various forces are responsible for the increased integration. Growth in international trade continuously outpaces the rise in national outputs. Transportation and communications are becoming faster, cheaper, and more widely accessible. The nature of value-adding activities is changing in the advanced countries from manufacturing to services and information manipulation. Such changes are a result of and are a force behind the rapid advancement in telecommunications and computers. Even developing nations, regardless of their political colors, have realized the importance of telecommunications and are attempting to improve their telecommunications infrastructure. The capital markets of the world are already integrated for all practical purposes, and this integration affects exchange rates, interest rates, investments, employment, and growth across the world. Multinational corporations have truly become the global operations in name and spirit that they were envisaged to be. In short, to repeat an old maxim, the world is becoming a global village. When Karl Marx said in 1848 that the world was becoming a smaller place, he could not have imagined how small it truly has become.

REVIEW QUESTIONS

1. What are some of the visible signs that reflect the current increased economic interdependence among countries? What are some reasons for this growth in interdependence and for the rise in global integration?

2. What is GATT, and what is its role in international transactions?

3. How is the WTO different from GATT? What functions is WTO expected to perform?

4. In what ways have the U.S. foreign direct investment and trade patterns changed over the past decade?

5. Cooperative inter-relationships between countries (regional groupings) can be classified into five broad categories. What are these categories, and how do they differ from each other?

6. Do current measures of balance of payments accurately reflect a country's transactions with the rest of the world? What are the concerns?

7. What challenges do the content creators and information providers face due to the advent and popularity of the electronic media? Are there current mechanisms to protect their rights? What are the macroeconomic implications for industrialized countries?

8. What are some of the forces influencing the increase in size of multinational corporations? Are there any forces that are influencing them to downsize?

DISCUSSION QUESTIONS

1. A justification of developing countries against product patents for pharmaceutical products has been that if they were enforced, life-saving drugs would be out of reach for all but the very rich. A similar argument is being used in a populist move in the U.S senate for reducing the patent lives of innovative drugs, in a bid to reduce health care costs. Some senators and the pharmaceutical industry leaders claim that this move would discourage medical innovation and slow down the development of drugs for the cure of such diseases as AIDS and cancer, and thereby increase the costs of taking care of current and future patients. How would you react to the arguments and counterarguments for reducing patent lives, and what would be your stance on this issue? In your opinion, what would be the international repercussions if this bill

were to pass? How do you think other developed and developing countries would react?

2. In 1990, Robert Reich, a Harvard professor (and ex-Labor Secretary in the Clinton administration) stated that multinational corporations (MNCs) have become so internationally oriented that what is good for U.S. multinationals may no longer be good for the United States. Therefore, the U.S. government should not treat U.S. MNCs any differently from foreign corporations' subsidiaries in the United States. Laura Tyson, then a professor at the University of California, Berkeley (and the chairperson of the Council of Economic Advisers in the Clinton administration), countered this by stating that U.S. MNCs still remained overwhelmingly American in terms of their highest-value production, and that economic and national security considerations required U.S. policy makers to differentiate between U.S.- and foreign-owned corporations. Whom would you agree with, and why? According to the International Automobile Manufacturers Association, foreign-owned auto plants in the United States contributed to 500,000 jobs and U.S.$10 billion in investments. Would this information influence your previous answer? How?

3. Information technology is having significant effects on the globalization activities of corporations. It was recently quoted in the *New York Times* (September 10, 1995) that Texas Instruments is now developing sophisticated chips in India. Motorola has set up programming and equipment design centers in China, India, Singapore, Hong Kong, Taiwan, and Australia. Similarly, a large number of U.S. and European corporations are looking at ways to transfer activities such as preparing tax returns, account statements, insurance claims, and other information processing work to Asia. Although until now it was only blue-collar employees in the industrialized countries who faced the threat of competition from low-wage countries (which could be countered to some extent through direct and indirect trade barriers), this new trend in movement of white-collar tasks may be a cause for concern to industrialized countries, as the sophistication of these tasks increases. This movement of white-collar jobs could be a cause for social concern in the near future. Do you foresee social pressures in developed countries having the potential of reversing the trend of movement of white-collar tasks to developing countries? Given the intangibility of information, are there any effective ways of controlling the movement of information across borders?

4. The effects of the formation of regional trade blocs on international trade could be interpreted in two ways. One way is to view regional blocs as one step forward in the process of ensuring completely free trade between countries on a global basis. On the other hand, the formation of regional blocs could be seen as a step backward toward an era of greater protectionism and greater trade tensions between the regions. Which view would you agree with, and why?

5. According to published reports, the total capital outflows from the United States for the year 1994 were U.S.$52.4 billion. Of this amount, $19.7 billion flowed to Europe, $15.8 billion to Asia/Pacific, and $13.4 billion to Latin America/Western Hemisphere. Do these relatively equitable capital flows across the Triad markets reflect a move toward regionalization of the world economy? Why or why not?

Further Readings ◆

Blecker, Robert A. *U.S. Trade Policy & Global Growth: New Directions in the International Economy.* Armonk, NY, 1996.

Bovard, James. "U.S. Trade Laws Harm U.S. Industries." *Regulation* 16 (4) (1993):47–53.

Emmerji, Louis. "Globalization, Regionalization and World Trade." *Columbia Journal of World Business,* 27 (2) (1992):6–13.

Harry, Michael G., and Laurie A. Lucas. "Intellectual Property Rights Protection: What MNC Managers Should Know About GATT." *Multinational Business Review,* 4 (1), (1996):77–93.

Irwin, Douglas A. "The GATT in Historical Perspective." *American Economic Review,* 85 (2) (May 1995):323–328.

Murphy, Louis J. "Successful Uruguay Round Launches Revitalized World Trading System." *Business America,* 115 (1) (1994):4–6.

Park, Seung Ho. "The Interfirm Collaboration in Global Competition." *Multinational Business Review,* 4 (1) (1996):94–106.

Qureshi, Asif H. "The Role of GATT in the Management of Trade Blocs: An Enforcement Perspective." *Journal of World Trade,* 27 (3), (1993):101–115.

FINANCIAL ENVIRONMENT

HAPTER OVERVIEW

1. HISTORICAL ROLE OF THE U.S. DOLLAR
2. THE GOLD STANDARD
3. THE INTERWAR YEARS: 1919–1939
4. DEVELOPMENT OF THE CURRENT INTERNATIONAL MONETARY SYSTEM
5. FIXED VERSUS FLOATING EXCHANGE RATES
6. FOREIGN EXCHANGE AND FOREIGN EXCHANGE RATES
7. BALANCE OF PAYMENTS

When international transactions occur, foreign exchange is the monetary mechanism allowing the transfer of funds from one nation to another. The existing international monetary system always affects companies as well as individuals whenever they buy or sell products and services traded across national boundaries. When individuals purchase a Toyota made in Japan, they pay the price in dollars and would not usually pay attention to the dollar–yen exchange rate. However, loyal Toyota buyers in the past few years have experienced a hefty increase in sticker prices at Toyota dealers in the United States feeling the full brunt of the yen's appreciation relative to the dollar. Similarly, many PC makers in the United States, including Compaq and Apple, have had to deal with a sudden increase in costs of LCD monitors they purchase from Japanese manufacturers, who control about 90 percent of the LCD market in the world. On the other hand, the depreciated dollar has also enabled those PC makers to export more PCs abroad, as the U.S.-made PCs have become less expensive in terms of foreign currencies. It is obvious that the current international monetary system has a profound impact not only on individuals and companies but also on the U.S. balance of payments at the aggregate level.

This chapter examines international trade in monetary terms. In fact, the international monetary system has changed rather drastically over the years. Given the drastic realignment in recent years of the exchange rates of major currencies, including the U.S. dollar, Japanese yen, and German mark, the current international monetary system may well be in for a major change. The possible move toward the adoption of a common currency (i.e., the ECU) in the European Union is just one example of the many changes to come. Although international marketers have to operate in a currently existing international monetary system for international transactions and settlements, they should understand how the scope and nature of the system has changed and how it has worked over time. Forward-looking international marketers need to be aware of the dynamics of the international monetary system.

◆ ◆ ◆ ◆ ◆ ◆ HISTORICAL ROLE OF THE U.S. DOLLAR

Trade settlements involve topics such as determination of foreign exchange rates, balance of payments, foreign exchange transactions, international financial flows, and international financial and trade institutions. All international transactions must take place within the context of an international monetary system, or a set of procedures for making and receiving international payments.

Each country also has its own currency through which it expresses the value of its products. An international monetary system is necessary because each country has a different monetary unit or currency that serves as a medium of exchange and store of value. The absence of a universal currency means that we must have a system that allows for the transfer of purchase power between countries with different national currencies. For international trade settlements, the various currencies of the world must be exchanged from one to another. This is accomplished through foreign exchange markets.

Periodically, a country must review the status of its economic relations with the rest of the world in terms of its exports and imports, its exchange of various kinds of services, and its purchase and sale of different types of capital assets and other international payments, receipts and transfers. In the post–World War II period, a number of institutions came into existence to monitor and assist countries as necessary in keeping their international financial commitments. As a result, a new system of international monetary relations emerged, which promoted increased international trade through the 1950s and 1960s. In the early 1970s, however, a weakening U.S. dollar caused the existing system to show strains and eventually break.

Following World War II, the United States agreed to exchange the dollar at $35 per ounce of gold. With the value of the dollar stabilized, countries could deal in dollars without being constrained by currency fluctuations. Thus, the dollar became the common denominator in world trade. Because of the weakening of the dollar and other issues, the monetary stability of the world became unsettled beginning with the 1970s and continuing into the early 1980s. As the 1980s advanced, the U.S. economy stabilized and the value of the dollar against other currencies climbed to an all-time high. This caused U.S exports to become costlier, and foreign imports to become cheaper, resulting in an adverse trade balance. In the fall of 1985, leading industrialized countries joined the United States effort to intervene in the foreign exchange markets to decrease the value of the dollar. The dollar fell and remained weak in the remaining years of the 1980s and early 1990s. There is no indication that the dollar is likely to strengthen appreciably in the remainder of the 1990s.

THE GOLD STANDARD ◆ ◆ ◆ ◆ ◆ ◆

Although there is no official starting date, the gold standard extended from the 1880s to the outbreak of World War I in 1914. Under the gold standard, the major nations of the world issued paper money backed by gold. Each country declared a par value for its currency in terms of this metal. For example, the British pound was valued at 7.3 pounds per ounce of fine gold and the dollar at $35 per ounce. Gold could be surrendered to the monetary authorities of these two nations in return for local currency at its respective value. The gold standard had three major features:

1. It established a system of fixed exchange rates between participating countries. Stable exchange rates were considered necessary in order to increase trade between nations.

2. The gold standard limited the rate of growth in a country's money supply. This was due to the fact that all money must be backed by gold, and the supply of gold in the world increased quite slowly during this period in history.

3. Gold served as an automatic adjustment tool for countries experiencing balance of payment problems. If a country was running a balance of payments deficit, gold would, by market forces, flow out of the country, decreasing economic activity and pushing the balance of payments back toward balance.

However, there were also problems with the gold standard. After World War I, the world was unable to get back on the gold standard because the gold supply was no longer growing and could not keep pace with the needs of commerce. Many believe the attempt to return to the International Gold Standard was a major contributing factor to the Great Depression, which for all intents and purposes buried it as a method for controlling inflation.[1]

Because under the gold standard each unit of currency was backed by gold, the supply of money in the country could not increase faster than the amount of gold. The slow growth in the gold supply effectively restricted how much government authorities in charge of monetary policy could increase their money supplies. This system thus limited governments' ability to decide their own independent monetary policies.

As just mentioned, the gold standard relied on the ability of gold to move freely from one nation to another. However, the onset of World War I put a halt to the free flow of gold across borders, and the world's currency markets were in substantial turmoil until the war's end in 1919.

THE INTERWAR YEARS: 1919–1939 ◆ ◆ ◆ ◆ ◆ ◆

The 1920s and 1930s were a tumultuous period for the international monetary system. The British pound sterling, which was the world's dominant currency prior to World War I, survived the war but in a greatly weakened state. Inflation in Britain after the war threatened the stability of the local economy, and the Bank of England, in

---

[1]Michael K. Evans, "Thumbs Down on the Gold Standard," *Modern Office Technology* (January 1988), pp. 12–13.

a move to restore stability, established the pound at its prewar parity of 4.2474 pounds per ounce of gold.

The U.S. dollar returned to the gold standard at the end of the war in June 1919. It was not until the Great Depression and the related bank failures in 1933 that the U.S. was forced to abandon gold convertibility again. With the Depression, many countries, including the United States, resorted to isolationist policies and protectionism. Markets were closed to foreign producers, and in the markets that remained open, exporting countries tried to undercut each other through continual currency devaluations. These devaluations served only to push many of the world's currencies beneath their true values and increased pressures for further nationalistic protectionist policies to shield domestic firms from unfair foreign competition. By the early days of World War II, international trade had ground to a halt.

◆ ◆ ◆ ◆ ◆ ◆ DEVELOPMENT OF TODAY'S INTERNATIONAL MONETARY SYSTEM

The Bretton Woods Conference

Post–World War II developments had long-range effects on international financial arrangements, the role of gold, and the problems of adjustment of balance of payments disequilibria. Following World War II, a keen awareness of the need to achieve economic prosperity grew among nations. The war years had shattered Europe and Japan, and they needed reconstruction. There was a feeling in many nations that the economically disastrous interwar period and the following World War had resulted from the harsh terms exacted upon Germany following World War I and a failure to properly coordinate economic policies since that time. There was a strong desire to avoid the mistakes of the past and adhere to goals that would bring economic prosperity and hopefully a long-term peace to the world.

The negotiations to establish the postwar international monetary system took place at the resort of Bretton Woods in New Hampshire in 1944. The negotiators at Bretton Woods recommended the following:[2]

1. Each nation should be at liberty to use macroeconomic policies for full employment. This ruled out a return to the gold standard.

2. Free floating exchange rates could not work. Their ineffectiveness had been demonstrated in the interwar years. The extremes of both permanently fixed and floating rates should be avoided.

3. A monetary system was needed that would recognize that exchange rates were both a national and international concern.

In order to avoid both the rigidity of a fixed exchange rate system and at the same time the chaos of freely floating exchange rates, the Bretton Woods Agreement provided for an adjustable peg. Under this system, currencies were to establish par values in terms of gold, but there was to be little, if any, convertibility of the currencies for gold. Each government was responsible for monitoring its own currency to see that it did not float beyond 1 percent above or below its established par value. As

---

[2]See, for example, Delbert Snider, *Introduction to International Economics*, 5th ed., (Homewood, Ill.: Richard D. Irwin, 1981), and Armand Van Dormael, *Bretton Woods* (New York: Holmes and Meier, 1978).

a nation's currency attained or approached either limit, its central bank intervened in the world financial markets to prevent the rate from passing the limit.

Under this system, a country experiencing a balance-of-payments deficit would normally experience devaluation pressure on its current value. The country's authorities would defend its currency by using its foreign currency reserves, primarily U.S. dollars, to purchase its own currency on the open market to push its value back up to its par value. A country experiencing a balance-of-payments surplus would do the opposite and sell its currency on the open market. An institution called the **International Monetary Fund (IMF)** was established at Bretton Woods to oversee the newly agreed upon monetary system. If a country experienced a fundamental or long-term disequilibrium in its balance of payments, it could alter its peg by up to 10 percent from its initial par value without approval from the International Monetary Fund. Adjustment beyond 10 percent required IMF approval.

In the 1960s, the United States began to experience sequential balance of payments deficits, resulting in downward pressure on the dollar. Since the U.S. government was obligated to maintain the dollar at its par value, it had to spend much of its gold and foreign currency reserves in order to purchase dollars on the world financial markets. In addition, the U.S. dollar was the reserve currency, convertible to gold under the Bretton Woods Agreement; the U.S. Treasury was obligated to convert dollars to gold upon demand by foreign central banks.

Furthermore, many central banks engaged in massive dollar purchases on the foreign exchange markets to counteract the downward pressure on the dollar and related upward pressure on their own currencies. The continued defense of the dollar left central banks around the world with massive quantities of dollars. These countries, knowing that the dollars they held were in fact convertible to gold with the U.S. Treasury, attempted to hold back, demanding gold in exchange. However, it became clear in 1971 that the dollar was quite overvalued, and devaluation of the dollar versus gold was inevitable. Central banks increasingly presented U.S. dollar balances to the U.S. Treasury for conversion to gold, and gold flowed out of the U.S. vaults at an alarming rate.

This situation led President Nixon to suspend the convertibility of the dollar to gold on August 15, 1971. This effectively ended the exchange rate regime begun at Bretton Woods more than twenty-five years earlier.

The International Monetary Fund

The International Monetary Fund (IMF) was created at Bretton Woods to oversee the newly created monetary system. The IMF was a specialized agency within the United Nations, established to promote international monetary cooperation and to facilitate the expansion of trade, and in turn to contribute to increased employment and improved economic conditions in all member countries.

Its purposes are defined in the following terms:[3]

1. To promote international monetary cooperation through a permanent institution, providing the machinery for consultations and collaboration on international monetary problems.

---

[3]International Monetary Fund, *The Role and Function of the International Monetary Fund* (Washington, D.C.: International Monetary Fund, 1985).

2. To facilitate the expansion and balanced growth of international trade, and to contribute thereby to the promotion and maintenance of high levels of employment and real income, and to the development of the productive resources of all members as primary objectives of economic policy.

3. To promote exchange stability, to maintain orderly exchange arrangements among members, and to avoid competitive exchange depreciation.

4. To assist in the establishment of a multilateral system of payments in respect to current transactions between members and in the elimination of foreign exchange restrictions that hamper the growth of world trade.

5. To give confidence to members by making the general resources of the fund temporarily available to them under adequate safeguards, thus providing them with the opportunity to correct maladjustments in their balance of payments without resorting to measures destructive of national or international prosperity.

6. In accordance with the above, to shorten the duration and lessen the degree of disequilibrium in the international balance of payments to members.

Today there are more than 150 members of the IMF. Its accomplishments include sustaining a rapidly increasing volume of trade and investment and displaying flexibility in adapting to changes in international commerce. To an extent, the fund served as an international central bank to help countries during periods of temporary balance of payments difficulties, by protecting their rates of exchange. This helped countries avoid the placement of foreign exchange controls and other trade barriers.

As time passed, it became evident that the IMF's resources for providing short-term accommodation to countries in monetary difficulties were not sufficient. To resolve the situation, and to reduce upward pressure on the U.S. dollar by countries holding dollar reserves, the fund created special drawing rights in 1969. **Special drawing rights (SDRs)**, are special account entries on the IMF books designed to provide additional liquidity to support growing world trade. The value of SDRs is determined by a weighted average of a basket of five currencies: the U.S. dollar, the Japanese yen, the French franc, the German deutsche mark, and the British pound. Although SDRs are a form of fiat money and not convertible to gold, their gold value is guaranteed, which helps to ensure their acceptability.

Participant nations may use SDRs as a source of currency in a spot transaction, as a loan for clearing a financial obligation, as security for a loan, as a swap against a currency, or in a forward exchange operation. A nation with a balance of payment problem may use its SDRs to obtain usable currency from another nation designated by the fund. By providing a mechanism for international monetary cooperation, working to reduce restrictions to trade and investment flows, and helping members with their short term balance of payment difficulties, the IMF makes a significant and unique contribution to economic stability and improved living standards throughout the world.

The International Bank for Reconstruction and Development

Another creation of the Bretton Woods Agreement was the International Bank for Reconstruction and Development, known as the **World Bank**. Although the International Monetary Fund was created to aid countries in financing their balance of payment difficulties and maintaining a relatively stable currency, the World Bank was initially intended for the financing of postwar reconstruction and development and

Various foreign currencies and gold coins, nuggets, and bars as means to measure and store economic value.

later for infrastructure building projects in the developing world. More recently, the World Bank has begun to participate actively with the IMF to resolve debt problems of the developing world, and it may also play a major role in bringing a market economy to the former members of the Eastern bloc.

Twin Crises: Oil Prices and Foreign Debt

In the 1970s, developing countries throughout the world began to suffer from rapid increases in the price of oil. The increased price of oil provoked a round of inflation at the same time principal commodities produced by these developing nations were falling in price. Many of these developing nations began to borrow heavily from international banks in order to finance routine expenses or, in some cases, grandiose development projects. Much of the funds lent out by banks to these developing nations were from the bank deposits of wealthy oil-producing nations, which had received this money from the developing nations as payment for petroleum shipments in the first place. So this truly represented a recycling of dollars from the developing nations back to them, but with the addition of hefty interest and finance charges in the interim.

Fixed Versus Floating Exchange Rates

Since the 1970s all major nations have had floating currencies. An IMF meeting in Jamaica in 1976 reached consensus on amendments to the IMF Articles of Agreement that accepted floating rates as the basis for the international monetary system. The amended agreement recognized that real rate stability can only be achieved through stability in underlying economic and financial conditions. Exchange rate stability cannot be imposed by adoption of pegged exchange rates and official intervention in the foreign exchange markets.

However, the supposed benefits of floating exchange rates have not been borne out in reality. For example:[4]

1. Floating exchange rates were supposed to facilitate balance of payments adjustments. However, not only have imbalances not disappeared, they have become worse.

2. Currency speculation was expected to be curtailed. But speculation has since been greater than ever.

3. Market forces, left to their own devices, were expected to determine the correct foreign exchange rate balance. But imbalances have become greater than ever, as have fluctuations in rates.

4. Autonomy in economic and monetary policy was hoped to be preserved, allowing each country free choice of its monetary policy and rate of inflation. But this has also been an illusion.

In March 1973, the major currencies began to float in the foreign exchange markets. The advocates for floating exchange regime argued that it would end balance of payments disequilibria because the value of each currency would float up or down to a point where supply equaled demand. It has not worked that way, at least in part due to the reluctance of governments to permit extreme changes in the value of their currencies. Governments have intervened in the currency markets to moderate or prevent value changes.

There are two kinds of currency floats, and these are referred to as free or managed or as clean or dirty. The **free (clean) float** is the closest approximation to perfect competition, because there is no government intervention and because billions of units of currency are being traded by buyers and sellers. Buyers and sellers may change sides on short notice as information, rumors, or moods change, or as their clients' needs differ.

A **managed float** allows for a limited amount of government intervention to soften sudden swings in the value of a currency. If a nation's currency enters into a rapid ascent or decline, that nation's central bank may wish to sell or buy that currency on the open market in a countervailing movement to offset the prevailing market tendency. This is for the purpose of maintaining an orderly, less-volatile foreign exchange market. An example of this has been Mexico, which since 1988 has allowed a gradual slide in the value of the peso in order to retain investor confidence, as well as to avoid rapid inflation and other negative effects of sudden devaluations. This strategy has worked, as hundreds of billions of investor dollars have entered the country since 1988.

Despite occasional problems and sharp changes in the relative values of currencies, the floating rates system has not collapsed. The volatility of exchange rate movements diminished after a period of uncertainty in 1973–74. This uncertainty was heightened by the sudden increase in the price of oil. The system again fluctuated wildly between 1977 and 1987. Beginning in June 1977, the U.S. dollar fell in value about 28 percent against the Swiss franc, 20 percent against the Japanese yen, and 15 percent against the German mark within a year! Many blamed the dollar's

---

[4]Subhash Jain, *International Marketing Management*. Belmont, CA: Wadsworth Publishing Co., 1993, p. 113.

EXHIBIT 3-1
FOREIGN EXCHANGE RATE FLUCTUATIONS OVER THE PAST 30 YEARS
(FOREIGN CURRENCY UNITS/U.S. DOLLAR)

Year	Japanese Yen	Deutsche Mark	British Pound	French Franc	Swiss Franc
1967	361.91	3.9990	0.4156	4.9371	4.3250
1968	357.70	3.9995	0.4194	4.9371	4.3020
1969	357.80	3.6899	0.4166	5.5542	4.3180
1970	357.65	3.6480	0.4178	5.5542	4.3160
1971	314.80	3.2685	0.3918	5.1158	3.9151
1972	302.00	3.2015	0.4259	5.1158	3.7741
1973	279.99	2.7029	0.4304	4.7083	3.2439
1974	300.94	2.4094	0.4258	4.4443	2.5399
1975	305.14	2.6222	0.4942	4.4854	2.6199
1976	292.80	2.3625	0.5874	4.9699	2.4496
1977	240.00	2.1050	0.5247	4.7050	2.0000
1978	194.60	1.8280	0.4915	4.1800	1.6200
1979	239.70	1.7316	0.4496	4.0201	1.5801
1980	203.00	1.9590	0.4193	4.5460	1.7635
1981	219.89	2.2547	0.5241	5.7478	1.7985
1982	235.00	2.3765	0.6194	6.7250	1.9946
1983	232.19	2.7237	0.6893	8.3471	2.1794
1984	251.10	3.1480	0.8647	9.5921	2.5850
1985	200.50	2.4613	0.6923	7.5612	2.0766
1986	159.10	1.9408	0.6782	6.4550	1.6234
1987	123.49	1.5814	0.5343	5.3398	1.2779
1988	125.85	1.7803	0.5526	6.0590	1.5040
1989	143.45	1.6978	0.6228	5.7879	1.5464
1990	134.40	1.4940	0.5187	5.1288	1.2955
1991	125.20	1.5160	0.5346	5.1801	1.3555
1992	124.75	1.6140	0.6614	5.5065	1.4560
1993	111.84	1.7263	0.6751	5.8953	1.4795
1994	99.74	1.5487	0.6400	5.3458	1.3115
1995	102.83	1.4335	0.6452	4.9000	1.1505
1996	93.96	1.5049	0.6407	5.1158	1.2361
1997	126.07	1.7135	0.6161	5.7785	1.4625

Sources: International Monetary Fund, *Balance of Payments Statistics Yearbook* (Washington, D.C.: U.S. Government Printing Office), and Federal Reserve Board, *Federal Reserve Bulletin* (Washington, D.C.: U.S. Government Printing Office, various issues).

weakness on American fiscal and monetary policies, especially the U.S. balance of payments and budget deficits.

Since then, international marketers have had to cope with the ever-fluctuating exchange rates (see Exhibit 3-1). Even a small fluctuation in exchange rates cannot be ignored, since it has an enormous impact on a company's operating profit. For example, a one-yen rise against the dollar cuts Honda's annual operating profit by a whopping 8 to 9 billion yen (or some $80 million to $90 million).[5]

---

[5]Mitsuo Suzuki, "Honda's Profits Plunge but It Sees Good Year Ahead," *The Reuter European Business Report* (May 20, 1994).

Currency Blocs

The U.S. dollar, Canadian dollar, German mark, Japanese yen, Swiss franc, British pound, and several other major currencies float in value against one another and against the European Currency Unit (ECU), a grouping of eight Western European currencies. Most currencies of developing countries are pegged (or fixed) to one of the major currencies or to a basket of major currencies such as the ECU, Special Drawing Rights, or some specially chosen currency mix. In general, developing countries that depend on their trading relationships with a major country, such as the United States, for economic growth tend to use the currency of the principal country.

Today, the global economy is increasingly dominated by three major currency blocs. The U.S. dollar, the Japanese yen, and the German deutsche mark each represent their "sphere of influence" on the currencies of other countries in the respective regions (i.e., North and South America, East Asia, and Europe respectively).[6] Although the U.S. dollar has lost some of its role as the international transaction currency, it remains a currency of choice that many Latin American companies use for operating purposes. The Japanese yen has increasingly become a regional transaction currency in Asia. Similarly, the German mark has become a reference currency of Europe, and its role will be further consolidated as Europe moves toward economic integration. In other words, U.S. companies will find it easier to do business with companies in Latin America as business planning as well as transactions are increasingly conducted in dollar denominations. On the other hand, those U.S. companies will increasingly have to accept yen-denominated business transactions in Asia and German mark-denominated transactions in Europe, thus being susceptible to exchange rate fluctuations. Considering increased trade volumes with Asian and European countries as well as with Latin American countries, it has become all the more important for U.S. marketing executives to understand the dynamic forces that affect exchange rates and predict the exchange rate fluctuations.

◆ ◆ ◆ ◆ ◆ ◆ FOREIGN EXCHANGE AND FOREIGN EXCHANGE RATES

Foreign exchange, as the term implies, refers to the exchange of one country's money for that of another country. When international transactions occur, foreign exchange is the monetary mechanism allowing the transfer of funds from one nation to another. In this section, we explore what factors influence the exchange rates over time and how the exchange rates are determined.

Purchasing Power Parity

One of the most fundamental determinants of the exchange rate is **purchasing power parity** (PPP), whereby the exchange rate between the currencies of two countries is in equilibrium when it equates the prices of a basket of goods and services in both countries. In other words, the value of a currency is determined by what it can buy.

---

[6]David K. Eiteman, Arthur I. Stonehill, and Michael H. Moffett, *Multinational Business Finance*, 6th ed., Reading (Mass.: Addison-Wesley, 1996), p. 39.

The following formula represents the relationship between inflation rates and the exchange rate:

$$R_t = R_0 \times \frac{(1 + \text{Infl}_{\text{Ger}})}{(1 + \text{Infl}_{\text{US}})}$$

where

R = the exchange rate quoted in DM/$,
Infl = inflation rate,
t = time period.

For example, if German inflation were 2 percent a year and U.S. inflation were 5 percent a year, the value of the dollar would be expected to fall by the difference of 3 percent, so that the real prices of goods in the two countries would remain fairly similar. If the current exchange rate (R_0) is 1.52 deutsche mark to the dollar (DM 1.52/$), then

$$R_t = 1.52 \times \frac{(1 + .02)}{(1 + .05)} = \text{DM } 1.48/\$.$$

In other words, the dollar is expected to depreciate from DM 1.52/$ to DM 1.48/$ in a year. The U.S. dollar will be able to buy slightly fewer deutsche marks.

In fact, the *Economist* publishes a PPP study every year based on McDonald's Big Mac hamburger, sold all over the world. It is known as the Big Mac Index to show whether currencies are at their "correct" exchange rate. Look at the recent Big Mac Index to see how actual exchange rates "deviate" from the Big Mac Index (See Exhibit 3-2). If the dollar is undervalued relative to a foreign currency (i.e., the foreign currency is overvalued relative to the dollar), people using that foreign currency will find it cheaper to buy goods from the United States. Conversely, people living in the United States will find it more expensive to import goods from a country with an overvalued currency.

Forecasting Exchange Rate Fluctuation

Actual exchange rates can be very different from the expected rates. Those deviations are not necessarily a random variation. As summarized in Exhibit 3-3, many interrelated factors influence the value of a floating currency. In particular, the nation's inflation rate relative to its trading partners, its balance of payments situation, and world political events are the three most fundamental factors.

Although accurately predicting the actual exchange rate fluctuations is not possible and it is not related directly to marketing executives' jobs, seasoned marketers can benefit from the knowledge. Exchange rate fluctuations have an enormous direct impact on the bottom line for the company—profitability. For example, of the pretax profit of 18 billion yen that Sony made for the third quarter of 1993 alone, 12 billion yen, or two-thirds of the pretax profit, was attributed to foreign exchange gains through successful currency hedging. In other words, almost two-thirds of Sony's pretax profit came from sources not directly related to its core business![7]

---

[7]"Nintendo Posts Decline in Pretax Profit; Sony's Rises on Currency-Hedging Gain," *Wall Street Journal* (November 19, 1993), p. 4E.

Exhibit 3-2
The Big Mac Index

	Big Mac prices		Implied PPP* of the dollar	Actual $ exchange rate 7/4/97	Local currency under (−)/over(+) valuation,† %
	In local currency	In dollars			
United States‡	$2.42	2.42	—	—	—
Argentina	Peso2.50	2.50	1.03	1.00	+3
Australia	A$2.50	1.94	1.03	1.29	−20
Austria	Sch34.00	2.82	14.0	12.0	+17
Belgium	BFr109	3.09	45.0	35.3	+28
Brazil	Real2.97	2.81	1.23	1.06	+16
Britain	£1.81	2.95	1.34††	1.63††	+22
Canada	C$2.88	2.07	1.19	1.39	−14
Chile	Peso1,200	2.88	496	417	+19
China	Yuan9.70	1.16	4.01	8.33	−52
Czech Republic	CKr53.0	1.81	21.9	29.2	−25
Denmark	DKr25.75	3.95	10.6	6.52	+63
France	FFr17.5	3.04	7.23	5.76	+26
Germany	DM4.90	2.86	2.02	1.71	+18
Hong Kong	HK$9.90	1.28	4.09	7.75	−47
Hungary	Forint271	1.52	112	178	−37
Israel	Shekel11.5	3.40	4.75	3.38	+40
Italy	Lire4,600	2.73	1,901	1,683	+13
Japan	¥294	2.34	121	126	−3
Malaysia	M$3.87	1.55	1.60	2.50	−36
Mexico	Peso14.9	1.89	6.16	7.90	−22
Netherlands	Fl5.45	2.83	2.25	1.92	+17
New Zealand	NZ$3.25	2.24	1.34	1.45	−7
Poland	Zloty4.30	1.39	1.78	3.10	−43
Russia	Rouble11,000	1.92	4,545	5,739	−21
Singapore	S$3.00	2.08	1.24	1.44	−14
South Africa	Rand7.80	1.76	3.22	4.43	−27
South Korea	Won2,300	2.57	950	894	+6
Spain	Pta375	2.60	155	144	+7
Sweden	SKr26.0	3.37	10.7	7.72	+39
Switzerland	SFr5.90	4.02	2.44	1.47	+66
Taiwan	NT$68.0	2.47	28.1	27.6	+2
Thailand	Baht46.7	1.79	19.3	26.1	−26

*Purchasing-power parity: local price divided by price in the United States.

†Against dollar

‡Average of New York, Chicago, San Francisco, and Atlanta

††Dollars per pound

Source: McDonald's. "Big MacCurrencies," *Economist*, April 12, 1997, p. 71.

Coping with Exchange Rate Fluctuations

When the fast-food operator KFC opens new restaurants in Mexico, for example, it often imports some of the kitchen equipment, including fryers, roasters, stainless steel counters, and other items for its stores from U.S. suppliers.

In order to pay for these imports, the Mexican subsidiary of KFC must purchase U.S. dollars with Mexican pesos through their bank in Mexico City. This is necessary

EXHIBIT 3-3
FACTORS INFLUENCING FOREIGN EXCHANGE RATES

MACROECONOMIC FACTORS

1. **Relative Inflation**: A country suffering relatively higher inflation rates than other major trading partners will cause depreciation of its currency.
2. **Balance of Payments**: Improvement (Deterioration) in the balance of payments for goods and services is an early sign of a currency appreciation (depreciation).
3. **Foreign Exchange Reserves**: A government may intervene in the foreign exchange markets to either push up or push down the value of its currency. The central bank can support (depreciate) the domestic currency by selling its foreign currency reserves to buy its own currency (selling its domestic currency to buy foreign currency).
4. **Economic Growth**: If the domestic economy is growing fast relative to major trading partners, the country's imports tends to rise faster than exports, resulting in deterioration of the trade balance and thus depreciation of its currency. However, if the domestic economic growth attracts a large amount of investment from abroad, it could offset the negative trade effect, thus potentially resulting in appreciation of the domestic currency.
5. **Government Spending**: An increase in government spending, particularly if financed through deficit spending, causes increased inflationary pressures on the economy. Inflation leads to domestic currency depreciation (as in 1).
6. **Money Supply Growth**: Many countries' central banks attempt to stave off recession by increasing money supply to lower domestic interest rates for increased consumption and investment. Increase in money supply usually leads to higher inflation rates and subsequently currency depreciation.
7. **Interest Rate Policy**: As in 6, the central bank may also control its discount rate (interest rate charged to banks) to raise domestic lending rates so as to control inflation. Higher interest rates discourage economic activity and tend to reduce inflation and also attract investment from abroad. Reduced inflation and increased investment from abroad both lead to currency appreciation.

POLITICAL FACTORS

1. **Exchange Rate Control**: Some governments have an explicit control on the exchange rate. The official rate for domestic currency is artificially overvalued, thereby discouraging foreign companies from exporting to such a country. However, as long as there is a genuine domestic demand for imported products, the black market tends to appear for foreign currency. Black market exchange rates for a domestic currency tend to be much lower than the government-imposed artificial rate. Thus, a wide spread between the official exchange rate and the black market rate indicates potential pressures leading to domestic currency devaluation.
2. **Election Year or Leadership Change**: Expectations about imminent government policy change influence exchange rates. In general, pro-business government policy tends to lead to domestic currency appreciation as foreign companies are willing to accept that currency for business transactions.

RANDOM FACTORS

Unexpected and/or unpredicted events in a country, such as assassination of political figures and sudden stock market crash, can cause its currency to depreciate for fear of uncertainty. Similarly, events such as sudden discovery of huge oil reserves and gold mines tend to push up the currency value.

Source: David K. Eiteman, Arthur I. Stonehill, and Michael H. Moffett, *Multinational Business Finance*, 7th ed. (see Exhibit 6-5). ©1996 by Addison-Wesley Publishing Company, Inc. Reprinted by permission of Addison-Wesley Longman, Inc.

because Mexican pesos are not readily accepted currency in the United States. Most likely, KFC–Mexico will pay for the imported merchandise via a bank cashier's check from its local bank in Mexico City, denominated in U.S. dollars. If the exchange rate on the date of purchase is 7.65 Mexican pesos per U.S. dollar and their debt is $10,000 dollars, then KFC–Mexico must pay 76,500 pesos, plus a commission to the bank, for the dollars it sends to the U.S. supplier. The bank in Mexico acquires the dollars on the open foreign exchange market or through other banks for the purpose of satisfying the foreign exchange needs of its customers.

This is the case when currency is freely convertible with minimal government foreign exchange controls, as is true in Mexico in the 1990s. However, this is not always the case. Governments have often limited the amount of domestic currency that can leave a country, in order to avoid capital flight and decapitalization. One example of this was South Africa in the 1980s, where it was illegal to buy foreign currency or take domestic currency out of the country without government approval. If a company in South Africa required foreign manufactured goods, it had to solicit authorization for the purchase of foreign exchange through the national treasury in order to make payment.

Even more rigid exchange controls existed in the former Soviet Union and other Eastern bloc countries prior to the fall of communism, where trade in foreign currency was a crime meriting harsh punishment. The problem with such tight exchange controls is that often they promote a black market in unauthorized trade in the controlled currency. In such cases, the official rate of exchange for a currency will tend to be *overvalued*, or in other words, possessing an officially stated value which does not reflect its true worth. The black market will more likely reflect its true worth on the street.

Another issue affecting foreign exchange concerns fluctuation in the rates of exchange, whereby currencies either *appreciate* or *depreciate* with respect to one another. Since the 1970s most of the world's currencies have been on a floating system, often fluctuating with wide variations. For example, in 1976, the Mexican peso traded at an exchange rate of 12.5 per dollar, but 11 years later in 1987 it had fallen to 2,300 pesos per dollar.

This peso devaluation reflected much greater inflation in Mexico compared to the United States, and the fear of political/financial instability in Mexico prompted Mexican residents to buy dollars for security. By 1993, the exchange rate had fallen to 3,200 pesos per dollar, and the Mexican government dropped three zeroes off the currency, creating a new peso (nuevo peso) worth 3.2 pesos per dollar. This rate climbed again with the devaluation that began in December 1994 to the 8 pesos per dollar range. On the other hand, in the early 1980s, the Japanese yen traded at approximately 250 yen per dollar, but by 1994 had appreciated to 97 yen per dollar (before losing value slightly to approximately 115 yen per dollar in 1997). This long-term devaluation of the dollar against the yen reflected continuing U.S. trade deficits with Japan, as well as a higher level of inflation in the United States relative to Japan.

Many countries attempt to maintain a lower value for their currency in order to encourage exports. The reason for this is that if the dollar devalues against the Japanese yen, for example, U.S. manufactured goods should become cheaper to the Japanese consumers, who find that their supply of yen suddenly purchases a greater quantity of dollars. The devaluation of a currency should then help to reduce a nation's deficit with its trading partners, in the absence of other countervailing factors.

Directly related to the issue of floating currency is the concept of transaction gain or loss on the import or export of merchandise. Returning to the example of

KFC–Mexico's import of $10,000 in kitchen equipment, if that company ordered the equipment in late 1996 (when the exchange rate was 7 pesos per dollar) for payment in April 1997 (when the exchange rate had fallen to 8 pesos per dollar), they would incur a foreign exchange transaction loss. This is because the company would have to buy dollars for payment in the month of December at a devalued rate, thus paying more pesos for every dollar purchased. Only if they had the foresight (or good luck) to buy the dollars in late 1996 at the more favorable rate could they avoid this foreign exchange loss. A more detailed illustration follows:

Cost of imported equipment in pesos at exchange rate in effect at order date (7 pesos per dollar)	70,000 pesos
Cost of imported equipment in pesos at exchange rate in effect at payment date (8 pesos per dollar)	80,000 pesos
Foreign exchange loss in pesos	10,000 pesos

Conversely, if the peso were to *revalue* (or appreciate) prior to the payment date, KFC–Mexico would have a transaction gain in foreign exchange.

Spot versus Forward Foreign Exchange

If payment on a transaction is to be made immediately, the purchaser has no choice other than to buy foreign exchange on the spot (or current) market, for immediate delivery. However, if payment is to be made at some future date, as was the case in the KFC–Mexico example, the purchaser has the option of buying foreign exchange on the spot market or on the **forward** market, for delivery at some future date. The advantage of the forward market is that the buyer can lock in an exchange rate and avoid the risk of currency fluctuations; this is called **hedging**, or protecting oneself against potential loss.

Many multinational corporations actively buy and sell the foreign currencies of the countries in which they do business.[8] For example, as in the case of Sony just described, Canadian Oil Sands Trust took advantage of an opportunity to reduce its exposure to foreign exchange fluctuations with a US$1.5 billion currency hedge over a 20 year period in 1996. Around 35 percent of the company's U.S. dollar exposure was attributable to sales of its production was hedged against the Canadian dollar at a rate of $0.6937 (US$/Cdn$). During 1996, this hedge resulted in an additional $0.09 per unit of distributable income to is shareholders. With the Canadian dollar averaging around US$0.74 so far in 1997, Canadian Oil Sands's currency hedge is continuing to have a positive effect.[9]

The sound management of foreign exchange in an environment of volatile floating rates requires an astute corporate treasurer and effective coordination with the purchasing or marketing functions of the business.[10] If they see their national cur-

---

[8]Timothy A. Luehrman, "Exchange Rate Changes and the Distribution of Industry Value," *Journal of International Business Studies*, Fourth Quarter 1991, pp. 619–649.

[9]"Canadian Oil Sands Trust Announces Fourth Quarter Results," *Canada NewsWire, Ltd.* (January 27, 1997).

[10]Raj Aggarwal and Luc A. Soenen, "Managing Persistent Real Changes in Currency Values: The Role of Multinational Operating Strategies," *Columbia Journal of World Business* (Fall 1989), pp. 60–67.

rency or the currency of one of their subsidiaries declining, they may purchase a stronger foreign currency as a reserve for future use. Often, if the corporation's money managers are savvy enough, significant income can be generated through foreign exchange transactions beyond that of normal company operations.[11]

Forward currency markets exist for the strongest currencies, including the British pound, Canadian dollar, German mark, Japanese yen, Swiss franc, and U.S. dollar. The terms of purchase are usually for delivery of the foreign currency in either thirty, sixty, or ninety days from the date of purchase. These aforementioned currencies are often called *hard currencies*, because they are the world's strongest and represent the world's leading economies.

Forward currency markets do not exist for the traditionally weaker currencies such as the Mexican peso or the Indian rupee, because there is no worldwide demand for such a market; nearly all international transactions are expressed in terms of a hard currency. Exhibit 3-4 illustrates the daily quotes for foreign exchange on the spot and forward markets. In the first two columns, the foreign currency is expressed in terms of how many dollars it takes to buy one unit. The third and fourth columns indicate the inverse, or how many units of the foreign currency it would take to purchase one dollar.

By custom, when quoting the value of a foreign currency, it is expressed in how many units of that currency it takes to buy one dollar. For example, on May 23, 1997, the value of the yen was expressed as 115.70 yen per dollar. The British pound is an exception to this, as its value is customarily expressed in terms of how many dollars it takes to purchase one pound. On the same day, May 23, 1997, the pound's value was expressed at $1.6360.

Exchange Rate Pass-Through

The dramatic swings in the value of the dollar since the early 1980s have made it clear that foreign companies charge different prices in the United States than in other markets.[12] When the dollar appreciated against the Japanese yen and the German mark in the 1980s, Japanese cars were priced fairly low in the United States, justified by the cheaper yen, while German cars became far more expensive in the United States than in Europe. In the 1990s, when the dollar began depreciating against the yen and the mark, Japanese and German auto makers had to increase their dollar prices in the United States. Japanese auto makers did not raise their prices nearly as much as German competitors. Obviously, they "price to market."[13] As a result, Japanese car makers did not lose as much U.S. market share as did German car makers.

One of the success factors for many Japanese companies in the U.S. markets seems to be in the way they used dollar–yen exchange rates to their advantage, known as the **target exchange rate**. Japanese companies, in particular, are known to employ a very unfavorable target exchange rate (i.e., hypothetically appreciated yen

---

[11]Ike Mathur, "Managing Foreign Exchange Risk Profitably," *Columbia Journal of World Business* (Winter 1982), pp. 23–30.

[12]Kenneth A. Froot and Paul D. Klemperer, "Exchange Rate Pass-Through When Market Share Matters," *American Economic Review*, 79 (September 1989), pp. 637–54.

[13]"Pricing Paradox: Consumers Still Find Imported Bargains Despite Weak Dollar," *Wall Street Journal* (October 7, 1992), p. A6.

EXHIBIT 3-4
EXCHANGE RATES (FRIDAY MAY 23, 1997)

The New York foreign exchange selling rates below apply to trading among banks in amounts of $1 million and more, as quoted at 4 p.m. Eastern time by Dow Jones and other sources. Retail transactions provide fewer units of foreign currency per dollar.

Country	U.S.$ equivalent		Currency per U.S. $	
	Fri	Thu	Fri	Thu
Argentina (Peso)	1.0014	1.0014	.9986	.9986
Australia (Dollar)	.7658	.7774	1.3058	1.2863
Austria (Schilling)	.08394	.08386	11.913	11.925
Bahrain (Dinar)	2.6525	2.6525	.3770	.3770
Belgium (Franc)	.02865	.02855	34.905	35.022
Brazil (Real)	.9323	.9345	1.0726	1.0701
Britain (Pound)	1.6360	1.6240	.6112	.6158
1-month forward	1.6350	1.6230	.6116	.6161
3-months forward	1.6332	1.6212	.6123	.6168
6-months forward	1.6304	1.6184	.6134	.6179
Canada (Dollar)	.7270	.7288	1.3756	1.3721
1-month forward	.7285	.7304	1.3726	1.3691
3-months forward	.7316	.7335	1.3669	1.3633
6-months forward	.7358	.7376	1.3591	1.3557
Chile (Peso)	.002384	.002389	419.40	418.60
China (Renminbi)	.1202	.1201	8.3223	8.3249
Colombia (Peso)	.0009256	.0009255	1080.43	1080.44
Czech. Rep. (Koruna)	. . .	. . .	. . .	. . .
Commercial rate	.03244	.03265	30.824	30.629
Denmark (Krone)	.1551	.1550	6.4475	6.4510
Ecuador (Sucre)	. . .	. . .	. . .	. . .
Floating rate	.0002574	.0002574	3885.00	3885.00
Finland (Markka)	.1957	.1959	5.1087	5.1055
France (Franc)	.1752	.1753	5.7085	5.7045
1-month forward	.1755	.1756	5.6973	5.6934
3-months forward	.1762	.1763	5.6751	5.6712
6-months forward	.1773	.1774	5.6399	5.6360
Germany (Mark)	.5904	.5902	1.6938	1.6943
1-month forward	.5916	.5915	1.6902	1.6907
3-months forward	.5942	.5941	1.6828	1.6832
6-months forward	.5984	.5982	1.6711	1.6717
Greece (Drachma)	.003696	.003701	270.57	270.23
Hong Kong (Dollar)	.1292	.1293	7.7400	7.7368
Hungary (Forint)	.005520	.005538	181.17	180.56
India (Rupee)	.02797	.02794	35.755	35.790
Indonesia (Rupiah)	.0004096	.0004095	2441.50	2442.00
Ireland (Punt)	1.5207	1.5076	.6576	.6633
Israel (Shekel)	.2943	.2941	3.3983	3.4001
Italy (Lira)	.0005998	.0005995	1667.20	1668.00
Japan (Yen)	.008643	.008618	115.70	116.03
1-month forward	.008681	.008657	115.19	115.52
3-months forward	.008758	.008733	114.18	114.50
6-months forward	.008876	.008853	112.66	112.96
Jordan (Dinar)	1.4094	1.4094	.7095	.7095

Continued

EXHIBIT 3-4 (continued)

Country	U.S.$ equivalent		Currency per U.S. $	
	Fri	Thu	Fri	Thu
Kuwait (Dinar)	3.3091	3.3091	.3022	.3022
Lebanon (Pound)	.0006484	.0006484	1542.25	1542.25
Malaysia (Ringgit)	.3994	.3995	2.5035	2.5033
Malta (Lira)	2.5974	2.5641	.3850	.3900
Mexico (Peso)	. . .	. . .	. . .	. . .
Floating rate	.1270	.1272	7.8750	7.8630
Netherlands (Guilder)	.5252	.5250	1.9040	1.9049
New Zealand (Dollar)	.6924	.6930	1.4443	1.4430
Norway (Krone)	.1416	.1416	7.0600	7.0618
Pakistan (Rupee)	.02508	.02508	39.880	39.880
Peru (new Sol)	.3773	.3774	2.6507	2.6497
Philippines (Peso)	.03791	.03791	26.378	26.375
Poland (Zloty)	.3113	.3110	3.2125	3.2150
Portugal (Escudo)	.005848	.005853	171.00	170.85
Russia (Ruble) (a)	.0001739	.0001738	5751.00	5754.00
Saudi Arabia (Riyal)	.2666	.2666	3.7505	3.7505
Singapore (Dollar)	.6988	.6983	1.4310	1.4320
Slovak Rep. (Koruna)	.03080	.03080	32.473	32.473
South Africa (Rand)	.2237	.2238	4.4710	4.4685
South Korea (Won)	.001123	.001122	890.85	891.35
Spain (Peseta)	.007000	.006998	142.86	142.90
Sweden (Krona)	.1316	.1316	7.6004	7.5995
Switzerland (Franc)	.7125	.7080	1.4035	1.4125
1-month forward	.7151	.7104	1.3985	1.4076
3-months forward	.7201	.7155	1.3887	1.3976
6-months forward	.7283	.7235	1.3730	1.3821
Taiwan (Dollar)	.03594	.03596	27.824	27.810
Thailand (Baht)	.03920	.03902	25.508	25.629
Turkey (Lira)	.00000723	.00000724	138235.00	138090.00
United Arab (Dirham)	.2723	.2723	3.6725	3.6725
Uruguay (New Peso)	. . .	. . .	. . .	. . .
Financial	.1076	.1076	9.2950	9.2950
Venezuela (Bolivar)	.002065	.002065	484.22	484.37
SDR	1.3946	1.3954	.7170	.7166
ECU	1.1530	1.1507	. . .	. . .

Special Drawing Rights (SDR) are based on exchange rates for the U.S., German, British, French, and Japanese currencies. Source: International Monetary Fund.

European Currency Unit (ECU) is based on a basket of community currencies.

Source: Wall Street Journal, May 27, 1997, p. C19.

environment) for their costing strategy to make sure they will not be adversely affected should the yen appreciate. Therefore, despite close to a twofold appreciation of the yen vis-à-vis the dollar from 240 yen/$ in to 110 yen/$ in a decade, the dollar prices of Japanese products have not increased nearly as much. The extent to which a foreign company changes dollar prices of its products in the U.S. market as a result of exchange rate fluctuations is called **exchange rate pass-through**. Although accurately estimating the average increase in dollar prices of Japanese products is almost impossible, our estimate suggests about 30 percent price increase, or pass-through, over the same period. If this estimate is accurate, Japanese companies must have somehow absorbed more than 70 percent of the price increase. This cost absorption could result from smaller profit margins, cost reductions, or both. According to Morgan Stanley Japan Ltd.'s estimate,[14] Toyota could break even at an unheard-of 52 yen to the dollar. In other words, as long as the Japanese currency does not appreciate all the way to 52 yen to the dollar, Toyota is expected to earn windfall operating profits. This pass-through issue will be elaborated on in Chapter 13 when we discuss global pricing issues.

BALANCE OF PAYMENTS

The balance of payments of a nation summarizes all the transactions that have taken place between its residents and the residents of other countries over a specified time period, usually a month, quarter, or year. The transactions are recorded in three categories: current account, capital account and official reserves. Sometimes, the capital account is broken down into two accounts—capital account and financial account. There is also an extra category for errors and omissions. Exhibit 3-5 shows the balance of payments for the United States (the historical trend of the U.S. balance of payments is presented earlier in Exhibit 1-2 in Chapter 1).

The balance of payments record is made on the basis of rules of debits and credits, similar to those in business accounting. Exports, like sales, are outflows of goods, and are entered as credits to merchandise trade. Imports, or inflows, are represented by debits to the same account. These exports and imports are most likely offset by an opposite entry to the capital account, reflecting the receipt of cash or the outflow of cash for payment.

When a German tourist visits the United States and spends money on meals and lodging, it is a credit to the U.S. trade in services balance reflecting the rendering of a service to a foreign resident. On the other hand, this transaction would represent a debit to the trade in services account of Germany, reflecting the receipt of a service from a foreign resident by a resident of Germany. If the foreign resident's payment is made in cash, the credit to trade in services is offset by a debit (inflow) to short-term capital. On the other hand, if a foreign resident purchases land in the United States, paying cash, this is represented on the United States balance of payments as a debit to short-term capital (representing the inflow of payment for the land) and a credit to long-term capital (representing the outflow of ownership of real estate).

This is based on the principle of double entry accounting, so theoretically every debit must be offset by a credit to some other account within the balance of payments statement. In other words, the balance of payments statement must always balance, because total debits must equal total credits. A deficit (debit balance) in one account will then be offset by a surplus (credit balance) in another account.

---

[14]Valerie Reitman, "Toyota Names a Chief Likely to Shake Up Global Auto Business," *Wall Street Journal* (August 11, 1995), p. A1, A5.

EXHIBIT 3-5
U.S. BALANCE OF PAYMENTS, 1980–1996.
(IN $MILLIONS. MINUS SIGN (−) INDICATES DEBITS)

Type of Transaction	1980	1985	1987	1988	1989	1990	1991	1992	1993	1994	1995	1996
Exports of goods and services[1]	**344,440**	**382,747**	**449,514**	**560,426**	**642,025**	**697,426**	**718,194**	**737,394**	**763,826**	**838,820**	**965,008**	**1,032,478**
Merchandise, excl. military[2,3]	224,250	215,915	250,208	320,230	362,120	389,307	416,913	440,352	456,823	502,485	574,879	611,669
Services	47,584	73,155	98,539	111,126	127,387	147,819	164,278	178,617	187,755	198,716	208,828	223,907
Transfers under U.S. military agency sales contracts	9,029	8,718	11,106	9,284	8,564	9,932	11,135	11,693	12,650	12,418	12,674	13,802
Travel	10,588	17,762	23,563	29,434	36,205	43,007	48,385	54,742	57,875	60,406	60,278	64,499
Passenger fares	2,591	4,411	7,003	8,976	10,657	15,298	15,854	16,618	16,611	17,477	18,213	19,579
Other transportation	11,618	14,674	17,471	19,811	21,106	22,745	23,331	23,691	23,983	26,078	28,553	29,115
Royalties and license fees	7,085	6,678	10,183	12,146	13,818	16,634	18,114	20,015	20,637	22,436	25,852	28,829
Current Account												
Other private services	6,276	20,035	28,688	30,812	36,450	39,535	46,770	50,997	55,101	59,022	62,488	67,268
U.S. Government misc. services	398	878	526	664	587	668	690	861	899	880	771	815
Income on U.S. assets abroad	72,606	93,677	100,767	129,070	152,517	160,300	137,003	118,425	119,248	137,619	181,301	196,902
Direct investment	37,146	30,547	39,608	52,092	55,368	58,740	52,198	51,912	61,579	67,702	91,195	98,260
Other private receipts	32,898	57,631	55,848	70,275	91,496	91,048	76,781	59,399	52,561	65,835	85,511	94,078
U.S. Government receipts	2,562	5,499	5,311	6,703	5,653	10,512	8,023	7,114	5,108	4,082	4,595	4,564
Imports of goods, services and income	**−333,774**	**−484,037**	**−592,745**	**−662,487**	**−719,758**	**−756,694**	**−732,486**	**−766,796**	**−829,668**	**−954,304**	**−1,087,827**	**−1,155,101**
Merchandise, excl. military[2,3]	−249,750	−338,088	−409,765	−447,189	−477,365	−498,337	−490,981	−536,458	−589,441	−668,584	−749,348	−799,343
Services	−41,491	−72,862	−91,678	−99,491	−103,535	−118,783	−119,614	−121,991	−129,979	−138,829	−145,777	−150,440
Direct defense expenditures	−10,851	−13,108	−14,950	−15,604	−15,313	−17,531	−16,409	−13,835	−12,202	−10,270	−9,864	−10,993
Travel	−10,397	−24,558	−29,310	−32,114	−33,416	−37,349	−35,322	−38,552	−40,713	−43,562	−45,496	−48,712
Passenger Fares	−3,607	−6,444	−7,283	−7,729	−8,249	−10,531	−10,012	−10,556	−11,313	−12,696	−13,385	−14,287
Other transportation	−11,790	−15,643	−19,057	−20,969	−22,260	−25,168	−25,204	−25,459	−26,558	−28,373	−29,505	−29,100
Royalties and license fees	−724	−1,170	−1,857	−2,601	−2,528	−3,135	−4,035	−5,074	−4,863	−5,666	−6,561	−7,036
Other private services	−2,909	−10,203	−17,328	−18,554	−19,898	−23,150	−26,516	−26,214	−31,999	−35,605	−38,147	−37,626
U.S. Government miscellaneous services	−1,214	−1,735	−1,893	−1,921	−1,871	−1,919	−2,116	−2,301	−2,331	−2,657	−2,818	−2,686
Income on foreign assets in the United States	−42,532	−73,087	−91,302	−115,806	−138,858	−139,574	−121,892	−108,346	−110,248	−146,891	−192,703	−205,318
Direct investment	−8,635	−7,213	−7,425	−11,693	−6,507	−2,871	3,433	−317	−5,250	−22,621	−32,062	−33,817
Other private payments	−21,214	−42,745	−57,659	−72,398	−93,987	−95,661	−83,796	−67,549	−63,437	−77,251	−99,362	−100,159
U.S. Government payments	−12,684	−23,129	−26,218	−31,715	−38,364	−41,042	−41,529	−40,480	−41,561	−47,019	−61,279	−71,342
Unilateral transfers (excl. military grants), net	**−8,349**	**−22,954**	**−23,107**	**−25,023**	**−26,106**	**−33,393**	**6,869**	**−32,148**	**−34,084**	**−35,761**	**−30,095**	**−42,472**
U.S. Government grants	−5,486	−11,268	−10,287	−10,513	−10,892	−17,417	24,194	−15,083	−16,311	−15,814	−11,027	−14,634
U.S. Government pensions	−1,818	−2,138	−2,221	−2,501	−2,516	−2,934	−3,461	−3,735	−3,785	−4,247	−3,114	−4,233
Private remittances and other transfers	−1,044	−9,549	−10,599	−12,009	−12,698	−13,042	−13,864	−13,330	−13,988	−15,700	−19,954	−23,605

Financial Account

U.S. Assets abroad, net (increase/capital outflow (−))	−306,830	−280,096	−125,851	−184,589	−65,875	−57,881	−74,011	−168,744	−100,087	−72,617	−39,889	−86,967
U.S. official reserve assets, net	6,668	−9,742	5,346	−1,379	3,901	5,763	−2,158	−25,293	−3,912	9,149	−3,858	−8,155
Special drawing rights	370	−808	−441	−537	2,316	−177	−192	−535	127	−509	−897	−16
Reserve position in the International Monetary Fund	−1,280	−2,466	494	−44	−2,692	−367	731	471	1,025	2,070	908	−1,667
Foreign currencies	7,578	−6,468	5,293	−797	4,277	6,307	−2,697	−25,229	−5,064	7,588	−3,869	−6,472
U.S. Govt. assets, other than official reserve assets, net	−665	−326	−322	−330	−1,661	2,911	2,307	1,259	2,967	1,006	−2,821	−5,162
U.S. credits and other long-term assets	−4,909	−4,744	−5,182	−6,299	−7,403	−12,874	−8,430	−5,590	−7,680	−6,506	−7,657	−9,860
Repayments on U.S. credits and other long-term assets	4,155	4,352	5,044	6,270	5,809	16,776	10,867	6,723	10,370	7,625	4,719	4,456
U.S. foreign currency holdings and U.S. short-term assets, net	89	66	−184	−301	−66	−992	−130	125	277	−113	117	242
U.S. private assets, net	−312,833	−270,028	−130,875	−182,880	−68,115	−66,555	−74,160	−144,710	−99,141	−82,771	−33,211	−73,651
Direct investments abroad	−88,304	−96,897	−49,370	−72,601	−42,640	−31,369	−29,950	−36,834	−16,175	−28,355	−14,065	−19,222
Foreign securities	−104,533	−93,769	−49,799	−141,807	−46,415	−45,673	−28,765	−22,070	−7,846	−5,251	−7,481	−3,568
U.S. claims on unaffiliated foreigners reported by U.S. nonbanking concerns	−31,777	−20,358	−32,621	1,531	45	11,097	−27,824	−27,646	−21,193	−7,046	−10,342	−4,023
U.S. claims reported by U.S. banks n.i.e.[8]	−88,219	−59,004	915	29,947	20,895	−610	12,379	−58,160	−53,927	−42,119	−1,323	−46,838
Foreign assets in the U.S. net (increase/capital inflow (+))	525,046	426,325	291,365	248,529	153,823	94,241	122,192	218,490	240,265	242,983	141,183	58,112
Foreign official assets in the U.S., net	122,778	110,483	39,409	72,146	40,466	17,389	33,910	8,503	39,758	45,387	−1,119	15,497
U.S. Government securities	115,482	72,507	36,748	53,014	22,403	16,147	30,243	1,532	43,050	44,802	−1,139	11,895
U.S. Treasury securities	111,151	68,773	30,723	48,952	18,454	14,846	29,576	149	41,741	43,238	−838	9,708
Other	4,331	3,734	6,025	4,062	3,949	1,301	667	1,383	1,309	1,564	−301	2,187
Other U.S. Government liabilities	1,404	1,814	2,211	1,706	2,180	1,367	1,868	160	−467	−2,326	844	615
U.S. liabilities reported by U.S. banks, n.i.e.[8]	4,614	32,896	2,923	14,841	16,571	−1,484	3,385	4,976	−319	3,918	645	−159
Other foreign official assets	1,278	3,266	−2,473	2,585	−688	1,359	−1,586	1,835	−2,506	−1,007	−1,469	3,145
Other foreign assets in the United States, net	402,268	315,842	251,956	176,383	113,358	76,853	88,282	209,987	200,507	197,596	142,301	42,615
Direct investments in the United States	83,950	74,701	49,448	41,108	17,600	22,004	47,915	67,736	57,278	58,219	20,010	16,918
U.S. Treasury securities	153,784	99,081	33,811	24,063	36,857	18,826	−2,534	29,618	20,239	−7,643	20,433	2,645
U.S. securities other than U.S. Treasury securities	131,682	94,576	58,625	79,864	29,867	35,144	1,592	38,767	26,353	42,120	50,962	5,457
U.S. liabilities to unaffiliated foreigners reported by U.S. nonbanking concerns	n.a.	27,578	−4,324	10,489	13,573	−3,115	45,133	22,086	32,893	18,363	9,851	6,852
U.S. liabilities reported by U.S. banks, n.i.e.[8]	−1,558	19,906	114,396	20,859	15,461	3,994	−3,824	51,780	63,744	86,537	41,045	10,743

Continued

EXHIBIT 3-5 (continued)

Type of Transaction	1980	1985	1987	1988	1989	1990	1991	1992	1993	1994	1995	1996
Allocations of special drawing rights	**1,153**	n.a.	n.a.	n.a.	n.a.	n.a.	n.a.	n.a.	n.a.	n.a.	n.a.	. . .
Discrepancy												
Statistical discrepancy	25,386	22,950	−4,028	−13,095	54,094	44,480	−28,936	−26,399	35,985	−14,269	6,684	−53,122
Summary statistics												
Balance on merchandise trade	−25,500	−122,173	−159,557	−126,959	−115,245	−109,030	−74,068	−96,106	−132,618	−166,099	−174,469	−187,674
Balance on services	6,093	294	6,861	11,635	23,853	29,037	44,664	56,626	57,777	59,887	63,052	73,467
Balance on investment income	30,073	20,590	9,465	13,264	13,659	20,725	1,511	10,079	9,000	−9,272	−11,402	−8,416
Balance on goods, services, and income	10,666	−101,290	−143,231	−102,060	−77,733	−59,268	−14,293	−29,402	−65,841	−115,484	−122,819	−122,623
Unilateral transfers, net	−8,349	−22,954	−23,107	−25,023	−26,106	−33,393	6,869	−32,148	−34,084	−35,761	−30,095	−42,472
Balance on current account	2,317	−124,243	−166,338	−127,083	−103,839	−92,661	−7,424	−61,549	−99,925	−151,245	−152,914	−165,095

− Represents zero

n.a. Not applicable

Sources: U.S. Bureau of Economic Analysis. *Statistical Abstract of the United States 1996*; *Survey of Current Business*, (June 1997 issue).

If the statement does not balance, an entry must be made to the errors and omissions account. But in reality, there is no national accountant making accounting entries for every international transaction. The U.S. Department of Commerce, which prepares the balance of payments statement, must gather information from a variety of sources, including banks and other business entities concerning the inflow and outflow of goods, services, gifts, and capital items. Since the information used by the Department of Commerce will come from a number of different sources, it is near certain that the statement will not balance like a balance sheet of a corporation, where double entries are made by corporate accountants for each transaction. Therefore, the errors and omissions category will reflect a significant dollar volume.

The balance of payments in goods account (**trade balance**, for short) shows trade in currently produced goods as well as unilateral transfers (private gifts) of merchandise. Trade balance is the most frequently used indicator of the health of a country's international trade position. The balance of payments in current account (**current account balance**) shows trade in currently produced goods and services, as well as unilateral transfers (private gifts and foreign aid) of merchandise. The goods or merchandise account deals with tangibles such as autos, grain, machinery, or equipment that can be seen and felt, as well as exported and imported. The services account deals with intangibles that are sold or bought internationally. Examples include dividends or interest on foreign investments, royalties on trademarks or patents abroad, food or lodging (travel expenses), and transportation. Unilateral transfers are transactions with no quid pro quo; some of these transfers are made by private individuals and institutions and some by government. These gifts are sometimes for charitable, missionary, or educational purposes, and other times they consist of funds wired home by migrant workers to their families in their country of origin. The largest unilateral transfers are aid, either in money or in the form of goods and services, from developed to developing countries.

The balance of payments in capital account (**capital account**) summarizes financial transactions and is divided into two sections, short- and long-term capital accounts. Long-term capital includes any financial asset maturing in a period exceeding one year, including equities. Subaccounts under long-term capital are direct investment and portfolio investment.

Direct investments are those investments in enterprises or properties that are effectively controlled by residents of another country. Whenever 10 percent or more of the voting shares in a U.S. company are held by foreign investors, the company is classified as a U.S. affiliate of a foreign company and therefore a foreign direct investment.[15] Similarly, if U.S. investors hold 10 percent or more of the voting shares of a foreign company, the entity is considered a foreign affiliate of a U.S. company.

Portfolio investment includes all long-term investments that do not give the investors effective control over the investment. Such transactions typically involve the purchase of stocks or bonds of foreign investors for investment. These shares are normally bought for investment, not control, purposes.

---

[15]Department of Commerce, *U.S. Direct Investment Abroad* (Washington, D.C.: Bureau of Economic Analysis, 1994).

◆ ◆

$\mathcal{G}$LOBAL PERSPECTIVE 3-1

BALANCE OF PAYMENTS AND COMPETITIVENESS OF A NATION

The Information Age characterizes the world we live in today, but some people do not seem to recognize it.

Each time the U.S. trade statistics are reported, we hear the dismal news of a trade deficit—the largest U.S. trade deficit ever of $172 billion in 1987, and the second largest trade deficit of upwards of $150 billion in 1994, despite a U.S. export boom. But when it comes to U.S. balance of payments, many people do not look beyond the "trade" statistics.

When we say *trade statistics*, we talk about exports and imports of *goods*. Trade of *services* is not included. When the United States incurred a $164 billion trade deficit in goods in 1994, its trade deficit was partly offset by a $60 billion trade *surplus* in services. Such services—the hallmark of the Information Age—include telecommunications, education, financial services, and a host of other intangibles.

These and other services did not only have just one good year. Around the world, service companies are expanding rapidly, ringing up sales at a fast pace. Indeed, worldwide, services now account for more than $600 billion in international trade.

Why, then, don't we notice this important development? It is primarily because many of us are still measuring our economic performance based on the facts of an earlier era, which meant apples, steel, sneakers and the like—tangible merchandise and nothing else. Many just do not realize a new day has dawned—one in which ad-vertising exports can mean as much as auto exports.

Take the Department of Commerce, which collects U.S. trade data. The department keeps track of more than 10,000 different kinds of tangible goods. But when it comes to services, the agency collects trade data for only a few service categories. Services excluded from Department of Commerce data, or addressed only partially, include such significant ones as public relations, management consulting, legal services, and many financial and information-related services. While accurate estimates are difficult, it is believed that exports of services would be 70 percent higher than reported in Department of Commerce trade data.

What is wrong with underplaying the importance of services? First, it misleads the public about the nation's true competitiveness. Second, it induces government officials to develop trade policy on mistaken premises. Third, and worst of all, the growth of services could be thwarted because many nontariff barriers to trade in services—such as discriminatory licensing and certification rules, and bans of the use of internationally known company names—do not get as much policy attention as tariffs on goods and thus could harm U.S. service companies trying to sell various services abroad.

There is also a word of caution. The increased importance of services in the U.S. balance of payments does not necessarily mean that the United States can ignore manufacturing businesses. First, exports of services have been historically too small to offset the staggering deficits in goods. Second, if the United States loses mastery and control of manufacturing, the high-paying and thus important service jobs that are directly linked to manufacturing—such as product designing, engineering, accounting, financing and insurance, and transportation—may also wither away. Manufacturing and those services are tightly linked and may not be separable.

Source: Based on Daniel J. Connors, Jr. and Douglas S. Heller, "The Good Word in Trade is 'Services'," *New York Times* (September 19, 1993), p. B1; Stephen S. Cohen and John Zysman, *Manufacturing Matters: The Myth of the Post-Industrial Economy* (New York: Basic Books, 1987); and trade figures adopted from the International Monetary Fund, *Balance of Payments Statistics Yearbook 1995*.

Short-term capital includes only those items maturing in less than one year, including cash. The official reserves account registers the movement of funds to or from central banks.

A key point to remember here is that the deficit or surplus is calculated based not on the aggregate of all transactions in the balance of payments, but on the net balance for certain selected categories.

There are three particularly important balances to identify on the balance of payments statement of a country, including the balance of the merchandise trade account, the current account (including merchandise trade, trade in services and unilateral transfers) and the basic balance (the current account and long term capital). Everyone knows about the U.S. deficit in merchandise trade, but what is less commonly known is that the U.S. regularly runs a surplus in trade in services. This surplus offsets a large part of the deficit in the merchandise account (see Global Perspective 3-1).

Many observers have commented that in the 1980s the United States was able to continue its import binge via the sale of long-term investments, including real estate and ownership in companies. This belief was heightened by the high-profile sale of such U.S. landmarks as Rockefeller Center and Columbia records to foreign investors. These foreigners invested in U.S. capital assets, paying in cash that was then recycled in payment for merchandise imports by U.S. residents. The criticism was made that the U.S. was selling off capital assets for short-term merchandise imports like a wealthy heir who sells off the family jewels to finance a profligate lifestyle. Meanwhile, others viewed the increase in foreign investment in the United States as proof of the nation's vitality and long-term attractiveness to investors.

The Internal and External Adjustments

According to the theory of international trade and balance of payments, a surplus or deficit in a country's basic balance should be self-correcting. This self-correction is accomplished through the internal and external market adjustments. The market adjustment mechanisms bring a nation's deficit or surplus within the basic balance back into equilibrium. This is a natural event where the economy of a nation corrects its prior excesses by moving back toward the middle.[16]

The **internal market adjustment** refers to the movement of prices and incomes in a country. The following is an example of such an adjustment in the case of a Current Account surplus country, such as Japan.

1. As Japan continues to export more than it imports resulting in a surplus in the Current Account, its internal money supply grows, the result of receiving payment from foreigners for their purchases of goods, services, and investments originating in Japan. The payments are made to Japanese residents and may be deposited in banks either in Japan or abroad, either in yen or foreign currency. But wherever and however payment is made, it becomes an asset of a Japanese resident.

2. As Japan's money supply increases, domestic residents of Japan spend more, because they have more money available to spend. Japan's money supply is increasing because foreigners are buying Japanese goods in greater quantities than Japanese are buying foreign goods.

3. As local residents in Japan spend more, domestic prices rise. In other words, inflation occurs. This results simply because Japanese residents have greater demand for products and services as a result of the prosperity generated by their current account surplus.

4. As domestic prices increase, Japanese residents find that foreign goods are relatively cheaper. This is because foreign countries are not experiencing the prosperity-induced inflation that Japan is.

---

[16]Franklin R. Root, *International Trade and Investment* (Cincinnati, Ohio: Southwestern Publishing Co., 1984).

5. Because the Japanese find foreign goods cheaper, they import more goods from abroad. This begins to reduce Japan's current account surplus and bring it back into balance.

The **external market adjustment** concerns exchange rates or a nation's currency and its value with respect to the currencies of other nations. The following is a description of the application of the external adjustment to a surplus nation, in this case again, Japan:

1. Japan exports more than it imports, resulting in a surplus in its current account. So, foreigners must pay Japanese residents for the goods they purchase from Japan. Payment will likely be made in Japanese yen.

2. Currency is a commodity like any other, whose market price rises and falls with relative supply and demand. Because Japanese residents export more than they import, there is more demand for yen by foreigners than demand for dollars by Japanese residents. This excess in relative demand for yen causes it to appreciate in value with respect to other currencies. Remember, it appreciates because foreigners must pay Japanese suppliers for their goods and services.

3. The appreciated yen causes Japanese goods, services, and investments to be more expensive to foreign residents who convert prices quoted in yen to their local currencies.

4. All other things being equal, this should cause foreigners to buy fewer Japanese goods and thus shrink Japan's trade surplus.

However, other factors, such as a country's taste for foreign goods and general habits of consumption, must be taken into account, as well as the quality and reputation of a country's manufactured goods. Many other factors beyond domestic prices and foreign exchange values affect Japan's trade balance with the United States, and these have become a topic of serious discussion between the governments of these two nations.

SUMMARY ◆

The international financial environment is constantly changing as a result of income growth, balance of payments position, inflation, exchange rate fluctuations, and unpredictable political events in various countries. The International Monetary Fund and World Bank also assist in the economic development of many countries, particularly those of developing countries, and promote stable economic growth in many parts of the world. In most cases, the change in a county's balance of payments position is an immediate precursor to its currency rate fluctuation and subsequent instability in the international financial market.

Thanks to the huge domestic economy and the international transaction currency role of the U.S. dollar, many U.S. companies have been shielded from the changes in the international financial market during much of the postwar era. However, as the U.S. economy depends increasingly on international trade and investment for its livelihood, few companies can ignore the changes.

Having been more dependent on foreign business, many European and Japanese companies have honed their international financial expertise as a matter of survival, particularly since the early 1970s. Accordingly, European countries and Japan have been better able to cope with foreign exchange rate fluctuations than the United States.

International marketers should be aware of the immediate consequences of exchange rate fluctuations on pricing. As increased cost pressure is imminent in an era of global competition, cost competitiveness has become an extremely important strategic issue to many companies. Astute companies have even employed an adverse target exchange rate for cost accounting and pricing purposes. Although ac-curate prediction is not possible, international mar-keters should be able to "guesstimate" the direction of exchange rate movements in major currencies. Some tools are available.

REVIEW QUESTIONS ❖

1. How did the U.S. dollar become the international transaction currency in the post–World War II era?

2. Which international currency or currencies are likely to assume increasingly a role of the international transaction currency in international trade? Why?

3. Why is a fixed exchange rate regime that promotes the stability of the currency value inherently unstable?

4. Discuss the primary roles of the International Mone-tary Fund and World Bank.

5. What is the managed float?

6. How does a currency bloc help a multinational com-pany's global operations?

7. Using the purchasing power parity argument, esti-mate whether the U.S. dollar is overvalued or under-valued relative to the German deutsche mark, the French franc, and the Japanese yen.

8. Describe in your own words how the knowledge of spot and forward exchange rate market helps interna-tional marketers.

9. Why is the exchange rate pass-through usually less than perfect (i.e., less than 100 percent)?

10. Define the four types of balance of payments measures.

DISCUSSION QUESTIONS ❖ ❖ ❖ ❖ ❖ ❖ ❖ ❖ ❖ ❖ ❖ ❖ ❖ ❖ ❖ ❖ ❖ ❖ ❖

1. The July 1996 issue of *Japan Economic Newswire* has quoted Fujitsu Limited as taking various steps to pre-vent wild foreign exchange fluctuations from affect-ing the company's business. One step being taken is the balancing of export and import contracts. In the year 1995, the company entered into $2.9 billion of export contracts and $2.3 billion of import contracts. For the year 1996, these figures are expected to be balanced. Explain how this measure would help the firm. What are the advantages and disadvantages of this measure? Are there any alternate courses of ac-tion that would give the same end results?

2. One feature of the Japanese business with companies of the rest of the world has been an insistence of en-tering into import contracts only in U.S. dollar de-nomination. There has been a reluctance on the part of Japanese companies to enter into import contracts in yen. One reason could be what has been cited in the Fujitsu case in the previous question. What could be the other reason/s?

3. The Big Mac Index of the *Economist* has been intro-duced as a guide in the popular press to whether cur-rencies are at their "correct" exchange rate. Although the merits of this index have been mentioned, this in-dex has various defects. Identify and explain the de-fects associated with this index.

4. Since the introduction of a new currency, Real, in Brazil in July 1994, the country has experienced more than a 50% domestic inflation over the period (i.e., at an annual rate of more than 15 percent). Yet, the value of Real relative to the U.S. dollar has remained relatively constant (1 Real in 1994 to 1.06 Real in mid-1997 per U.S. dollar). Brazil's trade deficit is ex-pected to increase to over 5 percent of the country's GDP by 1998 from a balanced position in 1994.[17] As a reference, the United States' largest trade deficit ever recorded in the country's history amounted to a mere 3 percent of its GDP in 1987. How would you advise companies such as Anheuser-Busch and Wal-Mart interested in further increasing their direct in-vestment in local operations?

5. A recent reflection of the perils of foreign exchange fluctuations is the steep depreciation in the value of the Mexican peso, initiated by a government move at

---

[17]Geoff Dyer, "Brazil Demands Fair Play on Deficit," *Financial Times* (April 9, 1997), p. 10.

the end of 1994 to prevent the country from a balance of payments crisis. The value of the Mexican peso plummeted from approximately 3.38 pesos to the dollar in 1994 to its value of approximately 8 pesos to the dollar in May 1997. Although the aggregate trade figures for the years 1995 and 1996 showed a large drop in U.S. exports to Mexico, compared to 1994 (although compared to 1993, U.S. exports to Mexico in 1995 were higher by approximately $5 billion), the drop was not uniform across industries. Certain industries have had little impact of this depreciation.

(a) You are preparing a report for the marketing manager of the generator division of an electrical equipment manufacturing company called ABC, based in the United States. In one section of the report, the marketing manager wants you to highlight the prospects of the Mexican peso for the subsequent year and how it would affect likely sales of a large-size generator (currently being manufactured by only three companies, including ABC, all of which are based outside Mexico).

(b) You are preparing the same report for the marketing manager of an automobile division of a company with manufacturing facilities in the United States (with no current facilities in Mexico). Would you change your forecast prospects for the firm's sales in the subsequent year?

FURTHER READINGS ◆

Athukorala, Premachandra, and Jayant Menon. "Pricing to Market Behavior and Exchange Rate Pass-Through in Japanese Exports." *Economic Journal*, 104 (423) (March 1994):271–81.

Cogue, Dennis E. "Globalization: First We Kill All the Currency Traders." *Journal of Business Strategy*, 17 (2) (March/April 1996):12–13.

Donnely, Raymond, and Edward Shuhi. "The Share Price Reaction of U.S. Exporters to Exchange Rate Movements: An Empirical Study." *Journal of International Business Studies*, 27 (1) (First Quarter 1996):157–65.

Genberg, Hans. *The International Monetary System: Its Institutions and Its Future*. New York: Springer, 1995.

Harvey, John T. "The International Monetary System and Exchange Rate Determination: 1945 to Present." *Journal of Economic Issues*, 29 (2) (June 1995):493–502.

Leondidas, Leonidou L. "Export Barriers: Non-Exporter's Perception." *International Marketing Review*, 12 (1) (1995): 4–25.

Miller, Cyndee. "Marketers Cautious, But Hopeful About Mexico." *Marketing News*, 29 (4) (February 13, 1994):1–2.

Rajgopal, Shan, and Kenneth N. Berhark. "Global Procurement: Motivations and Strategy." *Marketing Intelligence and Planning*, 12 (4) (1994):4–17.

GLOBAL CULTURAL ENVIRONMENT

<big>**4**</big>

CHAPTER OVERVIEW

1. DEFINING CULTURE
2. ELEMENTS OF CULTURE
3. CROSS-CULTURAL COMPARISONS
4. ADAPTING TO FOREIGN CULTURES
5. CROSS-CULTURAL NEGOTIATIONS

Buyer behavior and consumer needs are largely driven by cultural norms. Managers running a company in a foreign country need to interact with people from different cultural environments. Global business means dealing with consumers, strategic partners, distributors, and competitors with different cultural mindsets. Cultures often provide the cement between members of the same society. A given country could be an economic basketcase compared to the rest of the world, but its cultural heritage often provides pride and self-esteem to its citizens. Foreign cultures also intrigue. A stroll along Hong Kong's Nathan Road, Singapore's Orchard Road, or Tokyo's Roppongi reveals the appeal among Asian citizens of Western cuisine and dress codes. At the same time, cultures may also foster resentment, anxiety, or even division. When plans for Euro-Disney were revealed, French intellectuals referred to the planned themepark as a "cultural Chernobyl." The Uruguay Round of GATT negotiations almost got derailed because of the French government's efforts to protect the French movie industry against the Hollywood juggernaut.

In order to grasp the intricacies of foreign markets, it is imperative to get a deep understanding of cultural differences. From a global marketing perspective, the cultural environment matters for two main reasons. First and foremost, cultural forces are a major factor in shaping a company's global marketing mix program. Global marketing managers constantly face the issue of to what degree cultural differences should force adaptations of the firm's marketing strategy. Cultural blunders can easily become costly for MNCs. Some of the possible liabilities of *cultural faux pas* include embarrassment, lost customers, legal consequences, missed opportunities, damage control, and tarnished reputation.[1] Second, cultural analysis often pinpoints market opportunities. Companies that meet cultural needs that have been ignored so far by their competitors often gain a competitive edge. For instance, several Japanese diaper makers were able to steal market share away from Procter & Gamble by selling diapers that were much thinner than the ones marketed by P&G, thereby better meeting the desires of Japanese mothers.[2] Evolving trends, as mapped out by changes in cultural indicators, also lead to market opportunities that can be leveraged by savvy marketers. Consider for a moment the opportunities created by the "little emperors and empresses" in China, altogether a market of around 300 million children. Children in China impact consumption patterns in three ways: (1) spending power, (2) pester power, and (3) change agents. Giving pocket money to children is increasingly common in China. Chinese children—often without siblings, due to China's one-child policy—also have a tremendous amount of "pester power." Finally, children are for scores of new products important change agents, since they are often the first ones to be exposed (via friends, television) to the innovation. Capitalizing on these trends, Pepsi-Cola recently launched a new fruit drink (Fruit Magix) in China targeted toward children.[3] Global Perspective 4-1 on page 84 discusses how American-style fast-food restaurants grasped market opportunities in the Asian region.

To highlight the central role of culture, consider for a moment consumer behavior in the global marketplace. Within a given culture, consumption processes can be described via a sequence of four stages: access, buying behavior, consumption characteristics, and disposal (see Exhibit 4-1):[4]

- **Access.** Does the consumer have physical and/or economic access to the product/service?
- **Buying Behavior.** How is the decision to buy made by the consumers in the foreign market?
- **Consumption Characteristics.** What factors drive the consumption patterns?
- **Disposal.** How do consumers dispose of the product (in terms of resale, recycling, etc.)?

Each of these stages is heavily influenced by the culture in which the consumer thrives.

This chapter deals with the cultural environment of the global marketplace. We will first describe the concept of culture. Next, we explore various elements of cul-

---

[1]Tevfik Dalgic and Ruud Heijblom, "International Marketing Blunders Revisited—Some Lessons for Managers," *Journal of International Marketing*, 4 (1), (1996), pp. 81–91.

[2]Alecia Swasy, *Soap Opera. The Inside Story of Procter & Gamble* (New York: Random House, 1993).

[3]Amit Bose and Khushi Khanna, "The Little Emperor. A Case Study of a New Brand Launch," *Marketing and Research Today* (November 1996), pp. 216–21.

[4]P.S. Raju, "Consumer Behavior in Global Markets: The A-B-C-D Paradigm and its Application to Eastern Europe and the Third World," *Journal of Consumer Marketing*, vol. 12, no. 5, (1995), pp. 37–56.

◆ ◆

GLOBAL PERSPECTIVE 4-1

SELLING U.S.-STYLE FAST FOOD IN ASIA

At one time the skeptics said that Asians would never give up their diet for the blander tastes of American fast food. But the traditional corner coffee shop selling chicken, rice, and noodles is being replaced by McDonald's, Pizza Hut, or KFC. The taste of food is only one element in the success story. "Our marketing people tell us that people here (Malaysia) love the American way. People come to the stores not only for the food but to enjoy American style and American service," says Syed Ghazali, general manager in Malaysia of Kenny Rogers Roasters, a Florida-based fast-food chain. The region's economic success has created an increasingly affluent middle class. A plate of chicken and rice might only cost 95 cents in Kuala Lumpur, the capital of Malaysia. But more and more city dwellers have the money to pay twice or three times as much for a Roasters meal.

A vital ingredient in the attractiveness of U.S.-style fast food is that it caters to the family. Fast-food chains make some adjustments to local conditions. Kenny Rogers Roasters cost about half as much in Malaysia as in the United States. Some chains use local sauces and ingredients. Others insist that all supplies come from the United States. Tony Roma's, a Texas-based chain specializing in ribs, ships a container of U.S. pork ribs each month into Indonesia, the world's largest Moslem country.

Not everyone is happy about the U.S. invasion of Asia's high streets. There are suspicions that along with the food, U.S. values are being imported. Asia's leaders worry about a directionless, undisciplined younger generation lounging at eating joints.

Source: "Feast Your Eyes on an Asian Opportunity," *The Financial Times* (July 7, 1994), p. 6. Reprinted with permission.

---

ture. Cultures differ a great deal, but they also have elements in common. We will discuss several schemes that can be used to compare cultures. Cultural mishaps are quite likely when conducting global business. As a global business manager, you should be aware of your own cultural norms and other people's values. To that end, we will discuss several ways to adapt to foreign cultures. Finally, we examine a special form of cross-cultural interactions: international negotiations.

DEFINING CULTURE   ◆ ◆ ◆ ◆ ◆ ◆

Culture comes in many guises. A computer search of articles published in social science journals showed slightly more than 1,300 entries that contained the word *culture*. Recent books center on the *Culture of Contentment* (J.K. Galbraith) and *The Rise and Fall of Cattle Culture* (J. Rifkin). Given the manifold uses of the word *culture*, the concept becomes quite murky. The literature offers a host of definitions. The Dutch cultural anthropologist Hofstede defines culture as: "the collective programming of the mind which distinguishes the members of one group or category from those of another."[5] Terpstra and David offer a more business-oriented definition:[6]

---

[5]Geert Hofstede, *Cultures and Organizations: Software of the Mind* (London: McGraw-Hill, 1991), p. 5.

[6]Vern Terpstra and Kenneth David, *The Cultural Environment of International Business* (Cincinnati, Ohio: South-Western Publishing Co., 1991), p. 6.

Exhibit 4-1
The A-B-C-D Paradigm

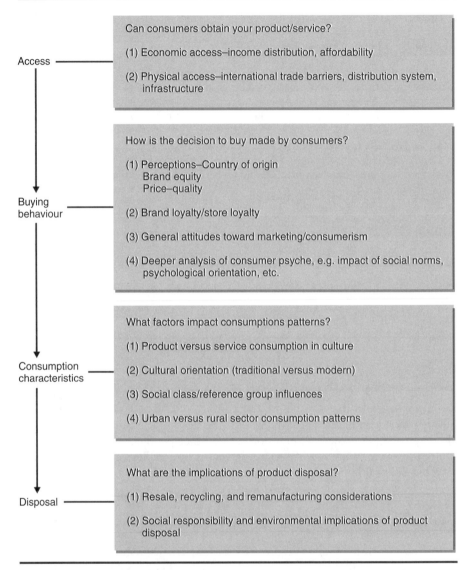

Source: P. S. Raju, "Consumer Behavior in Global Markets: The A-B-C-D Paradigm and Its Applications to Eastern Europe and the Third World," *Journal of Consumer Marketing,* 12, (5) (1995), p. 39. Reprinted with permission.

Culture is a learned, shared, compelling, interrelated set of symbols whose meanings provide a set of orientations for members of society. These orientations, taken together, provide solutions to problems that all societies must solve if they are to remain viable.

Despite the wide variety of definitions, common elements span the different formulations. First of all, culture is *learned* by people. In other words, it is not biologically transmitted via the genes (nurture, not nature). A society's culture is passed on ("cultivated") by various peer groups (family, school, youth organizations, and so forth) from one generation to the next one. The second element is that culture consists of many different parts that are all *interrelated* with one another. One element (say, one's social status) of a person's culture does have an impact on another part (say, the language that this person uses). So, a person's cultural mindset is not a random collection of behaviors. In a sense, culture is a complex jigsaw puzzle where all pieces hang together. Finally, culture is *shared* by individuals as members of society. You might speak Esperanto at home, but if other members of society do not share this habit, Esperanto is not part of your culture. These three facets—cultures being learned, shared, and composed of interrelated parts—spell out the essence of culture.

Cultures may be defined by national borders, especially when countries are isolated by natural barriers. Examples are island nations (e.g., Japan, Ireland, Taiwan) and peninsulas (e.g., Korea). However, most nations contain different subgroups (*subcultures*) within their borders. These subgroups could be defined along linguistic (Flemish versus Walloons in Belgium) or religious (Buddhist Sinhalese versus Hindu Tamils in Sri Lanka) lines. Few cultures are homogeneous. Typically, most cultures contain subcultures that often have little in common with one another. Needless to say, the wide variety of cultures and subcultures creates a tremendous challenge for global marketers.

ELEMENTS OF CULTURE

◆ ◆ ◆ ◆ ◆ ◆

Culture consists of many interrelated components. Knowledge of a culture requires a deep understanding of its different parts. In this section, we describe those elements that are most likely to matter to international marketers: material life, language, social interactions, religion, education, and values.

Material Life

A major component of culture is its material aspect. *Material life* primarily refers to the technologies that are used to produce, distribute, and consume goods and services within society. Differences in the material environment partly explain differences in the level and type of demand for many consumption goods. For instance, energy consumption is not only much higher in developed countries than in developing nations, but also relies on more advanced forms, such as nuclear energy. To bridge material environment differences, marketers are often forced to adapt their product offerings. Consider, for instance, the soft-drink industry. In many countries outside the United States, store shelf space is heavily restricted and refrigerators have far less capacity (smaller kitchens) compared to the United States. As a result, soft-drink bottlers sell one or one-and-a-half liter bottles rather than two-liter bottles. Also, in markets like China and India, the road infrastructure is extremely primitive, making distribution of products a total nightmare. In India, Coke uses large tricycles to distribute cases of Coke along narrow streets.[7]

Technology gaps also affect investment decisions. The poor transportation and distribution infrastructure in many developing countries forces companies to improvise and look for alternative ways to deliver their products. Governments in host nations often demand technology transfers as part of the investment package. Companies that are not keen on sharing their technology are forced to abandon or modify their investment plans. When the Indian government asked Coca Cola to share their recipe, Coke decided to jump ship and left the India marketplace in 1977 (Coke later re-entered India via a joint venture).

---

[7]"Coke Pours into Asia," *Business Week* (October 21, 1996), pp. 22–25.

The way things are—Despite urbanization, age-old culture remains in many parts of the world.

Language

Language is often described as the most important element that sets human beings apart from animals. Language is used to communicate and to interpret the environment. Two facets of language have a bearing on marketers: (1) the use of language as a communication tool within cultures, and (2) the huge diversity of languages across, and often within, national boundaries.

Let us first consider the communication aspect. As a communication medium, language has two parts: the **spoken** and the so-called **silent** language. Communication occurs through vocal sounds or written symbols. Silent language refers to the complex of nonverbal communication mechanisms that people use to get a message across. Examples include gestures, grimaces, body language, eye contact, and conversation distance.

Not surprisingly, a given gesture often has quite different meanings across cultures. In the United States, thumbs up is a sign of approval. In other countries, such as Greece or Brazil, such a gesture is grossly insulting. Other examples abound of silent language forms that are harmless in one society and risky in others. It is imperative that managers familiarize themselves with the critical aspects of a foreign culture's hidden language. Failure to follow this rule will sooner or later lead to hilarious or embarrassing situations.

The huge diversity of languages creates another headache for multinational companies. Language is often described as the mirror of a culture. Differences exist across and within borders. Not surprisingly, populous countries such as India contain many languages. Even small countries show a fair amount of language variety. Luxembourg, a tiny country of less than 400,000 people nestled between Belgium, France, and Germany, possesses three official languages (French, German, and Luxemburgian).

Even within the same language, meanings and expressions vary a great deal between countries that share the language. A good example is English. English words that sound completely harmless in one English-speaking country often have a silly or sinister meaning in another Anglo-Saxon country. Until a few years ago, Snickers candy bars were sold under the brand name Marathon in the United Kingdom. Mars felt that the Snickers name was too close to the English idiom for female lingerie (*knickers*). Cert, a London-based consultant, offers a few rules of thumb about talking in English to foreigners:[8]

1. Vocabulary. Go for the simplest words (e.g., use the word *rich* instead of loaded, affluent, or opulent). Treat colloquial words with care.

2. Idioms. Pick and choose idioms carefully (for instance, most non-U.S. speakers would not grasp the meaning of the expression *nickel-and-diming*).

3. Grammar. Express one idea in each sentence. Avoid subclauses.

4. Cultural references. Avoid culture-specific references (e.g., "Doesn't he look like David Letterman?").

5. Understanding the foreigner. This will be a matter of unpicking someone's accent. If you do not understand, make it seem that it is you, not the foreigner, who is slow.

Language blunders easily arise due to careless translation of advertising slogans or product labels. Techniques such as parallel (using multiple translators) and back translation (translate foreign version back into original language), used in global marketing research for proper translation of survey instruments (see Chapter 6), can also be applied to the translation of advertising messages, product labels, or brand names.

Firms doing business in multilingual societies need to decide what languages to use for product labels or advertising copy. Multilingual labels are fairly common now, especially in the Pan-European market. Advertising copy poses a bigger hurdle. To deal with language issues in advertising copy, advertisers might rely on local advertising agencies, minimize the spoken part of the commercial, or use subtitles. We will revisit these issues in more detail in Chapter 14.

Social Interactions

The movie *Iron & Silk* is a neat illustration of the cultural misunderstandings that arise in cross-cultural interactions. The movie is based on the true-life story of Mark Salzman, a Yale graduate who, after his studies, went to China to teach English in a Chinese village. During his first day of class, his students, out of respect for their teacher, insist on calling him "Mister Salzman." Mark prefers to be addressed on a first-name basis. Ultimately, students and teacher compromise on "teacher Mark."

A critical aspect of culture is the social interactions among people. Social interplay refers to the manner in which members of society relate to one another. Probably the most crucial expression of social interactions is the concept of kinship. This concept varies dramatically across societies. In most Western countries, the family unit encompasses the **nuclear family**, being the parents and the children. The relevant family unit in many developing countries is the **extended family** which comprises a much wider

---

[8]"When Fine Words Will Butter No Parsnips," *The Financial Times* (May 1, 1992).

group of often only remotely related family members. The way families are structured has important ramifications. Family units fulfill many roles, including economic and psychological support. For instance, Sri Lankan banks promote savings programs that allow participants to build up savings to support their parents when they reach retirement. Such saving programs would be unthinkable in the United States. An income-tax filer in Hong Kong can claim deductions for contributions made to support one's parents or grandparents. Major purchase decisions are agreed upon by many individuals in countries where extended families are the norm. Within such communities, members of an extended family will pool their resources to fund the purchase of big-ticket items (e.g., sewing machines). A Los Angeles radio contest targeting Hispanic families offered two tickets to Disneyland. The contest failed, largely because it demanded that Hispanics pick two family members out of their extended family.[9]

Countries also vary in terms of the scope of the decision-making authority. Exhibit 4-2 contrasts the purchase decision influence of husbands and wives in the United States and Venezuela. Although there are some similarities between the two countries (e.g., groceries), there are major differences for most product types. Compared to the United States, Venezuelan husbands delegate far less authority to their wives for purchases of furniture, major appliances, life insurance, and automobiles.

Another important aspect of social interactions is the individual's **reference groups**. Reference groups refer to the set of people to which an individual looks for guidance in values and attitudes. As such, reference groups will have an enormous impact on people's consumption behavior patterns. The consumer research literature[10] identifies three kinds of reference groups. Membership groups are those to which people belong. Anticipatory groups are groupings of which one would like to be part. Dissociative groups are groups with which individuals do not want to be associated. Reference groups are especially influential for consumer products that are socially visible, such as most status goods and luxury items. Knowledge on reference group patterns could provide an input in formulating product positioning strategies and devising advertising campaigns. One recent study showed the critical role of group-conformity pressure in Confucian cultures (e.g., Korea, Japan). Although U.S. subjects in the study primarily relied on their own personal attitudes regarding their purchase intentions of a new brand of sneakers, their Korean counterparts put much more emphasis on social norms.[11]

Religion

Religion plays a central role in many societies. To appreciate people's buying motives, customs, and practices, awareness and understanding of their religion is often crucial. Religion refers to a community's set of beliefs that relate to a reality that cannot be verified empirically.[12] These beliefs usually involve reflections about after-life, but not always.

---

[9]"Slips of the Tongue Result in Classic Marketing Errors," *Advertising Age International* (June 20, 1994), p. I-15.

[10]James F. Engel, Roger D. Blackwell, and Paul W. Miniard, *Consumer Behavior* (Hinsdale, Ill.: Dryden, 1986), pp. 318–24.

[11]Chol Lee and Robert T. Green, "Cross-Cultural Examination of the Fishbein Behavioral Intentions Model," *Journal of International Business Studies* (Second Quarter 1991), pp. 289–305.

[12]Terpstra and David, p. 73.

EXHIBIT 4-2
MEAN NUMBER OF PURCHASE
DECISIONS BY PRODUCT TYPE

Product	United States	Venezuela
Groceries		
Husband	.23	.23
Joint	.60	.69
Wife	3.20	3.08
Furniture		
Husband	.41	1.16
Joint	3.41	2.71
Wife	2.23	2.16
Major Appliances		
Husband	.98	1.97
Joint	3.21	2.10
Wife	.85	.93
Life Insurance		
Husband	2.65	3.38
Joint	1.23	.55
Wife	.15	.05
Automobiles		
Husband	2.59	4.16
Joint	3.06	1.42
Wife	.41	.40
Vacation		
Husband	1.00	1.51
Joint	3.68	3.18
Wife	.40	.41
Savings		
Husband	1.00	1.07
Joint	1.61	1.60
Wife	.44	.34
Housing		
Husband	.34	.87
Joint	2.47	1.82
Wife	.34	.39
Doctor		
Husband	.03	.10
Joint	.35	.42
Wife	.62	.49

Source: Robert T. Green and Isabella Cunningham,
"Family Purchasing Roles in Two Countries" *Journal of
International Business Studies* (Spring–Summer 1980), p. 95.
Reprinted with permission.

Exhibit 4-3 highlights the various influences of Islam on the marketing function. Religious taboos often force companies to adapt their marketing mix program. To cater to Hindu believers, McDonald's restaurants in India do not sell hamburgers that contain beef. Out of respect for the local Muslims, there is no pork on the menu. Global Perspective 4-2 describes in detail the efforts McDonald's undertook to respect local religious sensibilities in India. Elite Foods, a licensee of PepsiCo Foods International, ensured that Chee-tos met all religious specifications before launching

EXHIBIT 4-3
MARKETING IN AN ISLAMIC FRAMEWORK

Elements	Implications for Marketing
I. Fundamental Islamic concepts	
A. Unity (concept of centrality, oneness of God, harmony in life)	Product standardization, mass media techniques, central balance, unity in advertising copy and layout, strong brand loyalties, a smaller evoked size set, loyalty to company, opportunities for brand extension strategies.
B. Legitimacy (Fair dealings, reasonable level of profits)	Less formal product warranties, need for institutional advertising and/or advocacy advertising, especially by foreign firms, and a switch from profit maximizing to a profit satisfying strategy.
C. Zakaat (2.5 percent per annum compulsory tax bindings on all classified as "not poor.")	Use of "excessive" profits, if any, for charitable acts, corporate donation for charity, institutional advertising.
D. Usury (Cannot charge interest on loans. A general interpretation of this law defines "excessive interest" charged on loans as not permissible.)	Avoid direct use of credit as a marketing tool; establish a consumer policy of paying cash for low value products; for high value products, offer discounts for cash payments and raise prices of products on an installment basis; sometimes possible to conduct interest transactions between local/foreign firm in other non-Islamic countries; banks in some Islamic countries take equity in financing ventures, sharing resultant profits (and losses).
E. Supremacy of human life (Compared to other forms of life, objects, human life is of supreme importance.)	Pet food and/or products less important; avoid use of statues, bust-interpreted as forms of idolatry; symbols in advertising and/or promotion should reflect high human values; use floral designs and artwork in advertising as representation of aesthetic values.
F. Community (All Muslims should strive to achieve universal brotherhood—with allegiance to the "One God." One way of expressing community is the required pilgrimage to Mecca for all Muslims at least once in their lifetime, if able to do so.)	Formation of an Islamic Economic Community—development of an "Islamic consumer" served with Islamic-oriented products and services, for example, "kosher" meat packages, gifts exchanged at Muslim festivals, and so forth; development of community services—need for marketing or nonprofit organizations and skills.
G. Equality of people	Participative communication systems; roles and authority structures may be rigidly defined but accessibility at any level relatively easy.

Exhibit 4-3 (continued)

Elements	Implications for Marketing
H. Abstinence (During the month of Ramadan, Muslims are required to fast without food or drink from the first streak of dawn to sunset—a reminder to those who are more fortunate to be kind to the less fortunate and as an exercise in self-control.)	Products that are nutritious, cool, and digested easily can be formulated for Sehr and Iftar (beginning and end of the fast).
Consumption of alcohol and pork is forbidden; so is gambling.	Opportunities for developing nonalcoholic items and beverages (for example, soft drinks, ice cream, milk shakes, fruits juices) and nonchance social games, such as Scrabble; food products should use vegetable or beef shortening.
I. Environmentalism (The universe created by God was pure. Consequently, the land, air, and water should be held as sacred elements.)	Anticipate environmental, antipollution acts; opportunities for companies involved in maintaining a clean environment; easier acceptance of pollution-control devices in the community (for example, recent efforts in Turkey have been well received by the local communities).
J. Worship (Five times a day; timing of prayers varies.)	Need to take into account the variability and shift in prayer timings in planning sales calls, work schedules, business hours, customer traffic, and so forth.
II. Islamic culture A. Obligation to family and tribal traditions	Importance of respected members in the family or tribe as opinion leaders; word-of-mouth communication, customers referrals may be critical; social or clan allegiances, affiliations, and associations may be possible surrogates for reference groups; advertising home-oriented products stressing family roles may be highly effective, for example, electronic games.
B. Obligation toward parents is sacred	The image of functional products could be enhanced with advertisements that stress parental advice or approval; even with children's products, there should be less emphasis on children as decision makers.
C. Obligation to extend hospitality to both insiders and outsiders	Product designs that are symbols of hospitality, outwardly open in expression, rate of new product acceptance may be accelerated and eased by appeals based on community.

Continued

EXHIBIT 4-3 (continued)

Elements	Implications for Marketing
D. Obligation to conform to codes of sexual conduct and social interaction These may include the following:	
1. Modest dress for women in public	More colorful clothing and accessories are worn by women at home; so promotion of products for use in private homes could be more intimate—such audiences could be reached effectively through women's magazines; avoid use of immodest exposure and sexual implications in public settings.
2. Separation of male and female audiences (in some cases)	Access to female consumers can often be gained only through women as selling agents—salespersons, catalogs, home demonstrations, and women's specialty shops.
E. Obligations to religious occasions (For example, there are two major religious observances that are celebrated—Eid-ud-Fitr, Eid-ud-Adha.)	Tied to purchase of new shoes, clothing, sweets, and preparation of food items for family reunions, Muslim gatherings. There has been a practice of giving money in place of gifts. Increasingly, however, a shift is taking place to more gift giving; because lunar calendar, dates are not fixed.

Source: Mushtaq Luqmani, Zahir A. Quareshi, and Linda Delene, "Marketing in Islamic Countries: A Viewpoint," *MSU Business Topics* (Summer 1980), pp. 20–21. Reprinted with permission.

the snack brand in Israel.[13] Use of birth control devices is frowned upon in heavily Catholic countries such as the Philippines. Religious beliefs may also influence the siting and design of stores and office buildings. The design and location of many buildings in Hong Kong is affected by the laws of feng shui, literally "Wind and Water." For instance, the doors of the Mandarin Hotel were placed at an angle to the street to discourage the entry of evil spirits.[14]

Religion also drives the holiday calendar in many countries. A country like Sri Lanka, with several officially recognized religions (Hinduism, Buddhism), forces a careful examination of one's calendar whenever meetings are to be scheduled. Israel's national airline El Al is not allowed to fly on the Sabbath or on Jewish holidays. This government restriction reportedly cut El Al's profits by nearly 50 percent in 1992.[15] On the other hand, religious holidays often steer advertising campaigns

---

[13]"Ruffles Makes Waves in Israel," *Advertising Age International* (November 23, 1992), p. I-12.

[14]Jan Morris, *Hong Kong* (New York: Vintage Books), 1988, p. 132.

[15]"And You Thought U.S. Airlines Had It Tough," *Business Week* (October 12, 1992), p. 107.

◆ ◆

$\mathcal{G}$LOBAL PERSPECTIVE 4-2

THE GOLDEN ARCHES IN INDIA—NO PORK, NO BEEF

The morning the golden arches were unveiled on New Delhi's skyline, Ajay Seth and his two daughters braved the crowd at the first McDonald's in India to see how foreigners made one of the family's favorite snacks: the vegetable burger. "It's very important that the food has an Indian taste," said Seth before sinking his teeth into the sesame-seed bun sandwiching his vegetable patty. He was only mildly impressed.

McDonald's may yet have to refine some recipes for the spice-loving Indian palate. But its entry into India on October 13 after three years of discreet planning crowned an unprecedented effort to go "local" from the outset—a lesson for other multinational companies investing in this proud and often prickly market. That's good business and smart politics at a time when India's centrist-left government is trying delicately to build a consensus for greater foreign investment and free-market reforms, while preserving the coalition's "pro-poor" image.

McDonald's strategy to woo customers centers on the menu. To avoid insulting Hindus, who revere cows, it dropped beef for the first time. To cater to Muslims, there's no pork. Burgers are made from mutton, including the Big Mac, which has been rechristened the Maharaja Mac. To win over the strictest vegetarians, designated staffers prepare veggie dishes in a separate area of the kitchen, another first for McDonald's. To blunt nationalist opposition, McDonald's India projects itself as a local enterprise. It sources virtually all of its ingredients from local suppliers and claims to be guided by its 50–50 Indian partners in two restaurant ventures in New Delhi and Bombay. Foreign food and consumer-product companies have touched the deepest nerve since India opened its economy five years ago. But McDonald's entry indicates that the ground has shifted. The *Indian Express*, often critical of economic reforms, praised McDonald's in a lead editorial for respecting local culture and chastised the anti-multinational lobby for making food the "stuff of dubious politics."

Source: "Food for Politics," *Far Eastern Economic Review* (October 24, 1996), p. 72.

---

or may open up untapped market opportunities. In many Western European countries, Saint Nicholas (December 6) is the key event for toy companies and candy makers.

The role of women in society is sometimes largely driven by the local religion. In Islamic societies, conducting market research that involves women is extremely hard. For instance, mixing men and women in focus groups is prohibited in Saudi Arabia.[16]

Religious norms also influence advertising campaigns. In Iran, all ads need to be cleared by Islamic censors. This approval process can take up to three months. One print ad created for Chiquita was frowned upon by Iranian authorities because they considered showing only three bananas on a full-page ad a waste of space.[17] Also in Iran, Gillette's local advertising agency had a hard time placing an ad for the Gillette Blue II razor. Islam dictates that its followers refrain from shaving. Ultimately, Gillette's account executive was able to convince the advertising manager of one local

---

[16]"Programming Globally—With Care," *Advertising Age International* (September 18, 1995), p. I-14.

[17]"Multinationals Tread Softly While Advertising in Iran," *Advertising Age International* (November 8, 1993), p. I-21.

newspaper by using the argument that shaving sometimes becomes necessary, like in the case of head injuries resulting from a car accident.[18]

Education

Education is one of the major vehicles to channel culture from one generation to another. Two facets of education matter to international marketers: the level and the quality of education. The level of education varies a lot between countries. Most developed countries have mandatory education up to a certain age. In some countries, however, especially Muslim societies, education is largely the preserve of males. As a consequence, males are often far better educated than females in such societies. One powerful indicator of the education level is a country's illiteracy rate. Exhibit 4-4 gives you an overview of illiteracy levels around the world. In countries with low literacy levels, marketers need to exercise caution in matters such as product labeling, print ads, and survey research. One babyfood company attributed its poor sales in

EXHIBIT 4-4
EDUCATIONAL STATISTICS FOR A SAMPLE OF COUNTRIES

Country	Percentage of Illiterates (Age 15+)—1995 Estimates		Scientists and Engineers per Million Population
	Male	Female	
Africa:			
Egypt	36.4	61.2	458 (1991)
Nigeria	32.7	52.7	15 (1987)
South Africa	18.1	18.3	319 (1991)
Zaire	13.4	32.3	NA
South America:			
Brazil	16.7	16.8	391 (1985)
Chile	4.6	5.0	364 (1988)
Peru	5.5	17.0	273 (1981)
Venezuela	8.2	9.7	208 (1992)
Asia:			
China	10.1	27.3	1,128 (1992)
India	34.5	62.3	151 (1990)
Indonesia	10.4	22.0	181 (1988)
Iran	21.6	34.2 (1994)	65 (1985)
Thailand	4.0	8.4	173 (1991)
Europe:			
Italy	2.5	4.5 (1981)	1,366 (1990)
Russia	0.5	3.2 (1989)	5,930 (1991)
Spain	2.5	5.8 (1986)	956 (1990)

Source: UNESCO, 1995 Statistical Yearbook, Tables 1.2 and 5.1. Reproduced with permission from UNESCO.

---

[18]"Smooth Talk Wins Gillette Ad Space in Iran," *Advertising Age International* (April 27, 1992), p. I-40.

Africa to the product label that was used. The label's picture of a baby was mistakenly thought by the local people to mean that the jars contained ground-up babies.[19]

Companies are also concerned about the "quality" of education. Does education meet business needs? Does the labor force within a country possess the necessary skills to make the transition from labor-intensive to capital-intensive industries? Far Eastern countries tend to emphasize sciences and engineering much more than many Western countries. The last column of Exhibit 4-4 shows the number of scientists and engineers per million population. As you can see, there are some huge differences, even within countries with a similar level of economic development. Shortages in certain fields often force companies to employ expatriates or to bid up against one another for the scarce talent that is available. Many companies, such as Waste Management International, try to build up a local presence by hiring local people. However, a shortage of qualified people in the Asian marketplace forced Waste Management to rely on expatriates until local employees were properly trained.

Value Systems

All cultures have value systems that shape people's norms and standards. These norms influence people's attitudes toward objects and behavioral codes. Value systems tend to be deeply rooted. One study of the decision-making process made by executives from the People's Republic of China showed that even after almost four decades of communist philosophy, traditional Chinese values (e.g., saving face, long-term exchange relationships, respect for leaders) heavily influence market entry and product decisions.[20] The origins of many value systems are hidden in history. It is unlikely that people's value systems change in a short span of time.[21] Value systems vary enormously across cultures. A good example is the attitude toward time. Hall makes a distinction between cultures with a **monochronic** and **polychronic** notion of time.[22] Monochronic people do one thing at a time. Their agendas are very well organized; they tend to be punctual; they don't want to waste time. In short, they are "time is money" type of people. Polychronic people have an entirely different concept of time. They tend to do several things at once. They are less organized; less rigid regarding their schedule; less punctual. For them, business is a form of socializing, not the other way round. For instance, at business luncheon meetings in France it is considered rude not to while a couple of hours away and finish off at least one bottle of wine.[23]

Another important value distinction is a culture's attitude toward change. Societies that are resistant toward change are usually less willing to adopt new products or production processes. Terspstra and David (1991) suggest several useful guidelines that are helpful to implement innovations in cultures hostile toward changes:[24]

---

[19]David A. Ricks, *Blunders in International Business* (Cambridge, Mass.: Blackwell Publishers, 1993).

[20]David K. Tse, Kam-hon Lee, Ilan Vertinsky, and Donald A. Wehrung, "Does Culture Matter? A Cross-Cultural Study of Executives' Choice, Decisiveness, and Risk Adjustment in International Marketing," *Journal of Marketing*, 52 (4) (October 1988), pp. 81–95.

[21]J.E.B.M. Steenkamp, "Internationale Marketing en Consumentengedrag," Tijdschrift voor Economie en Management, vol. 38 (2) (1993), p. 130.

[22]Edward T. Hall, *Beyond Culture* (New York: Doubleday, 1977).

[23]"The Fall of Fun," *The New Yorker* (November 18, 1996), pp. 62–71.

[24]Terpstra and David, pp. 124–25.

1. Identify roadblocks toward change.
2. Determine which cultural hurdles can be met.
3. Test and demonstrate the innovation's effectiveness in the host culture.
4. Seek out those values that can be used to back up the proposed innovation.

Some cultures are quite open toward change. Russia's younger generation's desire for novel items spurred sales for snack foods such as Cheez Balls and Chips Ahoy! cookies that are viewed to represent change.[25]

From an international marketer's vantage point, a society's value system matters a great deal. Local attitudes toward foreign cultures will drive the product positioning and design decisions. In many countries, goods with American roots are strongly valued. U.S. companies are able to leverage on such sentiments by using Americana as a selling point. McIlhenny sells Tabasco with the same product label and formulation worldwide, emphasizing its American roots. In South Africa, Mars stresses the U.S. ties of Uncle Ben's rice with a "100% American" banner on its packaging.

Value systems often explain the dismal performance or phenomenal success of new product introductions. Despite Russia's low standard of living, canned pet food became very well accepted. Russians often pamper their pets, giving them choice cuts of meat. MasterFoods' marketing materials in Russia utilized a "more for your money" selling point by showing that canned pet food is more nutritious and cheaper than fresh food.[26]

Cultural norms might also dictate selling approaches. Dell's Japan operation uses a less aggressive tack to lure customers, because aggressiveness is not highly valued in Japan. In contrast, in the United States Dell vigorously promotes low computer prices, showing how direct selling leads to a lower price in.[27]

◆ ◆ ◆ ◆ ◆ ◆ CROSS-CULTURAL COMPARISIONS

Cultures differ from one another, but usually they share certain aspects. Getting a sense of the similarities and dissimilarities between your culture and the host country's culture is useful for scores of reasons. Cultural classifications allow the marketing manager to see how much overlap there can be between the marketing programs to be implemented in different markets. Several companies, such as McDonald's, use cultural similarity as a major country indicator for target market selection decisions. This section gives you an overview of the most common classification schemes.

High- versus Low-Context Cultures

One of the characters in the movie *Chan Is Missing* is a lawyer who describes a confrontation between her client who was involved in a traffic accident and a policeman at the scene of the accident. The client is a recent immigrant from mainland China.

---

[25]"Russians Go Nuts for Snacks as Planters, Frito Duke it Out," *Advertising Age International* (December 13, 1993), p. I-14.

[26]"How to Sell Pet Food in Russia," *Advertising Age International* (May 17, 1993), p. I-21.

[27]"Direct Mail Defies Japan's Ad Recession," *Advertising Age International* (April 18, 1994), p. I-8.

The policeman asks her client whether or not he stopped at the stop sign, expecting a yes or no for an answer. The Chinese man instead starts talking about his driving record, how long he has been in the United States, and other matters that he feels are relevant. The policeman, losing his patience, angrily repeats his question. The events described in the movie are a typical example of the culture clash that arises when somebody from a high-context culture (China) is faced with a person from a low-context culture (United States).

The notion of cultural complexity refers to the way messages are communicated within a society. The anthropologist Edward Hall makes a distinction between so-called **high-context** and **low-context** cultures.[28] The interpretation of messages in high-context cultures heavily rests on contextual cues. What is left unsaid is often as important (if not more) as what was said. Examples of contextual cues include the nature of the relationship between the sender and receiver of the message (for instance, in terms of gender, age, balance of power), the time and site of the communication, and so forth. Typical examples of high-context societies are Confucian cultures (China, Korea, Japan) and Latin America.

Low-context cultures, on the other hand, put most emphasis on the written or spoken word. What is meant is what is said. The context, within which messages are communicated, is largely discounted. The United States, Scandinavia, and Germany are all examples of low-context cultures. The distinction between high- and low-context cultures matters in many areas of international marketing. For example, in the field of personal selling, many U.S. companies like to rotate salespeople across territories. In high-context societies, where nurturing trust and rapport with the client plays a big role, firms might need to adjust such rotation policies. Research also indicates a faster rate of adoption of new products in high-context cultures than in low-context societies.[29] In the field of international advertising, campaigns that were developed with a high-context culture in mind are likely to be less effective when used in low-context cultures, and vice versa.

Cultural Homogeneity

Cultures differ enormously in their degree of homogeneity. At one extreme are **homophilous** cultures, where people share the same beliefs, speak the same language, and practice the same religion. Examples are the Koreas, Japan, and Scandinavian countries. Most countries are **heterophilous** cultures with a fair amount of differentiation. In general, less homogeneity demands a more individualized marketing approach. Failure to do so is usually a recipe for disaster. A case in point is China. Top Green International is a Hong Kong–based joint venture that holds the master franchise for TCBY ("The Country's Best Yogurt") in China. One of the joint venture partners notes that "Each city (in China) is very different; each province has its own culture. You can't just make one single television commercial and broadcast it across the country. You have to find out what the interest is in each city or province."[30] Differences in cultural homogeneity

---

[28]Edward T. Hall, *Beyond Culture* (New York: Doubleday, 1977).

[29]Hirokazu Takada and Dipak Jain, "Cross-National Analysis of Diffusion of Consumer Durable Goods in Pacific Rim Countries," *Journal of Marketing*, 55 (April 1991), pp. 48–54.

[30]"Frozen Assets. TCBY Takes a Scoop Out of the China Market," *Far Eastern Economic Review* (November 14, 1996), p. 68.

underlie differences in adoption rates for new products or services. There is strong evidence that new products diffuse more rapidly in homogeneous countries.[31]

Hofstede's Classification Scheme

The Dutch scholar Geert Hofstede has proposed several other cultural classification schemes.[32] His grid is based on a large-scale research project he conducted among employees of more than sixty IBM subsidiaries worldwide. The first dimension is termed **power distance**, referring to the degree of inequality which people of a country view acceptable. Societies that are high in power distance tolerate relatively high social inequalities. Members of such societies accept wide differences in income and power distribution. Examples of high power distance countries are the Arab countries, Mexico, and West Africa. On the other hand, low power distance societies tend to be more egalitarian. Low power distance countries are countries such as Germany, Great Britain and the United States.

The second dimension is labeled **uncertainty avoidance**, defined as the extent to which people in a given culture prefer structured situations with clear rules over unstructured ones. People tend to be more easygoing in countries with low degrees of uncertainty avoidance. Societies with high uncertainty avoidance tend to be rigid and risk averse. Examples of countries that score high on uncertainty avoidance are France, Japan, and Mexico.

The third dimension is called **individualism**. As the label suggests, this criterion describes the degree to which people prefer to act as individuals rather than group members ("me" versus "we" societies). In societies that are high on individualism, the focus is on people's own interests. In collectivist societies the interests of the group take center stage. This concept relates to the views about the "self" that people hold. In individualist societies, people tend to have an **independent** view of the self. The norm here is to discover and express one's unique attributes.[33] In collectivist societies, an **interdependent** view of the self prevails where people desire to be connected with other individuals.[34]

The fourth distinction, **masculinity**, considers the importance of "male" values such as assertiveness, success, competitive drive within society, and achievement, as opposed to "female" values like solidarity and quality of life. "Tough" societies are those in which male values dominate. Cultures where people favor values such as solidarity, preserving the environment, and quality of life, are more "feminine." Japan is viewed as a masculine society, while Indonesia is an example of a feminine culture.

Follow-up research of Hofstede's work in Asia led to a fifth dimension: **long-termism**.[35] This final criterion refers to the distinction between societies with a **long-**

---

[31]H. Takada and D. Jain, "Cross-National Analysis of Diffusion of Consumer Durable Goods in Pacific Rim Countries," *Journal of Marketing*, 55 (April 1991), pp. 48–54.

[32]Geert Hofstede, "Management Scientists are Human," *Management Science*, vol. 40, no. 1 (January 1994), pp. 4–13.

[33]Hazel R. Markus and Shinobu Kitayama, "Culture and the Self: Implications for Cognition, Emotion, and Motivation," *Psychological Review*, 98 (2) (1991), pp. 224–53.

[34]See also Harry C. Triandis, "The Self and Social Behavior in Differing Cultural Contexts," *Psychological Review*, 96 (3) (1989), pp. 506–20.

[35]Geert Hofstede and Michael H. Bond, "The Confucius Connection: From Cultural Roots to Economic Growth," *Organizational Dynamics*, 16 (4) (Spring 1988), pp. 4–21.

EXHIBIT 4-5(A)
UNCERTAINTY AVOIDANCE VERSUS POWER DISTANCE

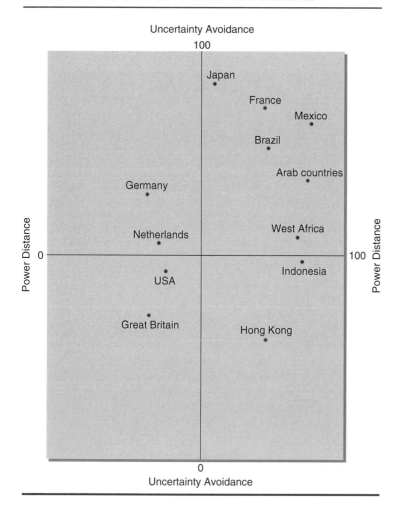

term orientation and those with a **short-term** focus. People in long-term-oriented societies tend to have values that center around the future (e.g., perseverance, thrift). On the other hand, members of short-term-oriented cultures are concerned about values that reflect the past and the present (e.g., respect for tradition). Countries like Hong Kong and Japan score high on the long-termism dimension, whereas West Africa, the United States, and Great Britain score very low on this criterion.

Exhibit 4-5 portrays how different countries score on the various dimensions. One must be cautious when applying these schemes to global buyer behavior. It is important to bear in mind that the five dimensions and the respective country scores that were derived in Hofstede's work were not determined in a consumption context. In fact, questions have been raised about the ability of these values to make meaningful predictions about consumption patterns.[36] Countries with the

---

[36]Marieke de Mooij, *Advertising Worldwide* (New York: Prentice-Hall, 1994), p. 159.

Exhibit 4-5(b)
Masculinity Versus Individualism

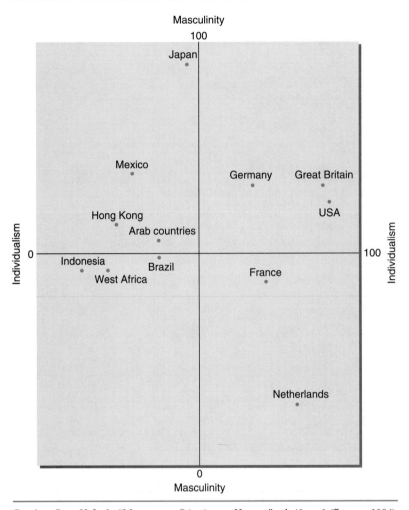

Based on: Geert Hofstede, "Management Scientists are Human," vol. 40 no. 1 (January 1994), pp. 4–13.

same scores may have entirely different buying behaviors. Likewise, countries that have completely different scores on a given cultural dimension could have very similar consumption patterns. To illustrate this point, consider the linkage between uncertainty avoidance and brand loyalty. Earlier we noted that perceived risk can be viewed as one of the indicators of uncertainty avoidance. Numerous consumer research studies in the United States have established a strong relationship between perceived risk and brand loyalty. That is, brand loyalty is one of the major risk reducers that consumers rely on when faced with a choice with a high level of perceived risk.[37] Given the overwhelming evidence for U.S. consumers,

---

[37]See, for instance, T. Roselius, "Consumer Rankings of Risk Reduction Methods," *Journal of Marketing*, 35 (1971), pp. 56–61

one would expect the same kind of relationship outside the United States: high levels of brand loyalty within societies where consumers tend to be high in perceived risk ("uncertainty avoidance"). However, a recent cross-cultural comparison found that outside the United States the relationship between the two measures is usually just flat (neither negative, nor positive).[38]

ADAPTING TO FOREIGN CULTURES   ◆ ◆ ◆ ◆ ◆ ◆

To function in the global marketplace, you need to become sensitive to cultural biases that influence your thinking, behavior, and decision-making. Given the diversity of cultures, cultural mishaps easily arise when global marketers interact with members of a "foreign" culture. Some of these cultural blunders are relatively harmless and easily forgiven. Unfortunately, many cultural mistakes put the company and its products in an unpleasant situation or even create permanent damage. There are numerous firms whose globalization efforts have been derailed by cultural mishaps.

Lack of cultural sensitivity takes many forms. Most of us hold cultural stereotypes that distort cultural assessments. Cultural blinders that occur at the subconscious level are hard to detect. When cultural misassessments do show up, it is usually after the fact. So cultural adaptation is absolutely necessary to make marketing decisions in line with the host culture. Such adaptation is hampered by the tendency to use a **self-reference criterion** (SRC), a term coined by J. A. Lee, a cultural anthropologist. The SRC refers to people's unconscious tendency to resort to their own cultural experience and value systems to interpret a given business situation. Lee outlined a four-step procedure that allows global marketers to identify cross-cultural

"I'm sorry you have to sit way over there. It's a Feng-Shui thing."

Cultural adaptation may be necessary when doing business abroad.

[38]Bronislaw J. Verhage, Ugur Yavas, and Robert T. Green, "Perceived Risk: A Cross-Cultural Phenomenon," *International Journal of Research in Marketing*, 7 (1990), pp. 297–303.

differences and take the necessary actions to cope with them. The four-step correction mechanism goes as follows:[39]

Step 1: Define the business problem or goal in terms of your own cultural traits, customs, or values.

Step 2: Define the business problem or goal in terms of the host culture's traits, customs, or values.

Step 3: Isolate the SRC influence in the problem and examine it scrupulously to see how it interferes with the business problem.

Step 4: Redefine the business problem, but this time without the SRC influence, and solve for the "optimal" business goal situation.

Even more dangerous than SRC-interference is to fall into the trap of **ethnocentrism**, the belief that one's own culture is superior to another culture.

Procter & Gamble's experience in Mexico exemplifies cultural adaptation. Ace detergent, launched in Mexico by P&G in the early 1950s, was clobbered by the local brands. Ace, developed for U.S. washing machines, had a low-suds formula. At that time, many Mexicans washed their clothes in the river. High-suds detergents were therefore preferable. Eventually, the formula was changed to have a higher suds content. P&G also adapted the packaging: smaller sizes, using plastic bags (to keep the detergent dry) instead of cardboard. Toymaker Mattel's experience with the Barbie doll in Japan is another nice illustration of adaptation.[40] Mattel first introduced a Barbie doll designed specifically for the Japanese market, called Moba Barbie. Moba's looks were supposedly akin to what Japanese consumers desired, bearing a close resemblance to the major competing doll. Mattel never conquered more than a 5–6 percent share of the Japanese doll market. After 8 years of lackluster sales, Mattel decided to reintroduce Barbie, taking on more Western looks. TV commercials also displayed Japanese girls playing with Barbies. Before the new campaign, most Japanese girls mistakenly believed that Moba Barbie was a display doll. As a result of these changes in Mattel's marketing strategy, the sales of Barbie dolls in Japan finally took off.

The lesson offered by the experience of marketing behemoths such as P&G and Mattel is that there is no magic bullet to avoid cultural mishaps. P&G mistakenly believed that what works in the United States would also find a market across the Rio Grande. Mattel, on the other hand, mistakenly tried to cater to "Japanese" desires. Although Lee's four-step SRC-correction procedure appears flawless, it is often hard to put into practice. For ages, travelers and scholars of various backgrounds have gathered material on peoples and shared it with others. Exhibit 4-6 summarizes some of the "Twenty-Seven Articles" that T. E. Lawrence ("Lawrence of Arabia") put down to assist others in coping with desert Arabs. Probably the most valuable piece of advice is given in Lawrence's introduction to his recommendations: "Handling Hejaz Arabs is an art, not a science, with exceptions and no obvious rules." The same piece of advice applies to any culture or subculture.

---

[39]J. A. Lee, "Cultural Analysis in Overseas Operations," *Harvard Business Review* (March–April 1966), pp. 106–14.

[40]"Western Barbie: Mattel Makes Japan Push with Revamped Doll," *Advertising Age* (October 7, 1991).

EXHIBIT 4.6
TWENTY-SEVEN ARTICLES BY T. E. LAWRENCE, AUGUST 1917

The following notes have been expressed in commandment form for greater clarity and to save words. They are, however, only my personal conclusions, arrived at gradually while I worked in the Hejaz and now put on paper as stalking horses for beginners in the Arab armies (. . .) They are of course not suitable to any person's need, or applicable unchanged in any particular situation. Handling Hejaz Arabs is an art, not a science, with exceptions and no obvious rules . . .

1. Go easy for the first weeks. A bad start is difficult to atone for, and the Arabs form their judgments on externals that we ignore.

2. Learn all you can about your Ashraf and Bedu. Get to know their families, clans, and tribes, friends and enemies, wells, hills and roads. Do all this by listening and by indirect enquiry. Do not ask questions. Get to speak their dialect of Arabic, not yours. . . . Be a little stiff at first.

3. In matters of business deal only with the commander of the army, column or party in which you serve. Never give orders to anyone at all, and reserve your directions or advice for the C.O. (commanding officer), however great the temptation of dealing direct with the underlings.

4. Win and keep the confidence of your leader. Strengthen his prestige at your expense before others when you can.

5. Remain in touch with your leader as constantly and unobtrusively as you can. . . . Formal visits to give advice are not so good as the constant dropping of ideas in casual talk. . . .

8. Your ideal position is when you are present and not noticed. Do not be too intimate, too prominent, or too earnest. . . .

11. The foreigner and Christian is not a popular person in Arabia. However friendly and informal the treatment of yourself may be, remember always that your foundations are very sandy ones.

12. Cling tight to your sense of humour. You will need it every day. . . . Reproof if wrapped up in some smiling form will carry further and last longer than the most violent speech. The power of mimicry or parody is valuable, but use it sparingly for wit is more dignified than humour. . . .

16. If you can, without being too lavish forestall presents to yourself. A well placed gift is often most effective in winning over a suspicious sheikh. Never receive a present without giving a liberal return. . . .

20. If you wear Arab things at all, go all the way. Leave your English friends and customs on the coast, and fall back on Arab habits entirely. . . .

25. In spite of ordinary Arab example avoid too free talk about women. It is as difficult a subject as religion, and their standards are so unlike your own, that a remark harmless in English may appear unrestrained to them . . .

27. The beginning and ending of the secret of handling Arabs is unremitting study of them. Keep always on your guard; never say an unconsidered thing, or do an unnecessary thing: watch yourself and your companions all the time: hear all that passes, search out what is going on beneath the surface, read their characters, discover their tastes and their weaknesses, and keep everything you find out to yourself.

Source: Abstracted from: Jeremy Wilson, *Lawrence of Arabia: The Authorized Biography of T. E. Lawrence,* New York: Atheneum, 1990, Appendix IV, pp. 960–965.

Still, there are a couple of techniques that companies can rely on to prepare managers for cross-cultural differences.[41] Foreign language training is one of the more common tools to foster cultural sensitivity. Language skills, though, are not sufficient to become a successful international manager. Other qualities like humility—willing to accept that you will not be as competent as in your own environment—also play an important role.[42] Numerous resources exist to familiarize managers with other aspects of the host country's cultural environment. A good example is the "Culturgram" series published by Brigham Young University that provides environmental briefings on the customs, values, and attitudes of individual countries. Many providers of cultural training programs (e.g., Berlitz International) offer a cultural orientation for executives. Such programs range from environmental briefings to "cultural assimilator" exercises where participants are exposed to various simulated settings that could arise during their assignment.[43]

◆ ◆ ◆ ◆ ◆ ◆ CROSS-CULTURAL NEGOTIATIONS

Conducting successful cross-cultural negotiations is a key ingredient for many international business transactions. International bargaining issues range from establishing the nuts and bolts of supplier agreements to setting up strategic alliances. Negotiation periods can run from a few hours to several months, if not years of bargaining. Bargaining taps many resources, skills, and expertise. Scores of books have been devoted to negotiation "dos and don'ts."[44] Cross-cultural negotiations are further complicated by divergent cultural backgrounds of the participants in the negotiation process. In this chapter, our focus will be on the cultural aspects of international negotiations. Chapter 15 will revisit cross-cultural bargaining in the personal selling context.

Stages of Negotiation Process

Roughly speaking, there are four stages encountered in most negotiation processes:[45] (1) nontask soundings, (2) task-related information exchange, (3) persuasion, and (4) concessions and agreement. Nontask soundings include all activities that are used to establish a rapport among the parties involved. Developing a rapport is a process that depends on subtle cues.[46] The second stage relates to all

[41]Howard Tu and Sherry E. Sullivan, "Preparing Yourself for an International Assignment," *Business Horizons* (January–February 1994), pp. 67–70.

[42]"Culture Shock for Executives," *The Financial Times* (April 5, 1995), p. 12.

[43]"Companies Use Cross-Cultural Training to Help Their Employees Adjust Abroad," *Wall Street Journal* (August 4, 1992), pp. B1, B6.

[44]See, for example, R. Fisher and W. Ury, *Getting to Yes: Negotiation Agreement Without Giving In* (New York: Penguin, 1981), and, G. Kennedy, *Negotiate Anywhere!* (London: Arrow Books, 1987).

[45]Graham, John L. and Yoshihiro Sano, "Across the Negotiating Table from the Japanese," *International Marketing Review*, 3 (Autumn 1986), pp. 58–71.

[46]Kathleen K. Reardon and Robert E. Spekman, "Starting Out Right: Negotiation Lessons for Domestic and Cross-Cultural Business Alliances," *Business Horizons* (January–February 1994), pp. 71–79.

 How do you order tea in Cairo? When do you bow in Bangkok? In 275 locations worldwide there's someone to clue you in on the customs. And AT&T USADirect® Service to bring you closer to home. Call 800-228-9290 or your travel agent for reservations. We believe:

 When you're comfortable you can do anything." **Marriott** HOTELS · RESORTS · SUITES

Cultural differences do exist. In many cases, your willingness to accept differences is a key to your success in business.

task-related exchanges of information. Once the information exchange stage is completed, the negotiation parties typically move toward the persuasion phase of the bargaining process. Persuasion is a give-and-take deal. The final step involves concession-making, hopefully resulting in a consensus. Not surprisingly, negotiation practices vary enormously across cultures. Japanese negotiators devote much more time to nurture a rapport than U.S. negotiators. For Americans, the persuasion stage is the most critical part of the negotiation process. Japanese bargainers prefer to spend most of their time on the first two stages so that little effort is needed for the persuasion phase. Japanese and American negotiators also differ in the way concessions are made. Americans tend to make concessions during the course of the negotiation process, whereas Japanese prefer to defer this toward the end of the bargaining.[47]

[47]John L. Graham, "Negotiating with the Japanese (Part 1)," *East Asian Executive Reports* (November 15, 1988), pp. 8, 19–21.

EXHIBIT 4-7
CULTURALLY RESPONSIVE STRATEGIES AND THEIR FEASIBILITY

High	Induce Counterpart to Follow One's Own Script	Improvise an Approach [Effect Symphony]
Counterpart's Familiarity with Negotiator's Culture	Adapt to the Counterpart's Script [Coordinate Adjustment of Both Parties]	
Low	Employ Agent or Adviser [Involve Mediator]	Embrace the Counterpart's Script
	Low High	
	Negotiator's Familiarity with Counterpart's Culture	

Brackets indicate a joint strategy, which requires deliberate consultation with counterpart. At each level of familiarity, a negotiator can consider feasible the strategies designated at that level and any lower level.

Reprinted from "Negotiating with "Romans—Part 1," by Stephen E. Weiss, *Sloan Management Review* (Winter 1994), pp. 51–61. Copyright 1994 by Sloan Management Review Association. All rights reserved.

Cross-Cultural Negotiation Strategies[48]

Exhibit 4-7 represents a framework of culturally responsive negotiation strategies, driven by the level of cultural familiarity that the negotiating parties possess about one another's cultures. Cultural familiarity is a measure of a party's current knowledge of his counterpart's culture and ability to use that knowledge competently. Depending on the particular situation, eight possible negotiation strategies could be selected. Let us briefly consider each one of them:

Employ an Agent or Advisor. Outside agents, such as technical experts or financial advisors, could be used when cultural familiarity is extremely low. These agents can be used to provide information and to advise on action plans.

Involve a Mediator. Whereas the previous strategy can be used unilaterally, both parties could also jointly decide to engage a mutually acceptable third party as a mediator. Successful mediation depends on maintaining the respect and trust of both parties.

Induce the Counterpart to Follow One's Own Negotiation Script. Effective negotiators proceed along a **negotiation script**—the rules, conduct, ends they target, means toward those ends, and so forth. When the counterpart's familiarity with

---

[48]Stephen E. Weiss, "Negotiating with "Romans—Part 1," *Sloan Management Review* (Winter 1994), pp. 51–61; Stephen E. Weiss, "Negotiating with "Romans—Part 2," *Sloan Management Review* (Spring 1994), pp. 85–99.

your culture is high, it might be feasible to induce the other party to follow your negotiation script. Inducement could be via verbal persuasion or subtle cues.

Adapt to Counterpart's Negotiation Script. With moderate levels of familiarity about the counterpart's cultural mindset, it becomes possible to adapt to his negotiation script. Adaptation involves a deliberate decision to adjust some common negotiation rules.

Coordinate Adjustment of Both Parties. When the circumstances lend themselves, both parties could jointly decide to arrive at a common negotiation approach that blends both cultures. Occasionally, they might propose to adopt the negotiation script of a third culture.

Embrace the Counterpart's Script. With this strategy, the negotiator volunteers to adopt his counterpart's negotiation approach. This demands a tremendous effort on part of the negotiator. It can only be effective when the negotiator possesses a great deal of familiarity about the other party's cultural background.

Improvise an Approach. This strategy constricts a negotiation script over the course of negotiating. This approach is advisable when both parties feel very comfortable with their counterpart's culture. It might be effective when bargaining with members from a high-context culture where mutual bonding and other contextual cues are at least as important (nontask-related aspects) as the immediate negotiation concerns.

Effect Symphony. The final strategy capitalizes on both parties' high cultural familiarity by creating an entirely new script or by following some other approach atypical to their respective cultures. For instance, the coordination might tap parts from both cultures.

The choice of a particular strategy partly depends on how familiar the negotiators are with the other party's culture. To pick a particular strategy, the following steps ought to be considered:

1. Reflect on your culture's negotiation practices. What negotiation model do you use? What is the role of the individual negotiator? What is the meaning of a satisfactory agreement?

2. Learn the negotiation script common in the counterpart's culture. This will help the negotiator to anticipate and interpret the other party's negotiating behaviors.

3. Consider the relationship and contextual clues. Different contexts necessitate different negotiating strategies. Contextual clues include considerations such as the life of the relationship, gender of the parties involved, balance of power.

4. Predict or influence the counterpart's approach. Prediction could be based on indicators like the counterpart's prenegotiation behavior, track record. In some cases, it is desirable to influence the other party's negotiation strategy via direct means (e.g., explicit request for a negotiation protocol) or through more subtle means (e.g., disclosing one's familiarity with the counterpart's culture).

5. Choosing a strategy. The chosen strategy should be compatible with the cultures involved, conducive to a coherent pattern of interaction, in line with the relationship and bargaining context, and ideally acceptable to both parties.

◆◆◆◆◆◆◆◆◆◆◆◆◆◆◆◆◆◆◆◆◆◆◆◆◆◆◆◆◆◆◆◆◆◆◆◆◆◆◆ NIGHTLY BUSINESS REPORT

⌒VIDEOBOX

CONSUMERS ACROSS BORDERS IN EUROPE

The European integration, which formed the European Union, is a political and economic success in the making. Now not only products but also people travel freely throughout the European Union. There is no denying that such a regional unification will enhance the gradual homogenization of product standards, industrial regulations, commercial codes, and fiscal and monetary policies in the long run. These factors will promote regional integration of corporate activities, such as standardizing products (or components) and services across national boundaries similar to the situation in the United States.

However, the video clip clearly shows that culture, taste, and lifestyle differences tend to remain as diverse as they have been across national borders in the European Union. Furthermore, as a result of the political and economic unification movement *forced* onto them, people of different nationalities may even try to emphasize their national heritage and cultural differences more than ever before. Such nationalistic needs may even create a more complex cultural diversity in an era of homogenization.

What implications do you draw for marketing research and segmentation from these two forces at work in the European Union?

SUMMARY ◆

Global marketing does not operate in a bubble. Culture is an intrinsic part of the global marketing environment. Cultural diversity brings along an immense richness. "Foreign" cultures may offer a breeding ground for new product ideas. Cultural changes typically open up new market opportunities. Cultural diversity also poses enormous challenges to international marketers and managers in general. Many cultural blunders are easily forgiven by members of the host culture. Occasionally, cultural mishaps create ill will and sometimes permanent damage to the firm's overseas business operations.

Preventive medicine is more effective than having to lick your wounds afterward. Dictums such as "When in Rome . . ." are nice catch-phrases but, unfortunately, it is seldom easy to learn what "do as the Romans" exactly means. Sensitivity to the host

culture is a nice attribute, but for most people it will always stay an ideal rather than an accomplishment. There simply are no tricks-of-the-trade or shortcuts. In fact, an often-fatal mistake is to overestimate one's familiarity with the host culture.

In this chapter we analyzed what is meant by culture. We examined several elements of culture in detail. Cultures have differences but also carry certain parallels. We provided several schemes that you can use to classify different cultures. Once you are aware of these differences and commonalities, the next task is to become sensitive to the host culture. We described several procedures to foster cultural adjustment. Finally, we gave some background on a very complex form of cultural interface: cross-cultural negotiations. Several strategies were introduced to assist you in international bargaining situations.

REVIEW QUESTIONS ◆

1. How does language complicate the tasks of global marketers?

2. Describe the importance of reference groups in international marketing.

3. What can marketers do to launch new products in countries that tend to resist change?

4. How do high-context cultures differ from low-context ones?

5. What are some possible issues in applying Hofstede's classification scheme in a global marketing context?

DISCUSSION QUESTIONS ◆ ◆ ◆ ◆ ◆ ◆ ◆ ◆ ◆ ◆ ◆ ◆ ◆ ◆ ◆ ◆ ◆

1. Focus group research conducted by advertising agencies like Leo Burnett shows that Asia's youngsters (the proverbial X-generation) mimic American trends but, at the same time, are pretty conservative. Gangsta rap, for instance, is extremely popular in Malaysia. But many of the values that Asian youths hold are quite traditional: family relations, respect for elders, marriage, and so on. Discuss this seeming contradiction.

2. What are some of the possible infrastructural roadblocks (e.g., in terms of transportation, storage) that ice cream manufacturers would face in Southeast Asia?

3. China's one-child policy has led to a league of "Little Emperors" and "Empresses." The chapter described how Pepsi-Cola exploited this development by launching a new fruit drink. What other sorts of companies might be able to tap into this market opportunity, and why?

4. One of the cultural dimensions singled out by Hofstede is the individualism/collectivism distinction. What would this categorization imply in terms of setting a sales force for international marketers? For instance, what incentive schemes might work in an individualistic culture? collectivistic?

5. Certain Muslim countries like Saudi Arabia do not allow advertisers to show a frontal picture of a woman with her hair. This creates a challenge for companies like Unilever or Procter & Gamble that want to advertise haircare products (e.g., shampoo). How would you tackle this challenge?

6. A lot of advertising efforts in Japan tend to establish a mood related to the product instead of convincing the viewer why s/he should buy brand X. What cultural traits might lie behind this so-called "soft-sell" approach toward advertising in Japan?

FURTHER READING ◆

Baligh, H. Helmy. "Components of Culture: Nature, Interconnections, and Relevance to the Decisions on the Organization Structure." *Management Science*, 40 (1) (1994): 14–27.

Barber, Benjamin R. *Jihad vs. McWorld. How Globalism and Tribalism are Reshaping the World*. New York: Ballantine Books, 1995.

Graham, John L., Alma T. Mintu, and Waymond Rodgers. "Explorations of Negotiation Behaviors in Ten Foreign Cultures Using a Model Developed in the United States." *Management Science*, 40 (1) (1994): 72–95.

Hall, Edward T. *Beyond Culture*. Garden City, N.Y.: Anchor Press, 1976.

Hofstede, Geert. *Culture's Consequences: International Differences in Work-Related Values*. Beverly Hills, Calif.: Sage Publications, 1980.

———. *Cultures and Organizations: Software of the Mind*. London: McGraw-Hill, 1991.

———. "Management Scientists Are Human." *Management Science*, 40 (1) (1994): 4–13.

Hofstede, Geert, and Michael Bond. "The Confucius Connection: From Cultural Roots to Economic Growth." *Organizational Dynamics*, (1988): 4–21.

Ricks, David A. *Blunders in International Business*. Cambridge, Mass.: Blackwell Publishers, 1993.

Terpstra, Vern, and Kenneth David. *The Cultural Environment of International Business*. Cincinnati, Ohio: South-Western Publishing Co., 1991.

Triandis, Harry C. "The Self and Social Behavior in Differing Cultural Contexts." *Psychological Review*, 96 (3), (1989): 506–520.

Tse, David K., Kam-hon Lee, Ilan Vertinsky, and Donald A. Wehrung. "Does Culture Matter? A Cross-Cultural Study of Executives' Choice, Decisiveness, and Risk Adjustment in International Marketing." *Journal of Marketing*, 52 (4) (October 1988): 81–95.

POLITICAL AND LEGAL ENVIRONMENT

5

HAPTER OVERVIEW

1. POLITICAL ENVIRONMENT—INDIVIDUAL GOVERNMENTS
2. POLITICAL ENVIRONMENT—SOCIAL PRESSURES AND POLITICAL RISK
3. INTERNATIONAL AGREEMENTS
4. INTERNATIONAL LAW AND LOCAL LEGAL ENVIRONMENT
5. ISSUES TRANSCENDING NATIONAL BOUNDARIES

Business has been considered an integral part of economic forces. Indeed, economics was once called *political economy*, and as such, business could not be conducted devoid of political and legal forces. Although we tend to take political and legal forces for granted most of the time in doing business domestically, they could become central issues in international business and cannot be ignored. It is human nature that we tend to look at other countries' political and legal systems as peculiar because they differ from ours. We might even make some value judgment that our own country's political and legal system is always superior to other countries' and that they should change their system to our way. This ethnocentrism, however, hinders our proper understanding of, and sensitivity to, differences in the system that might have major business implications. By the very nature of their jobs, international marketers cannot afford to be ethnocentric as they interact with a multitude of political and legal systems, including their own at home.

International marketers should be aware that the economic interests of their companies can differ widely from those of the countries in which they do business and sometimes even from those of their own home countries. Furthermore, there are various international agreements, treaties, and laws for them to abide by. In this chapter, we will examine political and legal forces that affect the company's international marketing activities from the following three perspectives: the political and legal climates of the host country, those of the home country, and the international agreements, treaties, and laws affecting international marketing activities transcending national boundaries. Although political and legal climates are inherently related and inseparable because laws are generally a manifestation of a country's political processes, we will look at political climate first, followed by legal climate.

◆ ◆ ◆ ◆ ◆ ◆   POLITICAL ENVIRONMENT—INDIVIDUAL GOVERNMENTS

Government affects almost every aspect of business life in a country. First, national politics affect business environments directly, through changes in policies, regulations, and laws. The government in each country determines which industries will receive protection in the country and which will face open competition. The government determines labor regulations and property laws. It determines fiscal and monetary policies, which then affect investment and returns. We will summarize those policies and regulations that directly influence the international business environment in a country.

Second, the political stability and mood in a country affect the actions a government will take—actions that may have an important impact on the viability of doing business in the country. A political movement may change prevailing attitudes toward foreign corporations and result in new regulations. An economic shift may influence the government's willingness to endure the hardships of an austerity program. We will discuss the strategic importance of understanding political risk in an international business context.

Home Country versus Host Country

Whenever marketing executives do business across national boundaries, they have to face the regulations and laws of both the home and host countries. A **home country** refers to a country the parent company is based in and operates from. A **host country** is a country in which foreign companies are allowed to do business in accordance with its government policies and within its laws. Therefore, international marketing executives should be concerned about the host government's policies and their possible changes in the future, as well as their home government's political climate.

Because companies usually do not operate in countries that have been hostile to their home country, many executives tend to take for granted the political environment of the host country in which they currently do business. Sweeping political upheavals, such as the Cuban crisis in the 1960s, the Iranian Revolution in the 1980s, the breakup of the Soviet Union in the late 1980s, and the Persian Gulf War in the 1990s have already made many business executives fully aware of dire political problems in some regions, and many companies have since stayed away from those areas. Despite the fact that those major political upheavals provide the largest single setting for an economic crisis faced by foreign companies, what most foreign companies are concerned about on a daily basis should be a much larger universe of low-key events that may not involve violence or a change in government regime but that do involve a fairly significant change in policy toward foreign companies.[1] In recent years, Vietnam has begun to attract foreign direct investment to spur its domestic economic growth and shift toward a more market-based economy.[2] Similarly, the end of apartheid in South Africa also signals foreign companies' cautious yet optimistic attitude toward resuming business relations with this African country.[3]

The intertwined nature of home and host government policies is illustrated by the U.S.–China diplomatic relationship having been re-established in the mid-1970s under the Nixon administration. As a result, the Chinese government finally opened its economy to foreign direct investment—mostly through joint ventures—in the 1980s. The first pioneer foreign companies have stood to gain from the host government policies designed to protect the domestic producers they teamed up with in China. Thus, the United States' Chrysler, Germany's Volkswagen, and France's Peugeot, with their respective Chinese partner companies, were such beneficiaries. However, the U.S.–China relationship has since been anything but smooth. The United States, in particular, has been openly critical of China's human rights "violations" since the Tiannanmen Square massacre of 1989 and has tried to make its trade policy with China contingent upon measurable improvements in China's human rights policy.

Reacting negatively to the U.S. pressure, and also because of China's own economic problems, however, the Chinese government announced a policy about-face in 1994, saying it would not approve any more joint ventures in automobiles for up to three years. Furthermore, new car-assembly plants will be approved only if they buy at least 40 percent of their components in China and increase this domestic content requirement to 60 percent in three years.[4] This new policy became a major setback to those automobile makers that had delayed their initial entry to the Chinese market.

International marketers must understand the fluid nature of the host country political climate in relation to the home country policies. Some countries are relatively stable over time; other countries experience different degrees of political volatility that make it difficult for international marketers to predict and plan ahead. Nonetheless, there are a few crucial political factors international executives should know that determines the nature of the host country's political climate.

Structure of Government

Ideology. One way to characterize the nature of government is by its socioeconomic ideology, ranging from communism and socialism to capitalism. Under strict **communism,** the government owns and manages all businesses and no private ownership is allowed. As the recent breakup of the Soviet Union shows, the strict govern-

---

[1]Stephen J. Kobrin, "Selective Vulnerability and Corporate Management," in Theodore H. Moran, ed., *International Political Risk Assessment: The State of the Art*, Landegger Papers in International Business and Public Policy, Georgetown University, Washington, D.C. 1981, pp. 9–13.

[2]Nick J. Freeman, "United States's Economic Sanctions against Vietnam: International Business and Development Repercussions," *Columbia Journal of World Business*, 28 (Summer 1993), pp. 12–22.

[3]"How Wrong Is It Going?" *Economist* (October 12, 1996), pp. 21–23.

[4]"Slow Car to China," *Economist* (April 16, 1994), pp. 71–72.

ment control not only strips its people of private incentives to work but also is an inefficient mechanism to allocate scarce resources across the economy. On the other hand, **capitalism** refers to an economic system in which free enterprise is permitted and encouraged along with private ownership. In a capitalistic society, free-market transactions are considered to produce the most efficient allocation of scarce resources. However, capitalism, if unfettered, may result in excessive production and excessive consumption, thereby causing severe air and water pollution in many parts of the world, as well as depleting the limited natural resources. Government roles would be limited to those functions that the private sector could not perform efficiently, such as defense, highway construction, pollution control, and other public services. **Socialism** generally is considered a political system that falls in between pure communism and pure capitalism. A socialistic government advocates government ownership and control of some industries considered critical to the welfare of the nation.

After the breakup of the communist Soviet Union, most East European countries have converted to capitalistic ideology.[5] China also seems to be in a transition stage, although many uncertainties still remain. There remain few countries that adhere to the extreme communist doctrine other than North Korea and Cuba. While many countries cherish capitalism and democracy, the extent of government intervention in the economy varies from country to country. (Both capitalistic and socialistic countries in which government planning and ownership play a major role are also referred to as **planned economies**).

Political Parties.   The number of political parties also influences the level of political stability. A one-party regime does not exist outside the communist country. Most countries have a number of large and small political parties representing different views and value systems of their population. In a **single-party-dominant** country, government policies tend to be stable and predictable over time. Although such a government provides consistent policies, they do not always guarantee a favorable political environment for foreign companies operating in the country. A dominant party regime may maintain policies, such as high tariff and nontariff barriers, foreign direct investment restrictions, and foreign exchange controls, that reduce the operational flexibility of foreign companies.

For example, in Mexico a few political parties have always existed, but one party, called the Institutional Revolutionary Party, had been dominant in the past seventy years. However, since 1994, Mexico's ruling party has lost its firm grip on its politics. Although the opening of the Mexican political system may eventually lead to a stronger democracy over time, it is believed that its economy will experience an unknown degree of political instability for the foreseeable future.[6] The social trauma followed by the collapse of one-party-dominant systems tends to be relatively large, as experienced also by the extreme of the Soviet Union to the less dramatic but still wrenching experience of Japan.[7]

In a **dual-party** system, such as the United States and Britain, the parties are usually not divided by ideology but rather have different constituencies. For example,

---

[5]Robert D. Russell, "The Emergence of Entrepreneurship in Eastern Europe: A Self-Organizing Perspective," *International Journal of Commerce and Management*, 6 (1-2), 1996, pp. 21–37.

[6]"PRI Loses a Mexico Governorship, but Clean Vote Could Help Image," *Economist* (February 14, 1995), p. 18; "The 5% Solution," *Economist*, (November 23, 1996), p. 48.

[7]"The Third Opening," *Economist* (March 9, 1996), p. 21.

in the United States, the Democrats tend to identify with working-class people and assume a greater role for the federal government while the Republicans tend to support business interests and prefer a limited role for the federal government. Yet both parties are strong proponents of democracy and capitalism. In such a dual-party system, the two parties tend to alternate their majority position over a relatively long period. In 1995, the Democrats finally relinquished control of Congress to the Republican majority after many years. We have begun to see some sweeping changes in government policy, ranging from environmental protection to affirmative action, usually in support of business interests.

The other extreme situation is a multiple-party system without any clear majority, found in Italy[8] and more recently in Japan. The consistency of government policies may be compromised as a result. Since there is no dominant party, different parties with differing policy goals form a coalition government. The major problem with a coalition government is a lack of political stability and continuity, and this portends a high level of uncertainty in the business climate. However, in the case of Japan, career bureaucrats, who are not political appointees, have been in virtual control of government policy development and execution; the changes in government leadership do not seem to pose any measurable policy change in the short run.[9] Turkey offers another interesting example. Although it is a multiple party system, the Islamic fundamentalist party gained popularity and formed a coalition party with a strong anti-Western rhetoric in 1996. While Prime Minister Necmettin Erbakan was turning his back on NATO, he seemed in fact to be practicing *realpolitik*, accommodating the anti-Western views of a vocal Turkish minority while trying not to alienate the United States and Europe. Despite his rhetoric, Erbakan was quietly maintaining many of Turkey's previous policies with the West.[10]

Government Policies and Regulations

It is the role of government to promote a country's interests in the international arena for various reasons and objectives. Some governments actively invest in certain industries that are considered important to national interests. Other governments protect fledgling industries in order to allow them to gain the experience and size necessary to compete internationally. In general, reasons for wanting to block or restrict trade are as follows:

1. National security
   - Ability to produce goods necessary to remain independent (e.g., self-sufficiency)
   - Not exporting goods that will help enemies or unfriendly nations
2. Developing new industries
   - Idea of nurturing nascent industries to strength in a protected market
3. Protecting declining industries
   - To maintain domestic employment for political stability

---

[8]"Italy Struggles for Stability," *Economist* (February 22, 1997), pp. 55–57.

[9]Jonathan Friedland, "Trouble in the Ranks," *Far Eastern Economic Review*, 157 (December 30, 1994), p. 83.

[10]John Doxey, "Turkey: Its Behavior Isn't as Ominous as It Looks," *Business Week* (September 30, 1996), p. 57.

For example, Japan's active industrial policy by the MITI (Ministry of International Trade and Industry) in the 1960s and 1970s is well known for its past success and has also been adopted by newly industrialized countries (NICs), such as Singapore, South Korea, and Malaysia.[11] Governments use a variety of laws, policies, and programs to pursue their economic interests. Later sections of this chapter will discuss the legal systems that produce and enforce a countries' laws. This section focuses on describing the various policies and laws that directly influence the international business environment in a country.

We must limit our discussion of government policies in some way. Almost any government decision can have an international impact if we consider enough subsequent effects. For example, a minimum wage increase can drive labor-intensive assembly plants overseas in search of lower wages, thus influencing the balance of trade, which can then affect public sentiments toward protectionism. This section will concentrate on describing those government programs, trade and investment laws, and macroeconomic policies, which have an immediate and direct impact on the international business in a country. We will discuss laws regulating business behavior—such as antitrust laws and anti-bribery laws—in a subsequent section on international legal environments.

Incentives and Government Programs. Most countries use government loans, subsidies, or training programs to support export activities and specific domestic industries. These programs are important for host-country firms, as well as for firms considering production in one country for export to others. In the United States, the International Trade Administration (ITA) has a national network of district offices in every state, offering export promotion assistance to local businesses. Furthermore, in light of federal budget cuts and as a supplement to the ITA's trade promotion efforts, state governments have significantly increased their staff and budgets, not only for export assistance, particularly in nurturing small local businesses,[12] but also for attracting foreign direct investment to increase employment in their respective states.[13] Thus, the major objectives of any state government support are (1) job creation and (2) improving the *state* balance of trade (as in any country). In any state, foreign companies that create jobs and export products abroad, as well as to other states, tend to enjoy a favorable political climate. State governments have a vested interest in ensuring their own economic growth and prosperity, independent of those of the nation as a whole.

[11]Masaaki Kotabe, "The Roles of Japanese Industrial Policy for Export Success: A Theoretical Perspective," *Columbia Journal of World Business,* 20 (Fall 1985), pp. 59–64; Mark L. Clifford, "Can Malaysia Take That Next Big Step?" *Business Week* (February 26, 1996), pp. 96–106.

[12]Masaaki Kotabe and Michael R. Czinkota, "State Government Promotion of Manufacturing Exports: A Gap Analysis," *Journal of International Business Studies,* 23 (Fourth Quarter 1992), pp. 637–658; and for the most recent comprehensive study, see Timothy J. Wilkinson, "American State Export Promotion Strategies for Entrepreneurs and Small- to Mid-Sized Businesses," A Ph.D. dissertation, Department of Political Science, University of Utah.

[13]Masaaki Kotabe, "The Promotional Roles of the State Government and Japanese Manufacturing Direct Investment in the United States," *Journal of Business Research,* 27 (June 1993), pp. 131–46.

Taiwan Innovalue℠ grabbed Peter Grose with a pen that reads.

As a successful biographer, Peter Grose has spent thousands of hours cross-referencing facts and documents, always longing for a faster compiling system.

Then, through a writer friend in Taiwan, he met the Primax DataPen. By running the head of the little scanner across a printed page, the text was transferred instantly to a computer, almost twenty times faster than the best typist.

At less than two hundred dollars, the DataPen represents Innovalue. That is, innovation in design and manufacturing that gives added value to so many Taiwan products.

These Innovalue products exist in all design areas. Including yours. To learn more, reach us by fax or the Internet. Taiwan's high end is soaring, not just with ideas and products, but also values that are VERY WELL MADE IN TAIWAN.

Selected Taiwan products carry this Symbol of Excellence. It is awarded by a panel of judges only to those products which excel in quality and innovation.

**TAIWAN.
Your Source
for Innovalue℠**

WWW: http://innovalue.cetra.org.tw
Our Fax Number: 886-2-723-5497
E-mail: mitnews@cetra.org.tw

The Primax DataPen scans the text directly into a computer, like the handsome Acer Aspire, another Gold Award Winner.

A government may set a high quality standard to actively promote its country's products abroad.

The state government's export promotion activities are more systematic, while its investment attraction activities are characterized by their case-by-case nature. Export promotion activities generally comprise (i) *export service programs* (e.g., seminars for potential exporters, export counseling, how-to-export handbooks, and export financing) and (ii) *market development activities* (e.g., dissemination of sales leads to local firms, sponsorship of foreign trade shows, preparation of market analysis, and export news letters).[14] Export promotion activities will be discussed in detail in Chapter 17.

---

[14]William C. Lesch, Abdolreza Eshghi, and Golpira S. Eshghi, "A Review of Export Promotion Programs in the Ten Largest Industrial States," in S. Tamer Cavusgil and Michael R. Czinkota, ed., *International Perspectives on Trade Promotion and Assistance* (New York: Quorum Books, 1990), pp. 25–37.

Although foreign investment attraction activities generally consist of seminars, various audio-visual and printed promotional materials, and investment missions, among others, investment missions and various tax and other financial incentives appear to play the most important role in investment promotional efforts. Investment missions are generally made by government officials, particularly by the governor of the state, visiting with potential investors. One study has shown that whether or not they are active in foreign investment attraction activities, state governments that are active in export promotion tend to attract more foreign companies' direct investment in their states than those state governments that are not.[15] Probably, export-active states may be more politically favorable and receptive to foreign companies operating there. A well-known example is that to attract a Nissan plant, Tennessee spent $12 million for new roads to the facility and provided a $7 million grant for training plant employees. The county provided a $10 million tax break to the Japanese company in 1985.[16] Similarly, Alabama provided a $253 million package of capital investments and tax breaks to lure Mercedes-Benz's sports utility vehicle production facility to the state.[17]

Most governments subsidize certain industries directly. Direct government subsidies are an important international consideration. In Europe, Airbus Industries was established with joint government subsidies from the governments of Britain, France, Germany, and Spain in 1970 to build a European competitor in the jet aircraft industry once dominated by U.S. companies, including Boeing and McDonnel-Douglas-Lockheed. The United States is no exception. When threatened by Japanese competition in the semiconductor industry in the 1980s, the Reagan administration decided to launch a Japanese-style government-industry joint industrial policy known as SEMATECH (Semiconductor Manufacturing Technology) in 1987. When SEMATECH was launched, the U.S. government initially agreed to subsidize half of its $200 million operating budget.[18] Thanks to SEMATECH, the U.S. semiconductor industry has finally recaptured the leading market share position by 1995, long lost to Japanese in the 1980s.

The point is to recognize how government support for particular industries or for exporting in general will affect which industries are competitive and which are not. International businesses can benefit by planning for and utilizing home-country and host-country government programs.

Government Procurement. The ultimate government involvement in trade is when the government itself is the customer. It engages in commercial operations through the departments and agencies under its control. The U.S. government ac-

---

[15]Masaaki Kotabe, "The Promotional Roles of the State Government and Japanese Manufacturing Direct Investment in the United States," *Journal of Business Research*, 27 (June 1993), pp. 131–46.

[16]"Tennessee's Pitch to Japan," *New York Times* (February 27, 1985), pp. D1 and D6.

[17]"Tax Freedom Day Index Would Be Keen Indicator," *Orlando Sentinel* (May 8, 1994), p. D1.

[18]Due to the U.S. government's gradual budget cut, SEMATECH became a technology consortium funded solely by member companies in 1998.

counts for a quarter of the total U.S. consumption, so the government has become the largest single consuming entity in the United States. Thus, the government procurement policy has an enormous impact on international trade. In the United States, the Buy American Act gives a bidding edge to domestic suppliers. For foreign suppliers to win a contract from a U.S. government agency, their products must contain at least 50 percent of U.S.-made parts, or they must undercut the closest comparable U.S. product by at least 6 percent.[19] This "buy domestic" policy orientation is not limited to the United States, but applies to all other nations. In other words, when a U.S. company tries to sell to any foreign government agency, it should always expect some sort of bidding disadvantage relative to local competitors.

Trade Laws. National trade laws directly influence the environment for international business. Trade controls can be broken into two categories—*economic* trade controls and *political* trade controls. Economic trade controls are those trade restraints that are instituted for primarily economic reasons, such as to protect local jobs. Both **tariffs** and **nontariff** barriers (NTB's) work to impede imports that might compete with locally produced goods. Tariffs tax imports directly, and also function as a form of income for the country that levies them. Average tariff rates on manufactured and mining products are 2.2 percent for Japan, 5.4 percent for the United States, and 5.7 percent for the European Union.[20] Nontariff barriers include a wide variety of quotas, procedural rules for imports, and standards set upon import quality that have the effect of limiting imports or making importing more difficult. A list of tariff and nontariff barriers is presented in Exhibit 5-1.

Political trade controls are those trade restraints that are instituted for national interests or for international political reasons. **Embargoes** and **sanctions** are country-based political trade controls. Political trade restraints have become an accepted form of political influence in the international community. They are coercive or retaliatory trade measures often enacted unilaterally with the hopes of changing a foreign government or its policies without resorting to military force. Embargoes restrict all trade with a nation for political purposes. The United States maintains an economic embargo on Cuba today in an effort to change the country's political disposition. Sanctions are more narrowly defined trade restrictions, such as the U.S. government's threat to impose a hefty 100 percent punitive tariff on Lexus, Infiniti, and other Japanese luxury cars imported from Japan in June 1995. While it was a politically motivated retaliatory action against Japan's recalcitrant huge trade surplus with the United States due mostly to its auto and auto parts trade imbalance, it would disrupt the price mechanism on the U.S. auto market, hurting many Lexus, Infiniti, and Accura dealers in the United States and probably benefiting other luxury car dealers selling competing models.[21]

---

[19]Sak Onkvisit and John J. Shaw, "Marketing Barriers in International Trade," *Business Horizons* (May-June 1988), pp. 64–72.

[20]"MITI Angered by U.S. View of Trade Practices," *Financial Times* (May 3, 1994), p. 6.

[21]Clay Chandler, "U.S. Turns Tough on Japan: Administration Renews Pressure in Trade Dispute over Auto, Auto Parts," *Washington Post* (March 30, 1995), p. D11.

EXHIBIT 5-1
TARIFF AND NONTARIFF BARRIERS

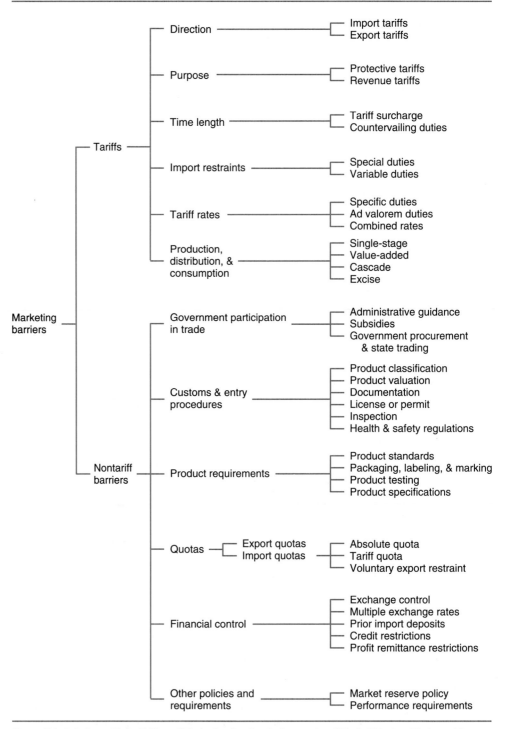

Source: Sak Onkvist and John J. Shaw, "Marketing Barriers in International Trade," *Business Horizons*, 31, May–June 1988, p. 66.

Export license requirements are product-based trade controls. All exports officially require a specific export license from the Export Administration of the Department of Commerce. However, most products that are not sensitive to national security or are in short supply in the country may be sent to another country using only a *general license*. The application process for more sensitive products, including much high-technology exports, is quite extensive and can include review by numerous government agencies and even by international review committees such as COCOM (see the description of COCOM later in this chapter).

International businesses have a number of reasons to be concerned with trade restrictions. First, trade restrictions may completely block a company's ability to export to a country. Even if the company can export its goods, restrictions such as quotas or local modification requirements may make the product so expensive that an otherwise lucrative market is eliminated. Some companies attempt to benefit from import restrictions by establishing production facilities inside the foreign market country. For example, Brazil suddenly raised a tariff on imported cars from 20 percent to 70 percent in late 1994. As a result, foreign auto makers Fiat and Ford, with operating plants in Brazil, enjoy a definite cost advantage over Chrysler, Toyota, Volvo, and others that still export cars to the country. This is one illustration of strategic reasons why firms sometimes have plants in various countries rather than rely solely on exporting from home. The average price of a Volvo in Brazil is a whopping $85,000! In this manner those companies, domestic or foreign, already manufacturing in the market can access the desired market with little competition from external producers.

However, trade restrictions are not necessarily good, even for companies inside a protected country. Trade restrictions often block companies from purchasing needed inputs at competitive prices. For example, in 1992 the U.S. International Trade Commission levied an import tariff on the flat panel display screens used in laptop computers in response to a complaint that foreign companies were dumping the screens below cost on the U.S. market. Although local producers of computer screens benefited from the protection from competition, U.S. producers of laptop computers, which relied mostly on imported screens, could no longer compete. Many laptop producers were forced to ship their assembly plants overseas in order to stay in the market.

If producers sold in a completely protected market, then their input costs would not matter much, because elevated input prices could be passed along to the consumer. However, very few companies sell in a completely protected home market. And if a company has any desire to produce for an international market, import restrictions on any of its inputs will place it at a disadvantage. Thus, trade policies can inhibit competitiveness—even if they appear to offer better sales to the protected firm.

At a more macro level, if trade laws harm other countries, they are likely to invoke retaliation. For example, wrangling over China's inability to enforce intellectual property protection laws against pirating, the U.S. government announced the largest trade sanctions in U.S. history in 1995, slapping 100 percent tariffs on $1.1 billion of Chinese exports such as cellular phones, sporting goods, and plastic articles. China responded angrily and promptly retaliated against U.S. exports of compact disks, video games, films, cigarettes, and alcohol.[22] Such a trade war also occurs

---

[22]Helene Cooper and Kathy Chen, "Sanctions Put U.S., China on Course to Trade War," *Wall Street Journal* (February 6, 1995), pp. A3, A11. Despite such bickerings, some improvement has also been observed. See, for example, "What's News—Worldwide," *Wall Street Journal* (April 30, 1997), p. 1.

frequently between seemingly friendly nations. For example, Canada has recently decided to knock an American-owned music video channel off the Canadian cable systems. Further, the United States imposes tariffs on Canadian sugar, while Canada has added tariffs on U.S. dairy and other food products. Both countries are opposed to each other's tariffs as unfairly restricting their respective industry's access to each other's market.[23]

However, trade wars, if left unchecked, harm all countries by limiting the ability of competitive firms to export and generate the benefits created by specialization. One thing is clear—government trade laws have a complex and dynamic impact on the environment for international business.

Investment Regulations.   International investments have been growing at a much faster pace than international trade. Much of these investments is being made by multinational corporations. Foreign direct investments are explained in terms of various market imperfections, including government imposed distortions, but governments also have a significant role in constructing barriers to foreign direct investment and portfolio flows. These barriers can broadly be characterized as ownership and financial controls.

Ownership Controls.   Most countries feel that some assets belong to the public—there is a sense of "national ownership" or "patrimony." In a highly nationalistic country, this sense could apply to the ownership of any company. In many countries, the natural resources (e.g., the land and mineral wealth) are viewed as part of the national wealth, not to be sold to foreigners. For example, in India, a ceiling of 25 percent has been stipulated on the divested shares of state-owned companies such as Indian Oil, Hindustan Petroleum, and Bharat Petroleum. Indian officials say the ceilings will ensure wide distribution of shares and thwart indirect ownership and control of the country's oil resources by individuals and private companies.[24]

The United States has very few restrictions on foreign ownership; however, for reasons of national security, limitations do exist. For example, the Federal Communications Commission limits the control of U.S. media companies to U.S. citizens only. This was one of the motivating factors for Rupert Murdoch to relinquish his Australian citizenship for U.S. citizenship in order to retain control of his media network, Fox Television. Similarly, the U.S. Shipping Act of 1916 limits noncitizen ownership of U.S. shipping lines. The Federal Aviation Act requires airlines to be U.S. citizens (defined as one where 75 percent of the voting rights of the firm are owned and controlled by U.S. citizens) in order to hold U.S. operating rights. The International Banking Act of 1978 limits interstate banking operations by foreign banks. Consequently, foreign banks cannot purchase or take over U.S. banks with interstate operations.

---

[23]"Pact to Expand Air Travel Caps Clinton Canada Visit," *Los Angeles Times* (February 29, 1995), p. A1; and "IDFA Panel Appointed to Resolve U.S.-Canada Trade Dispute," PR *Newswire* (February 6, 1996).

[24]"India Places Upper Limit on Private Ownership," *Platt's Oilgram News* (April 11, 1995), p. 2.

Financial Controls. Government-imposed restrictions can serve as strong barriers to foreign direct investments. Some common barriers include restrictions on profit remittances, and differential taxation and interest rates. Government-imposed restrictions can deter foreign investments. Restrictions of profit remittances can serve as a disincentive to invest, since returns cannot be realized in the home currency of the parent company. Although government controls on profit remittance are drawbacks in attracting investment, some governments also use such restrictions as a way to encourage foreign companies to increase exports from the host country. For example, Zimbabwe offers higher remittance rates—up to 100 percent—to foreign companies operating in that country that export significantly.[25]

Various multinational companies have been able to exploit legal loopholes to circumvent this problem to some extent. Tactics include currency swaps, parallel loans,[26] countertrade activities, and charging for management services, among others. Also, various countries treat operations of foreign companies differently from those of local companies. Two means through which local companies are supported are lower tax rates and lower interest rates for loans secured from local financial institutions. These differences can put foreign subsidiaries and/or companies at a significant disadvantage relative to domestic companies in that particular market, and can also act as a deterrent to foreign direct investments.

Macroeconomic Policies. Companies search internationally for stable growing markets where their profits will not be deteriorated by exchange loss or inflation. Government policies drive many economic factors such as the cost of capital, levels of economic growth, rates of inflation, and international exchange rates. Governments may directly determine the prime lending rate, or they may print or borrow the funds necessary to increase money supply. Governments may fix their currencies' exchange rates, or they may decide to allow the international currency market to determine their exchange rates. The monetary and exchange policies a government pursues will affect the stability of its currency—which is of critical concern to any company doing business abroad. Mexico kept the peso's exchange rate artificially high despite its increasing trade deficit in the early 1990s. One primary objective for such an exchange rate policy was to make it relatively easy for Mexico to import capital goods, such as machinery, from the United States for economic development. When Mexico's trade deficit rose to well over 8 percent of the country's GNP by 1994, Mexico could no longer hold on to an artificially high value of the peso and let it loose in December 1994. How serious was Mexico's trade deficit? Think, for a moment, that the United States had registered the largest trade deficit ever of $172 billion in 1987, which once ushered in a doomsday prophecy of the decline of U.S. competitiveness. Yet, the U.S. trade deficit was no more than 3 percent of the country's GNP then!

---

[25]Cris Chinaka, "Zimbabwe Announces Measures to Boost Investment," *Reuter Library Report* (April 27, 1993).

[26]For details, see Donald J. Smith and Robert A. Taggart, Jr., "Bond Market Innovations and Financial Intermediation," *Business Horizons*, 32 (November 1989), pp. 24–33.

Government fiscal policies also strongly influence macroeconomic conditions. The types of taxes a government employs will influence whether a particular type of business is competitive within a country. For example, if a government lowers long-term capital gains taxes or allows accelerated depreciation of corporate capital assets, it will encourage investment in manufacturing facilities. The Japanese government has been known for its pro-business tax abatement and depreciation policies that helped develop the world's leading manufacturing industries in Japan, ranging from steel and shipbuilding in the 1960s and 1970s, to machine tools, automobiles, and consumer electronics in the 1970s and 1980s, and to semiconductor and semiconductor manufacturing equipment in the 1980s and 1990s.

Although a government can play a role in a thriving economy and accessible capital, a number of other factors also determine a country's political environment. Historical considerations, social and political pressures, and the interests of particular constituencies will affect the political environment in important ways. For example, during the early 1990s China has been enjoying an unprecedented economic boom. However, companies that have tried to take advantage of China's open market policy have met with mixed results. The next section will discuss such nonpolicy political considerations for international business.

◆ ◆ ◆ ◆ ◆ ◆ POLITICAL ENVIRONMENT—SOCIAL PRESSURES AND POLITICAL RISK

The political environment in every country is regularly changing. New social pressures can force governments to make new laws or to enforce old policies differently. Policies that supported international investment may change toward isolationism or nationalism. In order to adequately prepare for international business or investment, the environment in each target country should be analyzed to determine its level of economic and political risk and opportunity. Global Perspective 5-1 shows a recent political change sweeping the Russian economy and subsequent business opportunities and risks.

Social Pressures and Special Interests

Governments respond to pressures from various forces in a country, including the public at large, lobbyists for businesses, the church, and sometimes the personal interests of the members of the government. In order to assess the political stability of a country, it is critical to evaluate the importance of major forces on the government of the country. Many developing countries have undertaken significant liberalization programs during the 1980s and 1990s.[27] Although these programs have been regularly promoted by the International Monetary Fund (IMF), their success during recent years must be attributed to a larger social acceptance of the potential benefits of necessary austerity measures. For example, one study has shown that the IMF's Structural Adjustment Program helped improve the economic efficiency of both do-

---

[27]Kate Gillespie and Dana Alden, "Consumer Product Export Opportunities to Liberalizing LDCs: A Life-Cycle Approach," *Journal of International Business Studies*, 20 (Spring 1989), pp. 93–112.

$\diamond$

$\mathcal{G}$LOBAL PERSPECTIVE 5-1

RUSSIA: ELECTION AND FOREIGN INVESTMENT

In the last two or three years multinational firms have invested in Russian brain power. Russian scientists are working on new technologies, from object-oriented programming tools to artificial diamonds to cardiac medicines. Investment opportunities seem reasonably low risk, because these assets could theoretically be removed to the West or, in the worst case, written off without great financial harm.

Companies like Rockwell, Rolls-Royce, Pratt & Whitney, Boeing, United Technologies, and McDonnell Douglas are developing space projects with Russian partners. Their opinion is that "every major space contractor who wants to be cost-effective should be thinking about relations with Russian partners," and that "by 2010 a quarter of the world's jet engines will be made in the former Soviet Union."

Russian science and technology are attractive for their bargain prices and their innovative ways, unknown in the West, as they have worked for a long period cut off from many discoveries and ways of doing research in the wider world. Companies like Sun Microsystems and Motorola have Russian research teams, and they believe the Russians can get more performance from every bit and byte.

Sources: Christopher Ogden, "Will Russia Turn Back the Clock?," *Fortune* (June 10, 1996), pp. 49–50; Craig Mellow, "Brain Rush: Why Western Business is Investing in Russian R&D," *Fortune*, (June 10, 1996), pp. 51-52.

Russia's command-and-control medical system makes it easy to round up test patients, and their top medical centers accept equipment donations as payment, creating a great interest among companies like Pfizer, Hoffmann-La Roche, Merck, and other pharmaceutical giants in working with them in clinical trials required for drug certification.

Westerners do not yet have total confidence in Russian follow-through. Besides, their way of working with a budget is different from world practice—if they run out of money, they just stop working. But what really worries foreign investors is the government ideology: communism. When Yeltsin took charge in 1991, he dissolved the central economic controls and began privatization, which has unleashed some 60 percent of the Russian economy into the profit-making, or at least profit-seeking sector.

They waited anxiously for the results of Russia's first wide-open presidential race, which took place on June 16, 1996. The candidates were Zyuganov and Yeltsin. Zyuganov tried to convince foreign investors that they would benefit from the order and predictability of a communist government, but did not succeed. He and his team were seen as nonmarket reformers. If he had won, investors' confidence would have collapsed and their money exited. Yeltsin won the presidential election along with the West's cautious optimism on Russian reforms, which began to attract a great deal of capital, especially in the energy field.

---

mestic and foreign companies operating in Nigeria in the 1980s.[28] The benefits of liberalization extend beyond the borders of the countries involved. Consider the liberalization in Mexico, where the privatization of the state telephone company (TelMex) led to large investments by Southwestern Bell. Similarly, private companies are moving rapidly to finance other large public projects. An international consortium composed of Mexico's Grupo Hermés, the United States's AES Corp., and the Japanese firm Nichimen have begun to construct Mexico's first independent power-producing plant in Yucatán State.[29] While liberalization may provide unprecedented

---

[28]Sam C. Okoroafo and Masaaki Kotabe, "The IMF's Structural Adjustment Program and Its Impact on Firm Performance: A Case of Foreign and Domestic Firms in Nigeria," *Management International Review*, 33 (2) (1993), pp. 139–156.

[29]"Mexico's Energy Infrastructure Expanding to Match Growth," *NAFTA Works* (February 1997), pp. 1–2.

opportunities, the forces of special interests or the backlash of public sentiment may also cause governments to limit or curtail entirely certain international business operations.

Feelings of national interest can act as a deterrent both to international trade and to foreign direct investments. As a manifestation of nationalistic sentiment, a *boycott* may be organized by an interest group or even by a government agency to refuse to buy a certain foreign product or products. A boycott represents an outburst of anger expressed by the interest group to protest a foreign company's activities that do not agree with the value system of the interest group. For example, abortion is a politically sensitive issue in the United States. An abortion pill, RU 486, developed by Hoechst AG (Germany's chemical and pharmaceutical giant) and its French subsidiary, Roussel Uclaf SA, was about to be introduced into the U.S. market. Stepping up its protest against the imminent arrival of the pill, a coalition of anti-abortion groups tried to boycott eleven prescription and over-the-counter drug products made by Hoechst and its affiliates in the United States, including the drug Allegra, which replaced the company's second-largest selling product, Seldane, a popular allergy medicine. Obviously, foreign companies have to be aware of the national sentiment of people in a foreign market.[30]

How should a manager evaluate the opportunities and risks a country presents? Obviously this depends upon too many factors to discuss them all. A manager should certainly consider the political history of the country, as well as the history of similar industries within the country. In the following section we will discuss a number of factors that international managers should consider when determining the economic and political risks associated with a country.

Managing the Political Environment

International managers must manage the political environment in which the international firm operates. This means, first and foremost, learning to follow the customs of the country in which the firm is operating. But managing the political environment also means knowing which facets of the foreign country must be carefully monitored, and which can be manipulated.

In order to make informed decisions, the marketing manager must understand the *political factors* of the country, and also must understand the *national strategies and goals* of the country. The political factors in a country include: the political stability, the predominant ideology toward business (and foreign business in particular), the roles that institutions have in the country (including the church, government agencies, and the legal systems), and the international links to other countries' legal and ideological structures.[31]

In order to be welcomed in a host country, the foreign firm has to offer some tangible benefits that the host government desires. Thus, it is critical that a manger recognize what the host country government's motivations and goals are. Most international business activities offer something to all parties involved. If the host

---

[30]Douglas Lavin, "Hoechst Will Stop Making Abortion Pill," *Wall Street Journal* (April 9, 1997), p. A3.

[31]James E. Austin, *Managing in Developing Countries: Strategic Analysis and Operating Techniques* (New York: Free Press, 1990).

EXHIBIT 5-2

GOVERNMENT POLICY AREAS AND INSTRUMENTS

Policy Areas Policy Instruments	Monetary	Fiscal	Trade	Foreign Investment	Incomes	Sectoral
Legal	• Banking reserve levels	• Tax rates • Subsidies	• Government import controls	• Ownership laws	• Labor laws	• Land tenure laws
Administrative	• Loan guarantee • Credit regulation	• Tax collection	• Import quotas • Tariffs • Exchange rates and controls	• Profit repatriation controls • Investment approvals	• Price controls • Wage controls	• Industry licensing • Domestic content
Direct market operations	• Money creation	• Government purchases	• Government imports	• Government joint ventures	• Government wages	• State-owned enterprises

Source: Adapted from James E. Austin, *Managing in Developing Countries: Strategic Analysis and Operating Techniques* (New York: Free Press, 1990), p. 89. Reprinted with permission.

country is actively pursuing job creation goals, then a foreign firm that can offer jobs has leverage for obtaining concessions against other problems. The manager will want to understand what national policies are being pursued, and what policy instruments the government typically uses to pursue its interests (see Exhibit 5-2).

It is important to carefully assess the political power structure and mood in a country before making decisions regarding business operations. By evaluating various environmental factors (see Exhibit 5-3), marketing managers can arrive at a more thorough understanding of the likelihood of various problems or opportunities in a country. As shown in Exhibit 5-4, managers can also purchase or subscribe to country risk ratings provided by various risk analysis agencies such as the *Economist*, Political Risk Services (formerly, Frost & Sullivan), and Business Environment Risk Intelligence (BERI).[32]

Irrespective of categories employed in their risk ratings, there are three general types of risks involved in operating in a foreign country: risks associated with changes in company *ownership*, risks associated with changes in company *operations*, and risks associated with changes in *transfers of goods and money*. Changes in ownership structure are usually due to dramatic political changes, such as wars or coups-de-état. A company may face the **expropriation** or **confiscation** of its property, or it may face the **nationalization** of its industry. Expropriation refers to foreign government's takeover of company goods, land, or other assets, with compensation that tends to fall short of their market value. Confiscation is an outright takeover of assets without compensation. Nationalization refers to foreign government's takeover for the pur-

---

[32]For excellent review of various countries risk analysis methods, see Llewellyn D. Howell and Brad Chaddick, "Models of Political Risk for Foreign Investment and Trade: An Assessment of Three Approaches," *Columbia Journal of World Business*, 29 (September 1994), pp. 70–91.

EXHIBIT 5-3
COUNTRY RISK ASSESSMENT CRITERIA

Index Area	Criteria
Political and economic environment	Stability of the political system
	Degree of control of economic system
	Constitutional guarantees
	Effectiveness of public administration
	Labor relations and social peace
Domestic economic conditions	Population size
	Per capita income
	Economic growth during previous 5 years
	Inflation during previous 2 years
	Accessibility of domestic capital market to foreigners
	Availability of high-quality local labor
	Possibility of giving employment to foreign nationals
	Legal requirements for environment
	Traffic system and communication channels
External economic relations	Restrictions imposed on imports
	Restrictions imposed on exports
	Restrictions imposed on foreign investments in the country
	Legal protection for brands and products
	Restrictions imposed on monetary transfers
	Revaluations of currency during previous 5 years
	Drain on foreign funds through oil or other energy imports
	Restrictions on the exchange of local money into foreign currencies

Source: Adapted from E. Dichtl and H. G. Koglmayr, "Country Risk Ratings," *Management International Review*, 26 (4) (1986), p. 6.

pose of making the industry a government-run industry. In nationalization, companies usually receive some level of compensation for their losses.

To reduce risk of expropriation or confiscation of corporate assets overseas, many companies use joint ventures with local companies or adopt a **domestication policy**. Joint ventures with local companies imply shared activities and tend to reduce nationalistic sentiment against the company operating in a foreign country. Domestication policy refers to a company gradually turning over management and operational responsibilities as well as ownership to local companies over time.

However, these risks have been reduced in recent years as countries around the world have realized the need for international support in order to receive the loans

EXHIBIT 5-4
EXAMPLES OF COUNTRY RISK RATINGS (1996)

Country*	Political Risk	Financial Risk	Economic Risk	Composite Risk
1. Switzerland	92	50	43	94
2. Germany	83	49	41	87
3. Japan	85	49	42	88
4. U.S.	83	49	38	85
5. Canada	83	46	39	84
6. U.K.	81	48	36	82
7. France	80	44	38	81
8. Italy	74	44	37	77
9. Mexico	68	32	28	64
10. Hong Kong	67	41	39	74
11. China	67	39	33	69
12. India	49	30	31	55
13. Argentina	62	23	21	53
14. Romania**	55	29	15	49.5
15. Liberia**	10	8	12	15

Note: *Lower scores represent higher risk (Highest Risk = 1 . . . 100 = Lowest Risk).

  **Data from 1991.

Source: Extracted from *International Country Risk Guide*, 1996, reprinted in Claude B. Erb, Campbell R. Harvey, and Tadas E. Viskanta, "Expected Returns and Volatility in 135 Countries," *Journal of Portfolio Management*, 22 (Spring 1996), p. 46.

and investment they need to prosper. Consequently, the number of privatizations of once government-owned industries has increased in the last decade.[33]

Other changes in operating regulations can make production unprofitable. For example, local-content requirements may force a company to use inputs of higher cost or inferior quality, making its products uncompetitive. Price controls may set limits on the sales price for a company's goods that are too low to recover investments made. Restrictions on the number of foreign employees may force a company to train local citizens in techniques that require years of specialization.

Shifts in regulations on the transfer of goods and money can also dramatically affect the profitability of operating in a country. These changes include exchange rate restrictions or devaluations, input restrictions, and output price fixing. If a country is experiencing a shortage of foreign capital, it may limit the sale of foreign currencies to companies that need to buy some inputs from abroad or repatriate profits back home. Faced with such foreign exchange restrictions, companies have developed creative, if not optimal, means to deal with the foreign exchange restrictions. **Countertrade** is a frequently used method that involves trading of products without involving direct monetary payments. For example, in order to expand its operations in Russia,

---

[33]Michael S. Minor, "The Demise of Expropriation as an Instrument of LDC Policy, 1980–1992," *Journal of International Business Studies*, 25 (First Quarter 1994), pp. 177–188; and Ravi Ramamurti, "Why are Developing Countries Privatizing?" *Journal of International Business Studies*, 23 (Second Quarter 1992), pp. 225–249.

the Russian subsidiary of PepsiCo needed to import bottling equipment from the United States. However, the Russian government did not allow the company to exchange rubles for dollars, so it exported Russian vodka to the United States to earn enough dollars to import the needed equipment.

◆ ◆ ◆ ◆ ◆ ◆ INTERNATIONAL AGREEMENTS

International politics has always been characterized by the predominance of strong ideological links, centered around, and dominated by, a relatively small number of large powers. After World War II, those links centered on the two contending superpowers, the United States and the Soviet Union. However, recently the hierarchical structure of world politics has been challenged by two processes.

First, the true independence of previously colonial countries has led to a much larger set of nations playing relatively independently on the international stage, entering into contracts and relations with new political and economic partners. Second, the loosening of the tight bipolarity in world politics, combined with the decline of the United States as the hegemonic state in the free world and the breakup of the Soviet Union that led the communist world, has created an increased level of ambiguity in geopolitical stability.[34]

While most nations guard their independence by maintaining the ability to produce critical products domestically, citizens around the world have learned to expect and demand the lifestyle that international trade provides. Thus, domestic politics cannot be isolated from international politics. Political actions in one country will eventually influence the actions of other countries. For example, Mexico's recent decision to devalue its currency caused U.S. exports to Mexico to decrease. If the industries that are harmed by the decrease in sales have enough political force, they might ask the U.S. government to pressure Mexico to invest in strengthening its currency or face trade repercussions.

Not only do nations react to each other's actions, they develop relationships and dependencies that determine their future actions. They form networks for achieving mutual goals, and they develop political and trade histories and dependencies which influence their perceptions of the world. Thus, the international political environment is determined by a dynamic process of the interactions of players each pursuing their own interests and working together for mutual interests. Coordination is required, for example, in order to establish and maintain a trade embargo as a viable alternative to military force. Similarly, coordination is required to avoid harmful currency devaluations or the financial insolvency of governments. The level at which governments rely on each other and are affected by each other's actions also leads to regular conflicts and tensions. Indeed, it is widely known throughout history that a war—an ultimate form of international conflicts and tensions—is less likely to occur between the two countries, the more trade they engage in with each other.[35]

The roles of the General Agreement on Tariffs and Trade (GATT) and the

---

[34]Tom Nierop, *Systems and Regions in Global Politics—An Empirical Study of Diplomacy, International Organization and Trade, 1950–1991* (New York: Wiley, 1994).

[35]Edward D. Mansfield, *Power, Trade, and War* (Princeton, NJ: Princeton University Press, 1994).

World Trade Organization that succeeded GATT in 1995 were explained earlier as part of the economic environment in Chapter 2. We limit our discussion to two major international agreements that have shaped and will reshape the political economies of the world.

G-7 (Group of Seven)

The **G-7 (Group of Seven)** is an economic policy coordination group made up of political leaders from Canada, England, France, Germany, Italy, Japan, and the United States (the name G-7 may have to be modified if current plans of trying to include Russia into this select group of countries materialize). The G-7 began during the economic crises of the mid-1970s.[36] Heads of state, senior economic ministers, and heads of central banks typically meet once a year to further economic coordination. G-7 meetings primarily deal with financial and macroeconomic issues, including an effort to help Mexico after its 1982 financial crisis, and efforts to stabilize world stock prices following the October 1987 stock market crash.

The G-7 provides a good example of the role and limitations of multinational agreements and economic groupings in the years to come. The 1990s have reflected some of the limitations of coordinated actions, especially at a micro level. Recent coordinated actions of the federal banks of the G-7 countries, in a bid to affect exchange rates, have had limited impact on the foreign exchange markets. At best, they have moderated the speed of the movements of exchange rates, rather than the extent of the movements. The primary reason is that the volume of foreign exchange traded on the exchanges worldwide far outstrips the combined resources of the federal banks. A recent report of the G-7 finance ministers acknowledged that federal banks can only play a limited role through direct intervention in the markets.

However, a role in which coordinated action is believed to be feasible and effective is in ensuring adherence to world accepted political agendas. One example is on the issue of protection of human rights. The United States has had limited success in ensuring protection of human rights in China. Unilateral measures and bilateral negotiations have resulted in little change of China's human rights record. However, the United States is now determined to use the G-7 forum to coordinate the action of the developed countries in linking China's trade status in all the seven countries to its human rights record.

COCOM (The Coordinating Committee for Multilateral Controls)

COCOM was founded in 1949 to stop the flow of Western technology to the Soviet Union. Australia, Japan, and the NATO countries (except Iceland) are members. For example, even when U.S. franchises were already operating in the Soviet Union, it was illegal to export personal computers for them to use! The initial emphasis of COCOM was on all technology products. Subsequently, the focus shifted to various types of dual-purpose hardware and software technology products—that is, products that could be used for civilian as well as military purposes. Two trends, however, started exerting pressure on the policies adopted by COCOM. First, technologies that had primarily mili-

---

[36]Philip G. Cerny, ed., *Finance and World Politics: Markets, Regimes and States in the Post-hegemonic Era* (Cambridge, England: University Press, 1993).

tary applications were increasingly finding more civilian applications. Satellites, computers, and telecommunication technologies were prime examples of this trend. Second, the trend of economic liberalization in the newly industrializing and developing countries put further competitive pressures on Western companies to share technologies that were until then privy to the Western world. U.S. firms were particularly adversely affected. Many U.S. companies, including the large telecommunications companies, complained to the government that the restrictions were outdated and that they were losing valuable contracts to competitors from countries without such restrictions.

In 1992, COCOM reevaluated its mission and loosened restrictions on exports of computers, telecommunications equipment, machine tools, and other materials that might assist the newly independent nations of Eastern Europe and the former Soviet Republics in their effort to develop market-driven economies. Due to the changed political and economic environment, COCOM ceased to exist in 1994. However, the spirit of the committee still lingers on. There is a move to establish a new multilateral system, tentatively addressed by the name *New World Forum*, to replace COCOM. Two issues of primary importance for being considered within this multilateral system are nuclear technologies and missile (especially ballistic missile) technologies. Besides COCOM, the United States has used domestic legislatures to control exports of dual-use technologies through the U.S. Export Administrative Act. The act officially expired as of November 1995, but restrictions have still been maintained in the spirit of the act. Even today, the United States forbids the export of such generally available technology as software for encoding electronic messages.

◆ ◆ ◆ ◆ ◆ ◆ INTERNATIONAL LAW AND LOCAL LEGAL ENVIRONMENT

International marketing managers should understand two legal environments—the legal environment in each country in which they do business, and the more general international legal environment. At a macro level, international law and the bodies that evaluate it affect high-level international disputes and influence the form of lower-level arbitration and decisions. Local laws and legal systems directly determine the legal procedures for doing business in a foreign country. Local laws also determine the settlement of most international business conflicts—the country whose laws are used is determined by the jurisdiction for the contract.

International Law

International law, or "the law of nations," may be defined as a body of rules or laws that is binding on states and other international persons in their mutual relations. Most nations and international bodies have voluntarily agreed to subjugate themselves to some level of constraint for the purpose of living in a world in which order, and not chaos, is the governing principle. In short, international law represents "gentlemen's agreements" among countries.

Although, technically speaking, there is no enforceable body of international law,[37] international customs, treaties, and court decisions establish a defined interna-

---

[37] The government of a sovereign nation stipulates its laws with policing authority. Since there is no supra-national government, no supra-national (i.e., international) laws are binding. Although the United Nations is the most comprehensive political body, made up of more than 100 member nations, it is not a sovereign state, and therefore, does not have enforceable laws that the member nations have to abide by other than voluntarily.

tional legal environment. International bodies and policies exist for arbitrating cases that cannot be settled fairly in any given country.

International law comes from three main sources—**customs**, international **treaties**, and national and international **court decisions**. Customs are usages or practices that have become so firmly accepted that they become rules of law. For example, nations have historically claimed sovereignty over the resources in their offshore continental shelves. This historical practice has developed into a consensus that amounts to an international law. Custom-based laws develop slowly.

Treaties and international contracts represent formal agreements among nations or firms that set down rules and obligations to govern their mutual relationships. Treaties and contracts are only binding on those who are members to them, but if a great number of treaties or contracts share similar stipulations, these may take on the character of a customer-based law or a *general rule*.

National courts often make rulings in cases that apply to international issues. When these rulings offer an unusually useful insight into the settlement of international cases, or when they develop into a series of interpretations consistent with other nations' courts, then national rulings may be accepted as international laws. If the issue of conflict is one where a national court is not acceptable to one or both parties, international courts and tribunals may rule. International tribunals may be turned to for **arbitration** if the parties agree to let the case be tried. The International Court of Justice was established by the United Nations to settle international conflicts between nations, not between individual parties (such as firms) across national boundaries. However it must be again noted that international court rulings do not establish precedent, as they might in the United States, but rather, apply only to the case at hand.

Local Legal Systems and Laws

Legal systems and the laws they create differ dramatically in countries around the world. Many legal systems do not follow the common law system followed in the United States. We discuss a number of different legal systems and the types of laws that govern contracts and business in each system. We also discuss the issue of jurisdiction, which determines the critical issue of what courts, and what laws, are used in deciding a legal question. For most business issues, international law is primarily a question of which national laws apply and how to apply them to cases involving international contracts, shipping, or parties.

The laws that govern behavior within a country, as well as the laws that govern the resolution of international contractual disputes, are primarily local, or municipal, laws. Foreign subsidiaries and expatriate employees live within the legal bounds of their host countries' legal systems. Although U.S. embassy property is considered U.S. territory no matter where it is located, in general, companies and their employees must live within the local country laws. The recent inability of the U.S. government to change the Singapore government's punishment by caning of Michael Fay, an American teenager charged of vandalism there, is a clear example of the sovereignty of each country's laws.[38] Laws and the legal systems that support them vary significantly across countries. The international marketing manager must be aware of the laws that will govern all business decisions and contracts.

---

[38]"Singapore's Prime Minister Denounces Western Society," *Wall Street Journal* (August 22, 1994), p. A8.

EXHIBIT 5-5
LEGAL ISSUES FACING THE COMPANY

Type of Decision	Issue
Pricing decisions	Price fixing
	Deceptive pricing
Packaging decisions	Pollution regulations
	Fair packaging and labeling
Product decisions	Patent protection
	Warranty requirements
	Product safety
Competitive decisions	Barriers to entry
	Anticompetitive collusion
Selling decisions	Bribery
	Stealing trade secrets
Production decisions	Wages and benefits
	Safety requirements
Channel decisions	Dealers' rights
	Exclusive territorial distributorships

Source: Adapted from Kottler, Philip and Gary Armstrong, *Principles of Marketing, 6th ed.* (Englewood Cliffs, N.J.: Prentice Hall), 1994.

Business Practices and the Legal System. Businesses face a myriad of legal issues every day. Questions relating to such issues as pricing policies and production practices must be clearly answered in order to avoid legal reproachment and punishment. Choices relating to legal industry constraints and various regulations on product specifications, promotional activities, and distribution must be understood in order to function efficiently and profitably. Legal systems in each country deal with these questions differently. For a brief summary of legal issues facing companies, see Exhibit 5-5.

For example, in many parts of the world, automobiles with engines larger than 2,000 cc displacement face a much stiffer commodity tax than those with smaller engines. Under the strict water purity law in Germany, foreign beers that contain any other additive or ingredient than the German law permits may not be exported to Germany. In China, the government allows passenger cars to be priced only in the range of $15,600 to $26,000. By law, foreign auto manufacturers can neither underprice their cars below $15,600 nor overprice them above $26,000. Due to recent cost inflation in China and due also to their low production volume, few foreign auto manufacturers can realize profits.[39] In Japan, the Large-Scale Retail Store Law, which regulates the retail store size, makes it difficult for large U.S. retailers, such as Toys 'Я' Us, to expand its retail distribution channel.

In some countries it is illegal to mention a competitor's name in an advertisement. In some countries that follow Islamic law, it is even illegal to borrow money or charge an interest! However, businesses need financial resources to grow; thus they must learn how to acquire the resources they need within the legal limits established by the country in which they are operating. For example, in Indonesia, credit card companies such as Visa and MasterCard receive collateral assets from card users in-

---

[39]"Where's That Pot of Gold?" *Business Week* (February 3, 1997), pp. 54–58.

stead of charging interest. An international business manager must understand the laws and the legal systems of various countries.

In recent years, some countries have started raising legal requirements for environmental protection. In Japan, the famed just-in-time delivery system, such as the one practiced by Toyota and 7-Eleven Japan, has been criticized as causing traffic congestion and air pollution. Laws are being considered to reduce the just-in-time practices. **Green marketing** has become fashionable in an increasing number of countries. It is marketers' reaction to governments' and concerned citizens' increased call for reduction of unnecessary packaging materials and increased recycling and recyclability of materials used in the products. Recent developments in the European Union threaten to utilize environmental standards to control internal and external trade in consumer products. Marketers who do not conform may be restricted from participation. Meanwhile, those marketers who do meet the requirements enjoy the benefits of reduced competition and growing market share.[40]

Types of Legal Systems.   Three principal legal "systems" are used in the majority of counties: common law systems, code law systems, and Islamic law systems. **Common law systems** base the interpretation of law on prior court rulings—that is, legal precedents and customs of the time. The majority of the states in the United States follow common law systems (Louisiana is an exception). **Code (written) law systems** rely on statutes and codes for the interpretation of the law. In essence, there is very little "interpretation" in a code law system—the law must be detailed enough to prescribe appropriate and inappropriate actions. The majority of the world's governments rely on some form of code law system. **Islamic law systems** rely on the legal interpretation of the Koran and the words of Mohammed. Unlike common and code law systems, which hold that law should be man-made and can be improved through time, Islamic legal systems hold that God established a "natural law" that embodies all justice.

Examples of Different Laws.   Legal systems address both criminal and civil law. **Criminal law** addresses stealing and other illegal activities. **Civil law** addresses the enforcement of contracts and other procedural guidelines. Civil laws regulating business contracts and transactions are usually called **commercial law.** International businesses are generally more concerned with differences in commercial laws across different countries. For example, who is responsible if a shipper delivers goods that are not up to standards and the contract fails to address the issue? What if the ship on which goods are being transported is lost at sea? What if goods arrive so late as to be worthless? What if a government limits foreign participation in a construction project after a foreign company has spent millions of dollars designing the project?

Sometimes the boundary between criminal and civil law will also be different across countries. For example, are the officers of a company liable for actions that take place while they are "on duty"? When a chemical tank leak in Bhopal, India, killed thousands of Indian citizens in 1984, it was not clear whether the officers of Union Carbide were criminally liable.[41]

---

[40]Barry N. Rosen and George B. Sloane, III, "Environmental Product Standards, Trade and European Consumer Goods Marketing: Processes, Threats and Opportunities," *Columbia Journal of World Business*, 30 (Spring 1995), pp. 74–86.

[41]Robert D. McFadden, "Labor and Class-Action Lawyer is Dead," *New York Times* (January 1, 1996), Section 1, p. 32.

EXHIBIT 5-6
THE NUMBER
OF LAWYERS PER
10,000 RESIDENTS

United States	307.4
Britain	102.7
Germany	82.0
Japan	12.1

Source: Michele Galen, Alice Cuneo, and David Greising, "Guilty," *Business Week* (April 13, 1992), pp. 60–65.

Cultural Values and Legal Systems. In Japan, legal confrontations are very rare. As shown in Exhibit 5-6, Japan's population of lawyers is low, which makes it difficult to obtain evidence from legal opponents. Also, rules against class-action suits and contingency-fee arrangements make it difficult to bring suit against a person or company. There are disadvantages to Japan's system, but it supports the cultural value of building long-term business ties based on trust.

In the United States, there is a strong belief in the use of explicit contracts and a reliance on the legal system to resolve problems in business. In other countries, such as China, a businessperson who tries to cover all possible problems or contingencies in a contract may be viewed as untrustworthy. Chinese culture values relationships and therefore relies more heavily on trust and verbal contracts than does U.S. culture. In Brazil, however, there is a value system different from both the United States' explicit contractual agreement and China's mutual trust and verbal contract. The Brazilian value system is known as *Jeitinho*, in which people believe that they can always find a solution outside the legal contract on a case-by-case basis.[42] If a culture does not respect the value of following through on an obligation, it will matter little whether the contract is written or verbal—no legal system will afford enough protection to make doing business easy.

Jurisdiction

Because there is no body of international law in the strictly legalistic sense, the key to evaluating an international contract is in determining *which* country's laws will apply, and *where* any conflicts will be resolved.

Planning Ahead. By far the easiest way to assure what laws will apply in a contract is to clearly state the applicable law in the contract. If both a home country producer and a foreign distributor agree that the producer's national laws of contracts will apply to a contract for the sale of goods, then both can operate with a similar understanding of the legal requirements they face. Similarly, to assure a venue that will interpret these laws in an expected manner, international contracts should stipulate the location of the court or arbitration system that will be relied upon for resolving conflicts that arise.

---

[42]Margaret Grieco and Richard Whipp, "Dismantling Logics of Action," *International Studies of Management and Organization*, 21 (Winter 1991), pp. 78–85.

If contacts fail to provide for the jurisdiction of the contract, it is not so clear which laws apply. Courts may use the laws where the contract is made. Alternatively, courts may apply the laws where the contract is fulfilled.

Arbitration and Enforcement. Due to the differences in international legal systems, and the difficulty and length of litigating over a conflict, many international contracts rely on a pre-arranged system of *arbitration* for settling any conflict. Arbitration may be by a neutral party, and both parties agree to accept any rulings.

However if one of the parties does not fulfill its contracted requirements and does not respond to or accept arbitration, there is little the injured party can do. There is no "international police" to force a foreign company to pay damages.

ISSUES TRANSCENDING NATIONAL BOUNDARIES ◆ ◆ ◆ ◆ ◆ ◆ ◆

ISO 9000

In a bid to establish common product standards for quality management, so as to obviate their misuse to hinder the exchange of goods and services worldwide, the International Standards Organization (based in Geneva, Switzerland) has instituted a set of process standards. Firms who conform to these standards are certified and registered with International Standards Organizations. This common standard is designated **ISO 9000**. The adoption of the ISO standards by member countries of the European Union has spurred widespread interest in companies worldwide to obtain this certification if they intend to trade with the European Union.

One of the reasons for the spurt of interest in ISO 9000 is the decision by the European Union to adopt ISO standards; the other main reason is the acknowledgment of the importance of quality by companies worldwide. It must be highlighted that ISO 9000 is not only concerned with standardized systems and procedures for manufacturing, but for all the activities of firms. These activities include management responsibility, quality systems, contract reviews, design control, document control, purchasing, product identification and tracing, (manufacturing) process control, inspection and testing, control of nonconforming products and necessary corrective actions, handling, storage, packaging and delivering, recordkeeping, internal quality audits, training, and servicing.

With the growing adoption of the ISO standards by firms worldwide, an ISO certification is likely to become an essential marketing tool for firms. Firms that have it will be able to convince prospective buyers of their ability to maintain strict quality requirements. Firms that do not have ISO certification will increasingly be at a disadvantage relative to other competitors, not only in Europe but in most parts of the world.

Intellectual Property Protection

Few topics in international business have attracted as much attention and discussion in recent years as intellectual property rights.[43] A recent Delphi study shows that one major reason is the heightened acknowledgment by policy makers, especially across the industrialized countries, about the competitive implications of the absence of

---

[43]Clifford J. Shultz III and Bill Saporito, "Protecting Intellectual Property: Strategies and Recommendations to Deter Counterfeiting and Brand Piracy in Global Markets," *Columbia Journal of World Business*, 31 (Spring 1996), pp. 19–27.

strict intellectual property protection laws, or the unsuccessful implementation of these laws in various other countries, especially developing countries.[44]

Intellectual property refers to "ideas that are translated into tangible products, writings, and so on, and that are protected by the state for a limited period of time from unauthorized commercial exploitation."[45] Intellectual property rights broadly include patents, trademarks, trade secrets, and copyrights. These ideas typically involve large investments in creative and investigative work to create the product, but fairly low costs of manufacturing. As such they are amenable to being duplicated readily by imitators. Imitation reduces the potential returns that would have accrued to the innovator, thereby limiting its ability to appropriate the large investments made. With increasing movements of goods and services across borders, the potential loss of revenues to innovator firms, most of which reside in industrialized countries, is significant. U.S. companies reportedly lose more than $50 billion a year as a result of inadequate protection from foreign infringement of intellectual property rights.[46] Governments of the developed countries, whose firms are losing the most, have been taking various steps at a bilateral level (e.g., Most Favored Nations status granted by the United States for imports of Chinese-made products being linked to the effective enactment and implementation of intellectual property rights, especially for entertainment products), as well as multilateral level (e.g., the agreement on Trade Related Aspects of Intellectual Property Rights, commonly known as the TRIPs agreement under the newly constituted World Trade Organization). An increasing number of developing countries have begun to endorse the TRIPs agreement in order to attract international investment through comprehensive and clear patent laws for ideas and innovation. For example, in 1996, Brazil signed into law the most far-reaching and forward-looking intellectual property protection of any nation in South America.[47]

Patent. Patent laws in the United States and Japan provide an example of the differences in laws across countries and their implications for corporations.[48] The most significant difference between the two countries is on the "first-to-file" and "first-to-invent" principles. While most countries follow the "first-to-file" principle, only the United States (along with the Philippines) follows the "first-to-invent" principle. In the majority of countries, the patent is granted to the first person filing an application for the patent. In the United States, however, the patent is granted to the person who first invented the product or technology. Any patents granted prior to the filing of the patent application by the "real" inventor would be reversed in order to protect rights of the inventor.

The marketing implications of this difference for U.S. companies as well as foreign companies are significant. To protect any new proprietary technologies, U.S.

---

[44]Michael R. Czinkota and Ilkka Ronkainen, "International Business and Trade in the Next Decade: A Report from a Delphi Study," A Working Paper, School of Business, Georgetown University, February 1997.

[45]Belay Sayoum, "The Impact Of Intellectual Property Rights on Foreign Direct Investment," *Columbia Journal of World Business*, 31 (Spring 1996), pp. 51–59.

[46]Maxine Lans Retsky, "Curbing Foreign Infringement," *Marketing News* (March 31, 1997), p. 10.

[47]"Pfizer Forum: Brazil's Landmark Intellectual Property Law," *Economist* (March 22, 1997), p. 63.

[48]Masaaki Kotabe, "A Comparative Study of U.S. and Japanese Patent Systems," *Journal of International Business Studies*, 23 (First Quarter 1992), pp. 147–168.

companies must ensure that their inventions are protected abroad through formal patent applications being filed in various countries, especially the major foreign markets and the markets of competitors and potential competitors. For foreign companies operating in the United States, the implications are that they must be extremely careful in introducing any technologies that have been invented in the United States. A "first-to-file" mentality could result in hasty patent applications and significant financial burden in the form of lawsuits that could be filed by competitors that claim to have invented the technology earlier.

Copyright. Copyrights protect original literary, dramatic, musical, artistic, and certain other intellectual works. A computer program, for example, is considered a literary work and is protected by copyright. A copyright provides its owner the exclusive right to reproduce and distribute the material or perform or display it publicly, although limited reproduction of copyrighted works by others may be permitted for fair use purposes. In the United States, registration is required for protection of intellectual works. However, many countries offer copyright protection without registration, while others offer little or no protection for the works of foreign nationals.[49]

Trademark. A trademark is a word, symbol, or device that identifies the source of goods and may serve as an index of quality. It is used primarily to differentiate or distinguish a product or service from another. Trademark laws are used to prevent others from offering a product or service with a confusingly similar mark. In the United States, registration is not mandatory, since "prior use" technically determines the rightful owner of a trademark. However, because determining who used the trademark prior to anyone else is difficult and subject to lawsuits, trademark registration is highly recommended. In most foreign countries, registration is mandatory for a trademark to be protected. In this sense, the legal principle that applies to trademarks is similar to the one that applies to patents: the "first-to-use" principle in the United States and the "first-to-file" principle in most other countries. Therefore, if companies are expected to do business overseas, their trademarks should be registered in every country in which protection is desired (also see Global Perspective 5-2 for how to keep copyright and trademark illegally used abroad from entering the United States).

Trade Secret. A trade secret is another means of protecting intellectual property and fundamentally differs from patent, copyright, and trademark in that protection is sought without registration. Therefore, it is not legally protected. However, it can be protected in the courts if the company can prove that it took all precautions to protect the idea from its competitors and that infringement occurred illegally by way of espionage or hiring employees with crucial working knowledge.

Although patent and copyright laws have been in place in the United States and other Western countries for well over a hundred years, laws on trademarks and trade secrets are of relatively recent vintage, having being instituted in the late nineteenth century and beginning of the twentieth century.[50] There are many international treaties to help provide intellectual property protection across national boundaries when, in fact, laws are essentially national. Two of the most important treaties are Paris Convention and Berne Convention.

---

[49]Subhash C. Jain, "Problems in International Protection of Intellectual Property Rights," *Journal of International Marketing*, 4 (1) (1996), pp. 9–32.

[50]Bruce A. Lehman, "Intellectual Property: America's Competitive Advantage in the 21st Century," *Columbia Journal of World Business*, 31 (Spring 1996), pp. 8–9.

◆ ◆

$\mathcal{G}$LOBAL PERSPECTIVE 5-2

HOW TO KEEP COPYRIGHTS AND TRADEMARKS ILLEGALLY USED ABROAD FROM ENTERING THE UNITED STATES

Infringement of intellectual property rights is not confined to the United States. Inadequate protection of intellectual property rights in foreign countries could also result in copyrights and trademarks illegally used abroad making their way back to the United States. In many industrialized countries, it is possible to stem illegally used copyrights and trademarks from entering the home country. For example, in the United States, the U.S. Customs Service provides protection to copyrights and trademarks.

Prior to receiving U.S. Customs protection, copyrights and trademarks have to be registered first with the U.S. Copyright Office and the U.S. Patent and Trademark Office, respectively. Then for U.S. Customs protection, each copyright and trademark must be recorded at the U.S. Customs Service Office. The fee is $190. Although there are no standard application forms, the application requirements for recording a copyright and a trademark are listed in Section 133.1–133.7 of the U.S.

Customs regulations. An application should include the following information: (1) a certified status copy and five photocopies of the copyright or trademark registration, (2) the name of its legal owner, (3) the business address of the legal owner, (4) the states or countries in which the business of the legal owner is incorporated or otherwise conducted, (5) a list of the names and addresses of all foreign persons or companies authorized or licensed to use the copyright or trademark to be protected, (6) a list of the names and addresses of authorized manufacturers of goods, and (7) a list of all places in which goods using the copyright or bearing the trademark are legally manufactured. Although it is not necessary to submit a separate application for protection of each copyright or trademark, the filing fee of $190 still applies to each and every copyright or trademark being recorded with the Customs Service.

Additional information can be obtained by contacting the U.S. Customs Service at the Intellectual Property Rights Branch, Franklin Court, 1301 Constitution Avenue, N.W., Washington, D.C. (Ph. 202-482-6960).

Source: Maxine Lans Retsky, "Curbing Foreign Infringement," *Marketing News* (March 31, 1997), p. 10.

Paris Convention. The Paris Convention was established in 1883, and the number of signatory countries currently stands at 93, including 51 developing countries. It is designed to provide "domestic" treatment to protect patent and trademark applications filed in other countries. Operationally, the convention establishes rights of priority that stipulate that once an application for protection is filed in one member country, the applicant has twelve months to file in any other signatory countries, which should consider such an application as if it were filed on the same date as the original application.[51] It also means that if an applicant does not file for protection in other signatory countries within a grace period of twelve months of original filing in one country, legal protection could not be provided. In most countries, other than the United States, the "first-to-file" principle is used for intellectual property protection. Lack of filing within a grace period in all other countries in which protection is desired could mean a loss of market opportunities to a competitor who filed for protection of either an identical or a similar type of intellectual property.

Berne Convention. The Berne Convention is the oldest and most comprehensive international copyright treaty. This treaty provides reciprocal copyright protection in each of the fifteen signatory countries. Similar to the Paris Convention, it establishes

---

[51]Subhash C. Jain, 1996.

EXHIBIT 5-7

RATINGS FOR THE LEVEL OF INTELLECTUAL PROPERTY PROTECTION IN VARIOUS COUNTRIES (MINIMUM = 0 . . . 10 = MAXIMUM)

Country	Patents	Copyrights	Trademarks	Trade Secrets
Argentina	3.8	5.7	7.1	4.4
Brazil	3.3	5.2	3.3	3.3
Canada	8.1	7.7	9.0	7.8
Chile	5.7	5.7	7.6	7.8
China	2.4	2.9	6.2	3.3
Germany	8.6	8.6	9.0	10.0
India	3.3	5.7	3.8	3.3
Israel	7.1	7.1	8.6	8.9
Mexico	3.3	7.6	3.8	3.3
New Zealand	7.1	8.1	9.5	7.8
Philippines	7.1	6.2	7.6	7.8
South Korea	3.3	4.8	3.8	3.3
Singapore	7.1	6.7	8.6	5.6
Thailand	2.4	4.8	6.7	5.6
United States	9.0	8.1	9.0	7.8

Source: Adapted from Belay Seyoum, "The Impact of Intellectual Property Rights on Foreign Direct Investment," *Columbia Journal of World Business,* 31 (Spring 1996), p. 56.

the principle of national treatment and provide protection without formal registration. The United States did not join the Berne Convention until 1989.[52]

Although there are separate laws to protect the various kinds of intellectual property, there appears to be a strong correlation between the levels of intellectual property in various countries. Exhibit 5-7 provides some of the results of a recently published academic study based on survey questionnaires administered to experts/ practitioners in the various countries.

A feature that corporations as well as individual managers have to deal with is the growing importance of intellectual property as a significant form of competitive advantage. The laws to deal with this issue are neither uniform across countries, nor are they extended across national boundaries (outside of the government pressure). Even if they are similar, the implementation levels vary significantly. Essentially, protection of intellectual property requires registration in all the countries in which a firm plans to do business. Managers need to be cognizant of this and take proactive measures to counteract any infringements.

Antitrust Laws of the United States[53]

The antitrust laws of the United States have their foundation in the Sherman Antitrust Act of 1890, the Clayton Act of 1914, the Federal Trade Commission Act of

---

[52]Subhash C. Jain, 1996.

[53]This section draws from Masaaki Kotabe and Kent W. Wheiler, *Anticompetitive Practices in Japan: Their Impact on the Performance of Foreign Firms* (Westport, CT: Praeger Publishers, 1996).

1914, and the Robinson Patman Act of 1936. U.S. antitrust laws have been, from the beginning, concerned with maximizing consumer welfare through the prevention of arrangements that increase market power without concurrently increasing social welfare through reduced costs or increased efficiency.

The Sherman Act specifically forbade every contract, combination, or conspiracy to restrain free and open trade, but it was soon argued that the law was intended to punish only unreasonable restraints. In the *Standard Oil* case of 1911, the courts ruled that an act must be an unreasonable restraint of trade for the Sherman Act to apply. Toward this end, a distinction developed between (1) cases in which a rule of reason should apply, and (2) cases considered to be *per se* violations of the law.

The Clayton Act strengthened the U.S. antitrust arsenal by prohibiting trade practices that were not covered by the Sherman Act. It outlawed exclusive dealing and price discrimination. Both are subject to the rule of reason—that is, they are unlawful only if the effect may be to substantially lessen competition. The word *may*, combined with the preamble's charge to "arrest the creation of trusts, conspiracies and monopolies in their incipiency," has led U.S. courts to judge "any imaginary threat to competition, no matter how shadowy and insubstantial" as reasonably probable of restraining trade."[54]

Concurrent with the enactment of the Clayton Act, Congress created the Federal Trade Commission (FTC) and empowered it to enjoin unfair methods of competition in commerce. Prior to the FTC, violations of antitrust laws were the jurisdiction of the Antitrust Division of the Justice Department. Since 1914, the organizations have pursued dual enforcement of the antitrust laws, with considerable, some argue inefficient, overlap. The Justice Department focuses largely on criminal price-fixing and merger review. The FTC, which does not handle criminal cases, concentrates about 60 percent of its total resources on merger review.

The U.S. antitrust laws were originally and primarily aimed at domestic monopolies and cartels, although the act expressly extends coverage to commerce with foreign nations. In the 1940s, the prosecution of Alcoa (*United States v. Aluminum Company of America*, 148 F. 2d 416 1945) resulted in a clear extension of U.S. antitrust laws to activities of foreign companies, even if those actions occur entirely outside the United States as long as they have a substantial and adverse effect on the foreign or domestic commerce and trade of the United States.

Successful extraterritorial enforcement, however, depends on effective jurisdictional reach. Detecting, proving, and punishing collusion and conspiracy to restrain trade among foreign companies is extremely difficult. From gathering evidence to carrying out retribution, the complexity of nearly every aspect of antitrust litigation is compounded when prosecuting a foreign entity. Issues of foreign sovereignty and diplomacy also complicate extraterritorial antitrust enforcement. If a foreign entity's actions are required by their own government, they are exempt from prosecution under U.S. law. Prior to the 1990s and the demise of the Soviet Union, U.S. trade and economic matters were typically a lower priority to defense and foreign policy concerns. This was particularly true with Japan. In nearly every major trade dispute over steel, textiles, televisions, semiconductors, automobiles, and so on, the Departments of State and Defense opposed and impeded retaliation against Japanese companies for violations of U.S. antitrust laws. A strong alliance with Japan and the strategic ge-

---

[54]Robert H. Bork, *The Antitrust Paradox* (New York: Basic Books, 1978), p. 48.

ographic military locations the alliance provided were deemed to be of more importance than unrestricted trade.

The extraterritorial application of U.S. antitrust laws has recently been subject to considerably more debate. In 1977 the Antitrust Division of the Justice Department issued its *Antitrust Guidelines for International Operations*, which, consistent with the precedent established in the Alcoa case, reaffirmed that U.S. antitrust laws could be applied to an overseas transaction if there were a direct, substantial, and foreseeable effect on the commerce of the United States. The Foreign Trade Antitrust Improvements Act of 1982 again reiterated this jurisdiction. There has been controversy, however, over the degree of U.S. commerce to which jurisdiction extends.

The 1977 Justice *Guidelines* suggested that foreign anticompetitive conduct injuring U.S. commerce raises antitrust concerns when either U.S. consumers or U.S. exporters are harmed. In a 1988 revision of the *Guidelines*, the reference to exporters was omitted. Later, in 1992, U.S. Attorney General William Barr announced that Justice would take enforcement action against conduct occurring overseas if it unfairly restricts U.S. exports, arguing that anticompetitive behavior of foreign companies that inhibits U.S. exports thereby reduces the economies of scale for U.S. producers and indirectly affects U.S. consumers through higher prices than might otherwise be possible.

Critics argue that comity concerns and the difficulties in gathering evidence and building a case around conduct occurring wholly within a foreign country make it unrealistic for the Justice Department to attempt such an extraterritorial application of U.S. laws. Perhaps the gravest concern, however, is that the policy may lead to prosecution of foreign business methods that actually promote U.S. consumer welfare, for it is predominantly believed in the U.S. economic and legal community that antitrust laws should be concerned solely with protecting consumer welfare. U.S. public opinion has also traditionally and strongly supported the government's role as the champion of consumer rights against commercial interests. U.S. antitrust laws have always reflected this grassroots backing. Such a tradition has not existed in Japan, and the development of antitrust laws there has been quite different.

Fully cognizant that there were many small- and medium-size firms with exportable products which were not currently exporting, the U.S. Congress passed the Export Trading Company legislation (ETC Act) in 1982 to encourage those firms to join forces to improve their export performance by exempting them from antitrust laws. Patterned after practices in Germany and Japan, the ETC Act also permits banks to own and operate export trading companies (ETCs) so that the export trading companies will have better access to capital resources, as well as market information through their banks.[55] As a result, the FTC Act assists in the formation of shippers' associations to reduce costs and increase efficiency, helps agribusiness firms achieve significant economies of scale by shipping and marketing their products together, covers technology–licensing agreements with foreign firms, and facilitates contact between producers interested in exporting and organizations offering export trade services. However, those trading companies are not allowed to join forces in their importing businesses, hence they are called export trading companies. In reality, many manufacturing companies import raw materials and in-process components

---

[55]Charles E. Cobb, Jr., John E. Stiner, "Export Trading Companies: Five Years of Bringing U.S. Exporters Together: The Future of the Export Trading Company Act," *Business America*, 10 (October 12, 1987), pp. 2–9.

from abroad and export finished products using those imported materials. Japanese trading companies handle both exports and imports, and have many manufacturing companies as captive customers for both exports and imports. However, in the United States, those trading companies certified as ETCs under the ETC Act may fully exploit economies of scale in their operation, because they cannot collectively handle manufacturing firms' imports.

U.S. Foreign Corrupt Practices Act of 1977

Among the many corrupt practices that international marketers face, bribery is considered the most endemic and murky aspect of conducting business abroad. However, special care must be taken to identify and accommodate the differences between international markets and those in the United States. Laws may vary widely from country to country, and these laws may on occasion conflict with one another. Bribery is a means for one party to get from another party (at the cost of a third party) some special treatment that would otherwise not normally be obtainable. However, what constitutes bribery may also differ, depending on local customs and practices.

In order to create the level playing field for U.S. companies to do business abroad and to establish a high ethical standard to be followed by foreign countries, the United States passed the Foreign Corrupt Practices Act (FCPA) in 1977. The FCPA was designed to prohibit the payment of any money or anything of value to a foreign official, foreign political party, or any candidate for foreign political office for purposes of obtaining, retaining, or directing business. FCPA sets a high ethical standard for U.S. firms doing business abroad, but it cannot keep foreign firms from engaging in bribery and other anticompetitive acts in foreign countries, potentially giving undue competitive advantage to foreign firms over U.S. firms. However, there is no hard evidence that U.S. firms have suffered competitive loss because of the FCPA.[56]

The FCPA, although silent on the subject, does not prohibit so called "facilitating" or "grease" payments, such as small payments to lower-level officials for expediting shipments through customs or placing a transoceanic telephone call, securing required permits, or obtaining adequate police protection—transactions that simply facilitate the proper performance of duties. These small payments are considered comparable to tips left for waiters. While some companies find such payments morally objectionable and operate without paying them, other companies do not prohibit such payments but require that employees seek advice in advance from their corporate legal counsel in cases where facilitating payments may be involved.[57]

The FCPA does not prohibit bribery payments to nongovernmental personnel, however. Nor does the United States have laws regulating other forms of payment that approach extortion. What constitutes bribery or extortion also becomes less transparent, and international marketers' ethical dilemma increases (see Global Per-

[56]Paul J. Beck, Michael W. Maher, and Adrian E. Tschoegl, "The Impact of the Foreign Corrupt Practices Act on U.S. Exports," *Managerial and Decision Economics*, 12 (August 1991), pp. 295–303.

[57]Mary Jane Sheffet, "The Foreign Corrupt Practices Act and the Omnibus Trade and Competition Act of 1988: Did They Change Corporate Behavior?" *Journal of Public Policy and Marketing*, 14 (Fall 1995), pp. 290–300.

spective 5-3). From an ethical point of view, the major questions that must be answered are:

1. Does such an act involve unfairness to anyone or violate anyone's right?
2. Must such an act be kept secret, such that it cannot be reported as a business expense?
3. Is such an act truly necessary in order to carry on business?

Unless the answer to the first two questions is negative and to the third positive, such an act is generally deemed unethical.[58] It is advised that multinational firms maintain good "corporate citizenship" wherever they do business, since long-term benefits tend to outweigh the short-term benefit gained from bribes for the same reasons just mentioned—for example, corporate contributions to humanitarian and environmental causes, such as the Save the Rain Forest project in Brazil, and moral stands on oppressive governments, such as Heineken's pullout from Burma to protest this Asian country's dictatorship regime.[59]

◆ ◆

Global Perspective 5-3

Cultural Relativism/Accommodation—Selling Out?

The following is an excerpt from an anonymous source circulating via e-mail on the GINLIST:

Cultural accommodation is an essential element in successful international and cross-cultural relationships. The question faced by the U.S. multinationals is whether to follow the advice, "When in Rome, do as the Romans do." Foreign firms operating in the U.S. are faced with a similar question, "When in America, should you do as the Americans do?" How far does an individual or a company go to accommodate cultural differences before they sell themselves out? . . . I will attempt to answer this question by looking at issues involving my personal core values, bribery and gift giving, and how these relate to the definitions presented. I will also discuss trust and credibility and how these qualities relate to the subject and present a case for marketplace morality. I will conclude by

Source: An anonymous source, distributed via e-mail on GINLIST, October 11, 1994.

presenting what I feel is the answer to the question posed above.

The primary issue . . . is one of cultural relativism and its place in cross-cultural encounters. Cultural relativism is a philosophical position which states that ethics is a function of culture. . . . Ethical relativism is the belief that nothing is objectively right or wrong, and that the definition of right or wrong depends on the prevailing view of a particular individual, culture, or historical period.

Cultural or ethical relativists will find themselves in a constant state of conflict within their own society. By definition, it would be impossible to reach an agreement on ethical rights and wrongs for the society. An ethical relativist believes that whatever an individual (any individual) believes to be right or wrong is in fact correct. The only cultural norm would be one of chaos since it would be impossible to hold anyone accountable to a prevailing or arbitrary ethos due to the accepted fact that all is relative and all is correct by definition.

---

[58]Richard T. De George, *Business Ethics*, 4th ed. (Englewood Cliffs, N.J.: Prentice Hall, 1995), pp. 511–512.

[59]"Heineken out of Burma," http:/www.antenna.nl/aseed/burma/index.html, accessed June 12, 1997.

As an example, imagine trying to hold Hitler's Nazi government accountable for their crimes during World War II from this perspective. If ethics is relative and that right and wrong are defined by the prevailing view of a particular individual, culture, or historical period, then Hitler's policies of racial purification were ethically correct. However, according to my ethical beliefs (and those of the world's representatives who presided over the Neurenburg Trials), that conclusion is completely unacceptable. There are some things that are moral and ethical absolutes. . . .

As we adapt to the differences in cultures, each individual and culture must still determine where the line is (which defines) the clear violations of moral absolutes. In pursuing this objective, understanding who we are and what we stand for are essential in identifying the sell-out point. We must come to terms with our core values and how they match up with both the company ethos and that of the host and home countries. . . .

There is an art to giving gifts in Japan. Every time my wife, Yuriko, and I go back to Japan, at least one or more suitcases are full of gifts for the in-laws and friends. When her family comes to see us, their luggage is full of gifts for us and our friends. . . . Benedict in *The Chrysanthemum and The Sword* explains the gift-giving tradition as a form of repayment on a debt incurred by the giver. The debt may be a result of a favor, a previous gift, or in anticipation of a debt. It is interesting to note that some debts can never be repaid. Examples of these are debts to parents for the care and sacrifices made to raise the child, as well as to a teacher for the education provided. The result of this eternal debt is a lifetime of respect for these individuals. . . . (Also,) there are some people who intentionally create more debt than a situation calls for with the intention of calling in the favor at a later time. The difference between the traditional gift giving and this type of action is the intention. This is similar to our view of a bribe. It is also where I draw the line between participating in the cultural tradition and committing an ethical violation.

It is interesting to note the Catch 22 that an international company can find itself in on this subject. In reference to China, if the company tries to avoid the appearance of a bribe by not participating in a culture's gift giving custom and just say "thanks," they may be seen as using the "verbal thanks as getting out of their obligation." The international manager must not only understand and respect the cultural subtleties, but know how to find the limits of the ethical behavior. One specific limit put in place by the U.S. Government is the Foreign Corrupt Practices Act (FCPA). This Act was passed in reaction to a "rash of controversial payments to foreign officials by American business in the 1970s." The Act specifically calls for "substantial fines for both corporations and individual corporate officers who engage in the bribery of foreign government officials."

U.S. firms are restricted from bribing; however, many companies in other countries engage in this practice routinely. American firms allege that restricting them from this practice puts them at a serious disadvantage to other nations' firms. In the short term, this may be true. Consider what would happen if every firm bribed. The cost of a project would be driven up so high that the country itself could no longer afford it. The bribe is not free and is always paid either by a higher contract price or through shortcuts in quality and material which may result in serious social costs. Consider a freeway overpass or a bridge not built to adequate safety standards or with poor quality materials. The result could be a collapsed bridge, resulting in loss of both life and property. The bribe also undermines the competitive process so that the purchaser pays more than the competitive price and erodes the trust in the public officials and the firm.

Is there a morality separate from the individual and from the culture? . . . A multinational corporation doing business in societies with differing moral norms must subscribe to a morality of the marketplace which is based on trust and credibility. Violating such norms would be self defeating. Companies engaging in business practices that result in a loss of trust or credibility will eventually lose their share of the market.

Supplier and customer relationships are built on a foundation of trust and credibility. A supplier who bribes a customer for the immediate business dooms him or herself to long-term failure. Individuals are affected by this as well. A person who approaches the world from a cultural relativist perspective will change his or her position and standards depending on the prevailing view of the culture or sub-culture that person is in. Trust and credibility can neither be built nor retained from such a position. International or domestic businessmen want to know who they are dealing with. They want to know if they can trust the person and/or company they are about to join together with. . . .

Where is the line drawn that separates accommodation from selling out? In a large part it depends on the individual's value system, since what they're selling out on is really their own core values, trust, and credibility. There are moral absolutes, which, if violated, are always examples of stepping across the line.

SUMMARY ◆

When doing business across national boundaries, international marketers almost always face what is perceived to be political and legal barriers. It is due to the fact that government policies and laws can be very different from country to country. In most cases, a foreign company has to accept a host country's government policies and laws, as they are usually outside its control. Some large multinational firms, if backed by their home country government, may sometimes influence the host country's policies and laws. However, such an extraterritorial interference may have negative consequences in the long run for a short-term gain.

Despite various international agreements brought about by such international organizations as WTO, G-7, and COCOM, which collectively strive toward freer and more equitable world trade, every nation is sovereign and maintains its special interests, which may occasionally clash with those of the international agreements. Although the world has been moving toward a freer trade and investment environment, the road has not necessarily been smooth. When considering entry or market expansion in foreign countries, their country risks need to be assessed. Multinational firms need to be aware of political risks arising from unstable political parties and government structure, changes in government programs, and social pressures and special interest groups in a host country. Political risks are further compounded by economic and financial risks. When disputes arise across national boundaries, they will most likely have to be settled in one country. Therefore, careful planning for establishing the jurisdictional clause in the contract is needed before the contract is entered into.

Although government policies and laws of a country usually affect business transactions involving that country, increased business activities transcending national boundaries have tested the territoriality of some policies and laws of a country. The United States frequently applies its laws, such as antitrust laws and the Foreign Corrupt Practices Act outside its political boundary to the extent U.S. businesses are affected or to the extent that its legal value system can be extended. On the other hand, despite the importance of intellectual property in international business, protection of intellectual property in foreign countries is granted essentially by registration in those countries. International marketing managers should be aware that domestic protection usually cannot be extended beyond their national boundary.

REVIEW QUESTIONS ◆

1. Describe with examples the role of governments in promoting national interests pertaining to business activities.

2. What different types of trade controls influence international business? What are their intended objectives?

3. How do host country macroeconomic and fiscal policies affect foreign company operations?

4. What are the factors that international managers should consider in determining the economic and political risks associated with a country?

5. International law is derived from three sources. What are these three? Compare and contrast them.

6. Briefly describe the various types of local legal systems. How do differences in these legal systems affect international business?

7. Enumerate some of the legal issues that international business managers need to take cognizance of in host countries.

8. Describe the various types of barriers to international trade and investment.

DISCUSSION QUESTIONS ✦

1. Various foreign companies operating in Russia, especially in the oil and gas exploration business, have had to face the vagaries of Russian legislations, which change frequently, making it difficult to plan activities. Besides being heavily taxed, foreign firms have had to face a change in export duties of crude oil over a dozen times in the past few years. Yet most companies continue to negotiate for making investments worth billions of dollars. Discuss some of the possible reasons for the actions of these companies. Companies take various steps to manage political risk. If you were representing a company negotiating investments in Russia, what steps would you take to manage (and/or reduce) the political risk associated with these investments?

2. (a) Pepsi International's humorous global ad campaign fronted by model Cindy Crawford, which includes the use of a Coke can, will not be seen in Germany because German regulations forbid the use of comparative advertising.

   (b) Advertising laws in China have restricted the use of Budweiser posters, featuring young attractive women in Budweiser swimsuits, by Anheuser-Busch to bars and stores with adult clientele only. Furthermore, when Anheuser-Busch wanted models to wear swimsuits for a beer festival, the mothers of the models used insisted on the girls wearing T-shirts beneath the swimsuits.

   (c) An Austin, Texas-based designer of computer games wants to market a game that involves humans fighting against aliens from different planets. One aspect of the game is that if the humans are shot, blood is shown to come out of their bodies. German laws, however, do not permit any depiction of red blood in computer games. The company wants to market this game in Germany, which is a huge market. One suggestion the company is working on is the use of an alternate color to depict human blood. However, it risks the prospect of making the game less realistic— "What would children make out of green liquid coming out of the human figure on being shot?"

   These examples highlight the impact of differences in laws and social norms on various aspects of the marketing program. What are the implications of such differences for using standardized product or advertising strategies (or using standardized advertising themes)?

3. KFC, a fast-food operator, faced immense resistance from some politically active consumer groups when it opened its operations in India. One group proclaimed that opening KFC outlets in the country would propagate a "junk-food" culture. Others proclaimed that this was "the return of imperialistic powers" and was an attempt to "Westernize the eating habits" of Indians. Overzealous local authorities in the city of Bangalore used a city law restricting the use of MSG (a food additive used in the chicken served by KFC) over a certain amount as a pretext for temporarily closing down the outlet, despite the fact that the authorities did not even have the equipment to measure the MSG content in the proportions stated in the law. In the capital city of New Delhi, a KFC outlet was temporarily closed down because the food inspector found a "house-fly" in the restaurant. While both of these issues got resolved through hectic consultations with these consumer groups and through legal orders issued protecting the interests of the outlets, they do reflect how political and social concerns of even a small segment of the population can adversely affect the operations of companies in foreign markets. If you were the country manager of KFC in India, what steps would you have taken to avoid these problems?

4. Enactment of intellectual property laws and their effective enforcement by developing countries, especially the newly industrializing countries and the high-growth economies of Asia, have been a prime concern of various Western countries. The academic literature has seen a dramatic increase in the discussion about the loss of revenue through infringement of intellectual property rights and the proactive steps that can be taken by companies to reduce their adverse effects. However, when the vice-president of international operations for one of the divisions of a highly innovative and respected U.S.-headquartered multibillion-dollar multinational company was asked about the steps taken by the firm in China to prevent intellectual property right infringements, the executive's response was that the company did not take any specific measures. The company just could not do anything about it. At best it could approach the pirate company and think about collaborating with it to make the product legally for the multinational company. According to this executive, companies can do little to control intellectual property rights infringements, besides influencing, to some extent, their home governments to put political pressure on the governments of the host countries. Do you agree with the arguments of this executive, or do you consider them to be more a matter of exception rather than the rule? Give reasons for why you do or don't agree.

5. An extension of the antitrust laws into the arena of international trade has taken the form of anti-dumping laws, which have been enacted by most Western countries, and which are increasingly being enacted by developing countries. On the surface, most of the anti-dumping laws across the various countries seem to be similar to each other. However, since much of the content of these laws is open to interpretation, the results of these laws could vary significantly. The bottom line for the initiation of any anti-dumping investigation is that if a foreign manufacturer gets an "undue" advantage while selling its products (either through pricing its products higher in other protected markets or through government subsidies) in another country relative to the domestic manufacturer and hurts the domestic industry, the company is resorting to unfair competition and should be penalized for it. While large firms are relatively more aware of the nuances of antidumping laws and have the resources, especially legal ones, to deal with this issue, it is the smaller firms, who often depend on governmental export assistance in various forms, that are the most susceptible to it.

One of your friends is planning to start exporting an industrial product to various countries in Europe. To help finance his export endeavor, he plans to utilize concessional export credit provided by the U.S. government to small exporters. This product is highly specialized, and caters to an extremely small niche market. Europe is a large market for this product. There are only two other manufacturers of this product, both based in Europe. One of these manufacturers is a $100-million company, which manufactures various other products besides the product in question. What would be your advice to your friend in terms of the significance of antidumping laws? What specific steps, if any, would you encourage your friend to take, especially in context of his limited financial resources?

FURTHER READING ✦

Anonymous. "The Myth of the Powerless State." *Economist* (October 7, 1995):15–16.

Boddewyn, Jean J., and Thomas L Brever. "International-business Political Behavior: New Theoretical Directions." *Academy of Management Review*, 19 (1) (1994):119–43.

Gillespie, Kate and J. Brad McBride, "Smuggling in Emerging Markets: Global Implications." *Columbia Journal of World Business*, 31 (Winter 1996):40–54.

Kotabe, Masaaki and Kent W. Wheiler, *Anticompetitive Practices in Japan: Their Impact on the Performance of Foreign Firms*, Westport, CT: Praeger Publishers, 1996.

Litka, Michael P. *International Dimensions of the Legal Environment of Business*. Boston, Mass.: PWS-Kent Pub. Co., 1988.

Makhija, Mona Verma. "Government Intervention in the Venezuelan Petroleum Industry: An Empirical Investigation of Political Risk." *Journal of International Business Studies*, 24 (3) (1993):531–55.

Osland, Gregory E., and S. Tamer Cavusgil. "Performance Issues in US-China Joint Ventures," *California Management Review*, 38 (2) (1996):106–30.

Prasad, V. Kanti, and G. M. Naidu. "Perspectives and Preparedness Regarding ISO-9000 International Quality Standards." *Journal of International Marketing*, vol. 2 (1994) pp. 81–98.

Sheffet, Mary Jane. "The Foreign Corrupt Practices Act and the Omnibus Trade and Competition Act of 1988: Did They Change Corporate Behavior." *Journal of Public Policy and Marketing*, 14 (2) (Fall 1995):290–300.

Stephanie, Ann Leeway. *The Politics of U.S. International Trade: Protection, Expansion, and Escape*, Boston, Mass.: Pitman, 1985.

GLOBAL
MARKETING RESEARCH

6

CHAPTER OVERVIEW

Given the complexity of the global marketplace, solid marketing research is critical for a host of global marketing decisions. Skipping the research phase in the international marketing decision process can often prove a costly mistake. The following anecdotes illustrate that even marketing behemoths such as Procter & Gamble sometimes fail to live up to the "Test, Test, Test" maxim:[1]

- Procter & Gamble launched Pampers diapers in Japan in the late 1970s. Initially, sales were fairly promising, showing a 10 percent growth rate. However, Pampers proved far too bulky for Japanese mothers, who change diapers twice as frequently as Americans. Given the lack of storage space, Japanese mothers desired thin diapers. A Japanese competitor was able to meet these desires for thinner diapers, grabbing market share away from Procter & Gamble.

- Also in Japan, Procter & Gamble stumbled into a cultural minefield by showing a Camay commercial that featured a man walking into the bathroom while his

---

[1]Alecia Swasy, *Soap Opera. The Inside Story of Procter & Gamble* (New York: Random House, 1993).

spouse was taking a bath. This spot raised eyebrows in Japan, where a husband is not supposed to impose on his wife's privacy in the bathroom.

Most of such cultural blunders stem from inadequate marketing research. Market research assists the global marketing manager in two ways:[2] (1) by making better decisions that recognize cross-country similarities and differences, and (2) by gaining support from the local subsidiaries for proposed marketing decisions.

To some degree, the procedures and methods that are followed to conduct global marketing research are close to those used in standard domestic research. Most of the marketing research tricks-of-the-trade available for the domestic market scene (e.g., questionnaire design, focus group research, multivariate techniques such as cluster analysis, conjoint measurement) are fruitfully employed in the global marketplace. Also, the typical sequence of a multicountry market research process follows the familiar pattern used in domestic marketing research. In particular, the steps to be followed to conduct global market research are:

1. Define the research problem(s)
2. Develop a research design
3. Determine information needs
4. Collect the data (secondary and primary)
5. Analyze the data and interpret the results
6. Report and present the findings of the study

A typical example of a multi-country market research project is summarized in Exhibit 6-1. At each of these six steps, special problems may arise when the research activity takes place in foreign markets. The major challenges that global marketing researchers need to confront are:[3]

1. Complexity of research design due to environmental differences
2. Lack and inaccuracy of secondary data
3. Time and cost requirements to collect primary data
4. Coordination of multi-country research efforts
5. Difficulty in establishing comparability across multi-country studies

In this chapter, you will learn about the major issues that complicate cross-country research. We will also show ways to cope with these roadblocks. We then describe several useful techniques for market demand assessment. During the last two decades new market information technologies have emerged. We will discuss the impact of these new technologies on the marketing research function. Finally, we will consider several issues that concern the management of global market research.

---

[2]Kamran Kashani, "Beware the Pitfalls of Global Marketing," *Harvard Business Review* (Sept.-Oct. 1989), p. 97.

[3]Susan P. Douglas and C. Samuel Craig, *International Marketing Research* (Englewood Cliffs, N.J.: Prentice-Hall, 1983).

Exhibit 6-1

A Multi-Country Marketing Research Project at Eli Lilly: Estimating
the Market Potential for a Prescription Weight-Loss Product

Research Problem:

Estimate the dollar potential for a prescription weight-loss product in the U.K., Spain,
Italy, and Germany.

Research Hypothesis:

Patients would be willing to pay a premium price for the product even without reimbursement by the government.

Secondary Data Research:

-Market share of a similar product (Isomeride)

-Incidence of overweight and obesity in Europe*

Primary Data Research:

-Sample size: 350 physicians from the U.K., Italy, Spain, and Germany

-Sampling procedure: random selection from a high prescribers doctor list based on company data

-Data Collected:

   (1) Diary kept by physicians for 2 weeks

   (2) Questionnaires completed by patients who were judged to be prospect for the product by physician

   (3) Pricing study done based on 30 additional phone interviews with physicians in the U.K., Italy and Spain to measure price sensitivity

Source: Based on William V. Lawson, "The "Heavyweights"—Forecasting the obesity market in Europe
for a new compound," *Marketing and Research Today* (November 1995), pp. 270–274.

*Overweight are people whose body weight is 25–29 percent more than recommended weight; obese are
people whose weight is more than 30 percent more than their ideal weight.

RESEARCH PROBLEM FORMULATION   ◆ ◆ ◆ ◆ ◆ ◆ ◆

Any research starts off with a precise definition of the research problem(s) to be addressed. The cliché of a well-defined problem being a half-solved problem definitely applies in a global setting. Fancy data-analytical tools will not compensate for wrong problem definitions. Once the nature of the research problem becomes clear, the research problem needs to be translated in specific research questions. The scope of market research questions extends to both strategic and tactical marketing decisions. For example, a recent positioning study carried out for BMW in the European market centered around the following three issues:[4]

1. What does the motorist in the country concerned demand of his/her car?

2. What does s/he believe s/he is getting from various brands?

3. What does that imply with regard to positioning the BMW brand across borders?

---

[4]Kern Horst, Hans-Christian Wagner and Roswitha Hassis, "European Aspects of a
Global Brand: The BMW Case," *Marketing and Research Today* (February 1990), pp. 47–57.

In an international context, the marketing research problem formulation is hindered by the self-reference criterion—that is, people's habit to fall back on their own cultural norms and values (see Chapter 4). This tendency could lead to wrong or narrow problem definitions. In a multicountry research process, the self-reference criterion also makes a meeting-of-the-minds between headquarters and local people an immensely formidable task. To avoid such mishaps, market researchers must try to view the research problem from the cultural perspective of the foreign players and isolate the influence of the self-reference criterion. At any rate, local subsidiaries should be consulted at every step of the research process if the study will affect their operations, including the first step of the problem definition.

A major difficulty in formulating the research problem is the unfamiliarity with the foreign environment. Lack of familiarity may lead to false assumptions, misdefined research problems, and, ultimately, misleading conclusions about the foreign markets. To reduce part of the uncertainty, some exploratory research at the early stage of the research process is often fruitful. A useful vehicle for such preliminary research is an **omnibus survey.** Omnibuses are conducted by research agencies at regular intervals. The survey contains a plethora of consumer-related questions. The surveys are administered to a very large sample of consumers, usually a panel owned by the agency. In most cases, clients are able incorporate their own questions. The prime benefit of an omnibus survey is cost, since expenses are shared with other subscribers. A major disadvantage is that only a limited amount of company-relevant information is obtainable through an omnibus. Also, the panel is usually not representative of the firm's target market profile. Still, an omnibus survey is probably the most economical way to gather preliminary information on target markets. Findings from an omnibus may assist managers and researchers in fine-tuning the research problem(s) to be tackled. Omnibuses conducted on a regular basis can also be useful as a tracking tool to spot changes in consumer attitudes or behaviors. Exhibit 6-2 presents the key features of A. C. Nielsen SRG's China omnibus.

Once the research issues have been stated, management needs to determine the information needs. Some of the information will be readily available within the company or in publicly available sources. Other information must be collected from scratch.

◆ ◆ ◆ ◆ ◆ ◆ SECONDARY GLOBAL MARKETING RESEARCH

Assessing the information needs is the next step after the research problem definition. Some pieces of information will already be available. That sort of information is referred to as **secondary data**. When the information is not useful, or simply does not exist, the firm will need to collect the data. **Primary data** are data collected specifically for the purpose of the research study. Researchers will first explore secondary data resources, since that kind of information is usually much cheaper and less time-consuming to gather than primary data. Both forms of data collection entail numerous issues in an international marketing setting. We will first touch on the major problems concerning secondary data research.

Secondary Data Sources

Market researchers in developed countries are spoiled with the wealth of data that are gathered by government agencies. Unfortunately, the equivalents of such databanks are often missing outside the developed world. Even when the information is

EXHIBIT 6-2
A. C. NIELSEN SRG's CHINA OMNIBUS
_____

Geographical Coverage:
    (a) Key cities: Guangzhou, Shanghai, Beijing
    (b) Two to three other cities (out of twelve secondary cities) per round, depending on client interest

Timing:
Four rounds per year—March, June, September and December

Sample Size:
    (a) 1,000 interviews in each key city
    (b) 500 interviews in each secondary city

Sampling:
Random probability sampling with face-to-face interviews

Deliverables:
Self-explanatory charts and computer tables. Computer tables are presented by city and cross-tabulated by sex, age, monthly household/personal income, occupation, and education.

Examples of Omnibus Questions:
-Do you use X?
-How often do you use X?
-What do you like/dislike about X?
-How much did you pay for X?
-Have you seen any ad for Y?

Cost:
Total cost depends on:
    (a) Number of questions
    (b) Nature of question: open-ended versus close-ended
    (c) Sample option (e.g., all adults; only males)
    (d) Number of cities
Minimum cost (three close-ended questions; all adults; one secondary city): US$3,050
_____

Source: Based on information provided by SRG China.

available, it may be hard to track down. A starting point for data collection is a computerized service such as Lexis/Nexis that provides real-time on-line access to information resources based on user-provided keywords. Another example of an electronic databank is FINDEX, which offers a worldwide directory of market research intelligence reports. Exhibit 6-3 shows the wide variety of secondary data resources available to global market researchers. Also, a wealth of international business resources can be accessed via the Internet. One of the most comprehensive resources is the National Trade Data Bank (NTDB), maintained by the U.S. Department of Commerce (http://www.stat-usa.gov).[5] The NTDB includes market research reports, information on export opportunities, how-to-market guides, and so forth.[6] One of the nice features is a search engine that allows users to retrieve any information that is available on the NTDB for a given topic. Another valuable on-line resource is the International Business Resources Directory maintained by the CIBER center at Michigan State University (http://ciber.bus.msu.edu/busres.htm). This on-line re-

_____

[5]The National Trade Data Bank information is also available on CD-ROM.

[6]Though not free, at an annual subscription rate of US$150 (individual rate), the information provided by the NTDB is a definite bargain.

EXHIBIT 6-3
RESOURCES FOR SECONDARY DATA

International Trade
- *Yearbook of International Trade Statistics* (United Nations)
- *US Imports* (U.S. Bureau of the Census)
- *US Exports* (U.S. Bureau of the Census)
- *Exporters' Encyclopaedia* (Dun and Bradstreet)

Country Information (Socioeconomic & Political Conditions)
- *Yearbook of Industrial Statistics* (United Nations)
- *Statistical Yearbook* (United Nations; Updated by *Monthly Bulletin of Statistics*)
- *Europa Yearbook*
- *OECD Economic Survey*
- *Country Reports* (The Economist Intelligence Unit)
- *Demographic Yearbook* (United Nations)
- *Statistical Yearbook* (United Nations)
- *UNESCO Statistical Yearbook*
- *World Factbook* (Central Intelligence Agency)

International Marketing
- *European Marketing Data and Statistics* (Euromonitor)
- *International Marketing Data and Statistics* (Euromonitor)
- *Consumer Europe* (Euromonitor)
- *European Advertising Marketing and Media Data* (Euromonitor)
- *Advertising Age International*
- *FINDEX: The Worldwide Directory of Market Research Reports, Studies & Surveys* (Cambridge Information Group Directories)
- *A Guide to Selling Your Service Overseas* (Northern California District Export Council)

Chambers of Commerce
See http://www.worldchambers.com/chambers.html on the World Wide Web for a global index

Directories of Foreign Firms
- *D & B Europa* (Dun & Bradstreet)
- *Directory of American Firms Operating in Foreign Countries* (World Trade Academy Press)
- *Directory of Foreign Firms Operating in the United States* (World Trade Academy Press)
- *Europe's 15,000 Largest Companies* (E L C Publishing)
- *International Directory of Importers: Europe* (Interdata)
- *Mailing Lists of Worldwide Importing Firms* (Interdata)
- *Moody's International Manual* (Moody's Investors Service)
- *Principal International Businesses; The World Marketing Directory* (Dun & Bradstreet)

source is an extremely well-organized directory that provides linkages to hundreds of on-line international business resources on the Internet.

Researchers will first tap information resources available within the company. Many companies have their own libraries that provide valuable data sources. Large companies typically compile enormous databanks on their operations. Government publications sometimes offer information on overseas markets. In the United States, the U.S. Department of Commerce offers detailed country reports and industry surveys. Many countries have a network of government-sponsored commercial delegations (e.g., Chambers of Commerce, the Japanese External Trade Organization—JETRO). These agencies will often provide valuable information to firms that desire to do business in their country, despite the fact that the raison-d'-être of most of these agencies is to assist home-grown companies in the foreign market.

Besides government offices, international agencies such as the World Bank, the OECD, the International Monetary Fund, and the United Nations gather a humongous amount of data. Reports published by these organizations are especially useful for demographic and economic information. Given that most of these documents report information across multiple years, their data can be used to examine trends in socioeconomic indicators. Unfortunately, reports published by such international agencies cover only their member states.

Several companies specialize in producing business-related information. Such information is usually far more expensive than government-based data. However, this sort of information often has more direct relevance for companies. Two prominent examples are the Economist Intelligence Unit (E.I.U.) and Euromonitor. One of the most useful resources put together by the E.I.U. are the country reports that appear on a quarterly basis. These country reports give a detailed update on the major *political* and economic trends in the countries covered. Euromonitor has several publications that are extremely useful to global marketers. Two well-known reports are the *European Marketing Data and Statistics* and *International Marketing Data and Statistics*, annual volumes covering Europe and the global marketplace outside Europe, respectively.

A more recent form of secondary data sources is the syndicated datasets sold by market research companies like A. C. Nielsen and Information Resources Inc. These firms acquire datasets that cover purchase transactions from retail outlets whose cash registers are equipped with optical scanning equipment. Until about a decade ago, such datasources were only available in the United States. Optical scanners are now well entrenched in most developed countries. Both giants in the syndicated data business, A. C. Nielsen and Information Resources Inc., have a major international presence now.

As firms move from government publications to syndicated data, the richness of the information increases enormously. At the same time, the cost of collecting and processing data goes up. Just as in a domestic marketing context, firms planning research in the global marketplace have to decide on the value added of additional information and make the appropriate trade-offs.

Problems with Secondary Data Research

In the global market scene, some of the information sought by market researchers does not exist. When data are missing, the researcher needs to infer the data by using proxy variables or values from previous periods. Even if the datasets are complete, the researcher will usually encounter many problems:

Accuracy of Data. The accuracy of secondary data is often questionable, for various reasons. The definition used for certain indicators often differs across countries. The quality of information may also be compromised by the mechanisms that were used to collect them. Most developed countries use sophisticated procedures to assemble data. Due to the lack of resources and skills, many developing countries have to rely on rather primitive mechanisms to collect data. The purpose for which the data were collected could affect their accuracy. International trade statistics do not cover cross-border smuggling activities. Such transactions are, in some cases, far more significant than legitimate trade.

Age of Data. The desired information may be available but outdated. Many countries collect economic activity information on a far less frequent basis than the United States. The frequency of census taking also varies from country to country. In the United States, a census is taken once every decade. In many LDCs census-taking seldom takes place.

Reliability Over Time. Often companies are interested in historical patterns of certain variables to spot underlying trends. Such trends might indicate whether a market opportunity opens up or whether a market is getting saturated. To study trends, the researcher has to know to what degree the data are measured consistently over time. Sudden changes in the definition of economic indicators are not uncommon. Juggling with economic variable measures is especially likely for variables that have political ramifications, such as unemployment and inflation statistics. For instance, government authorities may adjust the basket of goods used to measure inflation to produce more favorable numbers. Market researchers should be aware of such practices and, if necessary, make the appropriate corrections.

Comparability of Data. Cross-country research often demands a comparison of indicators across countries. Different sources on a given item often produce contradictory information. The issue then is how to reconcile these differences. One way to handle contradictory information is to **triangulate**—obtain information on the same item from at least three different sources and speculate on possible reasons behind these differences.[7] For instance, suppose you want to collect information on the import penetration of wine as a percentage of total consumption in various European countries. Triangulation might show that some of the figures you collected are based on value, while others are based on volume. It might also reveal that some sources include champagne and others do not.

Comparability may also be hindered by the lack of **functional** or **conceptual equivalence**.[8] Functional equivalence refers to the degree to which similar activities or products in different countries fulfill similar functions. Many products perform very different functions in different markets. In the United States bicycles are primarily used for leisure. In countries such as the Netherlands and China, bicycles are a major means of transportation. Absence of conceptual equivalence is another factor that undermines comparability. Conceptual equivalence reflects the degree to which a given concept has the same meaning in different environments. Many concepts have totally different meanings or may simply not exist in certain countries. The concept of "equal rights" for women is unfamiliar in many Muslim societies. Likewise, the notion of "privacy" is unknown in many non-Western societies.

The comparison of money-based indicators (e.g., income figures, consumer expenditures, trade statistics) is hampered by the need to convert such figures into a common currency. The key issues are what currency to use and at what exchange rate (beginning of the year, year-end or year-average). A further complication is that exchange rates do not always reflect the relative purchasing power between coun-

---

[7]S. C. Williams, "Researching Markets in Japan—A Methodological Case Study," *Journal of International Marketing* 4(2) (1996), pp. 87–93.

[8]Yusuf A. Choudhry, "Pitfalls in International Marketing Research: Are You Speaking French Like a Spanish Cow?" *Akron Business and Economic Review*, 17(4) (Winter 1986), pp. 19–20.

tries. As a result, comparing economic indicators using market exchange rates can be misleading.

Lumping of Data. Official datasources often group statistics on certain variables in very broad categories. This compromises the usefulness and the interpretation of such data for international market researchers. Managers should check what is included in certain categories.[9]

Given the hurdles posed by secondary data, it is important to verify the quality of collected information. To assess the quality of data, the researcher should seek answers to the following checklist:

1. When were the data collected? Over what time frame?
2. How were the data collected?
3. Have the variables been redefined over time?
4. Who collected the data?
5. For what purpose were the data gathered?

Of course, satisfactory answers to each of these questions does not assure total peace of mind. Researchers and managers should always be on guard regarding the quality of secondary data.

PRIMARY GLOBAL MARKETING RESEARCH

Seldom will secondary data prove satisfactory for market research studies. The next step in the research process is to collect primary data specifically for the purpose of the research project. Primary data can be collected in several ways: (1) focus groups, (2) survey research, or (3) test markets. In this section we will concentrate on focus group and survey research. Test marketing is discussed in Chapter 11 on global new product development.

Focus Groups

Before embarking on large-scale quantitative market research projects, most firms will conduct exploratory research. One of the most popular tools at this stage is the focus group. A focus group is a loosely structured free-flowing discussion among a small group (eight to twelve people) of target customers facilitated by a professional moderator. They can be used for many different purposes: to generate information to guide the quantitative research projects, to reveal new product opportunities, to test out new product concepts, and so forth.

The rules for designing and running focus groups in a domestic marketing setting also apply for global market research projects.[10] Hiring well-trained moderators is critical in conducting focus groups for international market research. Moderators should be familiar with the local language and social interaction patterns. Cultural sensitivity is an absolute must with focus groups. For instance, Japanese consumers

[9]Williams, p. 90.

[10]See, for example, Thomas C. Kinnear and James R. Taylor, *Marketing Research* (New York, NY: McGraw-Hill, Inc., 1996), Chapter 10.

Some marketing research companies focus on international marketing research with branch offices strategically located around the world.

tend to be much more hesitant to criticize new product ideas than their Western counterparts.[11] Also, many Asian societies like Japan are highly collective ("Confucian"). Strangers outside the group are excluded. As a result, getting the desired group dynamics for focus groups within such cultures is often very hard. To stimulate group dynamics, the following steps should be taken:[12]

• Be precise in recruitment to ensure group homogeneity and ease of bonding.

• Hire moderators who are able to develop group dynamics quickly through warm-ups, humor, group-playing.

• Hire moderators who can spot and challenge "consensus"-claimed behaviors and attitudes.

When analyzing and interpreting focus group findings, market researchers should also concentrate on the nonverbal cues (e.g., gestures, voice intonations).[13]

---

[11]David B. Montgomery, "Understanding the Japanese as Customers, Competitors, and Collaborators," *Japan and the World Economy*, 3(1) (1991), pp. 61–91.

[12]Chris Robinson, "Asian Culture: The Marketing Consequences," *Journal of the Market Research Society*, 38(1) (1996), pp. 55–62.

[13]Naresh K. Malhotra, James Agarwal, and Mark Peterson, "Methodological Issues in Cross-Cultural Marketing Research. A State-of-the-Art Review," *International Marketing Review*, 13(5) (1996), pp. 7–43.

Information provided by these nonverbal cues is often as important as the verbal content of the focus groups.

Survey Methods for Cross-Cultural Marketing Research

Questionnaires are the most common vehicle to gather primary data in marketing research. Survey research begins with the design of a questionnaire. The next step is to develop a sampling plan to collect the data. Once these two tasks have been accomplished, the researcher moves to the next phase, the physical collection of information to the questionnaires. Each stage may lead to major headaches.

Questionnaire Design. By far the most popular instrument to gather primary data is the questionnaire. Preparing questionnaires for global market research poses tremendous challenges. Just like in domestic marketing, care should be exercised with the wording and the sequencing of the questions. Further care is needed to assure comparability of survey-based results across frontiers. Measurement issues in cross-country research center around the question: "Are the phenomena in countries A and B measured in the same way?" Absence of measurement equivalence will render cross-country comparisons meaningless. Earlier we discussed the need for **conceptual** and **functional equivalence** of secondary data. The same requirements apply to primary data in order to avoid cultural biases. Cross-country survey research needs to fulfill two further criteria: **translation** and **scalar equivalence.**

The first aspect deals with the translation of the instrument from one language into another one. Cross-cultural research, even within the same country or parent language (e.g., English, Spanish), demands adequate translations from the master questionnaire into other languages. Careless translations of questionnaires can lead to embarrassing mistakes. Good translations are hard to accomplish. Several methods exist to minimize translation errors. Two procedures often used in practice to avoid sloppy translations are **back-translation** and **parallel translation**. The back-translation method is a two-phase process. Suppose a company wants to translate a questionnaire from English into Arab. In the first step, the master questionnaire is translated into Arabic. In the second stage, the Arab version is translated back into English by another interpreter. This version is then compared with the original survey to spot any bugs or translation errors. The process is reiterated until an acceptable degree of convergence is achieved. Parallel translation consists of using multiple interpreters who translate the same questionnaire independently. Alternative versions are compared by a committee of translators and differences are reconciled.

Most surveys typically have a battery of questions or "Agree/Disagree" statements with a (e.g., 7-point) scale to record responses. To make the findings of cross-country market research projects meaningful, it is paramount to pursue **scalar equivalence**: scores from subjects of different countries should have the same meaning and interpretation.[14] The standard format of scales used in survey research differs across countries. In the United States, a five- or seven-point scale is most common. In France twenty-point scales prevail in survey research. Keep in mind that high scores in one country are not necessarily high scores elsewhere. In some cases, you may also need to adjust the anchors of the scale. One recent study that measured attitudes of Japanese managers adopted scales that included "definitely true," "somewhat

---

[14]Ibid., p. 15.

true," and "not all true." A pretest of the survey showed that the Japanese respondents had trouble with the concept of "agree/disagree."[15] To make cross-country comparisons meaningful, it is advisable to adjust responses in each country by, for instance, taking deviations from country-averages on any given question. By the same token, in some societies people are cued to view "1" as best and the other endpoint of the scale as worst, while in others "1" is considered the worst, regardless of how the scale is designated.

Survey research in developing nations is further compounded by low levels of education. Specially designed visual scales like the Funny Faces scale (see Exhibit 6-4) are sometimes used to cope with illiteracy. In developing countries, market re-

EXHIBIT 6-4
THE FUNNY FACES SCALE

Very happy

Happy

Not happy but also not unhappy

Unhappy

Very unhappy

Source: C. K. Corder, "Problems and Pitfalls in Conducting Marketing Research in Africa." in *Marketing Expansion in a Shrinking World.* ed. Betsy Gelb. Proceedings of American Marketing Association Business Conference. (Chicago: AMA 1978), pp. 86–90.

[15]Jean L. Johnson, Tomoaki Sakano, Joseph A. Cote, and Naoto Onzo, "The Exercise of Interfirm Power and Its Repercussions in U.S.-Japanese Channel Relationships," *Journal of Marketing*, 57, (2) (April 1993), pp. 1–10.

searchers should also try to reduce the verbal content and use visual aids. In countries that are unfamiliar with survey research (e.g., former Eastern Bloc countries), it is advisable to avoid lengthy questionnaires or open-ended questions.[16]

Regardless of whether the survey is to be administered in Singapore, Erps-Kwerps or Dar es-Salaam, it is absolutely imperative to pretest the questionnaire. Pretesting is the only foolproof way to debug the questionnaire and spot embarrassing, and often expensive, mistakes. Speed is often critical when collecting data. However, rushing into the field without a thorough pretest of the questionnaire is highly risky.

Sampling. To collect data, the researcher has to draw a sample from the target population. A sampling plan basically centers around three issues:[17]

1. Who should be surveyed? What is our target population (**sampling unit**)?

2. How many people should be surveyed (**sample size**)?

3. How should prospective respondents be chosen from the target population (**sampling procedure**)?

Decisions on each of these issues will be driven by balancing costs, desired reliability, and time requirements. In multicountry research, firms also need to decide what countries should be researched. There are two broad approaches. The first approach starts off with a large-scale exploratory research project covering many countries. This step might take the form of an omnibus survey. The alternative approach focuses on a few key countries. To choose these countries, a firm might group countries (e.g., along sociocultural indicators) and pick one or two representative members from each cluster. Depending on the findings coming from this first pool of countries, the research process is extended to cover other countries of interest.

The preparation of a sampling plan for multicountry research is often a daunting task. When drawing a sample, the researcher needs a sampling frame, that is, a listing of the target population (e.g., a telephone directory). In many countries, such listings simply do not exist or may be very inadequate. In countries like Saudi Arabia, telephone directories are incomplete and out of date.[18] The proportion of individuals meeting the criteria of the target population could vary considerably. This forces the researcher to be flexible with the sampling methods employed in different countries.[19]

Computing the desired sample size in cross-country market research often becomes at best guesswork because the necessary pieces of information are missing. Sample sizes may also vary across cultures. Typically, heterogeneous cultures (e.g., India) demand bigger samples than homogeneous cultures (e.g., South Korea, Thailand).[20]

Most researchers prefer some form of probabilistic sampling that enables them to make statistical inferences about the collected data. The absence of sampling

---

[16]Erderer, Kaynak, *Marketing in the Third World* (New York: Praeger, 1982), Chapter 4.

[17]See, for example, Naresh K. Malhotra, *Marketing Research. An Applied Orientation* (Englewood-Cliffs, N.J.: Prentice-Hall, 1993), Chapter 13.

[18]Secil Tuncalp, "The Marketing Research Scene in Saudi Arabia," *European Journal of Marketing*, 22(5) (1988), pp. 15–22.

[19]D. N. Aldridge, "Multi-Country Research," in *Applied Marketing and Social Research*, U. Bradley, Ed., 2d ed. (New York: John Wiley, 1987), pp. 364–65.

[20]Malhotra et al., p. 27.

Exhibit 6-5

Comparison of European Data Collection Methods

	France	The Netherlands	Sweden	Switzerland	U. K.
Mail	4%	33%	23%	8%	9%
Telephone	15	18	44	21	16
Central location/streets	52	37	—	—	—
Home/work	—	—	8	44	54
Groups	13	—	5	6	11
Depth interviews	12	12	2	8	—
Secondary	4	—	4	8	—

Source: Emanuel H. Demby, "ESOMAR Urges Changes in Reporting Demographics, Issues Worldwide Report, *Marketing News* (January 8, 1990), p. 24. Reprinted by permission of the American Marketing Association.

frames and various cultural hurdles (e.g., inapproachability of women in Muslim societies) make a nonprobabilistic sampling procedure, such as convenience sampling, the only alternative, especially in LDCs. Such handicaps do not apply to all LDCs. For instance, Chinese cities are divided into Administrative Districts, Administrative Streets, and Resident Committees. Every household has to register with its Resident Committee. One recent omnibus survey randomly picked ten Resident Committees in each target city. From each of the chosen committees, one thousand households were drawn at random to be interviewed.[21]

Contact Method. When preparing a sampling plan, you also need to decide how to contact prospective subjects for the survey. The most common choices are mail, telephone, or person-to-person interviews (e.g., shopping mall intercepts). Exhibit 6-5 contrasts the usage of data collection methods in five European countries. There are several factors that explain why some methods prevail in some countries and are barely used elsewhere. Cultural norms often rule out certain data collection methods. Germans tend to show greater resistance to telephone interviewing than other Europeans.[22] By the same token, daytime phone calls will not work in Saudi Arabia, since social norms dictate that housewives do not respond to calls from strangers.[23] Cost differentials will also favor some methods over others. In many developing countries, the state of the infrastructure will make certain contact methods unattractive. In countries like Brazil, a significant portion of the mail faces large delays or never gets delivered. Lack of decent phone service in many LDCs creates a challenge for phone surveys. In China, researchers have to rely on very basic interviewing techniques because of poor phone coverage (about 7 percent versus 93 percent in the United States) and low response rates with mail surveys.[24] These and other challenges mean that market researchers must often improvise and settle for the second best alternative.

[21]Henry C. Steele, :"Marketing Research in China: The Hong Kong Connection," *Marketing and Research Today* (August 1990), pp. 155–64.

[22]D. N. Aldridge, "Multi-Country Research," p. 365.

[23]Tuncalp, p. 19.

[24]Cyndee Miller, "China Emerges as Latest Battleground for Marketing Researchers," *Marketing News* (February 14, 1994), pp. 1–2.

Collecting the Information. Once the design of your questionnaire and your sampling plan is completed, you need to collect the data in the field. This field will be covered with landmines, some of them fairly visible, others invisible. Primary data collection may be hindered by respondent and/or interviewer related biases.

Probably the most severe problem is nonresponse due to a reluctance to talk with strangers, fears about confidentiality, or other cultural biases. In many cultures, the only way to cope with nonresponse is to account for it when determining sample sizes. In China, surveys that are sanctioned by the local authorities will lead to a higher response rate.[25]

The **courtesy bias** refers to a desire to be polite toward the other person. This bias is fairly common in Asia and the Middle East.[26] The subject feels obliged to give responses that hopefully will please the interviewer. Another snag in survey research are biases towards **yea-** or **nay-saying.** In Russia, limited experience with brands could result in low ratings because the consumer only prefers those brands with which he is familiar.[27] In some countries, responses may reflect a **social desirability bias** where the subject attempts to reflect a certain social status in his responses. Topics such as income or sex are simply taboo in some regions. There are no panaceas to handle these and other biases. Measures such as careful wording and thorough pretesting of the survey, adequate training of the interviewer, will minimize the incidence of such biases. In some cases, it will be worthwhile to incorporate questions that measure tendencies such as social desirability. Another option to handle cultural biases is **ipsatizing** the responses. This is a procedure that basically converts the response ratings into rankings.

House-to-house or shopping mall survey responses could also be scrambled by interviewer related biases. Availability of skilled interviewers can be a major bottleneck in cross-country research, especially in LDCs and the former Eastern Bloc countries. Lack of supervision or low salaries will tempt interviewers in some countries to cut corners by filling out surveys themselves or ignoring the sampling procedure. In many cultures, it is advisable to match interviewers to respondents. Disparities in cultural backgrounds may lead to misunderstandings.[28] Survey-takers in some societies (e.g., Latin-America) are regarded with suspicion by the local population.[29] Obviously, adequate recruiting, training, and supervision of interviewers will lessen interviewer-related biases in survey research. In countries where survey research is still in an early stage and researchers have little expertise, questionnaires should not be overcomplex.[30] When developing a survey instrument like a questionnaire for a global market research project, it is also helpful to have **redundancy:** ask the same question in different ways and parts of the questionnaire. That way, the researcher can cross-check the validity of the responses.[31]

---

[25]Steele, p. 160.

[26]Kaynak, p. 171.

[27]J. Stafford and N. Upmeyer, "Product Shortages Hamper Research in Soviet Union," *Marketing News* (September 3, 1990), pp. 6, 40.

[28]Aldridge, p. 371.

[29]Douglas and Craig, p. 227.

[30]J. Stafford and N. Upmeyer, p. 40.

[31]Naghi Namakforoosh, "Data Collection Methods Hold Key to Research in Mexico," *Marketing News* (August 29, 1994), p. 28.

◆ ◆

$\mathcal{G}$LOBAL PERSPECTIVE 6-1

ONE MAN'S JUNK IS ANOTHER MAN'S TREASURE

Never mind research giant A. C. Nielsen's push in South America. A consulting firm here has found garbage-digging the way to the top of the local research heap.

After studying the curbside contributions of 400 homes in Buenos Aires, the Dynamic Group consulting company is expanding its aptly named Garbage Data Dynamics study to 1,650 more residences in the greater metropolitan area. The hope: that the saying, "one man's junk is another man's treasure" continues to ring true.

The company has already racked up its share of heavy-weight clients for the study, including Coca-Cola de Argentina, Mastellone Hermanos, Argentina's largest dairy products marketer; pasta marketer Matarazzo; and

two large wine and meat marketers, which pay $4,500 a month for garbage analysis.

What's the advantage to studying garbage?

"By analyzing the disposable containers we can certify that this is real consumption and not what somebody felt like saying or what they "thought" was right for a survey," said Market Dynamics Director Mario Haiquel. "The people in this study don't know that we are studying their garbage, so the information is totally objective," added Mr. Haiquel.

Mr. Haiquel claims that his organization can provide data on brand share gain and loss, key competitors and customer loyalty, associated consumption, the effect of ad campaigns. Discarded newspapers, magazines and cable TV guides can help advertisers with their media schedules. One of the more fascinating finds has been on people's recreational habits: poor people tend to buy more expensive wines and champagnes on weekends.

What happens to the garbage after the study? "It all gets thrown out. None of it is saved or recycled," said Mr. Haiquel.

Source: "Turning Trash to Research Treasure," p. I–16. Reprinted with permission from the April 17, 1995 issue of Advertising Age. Copyright, Crain Communications Inc. 1995.

Although most data collection procedures involve mail surveys, door-to-door interviewing, or phone interviews, observational methods often prove to be very insightful. **Global Perspective 6-1** describes how one market research company in Argentina uses garbage-digging to probe consumer behavior.

◆ ◆ ◆ ◆ ◆ ◆   MARKET SIZE ASSESSMENT

When deciding whether to enter a particular country, one of the key drivers is the market potential. In most developed countries, a fairly accurate estimate of the market size for any particular product is easily obtainable. For many frequently purchased consumer goods, information suppliers like A. C. Nielsen are able to give an up-to-date estimate of category volume and market shares based on scanning technology. Such information, however, does not come cheap. Before investing a substantial amount of money, you might consider less costly ways to estimate market demand. For many industries and developing countries, information on market demand is simply not readily available. Under such circumstances, there is a need to come up with a market size estimate, using "simple" ingredients.

Below we introduce four methods that can be fruitfully employed to assess the size of the market for any given product. All of these procedures can be used when very little data are available and/or the quality of the data is dismal, such as typically will be the case for many LDCs and former East Bloc countries. All four methods allow you to make a reasonable guesstimate of the market potential without necessitating intensive data-collection efforts. Market size estimates thus derived prove useful for country selection at the early stage. Countries that do not appear to be viable opportunities are weeded out. After this preliminary screening stage, richer data regarding market size and other indicators are collected for the countries that remain in the pool.

Method of Analogy

The first technique, the **analogy method,** starts by picking a country that is at the same stage of economic development as the country of interest and for which the market size is known. The method is based on the premise that the relationship between the demand for a product and a particular indicator, for instance, the demand for a related product, is similar in both countries.

Let us illustrate the method with a brief example. Suppose that a consumer electronics company wants to estimate the market size for VCRs in Poland. For the base country, we take another Central European country, say Hungary, for which we know the sales of VCRs. We also need to choose a proxy variable that correlates highly with the demand for VCRs. In this case, we decide to choose color TV sales as an indicator. So, in this example, we assume that the ratio of VCR ownership to color-TV ownership in Hungary and Poland is roughly equivalent:

$$\frac{\text{VCR Demand}_{\text{Poland}}}{\text{Color TV Demand}_{\text{Poland}}} = \frac{\text{VCR Demand}_{\text{Hungary}}}{\text{Color TV Demand}_{\text{Hungary}}}$$

Since we are interested in the demand for VCRs in Poland, we can derive an estimate based on the following relationship:

$$\text{VCR Demand}_{\text{Poland}} = \text{Color TV Demand}_{\text{Poland}} \left(\frac{\text{VCR Demand}_{\text{Hungary}}}{\text{Color TV Demand}_{\text{Hungary}}} \right)$$

For this specific example we collected the following pieces of information:

	Annual Retail Color TV (000s)	Sales VCR (000s)
Hungary	455	177
Poland	634	???

Source: European Marketing Data and Statistics 1992 (London: Euromonitor, 1992), Table 1416.

Plugging in those numbers, we get:

Estimate VCR Demand$_{\text{Poland}}$ (Annual Retail Sales) = 634 (177/455) = 246.6.

The critical part is finding a comparable country and a good surrogate measure (in this case, the demand for color television sets). In some cases, the analogy exists between different time periods. So, the stage of economic development in country A ten years back is similar to the current state of the economy in country B. In the same fashion as above, we can derive an estimate for the product demand in country B, but this time you would apply the ratio between product demand and the surrogate measure in country A that existed ten years ago:

$$M_B^{1998} = X_B^{1998} \times (M_A^{1988}/X_A^{1988})$$

where the Ms refer to the market size for the product of interest and the Xs are the surrogate measures. This variant is sometimes referred to as the **longitudinal method of analogy.**

Use of either approach will produce misleading estimates whenever:[32]

1. Consumption patterns are not comparable across countries due to strong cultural disparities

2. Other factors (competition, trade barriers) cause actual sales to differ from potential sales

3. Technological advances allow use of product innovations in a country at an earlier stage of economic development ("leapfrogging")

McDonald's uses a variation of the analogy method to derive market size estimates:[33]

$$\left(\frac{\text{Population of Country } X}{\substack{\text{No. Of People Per McDonald's} \\ \text{in United States (21,814)}}} \right) \left(\frac{\text{Per Capita Income of Country } X}{\substack{\text{Per Capita Income of U.S.} \\ \text{(\$25,850)}}} \right)$$

$$= \text{Potential Penetration in Country X}$$

This method is illustrated in Exhibit 6-6, which contrasts the number of restaurants McDonald's could build with its current number of outlets for several countries. According to this formula, the worldwide market potential of McDonald's would be 42,000 restaurants. Currently, McDonald's has about 21,000 restaurants in 101 different countries[34] ("on any given day, 99 percent of the world's population does not eat at McDonald's yet..."[35]), out of which almost 9,000 are located outside the United States.

Trade Audit

An alternative way to derive market size estimates is based on local production and import and export figures for the product of interest. The logic is very straightforward—take the local production figures, add imports, and subtract exports:

$$\text{Market Size in Country } A = \text{Local Production} + \text{Imports} - \text{Exports}$$

Strictly speaking, one should also make adjustments for inventory levels. While the procedure is commonsensical, the hard part is finding the input data. For many LDCs (and even developed countries), such data are missing, inaccurate, outdated, or collected at a very aggregate level in categories that are too broad for the company's purposes.

---

[32]Lyn S. Amine and S. Tamer Cavusgil, "Demand Estimation in Developing Country Environment: Difficulties, Techniques and Examples," *Journal of the Market Research Society*, 28(1), (1986), pp. 43-65.

[33]"How Many McDonald's Can He Build?" *Fortune* (October 17, 1994), p. 104. Figures are based on 1995 estimates as reported in the *CIA World Factbook 1996/7*.

[34]See http://www/mcdonalds.com.

[35]McDonald's Corp., *1995 Annual Report*, p. 7.

EXHIBIT 6-6
MARKET POTENTIAL ESTIMATES FOR MCDONALD'S

Country	Current Number of Restaurants (1996)	Market Potential (in terms of number of restaurants)
Japan	2,004	4,496
Canada	992	1,146
Germany	743	2,391
Britain	650	1,859
Australia	608	673
France	541	1,933
Brazil	337	1,591
Taiwan	163	460
Netherlands	151	492
Italy	147	1,775
Sweden	129	291
Hong Kong	125	241
Spain	121	917
New Zealand	120	101
Mexico	112	1,317
China	62	5,333

Sources: "How Many McDonald's Can He Build?" *Fortune* (October 17, 1994), p. 104, *CIA World Factbook 1996/7,* and http://www.mcdonalds.com/a_system/press_release/ Press_Release2624427.

Chain Ratio Method

The chain ratio method starts with a very rough base-number as an estimate for the market size (e.g., the entire population of the country). This base estimate is systematically fine-tuned by applying a string ("chain") of percentages to come up with the most meaningful estimate for total market potential.

To illustrate the procedure, let us use a simple example. Consider a firm that makes baby monitors and is planning to expand into China and/or India. Baby monitors are devices that track the baby's breathing while the baby is asleep. If for some reason the baby's breathing stops, an alarm will go off. The company wants to focus on urban areas, which are easier to access than the countryside. For the base number, we start with the overall population. Using the chain ratio method, you can compute a rough estimate of the market potential:[36]

	China	India	
Base Number—			
Total Population:	1,207.4	921.5	A
Urbanization Rate:	30.3%	26.8%	B
Urban Population:	365.8	247.0	$C = A \times B$
Birth Rates per 000s Population:	17.8	28.4	D
Market Potential Estimate:	6.5 mln	7.0 mln	$E = C \times D$

---

[36]The numbers for this illustration are taken from various tables in *International Marketing Data and Statistics 1997.* All numbers are in millions.

Evidently, these estimates could be refined even further, accounting for buying power, size of dwellings, and so forth, assuming the information is available.

Cross-Sectional Regression Analysis

Statistical techniques such as cross-sectional regression can be used to produce market size estimates. With regression analysis, the variable of interest (in our case "market size") is related to a set of predictor variables. To apply regression, you would first choose a set of indicators that are closely related to demand for the product of interest. You would then collect data on these variables and product demand figures for a set of countries (the *cross-section*) where the product has already been introduced. Given these data, you can then fit a regression that will allow you to predict the market size in countries in your consideration pool.[37]

Again, let us illustrate the procedure with a simple example. Suppose a pharmaceutical company XYZ would like to introduce an antidepressant in Central and Eastern Europe. As predictor variables, we picked two indicators: per capita income (economic wealth) and suicide rate (number of suicides per thousand). The latter variable is chosen as a proxy for a country's "mental" well-being. We collected data on these two measures and per-capita consumption (in U.S. dollars) of analgesics in thirteen Western European countries.[38] Using these data as inputs, we come up with the following regression model:

$$\text{Per Capita Consumption of Analgesics (in US\$)} = 0.72 + (0.000022 \times \text{per capita income})$$

$$+ (0.17 \times \text{suicide rate})$$

$$\text{Goodness of Fit: } R^2_{adj} = 0.49.^{[39]}$$

The fit of the regression is fairly decent, especially since we only consider two predictor variables (see Exhibit 6-7). Based on this regression, we are able to predict the market size (in terms of per-capita consumption in U.S. dollar) for analgesics in the Central and Eastern European markets. We plug in the income and suicide figures for the respective countries in this equation, with the following results:

Bulgaria:	$ 3.40
Czech Rep. & Slovakia:	$ 3.85
Hungary:	$12.54
Romania:	$ 4.36
Former Soviet Union:	$ 3.76

From a per-capita consumption perspective, it appears that Hungary is the most appealing market. Obviously, in overall market size, the former Soviet Union countries offer the most attractive market opportunities.

---

[37]For further details, see, for example, David A. Aaker, V. Kumar, and George S. Day, *Marketing Research* (New York, NY: John Wiley & Sons, 1995), Chapter 18.

[38]Our source for the data is *European Marketing Data and Statistics 1992.*

[39]The R^2_{adj} is a measure for the goodness of fit of the regression: the closer to 1.0, the better the fit.

EXHIBIT 6-7
CROSS-SECTIONAL REGRESSION MODEL FOR ANALGESICS

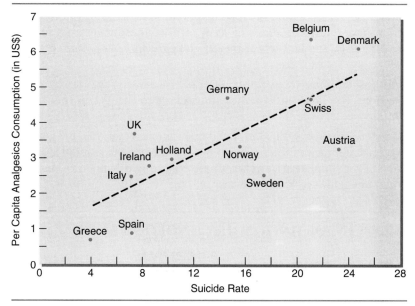

When applying regression to come up with a market size estimate, you should be careful in interpreting the results. For instance, caution is warranted whenever the range of one of the predictors for the countries of interest is outside the range of the countries used to calibrate the regression. In fact, in the previous application, the suicide rates for the Central and Eastern European countries were far above the rates reported for the Western European countries. So, strictly speaking, we should be careful when using our results for decision making. Having said this, regression is probably one of the most handy tools to estimate market sizes, keeping in mind its constraints.

The methods we described are not the only procedures you can use. Other, more sophisticated, procedures exist. Finally, some words of advice. Look at the three estimates for the size of the wallpaper market (in terms of number of rolls) in Morocco, based on different market-size estimation techniques:[40]

Chain Ratio Method:	484,000
Method by Analogy:	1,245,000
Trade Audit:	90,500

You immediately notice a wide gap between the different methods. Such discrepancies are not uncommon. When using market size estimates, keep the following rules in mind:

1. Whenever feasible, use several different methods that possibly rely on different data inputs.

---

[40]Amine and Cavusgil, Table 4.

2. Don't be misled by the numbers. Make sure you know the reasoning behind them.

3. Don't be misled by fancy methods. At some point, increased sophistication will lead to diminishing returns (in terms of accuracy of your estimates), not to mention negative returns. Simple back-of-the-envelope calculations are often a good start.

4. When many assumptions are to be made, do a sensitivity analysis by asking what-if questions. See how sensitive the estimates are to changes in your underlying assumptions.

5. Look for interval estimates with a lower and upper limit rather than for point estimates. The range indicates the precision of the estimates. The limits can later be used for market simulation exercises to see what might happen to the company's bottom line under various scenarios.

◆ ◆ ◆ ◆ ◆ ◆ NEW MARKET INFORMATION TECHNOLOGIES

These days almost all packaged consumer goods come with a bar code. For each purchase transaction, scanner data are gathered at the cash registers of stores that are equipped with laser scanning technology. The emergence of scanner data, coupled with rapid developments in computer hardware (e.g., workstations) and software has led to a revolution in market research. Although most of the early advances in this information revolution took place in the United States, Europe and Japan rapidly followed suit. Exhibit 6-8 illustrates the penetration of scanning technology worldwide. Scanning technology has spurred several sorts of databases. The major ones include:[41]

EXHIBIT 6-8
1993 WORLDWIDE SCANNING PENETRATION (PERCENT ACV[1] SCANNED)

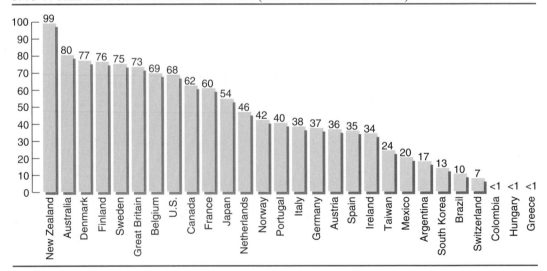

[1]ACV = All Commodity Volume
Source: A. C. Nielsen

---

[41]See, for example, Del I. Hawkins and Donald S. Tull, *Essentials of Marketing Research* (New York: MacMillan Publishing Company, 1994), pp. 115–21.

- **Point-of-Sale (POS) Store Scanner Data.** Companies like A.C. Nielsen and Information Resources obtain sales movement data from the checkout scanner tapes of retail outlets. These data are processed to provide instant information on weekly sales movements and market shares of individual brands, sizes, and product variants. Shifts in sales volume and market shares can be related to changes in the store environment (retail prices, display, and/or feature activity) and competitive moves. In the past, sales tracking was based on store audits or warehouse withdrawal. The advantage of POS scanner data over these traditional ways of data-gathering is obvious: far better data quality.[42] The data are collected on a weekly basis instead of bi-monthly. Further, they are gathered at a very detailed UPC-level, not just the brand level.

- **Consumer Panel Data.** Market research companies such as A.C. Nielsen and Information Resources have consumer panels who record their purchases. There are two approaches to collect household level data. Under the first approach, panel members present an ID card when checking out at the cash register. That information is entered each time the household shops. The alternative approach relies on at-home scanning. Each time the panel member returns from a shopping trip, s/he scans the items that s/he bought. The home-scanning method is favored in Japan for two reasons:[43]

  - Japanese supermarket chains are not very cooperative to install external scanner terminals.
  - Japanese shoppers are highly mobile and shop a lot outside their "designated" panel area.

- **Single-Source Data.** Single source data are continuous data that combine for any given household member TV viewing behavior with purchase transaction (product description, price, promotion, etc.) information. TV viewing behavior is tracked at the panel member's home via so-called people meters. The TV audience measurement system usually requires cooperation of the panel member. Each time the family member watches a program, s/he has to push a button to identify him/herself. More advanced systems involve a camera that records which members of the household are watching TV. Single-source data allow companies to measure, among other things, the effectiveness of their advertising policy.

  Outside the United States, most of the scanning data are store scanning data. Household level data are available in some countries, such as France and Japan, but are still in an infancy stage. Nielsen launched its retail tracking system ScanTrack in Japan in 1993, with plans to add a panel to track consumer behavior and media exposures.[44] In Europe, Nielsen set up a partnership with the U.K. Safeway supermarket chain that allows companies access to scanning data on all categories from all of the chain's 322 outlets.[45] Companies like Nestlé are also

---

[42]Gerry Eskin, "POS Scanner Data: The State of the Art, in Europe and the World," *Marketing and Research Today* (May 1994), pp. 107–17.

[43]Hotaka Katahira and Shigeru Yagi, "Marketing Information Technologies in Japan," in *The Marketing Information Revolution*, ed. R.C. Blattberg, R. Glazer, and J.D.C. Little (Boston, Mass: Harvard Business School, 1994), pp. 306–27.

[44]"Nielsen's Int'l Push for ScanTrack Reaches Japan," *Advertising Age International* (May 17, 1993), p. I-20.

[45]"IRI vs. Nielsen," *Advertising Age* (October 12, 1992), p. 50.

putting together their own databases. These innovations in marketing decision support systems have spurred several major developments in the marketing area:

- **Shift from mass to micro marketing.**[46] Better knowledge on shopping and viewing behavior has moved the focus from mass marketing to the individual. New information technologies enable firms to tailor their pricing, product line, advertising and promotion strategies to particular neighborhoods or even individuals. Database marketing gives companies an opportunity to enter into direct contact with their customers. Nestlé's strategy for its Buitoni pasta brand offers a good example of the power of database marketing in a Pan-European context. In the United Kingdom, Nestlé built up a database of people who had requested a free recipe booklet. The next step was the launch of a Casa Buitoni Club. Members of the club receive a magazine and opportunities to win a trip for cooking instruction. The goal of the strategy is to build a long-term commitment to the Buitoni brand.[47]

- **Continuous monitoring of brand sales/market share movements.** Sales measurement based on scanner data are more accurate and timely than, for instance, data from store audits. In Japan, thousands of new products are launched continuously. Accurate tracking information on new brand shares and incumbent brand shares is crucial information for manufacturers and retailers alike.[48]

- **Scanning data are used by manufacturers to support marketing decisions.** Initially, most scanning data were simply used as tracking devices. This has changed now. Scanning data are increasingly used for tactical decision support. The databases are used to assist all sorts of decisions in inventory management, consumer/trade promotions, pricing, shelf space allocation and media advertising. Scanning data are also increasingly used for category management.

- **Scanning data are used to provide merchandising support to retailers.** Many manufacturers also employ information distilled from scanning data to help out retailers with merchandising programs. Such support helps to build up a long-term relationship with retailers. Scanning data help manufacturers to show the "hard facts" to their distributors.

Richer market information should help global marketers to improve marketing decisions that have cross-border ramifications. Scanning data from the Pan-European region allows marketers to gauge the effectiveness of Pan-European advertising campaigns, branding decisions, distribution strategies, and so forth. The information can also be used to monitor competitors' activities. With the emergence of consumer panel data, marketers are able to spot cross-border similarities and disparities in cross-border consumer behavior. In sum, the consequences of new market research systems appear dramatic. Several environmental forces (e.g., single European market, cultural trends) promote the so-called "global village" with a convergence in tastes, preferences leading to "universal" segments. On the other hand, the new information technologies will ultimately allow marketers to enter into one-to-one relationships with their individual customers.

---

[46]Tim Bowles and Claude Charbit, "Can scanner data achieve their potential in Europe? New questions, new solutions," *Marketing and Research Today*, (May 1997), pp. 121–4.

[47]Stan Rapp and Thomas L. Collins, *Beyond Maxi-Marketing: The New Power of Caring and Sharing* (New York: McGraw-Hill, Inc., 1994).

[48]Katahira and Yagi, p. 310.

Despite the promises of scanner databases, their full potential is not yet exploited in many European countries. Many users still simply view scanner data as an instrument to track market share. Two factors are behind this state of affairs. One reason is the conservatisms of the users of the data. Another factor is the attitude of local retailers toward data access. In countries like the U.K., retailers are reluctant to release their data because they fear that by doing so they might inform their competition. Rivals are not just other retailers but in many cases the manufacturers who compete with the retailer's store brands.

State-of-the-art marketing research tools are also being developed to track the effectiveness of newer marketing mix media vehicles such as the Internet. For instance, the WebAudit is a package designed by ACNielsen Australia that allows subscribers to evaluate the performance of their Web site. Subscribers to the service receive information on user profiles by region, most requested pages, most downloaded files, and so on. The ultimate goal is to establish a "Nielsen rating" for Worldwide Web sites similar to the ratings A.C. Nielsen currently provides for television programming.[49]

MANAGING GLOBAL MARKETING RESEARCH   ◆ ◆ ◆ ◆ ◆ ◆

Global marketing research projects have to cater to the needs of various interest groups: global and regional headquarters, and local subsidiaries. Different requirements will lead to tension among the stakeholders. In this section we center on two highly important issues in managing global marketing research: (1) who should conduct the research project, and (2) coordination of global marketing research projects.

Selecting a Research Agency

Even companies with in-house expertise often employ local research agencies to assist with a multi-country research project. The choice of a research agency to run a multicountry research project is made centrally by headquarters or locally by regional headquarters or country affiliates. Reliance on local research firms is an absolute must in countries such as China, both to be close to the market and to get around government red tape.[50] Local agencies may also have a network of contacts that give access to secondary datasources. Whatever the motive for using a local research agency, selection of an agency should be based on careful scrutiny and screening of possible candidates. The first step is to see what sort of research support services are available to conduct the research project. Each year *Marketing News* (an American Marketing Association publication) puts together a directory of international marketing research firms.

Several considerations enter the agency selection decision. Agencies that are partners or subsidiaries of global research firms are especially useful when there is a strong need for coordination of multicountry research efforts. The agency's level of expertise is the main ingredient in the screening process: What are the qualifications of the staff? the fieldworkers? The track record of the agencies is also a key factor:

---

[49]"Benchmark Standards for Worldwide Web Sites," *ACNielsen SRG News* (October 1996), p. 3.

[50]Steele, p. 158.

How long has the agency been in business? What sort of research problems has it dealt with? What experience does the agency have in tackling our type of research problem(s)? What clients has it worked for? In some cases, it is worthwhile to contact previous or current clients and explore their feelings about the prospective research supplier.

When cross-border coordination is an issue, companies should also examine the willingness of the agency to be flexible and be a good team-player. Communication skills is another important issue. When secrecy is required, it is necessary to examine whether the candidate has any possible conflicts of interest. Has the agency any ties with one of our (potential) competitors? Does it have a good reputation in keeping matters confidential? Again, a background check with previous clients may provide the answer.

Cost is clearly a crucial input in the selection decision. Exhibit 6-9 shows cost indices of doing market research for different types of studies in various places. It illustrates that costs vary substantially, depending on the nature (e.g., telephone tracking versus usage survey) and the place of the study. For instance, attitude surveys, are on average, cheaper in the Pacific Rim countries (87) than in Western Europe (100 = Swiss Francs 40,800). On the other hand, in-home product tests tend to be more expensive in the Pacific Rim countries (144) than in Western Europe (100 = Swiss Francs 12,750). Budget constraints may force firms to go for a second-tier agency. Quality standards can vary a lot. One golden rule needs to be observed though: Beware of agencies that promise the world at a bargain price. Inaccurate and misleading information will almost certainly lead to disastrous decisions.

William Lawson, a marketing manager with the pharmaceutical company Eli Lilly, offers the following tips on how to use market research agencies more productively for global market research projects:[51]

- Use your agency creatively. For example, to "sell" the research findings to the local subsidiaries, market research managers might consider asking the agency to present the results. A third "neutral" party might have more credibility among the local affiliates.

- Take your agency into 100 percent confidence and share everything. Create a partnership.

- Use your agency strategically. Ask for their input, opinions, and their views on the implications of the study's findings.

Coordination of Multi-Country Research

Multi-country research projects demand careful coordination of the research efforts undertaken in the different markets. The benefits of coordination are manifold.[52] Coordination facilitates cross-country comparison of results whenever such comparisons are crucial. It also can have benefits of timeliness, cost, centralization of communication and quality control. Coordination brings up two central issues: (1) who should do the coordinating? and (2) what degree of coordination? In some cases, co-

---

[51]William V. Lawson, "The "Heavyweights"—Forecasting the Obesity Market in Europe for a New Compound," *Marketing and Research Today* (November 1995), pp. 270–74.

[52]Aldridge, p. 361.

EXHIBIT 6-9

CROSS-COUNTRY COST COMPARISON
FOR MARKET RESEARCH STUDIES

Usage & Attitude Survey

Western Europe (SwFrs 40,800)	100	
North America	220	
U.S.A.		234
Canada		202
Japan	181	
Australia	136	
Central/South America	100	
Brazil		114
Argentina		105
Mexico		92
Colombia/Chile/Venezuela		67
South Africa	102	
Middle East	96	
Saudi Arabia		106
U.A.E.		84
Pacific Rim	87	
Hong Kong		140
Indonesia		63
Taiwan/S. Korea		92
Eastern Europe	61	
Hungary		48
Czechoslovakia		65
Poland		62
Russia		81
North Africa	50	
Egypt		49
Turkey	45	
India	13	

Telephone Tracking Study

U.S.A. (SwFrs 36,120)	100
Canada	106
Japan	103
U.S.A.	100
Australia	80
Taiwan	78
Brazil	59
Hong Kong	48
South Africa	47
Argentina	34
Hungary	27
Turkey	26

In-Home Product Test

Western Europe (SwFrs 12,750)	100	
North America	318	
U.S.A.		283
Canada		362
Japan	297	
Central/South America	190	
Brazil		228
Mexico		150
South Africa	188	
Australia	157	
Middle East	151	
Saudi Arabia		165
U.A.E.		129
Pacific Rim	144	
Hong Kong		152
Indonesia		73
Taiwan/S. Korea		187
Eastern Europe	119	
Hungary		94
Czechoslovakia		111
Poland		127
Russia		155
North Africa	100	
Egypt		102
Turkey	77	
India	25	

Four Group Discussions

Western Europe (SwFrs 15,061)	100	
Japan	194	
North America	129	
U.S.A.		135
Canada		115
Pacific Rim	90	
Hong Kong		92
Indonesia		53
Taiwan/S. Korea		133
Central/South America	82	
Brazil		107
Argentina		53
Colombia/Chile/Venezuela		51
Mexico		83
Australia	74	
Middle East	70	
Saudi Arabia		72
U.A.E.		69
South Africa	51	
Eastern Europe	50	
Hungary		51
Czechoslovakia		53
Poland		48
Russia		45
North Africa	33	
Egypt		32
Turkey	51	
India	17	

Source: ESOMAR. Permission for using this material has been granted by (E.S.O.M.A.R.) The European Society for Opinion and Marketing Research J. J. Viottastraat 29, 1071 JP, Amsterdam, The Netherlands

ordination is implemented by the research agency that is hired to run the project. When markets differ a lot or when research agencies vary from country to country, the company itself will prefer to coordinate the project.[53]

The degree of coordination centers around the conflicting demands of various users of marketing research: global (or regional) headquarters and local subsidiaries. Headquarters favor standardized data collection, sampling procedures, survey instruments. Local user groups prefer country-customized research designs that recognize the peculiarities of their local environment. This conflict is referred to as the **emic** versus **etic** dilemma.[54] The **emic** school focuses on the peculiarities of each country. Attitudinal phenomena and values are so unique in each country that they can only be tapped via culture-specific measures. The other school of thought, the etic approach, emphasizes universal behavioral and attitudinal traits. To gauge such phenomena requires culturally unbiased measures.

In cross-cultural market research, the need for comparability favors the **etic** paradigm with an emphasis on the cross-border similarities and parallels. Nevertheless, in order to make the research study useful and acceptable to local users, companies need to recognize the peculiarities of local cultures. So, ideally, survey instruments that are developed for cross-country market research projects should encompass both approaches—*emic* and *etic*.[55] There are several approaches to balance these conflicting demands. In a Pan-European positioning study conducted for BMW, coordination was accomplished via the following measures:[56]

1. All relevant parties (users at headquarters and local subsidiaries) were included from the outset in planning the research project.
2. All parties contributed in funding the study.
3. Hypotheses and objectives were deemed to be binding at later stages of the project.
4. Data collection went through two stages. First, responses to a country-specific pool of psychographic statements were collected. The final data collection in the second stage used a mostly standardized survey instrument containing a few statements that were country-customized (based on findings from the first run).

The key lessons of the BMW example are twofold. First, coordination means that all parties (i.e., user groups) should get involved. Neglected parties will have little incentive to accept the results of the research project. Second, multi-country research should allow some leeway for country peculiarities. For instance, questionnaires should not be overstandardized but may include some country-specific items. This is especially important for collecting so-called "soft" data (e.g., lifestyle/attitude statements).

---

[53]"Multi-Country Research: Should You Do Your Own Coordinating?" *Industrial Marketing Digest*, 1985, pp. 79–82.

[54]Douglas and Craig, pp. 132–37.

[55]Malhotra, Agarwal, and Peterson, p. 12.

[56]Kern, Wagner, and Hassis, pp. 49–50.

SUMMARY ❖

Whenever you drive to an unknown destination, you will probably use a road map, ask for instructions to get there, and examine the road signals. If not, you risk getting lost. By the same token, whenever you need to make marketing decisions in the global marketplace, market intelligence will guide you in these endeavors. Shoddy information invariably leads to shoddy decision making. Good information will facilitate solid decision making. In this day and age, having timely and adequate market intelligence also provides a competitive advan-

tage. This does not mean that global marketers should do research at any cost. As always, it is important to examine at each step the incremental costs and the value added of having more information. Usually it is not hard to figure out the costs of gathering market intelligence. The hard part is the benefit component. Views on the benefits and role of market research sometimes differ between cultures. Global Perspective 6-2 highlights the peculiarities of Japanese firms' approach to marketing research.

GLOBAL PERSPECTIVE 6-2

HOW DOES JAPANESE MARKET RESEARCH DIFFER?

There is a philosophical difference in the role of marketing research between U.S./European and Japanese executives. Marketing researchers in the United States (and also to some extent within Europe) believe that various dimensions of consumer attitudes and behaviors can be measured with statistical tools. Japanese marketing researchers, however, believe that those tools are not sufficient to gauge the vagrant nature of consumer attitudes. As a result, Japanese marketing researchers rely far less on statistical techniques than their U.S. counterparts.

Toru Nishikawa, marketing manager at Hitachi, lists five reasons against "scientific" market research in the area of new product development:

1. Indifference of respondents. Careless random sampling leads to mistaken judgments, because some people are indifferent toward the product in question.

2. Absence of responsibility. The consumer is most sincere when spending, not when talking.

3. Conservative attitudes. Ordinary consumers are

conservative and tend to react negatively to new product ideas.

4. Vanity. It is part of human nature to exaggerate and put on a good appearance.

5. Insufficient information. The research results depend on information about product characteristics given to survey participants.

Japanese firms prefer more down-to-earth methods of information gathering. Instead of administering surveys, Japanese market researchers will go into the field and observe how consumers use the product. For example, Toyota sent a group of engineers and designers to Southern California to observe how women get into and operate their cars. They found that women with long fingernails have trouble opening the door and handling various knobs on the dashboard. Consequently, Toyota altered some of their automobiles' exterior and interior designs.

Hands-on market research does not negate the importance of conventional marketing research. In fact, scores of Japanese firms assign more people to information gathering and analysis than U.S. firms. What is unique about Japanese market research is that Japanese research teams include both product engineers and sales and marketing representatives. Engineers gain insights from talking with prospective customers as much as their marketing peers. They can directly incorporate user comments into product specifications.

Sources: Michael R. Czinkota and Masaaki Kotabe, "Product Development the Japanese Way," *Journal of Business Strategy*, 11 (Nov./Dec. 1990), pp. 31–36, and Johny K. Johansson and Ikujiro Nonaka, *Relentless: The Japanese Way of Marketing* (New York: Harper Business, 1996).

The complexities of the global marketplace are stunning. They pose a continuous challenge to market researchers. Hurdles are faced in gathering secondary and primary data. Not all challenges will be met successfully. Mistakes are easily made. One American toiletries manufacturer conducted its market research in (English-speaking) Toronto for a bar soap to be launched in (French-speaking) Québec. The whole venture became a sad soap opera with a tragic ending.[57] In this chapter we discussed the intricacies in developing and implementing a market research project in a cross-national setting. We also reviewed several techniques that prove useful to estimate the market size whenever few or only poor-quality data are at your disposal.

To make cross-country comparisons meaningful, companies need to adequately manage and coordinate their market research projects with a global scope. Inputs from local users of the research are desirable for several reasons. When the locals feel that they have been treated stepmotherly, it will be hard to "sell" the findings of the research project. As a result, getting their support for policies based on the study's conclusions becomes a formidable task. Local feedback also becomes necessary to uncover country-specific peculiarities that cannot be tapped with overstandardized measurement instruments.

REVIEW QUESTIONS ◆

1. What are the major benefits and limitations of omnibus surveys?

2. What is the notion of "triangulation" in global market research?

3. Discuss the major issues in running focus group discussions in an international context.

4. Discuss why market size estimates may differ, depending on the method being used. How can such differences be reconciled?

5. Contrast the emic versus the etic approach in international marketing research.

DISCUSSION QUESTIONS ◆

1. Chapter 6 suggests two ways to select countries for multicountry market research projects: (1) start with a preliminary research in each one of them, or (2) cluster the countries and pick one representative member from each cluster. Under what circumstances would you prefer one option over the other one?

2. Refer to Exhibit 6–6, which presents McDonald's market potential based on the formula given on page 168.

   (a) Using the same formula, estimate what McDonald's market potential would be for the following Pacific-Rim countries: Indonesia, Malaysia, Myanmar, the Philippines, Singapore, South Korea, Taiwan, and Thailand.

   (b) Which of these markets looks most appealing in terms of market size?

   (c) What factors are missing in the formula that McDonald's uses?

3. In most cases, standard data collection methods are still mail, phone, or personal interviewing. Tokyu Agency, Tokyo, a Japanese ad agency, has started using the Internet to find out how Japanese youngsters spend their money and what their views are on various issues (e.g., environment). What opportunities does the Internet offer as a data-gathering tool in international market research? What are its merits and disadvantages in this regard?

4. Clarion Marketing and Communications, a Connecticut-based marketing research firm, recently launched Global Focus, a technique that allows companies to run focus groups in different countries who interact with each other. The focus groups are held in videoconference centers in the different cities

---

[57]Sandra Vandermerwe, "Colgate-Palmolive: Cleopatra," Case Study, Lausanne: IMD, 1990.

(e.g., one in New York; one in London) with a moderator in each location. Do you see a need for "global focus groups"? Why ? (or why not?) What are potential benefits? concerns?

5. Imagine that Nokia plans to expand its market in South America. Use the chain-ratio method to come up with market size estimates for cellular phones in the following four countries: Argentina, Brazil, Chile, and Peru.

6. When developing a survey instrument for a cross-country study, market researchers often need to construct a scale (e.g., a 7-point disagree/agree scale). What major items should one be concerned about when building such scales?

FURTHER READINGS ◆

Aldridge, D. N. "Multi-Country Research." In *Applied Marketing and Social Research*, ed. U. Bradley, 2d ed. New York: John Wiley & Sons, 1987.

Amine, S. Lyn, and S. Tamer Cavusgil. "Demand Estimation in a Developing Country Environment: Difficulties, Techniques and Examples." *Journal of the Market Research Society*, 28(1) (1986): 43–65.

Choudhry, Yusuf A. "Pitfalls in International Marketing Research: Are You Speaking French Like a Spanish Cow?" *Akron Business and Economic Review*, 17(4): (Winter 1986), 18–28.

Douglas, Susan P., and C. Samuel Craig. *International Marketing Research*. Englewood Cliffs, N.J.: Prentice Hall, 1983.

Eskin, Gerry. "POS Scanner Data: The State of the Art, in Europe and the World." *Marketing and Research Today* (May 1994): 107–17.

Hibbert, Edgar. "Researching International Markets—How Can We Ensure Validity of Results?" *Marketing and Research Today* (November 1993): 222–28.

Johansson, K. Johny, and Ikujiro Nonaka. "Market Research the Japanese Way." *Harvard Business Review* (May-June 1987): 16–22.

Malhotra, Naresh K., James Agarwal, and Mark Peterson. "Methodological Issues in Cross-Cultural Marketing Research. A State-of-the-Art Review." *International Marketing Review*, 13(5) (1996): 7–43.

Steele, Henry C. "Marketing Research in China: The Hong Kong Connection." *Marketing and Research Today* (August, 1990): 155–64.

Tuncalp, Secil. "The Marketing Research Scene in Saudi Arabia." *European Journal of Marketing*, 22(5) (1988): 15–22.

Williams, S. C. "Researching Markets in Japan—A Methodological Case Study." *Journal of International Marketing*, 4(2) (1996): 87–93.

GLOBAL SEGMENTATION AND POSITIONING

7

HAPTER OVERVIEW

1. REASONS FOR INTERNATIONAL MARKET SEGMENTATION
2. INTERNATIONAL MARKET SEGMENTATION APPROACHES
3. BASES FOR COUNTRY SEGMENTATION
4. COUNTRY SEGMENTATION TOOLS
5. ISSUES IN INTERNATIONAL MARKET SEGMENTATION
6. INTERNATIONAL POSITIONING STRATEGIES

Few companies can be all things to all people. Instead of competing across the board, most companies will identify and target the most attractive market segments that they can serve effectively. Variation in customer needs is the primary motive for market segmentation. When consumer preferences vary, marketers can design a marketing mix program that is tailored toward the needs of the specific segments that the firm targets. Marketers select one or more segmentation bases (e.g., age) and slice up their prospective customer base according to the chosen criteria. Marketing programs are then developed that are in tune with the particular needs of each of the segments that the companies want to serve.

In global marketing, market segmentation becomes especially critical, given the sometimes incredibly wide divergence in cross-border consumer needs and preferences. In this chapter we will first focus on the motivations for international market segmentation. Given information on the segmentation criteria you plan to use, there are several country segmentation approaches you might take. We describe in detail two perspectives. We then consider several bases that marketers might consider for country segmentation. To assist you with implementing a segmentation analysis, we discuss some useful tools. We will also highlight the major pitfalls you might encounter when doing a cross-country segmentation. The final section focuses on possible international positioning strategies.

◆ ◆ ◆ ◆ ◆ ◆ REASONS FOR INTERNATIONAL MARKET SEGMENTATION

The goal of market segmentation is to break down the market for a product or a service into different groups of consumers that differ in their response to the firm's marketing mix program. That way, the firm can tailor its marketing mix to each individual segment, and, hence, do a better job in satisfying the needs of the target segments. This overall objective also applies in an international marketing context. In that sense, market segmentation is the logical outgrowth of the marketing concept.[1]

The requirements for effective market segmentation in a domestic marketing context also apply in international market segmentation. In particular, segments ideally should possess the following set of properties:[2]

1. **Measurable.** The segments should be easy to define and to measure. This criterion is easily met for "objective" country traits such as socioeconomic variables (e.g., per capita income). However, the size of segments based on cultural or lifestyle indicators is typically much harder to gauge.

2. **Sizable.** The segments should be large enough to be worth going after. Note that flexible manufacturing technologies enable companies to relax this criterion. In fact, many segments that might be considered too small in a single-country context become attractive once they are lumped across borders.

3. **Accessible.** The segments should also be easy to reach via the media. Differences in the quality of the media infrastructure (e.g., absence or presence of commercial television) imply that a given segment might be hard to reach in some countries and easy to target in other marketplaces.

4. **Actionable.** For market segmentation to be meaningful, it is important that effective marketing programs (the four Ps) can be developed to evoke the desired response from the target segment. When segments do not respond differently to the firm's marketing mix, there is basically no need to segment the market.

5. **Competitive Intensity.** Preferably, the segments are not preempted by the firm's competition. In fact, in global marketing, small companies often use competitive pressure as one of their segmentation criteria when assessing international markets.

6. **Growth Potential.** Finally, segments should hopefully have a significant growth potential. In practice, identifying market segments with promising growth prospects and low competitive pressure is quite challenging. Typically, marketers face a trade-off between competitive intensity and growth prospects.

Let us consider now the major reasons why international marketers implement international market segmentation.

---

[1]Yoram Wind and Susan P. Douglas, "International Market Segmentation," *European Journal of Marketing*, 6(1) (1972), pp. 17–25.

[2]See, for instance, R. E. Frank, W. F. Massy and Y. Wind, *Market Segmentation* (Englewood-Cliffs, N.J.: Prentice-Hall, 1971).

Country Screening

Companies usually do a preliminary screening of countries before identifying attractive market opportunities for their product or service. For preliminary screening, market analysts rely on a few indicators, for which information can easily be gathered from secondary data sources. At this stage, the international market analyst might classify countries in two or three piles. Countries that meet all criteria will be grouped in the "Go" pile for further consideration at the next stage. Countries that fail to meet most of the criteria will enter the "No Go" pile. The third set of countries are those that meet some of the criteria but not all of them. In a sense, these countries are in a *twilight zone*—the "On" pile. They may become of interest in the future, but probably not in the short term.

Companies will use different sets of criteria to screen countries, depending on the nature of the product. For example, Kellogg uses the population size to classify candidate markets. Jordan, a small Norwegian toothbrush maker, groups countries based on competitive intensity and growth potential (measured via per-capita consumption of toothbrushes). Given its small size, the firm's strategy is to be a niche-player shooting for markets with low competitive pressure and favorable growth opportunities.[3]

Global Market Research

Country segmentation also plays a role in global marketing research. Companies increasingly make an effort to design products or services that meet the needs of customers in different countries. Certain features might need to be added or altered, but the core product is largely common across countries. Other aspects of the marketing mix program such as the communication strategy might also be similar. The benefits of a standardization approach often outweigh the possible drawbacks. Yet in order to successfully adopt this approach, companies need to do sufficient market research. Given the sheer number of countries in which many companies operate, doing market research in each one of them is often inefficient. Especially at the early stage, companies are likely to focus on a select few countries. The key question, then, is which countries to choose. One approach is to start grouping prospective markets into clusters of homogeneous countries. Out of each group, one prototypical member is chosen. Research efforts will be concentrated on each of the key members, at least initially. Presumably, research findings for the selected key member countries can then be projected to other countries belonging to its cluster. For example, Heineken chose four countries to do market research for Buckler, a nonalcoholic beer: the Netherlands, Spain, the United States, and France. The Dutch brewer wanted to assess the market appeal of Buckler and the feasibility of a Pan-European marketing strategy.[4]

---

[3]Per V. Jenster and Kamran Kashani, "Jordan A/S," Case Study, International Institute for Management Development, Lausanne, Switzerland, 1991.

[4]Sandra Vandermerwe, "Heineken NV: Buckler Nonalcoholic Beer," Case Study, International Institute for Management Development, Switzerland, 1991.

Entry Decisions

When a product or service does well in one country, firms often hope to replicate their success story in other countries. The strategic logic is to launch the product in countries that in some regards are highly similar to the country where the product has already been introduced.[5] For example, Cadbury-Schweppes was confident about launching Schweppes tonic water in Brazil, given that the beverage was well accepted in culturally similar countries such as Mexico.

It is important, though, to realize that a host of factors make or break the success of a new product launch. Tabasco sauce is very popular in many Asian countries with a strong liking for spicy dishes. Hence, McIlhenny, the Louisiana-based maker of Tabasco sauce, might view entering Vietnam and India, two of the emerging markets in Asia with a palate for hot food, as the logical next step for its expansion strategy in Asia. Other factors, however, such as buying power, import restrictions, or the shoddy state of the distribution and media infrastructure, might lessen the appeal of these markets.

Positioning Strategy

Segmentation decisions are also instrumental in setting the company's product positioning strategy. Once the firm has selected the target segments, management needs to develop a positioning strategy to embrace the chosen segments. Basically, the company must decide on how it wants to position its products or services in the mind of the prospective target customers. Environmental changes or shifting consumer preferences often force a firm to rethink its positioning strategy. Cathay Pacific's recent repositioning strategy is a good example. The Hong Kong–based airline carrier realized that its product offerings failed to adequately meet the needs of its Asian clients, who represent 80 percent of its customer base. To better satisfy this target segment the airline repositioned itself in the fall of 1994 to become the preferred airline among Asian travelers. To that end, Cathay wanted to project an Asian personality with a personal touch. Cathay now offers a wide variety of Asian meals and entertainment. Other measures include a new logo (by some people referred to as a shark-fin), new colors, repainted exteriors, and redesigned cabins and ticket counters. To communicate these changes to the public, Cathay launched a heavy advertising campaign with the slogan "The Heart of Asia."[6]

Marketing Mix Policy

In domestic marketing, segmentation and positioning decisions will dictate a firm's marketing mix policy. By the same token, country segmentation will guide the global marketer's mix decisions. A persistent problem faced by international marketers is how to strike the balance between standardization and customization. International market segmentation could shed some light on this issue. Members falling in the same segment might lend themselves to a standardized marketing mix strategy. The same product design, an identical pricing policy, similar advertising messages and

[5]Johny K. Johansson and Reza Moinpour, "Objective and Perceived Similarity for Pacific-Rim Countries," *Columbia Journal of World Business* (Winter 1977), pp. 65–76.

[6]John Pies, Cathay Pacific, private communication, 1996.

EXHIBIT 7-1
"THINK" AND "FEEL" COUNTRY CLUSTERS

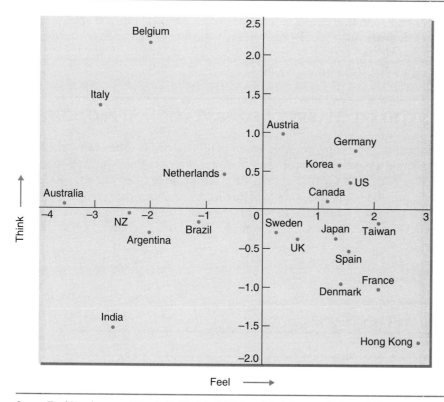

Source: Fred Zandpour and Katrin R. Harich, "Think and Feel Country Clusters: A New Approach to International Advertising Standardization," *International Journal of Advertising*, 15 (1996) p. 341. Copyright Advertising Association.

media, and the same distribution channels could be used in these markets. Of course, marketers need to be very careful when contemplating such moves. There should be a clear linkage between the segmentation bases and the target customers' responsiveness to any of these four Ps. Usually, it is very hard to establish a linkage between market segments and all four elements of the marketing mix. For instance, countries with an underdeveloped phone infrastructure (e.g., Eastern Europe, China, Thailand) are typically prime candidates for mobile phone technologies. However, many of these countries dramatically differ in terms of their price sensitivities, given the wide gaps in purchasing power. So, treating them as one group as far as the pricing policy goes might lead to disastrous consequences.

Exhibit 7-1 illustrates how country segmentation can be applied in developing international advertising strategies.[7] The mapping comes from a recent study that predicted the preference of a country in terms of rational ("think") and emotional

[7]Fred Zandpour and Katrin R. Harich, "Think and Feel Country Clusters: A New Approach to International Advertising Standardization," *International Journal of Advertising*, 15 (1996), pp. 325–44.

("feel") appeals based on the country's cultural and advertising industry environment (e.g., level of government regulation, per-capita ad spending, media characteristics). The "think" strategy uses argumentation and the lecture format to address the target audience. "Feel" appeals are centered around emotions (psychological appeals) often phrased in a dramatic format. The map shows four distinctive clusters. For instance, five countries (Austria, Canada, Germany, South Korea, and the United States) fall into the "high feel"/ "high think" region.

◆ ◆ ◆ ◆ ◆ ◆ INTERNATIONAL MARKET SEGMENTATION APPROACHES

Global marketers approach the segmentation process from different angles. The standard country segmentation procedure classifies prospect countries on a single dimension (e.g., per capita Gross National Product) or on a set of multiple socioeconomic, political, and cultural criteria available from secondary data sources (e.g., the World Bank, UNESCO, OECD). Exhibit 7-2 presents a list of various general country characteristics that analysts might consider for classifying countries in distinct

EXHIBIT 7-2
MACRO-LEVEL COUNTRY CHARACTERISTICS

Construct	Items
1. Aggregate Production and Transportation (Mobility)	Number of air passengers/km
	Air cargo (ton/km)
	Number of newspapers
	Population
	Cars per capita
	Motor gasoline consumption per capita
	Electricity production
2. Health	Life expectancy
	Physicians per capita
	Political stability
3. Trade	Imports/GNP
	Exports/GNP
4. Lifestyle	GDP per capita
	Phones per capita
	Electricity consumption per capita
5. Cosmopolitanism	Foreign visitors per capita
	Tourist expenditures per capita
	Tourist receipts per capita
6. Miscellaneous	Consumer price index
	Newspaper circulation
	Hospital beds
	Education expenditures/Government budget
	Graduate education in population per capita

Source: Kristiaan Helsen, Kamel Jedidi and Wayne S. DeSarbo, "A New Approach to Country Segmentation Utilizing Multinational Diffusion Patterns," *Journal of Marketing* 57(4) (October 1993), p. 64.

Reprinted with permission from the *Journal of Marketing*, published by the American Marketing Association.

EXHIBIT 7-3
TWO- AND THREE-SEGMENT SOLUTIONS

A. Two-Segment Solution

Segment 1	Segment 2
Austria	Japan
Belgium	Sweden
Denmark	U.S.
France	
Finland	
Holland	
Norway	
Switzerland	
U.K.	

B. Three-Segment Solution

Segment 1	Segment 2	Segment 3
Holland	Austria	U.S.
Japan	Belgium	
Sweden	Denmark	

Source: Kristiaan Helsen, Kamel Jedidi, and Wayne S. DeSarbo, "A New Approach to Country Segmentation Utilizing Multinational Diffusion Patterns," *Journal of Marketing*, 57(4) (October 1993), p. 66.

Reprinted with permission from the *Journal of Marketing*, published by the American Marketing Association.

segments. When there are numerous country traits, the segmentation variables are usually first collapsed into a smaller set of dimensions using data reduction techniques such as factor analysis. For instance, the set of variables listed in Exhibit 7-2 can be summarized via four constructs: mobility ("aggregate production and transportation"), health, trade, lifestyle, and, cosmopolitanism.[8] The countries under consideration are then classified into homogeneous groups using statistical algorithms such as cluster analysis.

Exhibit 7-3 presents the results for a three-cluster country segmentation along the five constructs listed in Exhibit 7-2. Note that the U.S. forms a cluster of its own. We also observe that Japan is grouped with some of the European countries. In general, macro-level segments seldom match geographic groupings. The problem with macro-level segmentation is that the resulting country groupings do not necessarily correspond to market response measures (e.g., penetration rate, purchase intention, willingness-to-pay).

From a marketer's perspective, the practical usefulness of macro-level segments is questionable. To address this shortcoming of the standard country segmentation

---

[8]Arguably, the labeling of these constructs is somewhat subjective. Factor analysis solutions are seldom clear-cut.

approach, an alternative procedure could be considered. This method proceeds as follows:[9]

Step 1 *Criteria Development:* Determine your cut-off criteria. For example, for Waste Management International, one of the requirements is the convertibility of the local currency. The criteria will be driven by product and company characteristics.

Step 2 *Preliminary Screening:* Examine which countries meet the thresholds for the criteria set forward in Step 1. Countries that do meet the cut-off will be retained. Those that fail to make the cut are thrown out.

Step 3 *Microsegmentation:* Develop microsegments in each of the countries that are still in your consideration set. There are two ways to come up with these segments:

1. Derive microsegments in each country individually. Survey data collected from prospect customers in each of the countries are used as inputs. The nature of the variables is similar to the ones used in domestic segmentation applications (e.g., demographics, lifestyle). In the next step, the analyst consolidates the microsegments across countries, based on similarities across the microsegments in the prospect countries.

2. Alternatively, you could jointly group individuals in all the prospect countries to come up directly with cross-border segments.

Marketing practitioners are more likely to benefit from the second approach, since it is in tune with the marketing concept. For any given product country, each country might consist of several consumer groupings that cross borders. This phenomenon is illustrated in Exhibit 7-4 where we have one universal segment ("A") while the other segments are either unique to the country or exist in only two of the three countries.

EXHIBIT 7-4
DIFFERENT SEGMENT SCENARIOS

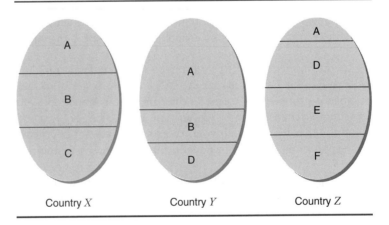

Country *X*   Country *Y*   Country *Z*

---

[9]Sudhir H. Kale and D. Sudharshan, "A Strategic Approach to International Segmentation," *International Marketing Review* (Summer 1987), pp. 60–70.

Global marketers have three choices in terms of their target marketing strategies, namely universal segments, diverse segments, and a mixture of the two:[10]

Universal Segments. Concentrate on cross-border segments that transcend national boundaries. Marketers appealing to universal segments have two approaches to reach their targets. One option is to adopt a largely standardized strategy. Alternatively, they might go for a country-tailored strategy that recognizes differences between the various countries. The undifferentiated approach will lead to scale economies. Differentiated strategies, however, that in a sense *globalize*—by pursuing global segments—and *localize*—by allowing for local peculiarities within the universal segment—often create more demand, being more market-oriented.[11] The Nokia 9000 Communicator exemplifies a product that is targeted toward a universal segment, in this case the business traveler. The product ($1,500) combines phone, fax, e-mail, and Internet functions and weighs less than a pound. To roll out the innovation, Nokia used a global campaign with the slogan "Everything. Everywhere."[12]

Diverse Segments. The second approach focuses on local segments that differ from country to country. The same product reaches different segments in each target market. Other elements of the marketing mix strategy (e.g., positioning, communication strategy, and pricing) are usually also differentiated. A case in point is the Canon AE-1 camera. In Japan, Canon focused on young replacement buyers. In the United States, the target was upscale, first-time buyers of 35mm single-lens reflex cameras.

Mixture of Universal and Diverse Segments. Multinational companies (MNCs) with the wherewithal do not need to settle for an either-or question. Instead, they can pursue both universal and local segments. Many large consumer goods companies like Unilever, Procter & Gamble, and PepsiCo sell a mixture of global (or pan-regional) brands and local brands.

A typical example of a universal consumer segment is the "global teenagers" segment. Although similarities exist within the youth market, there are also major differences, sometimes even within a single region. For instance, according to the results of one survey of the Pan-European youth market, feminism is in vogue in Norway but out of fashion in the United Kingdom. Other idiosyncrasies of the youth market in Europe are highlighted in Exhibit 7-5. Another important problem with this particular segment is that it tends to be a very volatile market with fickle tastes. To keep in touch with the teenager segment, consumer-goods marketers spend more on in-house research and experiment with new media vehicles (e.g., the Internet).[13]

---

[10]Hirotaka Takeuchi and Michael E. Porter, "Three Roles of International Marketing in Global Strategy," in *Competition in Global Industries*, ed. M. E. Porter (Boston, Mass.: Harvard Business School Press, 1986).

[11]Ugur Yavas, Bronislaw J. Verhage, and Robert T. Green, "Global Consumer Segmentation versus Local Market Orientation," *Management International Review*, 32(3) (1992), pp. 265–272.

[12]"Nokia Trying to Lighten Business Traveler's Load," *Advertising Age International* (October 1996), p. I-3, I-4

[13]"Tracking What's Trendy, Hot Before It's Old," *Advertising Age International* (May 1996), p. I-30.

EXHIBIT 7-5
WHAT MATTERS TO YOUNG EUROPEANS

Country	What's In
Austria	Snowboarding
Germany	Anything goes; be more liberal and individualistic
Italy	Music and films; do-it-yourself
Netherlands	Get a tattoo, pierce your body, shave your head, or stripe your hair in different colors
Norway	Join feminist movement; surf the Internet; be ecologically aware
U.K.	Be sexually aware; chauvinism

Source: Magic Hat, youth research arm of Mc-Cann Erickson, London.

◆ ◆ ◆ ◆ ◆ ◆ BASES FOR COUNTRY SEGMENTATION

The first step in doing international market segmentation is deciding which criteria to use in the task. Just as in a domestic marketing context, the marketing analyst faces an embarrassment of riches. Literally hundreds of country characteristics could be used as inputs. In a sense, you can pick and choose variables. However, for the segmentation to be meaningful, there should be a linkage between the market segments and the response variable(s) the company is interested in. Usually it is not a trivial exercise to figure out beforehand which variables will contribute to the segmentation. Instead, the marketing analyst will need to do some experimentation to find the "right" ingredients. Further, information on several segmentation criteria is typically missing, inaccurate, or outdated for some of the countries to be grouped.

We now briefly discuss different types of country variables that are most commonly used for country segmentation purposes. Most of these criteria can be used for the two segmentation approaches that we discussed earlier. For instance, one could use a socioeconomic variable like "per capita income" as a segmentation base to group countries. However, one could also use this dimension to segment consumers within country first and then derive pan-regional or global segments (e.g., pan-Asian middle class).

Demographics

Demographic variables are among the most popular segmentation criteria. They are easy to assess (recall the "measurability" requirement for effective market segmentation). Moreover, information on population variables is mostly reasonably accurate and readily available. Possible segmentation bases include population size, age structure, urbanization degree, ethnic composition, and birth/death rates. For many consumer goods, especially low-ticket items, population size is a good proxy for market potential.

Countries with an aging population clearly offer market opportunities for consumer goods and services that cater to the elderly. Examples are geriatric care, travel-related services, leisure items, and medicines. Societies that are highly urbanized share many problems, such as traffic congestion, environmental pollution, and criminality, to mention a few. By the same token, countries with high birth rates have

similar buying patterns. Examples of goods and services with high potential in such countries include babyfood and clothing, toys, prenatal care services, and birth-control devices. Global Perspective 7-1 focuses on the buying habits of the Asian teenagers segment.

Socioeconomic Variables

If you draw a circle with a 250-mile radius around the German city Cologne, you cover 50 million of the wealthiest consumers in the Pan-European market.[14] This so-called "Golden Circle" offers tremendous opportunities to marketers of luxury goods (e.g., LVMH, BMW), high-end services (e.g., resorts, Internet access, mutual funds) and leisure-activity-related goods.

Consumption patterns for many goods and services are largely driven by the consumer wealth or the country's level of economic development in general. Consumers from countries at the same stage of economic development often show similar needs in terms of the per-capita amount and types of goods they desire. One well-known income-based schema considers five stages of economic development:[15]

---

[14]Graham Hinton and Jane Hourigan, "The Golden Circles: Marketing in the New Europe," *The Journal of European Business*, 1(6) (July/August 1990), pp. 5–30.

[15]W. W. Rostow, *The Stages of Economic Growth* (London: Cambridge University Press, 1960).

1. **Traditional societies.** Countries at this stage are viewed as economic basket cases. Most of them remain in a relentless quagmire of enormous poverty, low productivity, high illiteracy, and low levels of technology. Many Sub-Saharan African countries belong to this group.

2. **Preconditions for take-off.** The second stage includes countries that are making the transition to the take-off phase. Advances in science and technology enter the agricultural sector. Examples of countries belonging to this group are the Philippines, Myanmar, Vietnam, Albania, and Romania. The first steps are taken to develop the infrastructure needed for industrialization, leading to the next stage:

3. **The take-off.** At this step, the infrastructure is mainly in place, spurring city-centered industries. Most of the ASEAN countries, such as Thailand, Malaysia, and Indonesia, can be considered as take-off economies. Modernization leads to rapid development in all sectors of the country's economy.

4. **The drive to maturity.** Countries entering this stage are able to produce a wide variety of products. The service sector gains prominence. Most Central European countries (e.g., Hungary, Poland, Czech Republic) and countries such as Singapore and South Korea have reached this stage.

5. **High mass-consumption.** The final stage includes countries that have a sizable middle class with significant discretionary incomes. The economies of these countries have a highly developed service sector. Most of these countries are major players in international trade. In fact, they have formed their own "club" so to speak: the OECD (Organization for Economic Cooperation and Development).

Not surprisingly, many consumer-good marketers view per-capita income, or a comparable measure, as one of the key criteria in grouping international markets. The usual caveats in using per capita income as an economic development indicator apply also when this measure is used for country segmentation:[16]

- **Monetization of transactions within a country.** To compare measures such as per-capita GNP across countries, figures based on a local currency need to be translated into a common currency (e.g., the U.S. dollar or the ECU). However, official exchange rates seldom reflect the purchasing power parity (PPP) of a currency. So, income figures based on GNP or GDP do not really tell you how much a household in a given country is able to buy.

- **Gray and black sectors of the economy.** National income figures only record transactions that arise in the legitimate sector of a country's economy. Many countries have a sizable *gray* sector, consisting of largely untaxed (or under-taxed) exchanges that often involve barter transactions. In cities like Moscow, many professors make ends meet by driving a taxi. In exchange for a dental checkup, a television repairman might fix the dentist's television set. Many societies also thrive on a substantial *black sector*, involving transactions that are

---

[16]Vern Terpstra and Kenneth David, *The Cultural Environment of International Business* (Cincinnati, Ohio: South-Western Publishing Co., 1991).

outright illegal. Examples of such activities include the drug trade, smuggling, racketeering, gambling, and prostitution.

- **Income disparities.** Quantities such as the per-capita GNP only tell part of the story. Such measures are misleading in countries with wide income inequalities. India, for example, has a sizable group of upscale consumers, despite its low per-capita income.

To protect against these shortcomings of standard "per-capita income" segmentation exercises, marketers might consider other methods to group consumers in terms of their buying power.[17] One alternative is to use PPP (Purchasing Power Parity) as a criterion. PPP reflects how much a household in each country has to spend (in U.S. dollars equivalent) to buy a standard basket of goods. The World Bank publishes PPP statistics every year in its *World Bank Atlas*.

Another alternative to analyze buying power in a set of countries is via a Socio-Economic Strata (SES) analysis. For instance, Strategy Research Corporation recently applied an SES-analysis for Latin American households using measures like the number of consumer durables in the household, education level, and so on. Each country was stratified into five socioeconomic segments, each one designated with a letter: upper-class (A), middle- to upper-class (B), middle-class (C), lower-class (D), and poverty level (E). Exhibit 7-6 shows the relative sizes of the various SES segments (D and E are combined) in several Latin American countries.

EXHIBIT 7-6

LATIN-AMERICAN MARKETS: MANY LATIN HOUSEHOLDS HAVE LOTS OF SPENDING MONEY. (PERCENT DISTRIBUTION OF SELECTED LATIN-AMERICAN COUNTRIES BY SES SEGMENTS, 1994)

	upper class	*middle-to-upper class*	*middle class*	*lower class and subsistence level*
Argentina	2%	9%	35%	55%
Brazil	3	16	29	53
Chile	2	6	42	50
Colombia	2	8	37	53
Ecuador	2	15	22	61
Mexico	2	12	30	56
Paraguay	3	12	34	51
Peru	3	8	33	56
Uruguay	8	20	36	36
Venezuela	1	4	36	59

Note: Class designations correspond to Socioeconomic Strata (SES) segments.

Source: Chip Walker, "The Global Middle Class," *American Demographics*, Sept. 1995, pp. 40–46. Reprinted with permission. ©1995 American Demographics.

---

[17]Chip Walker, "The Global Middle Class," *American Demographics* (September 1995), pp. 40–46.

Culture

Cultural traits provide another basis to classify countries. Culture covers a broad range of factors. Some of these variables, such as religion, language, and education are easy to measure. The more interesting cultural factors are much harder to establish. For instance, the aesthetic preferences of a society clearly have ramifications for product design and the creative aspects of an advertising campaign. Unfortunately, the marketer faces an enormous task in developing reliable measures that tap into this particular cultural dimension.

In some instances, marketers could rely on well-established measurement scales for culture-based market segmentation. Research done by the Dutch scholar Hofstede[18] has led to the development of four cultural dimensions along which countries are classified (see Chapter 4 for a more detailed discussion):

1. **Individualism versus collectivism (IND).** Individualism refers to how members of a given culture relate to one another. In societies that are high on collectivism, the group is the major focus. Such societies stress group ties and social cohesion. In countries where individualism is highly praised, people prefer to act as individuals and look after their own self-interests.

2. **Power distance (PD).** Power distance refers to how a society handles inequality among its members. At one end of the spectrum are societies high in power distance. They accept inequities in the area of power and wealth. At the other end are low PD communities that find such inequalities unacceptable and are much more egalitarian-oriented.

3. **Uncertainty avoidance (UA).** People from cultures high on the uncertainty avoidance dimension tend to feel threatened by uncertainties and ambiguities. Generally speaking, members of high UA societies tend to be quite risk-averse and dogmatic. In low UA cultures, people are much more easygoing, willing to take risk and tolerant of different opinions.

4. **Masculinity–Feminity (MA).** Values traditionally regarded as masculine (e.g., competitiveness, ambition, making money, performance) are held in high respect in so-called "masculine" societies. In low MA-societies, feminine values like "quality of life," solidarity, nurturing warm personal relationships dominate.

Exhibit 7-7 gives the results of grouping seventeen European countries based on the four cultural dimensions just described. Apparently, there are three distinctive "Euroclusters," ranging in size from 37 million (Cluster 3) up to 203 million consumers (Cluster 1). The last column suggests some marketing strategy implications for each of the three clusters. Cluster 3, for instance, which entirely consists of Scandinavian countries, is low in terms of uncertainty avoidance. This would imply that consumers within this cluster are open to new ideas and are willing to try out new products. The low level of masculinity suggests that "green" products and a socially conscious positioning will evoke a positive response among consumers in these countries.[19] For instance, in terms

---

[18]Geert Hofstede, *Culture's Consequences: International Differences in Work-Related Values* (Beverly Hills, Calif.: Sage Publications, 1984).

[19]Sudhir H. Kale, "Grouping Euroconsumers: A Culture-Based Clustering Approach," *Journal of International Marketing*, 3(3) (1995), pp. 35–48.

EXHIBIT 7-7
CULTURE-BASED CLUSTERING OF EUROCONSUMERS

	Size (Million)	Cultural Characteristics				Illustrative Marketing Implications
		Power Distance	Uncertainty Avoidance	Individualism	Masculinity	
Cluster 1 Austria, Germany Switzerland, Italy, Great Britain, Ireland	203	Small	Medium	Medium-High	High	Preference for "high-performance" products, use "successful-achiever" theme in advertising, desire for novelty, variety and pleasure, fairly risk-averse market.
Cluster 2 Belgium, France Greece, Portugal Spain, Turkey	182	Medium	Strong	Varied	Low-Medium	Appeal to consumer's status and power position, reduce perceived risk in product purchase and use, emphasize product functionality.
Cluster 3 Denmark, Sweden Finland, Netherlands Norway	37	Small	Low	High	Low	Relatively weak resistance to new products, strong consumer desire for novelty and variety, high consumer regard for "environmentally friendly" marketers and socially conscious firms.

Source: Sudhir H. Kale, "Grouping Euroconsumers: A Culture-Based Clustering Approach," p. 42.

This article originally appeared in *Journal of International Marketing*, Volume 3, Number 3, 1995 published by Michigan State University Press.

of promotional strategies, companies doing business within these countries should consider event sponsorships instead of couponing campaigns or sweepstakes, which might be viewed as wasteful and alienate local consumers.

Political Conditions

Political variables form another basis for country segmentation. Countries can be grouped according to their economic system: free market, mixed or centrally planned (currently, an endangered species) economies. Obviously, political risk is also a criterion to group prospective target markets. Political factors especially play a role for industrial goods and services. Waste Management International, for example, views environmental regulation and the enforcement of such laws as two of the key factors in selecting international market opportunities. With government procurement contracts, local authorities often tend to favor home-grown companies.

Political risk only matters to the extent that it is likely to have an impact on the company's business. A case in point is Singapore. Political risk surveys like BERI's Political Risk Index consistently classify Singapore as one of the politically most stable countries. However, for Wrigley, the world's leading chewing-gum maker, Singapore turned out to be an unappealing market when the Singaporean government imposed a total ban on the sale and consumption of chewing gum in a drive to clean up the city.

Behavior-Based Segmentation

Just as in domestic marketing, segments can also be formed based on behavioral response variables. Behavioral segmentation criteria include degree of brand/supplier loyalty, usage rate (based on per capita consumption), product penetration (that is, the percentage of the target market that uses the product), and benefits sought after. Exhibit 7-8 shows a behavior-based classification of European markets for a personal care company. Note that this particular company divides its markets into three groups: established markets, developmental markets and underdeveloped markets. Two segmentation variables are used: sales per capita and amount of advertising done by the local distributor.

For new products, firms might consider segmenting countries on the basis of the new product diffusion pattern observed in the countries of interest. Diffusion based criteria could relate to country traits such as the speed of adoption, the time-of-sales peak, and the propensity to innovate. Exhibit 7-9 shows the groupings of a broad range of countries based on the diffusion patterns observed in each of these markets for three consumer durables: color televisions, VCRs and CD-players.

Note that the respective country groupings have little in common in terms of the number of segments and their composition. In fact, the only countries that consistently fall into the same grouping for all three consumer durables are Belgium and Denmark.

EXHIBIT 7-8
EUROPEAN MARKET CLASSIFICATIONS
AS OF DECEMBER 31, 1994

Established Markets	Developmental Markets	Underdeveloped Markets
England	Austria	Czech Republic
Finland	Belgium	Denmark
Germany	Ireland	France
Holland	Italy	Hungary
Israel		Portugal
Norway		Spain
Switzerland		

Established = Above average sales/capita plus advertising

Developmental = Average sales/capita; may or may not be advertising

Underdeveloped = Below average sales/capita; no significant advertising

EXHIBIT 7-9
SEGMENT ASSIGNMENTS BASED ON NEW PRODUCT PENETRATION PATTERNS

Consumer Durable	Segment I	Segment II	Segment III
Color TV	Austria	Finland, France, the Netherlands, Sweden, Switzerland, United Kingdom, United States	Belgium, Denmark, Japan, Norway
VCR	Austria, France Japan, the Netherlands, Switzerland	Norway, United Kingdom, United States	Belgium, Denmark, Finland Sweden
CD-players	Austria, Belgium, Denmark, Finland, France, Japan, the Netherlands, United Kingdom	Norway, Sweden, Switzerland, United States	

Source: Kristiaan Helsen, Kamel Jedidi, and Wayne S. DeSarbo, "A New Approach to Country Segmenation Utilizing Multinational Diffusion Patterns," *Journal of Marketing,* 57 (October 1993), p. 67.

Reprinted with permission from the *Journal of Marketing,* published by the American Marketing Association.

Lifestyle

Marketers can group consumers according to their lifestyle, that is, their attitudes, opinions, and values. Lifestyle segmentation is especially popular in advertising circles. Many of the segmentation schemes are very general and not related to a specific product category. Others are derived for a specific product field. Distinctions can also be made between whether a given typology was prepared for a specific country or a given region.

An example of the general-type of lifestyle segmentation is the ACE-typology (Anticipating Change in Europe) that was developed by the research agency RISC. It consists of six Eurotypes. The percentages indicate the relative size of each cluster:[20]

Traditionalists	18 percent
Homebody	14 percent
Rationalist	23 percent
Pleasurist	17 percent
Striver	15 percent
Trendsetter	13 percent

Exhibit 7-10 exemplifies the product-specific approach. It shows a typology that was derived for the Pan-European car market. The distribution of the different types varies from country to country. Some of the types (e.g., the "prestige-oriented sporty driver") are more or less uniformly distributed. Other types, though (e.g., the "un-

---

[20]Marieke de Mooij, *Advertising Worldwide,* 2d ed. (Englewood Cliffs, N.J.: Prentice-Hall, 1994), p. 167.

EXHIBIT 7-10
TYPOLOGY OF EUROPEAN CAR MARKET

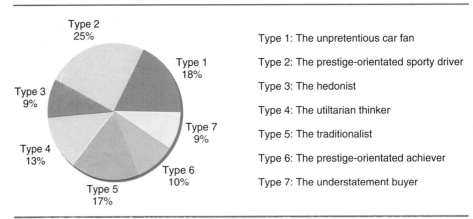

Type 1: The unpretentious car fan

Type 2: The prestige-orientated sporty driver

Type 3: The hedonist

Type 4: The utiltarian thinker

Type 5: The traditionalist

Type 6: The prestige-orientated achiever

Type 7: The understatement buyer

Source: Horst Kern, Hans-Christian Wagner, and Roswitha Hassis, "European Aspects of a Global Brand: The BMW Case," *Marketing and Research Today* (February 1990), p. 54.

Permission for using this material which was originally published in *Marketing and Research Today* has been granted by (E.S.O.M.A.R.) The European Society for Opinion and Marketing Research J.J. Viottastraat 29, 1071 JP, Amsterdam, The Netherlands.

derstatement" buyer), are prominent in some countries but far less visible in other countries.[21]

Lifestyle segmentation has been applied for the positioning of new brands, the repositioning of existing ones, identifying new product opportunities, and the development of brand personalities.[22] Several concerns have been raised by practitioners and academics alike about the use of lifestyle segmentation:[23]

- Values are too general to relate to consumption patterns or brand choice behavior within a specific product category. As a result, lifestyle segmentation is not very useful as a tool to make predictions about consumers' buying responsiveness. Obviously, this criticism only applies to the general value schemes.

- Value-based segmentation schemes are not always "actionable." Remember that one of the requirements for effective segmentation is actionability. Lifestyle groupings do not offer much guidance in terms of what marketing actions should be taken. Also, many of the typologies have too many different types to be useful for practical purposes.

- Value segments are not stable, since values typically change over time.

- Their international applicability is quite limited, since lifestyles, even within the same region, often vary from country to country.

Aside from the criteria just discussed, many other country characteristics may form a basis for segmentation. The proper criteria largely depend on the nature of the product and the objectives of the segmentation exercise.

---

[21]Horst Kern, Hans-Christian Wagner and Roswitha Hassis, "European Aspects of a Global Brand: The BMW Case," *Marketing and Research Today* (February 1990), pp. 47–57.

[22]de Mooij, p. 160.

[23]Peter Sampson, "People are People the World Over: The Case for Psychological Market Segmentation," *Marketing and Research Today* (November 1992), pp. 236–44.

Country Segmentation Tools[24]   ◆ ◆ ◆ ◆ ◆ ◆

In this section we focus on segmentation tools that can be used to do a country segmentation. A huge variety of segmentation methodologies has been developed in the marketing literature. Many of these techniques are quite sophisticated. We will just give you the flavor of two of the most popular tools without going through all the technical nitty-gritty.

When only one segmentation variable is used, classifying countries in distinct groups is quite straightforward. You could simply compute the mean (or median) and split countries into two groups based on the value (above or below) on the criterion variable compared to the mean (or median). When more than two groups need to be formed, one can use other quantiles. Things become a bit more complicated when you plan to use multiple country segmentation variables. Typically, the goal of market segmentation is to relate, in some manner, a battery of descriptive variables about the countries to one or more behavioral response variables:

$$\text{Response} = F(\text{Descriptor}_1, \text{Descriptor}_2, \text{Descriptor}_3, \ldots)$$

For instance, the response variable might be the per-capita consumption of a given product. The descriptor variables could be the stage in the product life cycle, per-capita GNP, literacy level, and so on. We now describe two methods that can help you in achieving this goal: cluster analysis and regression.

Cluster Analysis

Cluster analysis is an umbrella term that embraces a collection of statistical procedures for dividing objects into groups (*clusters*). The grouping is done in such a manner that members belonging to the same group are similar to one another but quite distinct from members of other groups.

Suppose information was collected for a set of countries on two variables, X and Y. The countries are plotted in Exhibit 7-11. Each dot corresponds to a country. In this case, the clusters are quite obvious. Just by eyeballing the graph, you can distinguish two clear-cut clusters, namely C_1 and C_2. Unfortunately, in real-world applications, clustering is seldom so easy. Consider Exhibit 7-12.[25] This exhibit plots the values of chocolate volume growth rate and market concentration in eight countries. For this example, it is far less obvious how many clusters there are, let alone how they are composed. In addition, most country segmentations involve many more than two criteria.

Luckily, many statistical algorithms are available to do the job for you. The basic notion is to group countries together that are "similar" in value for the segmentation bases of interest. Similarity measures come under many guises. The most popular way is to use some type of distance measure:

$$\text{Distance}_{\text{country }A \text{ vs. } B} = (X_{\text{country }A} - X_{\text{country }B})^2 + (Y_{\text{country }A} - Y_{\text{country }B})^2$$

where X and Y are the segmentation variables. These distances[26] would be computed

---

[24]This section is a bit more technical than the rest of the chapter. It can be skipped in less advanced classes.

[25]Measured via the combined market shares of the three largest competitors—Cadbury, Mars, and Nestlé.

[26]Strictly speaking, these are "squared" distances.

EXHIBIT 7-11
PRINCIPLES OF CLUSTER ANALYSIS

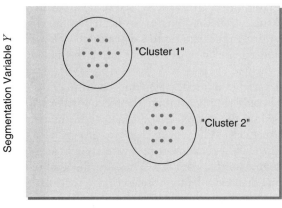

• *Indicates location of country given its value for "X" and "Y"*

EXHIBIT 7-12
PLOT OF CONCENTRATION VERSUS CATEGORY GROWTH
CHOCOLATE MARKET

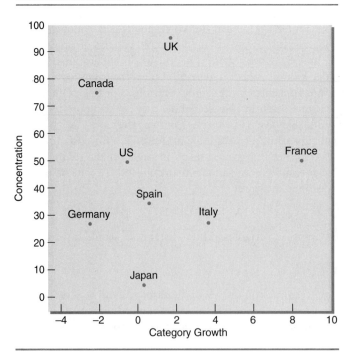

for each pair of countries in the set. The clustering algorithm takes these distances and uses them as inputs to generate the desired number of country groupings. Most "canned" statistical software packages (e.g., SAS, SPPS-X) have at least one procedure that allows you to run a cluster analysis. Exhibit 7-13 provides the two- and three-cluster solutions for the chocolate market example.

Regression

Alternatively, you might consider using regression analysis to classify countries. In regression, one assumes that there exists a relationship between a response variable, Y, and one or more so-called predictor variables, X_1, X_2 and so on:

$$Y = a + b_1 X_1 + b_2 X_2 + b_3 X_3 + \dots$$

The first term, a, is the intercept. It corresponds to the predicted value of Y when all the Xs are equal to 0. The other parameters, the bs, are the slope coefficients. For example, b_1 tells you what the predicted change in Y will be for a unit change in X_1.

In our context, the dependent variable, Y, would be a behavioral response variable (e.g., per capita consumption) and the predictor variables would be a collection of country characteristics that are presumed to be related to the response measure. For given values of the parameters, you can compute the predicted Y-values, $\hat{Y}$. Very seldom, these predicted values will match the observed Ys. The goal of regression is to find estimates for the intercept, a, and the slope coefficients, the bs, that provide the "best" fit by minimizing the prediction errors, $Y - \hat{Y}$, between the predicted and observed values of Y. The most common regression procedure, ordinary least squares (OLS), minimizes the sum of the squared differences of these prediction errors.

For each of the parameter estimates, the regression analysis will also produce a standard error. Dividing the parameter estimate by the standard error yields the t-ratio. This ratio tells you whether or not the predictor variable has a "significant" (statistically speaking) relationship with the dependent variable. As a rule of thumb, a t-ratio (in absolute value) larger than 2.0 would indicate a significant effect of the predictor variable on the response variable. The overall goodness of fit is captured via the R^2 statistic. The higher the R^2 value, the better the fit to the data.

To illustrate the use of regression analysis as a segmentation tool, let us look at a numerical example. Consider a microwave oven maker who wants to explore market opportunities in the European market. Data were collected for several European countries on the penetration of microwave ovens (as percentage of households owning a microwave). Data were also gathered on three potential segmentation variables: income (per-capita GDP), participation of women in the labor force, and per capita consumption of frozen foods.[27] Using these data as inputs, the following results were obtained (t-ratios in parentheses):

MICROWAVE OWNERSHIP =
$\qquad$ −76.7 − 0.5 FROZEN FOOD + 2.7 WOMEN − 0.03 PER CAP GDP
$\qquad$ (−2.2) (−1.3) $\qquad\qquad$ (2.9) $\qquad\quad$ (−0.04)
$\qquad\qquad$ $R^2 = 0.52$

Note that, apparently, the only meaningful segmentation base is the participation of women in the labor force: microwave ownership increases with the propor-

---

[27]The data for this example were collected from the *European Marketing Data and Statistics 1992*, London: Euromonitor.

EXHIBIT 7-13
CLUSTER ANALYSIS TWO-CLUSTER SOLUTION

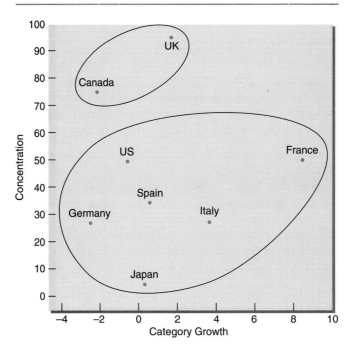

THREE-CLUSTER SOLUTION

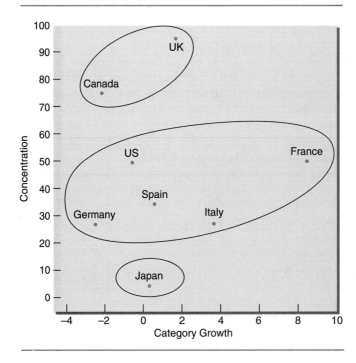

tion of women in the labor force. Since microwaves are a time-saving appliance, this result intuitively makes sense. The other variables appear to have (statistically speaking) not much impact on the adoption of microwave ovens. Somewhat surprisingly, high consumption of frozen foods does not lead to an increased ownership of microwave ovens. There is also no relationship with income. Thus, in this case, the European marketing manager could group countries simply on the basis of the degree of participation of women in the labor force.

Aside from these two commonplace tools, there are many other multivariate statistical procedures that can be used to do country segmentation analysis (e.g., latent class analysis, discriminant analysis, Automatic Interaction Detection).

ISSUES IN INTERNATIONAL MARKET SEGMENTATION ◆ ◆ ◆ ◆ ◆ ◆

By now, you should realize that international market segmentation provides a powerful ingredient for formulating global marketing strategies. Given the fancy toys at the disposal of marketers, it is easy to get carried away and to regard segmentation as a research tool and the preserve of your marketing research staff. The adage of "war being too important to be left to generals" also applies in this context. Extreme care is needed. We now highlight some of the issues you might encounter when doing a country segmentation in practice. We start with troublespots that are mostly technical in nature. In principle they should be addressed by the firm's marketing research staff. It is important, though, to be aware of them, since they are often overlooked in country segmentation applications. The second set of issues that we describe are the managerial ones. These primarily relate to the interpretation and usefulness of country segmentation results.

Technical Issues

Let us look first at some of the technical issues that you may encounter when doing cross-country segmentation.

Poor Data Quality. To do a country segmentation study, you need to collect data on scores of variables. Some of these data are collected via surveys. Macroeconomic data are retrieved from secondary data sources. The problems encountered in global marketing research also arise here: some pieces of information are missing, while others are available but hopelessly outdated, unreliable, or inaccurate. There are no easy cures to address these problems. We refer to Chapter 6 (Global Marketing Research) for a further discussion of this issue.

"Noisy" Variables. Somewhat related to the previous problem is the issue of "noisy" variables. Data for many of the variables that you collect may suffer from *noise* because of reporting errors, sampling mistakes, and so on. Variables with a substantial noise will not contribute much to the clustering solution. Moreover, they create a lot of havoc by scrambling your cluster or regression analysis.[28] The amount of harm will depend on many factors, but the upshot is that your cluster solution can be very unstable. In global marketing settings, one would expect this problem to be paramount.

---

[28]Kristiaan Helsen and Paul E. Green, "A Computational Study of Replicated Clustering with an Application to Market Segmentation," *Decision Sciences*, 22 (Nov./Dec. 1991), pp. 1124–41.

Presence of Outliers. Datasets may contain one or more outlying observations. Although there is some disagreement on the exact meaning of *outliers*, the term typically refers to datapoints that deviate from the general pattern followed by the bulk of the data. Outliers are not harmless. When a fair amount of the dataset consists of outliers (say 25 percent or even more), most cluster solutions are usually very unstable.

The upshot is that managers should be careful in interpreting country segmentation analyses. Under many circumstances, the results may not be very robust, due to the presence of outliers, "noisy" variables, or other complicating factors. Unfortunately, as of yet, there are no foolproof solutions.

Managerial Issues

Besides the technical problems, there are several managerial concerns. Country segmentation analyses could be hampered by one or more of the following pitfalls.

Stability of Segments over Time. Ideally, country segments should be stable over time. The size and composition of country segments is not always a given. Segments change over time. Seldom are such changes predictable. Segmentation analyses are nearly always based on historical information distilled from secondary (or sometimes primary) datasources. In a volatile environment, analyses based on past data could be misleading. Market segments *do* evolve over time: their size changes, new segments emerge. Such changes dictate a reassessment of the firm's segmentation and positioning strategy.

Managerial Usefulness. Country segmentation is a strategic tool to meet certain managerial objectives. One objective might be to explore the possibility of introducing the firm's product in other countries. A natural approach is to launch the product in markets that, in some regards, are "similar" to the countries that have already been penetrated.[29] To be useful, one would hope that a given country classification corresponds to the country groupings based on actual product penetration patterns. Unfortunately, this is seldom the case. In fact, empirical evidence shows that country segmentations based on macroeconomic aggregates seldom bear any resemblance to sales-pattern-based groupings.[30]

◆ ◆ ◆ ◆ ◆ ◆ INTERNATIONAL POSITIONING STRATEGIES

Segmenting international markets is only part of the game. Once the MNC has segmented its international markets for a particular product or service, the firm needs to decide which segments to pursue and what positioning strategy to use to reach the chosen segment(s). Developing a positioning theme involves the quest for a unique selling proposition (USP). In the global marketing scene, the positioning question boils down to the battle of the mind of your target customers, located not just within a certain country but, in some cases, worldwide.

---

[29]Johansson and Moinpour, p. 66.

[30]Kristiaan Helsen, Kamel Jedidi and Wayne S. DeSarbo, "A New Approach to Country Segmentation Utilizing Multinational Diffusion Patterns," *Journal of Marketing*, 57 (October 1993), pp. 60–71.

EXHIBIT 7-14
GLOBAL POSITIONING AND
SEGMENTATION STRATEGIES

	Universal Segment	Different Segments (case-by-case)
Uniform Positioning Theme	①	②
Different Positioning Themes	③	④

Consider the target market selection first. Roughly speaking, MNCs have two choices: target a universal segment across countries or pursue different segments across countries.[31] A similar split also arises for the selection of a positioning theme: the same positioning worldwide or positioning themes that are tailored to individual markets. So, in principle, by combining the available options along these two dimensions—target market and positioning theme—one gets to four possible choices, as summarized in Exhibit 7-14. Note, though, that option 3—country-tailored target markets/uniform positioning theme—is quite uncommon.

Universal Segment/Uniform Positioning Theme

With this option, the MNC pursues a universal segment and uses the same positioning theme to appeal to this particular segment. The challenge is to come up with a selling proposition that makes consumers tick everywhere and that transcends local peculiarities. For low-margin products, the uniform segment/positioning strategy is only viable when the cross-border segment that is chosen represents a sizable group of consumers. Typical examples of such segments include global teenagers, the global X-generation (20-somethings), the global middle-class, and global elites. To appeal to these segments, the same positioning theme is chosen. This strategy is especially viable for goods that are affordable and feel like little treats (e.g., fast food, soft drinks, Benetton clothing). Union Bank of Switzerland (UBS) launched a communication campaign that followed this strategy. Their target market is financial decision makers worldwide. Given the characteristics of their clients and the usage of a single brand name, a global communications campaign with a consistent theme is UBS's strategy of choice. The positioning theme that was ultimately selected—"Here Today. Here Tomorrow"—centers around the "long-term relationship" benefit that UBS provides for its corporate clients.[32]

---

[31]Strictly speaking, as we pointed out earlier, there is a third choice: namely, combine universal and country-specific segments.

[32]Christof Buri and Andrew Findlay, "Here Today, Here Tomorrow, the Contribution of Marketing Research to the Making of UBS' Global Brand Campaign," *Marketing and Research Today* (November 1996), pp. 208–15.

Universal Segment/Different Positioning Themes

Companies might pursue a universal target segment but adapt the positioning themes to the local markets. There may be plenty of reason (e.g., cultural differences, legal restraints, competitive factors) to choose country-tailored positioning strategies. While the cross-border target market is similar in terms of their demographics, the benefits sought for a particular product or service may well differ.

Different Segment/Different Positioning Themes

Adaptation of positioning and target is another possibility, especially for products that are marketed in developed countries and emerging markets. Scores of products target the mass market in developed markets and the upscale segment in developing countries. A case in point is the Ford Escort: although the car is sold as a mainstream passenger car in the United States and Europe, the Escort is perceived as a premium car in India because of its price tag. It is not uncommon to see a chauffeur-driven Escort there.[33]

Many firms position a brand that is *mainstream* in its home market as a premium brand in their overseas markets, thereby targeting a narrower segment that is willing to pay a premium for imports. Examples of brands that are "mainstream" in their home market but perceived as premium in the international marketplace are Heineken, Levi's, and Budweiser. This strategy is especially effective in product categories where the local brands already are very well-entrenched (like beer in most countries) and imported brands have a potential to leverage the cachet of being "imported." By targeting the masses, the firm would fall in the trap of the "majority fallacy": go for the mass market, which is already preempted by local competitors. The latter usually enjoy a pioneering advantage by the fact of being the first ones in the market. Therefore, instead of competing head-on with the local competition, foreign brands (despite the fact that they are a mainstream brand in their home market) are mostly better off by targeting the upscale segment. Though smaller in numbers, this segment is willing to pay a substantial premium price.

◆ ◆

↺IDEOBOX

CATHAY PACIFIC'S CORPORATE IDENTITY MAKEOVER

Cathay Pacific, headquartered in Hong Kong, is one of the world's most profitable airlines. For many years, most of its customers were Western expatriates. In recent years, the number of Asian passengers steadily increased and the competition from other Asian carriers like Singapore Airlines and Thai Airways intensified. In the wake of these environmental changes, Cathay needed to alter its corporate identity.

The challenge that Cathay faced was to come up with an Asian personality in line with its Asian passengers. In the Fall of 1994, Cathay kicked off a new communication campaign with the tagline "The Heart of Asia." Other repositioning initiatives included a new "brushwing" logo, more Asian meals and entertainment options, repainted exteriors, redesigned cabins, and so forth.

What does it take to adopt a more "Asian" identity? What are the possible downsides of Cathay's repositioning strategy?

---

[33]"GM, Ford Think Globally for Branding Strategies," *Advertising Age* (January 6, 1997), p. 35.

To determine the proper positioning theme(s), marketers need to factor in their firm's corporate culture and mission, core skills, the perceptions of their target customers in the various countries (are they consistent across borders or not?), positioning themes used in the past (for existing brands), and positioning strategies used by competitors.

SUMMARY ◆

A common theme in many writings on global marketing is the growing convergence of consumer needs.[34] This phenomenon of increasing globalization is especially visible for many upscale consumer goods and a variety of business-to-business goods and services that are bought by multinational customers. At the same time, new technological advances in interactive marketing open up heretofore untapped opportunities for increasingly refined segmentation.[35] This paradox, the increasing homogenization of customer needs versus the possibilities offered by micromarketing, offers a challenge to global marketers entering the twenty-first century.

Global marketers have a continuum of choices to segment their customer base. At one end of the spectrum, the firm might pursue a "universal" segment. Essentially the same product is offered, using a common positioning theme. Most likely there are a few, mostly minor, adaptations of the marketing mix program to recognize cross-border differences. At the other end, the firm might consider treating individual countries on a case-by-case basis. In some circumstances, marketers might be able to offer the same product in each country, provided that the positioning is customized. However, typically, the product will need to be modified or designed for each country separately. In between these two extremes, there are bound to be many other possibilities.

We concur with Abell that market segmentation is a "craft" rather than a "science."[36] The guidelines that Abell suggests for market segmentation also apply to country segmentation:

1. **Keep things simple.** There is no need to exhaust each possible permutation and combination of country variables. Ultimately, the goal is to come up with a viable set of target markets that will allow your company to pursue its goals effectively.

2. **Consider several levels of aggregation, not just one.** As you consider more disaggregate levels of aggregation, a wider range of possible segmentation schemes opens up.

3. **Two ways to fine-tune an existing segmentation scheme.** Realize that there are always two ways to augment precision: either subdivide an existing variable (e.g., low/high income becomes low/medium/high income) or introduce a new segmentation variable.

4. **Pursue "creative" ways to segment your market.** Look for segmentation schemes that are hard to imitate by your competition, and, that, ideally, offer a sustainable competitive edge. Especially in countries where the marketplace is crowded with brands, it is important to stand out of the crowd. Rather than doing what everybody else does ("borrow thy neighbor" segmentation), one would like to come up with a segmentation schema that "breaks through the clutter." Admittedly, this is a hard nut to crack.

---

[34]Theodore Levitt, "The Globalization of Markets," *Harvard Business Review* 61 (May-June 1983), pp. 92–102.

[35]Robert C. Blattberg and John Deighton, "Interactive Marketing: Exploiting the Age of Addressability," *Sloan Management Review* (Fall 1991), pp. 5–14.

[36]Derek F. Abell, *Managing with Dual Strategies. Mastering the Present, Preempting the Future* (New York: The Free Press), 1993, Chapter 4.

REVIEW QUESTIONS ✦ ✦ ✦ ✦ ✦ ✦ ✦ ✦ ✦ ✦ ✦ ✦ ✦ ✦ ✦ ✦ ✦ ✦ ✦

1. Under what conditions should companies pursue universal market segments?

2. What are the major issues in using per capita GDP or GNP as a country segmentation criterion?

3. Discuss the weaknesses of lifestyle-based segmentation schemes. For what kind of applications would lifestyle segmentation be appropriate?

DISCUSSION QUESTIONS ✦ ✦ ✦ ✦ ✦ ✦ ✦ ✦ ✦ ✦ ✦ ✦ ✦ ✦ ✦ ✦ ✦ ✦

1. Peter Sampson, a managing director of Burke Marketing Research, points out that "lifestyle and value-based segmentations are too general to be of great use in category-specific studies . . . their international application is too limited as lifestyles vary internationally." Do you agree or disagree with his comment?

2. In a host of emerging markets (e.g., India, Brazil, Thailand), 50 percent-plus of the population is under 25. One marketer observes that: "teenagers are teenagers everywhere and they tend to emulate U.S. teenagers" (*Advertising Age International*, October 17, 1994, p. I-15). Is there a global teenager segment? Do teenagers in, say, Beijing really tend to emulate L.A. teenagers? Discuss.

3. Assignment: Select a particular consumption product (e.g., ice-cream). Try to come up with at least two variables that you believe might be related to the per-capita demand for the chosen product. Collect data on the per-capita consumption levels for your chosen product and the selected variables for several countries. Segment the countries using, for example, cluster analysis (SAS users might consider PROC FAST-CLUS). Derive two- and three-cluster solutions. Discuss your findings.

4. A recent phenomenon in scores of emerging markets is a rising middle class. In a recent *Ad Age International* article (October 17, 1994) on the global middle class, one analyst referred to this phenomenon as the Twinkie-ization of the world (*Twinkie* being the brand name of a popular snack in the United States): "It's the little things that are treats and don't cost much and feel like a luxury." What are these "little things"? Do you agree with this statement?

FURTHER READINGS ✦ ✦ ✦ ✦ ✦ ✦ ✦ ✦ ✦ ✦ ✦ ✦ ✦ ✦ ✦ ✦ ✦ ✦ ✦

Hassan, Salah S., and Lea P. Katsanis. "Identification of Global Consumer Segments." *Journal of International Consumer Marketing*, 3(2) (1991): 11–28.

Helsen, Kristiaan, Kamel Jedidi, and Wayne S. DeSarbo. "A New Approach to Country Segmentation Utilizing Multinational Diffusion Patterns." *Journal of Marketing*, 57 (October 1993): 60–71.

Hinton, Graham, and Jane Hourigan. "The Golden Circles: Marketing in the New Europe." *Journal of European Business*, 1(6) (July/August 1990): 5–30.

Johansson, Johny K., and Reza Moinpour. "Objective and Perceived Similarity for Pacific-Rim Countries." *Columbia Journal of World Business* (Winter 1977): 65–76.

Kale, Sudhir. "Grouping Euroconsumers: A Culture-Based Clustering Approach." *Journal of International Marketing*, 3(3) (1995): 35–48.

Kale, Sudhir, and D. Sudharshan. "A Strategic Approach to International Segmentation." *International Marketing Review* (Summer 1987): 60–70.

Sampson, Peter. "People Are People the World Over: The Case for Psychological Segmentation." *Marketing and Research Today* (November 1992): 236–44.

Yavas, Ugur, Bronislaw J. Verhage, and Robert T. Green. "Global Consumer Segmentation versus Local Market Orientation: Empirical Findings." *Management International Review*, 32(3) (1992): 265–72.

GLOBAL COMPETITIVE ANALYSIS

CHAPTER OVERVIEW

1. INFORMATION TECHNOLOGY AND GLOBAL COMPETITION
2. GLOBAL STRATEGY
3. GLOBAL MARKETING STRATEGY
4. REGIONALIZATION OF GLOBAL MARKETING STRATEGY
5. COMPETITIVE ANALYSIS

On a political map, country borders are clear as ever. But on a competitive map, financial, trading, and industrial activities across national boundaries have rendered those political borders increasingly irrelevant. Of all the forces chipping away those boundaries, perhaps the most important is the flow of information—information that governments previously monopolized, cooking it up as they saw fit and redistributing it in forms of their own devising. Their information monopoly on events happening around the world enabled them to fool, mislead, or even control the people, because only the government possessed the facts in detail.[1]

Today people can see for themselves what tastes and preferences are like in other countries. For instance, people in India watching CNN and Star TV now know instantaneously what is happening in the rest of the world. A farmer in a remote village in Rajasthan in India asks the local vendor for Surf (the detergent manufactured by Unilever) because he has seen a commercial on TV. More than 10 million Japanese traveling abroad every year are exposed to larger-size homes and much lower consumer prices abroad. Such information access creates demand that would not have existed before and it restricts the power of governments to influence consumer choice.

The availability and explosion of information technology such as telecommunications has forever changed the nature of global competition. Geographical bound-

---

[1]Kenichi Ohmae, *The Borderless World* (London: Harper Collins, 1990).

aries and distance have become less of a constraint in designing strategies for the global market. The other side of the coin is that not only firms that compete internationally but also those whose primary market is considered domestic will be affected by competition from around the world. In this chapter, we explain the nature of global competition and examine various ways to gain competitive advantage for the firm facing global competition.

♦ ♦ ♦ ♦ ♦ ♦ INFORMATION TECHNOLOGY AND GLOBAL COMPETITION

The development of transportation technology, including jet air transportation, cold storage containers, and large ocean carriers, changed the nature of world trade in the fifty years after the Second World War. Since the 1980s, the explosion of information technology, particularly telecommunications, has forever changed the nature of competition around the world. Geographical distance has become increasingly less relevant in designing global strategy.

In the 1980s telecommunications grew by more than 600 percent, and a similar level of growth has taken place in the 1990s. We are observing the emergence of a *Gross Information Product*, and it dwarfs the Gross Domestic Product. In 1996, the total value of physical exports of the United States, Germany, and Japan combined amounted to $1.05 trillion a year; in one *week* London's international *electronic* transactions in the form of foreign exchange, securities, funds transfer, and credit card transactions amounted to that much. The power of telecommunications was apparent during the Gulf War, when news about the war was in real time.

Real-Time Management

Information that managers have about the state of the firm's operations is almost in real time. Routinely, the chief executive officer of a firm can know the previous day's sales down to a penny, and can be alerted to events and trends now instead of in several months, when it may be too late to do anything about them.

Top retailers such as Wal-Mart and Toys "Я" Us get information from their stores around the world every two hours via telecommunications.[2] Industry analysts say that former leader K-Mart fell behind due to the delay in installing point-of-sale information technology, which would have enabled it to get faster and more accurate information on inventories and shelf movement of products. Such access is now possible because advances in electronic storage and transmission technology have made it possible to store twenty-six volumes of *Encyclopaedia Britannica* on a single chip and transmit that material in a second; these figures are expected to improve by a factor of ten by the end of the decade.

The combination of information technology, access tools, and telecommunication has squeezed out a huge chunk of organizational slack from corporate operations that were previously inherent due to the slow and circuitous nature of information flow within the firm, with holdups due to human "switches." Ordering and purchasing of components, which was once a cumbersome, time-consuming process,

---

[2]Peter G. W. Keen and J. Michael Cummins, *Networks in Action* (Belmont, Calif.: Wadsworth Publishing Company, 1994).

is now done by Electronic Data Interchange (EDI), reducing the time involved in such transactions from weeks to days and eliminating a considerable amount of paperwork. Levi-Strauss uses LeviLink, an EDI service for handling all aspects of order and delivery. Customers can even place small orders as needed, say, every week, and goods are delivered within two days. One of Levi-Strauss's customers, Design p.l.c., with a chain of sixty stores, was able to entirely eliminate its warehouses, which were used as a buffer to deal with the long lead times between order and delivery. Caterpillar's "plant with a future" is built around an integrated global production process, which itself is built around a global information network utilizing the latest advances in telecommunications and information technology.

On-Line Communication

Sales representatives on field calls who were previously, in effect, tied to the regional or central headquarters due to lack of product information and limited authority, are now able to act independently in the field, because laptop computers, faxes, and satellite uplinks enable instant access to data from the company's central database. Changes in prices due to discounts can now be cleared on-line from the necessary authority. This reduces reaction time for the sales representative and increases productivity. Monitoring problems for the firm are also reduced, as is paperwork.

Multiple design sites around the world in different time zones can now work sequentially on the same problem. A laboratory in California can close its day at five local time when the design center in Japan is just opening the next day. That center continues work on the design problem and hands it over to London at the end of its day, which continues the work and hands over the cumulated work of Japan and London back to California. Finally, the use of telecommunications improves internal efficiency of the firm in other ways. For instance, when Microsoft came up with an upgrade on one of its applications that required some customer education, a customer, using video conferencing on its global information network, arranged a single presentation for the relevant personnel, dispersed across the world, obviating travel and multiple presentations.

"Internet" Organization

The ultimate effect of information networks within the multinational firm is expected to be on the nature of its organizational structure. As information flows faster across the organization and the number of "filtering" points between the source of information (e.g., point-of-sale information or market and industry analysis) and the user of the information (e.g., the brand manager or the chief executive officer) decreases, the nature of the organization chart in the multinational firm changes drastically. An increasing number of multinational firms have begun to use internal Web servers on the Internet to facilitate communications and transactions among employees, suppliers, independent contractors, and distributors.[3]

An assembly-line worker in a Procter & Gamble plant, for instance, knows from his computer that stores have been selling a particular brand of facial cream more briskly than anticipated, and, having this information, can change production schedul-

---

[3]John A. Quelch and Lisa R. Klein, "The Internet and International Marketing," *Sloan Management Review*, 37 (Spring 1996), pp. 60–75.

ing on his own, by giving the computer necessary instructions to cut down on some other brands and to increase the production of the brand in question. The foreman and the section manager of a conventional plant are no longer required. Similarly, a Xerox salesperson uploads and downloads sales-related data directly from the central database of the company using a laptop computer that communicates directly with the central computer. The information so obtained can be analyzed directly—the conventional functions of regional offices and the associated overheads decrease considerably.

Faster Product Diffusion

The obvious impact of information technology is the faster dispersion of technology and the shorter product lifecycles in global markets than ever before. It suggests that the former country-by-country sequential approach to entering markets throughout the world, described in the international product cycle model in Chapter 1, is increasingly untenable.

This trend is reflected in many product markets already. The time lag for color television between the United States on one hand and Japan and Europe on the other was six years. With compact discs the household penetration rates had come down to one year. For Pentium-based computers, Taiwan, India, Japan, and U.S.-based companies released computers at about the same time in their respective national markets. Thus, a firm selling personal computers would have to launch a new product on a worldwide basis in order not to fall behind in the global sweepstakes. This issue will be further discussed later when we discuss new product development in Chapter 11.

Global Citizenship

Another important contributing factor in the globalization of markets is the spread of English as *the* language of international business. The transformation of the European Community into a union has already taken place in language terms, even though the monetary union plans have failed so far. *Global citizenship* is no longer just a phrase in the lexicon of futurologists. It has already become every bit as concrete and measurable as changes in GNP and trade flows. In fact, conventional measures of trade flows may have outlived their usefulness, as we will discuss later.

The global environment thus demands a form of strategy that encompasses numerous national boundaries and tastes, and that integrates a firm's operations across the national borders. This strategy is truly global in nature and has gone beyond the home-country-focused ethnocentric orientation or the multicountry focused polycentric orientation of many multinational firms in the middle of the twentieth century. The firm thus needs to adopt a geocentric orientation, where the entire world is viewed as a potential market and firm activities are integrated on a global basis.[4]

---

[4]Jaishankar Ganesh, "Competitive Marketing Strategies of Firms in Multidomestic and Global Industries: An Empirical Investigation of the Strategy-Performance Relationship," a Ph.D. dissertation, University of Houston, 1995; Yoram Wind, Susan P. Douglas and Howard V. Perlmutter, "Guidelines for Developing International Marketing Strategies," *Journal of Marketing*, 37 (April 1973), pp. 14–23.

GLOBAL STRATEGY ◆ ◆ ◆ ◆ ◆ ◆ ◆

The acid test of a well-managed company is being able to conceive, develop, and implement an effective global strategy. Because of its inherent difficulties, global strategy development presents one of the stiffest challenges for managers today. Companies that operate on a global scale need to integrate their worldwide strategy, in contrast to the earlier multinational or multidomestic approach. The earlier strategies would more truly be categorized as multidomestic strategies rather than as global strategies.

Global Industry

We approach the issue of global strategy through various conceptualizations—the first conceptualization is that of a global industry.[5] Global industries are defined as *those where a firm's competitive position in one country is affected by its position in other countries, and vice versa.* Therefore, we are talking about not just a collection of domestic industries, but a series of interlinked domestic industries in which rivals compete against one another on a truly worldwide basis. For instance, part of the reason that General Motors managed to keep afloat during the late 1980s and early 1990s was the strength of its European operations. Its North American operations bled red ink for most of this period.

Therefore, the first question that faces managers is the extent of globalization of their industry. Assuming that the firm's activities are indeed global or, alternatively, that the firm wishes to grow toward global operations and markets, managers must design and implement a global strategy. This is because virtually every industry has global or potentially global aspects—some industries have more aspects that are global and more intensely so. Indeed, a case has been made that the globalization of markets has already been achieved, that consumer tastes around the world have converged, and that the global firm attempts, unceasingly, to drive consumer tastes toward convergence.[6] Four major forces determining the globalization potential of industry are presented in Exhibit 8-1.

The implications of a distinction between multidomestic and global strategy are quite profound. In a multidomestic strategy, a firm manages its international activities like a portfolio. Its subsidiaries or other operations around the world each control all the important activities necessary to maximize their returns in their area of operation independent of the activities of other subsidiaries in the firm. The subsidiaries enjoy a large degree of autonomy, and the firm's activities in each of its national markets is determined by the competitive conditions in that national market. In contrast, a global strategy integrates the activities of a firm on a worldwide basis to capture the linkages among countries and to treat the entire world as a single, borderless market. This requires more than the transferring of intangible assets between countries.

---

[5]Michael E. Porter, ed., *Competition in Global Industries* (Boston, Mass.: Harvard University Press, 1986).

[6]Theodore Levitt, "The Globalization of Markets," *Harvard Business Review,* 61 (May-June 1983), pp. 92–102.

EXHIBIT 8-1
INDUSTRY GLOBALIZATION DRIVERS

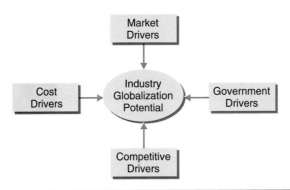

Market Globalization Drivers

Market drivers depend on the nature of customer behavior and the structure of channels of distribution. Some common market drivers are:

1. ***Common Customer Needs.*** Factors that affect whether customer needs are similar in different countries include economic development, climate, physical environment, and culture.

2. ***Global Customers and Channels.*** Global customers buy on a centralized or coordinated basis for decentralized use. Their existence affects the opportunity or need for global market participation, global products and services, global activity location, and global marketing.

3. ***Transferable Marketing.*** Certain elements of the marketing mix, e.g., brand name, pricing strategy, etc., may be transferable across markets. The implications are that these elements can be effectively used both for increasing as well as reducing barriers.

4. ***Lead Countries.*** Lead countries represent countries where innovations in particular industries are prone to take place, e.g., Japan for consumer electronics, Germany for industrial control equipment, and the United States for computer software.

Cost Globalization Drivers

Cost drivers depend on the economics of the business. These drivers particularly affect production location decisions, as well as global market participation and global product development decisions. Some of these cost drivers are:

1. ***Global Economies of Scale and Scope.*** Global economies of scale apply when single-country markets are not large enough to allow competitors to achieve optimum scale. One of the most visible examples of this has been in the electronics industry. In many cases, economies of scope may be available by using facilities and processes in a single operating unit to produce a larger variety of good or services with or without the presence of scale economies. Areas where economies of scope may be visible include consumer research, product development, and the creation of marketing programs.

2. ***Steep Experience Curve.*** Besides economies of scope and scale, steep learning activity associated with concentration of activities can result in significant cost advantages.

3. ***Global Sourcing Efficiencies.*** Efficiencies arise out of coordination of procurement activities of raw materials and components.

4. ***Favorable Logistics.*** A favorable ratio of sales value to transportation cost increases the ability to concentrate production and take advantage of economies of scale. Other logistic factors that have a bearing on global strategy development are nonperishability of products, absence of time urgency, and little need for location close to customer facilities.

EXHIBIT 8-1 (*Continued*)

5. ***Differences in Country Costs.*** This is based on the classical theories of differences in factor costs that do exist and can be exploited by firms to achieve comparative advantage. Besides factor cost differences, exchange rate differences also have a significant bearing on the absolute costs and the stability of costs.

6. ***High Product Development Costs.*** High product development costs relative to the size of national markets act as a driver to globalization. These costs can be reduced by developing few global or regional products.

7. ***Fast-Changing Technology.*** Fast-changing technologies in products or processes lead to high product development costs, which increase their globalization potential.

Government Globalization Drivers

Rules set by national governments can affect the use of global strategic decision-making. Some of these rules/policies include:

1. ***Favorable Trade Policies.*** Import tariffs and quotas, nontariff barriers, export subsidies, local content requirements, currency and capital flow restrictions, ownership restrictions, and requirements on technology transfer are some means governments can use to influence firm behavior. These policies can have a significant negative impact on standardization of products and programs.

2. ***Compatible Technical Standards.*** Differences in technical standards among countries also affect the extent of product standardization.

3. ***Common Marketing Regulations.*** Restrictions on various marketing activities can also act as a barrier to the use of uniform marketing approaches. For example, restrictions on the use of certain kinds of media for advertisements, differences in ad content like the use of sex and comparative advertising, and so on.

4. ***Government-Owned Competitors.*** The presence of government-owned competitors spurs the development of global plans as a means of counteracting the advantages of protected home markets.

5. ***Government-Owned Customers.*** Presence of government-owned customers could provide a barrier to globalization since such customers usually favor national suppliers.

Competitive Globalization Drivers

Competitive drivers raise the globalization potential of their industry and spur the need for a response on the global strategy levels. The common competitive drivers include:

1. ***High Exports and Imports.*** The level of exports and imports of final and intermediate products and services, i.e., the extent of interaction between countries, has a significant bearing on the use of a global strategy.

2. ***Competitors from Different Continents and Countries.*** Global competition among rivals from different continents tends to be more severe.

3. ***Interdependent Countries.*** Competitive interdependence among countries through shared business activities can help such firms to subsidize attacks on competitors in different countries. This can spur greater coordination of efforts by competitors to counterattack these subsidies.

4. ***Globalized Competitors.*** When a business's competitors use global strategy to exploit industry globalization potential, the business needs to match or preempt these competitors.

Source: Adapted from George S. Yip, *Total Global Strategy: Managing for Worldwide Competitive Advantage* (Englewood Cliffs, N.J.: Prentice Hall, 1992), pp. 223–231.

◆ ◆

$\mathcal{G}$LOBAL PERSPECTIVE 8-1

GLOBALIZING THE MULTIDOMESTIC CORPORATE CULTURE

In Unilever, three main groups are involved in strategic management: operating companies, management groups that oversee them, and the corporation as a whole. To be a successful global company, the strategies at different levels need to interrelate, considering bottom-up and top-down approaches. The dilemma is to find the right equilibrium between instructions from the top and inputs from the bottom in order not to stifle management creativity at the bottom as well as to provide sufficient direction to achieve the interests of all the corporation's stakeholders.

The company's culture and philosophy influence this equilibrium. Unilever, for example, used to be highly decentralized, with individual operating companies, with their own identity, linked by a common corporate culture and

some common services such as research, finance, and management development. After having experimented with various organizational structures to encourage global strategic management, Unilever has adopted a full-time Corporate Development board member, who is on staff with an advisory role, free from major line responsibilities.

Unilever's culture still emphasizes the relative independence of operating companies, where headquarters imposes changes only when there are clear advantages. As the problems faced by Unilever did not require an immediate strong reaction, the senior managers could proceed comparatively gradually, having the opportunity to feel a part of the strategy process. The gradual change in strategy orientation fit the company's corporate culture, demanding a gradual dosage rather than a sudden shock, with senior managers being able to feel a greater sense of commitment to the company's strategy.

Source: F.A. Maljers, "Strategic Planning and Intuition in Unilever," Long Range Planning, 23 (2) (1990), pp. 63–68.

In effect, the firm that truly operationalizes a global strategy is a geocentrically oriented firm. It considers the whole world as its arena of operation, and its managers maintain *equidistance* from all markets and do not permit any intrinsic national preferences to influence decisions concerning the global firm. This is in contrast to an ethnocentric orientation, where managers operate under the dominant influence of home country practices, or a polycentric orientation, where managers of individual subsidiaries operate independently of each other—the polycentric manager in practice leads to a multidomestic orientation, which prevents integration and optimization on a global basis. Until the early 1980s the global operations of Unilever were a good example of a multidomestic approach. Unilever's various country operations were largely independent of each other, with headquarters restricting itself to data collection and helping out subsidiaries when required. As presented in Global Perspective 8-1, Unilever has begun to add some geocentric dimensions to its global strategy.

Competitive Structure

A second aspect of global strategy is the nature of competitive industry structure. Customized flexible manufacturing as a result of CAD/CAM (computer-aided design and computer-aided manufacturing) technology has shown some progress. However, it proved to be more difficult operationally than was thought, so economies of scale still remain the main feature of market competition. The theory is that the greater the economies of scale, the greater the benefits to those firms with a larger market share. As a result, many firms try to jockey for larger market shares than their competitors. Economies of scale come about because larger plants are more efficient to run, and their per-unit cost of production is less as overhead costs are allocated across large volumes of production. Further economies of scale also result from learning effects: the firm learns more efficient methods of production with increasing cumulative experience in production over time. All of these effects tend to intensify competition. Once a high level of economies of scale is achieved, it provides the firm strong barriers against new entrants to the market. The firm that builds its competitive advantage on economies of scale is known as a **cost leader**. In the 1970s and early 1980s, many Japanese companies became cost leaders in such industries as automobiles and consumer electronics.

However, there is no guarantee that cost leadership will last. Until flexible manufacturing and customized production becomes fully operational, cost leaders may be vulnerable to firms that use **product differentiation** to better serve the exact needs of customers. Although one could argue that lower cost will attract customers away from other market segments, some customers are willing to pay a premium price for unique product features that they desire. Uniqueness may come in the form of comfort, product performance, and aesthetics, as well as status symbol and exclusivity. Despite the Japanese juggernaut in the automobile industry in the 1970s and 1980s, Mercedes-Benz of Germany and Volvo of Sweden, for example, managed to maintain their competitive strengths in the high-end segments of the automobile market. Smaller companies may pursue a limited differentiation strategy by keeping a niche in the market. Firms using a **niche** strategy focus exclusively on a highly specialized segment of the market and try to achieve a dominant position in that segment. Again in the automobile industry, Porsche and Saab maintain their competitive strengths in the high-power sports car enthusiast segment. However, particularly in an era of global competition, niche players may be vulnerable to large-scale operators due to sheer economies of scale needed to compete on a global scale.

Competition is not limited to the firms in the same industry. As just discussed, companies may adopt different strategies for different competitive advantage. If firms in an industry collectively have insufficient capacity to fulfill demand, the incentive is high for new market entrants. However, such entrants need to consider the time and investment it takes to develop new or additional capacity, the likelihood of such capacity being developed by existing competitors, and the possibility of changes in customer demand over time. Indirect competition also comes from suppliers and customers, as well as substitute products or services. A conceptual framework that portrays the multidimensional nature of competitive industry structure is presented in Exhibit 8-2.

1. **Industry competitors** determine the rivalry among existing firms.

2. **Potential entrants** may change the rule of competition but can be deterred through entry barriers. For example, Hyundai and Kia, two large Korean automobile manufacturers, and now Samsung, a brand-new entrant into the already crowded automobile industry,[7] may change the nature of competition in the U.S. automobile industry. However, they have also been kept at bay by existing domestic and foreign automakers operating in the United States.

3. The **bargaining power of suppliers** can change the structure of industries. Intel has become a dominant producer of microprocessors for personal computers. Its enormous bargaining power has caused many PC manufacturers to operate on wafer-thin profit margins, making the PC industry extremely competitive.

---

[7]Louis Kraar, "Behind Samsung's High-Stakes Push into Cars," *Fortune* (May 12, 1997), pp. 119–120.

EXHIBIT 8-2
NATURE OF COMPETITIVE INDUSTRY STRUCTURE

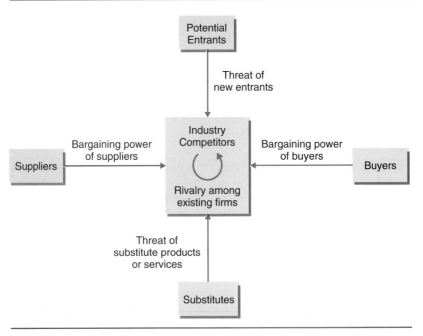

Source: Reprinted with the permission of the Free Press, a division of Simon & Schuster from *COMPETITIVE STRATEGY: Techniques for Analyzing Industries and Competitors* by Michael E. Porter, p. 4. Copyright © 1980 by The Free Press.

4. The **bargaining power of buyers** may affect the firm's profitability. It is particularly the case when governments try to get price and delivery concessions from foreign firms. Similarly, Nestlé, whose subsidiaries used to make independent decisions on cocoa purchase, has centralized its procurement decision at its headquarters to take advantage of its consolidated bargaining power over cocoa producers around the world.

5. The threat of **substitute products or services** can restructure the entire industry above and beyond the existing competitive structure. For example, OPEC learned in the 1970s that it could not raise crude oil prices artificially high without driving buyers to substitute sources of fuel such as alcohol and natural gas.

Hypercompetition[8]

In any given industry, firms jockey among themselves for better competitive position, given a set of customers and buyers, the threat of substitutes, and the barriers to entry in that industry. However, Exhibit 8-2 represents a description of a situation without any temporal dimension; there is no indication as to how a firm should act so

---

[8]Richard D'Aveni, *Hypercompetition: Managing the Dynamics of Strategic Maneuvering* (New York: The Free Press, 1994).

as to change the situation to its advantage. For instance, it is not clear how tomorrow's competitor may differ from today's. A new competitor may emerge from a completely different industry given the convergence of industries. Ricoh, a facsimile and copier maker, has now come up with a product that records moving images digitally, which is what a camcorder and a movie camera do using different technologies. This development potentially pits Ricoh as a direct competitor to camcorder and movie camera makers—something not possible ten or twenty years ago.

Such shifts in competition may be said to be *Schumpeterian*. The Schumpeterian view of creative destruction assumes continuous change, which is a basic assumption behind the concept of hypercompetitive strategy, where the firm's focus is on disrupting the market. In a hypercompetitive environment, a firm competes on the basis of price–quality, timing, and know-how, creating strongholds in the markets it operates in (this is akin to entry barriers), and financial resources to outlast one's competitors.

The basic premise of hypercompetition is that all firms are faced with a form of aggressive competition that is tougher than oligopoly or monopolistic competition, but is not perfect competition, where the firm is atomistic and cannot influence the market at all. This form of competition is pervasive not just in fast-moving high-technology industries like computers and deregulated industries like airlines, but also in industries which have traditionally been considered more sedate, like processed foods. The central thesis of this argument is that no type of competitive advantage can last—it is bound to get eroded.

For many firms, technology is the key to success in markets where significant advances in product performance are expected. A firm uses its technological leadership for rapid innovation and introduction of new products. The timing of such introductions in the global marketplace is an integral part of the firm's strategy. However, the dispersion of technological expertise means that any technological advantage is temporary, so the firm should not rest on its laurels. The firm needs to move on to its next source of temporary advantage to remain ahead. In the process, firms that are able to continue creating a series of temporary advantages are the ones that survive and thrive.

Hypercompetition postulates that firms compete in the following four arenas of competition.

Cost and Quality. The first arena is that of **cost** and **quality**. Japanese firms, in particular, have made U.S. and other Western competitors keenly aware that low cost and high quality can be achieved simultaneously. In the first arena, firms compete on price and quality—analogous to cost leadership, differentiation, and niche strategy, discussed earlier. As time goes by, the firms that are successful and that are still players in the market tend to become closer to one another in terms of price and quality. In other words, more firms become similar and the categorization of cost leadership and differentiation breaks down as firms attempt to deliver higher quality for lower cost. In effect, as shown in Exhibit 8-3, all firms attempt to move toward the ultimate value point—higher quality at lower costs. Improvements in manufacturing technology have enabled more firms to access this strategy than before.

Timing and Know-how. The second arena of competition is that of **timing** and **know-how**. They refer to factors such as being first to the market and technological leadership. Once competition shifts to the arena of timing and know-how, the tech-

EXHIBIT 8-3
THE PRICE/QUALITY TRADE-OFF AND THE
ULTIMATE VALUE POINT

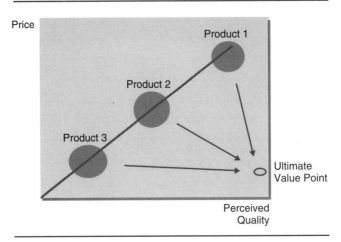

Source: Reprinted with the permission of The Free Press, a division of
Simon & Schuster from *TRIAD POWER: Hypercompetition: Managing
the Dynamics of Strategic Maneuvering,* p. 62. Copyright © 1994 by
Richard A. D'Aveni.

nology, marketing skills, and other assets that a firm possesses become its weapons to
gain advantages in time over its competitors. The firm now attempts to be among
the pioneers, or first-movers, in the market for the product categories that it operates
in.[9] Sony offers an excellent example of a company in constant pursuit of first-mover
advantage with Trinitron color television, Betamax videorecorder, Walkman, and
8mm videorecorder, although not all of its products succeeded in the market.

Strongholds. The third arena of competition is that of **strongholds**, referring to
geographic and other market segments where the firm is strong (through, for example, the creation of barriers). A strong competitive position in some market segments
provides the firm with the capability for attacking a competitor in another segment.
Here again, many Japanese companies built their initial competitive strengths by becoming strong domestic competitors in the large Japanese market, which constitutes
approximately two-thirds the size of the U.S. market and which is known for quality-
conscious, demanding customers.[10]

Financial Resources. The final arena of competition is the firm's **financial resources** that are used to make or purchase the latest technological advances or to
monitor its competitors anywhere they compete, eliminating surprises. For example,

---

[9]Gerard J. Tellis and Peter N. Golder, "First to Market, First to Fail?: Real Causes of Enduring Market Leadership," *Sloan Management Review,* 37 (Winter 1996), pp. 65–75.

[10]Michael E. Porter, "The Competitive Advantage of Nations," *Harvard Business Review,*
68 (March-April, 1990), pp. 73–93.

the merger of Asea of Sweden and Brown-Boveri of Switzerland has created a global company that can compete with General Electric in any part of the world on basis of its resources and global reach. Competition among firms now takes place, simultaneously or sequentially, through attempts to develop strongholds and to utilize the financial resources of the firm.

Black & Decker, a U.S.-based manufacturer of hand tools, switched to a global strategy using its strengths in the arenas of cost and quality and timing and know-how. In the 1980s Black & Decker's position was threatened by a powerful Japanese competitor, Makita. Makita's strategy of producing and marketing globally standardized products worldwide made it into a low-cost producer and enabled it to steadily increase its world market share. Within the company, Black & Decker's international fiefdoms combined with nationalist chauvinism to stifle coordination in product development and new product introductions, resulting in lost opportunities.

Then, responding to the increased competitive pressure, Black & Decker moved decisively toward globalization. It embarked on a program to coordinate new product development worldwide in order to develop core standardized products that could be marketed globally with minimum modification. The streamlining of R & D also offered scale economies and less duplication of effort—and new products could be introduced faster. Its increased emphasis on design made it into a global leader in design management. It consolidated its advertising into two agencies worldwide in an attempt to give a more consistent image worldwide. Black & Decker also strengthened the functional organization by giving the functional manager a larger role in coordinating with the country management. Finally, Black & Decker purchased General Electric's small appliance division to achieve world-scale economies in manufacturing, distribution, and marketing.

The global strategy initially faced skepticism and resistance from country managers at Black & Decker. The chief executive officer took a visible leadership role and made some management changes to start moving the company toward globalization. These changes in strategy helped Black & Decker increase revenues and profits by as much as 50 percent from 1986 to 1996.[11]

However, a word of caution is in order. A sudden strategy shift from a multidomestic to a global orientation could be more harmful than beneficial. A classic example of a failure is Parker Pen, as illustrated in Global Perspective 8-2. Indeed, it was not a global strategy that was at fault, but rather, implementation of the global strategy—it was too quick and too sudden, without due consideration of the company's organizational inertia.

Another on-going example is Intel, which, having established a premier position in microprocessors, is now attempting to create a stronghold in that area by adding more and more components to the basic microprocessor design, such as video and graphic controllers. Intel is also utilizing its financial muscle to create powerful brand-name recognition for a product that is not really an end-product that consumers buy but only a component in the end-product—albeit a critical one. Competition based on financial resources is akin to the utilization of a large war chest by a country to win a war. As more firms attempt to compete on this basis, status quo again reigns with no basic differentiation among firms. Firms may then shift again to cost- and quality-based competition.

---

[11]Black & Decker, various annual reports.

◆ ◆

$\mathcal{G}$LOBAL PERSPECTIVE 8-2

ROME COULD NOT BE BUILT IN A DAY AT PARKER PEN COMPANY

Parker Pen was a successful company until the early 1980s. It used to be a completely decentralized company, whose country managers had a great degree of operational flexibility. Parker Pen's subsidiaries used to develop their own marketing strategies, independently deciding what products to produce and selecting their own advertising agencies. Parker Pen was proud of its decentralized operational structure.

The Parker name was strongly associated with pens, having a strong reputation for quality and style. The company was able to charge premium prices in the past when pens were considered as a gift item.

In the 1960s, however, a fundamental change occurred in the market: the development of the disposable, ball-point market. Despite this trend, Parker Pen had remained in the upper end of the market with high-priced pens. When Parker Pen decided to enter the lower end of the market, however, it failed, because its management team did not know how to market the product in this new market segment.

When the U.S. dollar rose in the early 1980s, Parker Pen began to see its operational inefficiencies and consequently lower profits due to its fragmented production and marketing around the world. To address this issue, a new management team was brought in with James Peterson as president and chief executive officer. Peterson decided to go "global," standardizing product and promotion strategies.

As a result, the product line was slashed from 500 to the 100 most profitable items. The company began to use Ogilvy & Mather as its sole global advertising agency; its manufacturing facilities were updated—especially the one used to produce the lower-end product: the Vector, a roller-ball pen.

Peterson believed that his global marketing effort could save Parker Pen, and decided to enter in every viable segment. Peterson intensified the identical global advertising, forgetting that pens could mean different things to different people. His strategy backfired.

Parker Pen's global marketing strategy also failed because Peterson tried to transform his managers abroad from independently operating executives into simple implementers of the global marketing strategy. With the abrupt change imposed on the country managers, Peterson failed to consider the corporate culture and its organizational inertia.

Source: Laurie Freeman, "Parker Pen Dropping Its Global Plans," *Advertising Age* (May 13, 1985), p. 66.

In essence, competitive advantage goes to firms that disrupt the existing status quo in the market and take advantage of the disruption. Managers, therefore, seek actively to create a market disequilibrium and then profit from it. In this scenario, the traditional economists' market equilibrium cannot exist because the market is continuously lurching from one 'equilibrium' to another. The manager's job is to manage these continuous transitions so that the firm makes profits and gains on market share.

To disrupt the market, the firm must have its ear close to the ground so that it picks up customer requirements early enough to take advantage of market feedback ahead of its competitors. In other words, the firm needs to be market- and customer-oriented. Market orientation has been defined to be the organization-wide generation, dissemination, and responsiveness to the intelligence from customers and the market. If a firm is to maintain a market orientation consistently, it requires leadership from top executives in the organization who have to send the correct signals to personnel in the organization.

There appear to be primarily two approaches to gaining competitive advantage. The competitor-centered approaches involve comparison with the competitor on costs, prices, technology, market share, profitability, and other related activities. Such an approach may lead to a preoccupation with some activities, and the firm may lose sight of its customers and various constituents. Customer-focused approaches to gaining competitive advantage emanate from an analysis of customer benefits to be delivered. In practice, finding the proper links between required customer benefits and the activities and variables controlled by management is needed. Besides, there is evidence to suggest that listening too closely to customer requirements may cause a firm to miss the bus on innovations, because current customers might not want innovations that require them to change how they operate.

Interdependency

A fourth aspect of global strategy is interdependency of modern companies. Recent research has shown that the number of technologies used in a variety of products in numerous industries is rising.[12] Access to resources limit how many distinctive competencies a firm can gain, so firms must draw on outside technologies to be able to build a state-of-the-art product. Since most firms operating globally are limited by a lack of all required technologies, it follows that for firms to make optimal use of outside technologies, a degree of components standardization is required. Such standardization would enable different firms to develop different end products, using, in a large measure, the same components.[13] Research findings do indicate that *technology intensity*—that is, the degree of R & D expenditure a firm incurs as a proportion of sales—is a primary determinant of cross-border firm integration.[14]

The computer industry is a good instance of a case where firms use components from various sources. Compaq, Dell, and Acer all use semiconductor chips from Intel, AMD, or Cyrix, hard drives from Seagate or Conner, and software from Microsoft. The final product—in this case, the personal computer—carries some individual idiosyncrasies of Compaq, Dell, or Acer, but at least some of the components are common and, indeed, are portable across the products of the three companies.

In the international context, governments also tend to play a larger role and may, directly or indirectly, affect parts of the firm's strategy. Tariffs and nontariff barriers such as voluntary export restraints and restrictive customs procedures might change cost structures so that a firm may need to change its production and sourcing decisions. It is possible, however, that with the end of the Cold War and the spread of capitalism to previously socialist economies, such factors may decrease in importance. The successful completion of the Uruguay Round of GATT talks in December 1993 and the signing of the agreement in April 1994 is an encouraging sign because it leads to greater harmonization of tariff rules and less freedom for national governments to make arbitrary changes in tariff and nontariff barriers and in intellectual property laws.

---

[12]Ove Granstrand, Erik Bohlin, Christer Oskarsson, and Niklas Sjoberg, "External Technology Acquisition in Large Multitechnology Corporations," *R & D Management*, 22 (2) (1992), pp. 111–133.

[13]Masaaki Kotabe, Arvind Sahay, and Preet S. Aulakh, "Emerging Roles of Technology Licensing in Development of Global Product Strategy: A Conceptual Framework and Research Propositions," *Journal of Marketing*, 60 (January 1996), pp. 73–88.

[14]Stephen Kobrin, "An Empirical Analysis of the Determinants of Global Integration," *Strategic Management Journal*, 12 (1991), pp. 17–31.

GLOBAL MARKETING STRATEGY ◆ ◆ ◆ ◆ ◆ ◆

Multinational companies increasingly use global marketing and have been highly successful, such as Nestlé with its common brand name applied to many products in all countries, Coca Cola with its global advertising themes, Xerox with its global leasing policies, and Dell Computer's "sell-direct" strategy.[15] But global marketing is not about standardizing the marketing process on a global basis. Although every element of the marketing process—product design, product and brand positioning, brand name, packaging, pricing, advertising strategy and execution, promotion and distribution—may be a candidate for standardization, standardization is one part of a global marketing strategy and it may or may not be used by a company, depending on the mix of the product-market conditions, stage of market development, and the inclinations of the management of the multinational firm. For instance, a marketing element can be global without being 100 percent uniform in content or coverage. Exhibit 8-4 illustrates a possible pattern.

Let us take an instance from Exhibit 8-4 and look at distribution with a magnitude of less than 50 percent on both coverage of world market and on extent of uniform content. If we assume that the firm in question (represented in the diagram) does not have a manufacturing facility in each of the markets it serves, then to the extent that various markets have a uniform content, and presumably similar operations, there is a requirement for coordination with manufacturing facilities elsewhere in the firm's global network. Also, where content is not uniform, any change requirements for the nonuniform content of distribution require corresponding changes in the product and/or packaging. Thus, a consequence of a global marketing strategy is more intimate linkages with a firm's other functions, such as research and development, manufacturing, and finance.[16]

In other words, a global marketing strategy is but one component of a global strategy. For an analogy, you may think of a just-in-time inventory and manufacturing system that works for a single manufacturing facility to optimize production. Extend this concept now to finance and marketing, and include all subsidiaries of the firm across the world as well. One can imagine the magnitude and complexity of the task when a manager is attempting to develop and implement a global strategy. One implication is that without a global strategy for R & D, manufacturing, and finance that meshes with the various requirements of its global *marketing* strategy, a firm cannot best implement that global marketing strategy.

Benefits of Global Marketing

Global marketing strategy can achieve one or more of four major categories of potential globalization benefits: cost reduction, improved quality of products and programs, enhanced customer preference, and increased competitive advantage.[17]

---

[15]Silvia Ascarelli, "Dell Finds U.S. Strategy Works in Europe," *Wall Street Journal* (February 3, 1997), p. A8; Eryn Brown, "Could the Very Best PC Maker Be Dell Computer?" *Fortune* (April 14, 1997), p. 26.

[16]Masaaki Kotabe, *Global Sourcing Strategy: R & D, Manufacturing, and Marketing Interfaces* (New York: Quorum Books, 1992).

[17]George S. Yip, *Total Global Strategy: Managing for Worldwide Competitive Advantage* (Englewood Cliffs, N.J.: Prentice Hall, 1992), pp. 21–23.

EXHIBIT 8-4
VARIATION IN CONTENT AND COVERAGE OF
GLOBAL MARKETING

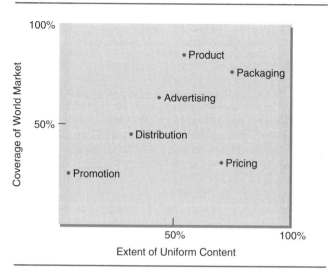

Source: George S. Yip, *Total Global Strategy: Managing for Worldwide Competitive Advantage* (Englewood Cliffs, NJ: Prentice Hall, 1992), p. 136.

General Motors and Ford approach global marketing somewhat differently; such a strategic difference suggests that the two U.S. automakers are in search of different benefits of global marketing (see Global Perspective 8-3).

Cost Reduction. This arises from savings in both work force and materials. When multiple national marketing functions are consolidated, personnel outlays are reduced through the avoidance of duplicating of activities. Costs are also saved in producing global advertisements and commercials and producing promotional materials and packaging. Savings from standardized packaging includes reduction in inventory costs. With typical inventory carrying costs at 20 percent of sales, any reduction in inventory can significantly impact sales. With the availability of a global span of coverage by various forms of modern communication media, multicountry campaigns capitalizing on countries' common features would also reduce advertising costs considerably. Exxon's "Put a Tiger in Your Tank" campaign is a good example of a campaign that used the same theme across much of the world, taking advantage of the fact that the tiger is almost universally associated with power and grace.

Cost savings can also translate into increased program effectiveness by allowing more money and resources into a smaller number of more focused programs. British Airways was able to afford spectacular and expensive special effects for its highly memorable "Manhattan Landing" global television commercial, in which Manhattan was shown landing on a small English village.

Improved Products and Program Effectiveness. This may often be the greatest advantage of a global marketing strategy. Good ideas are relatively scarce in the business arena. So a globalization program that overcomes local objections to allow the spread of a good marketing idea can often raise the effectiveness of the program

◆◆

𝒢LOBAL PERSPECTIVE 8-3

GM AND FORD PURSUE DIFFERENT BENEFITS FROM GLOBAL MARKETING

Ford and General Motors approach globalization differently. In its quest for a "world car," Ford has developed the so-called Ford 2000 program by creating five new vehicle centers—four in the United States and one in Europe—each responsible for designing and developing a different type of car worldwide. Ford's plan was put to test when it built a midsize world car in 1993 known as the Mondeo in Europe and the Ford Contour in North America. Its plan was to manufacture 700,000 cars a year in Europe and North America for nearly a decade with only a "refreshing" after four or five years. Ford executives say they can no longer afford to duplicate efforts and they want to emulate the Japanese, who develop cars that with minor variations can be sold around the world. While the Mondeo/Contour sold 642,000 units in the first two years in Europe, it had disappointing sales in the United States, attributed to its comparably higher price relative to the car's predecessors. Successful product development efforts require that the company avoid two problems that can arise from pursuing global design. First, the high cost of designing products or components that are acceptable in many settings could negatively affect efficiency. Second, the product, in this case a "world car," may be low cost but meet the lowest common denominator of taste in all countries.

Alternatively, General Motors has taken a more regional tack by retaining strong regional operations that develop distinctly different cars for their own. If a car has a strong crossover potential, engineers and marketers cross the Atlantic to suggest customization. Thus, Cadillac got an Americanized version of the Opel Omega small luxury sedan developed by GM's Opel subsidiary in Germany. GM managers contend that *ad hoc* efforts are cheaper and more flexible. John Oldfield, vice president of new product programs at Ford of Europe, counters that "doing two conventional car programs would have cost substantially more than doing one global program. If we did it again, we could do it in 3½ years."

The two automakers' contrasting product development and marketing programs illustrate the traditionally viewed tradeoffs of efficiency and adaptiveness, global standardization versus customization, market segmentation versus product differentiation, and product orientation versus customer orientation. These debates are framed by the tension between bending demand to the will of supply (i.e., driving the market) versus adjusting to market demand (i.e., driven by the market).

It is difficult to conclude that one strategy is genuinely better than the other. One has to be reminded that while the Ford Mondeo/Contour project cost $6 billion and took six years to develop, potential cost savings could also be enormous for years to come from the global strategy. On the other hand, GM's regional strategy could also make sense if regional taste differences remain so large that a Ford-style global strategy could, indeed, end up producing a "blandmobile" that hits the lowest common denominator of taste in different markets.

Source: "Ford: Alex Trotman's Daring Global Strategy," *Business Week*, (April 3, 1995), pp. 94–104.

---

when measured on a worldwide basis. Traditionally, R & D has been concentrated in the headquarters country of a global company. This has sometimes circumscribed a possible synergy from amalgamation of good ideas from around the world.

Procter & Gamble has solved this problem by setting up major R & D facilities in each of its major markets in the Triad—North America, Japan, and Western Europe—and by putting together the pertinent findings from each of the laboratories. As in the saying, "Necessity is the mother of invention," different needs in different parts of the world may lead to different inventions. For example, Procter & Gamble's Liquid Tide laundry detergent was an innovative product developed in an innovative way by taking advantage of both the company's technical abilities and various market requirements in the key markets around the world. Germans had been extremely concerned about polluting rivers with phosphate, a key whitening ingredient in the traditional detergent. To meet the German customer demand, Procter & Gamble in Germany had developed fatty acid to replace phosphate in the detergent. Similarly, Procter & Gamble Japan had developed surfactant to get off grease effectively in tepid water that Japanese use in washing their clothes. In the United States, Procter & Gamble in Cincinnati, Ohio, had independently developed "builder" to keep dirt from settling on clothes. Putting all these three innovations together, the company introduced Liquid Tide and its sister products around the world.

Three benefits followed from this multiple R & D location strategy. By being able to integrate required product attributes from three separate markets, P & G was able to introduce a much better product than would otherwise be possible and increase its chances of success. Second, its development costs were spread over a much larger market—a market that was more inclined to receive the product favorably because of the incorporation of the product features described. Third, it increased the sources from which product ideas are available to it. Thus, not only does P & G have immediate returns, but also it has secured for itself a reliable resource base of future products.

Enhanced Customer Preference. Awareness and recall of a product on a worldwide basis increase its value. A global marketing strategy helps build recognition that can enhance customer preferences through reinforcement. With the rise in the availability of information from a variety of sources across the world and the rise in travel across national borders, more and more people are being exposed to messages in different countries. So a uniform marketing message, whether communicated through a brand name, packaging, or advertisement reinforces the awareness, knowledge, and attitudes of people toward the product or service. Pepsi has a consistent theme in its marketing communication across the world—that of youthfulness and fun as a part of the experience of drinking Pepsi anywhere in the world.

Increased Competitive Advantage. By focusing resources into a smaller number of programs, global strategies magnify the competitive power of the programs. Although larger competitors might have the resources to develop different high-quality programs for each country, smaller firms might not. Using a focused global marketing strategy could allow the smaller firm to compete with a larger competitor in a more effective manner. However, the most important benefit of a global strategy may be that the entire organization gets behind a single idea, thus increasing the chances of the success of the idea. Avis created a global campaign communicating the idea that "We are number two, therefore we try harder," not only to customers, but also to its employees. As a result the entire organization pulled together to deliver on a global promise, not just in marketing but in all activities which directly or indirectly affected the company's interface with the customer.

Equally if not more important, are the benefits of market and competitive intelligence provided by the increased flow of information due to the worldwide coordination of activities. As the global firm meshes the different parts of the organization into the framework of a focused strategy, information flow through the organization improves and enables the functioning of the strategy. A byproduct is that the organization as a whole becomes much better informed about itself and about the activities of its competitors in markets across the world. Access to more and timely information results in the organization being more prepared and able to respond to signals from the marketplace.

Limits to Global Marketing

Although national boundaries have begun losing their significance both as a psychological and as a physical barrier to international business, the diversity of local environments, particularly cultural, political, and legal environments, still plays an important role not as a facilitator, but rather as an inhibitor, of optimal global marketing strategy development. Indeed, we still debate the very issue raised more than twenty years ago: counteracting forces of "unification versus fragmentation" in developing operational strategies along the value chain. As early as 1969, Fayerweather wrote emphatically:

> What fundamental effects does (the existence of many national borders) have on the strategy of the multinational firm? Although many effects can be itemized, one central theme recurs; that is, their tendency to push the firm toward adaptation to the diversity of local environments which leads toward fragmentation of operations. But there is a natural tendency in a single firm toward integration and uniformity which is basically at odds with fragmentation. Thus the central issue . . . is the conflict between unification and fragmentation—a close-knit operational strategy with similar foreign units versus a loosely related, highly variegated family of activities.[18]

The same counteracting forces have since been revisited by many authors in such terms as "standardization versus adaptation" (1960s), "globalization versus localization" (1970s), "global integration versus local responsiveness" (1980s), and most recently, "scale versus sensitivity" (1990s).[19] Terms have changed, but the quintessence of the strategic dilemma that multinational firms face today has not changed and will probably remain unchanged for years to come.

Now the question is to what extent successful multinational firms can circumvent the impact of local environmental diversity. In some industries, product standardization may result in a product that satisfies customers nowhere. For processed foods, for example, national tastes and consumption patterns differ sufficiently to make standardization counterproductive. In Latin America, a variety of canned spicy peppers, such as jalapeño peppers, is a national staple in Mexico, but is virtually unheard of in Brazil and Chile. Obviously, firms cannot lump together the whole of Latin America as one regional market for condiments.

On the other hand, Merck, the world's second largest pharmaceutical company, faces a different kind of problem with global marketing. The company can market the same products around the world for various ailments, but cultural and political differences make it very difficult to approach different markets in a similar way. Merck, which operates internationally as MSD, has to increase public awareness of health care issues in Mexico, Central America, and much of South America by bringing top journalists from these countries together on a regular basis to meet with health care experts ranging from physicians to government officials. In the Pacific Rim, the company is trying to change the way it does business there. It used to operate through local distributors and licensees, never learning the local quirks of pharmaceutical business. Now, the company is creating subsidiaries in nearly all main Asian countries, including Korea, China, the Philippines, Taiwan, Singapore, and Malaysia, in order to learn what goes on inside those markets. In Eastern Europe, Merck is starting from scratch, as its entry had been previously barred under the region's strict communist control. For example, in Hungary, the company has devoted

---

[18]John Fayerweather, *International Business Management: Conceptual Framework* (New York: McGraw-Hill, 1969), pp. 133–34.

[19]Martin Sorrell, Group Chief Executive, WPP Group, "Globalization: Scale versus Sensitivity," A speech, Joint Conference of the Korean Marketing Association and the American Marketing Association, May 14–17, 1995.

its initial investment to establishing resource centers that are affiliated with local hospitals and universities in order to create a special image for Merck.[20]

However, despite such cultural and political constraints in the markets, Nestlé, for example, has managed to integrate procurement functions in order to gain bargaining power in purchasing common ingredients such as cocoa and sugar. In other industries, such as computers and telecommunications, consumption patterns are in the process of being established and the associated cultural constraint is getting less prominent. Also, the simultaneous launch of most products in these categories across the world precludes large differences. For these products, governments frequently attempt to exert national control over technological development, the products or the production process.[21] However, while it is the multinational firms that are the vehicle through which technology, production and economic activity in general are integrated across borders, *it is the underlying technology and economic activity that are global.* National markets, regardless of how they are organized economically, are no longer enough to support the development of technology in many industries. See Exhibit 8-5 for some generalizations about the degree of product standardization around the world.

Thus, if critical technologies are transnational, then, to an extent, meanings of borders, sovereignty, and nation-states themselves are compromised. More specifically, terms such as *national control of technology* and *national industrial competitiveness* lose some of their meaning—the more so because national governments, which represent nations, do not "produce" anything or sell any of "their" product. Indeed, governments may then make themselves more useful by finding ways to provide the means to enhance the strengths and to access appropriate partners for the areas of weakness of the firms which call that government the home country government.

REGIONALIZATION OF GLOBAL MARKETING STRATEGY

◆ ◆ ◆ ◆ ◆ ◆

Some firms, such as General Motors, may have difficulty in organizing, or may not be willing to organize, operations to maximize flexibility and encourage integration across national borders. Beyond various cultural, political, and economic differences across national borders, organizational realities also impair the ability of multinational firms to pursue global marketing strategies. Not surprisingly, integration has often been opposed by foreign subsidiaries eager to protect their historical relative independence from their parent companies. As described earlier, the successful and gradual adoption of global orientation in Global Perspective 8-1 and the debacle of Parker Pen's attempt to shift to globally uniform marketing in Global Perspective 8-2 offer good contrasting examples.

In finding a balance between the need for greater integration and the need to exploit existing resources more effectively, many companies have begun to explore the use of regional strategies in Europe, North America, and the Pacific Rim. Regional

---

[20]Fannie Weinstein, "Drug Interaction: Merck Establishes Itself, Country by Country, in Emerging Markets," *Profiles* (September 1996), pp. 35–39.

[21]C. K. Prahalad and Yves L. Doz, *The Multinational Mission* (New York: The Free Press, 1987).

EXHIBIT 8-5
DEGREE OF STANDARDIZABILITY OF PRODUCTS IN WORLD MARKETS

Local → Universal

Factors limiting universality	Culture/ habits	Design taste	Language	Size/package	Technical system	User/ application	None
Example	• Fish sausage • Root beer • Boxer shorts • Rice cooker	• Furniture • Refrigerator • Processed food	• Word processor • Computer	• Textile • Automotive (seat size) • Soft drinks	• Color TV (PAL system in European voltage)	• Portable radio/cassette player (youths in U.S.) • While liqueur (young females in Japan)	• Watch • Motorcycle • Petrochemical products • Piano • Money (capital market)

Key functions:
- Marketing concept
- Technology
- Product application
- Product concept

☐ Must modify locally ☐ Could be shared globally

Source: Reprinted with the permission of The Free Press, a division of Simon & Schuster from *TRIAD POWER: The Coming Shape of Global Competition* by Kenichi Ohmae, p. 193. Copyright © 1985 by Kenichi Ohmae and McKinsey & Company, Inc.

GLOBAL PERSPECTIVE 8-4

NIKE AND REEBOK BATTLING FOR GLOBAL DOMINANCE

Sneakers have become an obsession—from sports enthusiasts to people concerned about health to junior executives, and to people who follow fashion, and housewives. Two giants dominate this market: Nike and Reebok. Nike was founded thirty years ago by Philip Knight, a University of Oregon track star, who began importing high-quality running shoes to the United States. Reebok, originally a British-made sneaker with a line of white-leather women's aerobic shoes, had its North American rights acquired in 1979 by Paul Fireman for his family's sporting-goods business.

Nike's first years were spent shuttling across the Pacific in search of capital and cheap labor from Japan to Korea to Taiwan. But the force that made this company fly was Knight's ability to attract popular sports heroes, the most dominant and charismatic, to his cause and then build new product lines and marketing campaigns around them. This formula had a great success—for a decade the company revenues grew at nearly triple-digit rates: they created a need.

By 1976 the jogging craze took off across the United States, and people desired a pricey pair of sneakers. In 1980s Nike was the market leader in the United States and went public. The global dominance of German manufacturers Puma and Adidas was threatened.

In the mid-1980s the jogging fever suddenly broke. Reebok's sales exploded through the 1980s, as more women got into exercise and more people began to use good sneakers for several activities besides sports. In 1984 Fireman bought out the parent company and in 1985 the company went public. When it passed Nike in annual sales in 1987, Knight decided to return to his core strategy—building new products around a popular athlete, this time with Michael Jordan. Nike's ad campaigns are legendary and have changed sports marketing forever, redefining what is celebrity, and positioned Nike as the brand of athletic performance.

The Air Jordan line of footwear and apparel put Nike back on track. By 1990 it was the leader again—and still is. Reebok remains a great competitor, and the two companies together have more than half the share of the U.S.

market, and also control more than 40 percent of the global market. In the global arena Adidas is the only significant competitor with a 10 percent share of the global sales.

Until the 1990s Reebok had Nike's attention but was perceived to be a different company, whose main market was women's fitness, with a product line including a range of lower-priced casual shoes. Nike's strategic focus was to deliver high-quality, high-priced products to male athletes and wannabes. Their similarities were to act in the athletic footwear and apparel business, and both maintained the bulk of their manufacturing base in low-cost countries.

Around 1990 Fireman had launched sallies into men's team sports, boosted product development budget and tried to broaden his products' appeal. He started using Nike's core strategy, then the two companies began to compete by sport heroes. Both companies know that their success heavily depends on celebrity marketing and consumer fad. That is also the reason they are trying to diversify. Nike is in retail with outlets called Nike Towns—conceived as sports museums—and Reebok has a fitness-club business and videos. They target every sport activity that can interest the under-18-year-old crowd.

In the future the main arena will be outside the United States. Reebok makes half its sales overseas, and Nike sells about 40 percent of its goods abroad. The most important global battleground is soccer, an arena dominated by Adidas, with some 300 million people playing the game worldwide. Reebok has been chipping away at Adidas for several years, using sponsorship, signing global superstars, and marking its presence in important championships such as World Cup. Nike entered this market more recently, but is already shaking up the sport—sponsoring men's and women's U.S. national teams, besides the Italian national team, and putting together a lineup of superstar endorsers, from Italy to Brazil.

Reebok's global strategy is to find a place in minor sports, by identifying the one that has an emotional appeal in a particular country—for example, handball in Denmark, cricket in Great Britain, and baseball in Japan. For Nike, its marketing power—sports celebrities—is no longer a secret. And both companies may have problems in the future with the overuse of heroes and emotions by so many advertisers.

Source: Kenneth Labaich, "Nike vs. Reebok—A Battle for Hearts, Minds & Feet," *Fortune* (September 18, 1995), pp. 58–69.

strategies can be defined as the cross-subsidization of market share battles in pursuit of regional production, branding, and distribution advantages.[22] Regional strategies in Europe and North America have been encouraged by the economic, political, and social pressures resulting from the development of regional trading blocs, such as European Union, North American Free Trade Agreement (NAFTA), and Southern Common Market (MERCOSUR).[23]

There are two favorable effects of the formation of regional trading blocs. First, the volatility of foreign exchange rates within a bloc seems to be reduced.[24] Second, with the growing level of macroeconomic integration with regions, there is also a trend toward greater harmonization of product and industry standards, pollution and safety standards, and environmental standards, among other things.[25] These regional commonalities further encourage firms to develop marketing strategies on a regional basis.[26] Global marketing strategy cannot be developed without considering competitive and other market forces from different regions around the world. To face those regional forces proactively, three additional strategies need to be considered at the firm level. These are *cross subsidization of markets, identification of weak market segments,* and *the lead market concept.*[27] See also Global Perspective 8-4 for an example of global competition between Nike and Reebok, employing these three strategies on an ongoing basis.

Cross-Subsidization of Markets

For example, Michelin used its strong profit base in Europe to attack the home market of Goodyear in the United States. Reducing prices in its home market (by Goodyear) would have meant that Goodyear would have reduced its own profits from its largest and most profitable market without substantially affecting Michelin's bottom line, because Michelin would have exposed only a small portion of its worldwide business by competing with Goodyear in the United States. Goodyear chose to strike back by expanding operations and reducing prices in Europe.

Kodak's ongoing rivalry with Fuji in the photographic film market provides another example of the importance of not permitting a global competitor unhindered operation in its home market. Kodak did not have a presence in Japan until the early 1980s. In this omission, Kodak was making the same mistake that many other West-

---

[22]Allen J. Morrison and Kendall Roth, "The Regional Solution: An Alternative to Globalization," *Transnational Corporations,* 1 (August 1, 1992), pp. 37–55.

[23]Maria Cecilia Coutinho de Arruda and Masaaki Kotabe, "MERCOSUR: An Emergent Market in South America," in Masaaki Kotabe, *MERCOSUR and Beyond: The Imminent Emergence of the South American Markets,* Center for International Business Education and Research, The University of Texas at Austin, 1996.

[24]Marc Hendriks, "Prospects for the European Financial System," *Business Economics,* 30 (July 1995), pp. 11–16; Alan David MacCormack, Lawrence James Newmann, and Donald B. Rosenfield, "The New Dynamics of Global Manufacturing Site Location," *Sloan Management Review,* 35 (Summer 1994), pp. 69–80.

[25]Edmund W. Beaty, "Standard Regionalization: A Threat to Internetworking?" *Telecommunications,* Americas Edition, 27 (May 1993), pp. 48–51.

[26]Maneesh Chandra, "The Regionalization of Global Strategy," A paper presented at 1997 Academy of International Business Annual Meeting, Monterrey, Mexico, October 8–12, 1997.

[27]Gary Hamel and C.K. Prahalad, "Do You Really Have a Global Strategy?" *Harvard Business Review* (July–August 1985), pp. 139–148.

ern companies have done—*avoiding Japan as unattractive on a stand-alone basis, while not seeing its strategic importance as the home base of a global competitor and a source of ideas.*

Identification of Weak Market Segments

The second strategy that firms should always keep an open eye for is the identification of weak market segments not covered by a firm in its home market. Small-screen portable TVs were used by Japanese TV makers to get a foot in the door of the large U.S. market for TVs. RCA and Zenith did not think this segment attractive enough to go after. Another classic example is Honda's entry into the U.S. motorcycle market in the 1960s. Honda offered small, lightweight machines that looked safe and cute, attracting families and an emerging leisure class with an advertising campaign, "You can meet the nicest people on a Honda." Prior to Honda's entry, the U.S. motorcycle market was characterized by the police, military personnel, aficionados, and scofflaws like Hell's Angels and Devil's Disciples. Honda broke away from the existing paradigms about motorcycles and the motorcycle market, and successfully differentiated itself by covering niches that did not exist before.[28] Once the Japanese companies were established in the small niche they had a base to expand on to larger and more profitable product lines. More recently in 1996, Labatt International of Canada took advantage of freer trading relationships in NAFTA and Canadian consumers awakening to things Mexican by importing a Mexican beer, Sol, brewed by Cerveceria Cuauhtemoc Moctezuma, to fill a newly found market segment in Canada. Thus, firms should avoid pegging their competitive advantage entirely on one market segment in their home market.

What directions can this lead to in terms of a global product strategy—or a worldwide distribution, pricing, or promotion strategy? Let us discuss some aspects of a global product strategy for an automobile company. Suppose market data tell the managers that four dozen different models are required if the company desires to design separate cars for each distinct segment of the Triad market. But the company has neither the financial nor the technological resources to go in for so many product designs. Also, there is no single global car that will solve the problems for the entire world. The United States, Japan, and Europe are different markets, with different mixes of needs and preferences. Japan requires right-hand drive cars with frequent inspections, while many parts of Europe need smaller cars as compared to the United States. As a top manager of an automobile company the option of leaving out a Triad market would not be a good one. The company needs to be present in, at least, all of these three markets with good products.

"Lead Market" Concept

The solution may be to look at the main requirements of each "key" market in turn. In the United States, a sporty model as well as a four-door family car is required. Tax policies in Britain may require development of a car that is suitable for corporate fleet sales. As indicated earlier, this is a strategic response to the emergence of lead countries as a market globalization driver. Each can be a **lead country model**—a product carefully tailored to meet distinct individual needs. With a short list of lead country models in hand, minor modifications may enable a fair amount of sales in

---

[28]Oren Harari, "The Secret Competitive Advantage," *Management Review*, 83 (January 1994), pp. 45–47.

other Triad markets and elsewhere. This will halve the number of basic models required to cover the global markets and, at the same time, cover a major proportion of sales with cars designed for major markets. Additional model types could be developed through adaptation of the lead country models for specific segments. This approach in each of the largest core markets permits development of a pool of supplemental designs that can be adapted to local preferences.

In line with our earlier example of Procter & Gamble, it is not necessary that the design and manufacturing of a lead country model be restricted to one R & D and manufacturing facility. Ford has now integrated the design and manufacturing process on a global basis. It has design centers at Dearborn (Michigan), England, Italy, and Japan, which are connected by a satellite uplink. Designers using fast workstations and massively parallel computers simulate a complete model and the working of the model for various conditions. Separate parts of the car are simulated at different facilities. Thereafter, the complete design for a lead country is integrated in the facility assigned for the purpose. For instance, the complete design for the new Ford Mustang was put together in Dearborn, but it incorporated some significant changes in body design that were made in England based on designs of Jaguar, which Ford had acquired. Similarly, different components of an automobile may be sourced from different parts of the global network of the firm or even from outside the firm. As firms move toward concentrating on developing expertise in a few core competencies,[29] they are increasingly outsourcing many of the components required for the total product system that constitutes the automobile.

This increase in outsourcing raises another question for firms that practice it. How can firms ensure uninterrupted flow of components when the component makers are independent companies? The answer to this question and the set of issues that it raises takes us into the area of cooperation between firms and strategic alliances, which will be discussed in Chapter 9.

◆ ◆ ◆ ◆ ◆ ◆ COMPETITIVE ANALYSIS

As we have discussed so far, a firm needs to broaden the sources of competitive advantage relentlessly over time. However, careful assessment of a firm's current competitive position is also required. One particularly useful technique in analyzing a firm's competitive position relative to its competitors is referred to as **SWOT** (Strengths, Weaknesses, Opportunities, Threats) **analysis**. A SWOT analysis divides the information into two main categories (internal factors and external factors) and then further into positive aspects (strengths and opportunities) and negative aspects (weaknesses and threats). The internal factors that may be viewed as strengths or weaknesses depend on their impact on the firm's positions; that is, they may represent a strength for one firm but a weakness, in relative terms, for another. They include all of the marketing mix (product, price, promotion, and distribution strategy); as well as personnel and finance. The external factors, which again may be threats to one firm and opportunities to another, include technological changes, legislation, sociocultural changes, and changes in the marketplace or competitive position.

The framework for a SWOT analysis is illustrated in Exhibit 8-6.

---

[29]C. K. Prahalad and Gary Hamel, "The Core Competence of the Corporation," *Harvard Business Review*, 68 (May–June 1990), pp. 79–91.

EXHIBIT 8-6
SWOT ANALYSIS

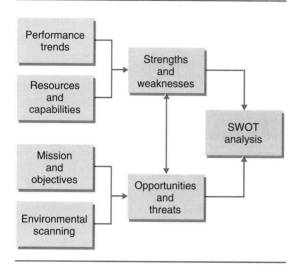

You should note, however, that SWOT is just *one* aid to categorization. It is not the only technique. One drawback of SWOT is that it tends to persuade companies to compile lists rather than think about what is really important to their business. It also presents the resulting lists uncritically, without clear prioritization; so that, for example, weak opportunities may appear to balance strong threats. Furthermore, using the company's strengths against its competitors' weaknesses may work once or twice, but not over several dynamic strategic interactions, as its approach becomes predictable and the competitors may begin to learn and outsmart it.

The aim of any SWOT analysis should be to isolate the key *issues* that will be important to the future of the firm and that subsequent marketing strategy will address.

$\mho$IDEOBOX

AUTOMOBILE COMPETITION IN THE EMERGING MARKETS

Japan remains one of the toughest markets for foreign automakers since there are eight domestic car makers vying for the market share, led by Toyota, Nissan, Honda, Mazda, and Mitsubishi. Among foreign imports, Mercedes-Benz, BMW, Ford, and Chrysler, among others, have also established their niches in the already congested auto market in Japan.

Now attracted to the growing Asian markets, many U.S., European, and Japanese automakers are hastily expanding their operations in those emerging markets through wholly owned subsidiaries and joint ventures with local partners. Despite economic and political uncertainties, China remains the single most attractive market with virtually unlimited demand potential for automobiles.

Discuss how the nature of competition may change over time in the automobile industry in Asia.

SUMMARY ◆

Market-oriented firms, facing greater competitiveness in world markets, find it essential to assume a global perspective in designing and implementing their marketing strategies. Cost containment, rising technology costs and the dispersal of technology, a greater number of global competitors in many industries, and the advent of hypercompetition in many markets mean that international business practices need to undergo continuous refinement in order to keep them aligned with company goals.

Strategic planning and the integration of the global activities into one coherent whole needs to be implemented for a firm to maximize its activities and for the firm to remain a viable player in international markets. In doing so, the multinational firm needs to mesh in information technology and telecommunications with its global operations in order to make relevant data available to managers in real time. In the end a global strategy of any kind has to resolve a number of apparent contradictions. Firms have to respond to national needs, yet seek to exploit know-how on a worldwide basis, while at all times striving to produce and distribute goods and services globally as efficiently as possible.

In recent years, however, as a result of the formation of regional trading blocs, an increasing number of companies have begun to organize their marketing strategies on a regional basis by exploiting emerging regional similarities. Globally minded, proactive firms increasingly exploit their competitive position in some regions by funneling abundant resources and regionally successful marketing programs to other regions where they do not necessarily occupy a strong market position. SWOT analysis helps isolate the key issues that will be important to the competitiveness of the firm and that its subsequent marketing strategy will address.

REVIEW QUESTIONS ◆

1. How are the developments in information technology impacting the global strategies of firms?

2. What are the various factors/forces/drivers that determine the globalization potential of industries? How are global industries different from multidomestic industries?

3. What do you understand by the term *hypercompetition*? What, according to hypercompetition, are the various arenas of competition?

4. How are the concepts *interdependency* and *standardization* related? What are the implications for global strategy?

5. How is a global marketing strategy distinct from standardization?

6. What are the benefits and limitations of global marketing strategies?

7. How are regional and global strategies different? What are some advantages and disadvantages of a regional strategy?

DISCUSSION QUESTIONS ◆ ◆ ◆ ◆ ◆ ◆ ◆ ◆ ◆ ◆ ◆ ◆ ◆ ◆ ◆ ◆ ◆ ◆

1. Food habits have been known to vary considerably across countries and regions. Would you describe the food industry as primarily multidomestic or global in nature? Use the fast-food chain McDonald's as a case example to explain your answer. Note that while there are certain similarities in all of the McDonald's outlets around the world, there are differences, especially in the menu, in various countries. Can the McDonald's example be generalized across the food industry?

2. In the summer of 1995, Procter & Gamble, the U.S. multinational giant, announced that it would be modifying its global operational structure. Its new structure would include a top-tier management team

consisting of four vice-presidents, each representing a particular region, namely North America, Europe (and also to include the Middle East and Africa), Asia (and Pacific Rim), and Latin America. One of the main reasons cited for this organizational change was the elimination of duties and regulations that now allows P & G to distribute its products to foreign consumers cheaper and quicker. While acknowledging that over 50 percent of the company's sales come from North America, and so, too, a bulk of its profits, the top management mentioned that it took care not to emphasize a particular region over the other. Yet, there is no doubt that most of the company's new products originated in the United States. Few dominant products and brands have been originated from its foreign subsidiaries. There are, however, examples of brands, such as Tide which involved the cross-fertilization of ideas and technologies from its operations around the world.

Based on the facts provided, and any popular press information about P & G you have been exposed to, what would you consider to be P & G's predominant international strategy—global (integrated on a worldwide basis), regional (integrated on a regional level), ethnocentric (predominantly influenced by its operations in North America), or polycentric (primarily independent and autonomous functioning of its international subsidiaries)?

3. Since the early 1980s, the benefits of globalization have been acknowledged by researchers in academia and by business practitioners. However, practitioners have continually indicated the constraints on human management resources in actually implementing global strategies—to implement a global strategy, you need globally thinking managers. In your opinion, are business schools making progress in developing more global managers? Are corporations doing a good job of training their managers to think globally? What are the deficiencies? What are some of the steps that you would recommend to business schools as well as corporations in order to promote the development of executives who think globally?

4. One of the many advantages of globalization suggested are economies of scale and scope. There is, however, a counterargument to this advantage. Mass customization production techniques could lead to an erosion of scale and scope economies with the added advantage of being able to customize products, if not for individual customers, definitely for individual markets. Discuss the strengths and weaknesses of this counterargument.

5. Present-day business competition is increasingly being characterized by two opposite perspectives. On the one hand, the reduced trade barriers and duty reductions are making competition more global in nature. An example are the multinational consumer nondurable manufacturing corporations such as Unilever, Procter & Gamble, and Colgate-Palmolive, which are integrating their activities at a regional and global level. At the same time, these companies are being faced with the problem of losing market share to in-store brands. Are these perspectives really opposite to each other? What are the implications of these market drivers for the retail chains such as Wal-Mart? What are the implications for the consumer nondurable goods manufacturers?

FURTHER READINGS ✦ ✦ ✦ ✦ ✦ ✦ ✦ ✦ ✦ ✦ ✦ ✦ ✦ ✦ ✦ ✦ ✦ ✦ ✦

Bartlett, Christopher, and Sumantra Ghoshal. "What Is A Global Manager?" *Harvard Business Review*, 70 (5) (September/October, 1992):124–132.

Douglas, Susan P., and C. Samuel Craig. *Global Marketing Strategy*. New York: McGraw-Hill, 1995.

Edgington, David W. "The Globalization of Japanese Manufacturing Corporations." *Growth and Change*, 24 (1) (1993):87–106.

Emmerji, Louis. "Globalization, Regionalization, and World Trade." *Columbia Journal of World Business*, 27 (Summer 1992):6–13.

Erdener, Kaynak. *The Global Business: Four Key Marketing Strategies*. New York: International Business Press, 1993.

Lovelock, Christopher H., and George S. Yip. "Developing Global Strategies for Service Businesses." *California Management Review*, 38 (Winter 1996):64–86.

O'Brian, Richard. *Global Financial Integration: The End of Geography*. New York: Council on Foreign Relations Press, 1992.

Yip, George S. "Toward a New Global Strategy." *Chief Executive* (January/February, 1996):66–67.

GLOBAL MARKET ENTRY STRATEGIES

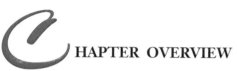

HAPTER OVERVIEW

1. TARGET MARKET SELECTION
2. CHOOSING THE MODE OF ENTRY
3. EXPORTING
4. LICENSING
5. FRANCHISING
6. CONTRACT MANUFACTURING
7. JOINT VENTURES
8. WHOLLY OWNED SUBSIDIARIES
9. CROSS-BORDER STRATEGIC ALLIANCES

The opening bid in a game of contract bridge is, strategically speaking, one of the most important moves in the whole game. It sends a strong signal to your partner and the other players on the suit that you hold in your hand. Making the "wrong" opening bid is often a recipe for disaster once the game progresses. On the other hand, the "right" opening bid is no guarantee for victory. Many things could go wrong: the other team holds better cards, your partner misinterprets your signal, or either you or your partner commit some unforgivable blunders. To some degree, there is a parallel between the opening bid in a game of bridge and the entry strategies for international markets. Making the "right" (or if you want, the "wrong") entry decisions will heavily impact the company's performance in global markets. Granted, other strategic marketing mix decisions also play a big role. A major difference here is that many of these other decisions can easily be corrected, sometimes even overnight (e.g., pricing decisions), while entry decisions are far more difficult to redress.

We can hardly overemphasize the need for a solid market entry strategy. Entry decisions will heavily influence the firm's other marketing mix decisions. Several decisions need to be made. The firm has to decide on: (1) the target product/market, (2) the goals of the target markets, (3) the mode of entry, (4) the time of entry, (5) a marketing mix plan, and (6) a control system to monitor the performance in the entered market.[1] This chapter will cover the major decisions that constitute market entry strategies. It starts with the target market selection decision. We then consider the different criteria that will affect the entry mode choice. Following that, we will concentrate on the various entry strategy options that MNCs might look at. Each of these will be described in some detail and evaluated. The final section focuses on cross-border strategic alliances.

◆ ◆ ◆ ◆ ◆ ◆ TARGET MARKET SELECTION

A crucial step in developing a global expansion strategy is the selection of potential target markets. Companies adopt many different approaches to pick target markets. A flowchart for one of the more elaborate approaches is given in Exhibit 9-1.

To identify market opportunities for a given product (or service) the international marketer usually starts off with a large pool of candidate countries (say, all Central European countries). To narrow down this pool of countries, the company will typically do a preliminary screening. The goal of this exercise is twofold: you want to minimize the mistakes of (1) ignoring countries that offer viable opportunities for your product, and (2) wasting time on countries that offer no or little potential.[2] Those countries that make the grade are scrutinized further to determine the final set of target countries. Here is a four-step procedure that you can employ for the initial screening process:

Step 1: *Indicator selection and data collection*

First, you need to pick a set of socioeconomic and political indicators you believe are critical. The indicators that a company selects are to a large degree driven by the strategic objectives spelled out in the company's global mission. Colgate-Palmolive, for instance, views per-capita purchasing power as a major driver behind market opportunities.[3] Nestlé sees prospects in countries with population and buying power growth.[4] McDonald's starts with countries that are similar to the United States in lifestyle, with a large proportion of women working, and shorter hours for lunch.[5] Information on these country indicators can easily be gathered from publicly available data sources. Typically, countries that do well on one indicator (say, market size) rate poorly on other indicators (say, market growth). Somehow, you need to combine your information to come up with an overall measure of market attractiveness for these candidate markets.

---

[1]Franklin R. Root, *Entry Strategies for International Markets* (New York: Lexington Books, 1994), p. 23.

[2]Root, p. 55.

[3]"Tangney is Bullish on L. America," *Advertising Age International* (May 17, 1993), p. I-23.

[4]"Nestlé Chairman Says Brands Must Prove Themselves," *Advertising Age International* (October 11, 1993), p. I-23.

[5]"Lifestyle Flux Lures McD's to Mideast," *Advertising Age International* (November 21, 1994), p. I-20.

EXHIBIT 9-1
A LOGICAL FLOW MODEL OF THE ENTRY DECISION PROCESS

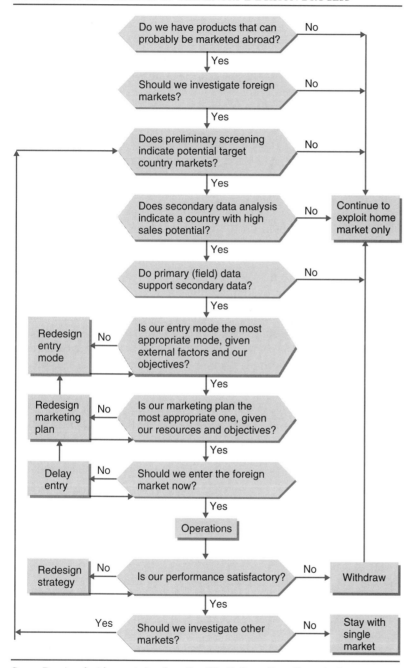

Step 2: *Determine importance of country indicators*

The second step is to determine the importance weights of each of the different country indicators identified in the previous step. One common method is the "constant-sum" allocation technique. Here, you simply allocate one hundred points across the set of indicators according to their importance in achieving the company's goals (e.g., market share). So, the more critical the indicator, the higher the number of points it gets assigned. The total number of points should add up to 100.

Step 3: *Rate the countries in the pool on each indicator*

Next, you give each country a score on each of the indicators. For instance, you could use a 100-point scale (0 meaning very unfavorable; 100 meaning very favorable). The better the country does on a particular indicator, the higher the score.

Step 4: *Compute overall score for each country*

The final step is to derive an overall score for each prospect country. To that end, simply sum up the weighted scores that the country obtained on each indicator. The weights are the importance weights that were assigned to the indicators in the second step. Countries with the highest overall scores are the ones that are most attractive. An example of this four-step procedure is given in Exhibit 9-2.

Sometimes, the company might desire to weed out countries that do not meet a cut-off for criteria that are of paramount importance to the company. For instance, Wrigley, the U.S. chewing gum maker, was not interested in Latin America until recently because many of the local governments imposed ownership restrictions.[7] In that case, the four-step procedure would be done only for the countries that stay in the pool.

When the product has already been launched in some regions, the firm can substantially reduce the subjectivity by using a variant of the screening procedure just described. The alternative method leverages the experience the firm gathered in its existing markets. It works as follows: Suppose the MNC currently does business in Europe and is now considering an expansion into Asia.

EXHIBIT 9-2
METHOD FOR PRE-SCREENING MARKET OPPORTUNITIES: EXAMPLE

Country	Per-Capita Income	Population	Competition	Political Risk	Score
A	50	25	30	40	3400[6]
B	20	50	40	10	3600
C	60	30	10	70	3650
D	20	20	70	80	3850
Weights	25	40	25	10	

[6]$(25 \times 50) + (40 \times 25) + (30 \times 35) + (40 \times 10) = 3400$.

[7]"Guanxi spoken here," *Forbes* (November 8, 1993), pp. 208–210.

Step 1: *Collect historical data on European market*

Go back to your files and collect the historical data for the European markets on the indicators you plan to use to assess the market opportunities for the Asian region. Let us refer to these pieces of information as X_{iec}, that is, the score of European country ec on indicator i;

Step 2: *Evaluate the MNC's post-entry performance in each of its existing European markets*

Assess the MNC's post-entry performance in each European country by assigning a success score (e.g., on a 10-point scale). If performance is measured on just one indicator, say, market-share achieved five years after entry, you could also simply use that indicator as a performance measure. Let us refer to the performance score for country ec as S_{ec}.

Step 3: *Derive weights for each of the country indicators*

The next step is to come up with importance weights for each of the country indicators. For this, you could run a cross-sectional regression using the European data gathered in the previous two steps. Our dependent variable is the post-entry success score (S_{ec}) while the predictor variables are the country indicators (X_{iec}):

$$S_{ec} = a + w_1 X_{1ec} + w_2 X_{2ec} + \ldots + w_I X_{Iec} \qquad ec = 1,2,\ldots, EC$$

By running a regression of the success scores, S_{ec}, on the predictor variables, X_{iec} ($i = 1, \ldots, I$), you can derive estimates for the importance weights of the different indicators.

Step 4: *Rate the Asian countries in the pool on each indicator*

Each of the Asian candidate markets in the pool is given a score on each of the indicators that are considered: X_{iac}.

Step 5: *Predict performance in prospect Asian countries*

Finally, predict the post-entry performance in the prospective Asian markets by using the weights estimated in the previous step and data collected on each of the indicators (the X_{iac}'s) for the Asian countries. For instance, the regression estimates might look like:

Performance = $-0.7 + 6.0$(Market Size) $+ 2.9$(Growth) $- 1$(Competition)

By plugging in the ratings (or actual values) for the Asian markets in this equation, you can then predict the MNC's performance in each of these countries.

Other far more sophisticated methods exist to screen target markets. Kumar and colleagues, for example, developed a screening methodology that incorporates multiple objectives of the firm, resource constraints, and its market expansion strategy.[8] Exhibit 9-3 shows the opportunity matrix for the Asia-Pacific division of Henkel, a German conglomerate. The shaded area highlights the countries that look most promising from Henkel's perspective.

---

[8]V. Kumar, A. Stam and E. A. Joachimsthaler, "An Interactive Multicriteria Approach to Identifying Potential Foreign Markets," *Journal of International Marketing*, 2, (1) (1994), pp. 29–52; see also Lloyd C. Russow and Sam C. Okoroafo, "On the Way Towards Developing a Global Screening Model," *International Marketing Review*, 13 (1) (1996), pp. 46–64.

EXHIBIT 9-3
OPPORTUNITY MATRIX FOR HENKEL IN ASIA PACIFIC

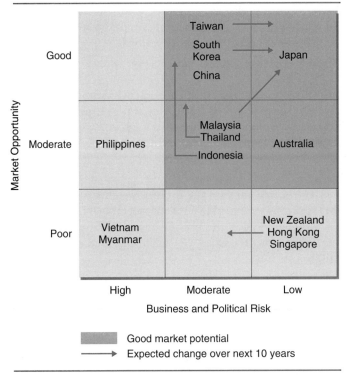

Source: Reprinted from Hellmut Schütte, "Henkel's Strategy for Asia Pacific," *Long Range Planning*, vol. 28, no. 1, p. 98. Copyright 1995, with kind permission from Elsevier Science Ltd., The Boulevard, Langford Lane, Kidlington OX5 1GB, UK.

◆ ◆ ◆ ◆ ◆ ◆ CHOOSING THE MODE OF ENTRY

Decision Criteria for Mode of Entry

Several decision criteria will influence the choice of entry mode. Roughly speaking, two classes of decision criteria can be distinguished: internal (firm-specific) criteria and external (environment-specific) criteria. Let us first consider the major external criteria.

Market Size and Growth. In many instances, the key determinant of entry choice decisions is the size of the market. Large markets justify major resource commitments in the form of joint-ventures or wholly owned subsidiaries. Market potential can relate to the current size of the market. However, future market potential as measured via the growth rate is often even more critical, especially when the target markets include emerging markets.

Risk. Another major concern when choosing entry modes is the risk factor. Risk relates to the instability in the political and economic environment that may impact the company's business prospects. Generally speaking, the greater the risk factor, the less eager companies are to make major resource commitments to the country (or region) concerned. Evidently, the level of country risk changes over time. For instance, the peace process in the Middle East and the abolishment of the apartheid regime in South Africa have lured many MNCs to these regions. Many companies opt to start their presence with a liaison office in markets that are high-risk but, at the same time, look very appealing because of their size or growth potential. For instance, Apple Computer used a liaison office in India and China. A liaison office functions as a low-cost listening initially to gather market intelligence and establish contacts with potential distributors.

Government Regulations.   Government requirements are also a major consideration in entry mode choices. In scores of countries, government regulations heavily constrain the set of available options. Trade barriers of all different kinds restrict the entry choice decision. In the car industry, local content requirements in countries such as France and Italy played a major role behind the decision of Japanese carmakers like Toyota and Nissan to build up a local manufacturing presence in Europe.

Competitive Environment.   The nature of the competitive situation in the local market is another driver. The dominance of Kellogg Co. as a global player in the ready-to-eat cereal market was a key motivation for the creation in the early 1990s of Cereal Partners Worldwide, a joint venture between Nestlé and General Mills. The partnership gained some market share (compared to the combined share of Nestlé and General Mills prior to the linkup) in some of the markets, though mostly at the expense of lesser players like Quaker Oats and Ralston Purina.

Local Infrastructure.   The physical infrastructure of a market refers to the country's distribution system, transportation network, and communication system. In general, the poorer the local infrastructure, the more reluctant the company is to commit major resources (monetary or human).

All these factors combined determine the overall market attractiveness of the countries being considered.[9] Markets can be classified in five types of countries based on their respective market attractiveness:[10]

- **Platform** countries that can be used to gather intelligence and establish a network. Examples include Singapore and Hong Kong.
- **Emerging** countries like Vietnam and the Philippines. Here the major goal is to build up an initial presence for instance via a liaison office.
- **Growth** countries like China and India. Early mover advantages often push companies to build up a significant presence in order to capitalize on future market opportunities.
- **Maturing** and **established** countries like South Korea, Taiwan, and Japan. These countries have far fewer growth prospects than the other types of markets. Often times, local competitors are well-entrenched. On the other hand, these markets have a sizable middle class and solid infrastructure. The prime task here is to look

---

[9]Philippe Lasserre, "Corporate Strategies for the Asia Pacific Region," *Long Range Planning*, 28, (1) (1995), pp. 13–30.

[10]Though the examples relate to Asian countries, the country classification can also be applied to other regions.

EXHIBIT 9-4
ENTRY MODES AND MARKET DEVELOPMENT

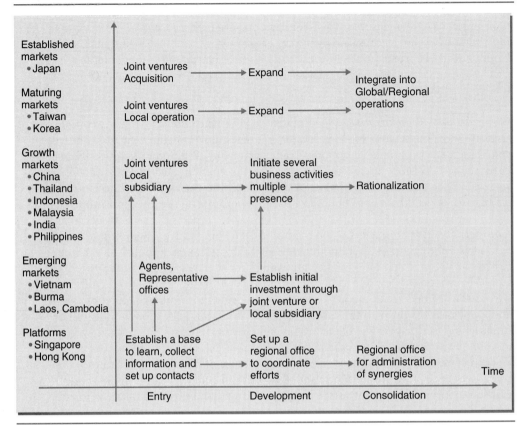

Source: Reprinted from Philippe Lasserre, "Corporate Strategies for the Asia Pacific Region," *Long Range Planning,* vol. 28, no. 1, p. 21. Copyright 1995, with kind permission from Elsevier Science Ltd., The Boulevard, Langford Lane, Kidlington OX5 1GB UK.

for ways to further develop the market via strategic alliances, major investments or acquisitions of local or smaller foreign players. A case in point is GE, the American megacorporation. In the hope of achieving big profits in Europe, GE has invested more than $10 billion from 1989 until 1996, half of it for building new plants and half for almost fifty acquisitions, despite the fact that Europe is a fairly mature market.[11]

Different types suggest different expansion paths as shown in Exhibit 9-4, though deviations cannot be ruled out.

We now give an overview of the key internal criteria.

Company Objectives. Corporate objectives are a key influence in choosing entry modes. Firms that have limited aspirations will typically prefer entry options that entail a minimum amount of commitment (e.g., licensing). Proactive companies with

---

[11]"If Europe's Dead, Why is GE Investing Billions There?" *Fortune* (September 9, 1996) pp. 114–118.

ambitious strategic objectives, on the other hand, will usually pick entry modes that give them the flexibility and control they need to achieve their goals. Bridgestone, the Japanese tiremaker, needed a strong foothold in the U.S. market to become a leading firm in the tire industry. To that end, Bridgestone entered into a bidding war with Pirelli to acquire Firestone. More recently, the company is setting up factories in Central Europe and China and a joint venture in India with Tata, a major truck company to achieve its goal of a 20 percent market share of the global tire market.[12]

Need for Control. Most MNCs would like to possess a certain amount of control over their foreign operations. Control may be desirable for any element of the marketing mix plan: pricing, advertising, the way the product is distributed, and so forth. To a large degree, the level of control is strongly correlated with the amount of resource commitment: the smaller the commitment, the lower the control. So, most firms face a trade-off between the degree of control over their foreign operations and the level of resource commitment they are willing to take.

Internal Resources, Assets and Capabilities. Companies with tight resources (human and/or financial) or limited assets are constrained to low commitment entry modes such as exporting and licensing that are not too demanding on their resources. Even large companies should carefully consider how to allocate their resources between their different markets, including the home-market. In some cases, major resource commitments to a given target market might be premature given the amount of risk. On the other hand, if a firm is overly reluctant with committing resources, the firm might miss the boat by sacrificing major market opportunities. Internal competencies also influence the choice-of-entry strategy. When the firm lacks certain skills that are critical for the success of its global expansion strategy, the company can try to fill the gap by forming a strategic alliance.

Flexibility. An entry mode that looks appealing today is not necessarily attractive five or ten years down the road. The local environment changes constantly. New market segments emerge. Local customers become more demanding or more price conscious. Local competitors become more sophisticated. To cope with these environmental changes, global players need a minimum amount of flexibility. The flexibility offered by the different entry mode alternatives varies a great deal. Given their very nature, contractual arrangements like joint ventures or licensing tend to provide very little flexibility. When major exit barriers exist, wholly owned subsidiaries are hard to divest, and, therefore offer very little flexibility compared to other entry alternatives.

Mode-of-Entry Choice: A Transaction Cost Explanation[13]

Although some of the factors listed above favor high-control entry modes, other criteria suggest a low-control mode. The different modes of entry can be classified according to the degree of control they offer to the entrant from low-control (e.g., indirect exporting) to high control modes (e.g., wholly owned subsidiary, majority stake partnerships). To some extent, the appropriate entry-mode decision boils down

---

[12]"The Buck Stops Here," *Forbes* (March 10, 1997), p. 44.

[13]Erin Anderson and Hubert Gatignon, "Modes of Foreign Entry: A Transaction Cost Analysis and Propositions," *Journal of International Business Studies*, 11 (Fall 1986), pp. 1–26.

to the issue of how much control is desirable. Ideally, the entrant would like to have as much control as possible. However, entry modes that offer a large degree of control also entail substantial resource commitments and huge amounts of risk. Therefore, the entrant faces a trade-off between the benefits of increased control and the costs of resource commitment and risk.

One useful framework to resolve this dilemma is the so-called **Transaction-Cost Analysis (TCA)** perspective. A given task can be looked at as a "make-or-buy" decision: either the firm contracts the task out to outside agents or partners (low-control modes) or does the job internally (high control modes). TCA argues that the desirable governance structure (high- versus low-control mode) will depend on the comparative transaction costs, that is, the cost of running the operation.

The TCA approach begins with the premise that markets are competitive. Therefore, market pressure minimizes the need for control. Under this utopian scenario, low-control modes are preferable, since the competitive pressures force the outside partner to comply with his contractual duties. When the market mechanism fails, high-control entry modes become more desirable. From the TCA angle, market failure typically happens when **transaction-specific assets** become valuable. These are assets that are only valuable for a very narrow range of applications. Examples include: brand equity, proprietary technology, know-how. When these types of assets become very important, the firm might be better off adopting a high-control entry mode to protect the value of these assets against opportunitistic behaviors and uncertainty.

An empirical study of entry decisions made by the 180 largest MNCs over a fifteen-year period found that MNCs are most likely to enter with wholly owned subsidiaries when one of the following conditions holds:[14]

- the entry involves an R & D-intensive line of business
- the entry involves an advertising-intensive line of business (high brand-equity)
- the MNC has accumulated a substantial amount of experience with foreign entries

On the other hand, MNCs are most likely to prefer a partnership when one of these holds:

- the entry is in a highly risky country
- the entry is in a socioculturally distant country
- there are legal restrictions on foreign ownership of assets

---

◆ ◆ ◆ ◆ ◆ ◆ EXPORTING

Most companies start their international expansion with exporting. For many small businesses, exporting is often the sole alternative for selling their goods in foreign markets. A fair number of Fortune 500 companies, such as Boeing and Caterpillar, also generate a major part of their global revenues via export sales. In 1995 Caterpillar's exports from the United States were a record $5.13 billion: around $300,000 per

---

[14]Hubert Gatignon and Erin Anderson, "The Multinational Corporation's Degree of Control over Foreign Subsidiaries: An Empirical Test of a Transaction Cost Explanation," *Journal of Law, Economics, and, Organization*, 4 (2), (Fall 1988), pp. 305–336.

Caterpillar job in the United States.[15] In 1995 Philip Morris's tobacco-related exports and royalties lessened the U.S. trade deficit by almost $6 billion.[16] Chapter 17 discusses in detail the export and import function. In this chapter we will give you a snapshot overview of exporting as an entry mode. Companies that plan to engage in exporting have a choice between three broad options: **indirect**, **cooperative**, and **direct exporting**. Indirect exporting means that the firm uses a middleman based in its home market to do the exporting. With cooperative exporting, the firm enters into an agreement with another company (local or foreign) where the partner will use its distribution network to sell the exporter's goods. Direct exporting means that the company sets up its own export organization within the company and relies on a middleman based in a foreign market (e.g., a foreign distributor).

Indirect Exporting

Indirect exporting happens when the firm sells its products in the foreign market via an intermediary located in the firm's home country. The middleman could be an export management company (EMC), a trading house, or simply a broker.

Indirect exporting offers several advantages to the exporting company compared to other entry modes. The firm gets instant foreign market expertise. Very little risk is involved. Generally speaking, no major resource commitments are required.

There are some downsides with indirect exporting. The company has little or no control over the way its product is marketed in the foreign country. Lack of adequate sales support, wrong pricing decisions, or poor distribution channels will inevitably lead to poor sales. Ill-fated marketing mix decisions made by the intermediary could also damage the company's corporate or brand image. The middleman may have very limited experience with handling the company's product line.

Given the low commitment, indirect exporting is often seen as a good beach-head strategy for "testing" the international waters: once the demand for the product takes off, the manufacturer can switch to another, more proactive, entry mode.

Cooperative Exporting

Companies that are not willing to commit the resources to set up their own distribution organization but still want to have some control over their foreign operations should consider cooperative exporting. One of the most popular forms of cooperative exporting is **piggyback exporting**. With piggybacking, the company uses the overseas distribution network of another company (local or foreign) for selling its goods in the foreign market. Wrigley, the U.S. chewing gum company, recently entered India by piggybacking on Parrys, a local confectionery firm. Through this tie-in, Wrigley is able to plug into Parrys' distribution network, thereby providing Wrigley immediate access to 250,000 retail outlets. The two major attractions that Parrys' network offered to Wrigley was the overlap in product category and the size of the distribution network. The quality of the distribution network might also play a role. Gillette tied in with Bangalore-based TTK, an Indian manufacturer of pressure cookers and kitchenware for the distribution of Braun products, despite the fact that Gillette has its own distribution network in India. Gillette needed department-store

---

[15]Caterpillar, *1995 Annual Report*, p. 25.

[16]Philip Morris Companies Inc., *1995 Annual Report*, p. 9.

type outlets for its Braun product range, precisely the type of distribution channels that TTK uses for the distribution of its merchandise.[17]

Direct Exporting

Under direct exporting, the firm sets up its own exporting department and sells its products via a middleman located in the foreign market. Once the international sales potential becomes substantial, direct exporting often looks far more appealing than indirect exporting. To some degree, the choice between indirect and direct exporting is a "make-or-buy" decision: should we as a company perform the export task, or are we better off delegating the task to outsiders? Compared to the indirect approach, direct exporting has a number of pluses. The exporter has far more control over its international operations. Hence, the sales potential (and profit) is often much more significant than under indirect exporting. It also allows the company to build up its own network in the foreign market and get better market feedback.

There is a price to be paid, though. Given that the responsibility for the exporting tasks is now in the hands of the company, the demands on resources—human and financial—are much more intense than with indirect exporting. Besides the marketing mix tasks, these tasks involve choosing target market, identifying and selecting representatives in the foreign market, and scores of logistics functions (e.g., documentation, insurance, shipping, packaging).

◆ ◆ ◆ ◆ ◆ ◆ LICENSING

Companies can also penetrate foreign markets via a licensing strategy. Licensing is a contractual transaction where the firm—the **licensor**—offers some proprietary assets to a foreign company—the **licensee**—in exchange for royalty fees. Examples of assets that can be part of a licensing agreement include trademarks, technology know-how, production processes, patents. Royalty rates range between one-eighth of 1 percent and 15 percent of sales revenue.[18] For instance, Tokyo Disneyland is owned and operated by Oriental Land Company under license from Disney. In return for being able to use the Disney name, Oriental Land Company pays royalties to Disney.

Benefits

For many companies, licensing has proven to be a profitable means for penetrating foreign markets. In most cases, licensing is not very demanding on the company's resources. Therefore, it is especially appealing to small companies that lack the resources and the wherewithal to invest in foreign facilities. One licensing expert notes that overseas licensing accounts for up to a third of the profits of some small companies.[19]

---

[17]"India—Distribution Overview," IMI960321, U.S. Department of Commerce, International Trade Administration, 1996.

[18]"Licensing May be Quickest Route to Foreign Markets," *Wall Street Journal* (September 14, 1990), Sec. B, p. 2.

[19]Ibid.

Compared to exporting, another low-commitment entry mode, licensing allows the licensor to navigate around import barriers or get access to markets that are completely closed to imports. For instance, several foreign tobacco companies in China use licensing agreements to avoid the 240 percent import tax levied on imported cigarettes.[20] Local governments may also favor licensing over other entry modes.

Companies that use licensing as part of their global expansion strategy lower their exposure to political or economic instabilities in their foreign markets. The only volatility that the licensor faces is the ups and downs in the royalty income stream. Other risks are absorbed by the licensee.

In high-tech industries, technology licensing has two further appeals. In highly competitive environments, rapid penetration of global markets allows the licensor to define the leading technology standard and to rapidly amortize R & D expenditures.[21] A case in point is Motorola's licensing of proprietary microprocessor technology to Toshiba.

Caveats

Licensing has some caveats, though. Revenues coming from a licensing agreement may be dwarfed by the potential income that other entry modes such as exporting could have generated. Another possible disadvantage is that the licensee may not be fully committed to the licensor's product or technology. Lack of enthusiasm on the part of the licensee will greatly limit the sales potential of the licensed product. When the licensing agreement involves a trademark, there is the further risk that misguided moves made by the licensee tarnish the trademark covered by the agreement.

The biggest danger is that a licensing arrangement could nurture a future competitor: Today's comrade-in-arms often becomes tomorrow's villain. The licensee can leverage the skills it acquires during the licensing period once the agreement expires. Global Perspective 9-1 chronicles the mishaps that Borden went through when its relationship with Meiji Milk, its licensee in Japan, turned sour.

There are several moves companies can make to protect themselves against the risks of licensing arrangements.[22] If doable, the company should seek patent or trademark protection abroad. A thorough profitability analysis of a licensing proposal is an absolute must. Such an analysis must single out all the costs that are entailed by the venture, including the opportunity costs that stem from revenues that need to be sacrificed. Careful selection of prospective licensees is extremely important. Once a partner has been singled out, the negotiation process starts, which, if successful, will produce a licensing contract. The contract will cover parameters like: the technology package, use conditions (including territorial rights and performance requirements), compensation, and provisions for the settlement of disputes.

---

[20]"Smoke Signals Point to China Market Opening," *South China Sunday Post* (October 6, 1996), p. 5.

[21]Masaaki Kotabe, Arvind Sahay, and Preet S. Aulakh, "Emerging Role of Technology Licensing in the Development of a Global Product Strategy: Conceptual Framework and Research Propositions," *Journal of Marketing*, 60 (1) (January 1996), pp. 73–88.

[22]Root, Chapter 5.

◆ ◆

𝒢LOBAL PERSPECTIVE 9-1

THE BORDEN–MEIJI MILK SAGA: THE MELTDOWN OF LADY BORDEN

When Borden, the U.S. multinational food company, entered Japan in 1971, it decided to link up with Meiji Milk. Borden's licensing agreement with Meiji Milk, Japan's leading dairy company, was the envy of many companies. Borden could benefit from Meiji Milk's vast distribution network. Meiji Milk, in turn, was able to acquire the expertise to manufacture various kinds of dairy products. The partnership also developed the premium ice cream market in Japan with its Lady Borden brand.

But the venture was not a fairy tale. Other brands entered the market, and Lady Borden's market share started to flounder. As a result, Borden wanted to dissolve its partnership with Meiji Milk, marketing Lady Borden on its own. Borden wanted to have more control over the

marketing of its products in Japan so that it could respond more rapidly to the competitive challenges. Meiji Milk retaliated by rolling out two ice cream brands of its own, one of which, Lady Breuges, was in direct competition with Lady Borden. When Borden cut its ties with Meiji Milk, it also lost access to Meiji Milk's distribution channels. The company hoped that brand clout would pull Japanese customers to the Lady Borden brand, but the pull of the Borden brand name did not make up for the loss of Meiji Milk's distribution muscle.

In June 1994, Borden, in a desperate move, licensed its trademarks and formulations for the Lady Borden brand to the confectionery maker Lotte Co. When Borden broke with Meiji Milk in 1991, its share of Japan's premium ice cream market was around 50 percent. Three years later, when a Japanese newspaper compiled a scorechart of the ice cream market, Meiji had 12 percent, while Borden's share was so negligible that it didn't make the list.

Sources: "Borden's Breakup with Meiji Milk Shows How a Japanese Partnership Can Curdle," *The Wall Street Journal* (February 21, 1991), p. B1, B4, and, "Borden's Hopes Melt in Japanese Market," *Advertising Age* (July 18, 1994), p. 38.

◆ ◆ ◆ ◆ ◆ ◆ ## FRANCHISING

Scores of service industry companies use franchising as a means for capturing opportunities in the global marketplace. For instance, of the 8,000 PepsiCo restaurants around the world, about 4,400[23] are franchised. Franchising is to some degree a "cousin" of licensing: it is an arrangement whereby the **franchisor** gives the **franchisee** the right to use the franchisor's business concept and product tradename in exchange for royalty payments. The package might include the marketing plan, operating manuals, standards, training, and quality monitoring.

To snap up opportunities in foreign markets, the method of choice is often **master franchising**. With this system, the franchisor gives a master franchise to a local entrepreneur, who will, in turn, sell local franchises within his territory. The territory could be a certain region within a country or a group of countries (e.g., Greater China).

Benefits

The benefits of franchising are clear. First and foremost, companies can capitalize on a winning business formula by expanding overseas with a minimum of investment. Just as with licensing, political risks for the rights-owner are very limited. Further,

---

[23]PepsiCo, Inc., *1995 Annual Report*, p. 10.

since the franchisees' profits are directly tied to their efforts, franchisees are usually highly motivated. Finally, the franchisor can also capitalize on the local franchisees' knowledge of the local market place. They usually have a much better understanding of local customs and laws than the foreign firm.

Caveats

Franchising carries some risks, though. As in the case of licensing, the franchisor's income stream is only a fraction of what it would be if the company held an equity stake in the foreign ventures. A major concern is the lack of control over the franchisees' operations. Dissatisfied with the performance of its franchisees in Mexico and Brazil, Blockbuster Video changed tracks in 1995. The entertainment company decided to set up joint ventures and equity relations in Mexico and Brazil to replace the franchising arrangements held there, thereby getting more control and oversight.[24] Given the largely intangible nature of many franchising systems, cultural hurdles can also create problems. In fact, a recent study shows that cultural and physical proximity are the two most popular criteria used by companies for picking international markets in franchising.[25]

CONTRACT MANUFACTURING   ◆ ◆ ◆ ◆ ◆ ◆ ◆

With contract manufacturing, the company arranges with a local manufacturer to manufacture parts of the product or even the entire product. The marketing of the products is still the responsibility of the international firm.

Benefits

Cost savings are the prime motivation behind contract manufacturing. Significant cost savings can be achieved for labor-intensive production processes by sourcing the product in a low-wage country. Typically, the countries of choice are places that have a substantial comparative labor cost advantage. Labor cost savings are not the only factor. Savings can also be achieved via taxation benefits, lower energy costs, raw materials costs, or overhead.

Some of the benefits listed for the previous entry modes also apply here. Subcontracting leads to a small amount of exposure to political and economic risks for the international firm. It is also not very demanding on the company's resources. Contract manufacturing also allows access to markets that, because of import barriers, would otherwise be closed.

Caveats

Contract manufacturing is not without drawbacks though. The "nurture-a-future-competitor" concern raised for licensing and franchising also applies here. Because of this risk, many companies prefer to make high-value items or products that involve

---

[24]"Blockbuster's Fast-Forward," *Advertising Age International* (September 18, 1995), p. I-32.

[25]John F. Preble and Richard C. Hoffman, "Franchising Systems Around the Globe: A Status Report," *Journal of Small Business Management* (April 1995), pp. 80–88.

proprietary design features in-house. A fixation with low labor costs can often have painful consequences. Low-labor-cost countries typically have very low labor productivity. Some of these countries, such as India and South Korea, also have a long history of bad labor relations. Too much reliance on low-cost labor could also create a backlash in the company's home-market among its employees and customers. Monitoring quality and production levels is a must, especially during the start-up phase, when "teething problems" are not uncommon.

When screening foreign subcontractors, the ideal candidate should meet the following criteria:[26]

- Flexible and geared toward just-in-time delivery
- Able to meet quality standards and implement Total Quality Management
- Solid financial footing
- Able to integrate with company's business
- Have contingency plans to handle sudden changes in demand

◆ ◆ ◆ ◆ ◆ ◆ JOINT VENTURES

For many MNCs who want to expand their global operations, joint ventures prove to be the most viable way to enter foreign markets, especially in emerging markets. For instance, in 1991 almost 65 percent of the approved foreign investment projects in China were equity joint ventures.[27] With a joint venture, the foreign company agrees to share equity and other resources with other partners to establish a new entity in the target country. The partners typically are local companies, but they can also be local government authorities, other foreign companies, or a mixture of local and foreign players. Depending on the equity stake, three forms of partnerships can be distinguished: majority (more than 50 percent ownership), fifty–fifty, and minority (50 percent less than ownership) ventures. Huge infrastructure or high-tech projects that demand a large amount of expertise and money often involve multiple foreign and local partners.

Benefits

A major advantage of joint ventures, compared to lesser forms of resource commitment such as licensing, is the return potential. With licensing, for instance, the company solely gets royalty payments instead of a share of the profits. Joint ventures also entail much more control over the operations than most of the previous entry modes we discussed so far. MNCs that like to maximize their degree of control prefer full ownership. However, in many instances, local governments (e.g., China) discourage or even forbid wholly owned ventures in certain industries. Under such circumstances, partnerships are a second-best or temporary solution.

Apart from the benefits just listed, the **synergy** argument is another compelling reason for setting up a joint venture. Partnerships not only mean a sharing of capital and risk. Possible contributions brought in by the local partner include: land, raw

[26]E. P. Hibbert, "Global Make-or-Buy Decisions," *Industrial Marketing Management*, 22 (1993), pp. 67–77.

[27]Yigang Pan and Wilfried R. Vanhonacker, "Equity Sharing Arrangements and Joint Venture Operation in the People's Republic of China," Working Paper, February 1994, H.K.U.S.T., Department of Marketing.

materials, expertise on the local environment (culture, legal, political), access to a distribution network, personal contacts with suppliers, government officials, and so on. Combined with the skills and resources owned by the foreign partner, these inputs offer the key to a successful market entry.

Caveats

For many MNCs, lack of full control is the biggest shortcoming of joint ventures. There are a number of ways for the MNC to gain more leverage. The most obvious way is via a majority equity stake. However, government restrictions often rule this option out. Even when for some reason majority ownership is not a viable alternative, MNCs have other means at their disposal to exercise control over the joint venture. MNCs could deploy expatriates in key line positions thereby controlling financial, marketing and other critical operations of the venture. MNCs could also offer various types of outside support services to back up their weaker joint ventures in areas such as marketing, quality control, customer service.[28]

Lack of trust and mutual conflicts can turn an international joint venture into a marriage from hell. Conflicts could arise over matters such as strategies, resource allocation, transfer pricing, ownerships of critical assets like technologies and brand names. In many cases, the seeds for trouble exist from the very beginning of the joint venture. Exhibit 9-5 contrasts the mutually conflicting objectives that the foreign

EXHIBIT 9-5
CONFLICTING OBJECTIVES IN CHINESE JOINT VENTURES

	Foreign Partner	Chinese Partner
Planning	retain business flexibility	maintain congruency between the venture and the state economic plan
Contracts	unambiguous, detailed and enforceable	ambiguous, brief and adaptable
Negotiations	sequential, issue by issue	holistic and heuristic
Staffing	maximize productivity; fewest people per given output level	employ maximum number of local people
Technology	match technical sophistication to the organization and its environment	gain access to the most advanced technology as quickly as possible
Profits	maximize in long term; repatriate over time	reinvest for future modernization; maintain foreign exchange reserves
Inputs	minimize unpredictability and poor quality of supplies	promote domestic sourcing
Process	stress high quality	stress high quantity
Outputs	access and develop domestic market	export to generate foreign currency
Control	reduce political and economic controls on decision-making	accept technology and capital but preclude foreign authority infringement on sovereignty and ideology

Reprinted from M. G. Martinsons and C.-S. Tsong, "Successful Joint Ventures in the Heart of the Dragon," *Long Range Planning*, vol. 28, no. 5, p. 5. Copyright 1995, with kind permission from Elsevier Science Ltd., The Boulevard, Langford Lane, Kidlington OX5 1GB UK.

---

[28]Johannes Meier, Javier Perez, and Jonathan R. Woetzel, "Solving the Puzzle—MNCs in China," *The McKinsey Quarterly*, 2, (1995) pp. 20–33.

partner and the local Chinese partner may hold when setting up a joint venture in China. Cultural strains between partners often spur mistrust and mutual conflict, making a bad situation even worse. Autolatina, a joint venture set up by Ford Motor Co. and Volkswagen AG in Latin America, was dissolved after seven years in spite of the fact that it remained profitable to the very end. Cultural differences between the German and American managers were a major factor. One participating executive noted that "there were good intentions behind Autolatina's formation but they never really overcame the VW–Ford culture shock."[29]

When trouble undermines the joint venture, the partners can try to resolve the conflict via mechanisms built into the agreement. If a mutually acceptable resolution is not achievable, the joint venture is scaled back or dissolved. For instance, a joint venture between Unilever and AKI in South Korea broke up after seven years following disagreements over brand strategies for new products, resource allocation, advertising support, and brand ownership.[30]

Drivers Behind Successful International Joint Ventures

There are no magic ingredients to foster the stability of joint ventures. Yet, there are some important lessons that can be drawn from past jv fairy tales and horror stories:

Pick the Right Partner. Most joint venture marriages prosper by choosing a suitable partner. That means that the MNC should invest the time in identifying proper candidates. A careful screening of the joint venture partner is an absolute necessity. Michael Bonsignore, CEO of Honeywell, observes: "Nothing reinforces our success more than choosing the right partner. We pick well."[31] It is not easy to sketch a profile of the "ideal" partner. The presence of complementary skills that lead to synergies is one characteristic of successful joint ventures. Some evidence indicates that partners should be similar in terms of size and resources. Partners with whom the MNC has built up an existing relationship (e.g., customers, suppliers) also facilitate a strong relationship.[32] One issue that latecomers in a market often face is that the "best" partners have already been snapped up. Note, though, that the same issue arises with acquisition strategies.

Establish Clear Objectives from the Beginning.[33] It is important to clearly spell out the objectives of the joint venture from day one. Partners should know what their respective contributions and responsibilities are before signing the contract.[34] They should also know what to expect from the partnership.

---

[29]"Why Ford, VW's Latin Marriage Succumbed to 7-year Itch," *Advertising Age International* (March 20, 1995), p. I-22.

[30]"How Unilever's South Korean Partnership Fell Apart," *Advertising Age*, Aug. 31, 1992, p. 3, 39.

[31]"Investing in Emerging Asia," *Asiaweek* (December 20, 1996), p. 54.

[32]Karen J. Hladik, "R & D and International Joint Ventures," in *Cooperative Forms of Transnational Corporation Activity*, P. J. Buckley (London: Routledge, 1994).

[33]Dominique Turpin, "Strategic Alliances with Japanese Firms: Myths and Realities," *Long Range Planning*, 26 (4), (1993), pp. 11–16.

[34]Maris G. Martinsons and Choo-sin Tseng, "Successful Joint Ventures in the Heart of the Dragon," *Long Range Planning*, 28 (5) (1995), pp. 45–58.

Bridge Cultural Gaps. Many joint venture disputes stem from cultural differences between the local and foreign partners. A lot of agony and frustration can be avoided when the foreign investor makes an attempt to bridge cultural differences. For instance, when setting up joint ventures in China, having an ethnic Chinese or an "old China hand" as a middleman often helps a great deal. The problem is that knowledgeable people who share the perspectives of both cultures are often very hard to find.[35]

Top Managerial Commitment and Respect. Short of a strong commitment from the parent companies' top management, most international joint ventures are doomed to become a failure. The companies should be willing to assign their best managerial talent to the joint venture. Venture managers should also have complete access to and support from their respective parent companies.[36]

Incremental Approach Works Best. Rather than being overambitious, an incremental approach toward setting up the international joint venture appears to be much more effective. The partnership starts on a small scale. Gradually, the scope of the joint venture is broadened by adding other responsibilities and activities to the joint venture's charter.

WHOLLY OWNED SUBSIDIARIES

◆ ◆ ◆ ◆ ◆ ◆ ◆

Multinational companies often prefer to enter new markets with 100 percent ownership. Ownership strategies in foreign markets can essentially take two routes: **acquisitions**, where the MNC buys up existing companies, or **greenfield operations** that are started from scratch. As with the other entry modes, full ownership entry entails certain benefits to the MNC but also carries substantial risks.

Benefits

Wholly owned subsidiaries give MNCs full control of their operations. It is often the ideal solution for companies that do not want to be saddled with all the risks and anxieties associated with partnerships like joint venturing. Full ownership means that all the profits go to the company. Fully owned enterprises allow the investor to manage and control its own processes and tasks in terms of marketing, production and sourcing decisions. Setting up fully owned subsidiaries also sends a strong commitment signal to the local market. In some markets—China, for example—wholly owned subsidiaries can be erected much faster than joint ventures with local companies, which may consume years of negotiations before their final take-off.[37] The latter point is especially important when there are substantial advantages of being an early entrant in the target market.

---

[35]Ibid., p. 56.

[36]Turpin, p. 15.

[37]Wilfried Vanhonacker, "Entering China: An Unconventional Approach," *Harvard Business Review* (March-April 1997), pp. 130–140.

Caveats

Despite the advantages of 100 percent ownership, many MNCs are quite reluctant to choose this particular mode of entry. The risks of full ownership cannot be easily discounted. Complete ownership means that the parent company will have to carry the full burden of possible losses. Developing a foreign presence without the support of a third party is also very demanding on the firm's resources. Obviously, apart from the market-related risks, substantial political risks (e.g., nationalization) must be factored in.

Companies that enter via a wholly owned enterprise are sometimes also perceived as a threat to the cultural and/or economic sovereignty of the host country. Shortly after Daewoo's initially successful bid for the multimedia arm of the French group Thomson–CSF in the fall of 1996, the deal sparked controversy among French trade unions and the media. In the end, the French government vetoed the sale of the Thomson group, following the negative opinion of the French privatization commission.[38]

One way to address hostility to foreign acquisitions in the host country is by "localizing" the firm's presence in the foreign market by hiring local managers, sourcing locally, developing local brands, sponsoring local sports or cultural events and so forth.[39] Global Perspective 9-2 describes how Reebok entered Russia through wholly owned subsidiaries.

◆ ◆

$\mathcal{G}$LOBAL PERSPECTIVE 9-2

REEBOK'S ENTRY STRATEGY IN RUSSIA

Reebok, a manufacturer and distributor of footwear and other clothing items, entered Russia in 1992 by creating wholly owned subsidiaries known as *Reebok Russia*. These subsidiaries are managed by corporate personnel with a very strong emphasis on the use of Russian nationals in local support of the company.

According to George Elbaum, managing director of Reebok Russia, capital investment was minimal, while extensive labor was utilized to achieve the entrance.

Reebok initially offered low-priced products, but as demand has increased, they have begun to offer more higher-priced premium products. Past sales have been approximately $10 million since inception.

Reebok Russia is a growing subsidiary that is creating goodwill by donating $50,000 worth of products to highly visible outlet sources such as public schools, orphanages,

and the Russian Olympic Team. By aligning themselves with such popular concepts as school sports and the Olympics, Reebok Russia hopes to gain acceptance as a premier product to the people of Russia.

"Entering the market in Russia is a long bureaucratic nightmare," said Mr. Elbaum. Politicians are not too eager to allow the expansion of new enterprises into Russia. Reebok Russia was able to become successful because their venture brought the promise of capital infusion into a suffering and weak economy. In evaluating the risk, the prime concern for Reebok Russia is the political uncertainty in Russia. To manage this risk, Reebok Russia minimizes the amount of hard currency it holds in the country. Additionally, Reebok Russia utilizes a large number of nationals in its operations. This has a significant impact on the elimination of the "Western bad guy" image that so many Russians hold about the West and capitalism in general.

Future plans for Reebok Russia include continued expansion throughout Russia. Many cities are selected for the introduction of the Reebok concept stores. As the economy continues to grow, so will the presence of Reebok.

Source: Avraham Shama, "Entry Strategies of U.S. Firms to the Newly Independent States, Baltic States, and Eastern European Countries," *California Management Review*, 37 (3), (Spring 1995), pp. 105–6. Copyright ©1995, by The Regents of the University of California, Vol. 37, No. 3. By permission of The Regents.

---

[38]http://www.asiatimes.com/96/12/05/05129601
[39]Vanhonacker, pp. 130–40.

Acquisitions (and Mergers)

Companies such as Sara Lee have built up strong global competitive positions via cleverly planned and finely executed acquisition strategies. MNCs choose acquisition entry to expand globally for a number of reasons. First and foremost, when contrasted with greenfield operations, acquisitions provide a rapid means to get access to the local market. For relative latecomers in an industry, acquisitions are also a viable option to obtain well-established brand names, instant access to distribution outlets, or technology. In recent years, some of the South Korean *chaebols* have used acquisition entries in foreign markets to gain a foothold in high-tech industries. Highly visible examples include Samsung's acquisition of the American computer maker AST and LG Electronics' takeover of Zenith. LG would have needed to invest more than $1 billion to build up a strong global TV brand from scratch.[40]

Sara Lee, a U.S. conglomerate, has been extremely successful in building up growth via well-chosen acquisitions. Instead of milking the acquired local brands and replacing them with a global brand, Sara Lee heavily invests in its local brand assets in the hope that one day they can be converted into prestigious regional or even global brand names. Success stories of local brands that became leading European brands include Douwe Egberts in coffee, Pickwick in tea, and Dim in hosiery. Sara Lee is also following the acquisition path in emerging markets with an equal amount of success.

Expansion via acquisitions or mergers carries substantial risks, though. Differences in the corporate culture of the two companies between managers are often extremely hard to bridge. A well-publicized example of a company that has been plagued with corporate culture disease is Pharmacia & Upjohn, a pharmaceutical company that was formed in 1995 via the merger of Sweden-based Pharmacia AB and the American drug firm Upjohn. Swedish managers were stunned by the hard-driving, mission-oriented approach of Upjohn executives. Their U.S. counterparts were shocked by European vacation habits.[41]

The assets of the acquisition do not always live up to the expectations of the acquiring company. Outdated plants, tarnished brand names, or an unmotivated work force are only a few of the many possible disappointments that the acquiring company could face. The local government might also attach certain conditions to the acquisition. Daewoo, for instance, promised the French government to hire 5,000 more people when it was bidding for the consumer electronics division of Thomson. A careful screening and assessment of takeover candidates can avoid a lot of heartburn on the part of the acquiring company. Another drawback is that acquisition entry can be a very costly global expansion strategy. Good prospects are usually unwilling to sell themselves. If they are, they do not come cheap. Other foreign or local companies are typically interested too, and the result is often a painful bidding war. Apart from that, the acquired company could be saddled with huge debts.

Greenfield Operations

Acquisition strategies are not always feasible. Good prospects may already have been nabbed by the company's competitors. In many emerging markets, acceptable acquisition candidates often are simply not available. Overhauling the facilities of possible

---

[40]"Guess Who's Betting on America's High-Tech Losers?" *Fortune* (October 28, 1996).

[41]"A Case of Corporate Culture Shock in the Global Arena," *International Herald Tribune* (April 23, 1997), pp. 1, 11.

candidates is sometimes much more costly than building an operation from scratch. In the wake of these downsides, MNCs often prefer to enter foreign markets through greenfield operations that are established from scratch. Greenfield operations offer the company more flexibility than acquisitions in areas such as human resources, suppliers, logistics, plant layout, or manufacturing technology. Greenfield investments also avoid the costs of integrating the acquisition into the parent company.[42] Another motivation is the package of goodies (e.g., tax holidays) that host governments sometimes offer to whet the appetite of foreign investors. A major disadvantage, though, of greenfield operations is that they require enormous investments of time and capital.

◆ ◆ ◆ ◆ ◆ ◆ CROSS-BORDER STRATEGIC ALLIANCES

A distinctive feature of the activities of global corporations today is that they are using cooperative relationships like licensing, joint ventures, R & D partnerships, and informal arrangements—all under the rubric of alliances of various forms—on an increasing scale. More formally, strategic alliances can be described as *a coalition of two or more organizations to achieve strategically significant goals that are mutually beneficial.*[43] The business press reports like clockwork the birth of strategic alliances in various kinds of industries. Eye-catching are especially those partnerships between firms that have been arch-enemies for ages. A principal reason for the increase in cooperative relationships is that firms today no longer have the capacity of a General Motors of the 1940s which developed all its technologies in-house. As a result, firms, especially those operating in technology-intensive industries, may not be at the forefront of all the required critical technologies.[44] This implies that there should be a rise in cooperative relationships, and this is indeed the case. Firms are also adopting some of the practices of Japanese *keiretsu*, which use a network of cross shareholdings, inter-company movement of personnel, R & D partnerships, and regular meetings between top managers of the member companies of the *keiretsu* to work together as a team; at the same time the members of the group do not foreclose the option of dealing with outside companies.

Types of Strategic Alliances

Strategic alliances come in all kinds of shapes. At one extreme alliances can be based on a simple licensing agreement between two partners. At the other extreme, they may consist of a thick web of ties like the RISC[45] alliance groups shown in Exhibit 9-6. The

[42]Jiatao Li, "Foreign Entry and Survival: Effects of Strategic Choices on Performance in International Markets," *Strategic Management Journal*, 16 (1995), pp. 333–51.

[43]Edwin A. Murray, Jr. and John F. Mahon, "Strategic Alliances: Gateway to the New Europe?" *Long Range Planning* (August 1993), pp. 102–11.

[44]Capon, Noel and Rashi Glazer, "Marketing and Technology: A Strategic Co-alignment," *Journal of Marketing*, 51(July 1987), pp. 1–14.

[45]RISC (Reduced Instruction-Set Computing) chips have a streamlined design with less circuitry.

EXHIBIT 9-6
RISC ALLIANCE GROUPS, EARLY 1992.

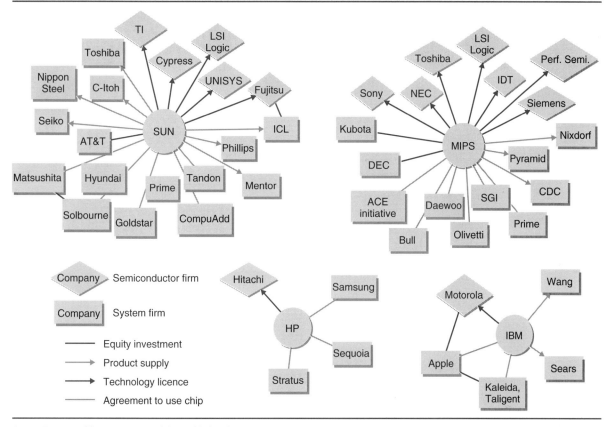

Source: Reprinted by permission of the publisher from THE ALLIANCE REVOLUTION: THE NEW SHAPE OF BUSINESS RIVALRY by Benjamin Gomes-Casseres, Cambridge, Mass.: Harvard University Press, Copyright © 1996 by the President and Fellows of Harvard College.

nature of alliances also varies, depending on the skills brought in by the partners. Most alliances in high-tech industries are based on technology swaps. Given the gyrating costs of new product development, strategic alliances offer a means for companies to learn and develop new technologies or products in a more cost-efficient manner. Exhibit 9-7 gives an overview of cross-border strategic alliances that were established in several high-tech industries. A second type of cross-border alliances involves marketing-based assets and resources such as access to distribution channels or trademarks. A case in point is the partnership established by Coca-Cola and Nestlé to market ready-to-drink coffees and teas under the Nescafé and Nestea brand names. This deal allowed the two partners to combine a well-established brand name with access to a vast, proven distribution network. Alliances may also be situated in the operations and logistics area. In their relentless search for scale economies for operations/logistics activities, companies may decide to join forces by setting up a partnership. Often, operations-based alliances are also driven by a desire to transfer manufacturing know-how. A classic example is the NUMMI joint venture set up by Toyota and General Motors to swap car-manufacturing expertise.

EXHIBIT 9-7
CROSS-BORDER TECHNOLOGY-BASED STRATEGIC ALLIANCES

Consumer Electronics

GE-Hitachi (TVs)

Westinghouse-Toshiba (TVs)

GE-Samsung (Microwave ovens)

GE-Matsushita
  (Room air conditioners)

RCA-Matsushita (VCRs)

Kodak-Canon
  (Photographic equipment)

Kodak-Matsushita (Camcorders)

Kodak-Philips (Photo-CD players)

Heavy Machinery

Allis Chalmers-Fiat-Hitachi
  (Construction equipment)

Ford-Fiat (Farm equipment)

Caterpillar (Growing outsourcing)

Dresser-Komatsu
  (Construction equipment)

Deere-Hitachi (Farm equipment)

Clark-Samsung (Forklift trucks)

Power Generation Equipment

Westinghouse-ABB
  (Heavy power equipment)

GE-Toshiba (Nuclear equipment)

GE-Hitachi (Nuclear equipment)

GE-Mitsubishi (Steam turbines)

Westinghouse-Mitsubishi (Motors)

Westinghouse-Komatsu
  (Motors, Robotics)

ABB-Combustion Engineering
  (Power equipment)

Composite Materials

GE-Asahi Diamond
  (Industrial diamonds)

Corning Glass-NGK Insulators
  (High energy ceramics)

Hercules-Toray (Specialized chemicals)

Armco-Mitsubishi Rayon
  (Composite plastics)

Factory Equipment

GE-Fanuc (Controllers)

GM-Fanuc (Robotics)

GM-Hitachi (Robotics)

Bendix-Murata (Machine tools)

Cincinnati Milacron (Semiconductors,
  automated equipment)

Kawasaki-Unimation (Robotics)

Fujitsu-McDonnell Douglas
  (CAD/CAM systems)

IBM-Sankyo Seiki (Robotics)

Houdaille-Okuma (Machine tools)

Allen Bradley-Nippondenso
  (Programmable controls)

Bendix-Yasegawa Tools (Robotics)

Office Equipment

AT&T-Ricoh (Fax machines)

Kodak-Canon (Mid-range copiers)

Fuji-Xerox (Small copiers)

3M-Toshiba (Copiers)

Apple-Toshiba (Printers)

RCA-Hitachi (PBX controls)

Hewlett Packard-Canon (Laser printers)

Xerox-Sharp (Low-end copiers)

The Logic Behind Strategic Alliances

The strategic pay-offs of cross-border alliances are alluring, especially in high-tech industries. Lorange and colleagues[46] suggest that there are four generic reasons for forming strategic alliances: defense, catch-up, remain, or restructure (see Exhibit 9-8).

---

[46]Peter Lorange, Johan Roos, and Peggy S. Brønn, "Building Successful Strategic Alliances," *Long Range Planning*, 25 (6), (1992), pp. 10–17.

Exhibit 9-8
GENERIC MOTIVES FOR STRATEGIC ALLIANCES

		Business' Market Position	
		Leader	Follower
Strategic Importance in Parent's Portfolio	Core	Defend	Catch Up
	Peripheral	Remain	Restructure

Source: Reprinted from P. Lorange, J. Roos and P. S. Brønn, "Building Successful Strategic Alliances," *Long Range Planning*, vol. 25, no. 6, p. 10. Copyright 1992, with kind permission from Elsevier Science Ltd., The Boulevard, Langford Lane, Kidlington OX5 1GB, UK.

Their scheme centers around two dimensions: the strategic importance of the business unit to the parent company and the competitive position of the business.

- **Defences.** Companies create alliances for their core businesses to defend their leadership position. Basically, the underlying goal is to sustain the firm's leadership position by learning new skills, getting access to new markets, developing new technologies, or finessing other capabilities that help the company to reinforce its competitive advantage.[47]

- **Catch-Up.** Firms may also shape strategic alliances to catch up. This happens when companies create an alliance to shore up a core business in which they do not have a leadership position. Nestlé and General Mills launched Cereal Partners Worldwide to attack the Kelloggs-dominated global cereal market. PepsiCo and General Mills, two of the weaker players in the European snack-food business, set up a joint venture for their snack-food business to compete more effectively in the European market.

- **Remain.** Firms might also enter a strategic alliance to simply remain in a business. This might occur for business divisions where the firm has established a leadership position but that only play a peripheral role in the company's business portfolio. That way, the alliance enables the company to get the maximum efficiency out of its position.

- **Restructure.** Lastly, a firm might also view alliances as a vehicle to restructure a business that is not core and in which it has no leadership position. The ultimate intent here is that one partner uses the alliance to rejuvenate the business, thereby turning the business unit into a "presentable bride," so to speak. Usually, one of the other partners in the alliance will end up acquiring the business unit.

---

[47]See also David Lei and John W. Slocum, Jr., "Global Strategy, Competence-Building and Strategic Alliances," *California Management Review* (Fall 1992), pp. 81–97.

Cross-Border Alliances that Succeed

The formula for a successful strategic alliance will probably never be written. Still, a number of studies done by consulting agencies and academic scholars have uncovered several findings on what distinguishes enduring cross-border alliances from the floundering ones. A recent analysis of cross-border alliances done by McKinsey came up with the following recommendations:[48]

- **Alliances between strong and weak partners seldom work.** Building ties with weak partners is a recipe for disaster. The weak partner becomes a drag on the competitiveness of the partnership.

- **Autonomy and flexibility.** Autonomy and flexibility are two key ingredients for successful partnerships. Autonomy might mean that the alliance has its own management team and its own board of directors. This speeds up the decision-making process. Autonomy also makes it easier to resolve conflicts that arise. To cope with environmental changes over time, flexibility is essential. Market needs change, new technologies emerge, competitive forces regroup. Being flexible, alliances can more easily adapt to these changes by revising their objectives, the charter of the venture, or other aspects of the alliance.

- **Equal ownership.** Fifty–fifty ownership means that the partners are equally concerned about the other's success. Both partners should contribute equally to the alliance.[49] Thereby, all partners will be in a win–win situation where the gains are equally distributed. However, fifty–fifty joint ventures between partners from developed countries and LDCs are more likely to get bogged down in decision-making deadlocks. One recent study of equity joint ventures in China found that partnerships with minority foreign equity holding run much more smoothly than other equity sharing arrangements. Fifty–fifty partnerships ran into all sorts of internal managerial problems like joint decision-making and coordination with local managers. Majority foreign equity ventures had fewer internal problems but encountered many external issues such as lack of local sourcing and high dependence on imported materials.[50]

To these we would like to add a few more success factors. Stable alliances have the commitment and support of the top of the parents' organization. Strong alliance managers are key.[51] Alliances between partners that are related (in terms of products, markets, and/or technologies) or have similar cultures, assets sizes, and venturing experience levels tend to be much more viable.[52] Finally, a shared vision on the goals and the mutual benefits is the hallmark of viable alliances.

---

[48]Joel Bleeke and David Ernst, "The Way to Win in Cross-Border Alliances," *Harvard Business Review* (November-December 1991), pp. 127–135.

[49]Godfrey Devlin and Mark Bleackley, "Strategic Alliances—Guidelines for Success," *Long Range Planning*, 21 (5) (1988), pp. 18–23.

[50]Yigang Pan and Wilfried R. Vanhonacker, "Equity Sharing Arrangements and Joint Venture Operation in the People's Republic of China," Working Paper, February 1994, Hong Kong University of Science & Technology.

[51]Devlin and Bleackley, pp. 18–23.

[52]Kathryn R. Harrigan, "Strategic Alliances and Partner Asymetries," in *Cooperative Strategies in International Business*, F. J. Contractor and P. Lorange, eds. (Lexington, Mass.: Lexington Books, 1988).

◆◆◆◆◆◆◆◆◆◆◆◆◆◆◆◆◆◆◆◆◆◆◆◆◆◆◆◆◆◆◆◆◆◆◆◆◆

$\mathcal{U}$IDEOBOX

Baby Bells Offering Cable TV in the United Kingdom

A relaxed regulatory climate in the British telecom market has opened up opportunities for American local phone companies such as NYNEX, US West and Southwestern Bell. These so-called Baby Bells are heavily investing in the cable TV industry in Britain. Why? Their ultimate goal is to gain a foothold in the British telecom market. They plan to offer telephony services such as local phone, teleconferencing and video-text services along with entertainment.

The Baby Bells' strategy is to compete with British Telecom (BT) by offering cheaper phone service and inno-vations that BT cannot provide. BT is barred for several years from entering the cable TV market in Britain. With less than 12% of British homes and businesses hooked up to cable, the Baby Bells will have to wait for at least a decade before their operations will start making profits. Part of the pay-off will also be the expertise that the Baby Bells hope to gain in the new businesses and can apply back to their homebase once regulations in the United States ease.

Discuss the strategy followed by the Baby Bells. What competitive responses might BT consider to retaliate?

Summary ◆

Companies have a smorgasbord of entry strategy choices to implement their global expansion efforts. Each alternative has its pros and cons. No shoe fits all sizes. Many firms use a hodgepodge of entry modes. Motorola established a $300 million-plus manufacturing venture in Tianjin (China), which is a fully owned enterprise. However, the marketing and sales of the products is to be done via a range of equity joint ventures with local part-ners.[53] Companies often adopt a phased entry strategy: they start off with a minimal-risk strategy; once the perceived risk declines they switch to a higher commitment mode, such as a wholly owned venture. Caterpillar, Inc., the U.S.-based manufac-turer of earth-moving and construction equipment, entered the former Soviet bloc in 1992 via direct exporting to minimize its financial risk exposure. Once sales took off, Caterpillar upped the ante by establishing joint ventures with Russian and Amer-ican firms.[54]

As this chapter made clear, a broad range of variables impact the entry mode choice. The three major dimensions include the resource commitment the firm is willing to make, the amount of risk (po-litical and market) the firm is willing to take, and the degree of control that is desirable.

To compete more effectively in the global arena, more and more companies use cross-border strategic alliances to build up their muscle. Depending on the strategic role and the competitive position of the busi-ness unit involved, the goal of the alliance could be to defend, strengthen, sustain, or restructure the SBU. The benefits that the partners can derive from the syn-ergies of the alliance often downplay the concerns the parent companies might have about the partnership. Still, the formation of the alliance should always be preceded by a meticulous analysis of questions like:[55]

- What are the mutual benefits for each partner?
- What learning can take place between firms?
- How can the parties complement each other to create joint capabilities?
- Are the partners equal in strength, or is this the case of the "one-eyed guiding the blind"?

Satisfactory answers to these questions improve the chances of the cross-border alliance becoming a win–win situation for all partners involved.

---

[53]Vanhonacker, pp. 130–40.

[54]Avraham Shama, "Entry Strategies of U.S. Firms to the Newly Independent States, Baltic States, and Eastern European Countries," *California Management Review*, 37 (3) (Spring 1995), pp. 90–109.

[55]Lorange, Roos, and Brønn, pp. 12–13.

REVIEW QUESTIONS ◆ ◆ ◆ ◆ ◆ ◆ ◆ ◆ ◆ ◆ ◆ ◆ ◆ ◆ ◆ ◆ ◆

1. Why do some MNCs prefer to enter certain markets with a liaison office first?

2. What are the possible drawbacks of fifty–fifty joint ventures?

3. Draw up a list of the respective pros and cons of licensing.

4. What are the respective advantages and disadvantages of greenfield operations over acquisitions?

5. What mechanisms can firms use to protect themselves against ill-fated partnerships?

EXHIBIT 9-9
GLOBAL EXPANSION PATH OF CPC INTERNATIONAL

1920
France

1923
Switzerland

1926
Italy

1928
Argentina

1929
Brazil

1930
Mexico

1931
India

1932
Ireland

1933
Colombia

1954
Spain

1955
Philippines

1957
Hong Kong
Malaysia

1958
Uruguay

1960
Austria
Sweden
Venezuela

1961
Chile
Peru

1962
Pakistan

1963
Japan

1964
Portugal
Guatemala

1966
Singapore
Thailand

1968
Greece
Finland
Norway

1970
Ecuador
Morocco
Taiwan

1971
Kenya

1973
Honduras

1979
South Korea

1983
Panama

1984
Tunisia

1985
Turkey

1987
Bolivia

1989
Saudi Arabia

1991
Costa Rica
Dominican Republic
Hungary
Indonesia

1992
Czech Republic
Israel
Paraguay
Poland

1993
China
Russia
Slovak Republic
Sri Lanka
Vietnam

1994
South Africa

1995
Bulgaria
Jordan
Romania

Source: CPC International 1995 *Annual Report.*

DISCUSSION QUESTIONS ✦ ✦ ✦ ✦ ✦ ✦ ✦ ✦ ✦ ✦ ✦ ✦ ✦ ✦ ✦ ✦ ✦ ✦ ✦

1. Exhibit 9-9 shows the global expansion path of CPC International, a U.S. food company that owns brands like Knorr, Skippy, and Hellman's. Discuss the company's expansion path. What patterns do you recognize? What might be the reasons behind the patterns you observe?

2. Waste Management International relies heavily on acquisitions in Europe. In Asia, though, the company follows an entirely different entry strategy. What could be the reasons why companies use different entry choices in different regions?

3. Assignment: Check some recent issues of the *Wall Street Journal* and/or the *Financial Times*. Look for articles on cross-border strategic alliances. Pick one or two examples and find out more about the alliances you chose via a search on the Internet. Why were the alliances formed? What do the partners contribute to the alliance? What benefits do they anticipate? What concerns/issues were raised?

4. Helmut Maucher, former chairman of Nestlé was quoted saying: "I don't share the euphoria for alliances and joint ventures. First, very often they're an excuse, and an easy way out when people should do their own homework. Secondly, all joint ventures create additional difficulties—you share power and cultures, and decisions take longer." Comment.

FURTHER READING ✦ ✦ ✦ ✦ ✦ ✦ ✦ ✦ ✦ ✦ ✦ ✦ ✦ ✦ ✦ ✦ ✦ ✦ ✦

Anderson, Erin, and Hubert Gatignon. "Modes of Foreign Entry: A Transaction Cost Analysis and Propositions." *Journal of International Business Studies*, 11 (Fall 1986):1–26.

Bleeke, Joel, and David Ernst. "The Way to Win in Cross-Border Alliances." *Harvard Business Review* (Nov.–Dec. 1991):127–135.

Devlin, Godfrey, and Mark Bleackley. "Strategic Alliances—Guidelines for Success." *Long Range Planning*, 21 (5) (1988):18–23.

Kumar, V., A. Stam, and E. A. Joachimsthaler. "An Interactive Multicriteria Approach to Identifying Potential Foreign Markets," *Journal of International Marketing*, 2, (1) (1994), pp. 29–52.

Lorange, Peter, Johan Roos, and Peggy S. Brønn, "Building Successful Strategic Alliances." *Long Range Planning*, 25 (6) (1992):10–17.

Martinsons, M. G. and C.-S. Tseng. "Successful Joint Ventures in the Heart of the Dragon." *Long Range Planning*, 28 (5) (1995):45–58.

Ostland, Gregory E., and S. Tamer Cavusgil. "Performance Issues in U.S.–China Joint Ventures." *California Management Review*, 38 (2) (Winter 1996):106–130.

Preble, John F., and Richard C. Hoffman. "Franchising Systems Around the Globe: A Status Report," *Journal of Small Business Management* (April 1995):80–88.

Root, Franklin R. *Entry Strategies for International Markets*. New York, N.Y.: Lexington Books, 1994.

Shama, Avraham. "Entry Strategies of U.S. Firms to the Newly Independent States, Baltic States, and Eastern European Countries." *California Management Review*, 37 (3) (Spring 1995):90–109.

Turpin, Dominique. "Strategic Alliances with Japanese Firms: Myths and Realities." *Long Range Planning*, 28 (5) (1993):45–58.

GLOBAL SOURCING STRATEGY: R & D, MANUFACTURING, AND MARKETING INTERFACES

10

HAPTER OVERVIEW

1. EXTENT AND COMPLEXITY OF GLOBAL SOURCING STRATEGY
2. TRENDS IN GLOBAL SOURCING STRATEGY
3. VALUE CHAIN AND FUNCTIONAL INTERFACES
4. LOGISTICS OF SOURCING STRATEGY
5. COSTS AND CONSEQUENCES OF GLOBAL SOURCING

During the last decade or so, international business has experienced a major metamorphosis of an irreversible kind. Gone are the days when international business meant the one-way expansion of U.S. companies to the rest of the world. Also gone are the days when European and Japanese companies simply exported to, or manufactured in, the United States. Today, executives of the same companies have come to accept a new reality of global competition and global competitors. An increasing number of companies from around the world, particularly from the United States, Western Europe, and Japan, are competing head-on for global dominance. Global competition suggests a drastically shortened life cycle for most products, and no longer permits companies a polycentric, country-by-country approach to international business. If companies that have developed a new product do follow a country-by-country approach to foreign market entry over time, a globally oriented competitor will likely overcome their initial competitive advantages by blanketing the world markets with similar products in a shorter period of time.

A frequently used framework to describe cross-national business practices is the international product cycle theory (see Appendix to Chapter 1). The theory has provided a compelling description of dynamic patterns of international trade of manufactured products and direct investment as a product advances through its life cycle. According to the theory, changes in inputs and product characteristics toward standardization over time determine an optimal production location at any particular phase of the product's life cycle.

However, three major limitations of the international product cycle theory must be borne in mind:

1. **The trend toward an increased pace of new product introduction and reduction in innovational lead time** deprives companies of the age-old polycentric approach to global markets.

2. **Ability to preempt the product life cycle—predictable sourcing development during the product cycle—**permits a shrewd company to outmaneuver competition.

3. **More active management of locational and corporate resources on a global basis** gives a company a preemptive first-mover advantage over competition.

One successful example of a globally oriented strategist is Sony. Sony developed transistorized solid-state color TVs in Japan in the 1960s and marketed them initially in the United States before they were introduced in the rest of the world, including the Japanese market. Mass marketing initially in the United States and then throughout the world in a short time period had given this Japanese company a first-mover advantage, as well as economies of scale advantages.

In contrast, EMI provides a historic case example of the failure to take advantage of global opportunities. This British company developed and began marketing CAT (computer-aided tomography) scanners in 1972, for which its inventors, Godfrey Houndsfield and Allan Cormack, won a Nobel Prize. Despite an enormous demand for CAT scanners in the United States, the largest market for state-of-the-art medical equipment, EMI failed to export them to the United States immediately and in sufficient numbers. Instead, the British company slowly, and probably belatedly, began exporting them to the United States in the mid-1970s, as if to follow the evolutionary pattern suggested by the international product cycle model. Some years later, the British company established a production facility in the United States, only to be slowed down by technical problems. By then, EMI was already facing stiff competition from global electronics giants including Philips, Siemens, General Electric, and Toshiba. Indeed, it was General Electric that, in a short period of time, blanketed the U.S. market and subsequently the rest of the world with its own version of CAT scanners, which were technologically inferior to the British model.[1]

In both cases, technology diffused quickly. Today, quick technological diffusion is virtually assured. Without established sourcing plans, distribution, and service networks, it is extremely difficult to exploit both emerging technology and potential markets around the world simultaneously. General Electric's swift global reach could not have been possible without its ability to procure crucial components internally and on a global basis. As a result, the increased pace of new product introduction and reduction in innovational lead time calls for more proactive management of locational and corporate resources on a global basis. In this chapter, we emphasize logistical management of the **interfaces** of R & D, manufacturing, and marketing activities on a global basis—which we call **global sourcing strategy**—and also the importance of the ability to procure major components of the product in-house, such that companies can proactively standardize either components or products. Global

---

[1]Fillipo Dell'Osso, "Defending a Dominant Position in a Technology Led Environment," *Business Strategy Review* (Summer 1990), pp. 77–86.

sourcing strategy requires a close coordination among R & D, manufacturing, and marketing activities across national boundaries.[2]

Differing objectives tend to create a "tug-of-war"-like situation among R & D, manufacturing, and marketing. For example, the demands of marketing for repeated product modification and proliferation for the sake of satisfying the ever-changing customer needs may be contrary to the objectives of manufacturing of lowering costs, since repeated modifications lead to increased costs and loss of production efficiencies. Similarly, designing products and features as desired by customers may indeed be innovative, but might not be conducive to efficient manufacturing. An exception to this situation would be a perfectly flexible computer-aided design (CAD) and computer-aided manufacturing (CAM) facility, which would allow various modifications to be made in the products without significantly increasing the associated manufacturing costs. (One must note, however, that while CAD/CAM technology has improved tremendously in recent years, the full benefit of flexible manufacturing is still many years away).[3] Contrarily, excessive product standardization for the sake of lowering manufacturing costs will also be likely to result in unsatisfied or undersatisfied customers. Therefore, topics, such as product design for manufacturability and components/product standardization have become increasingly important strategic issues today. It has become imperative for many companies to develop a sound sourcing strategy in order to exploit most efficiently R & D, manufacturing, and marketing on a global basis.

EXTENT AND COMPLEXITY OF GLOBAL SOURCING STRATEGY

◆ ◆ ◆ ◆ ◆ ◆

In this chapter, we introduce you to subject matters not ordinarily covered in a marketing textbook. It is our strong belief that marketing managers should understand and appreciate the important roles that product designers, engineers, production managers, and purchasing managers, among others, play in marketing decision making. Marketing decisions cannot be made in the absence of these people. The overriding theme throughout the chapter is that successful management of the interfaces of R & D, manufacturing, and marketing activities determines a company's competitive strengths and consequently its market performance. Now we will look at logistical implications of this interface management.

One successful interface management is illustrated by Toyota's global operations. The Japanese carmaker is equiping its operations in the United States, Europe, and Southeast Asia with integrated capabilities for creating and marketing automobiles. The company gives the managers at those operations ample authority to accommodate local circumstances and values without diluting the benefit of integrated global operations. Thus, in the United States, Calty Design Research, a Toyota subsidiary in California, designs the bodies and interiors of new Toyota models, including Previa and Lexus, for production in the United States. Toyota has technical centers in the United States and in Brussels to adapt engine and vehicle specifications to local needs. Toyota operations that make automobiles in Southeast Asia supply each other

---

[2]Masaaki Kotabe, *Global Sourcing Strategy: R & D, Manufacturing, and Marketing Interfaces* (New York: Quorum Books, 1992).

[3]"A Survey of Manufacturing Technology," *Economist* (March 5, 1994), pp. 3–18.

with key components to foster increased economies of scale and standardization in those components—gasoline engines in Indonesia, steering components in Malaysia, transmissions in the Philippines, and diesel engines in Thailand.

Undoubtedly, these multinational companies, including Toyota, not only facilitate the flow of capital among various countries through direct investment abroad, but also significantly contribute to the world trade flow of goods and services. Multinational companies combine this production and distribution to supply those local markets hosting their foreign subsidiaries, and then export what remains to other foreign markets or back to their parent's home market.

Let us revisit the significance of multinational companies' foreign production relative to their exports from their home base. U.S. multinational companies are the most experienced in the industrialized world, and sell more than three times as much overseas through their subsidiaries than they export to the world. For U.S. multinationals, the 3:1 ratio of foreign sales to exports has remained largely unchanged since mid-1960s. This ratio for European multinationals has grown from 3:1 in the 1970s to 5:1 by 1990. Similarly, the ratio for Japanese multinationals has increased from 1:1 in mid-1970s to 2.5:1 by 1990. Also, both American and Japanese subsidiaries sell more than 20 percent of their foreign sales in third-country markets (third-country markets defined as markets other than the country where the parent company is based and the country where the particular manufacturing facility is based), including their home markets, while European subsidiaries in the United States and Japan sell approximately 10 percent in third-country markets.[4]

This intra-firm trade, through the management of foreign production by multinational firms, is one of the primary factors leading to the total volume of international trade among the Triad regions (i.e., the United States, European Community, and Japan) increasing more than tenfold in twenty years—to $514.7 billion in 1995 from $44.4 billion in 1970—or by more than four times in real terms.

Two notable changes have occurred in international trade. First, the last thirty years have observed a secular decline in the proportion of trade between the European Community and the United States in the Triad regions, and conversely an increase in trade between the United States and Japan, and in particular, between the European Community and Japan. It strongly indicates that European countries and Japan have found each other as increasingly important markets above and beyond their traditional market of the United States. Second, newly industrialized countries (NICs) in Asia, including South Korea, Taiwan, Hong Kong, and Singapore, have dramatically increased their trading position relative to the rest of the world. Not only have these NICs become prosperous marketplaces, but more significantly, they have become important manufacturing and sourcing locations for many multinational companies.

From the sourcing perspective, U.S. and other multinational companies were procuring a less expensive supply of components and finished products in NICs for sale in the United States and elsewhere. As a result, U.S. bilateral trade with NICs has increased more than eightyfold, to an estimated $150 billion in 1996 from $1.8 billion in 1970. Trade statistics, however, do not reveal anything other than the amount of bilateral trade flows between countries. It is false to assume that trade is always a business transaction between independent buyers and sellers across national boundaries. It is equally false to assume that a country's trade deficit in a certain *industry* equates with the

---

[4]Dennis J. Encarnation, "Transforming Trade and Investment, American, European, and Japanese Multinationals Across the Triad," a paper presented at the Academy of International Business Annual Meetings, November 22, 1992.

decline in the competitiveness of *companies* in that industry. For example, Honda's production and sourcing network is presented in Exhibit 10-1. Clearly, an increasing segment of international trade of components and finished products is strongly influenced by multinational companies' foreign production and sourcing investment activities.

TRENDS IN GLOBAL SOURCING STRATEGY ◆ ◆ ◆ ◆ ◆ ◆ ◆

Over the last twenty years or so, gradual yet significant changes have taken place in global sourcing strategy. Most of the changes are in the way business executives think of the scope of global sourcing for their companies and exploit various resultant opportunities as a source of competitive advantage. Peter Drucker, a famed management guru and business historian, once said that sourcing and logistics would remain "the darkest continent of business"—the least exploited area of business for competitive advantage. Naturally, many companies that have a limited scope of global sourcing are at a disadvantage over those that exploit it to their fullest extent in a globally competitive marketplace. Five trends in global sourcing are identified.[5] Exhibit 10-2 shows various factors that affect the scope of global sourcing strategy.

Trend 1: The Decline of Exchange Rate Determinism of Sourcing

Since the 1970s, exchange rates have fluctuated rather erratically. If the dollar appreciates, U.S. companies find it easy to procure components and products from abroad. Such was the case in the first half of the 1980s when the dollar appreciated precipitously. The appreciation of the dollar was reflected in the surge of U.S. imports. Contrarily, if the dollar depreciates, U.S. companies would find it increasingly difficult to depend on foreign supplies, as they have to pay higher dollar prices for every item sourced from abroad. In these scenarios, companies consider the exchange rate determining the extent to which they can engage in foreign sourcing.

However, this exchange rate determinism of sourcing is strictly based on the price factor. Indeed, a recent study shows that exchange rate fluctuations have little impact on the nature of sourcing strategy for crucial components.[6] Foreign sourcing also occurs for noncost reasons such as quality, technology, and so on. First of all, since it takes time to develop overseas suppliers for noncost purposes, purchasing managers cannot easily drop a foreign supplier when exchange rate changes have an adverse effect on the cost of imported components and products. Second, domestic suppliers are known to increase prices to match rising import prices following exchange rate changes. As a result, switching to a domestic supplier may not ensure cost advantages. Third, many companies are developing long-term relationships with international suppliers—whether those suppliers are their subsidiaries or independent contractors. In a long-term supply relationship, exchange rate fluctuations may be viewed as a temporary problem by the parties involved. Finally, some companies with global operations are able to shift supply locations from one country to another to overcome the adverse effects of exchange rate fluctuations.

---

[5]This section draws from Paul M. Swamidass, "Import Sourcing Dynamics: An Integrative Perspective," *Journal of International Business Studies*, 24 (Fourth Quarter 1993), pp. 671–91.

[6]Janet Y. Murray, "A Currency Exchange Rate-Driven vs. Strategy-Driven Analysis of Global Sourcing," *Multinational Business Review*, 4 (Spring 1996), pp. 40–51.

EXHIBIT 10-1
HONDA'S WORLDWIDE PRODUCTION AND SOURCING NETWORK

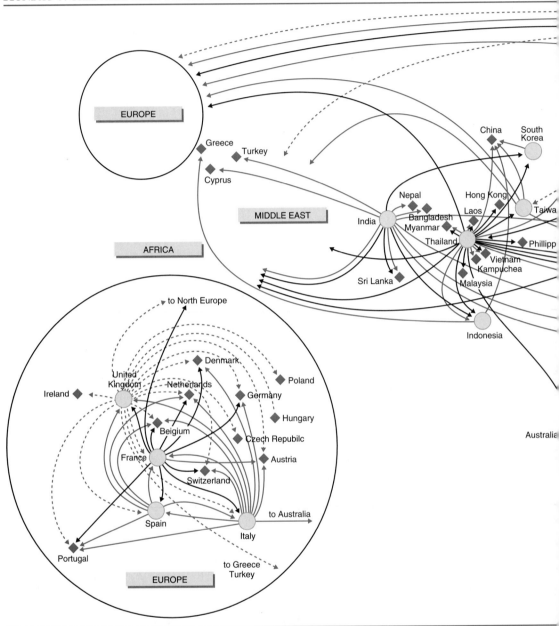

Source: Honda Motor Company Annual Report 1996.

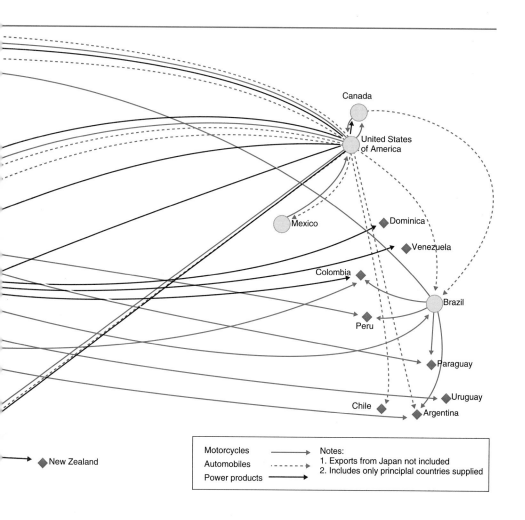

EXHIBIT 10-2
FACTORS THAT AFFECT GLOBAL SOURCING STRATEGY

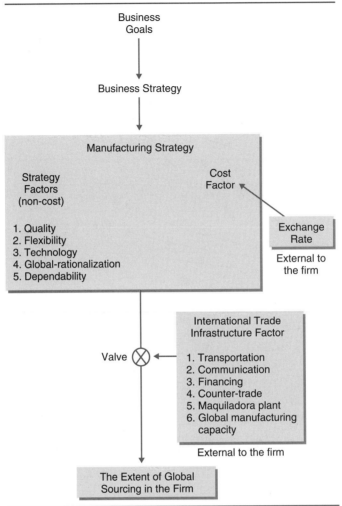

Source: Paul M. Swamidass, "Import Sourcing Dynamics: An Integrative Perspective," *Journal of International Business Studies* (Fourth Quarter 1993), p. 682.

Trend 2: New Competitive Environment Caused by Excess Worldwide Capacity

The worldwide growth in the number of manufacturers has added excess production capacity in most industries. The proliferation of manufacturers around the world in less sophisticated, less capital-intensive manufactured products, such as cement, is much greater than in more complex, knowledge-intensive products such as computers. Thus, there has been tremendous downward pressure on prices of many components and products around the world. Although the ability to deliver a high volume of products of satisfactory quality at a reasonable price was once the hallmark of many successful U.S. companies, an increasing number of global suppliers have effectively rendered the delivery of volume in an acceptable time no longer a competitive

EXHIBIT 10-3
KEY FACTORS FOR SOURCING FROM ABROAD

Factor

Very Important
1. Better quality
2. Lower price
3. Unavailability of items in the United States

Important
4. More advanced technology abroad
5. Willingness to solve problems
6. More on-time delivery
7. Negotiability
8. Association with foreign subsidiary

Neutral
9. Geographical location
10. Countertrade requirements
11. Government assistance

Source: Adapted from Hokey Min and William P. Galle, "International Purchasing Strategies of Multinational U.S. Firms," *International Journal of Purchasing and Materials Management* (Summer 1991), p. 14.

weapon. There has since occurred a strategic shift from *price* and *quantity* to *quality* and *reliability* of products as a determinant of competitive strength.[7] According to a recent survey (see Exhibit 10-3), better product and component quality, lower price, unavailability of item in the United States, and more advanced technology abroad are among the most important reasons for increased sourcing from abroad.

Trend 3: Innovations in and Restructuring of International Trade Infrastructure

Advances in structural elements of international trade have made it easier for companies to employ sourcing for strategic purposes. The innovations and structural changes that have important influences on sourcing strategy are (1) the increased number of purchasing managers experienced in sourcing, (2) improvements made in transportation and communication (e.g., fax), (3) new financing options, including countertrade (barter that includes all variations of exchange of goods for goods), offering new incentives and opportunities for exports from countries without hard currency, (4) manufacturing facilities diffused throughout the world by globally minded companies, and (5) *maquiladora* plants (Mexican version of free-trade-zone manufacturing facilities, mostly located close to the U.S.–Mexico border) on the Mexican side of the border providing a unique form of sourcing options to manufacturers operating in the United States.

---

[7]Martin K. Starr and John E. Ullman, "The Myth of Industrial Supremacy," in Martin K. Starr, ed., *Global Competitiveness* (New York: W. W. Norton and Co., 1988).

Trend 4: Enhanced Role of Purchasing Managers

During the last ten to fifteen years, U.S. manufacturers were under pressure to compete on the basis of improved cost and quality as just-in-time (JIT) production was adopted in the United States by a growing number of companies. JIT production requires close working relationships with component suppliers, and places an enormous amount of responsibility on purchasing managers. Furthermore, sourcing directly from foreign suppliers requires greater purchasing know-how and is riskier than other alternatives that use middlemen, who are generally U.S.-based wholesalers and representatives. Middlemen based in the United States are subject to U.S. laws and assume some of the currency risk associated with importing. However, now that purchasing managers are increasingly making long-term commitments to foreign suppliers, dealing directly with suppliers is justified. According to one major survey, the dominant form of purchasing from abroad was to buy directly from foreign sources.[8] The finding suggests that U.S. purchasing managers are confident about their international know-how and that they may be seeking long-term sourcing arrangements. The key to achieving effective global sourcing is securing management involvement at both the strategic (top), and the tactical (middle) levels.[9]

Trend 5: Trend Toward Global Manufacturing

During the 1980s, while U.S. companies continued to locate their operations in various parts of the world, companies from other countries such as Japan, Germany, and Britain expanded the magnitude of their foreign manufacturing operations at a much faster pace. The share of foreign-owned companies in U.S.-based manufacturing activities has increased from 5.2 percent in 1977 to close to 15 percent recently. As a global company adds another international plant to its network of existing plants, it creates the need for sourcing of components and other semi-processed goods to and from the new plant to existing plants (see Global Perspective 10-1). Global manufacturing adds enormously to global sourcing activities, either within the same company across national boundaries or between independent suppliers and new plants.

In the late 1980s, statistical trends clearly show that U.S. companies have increased sourcing from abroad, despite the depreciation of the U.S. dollar. Their continued sourcing from abroad represents a strategic expansion and rationalization over time. In response to slow productivity growth in the United States relative to other major trading nations in the 1980s, U.S. parent companies' technology has been increasingly transferred directly to their foreign affiliates for production instead of in the form of equipment and components for local modification in the foreign markets. Mature companies are increasingly assigning independent design and other R & D responsibilities to satellite foreign units so as to design a regional or world product.[10]

---

[8]Somerby Dowst, "International Buying: The Facts and Foolishness," *Purchasing* (June 25, 1987).

[9]S. Tamer Cavusgil, Attila Yaprak, and Poe-lin Yeoh, "A Decision-making Framework for Global Sourcing," *International Business Review*, 2 (2) (1993), pp. 143–56.

[10]Robert M. Monczka and Robert J. Trent, "Global Sourcing: A Development Approach," *International Journal of Purchasing and Materials Management*, 27 (Spring 1991), pp. 2–8.

$\mathcal{G}$LOBAL PERSPECTIVE 10-1

TRADE FOLLOWS INVESTMENT

"Trade follows investment in the '90s. . . . If you can't invest, you can't trade." The Commerce data support that argument. More than 80 percent of all Japanese imports are bought by U.S. affiliates of Japanese multinationals. That's almost double the norm for other foreign multinationals. Meanwhile, parts now account for almost half the value of all Japanese imports, up from 10 percent in the mid-1980s. . . . (Similarly, U.S.) companies such as Mo-

torola . . . that want to expand distribution networks in Japan . . . would likely bring in more U.S.-made components. "If there are no American companies (abroad), there's nothing to pull other U.S. goods in."

Japanese high-tech firms shipped $20 billion worth of integrated circuits and other electronic components into the United States in 1993. Shipments from Japan-based purchasing offices of U.S. companies made up a hefty chunk of that. Companies such as Texas Instruments, Apple Computer, and Digital Equipment now have big purchasing operations in Japan.

Source: "The Secret of Weapon that Won't Start a Trade War," *Business Week* (March 7, 1994), p. 45.

As a result, foreign affiliates have also developed more independent R & D activities to manufacture products for the U.S. markets in addition to expanding local sales.[11]

VALUE CHAIN AND FUNCTIONAL INTERFACES

The design of global sourcing strategy is based on the interplay between a company's competitive advantages and the comparative advantages of various countries. **Competitive advantage** influences the decision regarding *what* activities and technologies a company should concentrate its investment and managerial resources in, relative to its competitors in the industry. **Comparative advantage** affects the company's decision on *where* to source and market, based on the lower cost of labor and other resources in one country relative to another.[12] As shown in Exhibit 10-4, the **value chain concept** offers a general framework for understanding what it takes to manage the interrelated value-adding activities of a company on a global basis.[13] A company is essentially a collection of activities that are performed to design, manufacture, market, deliver, and support its product. This set of interrelated corporate activities is called the value chain. Therefore, to gain competitive advantage over its rivals in the marketplace, a company must perform these activities either at a lower cost or in such a way as to offer differentiated products and services, or accomplish both. For example, Daewoo, Korea's new entrant into the automobile industry, introduced a

---

[11]Masaaki Kotabe and K. Scott Swan, "Offshore Sourcing: Reaction, Maturation, and Consolidation of U.S. Multinationals," *Journal of International Business Studies*, 25 (First Quarter 1994), p. 1-27.

[12]Bruce Kogut, "Designing Global Strategies: Comparative and Competitive Value-Added Chains," *Sloan Management Review*, 26 (Summer 1985), pp. 15–28.

[13]Michael E. Porter, *Competition in Global Industries* (Cambridge, Mass.: Harvard Business School Press, 1986).

EXHIBIT 10-4
VALUE CHAIN CONCEPT

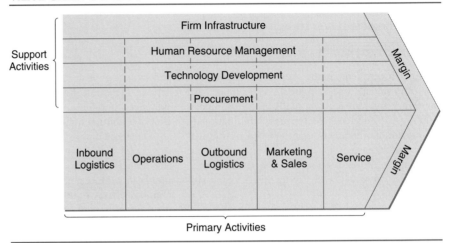

Source: Reprinted with the permission of The Free Press, a division of Simon & Schuster from
COMPETITIVE ADVANTAGE: Creating and Sustaining Superior Performance by Michael E. Porter,
p. 37. Copyright © 1985 by Michael E. Porter.

successful Lanos model whose prototype was developed at its Worthing Technical
Center in Britain and styled at Italdesign, a creative Italian design firm, with help
from Daewoo's new Design Forum in Korea. It was manufactured in Korea for export to the European market.[14]

The value chain can be divided into two major activities performed by a company: (1) **primary activities** consisting of inbound logistics (procurement of raw materials and components), manufacturing operations, outbound logistics (distribution),
sales, and after-sale service, and (2) **support activities** consisting of human resource
management, technology development, and other activities that help promote primary activities. Competing companies constantly strive to create value across various
activities in the value chain. Of course, the value that a company creates is measured
ultimately by the price buyers are willing to pay for its products. Therefore, the value
chain is a useful concept that provides an assessment of the activities that a company
performs to design, manufacture, market, deliver, and support its products in the
marketplace.

Five continuous and interactive steps are involved in developing a global sourcing strategy along the value chain.[15]

1. Identify the separable links (R & D, manufacturing, and marketing) in the company's value chain.

2. In the context of those links, determine the location of the company's competitive advantages, considering both economies of scale and scope.

---

[14]Michael Schuman, "Daewoo Lifts Its Sights to U.S. and Europe," *Wall Street Journal*
(March 4, 1997), p. A15.

[15]Richard D. Robinson, ed., *Direct Foreign Investment: Costs and Benefits* (New York:
Praeger Publishers, 1987).

3. Ascertain the level of transaction costs (e.g., cost of negotiation, cost of monitoring activities, and uncertainty resulting from contracts) between links in the value chain, both internal and external, and select the lowest cost mode.

4. Determine the comparative advantages of countries (including the company's home country) relative to each link in the value chain and to the relevant transaction costs.

5. Develop adequate flexibility in corporate decision making and organizational design so as to permit the company to respond to changes in both its competitive advantages and the comparative advantages of countries.

In this chapter, we focus on the three most important interrelated activities in the value chain: namely, R & D (i.e., technology development, product design, and engineering), manufacturing, and marketing activities. Management of the interfaces, or linkages, among these value-adding activities is a crucial determinant of a company's competitive advantage. A basic framework of management of R & D, manufacturing, and marketing interfaces is outlined in Exhibit 10-5. Undoubtedly, these value-adding activities should be examined as holistically as possible, by linking the boundaries of these primary activities. Thus, global sourcing strategy encompasses management of (1) the interfaces among R & D, manufacturing, and marketing on a global basis and (2) logistics identifying which production units will serve which particular markets and how components will be supplied for production. As presented in Global Perspective 10-2, linking R & D and manufacturing with marketing provides enormous direct and indirect benefits to companies operating in a highly competitive environment.

R & D/Manufacturing Interface

Technology is broadly defined as know-how. Technology can be classified based on the nature of know-how—know-how composed of product technology (the set of ideas embodied in the product) and process technology (the set of ideas involved in the manufacture of the product or the steps necessary to combine new materials to

EXHIBIT 10-5
INTERFACES AMONG R & D, MANUFACTURING, AND MARKETING

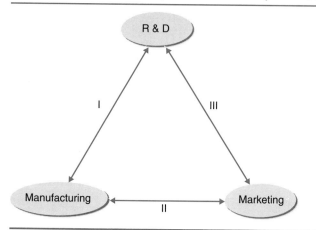

I. R & D / MANUFACTURING INTERFACE
   • Product innovation
   • Designing for manufacturability
   • Manufacturing process innovation
   • Components sourcing

II. MANUFACTURING / MARKETING INTERFACE
   • Product and component standardization
   • Product modification

III. MARKETING / R & D INTERFACE
   • New product development
   • Product positioning

◆ ◆

$\mathcal{G}$LOBAL PERSPECTIVE 10-2

POWER OF GOOD LINKAGE MANAGEMENT

In today's world of global competition and high speed product development, linkage among R & D, manufacturing and marketing is more vital to successful business than ever before. Delivering a competitive product to the market at the right time, with the right specifications and feature benefits, all at a manufacturing cost that allows for profit is one tough assignment. Add to this the global complexity of marketing, R & D, and manufacturing not being co-located in the same place, competing in an environment where world-class product development time is under fifty weeks, and you have a challenge that few companies are dealing with appropriately today.

International marketing executives can no longer have the luxury of time to consider R & D and manufacturing as activities remotely related and remotely relevant to them. They have to deal with all of this complexity and be fully aware that without adequate understanding of the linkages necessary among R & D, manufacturing, and marketing, their businesses run a very high risk of failure.

John A. Bermingham, who has worked as executive vice president at Sony Corporation of America, president and CEO of AT&T Smart Cards Systems, and most recently as president and CEO of Rolodex Corporation, has a keen appreciation of how important and beneficial it is to manage linkages among R & D, manufacturing, and marketing activities on a global basis. The following is his advice:

When marketing determines a product need, the very first thing that marketing managers must do is to bring R & D and manufacturing together to establish a powerful linkage for the duration of the project. Marketing should also include finance, sales, and operations in this project, but the key linkage for the purpose of the product development is among marketing, R & D and manufacturing.

According to John Bermingham, good linkage management has many benefits for these teams.

- *A powerful linkage develops the requisite personal/business relationship* needed among the three groups that allows for the understanding and empathy for each other's responsibilities. These relationships cannot be fos-

Source: John A. Bermingham, "Executive Insights: Roles of R & D and Manufacturing in Global Marketing Management," *Journal of International Marketing*, 4 (4) (1996), pp. 75–84.

tered via faxes and teleconferences. They need to be developed on a face-to-face basis as well as throughout the project, especially if the marketing, R & D and manufacturing teams are in different countries.

- *A powerful linkage is necessary to ensure that issues are on top of the table* at the beginning of the project and also as they develop throughout the project. Marketing must ensure that R & D and manufacturing are aware of the marketing strategy, competitive environment, and global implications. Any situations arising during the project must be discussed openly and positively with mutual understanding and with decisions being made to minimize impairment to the project with full understanding among the teams.

- *A powerful linkage allows for speed.* When you consider that world-class product development time is less than fifty weeks, and some say it will be less than forty weeks in the not too distant future, a powerful linkage is imperative. Teams must be working a series parallel effort. While certain things have to happen before others, certain things can be accomplished simultaneously. but this can only be accomplished with linkage.

- *A powerful linkage develops a high sense of urgency.* Teams really begin to understand how important speed is in this type of environment when they go past understanding their own needs and problems and begin to understand the other linked teams' needs and problems. Hence, urgency surrounds everything that these linked teams set out to accomplish. They see their linkage to the others and want to meet the needs of the entire team.

- *A powerful linkage fosters mutual ownership individually and collectively.* It is very important that there be individual ownership in the project, but it is just as important that the teams understand and accept collective ownership in the project. A tight linkage across the teams develops this collective ownership.

- *A powerful linkage develops a true team environment* that is essential and obligatory for success. Therefore, one of the most important roles for today and for the future for R & D and manufacturing in global marketing management is to ensure that these powerful linkages are established and strengthened.

produce a finished product). However, executives tend to focus solely on product-related technology as the driving force of the company's competitiveness. Product technology alone may not provide the company a long-term competitive edge over competition unless it is matched with sufficient manufacturing capabilities.[16]

The earlier example of EMI's CAT (computer-aided tomography) scan technology represents a classic case of such a product technology orientation. Similar cases exist throughout history. The British discovered and developed penicillin, but it was a small U.S. company, Pfizer, that improved on the fermentation (i.e., manufacturing) process and, as a result, became the world's foremost manufacturer of penicillin. The first jet engine was developed in Britain and Germany, but it was again U.S. companies, Boeing and Douglas, that improved on the technology and eventually dominated the jet plane market.

Ignoring manufacturing as a strategic weapon, many U.S. companies have historically emphasized product innovations (i.e., product proliferation and modifications). However, U.S. technological lead over foreign competition has virtually evaporated, so there will be fewer products that U.S. companies can export simply because no one else has the technology to manufacture the products.[17] Stressing the historical linkage of imitation and product innovations, it is contended that imitation (manufacturing process learning), followed by more innovative adaptation, leading to pioneering product design and innovation, forms the natural sequence of industrial development.[18] In other words, product innovation and manufacturing activities are intertwined, such that continual improvement in manufacturing processes can enable the company not only to maintain product innovation-based competitiveness, but also to improve its product innovative abilities in the future.[19]

These examples amply suggest that manufacturing processes should also be innovative. To facilitate the transferability of new product innovations to manufacturing, a team of product designers and engineers should strive to design components such that they are conducive to manufacturing without undue retooling required and that components may be used interchangeably for different models of the product. Low levels of retooling requirements and interchangeability of components are necessary conditions for efficient sourcing strategy on a global scale. If different equipment and components are used in various manufacturing plants, it is extremely difficult to establish a highly coordinated sourcing plan on a global basis.

Manufacturing/Marketing Interface

There exists a continual conflict between manufacturing and marketing divisions. It is to the manufacturing division's advantage if all the products and components are standardized to facilitate for standardized, low-cost production. The marketing divi-

---

[16]Bruce R. Guile and Harvey Brooks, ed., *Technology and Global Industry: Companies and Nations in the World Economy* (Washington, D.C.: National Academy Press, 1987).

[17]Lester C. Thurow, *The Management Challenge* (Cambridge, Mass.: MIT Press, 1985).

[18]Starr and Ullman, 1988.

[19]Harvey Brooks, "Japanese Technological Advances and Possible United States Responses Using Research Joint Ventures," presented at House Subcommittee on Investigations and Oversight and the Subcommittee on Science, Research, and Technology of the Committee on Science and Technology, 98th Congress, 1st session, June 29–30, 1983.

sion, however, is more interested in satisfying the diverse needs of customers, requiring broad product lines and frequent product modifications adding cost to manufacturing. How have successful companies coped with this dilemma?

Recently, there has been an increasing amount of interest in the strategic linkages between product policy and manufacturing long ignored in traditional considerations of global strategy development. With aggressive competition from European and Japanese multinational companies emphasizing corporate product policy and concomitant manufacturing, many companies have realized that product innovations alone cannot sustain their long-term competitive position without an effective product policy linking product and manufacturing process innovations.

Four different ways of developing a global product policy are generally considered an effective means to streamline manufacturing, thus lowering manufacturing cost, without sacrificing marketing flexibility: (1) core components standardization, (2) product design families, (3) universal product with all features, and (4) universal product with different positioning.[20]

Core Components Standardization. Successful global product policy mandates the development of universal products, or products that require no more than a cosmetic change for adaptation to differing local needs and use conditions. A few examples illustrate the point. Seiko, a Japanese watchmaker, offers a wide range of designs and models, but they are based on only a handful of different operating mechanisms. Similarly, the best-performing German machine tool-making companies have a narrower range of products, use up to 50 percent fewer parts than their less successful rivals, and make continual, incremental product and design improvements, with new developments passed rapidly on to customers.

Product Design Families. This is a variant of core component standardization. For companies marketing an extremely wide range of products due to cultural differences in product-use patterns around the world, it is also possible to reap economies of scale benefits. For example, Toyota offers several car models based on a similar family design concept, ranging from Lexus models to Toyota Avalons, Camrys, and Corollas. Many of the Lexus features well received by customers have been adopted into the Toyota lines with just a few minor modifications (mostly downsizing). In the process, Toyota has been able to cut product development costs and meet the needs of different market segments. Similarly, Electrolux, a Swedish appliance manufacturer, has adopted the concept of "design families," offering different products under four different brand names, but using the same basic designs. A key to such product design standardization lies in standardization of components, including motors, pumps, and compressors. Thus, White Consolidated in the United States and Zanussi in Italy, Electrolux's subsidiaries, have the main responsibility for components production within the group for worldwide application.

Universal Product with All Features. As just noted, competitive advantage can result from standardization of core components and/or product design families. One variant of components and product standardization is to develop a universal product

---

[20]Hirotaka Takeuchi and Michael E. Porter, "Three Roles of International Marketing in Global Strategy," *Competition in Global Industries*, Michael E. Porter, ed. (Boston, Mass.: Harvard Business School Press, 1986), pp. 111–46.

with all the features demanded anywhere in the world. Japan's Canon has done so successfully with its AE-1 cameras and newer models. After extensive market analyses around the world, Canon identified a set of common features customers wanted in a camera, including good picture quality, ease of operation with automatic features, technical sophistication, professional looks, and reasonable price. To develop such cameras, the company introduced a few breakthroughs in camera design and manufacturing, such as use of an electronic integrated circuitry brain to control camera operations, modularized production, and standardization and reduction of parts.

Universal Product with Different Positioning.   Alternatively, a universal product can be developed with different market segments in mind. Thus, a universal product may be positioned differently in different markets. This is where marketing promotion plays a major role to accomplish such a feat. Product and/or components standardization, however, does not necessarily imply either production standardization or a narrow product line. For example, Japanese automobile manufacturers have gradually stretched out their product line offerings, while marketing them with little adaptation in many parts of the world. This strategy requires manufacturing flexibility. The crux of global product or component standardization, rather, calls for proactive identification of homogeneous segments around the world, and is different from the concept of marketing abroad a product originally developed for the home market. A proactive approach to product policy has gained momentum in recent years as it is made possible by intermarket segmentation.[21] In addition to clustering of countries and identification of homogeneous segments in different countries, targeting different segments in different countries with the same products is another way to maintain a product policy of standardization.

For example, Honda has marketed almost identical Accord cars around the world by positioning them differently from country to country. Accord has been promoted as a family sedan in Japan, a relatively inexpensive sports car in Germany, and a reliable commuter car in the United States. In recent years, however, Honda has begun developing some regional variations of the Accord for the United States, European, and Japanese markets. Nonetheless, Honda adheres to a policy of *core component standardization* such that at least 50 percent of the components, including the chassis and transmission, are shared across the variations of the Accord.

Marketing/R & D Interface

Both R & D and manufacturing activities are technically outside marketing managers' responsibility. However, marketing managers' knowledge of the consumers' needs is indispensable in product development. Without a good understanding of the consumers' needs, product designers and engineers are prone to impose their technical specifications on the product, rather than fitting them to what consumers want. After all, consumers, not product designers or engineers, have the final say in deciding whether or not to buy the product.

Japanese companies, in particular, excel in management of the marketing/R & D interface.[22] Indeed, their source of competitive advantage often lies in marketing and

---

[21]Theodore Levitt, "The Globalization of Markets," *Harvard Business Review*, 61 (May-June 1983), pp. 92–102.

[22]Michael R. Czinkota and Masaaki Kotabe, "Product Development the Japanese Way," *Journal of Business Strategy*, 11 (November/December 1990), pp. 31–36.

R & D divisions' willingness to coordinate their respective activities concurrently. In a traditional product development, *either* a new product was developed and pushed down from the R & D division to the manufacturing and to the marketing division for sales *or* a new product idea was pushed up from the marketing division to the R & D division for development. This top-down or bottom-up new product development takes too much time in an era of global competition, when a short product development cycle is crucial to meet constant competitive pressure from new products introduced by rival companies.

R & D and marketing divisions of Japanese companies are always on the lookout for use of emerging technologies initially in existing products to satisfy customer needs better than their existing products and their competitors'. This affords them an opportunity to gain experience, debug technological glitches, reduce costs, boost performance, and adapt designs for worldwide customer use. As a result, they have been able to increase the speed of new product introductions, meet the competitive demands of a rapidly changing marketplace, and capture market share.

In other words, *the marketplace becomes a virtual R & D laboratory for Japanese companies to gain production and marketing experience, as well as to perfect technology.* This requires close contact with customers, whose inputs help Japanese companies improve upon their products on an ongoing basis.

In the process, they introduce new products one after another. Year after year, Japanese companies unveil not-entirely new products that keep getting better in design, reliability, and price. For example, Philips marketed the first practical VCR in 1972, three years before Japanese competitors entered the market. However, Philips took seven years to replace the first generation VCR with the all-new V2000, while the late-coming Japanese manufacturers launched an onslaught of no fewer than three generations of improved VCRs in this five-year period.

Another example worth noting is the exploitation of the so-called "fuzzy" logic by Hitachi and others.[23] When fuzzy logic was conceived in the mid-1960s by Lotfi A. Zadeh, a computer science professor at the University of California at Berkeley, nobody other than several Japanese companies paid serious heed to it for its potential application in ordinary products. The fuzzy logic allows computers to deal with shades of gray or something vague between 0 and 1—no small feat in a world of the binary computers that exist today. Today, Hitachi, Matsushita, Mitsubishi, Sony, and Nissan Motors, among others, use fuzzy logic in their products. For example, Hitachi introduced a "fuzzy" train that automatically accelerates and brakes so smoothly that no one reaches for the hanging straps. Matsushita, maker of Panasonics, began marketing a "fuzzy" washing machine with only one start button that automatically judges the size and dirtiness of the load and decides the optimum cycle times, amount of detergent needed, and water level. Sony introduced a palm-size computer capable of recognizing written Japanese, with a fuzzy circuit to iron out the inconsistencies in different writing styles. Now fuzzy circuits are put into the autofocus mechanisms of video cameras to get constantly clear pictures. By the beginning of 1990, fuzzy chips were appearing at a fast pace in a wide range of consumer products.

The continual introduction of *newer* and *better designed* products also brings a greater likelihood of market success.[24] Ideal products often require a giant leap in

---

[23]Larry Armstrong, "Why 'Fuzzy Logic' Beats Black-or-White Thinking," *Business Week* (May 21, 1990), pp. 92–93.

[24]Michael R. Czinkota and Masaaki Kotabe, "Product Development the Japanese Way," *Journal of Business Strategy*, 11 (November/December 1990), pp. 31–36.

technology and product development, and naturally are subject to a much higher risk of consumer rejection. Not only does the Japanese approach of incrementalism allow for continual improvement and a stream of new products, but it also permits for quicker consumer adoption. Consumers are likely to accept improved products more quickly than very different products, since the former are more compatible with the existing patterns of product use and lifestyles.

LOGISTICS OF SOURCING STRATEGY

Sourcing strategy includes a number of basic choices companies make in deciding how to serve foreign markets. One choice relates to the use of imports, assembly, or production within the country to serve a foreign market. Another decision involves the use of internal or external supplies of components or finished goods.

Sourcing decision making is multifaceted and entails both contractual and locational implications. From a contractual point of view, the sourcing of major components and products by multinational companies takes place in two ways: (1) from the parents or their foreign subsidiaries on an "intra-firm" basis and (2) from independent suppliers on a "contractual" basis. The first type of sourcing is known as **intra-firm sourcing**. The second type of sourcing is referred to commonly as **outsourcing**. Similarly, from a locational point of view, multinational companies can procure components and products either (1) domestically (i.e., *domestic sourcing*) or (2) from abroad (i.e., *offshore sourcing*). Therefore, as shown in Exhibit 10-6, four possible types of sourcing strategy can be identified.

EXHIBIT 10-6
TYPES OF SOURCING STRATEGY

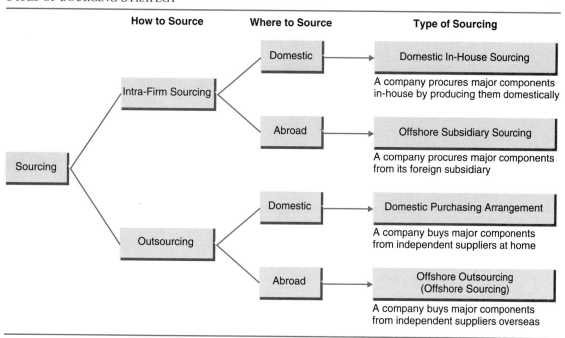

In developing viable sourcing strategies on a global scale, companies must consider not only manufacturing costs, the costs of various resources, and exchange rate fluctuations, but also availability of infrastructure (including transportation, communications, and energy), industrial and cultural environments, the ease of working with foreign host governments, and so on. Furthermore, the complex nature of sourcing strategy on a global scale spawns many barriers to its successful execution. In particular, logistics, inventory management, distance, nationalism, and lack of working knowledge about foreign business practices, among others, are major operational problems identified by both U.S. and foreign multinational companies engaging in international sourcing.

Many studies have shown, however, that despite, or maybe as a result of, those operational problems, *where* to source major components seems much less important than *how* to source them. Thus, when examining the relationship between sourcing and competitiveness of multinational companies, it is crucial to distinguish between sourcing on a "contractual" basis and sourcing on an "intra-firm" basis, for these two types of sourcing will have a different impact on their long-run competitiveness.

Intra-Firm Sourcing

Multinational companies can procure their components in-house within their corporate system around the world. They produce major components at their respective home base and/or at their affiliates overseas to be incorporated in their products marketed in various parts of the world. Thus, trade takes place between a parent company and its subsidiaries abroad, and also between foreign subsidiaries across national boundaries. This is often referred to as **intra-firm sourcing**. If such in-house component procurement takes place at home, it is essentially **domestic in-house sourcing**. If it takes place at a company's foreign subsidiary, it is called **offshore subsidiary sourcing**. Intra-firm sourcing makes trade statistics more complex to interpret, since part of the international flow of products and components is taking place between affiliated companies within the same multinational corporate system, which transcends national boundaries. As you recall from Chapter 1, about 30 percent of U.S. exports is attributed to U.S. parent companies transferring products and components to their affiliates overseas, and about 40 percent of U.S. imports is accounted for by foreign affiliates exporting to their U.S. parent companies. For both Japan and Britain, intra-firm transactions account for approximately 30 percent of their total trade flows (exports and imports combined), respectively.[25] Although statistics on intra-firm trade between foreign affiliates are limited to U.S. firms, the share of exports to other foreign affiliates in intra-firm exports of foreign affiliates rose from 37 percent in 1977 to 60 percent in 1993, also suggesting the increased role of foreign affiliates of U.S. multinational firms outside the United States.[26]

---

[25]United Nations Center on Transnational Corporations, *Transnational Corporations in World Development: Trends and Perspectives* (New York: United Nations, 1988).

[26]*World Investment Report 1996: Investment, Trade, and International Policy Arrangements,* (New York: United Nations, 1996), pp. 13–14.

Outsourcing

In the 1970s, foreign competitors gradually caught up in a productivity race with U.S. companies, which had once commanded a dominant position in international trade. It coincided with U.S. corporate strategic emphasis drifting from manufacturing to finance and marketing. As a result, manufacturing management gradually lost its organizational influence. Production managers' decision-making authority was reduced, such that R & D personnel prepared specifications with which production complied and marketing imposed delivery, inventory, and quality conditions. Productivity considerations were ignored. In a sense, production managers gradually took on the role of outside suppliers within their own companies.[27]

Production managers' reduced influence in the organization further led to an erroneous belief that manufacturing functions could, and should, be transferred easily to independent operators and subcontractors, depending on the cost differential between in-house and contracted-out production. A company's reliance on domestic suppliers for major components and/or products[28] is basically a **domestic purchase arrangement**. Furthermore, in order to lower production costs under competitive pressure, U.S. companies turned increasingly to **outsourcing** of components and finished products from abroad, particularly from newly industrialized countries including Singapore, South Korea, Taiwan, Singapore, Hong Kong, Brazil, and Mexico. Initially, subsidiaries were set up for production purposes (i.e., *offshore subsidiary sourcing*), but gradually, independent foreign suppliers took over component production for U.S. companies. This latter phenomenon is usually called *offshore outsourcing* (or *offshore sourcing*, for short).

Component procurement from overseas (i.e., *offshore subsidiary sourcing* and *offshore outsourcing*) is receiving an increasing amount of attention, as it not only affects domestic employment and economic structure but also sometimes raises ethical issues (see Global Perspective 10-3). U.S. companies using such strategy have been described pejoratively as **hollow corporations**.[29] It is occasionally argued that those companies are increasingly adopting a "designer role" in global competition—offering innovations in product design without investing in manufacturing process technology.

This widespread international sourcing practice could have a deleterious impact on the ability of U.S. companies to maintain their initial competitive advantage based on product innovations.[30] Indeed, keeping abreast of emerging technology through continual improvement in R & D and manufacturing is essential for the company's continued competitiveness.

[27]Stephen S. Cohen and John Zysman, "Why Manufacturing Matters: The Myth of the Post-Industrial Economy," *California Management Review*, 29 (Spring 1987), pp. 9–26.

[28]Rodney Ho, "Small Product-Development Firms Show Solid Growth," *Wall Street Journal* (April 22, 1997), p. 32: This article shows that entrepreneurial companies have begun to fill a void of new product development role as large companies trim their internal R & D staff and expenditures in the United States. Although it makes financial sense, at least in the short term, those outsourcing companies will face the same long-term concern as explained in this chapter.

[29]"Special Report: The Hollow Corporation," *Business Week* (March 3, 1986), pp. 56–59.

[30]Constantinos Markides and Norman Berg, "Manufacturing Offshore is Bad Business," *Harvard Business Review*, 66 (September-October 1988), pp. 113–20.

◆◆

$\mathcal{G}$LOBAL PERSPECTIVE 10-3

OFFSHORE SOURCING AND SWEATSHOPS OVERSEAS

The rapid globalization linking manufacturing companies, investors, and consumers around the world has touched off some ethical questions in recent years. Offshore sourcing is the practice of companies manufacturing or contracting out all or parts of their products abroad. Outsourcing makes it possible for those companies to procure products and components much more cheaply than manufacturing them in their home country. In many cases, labor cost savings are a strong motive for companies to engage in offshore sourcing. For example, Nike, the leading U.S. footwear company, has subcontractors in Taiwan, South Korea, and Indonesia, which collectively run twelve factories in Indonesia, producing 70 million pairs of Nike sneakers a year. Like any other footwear factories everywhere in Asia, work conditions are tough, with mandatory overtime work and constant exhaustion. While these factories may be modern, they are drab and utilitarian, with vast sheds housing row upon row of mostly young women

working many hours. The basic daily wage in Indonesia for these workers is a mere $2.23 a day. Here a pair of Pegasus running shoes costs about $18 to put together, and retails for $75 once shipped to the United States. The condition is similar in Vietnam, where 35,000 workers producing Nike shoes at five plants put in twelve hours a day to earn $1.60—less than the $2 or so it costs to buy three meals a day.

While the working conditions at these subcontractors' factories have improved over time at Nike's initiatives, the company has a long way to go before it lives up to its stated goal of providing a fair working environment for all its workers. In Indonesia, police and factory managers have a not-so-subtle cozy relationship where police help keep workers under control. Despite its strong political clout, Nike has not challenged the Indonesian government's control over labor. Nike's code of conduct seems to remain vague, despite its intentions.

Multinational companies cannot claim ignorance about the workers who produce the products they buy or the conditions in which they work. Large companies have the resources to investigate those with whom they do business. Ethically speaking, they should set standards that their contractors have to meet in order to continue their contracts.

Source: "Report Alleges Abuses by Nike Contractors," *Austin-American Statesman* (March 28, 1997), p. D8; "Pangs of Conscience: Sweatshops Haunt U.S. Consumers," *Business Week* (July 29, 1996), pp. 46–47; Richard T. De George, *Business Ethics*, 4th ed., (Englewood Cliffs, N.J.: Prentice Hall, 1995), pp. 525–26.

◆ ◆ ◆ ◆ ◆ ◆   COSTS AND CONSEQUENCES OF GLOBAL SOURCING

Need for Coordination

Global sourcing strategy requires close coordination of R & D, manufacturing, and marketing activities, among others, on a global basis. In Chapter 8, we discussed the two fundamental forces that have shaped the nature of competition for firms across national boundaries over the years: the firm's desire to integrate and streamline its operations and the diversity of markets. One thing that has changed, however, is the *ability* and *willingness* of these companies to integrate various activities on a global basis in an attempt either to circumvent or to nullify the impact of differences in local markets to the extent possible. It may be *more* correct to say that these companies have been increasingly compelled to take a global view of their businesses, due primarily to increased competition particularly among the Triad regions of the world: namely, the United States, Western Europe, and Japan. Remember "If you don't do it . . . , somebody else will . . . at your expense."—a contemporary view of competitive urgency that is shared by an increasing number of executives of multinational firms, irrespective of nationality.

The lack of competitive urgency can indeed be a problem. In his *Business Not As Usual,* for instance, Mitroff[31] was critical about the lack of this competitive urgency in the U.S. automobile industry in the 1970s and 1980s. He argued that the automobile industry minimized the need for constant innovation and its adoption into the working design of cars until those things were forced on it by foreign competition. Not surprisingly, the result was extreme isolation from the rest of the world—"a tunnel vision of the worst kind."[32] This is not an isolated incident, however. Mitroff's indictment arguably applies to other industries, such as machine tool and electronics, in the United States.

In contrast, the last thirty years have seen a tremendous growth and expansion of European and Japanese multinational companies encroaching on the competitive strengths of U.S. multinational companies in almost all the markets around the world. While U.S. multinational companies have subsidiaries all over the world, they have been somewhat reluctant to develop an integrated and well-coordinated global strategy that successful European and Japanese multinational companies have managed to establish. At the core of an integrated global strategy lies the company's ability to coordinate manufacturing activities with R & D, engineering, and marketing on a global basis. Indeed, European and Japanese multinational companies have heavily invested in, and improved upon, their strengths in manufacturing that many U.S. multinational companies have ignored. As a result, many U.S. companies tend to have an ill-coordinated manufacturing strategy that results in a poor match between their manufacturing system capability and markets.

Functional Mismatch

This functional mismatch has been traced to U.S. management's strategic emphasis having drifted away from manufacturing to marketing and to finance over the years.[33] U.S. management's attention was focused on marketing in the 1960s, followed by a preoccupation with finance in the 1970s, culminating in the merger and acquisition craze of the 1980s—aptly called *paper entrepreneurship.*[34]

As a result, manufacturing management gradually lost its influence in the business organization. Production managers' decision-making authority was reduced, such that R & D personnel prepared specifications with which production complied and marketing imposed its own delivery, inventory, and quality conditions, but not productivity considerations. In a sense, production managers gradually took on the role of outside suppliers within their own companies. Production managers' reduced influence in the organization led to a belief that manufacturing functions could be transferred easily to independent operators and subcontractors, depending on the cost differential between in-house and contracted-out production. Thus, in order to lower production costs under competitive pressure, U.S. multinational companies

[31]Ian I. Mitroff, *Business Not As Usual: Rethinking Our Individual, Corporate, and Industrial Strategies for Global Competition* (San Francisco, Calif.: Jossey-Bass, Inc, 1987).

[32]Ibid., p. 84.

[33]Elwood S. Buffa, "Making American Manufacturing Competitive," *California Management Review,* 26 (Spring 1984), pp. 29–46.

[34]Robert Reich, *The Next American Frontier* (New York: Times Books, 1983).

turned increasingly to *outsourcing* of components and finished products from newly industrializing countries such as South Korea, Taiwan, Singapore, Hong Kong, Brazil, and Mexico, among others. Akio Morita, a co-founder of Sony, a highly innovative Japanese electronics company, chided such U.S. multinational companies as hollow corporations that simply put their well-known brand names on foreign-made products and sold them as if the products were their own.[35] The main characteristics of hollow corporations are illustrated in Global Perspective 10-4.

However, we should not rush to a hasty conclusion that outsourcing certain components and/or finished products from foreign countries will diminish a company's competitiveness. Many multinational companies with plants in various parts of the world are exploiting not only their own competitive advantages (e.g., R & D, manufacturing, and marketing skills) but also the locational advantages (e.g., inexpensive labor cost, certain skills, mineral resources, government subsidy, and tax advantages) of various countries. Thus, it is also plausible to argue that these multinational companies are in a more advantageous competitive position than are domestic-bound companies.

Then, isn't the "hollowing-out" phenomenon indicative of a superior management of both corporate and locational resources on a global basis? What is wrong, if at all, with Caterpillar Tractor Company procuring more than 15 percent of components for its tractors from foreign suppliers? How about Honeywell marketing in the United States the products manufactured in its European plants? Answers to these questions hinge on a company's ability and willingness to integrate and coordinate various activities.

Long-Term Consequences

There are two opposing views of the long-term implications of offshore sourcing. One school of thought argues that many successful companies have developed a dynamic organizational network through increased use of joint ventures, subcontracting and licensing activities across international borders.[36] This flexible network system is broadly called **strategic alliances**. Strategic alliances allow each participant to pursue its particular competence. Therefore, each network participant can be seen as complementing rather than competing with the other participants for the common goals. Strategic alliances may even be formed by competing companies in the same industry in pursuit of complementary abilities (new technologies or skills) from each other. The other school of thought argues, however, that while this may be true in the short run, there could also be negative long-term consequences resulting from a company's dependence on independent suppliers and subsequently the inherent difficulty for the company to keep abreast of constantly evolving design and engineering technologies without engaging in those developmental activities. These two opposing arguments will be elaborated here.

---

[35]"Special Report: The Hollow Corporation," *Business Week* (March 3, 1986), pp. 56–59.

[36]Raymond E. Miles, and Charles C. Snow, "Organizations: New Concepts for New Forms," *California Management Review*, 28 (Spring 1986), pp. 62–73.

GLOBAL PERSPECTIVE 10-4

HOLLOW CORPORATIONS

By shifting production overseas or shopping abroad for parts and components, U.S. companies are whittling away at the critical mass essential to a strong industrial base. For example,

- General Electric Co. spent $1.4 billion in 1995 to import products sold in the U.S. under the GE label. Virtually all of its consumer electronics goods are already made in Asia. By the end of summer, the company plans to shut down its last domestic color-TV plant. In appliances, GE now buys its microwave ovens from Japan and began going offshore for room air conditioners in 1987.

- Eastman Kodak Co. is counting on foreign-made products to fuel much of its growth. To diversify from the stagnant film business, Kodak is buying video camera recorders and videotape from Japan, along with its midsize copying machines. It also imports floppy disks from a Kodak factory in Britain.

- Honeywell Inc. gets the central processing "brain" for its biggest mainframe computer from a Japanese manufacturer, and two other mainframes that Honeywell sells in the U.S. are imported as finished products from Europe. The Minneapolis company also goes abroad for a host of components used in its factory-automation equipment and commercial air-conditioning systems.

If this trend continues, warns Jack D. Kuehler, senior vice-president of International Business Machines Corp., companies will gradually become less adept at understanding how new technology can be exploited and eventually "lose the ability to design." Adds Robert A. Lutz, chairman of Ford of Europe Inc.: "You're seeing a substantial deindustrialization of the U.S., and I can't imagine any country maintaining its position in the world without an industrial base." Only now U.S. companies are also shifting far more valuable things overseas: fundamental technology, management functions, and even the design and engineering skills that are crucial to innovation.

Backing Away. When Sony Corp. unveiled the first VCRs in 1975, they carried price tags of more than $1,000, so most U.S. companies dismissed them as too expensive and complex ever to command a major market. Besides, they were already backing away from tape recorders, the source of the technology that went into the VCR. Now, with product simplification and automated production, VCRs are selling—like hotcakes—at less than $300.

Here, too, not one is made in the U.S., although Sony plans to start building a U.S. VCR factory this year. And now it has spun off its VCR technology into the so-called camcorder, a combination video camera recorder that promises to be the last straw for movie cameras and film. Alarmed, Kodak has jumped into the video market—with a camcorder made by Matsushita Electric Industrial Co.

However, as RCA has learned, selling goods made by a foreign competitor can be a rocky partnership. RCA has leveraged its name and distribution resources to grab the biggest share of domestic VCR sales, an estimated 20 percent. Its machines now get stamped with the RCA logo in a Hitachi Ltd. factory. Matsushita used to do that for RCA. But in 1984, with Matsushita gaining market share by undercutting RCA's prices with Panasonic VCRs that were clones of RCA's units, RCA turned to Hitachi. RCA suspects the deal with Hitachi will also prove temporary. "You can only source for a limited time," admits Jack K. Sauter, an RCA group vice-president. But RCA, GE, and Zenith are compelled to endure the situation. Not only do the profits from VCRs help subsidize their manufacturing losses on color TV sets, but also they lack the expertise to produce competitively.

Waiting in the Wings. Of course, not all companies are oblivious to the implications of deindustrialization. A small but growing band is feverishly working to develop the technologies that will be used in the totally automated factory. Caterpillar has launched a major effort to automate production, both in the U.S. and abroad. And Cat is encouraging managers to think long term, planning ten years ahead. "That's a dramatic difference" in philosophy, says Caterpillar's Ranney.

Source: "Even American Knowhow is Headed Abroad," *Business Week* (March 3, 1986), p. 60–63.

Strategic Alliances. The advantage of forming a strategic alliance is claimed to be its structural flexibility. Strategic alliances can accommodate a vast amount of complexity while maximizing the specialized competence of each member, and provide much more effective use of human resources that would otherwise have to be accumulated, allocated, and maintained by a single organization. In other words, a company can concentrate on performing the task at which it is most efficient. This approach is increasingly applied on a global basis with countries participating in a dynamic network as multinational companies configure and coordinate product development, manufacturing, and sourcing activities around the world.

First, due to the need for fast internationalization and related diversification, strategic alliances provide a relatively easy option to access the world markets and to combine complementary technologies. Thus, AT & T needed Olivetti's established European network to enter the European market for telephone switchboard equipment. Similarly, Toyota established a joint venture with General Motors so that the Japanese car maker could learn to work with UAW union members while General Motors could learn just-in-time inventory management from Toyota.

Second and more relevant to sourcing issues, an increasing number of companies have funneled out manufacturing functions to independent partners. In 1989, for example, Apple Computer enlisted Sony to design and manufacture a new notebook-size Macintosh computer called the PowerBook 100. In this arrangement, Apple gave Sony the basic blueprint, and Sony engineers, who had little experience building personal computers, developed Apple's smallest and lightest machine from drawing board to factory floor in less than thirteen months.[37] This is a strategic alliance in which Apple's basic design ability was complemented by Sony's miniaturization technology. The result has been a spectacular success for Apple that could not have materialized without Sony's participation.

However, it has also become apparent that Apple could lose manufacturing capabilities for the next generations of notebook-size computers without Sony's participation. On the other hand, Sony, having mastered engineering and manufacturing of Apple's notebook computers, gradually increased its role upstream to assisting Apple in product designing. Such a relationship could prove to be detrimental to Apple's competitiveness if Sony were able to take over most of what it takes to develop a notebook computer. Later, being concerned about this, Apple decided to sever its relationship with Sony.

Dependence. Companies that rely on independent external sources of supply of major components tend to forsake part of the most important value-creating activities to, and also become dependent on, independent operators for assurance of component quality. Furthermore, those multinational companies tend to promote competition among independent suppliers, ensure continuing availability of materials in the future, and exploit full benefits of changing market conditions. However, individual suppliers are forced to operate in an uncertain business environment that inherently necessitates a shorter planning horizon. The uncertainty about the potential loss of orders to competitors often forces individual suppliers to make operating decisions that will likely increase their own long-term production and materials costs. In the process, this uncertain business environment tends to adversely affect the multinational companies sourcing components and/or finished products from independent suppliers.

---

[37]Brenton R. Schlender, "Apple's Japanese Ally," *Fortune* (November 4, 1991), pp. 151–52.

The decline of IBM in the personal computer market in recent years offers the most vivid example of the problems caused by its dependence on independent suppliers for crucial components in the personal computer market.[38] As a relatively late entrant into the burgeoning personal computer market in early 1980s, IBM decided, contrary to its long-held policy of developing proprietary technology in-house, to rely on microprocessors from Intel and operating software from Microsoft. Given its massive size and marketing abilities, IBM was able to become a market leader in the personal computer business in a short period of time. However, Intel and Microsoft were also free to market their wares to any other companies. As a result, many small and nimble personal computer companies rushed into the personal computer market and began marketing IBM-compatible personal computers at the cost of IBM's market share position. Yet, being slow to respond to this competition, IBM has already lost its dominant position and subsequently control of the personal computer market that it had helped create a decade ago.

Gradual Loss of Design and Manufacturing Abilities.

Multinational companies that depend heavily on independent suppliers could also lose sight of emerging technologies and expertise in the long run that could be incorporated into the development of new manufacturing processes as well as new products. Apple–Sony and IBM–Intel–Microsoft alliances may be illustrative of such possibilities. Thus, continual sourcing from independent suppliers is likely to forebode those companies' long-term loss of the ability to manufacture at competitive cost and, as a result, loss of their global competitiveness. However, if technology and expertise developed by a multinational company are exploited within its multinational corporate system (i.e., by its foreign affiliates and by the parent company itself), the company can retain its technological base without unduly disseminating expertise to competitors. The benefit of such internalization is likely to be great, particularly when technology is highly idiosyncratic or specific with limited alternative uses, or when it is novel in the marketplace. For such a technology, the market price mechanism is known to break down, as a seller and potential buyers of the technology tend to see its value very differently. Potential buyers, who do not have perfect knowledge of how useful the technology will be, tend to undervalue its true market value. As a result, the seller of the technology is not likely to get a full economic benefit of the technology by selling it in the open market.

In a relationship with a foreign supplier, it is particularly essential that a lead company devise methods to ensure the continued product and service quality. For example, in entering the Chinese industrial tire market recently, Industrial Tires Co. (ITL), Canada's top industrial tire maker, continues to provide technology, patterns, compounds, and trade names, takes care of equipment selection and process and product engineering, and maintains a high-level quality assurance program for Yantai, a manufacturing and marketing partner in China.[39]

In addition, by getting involved in design and production on its own, the multinational company can keep abreast of emerging technologies and innovations originating anywhere in the world for potential use in the future. Furthermore, management of the quality of major components is required to retain the goodwill and

---

[38]Bruce Lloyd, "IBM: Decline or Resurrection?" *Management Decision*, 32 (8), 1994, pp. 5–10.

[39]Bruce Meyer, "ITL Building on Global Strategy," *Rubber and Plastics*, July 4, 1994.

confidence of consumers in the products. As a result, "intra-firm" sourcing of major components and finished products between the parent company and its affiliates abroad and between its foreign affiliates themselves would more likely enable the company to retain a long-term competitive edge in the world market.

✪IDEOBOX

NAFTA AND ITS SOURCING IMPLICATIONS

The North American Free Trade Agreement (NAFTA) is the free trade agreement among Canada, the United States, and Mexico. It promises to eliminate all tariffs on industrial products traded between Canada, Mexico, and the United States by the end of year 2003. A freer trading region will result. As comparative advantage theory (see the Appendix to Chapter 1) predicts, competitive industries will benefit from freer access to the neighboring markets across national boundaries, while uncompetitive industries will experience an inevitable gradual decline.

This video clip presents both views: an argument for and an argument against NAFTA, based upon the creation/loss and relocation of jobs in the NAFTA member countries. While both arguments have merit, history has shown that a freer and larger market economy promotes healthy competition among companies. As shown in the video, NAFTA prompts many companies, including Wal-Mart, Microsoft, and U.S. automakers, to develop more efficient and technologically advanced procurement, production, and/or logistics operations.

For example, Wal-Mart in Mexico clearly benefited from the NAFTA. However, you should also be warned that the larger, integrated economy does not necessarily mean stable exchange rates. The Mexican peso plummeted in value against the U.S. dollar in December 1994. Discuss what happened to Wal-Mart importing some 40% of its merchandise from the United States, and offer sourcing implications for other companies to follow.

SUMMARY

The scope of global sourcing has expanded over time. Whether or not to procure components or products from abroad was once determined strictly on price and thus strongly influenced by the fluctuating exchange rate. Thus, the appreciation of the dollar prompted companies to increase offshore sourcing, while the depreciation of the dollar encouraged domestic sourcing. Today many companies consider not simply price but also quality, reliability, and technology of components and products to be procured. Those companies design their sourcing decision based on the interplay between their competitive advantages and the comparative advantages of various sourcing locations for long-term gains.

Trade and foreign production managed by multinational companies are very complex. In growing global competition, sourcing of components and finished products around the world within the multinational company has increased. The development of global sourcing and marketing strategies across different foreign markets has become a central issue for many multinational companies. Traditionally, a polycentric approach to organizing operations on a country-by-country basis allowed each country manager to tailor marketing strategy to the peculiarities of local markets. As such, product adaptations were considered a necessary strategy to better cater to the different needs and wants of customers in various countries. Product adaptation tends to be a reactive, rather than a proactive, strategic response to the market. A high level of product adaptation may make it difficult for multinational companies to reap economies of scale in production and marketing and to coordinate their networks of activities on a global scale.

Global sourcing strategy requires close coordination of R & D, manufacturing, and marketing activities on a global basis. Managing geographically separated R & D, manufacturing, and marketing activities, those companies face difficult coordination problems of integrating their operations and adapting them to different legal, political, and cultural environments in different countries. Furthermore, separation of manufacturing activities involves an inherent risk that manufacturing in the value chain will gradually become neglected. Such a neglect can be costly, as continued involvement in manufacturing leads to pioneering product design and innovation over time. An effective global sourcing strategy calls for continual efforts to streamline manufacturing without sacrificing marketing flexibility. To accomplish this, a conscious effort to develop either core components in house or develop product design families or universal products is called for.

A caveat should be also noted. Although a company's ability to develop core components and products and market them in the world markets on its own is preferred, the enormousness of such a task should be examined in light of rapid changes in both technology and customer needs around the world. Those changes make the product life cycle extremely short, sometimes too short for many multinational companies to pursue product development, manufacturing, and marketing on a global basis without strategic alliance partners. Benefits of maintaining an independent proprietary position should always be weighed against the time cost of delayed market entry.

REVIEW QUESTIONS ◆

1. Discuss the reasons why trade statistics do not capture the intricasies of global sourcing.

2. Discuss the trends in global sourcing strategy. Why is it necessary for companies to keep up with those trends?

3. Why was manufacturing ignored by U.S. multinational companies in the 1980s?

4. Discuss the relationships between paper entrepreneurship and hollow corporations.

5. How do multinational companies exploit the value chain on a global basis?

6. What are inherent difficulties in coordinating (a) R & D/manufacturing, (b) manufacturing/marketing, and (c) marketing/R & D interfaces?

7. What are strategic motivations for standardizing either components or products or both?

8. Under what conditions can a company develop its global sourcing strategy without an alliance partner?

DISCUSSION QUESTIONS ◆ ◆ ◆ ◆ ◆ ◆ ◆ ◆ ◆ ◆ ◆ ◆ ◆ ◆ ◆ ◆ ◆ ◆ ◆

1. Sirena Apparel Group Inc. is a manufacturer and distributor of men's and women's clothing items. Recently, it decided to establish its own manufacturing facility in San Luis Rio Colorado, Mexico. The reason was the intense cost pressures that it faced from foreign imports. The establishing of this manufacturing facility in Mexico would, according to the company, give it the edge in competing effectively with other foreign manufacturers. Sirena is not an isolated example. It is just one of the many companies that have been establishing manufacturing facilities across the border. Would you consider the move by the company as one step toward the hollowing out of the company? Why or why not? Hewlett–Packard is one of the many personal manufacturers which has established its own manufacturing facilities abroad, especially in Southeast Asia. Are these companies being hollowed out?

2. According to Nobuhiko Kawamoto, the President of Honda Motor Company, its global sourcing strategy can help the company considerably in its new emphasis on the Japanese market. Until recently, Honda has been one of the star performers among foreign automobile manufacturers in the United States. However, its position in the domestic Japanese market has been less formidable. It continues to hold a less impressive fifth position in sales of automobiles in Japan. As part of its strategy, Honda Motor Company plans to introduce more than 15 new models of cars in a short span of time. The high costs involved would in part be met by 'skimming' more models off fewer platforms and with fewer parts. Lower costs due to more efficient sourcing of components and sub-assemblies are expected to reduce manufacturing costs to counter some of the high costs involved with the

strategy. Skeptics point out that overemphasis on common platforms may lead to coming out with products that might not be well received by the domestic customers, who are known to be extremely discerning and are becoming more style conscious. Would you agree with the view of the skeptics?

3. There has been considerable emphasis on the declining productivity of U.S. manufacturing firms since the early 1980s when Japanese and Korean manufacturers made their presence felt in the United States. An argument could be made that this emphasis on manufacturing activity may be slightly misplaced, especially given the fact that today only 25 percent of the GNP of the United States comes from manufacturing activities, while nearly 70 percent of the GNP is attributable to service activities. Do you agree with this argument? Why or why not?

4. The integration–adaptiveness dichotomy has long plagued international marketers as two opposing forces in the formulation of international strategies. The pressures for integrated strategies include the importance of multinational customers and competitors, high investment intensity, high technology intensity, pressure for reducing costs, universal customer needs, and access to raw materials and energy. The pressures of adaptiveness include differences in customer needs, differences in markets structure, differences in distribution channels, availability of substitutes and need to adapt, and host government demands. What are the implications of these opposing pressures on the sourcing strategy chosen by the firm? Describe two industries in which a global and integrated sourcing strategy would seem more appropriate. Describe two industries in which a local decentralized sourcing strategy may be more appropriate. Which sourcing strategy would be more appropriate for the microprocessor (semiconductor) industry?

5. An important impediment to the implementation of global sourcing strategies is the fluctuations in the foreign exchange rates. You are the executive assistant to the vice-president of the international operations of a multibillion-dollar and multinational manufacturer of earth-moving equipment. The company has manufacturing facilities in all three countries in North America, in seven countries in Europe, in three countries in South America, and in six countries in East and Southeast Asia. Approximately 50 percent of the components of each manufacturing facility come from one of the other manufacturing facilities (25 percent from within the same continent and 25 percent from a different continent). The vice-president would like you to suggest ways in which the risks of foreign exchange rate fluctuations can be reduced and yet the benefits of an integrated sourcing strategy can be derived. What are some of the suggestions that you would make?

FURTHER READING ◆ ◆ ◆ ◆ ◆ ◆ ◆ ◆ ◆ ◆ ◆ ◆ ◆ ◆ ◆ ◆ ◆

S. Tamer Cavusgil, Attila Yaprak, and Poe-lin Yeoh. "A Decision-making Framework for Global Sourcing." *International Business Review*, 2 (2) (1993):143–56.

Cohen, Stephen S., and John Zysman. "Why Manufacturing Matters: The Myth of the Post-Industrial Economy." *California Management Review*, 29 (Spring 1987): 9–26.

Guile, Bruce R., and Harvey Brooks, ed. *Technology and Global Industry: Companies and Nations in the World Economy*. Washington, D.C.: National Academy Press, 1987.

Kotabe, Masaaki, and K. Scott Swan. "Offshore Sourcing: Reaction, Maturation, and Consolidation of U.S. Multinationals." *Journal of International Business Studies*, 25 (First Quarter 1994):115–40.

Kotabe, Masaaki. *Global Sourcing Strategy: R & D, Manufacturing, and Marketing Interfaces*. New York: Quorum Books, 1992.

Markides, Constantinos, and Norman Berg. "Manufacturing Offshore is Bad Business." *Harvard Business Review*, 66 (September-October 1988):113–20.

Monczka, Robert M., and Robert J. Trent. "Global Sourcing: A Development Approach." *International Journal of Purchasing and Materials Management*, 27 (Spring 1991): 2–8.

Murray, Janet Y., Masaaki Kotabe, and Albert R. Wildt. "Strategic and Financial Performance Implications of Global Sourcing Strategy: A Contingency Analysis." *Journal of International Business Studies*, 26 (First Quarter 1995):181–202.

Porter, Michael E. *Competition in Global Industries*. Cambridge, Mass.: Harvard Business School Press, 1986.

Reich, Robert. *The Next American Frontier*. New York: Times Books, 1983.

Starr, Martin K., and John E. Ullman. "The Myth of Industrial Supremacy." In Martin K. Starr, ed., *Global Competitiveness*. New York: W. W. Norton and Co., 1988.

GLOBAL PRODUCT POLICY DECISIONS I: DEVELOPING NEW PRODUCTS FOR GLOBAL MARKETS

11

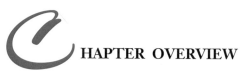

CHAPTER OVERVIEW

1. GLOBAL PRODUCT STRATEGIES
2. STANDARDIZATION VERSUS CUSTOMIZATION
3. MULTINATIONAL DIFFUSION
4. DEVELOPING NEW PRODUCTS FOR GLOBAL MARKETS
5. GLOBAL NPD AND CULTURE

A cornerstone of a global marketing mix program is the set of product policy decisions that multinational companies (MNCs) constantly need to formulate. The range of product policy questions that need to be tackled is mindboggling: What new products should be developed for what markets? What products should be added, removed, or modified for the product line in each of the countries in which the company operates? What brand names should be used? How should the product be packaged? serviced? and so forth. Clearly, product managers in charge of the product line of a multinational company have their work cut out for them.

Improper product policy decisions are easily made, as the following anecdotes illustrate:

* *Ikea in the United States.* Ikea, the Swedish furniture chain, insists that all its stores carry the basic product line with little room for adaptation to local tastes. In the United States, Ikea was initially puzzled by the reluctance of customers to buy its beds and bed linen. Eventually, the firm uncovered that Americans liked bigger beds than Swedes. Ikea remedied the situation by ordering larger beds and sheets from its suppliers.[1]

---

[1]Hugh Carnegy, "Struggle to Save the Soul of Ikea," *Financial Times* (March 27, 1995), p. 12.

- *Procter & Gamble in Australia and Japan.* Rather than manufacturing disposable diapers locally in Australia like its major competitor in that market, Kimberly-Clark (the maker of Huggies) P & G decided to import them. The size of the Australian and New Zealand markets did not warrant local manufacturing, according to P & G. Unfortunately, by using packaging designed for the Asian region with non-English labeling, P & G alienated its customers in Australia.[2] In Japan, Pampers were found to be too thick and bulky for Japanese mothers. Japanese mothers change diapers much more often than their American counterparts. They wanted diapers that were easy to store and use. For that reason, many Japanese prospective customers of Pampers switched to Moony, a superabsorbent thin diaper, that gained 23 percent market share, despite the fact that it was much more expensive than Pampers.[3]

- *Wal-Mart in Hong Kong.* When Wal-Mart, the U.S.-based mega-retailer, first entered Hong Kong it stocked basketball court backboards, an item not featured on the shopping list of many Hong Kong people, who mostly live in tiny apartments. After a year of lackluster sales, Wal-Mart called it quits and decided to focus on China.[4]

- *U.S. carmakers in Japan.* Historically, U.S. car sales in Japan have been pretty dismal. Many commentators have blamed import barriers and the fact that most U.S.-made cars were originally sold with the steering wheel on the left-hand side. There are other factors at play, though. Sales of Chrysler's Neon car during the first year of introduction in Japan were far below target. Japanese carbuyers disliked the Neon's roundy curves; they preferred boxier designs. The sales of Ford's Taurus in Japan were also lackluster. Part of the problem was that, initially, the Taurus did not fit in Japanese parking spaces. In order for a car to be registered in Japan, the police must certify that it will fit in the customer's parking lot.[5]

- *Ford in Brazil.* When Ford introduced the Pinto model in Brazil, it was unaware that *Pinto* stands for small male genitals in Brazilian slang. Sales of the Pinto, not surprisingly, were pretty dismal. Once Ford figured out why sales for the Pinto model were so low, it renamed the model Corcel, meaning horse.[6]

These anecdotes amply show that even seasoned blue-chip companies commit the occasional "blunder" when making product decisions in the global marketplace. Product blunder stories, aside from being entertaining (at least for outsiders), sometimes teach valuable lessons. Lessons can also be drawn from success stories. Global Perspective 11-1 chronicles the development efforts behind "Fruit Magix," a new fruit beverage that Pepsi-Cola International launched in South China. This chapter

[2]Geoffrey Lee Martin, "P&G Puts Nappies to Rest in Australia," *Advertising Age International* (September 19, 1994), p. I-31.

[3]Alecia Swasy, *Soap Opera. The Inside Story of Procter & Gamble* (New York: Random House, 1993).

[4]"New Markets Lure Retailers Wanting Growth," *Advertising Age International* (October 1996), pp. I-18, I-21.

[5]"Success Continues to Elude U.S. Car Makers in Japan," *The Asian Wall Street Journal* (January 10–11, 1997), pp. 1, 7.

[6]Jack Mingo, *How the Cadillac Got its Fins* (New York: Harper Business, 1994).

GLOBAL PERSPECTIVE 11-1

THE LAUNCH OF "FRUIT MAGIX"

WINDOW OF OPPORTUNITY:

- China has more than 300 million kids aged 4–12
- Parents spend much more on kids than they used to (one-child policy; growth of buying power)
- Power of kids (spending power; pester power; change agents)
- No fruit drink brands targeted toward kids

MARKETING GOAL:

- To develop a juice drink brand for the "Little Emperors" and "Empresses"

MARKET RESEARCH:

- A pack-price trade-off analysis among mothers to determine "optimal" price and packaging form

Sources: Olivia Kan, Senior Executive, Pepsi-Cola International and A. Bose and K. Khanna, "The Little Emperor. A Case Study of a New Brand Launch," *Marketing and Research Today* (November 1996), pp. 216–21.

- Quantitative taste test among 300 children each in Guangzhou, Shanghai, and Beijing
- Two rounds of focus groups in Shanghai and Guangzhou amongs boys and girls aged 7 to 10 years to identify: relevant icon, key brand property, and most effective style/tone of communication

NEW PRODUCT INTRODUCTION LAUNCH PLAN:

Brand Name:	Fruit Magix
Brand Device:	Fruitman
Product Variants:	Orange, Strawberry/Grapes and Mango (10% juice)
Package:	250 ml. Tetra Pak
Price:	RMB 2.00 per pack (approx. U.S.$0.25)
Target Audience:	Primary—kids aged 6-12; Secondary—mothers
Positioning:	"Fruit Magix is delicious and fun fruit drink for cool kids of today"

focuses on new product development strategies for global markets. Fostering the development of new products that satisfy or even amaze consumers worldwide is the major ingredient of many global success stories. The first part of this chapter looks at the product strategic issues that MNCs face. The second part gives an overview of new product development process in a global setting.

GLOBAL PRODUCT STRATEGIES

◆ ◆ ◆ ◆ ◆ ◆

Companies can pursue three global strategies to penetrate foreign markets.[7] Some firms will simply adopt the same product or communication policy used in their home market. They **extend** their home-grown product/communication strategies to their foreign markets. Other companies prefer to adapt their strategy to the local

---

[7]Warren J. Keegan, "Multinational Product Planning: Strategic Alternatives," *Journal of Marketing*, 33 (January 1969), pp. 58–62.

EXHIBIT 11-1
GLOBAL EXPANSION STRATEGIES

Strategy	Product function or need satisfied	Conditions of product use	Ability to buy product	Recommended product strategy	Recommended communications strategy	Rank order from least to most expensive	Product examples
1	Same	Same	Yes	Extension	Extension	1	Soft drinks
2	Different	Same	Yes	Extension	Adaptation	2	Bicycles, motorscooters
3	Same	Different	Yes	Adaptation	Extension	3	Gasoline, detergents,
4	Different	Different	Yes	Adaptation	Adaptation	4	Clothing, greeting cards
5	Same	—	No	Invention	Develop new communications	5	Hand-powered washing machines

Source: From Warren J. Keegan, "Multinational Product Planning: Strategic Alternatives." Reprinted from *Journal of Marketing*, vol. 33, January 1969, pp. 58–62, published by the American Marketing Association.

marketplace. This strategy of **adaptation** enables the firm to cater to the needs and wants of its foreign customers. A third alternative is to adopt an **invention** strategy, where products are designed from scratch for foreign customers. These three basic strategies can be further finessed into five strategic options, as shown in Exhibit 11-1.

Let us look at each one of these options in greater detail:

Strategic Option 1: Product and Communication Extension—Dual Extension

At one extreme, a company might choose to market a standardized product using a uniform communications strategy. Early entrants in the global arena will often opt for this approach. Also, small companies with few resources typically prefer this option. For them, the potential payoffs of customized products and/or advertising campaigns usually do not justify the incremental costs of adaptation. Dual extension might also work when the company targets a "global" segment with similar needs. Blistex's marketing efforts for its namesake product in Europe is a typical example. The product, a lipbalm, offers identical needs in each of the various European markets. Except for some minor modifications (e.g., labeling), the same product is sold in each country. Starting in 1995, Blistex ran a uniform European advertising campaign, using identical positioning ("Care-to-Cure") and advertising themes across countries.[8]

Generally speaking, a standardized product policy coupled with a uniform communication strategy offers substantial savings coming from economies of scale. This strategy is basically product-driven rather than market-driven. The downside is that it is likely to alienate foreign customers, who might switch to a local or another foreign competing brand that is more in tune with their needs. In many industries,

---

[8]Mark Boersma, Supervisor International Operations, Blistex, Inc., personal communication, 1995.

modern production processes such as CAD/CAM[9] manufacturing technologies obviate the need for large production batch sizes.

Strategic Option 2: Product Extension—Communications Adaptation

Due to differences in the cultural or competitive environment, the same product often is used to offer benefits or functions that dramatically differ from those in the home market. Such gaps between the foreign and home market drive companies to market the same product using customized advertising campaigns. Although it retains the scale economies on the manufacturing side, the firm sacrifices potential savings on the advertising front. Wrigley, the Chicago-based chewing gum company, is a typical practitioner of this approach. Most of the brands marketed in the United States are also sold in Wrigley's overseas markets. Wrigley strives for a uniformly superior quality product. To build up the chewing-gum category, Wrigley sells its products at a stable and low price. Given that chewing gum is an impulse item, Wrigley aims for mass distribution. The company sees an opportunity to sell its product at any place where money changes hands. Despite these similarities in Wrigley's product and distribution strategies, there are wide differences in its communication strategy. The benefits that are promoted in Wrigley's advertising campaigns vary from country to country. In the United States, Wrigley has capitalized on smoking regulations by promoting chewing gum as a substitute for smoking. In several Western countries, dental benefits of chewing gum are highlighted. In the Far East, Wrigley uses the benefit of facial fitness as a positioning theme in its advertising campaigns.[10]

Strategic Option 3: Product Adaptation—Communications Extension

Alternatively, firms might adapt their product but market it using a standardized communications strategy. Local market circumstances often favor the case of product adaptation. Government regulations leave most companies two options: either accept the restrictions and adapt your product or abandon this particular market. Another source behind product adaptation is the company's expansion strategy. Many companies add brands to their product portfolio via acquisitions of local companies. To leverage the existing brand equity enjoyed by the acquired brand, the local brand is usually retained. Although these factors lead to product adaptation, cultural similarities that stretch to consumers using the product present an opportunity for a harmonized communications strategy. Within such a context, clever marketing ideas can be transferred from one country to another country, despite the product-related differences. For instance, a Taiwan-produced commercial for P & G's Pantene shampoo was successfully transferred with a few minor changes to Latin America. Likewise, an ad campaign developed in Mexico for Vicks Vaporub was used throughout Latin America.[11]

---

[9]Computer-Aided-Design/Computer-Aided-Manufacturing.

[10]Doug Barrie, Group Vice-President International, Wrigley Cy., personal communication, 1995.

[11]"P&G Sees Success in Policy of Transplanting Ad Ideas," *Advertising Age International* (July 19, 1993), p. I-2.

Strategic Option 4: Product and Communications Adaptation—Dual Adaptation

Differences in *both* the cultural and physical environment across countries call for a dual adaptation strategy. Under such circumstances, adaptation of the company's product and communication strategy is the most viable option for international expansion.

Slim-Fast adapts both product and advertising to comply with varying government regulations for weight-loss products. When Slim-Fast was first launched in Germany, its ads used a local celebrity. In Great Britain, testimonials for diet aids are not allowed to feature celebrities. Instead, the British introduction campaign centered around teachers, an opera singer, a disk jockey, and others. Also, the product gets adapted to the local markets. In the United Kingdom, banana is the most popular flavor, but it is not available in other countries.[12]

Strategic Option 5: Product Invention

Genuinely global marketers try to figure out how to create products with a global scope rather than just for a single country. Instead of simply adapting existing products or services to the local market conditions, their mindset is to zero in on global market opportunities. Black & Decker is a good example of a company that adopts the **product invention** approach to global market expansion. Black & Decker aims to bring out new products that cater to common needs and opportunities around the world. To manage this global product development process, the company has set up a Worldwide Household Board. This steering committee approves global plans, allocates resources, and gives direction and support, among other tasks. One of the product innovations flowing from this global product planning approach is the SnakeLight Flexible Flashlight. The SnakeLight was first launched in North America, and then, six months later, in Europe, Latin America, and Australia. The product addresses a global need for portable lighting. Since flashlights are powered by alkaline batteries, there is no need for product modifications. The SnakeLight proved to be phenomenally successful around the world.[13]

Other companies increasingly adhere to the invention strategy. In the past, Procter & Gamble Europe was a patchwork of country-based operations, each with its own business. These days, P & G aims to develop products that appeal to the entire European region. Many automotive companies also recently jumped on the "produce globally, market locally" bandwagon. Ford's Mondeo model was developed for the European market. Give and take a few minor alterations, the Mondeo is largely the same across Europe. As one of Ford's European marketing managers commented: "A Mondeo in Spain is the same as the Mondeo you buy in Norway. You might find that one country has an air conditioner as standard and one has a sun roof as standard."[14]

---

[12]"Slim-Fast Beefs up in Europe," *Advertising Age International* (May 17, 1993), p. I-4.

[13]Don R. Garber, "How to Manage a Global Product Development Process," *Industrial Marketing Management*, 25 (1996), pp. 483–89.

[14]"Auto Marketers Gas Up for World Car Drive," *Advertising Age International* (January 16, 1995), p. I-16.

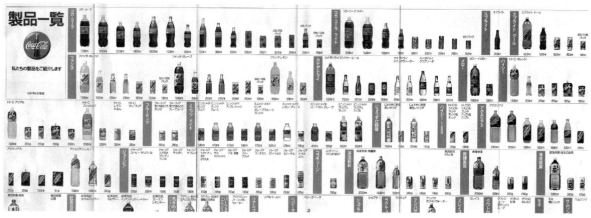

Coca-Cola Japan boasts a larger number of product types than any other Coca-Cola subsidiaries in the world. It is Coca-Cola's response to the highly competitive beverage market in Japan where competitors introduce a new drink almost weekly.

STANDARDIZATION VERSUS CUSTOMIZATION

♦ ♦ ♦ ♦ ♦ ♦

A recurrent theme in global marketing is whether companies should aim for a standardized or country-tailored product strategy. **Standardization** means offering a uniform product on a regional or worldwide basis. Minor alternations are usually made to meet local regulations or market conditions (for instance, voltage adjustments). However, by and large, these changes only lead to minor cost increases. A uniform product policy capitalizes on the commonalities in customers' needs across countries. The goal is to minimize costs. These cost savings are passed through to the company's customers via low prices. **Customization**, on the other hand, leverages cross-border differences in needs and wants of the firm's target customers. Under this regime, appropriate changes are made to match local market conditions. While standardization has a product-driven orientation—lower your costs via mass-production—customization is inspired by a market-driven mindset—increase customer satisfaction by adapting your products to local needs.

Forces that favor a globalized product strategy are:

1. **Common customer needs.** For many product categories, consumer needs are very similar in different countries. The functions for which the product is used might be identical. Likewise, the usage conditions or the benefits sought might be similar. An example of a product that targets a global segment is Pepsi Max, a sugar-free cola that Pepsi rolled out in 1993. Pepsi Max is a one-calorie soda with the "mouth-feel" of a regular cola. The product caters to consumers who shunned traditional diet drinks because of taste.[15] Many product categories also show a gradual but steady convergence in consumer preferences. Exhibit 11-2 portrays changes over time in worldwide alcohol consumption patterns. There is apparently a shift in the consumption mix toward one focal point: 20 percent spirits/40 percent wine/40 percent beer. Growing similarities in consumer pref-

---

[15]"Double Entendre: The Life and the Life of Pepsi Max," *Brandweek* (April 18, 1994), p. 40.

EXHIBIT 11-2
CONVERGENCE IN DRINKING PATTERNS

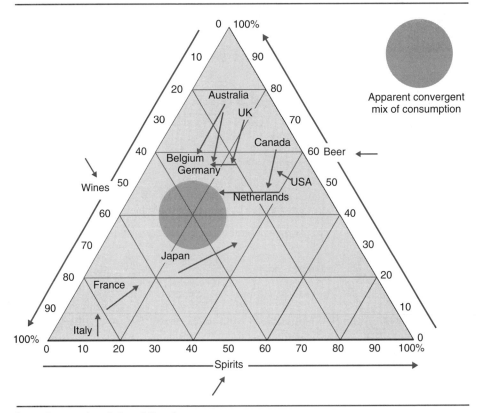

Source: Brewers Association of Canada.

erences have also been observed in the car industry.[16] In the Triad markets (Japan, Europe, and the United States) the preferred car size in terms of length-by-width has shifted toward a space of 7 to 9 squared meters. The size of cars in Europe has not changed much during the last two decades. In the United States fuel conservation efforts following the 1973 oil crisis spurred a move to more compact cars. On the other hand, Japan witnessed an increase in the demand of large cars driven by changes in the tax regime and consumer preferences (see Exhibit 11-3). The outlook on cars in the Triad markets is also becoming increasingly alike. Marketing research done by Nissan showed that car buyers in all three Triad markets rank self-expression, pleasantness of operation, and comfort among their top values. Obviously, the importance of such similarities should not be exaggerated. Despite a convergence of consumer needs in some regards, cultural differences persist and should not be overlooked. A multicountry market research project carried out for BMW underscored the importance of market

---

[16]Takashi Hisatomi, "Global Marketing by the Nissan Motor Company Limited—A Simultaneous Market Study of Users' Opinions and Attitudes in Europe, USA and Japan," *Marketing and Research Today* (February 1991), pp. 56–61.

Exhibit 11-3
Transitions of Body Size

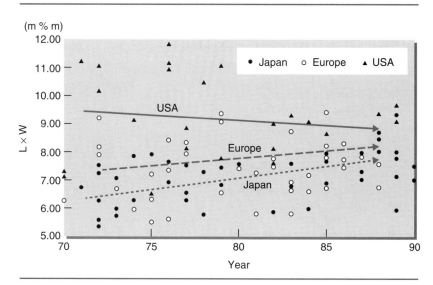

Source: Takashi Hisatomi, "Global Marketing by the Nissan Motor Company Limited—A Simultaneous Market Study of Users' Opinions and Attitudes in Europe, USA and Japan," *Marketing and Research Today* (February 1991), pp. 56–61.

Permission for using this material which was originally published in *Marketing and Research Today*, has been granted by (E.S.O.M.A.R.) The European Society for Opinion and Marketing Research J. J. Viottastraat 29, 1071 JP, Amsterdam, The Netherlands.

peculiarities.[17] European motorists have a common desire for reliability, safety, quality, and advanced technology. These are the basic criteria that any decent car should meet. However, once you go beyond these basic requirements, there are a set of other requirements that differ from country to country (see Exhibit 11-4). In Austria prestige is key: a car is expected to reflect "who" the owner is. Italian car drivers, on the other hand, attach importance to dynamic driving perfor-mance, design, and aesthetic qualities.

2. **Global Customers.** In business-to-business marketing, the shift toward global-ization means that for many companies a significant part of their business comes from MNCs that are essentially global customers. Buying and sourcing decisions are commonly centralized, or at the least regionalized. As a result, such cus-tomers typically require services or products that are harmonized worldwide.

3. **Scale Economies.** Scale economies in the manufacturing, and distribution, of globalized products is in most cases the key driver behind standardization moves. Savings are also often realized because of sourcing efficiencies or lowered R & D expenditures. These savings can be passed through to the company's end-cus-tomers via lower prices. Scale economies offer global competitors a tremendous competitive advantage over local or regional competitors. In many industries

---

[17]Horst Kern, Hans-Christian Wagner, and Roswitha Hassis, "European Aspects of a Global Brand: The BMW Case," *Marketing and Research Today* (February 1990), pp. 47–57.

EXHIBIT 11-4
DIFFERENCES IN CAR REQUIREMENTS FOR VARIOUS
EUROPEAN COUNTRIES

Country	Requirements
Netherlands	• Understatement • High reputation of brand
France	• Self-confident posture • Good road-holding ability
Switzerland	• Demanding but discreet
Austria	• Prestige thinking • Car for presenting oneself to the outside world
Italy	• In accordance with personal style • Dynamic driving • Road holding

Source: Horst Kern, Hans-Christian Wagner and Roswitha Hassis, "European Aspects of a Global Brand: The BMW Case," *Marketing and Research Today,* February 1990, p. 53.
Permission for using this material which was originally published in *Marketing and Research Today* has been granted by (E.S.O.M.A.R.) The European Society for Opinion and Marketing Research J. J. Viottastraat 29, 1071 JP, Amsterdam, The Netherlands.

though, the "economies of scale" rationale has lost some of its allure. Production procedures such as flexible manufacturing and just-in-time production have shifted the focus from size to timeliness. CAD/CAM techniques allow companies to manufacture customized products in small batch sizes at reduced cost. Although size often leads to lower unit costs, the diseconomies of scale also should not be overlooked. Hidden costs associated with size can often be ascribed to bureaucratic bloat and shop-floor alienation.[18]

4. **Time-to-Market.** In numerous industries being innovative is not enough to be competitive. Companies must also seek ways to shorten the time to bring new products to the market. By centralizing research and consolidating new product development efforts on fewer projects, companies are often able to reduce the time-to-market cycle. Procter & Gamble notes that a recent Pan-European launch of liquid laundry detergents could be done in 10 percent of the time it took in the early 1980s, when marketing efforts were still very decentralized.[19]

5. **Europe 1992 and Other Regional Market Agreements.** The formation of regional market agreements such as the Single European Market encourages companies to launch regional (e.g., Pan-European) products or redesign existing products as Pan-European brands. The legislation leading to the creation of the Single European Market in January 1993 aimed to remove most barriers to trade within the European Union. It also provided for the harmonization of technical standards in many industries. These moves favor Pan-European product strategies. Mars, for instance, now regards Europe as one giant market. It modified

---

[18]"Big is Back. A Survey of Multinationals," *The Economist* (June 24, 1995), p. 4.
[19]Procter & Gamble, *Annual Report 1993.*

the brand names for several of its products, turning them into Pan-European brands. Marathon in the United Kingdom became Snickers, the name used in Continental Europe. The Raider bar in Continental Europe was renamed Twix, the name used in the United Kingdom.[20]

Whether firms should strive for standardized or localized products is a bogus question. The issue should not be phrased as an either-or dilemma. Instead, product managers should look at it in terms of degree of globalization: What elements of my product policy should be tailored to the local market conditions? Which ones can I leave unchanged? At the same time, there are strategic options that allow firms to modify their product while keeping most of the benefits flowing from a uniform product policy. Two of these product design policies are the **modular** and the **core-product** approach:[21]

Modular Approach. The first approach consists of developing a range of product parts that can be used worldwide. The parts can be assembled into numerous product configurations. Scale economies flow from the mass-production of more-or-less standard product components at a few sites. This approach is very popular in the automotive industry. General Motor's chief executive notes that "it makes little sense to build duplicate components or near-duplicate platforms for different regional market segments, when one region can adapt or tailor what is being developed for another."[22] Global Perspective 11-2 describes how Volvo's Truck division uses modular design for one of its recent model launches.

Core-Product Approach. As discussed in Chapter 10, the core-product approach starts with the design of a mostly uniform core-product. Attachments are added to the core product to match local market needs. Savings are achieved by centralizing the manufacturing of the core product. At the same time companies adopting this approach have the flexibility that allows them to modify the product easily. The French carmaker Renault's model design procedures exemplify this approach. More than 90 percent of Renault's sales revenues comes from the European market. The body, engines, transmissions, and chassis of a given model are the same in the different markets. Minor changes, such as stronger heaters in Nordic countries or better air-conditioning for cars sold in Southern Europe, are easily implemented.[23]

The balancing act between standardization and adaptation is very tricky. One scholar[24] describes **overstandardization** as one of the five pitfalls that global marketers could run into. Too much standardization stifles initiative and experimentation at the local subsidiary level. However, one should not forget that there is also a risk of **overcustomization**. Part of the appeal of imported brands is often their *foreigness*. By adapting too much to the local market conditions, an import runs the risk of losing that cachet and simply becoming a me-too brand, barely differentiated from the local brands. Such

---

[20]Dale Littler and Katrin Schlieper, "The Development of the Eurobrand," *International Marketing Review*, 12 (2) (1995), pp. 22–37.

[21]Peter G. P. Walters and Brian Toyne, "Product Modification and Standardization in International Markets: Strategic Options and Facilitating Policies," *Columbia Journal of World Business*, 24 (Winter 1989), pp. 37–44.

[22]"Making its Marque All Over the World," *The Financial Times* (May 26, 1994), p. 17.

[23]"Auto Marketers Gas up for World Car Drive," *Advertising Age International* (January 16, 1995), p. 1-16.

[24]Kamran Kashani, "Beware the Pitfalls of Global Marketing," *Harvard Business Review* (September-October 1989).

* *

𝒢LOBAL PERSPECTIVE 11-2

GLOBAL TAKE-OFF FOR VOLVO FH

Volvo Truck, the truck division of Volvo, the Swedish car-maker, designed the FH model with the idea that the FH would be sold globally. The model had to meet all prevailing technical specifications as well as the toughest demands made by customers throughout the world.

The FH series is designed for rational assembly and a high degree of cost-effectiveness in production. As a result of the global supply of components, and substantial standardization of them, the number of parts has been cut down. This method of operation cuts lead time and increases production flexibility.

Source: Volvo, *1995 Annual Report,* pp. 22–23.

The focus is that assembly should be close to the customer. Accordingly, the FH series is assembled in plants around the world. In addition to Göteborg, assembly is carried out in Volvo Trucks' plants in Ghent (Belgium), Irvine (Scotland), Wroclaw (Poland) and Brisbane (Australia).

The new model was launched in 1993. The orders received show that the FH series has obtained high marks in the marketplace. In 1995 the FH model accounted for nearly 40 percent of the total number of orders. In Europe, where the FH model was first introduced, it helped to boost Volvo's share of heavy trucks from 12.1 percent in 1993 to 16.3 percent in 1995. Volvo thereby consolidated its position as the second largest make in the heavy-truck class in Europe.

---

a mistake was made by Carlsberg when it entered Thailand. Carlsberg tried to imitate Singha, the leading local brand. It raised the alcohol level to 6 percent for its flagship brand, thereby matching Singha's level. It launched a second brand, Chang, as a "local" beer. Prices were set at par with Singha. As a result, Thai beer drinkers had little reason to switch to Carlsberg's offerings. Dealers tried to get rid of their inventory by lowering the price, thereby cheapening Carlsberg's brand image.[25]

◆ ◆ ◆ ◆ ◆ ◆ MULTINATIONAL DIFFUSION

In spite of rapid adoption in their home market, many product innovations penetrate foreign markets very slowly. The speed and pattern of market penetration for a given product innovation usually differs substantially between markets. This point is illustrated in Exhibit 11-5, which portrays the penetration of VCRs in five countries.

By the same token, it is not uncommon for new products that were phenomenally successful in one country to turn out to be turkeys in foreign markets. For example, dry beers rejuvenated the beer market in Japan during the late 1980s but never gained a foothold in the United States and Europe. In this section we will introduce several concepts and insights from multinational new product diffusion research. These explain some of the differences in new product performance between different countries.

In general, the adoption of new products is driven by three types of factors: individual differences, personal influences, and product characteristics. Individuals differ in terms of their willingness to try out new products. Early adopters are eager to experiment with new ideas or products. Late adopters take a wait-and-see attitude. Early adopters differ from laggards in terms of socioeconomic traits (income, education, social status), personality, and communication behavior. A prominent role is also played by the influence of prior adopters. Word-of-mouth spread by previous

---

[25]"Foreigners Go Home," *Forbes* (October 9, 1995), p. 68.

EXHIBIT 11-5
VCR SALES IN VARIOUS COUNTRIES

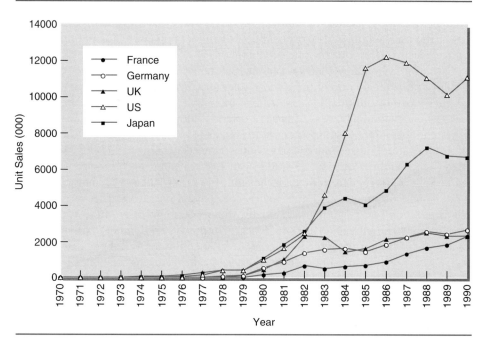

Source: Based on data provided by Philips.

adopters often has a much more significant impact on the adoption decision than nonpersonal factors such as media advertising. For many product categories, peer pressure will often determine whether (and when) a person will adopt the innovation. The third set of factors relates to the nature of the product itself. Five product characteristics are key:[26]

1. **Relative advantage.** To what extent does the new product offer more perceived value to potential adopters than existing alternatives?

2. **Compatibility.** Is the product consistent with existing values and attitudes of the individuals in the social system? Are there any switching costs that people might incur if they decide to adopt the innovation?

3. **Complexity.** Is the product easy to understand? Easy to use?

4. **Triability.** Are prospects able to try out the product on a limited basis?

5. **Observability.** How easy is it for possible adopters to observe the results or benefits of the innovation? Can these benefits easily be communicated?

Aside from these variables, several country characteristics can be used to predict new product penetration patterns. Communication leading to the transfer of ideas tends to be easier when it happens between individuals who have a similar cultural mindset. Therefore, the adoption rate for new products in countries with a **homogeneous** population (e.g., Japan, South Korea, Thailand) is usually faster than in countries with a highly diverse culture. When a new product is launched at different time in-

---

[26]Thomas S. Robertson, *Innovative Behavior and Communication* (New York: Holt, Rinehart and Winston, 1971).

tervals, there will be **lead-countries**, where it is introduced first, and **lag-countries**, that are entered afterward. Generally, adoption rates seem to be higher in lag-countries than in the lead-country. Potential adopters in lag-countries have had more time to understand and evaluate the innovation's perceived attributes than their counterparts in the lead-country. Also, over time, the product's quality tends to improve and its price usually lowers due to scale economies.[27]

One research study that looked at the penetration patterns for consumer durables in Europe identified three more relevant country characteristics.[28] The first variable is **cosmopolitanism**. *Cosmopolitans* are people who look beyond their immediate social surroundings, while *locals* are oriented more toward their immediate social system. The more cosmopolitan the country's population, the higher the propensity to innovate. The second country trait is labeled **mobility**. Mobility is the ease with which members of a social system can move around and interact with other members. It is largely determined by the country's infrastructure. Mobility facilitates interpersonal communication, and, hence does have a positive impact on the product's penetration in a given market. Finally, the **percentage of women in the labor force** impacts the spread of certain types of innovations. Higher participation of women means higher incomes and hence more spending power. Time-saving products (such as washing machines, dishwashers) appeal to working women. By the same token, time-consuming durables will be less valued in societies where working women form a substantial portion of the labor force.

Recent research has also identified a strong relationship between two of Hofstede's (see Chapter 4) cultural dimensions, individualism and uncertainty avoidance, and national innovativeness (see Exhibit 11-6).[29] Individualistic cultures value autonomy. They also tend to be more hedonistic and materialistic than group-oriented cultures. Empirical findings show a positive relationship between individualism and an index of national innovativeness, meaning: the more individualistic the nation's culture, the higher national innovativeness. Members from societies that score high on uncertainty avoidance are less inclined to take risk or experiment. Since new product adoption involves some degree of risk taking, one would expect lower rates of new product adoption in countries with high levels of uncertainty avoidance. The data show indeed that there is a negative association between a country's innovativeness and uncertainty avoidance.

◆ ◆ ◆ ◆ ◆ ◆ DEVELOPING NEW PRODUCTS FOR GLOBAL MARKETS

For most companies, new products are the bread-and-butter of their growth strategy. Unfortunately, developing new products is time-consuming and costly, with immense challenges. The new product development process becomes especially a major headache for multinational organizations that try to coordinate the process on a regional or sometimes even worldwide basis. The steps to be followed in the global new product development (NPD) process are by-and-large very similar to domestic marketing situations (see Exhibit 11-7). In this section, we will focus on the unique

---

[27]Hirokazu Takada and Dipak Jain, "Cross-National Analysis of Diffusion of Consumer Durable Goods in Pacific Rim Countries," *Journal of Marketing*, 55 (2) (April 1991), pp. 48–54.

[28]Hubert Gatignon, Jehoshua Eliashberg, and Thomas S. Robertson, "Modeling Multinational Diffusion Patterns: An Efficient Methodology," *Marketing Science*, 8 (3) (Summer 1989), pp. 231–47.

[29]Michael Lynn and Betsy D. Gelb, "Identifying Innovative National Markets for Technical Consumer Goods," *International Marketing Review*, 13 (6) (1996), pp. 43–57.

EXHIBIT 11-6
NATIONAL INNOVATIVENESS VS. INDIVIDUALISM

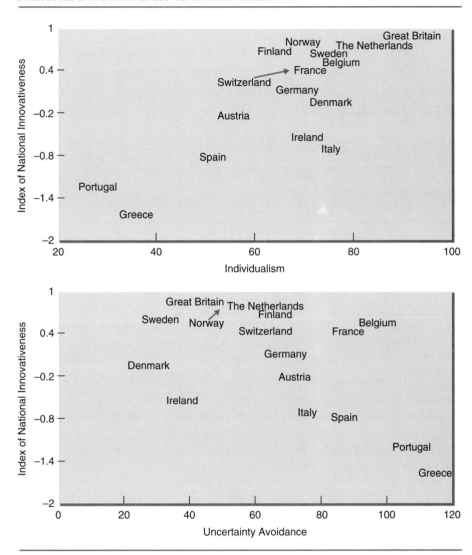

Source: Michael Lynn and Betsy D. Gelb, "Identifying Innovative National Markets for Technical Consumer Goods," *International Marketing Review,* 13 (6) 1996, pp. 43–57.

aspects that take place when innovation efforts are implemented on a global scope. Global Perspective 11-3 describes how one multinational consumer goods company, Colgate-Palmolive, manages its innovation efforts.

Identifying New Product Ideas

Every new product starts with an idea. Sources for new product ideas are manifold. Companies can tap into any of the so-called 4 C's—*C*ompany, *C*ustomers, *C*ompetition and *C*ollaborators (e.g., distribution channels, suppliers)—for creative new product ideas. Obviously, many successful new products originally started at the R & D labs. Other internal sources include salespeople, employees, and market researchers. Multinational companies often capitalize on their global know-how by transplanting

EXHIBIT 11-7
GLOBAL NEW PRODUCT DEVELOPMENT PROCESS

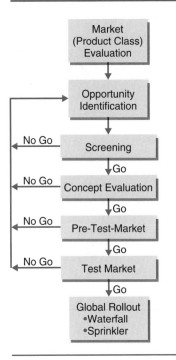

new product ideas that were successful in one country to other markets. A good example of this practice is the Dockers line of casual slacks. This product was introduced in Japan by Levi Strauss Japan in 1985. The line became incredibly successful in Japan. As a result, Levi Strauss subsequently decided to launch the line in the United States and Europe as well.[30]

These days many MNCs create organizational structures to foster global (or regional) product development. Global Perspective 11-3 chronicles the efforts that were made by Colgate-Palmolive to come up with new product ideas that have a worldwide market potential. Unilever set up a network of worldwide innovation centers (ICs) for personal care and food products. Each IC unit consists of marketing, advertising agency, and technical people and is headed by the company chairman of the country subsidiary where the IC is based. The centers are responsible for developing product ideas and research, technology, and marketing expertise. One example of an innovation spurred by an IC is a new formula developed for Timotei, one of Unilever's leading shampoo brands. A change in women's hairstyles required a shampoo that was more nourishing. Unilever's haircare IC came up with a new formula for Timotei that offered a solution.[31] Black & Decker sets up business teams to develop global products. Each team is headed by a Product General Manager and has representatives from the various geographic regions. The charter of the teams is to develop new products with "the right degree of commonality and the right amount

[30]"The Jeaning of Japan," *Business Tokyo* (February 1991), pp. 62–63.

[31]"Fanning Unilever's Flame of Innovation," *Advertising Age International* (November 23, 1992), pp. I-3, I-13.

$\mathcal{G}$LOBAL PERSPECTIVE 11-3

COLGATE-PALMOLIVE'S GLOBAL NEW PRODUCT DEVELOPMENT APPROACH

GLOBAL PRODUCT DEVELOPMENT

Colgate researchers create products for the world—not for a single country. The process begins with consumer research in multiple countries with a broad range of economic and cultural characteristics. Once products with potential global appeal are identified, development work begins. Here, Colgate's global marketing experts and global scientists work in team—organized around the specific core consumer business and its strategic growth plan.

MULTIYEAR ACTIVITY GRIDS

In the late stages of development, regional and country managers prioritize and plan all aspects of the launch using a three-year horizon. That way, everything—from raw materials to manufacturing to distribution to media advertising—is most efficiently coordinated.

COUNTRY—NOT CITY—TEST MARKETS

Concurrent test marketing begins with anywhere from one to six countries to identify the best plan to use for the

Source: Colgate-Palmolive, *1993 Annual Report*, p. 17.

subsequent rapid global rollout. For example, early results from introduction in Australia, the Philippines, New Zealand, Greece, Portugal, and Colombia indicated that Colgate Total, a new toothpaste containing a long-lasting antibacterial formula that fights plaque, tartar and cavities, would be a popular addition to the Colgate product line throughout the world.

"BUNDLE BOOKS" LEAVE NOTHING TO CHANCE

Modifications suggested by lead country testing are then incorporated into a "Bundle Book," a detailed manual explaining everything a country manager needs to know about a product—its formula, packaging, marketing strategy, and advertising—to launch it quickly and successfully.

WORLDWIDE PRODUCT EXPANSION

The final stage of taking Colgate's products from development to market involves the managers of a specific country orchestrating the product launch. Local Colgate experts, from manufacturing to marketing, working with the original global product development team, execute the launch strategy consistent with the unique characteristics of the particular market.

of local market uniqueness." Project leadership is assigned to that country or region that has a dominant category share position.[32]

Screening

Evidently not all new product ideas are winners. Once new product ideas have been identified, they need to be screened. The goal here is to weed out ideas with little potential. This filtering process can take the form of a formal scoring model. One example of a scoring model is NewProd, which was based on almost two hundred projects from a hundred companies.[33] Each of the projects was rated by managers on about fifty screening criteria and judged in terms of its commercial success. A regression model was derived using these managerial judgments as data points. The results of the regression are shown in Exhibit 11-8. The regression can be used as a bench-

---

[32]Don R. Graber, "How to Manage a Global Product Development Process," *Industrial Marketing Management*, 25 (1996), pp. 483–89.

[33]Robert G. Cooper, "Selecting New Product Projects: Using the NewProd System," *Journal of Product Innovation Management*, 2 (1) (March 1985), pp. 34–44.

EXHIBIT 11-8
NEWPROD SCREENING MODEL

Key Dimensions (factor name)	Regression Coefficient (weight of factor)	F-Value	Variables or Items Loading on Factor
Product superiority, quality, and uniqueness	1.744	68.7	Product: is superior to competing products has unique features for user is higher quality than competitors' does unique task for user reduces customers' costs is innovative—first of its kind
Overall project/resource compatibility	1.138	30.0	A good "fit" between needs of project and company resource base in terms of: managerial skills marketing research skills salesforce/distribution resources financial resources engineering skills production resources
Market need, growth, and size	0.801	12.5	High need level customers for product class Large market (S volume) Fast growing market
Economic advantage of product to end user	0.722	10.2	Product reduces customers' costs Product is priced lower than competing products
Newness to the firm (negative)	−0.354	2.9	Project takes the firm into new areas for the firm such as: new product class to company new salesforce/distribution new types of users' needs served new customers to company new competitors to company new product technology to firm new production process to firm
Technology resource compatibility	0.342	2.5	A good "fit" between needs of project and company resource base in terms of: R & D resources and skills engineering skills and resources
Market competitiveness (negative)	−0.301	2.0	Intense price competition in market Highly competitive market Many competitors Many new product intros into market Changing user needs
Product scope	0.225	0.9	Market-driven new product idea Not a custom product, i.e., more mass appeal A mass market for product (as opposed to one or a few customers)
Constant	0.328		

Source: Robert G. Cooper, "Selecting New Product Projects: Using the NewProd System," *Journal of Product Innovation Management*, 2 (1) (March 1985), p. 39.

mark to predict the potential of new product ideas. The model has been validated in North America, Scandinavia, and the Netherlands.[34]

Concept Testing

Once the merits of a new product idea have been established, it must be translated into a product concept. A product concept is a fairly detailed description, verbally or sometimes visually, of the new product or service. To assess the appeal of the product concept, companies rely on focus group discussions. Focus groups are a small group of prospective customers, typically with one moderator. The focus group members discuss the likes and dislikes of the proposed product and the current competing offerings. They also state their willingness to adopt the new product if it were to be launched in the market.

A more sophisticated procedure to measure consumer preferences for product concepts is **conjoint analysis** (sometimes also referred to as trade-off analysis). Most products and services are a bundle of product attributes. The starting premise of conjoint analysis is that people make trade-offs between the different product attributes when they evaluate alternatives (e.g., brands) from which they have to pick a choice. The purpose, then, of conjoint is to gain an understanding of the trade-offs that consumers make. The outcome of the exercise will be a set of utilities (partworths) for each attribute level, derived at the individual household or consumer segment level. This information allows the company to answer questions such as how much their customers are willing to pay extra for additional product features or superior performance. The tool can also be used to examine to what degree a firm should customize the products it plans to launch in the various target markets.

To illustrate the use of the conjoint for the design of products in an international setting, let us look at a hypothetical example. In what follows, we focus on the use of conjoint analysis in the context of global NPD.[35] Imagine that company XYZ considers selling satellite TV dishes in two Southeast Asian countries: Thailand and Malaysia.

The first step is to determine the salient attributes for the product (or service). Exploratory market research (e.g., a focus group discussion) or managerial judgment can be used to figure out the most critical attributes. At the same time, we also need to consider the possible levels ("values") that each of the attributes can take. In our example (see Exhibit 11-9) four attributes are considered to be important: (1) the number of channels, (2) the purchase price,[36] (3) the installation cost, and (4) the size of the dish (in terms of inches). Each of the attributes has three possible levels.

For instance, the diameter of the dish could be 18, 25, or 30 inches. The next step is to construct product profiles by combining the various attribute levels. Each profile would represent a hypothetical product configuration. In most applications it is unrealistic to consider every possible combination, since the number of possibilities rapidly explodes. Instead, one uses an experimental design to come up with a small but manageable number of product profiles. This number varies from study to

---

[34]Robert G. Cooper, "The NewProd System: The Industry Experience," *Journal of Product Innovation Management*, 9 (2) (June 1992), pp. 113–27.

[35]Those who are interested in the technical background should consult Paul E. Green and Yoram Wind, "New Ways to Measure Consumers' Judgments," *Harvard Business Review*, 53 (1975), pp. 107–17.

[36]In the example we assume that no middlemen will be used, so the retail price is the same as the ex-factory price.

EXHIBIT 11-9

SALIENT ATTRIBUTES AND ATTRIBUTE
LEVELS FOR SATELLITE DISHES

Product Attributes	Attribute Levels
Number of Channels	(1) 30
	(2) 50
	(3) 100
Selling Price	(1) $500
	(2) $600
	(3) $700
Installation Fee	(1) Free
	(2) $100
	(3) $200
Size of Dish	(1) 18"
	(2) 25"
	(3) 30"

study. Obviously, the number of profiles will depend not only on the number of attributes and attribute levels, but also on other factors like the amount of information you want to collect. In most studies, the number of profiles ranges between 18 and 32. An example of such a profile is given in Exhibit 11-10.

Once the profiles have been finalized, you can go into the field and gather the desired information. In each country several prospective target customers will be contacted. Every subject in your sample is shown each of the product profiles and asked to state his or her preferences. For instance, you might ask the respondent to rank the product profiles from most to least preferred. In addition, other data (e.g., demographics, lifestyle) are collected that often prove useful for benefit segmentation purposes.

Once you have collected the preference data, you need to analyze them using a statistical software package. The outcome of the analysis will be a set of "utilities" that each segment (or respondent) derives from each of the attribute levels. Hypothetical results for our example are shown in Exhibit 11-11. Each country has two segments: a price-sensitive and quality-sensitive segment. The entries in the columns represent the utilities (part-worths) for the respective attribute levels. For instance, the utility of 100 channels in Thailand would be 5.6 for segment II, compared to 2.5 for Malaysia's performance segment II. The results can be used to see which attributes matter most to each of the segments in the different target markets. The relative range of the utilities signals the attribute importances. In this example, price is most critical for the first Thai segment (utility range: 0 to −4.6), whereas the number of channels (utility range: 0 to 5.6) matters most

EXHIBIT 11-10

EXAMPLE OF A
PRODUCT PROFILE

Product Profile 18:

(1) Number of Channels: 30
(2) Price: $500
(3) Installation Fee: $100
(4) Size of Dish: 25"

EXHIBIT 11-11
RESULTS OF CONJOINT ANALYSIS FOR SATELLITE DISHES

Attributes	Thailand Segment I	Thailand Segment II	Malaysia Segment I	Malaysia Segment II
Number of Channels:				
30	0.0	0.0	0.0	0.0
50	1.5	3.4	1.4	1.8
100	3.2	5.6	3.0	2.5
Purchase Price:				
$500	0.0	0.0	0.0	0.0
$600	−3.2	−1.5	−2.8	−2.5
$700	−4.6	−2.0	−4.8	−3.0
Installation:				
Free	0.0	0.0	0.0	0.0
$100	−1.5	−0.2	−1.4	−1.0
$200	−1.8	−0.4	−2.1	−1.7
Size of Dish (Diameter):				
18"	0.0	0.0	0.0	0.0
25"	−0.5	−1.0	−0.4	−2.0
30"	−0.8	−1.5	−1.0	−5.0
Size of Segment	12,000	28,000	15,000	16,000

for the second Thai segment. The technical nitty-gritty is less important here, but we would like you to get a flavor of how conjoint can be used to settle product design issues in a global setting. Let us consider the standardize versus customize issue.

To standardize or not to standardize. For the sake of simplicity, suppose that currently there is one incumbent competitor, ABC, in the satellite dish industry in Thailand and Malaysia. The ABC brand has the following features:

Number of Channels: 30
Selling Price: $500
Installation Fee: Free
Size of Dish: 30"

XYZ is looking at two possibilities: (1) sell a uniform product (model XYZST) or (2) launch a customized product for each of the two markets (models XYZTH and XYZMA). The standardized product (XYZST) has the following profile:

Number of Channels: 50
Selling Price: $600
Installation: $100
Size of Dish: 25"

The customized products would have the following characteristics:

Attribute	Product XYZTH (Thailand)	Product XYZMA (Malaysia)
Nr. of Channels	100	30
Price	$700	$700
Installation	$200	Free
Size of Dish	25"	18"

In this example, the selling price for the standardized product is less than the price for the customized product because of scale economies. By computing the overall utility for each of the alternatives we are able to estimate the market share that each product would grab in the two countries. This overall score is simply the sum of the utilities for the attribute levels. The respective utilities for the various product configurations are shown in Exhibit 11-12.

Assuming that each customer will pick the alternative that gives the highest overall utility, we can derive market share estimates in the two countries for the two product alternatives. For instance, looking at the uniform dish in Thailand, we find that customers in the quality segment II would prefer it over the competing model (since $0.7 > -1.5$). On the other hand, the first segment in Thailand would pick ABC (since $-3.7 < -0.8$). Hence, the market share for the standardized model (XYZST) in the Thai market would equal 70 percent: the number of households in the quality segment, 28,000—see bottom row of Exhibit 11-11—divided by the entire market size for satellite dishes in Thailand, 40,000. In the same manner, we can compute XYZ's market share for the standardized model in Malaysia and for the customized models in the two countries:

Market share standardized product XYZST in Malaysia = 51.6% (16,000/31,000)

Market share customized product XYZTH in Thailand = 70% (28,000/40,000)

Market share customized product XYZMA in Malaysia = 51.6% (16,000/31,000)

Exhibit 11-12
Utilities for Respective Alternatives Derived Via Conjoint Study

Alternative	Thailand Segment I	Thailand Segment II	Malaysia Segment I	Malaysia Segment II
ABC (Competitor)	−0.8	−1.5	−1.0	−5.0
XYZST (Standardized)	−3.7[1]	0.7	−3.2	−3.7
XYZTH (Customized for Thailand)	−4.0	2.2	Not offered	Not offered
XYZMA (Customized for Malaysia)	Not offered	Not offered	−4.8	−3.0

[1] $1.5 + (-3.2) + (-1.5) + (-0.5) = -3.7$

In our example, the market share estimates for the two alternatives (standardized versus customized) end up being equal. Once we have cost estimates for the manufacturing and marketing of the different alternatives, we can come up with an estimate of their expected profits. For instance, let us assume that the variable costs are equal (say, $400 per unit) but the fixed costs (combined across the two markets) differ: $5 million for the standardized product option as opposed to $10 million for the customized product option. Plugging in our market share estimates and these cost estimates, we can assess the profit potential of the various options:

Profits for standardized product approach (combined across the two countries) =
    (Unit Sales Thailand + Unit Sales Malaysia) (unit contribution) − (Fixed Costs)

or

$$(28,000 + 16,000) \times (\$600 + \$100 - \$400) - \$5,000,000 = \$8.2 \text{ million}[37]$$

Profits for the customized product strategy:

$$(28,000 + 16,000) \times (\$700 + \$0 - \$400) - \$10,000,000 = \$8.8 \text{ million.}$$

Given the higher profit potential for the second alternative, launching two customized models (model XYZTH targeted toward Thailand and model XYZMA toward Malaysia) is clearly the winning option here. Obviously, aside of the economics, other factors need to be taken into consideration before settling such issues.

Test Marketing

In many Western countries, test marketing new products before the full-fledged rollout is common. Test marketing is essentially a field experiment where the new product is marketed in a select set of cities to assess its sales potential and scores of other performance measures. In a sense, a test market is the dress rehearsal prior to the product launch (assuming the test market results support a "GO" decision). There are several reasons why companies would like to run a test market before the rollout. It allows them to make fairly accurate projections of the market share, sales volume, and penetration of the new product. In countries where household scanning panels are available, firms can also get insights into likely trial, repeat purchase, and usage rates for the product. Another boon of test marketing is that companies can contrast competing marketing mix strategies to decide which one is most promising in achieving the firm's objectives.

Despite these merits, test markets also have several shortcomings. They are typically time-consuming and costly. Apart from the direct costs of running the test markets, there is also the opportunity cost of lost sales that the company would have achieved during the test market period in case of a successful global rollout. Moreover, test market results can be misleading. It may be difficult to replicate test market conditions with the final rollout. For instance, certain communication options that were available in the test market cities are not always accessible in all of the final target markets. Finally, there is also a strategic concern: test markets might alert your competitors, allowing them to pre-empt you.

In light of these drawbacks, MNCs often prefer to skip the test market stage. Instead, they use a market simulation or immediately launch the new product. In fact, one survey indicated that Pan-European financial institutions conducted test markets

---

[37]The unit contribution in this example is: selling price + installation fee − variable cost.

less than 20 percent of the time.[38] One alternative to test marketing is the laboratory test market. Prospective customers are contacted and shown commercials for the new item and existing competing brands. After the viewing, they are given a small amount of money and are invited to make a purchase in the product category in a simulated store setting ("lab"). Hopefully, some of the prospects will pick your new product. Those who purchase the new product, take it home and consume it. Those who choose a competing brand are given a sample of the new product. After a couple of weeks the subjects are contacted again via the phone. They are asked to state their attitude toward the new item in terms of likes and dislikes, satisfaction, and whether they would be willing to buy the product again.

Such procedures, though relatively cheap, still give valuable insights about the likely trial and repeat buying rates, usage, and customer satisfaction for the new product, price sensitivities, and the effectiveness of sampling. The collected data are often used as inputs for a marketing computer simulation model to answer "what if" questions.

Another route that is often taken is to rely on the sales performance of the product in one country, the lead market, to project sales figures in other countries that are considered for a launching decision. In a sense, an entire country is used as one big test market. A practitioner of this approach is Colgate-Palmolive. For example, Colgate used Thailand as a bellwether for the worldwide introduction of Nouriché, a treatment shampoo.[39] Thailand was chosen as a springboard because of the size and growth potential of its haircare market. In Canada, Pepsi launched Pepsi Max, a mid-calorie cola.[40] The product offers a compromise to customers who do not like the taste of diet colas but want to avoid the calories of regular colas. Pepsi views Canada as a "big test market" to assess the viability of a mid-calorie soft drink in the United States.[41] Miller, the U.S. beer brewer, also employed Canada as a test market for Red Dog for the United States.[42] The brand is red in color, low in carbonation, and easy to drink. Miller planned to position Red Dog as interactive, liberating, nonconformist, and confident. The new product strategy for Red Dog was first implemented and tested in Canada. After the successful launch in Canada, Red Dog was introduced in the United States in 1994. By and large, the segmentation and positioning strategies used in Canada were replicated for the U.S. rollout. Some changes were made, though, to allow for the peculiarities of the American beer market. Other recent cases of the use of an entire country as a test market are summarized in Exhibit 11-13.

Using a country as a test market for other markets raises several issues. How many countries should be selected? What countries should be used? To what degree can sales experience garnered in one country be projected to other countries? Generally speaking, cross-cultural and other environmental differences (e.g., the competitive climate) turn cross-country projections into a risky venture. The practice is only recommendable when the new product targets cross-border segments.

---

[38]Aliah Mohammed-Salleh and Chris Easingwood, "Why European Financial Institutions Do Not Test-Market New Consumer Products," *International Journal of Bank Marketing*, 11 (3) (1993), pp. 23–27.

[39]"Colgate Tries Thai for Global Entry," *Advertising Age International* (May 16, 1994), p. I-22.

[40]Outside Canada, Pepsi Max was launched as a one-calorie product.

[41]"Double Entendre: The Life and the Life of Pepsi Max," *Brandweek* (April 18, 1994), p. 40.

[42]Donna J. Neal, "Crossing Borders with New Brand Introductions," in *Brand Equity and the Marketing Mix: Creating Customer Value*, Sanjay Sood, ed., Marketing Science Institute, Report No. 95-111, September 1995.

EXHIBIT 11-13
EXAMPLES OF TEST MARKET COUNTRIES

Company	Product	Test Market Used	Geographic Coverage
Colgate-Palmolive	Nouriché (shampoo)	Thailand	World
Unilever	Organics (shampoo)	Thailand	World
Procter & Gamble,			
Colgate-Palmolive		Brazil	Latin America
Procter & Gamble		Ireland	Europe
Miller	Red Dog (beer)	Canada	North America
KFC	Breakfast menu	Singapore	World
Fiat	Palio (car)	Brazil	World

Timing of Entry: Waterfall versus Sprinkler Strategies

A key element of a global product launch strategy is the entry timing decision: When should we launch the new product in the target markets? Roughly speaking, there are two broad strategic options: the **waterfall** and the **sprinkler model** (see Exhibit 11-14).[43] The first option is the global phased rollout or **waterfall** model, where new products trickle down in a cascade-like manner.[44] The typical pattern is to introduce the new product first in the company's home market. Next, the innovation is launched in other advanced markets. In the final phase, the multinational firm markets the product in less advanced countries. This whole process of geographic expansion may last several decades. The time span between the U.S. launch and the foreign launch was twenty-two years for McDonald's, twenty years for Coca-Cola, and thirty-five years for Marlboro.[45] Samsonite's Italian-made shoes were first launched in Italy in September 1994. Samsonite's entry strategy dictated that the shoes would be launched in Germany, Austria, and Switzerland in January 1995. Six months later, four other European markets were to be added: France, Spain, Belgium, and the Netherlands. A move into the U.S. market was planned for 1996.[46] The prime motive for the waterfall model is that customization of the product for the foreign market launch is time-consuming.

The second timing decision option is the **sprinkler** strategy of simultaneous worldwide entry. Under this scenario, the global rollout takes place within a period of one to two years. The growing prominence of universal segments and concerns about competitive pre-emption in the foreign markets are the two major factors behind this expansion approach. Microsoft launched Windows 95 worldwide in August 1995. The entry was backed up with a multimillion-dollar mass-market advertising campaign that ran in more than twenty countries. Between 4 and 6 million customers worldwide bought the operating system in the first three weeks after the launch date.[47]

---

[43]Hajo Riesenbeck and Anthony Freeling, "How Global Are Global Brands?" *The McKinsey Quarterly*, 4 (1991), pp. 3–18.

[44]Kenichi Ohmae, "The Triad World View," *Journal of Business Strategy*, 7 (Spring 1985), pp. 8–19.

[45]Riesenbeck and Freeling.

[46]"Samsonite Packing Shoes for World Tour," *Advertising Age International* (July 18, 1994), p. I-4.

[47]"Eighth Wonder of the World," *Advertising Age International* (September 18, 1995), p. I-3.

EXHIBIT 11-14
"WATERFALL" VERSUS "SPRINKLER" MODEL

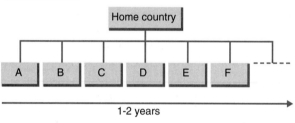

"Waterfall" model

Home country

A

B

C

D

> 3 years

"Sprinkler" model

Home country

A B C D E F

1-2 years

Source: Reprinted by special permission from 'The McKinsey Quarterly' 1991 Number 4. Copyright © 1991 McKinsey & Company. All rights reserved.

The waterfall strategy of sequential entry is preferable over the sprinkler model when:[48]

1. The lifecycle of the product is relatively long

2. Nonfavorable conditions govern the foreign market, such as:
   - small foreign markets (compared to the home market)
   - slow growth
   - high fixed costs of entry

3. Weak competitive climate exists in the foreign market, because of such things as:
   - very weak local competitors
   - competitors willing to cooperate
   - no competitors

---

[48]Shlomo Kalish, Vijay Mahajan and Eitan Muller, "Waterfall and Sprinkler New-Product Strategies in Competitive Global Markets," *International Journal of Research in Marketing*, 12 (July 1995), pp. 105–19.

GLOBAL NPD AND CULTURE   ◆ ◆ ◆ ◆ ◆ ◆

In this final section we touch on the linkages between the new product development process and national cultures. Cultural differences heavily influence the NPD process. A recent study that contrasted European and North American new product programs led to the following conclusions:[49]

- The NPD process among European firms is much more formalized.

- European Go/No Go standards tend to be far stricter than American norms.

- In terms of organization, NPD projects within European firms more likely have a well-defined project leader and an assigned team of players than projects run by North American companies. Also, when teams do exist, they are much more multifunctional than American teams.

- Incentive schemes also differ. Compared to American firms, European companies punish project leaders less in case of failure, reward intrapreneurs more generously, and offer more seed money for pet projects.

Another study contrasted the trade-offs that German and U.S. new product managers make.[50] The study showed that U.S. managers put the greatest emphasis on meeting the product development budget. Least important is beating the development schedule. For German companies, the priorities are reversed: their top priority is meeting the product development schedule.

Peculiarities have also been observed for the Japanese NPD process. The Japanese approach takes an incremental perspective with the emphasis being on continuous technological improvements.[51] One of the consequences of this "incrementalist" approach is parallel new product development.[52] While developing the first generation of a new product, Japanese firms will work on the second and third generation products. Thereby, as soon as competitors launch a me-too product, the Japanese firm can counter by introducing the next generation product.[53] Japanese companies also strongly believe in **product churning**: they rush new products to the market with little or no market research and then gauge the market's reaction.[54] Another characteristic of Japanese NPD is the close and ongoing linkage with the customer. Japanese NPD managers constantly listen to the "voice of the customer."[55]

---

[49]E. J. Kleinschmidt, "A comparative analysis of new product programmes," *European Journal of Marketing*, 28 (7) (1994), pp. 5–29.

[50]Ashok K. Gupta, Klaus Brockhoff and Ursula Weisenfeld, "Making Trade-Offs in the New Product Development Process: A German/US Comparison," *Journal of Product Innovation Management*, 9 (March 1992), pp. 11–18.

[51]Michael Czinkota and Masaaki Kotabe, "Product Development the Japanese Way," *Journal of Business Strategy* (Nov./Dec. 1990), pp. 31–36.

[52]R. B. Kennard, "From Experience: Japanese Product Development Process," *Journal of Product Innovation Management*, 8 (September 1991), pp. 184–88.

[53]Paul A. Herbig and Fred Palumbo, "A Brief Examination of the Japanese Innovative Process: Part 2," *Marketing Intelligence & Planning*, 12 (2) (1994), pp. 38–42.

[54]David McHardy Reid, "Perspectives for International Marketers on the Japanese Market," *Journal of International Marketing*, 3 (1) (1995), pp. 63–84.

[55]Kennard.

The precise role of culture depends on the stage of the NPD process. We can make a distinction between the "initiation" (idea generation, screening, concept development) and "implementation" (test marketing, product launch) stages of global NPD.[56] Decentralization, often found in egalitarian (low power distance—see chapter 4) cultures, encourages idea generation and feedback. On the other hand, a centralized structure (high power distance) is probably a strength for the implementation steps of the NPD when rigor and control become more critical. Cultures with low uncertainty avoidance—characterized with risk taking and little need for planning and structure—are probably beneficial for the initial steps of the NPD process. At later stages, risk avoidance and planning become more desirable. These traits are typically found in cultures with high uncertainty avoidance. Similar contrasts can be made for other cultural dimensions. To tap into the benefits of differing cultural mindsets, MNCs like Baxter International, Black & Decker, Procter & Gamble, and Colgate-Palmolive increasingly opt for cross-cultural new product project teams.

SUMMARY ✦

Global product policy decisions are tremendously important for the success of an MNC's global marketing strategies. In this chapter, the focus was on managing the new product development process in a global context. We first gave an overview of the different product strategy options that companies might pursue. Roughly speaking, a multinational company has three options: **extension** of the domestic strategy, **adaptation** of home-grown strategies, or **invention** by designing products that cater to the common needs of global customers. One of the major issues firms wrestle with is the standardization-versus-customization issue. By now, you should realize that this issue should not be stated in "either-or" terms. Instead, it is a matter of "degree": To what extent should we adapt (or if you want: standardize) our product strategy? We described the major forces that favor a globalized (or regionalized) product strategy. At the same time, there will always be forces that push your product strategy in the direction of customization.

Ideally, companies strike a neat balance between product standardization and adaptation. We described two product design approaches that enable a firm to capture the benefits of either option: the **modular** and the **core-product** approach. By adopting these approaches or their variants, firms minimize the risk of over-standardizing their product offerings while still grabbing the scale economies benefits that flow from a uniform product policy. We also demonstrated how you can use one market research tool—conjoint analysis—to make global product design decisions in practice.

The last part of this chapter highlighted the different stages in the new product development process. By and large, the pattern is similar to the steps followed in developing new products for the home market. However, there are a number of complicating factors that need to be handled: How do we coordinate global NPD efforts across different cultures? What mechanisms and communication channels can we use to stimulate idea exchanges? What alternatives do we have when certain steps of the NPD sequence are not doable (e.g., test marketing)?

Finally, we showed how cultural differences translate into different NPD approaches. It is fitting to conclude this chapter with the insights of a seasoned practitioner. In a recent speech Don Graber, president of Worldwide Household Products at Black & Decker, offered the following set of guidelines on global product development:[57]

---

[56]Cheryl Nakata and K. Sivakumar, "National Culture and New Product Development: An Integrative Review," *Journal of Marketing*, 60 (1) (January 1996), pp. 61–72.

[57]Don R. Graber, "How to Manage a Global Product Development Process," *Industrial Marketing Management*, 25 (1996), pp. 483–89.

- Start with the consumer. Understand the commonalities and differences in regional needs.
- Do not try to make a product more global than it really is. A good, well-executed regional product is better than a "poorly executed" global product.

- Global business teams that are multifunctional and multigeographic are very helpful in supporting a global product program.
- Top managerial commitment and support is absolutely essential.

REVIEW QUESTIONS

1. Under what conditions is a dual extension strategy advisable? When is product invention more appropriate?

2. Explain the difference between the modular and core-product approaches.

3. Discuss the forces that favor a globalized product design strategy.

4. In what sense is the "standardize versus customize" question in global product design a bogus issue?

5. MNCs tend to move more and more toward a sprinkler strategy in terms of their global launch timing decisions. What forces lie behind this trend?

6. What are the major dangers in using an entire country as a "test market" for new products that are to be launched globally (or regionally)?

DISCUSSION QUESTIONS

1. Do you agree/disagree with the following statement recently made by John Dooner, chairman-CEO of McCann-Erickson Worldwide, a global advertising agency (*Advertising Age International*, September 1996, p. I-21):

   "The old global view was that a centrally developed brand idea could be made relevant in just about any market, depending on how it was adapted. The reality of the new globalism is that a brand viewpoint that starts out being relevant in one market can become relevant in others, because of the nature of converging consumers. Creative ideas literally can come from anywhere, as long as there is a coordinated system for recognizing and disseminating these ideas. Countries that were once thought of as only being on the receiving end of global ideas can now also be the creators and exporters of these ideas."

2. The median income of consumers in emerging markets like India, Vietnam, and the Philippines is a small fraction of the median income level in developed markets. Given the low buying power, the price charged in Western countries for many impulse items would represent a major expense in developing countries. The retail price for a pack of Wrigley chewing gum in the United States is a quarter for a five-stick package. What product policy options might Wrigley consider to make its product more affordable to local consumers in, say, the Philippines?

3. A few years ago, Discovery Communications, the parent company of the Discovery Channel, made a decision to create a global TV brand. It now reaches almost 90 million subscribers in ninety countries. The Discovery Channel's programming includes history, nature, science, travel, and technology. In light of McLuhan's "global village" do you feel that there is potential for simply offering the U.S. program schedule, or should the Discovery Channel adapt its product to local markets?

4. Recently, Whirlpool's Swedish division developed the VIP microwave oven. This microwave oven uses state-of-the-art technology and has several advanced features. Imagine that Whirlpool would like to introduce this new model in Asia. In its 1995 Annual Report, Whirlpool notes that microwave ovens have become "global products." Would Whirlpool be able to launch the VIP as a truly "global product," or do you think they probably would need to adapt the product?

5. Many Japanese companies do not follow the typical new product development process (idea generation → screening → . . . → commercialization). Instead, they practice "product churning": make a batch of the new product and then see whether Japanese consumers buy the product. After the product is launched, other entrants often introduce me-too versions. What are the possible benefits of this approach compared to the Western NPD model?

6. What particular challenges do you see for companies introducing product categories that are truly new—recent examples include frozen yogurt (TCBY) and breakfast cereals (Kellogg's) in China; iced tea (Snapple) in Europe—into the foreign market? How might the marketing mix strategies used by the companies involved differ from the strategies used in the more developed markets?

7. *Assignment.* Most annual reports have some discussion on the product strategies that are used. Get a recent annual report of at least two multinational companies in the same industry (many companies now put their annual report on the World Wide Web). How do their global product strategies differ? What do they have in common? How do the companies organize their global product development efforts?

FURTHER READINGS ◆

Bose, Amit, and Khushi Khanna. "The Little Emperor. A Case Study of a New Brand Launch." *Marketing and Research Today* (November 1996):216–21.

Czinkota, Michael, and Masaaki Kotabe. "Product Development the Japanese Way." *Journal of Business Strategy* (Nov./Dec. 1990):31–36.

Garber, Don. "How to Manage a Global Product Development Process." *Industrial Marketing Management*, 25 (1996):483–89.

Gatignon, Hubert, Jehoshua Eliashberg, and Thomas S. Robertson. "Modeling Multinational Diffusion Patterns: An Efficient Methodology." *Marketing Science*, 8 (Summer 1989):231–47.

Gupta, Ashok K., Klaus Brockhoff, and Ursula Weisenfeld. "Making Trade-Offs in the New Product Development Process: A German/US Comparison." *Journal of Product Innovation Management*, 9 (1992):11–18.

Herbig, Paul A., and Fred Palumbo. "A Brief Examination of the Japanese Innovative Process: Part 2." *Marketing Intelligence & Planning*, 12 (2) (1994):38–42.

Kalish, Shlomo, Vijay Mahajan, and Eitan Muller. "Waterfall and Sprinkler New-Product Strategies in Competitive Global Markets." *International Journal of Research in Marketing*, 12 (July 1995):105–19.

Keegan, Warren J., and C.S. Mayer, (eds.) *Multinational Product Management.* Chicago: American Marketing Association, 1977.

Kleinschmidt, E. J. "A Comparative Analysis of New Product Programmes." *European Journal of Marketing*, 28 (7) (1994):5–29.

Lynn, Michael, and Betsy D. Gelb. "Identifying innovative national markets for technical consumer goods." *International Marketing Review*, 13 (6) (1996):43–57.

Nakata, Cheryl, and K. Sivakumar. "National Culture and New Product Development: An Integrative Review." *Journal of Marketing*, 60 (January 1996):61–72.

Song, X. Michael, and Mark E. Parry. "The Dimensions of Industrial New Product Success and Failure in State Enterprises in the People's Republic of China." *Journal of Product Innovation Management*, 11 (2) (1994):105–18.

Song, X. Michael, and Mark E. Parry. "The Determinants of Japanese New Product Sucesses." *Journal of Marketing Research* (February 1997):64–76.

Takada, Hirokazu, and Dipak Jain. "Cross-National Analysis of Diffusion of Consumer Durable Goods in Pacific Rim Countries." *Journal of Marketing*, 55 (April 1991):48–54.

Walters, Peter G. P., and Brian Toyne. "Product Modification and Standardization in International Markets: Strategic Options and Facilitating Policies." *Columbia Journal of World Business*, 24 (Winter 1989):37–44.

POPULATION

Note: Size of each country is proportional to population.

Tints indicate rate of natural increase.

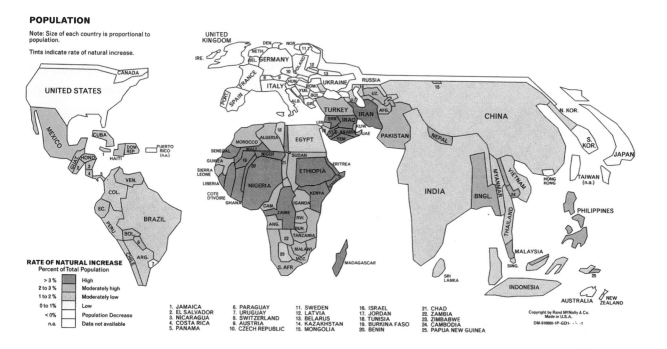

RATE OF NATURAL INCREASE
Percent of Total Population

> 3 %	High
2 to 3 %	Moderately high
1 to 2 %	Moderately low
0 to 1%	Low
< 0%	Population Decrease
n.a.	Data not available

1. JAMAICA
2. EL SALVADOR
3. NICARAGUA
4. COSTA RICA
5. PANAMA
6. PARAGUAY
7. URUGUAY
8. SWITZERLAND
9. AUSTRIA
10. CZECH REPUBLIC
11. SWEDEN
12. LATVIA
13. BELARUS
14. KAZAKHSTAN
15. MONGOLIA
16. ISRAEL
17. JORDAN
18. TUNISIA
19. BURKINA FASO
20. BENIN
21. CHAD
22. ZAMBIA
23. ZIMBABWE
24. CAMBODIA
25. PAPUA NEW GUINEA

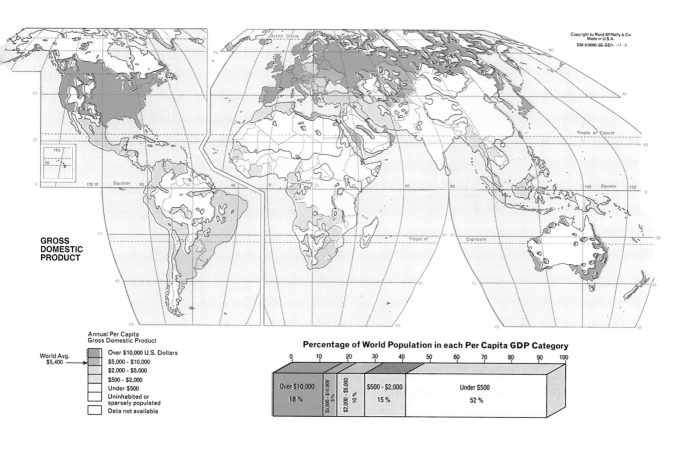

GROSS DOMESTIC PRODUCT

Annual Per Capita Gross Domestic Product

World Avg. $5,400 →

	Over $10,000 U.S. Dollars
	$5,000 - $10,000
	$2,000 - $5,000
	$500 - $2,000
	Under $500
	Uninhabited or sparsely populated
	Data not available

Percentage of World Population in each Per Capita GDP Category

Over $10,000 18 %	$5,000-$10,000 5%	$2,000-$5,000 10 %	$500 - $2,000 15 %	Under $500 52 %

All maps used with permission from Goode's World Atlas, 19th edition. Copyright © 1995 Rand McNally.

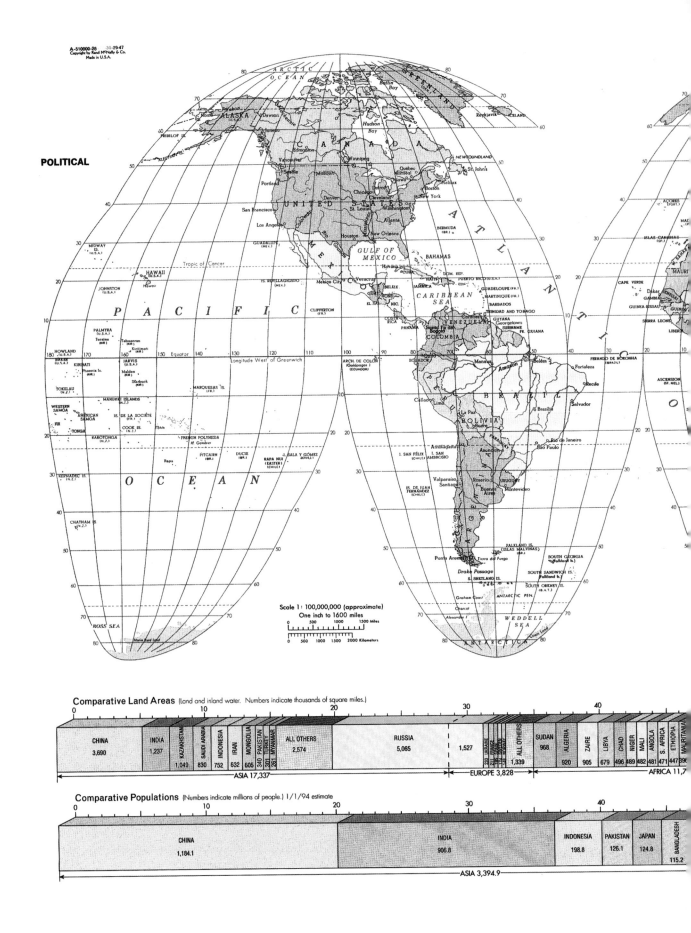

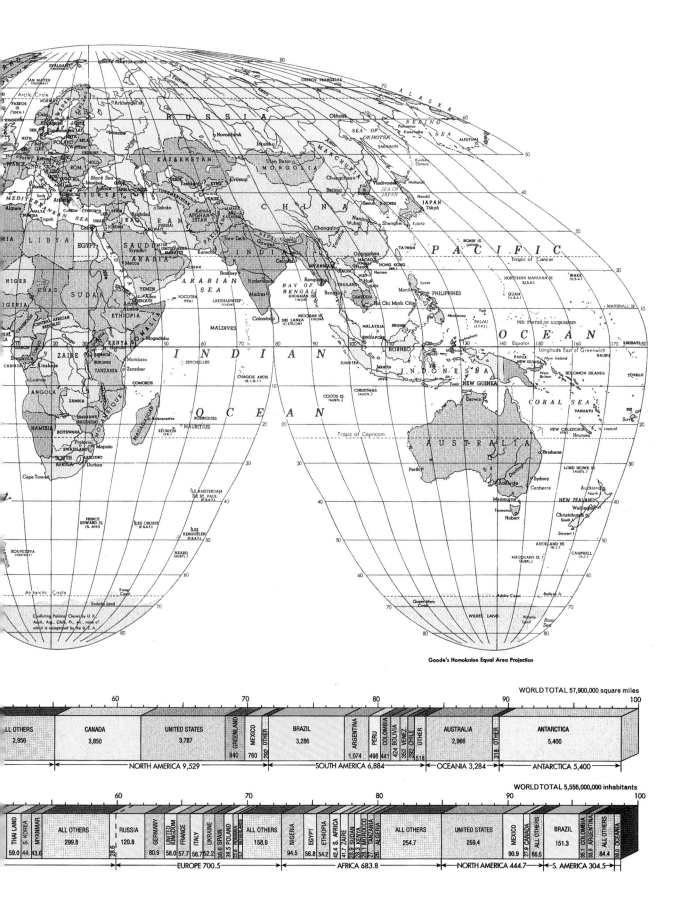

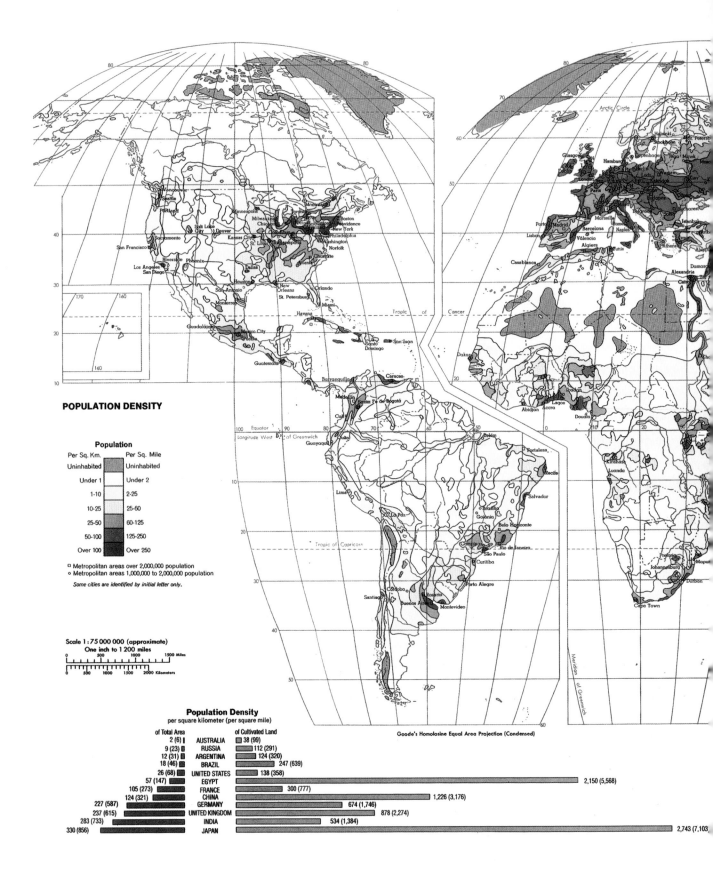

POPULATION DENSITY

Population

Per Sq. Km.		Per Sq. Mile
Uninhabited		Uninhabited
Under 1		Under 2
1-10		2-25
10-25		25-60
25-50		60-125
50-100		125-250
Over 100		Over 250

□ Metropolitan areas over 2,000,000 population
○ Metropolitan areas 1,000,000 to 2,000,000 population

Some cities are identified by initial letter only.

Scale 1 : 75 000 000 (approximate)
One inch to 1 200 miles

0   500   1000   1500 Miles

0   500   1000   1500   2000 Kilometers

Population Density
per square kilometer (per square mile)

of Total Area		of Cultivated Land
2 (6)	AUSTRALIA	38 (99)
9 (23)	RUSSIA	112 (291)
12 (31)	ARGENTINA	124 (320)
18 (46)	BRAZIL	247 (639)
26 (68)	UNITED STATES	138 (358)
57 (147)	EGYPT	2,150 (5,568)
105 (273)	FRANCE	300 (777)
124 (321)	CHINA	1,226 (3,176)
227 (587)	GERMANY	674 (1,746)
237 (615)	UNITED KINGDOM	878 (2,274)
283 (733)	INDIA	534 (1,384)
330 (856)	JAPAN	2,743 (7,103)

Goode's Homolosine Equal Area Projection (Condensed)

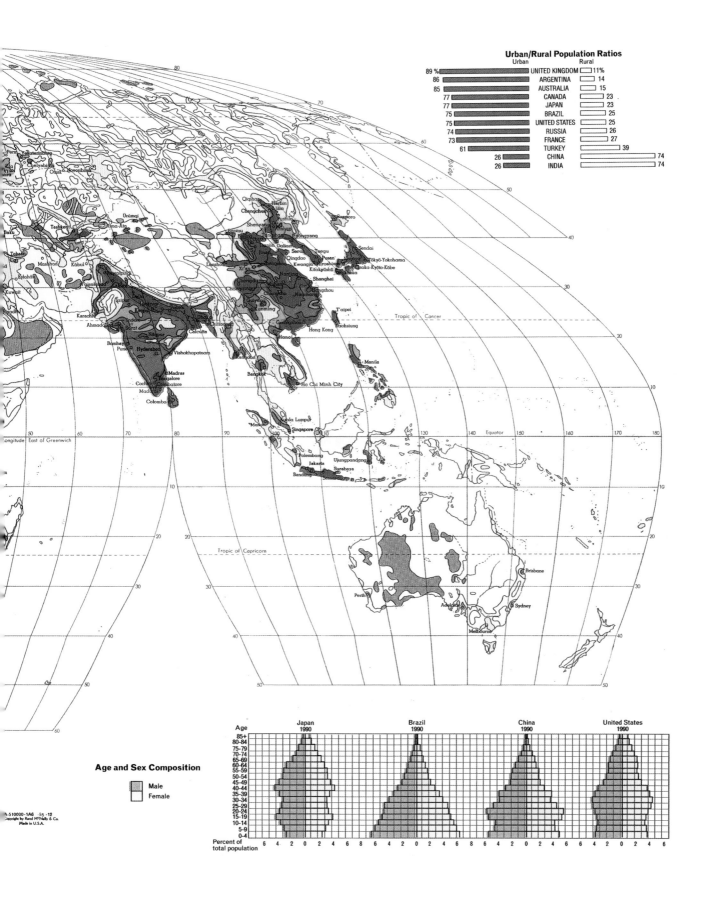

Urban/Rural Population Ratios

	Urban		Rural
89 %		UNITED KINGDOM	11%
86		ARGENTINA	14
85		AUSTRALIA	15
77		CANADA	23
77		JAPAN	23
75		BRAZIL	25
75		UNITED STATES	25
74		RUSSIA	26
73		FRANCE	27
61		TURKEY	39
26		CHINA	74
26		INDIA	74

Age and Sex Composition

Male
Female

Japan 1990 Brazil 1990 China 1990 United States 1990

Age
85+
80-84
75-79
70-74
65-69
60-64
55-59
50-54
45-49
40-44
35-39
30-34
25-29
20-24
15-19
10-14
5-9
0-4
Percent of
total population

6 4 2 0 2 4 6 8   6 4 2 0 2 4 6 8   6 4 2 0 2 4 6   6 4 2 0 2 4 6

A-510000-1A6 85 -12
Copyright by Rand M°Nally & Co.
Made in U.S.A.

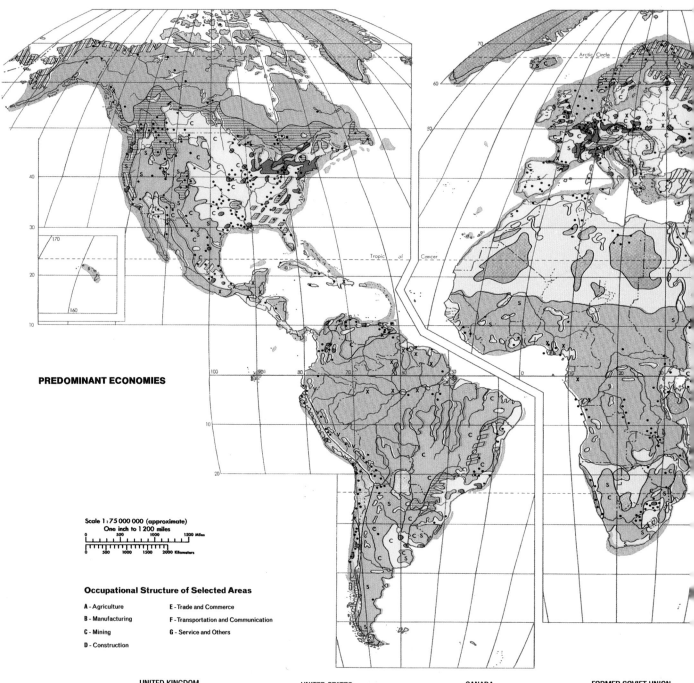

PREDOMINANT ECONOMIES

Scale 1 : 75 000 000 (approximate)
One inch to 1 200 miles

Occupational Structure of Selected Areas

A - Agriculture   E - Trade and Commerce

B - Manufacturing   F - Transportation and Communication

C - Mining   G - Service and Others

D - Construction

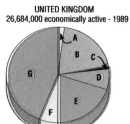

UNITED KINGDOM
26,684,000 economically active - 1989

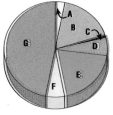

UNITED STATES
116,877,000 economically active - 1991

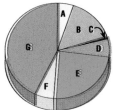

CANADA
12,340,000 economically active - 1991

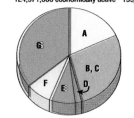

FORMER SOVIET UNION
124,971,000 economically active - 199

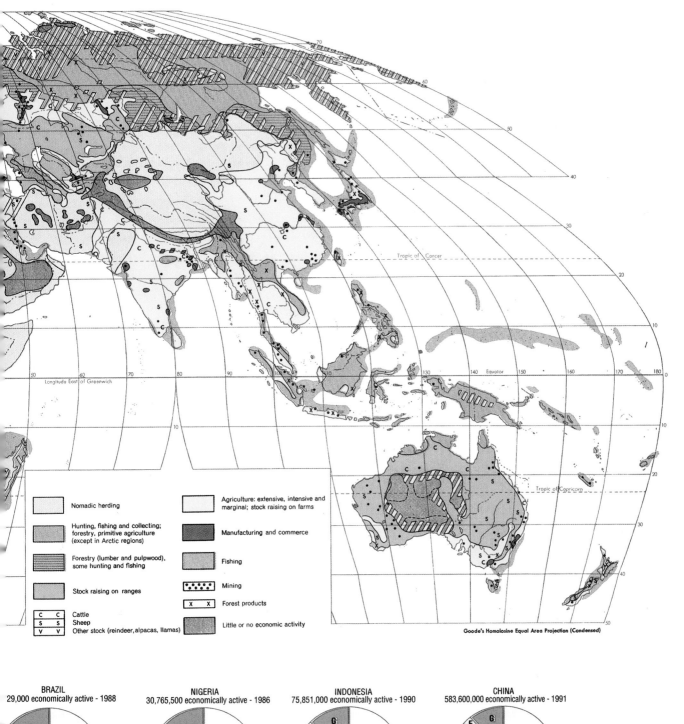

Nomadic herding

Hunting, fishing and collecting; forestry, primitive agriculture (except in Arctic regions)

Forestry (lumber and pulpwood), some hunting and fishing

Stock raising on ranges

C	C	Cattle
S	S	Sheep
V	V	Other stock (reindeer, alpacas, llamas)

Agriculture: extensive, intensive and marginal; stock raising on farms

Manufacturing and commerce

Fishing

• • • • • Mining

X   X Forest products

Little or no economic activity

Goode's Homolosine Equal Area Projection (Condensed)

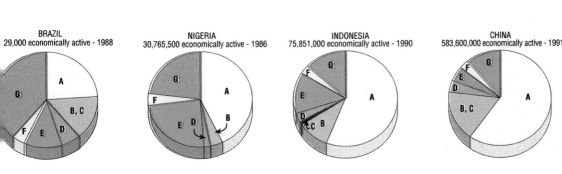

BRAZIL
29,000 economically active - 1988

NIGERIA
30,765,500 economically active - 1986

INDONESIA
75,851,000 economically active - 1990

CHINA
583,600,000 economically active - 1991

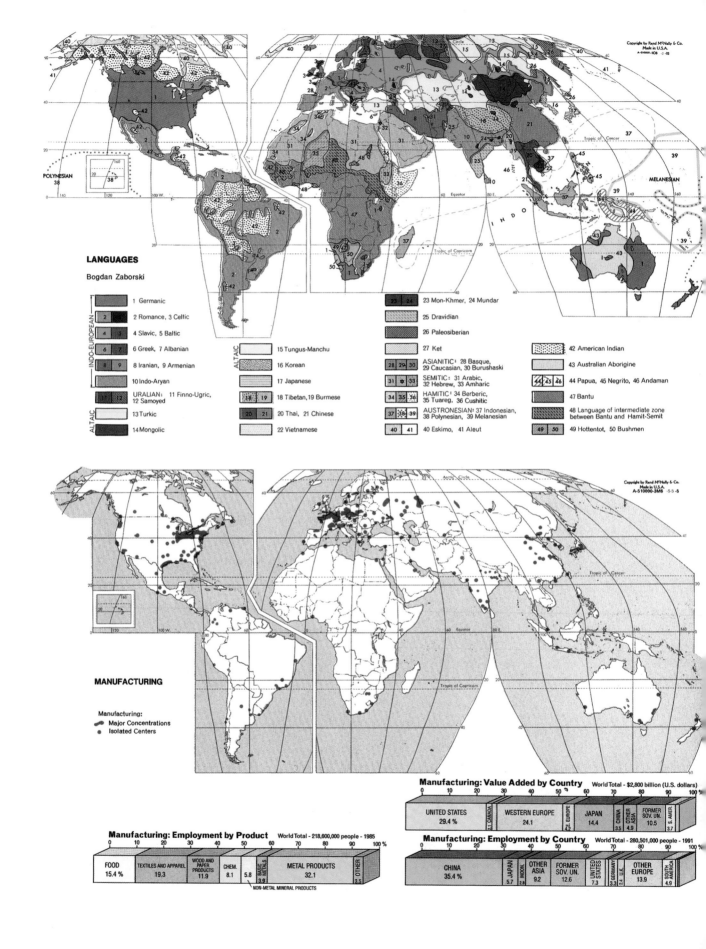

LANGUAGES

Bogdan Zaborski

INDO-EUROPEAN
- 1 Germanic
- 2 Romance, 3 Celtic
- 4 Slavic, 5 Baltic
- 6 Greek, 7 Albanian
- 8 Iranian, 9 Armenian
- 10 Indo-Aryan

URALIAN: 11 Finno-Ugric, 12 Samoyed

ALTAIC
- 13 Turkic
- 14 Mongolic
- 15 Tungus-Manchu
- 16 Korean
- 17 Japanese
- 18 Tibetan, 19 Burmese
- 20 Thai, 21 Chinese
- 22 Vietnamese

- 23 Mon-Khmer, 24 Mundar
- 25 Dravidian
- 26 Paleosiberian
- 27 Ket
- ASIANITIC: 28 Basque, 29 Caucasian, 30 Burushaski
- SEMITIC: 31 Arabic, 32 Hebrew, 33 Amharic
- HAMITIC: 34 Berberic, 35 Tuareg, 36 Cushitic
- AUSTRONESIAN: 37 Indonesian, 38 Polynesian, 39 Melanesian
- 40 Eskimo, 41 Aleut

- 42 American Indian
- 43 Australian Aborigine
- 44 Papua, 45 Negrito, 46 Andaman
- 47 Bantu
- 48 Language of intermediate zone between Bantu and Hamit-Semit
- 49 Hottentot, 50 Bushmen

MANUFACTURING

Manufacturing:
- Major Concentrations
- Isolated Centers

Manufacturing: Value Added by Country
World Total - $2,800 billion (U.S. dollars)

UNITED STATES 29.4 %	CANADA	WESTERN EUROPE 24.1	CE. EUROPE	JAPAN 14.4	CHINA 3.5	OTHER ASIA 4.9	FORMER SOV. UN. 10.5	S. AMER.

Manufacturing: Employment by Product
World Total - 218,600,000 people - 1985

FOOD 15.4 %	TEXTILES AND APPAREL 19.3	WOOD AND PAPER PRODUCTS 11.9	CHEM. 8.1	5.8	BASIC METALS 3.9	METAL PRODUCTS 32.1	OTHER 3.5

NON-METAL MINERAL PRODUCTS

Manufacturing: Employment by Country
World Total - 280,501,000 people - 1991

CHINA 35.4 %	JAPAN 5.7	INDON. 2.8	OTHER ASIA 9.2	FORMER SOV. UN. 12.6	UNITED STATES 7.3	GERMANY 3.3	U.K. 2.4	OTHER EUROPE 13.9	SOUTH AMERICA 4.9

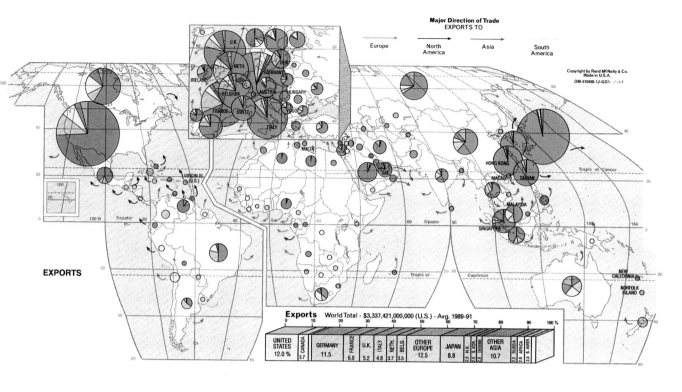

Copyright by Rand McNally & Co.
Made in U.S.A.
DM-515400-1J-GD1- -i-1-1

Major Direction of Trade
EXPORTS TO

Europe   North   Asia   South
          America   America

EXPORTS

Exports World Total - $3,337,421,000,000 (U.S.) - Avg. 1989-91

UNITED STATES 12.0 %	CANADA 3.7	GERMANY 11.5	FRANCE 6.0	U.K. 5.2	ITALY 4.8	NETH. 3.7	BELG. 3.5	OTHER EUROPE 12.5	JAPAN 8.8	H.K. 2.5	S. KOR 2.1	TAIWAN 2.0	OTHER ASIA 10.7	RUSSIA 2.2	AFRICA 2.6	S. AMER. 2.5

Volume of Trade
(in millions of U.S. dollars - Avg. 1989-91)

500,000
200,000
100,000
50,000
20,000
10,000
500 - 2,000

If volume of trade is less than 10 billion dollars, color
indicates major class only. If no symbol is shown,
volume of trade is less than 500 million dollars.

Composition of Trade

Manufactured   Food, Beverages,   Raw   Fuel &   All other or
Articles   & Tobacco   Materials   Related Products   undifferentiated

Major Direction of Trade
IMPORTS FROM

Europe   North   Asia   South
          America   America

Copyright by Rand McNally & Co.
Made in U.S.A.
DM-515400-1Q-GD1- -i-1-1

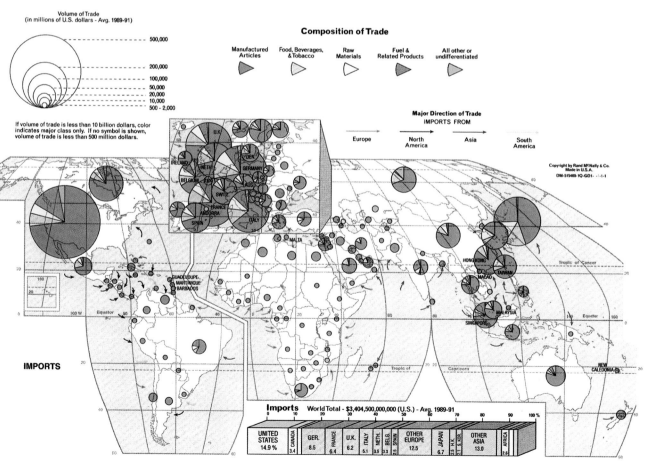

IMPORTS

Imports World Total - $3,404,500,000,000 (U.S.) - Avg. 1989-91

UNITED STATES 14.9 %	CANADA 3.4	GER. 8.5	FRANCE 6.4	U.K. 6.2	ITALY 5.1	NETH. 3.5	BELG. 3.3	SPAIN	OTHER EUROPE 12.5	JAPAN 6.7	H.K. 2.5	S. KOR 2.1	OTHER ASIA 13.0	AFRICA 2.6

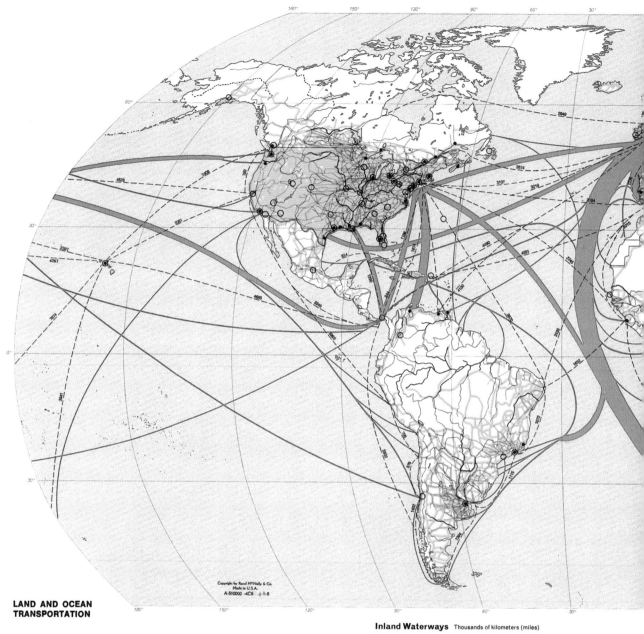

LAND AND OCEAN TRANSPORTATION

Vehicles Per kilometer (mile) of motorable road

INDIA	1.5 (2.5)
CHINA	5.8 (8.8)
FORMER SOV. UN.	24.4 (39.3)
ARGENTINA	25.2 (40.6)
UNITED STATES	29.4 (47.3)
FRANCE	32.6 (52.4)
UNITED KINGDOM	56.8 (91.5)

Persons per Vehicle

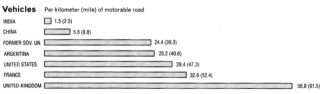

UNITED STATES	1.3
FRANCE	2.0
UNITED KINGDOM	2.2
ARGENTINA	5.6
FORMER SOV. UN.	11.9
INDIA	179.1
CHINA	186.7

Inland Waterways Thousands of kilometers (miles)

ARGENTINA	3.2 (2.0)
UNITED KINGDOM	4.2 (2.6)
INDIA	8.2 (5.1)
FRANCE	10.3 (6.4)
CHINA	40.2 (25.0)
UNITED STATES	46.7 (29.0)
FORMER SOV. UN.	140.0 (87

Railroads and Motorable Roads Kilometers per 100 square kilometers (miles per 100 square miles)

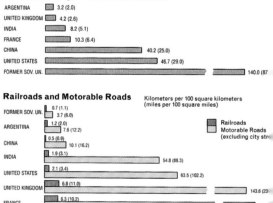

	Railroads	Motorable Roads (excluding city stre
FORMER SOV. UN.	0.7 (1.1)	3.7 (6.0)
ARGENTINA	1.2 (2.0)	7.6 (12.2)
CHINA	0.5 (0.9)	10.1 (16.2)
INDIA	1.9 (3.1)	54.8 (88.3)
UNITED STATES	2.1 (3.4)	63.5 (102.2)
UNITED KINGDOM	6.8 (11.0)	143.6 (23
FRANCE	6.3 (10.2)	147

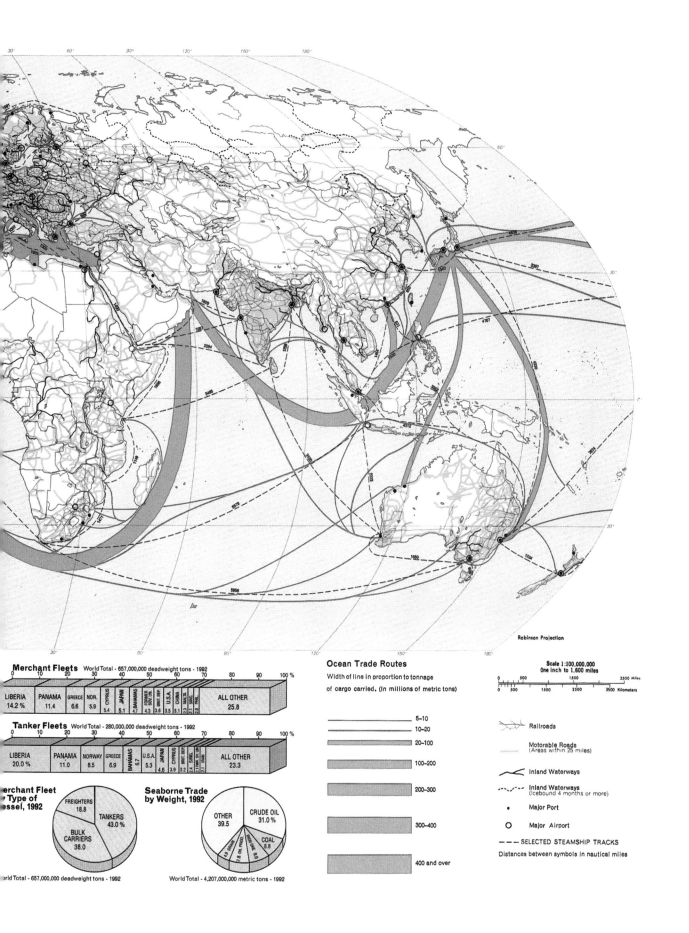

Robinson Projection

Merchant Fleets
World Total - 657,000,000 deadweight tons - 1992

	0 10 20 30 40 50 60 70 80 90 100 %

LIBERIA 14.2%	PANAMA 11.4	GREECE 6.6	NOR. 5.9	CYPRUS 5.4	JAPAN 5.1	BAHAMAS 4.7	FORMER SOV. UN. 4.3	BRIT. REP. 3.6	U.S.A. 3.5	CHINA 3.1	MALTA 2.3	SING. 2.9	PHIL.	ALL OTHER 25.8

Tanker Fleets
World Total - 280,000,000 deadweight tons - 1992

	0 10 20 30 40 50 60 70 80 90 100 %

LIBERIA 20.0%	PANAMA 11.0	NORWAY 8.5	GREECE 6.9	BAHAMAS 6.7	U.S.A. 5.3	JAPAN 4.6	CYPRUS 3.9	BRIT. REP. 3.2	FMR. SV. UN. 2.4	IRAN 2.1	ALL OTHER 23.3

Merchant Fleet by Type of Vessel, 1992

- FREIGHTERS 18.8
- TANKERS 43.0%
- BULK CARRIERS 38.0

World Total - 657,000,000 deadweight tons - 1992

Seaborne Trade by Weight, 1992

- OTHER 39.5
- CRUDE OIL 31.0%
- COAL 8.8
- IRON ORE 8.0
- OIL PROD. 7.8
- GRAIN 4.9

World Total - 4,207,000,000 metric tons - 1992

Ocean Trade Routes

Width of line in proportion to tonnage
of cargo carried. (In millions of metric tons)

————	5–10
————	10–20
————	20–100
▬▬▬▬	100–200
▬▬▬▬	200–300
▬▬▬▬	300–400
▬▬▬▬	400 and over

Scale 1:100,000,000
One inch to 1,600 miles

0 500 1500 2500 Miles
0 500 1500 3500 Kilometers

- ⟋⟍ Railroads
- Motorable Roads (Areas within 25 miles)
- ⟋⟍ Inland Waterways
- – – – Inland Waterways (Icebound 4 months or more)
- • Major Port
- ○ Major Airport
- – – – SELECTED STEAMSHIP TRACKS

Distances between symbols in nautical miles

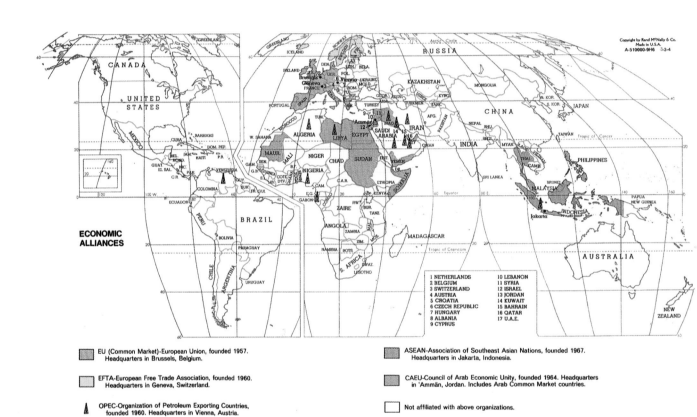

ECONOMIC ALLIANCES

1 NETHERLANDS	10 LEBANON
2 BELGIUM	11 SYRIA
3 SWITZERLAND	12 ISRAEL
4 AUSTRIA	13 JORDAN
5 CROATIA	14 KUWAIT
6 CZECH REPUBLIC	15 BAHRAIN
7 HUNGARY	16 QATAR
8 ALBANIA	17 U.A.E.
9 CYPRUS	

EU (Common Market)-European Union, founded 1957. Headquarters in Brussels, Belgium.

EFTA-European Free Trade Association, founded 1960. Headquarters in Geneva, Switzerland.

OPEC-Organization of Petroleum Exporting Countries, founded 1960. Headquarters in Vienna, Austria.

ASEAN-Association of Southeast Asian Nations, founded 1967. Headquarters in Jakarta, Indonesia.

CAEU-Council of Arab Economic Unity, founded 1964. Headquarters in 'Ammän, Jordan. Includes Arab Common Market countries.

Not affiliated with above organizations.

Copyright by Rand McNally & Co.
Made in U.S.A.
A-510000-9H6 3-3-4

GLOBAL PRODUCT POLICY DECISIONS II: MARKETING PRODUCTS AND SERVICES

12

HAPTER OVERVIEW

1. GLOBAL BRANDING STRATEGIES
2. MANAGING MULTINATIONAL PRODUCT LINES
3. PRODUCT PIRACY
4. COUNTRY OF ORIGIN STEREOTYPES
5. GLOBAL MARKETING OF SERVICES

The previous chapter focused on new product development in the global arena. Managing the new product development process is only one part (albeit a crucial part) of the responsibilities of global product policy makers. In this chapter we continue with our discussion of international product policy decisions. The topics considered in this chapter relate to managing a multinational product portfolio.

Companies that brand their products have various options when they sell their goods in multiple countries. More and more companies see global (or at least regional) branding as a must. Nevertheless, quite a few firms still stick to local branding strategies. In between these two extreme alternatives, there are scores of variations. This chapter will consider and assess different global branding approaches. Next, we shift our attention to the managing of an international product line. Multinational product-line management entails issues such as: What product assortment should the company launch when it first enters a new market? How should the firm expand its multinational product line over time? What product lines should be added or dropped?

Another concern that global marketers face is the issue of product piracy. In this chapter we will suggest several approaches that can be employed to tackle counterfeiting. A lot of research has investigated the impact of country-of-origin effects on consumer attitudes toward a product. We will explore the major findings of this research stream and examine different strategies that firms can use to handle negative country-of-origin stereotypes. The balance of this chapter covers the unique problems of marketing services internationally. Services differ from tangible products in many respects. What these differences imply in terms of market opportunities, challenges, and marketing strategies will be discussed in the last section.

◆ ◆ ◆ ◆ ◆ ◆   GLOBAL BRANDING STRATEGIES

Sara Lee, a U.S. Fortune 500 company, has 25,000 trademarks registered worldwide, 80 percent of which are in current use.[1] One of the major tasks that international marketers like Sara Lee face is the management of their company's brand portfolio. For many firms the brands they own are their most valuable assets. A brand can be defined as "a name, term, sign, symbol, or combination of them which is intended to identify the goods and services of one seller or group of sellers and to differentiate them from those of competitors."[2] Linked to a brand name is a collection of assets and liabilities—the **brand equity** tied to the brand name. These include brand-name awareness, perceived quality, and any other associations invoked by the brand name in the customer's mind. The concerns that are to be addressed when building up and managing brand equity in a multinational setting include:[3]

- How do we strike the balance between a global brand that shuns cultural barriers and one that allows for local requirements?
- What aspects of the brand policy can be adapted to global use? Which ones should remain flexible?
- Which brands are destined to become "global" mega-brands? Which ones should be kept as "local" brands?
- How do you condense a multitude of local brands (like in the case of Sara Lee) into a smaller, more manageable number of global (or regional) brands?
- How do you execute the changeover from a local to a global brand?
- How do you build up a portfolio of global mega-brands?

Suffice it to say, there are no simple answers to these questions. In what follows, we will touch on the major issues regarding international branding.

Global Brands

Reflect on your most recent trip overseas and some of the shopping expeditions that you undertook. Several of the brand names that you saw there probably sounded quite familiar: McDonald's, Coca-Cola, Levi Strauss, Canon, Rolex. On the other hand, there were most likely some products that carried brand names that you had never heard of before, or that were slight (or even drastic) variations of brand names

---

[1] Keith Alm, formerly Senior Vice-President Pacific Rim, Sara Lee, private communication, 1994.

[2] Philip H. Kotler, *Marketing Management: Analysis, Planning and Control*, 8th ed. (Englewood Cliffs, N.J.: Prentice-Hall, 1991).

[3] Jean-Noel Kapferer, *Strategic Brand Management. New Approaches to Creating and Evaluating Brand Equity* (London: Kogan Page, 1992), p. 148.

with a more familiar ring. A key strategic issue that appears on international marketers' agendas is whether or not there should be a **global brand.** What conditions favor launching a product with a single brand name worldwide? the same logo? maybe even the same slogan? When is it more appropriate to keep brand names local? In between these two extremes, you might consider several other options. For instance, some companies use local brand names but at the same time put a corporate banner brand name on their products (e.g., "Findus by Nestlé").

Exhibit 12-1 gives an overview of the top twenty-five brands in the Triad markets. The rankings are based on a survey that measured share-of-mind ("SOM")—meaning brand awareness—and esteem for each of the brands listed. Eyeballing the table, you can spot several brands that show up in all four rankings: Coca-Cola, Sony, among others. However, the majority of the brands appear in only two (e.g., Mercedes in Europe and Japan, Disney in the United States and Japan) or even one of the rankings. This indicates that "truly" global brands are still a rare phenomenon.

What is the case for global branding? One advantage of having a global brand name is obvious: economies of scale. First and foremost, the development costs for products launched under the global brand name can be spread over large volumes. This is especially a bonus in high-tech industries (e.g., pharmaceuticals, computing, chemicals, automobiles) where multibillion dollar R & D projects are the norm. Scale economies also arise in manufacturing, distribution (warehousing and shipping), and, possibly, promotion of a single-brand product. As we noted in the last chapter, computerized design and manufacturing processes allow companies to harvest the scale benefits of mass production while customizing the product to the needs of the local market. Even then, substantial scale advantages on the distribution and marketing front often strongly favor global branding.

The scale advantage is only one reason for using a global brand name.[4] Part of the task of brand managers is building up brand awareness. By its very nature, a global brand has much more visibility than a local brand. Prospective customers who travel around may be exposed to the brand both in their home country and in many of the countries they visit. Therefore, it is typically far easier to build up brand awareness for a global brand than for a local brand. A global brand can also capitalize on the extensive media overlap that exists in many regions. Cable-TV subscribers in Europe and many Asian countries have access to scores of channels from neighboring countries. Advertising a global brand on one or more of these channels can mean more bang-for-the-bucks.

A further benefit is the prestige factor. Simply stated, the fact of being *global* adds to the image of your brand: it signals that you have the resources to compete globally, it signals that you have the willpower and commitment to support your brand worldwide.[5] Positioning yourself as a global brand can be very effective if you are able to claim leadership in your home country, especially when there is a favorable match between the product and the country image. After years of an uphill struggle, Marlboro quickly became the leading cigarette brand in Hong Kong when it positioned itself as being the leading brand in the United States. Global brands that can claim worldwide leadership in their product category have even more clout: Colgate, Marlboro, Coca-Cola, and Nike, to mention just a few.

---

[4]David A. Aaker, *Managing Brand Equity. Capitalizing on the Value of a Brand Name* (New York: The Free Press, 1991), pp. 264–8.

[5]David A. Aaker, *Building Strong Brands* (New York: The Free Press, 1996), p. 130.

EXHIBIT 12-1
TOP 25 BRANDS IN THE UNITED STATES, EUROPE, JAPAN, AND WORLDWIDE

	United States			Europe			Japan			World		
	Brand	SOM	Esteem	Brand	SOM	Esteem	Brand	SOM	Esteem	Brand	SOM	Esteem
1	Coca-Cola	1	5	Coca-Cola	1	10	Sony	1	4	Coca-Cola	1	6
2	Campbell's	6	1	Sony	3	1	National	4	9	Sony	4	1
3	Disney	10	2	Mercedes-Benz	8	3	Mercedes-Benz	50	2	Mercedes-Benz	12	2
4	Pepsi-Cola	4	11	BMW	11	2	Toyota	9	18	Kodak	5	9
5	Kodak	8	4	Philips	2	6	Takashimaya	5	25	Disney	8	5
6	NBC	3	16	Volkswagen	4	7	Rolls Royce	100	1	Nestlé	7	14
7	Black & Decker	15	3	Adidas	6	9	Seiko	21	14	Toyota	6	23
8	Kellogg's	9	7	Kodak	7	8	Matsushita	18	20	McDonald's	2	85
9	McDonald's	2	84	Nivea	5	14	Hibachi	6	44	IBM	20	4
10	Hershey's	22	6	Porsche	18	4	Suntory	8	42	Pepsi-Cola	3	92
11	Levi's	18	10	Volvo	16	12	Porsche	118	3	Rolls Royce	23	3
12	GE	14	14	Colgate	9	24	Kirin	17	32	Honda	9	22
13	Sears	5	79	Rolls Royce	28	5	Hotel New Otani	78	8	Panasonic	17	10
14	Hallmark	32	9	Levi's	21	13	Fuji TV	7	81	Levi's	16	8
15	Johnson & Johnson	35	8	Ford	15	31	Snow Brand Milk	19	45	Kleenex	13	16
16	Betty Crocker	26	12	Jaguar	38	11	Imperial Hotel	109	7	Ford	10	24
17	Kraft	24	13	Fanta	10	51	Coca-Cola/Coke	3	119	Volkswagen	11	26
18	Kleenex	20	19	Nescafé	13	56	Mitsukoshi	20	48	Kellogg's	14	30
19	Jell-O	16	26	Black & Decker	25	20	Japan Travel Bureau	13	63	Porsche	27	11
20	Tylenol	28	18	Esso	17	42	Disney	55	19	Polaroid	15	44
21	AT & T	12	62	Michelin	29	21	Aunomoto	12	74	BMW	32	12
22	Crest	31	28	Lego	41	15	Kikkoman	14	70	Colgate	21	51
23	Duracell	39	20	Bosch	43	16	All-Nippon-Airlines	28	49	Seiko	33	15
24	IBM	46	17	Peugeot	19	50	Honda	30	50	Nescafé	19	64
25	Fruit of the Loom	25	41	Audi	36	22	Yamaha	38	34	Canon	35	17

Source: Stewart Owen, "The London ImagePower Survey®: A Global Assessment of Brand Strength," in *Brand Equity & Advertising: Advertising's Role in Building Strong Brands*, D.A. Aaker and A. L. Biel, eds. (Hillsdale, N. J.: Erlbaum Associates, 1993).

In some cases global brands are also able to leverage the country association for the product: McDonald's is U.S. fast food, Swatch is a Swiss watch, Nissin Cup is Japanese noodles, and so on. A desire to reflect its American roots also motivated Disney to change the name for its Paris themepark from Euro Disney to Disneyland Paris.[6] Of course, such positioning loses some of its appeal when your competition has the same heritage. For instance, Marlboro is an American cigarette brand, but so are Camel and Salem.

These arguments for global branding sound very powerful. Note, though, that, like many other aspects of global marketing, the value of a brand, its **brand equity,** usually varies a great deal from country to country. A large-scale brand assessment study done by the advertising agency DDB Needham in Europe illustrates this point:[7] brand equity scores for Kodak ranged from 104 in Spain to 130 in the United Kingdom and Italy.[8] Inter-country gaps in brand equity may be due to any of the following factors:

1. **History.** By necessity, brands that have been around for a long time tend to have much more familiarity among consumers than latecomers. Usually, early entrants also will have a much more solid brand image if they have used a consistent positioning strategy over the years.

2. **Competitive climate.** The battlefield varies from country to country. In some countries the brand faces only a few competitors. In others the brand constantly has to break through the clutter and combat scores of competing brands that nibble away at its market share.

3. **Marketing support.** Especially in decentralized organizations, the communication strategy used to back up the brand can vary a great deal. Some country affiliates favor marketing push, using trade promotions and other incentives targeted toward distributors. Others might prefer a pull strategy and thus focus on the end-consumers. It is not uncommon for the positioning theme used in the advertising messages to vary from country to country.

4. **Cultural receptivity to brands.** Another factor is the cultural receptivity to brands. Brand receptivity is largely driven by risk aversion. Within Europe, countries such as Spain and Italy are much more receptive toward brand names than Germany or France.[9] Asian societies tend to be very group-oriented. Being part of a group means sharing values and product experiences. As a result, this sense for collectivism leads to high levels of brand loyalty in Asian countries.

5. **Product category penetration.** A final factor is the salience of the product category in which the brand competes. Because of lifestyle differences, a given category will be established much more solidly in some countries than in others. In general, brand equity and product salience go together: the higher the product usage, the more solid will be the brand equity.

---

[6]"The Kingdom Inside a Republic," *The Economist* (April 13, 1996), pp. 68–69.

[7]Jeri Moore, "Building Brands Across Markets: Cultural Differences in Brand Relationships within the European Community," in *Brand Equity & Advertising: Advertising's Role in Building Strong Brands*, D.A. Aaker and A.L. Biel, eds (Hillsdale, N.J.: Erlbaum Associates, 1993), 31–49.

[8]The scores were derived via a multiplication formula: Brand Awareness × Brand Liking × Brand Perception.

[9]Moore, p. 44.

Local Branding

Although the advantages of a global brand name are numerous, there are also substantial benefits of using a local brand. In some cases legal constraints force the company to adopt a local brand name or "localize" an existing brand. In 1996 the Vietnamese government imposed new regulations that required that all brand names be localized. Billboards that did not comply with the new legislation were painted over.

In some cases, a local brand becomes necessary because the name or a very similar name is already used within the country in another (or even the same) product category. The U.S. beer brewer Anheuser-Busch had to modify the name for its flagship brand Budweiser in Europe: in most of Europe it chose the name Bud, in Germany Budweiser became Anheuser-Busch B. This name adaptation was due to the fact that the Budweiser brand name is owned by a Czech brewer in much of continental Europe.[10]

Cultural barriers also often justify local branding. Without localizing the brand name, the name might be hard to pronounce or may have undesirable associations in the local language. Soft drinks like the Japanese brew Pocari Sweat and the Dutch beverage Sisi would have a hard sell in Anglo-Saxon countries. Associations linked to the brand name often lose their relevance in the foreign market.[11] Brand names like "Snuggle," "Healthy Choice," "Weight Watchers" or "I Can't Believe It's Not Butter" don't mean much in non–English-speaking markets.

A local linkage can also prove helpful in countries where patriotism and buy-local attitudes matter. Under such circumstances, the local brand name offers a cue that the company cares about local sensitivities. U S West, an American telecom, drops the U S West name in its foreign market, the reason being that "It's better to build up a name suiting the local market."[12] America Online, the leading online service provider in the United States, decided to call itself AOL in its foreign markets in order not to be perceived as a U.S.-centered product.[13]

When the local brand name stems from an acquisition, keeping the local brand can be preferable to changing it into a global brand name. The brand equity built up over the years for the local brand can often be a tremendous asset. Thus, one motive for sticking with the local brand name is that the potential pay-offs from transforming it into a global brand name do not outweigh the equity that would have to be sacrificed.

Global or Local Brands?

By now you probably realize that there are no simple answers to the global-versus-local brand dilemma. Companies such as Nestlé and Sara Lee have a portfolio of local, regional, and global brands. Take Sara Lee, for example. The company[14] describes its brand portfolio as a "hierarchy" of brands (see Exhibit 12-2).

---

[10]"Anheuser-Busch Opts for Plan B," *Advertising Age International* (March 11, 1996), p. I-2.

[11]Rajeev Batra, "The Why, When, and How of Global Branding," in *Brand Equity and the Marketing Mix: Creating Customer Value*, Sanjay Sood, ed., Marketing Science Institute, Report No. 95-111, September 1995.

[12]"Telecom Marketing," *Advertising Age International* (January 15, 1996), pp. I-16, I-22.

[13]"We're not late to the party," *Business Week International* (April 28, 1997), p. 18.

[14]Alm, private communication.

EXHIBIT 12-2
SARA LEE'S HIERARCHY OF
BRANDS

Global
Brands

Regional Brands

Local Brands

The bottom layer consists of hundreds of local brands. These brands are generally quite successful in their homebase. They are typically one of the leading shareholders in their product category. The second set of brands are the regional ones. Examples of such brands include Douwe Egberts coffee in Europe and L'Eggs hosiery in the United States and Mexico. These brands enjoy solid regional recognition. In many of their markets they have established brand leadership. Sara Lee's mission for the regional brands is to nurture them through solid management, and to build up equity by sustained marketing investment and by providing the right value equation. At the top of the hierarchy are the "truly global" brands like Champion, the athletic sportswear brand, and the shoecare polish Kiwi, which is sold in almost 140 countries with the exact same formula in each can. Sara Lee's strategy is to nurture local brands into regional brands and ultimately global ones. Douwe Egberts, for example, is now also marketed in Thailand as a premium coffee. Global Perspective 12-1 describes the global branding strategy implemented by Nestlé, the Swiss consumer goods multinational.

$\mathcal{G}$LOBAL PERSPECTIVE 12-1

NESTLÉ'S BRAND-BUILDING STRATEGY

Nestlé, the Swiss multinational, now owns nearly 8,000 different brands worldwide. Of those 8,000 worldwide brands, only 750 are registered in more than one country, and only 80 are registered in ten. The company has ten worldwide corporate strategic brands (see Exhibit 12-3) such as Nescafé, Maggi, and Carnation. In addition, there are 45 different strategic worldwide brands (e.g., Kitkat, After Eight) that are managed at the strategic business unit level.

Sources: "Nestlé's Brand Building Machine," *Fortune* (September 19, 1994), pp. 137-141, and Andrew J. Parsons, "Nestlé: The Visions of Local Managers. An interview with Peter Brabeck-Letmathe, CEO elect, Nestlé," *The McKinsey Quarterly* (2)(1996), pp. 5–29.

At the next level are the twenty-five regional corporate strategic brands (e.g., Stouffer's) and around a hundred regional product brands (e.g., Taster's Choice). These are managed by the SBUs and regional headquarters. Ultimately, there are numerous local brands for which the local markets are responsible.

Nestlé has chosen two growth paths, neither of which involves global travel for most brands. In developed markets, the company gains economies of scale through big acquisitions—Carnation, Perrier, Stouffer's, to name three. In the developing world, it grows by manipulating ingredients, or processing technology for local conditions, and then slaps on the proper brand name. Sometimes the name is well-known, like Nescafé; generally a local one works fine—for instance, Bear Brand condensed milk in Asia.

EXHIBIT 12-3
NESTLÉ BRANDING TREE

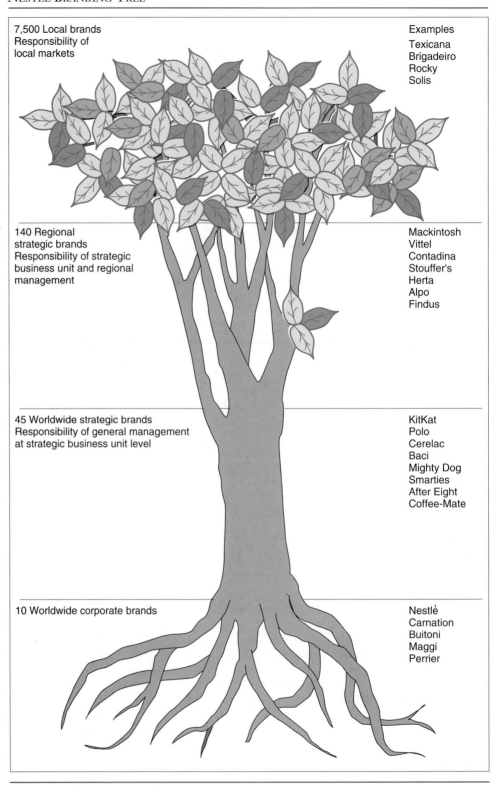

7,500 Local brands
Responsibility of local markets

Examples
Texicana
Brigadeiro
Rocky
Solis

140 Regional strategic brands
Responsibility of strategic business unit and regional management

Mackintosh
Vittel
Contadina
Stouffer's
Herta
Alpo
Findus

45 Worldwide strategic brands
Responsibility of general management at strategic business unit level

KitKat
Polo
Cerelac
Baci
Mighty Dog
Smarties
After Eight
Coffee-Mate

10 Worldwide corporate brands

Nestlé
Carnation
Buitoni
Maggi
Perrier

Although there is often a drive to build up global brands, there are solid reasons to make an in-depth analysis before converting local brands into regional or global ones. In fact, local brands sometimes have much more appeal among consumers than their global competing brands. This is especially true when there is not much benefit from being global. In the Polish detergent market, P & G launched Ariel and Unilever introduced Omo. The leading detergent brand, though, is Pollena 2000, a local brand owned by Unilever.[15]

David Aaker, a branding guru, offers the following checklist for analyzing globalization propositions:[16]

1. What is the cost of creating and maintaining awareness and associations for a local brand versus a global one?

2. Are there significant economies of scale in the creation and running of a communication program globally (including advertising, PR, sponsorships)?

3. Is there value to associations of a global brand or of a brand associated with the source country?

4. What local associations will be generated by the global name? symbol? slogan? imagery?

5. Is it culturally and legally doable to use the brand name, symbol, slogan across the different countries?

6. What is the value of the awareness and associations that a regional brand might create?

Exhibit 12-4 summarizes the findings of a field study that investigated the branding practices of six consumer goods MNCs. The figures clearly indicate that despite the mantras being chanted on global branding, local brands are still the norm, even for the major MNCs.

EXHIBIT 12-4
BRANDS OF SIX MULTINATIONAL COMPANIES IN 67 COUNTRIES

Company	Total Number of Brands	Brands found in 50% or more countries (%)	Brands marketed in only one country (%)
Colgate	163	6 (4%)	59 (36%)
Kraft GF	238	6 (3%)	104 (44%)
Nestlé	560	19 (4%)	250 (45%)
P & G	217	18 (8%)	80 (37%)
Quaker	143	2 (1%)	55 (38%)
Unilever	471	17 (4%)	236 (50%)
Total	1,792		

Source: Betsy V. Boze and Charles R. Patton, "The Future of Consumer Branding as Seen from the Picture Today," *Journal of Consumer Marketing,* 12(4) (1995), p. 22.

---

[15]"Unilever Chief: Refresh Brands," *Advertising Age International* (July 18, 1994), p. I-20.

[16]Aaker, pp. 267–8.

Brand Name Changeover Strategies

When the case for a transition from a local to a global (or regional) brand name is made, the firm needs to decide on how to implement the changeover in practice. Three broad strategic options exist:[17] fade-in/fade-out, transparent forewarning, and summary axing. With **fade-in/fade-out,** the new global brand name is somehow tied with the existing local brand name. After a transition period, the old name is dropped. A typical example is the brand name change that Disney implemented for its Paris theme park. It first shrunk the *Euro* part in Euro Disney and added the word *land.* In October 1994 the word *Euro* was dropped altogether and the themepark is now branded as *Disneyland Paris.*[18] One tactic that is sometimes employed is to have the local brand as an endorser brand. For example, Pedigree was launched in the late 1980s in France as "Pedigree by Pal." Another possibility is dual branding. When Whirlpool acquired the white goods division of Philips, the company initially employed a dual branding strategy—Philips and Whirlpool. After a transition period, the Philips brand name was dropped.

The second approach, **transparent forewarning,** alerts the customers about the brand name change. The forewarning can be done via the communication program, in-store displays, and product packaging. A good example is the transition made by Mars in the Pan-European market for Raider, one of its candy products. Mars launched a TV-advertising campaign to launch the change saying: "Now Raider becomes Twix, for it is Twix everywhere in the world." Far less common is the third practice, **summary axing,** where the company simply drops the old brand name and immediately replaces it with the global name.

To ensure a smooth transition, there are some rules that should be respected.[19] When the name is changed gradually, one of the key concerns is the proper length for the transition period. Coming back to the Philips–Whirlpool example, the two companies had agreed that Whirlpool could use the Philips brand name until 1999. In principle, the firm should allow sufficient time for the customers to absorb the name change. How long this process will take depends on the product and the strength of the image associated with the old brand name. For some product categories, the purchase cycle matters, too. Sometimes the phase-out can be done sooner than scheduled. Whirlpool discovered through its research that the Philips brand name could be dropped far ahead of the originally planned drop date.

It is also important that consumers who are exposed to the changeover messages, via advertising or product packaging or both, associate the new brand name with the old one. One of the primary goals of Whirlpool's advertising campaign was to maintain awareness of the Philips brand name while building up association with Whirlpool.[20]

To avoid negative spillovers on the global brand name, companies should also assure themselves that the local products have acceptable quality before attaching the global brand name to them. Otherwise, the goodwill of the global brand name could

---

[17]Kapferer, pp. 166–8.

[18]"The Kingdom Inside a Republic," p. 69.

[19]Marieke de Mooij, *Advertising Worldwide. Concepts, Theories and Practice of International, Multinational and Global Advertising* (Englewood Cliffs, N.J.; Prentice-Hall, 1994), p. 112.

[20]Jan Willem Karel, "Brand Strategy Positions Products Worldwide," *The Journal of Business Strategy* (May/June 1991), pp. 16–19.

be irreparably damaged. As a result, other products launched under the global brand name might be viewed with skepticism by consumers in the foreign market. Part of Whirlpool's geographic expansion in China involved a joint venture that makes air conditioners based on Japanese designs. The air conditioners, sold under a local brand name, Raybo, initially had about half the life expectancy of U.S.-made Whirlpool models. Whirlpool's president declared that his company would not put the Whirlpool name on the product until its quality problems were fixed.[21]

Finally, companies should monitor the marketplace's response to the brand name change with marketing research. Such tracking studies enable the firm to ensure that the change-over runs smoothly. They also assist firms in determining how long promotional programs that announce the name-change should last. Whirlpool tracked brand recognition and buying preference of consumers on a weekly basis during the brand-change period.

We now consider two other branding practices that companies use, namely private branding and corporate branding:

Private Label Branding ("Store Brands")

Heinz is one of the leading canned soup brands in the United Kingdom. The company also sells soup in the United States. In fact, Heinz has captured a 7 percent share of the overall soup category. But the soup that Heinz makes in the United States is not sold under the Heinz brand name.[22] Instead, it is sold under store brand names. Heinz has an 87 percent share of the private label soup market in the United States.[23]

One of the most visible retailing phenomena during the last decade is the spread of **private labels** ("store brands"). Private labels come under various guises. At one extreme are the generic products that are packaged very simply and sold at bottom prices. At the other extreme are premium store brands that deliver quality sometimes superior to national brands. Private labels have made big inroads in several European countries. They account for almost one-third of supermarket sales in the United Kingdom and one fourth in France.[24] In Japan and most other Asian countries, on the other hand, store brands are still marginal players. Consumers in this region tend to be extremely brand loyal.[25] Private labels, however, are definitely on the rise in the Japanese marketplace, as shown in Exhibit 12-5.

Several factors explain the success of private labels:[26]

1. **Improved quality of private-label products.** Many years ago private labels used to have a quality stigma: only cheapskates would buy a store brand. Today the quality gap between store brands and their brand-name competitors is gone

---

[21]"For Whirlpool, Asia Is the New Frontier," *The Wall Street Journal* (April 25, 1996), p. B1.

[22]Heinz once marketed canned soup under its own name in the United States.

[23]"Your Global Portfolio," Heinz, Corporate Affairs Department, 1995.

[24]Erich Joachimsthaler, "Marketing Metamorphosis: From Products to Brand to Consumers," *mimeo*, IESE, Barcelona, 1994.

[25]"No Global Private Label Quake—Yet," *Advertising Age International* (January 16, 1995), p. I-26.

[26]John A. Quelch and David Harding, "Brands Versus Private Labels: Fighting to Win," *Harvard Business Review* (January-February 1996), pp. 99–109.

EXHIBIT 12-5
MARKET SHARE (% VALUE) OF PRIVATE
LABELS IN JAPAN: 1990 AND 1994

	1990	1994
Dairy products	4.9	6.2
Chilled foods	4.5	5.7
Frozen foods	6.2	7.3
Fresh foods	—	—
Snack foods	4.4	5.2
Hot drinks	—	1.6
Non-alcoholic cold drinks	—	9.3
Alcoholic drinks	2.1	7.8
Tobacco	—	—
Toiletries	0.9	2.1
Cosmetics	—	—
Household cleaning agents	—	3.5
Textile washing products	—	6.1
Household paper products	4.3	9.6
Personal paper products	5.6	10.2
OTC healthcare	—	—
Footwear	1.9	3.4
Clothing	7.7	10.9
Electrical appliances	—	5.0
Consumer electronics	—	2.0
Furniture	2.1	4.6

Source: "Private Label in Japan," *Retail Monitor International* (Jan. 1996), p. 110. Reprinted with kind permission of Euromonitor.

in most countries. The improved quality image is probably the key success factor behind the spread of store brands. In many product categories, consumers now have the option to buy a good-quality store brand at a lower price than the brand-name alternative.

2. **Development of premium private-label brands.** Not only has the quality gap disappeared, but retailers in North America and Europe, in collaboration with private-label manufacturers, have developed private-label products that offer premium quality. In some cases, store brand products have even become far more innovative than the competing name brand products.

3. **Shift in balance of power between retailers and manufacturers.** A third factor is the shift in the balance of power from manufacturers to retailers. This reversal has been especially strong in Europe, where large-scale national chains dominate the retailing landscape. Italy is one of the few countries in Europe where private labels have made little progress. It is also a market where government regulations have dampened the development of big chain stores.

4. **Expansion into new product categories.** Private labels used to be limited to a small range of product categories. These days private labels are marketed in an ever-widening range of categories. This spread has helped to make private labels more acceptable among consumers.

5. **Internationalization of retail chains.** Another factor is the growing internationalization of large supermarket chains. In recent years, French hypermarchés like Carrefour invaded Spain, the German food-store chain Aldi entered the Benelux countries, France and the United Kingdom, and the Dutch retailer Ahold started to penetrate the U.S. market. Many of these international retailers plan to replicate their private-label program in the host country.

6. **Economic downturns.** When disposable income drops, consumers usually become more value-conscious and tend to switch from national brands to private labels.[27] Without doubt, the persistent economic malaise in many European countries has been a major driver behind the success of store brands in Europe.

As a branding strategy, private labeling is especially attractive to MNCs that face well-entrenched incumbent brands in the markets they plan to enter. Under such circumstances, launching the product as a store brand enables the firm to get the shelf space access it would otherwise be denied.

The private labels boom offers for many manufacturers an opportunity to penetrate markets that would otherwise be hard to crack. In Japan, manufacturers that do not have the resources to set up a distribution channel network have joined up with local retailers to penetrate the market. Agfa-Gevaert, the German/Belgian photo film maker agreed to supply a store brand film to Daiei, a major Japanese supermarket chain.[28] Eastman Kodak also decided to offer private-label film in Japan. Most of the distribution system is locked up by the local competitors, Fuji and Konica. Kodak hoped to grab a larger share of the Japanese film market by making a private-label film for the Japanese Cooperative Union, a group of 2,500 retail stores.[29]

Umbrella (Corporate) Branding

Umbrella branding is a system where a single banner brand is used worldwide, often with a sub-brand name, for almost the entire product mix of the company. Often times, the banner is the company's name: Sony, Kodak, Siemens, Virgin, to name a few. Some companies also use noncompany names. For example, Matsushita, the Japanese consumer electronics maker, employs banner brands like JVC and Panasonic. Umbrella branding is particularly popular among Japanese firms, though there are also quite a few non–Japanese companies that opt for this branding system. What is the appeal of corporate branding in a global marketing context? Researchers have identified several sources. First and foremost, in many cultures a good corporate image will have a strong positive impact on the evaluation of the attributes of the product endorsed by the banner brand. For the customers, the presence of the banner brand's logo on the product means trust, a seal of approval, a guarantee for quality and excellence.[30] The umbrella brand basically serves as a risk-reducing device for

---

[27]Stephen J. Hoch and Shumeet Banerji, "When Do Private Labels Succeed?" *Sloan Management Review* (Summer 1993), pp. 57–67.

[28]"Japan's Brands Feel the Pinch, Too," *Financial Times* (April 28, 1994), p. 9.

[29]"Kodak Pursues a Greater Market Share in Japan with New Private-Label Film," *Wall Street Journal* (March 7, 1995), p. B-4.

[30]Camillo Pagano, "The Management of Global Brands," in *Brand Power*, Paul Stobart, ed. (London: The MacMillan Press, Ltd., 1994).

the customer.[31] London International Group (LIG), the world's leading condom marketer, mentions this benefit as the reason behind its drive to make the Durex brand the umbrella for its condom business worldwide.[32] Local brand names are now tied with the Durex name. In Germany, the packaging was altered to say "From the house of Durex." One observer described the motives behind this move as follows:

> The idea behind it is that anywhere you go in the world, you will see the Durex name, rather than lots of sub-brands. People want security and safety when they are buying these products.

A second benefit is that umbrella branding facilitates brand building efforts over a range of products. Having a banner brand makes it easier to build up global share of mind and brand integrity.[33] Instead of splitting marketing dollars over scores of different brands, the advertising support focuses on a single umbrella brand. A case in point is Nokia, one of the leading makers of cellular phones. Nokia used to have scores of brand names. These days the company pushes the corporate brand name in the global marketplace where the Nokia brand is far less familiar than in Scandinavia. As one company official commented: "We had many brand names but now we believe it is better to stick to one brand."[34]

A final rationale is that a corporate branding system makes it easier to add or drop new products.[35] High-tech companies like Siemens and Motorola tend to rely heavily on product innovation to defend their market share. Nurturing a single strong banner brand is far more efficient than creating a distinct brand from scratch for every new product launch.

Protecting Brand Names

Visitors of Kathmandu who are getting tired of the Nepalese cuisine can always try out the local Pizza Hut. Just like Pizza Hut restaurants elsewhere in the world, it serves pizza. But except for the name and the main menu items, the Kathmandu Pizza Hut has nothing in common with a U.S. Pizza Hut. Exhibit 12-6 presents another example of trademark infringement: Pizza Domino, a pizza chain based in Israel with a logo (and name) that bears a striking resemblance to a well-known pizza chain.

Brands are vital assets to brand owners. The Coca-Cola trademark is valued around $39 billion, almost ten times the value of Coca-Cola's physical assets.[36] Given the strategic importance of brands, protection of the brand name is one of the major

---

[31]Cynthia A. Montgomery and Birger Wernerfelt, "Risk Reduction and Umbrella Branding," *Journal of Business*, 65(1) (1992), pp. 31–50.

[32]"LIG Stretches Durex Identity Around World," *Advertising Age International* (March 11, 1996), p. I4.

[33]Gary Hamel and C.K. Prahalad, *Competing for the Future* (Boston, Mass. Harvard Business School Press, 1994).

[34]"Scandinavia's Nokia Phones Japan," *Advertising Age International* (December 13, 1993), p. I6.

[35]Hiroshi Tanaka, "Branding in Japan," in *Brand Equity & Advertising: Advertising's Role in Building Strong Brands*, D.A. Aaker & A.L. Biel, eds. (Hillsdale, N.J.: L. Erlbaum Associates, 1993).

[36]The Coca-Cola Company, *1995 Annual Report*.

EXHIBIT 12-6
PIZZA DOMINO IN ISRAEL: TWIN BROTHER OF
DOMINO'S PIZZA?

Source: Courtesy Edmund Wong.

tasks faced by the brand owner. The protection challenge entails several questions: How should the brand be protected? Which aspects of the brand? When? Where? For what product classes? Answers to these questions are largely driven by an analysis of the costs and benefits of protecting the brand.

Consider the first issue: how? The most common way to seek protection is by legal registration. The first step is to hire legal counsel in each country where the brand should be protected. There are several international agreements in force that help this process. The oldest treaty is the Paris Convention for the Protection of Intellectual Property, supported by almost a hundred countries. The Paris Convention is based on the principle of reciprocity: (a) people of member states have the same rights that the state grants to its own nationals, and (b) foreigners have equal access to local courts to combat trademark infringement. In the European Union, the Single Market Act also had ramifications for brand protection: trademark registration in any of the EU member states is now effective for the entire European Union. One major stumbling block is the difference in opinion held by industrialized and developing countries on intellectual property protection. Developed countries view intellectual property right protection as the reward for innovativeness. Taking the protection away would mean that companies lose their incentive to invest in new product development. Many LDCs, on the other hand, regard intellectual property (IP) as a public good. Easy access to IP spurs economic development and, thereby, enables the developing country to narrow the gap with the developed world.[37] The two opposing views are summarized in Exhibit 12-7.

What should be protected? Many elements of the brand franchise may require protection. Obviously, one should register the brand name. But in some countries, you might also consider protecting the translation of the brand name, or even the transliteration equivalent—that is, representations in the local language that have the same "sound."[38] Other forms of intellectual property that might need protection in-

[37]Subhash C. Jain, "Problems in International Protection of Intellectual Property Rights," *Journal of International Marketing*, 4(1) (1996), pp. 9–32.

Exhibit 12-7
Differing Views on Intellectual
Property Protection

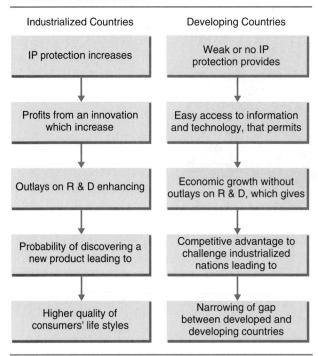

Industrialized Countries	Developing Countries
IP protection increases	Weak or no IP protection provides
Profits from an innovation which increase	Easy access to information and technology, that permits
Outlays on R & D enhancing	Economic growth without outlays on R & D, which gives
Probability of discovering a new product leading to	Competitive advantage to challenge industrialized nations leading to
Higher quality of consumers' life styles	Narrowing of gap between developed and developing countries

Source: Subhash C. Jain, "Problems in International Protection of Intellectual Property Rights," *Journal of International Marketing,* 4(1) (1996), pp. 9–32.

clude slogans, jingles, visual aspects (e.g., McDonald's golden arches)—in short, any distinctive elements that are part of the brand's imagery.

The "when" and "where" issues at first sight appear trivial: ideally, you would like to register the brand's trademarks in as many places and as soon as possible. But, there are some constraints here that enter the picture. The costs of registration itself are usually quite modest. But legal counsel fees are far more significant. However, the major cost item is often the use cost. In many countries, the company is obliged to "use" the trademarks in order to enjoy the protection benefits. *Use* means that the company has to sell commercially significant volumes of the product under the protected brand name. Most countries, however, give a grace period of several years (usually five) before the brand owner has to use the registered trademarks.

The last concern deals with the scope of the protection: What product classes should be covered? Many companies register their brands in virtually all product categories. A more sensible rule is to register the trademarks in all classes covering goods for which the brand is currently used and related classes.[39] The related classes are product categories that the company might enter in the future via brand extensions, using the protected brand name.

---

[38]Garo Partoyan, "Protecting Power Brands," in *Brand Power*, P. Stobart, ed. (London: MacMillan, 1994).

[39]Ibid.

MANAGING MULTINATIONAL PRODUCT LINES

◆ ◆ ◆ ◆ ◆ ◆

Most companies sell a wide assortment of products. The product assortment is usually described on two dimensions: the width and the length of the product mix.[40] The first dimension, the width, refers to the collection of different product lines marketed by the firm. For most companies these product lines are related. Heinz has a broad mix of product lines. Besides ketchup, Heinz's flagship product, the company sells baby food, pet food, and ice cream, for example. All these product lines, though, are food items. Other companies, especially Japanese and Korean ones, have a much more diverse product mix. Kao, one of Japan's biggest consumer goods manufacturers, has a product mix that covers personal care products, cosmetics, laundry products, and food items. But Kao also sells chemicals, floppy disks, and CD-ROMs. The second dimension, the length, refers to the number of different items that the company sells within a given product line. Thus, the product mix for a particular MNC could vary along the width and/or length dimension across the different countries where the firm operates.

When comparing the product mix in the company's host and home markets, there are four possible scenarios. The product mix in the host country could be: an extension of the domestic line, a subset of the home market's product line, a mixture of local and nonlocal product lines, or, lastly, a completely localized product line.

Small firms with a narrow product assortment will simply extend their domestic product line. Blistex, a tiny U.S. company that makes primarily lip-care products, has a very limited range of product lines that are marketed in all of its foreign markets. Companies that enter new markets carefully select a subset of their product mix. When Cadbury, the U.K.-based confectionery manufacturer, decided to re-enter the Middle East, the firm commissioned a market research study. One of the purposes of the project was to find out which of its products would be most popular in the Middle Eastern market.[41] Most MNCs have a product mix that is partly global (or regional) and partly home-grown. A typical example is presented in Exhibit 12-8, which gives an overview of the wordwide product mix of the American food company, CPC International.

Several drivers impact the composition of a firm's international product line. We briefly discuss the key factors:

Customer Preferences. In many product categories, consumer preferences vary from country to country. Especially for consumer packaged goods, preferences are still very localized. To cater to their distinctive customer needs, marketers may add certain items to the country's product lines that are not offered elsewhere. This point is illustrated in Exhibit 12-9, which shows the leading Campbell soup flavors for a sample of countries around the globe. Although there is some overlap ("Cream of Mushroom" is highly popular in the United Kingdom, the United States, and Mexico) some other popular flavors (e.g., "Cream of Pumpkin" in Australia) are not even offered in the U.S. market.

---

[40]See, for instance, Douglas J. Dalrymple and Leonard J. Parsons, *Marketing Management* (New York: John Wiley & Sons, Inc., 1995).

[41]Philip Parker, "Cadbury in the Middle East (A)," *mimeo*, INSEAD-CEDEP, 1989.

EXHIBIT 12-8
INTERNATIONAL PRODUCT MIX OF CPC INTERNATIONAL

Market Positions Worldwide

1 Leader in Market Share
2 Second in Market Share
• Present in the Market
◆ Technical or Licensing Agreement

	Soups*	Sauces*	Bouillons	Mealmakers*	Potato Products	Pasta	Mayonnaise	Pourable Dressings	Corn Oil	Foodservice**	Peanut Butter	Starches	Desserts (Ambient)	Premium Baking	Corn Refining
	Worldwide Businesses										*Key Businesses*				
North America, Caribbean															
Canada	2	2	1				1		1	•	2	1			1
United States	•	•	2	•	•	•	1	•	1	•	2	1	•	1	•
Dominican Republic	2		2				•		•	•	•				
Europe, Africa/Middle East															
Austria	1	2	1	1	1		•		1	•		1			
Belgium	1	1	1	1						•		1			
Bulgaria	•	•	•		•	•									
Czech Republic	•	•	•	•	•		1			•					
Denmark	1	1	1	1	2			2		•		1	•		
Finland	1	1	1	2						•		2			
France	1	2	2				2	2		•		1	1		
Germany	2	2	2	2	1		•		1	•		1	•		
Greece	1	1	1		2		1	1		•		2	2		
Hungary	1	1	1	1	•		2			•			•		
Ireland	1	1	1	1	1	•	1	2	•	•		2	•		
Italy	1	•	2	•	1		•		•	•		1			
Netherlands	2	1	•	2	•				•	•		1			
Norway	2	2	•	2						•		1			
Poland	1	1	2	1	1		2			•			•		
Portugal	1	•	1		2		1	2		•		1	2		
Romania	•	•	•		•					•					
Russia	1	1	2	1			•		•	•	•				
Slovak Republic	•	•	•	•	•		1								
Spain	2	•	•	•			•	•		•			1	2	
Sweden	1	2	1	1				•	1	•	•	1			
Switzerland	1	1	1	1				•	•	•		1			
United Kingdom	1	1	2	•		•	1	•	1	•		1	1	•	
Israel	1		2		•	•	1		1	•	1		2		
Jordan	•	•							•						
Kenya	1		1						•	•		1			1
Morocco	1	•	1							•		1	1		
Saudi Arabia							2		2	•	•	1			
South Africa	•	•								•	•	•			◆
Tunisia	1		1							•				•	
Turkey	1	2								•		1		•	
Latin America															
Argentina	1		1		1		1	•	1	•		1		•	1
Bolivia	1	•	•	•	•	•			•	•		1			
Brazil	2	2	1	2		•	1	•	2	•		1		•	1
Chile	•	•	•	•	•		1	•	1	•		•			1

EXHIBIT 12-8 (continued)

Market Positions Worldwide

1 Leader in Market Share
2 Second in Market Share
• Present in the Market
♦ Technical or Licensing Agreement

	Soups*	Sauces*	Bouillons	Mealmakers*	Potato Products	Pasta	Mayonnaise	Pourable Dressings	Corn Oil	Foodservice**	Peanut Butter	Starches	Desserts (Ambient)	Premium Baking	Corn Refining
	Worldwide Businesses										Key Businesses				
Latin America															
Colombia	2	2	2	2	•		1	•	1	•	1	1	•		1
Costa Rica	2		2				1		•	•	•	1			
Ecuador	2	2	2	2			•		1	•					
Guatemala							•		•	•	•	2			
Honduras							•		•	•	•	1			
Mexico	1		1	1			2		2	•	2	1	•		1
Panama	•		•				•					1			
Paraguay	1	1	1	1	1		1		1	•		1			
Peru	2	2	2	2	2	•	1	•	•	•	•	2			
Uruguay	1	1	1		2		1	•	2	•		1	•		
Venezuela	2		2	1			•			•					♦
Asia															
China		•	1				•				•	•	•		
Hong Kong	1		1				2		•	•		1	1	1	
India	2											1	1		♦
Indonesia	1	•	•				•	•	•	•	•				
Japan♦	1		1	1			2	2	1	•					♦
Malaysia	1		2				1	2	1	•		1		2	1
Pakistan	1		1	1		•	2		1	•		1	1		1
Philippines	1	•	1			2	1			•		1	1		
Singapore	1		1				1	•	•	•		1	1	1	
Sri Lanka	2	1	2							•					
Taiwan	1		1				2		•	•		1			
Thailand	1	1	1	2		1	1		1	•		1			♦
Vietnam	•		1				1			•					

* Dehydrated products only.
**CPC foodservice (catering) products hold leading share positions in many of the categories in which they compete.
Source: CPC International, *1996 Annual Report.*

Competitive Climate. Differences in the competitive environment often explain why a company offers certain product lines in some countries but not in others. A telling example is the canned soup industry. In the United States, the soup category is basically owned by Campbell Soup: eight out of every ten cans of soup sold is a Campbell brand.[42] Given the clout of the Campbell brand name, it is virtually impossible to penetrate the U.S. canned soup market. The picture is quite different in the United Kingdom, where Campbell was a relative latecomer. In the United Kingdom,

---

[42]Campbell Soup Company, *1995 Annual Report.*

EXHIBIT 12-9
TOP-SELLING CAMPBELL'S SOUPS AROUND THE WORLD

Country	Top-Selling Soup Flavour
United States	Chicken Noodle (No. 2: Cream of Mushroom; No. 3: Tomato)
Australia	Cream of Pumpkin
Canada	Tomato
Hong Kong	Cream Style Corn with Chicken
Mexico	Cream of Mushroom
U.K.	Cream of Mushroom

Source: Campbell Soup Company, *1995 Annual Report*, pp. 18–9

the leading canned soup brand is Heinz with a 36 percent share of the market.[43] Coca-Cola's product line strategy in Japan is also driven to a large degree by the local rivalry in the Japanese beverage market. One of the pillars of Coke's Japan-marketing strategy is to improve on its rivals' products. As a result, Coke sells beverages in Japan that are not available anywhere else such as: Sokenbicha, an Asian tea, Kochakaden, an English tea, Georgia, a coffee drink, and, Lactia, a fermented milk drink.[44]

Organizational Structure. Especially in MNCs that are organized on a country basis, product lines may evolve to a large degree independently in the different countries. The scope of the country manager's responsibility is increasingly being limited in many MNCs (see chapter 18). Nevertheless, country managers still have a great deal of decision-making autonomy in many functional areas, including product policy.

History. Product lines often become part of an MNC's local product mix following geographic expansion efforts. For example, Procter & Gamble, Heinz, and Sara Lee penetrate new and existing markets via acquisitions. Some of these acquisitions include product lines that are outside the MNC's core business. Rather than divesting these noncore businesses, a company often decides to keep them. As part of its growth strategy in Central Europe, in Hungary Heinz acquired Kecskemeti Konzervgyar, a formerly state-owned canning company. The company makes a broad range of food products, including baby food, ketchup, and pickles, which are staple items for Heinz, but also jams, and canned vegetables.

---

[43]H.J. Heinz Company, *1995 Annual Report*.

[44]"Coke Turns to Other Drinks to Win Back Sales in Japan," *The Asian Wall Street Journal* (January 20, 1997), pp. 1, 6.

Global marketers need to decide for each market of interest which product lines should be offered and which ones should be dropped. When markets are entered for the first time, market research can be very helpful for designing the initial product assortment. Market research is less useful for radically new products (e.g., frozen yogurt, electric vehicles) or newly emerging markets. In such situations, the company should consider using a "probing-and-learning" approach. Such a procedure has the following steps:

1. Start with a product line that has a minimum level of product variety.
2. Gradually adjust the amount of product variety over time by adding new items and dropping existing ones.
3. Analyze the incoming actual sales data and other market feedback.
4. Make the appropriate inferences.
5. If necessary, adjust the product line further.[45]

The gist of this procedure is to use the product line as a listening post for the new market to see what product items work best.

By and large, add/drop decisions should be driven by profit considerations. In the global marketing arena, it is crucial to look not just at profit ramifications within an individual country. Ideally, the profitability analysis should be done on a regional or even global basis. A good start is to analyze each individual country's product portfolio on a sales turnover basis. Product lines can be categorized as (1) core products, (2) niche items, (3) seasonal products, or (4) filler products.[46] Core products are the items that represent the bulk of the subsidiary's sales volume. Niche products appeal to small segments of the population, which might grow. Seasonal products have most of their sales during limited times of the year. Finally, filler products are items that account for only a small portion of the subsidiary's overall sales. These might include "dead-weight" items whose sales were always lackluster or prospective up-and-coming products. From a global perspective, a comparison of the product mix make-up across the various countries provides valuable insights. Such an analysis might provide answers to questions like:

- Could some of our "seasonal" products in country A be turned into "core" items in country B?

- Given our track record in country A, which ones of our filler products should be considered as up-and-coming in country B and which ones should be written off as dead-weight products?

- Is there a way to streamline our product assortment in country A by dropping some of the items and consolidating others, given our experience in country B?

PRODUCT PIRACY ◆ ◆ ◆ ◆ ◆ ◆

Sham Shui Po and Mong Kok are two of the hottest tourist attractions in Hong Kong. Yet, tourist guides barely mention the spots. Their appeal is a computer shopping center where you can buy the latest software on CD-ROMs at bargain prices—

---

[45]Anirudh Dhebar, "Using Extensive, Dynamic Product Lines for Listening in on Evolving Demand," *European Management Journal*, 13(2) (June 1995), pp. 187–92.

[46]John A. Quelch and David Kenny, "Extend Profits, Not Product Lines, *Harvard Business Review* (Sept.-Oct. 1994), pp. 153–60.

EXHIBIT 12-10
PIRACY AROUND THE WORLD
(MM = MILLION)

Leaders for motion picture losses

Italy	$ 321 MM
Japan	$ 156 MM
Russia	$ 145 MM
Saudi Arabia	$ 100 MM
Mexico	$ 74 MM

Leaders for music recordings losses

China	$ 345 MM
Russia	$ 300 MM
Bulgaria	$ 126 MM
United Arab Emirates	$ 72 MM
Germany	$ 70 MM

Leaders for software losses

Japan	$1,106 MM
Germany	$1,076 MM
China	$ 351 MM
Korea	$ 313 MM
Russia	$ 310 MM

Source: Reprinted with permission from the March 20, 1995 issue of *Advertising Age*. Copyright, Crain Communications Inc. 1995.

less than $10 apiece. Closer inspection quickly reveals that the merchandise is not the genuine product but pirated software, mostly imported from China.

Product piracy is one of the downsides that popular global marketers face. Any aspect of the product is vulnerable to piracy, including the brand name, the logo, the design, and the packaging.

The impact on the victimized company's profits is twofold. Obviously, there are losses stemming from lost sales revenues. The monetary losses due to piracy are potentially staggering (see Exhibit 12-10). Losses in sales revenues incurred by U.S. software manufacturers in China are estimated to be around $500 million. China is thought to have fifteen pirate CD plants with a total capacity of more than 50 million units, far above China's domestic demand (3m units).[47] Worldwide, the retail value of pirated music was assessed to be around $2.25 billion in 1994, or 6 percent of legitimate sales.[48] Counterfeiters also depress the MNC's profits indirectly. In many markets, MNCs often are forced to lower their prices in order to defend their market share against their counterfeit competitors.

Even more worrisome than the monetary losses is the damage that pirated products could inflict to the brand name. Pirated products tend to be of poor quality. As one Levi-Strauss official remarked: "If someone is buying a pair of what they assume are Levi's that fall apart after a day and a half, obviously that hurts our image."[49]

---

[47]"U.S. Seeks to Dog Chinese Copycats," *Financial Times* (February 16, 1994), p. 8.

[48]"Skull and CD," *The Economist* (Dec. 23 - Jan. 5, 1995), p. 78.

[49]"Modern Day Pirates a Threat Worldwide," *Advertising Age International* (March 20, 1995), pp. I-3, I-4.

Strategic Options Against Product Piracy

MNCs have several strategic options at their disposal to combat counterfeiters. The major weapons are as follows:

Lobbying Activities. Lobbying governments is one of the most common courses of action that firms use to protect themselves against counterfeiting. Lobbyists pursue different types of objectives. One goal is to toughen legislation and enforcement of existing laws in the foreign market. Another possible objective is to lobby the home government to impose sanctions against countries that tolerate product piracy. Intellectual property rights infringement has been one of the major stumbling blocks for China's application to the World Trade Organization (WTO) and renewal of "Most Favored Nation" (MFN) status by the U.S. government.[50] Lastly, MNCs might also lobby their government to negotiate for better trademark protection in international treaties such as the GATT agreement and NAFTA. During the Uruguay Round that led to the new GATT agreement, the U.S. pharmaceutical industry urged their government to press for more stringent drug patent protection. These efforts had a mixed outcome. The new GATT agreement now prohibits countries from excluding pharmaceutical MNCs from their patent protection regimes. However, developing countries have a grace period of eleven-and-a-half years.[51]

Legal Action. Prosecuting counterfeiters is another alternative that companies can employ to fight product piracy. China has set up special courts now to stamp out product piracy. In order to sue infringers, companies need to track them down first. In China, for example, MNCs can hire private agencies to help them with investigations of suspected infringers. Legal action has numerous downsides, though. A positive outcome in court is seldom guaranteed. The whole process is time-consuming and costly. Court action could also generate negative publicity.[52]

Product Policy Options. The third set of measures to cope with product piracy entail product policy actions. For instance, software manufacturers often protect their products by putting holograms on the product to discourage counterfeiters. But holograms are only effective when they are hard to copy. Microsoft learned that lesson the hard way when it found out that counterfeiters simply sold MS-DOS 5.0 knockoffs using counterfeit holograms.[53] LVMH, the French maker of a wide variety of upscale liquor brands, redesigned its bottles to make it harder for copycatters to re-use LVMH bottles for their own brews.[54]

Communication Options. Companies also use their communication strategy to counter rip-offs. Through advertising or public relations campaigns, companies warn their target audience about the consequences of accepting counterfeit merchandise. In Japan, LVMH distributed a million leaflets at three airports. The goal of this campaign was to warn Japanese tourists that the importation of counterfeit products is

---

[50]"U.S. Seeks to Dog Chinese Copycats," p. 8.

[51]"How Our Industry Gains with General Agreement on Tariffs and Trade," *Medical Marketing & Media* (May 1994), pp. 56–61.

[52]"Counter Feats," *The China Business Review* (Nov./Dec. 1994), pp. 12–15.

[53]"Catching Counterfeits," *Security Management* (December 1994), p. 18.

[54]Mr. Joël Tiphonnet, Vice-President LVMH Asia Pacific, personal communication, 1997.

against the law.[55] Victims of piracy can also try to educate consumers about the fact that without royalties producers have less incentive to innovate.[56] Anti-counterfeiting advertising campaigns that target end-consumers could also try to appeal to people's ethical judgment: a "good citizen" does not buy counterfeit goods.[57] The target of warning campaigns is not always the end-customer. Converse, the U.S. athletic shoe-maker, ran a campaign in trade journals throughout Europe alerting retailers to the legal consequences of selling counterfeits.[58]

◆ ◆ ◆ ◆ ◆ ◆ COUNTRY OF ORIGIN (COO) STEREOTYPES

Two of the biggest cosmetics companies in the world are Japanese: Kao and Shiseido. While successful in Japan and other Asian countries, Kao and Shiseido have had a hard time penetrating the European and American markets. Apparently, part of the problem is that they are Japanese. One image study conducted by a London-based advertising agency revealed that European consumers view Japanese-made products as "technically advanced and reliable, but short on soul."[59]

Country of Origin (COO) Influences on Consumers

There is ample evidence that shows that for many products, the "Made in" label matters a great deal to consumers. Consumers often seem to rely heavily on country-of-origin cues to evaluate products. Most of us greatly prefer a bottle of French champagne over a Chinese-made bottle, despite the huge price gap. As the Kao/Shiseido story tells us, consumers hold cultural stereotypes about countries that will influence their product assessments. At the same time, research studies of COO effects clearly show that the phenomenon is pretty complex. Some of the key research findings are:

- COO effects are not stable; perceptions change over time.[60] Country images will change when consumers become more familiar with the country, the marketing practices behind the product improve over time, or when the product's actual quality improves. A classic example is with Japanese-made cars, where COO effects took a 180°-turn during the last couple of decades, from a very negative to a very positive country image.[61]

---

[55]"Modern Day Pirates a Threat Worldwide," pp. I-3, I-4.

[56]Professor Allan Shocker, University of Minnesota, private communication, 1996.

[57]Alexander Nill and Clifford J. Shultz II, "The Scourge of Global Counterfeiting," *Business Horizons* (Nov.–Dec. 1996), pp. 37–42.

[58]"Converse Jumps on Counterfeit Culprits with Ad," *Marketing* (October 21, 1993), p. 11.

[59]"The Softer Samurai," *The Economist* (May 12, 1990), p. 73.

[60]John R. Darling and Van R. Wood, "A Longitudinal Study Comparing Perceptions of U.S. and Japanese Consumer Products in a Third/Neutral Country: Finland 1975 to 1985," *Journal of International Business Studies* (Third Quarter, 1990), pp. 427–50.

[61]Akira Nagashima, "A Comparison of Japanese and U.S. Attitudes Toward Foreign Products," *Journal of Marketing* (January 1970), pp. 68–74.

- In general, consumers prefer domestic products over imports. The no. 1 selling car is Renault in France, Toyota in Japan, Volkswagen in Germany, and Fiat in Italy. Not surprisingly, there is a COO bias against products coming from developing countries. For example, a recent study conducted in the Philippines found that products made in LDCs are only marketable when they are priced far less than products offered by regional or global competitors.[62]

- The critical factor appears to be the place of manufacture rather than the location of the company's headquarters.[63] Products sold by the Dutch consumer electronics firm Philips in the Far East suffer from an image problem, since Asian consumers suspect that Philips' products manufactured in China are of shoddy quality.

- Demographics make a difference. COO influences are particularly strong among the elderly,[64] less educated, and politically conservative.[65] Consumer expertise also makes a difference: novices tend to use COO as a cue in evaluating a product under any circumstances, experts only rely on COO stereotypes when product attribute information is ambiguous.[66]

- Consumers are likely to use the origin of a product as a cue when they are unfamiliar with the brand name carried by the product.[67]

- Finally, COO effects depend on the product category. Japan is strongly linked in consumers' minds with "high-tech" and performance type attributes but perceived poorly on attributes like "design," "hedonism" or "style." So, in Japan's case, a product-country match should occur for products like cars or consumer electronics, while COO effects would be less relevant for cosmetics or designer clothing. As shown in Exhibit 12-11, there are four possible outcomes, depending on (1) whether there is a match between the product and country, and, (2) whether or not the (mis-)match is favorable.[68]

---

[62]John Hulland, Honorio S. Todiño, Jr., and Donald J. Lecraw, "Country-of-Origin Effects on Sellers' Price Premiums in Competitive Philippine Markets," *Journal of International Marketing* 4(1) (1996), pp. 57–80.

[63]David K. Tse and Gerald J. Gorn, "An Experiment on the Salience of Country-of-Origin in the Era of Global Brands," *Journal of International Marketing*, 1, pp. 57–76, 1992.

[64]Terence A. Shimp and Subhash Sharma, "Consumer Ethnocentrism: Construction and Validation of the CETSCALE," *Journal of Marketing Research*, 24 (August 1987), pp. 280–289.

[65]Thomas W. Anderson and William H. Cunningham, "Gauging Foreign Product Promotion," *Journal of Advertising Research* (February 1972), pp. 29–34.

[66]Durairaj Maheswaran, "Country of Origin as a Stereotype: Effects of Consumer Expertise and Attribute Strength on Product Evaluations," *Journal of Consumer Research*, 21 (September 1994), pp. 354–365.

[67]Victor V. Cordell, "Effects of Consumer Preferences for Foreign Sourced Products," *Journal of International Business Studies* (Second Quarter 1992), pp. 251–269.

[68]Martin S. Roth and Jean B. Romeo, "Matching Product Category and Country Image Perceptions: A Framework for Managing Country-of-Origin Effects," *Journal of International Business Studies* (Third Quarter 1992), pp. 477–497.

EXHIBIT 12-11
PRODUCT-COUNTRY MATCHES AND MISMATCHES:
EXAMPLES AND STRATEGIC IMPLICATIONS

	Country Image Dimensions	
	Positive	*Negative*
Important	I Favorable Match Examples: • Japanese auto • German watch Strategic Implications: • Brand name reflects COO • Packaging includes COO Information • Promote brand's COO • Attractive potential manufacturing site	II Unfavorable Match Examples: • Hungarian auto • Mexican watch Strategic Implications: • Emphasize benefits other than COO • Non-country branding • Joint-venture with favorable match partner • Communication campaign to enhance country image
Not Important	III Favorable Mismatch Example: • Japanese beer Strategic Implications: • Alter importance of product category image dimensions • Promote COO as secondary benefit if compensatory choice process	IV Unfavorable Mismatch Example: • Hungarian beer Strategic Implications: • Ignore COO—such information not beneficial

Dimensions as Product Features (vertical axis label)

Source: Martin S. Roth and Jean B. Romeo, "Matching Product Category and Country Image Perceptions: A Framework for Managing Country-of-Origin Effects," *Journal of International Business Studies* (Third Quarter 1992), p. 495.

Strategies to Cope with COO Stereotypes

Before exploring strategic options to deal with COO, firms should conduct market research to investigate the extent and the impact of COO stereotypes for their particular product. Such studies would reveal whether the country of origin really matters to consumers and to what degree COO hurts or helps the product's evaluation. One useful technique makes use of a *dollar preference scale.* Participants are asked to indicate how much they are willing to pay for particular brand/country combinations.[69]

---

[69]Usually the respondents are also given an anchor point (e.g., "Amount above or below $10,000?"). For further details see: Johny K. Johansson and Israel D. Nebenzahl, "Multinational Production: Effect on Brand Value," *Journal of International Business Studies* (Fall 1986), pp. 101–126.

Country image stereotypes can either benefit or hurt a company's product. Evidently, when there is a favorable match between the country image and the desired product features, a firm could leverage this match by touting the origin of its product, provided its main competitors do not have the same (or better) origin. Our focus below is on strategies that can be used to counter negative COO stereotypes. The overview is organized along the four marketing mix elements: product policy, pricing, distribution, and communication.

Product Policy. A common practice to cope with COO is to select a brand name that disguises the country-of-origin or even invokes a favorable COO.[70] It is probably no coincidence that two of the more successful local apparel retailers in Hong Kong have Italian-sounding names (Giordano and Bossini). Another branding option to downplay negative COO feelings is to use private-label branding. A recent study that looked at COO influences on prices in the Philippines shows that marketers can overcome negative COO effects by developing brand equity.[71] Sheer innovation and a drive for superior quality will usually help firms to overcome COO biases in the long run.

Pricing. Selling the product at a relatively low price will attract value-conscious customers who are less concerned about the brand's country of origin. Obviously, this strategy is only doable when the firm enjoys a cost advantage. At the other end of the pricing spectrum, firms could set a premium price to combat COO biases. This is especially effective for product categories in which price plays a role as a signal of quality (e.g., wines, cosmetics, clothing).

Distribution. Alternatively, companies could influence consumer attitudes by using highly respected distribution channels. In the United Kingdom, Hungarian and Chilean wines are becoming increasingly popular. One reason for their success is that they are sold via prestigious supermarket chains in Britain, like Tesco and J. Sainsbury.[72]

Communication. Lastly, the firm's communication strategy can be used to alter consumer's attitudes toward the product. Such strategies could pursue two broad objectives: (1) improve the country image, or (2) bolster the brand image. The first goal, changing the country image, is less appealing, since it could lead to "free-rider" problems. Efforts carried out by your company to change the country image would also benefit your competitors from the same country of manufacture, even though they don't spend a penny on the country-image campaign. For that reason, country-image type of campaigns are mostly done by industry associations or government agencies. For instance, in the United States, Chilean wines were promoted with wine tastings and a print advertising campaign with the tag line: "It's not just a wine. It's a

[70]France Leclerc, Bernd H. Schmitt, and Laurette Dubé, "Foreign Branding and Its Effects on Product Perceptions and Attitudes," *Journal of Marketing Research*, 31 (May 1994), pp. 263–270.

[71]John Hulland et al., "Country-of-Origin Effects on Sellers' Price Premiums."

[72]"Non-traditional Nations Pour into Wine Market," *Advertising Age International* (May 15, 1995) p. I-4.

country". The $2–3 million campaign was sponsored by ProChile, Chile's Ministry of Foreign Affairs' trade group.[73] Seagram UK, on the other hand, developed a strategy to build up the Paul Masson brand image when the California wine was first launched in the United Kingdom.[74]

◆ ◆ ◆ ◆ ◆ ◆ GLOBAL MARKETING OF SERVICES

Most of the discussion in this chapter has focused on the marketing of so-called "tangible" goods. However, as countries grow richer, services tend to become the dominant sector of their economy. Looking at Asia, the service sector now accounts for more than half of the GDP in countries like Hong Kong (more than 60 percent there), Singapore, Taiwan, and Thailand.[75] Worldwide, the service sector accounts for more than 60 percent of the world output.[76] Global service exports totaled $2.4 trillion in 1994. These statistics show the increasing clout of services in global marketing.

In this section we will first focus on the challenges and opportunities that exist in the global service market. We will then offer a set of managerial guidelines that might prove fruitful to service marketers who plan to expand overseas.

Challenges in Marketing Services Internationally

Compared to marketers of *tangible* goods, service marketers face several unique hurdles on the road to international expansion. The major challenges include:

Protectionism. Trade barriers to service marketers tend to be much more cumbersome than for their physical goods counterparts. Many parts of the world are littered with service trade barriers coming under many different guises. An overview of the major stumbling blocks is given in Exhibit 12-12. Most cumbersome are the nontariff trade barriers, where the creativity of government regulators knows no limits. In the past, the service sector has been treated very stepmotherly in trade agreements. The rules of the GATT system, for instance, only applied to visible trade. Its successor, the World Trade Organization (WTO), now expands at least some of the GATT rules to the service sector.[77] Note, though, that government policies can be favorable for service businesses that create local jobs.

Immediate Face-to-Face Contacts with Service Transactions. The human aspect in service delivery is much more critical than for the marketing of tangible

---

[73]Ibid.

[74]Paul E. Breach, "Building the Paul Masson Brand," *European Journal of Marketing*, 23(9) (1989), pp. 27–30.

[75]"Asia, At Your Service," *The Economist* (February 11, 1995), p. 53.

[76]Joseph A. McKinney, "Changes in the World Trading System," *Baylor Business Review* (Fall 1995), p. 13.

[77]Ibid.

EXHIBIT 12-12
BARRIERS TO INTERNATIONAL MARKETING OF SERVICES

Type	Example	Impact
Tariff	Tax on imported advertising	Discriminates against foreign agencies
	Tax on computer service	Prices international service providers higher than domestic which stand alone
	Higher fees for university students from outside the country	Decreases foreign student enrollment
Nontariff		
Bilateral and multilateral country agreements	GATT multilateral lowering of barriers	Increases international market potential and competition
	U.S. Korean insurance	Lowers barriers to entry for U.S. companies
Buy national policies	U.S. government buying training service from only U.S. companies	Discriminates against foreign suppliers
Prohibit employment of foreigners	Canadian priority to citizens for available jobs	May prevent suppliers from going to buyers
Distance	International business education	Economies of bringing supplier to buyer, buyer to supplier, or both moving to a third location
Direct government competition	Indonesian monopoly on telecommunications	Must market services to government
Scarce factors of production	Lack of trained medical workers in Biafra	Limits production of services
Restrictions on service buyers or sellers	North Korea limited the number of tourists allowed to enter and exit the country	Limits the restricted industry

Source: Lee D. Dahringer, "Marketing Services Internationally: Barriers and Management Strategies," *The Journal of Services Marketing,* 5(3) (Summer 1991), p. 10.

goods. Services are *performed*. This performance feature has several consequences in the international domain. Given the intrinsic need for people-to-people contact, cultural barriers in the global marketplace are much more prominent for service marketers than in other industries. Being in tune with the cultural values and norms of the local market is essential to survive in service industries. As a result, services are typically standardized far less than are tangible products.[78] At the same time, service companies usually aspire to provide a consistent quality image worldwide. Careful screening and training of personnel to assure consistent quality is vital for international service firms. To foster the transfer of know-how between branches, many service companies set up communication channels such as regional councils.

The need for direct customer interface also means that service providers must often have a local presence. This is especially the case with support services such as advertising, insurance, accounting, law firms, or overnight package delivery. In order not to lose MNC customer accounts, many support service companies are obliged to follow in their clients' footsteps.

Difficulties Measuring Customer Satisfaction Overseas. Given the human element in services, monitoring consumer satisfaction is imperative for successful service marketing. Doing customer satisfaction studies in an international context is often frustrating. The hindrances to conducting market research surveys also apply here. In many countries, consumers are not used to sharing their opinions or suggestions. Instead of expressing their true opinions about the service, foreign respondents may simply state what they believe the company wants to hear (the "courtesy" bias).[79]

Opportunities in the Global Service Industries

Despite these challenges, many international service industries offer enormous opportunities to savvy service marketers. The major ones are given here:

Deregulation of Service Industries. While protectionism is still rampant in many service industries, there is a steady improvement in the international trade service climate. Some of the GATT rules that only applied to tangible goods are now extended to the international service trade under the new WTO regime. Several individual countries are taking steps to lift restrictions targeting foreign service firms. Even sectors that are traditionally off-limits to foreigners are opening up now in numerous countries. India and the Philippines, for example, recently opened up their telephone industry to foreign companies.[80]

Increasing Demand for Premium Services. Demand for premium quality services expands with increases in consumers' buying power. International service providers that are able to deliver a premium product often have an edge over their local competitors. There are two major factors behind this competitive advantage. One of the legacies of years of protectionism is that local service firms are typically unprepared for the hard

---

[78]B. Nicolaud, "Problems and Strategies in the International Marketing of Services," *European Journal of Marketing* 23(6) pp. 55–66, 1989

[79]Gaye Kaufman, "Customer Satisfaction Studies Overseas Can Be Frustrating," *Marketing News* (August 29, 1994), p. 34.

[80]"Asia, At Your Service," pp. 53–54.

laws of the marketplace. Notions such as customer orientation, consumer satisfaction, and service quality are marketing concepts that are especially hard to digest for local service firms that, until recently, did not face any serious competition. For example, local funeral companies in France invested very little in funeral homes. Prior to the de-monopolization of the industry, funeral business in France was basically a utility: firms bid for the right to offer funeral services to a municipality at fixed prices. Service Corp. International, a leading American funeral company, now plans to gain a foothold in France by selling premium products and upgraded facilities.[81]

Global service firms can also leverage their "global know-how" base. A major strength for the likes of Waste Management International, Federal Express, and AT & T is that they have a worldwide knowledge base into which they can tap instantly. Some of McDonald's American restaurants switched to a face-to-face ordering system for drive-in meals after their experience in Japan showed that customers preferred this system to placing orders via intercoms.[82]

Increased Value Consciousness.   As customers worldwide have more alternatives to choose from and become more sophisticated, they also grow increasingly value conscious. Service companies that compete internationally also have clout on this front versus local service providers, since global service firms usually benefit from scale economies. Such savings can be passed through to their customers. McDonald's apparently saved around $2 million by centralizing the purchase of sesame seeds.[83] In Thailand, Makro, the Dutch mega-retailer, uses computerized inventory controls and bulk selling to undercut its local rivals.[84] Given the size of its business, Toys "Я" Us, the U.S. discount toy retailer, was able to set up its own direct import company in Japan, allowing the firm to deliver merchandise straight from the docks to its warehouses, thereby bypassing distributors' margins.[85]

Global Service Marketing Strategies

To compete in foreign markets, service firms resort to a plethora of different strategies.

Capitalize on Cultural Forces in the Host Market.   To bridge cultural gaps between the home and host market, service companies often customize the product to the local market. Successful service firms grab market share by spotting cultural opportunities and setting up a service product around these cultural forces. Global Perspective 12-2 describes some of the selling tools used by AIG, an American insurance company, to conquer the insurance market in China.

Standardize and Customize.   As noted in the last chapter, one of the major challenges in global product design is striking the right balance between standardization and customization. By their very nature (service delivery at the point of consumption) most services do not need to wrestle with that issue. Both standardization and

---

[81]"Funereal prospects," *Forbes* (September 11, 1995), pp. 45–46.

[82]"Big Mac's Counter Attack," *The Economist* (November 13, 1993), pp. 71–72.

[83]Ibid.

[84]"Asia, At Your Service," pp. 53–54.

[85]"Revolution in Toyland," *The Financial Times* (April 8, 1994), p. 9.

◆ ◆

GLOBAL PERSPECTIVE 12-2

SELLING INSURANCE POLICIES IN CHINA

Miss Hua and more than 3,000 other agents are peddling life insurance door-to-door for American International Group (AIG), the first foreign company allowed to sell insurance directly in China. Using street smarts and traditional business practices, they are carving a solid niche in a fast-growing market.

Sales at AIG have grown from scratch to 20,000 policies a month since it began here in late 1992. Its experience in Shanghai illustrates how, with a simple strategy energetically executed, an American company can overcome the myriad bureaucratic and practical hurdles that make China a difficult market to crack.

Source: Reprinted with permission from *The New York Times* (April 4, 1995), p. D-1.

The strategy that is succeeding for AIG agents—easily identifiable on the street by their careful grooming and thick briefcases, even when they commute on bicycles—is to be aggressive but studiously polite as they approach customers to talk about the virtues of life insurance. They also send birthday cards, a light touch that seems to surprise and delight many customers.

Perhaps most important, agents figure out what works in China and then pursue it. They visit offices, where underemployed workers do not mind being interrupted. They sell to the boss first, so the authority-conscious employees know it is acceptable to buy. And they appeal to parents—many of them, abiding by the one-child policy, tend to be over-protective—to buy insurance for their children.

---

adaptation are doable. The core service product can easily be augmented with localized support service features that cater to local market conditions.[86]

Central Role of Information Technologies (IT). Information technology forms the second pillar of global service strategies. Service firms add value for their customers by employing technology such as computers, intelligent terminals, and state-of-the-art telecommunications. Many service firms have established Internet access to communicate with their customers and suppliers. IT is especially valued in markets that have a fairly underdeveloped infrastructure. Companies should also recognize the potential of realizing scale economies by centralizing their IT functions via "information hubs."[87]

Add Value by Differentiation. Services differ from tangible products by the fact that it is usually far easier to find differentiation possibilities. Service firms can appeal to their customers by offering benefits not provided by their competitors and/or lowering costs. Apart from monetary expenses, cost items include psychic costs (hassles), time costs (waiting time), and physical efforts.[88] Especially in markets where the service industry is still developing, multinational service firms can add value by providing premium products. AIG allows its customers in China to settle their bills by bank transfers. Local insurance companies required their customers to wait in line to pay the premiums in cash. Exhibit 12-13 describes the measures that Japanese service providers adopt to satisfy their customers.

---

[86]Christopher H. Lovelock and George S. Yip, "Developing Global Strategies for Service Businesses," *California Management Review*, 38(2) (Winter 1996), pp. 64–86.

[87]Ibid.

[88]"Services Go International," *Marketing News* (March 14, 1994), pp. 14–15.

EXHIBIT 12-13
JAPANESE PRACTICES TO ACHIEVE CUSTOMER SATISFACTION

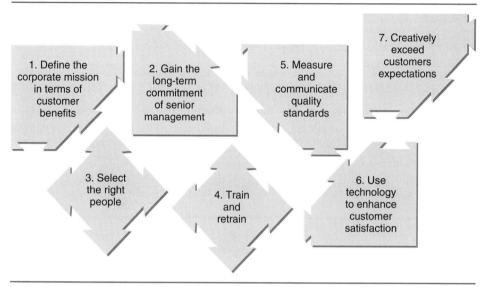

Source: Reprinted from Dominique V. Turpin, "Japanese Approaches to Customer Satisfaction: Some Best Practices," *Long Range Planning*, vol. 28, no. 3, pp. 84–90. Copyright 1995, with kind permission from Elsevier Science Ltd., Langford Lane, Kidlington OX5 1GB, UK.

Establish Global Service Networks. Service firms with a global customer base face the challenge of setting up a seamless global service network. One of the key questions is whether the company should set up the network on its own or use outside partners. Given the huge investments required to develop a worldwide network, more and more companies are choosing the latter route. In the international tele-

IDEOBOX

SARA LEE CORPORATION: BUILDING BRANDS WORLDWIDE

Back in the early 1980s, Sara Lee started its overseas expansion. Today, the company markets over one hundred well-known consumer brands across the globe. Non-U.S. businesses now generate 40% of Sara Lee's sales ($18 billion in 1995). Twelve of the largest brands—including Hanes (underwear), Douwe Egberts (coffee), Sara Lee (bakery products), and Playtex (apparel)—have annual sales of more than $250 million. Brands like Dim (hosiery), Zwitsal (babycare), and Kiwi (shoecare) are sold in 118 countries.

Sara Lee pursues global opportunities through five strategies:

- Build brands in new distribution channels and new ways. In many product lines, the firm uses hybrid channels. Apparel products, for instance, are distributed via department stores, catalogs and mass merchandisers.

- Achieve low-cost production worldwide. In most of its businesses, Sara Lee has the scale to maintain a low cost position.

- Make acquisitions that are strategic and complementary to Sara Lee's core positions.

- Concentrate investments on high-margin, value-added products.

- Focus on developing economies, especially in Asia and South America, with rapid growth and a high desire for U.S. brands.

Comment on Sara Lee's global expansion strategy.

phony market, telecom firms are setting up global alliances that target large MNC customers. Recent examples of such ventures include Concert, an alliance between MCI and British Telecom (the two partners recently merged), and, Global One, a threesome created by Sprint, France Télécom, and Deutsche Telekom.[89]

SUMMARY ◆

Mission statements in annual reports reflect the aspiration of scores of companies to sell their products to consumers worldwide. This push toward global expansion raises many tricky questions on the product policy front. Mastering these global product issues will yield success and, possibly, even worldwide leadership.

Companies need to decide what branding strategies they plan to pursue to develop their overseas business. There is plenty of ammunition to build a case for global brands. At the same time, many arguments can be put forward in favor of other branding strategies. Developing a global branding strategy involves tackling questions such as:

- Which of the brands in our brand portfolio have the potential to be globalized?
- What is the best route toward globalizing our brands? Should we start by acquiring local brands and developing them into regional brands, and, ultimately, if the potential is there, into a "truly" global brand?
- What is the best way to implement the changeover from a local to a global (or regional) brand?
- How do we foster and sustain the consistency of our global brand image?
- What organizational mechanisms should we as a company use to coordinate our branding strategies across markets? Should coordination happen at the regional or global level?

The ultimate reward of mastering these issues successfully is regional—or sometimes even worldwide—leadership in the marketplace, as companies such as Coca-Cola (see Exhibit 12-14) have been able to establish.

EXHIBIT 12-14
MARKET LEADERSHIP COCA-COLA

	Market Leader	Leadership Margin*	Second Place
Australia	Coca-Cola	3.9:1	Diet Coke
Belgium	Coca-Cola	7.7:1	Coca-Cola light
Brazil	Coca-Cola	3.3:1	Brazilian Brand
Chile	Coca-Cola	4.6:1	Fanta
France	Coca-Cola	4.3:1	French Brand
Germany	Coca-Cola	3.1:1	Fanta
Great Britain	Coca-Cola	1.9:1	Diet Coke
Greece	Coca-Cola	3.8:1	Fanta
Italy	Coca-Cola	3.1:1	Fanta
Japan	Coca-Cola	2.3:1	Fanta
Korea	Coca-Cola	2.1:1	Korean Brand
Norway	Coca-Cola	3.3:1	Coca-Cola light
South Africa	Coca-Cola	4.1:1	Sparletta
Spain	Coca-Cola	3.0:1	Spanish Brand
Sweden	Coca-Cola	3.8:1	Fanta

* Over second-place brand.
Source: The Coca-Cola Company, p. 33. *1995 Annual Report.*

[89]"The Lure of Distance," *The Economist* (April 6, 1996), pp. 67–68.

REVIEW QUESTIONS ◆ ◆ ◆ ◆ ◆ ◆ ◆ ◆ ◆ ◆ ◆ ◆ ◆ ◆ ◆ ◆ ◆ ◆

1. For what types of product/service categories would you expect global brand names? For which ones would you anticipate localized names?

2. Why is the market share of private labels much higher in Europe than in Asia?

3. Explain why the strength of a global brand may vary enormously from country to country.

4. What factors should MNCs consider when implementing a brand-name facelift in their foreign markets?

5. Describe the key success factors behind private labels in Europe.

6. What strategies can MNCs adopt to cope with product piracy?

7. How does the marketing of global services differ from marketing tangible goods worldwide?

DISCUSSION QUESTIONS ◆ ◆ ◆ ◆ ◆ ◆ ◆ ◆ ◆ ◆ ◆ ◆ ◆ ◆ ◆ ◆

1. The Advanced Photo System (APS) is a new digital photography system that was launched in 1996 by several companies in the camera industry. APS cameras have features like simple loading, adjustable print size, and the ability to download pictures onto computers. The major photo industry companies use quite different branding strategies. Kodak and Nikon use a global brand name: Advantix and Nuvis, respectively. Other competitors, such as Fuji and Canon, use several brand names for their APS camera and film products. Brand names used by Fuji, for example, are Endeavor in the United States, Fotonex in Europe, and Epion in Japan.

   Why would some competitors (e.g., Kodak) use a global brand name for this product while others (e.g., Fuji, Canon) use several brand names?

2. Coming up with the proper brand name is a key decision. What types of brand names or symbols "travel" across borders? Which ones don't?

3. What strategies might software makers consider to combat software piracy in terms of technological solutions, pricing, promotion, and distribution strategies?

4. As noted above, developing and industrialized countries hold different views about intellectual copyright protection. LDCs claim that stringent copyright protection does not enable them to close the gap with the industrialized world. Discuss what rewards developing countries might derive from intellectual property right protection.

5. Most of the luxury watches have a Swiss-made label. Consider strategies that a watch company whose product is made in India might consider if it wants to target the premium segment in the Western world.

6. Nestlé, the Swiss food conglomerate, has created a Nestlé Seal of Guarantee that it puts on the back of some of its products (e.g., Maggi sauces). The Seal of Guarantee is not used for many of its other products, such as pet food and mineral water. What might be Nestlé's motivations for adding or dropping its Nestlé Seal of Guarantee stamp to the brand name?

7. The intangible nature of many service businesses leads to uncertainty on the part of the customer. Describe how global service providers can lessen this uncertainty by marketing their services globally.

FURTHER READINGS ◆ ◆ ◆ ◆ ◆ ◆ ◆ ◆ ◆ ◆ ◆ ◆ ◆ ◆ ◆ ◆

Cordell, Victor V. "Effects of Consumer Preferences for Foreign Sourced Products." *Journal of International Business Studies* (Second Quarter 1992): 251–69.

Dahringer, Lee D. "Marketing Services Internationally: Barriers and Management Strategies." *The Journal of Services Marketing*, 5(3) (Summer 1991).

Darling, John R., and Van R. Wood. "A Longitudinal Study Comparing Perceptions of U.S. and Japanese Consumer Products in a Third/Neutral Country: Finland 1975 to 1985." *Journal of International Business Studies* (Third Quarter 1990): 427–50.

Harvey, Michael G., and Ilkka A. Ronkainen. "International Counterfeiters: Marketing Success Without the Cost and the Risk." *Columbia Journal of World Business* (Fall 1985): 37–45.

Jain, Subhash C. "Problems in International Protection of Intellectual Property Rights." *Journal of International Marketing*, 4(1) (1996): 9–32.

Kapferer, Jean-Noel, *Strategic Brand Management: New Approaches to Creating and Evaluating Brand Equity* (London: Kogan Page, 1992).

Leclerc, France, Bernd H. Schmitt, and Laurette Dubé. "Foreign Branding and Its Effects on Product Perceptions and Attitudes." *Journal of Marketing Research*, 31 (May 1994): 263–270.

Lovelock, Christopher H., and George S. Yip. "Developing Global Strategies for Service Businesses." *California Management Review*, 38(2) (Winter 1996): 64–86.

Martin, Ingrid M. and Sevgin Eroglu, "Measuring a Multi-Dimensional Construct: Country Image." *Journal of Business Research*, 28(3) (1993): 191–210.

Moore, Jeri, "Building Brands Across Markets: Cultural Differences in Brand Relationships Within the European Community." In *Brand Equity & Advertising: Advertising's Role in Building Strong Brands*. D.A. Aaker and A.L. Biel, eds. (Hillsdale, N.J.: Erlbaum Associates, 1993). pp. 31–49.

Pagano, Camillo. "The Management of Global Brands." In *Brand Power*, P. Stobart, ed. (London: The MacMillan Press, Ltd., 1994).

Partoyan, Garo. "Protecting Power Brands." In *Brand Power*, P. Stobart, ed. (London: The MacMillan Press, Ltd., 1994).

Roth, Martin S., and Jean B. Romeo. "Matching Product Category and Country Image Perceptions: A Framework for Managing Country-of-Origin Effects." *Journal of International Business Studies* (Third Quarter 1992), pp. 477–497.

Shultz, C., and B. Saporito. "Protecting Intellectual Property: Strategies and Recommendations to Deter Counterfeiting and Brand Piracy in Global Markets." *Columbia Journal of World Business* (Spring 1996): 18–28.

Tanaka, Hiroshi. "Branding in Japan." In *Brand Equity & Advertising: Advertising's Role in Building Strong Brands*, D.A. Aaker and A.L. Biel, eds. (Hillsdale, N.J.: Erlbaum Associates, 1993).

GLOBAL PRICING

CHAPTER OVERVIEW

1. DRIVERS OF FOREIGN MARKET PRICING
2. PRICE ESCALATION
3. PRICING IN INFLATIONARY ENVIRONMENTS
4. GLOBAL PRICING AND CURRENCY MOVEMENTS
5. TRANSFER PRICING
6. GLOBAL PRICING AND ANTIDUMPING REGULATION
7. COORDINATING PRICES
8. COUNTERTRADE

Global pricing is one of the most critical and complex issues that global firms face. Price is the only marketing mix instrument that creates revenues. All other elements entail costs. Thus, a company's global pricing policy may make or break its overseas expansion efforts. Furthermore, a firm's pricing policy is inherently a highly cross-functional process based on inputs from the firm's finance, accounting, manufacturing, tax, and legal divisions. Predictably, the interests of one group (say, marketing) may clash with the objectives of another group (say, finance).

Multinationals also face the challenge of how to coordinate their pricing policy across different countries. A lack of coordination will create gray market ("parallel imports") situations (see chapter 17). In gray markets, products marketed in low-priced countries are shipped and resold by unauthorized channels in high-priced markets. These imports will compete with the high-priced equivalent products offered by legitimate distributors. Efforts to trim big price gaps between countries may be hampered by stonewalling attempts of local country managers or distribution channels.

This chapter will focus on global pricing strategies. After giving an overview of the key drivers (customers, competition, company goals and costs, distribution channels, and government policies) of foreign market pricing, we will discuss several strategic international pricing issues. The chapter concludes with a discussion of countertrade, which is a form of noncash pricing.

◆ ◆ ◆ ◆ ◆ ◆ DRIVERS OF FOREIGN MARKET PRICING

Even within the same geographic area such as the Pan-European market, wide cross-border price differences are quite common. This is illustrated in Exhibit 13-1, which reports price variations for a wide range of consumer products based on a 1990 survey carried out in major European cities.[1] The second column shows the city where the lowest price was recorded, while the fourth column indicates the city where the highest price was registered for a given product. The third (fifth) column gives the lowest (highest) before- and after-tax prices in ECU (European Currency Unit). Of interest is the last column of Exhibit 13-1, which shows the ratio of the highest to the lowest pre-tax price. Gaps of two-to-one price disparities are apparently not very unusual. Not surprisingly, cross-border price comparisons will reveal even wider differentials when they are made across continents. In 1993, a pack of Marlboro sold for less than U.S.$2 in Russia ($0.62), South Korea ($1.00), Brazil ($1.25), and Chile ($1.25). However, the price of a pack was close to U.S.$3 in Germany ($2.90), Australia ($2.99), and the U.K. ($3.45).

Why these huge price variations? A potpourri of factors governs global pricing decisions. Some of the drivers are related to the so-called 4 C's: Company (costs, company goals), *Customers* (price sensitivity, segments), Competition (nature, intensity), and *Channels*. Aside from these, in many countries, multinationals' pricing decisions are often influenced by government policies. We now consider the main drivers that affect global pricing.

Company Goals

When developing a pricing strategy for its global markets, the firm needs to decide what it wants to accomplish with its strategy. These goals might include maximizing current profits or projecting a premium image. According to one study,[2] the most important pricing objectives of companies doing business in the United States (including foreign-based firms) are: (1) to achieve a satisfactory return on investment, (2) to maintain market share, and (3) to meet a specified profit goal (in that order). Company objectives will vary from market to market, especially in multinationals with a large degree of local autonomy. A pair of Levi 501 blue jeans may sell for up to $80 in Europe or Japan, versus $30 in the United States. In several European countries 501 jeans are regarded as fashion items. Hence, the Levi brand name enjoys much more prestige abroad than in the United States.[3] Company goals will also change over time. Initially, when a firm enters a country, it may set a relatively low price (compared to other countries) to penetrate the

---

[1]"Counting Costs of Dual Pricing in the Run-up to 1992," *The Financial Times*, (July 9, 1990), p. 4.

[2]Saeed Samiee, "Pricing in Marketing Strategies of U.S.- and Foreign-Based Companies," *Journal of Business Research*, 15 (1987), pp. 17–30.

[3]"The Levi Straddle," *Forbes* (January 17, 1994), p. 44.

EXHIBIT 13-1
HIGHEST AND LOWEST PRICES IN ECU OF PRODUCTS IN EU CITIES

	Lowest*		Highest*		Price coefficient**
Bosch 500-2 power drill	Brussels	70.94–56.75	Milan	99.34–83.48	1.47
Bosch 4542 washing machine	London	462.69–402.34	Milan	672.74–565.33	1.40
Braun Silencio hairdryer	London	18.44–16.03	Athens	50.60–43.62	2.72
Coca Cola, 1.5l bottle	Amsterdam	.82–.69	Copenhagen	2.04–1.45	2.10
Colgate toothpaste, 100ml	Athens	1.33–1.15	Milan	1.88–1.72	1.50
EMI Compact disc: Tina Turner "Foreign Affair"	Athens	14.39–12.41	Madrid	21.72–19.39	1.36
EMI cassette of same	London	8.7–7.57	Copenhagen	21.84–17.9	2.36
Financial Times	London	.67–.67	Copenhagen	1.54–1.54	2.30
Gillette Contour razor blades, 5-pack	Athens	1.99–1.72	Copenhagen	3.53–2.76	1.60
Heinz ketchup, 570gm	London	.86–.86	Madrid	2.04–1.92	1.98
Hitachi 630 videorecorder	London	452.17–393.19	Athens	749.64–551.21	1.40
Hoover 3726 vacuum cleaner	Luxembourg	118.31–105.63	Amsterdam	260.31–219.67	2.08
IBM 30-021 personal computer, 20MB, colour display	Athens	1629.21–1404.49	Copenhagen	4065.75–3332.58	1.60
Kelloggs cornflakes, 375 gm	Amsterdam	1.26–1.06	Cologne	1.95–1.82	1.72
Kodak 35mm Gold 100 film	Cologne	3.4–2.98	Copenhagen	5.98–4.90	1.64
Levi 501 jeans	London	50.01–43.49	Madrid	74.65–66.65	1.53
Mars Bar	London	.27–.27	Copenhagen	.67–.55	2.04
Nescafé, 200gm	Athens	3.67–3.16	Milan	7.78–7.14	2.26
Olivetti ET65 electronic typewriter	Brussels	331.37–278.46	Lisbon	638.37–545.62	1.96
Pampers, Midi 52, boy's	Dublin	10.47–8.51	Milan	11.70–10.73	1.26
Sony 2121 television	London	536.45–466.48	Copenhagen	1091.74–894.87	1.92
Timotel shampoo, 200ml	London	1.23–1.07	Amsterdam	2.09–1.76	1.64
Toblerone, 100gm	Amsterdam	.85–.72	Lisbon	1.49–1.38	1.92

*Prices in ECU. converted at rate of April 27, 1990. The first set of figures in each column is the retail price, the second the price before tax.

**Ratio of highest to lowest pre-tax prices. Data supplied by Runzheimer Mitchell Europe.

Source: "Counting Costs of Dual Pricing in the Run-up to 1992," *The Financial Times* (July 9. 1990), p.4. Reprinted by permission.

market. Once the firm is well entrenched, it may shift its objectives and bring them in line with the goals pursued in other countries.

Company Costs

Company costs figure prominently in the pricing decision. Costs set the floor: the company wants to set a price that will at least cover all costs needed to make and sell its products. Cost differentials between countries can lead to wide price gaps. It is important that management considers all relevant costs of manufacturing, marketing, and distributing the product. Company costs consist of two parts: variable costs, which change with sales volume, and fixed costs (e.g., overhead), which do not vary.

Export pricing policies differ depending on the way costs are treated.[4] The most

[4]S. Tamer Cavusgil, "Unraveling the Mystique of Export Pricing," *Business Horizons*, 31 (May-June 1988), pp. 54–63.

popular practice is **cost-plus pricing.** This approach adds international costs and a mark-up to the domestic manufacturing cost. At times, the company will offer discounts or rebates to reward its customer. An alternative approach is **dynamic incremental pricing.** This strategy arrives at a price after removing domestic fixed costs. The premise is that these costs have to be borne anyhow, regardless of whether or not the goods are exported. Only variable costs generated by the exporting efforts and a portion of the overhead load (the "incremental" costs) should be recuperated. Examples of exporting-related incremental costs include manufacturing costs, shipping expenses, insurance, and overseas promotional costs. Although the second approach is more kosher from an economic perspective, there are certain risks. Situations where the export list price is far below the domestic price could trigger dumping accusations in the export market.

When demand is highly price sensitive, the company needs to consider how it can reduce costs from a global perspective. Manufacturing scale economies provide an incentive to standardize product offerings or to consolidate manufacturing facilities. In some markets, logistics costs can be trimmed by centralizing distribution centers or warehouse facilities. By the same token, significant marketing costs may prompt a multinational operating in Europe to develop Pan-European advertising campaigns.

Customer Demand

Whereas costs set a floor, consumers' perceived value attached to your product will set a ceiling to the price. Consumer demand is a function of buying power, tastes, habits, and substitutes. These demand conditions will vary from country to country. For instance, Nescafé is fairly expensive in Italy, since the Italian demand for instant coffee is minor.[5]

Buying power is a key consideration in pricing decisions. Countries with low per-capita incomes pose a dilemma. Consumers in such countries are far more price-sensitive than in developed markets. Therefore, price premiums are often a major hurdle for most consumers in these markets. One option is to go for the mass market by adjusting the product. Firms might consider downsizing the product (smaller volume, size, fewer units per package) or lowering the product quality. In the Philippines, Wrigley markets tiny, individual pieces of chewing gum (rather than five-stick packages) while the quality is maintained (see Exhibit 13-2). Retailers charge customers one Philippine peso[6] for three pieces of chewing gum.[7] In Egypt, one of the moves that Procter & Gamble undertook to revitalize the sales of Ariel, its high-suds laundry detergent brand, was to downsize the package size from 200 grams to 150 grams, thereby lowering the cash outlay for ordinary consumers.[8] In Russia, Procter & Gamble chose the second route—lower quality—by rolling out an economy laundry detergent product carrying the Tide brand name—a premium U.S. brand.[9]

---

[5]"Counting Costs of Dual Pricing . . . ," *The Financial Times* (July 9, 1990), p. 4.

[6]25 Philippine Peso equals about $1.

[7]Douglas S. Barrie, Group Vice-President International, Wrigley Company, personal communication, 1994.

[8]Mahmoud Aboul-Fath and Loula Zaklama, "Ariel High Suds Detergent in Egypt—A Case Study," *Marketing and Research Today* (May 1992), pp. 130–35.

[9]"P & G Accelerates International Pace," *Advertising Age International* (March 21, 1994), pp. I-3, I-23.

EXHIBIT 13-2
AN EXAMPLE OF DOWNSIZING
WITH PRICE ADJUSTMENT

Another strategic option is to charge prices in the same range as Western prices and target the upper-end of the foreign market. In 1993, Masterfoods, a unit of Mars Inc., sold a 40-pound sack of Pedigree Pal dry dog food for $27.70 in Russia, far above the average monthly salary (about $22) around that time. The high price was advocated by a "more for your money" positioning strategy, claiming that the product is far more nutritious and cheaper to serve than fresh food.[10] Other Western multinationals also use a high price, premium positioning strategy in Central and Eastern Europe. Nabisco markets a broad range of products in Russia at retail prices in the Western European price range: Cheez Balls sell for $1–$2 (depending on the retail outlet), and a 340 gram package of Chips Ahoy! cookies sells for $2.50–$3.20.[11]

Generally speaking, a market consists of a quality-sensitive and a price-sensitive market segment. In some markets the quality segment dominates. In other countries, the price segment rules. Standard microeconomic theory suggests that companies should exploit differences in price sensitivity by price discrimination. One useful summary measure for price sensitivity is price elasticity: the percentage change in unit demand resulting from a one percentage point change in price. If competition does not play a role, we can apply a simple formula to find the optimal price (i.e., profit maximizing) in country i:

$$\text{optimal price}_i = [e_i/(1 + e_i)] * \text{marginal cost}_i$$

where e_i is the price elasticity in country i. Suppose the price elasticity in countries A and B is -2 (meaning that a 1 percent increase in price leads to a 2 percent demand decline) and -3, respectively. Marginal costs are $1 per unit in both countries. Under these conditions, the optimal unit prices to be charged are: $3.00 in the low-price-sensitive country A and $1.50 in the high-price-sensitive country B. So, significant cross-country differences in price sensitivities encourage a company to charge hugely different prices (in this particular case, 2-to-1). Wide gaps could create arbitrage opportunities (buy low in low-priced countries, sell high in high-priced countries) and

[10]"How to Sell Pet Food in Russia," *Advertising Age International* (May 17, 1993), p. I-21.

[11]"Russians Go Nuts for Snacks as Planters, Frito Duke It Out," *Advertising Age International* (December 13, 1993), pp. I-3, I-14.

lead to gray market situations. Another concern is that price sensitivities change over time. Economic recessions usually make households much more price-conscious. About one in four Japanese car buyers cited price as a key purchase consideration in 1993 when the Japanese economy was weak, compared to less than 12 percent in 1992.[12]

Typically, the nature of demand will change over time. In countries that were entered recently, the firm may need to stimulate trial via discounting or a penetration pricing strategy. In more mature markets, the lion's share of customers will be repeat buyers. Once brand loyalty has been established, price will play less of a role as a purchase criterion, and the firm may be able to afford the luxury of a premium pricing strategy. The success of such a pricing strategy will depend on the company's ability to differentiate its product from the competition.

Competition

Competition is another key factor in global pricing. Differences in the competitive situation across countries will usually lead to cross-border price differentials. Exhibit 13-3 contrasts the 1993 price of a Marlboro pack of cigarettes with the highest- and lowest-priced brands in several countries. Not surprisingly, the Marlboro price tends to be very low in markets where the competing brands are priced low, and vice versa in high-price markets.

The competitive situation may vary for a number of reasons. First, the number of competitors typically varies from country to country. In some countries, the firm faces very few competitors (or even enjoys a monopoly position), whereas in others, the company has to combat numerous competing brands. Also, the nature of competition will differ: global versus local players, private firms versus state-owned companies. Even when local companies are not state-owned, they often are viewed as "national champions" and treated accordingly by their local governments. Such a status entails subsidies or other goodies (e.g., cheap loans) that enable them to undercut their competitors. In some markets, firms have to compete with a knock-off version of their own product. The presence of counterfeit products could force the firm to lower its price in such markets. Also, in many emerging markets, legitimate distributors of global brands need to compete with smugglers. In China, for instance, industry analysts estimated that 100,000 cars were smuggled in 1996 from Japan and South Korea.[13] Smuggling operations put downward pressure on the price of the affected product. The strength of private labels (store brands) is another important driver. In countries where store brands are well entrenched, companies are forced to accept lower margins than elsewhere.

A company's competitive position typically varies across countries. Companies will be price leaders in some countries and price takers in other countries. Heinz's policy is to cut prices in markets where it is not the leading brand.[14] Finally, the rules of the game usually differ. Nonprice competition (e.g., advertising, channel coverage) may be favored in some countries. Elsewhere, price combats are a way of life. In

---

[12]"Recession Drives New Approaches," *Advertising Age International* (January 17, 1994), p. I-27.

[13]"Where's the Pot of Gold?" *Business Week* (*Asian Edition*) (February 3, 1997), pp. 14–15.

[14]"Counting Costs of Dual Pricing . . . ," p. 4.

EXHIBIT 13-3
THE COST OF A PACK OF MARLBORO CIGARETTES VS. THE HIGHEST- AND LOWEST-
PRICE BRANDS IN EACH MARKET

Country	Marlboro price (Marketer)	Highest-price cigarette (Marketer)	Lowest-price cigarette (Marketer)
Russia*	62¢ (Philip Morris)	87¢ Davidoff (Reemstma)	6¢ Dymok (Not available)
S. Korea	$1.00 (Philip Morris)	$2.50 Davidoff (Not available)	25¢ Chongja and Baekja (Korea Tobacco & Ginseng Corp.)
Brazil	$1.25 (Philip Morris)	$1.42 Capri (Souza Cruz)	64¢ Imperador (Philip Morris)
Chile	$1.25 (Facil SA)	$1.40 Barclay (Chile Tobacco)	65¢ Life (Chile Tobacco)
Mexico	$1.26 (Cigatam)	$1.35 Benson & Hedges (Cigatam)	35¢ Delicados (Cigatam)
Hungary	$1.36 (Philip Morris)	$1.57 Eve (Philip Morris)	51¢ Symphonia (Reemstma)
Japan	$2.20 (Japan Tobacco)	$2.48 Parliament (Philip Morris)	$1.76 Hope, Peace (Japan Tobacco)
France	$2.40 (Philip Morris)	$2.59 Dunhill (Rothman's)	$1.38 Gauloises Brunes (Seita)
Hong Kong	$2.80 (Philip Morris)	$3.50 Cartier (Rothman's Far East)	$2.00 Double Happiness (Nanyang Bros. Tobacco)
Germany	$2.90 (Philip Morris)	$3.13 Dunhill (Rothman's)	$2.68 West (Reemstma)
Australia	$2.99 (Philip Morris)	$3.24 Camel (R.J. Reynolds)	$4.86** Horizon (WD & HO Wills)
U.K.	$3.45 (Rothman's)	$3.45 Camel (R.J. Reynolds)	$2.70 Red Band (Nurdin & Peacock)

*800 rubies to the dollar.

**Sold in packs of 50 cigarettes.

Source: Advertising Age International. Reprinted with permission from the June 21, 1993, issue of
Advertising Age. Copyright, Crain Communications Inc. 1993.

France, a ban on cigarette advertising leaves price as the only competitive device to gain market share.[15]

Distribution Channels

Another driver behind global pricing is the distribution channel. The pressure exercised by channels can take many forms. Variations in trade margins and the length of the channels will influence the ex-factory price charged by the company. The balance of power between manufacturers and their distributors is another factor behind pricing practices. Countries such as France and the United Kingdom are characterized by large retailers who are able to order in bulk and to bargain for huge discounts with manufacturers. In the Pan-European market, several smaller retailers have formed cross-border co-ops to strengthen their negotiation position with their common suppliers. The power of large-scale retailers in Europe is visibly illustrated by the hurdles that several manufacturers faced in implementing everyday-low-pricing (EDLP). With EDLP, the manufacturer offers consistently lower prices to the retailer (and the ultimate shopper) instead of promotional price discounts and trade promotions. Several German supermarket chains delisted P & G brands like Ariel, Vizir and Lenor detergent products, and Bess toilet tissue when P & G introduced EDLP in Germany in early 1996. As a result, P & G Germany's sales slightly declined in 1996, but profits increased by 77 percent.[16]

Large cross-country price gaps open up arbitrage opportunities that lead to **parallel imports** from low-price countries to high-price ones. These parallel imports are commonly handled by unauthorized distributors at the expense of legitimate trade channels. To lessen parallel imports, firms might consider to narrow cross-border price disparities. Thus, pre-emption of cross-border bargain hunting is often times a strong motivation behind a company's pricing practices.

Government Policies

Government policies can have a direct or indirect impact on pricing policies. Factors that have a direct impact include sales tax rates (e.g., value added taxes), tariffs, and price controls. Sometimes government interference is very blatant. The Chinese government, for instance, fixes passenger car-prices between $15,600 and $26,000.[17]

An increase in the sales tax rate will usually lower overall demand. However, in some cases taxes may selectively affect imports. For instance, in the late 1980s, the U.S. government introduced a 10-percent luxury tax on the part of a car's price that exceeds $30,000. This luxury tax primarily affected the price of luxury import cars since few U.S. made luxury cars sell for more than the $30,000 threshold. Tariffs obviously will inflate the retail price of imports. Another concern is price controls. These either affect the whole economy (for instance, in high-inflation countries) or selective industries. In many countries, a substantial part of the health care costs are borne by the government. As a result, drug prices in many of these countries are ne-

---

[15]"Marlboro Price Cut Stays on Home Soil," *Advertising Age International* (June 21, 1993), p. I-18.

[16]"Heat's on Value Pricing," *Advertising Age International* (January 1997), pp. I-21, I-22.

[17]"Where's the Pot of Gold?"

gotiated with the host government. Many pharmaceutical companies face the dilemma of accepting lower prices for their drugs or having their drugs registered on a negative list, which contains drugs that the government will not reimburse.[18] Further, several governments heavily encourage the prescription on generics or stimulate parallel imports from low-price countries to put pressure on drug companies.

Aside from direct intervention, government policies can have an indirect impact on pricing decisions. For instance, huge government deficits spur interest rates (cost of capital), currency volatility, and inflation. The interplay of these factors will affect the product cost. Ultimately, the firm will have to decide to what degree cost increases should be passed through to its customers. Inflation might also impact labor costs in those countries (e.g., Belgium, Brazil) that have a wage indexation system. Such a system adjusts wages for increases in the cost of living.

We have pinpointed the main factors that will drive global pricing decisions. We now highlight the key managerial issues in global pricing.

MANAGING PRICE ESCALATION

Exporting involves more steps and substantially higher risks than domestic marketing. To cover the incremental costs (e.g., shipping, insurance, tariffs, margins of various intermediaries), the final foreign retail price will often be much higher than the domestic retail price. This phenomenon is known as price escalation. Price escalation raises two issues that management needs to confront: (1) will our foreign customers be willing to pay the inflated price for our product ("sticker shock")? and (2) will this price make our product less competitive? If the answer is negative, the exporter needs to decide how to cope with price escalation.

There are two broad approaches to deal with price escalation: (1) find ways to cut the export price, or (2) position the product as a (super) premium brand. Several options exist to lower the export price:[19]

1. **Rearrange the distribution channel.** Channels are often largely responsible for price escalation, either due to the length of the channel (number of layers between manufacturer and end-user) or due to exorbitant margins. In some circumstances, it is possible to shorten the channel. Alternatively, firms could look into channel arrangements that provide cost efficiencies. Recently, several U.S. companies have decided to penetrate the Japanese consumer market through direct marketing (e.g., catalog sales, telemarketing). This allows them to bypass the notorious Japanese distribution infrastructure and become more price-competitive.

2. **Eliminate costly features (or make them optional).** Several exporters have addressed the price escalation issue by offering no-frills versions of their product. Rather than having to purchase the entire bundle, customers can buy the core product and then decide whether or not they want to pay extra for optional features.

---

[18]Some countries have a "positive" list of drugs from which physicians can prescribe.

[19]S. Tamer Cavusgil, "Unraveling the Mystique of Export Pricing," *Business Horizons* (May-June 1988), p. 56.

3. **Downsize the product.**   Another route to dampen sticker shock is downsizing the product by offering a smaller version of the product or a lesser count. This option is only desirable when consumers are not aware of cross-border volume differences. To that end, manufacturers may decide to go for a local branding strategy.

4. **Assemble or manufacture the product in foreign markets.**   A more extreme option is to assemble or even manufacture the entire product in foreign markets (not necessarily the export market). Closer proximity to the export market will lower transportation costs. To lessen import duties for goods sold within European Union markets, numerous firms have decided to set up assembly operations in EU member states.

5 . **Adapt the product to escape tariffs or tax levies.**   Finally, a company could also modify its export product to bring it into a different tariff or tax bracket. When the United States levied a 10 percent tax on plus-$30,000 luxury cars, Land Rover increased the maximum weight of Range Rover models sold in America to 6,019 lbs. As a result, the Range Rover was classified as a truck (not subject to the 10 percent luxury tax) rather than a luxury car.

These measures are different ways to counter price escalation. Alternatively, an exporter could exploit the price escalation situation and go for a premium positioning strategy. LEGO, the Danish toymaker, sells building block sets in India that are priced between $6 and $223, far more than most other toys that Indian parents can purchase. To justify the premium price, LEGO uses a marketing strategy that targets middle-class parents and stresses the educational value of LEGO toys.[20] Of course, for this strategy to work, other elements of the export marketing-mix should be in tandem with the premium positioning. To return to the Levi example, in Japan and Europe, Levi Strauss sells its jeans mainly in upscale boutiques rather than in department stores.[21]

◆ ◆ ◆ ◆ ◆ ◆   **PRICING IN INFLATIONARY ENVIRONMENTS**

When McDonald's opened its doors in January 1990, a Big Mac meal (including fries and a soft drink) in Moscow cost 6 rubles.[22] Three years later, the same meal cost 1,100 rubles. Rampant inflation is a major obstacle to doing business in many countries. Double-digit annual inflation rates are not unusual in several Latin American and former East Bloc countries. Moreover, high inflation rates are usually coupled with highly volatile exchange rate movements. In such environments, price setting and stringent cost control become extremely crucial. Not surprisingly, in such markets, companies' financial divisions are often far more important than other departments.[23]

There are several alternative ways to safeguard against inflation.

---

[20]"LEGO Building Its Way to China," *Advertising Age International* (March 20, 1995), p. I-29.

[21]"The Levi Straddle," *Forbes* (January 17, 1994), p. 44.

[22]"Inflation Bites Russians, Who Still Bite into Big Mac," *Advertising Age International* (March 15, 1993), pp. I-3, I-23.

[23]"A Rollercoaster Out of Control," *The Financial Times* (February 22, 1993).

1. **Modify components, ingredients, parts and/or packaging materials.** Some ingredients are subject to lower inflation rates than others. This might justify a change in the ingredient mix. Of course, before implementing such a move, the firm should consider all its consequences (e.g., consumer response, impact on shelf life of the product).

2. **Source materials from low-cost suppliers.** Supply management plays a central role in high inflation environments. A first step is to screen suppliers and determine which ones are most cost-efficient without cutting corners. If feasible, materials could be imported from low-inflation countries. Note, though, that high inflation rates are coupled with a weakening currency. This will push up the price of imports.

3. **Shorten credit terms.** In some cases, profits can be realized by juggling around with terms of payment. For instance, a firm that is able to collect cash from its customers within fifteen days but has one month to pay its suppliers can invest its money during the fifteen-day grace period. Thus, firms strive to push up the lead time in paying their suppliers. At the same time, they also try to shorten the time to collect from their clients.[24]

4. **Include escalator clauses in long-term contracts.** Many business-to-business marketing situations involve long term contracts (e.g., leasing arrangements). To hedge their position against inflation, the parties will include escalator clauses that will provide the necessary protection.

5. **Quote prices in a stable currency.** To handle high inflation, companies often quote prices in a stable currency such as the U.S. dollar or the ECU.

6. **Pursue rapid inventory turnovers.** High inflation also mandates rapid inventory turnarounds. As a result, information technologies (e.g., scanning techniques, computerized inventory tracking) that facilitate rapid inventory turnovers or even just-in-time delivery will yield a competitive advantage.

7. **Draw lessons from other countries.** Operations in countries with a long history of inflation offer valuable lessons for ventures in other high-inflation countries. Cross-fertilization by drawing from experience in other high inflation markets often helps. Some companies—McDonald's[25] and Otis Elevator International,[26] for example—have relied on expatriate managers from Latin America to cope with inflation in the former Soviet Union.

Global Perspective 13-1 discusses how McDonald's copes with hyper-inflation. To combat hyper-inflation, governments occasionally impose price controls (usually coupled with a wage freeze). For instance, Brazil went through five price freezes over a six-year interval. Such temporary price caps could be selective, targeting certain products, but, in extreme circumstances, they will apply across-the-board to all consumer goods. Price freezes have proven to be very ineffective to dampen inflation, witness the experience of Brazil. Often, expectations of an imminent price freeze start off a rumor mill that will spur companies to implement substantial price increases, thereby setting off a vicious cycle. One consequence of price controls is that goods are diverted to the black market, leading to shortages in the regular market.

---

[24]"A Rollercoaster Out of Control," *The Financial Times* (February 22, 1993).

[25]"Inflation Lessons over a Big Mac," *The Financial Times* (February 22, 1993).

[26]"Russians Up and Down," *The Financial Times* (October 18, 1993), p. 12.

◆ ◆

$\mathcal{G}$LOBAL PERSPECTIVE 13-1

SELLING BURGERS IN HYPER-INFLATIONARY ENVIRONMENTS

As the site of boot camp for the shock troops in the battle to cope with Russian inflation, few places could outclass Brazil. That was the conclusion of the McDonald's Corporation. And that is why it sent a group of high-level trainees there for a crash course in how to brave inflation in a country where prices have risen by at least 400 percent a year since 1987. In 1992, Russia's rate of 1,450 percent was one of the few to top Brazil's astounding figure of 1,149 percent.

The contingent consisted of three Canadians, including the head of Russian operations, and a native Russian vice-president. The Canadian subsidiary controls the branch in Moscow, where the outlet on Pushkin Square is the fast-food company's busiest.

"They came in search of the tools needed to manage and operate in a hyper-inflationary environment," said Gerson Ferrari, finance director of McDonald's in Brazil. Ferrari led them to multinationals well-versed in adapting to rocketing prices—firms such as Cargill, Goodyear, and Kodak. Ferrari's lesson emphasized cash-flow management, control of raw materials, sales and price setting strategies, and how to hedge for potentially substantial distortions in the exchange rate.

The visitors learned that in Brazil McDonald's negotiates a separate inflation rate for each of its suppliers. It then uses those rates for monthly realignments, instead of applying the government's generic inflation figures across the board. The monthly adjustments for suppliers are "wedded" to periodic price increases for Big Macs.

Source: "Inflation Lessons Over a Big Mac," *The Financial Times* (February 22, 1993). Reprinted by permission.

Companies faced with price controls can consider several action courses:

1. **Adapt the product line.** To reduce exposure to a government-imposed price freeze, companies diversify into product lines that are relatively free of price controls.[27] Of course, before embarking on such a change-over, the firm has to examine the long-term ramifications. Modifying the product line could imply loss of economies of scale, an increase in overhead, and adverse reactions from the company's customer base.

2. **Shift target segments or markets.** A more drastic move is to shift the firm's target segment. For instance, price controls often apply to consumer food products, but not to animal-related products. So a maker of corn-based consumer products might consider a shift from breakfast cereals to chicken-feed products. Again, such action should be preceded by a thorough analysis of its strategic implications. Alternatively, a firm might consider using its operations in the high-inflation country as an export base for countries that are not subject to price controls.

3. **Launch new products or variants of existing products.** If price controls are selective, a company can navigate around them by systematically launching new products or modifying existing ones. Also here, the firm should con-

---

[27]Venkatakrishna V. Bellur, Radharao Chaganti, Rajeswararao Chaganti, and Saraswati P. Singh, "Strategic Adaptations to Price Controls: The Case of the Indian Drug Industry," *Journal of the Academy of Marketing Science*, 13(1) (Winter 1985), pp. 143–59.

sider the overall picture by answering questions such as: Will there be a demand for these products? What are the implications in terms of manufacturing economies? inventory management? How will the trade react? Further, if these products are not yet available elsewhere, this option is merely a long-term solution.

4. **Negotiate with the government.** In some cases, firms are able to negotiate for permission to adjust their prices. Lobbying can be done individually, but is more likely to be successful on an industry-wide basis.

5. **Predict incidence of price controls.** Some countries have a history of price freeze programs. Given historical information on the occurrence of price controls and other economic variables, econometric models can be constructed to forecast the likelihood of price controls. That information can be used by managers to see whether or not price adjustments are warranted, given the likelihood of an imminent price freeze.[28]

A drastic action course is simply to leave the country. Many consumer goods companies chose this option when they exited their South-American markets during the 1980s ("If you can't stand the heat, leave the kitchen."). However, companies that hang on and learn to manage a high-inflation environment will be able carry over their expertise to other countries. Further, they will enjoy a competitive advantage (due to entry barriers such as brand loyalty, channel and supplier ties) versus companies that re-enter these markets once inflation has been suppressed.

GLOBAL PRICING AND CURRENCY MOVEMENTS ◆ ◆ ◆ ◆ ◆ ◆ ◆

In May 1992, two of the most expensive car markets in the European Union were Spain and Italy. One year later, Italy and Spain were the two lowest-priced markets.[29] Currency volatility within the European Union was mostly responsible for these car price reversals. With a few exceptions (e.g., the Eastern Caribbean, some former French colonies in West Africa), most countries have their own currency. Exchange rates reflect how much one currency is worth in terms of another currency. Due to the interplay of a variety of economic and political factors, exchange rates continuously float up- or downward. Even membership in a monetary union does not guarantee exchange rate stability. In September 1992, the Italian lira and the pound sterling were forced to withdraw from the European Monetary System. At the same time, the bands within which the remaining currencies could move without intervention were broadened. In early 1994, the CFA, the currency unit shared by several former French African colonies, was devalued by 50 percent. Given the sometimes dramatic exchange rate movements, setting prices in a floating exchange rate world poses a tremendous challenge.[30] Exhibit 13-4 lists several exporter strategies under varying currency regimes.

---

[28]James K. Weekly, "Pricing in Foreign Markets: Pitfalls and Opportunities," *Industrial Marketing Management*, 21 (1992), pp. 173–79.

[29]"Fluctuating Exchange Rates Main Factor in European Car Price Comparisons," *The Financial Times* (July 5, 1993).

[30]Llewlyn Clague and Rena Grossfield, "Export Pricing in a Floating Rate World," *Columbia Journal of World Business* (Winter 1974), pp. 17–22.

EXHIBIT 13-4
EXPORTER STRATEGIES UNDER VARYING CURRENCY CONDITIONS

When domestic currency is WEAK . . .	*When domestic currency is* STRONG . . .
• Stress price benefits	• Engage in nonprice competition by improving quality, delivery and aftersale service
• Costly features expand product line and add more	• Improve productivity and engage in vigorous cost reduction
• Shift sourcing and manufacturing to domestic market	• Shift sourcing and manufacturing overseas
• Exploit export opportunities in all markets	• Give priority to exports to relatively strong-currency countries
• Conduct conventional cash-for-goods trade	• Deal in countertrade with weak-currency countries
• Use full-costing approach, but use marginal-cost pricing to penetrate new/competitive markets	• Trim profit margins and use marginal-cost pricing
• Speed repatriation of foreign-earned income and collections	• Keep the foreign-earned income in host country, slow collections
• Minimize expenditures in local, host country currency	• Maximize expenditures in local, host country currency
• Buy needed services (advertising, insurance, transportation, etc.) in domestic market	• Buy needed services abroad and pay for them in local currencies
• Minimize local borrowing	• Borrow money needed for expansion in local market
• Bill foreign customers in domestic currency	• Bill foreign customers in their own currency

Source: S. Tamer Cavusgil, "Unraveling the Mystique of Export Pricing," reprinted from *Business Horizons*, May-June 1988. Copyright 1988 by the Foundation for the School of Business at Indiana University. Used with permission.

Currency Gain/Loss Pass Through

Two major managerial pricing issues result from currency movements: (1) How much of a exchange rate gain (loss) should be passed through to our customers? and (2) In what currency should we quote our prices? Let us first address the pass-through issue. Consider the predicament of American companies exporting to Japan. In principle, a weakening of the U.S. dollar versus the Japanese yen will strengthen the competitive position of U.S.-based exporters in Japan. A weak dollar allows U.S.-based firms to lower the yen price of American goods exported to Japan. This enables American exporters to steal market share away from the local Japanese competitors without sacrificing profits. By the same token, a strengthening U.S. dollar will undermine the competitive position of American exporters. When the dollar appreciates versus the yen, we have the mirror picture of the previous situation: the retail price in yen of American exports goes up. As a result, American exporters might lose market share if they leave their ex-factory prices unchanged. To maintain their competitive edge, they may be forced to lower their ex-factory dollar prices. Of course, the ultimate impact on the exporter's competitive position will also depend on the impact of currency movement on the exporter's costs and the nature of the competition in the Japanese market. The benefits of a weaker dollar could be washed out when many parts are imported from Japan, since the weaker dollar will make these parts more expensive. When most of the competitors are U.S.-based manufacturers, changes in the dollar's exchange rate might not matter.

Let us illustrate these points with a numerical example. Consider the situation in Exhibit 13-5, which looks at the dilemmas that a hypothetical U.S.-based exporter to Japan faces when the exchange rate between the U.S. dollar and the Japanese yen changes. In the example we assume a simple linear demand schedule:

Demand (in units) in Japanese export market = 2,000 − 50 × yen price.

We also make an admittedly dubious assumption: Our exporter does not face any costs (in other words, total revenues equal total profits). Initially, one U.S. dollar equals 100 yen and the firm's total export revenue is $55.5 million. Suppose now that the U.S. dollar has strengthened by 30 percent versus the Japanese yen, moving from an exchange rate of 100 yen to one U.S.$ to a 130-to-1 exchange rate (row 2 in Exhibit 13-5). If the US$ ex-factory price remains the same (i.e., $30,000) Japanese consumers will face a 30 percent price increase. Total demand decreases (from 1,850 units to 1,805 units) and also US$ revenue goes down by $1.35 million. Our American exporter faces the problem of whether or not to pass through exchange rate losses, and if so, how much, of the loss he should absorb. If our exporter does not lower the U.S. dollar ex-factory price, he is likely to lose market share to his Japanese (or European) competitors in Japan. So, to sustain its competitive position, the U.S.-based manufacturer would be forced to lower its ex-factory price. In this situation, American exporters face the trade-off between sacrificing short-term profits (maintaining price) and sustaining long-term market share in export markets (cutting ex-factory price). For example, in the extreme case, the U.S. firm might consider sus-

EXHIBIT 13-5
A NUMERICAL ILLUSTRATION OF PASS-THROUGH AND LOCAL CURRENCY STABILITY

Demand in Japan (Units) = 2,000 − 50 × Price (in Yen)
Costs = $0.0

Panel A: 100% Pass-Through

Exchange Rate	Unit Price in US$	Unit Price in Yen	Units Sold	US$ Revenue
100 Yen = $1	$30,000	3.0m	1,850	$55.50m
130 Yen = $1	$30,000	3.9m	1,805	$54.15m
70 Yen = $1	$30,000	2.1m	1,895	$56.85m

Panel B: Local-Currency Price Stability

Exchange Rate	Unit Price in US$	Unit Price in YEN	Units Sold	US$ Revenue	Revenue Gain/(Loss) vs. 100% PT
100 Yen = $1	$30,000	3.0m	1,850	$55.50m	$0.00m
130 Yen = $1	$23,077	3.0m	1,850	$42.69m	($11.45m)
70 Yen = $1	$42,857	3.0m	1,850	$79.28m	$22.45m

taining the yen-based retail price (i.e., 3m yen). In that case, U.S.$ revenues would go down by $11.45 million.

Generally speaking, the appropriate action will depend on three factors, namely: (1) customers' price sensitivity, (2) the impact of the dollar appreciation on the firm's cost structure, and (3) the amount of competition in the export market. The higher consumers' price sensitivity in the export market, the stronger the case for lowering the ex-factory price. On the other hand, a decline in costs resulting from the strengthening of the U.S. dollar (e.g., when many parts are imported from Japan) broadens the price adjustment latitude. The more intense the competition in the export market, the stronger the pressure to cut prices. The bottom row of Exhibit 13-5 shows what happens when the U.S. dollar weakens by 30 percent. In that case we have the mirror picture of the previous scenario.

American exporters might lower their mark-ups much more in price-conscious export markets than in price-insensitive markets. Such destination-specific adjustments of mark-ups in response to exchange rate movements is referred to as **pricing-to-market (PTM).** PTM behaviors differ across source countries. One study of export pricing adjustments in the U.S. automobile market contrasted pricing decisions of Japanese and German exporters over periods where both the Japanese yen and the deutsche mark depreciated against the U.S. dollar.[31] The results of the study showed that there was much more pass-through (and less PTM) by German exporters than by their Japanese rivals (see Exhibit 13-6).

EXHIBIT 13-6

RETAIL PRICE CHANGES DURING DOLLAR APPRECIATIONS: JAPANESE AND GERMAN EXPORTS TO THE U.S. MARKET

Model	Real dollar appreciation	Real retail price change in US market
Honda Civic 2-Dr. Sedan	39%	−7%
Datsun 200 SX 2-Dr.	39	−10
Toyota Cressida 4-Dr.	39	6
BMW 320i 2-Dr. Sedan	42	−8
BMW 733i 4-Dr. Sedan	42	−17
Mercedes 300 TD Sta. Wgn.	42	−39

Note: The real dollar appreciation measures the movement of the U.S. producer price index relative to the Japanese and German producer price indices converted into dollars by the nominal exchange rate. The real retail price change measures the movement of the dollar retail price of specific auto models relative to the retail unit value of all domestically produced cars.

Source: Reprinted from Joseph A. Gagnon and Michael M. Knetter, "Markup Adjustment and Exchange Rate Fluctuations: Evidence from Panel Data on Automobile Exports," *Journal of International Money and Finance*, vol. 14, no. 2, p. 304. Copyright 1995, with kind permission from Elsevier Science Ltd., Langford Lane, Kidlington OX5 1GB, UK.

---

[31]Joseph A. Gagnon and Michael M. Knetter, "Markup Adjustment and Exchange Rate Fluctuations: Evidence from Panel Data on Automobile Exports," *Journal of International Money and Finance*, 14(2) (1995), pp. 289–310.

Playing the pricing-to-market game carries certain risks. Frequent adjustments of prices in response to currency movements will distress local channels and customers. When local currency prices move up, foreign customers may express their disapproval by switching to other brands. On the other hand, when prices go down, it will often be hard to raise prices in the future. Therefore, often times, the preferred strategy is to adjust mark-ups in such a way that local currency prices remain fairly stable. This special form of pricing-to-market has been referred to as **local-currency price stability (LCPS),** where mark-ups are adjusted to stabilize prices in the buyer's currency.[32] The bottom panel of Exhibit 13-5 reports the revenue losses or gains of an exporter who maintains LCPS. To pass through exchange rate gains from U.S. dollar devaluations, U.S.-based exporters could resort to temporary price promotions or other incentives (e.g., trade deals) rather than a permanent cut of the local currency regular price.

Currency Quotation

Another pricing concern rising from floating exchange rates centers on the currency unit to be used in international business transactions. Sellers and buyers usually prefer a quote in their domestic currency. That way, the other party will have to bear currency risks. The decision largely depends on the balance of power between the supplier and the customer. Whoever yields will need to cover currency exposure risk through hedging transactions on the forward exchange market. Some firms decide to use a common currency for all their business transactions, world- or region-wide. Dow Chemical embraces the deutsche mark for all its business dealings in Europe. A few companies have even gone a step further by using the European Currency Unit (ECU), Europe's basket currency, to settle payments in the Pan-European market. Most member states of the European Union plan to launch a common currency—the so-called euro—in 1999 that will be managed by a European central bank. So, starting in 1999, firms within the European Union might be able to use the euro as a currency to settle their transactions.

TRANSFER PRICING   ◆ ◆ ◆ ◆ ◆ ◆

Determinants of Transfer Prices

Most large multinational corporations have a network of subsidiaries spread across the globe. Sales transactions between related entities of the same company can be quite substantial, involving trade of raw materials, components, finished goods, or services. Transfer prices are prices charged for such transactions. Transfer pricing decisions in an international context need to balance off the interests of a broad range of stakeholders: (1) parent company, (2) local country managers, (3) host government(s), (4) domestic government, and (5) joint venture partner(s) when the transaction involves a partnership. Not surprisingly, reconciling the conflicting interests of these various parties can be a mind-boggling juggling act.

---

[32]Michael M. Knetter, "International Comparisons of Pricing-to-Market Behavior," *American Economic Review*, 83(3), pp. 473–486, 1993.

A number of studies have examined the key drivers behind transfer pricing decisions. One survey of U.S.-based multinationals found that transfer pricing policies were primarily influenced by the following factors (in order of importance):

1. Market conditions in the foreign country
2. Competition in the foreign country
3. Reasonable profit for foreign affiliate
4. U.S. federal income taxes
5. Economic conditions in the foreign country
6. Import restrictions
7. Customs duties
8. Price controls
9. Taxation in the foreign country
10. Exchange controls.[33]

Other surveys have come up with different rankings.[34] However, a recurring theme appears to be the importance of market conditions (especially, the competitive situation), taxation regimes, and various market imperfections (e.g., currency control, custom duties, price freeze). Generally speaking, MNCs should consider the following criteria when making transfer pricing decisions:[35]

- **Tax regimes.** Ideally, firms would like to boost their profits in low-tax countries and dampen them in high-tax countries. To shift profits from high-tax to low-tax markets, companies would set transfer prices as high as possible for goods entering high-tax countries and vice versa for low-tax countries. However, manipulating transfer prices to exploit corporate tax rate differentials will undoubtedly alert the tax authorities in the high-tax rate country and, in the worst case, lead to a tax audit. We will revisit the taxation issue shortly.

- **Local market conditions.** Another key influence is the local market conditions. Examples of market-related factors include the market share of the affiliate, the growth rate of the market, and the nature of local competition (e.g., non-price-versus price-based). To expand market share in a new market, multinationals may initially underprice intra-company shipments to a start-up subsidiary.[36]

- **Market imperfections.** Market imperfections in the host country, such as price freezes and profit repatriation restrictions hinder the multinational's ability to move earnings out of the country. Under such circumstances, transfer prices

[33]Jane Burns, "Transfer Pricing Decisions in U.S. Multinational Corporations," *Journal of International Business Studies*, 11(2) (Fall 1980), pp. 23–39.

[34]See, e.g., Seung H. Kim and Stephen W. Miller, "Constituents of the International Transfer Pricing Decision," *Columbia Journal of World Business* (Spring 1979), p. 71.

[35]S. Tamer Cavusgil, "Pricing for Global Markets," *Columbia Journal of World Business* (Winter 1996), pp. 66–78.

[36]Mohammad F. Al-Eryani, Pervaiz Alam, and Syed H. Akhter, "Transfer Pricing Determinants of U.S. Multinationals," *Journal of International Business Studies*, 21 (Third Quarter 1990), pp. 409–25.

can be used as a mechanism to get around these obstacles. Also, high import duties might prompt a firm to lower transfer prices charged to subsidiaries located in that particular country.

- **Joint venture partner.**   When the entity concerned is part of a joint venture, parent companies should also factor in the interests of the local joint venture partner. Numerous joint venture partnerships have hit the rocks because of disagreements over transfer pricing decisions.

- **Morale of local country managers.**   Finally, firms should also be concerned about the morale of their local country managers. Especially when performance evaluation is primarily based on local profits, transfer price manipulations might distress country managers whose subsidiary's profits are artificially deflated.

Setting Transfer Prices

There are two broad transfer pricing strategies: market-based transfer pricing, and nonmarket-based pricing. The first perspective uses the market mechanism as a cue for setting transfer prices. Such prices are usually referred to as **arm's length prices.** Basically, the company charges the price that any buyer outside the MNC would pay, as if the transaction had occurred between two unrelated companies (at "arm's length"). Tax authorities typically prefer this method over other transfer pricing approaches. Since an objective yardstick is used—the *market price*—transfer prices based on this approach are easy to justify to third parties (e.g., tax authorities). The major problem with arm's length transfer pricing is that an appropriate benchmark is often lacking, due to the absence of competition. This is especially true for intangible services. Many services are only available within the multinational. Payments of royalties and license fees within U.S.-based multinationals were $13 billion in 1990, far beyond the $4 billion paid between unrelated companies.[37]

Nonmarket-based pricing covers various policies that deviate from market-based pricing, the most prominent ones being: **cost-based pricing** and **negotiated pricing.**[39] Cost-based pricing simply adds a mark-up to the cost of the goods. Issues here revolve around getting a consensus on a "fair" profit split and allocation of corporate overhead. Further, tax authorities often do not accept cost-based pricing procedures. Another form of non-market based pricing is negotiated transfer prices. Here conflicts between country affiliates are resolved through negotiation of transfer prices. This process may lead to better cooperation among corporate divisions.[38]

A recent study shows that compliance with financial reporting norms, fiscal and customs rules, and anti-dumping regulations prompt companies to use market-based transfer pricing.[39] Government imposed market constraints (e.g., import restrictions, price controls, exchange controls) favor nonmarket-based transfer pricing methods. To the question, which procedure works best, the answer is pretty murky: there is no "universally optimal" system.[40] In fact, most firms use a mixture of market-based and nonmarket-pricing procedures.

---

[37]"Taxing Questions," *The Economist* (May 22, 1993), p. 73.

[38]R. Ackelsberg and G. Yukl, "Negotiated Transfer Pricing and Conflict Resolution in Organization," *Decision Sciences* (July 1979), pp. 387–98.

[39]M. F. Al-Eryani et al., p. 422.

[40]Jeffrey S. Arpan, "International Intracorporate Pricing: Non-American Systems and Views," *Journal of International Business Studies* (Spring 1972), p. 18.

Minimizing the Risk of Transfer Pricing Tax Audits[41]

Cross-country tax rate differentials encourage many MNCs to set transfer prices that shift profits from high-tax to low-tax countries to minimize their overall tax burden. At the same time, MNCs need to comply with the tax codes of their home country and the host countries involved. Noncompliance may risk accusations of tax evasion and lead to tax audits. So, the issue that MNCs face can be stated as follows: How do we as a company draw the line between setting transfer prices that maximize corporate profits and compliance with tax regulations?

To avoid walking on thin ice, experts suggest setting transfer prices that are as close as possible to the Basic Arm's Length Standard (BALS). This criterion is now accepted by tax authorities worldwide as the international standard for assessing transfer prices. In practice, there are three methods to calculate a BALS price: comparable/uncontrollable price, resale price, and cost-plus. The first rule—comparable/uncontrollable—states that the parent company should compare the transfer price of its "controlled" subsidiary to the selling price charged by an independent seller to an independent buyer of similar goods or services. The resale price method determines the BALS by subtracting the gross margin percentage used by comparable independent buyers from the final third-party sales price. Finally, the cost-plus method fixes the BALS by adding the gross profit mark-up percentage earned by comparable companies performing similar functions to the production costs of the controlled manufacturer or seller. Note that this rule is somewhat different from the cost method that we discussed earlier since, strictly speaking, the latter method does not rely on mark-ups set by third parties.

Exhibit 13-7 gives a flowchart that can be used to devise transfer pricing strategies that minimize the risk of tax audits. Decisions center around the following five questions:

1. Do comparable/uncontrolled transactions exist?
2. Where is the most value added? Parent? Subsidiary?
3. Are combined profits of parent and subsidiary shared in proportion to contributions?
4. Does the transfer price meet the benchmark set by the tax authorities?
5. Does the MNC have the information to justify the transfer prices used?

◆ ◆ ◆ ◆ ◆ ◆ GLOBAL PRICING AND ANTIDUMPING REGULATION

A potential minefield for global pricing policies are the antidumping laws that most governments use to counter dumping practices. Dumping occurs when imports are being sold at an "unfair" price. To protect local producers against the encroachment of low-priced imports, governments may levy countervailing duties or fines. Thus, it is important for exporters to realize that pricing policies, such as penetration pricing, may trigger antidumping actions. The number of antidumping initiatives has staggered in recent years. Most of the action takes place in the United States and the European Union. However, antidumping cases are increasingly initiated in Japan, India,

---

[41]This section is based on John P. Fraedrich and Connie Rae Bateman, "Transfer Pricing by Multinational Marketers: Risky Business," *Business Horizons* (Jan. - Feb. 1996), pp. 17–22.

EXHIBIT 13-7
DECISION MAKING MODEL FOR ASSESSING RISK OF TP STRATEGY

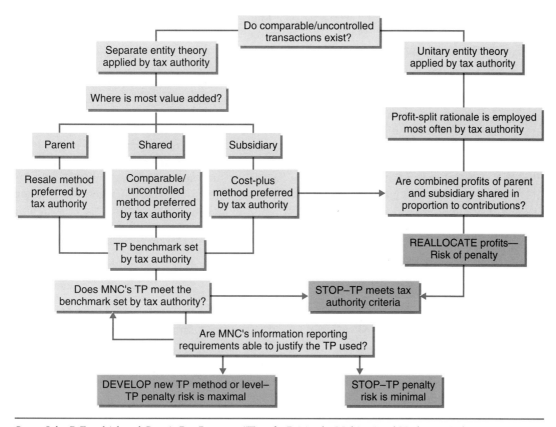

Source: John P. Fraedrich and Connie Rae Bateman, "Transfer Pricing by Multinational Marketers: Risky Business." Reprinted from *Business Horizons*, January-February 1996. Copyright 1996 by the Foundation for the School of Business at Indiana University. Used with permission.

and other developing countries. Economists often refer to this trend as a rise in protectionism.[42]

There are several possible reasons to explain the growing popularity of antidumping litigation. The removal of traditional trade barriers (tariffs, quotas) has encouraged several countries to switch to nontariff barriers such as antidumping to protect their local industries. A World Bank study showed that the impact of dumping duties in the U.S. manufactured goods sector has boosted average tariffs in that sector from a nominal 6 percent rate to 23 percent.[43] There is also a huge imbalance between plaintiffs (local producer(s)) and defendants (importer(s)) in antidumping cases. Plaintiffs typically face no penalties for frivolous complaints. Moreover, plaintiffs clearly have a home advantage (local legislation, local judge).[44] Allegedly, an-

[42]Jagdish Bhagwati, *Protectionism* (Cambridge, Mass.: The MIT Press, 1988), chapter 3.

[43]"Negotiators Down in the Dumps over U.S. Draft," *The Financial Times* (November 25, 1993), p. 6.

[44]Bhagwati, pp. 48–49.

tidumping action is often utilized as a tactical tool to foster voluntary export restraints (VER). Foreign competitors, faced with the prospect of antidumping action,
may decide to fall back on VERs as the lesser of two evils.[45] Finally, the concept of a
"fair" price is usually pretty murky. The U.S. trade law defines dumping to occur
when imports are sold below the home-country price (price discrimination) or when
the import price is less than the "constructed value" or average cost of production
("pricing below cost"). Either concept can be vague. In some situations, the imported
good is not sold in the home country, so no basis of comparison exists (absence of
domestic price). Determining the "true" cost for goods coming from centrally
planned economies is a vexing exercise.

Antidumping actions will persist in the future. The new GATT deal negotiated
at the latest round in Geneva will supposedly make it more difficult for countries to
use antidumping for trade harassment (e.g., duties should lapse after five years). On
the other hand, it will also make it harder for companies to escape duties by relocating. Multinationals need to take antidumping laws into account when determining
their global pricing policy. Aggressive pricing may trigger antidumping measures
and, thus, jeopardize the company's competitive position. Global companies should
also monitor changes in antidumping legislation and closely track antidumping cases
in their particular industry.

To minimize risk exposure to antidumping actions, exporters might pursue any
of the following marketing strategies:[46]

- **Trading-up.** Move away from low-value to high-value products via product
  differentiation. Most Japanese carmakers have stretched their product line upward to tap into the upper-tier segments of their export markets.

- **Service enhancement.** Exporters can also differentiate their product by
  adding support services to the core product. Both moves—trading up and service
  enhancement—are basically attempts to move away from price competition,
  thereby making the exporter less vulnerable to dumping accusations.

- **Distribution and communication.** Other initiatives on the distribution and
  communication front of the marketing mix include: (1) the establishment of
  communication channels with local competitors, (2) entering into cooperative
  agreements with them (e.g., strategic alliances), or (3) reallocation of the firm's
  marketing efforts from vulnerable products (that is, those most likely to be subjected to dumping scrutiny) to less sensitive products.

◆ ◆ ◆ ◆ ◆ ◆ **PRICE COORDINATION**

When developing a global pricing strategy, one of the thorniest issues is how much
coordination should exist between prices charged in different countries. This issue is
especially critical for global (or regional) brands that are marketed with no or very
few cross-border variations. Economics dictate that firms should price discriminate
between markets such that overall profits are maximized. So, if (marginal) costs are

---

[45]James E. Anderson, "Domino Dumping, I: Competitive Exporters," *American Economic
Review*, 82(1) (March 1992), pp. 65–83.

[46]Michel M. Kostecki, "Marketing Strategies between Dumping and Anti-dumping Action," *European Journal of Marketing*, 25(12), (1991), pp. 7–19.

roughly equivalent, multinationals would charge relatively low prices in highly price-sensitive countries and high prices in insensitive markets. Unfortunately, reality is not that simple. In most cases, markets cannot be perfectly separated. Huge cross-country price differentials will encourage gray markets where goods are shipped from low-price to high-price countries by unauthorized distributors. Thus, some coordination will usually be necessary. In deciding how much coordination, several considerations matter:

1. **Nature of customers.** When information on prices travels fast across borders, it is fairly hard to sustain wide price gaps. Under such conditions, firms will need to make a convincing case to their customers to justify price disparities. With global customers (e.g., multinational clients in business-to-business transactions), price coordination definitely becomes a must. In Europe, Microsoft sets prices that differ by no more than 5 percent between countries due to pressure from bargain-hunting multinational customers.[47]

2. **Nature of channels.** In a sense, distribution channels can be viewed as intermediate customers. So, the same logic applies here: price coordination becomes critical when price information is transparent and/or the firm deals with cross-border distribution channels. Pricing discipline becomes mandatory when manufacturers have little control over their distributors.

3. **Nature of competition.** In many industries, firms compete with the same rivals in a given region, if not worldwide. Global competition demands a cohesive strategic approach for the entire marketing mix strategy, including pricing. From that angle, competition pushes companies toward centralized pricing policies. On the other hand, price changes made by competitors in the local market often require a rapid response. Should the subsidiary match a given price cut? If so, to what extent? Local subsidiaries often have much better information about the local market conditions to answer such questions than corporate or regional headquarters. Thus, the need for alertness and speedy response to competitive pricing moves encourages a decentralized approach toward pricing decisions.

4. **Market integration.** When markets integrate (e.g., Single European Market), barriers (such as custom duties, paper work) to cross-border movement of goods are brought down. Given the freedom to move goods from one European Union–member state to another, the Pan-European market offers little latitude for perfect price discrimination.[48] Many of the transaction costs that once plagued parallel imports have now disappeared. In fact, the European Commission imposes heavy penalties against companies that try to limit gray market transactions. Dunlop Slazenger International was fined almost $6 million by the European Commission for limiting exports of tennis balls from the United Kingdom to other parts of the European Union.[49]

---

[47]"European Software-Pricing Formulas, Long Abstruse, Develop a Rationale," *The Wall Street Journal* (June 11, 1993).

[48]Wolfgang Gaul and Ulrich Lutz, "Pricing in International Marketing and Western European Economic Integration," *Management International Review*, 34(2) (1994), pp. 101–24.

[49]"Price Flaws Undermining EC's Single Market Hopes," *The Financial Times* (March 8, 1992).

Several multinationals doing business in the European Union harmonize their prices to narrow down price gaps between different member states. Mars and Levi Strauss aim to reduce Pan-European price gaps to no more than 10 percent.[50] In the same manner, Compaq limits price variations to 5 percent around a central price.

5. **Internal organization.** The organization setup is another important influence. Highly decentralized companies pose a hurdle to price coordination efforts. In many companies, the pricing decision is left to the local subsidiaries. Moves to take away some of the pricing authority from country affiliates will undoubtedly spark opposition and lead to bruised egos. Just as with other centralization decisions, it is important that performance evaluation systems are fine-tuned if necessary.

6. **Government regulation.** Government regulation of prices puts pressure on firms to harmonize their prices. A good example is in the pharmaceutical industry. In many countries, multinationals need to negotiate the price for new drugs with the local authorities. Governments in the European Union increasingly use prices set in other EU member states as a cue for their negotiating position. This trend has prompted several pharmaceutical companies, such as Glaxo, to negotiate a common EU-price for new drugs.

Aligning Pan-Regional Prices

Given that all indicators signal an increasing amount of globalization (especially in the Pan-European market), some degree of price coordination becomes absolutely necessary. In some cases, firms set a uniform pricing formula that is applied by all affiliates. Elsewhere, coordination is limited to general rules that only indicate the desired pricing positioning (e.g., premium positioning, middle-of-the road positioning).

Simon and Kucher[51] propose a three-step procedure to align prices in the Pan-European market. Pressure to narrow down price gaps could lead to two scenarios (see Exhibit 13.8). The disaster scenario (panel (A) in Exhibit 13-8) is a situation where all prices sink to the lowest price. At the other extreme, companies may try to sustain cross-border price gaps. The desired scenario (panel (B) in Exhibit 13-8) tries to find the middle ground by upping prices in low-price countries and cutting them in high-price countries. To pursue this scenario, firms should set a pricing corridor within the region.

The procedure works as follows:

Step 1: **Determine Optimal Price for Each Country.** Find out what price schedules will maximize overall profits. Given information on the demand schedule and the costs incurred in each market, managers are able to figure out the desirable prices in the respective markets.

---

[50]"Counting Costs of Dual Pricing in the Run-Up to 1992," *The Financial Times*, July 9, 1990, p. 4.

[51]Hermann Simon and Eckhard Kucher, "The European Pricing Time Bomb—And How to Cope With It," *Marketing and Research Today* (February 1993), pp. 25–36.

EXHIBIT 13-8
PAN-EUROPEAN PRICE COORDINATION

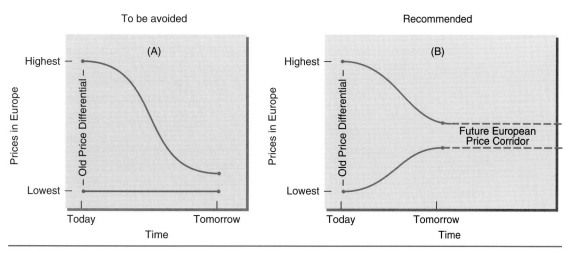

Source: Hermann Simon and Eckhard Kucher, "The European Pricing Time Bomb—and How to Cope with It," *Marketing and Research Today* (March 1992), pp. 3–14.

Permission for using this material which was originally published in Marketing and Research Today, has been granted by (E.S.O.M.A.R.) The European Society for Opinion Research J. J. Viottastraat 29, 1071 JP, Amsterdam, The Netherlands.

Step 2: **Find out whether parallel imports ("gray markets") are likely to occur at these prices.** Parallel imports arise when unauthorized distributors purchase the product (sometimes repackaged) in the low-price market and then ship it to high-price markets. The goal of step 2 is not to pre-empt parallel imports altogether, but to boost profits to the best possible degree. Given the "optimal" prices derived in the first step, the manager needs to determine to what extent the proposed price schedule will foster parallel imports. Parallel imports become harmful insofar as they inflict damage on authorized distributors. They could also hurt the morale of the local sales force or country managers. Information is needed on the arbitrage costs of parallel importers. For instance, in the European drug industry, parallel importers target drugs with more than 20 percent price differentials. Conceivably, firms might decide to abandon (or not enter) small, low-price markets, thereby avoiding pricing pressure on high price markets. MNCs should also consider the pros and cons of nonpricing solutions to cope with parallel imports. Possible strategies include: product differentiation, intelligence systems to measure exposure to gray markets, creating negative perceptions in the mind of the end-user about parallel imports.[52]

---

[52]Peggy A. Chaudhry and Michael G. Walsh, "Managing the Gray Market in the European Union: The Case of the Pharmaceutical Industry," *Journal of International Marketing*, 3(3) (1995), pp. 11–33.

Step 3: **Set a pricing corridor.** If the "optimal" prices that were derived in Step 1 are not sustainable, firms need to narrow the gap between prices for high-price and low-price markets. Charging the same price across-the-board is not desirable. Such a solution would sacrifice company profits. Instead, the firm should set a pricing corridor. The corridor is formed by systematically exploring the profit impact from lowering prices in high-price countries and upping prices in low-price countries, as shown in panel (B) of Exhibit 13-8. The narrower the price gap, the more profits the firm has to sacrifice. At some point, there will be a desirable trade-off between the size of the gray market and the amount of profits sacrificed.

Of course, this method is not foolproof. Competitive reactions (e.g., price wars) need to be factored in. Also, government regulations may restrict pricing flexibility. Still, the procedure is a good start when pricing alignment becomes desirable.

Implementing Price Coordination

Global marketers can choose from four alternatives to promote price coordination within their organization, namely:[53]

1. **Economic Measures.** Corporate headquarters are able to influence pricing decisions at the local level via the transfer prices that are set for the goods that are sold to or purchased from the local affiliates. Another option is rationing; that is, headquarters sets upper limits on the number of units that can be shipped to each country.

2. **Centralization.** In the extreme case, pricing decisions are made at corporate or regional headquarters level. Centralized price decision-making is fairly uncommon, given its numerous shortcomings. It sacrifices the flexibility that firms often need to respond rapidly to local competitive conditions.

3. **Formalization.** Far more common than the previous approach is formalization where headquarters spells out a set of pricing rules that the country managers should comply with. Within these norms, country managers have a certain level of flexibility in determining their ultimate prices.

4. **Informal Coordination.** Finally, firms can use various forms of informal price coordination. The emphasis here is on informing and persuasion rather than prescription and dictates. Examples of informal price coordination tactics include discussion groups, "best-practice" gatherings.

Which approach is most effective is contingent on the complexity of the environment in which the firm is doing business. When the environment is fairly stable and the various markets are highly similar, centralization is usually preferable over the other options. However, highly complex environments require a more decentralized approach.

---

[53]Gert Assmus and Carsten Wiese, "How to Address the Gray Market Threat Using Price Coordination," *Sloan Management Review* (Spring 1995), pp. 31–41.

COUNTERTRADE   ◆ ◆ ◆ ◆ ◆ ◆

Countertrade is an umbrella term used to describe unconventional trade-financing transactions that involve some form of noncash compensation. During the last decade, companies have increasingly been forced to rely on countertrade. The number of countries mandating countertrade jumped from about fifteen (mostly former East Bloc and developing countries) in 1975 to more than a hundred in 1991.[54] Estimates on the overall magnitude of countertrade vary, but the consensus estimate is that it covers 10 percent to 15 percent of world trade.[55] One of the most publicized deals was PepsiCo's $3 billion arrangement with the former Soviet Union to swap Pepsi for profits in Stolichnaya vodka and ocean freighters and tankers.[56] Given the growth of countertrade, global marketers should be aware of its nuts and bolts.

Forms of Countertrade

Countertrade comes in six guises: Barter, clearing arrangements, switch trading, buyback, counterpurchase, and offset. Exhibit 13-9 classifies these different forms of countertrade.

The main distinction is whether or not the transaction involves monetary compensation. Let us look at each form in more detail:[57]

- **Simple Barter.** Simple barter is a swap of one product for another product without the use of any money. Usually, no third party is involved to carry out the transaction. Though one of the oldest forms of countertrade, it is very seldom used these days. China's Farm Chemical Sales Promotion Group and the Moroccan government arranged a barter agreement in which $260 million worth of plant-protection chemicals were swapped for the equivalent value of Moroccan phosphate products.[58]

- **Clearing Agreement.** Under this form, two governments agree to import a set specified value of goods from one another over a given period. Each party sets up an account that is debited whenever goods are traded. Imbalances at the end of the contract period are cleared through payment in hard currency or goods. A recent clearing agreement between Indonesia and Iran specified that

---

[54]Kwabena Anyane-Ntow and Santhi C. Harvey, "A Countertrade Primer," *Management Accounting* (April 1995), pp. 47–49.

[55]Jean-François Hennart and Erin Anderson, "Countertrade and The Minimization of Transaction Costs," Working Paper no. 92-012R, The Wharton School, University of Pennsylvania, Philadelphia, Pennsylvania.

[56]"Worldwide Money Crunch Fuels More International Barter," *Marketing News* (March 2, 1992), p. 5.

[57]Costas G. Alexandrides and Barbara L. Bowers, *Countertrade. Practices, Strategies, and Tactics* (New York: John Wiley & Sons, 1987), chapter 1.

[58]Aspy P. Palia and Oded Shenkar, "Countertrade Practices in China," *Industrial Marketing Management*, 20, 1991, pp. 57-65.

Exhibit 13-9
Classification of Forms of Countertrade

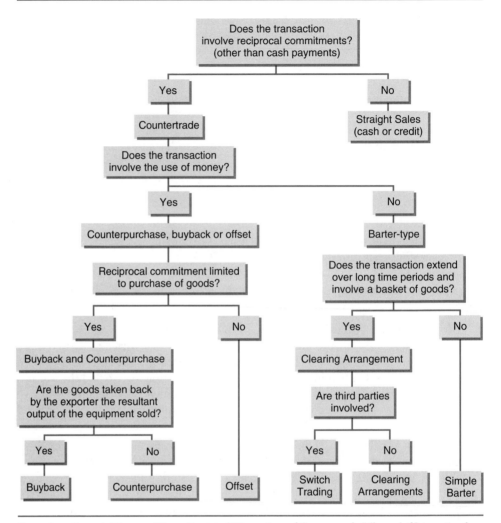

Source: Jean-François Hennart, "Some Empirical Dimensions of Countertrade," *Journal of International Business Studies* (Second Quarter 1990), p. 245.

Indonesia would supply paper, rubber, and galvanized sheets in exchange for 30,000 barrels per day of Iranian crude oil.[59]

- **Switch Trading.** This is a variant of clearing arrangements where a third party is involved. In such deals, rights to the surplus credits are sold to specialized traders (**switch traders**) at a discount. The third party then uses the credits to buy goods from the deficit country.

All these types described do not entail cash payment flows. The remaining forms involve some use of money. They lead to two parallel agreements: the original sales

[59]Aspy P. Palia, "Countertrade Practices in Indonesia," *Industrial Marketing Management*, 21 (1992), pp. 273–79.

agreement between the foreign customer and supplier, and a second contract where the supplier commits himself to purchase goods in the customer's country.

- **Buy-back (Compensation).** Buy-back arrangements typically occur with the sale of technology, turn-key plants, or machinery equipment. In such transactions, the seller provides the equipment and agrees to be paid (partially or fully) by the products resulting from using the equipment. Such agreements are much more mutually beneficial than the other forms of countertrade. A typical example of a buy-back contract is an agreement that was settled between PALMCO Holdings, Malaysia's biggest palm oil refiner, and Japan's Kao Corporation. The contract set up a $70 million joint venture to produce palm oil byproducts in Malaysia. Kao was to be compensated by 60 percent of the output, which it could use as inputs for producing detergents, cosmetics and toiletries.[60]

- **Counterpurchase.** Counterpurchase is the most popular form of countertrade. Similar to buy-back arrangements, two parallel contracts are set up. Each party agrees to buy a specified amount of goods from the other for hard currency over a set period. Contrary to buybacks, the products are unrelated. Typically, the importer will provide a shopping list from which the Western exporter can choose. In October 1992, PepsiCo set up a joint-venture in Ukraine with three local partners. Under the agreement, the partnership was to market Ukranian-built ships. Proceeds from the ship sales were to be used to buy soft-drink equipment, to build bottling plants, and to open Pizza Hut restaurants in Ukraine.[61]

- **Offset.** Offset is a variation of counterpurchase: the seller agrees to "offset" the purchase price by sourcing from the importer's country or transferring technology, to the other party's country. Offset is very common with defense contracts. An offset contract concluded between Indonesia and General Dynamics to buy F-16 aircraft stipulated that some of the parts would be supplied by PT Nusantara, an Indonesian manufacturer.

Motives Behind Countertrade

Companies engage in countertrade for a variety of reasons. The most commonly cited benefits are:

- **Gain access to new or difficult markets.** Countertrade in many ways is a "necessary evil." It can be very costly and risky. Nevertheless, being prepared to accept countertrade deals offers for many companies a competitive edge that allows them to penetrate markets with a lack of hard currency cash. Many exporters accept countertrade arrangements because their rivals offer it. A U.K. survey found that 80 percent of the exporters' competitors were also involved in countertrade.[62]

- **Overcome exchange rate controls or lack of hard currency.** Shortages of hard currency often lead to exchange controls. To navigate around government-

[60]Aspy P. Palia, "Countertrade Practices in Japan," *Industrial Marketing Management*, 22 (1993), pp. 125–32.

[61]"PepsiCo to Finance Ukraine Expansion with Ship Exports," *The Financial Times* (October 23, 1992).

[62]David Shipley and Bill Neale, "Industrial Barter and Countertrade," *Industrial Marketing Management*, 16 (1987), pp. 1–8.

imposed currency restrictions, firms use countertrade. Note that this motive only applies to barter-type agreements.[63]

- **Overcome low country credit worthiness.** This benefit applies to trade with parties located in countries with low credit ratings. Under such conditions, the other party faces high interest rates or difficult access to credit financing. Countertrade allows both parties to overcome such hurdles.

- **Increase sales volume.** Firms with a substantial amount of overhead face a lot of pressure to increase sales. Despite the risks and costs of countertrade, such deals provide a viable opportunity to achieve full capacity utilization. Also, companies often engage in countertrade to dispose of surplus or obsolete products.

- **Generate long-term customer goodwill.** A final payoff is that willingness to accept countertrade deals fosters long-term customer goodwill. Once the credit and/or currency situation in the client's country improves, sellers will be able to capitalize on the customer goodwill cemented over the years.

Among these marketing objectives, a recent survey of industrial firms located in twenty-three countries showed that the most important ones are: (1) sales increase (mean response of 3.91 on a 5-point scale), (2) increased competitiveness (3.90), and (3) entry to new markets (3.54).[64] Note that several of the motives listed are long-term oriented (e.g., gaining entry to new markets, generate goodwill), while some of the other motives are short-term oriented (e.g., use excess production capacity). Firms that are driven by long-term benefits tend to be much more proactive in soliciting countertrade business and pursuing countertrade transactions than short-term-oriented firms.[65] Whatever the motive for entering a countertrade agreement, it is important to realize the drawbacks of such arrangements.

Shortcomings of Countertrade

Not every exporter is willing to jump on the countertrade bandwagon. In many cases, the risks and costs of a countertrade deal far outweigh its potential advantages. Some of the shortcomings that have been identified by exporters include:[66]

- **No "in-house" use for goods offered by customers.** Exporters often face the problem of what to do with the goods they are offered. Goods that cannot be used in-house need to be resold. Getting rid of the goods can be a major headache, especially when the quality of the merchandise is poor or when there is an oversupply. Some firms will rely on specialist brokers to sell their goods.

- **Timely and costly negotiations.** Arranging a countertrade deal requires a time-consuming and complex bargaining process. A prospective customer with a long track record usually has a tremendous edge over an exporter with little negotiation skills. Parties will need to haggle over the goods to be traded, their respective valuation, the mixture cash/merchandise, the time horizon, and so on.

---

[63]J.-F. Hennart and E. Anderson, "Countertrade and the Minimization of Transaction Costs."

[64]Dorothy A. Paun, "An International Profile of Countertrading Firms," *Industrial Marketing Management*, 26(1) (1997), pp. 41–50.

[65]Dorothy A. Paun and Aviv Shoham, "Marketing Motives in International Countertrade: An Empirical Examination," *Journal of International Marketing*, 4(3) (1996), pp. 29–47.

[66]Shipley and Neale, pp. 5–6.

- **Uncertainty and lack of information on future prices.** When part of the traded goods involve commodities, firms run the risk that the price sinks before the goods can be sold. Apart from price uncertainty, there is uncertainty about the quality of the goods.

- **Transaction costs.** Costs flowing from countertrade quickly add up: cost of finding buyers for the goods (if there is no in-house use), commissions to middlemen (if any), insurance costs to cover risk of faulty or nondelivery, hedging costs to protect against sinking commodity prices.

Given the potential risks and costs an exporter might run, one of the key questions is whether to handle deals in-house or to use specialist middlemen. This decision will basically be driven by a trade-off of the benefits of using outsiders (reduction of risks and transaction costs) with the costs to be incurred (mainly commission).

Countertrade has probably reached its peak now. In fact, some former East Bloc countries are trying to avoid such trade in order to signal their commitment to free markets.[67] Still, countertrade will survive, as many countries remain strapped for hard-currency cash.[68] Finally, a few words of advice:[69]

1. Always evaluate the pros and cons of countertrade against other options.

2. Minimize the ratio of compensation goods to cash.

3. Strive for goods that can be used in-house.

4. Assess the relative merits of relying on middlemen versus an in-house staff.

5. Check whether the goods are subject to any import restrictions.

6. Assess the quality of the goods.

$\mathcal{V}$IDEOBOX

BARTERING PEPSI FOR VODKA AND TANKERS

In countries that do not have the resources to pay for their imports or with a non-convertible currency, firms oftentimes must look for alternative ways to repatriate their revenues. Countertrade is one mechanism that companies rely on to escape the hard currency crunch faced by their customers in many developing countries.

One of the most eye-catching barter deals in recent years was a transaction that Pepsi set up in the former Soviet Union to exchange Pepsi concentrated syrup for ocean freighters and tankers. For years Pepsi traded concentrated syrup for Stolichnaya vodka. The Pepsi/ship barter deal was expected to generate $3 billion over a ten-year period. While selling Pepsi for other beverages such as vodka is not that unusual, getting involved in the shipping brokerage business to sell Pepsi certainly is.

Discuss the possible motives behind Pepsi's barter deal described in the videoclip. Do you feel that the deal was a sensible move on Pepsi's behalf?

[67]"A Necessary Evil," *The Economist* (November 25, 1989), p. 79.

[68]"Worldwide Money Crunch Fuels More International Barter," *Marketing News* (March 2, 1992), p. 5.

[69]Based on Shipley and Neale, and J. R. Carter and J. Gagne, "The Dos and Don'ts of International Countertrade," *Sloan Management Review* (Spring 1988).

SUMMARY ✦

When setting the price in foreign markets, two kinds of mistakes could be made: pricing the product too high or pricing it too low. When the price is set too high, customers will stay away from the firm's products. As a result, profits will be far less than they might have been. For instance, in India, Procter & Gamble's Ariel detergent brand initially led to a flow of red ink, partly because P & G charged a retail price far higher than Unilever's Surf Ultra.[70] Setting prices too low might also generate numerous pains. Local governments may cry foul and accuse the firm of dumping. Local customers might interpret the low price as a signal of low quality and avoid your product. Local competitors might perceive the low price as an aggressive move to grab market share and start a price war. And when the price is far lower than in other markets, distributors (local and nonlocal) might spot an arbitrage opportunity and ship the product to your high-price markets, thereby creating a gray market situation. Making pricing decisions is one of the most formidable tasks international marketers face. Many different elements influence global pricing decisions. Aside of the roles played by the 4 C's (customers, competition, channels and company), marketers also need to factor in the impact of local government decisions.

In this chapter, we covered the major global pricing issues that matter to marketers: export price escalation, inflation, currency movements, antidumping regulations, and price coordination. In spite of the fact that pricing is typically a highly decentralized marketing decision, cross-border price coordination becomes increasingly a prime concern. We introduced several approaches through which international marketers can implement price coordination. Especially in industrial markets, firms increasingly become aware of the long-term rewards of countertrade as a way of doing business in the global arena. In many cases, countertrade is the sole means for gaining access to new markets. Companies that decide to engage in countertrade should bear in mind the numerous road bumps that these transactions involve.

REVIEW QUESTIONS ✦

1. What mechanisms can exporters use to curtail the risks of price escalation in foreign markets?

2. How does competition in the foreign market affect your global pricing decisions?

3. One recent study quoted in Chapter 13 reports that there was much more pass-through by German carmakers than their Japanese counterparts in the U.S. carmarket when both currencies depreciated against the U.S. dollar. What might explain these different responses?

4. Should MNCs always try to minimize their transfer in high corporate tax countries? Why (or why not)?

5. What measures might exporters consider to hedge themselves against antidumping accusations?

6. Explain why countertrade is often viewed as a necessary evil.

DISCUSSION QUESTIONS ✦ ✦ ✦ ✦ ✦ ✦ ✦ ✦ ✦ ✦ ✦ ✦ ✦ ✦ ✦ ✦ ✦ ✦ ✦

1. Many multinational companies that consider entering emerging markets face the issue that the regular price they charge for their goods (that is, the retail price in developed markets) is far beyond the buying power of most local consumers. What strategic options do these companies have to penetrate these markets?

---

[70]"Ariel Share Gain Puts P & G India Through the Wringer," *Advertising Age International* (November 8, 1993), pp. I-3, I-22.

2. Company XYZ sells a body-weight control drug in countries A and B. The demand schedules in the two countries are:

   Country A: Sales in A = $100 - 10 \times$ Price in A

   Country B: Sales in B = $100 - 6.67 \times$ Price in B

   The marginal costs are 4 in both countries. There are no fixed costs.

   (a) What prices should XYZ set in A and B if it optimizes the price in A and B individually? What would be total profits?

   (b) Suppose that due to parallel imports, prices in the high-price countries drop to the level of the low-price country? What would be total profits under that scenario?

   (c) Suppose now that the two countries are treated as one big market? What would be the optimal price then? What would be total profits?

   (d) Set a pricing corridor between A and B by completing the following table:

Price Corridor (in %)	Price in A	Price in B	Sales Revenue in A	Sales Revenue in B	Profits in A	Profits in B	Total Profit	Profit Sacrifice (in %)
0								
5								
10								
20								
25								

3. Countertrade accounts for a substantial proportion of international trade. Do you foresee that the share of countertrade will increase or decline? Why?

4. How will a weakening of the German mark versus the Japanese yen affect German carmakers such as BMW and Volkswagen in Japan? What measures do you suggest German carmakers might consider taking to cope with a weaker German mark?

5. How can local competitors use antidumping procedures as a competitive tool against foreign competitors?

6. In Russia, Procter & Gamble markets Tide, its U.S. premium laundry detergent brand, as an economy brand with the slogan "Tide is a guarantee of clean clothes." Except for the brand name and the product category, all aspects of the products (formula, price, positioning) are different between the U.S. and the Russian product. What might be the rationale behind this strategy? Was this strategy a good idea?

FURTHER READING ◆ ◆ ◆ ◆ ◆ ◆ ◆ ◆ ◆ ◆ ◆ ◆ ◆ ◆ ◆ ◆ ◆ ◆

Adler, Ralph A. "Transfer Pricing for World-Class Manufacturing." *Long Range Planning,* 29(1) (1996) 69–75.

Assmus, Gert, and Carsten Wiese. "How to Address the Gray Market Threat Using Price Coordination." *Sloan Management Review* (Spring 1995); 31–41.

Carter, Joseph R., and James Gagne. "The Dos and Don'ts of International Countertrade." *Sloan Management Review,* 29(3) (Spring 1988), 31–37.

Cavusgil, S. Tamer. "Unraveling the Mystique of Export Pricing." *Business Horizons* 31 (May-June 1988); 54–63.

Cavusgil, S. Tamer. "Pricing for Global Markets." *The Columbia Journal of World Business* (Winter 1996), 66–78.

Fraedrich, John P., and Connie Rae Bateman. "Transfer Pricing by Multinational Marketers: Risky Business." *Business Horizons* (Jan.-Feb. 1996); 17–22.

Gaul, Wolfgang and Ulrich Lutz, "Pricing in International Marketing and Western European Economic Integration." *Management International Review,* vol. 34, no. 2, 1994, pp. 101-124.

Kostecki, Michel M. "Marketing Strategies between Dumping and Anti-Dumping Action." *European Journal of Marketing,* 25(12) (1991); 7–19.

Paun, Dorothy. "An International Profile of Countertrading Firms." *Industrial Marketing Management,* 26 (1997); 41–50.

Paun, Dorothy, and Aviv Shoham. "Marketing Motives in

International Countertrade: An Empirical Examination." *Journal of International Marketing*, 4(3) (1996); 29–47.

Rabino, Samuel, and Kirit Shah. "Countertrade and Penetration of LDC's Markets." *The Columbia Journal of World Business* (Winter 1987); 31–38.

Samiee, Saeed. "Pricing in Marketing Strategies of U.S.- and Foreign-Based Companies." *Journal of Business Research* 15 (1987); 17–30.

Shipley, David, and Bill Neale. "Industrial Barter and Countertrade." *Industrial Marketing Management*, 16 (1987); 1–8.

Simon, Hermann, and Eckhard Kucher. "The European Pricing Time Bomb—and How to Cope with It." *Marketing and Research Today* (February 1993); 25–36.

Sims, Clive, Adam Phillips, and Trevor Richards. "Developing a Global Pricing Strategy." *Marketing and Research Today* (March 1992); 3–14.

Weekly, James K. "Pricing in Foreign Markets: Pitfalls and Opportunities." *Industrial Marketing Management*, 21 (1992); 173–79.

COMMUNICATING WITH THE WORLD CONSUMER

14

HAPTER OVERVIEW

1. CONSTRAINTS ON GLOBAL COMMUNICATION STRATEGIES
2. SETTING THE GLOBAL ADVERTISING BUDGET
3. MESSAGE STRATEGY
4. GLOBAL MEDIA DECISIONS
5. CHOOSING AN ADVERTISING AGENCY
6. COORDINATING INTERNATIONAL ADVERTISING
7. OTHER FORMS OF COMMUNICATION

A few years ago Chanel, the French fragrance house, ran a very popular Pan-European campaign for its Chanel No. 5 brand. The spot showed a French actress whispering hate words ("You hate me, don't you? Hate is a troubling emotion...") to an unseen man. After testing out the campaign for four months in Philadelphia, Los Angeles, and Boston, Chanel decided not to release the ad in the United States. Ironically, the ad did not travel well, because American viewers linked the words of hate with unacceptable violence.[1] Promotional strategies in the global marketplace easily misfire. The first part of this chapter will cover the major environmental challenges that multinational companies encounter in developing communication strategies. After considering the constraints in international advertising, we will examine the major international advertising planning decisions that marketers need to address. The steps in developing a promotional plan in international marketing are by and large similar to the sequence in domestic marketing:

---

[1]"Global Approach Doesn't Always Make Scents," *Advertising Age International* (January 17, 1994), pp. I-1, I-38. For a nice overview of numerous other promotional blunders, see: David A. Ricks, *Blunders in International Business* (Cambridge, Mass.: Blackwell Publishers, 1993, chapter 4.

1. Select target audience and positioning theme.
2. Set specific campaign objectives (strategic and operational).
3. Determine the promotional budget.
4. Develop a message strategy.
5. Decide on a media strategy.
6. Monitor and assess campaign effectiveness.

Exhibit 14-1 gives an example of these stages for a Pan-European ad campaign that UPS, the U.S.-based courier firm, recently ran to promote its services. In the first half of this chapter we will focus on the peculiarities of developing promotion campaigns within the global marketplace. Next we will turn to another important global advertising concern: advertising agency selection for foreign markets. When running regional or global campaigns, coordination of multicountry communication efforts becomes paramount. We will discuss several approaches that you can use to coordinate multicountry advertising campaigns. The final section will explore some other forms of communication tools that global marketers rely on.

◆ ◆ ◆ ◆ ◆ ◆ **CONSTRAINTS ON GLOBAL COMMUNICATION STRATEGIES**

The hurdles that advertisers face in the international scene are—to put it mildly—unsettling. Even the most seasoned advertisers sometimes fail to master the intricacies of the global marketplace. In what follows we will review five types of constraints that you might run into when communicating with customers overseas, namely: language barriers, cultural constraints, local attitudes toward advertising, poor media infrastructure, and advertising regulations.

Language Barriers

Language is one of the most formidable barriers that international advertisers need to surmount. Numerous promotional efforts have misfired because of language related mishaps. Given the bewildering variety of languages, advertising copy translation mistakes are easily made. One can identify three different types of translation errors: simple carelessness, multiple-meaning words, and idioms.[2] Some typical instances of translation blunders that can be ascribed to pure carelessness are the following examples:

Original slogan: "It takes a tough man to make a tender chicken."
Translation: "It takes a sexually excited man to make a chick affectionate."

Original slogan: "Body by Fisher."
Translation: "Corpse by Fisher."

Original slogan: "When I used this shirt, I felt good."
Translation: "Until I used this shirt, I felt good."

---

[2]David A. Ricks, *Blunders in International Business* (Cambridge, Mass.: Blackwell Publishers, 1993).

EXHIBIT 14-1
UNITED PARCEL SERVICE (UPS)'S PAN-EUROPEAN CAMPAIGN

- TARGET:
  - Senior executives
  - Shipping/office/mailroom managers
  - Receptionists

- POSITIONING:
  - Speed of delivery
  - "Courteous company"

- OBJECTIVES:
  - Increase public's awareness of UPS
  - Improve perception of UPS, a relative newcomer on the European package-delivery scene
  - Promote new service—"Worldwide Express Guarantee" that promises next-morning delivery to both Europe and the U.S. or your money back (none of UPS's rivals could match this offer)

- MESSAGE STRATEGY:
  - Show UPS drivers making their early morning deliveries, announcing their arrival with "Good morning," "Bon matin," "Guten Morgen" . . . depending on country in which spot was shown
  - One basic execution

- MEDIA STRATEGY:
  - Concentrate ad spending on TV
  - Pan-European and domestic channels:
    - CNN, *Business Week*, *Newsweek* (senior execs)
    - Eurosport, movies and sports programs on local TV (other targets)

- EVALUATION:
  - Perceived as No. 2 carrier (behind DHL); seen as no. 4 prior to campaign
  - Spontaneous awareness climbed, e.g.:
    - France 43% (vs. 24% pre-campaign)
    - Italy 59% (35%)
    - Spain 43% (26%)
  - Highest advertising recall among all carriers (33%)
  - Actual revenue exceeded estimates by up to 23%

Abstracted from: "McCann's Ad Campaign Speaks Volumes for UPS," *Advertising Age International* (October 1996), pp. A4, A14.

The second group of translation mishaps relates to words that have multiple meanings. Consider a campaign ran by the Parker Pen Company in Latin America. When entering Latin America, Parker used a literal translation of a slogan the company was using in the United States: "Avoid embarrassment—use Parker Pens." However, the Spanish word for "embarrassment" has also the meaning of pregnancy. As a result, Parker was unconsciously advertising its products as a contraceptive.[3]

---

[3]David A. Ricks, *Blunders in International Business*.

EXHIBIT 14-2
FIVE DIFFERENT WAYS FOR SAYING *TIRES* IN SPANISH

Spanish Word for Tires	Countries Using Each Word
Cauchos	Venezuela
Cubiertas	Argentina
Gomas	Puerto Rico
Llantas	Mexico, Peru, Guatemala, Colombia, and elsewhere in Central America
Neumaticos	Chile

Source: D.A. Hanni, J.K. Ryans, Jr. and I.R. Vernon, "Coordinating International Advertising—The Goodyear Case Revisited for Latin America." This article originally appeared in *Journal of International Marketing*, Volume 3, Number 2, 1995, published by Michigan State University Press, p. 84.

The third class of language-related advertising blunders stems from idioms or local slang. Idioms or expressions that use slang from one country may inadvertently lead to embarrassing meanings in another country. One U.S. advertiser ran a campaign in Britain that used the same slogan as the one that was used back home: "You can use no finer napkin at your dinner table." Unfortunately, in Britain, the word napkin is slang for "diapers."[4] Exhibit 14-2 lists the different words that Goodyear has singled out for saying *tires* in Spanish.

So, what are the solutions for overcoming language barriers? One obvious cure is to involve local advertising agencies in the development of your promotional campaigns. Their feedback and suggestions are often highly useful.

Another tactic is simply not to translate the slogan into the local language. Instead, the English slogan is used worldwide. The Swiss luxury watch maker TAG Heuer used the tag line "Don't crack under pressure" without translating it in each of its markets, even Japan, where over 60 percent of the audience had no clue of the slogan's meaning.[5] Other examples of universally used slogans that were left untranslated are "Coke is it" and "United Colors of Benetton." For TV commercials, one can add local subtitles to translate the "foreign" language like IBM did for its global "Subtitles" campaign.[6]

For radio or TV commercials, voice-overs that use the local slang often become necessary. However, this rule cannot be generalized. For instance, whereas Egyptian consumers prefer colloquial Egyptian Arabic in their advertising, usage of local slang is less advisable for Gulf Arabs.[7] Finally, meticulous copy research and testing should enable advertisers to pick up translation glitches.

---

[4]Ibid.

[5]"TAG Heuer: All Time Greats?" *Director* (April 1994), pp. 45–48.

[6]Wayne R. McCullough, "Global Advertising Which Acts Locally: The IBM Subtitles Campaign," *Journal of Advertising Research* (May/June 1996), pp. 11–5.

[7]"Peace Process Forges New Middle East Future," *Advertising Age International* (April 1996), p. I-13.

Cultural Barriers

Cultural gaps arguably pose the biggest stumbling block in international advertising. Many of the trickiest promotional issues center around the host country's religion. In Saudi Arabia, for example, only veiled women can be shown in TV commercials, except from the back. As you can imagine, such restrictions lead to horrendous problems for haircare advertisers. Procter & Gamble navigated around that constraint by creating a spot for Pert Plus shampoo that showed the face of a veiled woman and the hair of another woman from the back.

International advertisers should also be aware of other cultural aspects that may affect the target audience's attitude toward the advertisement and the product. In Eastern Europe, lifestyle ads are apparently far less effective than informative ads.[8] Eastern European consumers want to know the facts about the product. Over time, of course, these attitudes are likely to change.

One framework that helps with studying the influence of culture on global advertising is the cultural classification scheme developed by Geert Hofstede, a Dutch management theorist (see also chapter 4). The model classifies national cultures based on their value systems. Five dimensions were derived: power distance, uncertainty avoidance, individualism, masculinity, and long-termism.[9] This model can be used to assess the effectiveness of advertising campaigns.[10] The idea is that campaigns should reflect the cultural value systems of the target audience.

Let us consider each of these five cultural dimensions. Power distance refers to the degree of inequality that is seen as acceptable within the country. Ads that position products or services as status symbols are most likely to be effective in countries with large power distance (e.g., Arab countries, Indonesia, Mexico).

Uncertainty avoidance relates to the extent that people within the culture prefer structured situations with clear-cut rules and little ambiguity. Campaigns that center around the hard-sell approach (e.g., testimonials) are advisable for cultures with high uncertainty avoidance (e.g., France, Japan, Mexico). Countries that score high on individualism (e.g., Great Britain, U.S.A.) are societies where the members see themselves as individuals rather than part of a group. This cultural trait might determine whether ads should feature people alone or in a group setting.

Masculinity is an umbrella term that reflects typically "male" values such as performance, success, competition. Ad campaigns should recognize these values in highly "masculine" societies (e.g., Japan). The final dimension is the long-term versus short-term orientation of a society. Cultures with a long-term orientation are driven by future-directed values such as thrift, perseverance, longevity. Ads developed for audiences in countries that score relatively high on long-termism (e.g., Japan,

---

[8]"Lifestyle Ads Irk East Europeans," *Advertising Age* (October 8, 1990), p. 56.

[9]Geert Hofstede, "Managements Scientists Are Human," *Management Science*, 40 (1) (January 1994), pp. 4-13.

[10]"Individualism is Major Element in Effective Global Advertising," *Advertising Age International* (February 12, 1996), p. I-8.

Hong Kong) might consider projecting long-term-oriented values in their message appeals.

Although such categorizations are useful, it is important to bear in mind that value systems change over time. Otherwise you risk falling into the trap of cultural stereotypes. For instance, Japan has become much more family-oriented during the 1990s. This shift from materialism and status toward family values in Japan has spurred commercials that center around family life.[11]

Local Attitudes toward Advertising

Consumer feelings about advertising differ dramatically from country to country. A recent eight-question survey conducted by Gallup International in twenty-two countries tried to gauge consumers' views about the benefits of advertising.[12] In general, consumers hold quite favorable views on advertising, especially in the former East Bloc countries and Japan. More than three out of four of the respondents in Estonia, Bulgaria, and Latvia agreed with the statement: "If a product is legal to sell, it should also be legal to advertise." Almost 80 percent of the Japanese participants stated that they would miss advertising if it were banned tomorrow, far more than in most of the other countries covered in the survey (see Exhibit 14-3).

The most negative attitudes toward advertising were found in Egypt, where only 13 percent of the respondents agreed that advertising helps improve product quality by spurring competition among brands. The sponsors of the survey attributed these negative feelings to the rise of Islamic fundamentalism in Egypt.

Differing attitudes toward advertising partly explain the relative importance of advertising in shaping brand loyalty. Findings from a survey done by the advertising agency DMB&B showed that advertising is the prime factor that consumers in China use to choose a brand leader.[13] Advertising turns out to be more critical than quality, trust, or value (see Exhibit 14-4). China, however, is clearly an exception. In France and Italy, for example, advertising plays much less of a role in determining brand images.

Media Infrastructure

In Japan and the United States, where marketing is well-established, advertisers face an embarrassment of riches as far as the media landscape goes. The number of media vehicle possibilities are endless. New options emerge all the time. Given this abundance, the major issue marketers face is how to allocate their promotional dollars across these different media, while getting the biggest bang for their bucks. In many of the emerging markets, the media infrastructure is still fairly underdeveloped. Take China, for instance. No reliable statistics are available on media readership. There are no surveys on who reads what and where. Print quality of magazines and newspa-

---

[11]"It's All in the Family for Japan Ads," *Advertising Age International* (July 19, 1993), pp. I-3, I-22.

[12]"Major Global Study Finds Consumers Support Ads," *Advertising Age International* (October 11, 1993), pp. I-1, I-21.

[13]"Want to Be a Brand Leader in China? All You Need is to Advertise," *Advertising Age International* (June 20, 1994), p. I-23.

EXHIBIT 14-3
GLOBAL ATTITUDES TOWARD ADVERTISING

Responses to the statement, "If advertising were banned tomorrow, I would miss it."

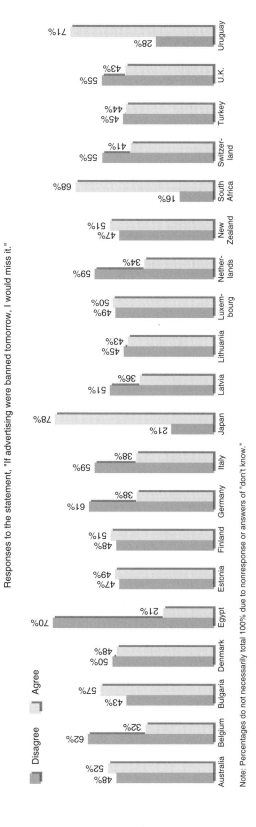

Disagree Agree

Note: Percentages do not necessarily total 100% due to nonresponse or answers of "don't know."

Source: Gallup International. Reprinted with permission.

407

EXHIBIT 14-4
RANKED RESPONSES FOR WHY CONSUMERS CHOOSE A BRAND LEADER

Reason	China	France	Italy	Spain	U.K.	U.S.
Advertising	1	6	10	6	7	7
Highest quality	2	3	2	2	3	4
Trust them	3	1	1	1	1	2
Stood test of time	4	1*	3*	3	2	1
Best value	5	5	5	4	4	6
Best service	6	4	3*	4*	6	3
Sells the most	7	7	7	8	8	8
Industry standard	8	8	6	7	4*	4*
Most innovative	9	9	9	10	9	9
Growing fastest	10	10	8	9	10	10

*Indicates tie.

Source: "Want to Be a Brand Leader in China? All You Need Is to Advertise." Reprinted with permission from the June 20, 1994 issue of *Advertising Age.* Copyright, Crain Communications Inc. 1994.

pers is poor. Advertising rates are not stable. Newspapers may demand full payment in advance when the order is booked and ask for additional money later on. There is no guarantee that newspapers will run your ad on the agreed date or TV broadcasters will show your spot. Paper shortages limit the amount of space available for print ads.[14] Sites for outdoor advertising are controlled by local media barons, who often discriminate against foreign marketers.[15]

Advertising Regulations

A major roadblock that global advertisers face is the bewildering set of advertising regulations in foreign markets. Advertising regulations are usually imposed by the local government bodies. In many countries the local advertising industry is also governed by some form of self-regulation. Self-regulation can take various forms.[16] One possibility is that local advertisers, advertising agencies, and broadcast media jointly agree on a set of rules. Alternatively, the local advertising industry and government representatives may decide on a code of advertising ethics. There are several reasons behind self-regulation of the advertising industry, including protection of consumers against misleading or offensive advertising, and protection of legitimate advertisers against false claims or accusations made by competitors. Another forceful reason to set up self-regulatory bodies is to prevent more stringent goverment-imposed regulation or control of the advertising industry.

Advertising regulations come in many guises. Below we summarize the major types of advertising regulations and offer some recent examples for each one of them:

---

[14]"Chinese Media Resist Call for Change," *Advertising Age International* (November 8, 1993), p. I-14.

[15]"Hard Sell," *The Economist* (March 4, 1995), p. 67.

[16]Marieke de Mooij, *Advertising Worldwide*, 2nd ed. (Englewood Cliffs, NJ, Prentice-Hall, 1994).

Advertising of "Vice Products" and Pharmaceuticals.   Tough restrictions, if not outright bans, apply to the advertising of pharmaceuticals and so-called *vice* products in many countries. Despite opposition of advertising agencies, advertisers and media rules on the advertising of tobacco and liquor products are becoming increasingly more severe. Several emerging markets are also curbing the advertising of vice products. The Polish government, for instance, recently banned tobacco advertising in cinemas, broadcast media, and youth publications.

Comparative Advertising.   Another area of contention is comparative advertising, where advertisers disparage the competing brand. While such advertising practices are commonplace in the United States, other countries heavily constrain or even prohibit comparative advertising. For example, until recently, advertisers in South Africa were forbidden to name competitors, show rival brands, or make comparisons that allude to the competing brand.[17] In other markets, such as Colombia, marketers that use comparative advertising must substantiate their claims.

Content of Advertising Messages.   The content of advertising messages could be subject to certain rules or guidelines. Dorf Industries, an Australian plumbing fixtures marketer, ran a campaign that featured a spurned lover getting even with her boyfriend by turning on all taps. The slighted girlfriend leaves the house which, in the mean time, is filling up with water. The spots were aired during an Australian drought. The campaign was banned by the Advertising Standards Council for its "wanton and irresponsible waste of water."[18] Also in Australia, Toyota was forced to withdraw a series of spots advertising the Celica model because of their content. One of the spots was a "Jaws" spoof in which shark-like Celicas speed down a jetty. The ad violated the Advertising Standards Council's guidelines on "dangerous behavior or illegal or unsafe road usage practices."[19]

In Vietnam, the Ministry of Trade, The Ministry of Culture and Information, the Customs department, and any single TV station or newspaper can censor ads. A pan-Asian campaign that San Miguel, the Philippine beer brewer, planned to run in Vietnam got nixed by the Ho Chi Minh City authorities. The campaign, showing a Western businessman who offered a San Miguel to an Asian colleague, used the slogan "San Miguel: A Sign of Friendship." The ad was banned because the local authorities claimed that beer couldn't be a sign of friendship.[20]

Ads may also be banned or taken off the air because they are offensive or indecent. For example, ads that show skin or revealing lingerie are banned from TV advertising in Singapore.[21] Many countries also have regulations against sexist advertising or ads with exaggerated ("puffery") or even false claims.

Advertising toward Children.   Another area that tends to be heavily regulated is advertising targeted toward children. Some markets, such as Québec, simply prohibit

---

[17]"Comparative Ads Mulled," *Advertising Age International* (March 15, 1993), p. I-6.

[18]"Aussie Ad Probe Comes to a Boil over Dorf Ads," *Advertising Age International* (February 20, 1995), I-6.

[19]"ASC Slams Brakes on Australian Toyota Ads," *Advertising Age International* (May 16, 1994), p. I-6.

[20]"Get My Censor Sensor," *Far Eastern Economic Review* (June 6, 1996), p. 61.

[21]"Sensitive Sensors," *Advertising Age International* (November 23, 1992), p. I-13.

TV stations from airing children's ads.[22] In Europe, rules on advertising to children are widespread. In Finland, for example, children cannot speak or sing the name of a product in commercials. In Turkey, children are only allowed to watch TV ads with "parental guidance." Italy bans commercials in cartoon programs that target children. China poses a series of rules that advertisers to children need to respect. Contrary to regulations in Western countries, most of the standards center around cultural values: respect for elders and discipline. For instance, one of the rules bans ads that "show acts that children should not be doing alone." This standard would conflict with Michelin's celebrated baby commercials.[23]

Scores of other sorts of advertising regulations usually litter the marketing landscape. Some countries only allow advertising in the local language or commercials that were produced with local talent. A number of countries view advertising also as an easy source to raise money: ad spending is taxed in countries like Italy and Colombia. China, Vietnam and other developing markets have a multi-tiered advertising rate structure—charging a local rate, a foreign rate and a joint venture rate.

While many ad regulations often sound frivolous, having a clear set of advertising rules and restrictions is a boon. If not, the law of the jungle applies. Marketers in Taiwan did not face any restrictions on ad claims until recently. Lack of regulation fostered a climate where advertisers misled consumers or even lied to them about their product's performance.[24]

How should marketers cope with advertising regulations? There are a couple of possible actions:

1. **Keep track of regulations and pending legislation.** Monitoring legislation and gathering intelligence on possible changes in advertising regulations is crucial. Bear in mind that advertising regulations change continuously. In many countries the prevailing mood is in favor of liberalization with the important exception of tobacco and alcohol advertising. European Union member states are also trying to bring their rules in line with EU regulations. Many companies have in-house legal counsels to assist them in handling pending advertising legislation.

2. **Lobbying activities.** A more drastic action is to lobby local governments or international legislative bodies such as the European Parliament. Lobbying activities are usually sponsored jointly by advertisers, advertising agencies and the media. As usual, too much lobbying carries the risk of generating bad publicity, especially when the issues at hand are highly controversial.

3. **Challenge regulations in court.** Advertisers may also consider fighting advertising legislation in court. In Chile, outdoor board companies, advertisers and sign painters filed suit in civil court when the Chilean government issued new

[22]"Group Wants Children's Ads in Québec," *Advertising Age International* (April 1996), p. I-10.

[23]Louisa Ha, "Concerns about Advertising Practices in a Developing Country: An Examination of China's New Advertising Regulations," *International Journal of Advertising* 15 (1996), pp. 91-102.

[24]"Taiwanese Consumer Law May Rein in Wild Ad Claims," *Advertising Age International* (June 20, 1994), p. I-6.

regulations that required outdoor boards to be placed several blocks from the road.[25] In European Union member states, advertisers have also been able to overturn local laws by appealing to the European Commission or the European Court of Justice. A French law that heavily restricted tobacco and liquor advertising was recently found incompatible by the European Commission with EU rules.[26]

4. **Adapt marketing mix strategy.** Tobacco marketers have been extremely creative in handling advertising regulations. A widely popular mechanism is to use the brand extension path to cope with tobacco ad bans. For instance, the Swedish Tobacco Co., whose brands have captured more than 80 percent of the Swedish cigarette market, started promoting sunglasses and cigarette lighters under the Blend name, its best-selling cigarette brand, to cope with a complete tobacco ad ban in Sweden.[27] In the United Kingdom, Hamlet, the leading cigar brand, shifted to other media vehicles following the ban on all TV tobacco advertising in the U.K. in October 1992. Hamlet started using outdoor boards for the first time, installing them at 2,250 sites. It ran a sales promotion campaign at a horse race where losing bettors got a free Hamlet cigar. It also developed a videocassette with about twenty of its celebrated commercials. The videotape was made available for purchase or rent.[28] South Korea is the only country where Virginia Slims is pitched as the succesful man's cigarette. Why? Because Korean law forbids advertising cigarettes to women and young adults.[29]

Global Perspective 14-1 summarizes some of the advertising regulations that were recently imposed in Vietnam.

SETTING THE GLOBAL ADVERTISING BUDGET ◆ ◆ ◆ ◆ ◆ ◆

One of the delicate decisions that marketers face when planning their communication strategy centers around the "money" issue: How much should we spend and how should we allocate our resources across our different markets? Exhibit 14-5 compares the advertising spending amounts of the major computer companies in several European countries. To make the cross-country comparisons more meaningful, Exhibit 14-5 also expresses the amounts in terms of "share-of-voice" (brand advertising versus industry advertising) for each of the advertisers.

Companies rely on different kinds of advertising budgeting rules:[30]

---

[25]"Chilean Fight for Outdoor Ads," *Advertising Age International* (April 27, 1992), p. I-8.

[26]"Ad Restrictions Back Under Fire," *Advertising Age International* (March 11, 1996), p. I-6.

[27]"Swedish Marketers Skirt Tobacco Ad Ban," *Advertising Age International* (June 20, 1994), p. I-2.

[28]"Hamlet Shifts to Other Media Since TV Spots are Banned," *Advertising Age International* (April 27, 1992), p. I-8.

[29]"Real Men May Not Eat Quiche... But in Korea They Puff Virginia Slims," *Asian Wall Street Journal* (December 27/28 1996), pp. 1, 7.

[30]See, for instance, Rajeev Batra, John G. Myers and David A. Aaker, *Advertising Management,* 5th ed, (Englewood Cliffs, N.J.: Prentice-Hall, 1996).

GLOBAL PERSPECTIVE 14-1

DO'S AND DON'TS FOR ADVERTISERS IN VIETNAM

Content. The content of advertising must be accurate, truthful and correctly reflect the function, effect, and quality of goods and services.

Language. The voice and words must be in Vietnamese, except if licensed business names, phrases and words cannot be replaced by Vietnamese words. When Vietnamese is used with another language, the Vietname words should be shown larger and above the foreign words.

National symbols. Use of national symbols such as the Vietnamese flag, anthem, leaders' pictures, and the "International" anthem are forbidden.

Media restrictions. No ads on the front page of newspapers or magazines. No ads inserted in news stories, television, or radio programs. Outdoor advertising that may affect traffic safety, cause difficulties to firefighting operations, and affect the aesthetic value of streetscapes, landscapes or structures is banned. Ad space should be no more than 10 percent of the total newspaper space and maximum 5 percent of a TV/Radio program.

Duration of ads. An ad cannot run more than five consecutive days for newspapers and radio, with no more than ten airings per day for radio spots. Limits for TV spots are eight days and five showings per day.

Source: "Advertising Industry Regulations to Help Boost Vietnam's Profile," *Media* (February 3, 1995), p. 14.

Percentage of Sales

This rule simply sets the overall advertising budget as a percentage of sales. The base is either past or expected sales revenues. The obvious appeal of this decision rule is its simplicity. Its biggest downside is that sales revenue (past or expected) drives advertising spending, whereas the purpose of advertising is to impact sales. The method is clearly not a sound strategy for markets that were recently entered, especially if the percentage base is historical sales revenues. A recent survey of advertising practices worldwide showed that the percentage-of-sales method was used by almost half of the respondents.[31]

Competitive Parity

The principle of the competitive parity rule is extremely simple: Use your competitors' spending as a benchmark, for instance, by simply matching their spending amounts. The rationale for this approach is that the competitors' collective wisdom signals the "optimal" spending amount. The rule also allows the company to sustain a minimum "share of voice" (brand advertising as a share of total industry advertising) without rocking the boat. Advertising scholars have pointed out several shortcomings of competitive parity as a budgeting norm. Obviously, the industry's spending habits may well be very questionable. Also, marketers that recently entered a new market probably should spend far more relative to the incumbent brands to break through the clutter.

[31]N. E. Synodinos, C. F. Keown and L. W. Jacobs, "Transnational Advertising Practices: A Survey of Leading Brand Advertisers in Fifteen Countries," *Journal of Advertising Research* (April/May 1989), pp. 43–50.

EXHIBIT 14-5
EUROPEAN COMPUTER ADVERTISING
AD SPENDING IN US$ (1000S) BY THE TOP 9 MARKETERS FOR JANUARY–DECEMBER 1992.

Company	Product	Germany	Spain	France	U.K.	Italy	Netherlands	Total Europe
IBM	Computers	13700	4520	12287	7864	12909	2795	69593
Apple Computer	Computers	8071	1022	5425	6124	4541	720	36128
Olivetti	Computers	3398	2286	2854	3846	13012	341	32075
Compaq Computer	Computers	5637	714	6686	3021	2166	900	23856
Amstrad	Computers	2030	1848	1318	8423	5282	262	19358
Siemens-Nixdorf	Software, Computers	9266	609	192	287	181	920	19050
Digital Equipment Co.	Computers	3866	1185	1469	3054	860	422	14247
Epson	Computers, printers	5691	707	2466	1667	602	39	12209
ICL	Computers	467	356	532	3094	477	733	9960
Total		52126	13247	33229	37380	40030	7132	236476

Share-of-Voice (%)

Company	Product	Germany	Spain	France	U.K.	Italy	Netherlands	Total Europe
IBM	Computers	26%	34%	37%	21%	32%	39%	29%
Apple Computer	Computers	15%	8%	16%	16%	11%	10%	15%
Olivetti	Computers	7%	17%	9%	10%	33%	5%	14%
Compaq Computer	Computers	11%	5%	20%	8%	5%	13%	10%
Amstrad	Computers	4%	14%	4%	23%	13%	4%	8%
Siemens-Nixdorf	Software, computers	18%	5%	1%	1%	0%	13%	8%
Digital Equipment Co.	Computers	7%	9%	4%	8%	2%	6%	6%
Epson	Computers, printers	11%	5%	7%	4%	2%	1%	5%
ICL	Computers	1%	3%	2%	8%	1%	10%	4%
Total		100%	100%	100%	100%	100%	100%	100%

Based on: "IBM Spends Big on European Ads," *Advertising Age International* (May 17, 1993), p. 1-15.
Includes TV spending in top 6 countries and print in 14 countries. Source: Adtrack.

Objective-and-Task

The most popular budgeting rule is the so-called objective-and-task method. Conceptually, this is also the most appealing budgeting rule: promotional efforts are treated here as a means to achieve the advertiser's stated objectives. This method was found to be used by almost two-thirds of the respondents in the same survey mentioned earlier.[32] The concept of this budgeting rule is very straightforward. The first step of the procedure is to spell out the goals of the communication strategy. The next step is to determine the tasks that are needed to achieve the desired objectives. The planned budget is then the overall costs that the completion of these tasks will amount to. The objective-and-task method necessitates a solid understanding of the relationship between advertising spending and the stated objectives (e.g., market share, brand awareness). One way to assess these linkages is to use field experiments. With experimentation, the advertiser systematically manipulates the spending

---

[32]Ibid.

amount in different areas within the country to measure the impact of advertising on the brand's awareness, sales volume, or market share.

Part of the budgeting process is also the allocation of the resources across the different countries. At one extreme—bottom-up planning—each country subsidiary independently determines how much should be spent within its market and then requests the desired resources from headquarters. Top-down budgeting is the opposite approach. Here headquarters sets the overall budget and then splits up the pie among its different affiliates. A third approach, which becomes increasingly more common, takes a regional angle. Each region decides the amount of resources that are needed to achieve its planned objectives and then proposes its budget to headquarters. A survey conducted by *Advertising Age International* in 1995 found that the most favored approaches are bottom-up (28 percent of respondents) or region-up budgeting (28 percent)—see Exhibit 14-6.[33] Only 20 percent of the responses indicated that the headquarters office has direct control over funding decisions. The survey also indicated substantial cross-industry differences in resource allocation practices.

◆ ◆ ◆ ◆ ◆ ◆ MESSAGE STRATEGY

The "Standardization" versus "Adaptation" Debate

One of the most thorny issues that marketers face when developing a communication strategy is the choice of a proper advertising theme. Companies that sell the same product in multiple markets need to establish to what degree their advertising campaign should be standardized. Standardization simply means that one or more elements of the communication campaign are kept the same. The major elements of a campaign are the message (strategy, selling proposition)—the "what should we say?" part—and the execution—the "how should we say it?" part. The degree of standardization can also refer to the geographic scope, that is, pan-regional (e.g., Pan-Asian), as opposed to global campaigns.

The issue of standardize-versus-adapt has sparked a fierce debate in advertising circles. "Truly" global campaigns are still quite uncommon. Global Perspective 14-2 describes the efforts recently made by Philips, the Dutch consumer electronics giant, to run a global image campaign.

Merits of Standardization

What makes the case of standardization so compelling in the eyes of many marketers? A variety of reasons have been offered to defend global, if not pan-regional advertising campaigns. The major ones are listed here.

Scale Economies. Of the factors encouraging companies to standardize their advertising campaigns, the most appealing one is the positive impact on the advertiser's bottom line. The savings coming from the economies of scale of a single cam-

---

[33]"Ad Decision-Makers Favor Regional Angle," *Advertising Age International* (May 15, 1995), p. I-3, I-16.

Exhibit 14-6
Survey on International Ad Budget Allocation Practices

Current Budget Allocation	Response By Industry						
	Total	Airlines	Automotive	Consumer products	High-tech/ telecom	Hotels	Luxury goods
Each pan-geographic region determines its own needs, petitioning headquarters for a budget	28%	46%	29%	30%	25%	23%	17%
Each individual market has a different strategy with a different means of funding advertising budgets	28%	8%	29%	45%	39%	14%	22%
Worldwide headquarters determines the total allocation, controlling the budget directly	20%	29%	11%	9%	25%	23%	26%
Several budget sources (e.g., corporate/worldwide and local budgets)	15%	13%	14%	6%	11%	32%	17%
Other allocation method	9%	4%	18%	9%	—	4%	17%
No answer	1%	—	—	—	—	4%	—

Source: "Ad Decision-Makers Favor Regional Angle." Reprinted with permission from the May 15, 1995 issue of *Advertising Age.* Copyright, Crain Communications Inc. 1995.

paign (as opposed to multiple country-level ones) can be quite eye-catching. Levi Strauss reportedly saved around £1.5 million (±$2.2 million) by shooting a single TV ad covering six European markets.[34] By the same token, advertising for Martini & Rossi, the Italian vermouth brand, would probably cost three times as much if the ads were to be developed on a country-by-country basis.[35] There are several factors behind such savings. Producing a single commercial is often far cheaper than making several different ones for each individual market. Savings are also realized because firms can assign fewer executives to develop the campaign at the global or pan-regional level.

Consistent Image. For many companies that sell the same product in multiple markets, having a consistent brand image is extremely important. Consistency was one of the prime motives behind the Pan-European campaign that Blistex, a U.S.-based lipcare manufacturer, started to run in 1995. Prior to the campaign, advertising themes varied from country to country, often highlighting only one item of Blistex's product line. The entire product range consists of three items, each one standing for a different need. In many of its markets, brand awareness was dismally

---

[34]"A Universal Message," *The Financial Times* (May 27, 1993).

[35]Rein Rijkens, *European Advertising Strategies* (London: Cassell), 1992.

◆ ◆

𝒢LOBAL PERSPECTIVE 14-2

"LET'S MAKE THINGS BETTER"—PHILIPS' FIRST GLOBAL IMAGE ADVERTISING CAMPAIGN

In the fall of 1995, Philips Electronics N.V. launched a new global advertising campaign with the theme "Let's make things better." The $40 million campaign was the company's first global image-building effort. Boonstra, executive vice-president of Philips, described the rationale behind the new theme as follows: "It is a carrier-wave for our communication, an attitude rather than a statement. It

is not technology but people who are the centre of things." The campaign was scheduled to run in three installments. The first part consisted of an ad featuring Jan Timmer, Philips's president, and ran in international publications such as *Time* and *The Wall Street Journal*. The second part consisted of a series of advertisements featuring Philips's employees from all over the world. The employees describe improvements in which they participated. The final set of advertising would be product advertising. The campaign was developed to motivate staff and, at the same time, to convince consumers that Philips offers superior products.

Sources: http://www-eu.philips.com/letsmake and "Philips Amplifies Marketing Efforts," *Advertising Age International* (September 18, 1995), p. I-4.

---

low. The objectives for the new Pan-European campaign were (1) to increase brand awareness, and (2) to have the same positioning theme by communicating the so-called "care-to-cure" concept behind Blistex' product line.[36] Campbell's pan-European advertising strategy for the Delacre cookie brand is also driven by a desire to establish a single brand identity across Europe. The brand's platform is that Delacre is a premium cookie brand with the finest ingredients based on French know-how. The same campaign is aired in English reaching 30 million people in more than twenty countries.[37] Message consistency matters a great deal in markets with extensive media overlap or for goods that are sold to "cosmopolitan" customers who travel the globe. Banking is a typical example: "Those customers span the global and travel the globe. They can only know one Chase in their minds, so why should we try to confuse them?"[38]

Global Consumer Segments. Cross-cultural similarities are a major impetus behind efforts toward a standardized advertising approach. The "global village" argument often pops up in discussions on the merits of global or pan-regional advertising campaign. The argument of cultural binding especially has clout with respect to product categories that appeal to the elites or youngsters, as pointed out by David Newkirk, a consultant with Booz Allen & Hamilton: "The young and the rich have very similar tastes the world over, and that's what's driving the convergences in advertising and media."[39] Bausch & Lomb's first Pan-Asian campaign for Ray-Ban sun-

---

[36]Mark Boersma, Blistex, personal communication, 1995.

[37]"Rebuilding in a Crumbling Sector," *Marketing* (February 18, 1993), pp. 28–29.

[38]"Ads Going Global," *Advertising Age*, (July 22, 1991), p. 42.

[39]"A Universal Message."

glasses is a good example. The campaign targets Asia's Generation X: 16-to-25 years old—young and trendy Asians with buying power. Loughlin, president for North Asia of Bausch & Lomb, observed that: "We are trying to talk to Asian youth in a language that they understand and relate to across the region. It's a language of music and fast-paced images." The campaign was built around a series of questions that youngsters ask. Each one of the spots ended with the tag line: "Whatever you're looking for. Ray-Ban the new look."[40]

Creative Talent. Creative talent among ad agencies is a scarce supply. It is not uncommon that the most talented people within the agency are assigned to big accounts, leaving small accounts with junior executives. The talent issue matters especially in countries that are plagued with a shortage of highly skilled advertising staff.

Cross-Fertilization. More and more companies try to take advantage of their global scope by fostering cross-fertilization. In the domain of advertising, cross-fertilization means that marketers encourage their affiliates to adopt, or at least consider, advertising ideas that have proven successful in other markets. This process of exploiting "good" ideas does not even need to be restricted to "global" brands. Nestlé used the idea of a serialized "soap-mercial" that it was running for the Nescafé brand in the United Kingdom for its Tasters Choice coffee brand in the United States. The campaigns, chronicling a relationship between two neighbors that centers around coffee, were phenomenally successful in both markets. Likewise, when Procter & Gamble introduced Pantene shampoo in Latin America, it used a spot that was originally produced in Taiwan. Only a few minor changes were made to allow for local cultural differences.[41] Coming up with a good idea typically takes a long time. Once the marketer has hit on a creative idea, it makes sense to try to leverage it by considering how it can be transplanted to other countries.[42]

Apart from these reasons, there are other considerations that might justify standardized multinational advertising. A survey conducted among ad agency executives found that the single brand image factor was singled out as the most important driver for standardizing multinational advertising (see Exhibit 14-7). Two other critical factors are time pressure and corporate organizational setup.[43] Obviously, developing a single campaign is less time-consuming than creating several ones.

Another crucial variable is the corporation's organizational setup. In general, if the advertiser is highly centralized, it is highly likely that theme development is standardized. Advertising is usually very localized in decentralized organizations. On the other hand, for many small companies, local advertising is the responsibility of local

[40]"Ray-Ban Ogles 16-25 Group in Southeast Asia Blitz," *Advertising Age International* (June 1996), p. I-30.

[41]"P&G Sees Success in Policy of Transplanting Ad Ideas," *Advertising Age International* (July 19, 1993), p. I-2.

[42]T. Duncan and J. Ramaprasad, "Standardizing Multinational Advertising: The Influencing Factors," *Journal of Advertising* 24(3) (Fall 1995), pp. 55–68.

[43]Ibid.

EXHIBIT 14-7
AGENCY SURVEY: MEAN IMPORTANCE OF REASONS FOR STANDARDIZING
MULTINATIONAL ADVERTISING

Reason	Western	Non-Western	Total
Create a single brand image in all markets	1.5*	1.7	1.5
Make full use of a proven, successful idea	1.9	2.1	2.0
Take advantage of the demographic/ psychographic similarity in target audience	2.2	2.0	2.1
Culture is similar between countries	2.3	2.1	2.2
Product usage is similar in all markets	2.2	2.7	2.4
Research has shown that one campaign will work	2.2	2.6	2.4
Product is standardized	2.3	2.7	2.5
Pressure from client's headquarters	2.6	2.9	2.7
Save money (one campaign costs less)	2.7	2.9	2.8
Pressure from other agency branches	3.8	3.6	3.7
Time pressure (one campaign takes less time)	3.9	3.5	3.7

*A 5-point scale was used. A lower score indicates greater importance.
Source: T. Duncan and J. Ramaprasad, "Standardizing Multinational Advertising: The Influencing Factors," *Journal of Advertising*, 24 (3) (Fall 1995), p. 62. Reprinted with permission.

distributors. The shift toward regional organizational structures is definitely one of the major drivers behind the growing popularity of regional campaigns.

Barriers to Standardization

Faced with the arguments just listed for standardization, advocates of adaptation can easily bring forward an equally compelling list to build up the case for adaptation. The four major barriers to standardization relate to: (1) cultural differences, (2) advertising regulations, (3) differences in the degree of market development, and (4) the "Not Invented Here" (NIH) syndrome.

Cultural Differences. Notwithstanding the "global village" headlines, cultural differences still persist for many product categories. Cultural gaps between countries may exist in terms of lifestyles, benefits sought, usage contexts, and so forth. As a result, many companies think twice before standardizing their multinational advertising campaigns, especially for culturally sensitive products such as food. Global Perspective 14-3 describes how Blue Diamond, a California-based cooperative of almond growers, tailors its advertising messages to each individual market.

Cultural gaps may even prevail for goods that cater toward global segments. A case in point are luxury goods that target global elites. The user benefits of cognac are by and large the same worldwide. The usage context, however, varies a lot: In the United States cognac is consumed as a stand-alone drink, in Europe, often as an af-

◆ ◆

*G*LOBAL PERSPECTIVE 14-3

BLUE DIAMOND—A WINNING MESSAGE IN THE U.S. DOES NOT TRAVEL

In the United States, Blue Diamond aired an award winning campaign showing farmer waist deep in almonds, begging viewers to buy "A can a week, that's all we ask." Despite the success of the spots in Blue Diamond's home market, the ads were never shown in the export markets. A pretest of the spot in Canada found that the ad was just too silly for Canadians' tastes. Also, Canadians would prefer buying their "can a week" from Canadian farmers. Instead, a series of local commercials were created in French and English with the tagline "Blue Diamond Almonds.

Adapted from: "Every Market Needs a Different Message," *IABC Communication World* (April 1990), pp. 16-18.

The Classic Snack." In Japan, where almonds were still a relatively novel item when Blue Diamond first entered the market, the main challenge was to educate the market. One commercial was aired that used animation, describing the nutritional value of almonds. Another ad illustrated the different possible uses of almonds.

The Korean commercial featured a guitar-player singing "Blue, Blue Diamond" to the tune of Blue Hawaii. In Hong Kong, "Ode to Almond" ads touted almonds' Californian roots, flavor and nutritional value. The spots used in Germany also emphasized Blue Diamond's California origin. Ads aired in the Middle East used a taste positioning theme: "The luxurious taste of Blue Diamond almonds in seven unique flavors."

---

ter-dinner drink, and in China it is consumed with a glass of water during dinner. As a result, Hennessy cognac, while promoting the same brand image, adapts its appeals according to local customs.[44] Even in industrial marketing, advertisers occasionally need to make allowances for cultural differences. A print ad originally created for Siemens in Germany to convey "energy" was deemed unsuitable for the Hong Kong market (see Exhibit 14-8). The German ad showed a crowd of enthusiastic youngsters at a pop concert. Audiences at Canto (or Mando)—pop concerts tend to be much more subdued than their Western counterparts. Instead of using the German print ad, Siemens Hong Kong came up with an ad that showed a fireworks display with a view of the Hong Kong skyline.[45]

Advertising Regulations. Local advertising regulations pose another barrier for standardization. Regulations usually affect the execution of the commercial. Coming back to the Ray-Ban example, whereas the theme that was used in the Pan-Asian campaign was the same across Asia, the execution sometimes differed due to local rules. In Malaysia, for instance, foreign-made commercials or ads featuring Caucasians are not allowed. Hence, Ray-Ban was forced to shoot local commercials for Malaysian TV.[46]

Market Maturity. Differences in the degree of market maturity also rule out a standardized strategy. Following the breakup of the former East Bloc, the prime challenge faced by Procter & Gamble, for example, in these new markets was to edu-

---

[44]"Cachet and Carry," *Advertising Age International* (February 12, 1996), p. I-18.

[45]Monika Sturm, Senior Communications Manager, Siemens Hong Kong Ltd., personal communication, 1996.

[46]"Ray-Ban Ogles 16-25 Group in Southeast Asia Blitz."

Exhibit 14-8
Adaptation of Siemens Print Ad

Print Ad used in Hong Kong   Print Ad used in Germany

cate consumers by giving them product information. Gaps in cross-market maturity levels mandate different advertising approaches. When Snapple, the U.S. based "New Age" beverage, first entered the European market, the biggest challenge was to overcome initial skepticism among consumers about the concept of "iced tea." Typically, in markets that were entered very recently, one of the main objectives is to create brand awareness. As brand awareness builds up, other advertising goals gain prominence. Products that are relatively new to the entered market also demand education of the customers.

"Not-Invented-Here" (NIH) Syndrome. Finally, efforts to implement a standardized campaign often need to cope with the NIH-syndrome. Stonewalling attempts to standardization may come from local subsidiaries and/or local advertising agencies. Local offices generally have a hard time accepting creative materials from other countries. Later on in this chapter we will suggest some guidelines that can be used to overcome NIH attitudes.

Approaches to Creating Advertising Copy

Marketers adopt several approaches to create multinational ads. At one extreme, the entire process may be left to the local subsidiary or distributor, with only a minimum of guidance from headquarters. At the other extreme, global or regional headquarters makes all the decisions, including all the nitty-gritty surrounding the development of ad campaigns. Most companies adopt an approach that falls somewhere in between these two extremes.

Export Advertising. With export advertising, the creative strategy is highly centralized. Universal copy is developed for all markets. The same positioning theme is used worldwide. Minor allowances are made for local sensitivities, but by and large the same copy is used in each of the company's markets. Obviously, export advertising delivers all the benefits of standardized campaigns: (1) the same brand image and identity worldwide, (2) no confusion among customers, (3) substantial savings, and (4) strict control over the planning and execution of your global communication strategy.[47] On the creative strategy front, a centralized message demands a universal positioning theme that travels worldwide. Exhibit 14-9 offers several examples of universal appeals.

Prototype (Pattern) Advertising. With prototype advertising, guidelines are given to the local affiliates concerning the execution of the advertising. These guidelines are conveyed via manuals or VCR tapes. Mercedes uses a handbook to communicate its advertising guidelines to the local subsidiaries and sales agents. Instructions are given on the format, visual treatment, print to be employed for headlines, and so on.[48] Likewise, the Swiss watchmaker TAG Heuer has a series of guidebooks covering all the nuts and bolts of their communication approach, including rules on business card design.[49] Wrigley, the Chicago-based chewing gum maker, has produced a videotape for its international advertising program that offers guidelines on ad execution, including minutiae such as: how the talent should put the gum in his or her mouth, the background of the closing shot, tips on the handling of the gum before the shooting of the commercial, and so forth.

Concept Cooperation Advertising. Guidelines usually center around the positioning theme to be used in the ads rather than the execution. Responsibility for the execution, on the other hand, is left to the local offices. Apple's European advertising

---

[47]M.G. Harvey, "Point of View: A Model to Determine Standardization of the Advertising Process in International Markets," *Journal of Advertising Research* (July/August 1993), pp. 57–64.

[48]Rijkens.

[49]"TAG Heuer: All Time Greats?"

EXHIBIT 14-9
EXAMPLES OF UNIVERSAL APPEALS

Case Histories. For instance, Philips uses case histories in some of its "Let's make things better campaign" print ads.

Superior Quality. Clearly, the promise of superior quality is a theme that makes any customer tick. A classic example here is the "Ultimate Driving Machine" slogan that BMW uses in many of its markets.

New Product/Service. A global rollout of a new product or service is often coupled with a global campaign announcing the launch. A recent example is the marketing hype surrounding the launch of Windows 95 by Microsoft.

Country-of-Origin. Brands in a product category with a strong country stereotype often leverage their roots by touting the "made in" cachet. This positioning strategy is especially popular among fashion and luxury goods marketers.

Heroes and Celebrities. Tying the product with heroes or celebrities is another form of universal positioning. A recurring issue on this front is whether advertisers should use "local" or "global" heroes. When sports heroes are used, most advertisers will select local, or at least regional, celebrities. Reebok International's advertising strategy in the Asian region heavily relies on Asian athletes such as tennis player Michael Chang, Indian cricketer Mohammed Azharuddin, or New Zealand rugby player Jonah Lomu.* With movie personalities the approach usually differs. Swiss watchmaker SMH International promoted its Omega brand with a TV commercial featuring the actor Pierce Brosnan after the release of the James Bond movie *GoldenEye*.

Lifestyle. The mystique of many global upscale brands is often promoted by lifestyle ads that reflect a lifestyle shared by target customers, regardless of where they live. As one media buyer commented: "It's not just a question of money. It's being able to afford it and having the lifestyle that lets you say, 'I need a pen worth $300.'"**

Global Presence. Many marketers try to enhance the image of their brands via a "global presence" approach—telling the target audience that their product is sold across the globe. Obviously, such a positioning approach can be adopted anywhere. The "global scope" pitch is often used by companies that sell their product or services to customers for whom this attribute is crucial. The concept is also used by other types of advertisers, though. Warner–Lambert created commercials for its Chiclets chewing gum brand that tried to project the cross-cultural appeal of the brand. One spot showed a young man in a desert shack rattling a Chiclets box. The sound of Chiclets triggers the arrival of a cosmopolitan group of eager customers.***

Market Leadership. Regardless of the country, being the leading brand worldwide or within the region is a powerful message to most consumers. For products that possess a strong country image, a brand can send a strong signal by making the claim that it is the most preferred brand in its home country.

Corporate Image. Finally, corporate communication ads that aspire to foster a certain corporate image also often lend themselves to a uniform approach.

---

*"Reebok Sets Strategy to Get Sales on Track in Fast-Growing Asia," p.12.
**"Cachet and Carry," p. I–15.
***"Chiclets Tries New Language," *Advertising Age International* (April 19, 1993), p. I–1, I–21.

strategy in the 1980s worked largely in this fashion. Local subsidiaries had to follow an internationally agreed positioning strategy. However, the execution of the strategy was decided upon by Apple's local affiliates, who could even choose their own advertising agency.[50] Seagram, the liquor marketer, took a **modular** approach for a cam-

---

[50]Rijkens.

paign it ran for Chivas Regal. After doing a copy test in seven countries, Seagram picked a campaign that consisted of a series of twenty-four ads, each using the slogan "There will always be a Chivas Regal." Marketing executives in each country, however, were able to cherry-pick the specific ads from the series for their market. Just as with the previous approach, instructions on proper positioning themes and concepts are shared with the local agencies and affiliates through manuals, videotapes or other means.

GLOBAL MEDIA DECISIONS

Another task that international marketers need to confront is the choice of the media in each of the countries where the company is doing business. In some countries, media decisions are much more critical than the creative aspects of the campaign. In Japan, for instance, media-buying is crucial, given the scarce supply of advertising space. Given the choice between an ad agency that possesses good creative skills and one that has enormous media-buying clout, most advertisers in Japan would pick the latter.[51]

International media planners have to surmount a wide range of issues. The media landscape varies dramatically across countries or even between regions within a country. Differences in the media infrastructure exist in terms of media availability, accessibility, media costs, and media habits.

Media Infrastructure

Some countries offer an incredibly rich and varied portfolio of media choices. In other countries the range of media possibilities is extremely limited. Many of the media vehicles that exist in the marketer's home country are simply not available in the foreign market. Government controls heavily restrict the access to mass media options such as television in a host of countries. For instance, advertising is not allowed on Saudi Arabian radio. In Germany, TV commercials are only allowed during a limited time of the day.

The media infrastructure differs dramatically from country to country, even within the same region. Whereas TV viewers in the West can surf an abundance of twenty-five TV channels or more, their Asian counterparts have access, on average, to a measly choice of 2.4 channels. The standard media vehicles such as radio, cinema, and TV are well established in most countries. New media such as cable, satellite TV and pay-TV are steadily growing. Given the media diversity, advertisers are forced to adapt their media schedule to the parameters set by the local environment. Exhibit 14-10 contrasts typical media allocation patterns in various countries.

Media Limitations

One of the major limitations in many markets is media availability. The lack of standard media options challenges marketers to use their imagination to come up with "creative" options. Intel, the U.S. computer chip maker, builds up brand awareness in China by distributing bike reflectors in Shanghai and Beijing with the words "Intel

---

[51]"The Enigma of Japanese Advertising," *The Economist* (August 14, 1993), pp. 59–60.

EXHIBIT 14-10

AD SPENDING BY MEDIUM

	Television	Newspapers	Magazines	Radio	Outdoor	Cinema	Others	Direct Mail/Catalogs
Brazil	57.0%	24.9%	9.0%	4.6%	4.5%			
Canada	19.2%	26.3%	3.4%	8.0%	8.6%		11.8%	22.7%
China	25.7%	29.7%	1.4%	2.1%			41.1%	
France	32.5%	24.3%	22.7%	7.7%	12.3%	0.5%		
Germany	20.5%	46.5%	25.3%	3.8%	3.0%	0.9%		
Italy	54.9%	21.1%	16.3%	3.8%	3.6%	0.3%		
Japan	43.0%	28.9%	8.8%	5.1%	14.2%			
South Korea	28.0%	40.0%	3.8%	4.1%			24.1%	
Spain	37.3%	34.4%	13.5%	9.4%	4.5%			
United Kingdom	31.7%	37.8%	22.8%	3.0%	4.1%	0.6%		
United States	22.8%	22.4%	7.7%	6.8%	1.0%		20.3%	19.0%

Source: Advertising Age International (June 1996), pp. I-19–I-24. *Media* (October 27, 1995), p. 28.

Inside Pentium Processor." Advertisers in Bangkok have taken advantage of the city's notorious traffic jams by using media strategies that reach commuters. Some of the selected media vehicles include outdoor advertising, traffic report radio stations, and three-wheeled taxis ("tuk-tuk").[52] Exhibit 14-11 illustrates some other forms of creative media venues that advertisers such as PepsiCo use in Vietnam.

Another important consideration are the media costs. For all kinds of reasons, media costs differ enormously between countries. Exhibit 14-12 gives some cost-per-thousand (CPM) estimates for the major media. In general, high CPMs are found in areas that have a high per-capita GNP. The amount of competition within the media market is another important factor. In the U.K. TV ad rates are relatively low because it is a mature market and there are many competing channels.[53]

In China, for example, advertising rates differ greatly across regions. Also, different TV advertising rates are charged to local firms, foreign companies, and joint ventures, though the gap is narrowing.[54]

A major obstacle in many emerging markets is the overall quality of the local media. In China, the print quality of many newspapers and magazines is appalling. Another recurring issue is the lack of reliable information on circulation figures and audience profiles. This situation will most likely improve with the installation of TV viewership monitors such as "people meters" (described later) by market research companies like ACNielsen's Survey Research Group.

In some countries, advertisers should also take into consideration the political orientation of the newspapers in which they plan to place advertisements.

---

[52]"Bangkok is Bumper to Bumper with Ads," *Advertising Age International* (February 20, 1996), p. I-4.

[53]"TV is Advertisers' Big Pick in Europe," *Advertising Age International* (June 21, 1993), p. I-19.

[54]"China TV Stations Narrow Pricing Gap," *Media* (March 15, 1996), p. 4.

EXHIBIT 14-11
MEDIA VEHICLES USED BY PEPSI INTERNATIONAL IN VIETNAM

Recent Developments
in the International Media Landscape

To illustrate the rapid changes in the media landscape, we would like to pinpoint six major trends:

- **Growing commercialization and deregulation of mass media.** One undeniable shift in scores of countries is the growing commercialization of the mass media, especially the broadcast media. Take Belgium: Ten years ago, commercial TV was basically nonexistent there. Advertisers who wanted to use TV as a medium either had to rely on cinema as a substitute or TV channels in neigh-

EXHIBIT 14-12
MEDIA ADVERTISING COSTS

Country	TV Peak Time	CPMs for Adults 15 and Older Radio Peak Time	Newspapers	Magazines
France	$9.49	$7.00	$21.63	$5.33
Germany	$13.31	$2.20	$7.41	$6.91
Italy	$11.62	$3.24	$5.80	$4.89
Japan	$4.91	N/A	$2.25	$4.08
Netherlands	$11.68	N/A	$4.84	$5.04
Spain	$7.99	$5.39	$6.63	$4.14
Switzerland	$23.72	$15.46	$9.28	$18.64
U.K.	$6.82	N/A	$4.16	$4.88
U.S.	$6.66	$1.53	$11.26	$4.91

CPM = Cost per Thousand

Source: "TV is Advertiser's Big Pick in Europe," Reprinted with permission from the June 21, 1993 issue of *Advertising Age.* Copyright, Crain Communications Inc. 1993.

boring countries. Following the introduction of several commercial TV stations, the situation is totally different now. Similar moves toward commercialization and the lifting of government restrictions on the local media can be observed in many other countries.

- **Shift from radio and print to TV advertising.** The rise of commercial TV has turned TV into the medium of choice for advertisers worldwide.[55] Some advertisers who traditionally focused mostly on print media are shifting some of their advertising dollars to television. Luxury goods marketers such as the Swiss watchmaker SMH have started to run ad campaigns on channels like CNN International and Star TV.[56] Television also offers novel ways of reaching target customers. TVSN ("Television Shopping Network") is a twenty-four-hour shopping network that is seen by satellite and cable TV viewers in Japan, Korea, Taiwan, Hong Kong, and the Philippines. Merchandise can be ordered via a toll-free number, paid for with a credit card, and delivered by courier.[57] Global marketers also increasingly recognize the power of infomercials as a selling tool. In Japan, for instance, infomercial marketers now have access to more than half of Japan's population. The head of one infomercial marketing firm underscores the opportunities available in international markets as follows: "Down the road we'll be able to put a product simultaneously into the homes of 300 to 500 million people around the globe. Now that's powerful."[58]

- **Rise of global media.** One of the most dramatic developments in the media world has been the proliferation of regional and global media. Several factors explain the appeal of global or regional media to international advertisers. In some countries it is hard to get access to the local media. By using international media, advertisers get a chance to target customers who would otherwise be hard to reach. International media also facilitate the launch of global or pan-regional ad campaigns. Campbell aired a Pan-European campaign for Delacre, a premium brand of cookies, on regional channels CNN and MTV. Another major asset is that most international media have well-defined background information on their audience reach and profile. In contrast to most local media, they tend to have a very well-defined audience. The major barrier to advertising on global media has been the cultural issue. Satellite TV broadcasters, for instance, initially planned to broadcast the same ads and programs globally. Because of that, viewership for many of the satellite channels was extremely low. As a result, very few advertisers were interested in airing spots on satellite TV. Lately, however, more and more satellite networks have started to customize the content of their programs. NBC Super Channel even broadcasts many of its programs in Europe with subtitles now or local voice-overs to overcome the language barrier. ESPN

---

[55]John M. Eger, "Global Television: An Executive Overview," *Columbia Journal of World Business* (Fall 1987), pp. 5–10.

[56]"Marketers at High End Try New Media Mixes," *Advertising Age International* (February 12, 1996), p. I-16.

[57]"As Advertised on TV," *Asiaweek* (July 12, 1996), p. 48.

[58]"Infomercial Audience Crosses Over Cultures," *Advertising Age International* (January 15, 1996), p. I-8.

Asia, the sports channel, plans to have seven subregional networks in Asia, each with its own fare to cater toward local sports preferences. Once the new setup is completed, ESPN will be able to bring Asian viewers their local sports and global sports. Advertisers will be offered packages that leverage on the new program portfolio.[59] A push toward localization also exists among many publishing houses of international magazine titles. In Japanese bookstores, magazine racks offer Japanese editions of titles such as *GQ*, *National Geographic*, and *Cosmopolitan*.

- **Growing importance of multimedia advertising tools.** More and more advertisers worldwide are experimenting with multimedia.[60] The most visible form is the Internet, though clearly interest in the Internet as an advertising vehicle is still very minimal.[61] While some markets, like Hong Kong, have scores of consultants that can assist marketers with the set-up and upkeep of a Web site, in most other countries such expertise is lacking. Access to and use of the Internet medium differs substantially across countries. In many countries, there is also a lot of skepticism about the cost efficiencies of the Internet as an advertising tool.[62]

- **Improved monitoring.** A few years ago, Speedo, a Kenyan pen maker, tried to boost its sales in Kenya during the Christmas season with a massive advertising campaign. The results were pretty discouraging. Follow-up on the campaign quickly pointed out the reason: none of the scheduled TV spots was ever broadcast.[63] Obviously, having an infrastructure in place that allows advertisers to monitor broadcast and print media is highly desirable to avoid these kinds of problems. Moreover, advertisers can track how much, when, and in what media their competitors advertise. Fortunately, in more and more countries, watchdog agencies exist that provide the wherewithal for monitoring the media landscape.

- **Improved TV-viewership measurement.** To plan a TV ad campaign, high quality viewership data are an absolute must for marketers. In many markets, measurement of TV viewership relied on diary data collected by a local market research agency from household panel members. Not surprisingly, the value of such data was highly questionable. The advent of new technologies has led to monitoring devices that allow far more precise data collection than past tools. The most advanced tool is the so-called people meter, a device hooked up to the TV set of a household panel member, that automatically registers viewing be-

[59]"ESPN Splits Asia into Subregions, Targeted Markets," *Advertising Age International* (March 20, 1996), p. I-14.

[60]"Scoping Out Europe's Interactive Activity," *Advertising Age International* (January 16, 1995), p. I-12.

[61]John A. Quelch and Lisa R. Klein, "The Internet and International Marketing," *Sloan Management Review* (Spring 1996), pp. 60–75.

[62]"Internet Foreign Turf to Some Marketers," *Advertising Age International* (March 11, 1996), p. I-12.

[63]"Watchdog Agency Monitors Ad Space in Kenya's Media," *Advertising Age International* (June 19, 1995), p. I-11.

Exhibit 14-13
How Switching to People Meters Affected TV Ratings Worldwide

Country	Ratings Change	Prior Ratings Method
Argentina*	Down 50% for popular programs. Down 20% to 25%	Meter/diary
Australia	Up 10% to 25%	Diary sweeps
Brazil	Down 25%	Diary
Canada	News, sports, networks, young viewers down	Diary
Chile	Smaller stations up, bigger stations down	Daily diaries
Finland	Slight increase	Diary panel
France	Prime down 10%, day down 5%	Meter/telephone
Greece	Down 20% to 40%	Diary sweeps
Ireland	No change	People meter
Mexico	Down 30%	Meter/diary
Netherlands	High-rated shows down, low-rated shows up	Diary panel
New Zealand	Slight increase overall (news down, but off-peak viewing up)	Diary sweeps
Philippines	Down 25%	Telephone coincidental
Puerto Rico	Down 4%	Meter/diary
Spain	Down 15%	Aided recall
Switzerland	Up before and after peak time	Readership survey
Thailand	Prime down	Diary sweeps
U.K.	Up 15% to 20%	Meter/diary
U.S.	Down 5% to 10%	Meter/diary

*Before people meters, Argentina had two ratings services with different methods.

Source: "People Meters Shake Up Global TV Ratings". Reprinted with permission from the July 18, 1994 issue of *Advertising Age*. Copyright, Crain Communications Inc. 1994.

havior. Exhibit 14-13 illustrates how the introduction of people meters in various countries affected TV ratings. Note that the previous ratings methods grossly overestimated TV ratings in most of the countries.

◆ ◆ ◆ ◆ ◆ ◆ **Choosing an Advertising Agency**

Although some companies like Benetton, Hugo Boss, and Chanel develop their advertising campaigns in-house, most firms heavily rely on the expertise of an advertising agency. In selecting an agency, the international marketer has several options:

1. Work with the agency that handles the advertising in the firm's home market.
2. Pick a purely local agency in the foreign market.
3. Choose the local office of a large international agency.
4. Select an international network of ad agencies that spans the globe.

When screening ad agencies, the following set of criteria can be used:

- **Market coverage.** Does the agency cover all relevant markets? What is the geographic scope of the agency?
- **Quality of coverage.** What are the core skills of the agency? Does the level of these skills meet the standards set by the company? Also, is there a match between the agency's core skills and the market requirements? For instance, in a

market such as Japan where media space is scarce, media buying skills are far more critical than creative development.

- **Expertise with developing a central international campaign.** When the intent of the marketer is to develop a global or pan-regional advertising campaign, expertise in handling a central campaign becomes essential.

- **Scope and quality of support services.** Most agencies are not just hired for their creative skills and media buying. They are also expected to deliver a range of support services, like marketing research, developing other forms of communication (e.g., sales promotions, public relations, event-sponsorships).

- **Desirable image ("global" versus "local").** The image—global or local—that the company wants to project with its communication efforts also matters a great deal. Companies that aspire to develop a "local" image often assign their account to local ad agencies. The Citrus Marketing Board of Israel uses local advertising agencies for precisely this reason: "We can't translate campaigns from Israel into another culture, so we get into these cultures by using local promoters."[64]

- **Size of the agency.** Generally speaking, large agencies have more power than small agencies. This is especially critical for media buying, where a healthy relationship between the media outlet and the ad agency is critical.

- **Conflicting accounts.** Does the agency already work on an account of one of our competitors? The risk of conflicting accounts is a major concern to many advertisers. There are two kinds of risks here. First of all, there is the confidentiality issue: marketers share a lot of proprietary data with their advertising agency. Second, there is the fear that superior creative talent might be assigned by the ad agency to the competing brand's account.

COORDINATING INTERNATIONAL ADVERTISING

◆ ◆ ◆ ◆ ◆ ◆

Global or pan-regional advertising approaches require a great deal of coordination across and communication among the various subsidiaries. In this section we discuss a number of mechanisms that can be used to facilitate this process.

Monetary Incentives (Cooperative Advertising)

Small companies often assign the advertising responsibility to their local distributors. In such a setup, the marketer might face two possible issues. First, relative advertising efforts may vary a great deal across the different distributors. Second, there is usually very little consistency in the message that is conveyed in each of the different markets where the product is sold. To tackle these concerns, marketers often provide monetary incentives to their respective distributors to get some level of coordination. Most often, the incentive takes the form of cooperative advertising where the firm contributes to the local distributor's advertising spending activities.

---

[64]"Using Culture to Promote Fruit," *Advertising Age International* (May 1996), p. I-4.

Blistex, an American maker of lipcare products, set up a cooperative advertising system to implement a Pan-European advertising campaign. One objective of the campaign was to get all distributors to advertise Blistex. The second major priority was to use a common advertising theme across all European markets. To achieve these goals, Blistex set up an advertising fund from which each distributor could withdraw money up to a certain amount to fund his advertising activities.[65]

Advertising Manuals

The use of an advertising manual or videotape to guide international advertising efforts is fairly common. Mercedes-Benz puts together a handbook that spells out its advertising guidelines for its European subsidiaries and sales agents. Likewise, Seiko, the Japanese watchmaker, guides its local affiliates and advertising agencies via an advertising manual.[66]

Feedback via the Internet

Scores of companies coordinate their international advertising by demanding feedback from their local affiliates. Olivetti, the Italian computer company, relies on the Internet to get feedback on proposed advertising strategies. Ads are sent to Olivetti's local managers via the Internet who return feedback via electronic Post-It Notes and Internet discussion forums.[67]

Lead-Country Concept

Colgate-Palmolive has implemented a lead-country system for its international advertising campaigns. For instance, for Colgate Tartar Control Formula, the lead-country was the United Kingdom. Aside from the lead-country, inputs are provided by the advertising agency and the global business development manager. The details of the campaign are summarized in a "bundle," which is sent to the various subsidiaries.[68]

Global or Pan-Regional Meetings

Scores of MNCs rely on global or pan-regional meetings to coordinate their international advertising. These meetings can be very informal. To create a new communication campaign for the Latin-American region, Goodyear, the US tiremaker, set up an informal two-day working conference in Miami. Participants included the marketing executives from each country, regional senior executives, and several key creative staff people from Leo Burnett's Latin American offices, the ad agency in charge

---

[65]Mark Boersma, Blistex Inc., private communication.

[66]Rein Rijkens, *European Advertising Strategies.*

[67]"Olivetti Puts All its Eggs in Basket of Advertising," *Advertising Age International,* (June 1996), p. I-13.

[68]Rijkens.

[69]D. A. Hanni, J. K. Ryans, Jr., and I. R. Vernon, "Coordinating International Advertising—The Goodyear Case Revisited for Latin America," *Journal of International Marketing,* 3(2) (1995), pp. 83–98.

EXHIBIT 14-14

FRAMEWORK FOR PAN-REGIONAL AD CAMPAIGN DEVELOPMENT AT GOODYEAR

1. Preliminary Orientation
September 1992
Subsidiary strategic information input on business and communications strategy on country-by-country basis.
Home Office Review

2. Regional Communications Strategy Definition
Strategy Definition Meeting
October 1992
Outputs: Regional positioning objective, communication objectives, and creative assignment for advertising agency.

3. Advertising Creative Review
Creative Review Meeting
November 12, 1992
Outputs: Six creative concepts (story boards). Research questions regarding real consumer concerns to guide research.

4. Qualitative Research Store
Qualitative Research
November–December 1992
Consistent research results across five countries on purchase intentions and consumer perceptions of safety.

5. Research Review
Research Review Meeting
January 15, 1993
Sharply defined "consumer proposition" identified and agreed upon with new creative assignment for agency.

6. Final Creative Review
Final Creative Review Meeting
March 12, 1993
Campaign Adoption

7. Budget Approval—Home Office
8. Campaign Execution—Media Buys Local Countries

Source: D.A. Hanni, J.K. Ryans, Jr. and I.R. Vernon, "Coordinating International Advertising—The Goodyear Case Revisited for Latin America."

This article originally appeared in *Journal of International Marketing*, Volume 3, Number 2, 1995, published by Michigan State University Press.

of the account.[69] The different steps behind the development of Goodyear's 1992 Latin American ad campaign are presented in Exhibit 14-14. Note that the entire process took about six months.

Robert Jordan, a senior advertising executive, offers six guidelines to implement a global or pan-regional advertising approach:[70]

---

[70]R. O. Jordan, "Going Global: How to Join the Second Major Revolution in Marketing. Commentary," *The Journal of Consumer Marketing*, 5(1) (Winter 1988), pp. 39–44.

1. Top management must be dedicated to going global.

2. A third party (e.g., the ad agency) can help sell key managers the benefits of a global advertising approach.

3. A global brief based on cross-border consumer research can help persuade managers to think in terms of global consumers.

4. Find product champions and give them a charter for the success of the global marketing program.

5. Convince local staff that they have an opportunity in developing a global campaign.

6. Get local managers on the global marketing team; have them do the job themselves.

◆ ◆ ◆ ◆ ◆ ◆ **OTHER FORMS OF COMMUNICATION**

For most companies, media advertising is only one part of the communication package. Although advertising is the most visible form, the other communication tools play a vital role in a company's global marketing mix strategy.

Sales Promotions

Sales promotions refer to a collection of short-term incentive tools that lead to quicker and/or larger sales of a particular product by consumers or the trade.[71] Examples of promotional tools include sampling, price-offs, coupons, sweepstakes, bonus packs, and trade allowances. For the majority of MNCs, the sales promotion policy is a local affair. Several rationales explain the local character of promotions:[72]

- **Economic development.**   Low incomes and poor literacy in developing countries make some promotional techniques unattractive but, at the same time, render other tools more appealing. One study of promotional practices in developing countries found above-average use of samples and price-off packs.[73]

- **Market maturity.**   For most product categories, there is a great deal of variation in terms of market maturity. In countries where the product is still in an early stage of the product life cycle, trial-inducing tools such as samples, coupons, and cross-promotions are appropriate. In more established markets, one of the prime goals of promotions will be to encourage repeat purchase. Incentives such as bonus packs, in-pack coupons, and trade promotions that stimulate brand loyalty tend to be favored.

- **Cultural perceptions.**   Cultural perceptions of promotions differ widely across countries. Some types of promotions (e.g., sweepstakes) may have a negative im-

---

[71]Philip Kotler, *Marketing Management: Analysis, Planning Implementation and Control*, 8th ed., (Englewood Cliffs, N. J.: Prentice-Hall, 1994).

[72]K. Kashani and J. A. Quelch, "Can Sales Promotions Go Global?" *Business Horizons*, 33(3) (May-June 1990), pp. 37–43.

[73]J. S. Hill and U. O. Boya, "Consumer Goods Promotions in Developing Countries," *International Journal of Advertising*, 6 (1987), pp. 249–264.

age in certain countries. Shoppers in Europe redeem far fewer coupons than their counterparts in the United States.[74]

- **Trade structure.** One of the major issues companies face is how to allocate their promotional dollars between consumer promotions—that are directly aimed at the end-user ("pull")—and trade promotions ("push")—that target the middlemen. Because of differences in the local trade structure, the balance of power between manufacturers and trade is tilted in favor of distributors in certain countries. When Procter & Gamble recently attempted to cut back on trade promotions by introducing every-day-low-pricing in Germany, several major German retailers retaliated by delisting P & G brands.[75] Differences in distributors' inventory space and/or costs also play a role in determining which types of promotions are effective.

- **Government regulations.** Probably the most critical factor in designing a promotional package is the local laws. Certain practices may be heavily restricted or simply forbidden. In Germany, for instance, coupon values cannot be more than 1 percent of the product's value. Vouchers, stamps, and coupons are banned in Norway.[76]

Kashani and Quelch suggest that MNCs appoint an international sales promotion coordinator. The coordinator's agenda would involve tasks such as:[77]

- Promote transfer of successful promotional ideas across units.
- Transplant ideas on how to constrain harmful trade promotional practices.
- Gather performance data and develop monitoring systems to evaluate the efficiency and effectiveness of promotions.
- Coordinate relations with the company's sales promotion agencies worldwide.

Event Sponsorships

Given the global appeal of sports, more and more MNCs are using sports sponsorships as their weapon of choice in their global battle for market share. Sponsorship also stretches to other types of events, such as concert tours and art exhibitions. A case in point is Heineken, the Dutch beer brewer. In 1995 Heineken pumped money into various sports activities worldwide, including the Rugby World Cup in South Africa, the Davis Cup, and the U.S. Open Tennis. However, the brewer also organized a Heineken Night of the Proms in the Netherlands, Spain, and Switzerland.[78]

Ideally, the sponsored event should reinforce the brand image that the company is trying to promote. TAG Heuer, a Swiss watchmaker, is a prime example of a company that relies on sponsorship to build up its brand reputation by being the official

[74]"Coupon FSIs Dropped," *Advertising Age International* (October 11, 1993), p. I-8.

[75]"Heat's on Value Pricing," *Advertising Age International* (January 1997), pp. I-21, I-22.

[76]"Coupon FSIs dropped."

[77]Kashani and Quelch, pp. 37–43.

[78]Heineken N.V., *Annual Report 1995*.

timekeeper of various Olympic games. The company spends about $10 million annually in sponsorship activities.[79] Likewise, United Distillers sponsors international golf events to reinforce the brand image of Johnnie Walker Black Label.[80]

There are three major risks with event sponsorship. The organizers of the event may let nonsponsors in, thereby discounting the value of the sponsorship to the official sponsors. They might also sell too many sponsorships, leading to clutter. The third risk is lack of adequate protection of the sponsorship. For example, some U.S. mail trucks still carried the Olympic rings years after the U.S. Post Office gave up its sponsorship of the Olympics.[81] Aside of these risks, there is also the issue of response measurement. In general, measuring the effectiveness of a particular sponsorship activity is extremely hard. Some firms have come up with creative procedures to do just that. In Asia, Reebok tested out a campaign on Star TV's Channel V music channel in which the veejays wear Reebok shoes. To gauge the impact of the campaign, TV viewers were directed to Reebok's Web site on the Internet. Once the viewer got access to Reebok's site, she or he was able to download a coupon that could be used for the next shoe purchase.[82]

Trade Shows

Trade shows are a vital part of the communication package for many international business-to-business marketers. Trade show spending accounts for almost one-fifth of the total communications budget of U.S. industrial firms and one-fourth for European companies.[83] Trade shows have a direct sales effect—the sales coming from visitors of the trade show booth—and indirect impacts on the exhibitor's sales.[84] Indirect sales effects stem from the fact that visitors become more aware of and interested in the participating company's products. The indirect effects matter especially for new products. Trade fairs are often promoted in trade journals. Government agencies—the U.S. Department of Commerce, for example—also provide detailed information on international trade fairs.

When attending an international trade show, the following guidelines might prove useful:[85]

- Decide on what trade shows to attend at least a year in advance. Prepare translations of product materials, price lists, and selling aids.

- Bring plenty of literature. Bring someone who knows the language or have a translator.

---

[79]"TAG Heuer: All Time Greats?" pp. 45–48.

[80]"Tiger Woods Played Here," *Forbes* (March 10, 1997), pp. 96–97.

[81]"Javelins Are Already Flying—at Billy Payne," *Business Week* (July 22, 1996), p. 43.

[82]"Reebok Sets Strategy to Get Sales on Track in Fast-Growing Asia," *The Asian Wall Street Journal* (May 31-June 1, 1996), p. 12.

[83]D. Jacobson, "Marketers Say They'll Boost Spending," *Business Marketing*, 75 (March 1990), pp. 31–32.

[84]S. Gopalakrishna, G. L. Lilien, J. D. Williams and I. K. Sequeira, "Do Trade Shows Pay Off?" *Journal of Marketing* 59 (July 1995), pp. 75–83.

[85]B. O'Hara, F. Palumbo and P. Herbig, "Industrial Trade Shows Abroad," *Industrial Marketing Management*, 22 (1993) pp. 233–237.

- Send out, ahead of time, direct-mail pieces to potential attendees.
- Find out the best possible space, for instance in terms of traffic.
- Plan the best way to display your products and to tell your story.

Finally, it is important to assess the impact of trade show participation on the company's bottom line.[86]

For most companies, advertising is only one element of their global communications efforts. In fact, more and more companies are pursuing an **integrated marketing communications (IMC)** program now. The goal of IMC is to coordinate the different communication vehicles—mass advertising, sponsorships, sales promotions, packaging, point-of-purchase displays, and so forth—to convey one and the same idea to the prospective customers with a unified voice. Rather than having the different promotional mix elements send out a mish-mash of messages, each and every one of them centers around a single key idea.

SUMMARY ◆

Global advertising is for many marketers one of the most daunting challenges they face. There are a multitude of decisions that must be carried out on the front of international advertising. This chapter gave you an overview of the major ones: creating advertising campaigns, setting and allocating the budget, selecting media vehicles to carry the campaign, choosing advertising agencies, coordinating cross-country advertising programs. The development of a global advertising plan involves many players—headquarters, regional and/or local offices, advertising agencies—which typically makes the entire process pretty frustrating. However, the potential rewards—in the form of increased market share and an improved profit picture—of a brilliant and well-executed international advertising strategy are tantalizing.

One of the front-burner issues that scores of international advertisers face is to what degree they should push for pan-regional or even global advertising campaigns. The arguments for standardizing campaigns are pretty compelling: (1) cost savings, (2) a coherent brand image, (3) similarity of target groups, and (4) transplanting of creative ideas. By now, you should also be quite familiar with the counterarguments: (1) cultural differences, (2) different markets having different degree of market maturity, (3) role of advertising regulations, and (4) and variations in the media environment. Despite years of debate, it is almost impossible to establish waterproof guidelines.

Overall, there seems to be a definite move toward more pan-regional (or even globalized) campaigns. Numerous explanations have been put forward to explain this shift: the "global" village rationale, the mushrooming of global and pan-regional media vehicles, and restructuring of marketing divisions and brand systems along global or pan-regional lines. Another important development is the emergence of new media outlets, including the Internet. Although we cannot gaze in a crystal ball and come up with concrete predictions, it is clear that international advertisers will face a drastically different environment ten years from now.

---

[86]See S. Gopalakrishna and G. L. Lilien, "A Three-Stage Model of Industrial Trade Show Performance," *Marketing Science*, 14(1) (Winter 1995), pp. 22–42 for a formal mathematical model to assess trade show effectiveness.

REVIEW QUESTIONS ◆

1. Most luxury products appeal to global segments. Does that mean that global advertising campaigns are most appropriate for such kind of products?

2. Discuss the major challenges faced by international advertisers.

3. Spell out the steps that international advertisers should consider to cope with advertising regulations in their foreign markets.

4. What factors entice international advertisers to localize their advertising campaigns in foreign markets?

5. What are the major reasons for standardizing an international advertising program?

6. What will be the impact of satellite TV on international advertising?

7. What do you see as the major drawbacks of the Internet as a communication tool from the perspective of an international advertiser?

8. What mechanisms should MNCs contemplate to coordinate their advertising efforts across different countries?

DISCUSSION QUESTIONS ◆

1. Poland recently imposed a ban on drinks advertising. How do you think brewers like United Distillers and Seagram should adjust their marketing mix strategy to cope with this ban?

2. The allocation of promotional dollars between "pull" (consumer promotions + media advertising) and "push" varies drastically for many advertisers across countries. What are the factors behind these variations?

3. Consider Exhibit 14-4 in this chapter. What does it suggest in terms of possible advertising strategies in the different countries listed there?

4. Assignment: For a particular brand, select at least three different print ads from different countries that came out during the same period. What do the ads have in common? How do they differ? Speculate about the reasons behind the commonalities and differences.

5. Look up the most recent ad spending figures of the top ten advertisers in five different European countries on the Web site of *Advertising Age* (http://www.adage.com/dataplace/index.html). Compare the spending figures of Procter & Gamble and Unilever. How do their advertising budgets differ across countries? Is there an overall picture? What might be the reasons behind the differences in ad spending across the different countries?

FURTHER READING ◆

Al-Makaty, Safran S., G. Norman van Tubergen, S. Scott Whitlow, and Douglas A. Boyd. "Attitudes toward Advertising in Islam." *Journal of Advertising Research* (May/June 1996); 16–26.

Davison, Andrew, and Erik Grab. "The Contributions of Advertising Testing to the Development of Effective International Advertising: The KitKat Case Study." *Marketing and Research Today* (February 1993); 15–24.

De Mooij, Marieke. *Advertising Worldwide*, 2nd ed. (Englewood Cliffs, NJ: Prentice-Hall, 1994).

Domzal, Teresa J., and Jerome B. Kernan. "Mirror, Mirror: Some Postmodern Reflections on Global Advertising," *Journal of Advertising*, 22(4) (December 1993); 1–20.

Duncan, Tom, and Jyotika Ramaprasad. "Standardizing Multinational Advertising: The Influencing Factors." *Journal of Advertising*, 24(3) (Fall 1995); 55–68.

Hanni, D. A., J. K. Ryans, Jr., and I. R. Vernon. "Coordinating International Advertising—The Goodyear Case Revisited for Latin America." *Journal of International Marketing*, 3(2) (1995); 83–98.

Harvey, M. G. "Point of View: A Model to Determine Standardization of the Advertising Process in International Markets," *Journal of Advertising Research* (July/August 1993); 57–64.

Hill, John S., and Unal O. Boya. "Consumer Goods Promotions in Developing Countries." *International Journal of Advertising*, 6 (1987); 249–64.

James, W. L., and J. S. Hill. "International Advertising Messages: To Adapt or Not to Adapt (That is the Question)." *Journal of Advertising Research* (June/July 1991); 65–71.

Johansson, Johny K. "The Sense of 'Nonsense': Japanese TV Advertising." *Journal of Advertising*, 23(1) (March 1994); 17–26.

Kashani, Kamran, and John A. Quelch. "Can Sales Promotions Go Global?" *Business Horizons*, 33(3) (May-June 1990); 37–43.

Kaynak, Erderer. *The Management of International Advertising* (New York: Quorum Books, 1989).

McCullough, Wayne R. "Global Advertising Which Acts Locally: The IBM Subtitles Campaign." *Journal of Advertising Research* (May/June 1996); 11–15.

Maynard, Michael L., and Charles R. Taylor. "A Comparative Analysis of Japanese and U.S. Attitudes toward Direct Marketing." *Journal of Direct Marketing*, 10 (Winter 1996); 34–44.

Mehta, Raj, Rajdeep Grewal, and Eugene Sivadas. "International Direct Marketing on the Internet: Do Internet Users Form a Global Segment?" *Journal of Direct Marketing*, 10 (Winter 1996); 45–58.

Mueller, Barbara. "An Analysis of Information Content in Standardized vs. Specialized Multinational Advertisements." *Journal of International Business Studies* (First Quarter 1991); 23–39.

O'Hara, B., F. Palumbo, and P. Herbig, "Industrial Trade Shows Abroad." *Industrial Marketing Management*, 22 (1993); 233–37.

Plummer, Joseph T. "The Role of Copy Research in Multinational Advertising." *Journal of Advertising Research* (Oct./Nov. 1986); 11–15.

Quelch, John A., and Lisa R. Klein. "The Internet and International Marketing." *Sloan Management Review* (Spring 1996); 60–75.

Rijkens, Rein. *European Advertising Strategies* (London: Cassell, 1992).

SALES MANAGEMENT

15

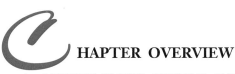

HAPTER OVERVIEW

1. MARKET ENTRY OPTIONS AND SALES FORCE STRATEGY
2. CULTURAL CONSIDERATIONS
3. IMPACT OF CULTURE ON SALES MANAGEMENT AND PERSONAL SELLING
4. EXPATRIATES

U.S. automakers still have great difficulty making inroads into the Japanese market, although Japan does not impose any tariffs on foreign cars and has eliminated nearly all non-tariff barriers to automobile trade. One major, yet little known, reason is in the way cars are sold in Japan. Unlike the United States where customers visit car dealers, a majority of cars are peddled by door-to-door salespeople in Japan, much the same way Avon representatives sell personal care and beauty products (see Global Perspective 15-1). This example vividly illustrates the importance of international sales management.

What does the salesperson do in a company? We can think of many different types of salespeople, from entry-level laborers who stand behind the counter at an ice cream store to industrial experts who work entirely within the offices of a corporate client. Some salespeople are selling products, others are selling services. Some are focused on the immediate sale, some are primarily concerned with building the confidence and goodwill of a client. Salespeople take orders, deliver products, educate buyers, build relationships with clients, and provide technical knowledge.

In all cases the salesperson is the front line for the company. The customer sees only the salesperson and the product. Through the salesperson, the customer develops an opinion of the company. And the success or failure of the company rests largely on the ability of the sales force. We cannot overstate the importance of making good decisions when those decisions affect the quality and ability of the com-

◆◆

$\mathcal{G}$LOBAL PERSPECTIVE 15-1

DIRECT MARKETING: CAR SALES DOOR-TO-DOOR—WHY THE BIG THREE HAVE DIFFICULTY CRACKING INTO THE JAPANESE MARKET

Autos are always a contentious issue in the U.S.–Japan trade relationship. Roughly two-thirds of the U.S. trade deficit with Japan is auto-related. Why can't U.S. auto makers crack into the Japanese market?

The answer is hidden in the way cars are sold. For example, Eiko Shiraishi, a Tokyo housewife, has never visited an auto dealership, kicked a tire, or taken a test drive. So how does she end up with a $30,000 gleaming silver Toyota in her driveway?

In Japan, a door-to-door salesperson peddles cars the way the Avon Lady sells cosmetics. Japanese cars may be high-tech, but Japanese salesmanship is very old-fashioned. The Japan Automobile Dealers Association estimates that half the cars sold in Japan are peddled by door-to-door salespeople. No wonder U.S. auto makers still have difficulty competing against Toyota, Nissan, Honda, and so on in Japan.

J. Michael Durrie, the head of General Motors Japan, sighs, "There isn't any silver bullet that would make it easier to sell products in this very competitive, very expensive marketplace." U.S. trade negotiators want the Japanese to assure that substantially more auto dealerships in Japan will stock U.S. vehicles. Even if Japanese auto dealerships did carry more U.S. cars on their lots, sales of U.S. cars would not materially increase . . . until, and unless, door-to-door salespeople were assigned to making the door-to-door rounds peddling U.S. cars in Japan.

Toyota alone boasts more than 100,000 door-to-door salespeople in Japan, the size of California. This figure amounts to half as many as the entire sales force in the United States for all domestic and foreign cars. "Indeed, Toyota's sales force is so strong that they just blow everybody else off the face of the earth," says Keith Donaldson, an auto analyst at Salomon Brothers Asia Ltd.

Ford Motor Co., the most aggressive of the Big Three in Japan, is trying to attract customers the American Way: mounting a media and advertising blitz aimed at bringing prospective buyers into the showroom. Ford dealers do not knock on doors, as such a sales tactic is too costly and inefficient. However, a Ford executive admits, "We need to come up with some ideas to sell more cars without door-to-door sales, but the reality is that we haven't come up with any."

Source: Summarized from Valerie Reitman, "In Japan's Car Market, Big Three Face Rivals Who Go Door-to-Door," *Wall Street Journal* (September 28, 1994), p. A1, A11.

---

pany's sales force. This chapter investigates how the processes of sales management and personal selling are changed when taken overseas into another culture.

So what is international about sales management and personal selling? First, we can break international sales management issues into two categories that provide a clarification of the use of the term *international:* (1) *international strategy considerations:* issues that analyze more than one country's assets, strengths, and situations, or that deal directly with cross-border coordination; and (2) *intercultural considerations:* issues that focus on the culture of the foreign country and its impact on operations within that country.

Although these two categories are not mutually exclusive, they help to clarify what makes international sales management considerations different from domestic sales management.

A list of examples appears in Exhibit 15-1.

In this chapter, we highlight issues related to the choice of market entry method and the sales management step to setting sales force objectives. In relating foreign entry choices to sales management, we provide a framework for thinking about the effects of various sales force management issues. Subsequently, we ask the student to carefully consider the cultural generalizations that influence international decisions and interactions. Poor generalizations will produce flawed sales management. Good

EXHIBIT 15-1
INTERNATIONAL SALES STRATEGY AND INTERCULTURAL CONSIDERATIONS

International Sales Strategy Issues	Intercultural Issues within the Foreign Country
Sales force skill availability	Motivation
Country image	Cultural sensivity
Expatriate recruiting	Ethical standards
Centralized training	Fairness
Home to host communications	Relationship building
	Selling style differences

tools for generalizing about cultures can help the international manager make decisions that accurately take into account cultural differences.

We also discuss how cultural differences, in general, will affect issues central to sales management. We consider cultural impacts on recruiting, training, supervising, and evaluating salespeople, as well as on the personal sales process. We evaluate the issues of recruiting, training, supervising, and evaluating the sales force with a focus on the host country, local salesperson.

Finally, we discuss the complex issues involved when a company sends its employees overseas. The successful use of expatriates gives a company significant advantages, but requires careful selection, training, supervision, and evaluation.

MARKET ENTRY OPTIONS AND SALES FORCE STRATEGY ◆ ◆ ◆ ◆ ◆ ◆

In the sales force management "process," we start with setting objectives and strategy. These steps include determining the goals and purposes of the sales force and the structure that will best meet those goals. To a large extent, these initial steps determine the requirements for the subsequent steps in the process—recruiting, training, supervising, and evaluating.

The question of *how to enter the market* is central to marketing. As a company decides what form its market entry will take, it is making a decision that limits and defines key underlying aspects of its future sales force management. For example, if a company decides to sell its products in the United States through a large, integrated distributor, it may only need a small, highly mobile sales force.

In international sales, the form of entry has even greater implications in international sales. The form of entry will determine how large the sales force needs to be, and will influence how much training it will require. It will also influence whether the sales force is predominantly local foreign citizens or whether it is primarily expatriates. This composition will then influence the compensation scale required. As we can see, the form of entry directly influences many of the *downstream* sales-force management options. This section reviews various options for entering a foreign market and summarizes the principle implications and questions each option raises.

The entry method we have been referring to is also termed the *level of integration* in the market. Forward integration refers to greater ownership and control of the distribution channel. For example, a company might begin its foreign sales by exporting through a merchant distributor who takes title to the product and performs all of the necessary foreign sales functions. Later, the company might integrate forward into the distribution channel by hiring its own commissioned sales agents in the foreign country. Still greater forward integration might consist of the company purchasing a sales subsidiary and establishing product warehouses abroad.[1]

Determining the best level of integration is an issue more appropriate for a chapter on international strategy than sales management. However in determining the entry form, the company must consider the subsequent influences it will have on their sales management options. In general, a greater forward integration is preferred when: (1) the operation is large enough to spread out the overhead costs of owning and maintaining infrastructure and training and supervising employees, or (2) an inability to enforce contractual obligations on outside intermediaries or some other need for greater control of the sales process requires a strong presence in the host country. Additionally, (3) sales of a service usually require a presence in the country earlier than would otherwise be considered.

A number of typical entry approaches and the sales management concerns each raises are presented in Exhibit 15-2.

EXHIBIT 15-2
DEGREE OF INVOLVEMENT AND SALES MANAGEMENT ISSUES

Degree of Involvement	Examples	Description	Sales Management Concerns
Limited Foreign Involvement and Visibility	Export Management Companies (EMC), Export Trading Companies (ETC), direct exporting, licensing	• Concerned with contract for sales from the U.S. No sales force or representatives abroad; little or no control over foreign marketing process	• Goals of the company may not take precedence • Low foreign image and stability • Impossibility of training sales force
Local Management and Sales Force	Piggybacking, selling through chains	• Little attempt to make foreign sales imitate U.S. sales culture; may "borrow" a sales force or sell via direct contracts from abroad with multidistributor outlets	• Ineffective customs (lack of influence) • Low product knowledge • Control (Trust, commitment) • Poor communications
Expatriate Management and Local Sales Force (Mixed)	Selling through chains with locals, direct selling with locals	• Expatriates oversee sales regions, lead training	• Perceptions of equality and fairness • Cultural interactions
Heavy to Complete Expatriate Sales Force	Traveling global sales force, high technology experts	• Client-by-client sales by expatriate sales force	• Lack of local understanding of insiders and market workings • High cost • Difficulty in recruiting expatriates • Country limits on expatriates or rules, such as taxes, which vary depending on foreign presence

[1]Saul Kline, Gary L. Frazier, and Victor J. Roth, "A Transaction Cost Analysis Model of Channel Integration in International Markets," *Journal of Marketing Research*, 27 (May 1990), pp. 196–208.

Selling through an Export Management Company (EMC) or an Export Trading Company (ETC) is considered a *low-involvement* approach to international sales. Export management companies, in general, serve the needs of their clients in entering a market or sourcing goods from a market. They are characterized by their "service" nature and efforts to interact with and meet the needs of the exporter client. Many EMCs have specific expertise in selecting markets abroad and finding customers due to their language capabilities, previous business experience in the country, or a network of their business contacts. The EMC works with an exporter in one of two ways. First, the EMC may act as an agent distributor performing marketing services for the exporter client, primarily responsible for developing foreign business and sales strategies and establishing contact abroad. For this prospecting role, the EMC earns its income from a commission on the products it sells on the exporter's behalf. Second, the EMC may alternatively act as a merchant distributor who purchases products from the domestic exporter, takes title, sells the product in its own name, and consequently assumes all trading risks. The domestic exporter selling directly to the merchant EMC receives its money without having to deal with the complexities and trading risks in the international market. On the other hand, the exporter is less likely to build its own international experience. Many inexperienced exporters use EMCs services mainly to test the international arena, with some desire to become direct participants once a foreign customer base has been established. This can cause conflict between the interests of the EMC and those of the client exporter.

Export trading companies are usually large conglomerates that import, export, countertrade, invest, and manufacture in the global arena. The ETC can purchase products, act as a distributor abroad, or offer services. Mitsubishi, Mitsui, Sumitomo, and Marubeni, among others, are major examples of an ETC, which are known in Japan as **sogoshosha**.[2] ETCs utilize their vast size to benefit from economies of scale in shipping and distribution. In the United States, the Export Trading Company Act of 1982 authorized an exemption from antitrust laws for ETCs.[3] The intent was to improve the export performance of small and medium-sized companies by allowing them joint participation with banks in an ETC. ETCs offer the exporting company a stable, known distributor, but they do not offer the exporting company much control over or knowledge about the international sales process.

Licensing also represents a low-involvement approach to foreign sales. The company licenses its product or technology abroad and allows the contracting foreign company to coordinate the production and foreign distribution of the product.

Limited involvement approaches to international market entry simplify sales management greatly by reducing it to a predominantly domestic activity. There is little need to recruit, train, supervise, or evaluate a foreign or expatriate sales force. However, companies that follow a limited involvement approach sacrifice the benefits that hiring and training their own sales force can provide. These benefits include the ability to motivate and monitor the sales force and to train them to better serve the customer, the customer loyalty which a dedicated sales force can generate,

---

[2]Masaaki Kotabe, "Changing Roles of the Sogo Shoshas, the Manufacturing Firms, and the MITI in the Context of the Japanese 'Trade or Die' Mentality," *Columbia Journal of World Business*, 19 (Fall 1984), pp. 33–42; Alan T. Shao, "The Future of Sogo Shosha in a Global Economy," *International Marketing Review*, 10 (December 1993), pp. 37–55.

[3]Daniel C. Bello and Nicholas C. Williamson, "The American Export Trading Company: Designing A New International Marketing Institution," *Journal of Marketing*, 49 (Fall 1985), pp. 60-69.

and the perception of permanence and commitment that a dedicated sales force conveys. Many foreign companies look for such an indication of stability and commitment when selecting suppliers.

Mid-level involvement approaches to foreign sales are those approaches in which the company controls some portion of the distribution process. Thus, the company must employ some management or sales force abroad. This work force may be either predominantly host country employees or it may include a large share of expatriates. In either case, the company will deal face to face with the foreign culture, and intercultural communication becomes a significant issue. Training can help reduce misunderstandings and miscommunications, and can provide both sides with tools to understand the perspectives of the others. For example, training helps the local salespeople better understand the company's policies by reviewing its history and goals. And training also helps the expatriates understand the local market by reviewing the norms of business within their industry and country.

The choice of whether to rely on expatriate involvement is not an easy one. Without expatriate involvement, the company might decide it is difficult to control the sales process, even though it owns part of the process. With expatriate involvement, local nationals may envy the expatriates' higher levels of pay or resent the limitations on their career opportunities with the company.

High involvement approaches are those in which the company substantially controls the foreign distribution channels. The company may own warehouses to store products. The company may own outlets where the products are sold, and it may manage a large, dedicated sales force abroad. Typically, if a U.S. company is highly involved in a foreign country, at least some of that presence will be expatriates. For some companies only the top officer abroad is an expatriate. For others the expatriate presence is much stronger.

The benefits of controlling distribution include the ability to recruit, train, and supervise a foreign sales force that can best represent the company abroad. However, controlling distribution requires that the sales volume be large enough to justify the costs, and it also requires enough experience to avoid costly errors.

Role of Foreign Governments

At the time the company is considering its entry strategy, it should take into consideration foreign government rules and practices. Many host country governments design regulations to protect local firms from international competition and ensure that local citizens benefit from experience in management positions at international companies. Thus, governments limit the number of international companies they allow to sell in the market, and they require that foreign companies fill a large number of positions with local citizens. Even the United States follows such practices. The U.S. Immigration and Naturalization Service does not let foreign managers enter the United States to work when it believes that there are U.S. citizens capable of performing the same jobs. Foreign countries often dictate who can enter, for how long, and for what jobs. These requirements may determine which entry strategy makes sense for a company.

A second issue in deciding the entry approach is the role expected of companies as "corporate citizens" in the country. If a company sets up a complete sales and distribution subsidiary, it may be expected to build local infrastructure or support local politicians or take part in local training initiatives. Such considerations will weigh in on the choice of the sales approach.

CULTURAL CONSIDERATIONS

◆ ◆ ◆ ◆ ◆ ◆

Personal Selling

At the level of personal selling there is little true *international* selling. The sales task tends to take place on a national basis. Generally, salespeople carry out the majority of their sales within one country—probably even within one region or area of a country. A salesperson selling big-ticket items, such as airplanes or dam construction, may sell to many countries. But even then, each sale is a sale within one country, and the entire sales process takes place in one country. Further, despite growing "international sales," salespeople typically work only in one region. Even in the European Union (EU), for example, where close borders and similar economies might encourage salespeople to work over larger areas, personal selling activities still remain bound mostly to a country or a region. Thus, an analysis of *international* personal selling is a study of how differences in culture impact the forms, rules, and norms for personal selling within each country.

Personal selling is predominantly a personal activity. It requires that the salesperson understand the needs and wants of the customer. The salesperson must understand local customs well enough to be accepted. And the salesperson must be able to form relationships with the customers. Do customers require a close, supportive relationship where the salesperson regularly checks up on them and knows the names of relatives? Does the customer expect some favors to "lubricate the process"? Each culture has different norms for the process of selling and buying.

Throughout this chapter, we refer to the need to adapt sales and management techniques to the local culture to be successful. It would be wonderful if a diagram

Bankers dealing with customers in different languages at an American bank operating in Riyadh, Saudi Arabia.

were available that could help managers plot the appropriate solutions for each country. While such a diagram is too much to hope for, we can take a look at some common generalizations and categorizations of cultural traits and think how they might affect our sales approach. We must take care, though, not to imply that any culture can be described accurately in a few words or categories.

Cultural Generalization

As an example of a cultural generalization with both helpful insights and misleading oversights, consider the foreign view of Germans. Germans are typically viewed as scientifically exacting and industrious people. We might therefore approach sales in Germany by building a small core of technically trained, independent sales agents. But if we think Germans look at work the same way Americans do, we will be misguided! The typical German manufacturing work week is only thirty hours. Also, Germans jealously guard their free time and show little interest in working more to earn more.[4]

We must also be careful not to group people from what may appear to us as very similar cultures, but who consider themselves, and react to situations, in a very distinct manner. Consider, for example, South Korea and Japan. We may think that Koreans would be accustomed to the same bottom-up, consensual decision-making approach the Japanese are known for. Korean workers, however, tend to work within a top-down, authoritarian leadership structure,[5] and require a higher level of definition in their job structure to avoid suffering from role conflict. A Korean salesperson might accept as normal a short-term position with few prospects for long-term progress, whereas a Japanese salesperson would not dream of it.[6]

As explained earlier in chapter 4, one of the most widely used tools for categorizing cultures for managerial purposes is Hofstede's scale of five cultural dimensions (see Exhibit 15-3). Hofstede's scale uses many questions to determine where countries stand on each dimension.

Corporate Culture

Companies also have their own distinct *cultures*. The culture at a company helps determine the norms of behavior and the mood at the workplace. This corporate culture acts in conjunction with national or country culture to set the values and beliefs that employees carry in the workplace.

The differences between the cultures of any two companies have been found to be determined significantly by the *practices* of those already in the company, especially the founders. By contrast, the differences between the cultures of companies in

---

[4]Daniel Benjamin and Tony Horwitz, "German View: You Americans Work Too Hard— And For What?" *Wall Street Journal* (July 14, 1994), p. B1.

[5]Hak Chong Lee, "Managerial Characteristics of Korean Firms," in K. H. Chung and H. C. Lee, eds. *Korean Managerial Dynamics* (New York: Praeger, 1989), pp. 147–62.

[6]Alan J. Dubinsky, Ronald E. Michaels, Masaaki Kotabe, Chae Un Lim, and Hee-Cheol Moon, "Influence of Role Stress on Industrial Salespeople's Work Outcomes in the United States, Japan, and Korea," *Journal of International Business Studies*, 23 (First Quarter 1992), pp. 77–99.

EXHIBIT 15-3
FIVE CULTURAL DIMENSIONS

Dimension	Definition	Examples
Power Distance	The concentration of power (physical and intellectual capabilities, power, and wealth) in certain groups and the acceptance of it	*High power distance:* Korea, India, Japan, Mexico *Low power distance:* Australia, United States, Germany
Individualism vs. Collectivism	The importance of the individual vs. the group; or the pursuit of self-interests vs. subordination to group interests (i.e., "I" vs. "we" orientation)	*High individualism:* United States, Australia, Great Britain, Canada *Low individualism:* Japan, Venezuela, China, Pakistan, Thailand, Mexico
Masculinity vs. Femininity	The need for achievement, assertiveness, and material success vs. the need for relationships and modesty (Masculine cultures have segregated roles, think big is beautiful, and need to show off. Feminine cultures care more for quality of life and environment than money.)	*Feminine:* Sweden, France, Netherlands *Masculine:* Japan, Mexico, Britain, Germany
Uncertainty Avoidance	Extent of ability to cope with uncertainty about the future without stress	*High uncertainty avoidance:* Japan, France, Mexico *Low uncertainty avoidance:* United States, Hong Kong, Great Britain
Long-Term Orientation	Values oriented toward the future, thrift, and perseverance	*Long-term orientation:* Hong Kong, Japan *Short-term orientation:* United States, Great Britain, Germany

Source: Geert H. Hofstede, *Cultures and Organizations: Software of the Mind* (New York: McGraw-Hill 1991).

two countries are based more in the ingrained cultural *values* of the employees.[7] Values are learned earlier in life and are much more difficult to change than practices. Consider an example of the difference in trying to modify each. We might expect to initiate novel work practices without strong negative reactions from the employees. For example, we might ask salespeople to report to a group instead of to a boss in an effort to instill a sense of group responsibility. However, if we attempt to change pro-

----

[7]Geert Hofstede, Bram Neuijen, Denise Daval Ohayv, and Geert Sanders, "Measuring Organizational Cultures: A Qualitative and Quantitative Study Across Twenty Cases," *Administrative Science Quarterly*, 35 (1990), pp. 286–316.

cedures that are strongly rooted in the values of a country's culture, we may be asking for a negative response. Consider the troubles we might encounter if we attempted to integrate men and women in the sales force in Saudi Arabia. At the very least we would not bring out the best the sales force has to offer.

Thus, while corporate cultures determine much about the working environment and even the success of an organization, the practices that characterize them are fairly malleable. Country cultures, and more specifically, the values people build at an early age in life, also greatly influence which management practices will succeed. However, cultural values are fairly fixed—do not underestimate the importance of cultural values and people's unwillingness to change them.[8]

Myers–Briggs Type Indicator

One popular tool for characterizing people that addresses their cognitive styles is the *Myers–Briggs Type Indicator* (MBTI). As shown in Exhibit 15-4, the MBTI is based on the following four personal dimensions: (1) extrovert versus introvert, (2) sensing versus intuitive, (3) thinking versus feeling, and (4) judging versus perceiving.

EXHIBIT 15-4
MYERS–BRIGGS TYPE INDICATOR OF PERSONAL CHARACTERISTICS

Personal Dimension	Description
Extrovert vs. Introvert	An *extrovert* tends to rely on the environment for guidance, be action-oriented, sociable, and communicate with ease and frankness.
	An *introvert* tends to show a greater concern with concepts and ideas than with external events, relative detachment, and enjoyment of solitude and privacy over companionship.
Sensing vs. Intuitive	A *sensing* person tends to focus on immediate experience, become more realistic and practical, and develop skills such as acute powers of observation and memory for details.
	An *intuitive* person tends to value possibility and meaning more than immediate experience, and become more imaginative, theoretical, abstract, and future oriented.
Thinking vs. Feeling	A *thinking* person tends to be concerned with logical and impersonal decision making and principles of justice and fairness, and is strong in analytical ability and objectivity.
	A *feeling* person tends to make decisions by weighing relative values and merits of issues, be attuned to personal and group values, and be concerned with human, rather than technical, aspects of a problem.
Judging vs. Perceiving	A *judging* person tends to make relatively quick decisions, be well planned and organized, and seek closure.
	A *perceiving* person tends to be open to new information, not move for closure to make quick decisions, and stay adaptable and open to new events or change.

Source: Neil R. Abramson, Henry W. Lane, Hirohisa Nagai, and Haruo Takagi, "A Comparison of Canadian and Japanese Cognitive Styles: Implications for Management Interactions," *Journal of International Business Studies,* 24 (Third Quarter 1993), pp. 575–87.

---

[8]Ibid.

Using this scale, Abramsom, Lane, Nagai, and Takagi[9] found significant cognitive distinctions between Canadian and Japanese MBA students. The Canadian students preferred intuition, judgment, and thinking, whereas the Japanese students preferred sensing, perceiving, and thinking, but were more feeling-oriented than the Canadian students. In summary, the Canadians displayed a logical and impersonal, or objective, style that subordinates the human element. The Japanese displayed a more feeling style, which emphasized the human element in problem solving—such as being sympathetic and friendly in human relations. Canadians have a tendency to seek fast decisions and rush to closure on data collection. The Japanese were found to resist fast decision making because of a preference to obtain large amounts of information.

Such differences in style must be taken into consideration whenever two cultures interact. In international sales, cross-cultural interaction takes place between the home office and the subsidiary, between expatriate managers and the sales force, or between an expatriate salesperson and the customer. If the cultural norms and cognitive styles of both sides are more clearly understood, it will help reduce misconceptions and miscommunications.

IMPACT OF CULTURE ON SALES MANAGEMENT AND PERSONAL SELLING PROCESS

♦ ♦ ♦ ♦ ♦ ♦

In general, human resource practices of multinational corporations (MNCs) closely follow the local practices of the country in which they operate.[10] These human resource practices include: time off, benefits, gender composition, training, executive bonuses, and participation of employees in management. However, human resource practices also depend on the strategy desired, the culture of the company, and even the country from which the company originated.

Thus, while we can say that the sales management process should adapt to the local environment,[11] we acknowledge the difficult give and take involved in adapting a U.S. company's culture and procedures with the sales and management practices of a foreign country.

> When host-country standards seem substandard from the perspective of the home country (manager), the manager faces a dilemma. Should the MNC implement home country standards and so seem to lack respect for the cultural diversity and national integrity of the host (country)? Or, should the MNC implement seemingly less optimal host country standards?[12]

---

[9]Neil R. Abramson, Henry W. Lane, Hirohisa Nagai, and Haruo Takagi, "A Comparison of Canadian and Japanese Cognitive Styles: Implications for Management Interactions," *Journal of International Business Studies*, 24 (Third Quarter 1993), pp. 575–87.

[10]Philip M. Rosenzweig, and Ritin Nohria. "Influences on Human Resource Management Practices in Multinational Corporations," *Journal of International Business Studies*, 25 (Second Quarter 1994), pp. 229–51.

[11]A recent study proves that when management practices are adapted to the national culture of a country in which the company operates, its financial performance tends to improve. See Karen L. Newman and Stanley D. Nollen, "Culture and Congruence: The Fit between Management Practices and National Culture," *Journal of International Business Studies*, 27 (Fourth Quarter 1996), pp. 753–79.

[12]Thomas Donaldson, "Multinational Decision-Making: Reconciling International Norma," *Journal of Business Ethics*, 4 (1985), pp. 357–66.

GLOBAL PERSPECTIVE 15-2

TGI FRIDAY'S, INC.

In setting up overseas operations, TGI Friday's:

Chooses a local development partner to guide it in negotiating government obstacles, hiring practices, and local business hurdles.

Concentrates on hiring employees that can "fit" the company's image—"fun" people willing to sing "Happy Birthday" to a customer.

Source: Adapted from Wallace Doolin, "Taking Your Business on the Road Again," *Wall Street Journal* (July 25), 1994, p. A16.

Entrusts the complete operations to the overseas operations once the business and its philosophy have been transferred.

Seeks out foreign nationals who may be on assignment or pursuing higher education in the U.S. and offers them an opportunity to return home. These individuals already understand U.S. business and service standards. But just as important, they are experts in the traditions, ethics, and ways of life of the customers (we) want to serve in foreign markets.

One good exemplary hiring policy is presented in Global Perspective 15-2.

The process of sales force management provides a framework for a closer look at the challenges involved in adapting management practices to a new culture. Sales force management consists of the following six steps:[13]

1. Setting sales force objectives
2. Designing sales force strategy
3. Recruiting and selecting salespeople
4. Training salespeople
5. Supervising salespeople
6. Evaluating salespeople

Sales Force Objectives

Setting sales force objectives is dependent on having already determined the larger, strategic objectives of the company. A company may have the strategic objective of adding value by providing the customer with more understanding of a product's use. Or the company may want to enter the market as the low-cost provider. Once such strategic objectives are decided upon, the company can evaluate what roles the sales force will play in reaching these goals. These roles are the sales force objectives. They explicitly state *what* the sales force will be asked to do, whether it is solving customer complaints or pushing for publicity of the product.

Sales force objectives will then influence much of the rest of the sales management process. If a sales force objective is to expand market share, then the sales force will be designed, recruited, trained, supervised, and evaluated using that objective as a guideline. Sales force objectives will guide how much sales force time and effort

---

[13]See Philip Kotler, *Marketing Management*, 9th ed. (Englewood Cliffs, NJ: Prentice-Hall, 1997), pp. 685–704.

will be required for digging up leads versus working with existing customers, or how much effort will be placed on new products versus older products, or how much effort will be spent on customer satisfaction compared to sales volume.

Setting sales force objectives will require a very similar approach internationally as it does domestically. In fact, many "international" sales force issues are really local issues in a foreign country. However, setting the best international sales force objectives will depend not only on the company goals, but also on an analysis of the culture and values of the country it is entering. The company might use a standardized approach for all countries, or it might customize its sales force management approach from the ground up for each country. Most companies will probably customize some aspects of each country's sales force objectives, but will follow previously held beliefs about the purpose of the sales force to decide most objectives. Once the objectives are known, the company can begin designing the structure of the proposed sales force.

Sales Force Strategy

With the sales force's objectives set, the company can concentrate on the strategies needed to achieve those objectives. Sales force strategy addresses the structure, size, and compensation of the sales force.

The structure determines the physical positioning and responsibilities of each salesperson. A company selling one product to a dispersed client base might consider a *territorial sales force*, with each salesperson responsible for a particular area, and reporting up the line to regional sales managers. Another company, with numerous, unrelated, complex products, might consider a *product sales force structure*, where each salesperson sells only one product or product line, even when selling to a single customer. A third company, which requires close contact with its customers to keep up on customer needs and build tight relationships, might employ a *customer sales force structure*, where account managers are responsible for particular clients. Each of these approaches has advantages and disadvantages. Internationally, choosing the most appropriate sales force strategy will require analyzing many of the same considerations as it does domestically. However, additional considerations might arise concerning the lack of capable local salespeople, the cultural expectations of clients, and the dramatically increased costs of maintaining expatriate personnel abroad.

The size of the sales force depends on the sales structure. The company often calculates how many salespeople are needed by determining how many visits or calls each type of customer should receive and how many salespeople will be needed to make the necessary number of visits. In a foreign culture, customers' distinct expectations may modify the calculations. Although a client in the United States might be satisfied with buying large quantities of a product and hearing from the salesperson every six months, the foreign client might expect a salesperson to be in regular contact and might want to buy smaller quantities more regularly. Such considerations will impact the sales force size.

Sales force compensation is the chief form of motivation for salespeople. However, companies do not pay sales forces equally in all countries. The purchasing power of the "same" quantity of money may not be the same. And more importantly, pay expectations, or the "going rate," varies dramatically from country to country. The company must carefully consider the social perceptions of its compensation scale. A commission-based compensation may not motivate salespeople in some other countries. A salary scale with large rewards for success may be viewed as unfair.

The company must evaluate the impact the compensation system will have on the employees, and then consider what impact the system will also have on the final customer. The pay system must motivate salespeople to leave customers with the appropriate, desired perceptions of the company.

Recruiting and Selecting

In order to successfully recruit and select salespeople, the company must understand what it wants in its salespeople and know how to find and attract people with the necessary skills. The first decision is whether the company will recruit from the local, foreign labor force for the jobs it is creating or whether it will fill them by sending U.S. employees overseas. The company may find a strong cultural bias against salespeople in the local market and find it difficult to recruit the necessary talent. Even if it can recruit "talented" people, the company may not clearly know what skills and character traits will work the best in the unfamiliar culture. If the company tries to recruit employees at home, it may have a tough time convincing salespeople or managers with the necessary skills to take the time off from the "fast track" at home.

Complicating the search for talent is that the desired skills and characteristics are not as clear as it first appears. Employers may base their expectations for salespeople on U.S. standards. For example, the employer may look for candidates with an outgoing attitude. However, in some cultures it requires a quieter, more patient approach to truly maximize sales. The skills required for success as a salesperson depend on the culture in which the sales take place.

Finally, the employer must consider the strong influences of tribal, religious, or other group relations within a country. A Hindu might not want to make purchases from a Muslim. English companies might do better to hire Irish salespeople to make sales in Ireland. History may give one group a distinct advantage, especially where they have become accepted as a strong business force. For example, the Parsees in India manage an unusually large portion of the nation's business, and Chinese salespeople, the descendants of the Chinese merchant clan, are prominent throughout Asia.[14] A wise sales manager will look for and recruit a sales force that takes advantage of each country's natural distinctions.

One way for the company to accelerate the difficult process of building a sales force from scratch is to establish a joint venture with or acquire a local company that already has a functional sales force. For example, when Merck wanted to expand its pharmaceutical business in Japan, it acquired Banyu Pharmaceutical instead of building its subsidiary and distribution channel from scratch. Merck had immediate access to Banyu's field sales force of more than 1,000. In Japan, where personal relationships probably weigh in importance more than the quality of products per se, personal selling is all the more critical in relationship-building and -maintaining purposes.

Training

Most sales training takes place in the country where the salespeople reside. The company determines how much technical, product knowledge, company history and culture, or other training its sales force requires. IBM puts its sales force through an initial training of thirteen months and expects all salespeople to spend 15 percent of

---

[14]See an excellent treatise, Min Chen, *Asian Management Systems: Chinese, Japanese and Korean Styles of Business* (London: Routledge, 1995), pp. 69–83.

their time each year in additional training.[15] International training can require trainers who speak the appropriate foreign languages. It may require building training facilities in the host country.

An additional consideration of international sales training is adapting the training to the needs of the local market. For example, a computer salesperson in Japan may need an exceptionally detailed technical understanding of his product to make the sale, whereas in Paraguay a salesperson may benefit more from training about company values and warranty procedures. The training the sales force receives must reflect cultural differences in purchasing patterns, values, and perspective of the selling process.

For some high-technology or highly standardized global products, sales training may be held at the international or regional level. Training for such products may require expensive training tools or materials, and is probably more similar across countries than training in sales techniques, so it makes more sense to centralize training. IBM, for example, has a European training center with average attendance of 5,000 people a day. Another good example is McDonald's Hamburger University in the outskirts of Chicago, where all franchisees from around the world have to receive centralized training.

While international companies often benefit in the local market by offering their employees better training than local competitors, they face the problem of protecting their investment in their employees. Companies with well-trained sales forces are often "raided" for employees by national companies. In order to protect their investments, the MNCs must offer higher compensation than their competitors.

Supervising

Supervising the sales force means directing and motivating the sales force to fulfill the company's objectives and it means providing the resources that allow them to do so. The company may set norms concerning how often a salesperson should call each category of customer, and how much of his or her time the salesperson should spend with each of various activities. The company may motivate the salesperson by establishing a supportive, opportunity-filled organizational climate, or by establishing sales quotas or positive incentives for sales. The company often provides the salesperson with tools, such as portable computers or research facilities, so as to provide better chances to achieve his or her goals. International sales management addresses how each of these supervising approaches will be received by the sales force, and what the cultural implications are. For example, cultures that cherish group identity over individuality will probably not respond well to a sales contest as a motivator.

Motivation and Compensation. Financial compensation is one of the key motivators for employees in all cultures. However, successful sales programs make use of a wide variety of motivators. The sales manager will want to adapt the incentive structure to best meet local desires and regulations. The use of commissions in motivating salespeople is not publicly acceptable in many countries. Commissions reinforce the negative image of the salesperson benefiting from the sale, with no regard for the purchaser's well-being. Salary increases may substitute for commissions to motivate salespeople to consistently perform highly. However, under certain circum-

---

[15]"How IBM Teaches Techies to Sell," *Fortune* (June 6, 1988), pp. 141–46.

stances, large salary discrepancies between employees are also not acceptable. Strong unions may tie a company's hands in setting salaries. Or the "collectivist" culture of a country like Japan may not accept that one person should earn substantially more than another in the same position. Koreans, for example, are used to working under conditions where compensation is not directly contingent on performance, but rather, on seniority. When financial rewards are not acceptable, the company must rely more heavily on nonfinancial rewards, such as recognition, titles, and perquisites for motivation.

Foreign travel is another reward employed by international companies. For example, Electrolux rewards winning sales teams in Asia with international trips. When necessary, companies can combine an international trip with training and justify it as an investment in top salespeople.

Management Style. Management style refers to the approach the manager takes in supervising employees. The manager may define the employee's roles explicitly and require a standardized sales pitch. Or the manager may set broad, general goals that allow each salesperson to develop their own skills. A number of studies have found that the best management approach varies by culture and country. For example, Dubinsky et. al.[16] found that role ambiguity, role conflict, job satisfaction, and organizational commitment were just as relevant to salespeople in Japan and Korea as in the United States, and that role conflict and ambiguity have deleterious effects on salespersons in any of the countries. However, specific remedies for role ambiguity, such as greater job formalization (or more hierarchical power, defined rules, and supervision), have a distinct effect on the salespeople in different countries.

One fair generalization is that greater formalization invokes negative responses from the sales force in countries in which the power distance is *low* and the individualism is *high* (such as in the United States). And greater formalization invokes positive responses from the sales force in countries in which the power distance is *high* and the individualism is *low* (such as in India).[17]

Ethical Perceptions. Culture, or nationality, also influences salespeople's beliefs about the ethics of common selling practices and the need for company policies to guide those practices. Why is this important? Salespeople need to stay within the law, of course. But more importantly, in order to maintain the respect of customers, salespeople must know what is ethically acceptable in a culture. For example, in the United States, giving a bribe is tantamount to admitting that your product cannot compete without help. However, in many cultures, receiving a bribe is seen as a privilege of having attained a position of influence. An understanding of the ethical norms in a culture will help the company maintain a clean image and will also help the company create policies that keep salespeople out of the tense and frustrating situations where they feel they are compromising their ethical standards.

[16]Dubinsky et al., pp. 77–99.

[17]Sanjeev Agarwal, "Influence of Formalization on Role Stress, Organizational Commitment, and Work Alienation of Salespersons: A Cross-National Comparative Study," *Journal of International Business Studies*, 24 (Fourth Quarter 1993), pp. 715–40.

As an example of differences in ethical perceptions, consider the results of a study by Dubinsky et. al.[18] The study presented salespeople in Korea, Japan, and the United States with written examples of "questionable" sales situations. Examples of the situations used are:

- having different prices for buyers for which you are the sole supplier
- attempting to circumvent the purchasing department and reach other departments directly when it will help sales
- giving preferential treatment to customers who management prefers or who are also good suppliers

The salespeople were asked to rate to what extent it was unethical to take part in the suggested activity. The results indicated that in general, U.S. salespeople felt the situations posed *less* ethical problems than did salespeople from Japan and Korea. Another interesting finding of the study—the assumption that Japanese "gift-giving" would extend into the sales realm was found to be untrue. In fact, Japanese felt it was more of an ethical problem to give free gifts to a purchaser than did U.S. salespeople. For Koreans, however, gift-giving was less of an issue.

Paradoxically, U.S. salespeople indicated that they wanted their companies to have more policies explicitly addressing these ethical questions. Why? Apparently, salespeople in the United States feel more comfortable when the ethical guidelines are explicitly stated, whereas in other countries (Korea and Japan here), the cultural exchange of living in a more community-oriented society provides the necessary guidelines.

Evaluating

Evaluating salespeople includes requiring that salespeople justify their efforts and provide the company with information about their successes, failures, expenses, and time. Evaluations are important to motivate the sales force, to correct problems, and to reward and promote those who best help the company achieve its goals. Two types of evaluations are common: *quantitative* evaluations and *qualitative* evaluations. Examples of quantitative evaluations are comparisons of sales, of sales percents, or increases in sales. Examples of qualitative evaluations include tests of the knowledge and manner of the salesperson. Since net profit is often the company's primary objective, evaluations should serve to promote long-term net profits. In some foreign cultures, however, evaluations may be seen as an unnecessary waste of time, or they may invade the sense of privacy of salespeople.

Evaluations help management keep up on sales progress, and they help employees receive feedback and set goals. International sales force evaluations must take into consideration the culture's built-in ability to provide feedback to employees. For example, in Japan the "collectivist" nature of the culture may provide the salesperson with much more sense of performance feedback than the "individualistic" culture in the U.S. would. Thus, it makes sense that U.S. sales managers use more regular,

[18]Alan J. Dubinsky, Marvin A. Jolson, Masaaki Kotabe, and Chae Un Lim, "A Cross-National Investigation of Industrial Salespeople's Ethical Perceptions," *Journal of International Business Studies*, 22 (Fourth Quarter 1991), pp. 651–70.

short-term performance evaluations than Japanese sales managers in order to provide their sales force with more feedback.[19]

Evaluations in international sales management can provide useful information for making international comparisons. Such comparisons can help management identify countries where sales are below average and refine the training, compensation, or sales force strategy as necessary to improve performance.

◆ ◆ ◆ ◆ ◆ ◆   EXPATRIATES

Most companies with a sales force abroad will, at the very least, send a few expatriates abroad as operations begin in a new country. **Expatriates** are home country personnel sent overseas to manage local operations in the foreign market. The general trend of the last decade has been a decreasing use of expatriate managers overseas and an increasing reliance on local foreign talent.[20] This trend reflects the increasingly international perspective of MNCs, increasing competence of foreign managers, and the relatively increasing competitive disadvantage of the cost of maintaining Americans abroad. Despite the relative decline, there are more employees than ever involved in international assignments due to the increase in international sales and production.[21] Expatriates have a number of advantages over foreign nationals for companies that sell their products internationally.

Advantages of Expatriates

Better Communication.   Expatriates understand the home office, its politics, and its priorities. They are intimately familiar with the products being sold and with previously successful sales techniques. Expatriates may be able to rely on personal relationships with home office management, which increases trust on both sides of the border and may give the expatriate an ability to achieve things that a third-country national or a host-country national could not achieve. With an expatriate abroad, communications with the home country will be easier and more precise due to the groundwork of cultural and corporate understanding. And the expatriate will give the home office the sense that they have someone in place who they can be sure understands the company intent and expectations.

Development of Talent.   Sending employees overseas provides the company with another advantage that hiring foreign locals may not provide: The company develops future managers and executives who can later use their international perspective in management. The expatriate executive will need to understand the workings of the home office, as well as the cultural distinctions of doing business in Brazil or in France. He or she will weave personal contacts abroad with an understanding of pro-

---

[19]Ueno Susumu, and Uma Sekaran, "The Influence of Culture on Budget Control Practices in the U.S. and Japan: An Empirical Study," *Journal of International Business Studies*, 23 (Fourth Quarter 1992), pp. 659–74.

[20]Stephen J. Kobrin, "Expatriate Reduction and Strategic Control in American Multinational Corporations," *Human Resource Management*, 27(1), pp. 63–75.

[21]Michael Harvey, "Empirical Evidence of Recurring International Compensation Problems," *Journal of International Business Studies*, 24 (Fourth Quarter 1993), pp. 785–99.

duction techniques.[22] As a Whirlpool Corporation executive was quoted saying, "The CEO in the twenty-first century must have multienvironment, multicountry, multifunctional, and maybe even multi-company, multi-industry experience." Indeed, of the eight members of Whirlpool's executive committee, five had international experience, and four of those have had international postings within the last three years.[23] Thus, by sending their most promising rising stars overseas, companies are sowing the seeds to harvest the next generation of executives.

Difficulties of Sending Expatriates Abroad

Cross-Cultural Training. As with so many other complex situations in life, a little shared understanding goes a long way. In the case of the expatriate, training can significantly help in understanding the cultural differences of the foreign country. Such "cultural sensitivity training" used to be overlooked by U.S. companies; expatriates were expected to "pick it up as they go."

However, the impact of cultural misunderstandings can be large. As a result, cross-cultural training is on the rise in recent years as more globally oriented companies moving fast-track executives overseas want to curb the cost of failed expatriate stints, estimated at $2 billion to $2.5 billion a year.[24] Now nearly half of major U.S. companies provide formal cross-cultural training programs before foreign transfers, compared with a mere 10 percent a decade ago. On average, a cross-cultural training program costs $3,000 to $6,000 per expatriate-to-be. Although cultural orientation and foreign language training are two of the most important parts of the cross-cultural training program, a recent survey reported that companies needed cultural orientation (including culture, history, and background of country) more than foreign-language training.[25]

Once the expatriate is overseas, training becomes more difficult to provide, but it is even more important. The expatriates are not in constant contact with colleagues, and may not be picking up the newest technology in their company's field. They may be missing out on important policy or procedural changes that the company is undertaking. Ongoing training, whether in country or back in the United States, can make a huge difference in the success of an overseas assignment.

It is advised that the more different the culture into which people are venturing, the more specific and rigorous the training needs to be, and the more the training needs to incorporate such experiential tactics such as simulations and role plays aimed at specific differences.[26]

However, the expatriates must recognize that within a two- to four-year average time frame abroad they will never internalize enough of the local culture to over-

---

[22]Amanda Bennett, "The Chief Executives in Year 2000 Will Be Experienced Abroad," *Wall Street Journal* (February 27, 1990), p. A1.

[23]"GE Redesigns Rungs of Career Ladder," *Wall Street Journal* (March 15, 1993), p. B1, B7.

[24]Joann S. Lublin, "Companies Use Cross-Cultural Training to Help Their Employees Adjust Abroad," *Wall Street Journal* (August 4, 1992), p. B1, B6.

[25]Lublin, 1992.

[26]J. Stewart Black, Mark Mendenhall, and Gary Oddou, "Toward a Comprehensive Model of International Adjustment. An Integration of Multiple Theoretical Perspectives," *Academy of Management Review*, 16 (April 1991), pp. 291–317.

come all social and communication concerns. Even with appropriate training, the expatriates are the product of their home culture. They will eat with a fork when a hand is more polite, shake on a deal and thereby show their lack of faith, or require that a contract with all possible legal contingencies spelled out be signed in triplicate when honor and trust dictate that the deal go through on a shared local drink. These may appear small social problems, but such social problems may keep the expatriate out of important deals. As Black and Porter[27] noted in their article title, "a successful manager in Los Angeles may not succeed in Hong Kong." The expatriate may find, after some time, that the best place to make sales is not his or her client's offices but sitting at the bar watching soccer with other executives.

Motivation. Motivating expatriates to accept and succeed at positions abroad requires a combination of carefully planned policies and incentives. Appropriate policies help make the prospects of going overseas attractive before, during, and after it takes place. Expatriates often express concern that their stints abroad not hinder their career progress. Companies should set up and publicize career paths that reward and make use of skills expatriates acquire overseas. Additionally, while the expatriate is overseas, regular communication with the home office will help allay fears that "out of sight, out of mind" will hinder his career progress.[28]

EXHIBIT 15-5
THE PRICE OF AN EXPATRIATE

An employer's average first-year direct cost of sending a U.S. executive to Britain, with a $100,000 salary and a family of four:

Direct Compensation Costs

Base salary	$100,000
Foreign assignment premium	15,000
Cost of living adjustment	21,000
Housing costs	39,000

Transfer Costs

Relocation allowance	$5,000
Airfare to London	2,000
Moving expenses	25,000

Other Costs

Company car	15,000
Schooling for two children	20,000
Annual home leave (four people)	4,000
U.K. personal income tax	56,000
TOTAL	**$302,000**

Source: Organization Resource Counselors, Inc., 1997.

---

[27]J. Stewart Black and Lyman W. Porter, "Managerial Behaviors and Job Performance: A Successful Manager in Los Angeles May Not Succeed in Hong Kong," *Journal of International Business Studies*, 22 (First Quarter 1991), pp. 99–113.

[28]Thomas F. O'Boyle, "Little Benefit to Careers Seen in Foreign Stints," *Wall Street Journal* (December 11, 1989), p. B1, B4.

Compensation. As presented in Exhibit 15-5, estimates are that the cost of sending a home country employee abroad is, on average, 2.5 to 3 times his or her base salary.[29] Compensation packages may include overseas premiums, housing allowances, cost-of-living allowances, tax equalizations, repatriation allowances, all-expense-paid vacations, and performance-based bonuses. Yet despite this, a recent survey found 77 percent of expatriates were dissatisfied with their expatriation salaries and benefits and their international compensation packages in general. In fact, more than 25 percent were contemplating leaving their company.[30] How much should overseas assignments pay?

One approach has been to pay expatriates a premium for their willingness to live in adverse conditions. Such special "hardship packages" can cause problems, however. Overseas employees may notice the discrepancy in remuneration between expatriates, local nationals, and third-country nationals. An expatriate sales manager in Japan may be motivated by an incentive system through which he or she would earn a higher salary for stellar performance. However, such an individual approach would not sit well with Japanese colleagues, who subscribe to a collective approach that does not favor standing out from others of similar seniority. Furthermore, expatriates who receive a generous compensation package while abroad may lose motivation upon returning home to a previous salary scale.[31] A more recent approach has been to consider the overseas assignment a necessary step for progress within the company, viewed more as a learning experience than as a hardship.[32]

The company must also consider the impact of family life cycle on compensation.[33] Expatriates with spouses and children encounter higher needs abroad, including the need to make up for the loss of a spouse's income and the cost of enrolling children in private schools. A program must be flexible enough to adjust to the varying needs of different employees.

Family Discord. The typical candidate for an international assignment is married, has two school-aged children, and is expected to stay overseas for three years. In the age of two-career families, an international assignment means that a spouse may have to suspend a stateside career. Thus, many employees are reluctant to move abroad. Others who accept transfers grow frustrated as they find that their spouses cannot get jobs or even work permits abroad. Schools where English is spoken must be found, or children must learn the local language. Concerns about the safety and happiness of family members may keep the candidate from accepting an overseas position. Given such complexities, it is clear why it might be difficult to motivate typical candidates to accept an overseas stint.[34]

Unsuccessful family adjustment is the single most important reason for expatriate dissatisfaction compelling an early return home. Expatriates as well as their fam-

---

[29]Hoann Lubin, "Companies Try to Cut Subsidies for Employees," *Wall Street Journal* (December 11, 1989), p. B1.

[30]J. Stewart Black, "Returning Expatriates Feel Foreign in Their Native Land," *Personnel*, 68 (August 1991), p. 17.

[31]Harvey.

[32]*Wall Street Journal* (March 15, 1993), p. B1, B7.

[33]Harvey 1993.

[34]Lublin 1992.

◆ ◆

GLOBAL PERSPECTIVE 15-3

SCREENING CANDIDATES FOR EXPATRIATION

An increasing number of companies are screening prospective expatriates and their spouses for cross-cultural adaptability. The following are some of the questions asked at AT & T.

1. Would your spouse's career be put on hold to accompany you on an international assignment? If so, how would this affect your spouse and your relationship with each other?

2. Would you enjoy the challenge of making your own way in new environments?

Source: Adapted from Gilbert Fuchsberg, "As Costs of Overseas Assignments Climb, Firms Select Expatriates More Carefully," *Wall Street Journal* (January 9, 1992), p. B1.

3. How would you feel about the need for networking and being your own advocate to secure a job upon return from your foreign assignment?

4. How willing and able are you in initiating and building new social contacts abroad?

5. Could you live without television?

6. How important is it for you to spend a significant amount of time with people of your own ethnic, racial, religious, and national background?

7. Have you ever been genuinely interested in learning about other peoples and cultures?

8. Do you like vacationing in foreign countries?

9. Do you enjoy ethnic and foreign cuisines?

10. How tolerant are you of having to wait for repairs?

ily members are in crisis because of culture shock and stress. As a result, marriages break up and some people become alcoholic.

Thus, international companies try to cut costs by reducing the problems that can hurt expatriates' job satisfaction and performance. For example, AT & T has begun putting prospective expatriates through management interviews, a written test, and a self-assessment checklist of "cultural adaptability," as well as interviews with a psychologist (see Global Perspective 15-3). To help spouses find jobs abroad, Philip Morris Company hired an outplacement firm to provide career counseling and job leads.[35]

The Return of the Expatriate—Repatriation. Repatriation is the return of the expatriate employee from overseas. Although efforts are being made by companies, many returning expatriates have difficulty finding good job assignments when their foreign positions end. The post-return concern that an overseas assignment can damage a career back home will discourage employees to take up a foreign position. According to one 1989 study, 65 percent of personnel managers surveyed indicated that expatriates' foreign assignments are not integrated into their overall career planning; and worse yet, 56 percent of them felt that a foreign assignment could be either detrimental to or immaterial in one's career.[36] The most recent extensive study conducted by the Conference Board in 1996 shows an equally deplorable picture. Only 38 percent of U.S. companies offer expatriates a written guarantee of a return posi-

---

[35]Gilbert Fuchsberg, "As Costs of Overseas Assignments Climb, Firms Select Expatriates More Carefully," *Wall Street Journal* (January 9, 1992), B1, B4.

[36]O'Boyle, 1989.

tion, compared to 74 percent of companies in continental Europe that do.[37] In the past two decades, U.S. companies have failed to make any measurable improvement in their repatriation policies.

Repatriation is distinct from other forms of relocation. After an average absence of 3.5 years, expatriates themselves have changed, adopting certain values, attitudes, and habits of their host countries. And the United States has changed, politically, economically, and technologically. The results of poor handling of repatriation are poor employee performance and high employee turnover—both very costly to the organization.[38]

Expatriates face a long list of difficulties upon returning home. Their standard of living often declines. And they often face a lack of appreciation for the knowledge they gained overseas. Without a clear use for their skills, returned expatriates often suffer from a lack of direction and purpose. New stateside assignments often do not give the repatriated employee the same responsibility, freedom, or respect that was enjoyed overseas. It is difficult to adjust to being just another middle manager at home. And poor communications with the home office while abroad leave the returnee cut off from the internal happenings and politics of the company, limiting opportunities for career growth.

Black, Gregersen, and Mendenhall[39] proposed a number of suggestions for enhancing repatriation adjustment. These include (1) post-arrival training, (2) a repatriation center to help employees reform their objectives with the company, (3) spouse adjustment assistance, (4) pre-return training, (5) increased contact with the home office while abroad, and (6) setting up a "sponsor" or partner back in the home office to keep the expatriate up to date and in touch. Pre-trip training should lay out the details for the candidate, including future training expected, help the company will provide, and, importantly, the career path that the move will help. The effort and cost of such comprehensive planning sends a strong signal of the importance of foreign assignments to expatriate candidates.[40]

Generalizations About When Expatriates Are Good/Bad

Expatriates are important whenever communication with the home country office is at a premium. Communication is facilitated among managers of the same nationality.[41] Thus, the company is better off with a stronger expatriate base abroad when the overseas situation puts pressure on communications with the home office. Thus, expatriates are especially important in complex operating environments, or when elevated political risk requires constant monitoring, or when a high cultural distance separates the home and host countries. On the other hand, in very competi-

---

[37]Valerie Frazee, "Repatriates Fight the Out-of-Sight, Out-of-Mind Mentality," *Workforce*, 2 (Global Workforce Supplement, January 1997), p. 10.

[38]J. Stewart Black, Hal B. Gregersen, and Mark E. Mendenhall, "Toward a Theoretical Framework of Operational Adjustment," *Journal of International Business Studies*, 23 (Fourth Quarter 1992), pp. 737–60.

[39]Ibid.

[40]*Wall Street Journal* (March 15, 1993), p. B1, B7.

[41]Nakiye Boyacigiller, "The Role of Expatriates in the Management of Interdependence, Complexity and Risk in Multinational Corporations," *Journal of International Business Studies*, 21 (Third Quarter 1990), pp. 357–81.

tive environments, local nationals may provide important links to the local business community and perhaps play a key strategic role in gaining business.[42]

SUMMARY ◆

No matter how global a company becomes, its sales force remains the front line for the company. On the other hand, actual sales activities are truly local activities, far detached from decision making at headquarters. An effective sales force management is most elusive, yet crucial in developing a coherent international marketing and distribution strategy.

Because sales activities are local activities, they tend to be strongly affected by cultural differences (e.g., shopping habit, negotiation style) around the world, making it difficult, if not impossible, for the international marketing manager to integrate overseas sales operations. Many companies rely on merchant distributors at home or sales agents in the foreign market who have more intimate knowledge of the marketplace. As sales increase, these companies begin to increase their commitment to developing their own distribution and sales force in the foreign market.

The development of an effective sales organization requires sales force objectives and sales force strategy adapted to local differences and calls for careful recruiting, training, supervising, motivating, and compensating of local salespeople. Furthermore, an increasing number of expatriate managers are sent to overseas posts to directly manage the company's local sales force. Expatriate managers function as a bridge between headquarters and local operations, and have to be culturally adaptive and versatile.

Although international assignments have increasingly become a necessary requirement for fast-track managers, cultural adaptability is not always an inborn qualification of many expatriate managers. Cross-cultural training is crucial, as failed expatriate assignments cost the company dearly in terms of lower business performance and dejected employee morale. Recently, companies have begun to develop a repatriation program to ease returned expatriates back into their stateside positions. Such a well-organized repatriation program is important to encourage managers to take up expatriate assignments.

REVIEW QUESTIONS ◆

1. In what ways does international sales management differ from domestic sales management?

2. Discuss why mode of entry and sales management are closely related.

3. For what type of business does a company employ a traveling global sales force?

4. How might foreign government affect a company's sales force management?

5. Why is it generally considered difficult to adopt a U.S.-style commission-based sales force management in such countries as Japan and Mexico?

6. Discuss why expatriate managers are important to a parent company, despite the enormous cost of sending them overseas.

7. Suppose you are developing a cultural training program for employees to be sent to overseas posts. What courses would you include in your two-week program? Why?

---

[42]Ibid., p. 371.

DISCUSSION QUESTIONS ✦

1. Domino's Pizza International, the Ann Arbor, Michigan, based pizza chain, is known worldwide for its delivery service. Its policy of giving away its pizza free if not delivered within half an hour was a legendary service theme, and it earned them a unique position in the consumer's mind. However, recently, the company's foray into Poland in 1994 proved how modifications to positioning strategies might become essential in certain international markets. In 1994, the company wanted to open franchises in Poland. It was keen on opening delivery units as it has in most other countries. However, the lack of reliable and appropriate infrastructure in terms of telephone service in Poland posed a problem. "Its delivery concept wouldn't ride very far if potential customers couldn't phone in their orders." So, in stark contrast to its policy in other countries, Domino opened a sit-in restaurant in Poland in March 1994, followed by another one a couple of months later. Only after some time did it open its standard delivery unit. While this was one way of tiding over the selling constraints peculiar to this market, there was the risk that they were deviating from their most salient positioning theme. Do you think the strategy adopted by Domino's was a wise one? If so, give reasons. If not, provide an alternate strategy, giving your justification for the same.

2. One feature in international selling that is becoming more common is the idea of *piggybacking*; i.e., tying up with existing sales channels to distribute and sell your products. Examples include Dunkin Donuts (as the name suggests, the confectionery chain) combining with Baskin-Robbins (the ice-cream chain) units to sell in Canada, Mexico, and Indonesia. According to business proponents of piggybacking, it allows a significant reduction in costs and risks by the ability to share resources such as dining space, staff, etc., leading to better profitability. However, the concern is that a foreign partner, who is often chosen as the piggybacking partner (unlike the example just stated) may devote less attention to the foreign product. If the piggybacking is with a unit in the same business, considerable cannibalization can also take place. Discuss the conditions under which a piggyback strategy would be appropriate and under which conditions it would not be appropriate.

3. A trend that has been worrying most manufacturers, especially of consumer nondurable products, is the increasing transfer of power from the manufacturers to large and multinational retailing chains. Manufacturers now have relatively less control on how to sell a product to the consumers—less say in in-store displays and pass-through of discounts, for example. A case example of this problem is the recent standoff between a multibillion-dollar retail chain and a multinational, multibillion-dollar food specialty giant. The retailer insisted that it be given certain discounts (which it deemed reasonable) for a certain product sold in China, given the strong relationship between these firms in the U.S. market. The Chinese subsidiary of the manufacturer refused to give these discounts. The retailing giant retaliated by saying that for each subsequent week that it did not receive a discount in China, it would remove one selling unit (brand) from all of the retailer's stores in the United States. Given the size of the U.S. market, the manufacturer finally gave in and accepted giving the discounts. Ten years back, no retailer would have dared using the same tactic with such a large manufacturer. Another troubling fact is that many of these retailing chains are promoting their own brands (e.g., WalMart promoting the Sam's brand), and various grocery chains are promoting their own brands. What are the implications of these changes for the manufacturers of these consumer nondurable products? What 'proactive' steps can manufacturing firms take to counter this trend?

4. Many firms have followed an incremental approach in the past to the sales channels used in international markets. Typically, these companies started by selling in foreign markets through sales agents or distributors. This was followed by opening of liaison offices to assist and monitor the activities of the appointed distributors. With subsequent growth in business, the company would set up its own sales subsidiary to manage sales and customer service. This incremental strategy has worked quite effectively for many companies in the past. In your opinion, would the current emphasis being placed on globalization have any bearing on the effectiveness of this incremental strategy? If so, what would this effect be, and why?

FURTHER READINGS ◆

Cook, Roy A., and Joel Herche. "Assessment Centers: An Untapped Resource for Global Salesforce Management." *Journal of Personal Selling and Sales Management,* 12 (Summer (1992): 31–37.

Maggiori, Herman J. *How to Make the World Your Market: The International Sales and Marketing Handbook.* Los Angeles: Burning Gale Press, 1992.

Scheneider, Fred. "Shopping on the Information Superhighway" *International Journal of Retail and Distribution Management* (Spring 1995): 9–10.

Segal-Horn, Susan, and Heather Davison. "Global Markets, The Global Consumer, and International Retailing." *Journal of Global Marketing,* 5(3) (1992): 31–61.

Solomon, Charlene Marmer. "HR's Helping Hand Plus Global Inpatriates Onbound." *Personnel Journal,* 74 (November 1995): 40.

Shumansky, Noel J. "Keeping Track of Global Managers." *Human Resource Professional,* 5 (Spring 1993): 6–9.

Sullivan, Sherry E., and Howard S. Tu. "Training Managers for International Assignments." *Executive Development,* 6(1) (1993): 25–28.

Talbott, Shannon Peters. "Building a Global Workforce Starts with Recruitment." *Personnel Journal,* 75 (March 1996): 59.

"Towards an International Salesforce." *Journal of Management Development,* 14(9) (1995): 6–8.

GLOBAL LOGISTICS AND DISTRIBUTION

16

CHAPTER OVERVIEW

1. DEFINITION OF GLOBAL LOGISTICS
2. MANAGING GLOBAL LOGISTICS
3. FREE TRADE ZONES
4. MAQUILADORA OPERATION
5. U.S. SPECIAL IMPORT TARIFF PROVISIONS
6. GLOBAL RETAILING

Global logistics and distribution have played a critical role in the growth and development of world trade and in the integration of manufacturing on a worldwide scale. In fact, the level of world trade in goods, and to an extent services, depends to a significant degree on the availability of economical and reliable international transportation services. Decreases in transportation costs and increases in performance reliability expand the scope of manufacturing operations and increase the associated level of international trade and competition.[1] The use of appropriate distribution channels in international markets increases the chances of success dramatically. Coca-Cola succeeded in Japan, in part, because it spent the time and the money to set up its own bottlers and distribution.

The concept of business logistics is relatively new. John F. Magee is generally credited with publishing the first article on logistics theory in 1960.[2] As far back as 1954, Peter Drucker had said that logistics would remain "the dark continent of

---

[1] John H. Dunning, "Reappraising the Eclectic Paradigm in an Age of Alliance Capitalism," *Journal of International Business Studies*, 26 (Third Quarter 1995), pp. 461–91.

[2] John F. Magee, "The Logistics of Distribution," *Harvard Business Review*, 38 (July 1960), pp. 89–101.

business"[3] and underdeveloped, and his prediction proved true until well in the 1980s. It is not too difficult to demonstrate the importance of the physical handling, moving, storing, and retrieving of material. In almost every product, more than 50 percent of product cost is material related, while less than 10 percent is labor. Yet, over the years this fact has not received much attention. In the United States, the total logistics cost is estimated to amount to 10 percent to 11 percent of the country's GNP, or about $600 billion, roughly four to five times as large as the current U.S. trade deficit.[4]

In the 1990s, a variety of issues are driving the increased emphasis on logistics and distribution management. It was epitomized by General Motors' recent lawsuit against Volkswagen over the defection of José Ignacio Lopez, the former vice president of purchasing at General Motors and one of the most renowned logistics managers in the automobile industry.[5] His expertise is said to have saved General Motors millions and millions of dollars from its purchasing and logistic operations, which would directly affect the company's bottom line.

As firms start operating on a global basis, logistics managers need to manage shipping of raw materials, components, and supplies among various manufacturing sites at the most economical and reliable rates. Simultaneously, they need to ship finished goods to customers in markets around the world at the desired place and time. The development of intermodal transportation and electronic tracking technology has caused a quantum jump in the efficiency of the logistic methods employed by firms. Intermodal transportation refers to the seamless transfer of goods from one mode of transport (e.g., aircraft or ship) to another (e.g., truck) and vice versa without the hassle of unpacking and repackaging of goods to suit the dimensions of the mode of transport being used. Tracking technology refers to the means for keeping continuous tabs on the exact location of the goods being shipped in the logistic chain—this enables quick reaction to any disruption in the shipments because (a) the shipper knows exactly where the goods are in real time and (b) the alternative means can be quickly mobilized.

◆ ◆ ◆ ◆ ◆ ◆ DEFINITION OF GLOBAL LOGISTICS

Global logistics is defined as the design and management of a system that directs and controls the flows of materials into, through and out of the firm across national boundaries to achieve its corporate objectives at a minimum total cost. As shown in Exhibit 16-1, it encompasses the entire range of operations concerned with products or components movement, including both exports and imports simultaneously. Global logistics, like domestic logistics, encompasses materials management and physical distribution.[6]

Materials management refers to the inflow of raw materials, parts, and supplies in and through the firm. This topic has been explored earlier in Chapter 10 in the

---

[3]Peter F. Drucker, *The Practice of Management* (New York: Harper & Brothers, 1954).

[4]Perry A. Trunick, "Logistics Results in Excellence," *Transportation and Distribution*, 36 (September 1995), p. 29.

[5]"GM-VW Battle: Blood Feud," *Fortune* (April 14, 1997), pp. 90–102.

[6]Donald F. Wood, *International Logistics* (New York: Chapman & Hall, 1995).

EXHIBIT 16-1
GLOBAL LOGISTICS

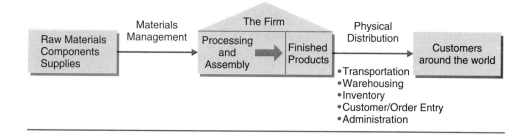

context of global sourcing strategy, or management of R & D, manufacturing, and marketing interfaces. **Physical distribution** refers to the movement of the firm's finished products to its customers, consisting of transportation, warehousing, inventory, customer service/order entry, and administration. In this chapter, we focus on physical distribution management.

Although the functions of physical distribution are universal, they are affected differently by the tradition, culture, economic infrastructure, laws, and topography, among others, in each country and each region. In general, in geographically large countries, such as the United States, where products are transported for a long distance, firms tend to incur relatively more transportation and inventory costs than in smaller countries. On the other hand, in geographically concentrated countries, such as Japan and Britain, firms tend to incur relatively more warehousing, customer service/order entry, and general administrative costs than in geographically larger countries. It is primarily because a wide variety of products with different features have to be stored to meet the variegated needs of customers in concentrated areas. The results of a recent survey of physical distribution costs in various European countries relative to the United States are presented in Global Perspective 16-1. Although it is possible to attribute all cost differences to topography, customs, laws of the land, and other factors, the cost differences could also reflect how efficiently or inefficiently physical distribution is managed in various countries and regions.

MANAGING GLOBAL LOGISTICS   ◆ ◆ ◆ ◆ ◆ ◆ ◆

Logistics management is inextricably tied with international trade and multinational manufacturing and sourcing of raw materials, components, and supplies. World trade in goods grew by 9 percent per annum in recent years, compared to an increase of only 3.5 percent in the output of goods. Global logistics, however, is considerably more complex, more costly, and as a result, more important for the success of a firm. A variety of factors contribute to the increased complexity and cost of global logistics, as compared to domestic logistics.

• **Distance.** The first fundamental difference is distance. Global logistics frequently require transportation of parts, supplies, and finished goods over much longer distances than is the norm domestically. A longer distance generally suggests higher direct costs of transportation and insurance for damages, deterioration, and pilferage in transit and higher indirect costs of warehousing and inventory.

◆◆◆

GLOBAL PERSPECTIVE 16-1

REGIONAL VARIATIONS IN PHYSICAL DISTRIBUTION COSTS IN EUROPE

Despite the allegedly more integrated and more efficient European economy under the aegis of the European Union, physical distribution costs in Europe have not declined yet, and worse yet, seem to have increased. According to Herbert W. Davis and Company's estimate, the Europeans paid 9.17 percent of revenue for physical distribution in 1993, up from 8.1 percent in 1992. The comparable rate for the United States was 8.07 percent in 1993.

Regional variations exist, however. Germany experienced a slight drop in distribution cost from 10.4 percent to 10.1 percent, while its average was still above the continental average. Costs in the Netherlands declined from 9.7 percent to 9.0 percent in the same period. The United Kingdom registered the highest increase from 6.8 percent to 8.0 percent, but still enjoyed the lowest in the continent. Similarly, French distribution costs went up to 8.3 percent from 7.3 percent. Sweden remained the highest distribution-cost country in the European Union, registering at 11.3 percent.

The physical distribution costs consist of transportation, warehousing, inventory, customer service/order entry, and administration. Let us make a comparison in terms of these components of the distribution costs between the two continents across the Atlantic. The following table shows cost comparisons (as a percentage of revenue).

The largest disparity was in warehousing, where European costs measured 3.03 percent, almost a third of total distribution costs, compared to 1.98 percent in the United States. These expenses are the cost of both plant and field warehouses including labor, space, direct materials, etc. Similarly, a large difference was observed in cus-

	European Union	The United States
Transportation	2.79%	3.23%
Warehousing	3.03%	1.98%
Inventory	1.73%	1.93%
Customer Service/ Order Entry	0.83%	0.49%
Administration	0.79%	0.44%
Total	9.17%	8.07%

tomer service/order entry—the cost of people, space and materials needed to take orders and handle inquiries—with 0.83 percent in Europe, compared to 0.49 percent in the United States.

These disparities mean opportunities to logisticians involved with Europe. They are hopeful of the promises of the single market for the continent's distribution industry by erasing national borders, deregulating industries, establishing a common currency, etc., over time.

As Herbert W. Davis, president of Davis and Company, notes, "Logistics, logically, would respond by a significant shift toward continent-wide manufacturing and would establish new distribution strategies based on freer cross-border freight movement." Also, retailers and wholesalers would shed nationalistic tendencies resulting in European-wide pricing and service over time. Indeed, manufacturing plants and associated logistics facilities have increased the amount of product shipped directly to customers, displacing many of the small, product-line, country-oriented plants that have closed.

As a result, the European physical distribution system is increasingly based on more direct flow from worldwide manufacturing sites to the countries where the sales take place. A growing number of multinational companies, many U.S.-based, have also kept up with the developments in Europe, responding to market conditions and cutting distribution costs.

Source: Adapted from James Thomas, "Mountain High, River Wide; Physical Distribution Costs in Europe," *Distribution*, 93 (May 1994), pp. 62–65.

- **Exchange Rate Fluctuation.** The second difference pertains to currency variations in international logistics. The corporation must adjust its planning to incorporate the existence of currencies and changes in exchange rates. For example, as the U.S. dollar depreciated while the Japanese yen soared in value in the last decade, Honda found it much cheaper to ship its Accord models to Europe from its U.S. plant in Marysville, Ohio, rather than from its plants in Japan.

- **Foreign Intermediaries.** Additional intermediaries participate in the global logistics process because of the need to negotiate border regulations of countries and deal with local government officials and distributors. Although home country export agents, brokers, and export merchants work as middlemen providing an exporting service for manufacturing firms, those home-based middlemen may not have sufficient knowledge about the foreign countries' market conditions or sufficient connections with local government officials and distributors. In Oriental countries such as Japan, Korea, and China, personal "connections" of who knows whom frequently seem to outweigh the Western economic principle of profit maximization or cost minimization in conducting business.[7] Therefore, working with the local distributors has proved very important in building initial connections with the local business community as well as local government regulators.

Modes of Transportation

The global logistics manager must understand the specific properties of the different modes of transport in order to use them optimally. The three most important factors in determining an optimal mode of transportation are the value-to-volume ratio and perishability of the product and the cost of transportation. The **value-to-volume** ratio is determined by how much value is added to the materials used in the product. **Perishability** of the product refers to the quality degradation over time and/or product obsolescence along the product life cycle. The **cost of transportation** should be considered in light of the value-to-volume and perishability of the product.

Ocean Shipping. Ocean shipping offers three options. **Liner service** offers regularly scheduled passage on established routes. **Bulk shipping** normally provides contractual service for prespecified periods of time, while the third category is for **irregular runs**. Container ships carry standardized containers that greatly facilitate the loading and unloading of cargo and intermodal transfer of cargo. Ocean shipping is used extensively for the transport of heavy, bulky, and/or nonperishable products, including crude oil, steel, and automobiles. Although most manufacturers rely on existing international ocean carriers, some large exporting companies, such as Toyota and Hyundai, have their own fleets of cargo ships. Over the years, shipping rates have been falling as a result of a price war among shipping lines. For example, an average rate for shipping a forty-foot container from Asia to the United States fell from $4,000 in 1992 to $3,500 in 1996. However, in a move to reclaim its power to set prices on the biggest American ocean trade line, a shipping cartel is trying to raise rates on goods imported from Asia to the United States.[8] Such a move, known as the Trans-Pacific Stabilization Agreement, by the shipping cartel may encourage large companies with a major stake in trans-Pacific trade to purchase their own fleets of cargo ships.

---

[7]See, for example, Jean L. Johnson, Tomoaki Sakano, and Naoto Onzo, "Behavioral Relations in Across-Culture Distribution Systems: Influence, Control, and Conflict in U.S.-Japanese Marketing Channels," *Journal of International Business Studies*, 21 (Fourth Quarter 1990), 639–55; and Min Chen, *Asian Management Systems: Chinese, Japanese, and Korean Styles of Business* (New York: Routledge, 1995).

[8]Anna W. Mathews, "Shipping Cartel to Raise Rates on Asian Imports," *Wall Street Journal* (February 21, 1997), A2, A5.

Air Freight.　Shipping of goods by air has seen rapid growth over the last thirty years. Although the total volume of international trade using air shipping remains quite small—it still constitutes less than 2 percent of international trade in goods—it represents more than 20 percent of the value of goods shipped in international commerce. High-value goods are more likely to be shipped by air, especially if they have a high value-to-volume ratio. Typical examples are semiconductor chips, LCD screens, and diamonds. Perishable products like produce and flowers also tend to be air-freighted. Changes in aircraft design have now enabled air transshipment of relatively bulky products. Three decades ago, a large propeller aircraft could hold only 10 tons of cargo. Today's cargo jumbo jets carry more than 30 tons, and medium- to long-haul transports planes like the C-130 and the AN-32 can carry more than 80 tons of cargo. In terms of sheer bulk, however, this is dwarfed by the million-ton-plus tankers that ferry crude oil from the Gulf to the United States and Japan.

Intermodal Transportation. More than one mode of transportation is usually employed. Naturally, when shipments travel across the ocean, surface or air shipping is the initial mode of transportation crossing national borders. Once landed, they may be further shipped by truck, barge, railroad, or air. Even if countries are contiguous, such as Canada, the United States, and Mexico, for example, various domestic regulations prohibit use of the same trucks between and across the national boundaries. When different modes of transportation are involved, or even when shipments are transferred from one truck to another at the national border, it is important to make sure that cargo space is utilized at full load so that the per-unit transportation cost is minimized.

　　Managing shipments so that they arrive in time at the desired destination is critical in modern-day logistics management. Due to low transit times, greater ease of

Depending upon a local market's stage of economic development and infrastructural conditions, a foreign company may need to adjust its mode of transportation drastically.

unloading and distribution, and higher predictability, many firms use air freight, either on a regular basis or as a backup to fill in when the regular shipment by an ocean vessel gets delayed. For footwear firms Reebok and Nike, and for fashion firms such as Pierre Cardin, use of air freight is becoming almost a required way of doing business, as firms jostle to get their products first into the U.S. market from their production centers in Asia and Europe. The customer in a retail store often buys a product that may have been air-freighted in from the opposite end of the world the previous day or even the same day. Thus, the face of retailing is also changing as a result of advances in global logistics.

Distance between the transacting parties increases transportation costs and requires longer-term commitment to forecasts and longer lead times. Differing legal environments, liability regimes, and pricing regulations affect transportation costs and distribution costs in a way not seen in the domestic market. Trade barriers, customs problems, and paperwork tend to slow the cycle times in logistics across national boundaries. Although this is true, the recent formation of regional trading blocs, such as the European Union, the North American Free Trade Agreement, and the MERCOSUR (The Southern Cone Free Trade Area), is also encouraging integration and consolidation of logistics in the region for improved economic efficiency and competition (see Global Perspective 16-2).

Warehousing and Inventory Management

The international strategy for logistics management that a firm chooses depends, in part, on the government policy and, in part, on the infrastructure and logistic services environment available. The traditional logistics strategy involves anticipatory demand management based on forecasting and inventory speculation.[9] In this scenario, a multinational firm estimates the requirements for supplies as well as the demand from its customers and then attempts to manage the flow of raw materials and components in its worldwide manufacturing system and the flow of finished products to its customers in such a manner as to minimize the holding of inventory without jeopardizing manufacturing runs and without losing sales due to stockouts.

In the past, the mechanics and reliability of transportation and tracking of the flow of goods was a major problem. With the increasing use of information technology, electronic data interchange and intermodal transportation, the production, scheduling and delivery of goods across national borders is also becoming a matter of just-in-time delivery while some structural problems still remain. For instance, the current restrictions on U.S.-Canada air freight services, and U.S.-Mexico cross border trucking restrict the speed of flow of goods and add to the lead times and are examples of government restrictions which need to be changed to facilitate faster movement of goods across borders.

Despite those restrictions, forward-looking multinational firms can still employ near just-in-time inventory management. For example, Sony has an assembly plant in Nuevo Laredo, Mexico just across the Texas border, importing components from its U.S. sister plants in the United States. While cross-border transportation across the U.S.–Mexico international bridges experiences traffic congestion and occasionally

---

[9]Louis P. Bucklin, "Postponement, Speculation and the Structure of Distribution Channels," *Journal of Marketing Research*, 2 (February 1965), pp. 26–31.

◆ ◆

$\mathcal{G}$LOBAL PERSPECTIVE 16-2

REDESIGNING LOGISTICS IN THE EMERGENCE OF THE EUROPEAN UNION

European governments have begun to privatize transportation services. Since January 1, 1993, the European Union (EU) movement presents opportunities for reducing logistics costs and boosting efficiency. And it is not just Europeans but also foreign manufacturers, including those in North America, who are finding that political changes in Europe have created opportunities for greater efficiency and lower costs in their logistics.

However, there still are many political, legal, and technical issues to be settled before Europe truly is unified. Thus, logistics managers must plan how to respond to changes as they occur. Here are some of the many changes reshaping European logistics strategies:

Customs procedures. For the most part, customs check points as a shipment crosses each nation's border have been eliminated. Duties and trade statistics now are a matter strictly between the originating and destination countries, and intermediate countries no longer are involved. Consequently, transit times and paperwork between EU countries, particularly for truck traffic, are steadily being reduced.

Harmonized product standards. Prior to unification, each European country had its own manufacturing, packaging, labeling, and safety standards for almost every item sold within its borders. Under the European Union, Pan-European harmonized standards are being developed and replacing most of those country-by-country regulations. As a result, companies can manufacture a single version of a product for sale in all parts of the EU, rather than design and manufacture different versions of the same item for each member country. Product harmonization will allow shippers to redesign not only their distribution patterns and facilities, but also their customer-service strategies.

Transportation deregulation. The European Commission is deregulating transportation in Europe in order to open markets in member states to competition and to eliminate conflicting regulations that impede the flow of traffic between EU countries. The deregulation promises to promote the development of efficient, cost-effective services in all modes.

Transportation infrastructure. As in Japan and the United States, growing demand for just-in-time deliveries increase traffic and exacerbates transportation bottlenecks (particularly, inter-regional trucking). The European Commission and individual governments are actively encouraging private development of rail and water alternatives.

Source: Adapted from "Logistics Strategies for a New Europe, *Traffic Management,* 33, (August, 1994), p. 49A.

causes delays in shipment, Sony has been able to manage just-in-time inventory management with a minimum of safety stock in its warehouse.

Hedging against Inflation and Exchange Rate Fluctuations.   Multinational corporations can also use inventory as a strategic tool in dealing with currency fluctuations and as a hedge against inflation. By increasing inventories before imminent depreciation of a currency instead of holding cash, the firm may reduce its exposure to currency depreciation losses. High inventories also provide a hedge against inflation, because the value of the goods/parts held in inventory remains the same compared to the buying power of a local currency, which falls with a devaluation. In such cases the international logistics manager has to coordinate operations with that of the rest of the firm, so that the cost of maintaining an increased level of inventories is more than offset by the gains from hedging against inflation and currency fluctuations. Many countries, for instance, charge a property tax on stored goods. If the increase in the cost of carrying the increased inventory along with the taxes exceeds the saving from hedging, then the increased inventory may not be a good idea.

Benefiting from Tax Differences. There are creative ways in which costs can be written off before taxes so that internal transit arrangements can actually make a profit. This implies that what and how much a firm transfers within its global manufacturing system is a function of the tax systems in various countries to and from which the transfers are being made. When the transfer of a component A from country B to country C is tax-deductible in country B (as an export) and gets credit in country C for being part of a locally assembled good D, then the transfer makes a profit for the multinational firm. Access to and use of such knowledge is the forte of logistics firms that sell these services to the multinational firm interested in optimizing its global logistics.

Logistic Integration and Rationalization. More dramatic changes are taking place in the wake of the European Union. According to a recent study conducted by Andersen Consulting and the U.K.'s Cranfield School of Management, an increasing number of European firms have begun to integrate European operations, rationalize those operations, or do both.[10] **Logistic integration** refers to coordinating production and distribution across geographic boundaries—a radical departure from the traditional country-by-country–based structure consisting of separate sales, production, warehousing, and distribution organizations in each country. **Rationalization,** on the other hand, means reducing resources to achieve more efficient and cost-effective operations. Although conceptually separate, most companies' strategies include both aspects of the logistics strategy.

For example, Baxter Healthcare, a U.S. medical-supplies manufacturer, has recently reorganized its production and logistics management by product lines for all of Europe. Previously, the company had separate organizations in each country, offering a full range of products. Now, each of its manufacturing, distribution, and administrative facilities specializes in one type of product and markets that product throughout Europe (integration). Furthermore, the company may consolidate warehouses so that it serves the entire region from one or a few strategically located distribution centers (rationalization). The cost savings as a result of redesigning European logistics systems has been reported to amount, on average, to as much as 40 percent to 50 percent from the current country-by-country–based approach.[11]

It must be remembered, however, that while the laws of the European Union point toward economic integration, there still are and will continue to be political, cultural, and legal differences among countries. Similarly, as shown in Global Perspective 16-3, the North American Free Trade Agreement is not free of arcane regulations, either. Consequently, despite the promised benefit of logistics integration and rationalization, international marketers as well as corporate planners have to have specialized local knowledge to ensure smooth operations. Particularly, customer service strategies need to be differentiated, depending on the expectations of local consumers. For example, German buyers of personal computers may be willing to accept Dell Computer's mail-order service or its Web site ordering service,[12] but French and Spanish customers may assume that a delivery person will deliver and install the products for them.

---

[10] This section draws from "Logistics Strategies for a "New Europe," *Traffic Management*, 33 (August, 1994), p. 49A.

[11] Ibid., p. 49A

[12] Silvia Ascarelli, "Dell Finds U.S. Strategy Works in Europe," *Wall Street Journal* (February 3, 1997), p. A8; Eryn Brown, "Could the Very Best PC Maker Be Dell Computer?" *Fortune* (April 14, 1997), p. 26.

* *

$\mathcal{G}$LOBAL PERSPECTIVE 16-3

CABOTAGE

Cabotage refers to the right of a trucker to be able to carry goods in an assigned territory. Traditionally, countries have restricted cabotage rights of foreign truckers. For instance, until 1992, a trucker delivering Opel sedans from Germany to Spain, having delivered the cars in

Madrid, could not carry goods originating in Spain back to Germany and had to drive back an empty truck. Similarly, an American trucker, even today, after delivering goods in Toronto, cannot pick up another load and deliver it in Ottawa—that is a violation of current cabotage rules. If the American trucking company has a scheduled load to the United States from Toronto, then the truck may carry the load but the driver must be Canadian. Mercifully, trucking interests in the United States and Canada are working to improve the antiquated cabotage laws, which predate the North American Free Trade Agreement.

Source: "Trucking Groups Near Agreement on Cabotage Deal," *Inside DOT and Transportation Week*, 6 (20) (May 19, 1995); and "Survey of World Commercial Vehicles," *Financial Times* (December 13, 1995), p. V.

Intra-Company versus Inter-Company (Third Party) Logistic Management

International shipping between a company's own facilities can be as tricky as dealing with an outside company. The trend seems to be decentralization, in varying degrees, accompanied, paradoxically, by a degree of centralization, as suggested by sourcing and logistics executives at some larger U.S. multinationals like General Motors, AT & T, Du Pont, Dow Chemical, and Westinghouse.

A survey conducted in 1994 by Robert C. Lieb, professor at Boston's Northeastern University, and Hugh Randall, group vice president of Mercer Consulting, found that 38 percent of Fortune 500 firms were using third-party logistics companies and that a further 27 percent were considering using third-party logistic firms. Also, of those using third-party logistics firms, 61 percent of the respondents were satisfied with the third-party logistics firm and 37 percent were very satisfied. Within the United States, the market for contract logistics is expected to expand from $16 billion in 1994 to $25 billion by 1997—spurred largely by the globalization of business.[13] To stay with the trend, information technology companies such as IBM have established a consulting group selling supply chain management services to other manufacturing firms (see Global Perspective 16-4).

This trend toward third-party logistics may be a result of concentrating on core competencies. Core competencies refer to the mix of skills and resources that a firm possesses that enable it to produce one set of goods and/or services in a much more effective manner than another. Also, competent logistic firms can save money for a multinational firm shipping components between its facilities in different countries, because shipping costs paid internally can vary according to the fluctuation of foreign currencies. There is much diversity in how payments are made, in whether ship-

---

[13]Daniel P. Bearth, "Ryder Ties Growth Strategy to Worldwide Logistics Market," *Transport Topics* (March 13, 1995), p.27; and James A. Cooke, "On the Up and Up and Up!: Logistics Outsourcing Report," *Traffic Management*, 35 (January 1996), pp. 49–51.

◆ ◆

GLOBAL PERSPECTIVE 16-4

IBM INTERNATIONAL TRADE MANAGEMENT SERVICES (ITMS)

IBM is one of the top importing and exporting companies in the United States. Like a number of large shippers, Big Blue has turned its expertise in global logistics into a profit-making, third-party service. Part of IBM's consulting group, ITMS's forte is global supply chain management, and the Boulder, Colorado, center processes about $15 billion worth of trade volume annually.

Some years ago, Kmart was making plans to move into Mexico. While Kmart had a state-of-the-art softlines distribution center in Sunnyvale, Texas, and another for hardlines in Corsicana, Texas, both the distribution centers were designed to ship products to U.S. stores only. K-mart turned to ITMS's expertise to help it bring its Mexico stores on line within schedule. ITMS developed compliant processes for cross-border goods, information, and financial flows for five different supply options, cover-

Source: William McKee, "Invitation to a Third Party," *Distribution*, 93 (December 1994), pp. 50–53.

ing all U.S. and Mexican trade requirements. ITMS designed a state-of-the-art trade system that preclassifies goods, provides Spanish descriptions and interfaces with the government systems to generate Special Economic Zone Documents and invoices. This involved coordination between fifteen different client, supplier, government and consultant organizations to enable correct information flow from Kmart's systems to trade and merchandising systems. Kmart's two super stores in Mexico City opened on time with all imported goods on the shelves.

Arrow Electronics, a $4 billion electronics distributor with operations in twenty-one countries asked ITMS to assess their U.S. order fulfillment and distribution system and what it would take to expand the system globally. ITMS developed an operational model diagramming all the functions a distribution company requires to operate in any country, including purchasing, inbound logistics, order fulfillment, value added activities, and outbound logistics. Arrow avoided the mistake that many companies make trying to plug a U.S. system into another country.

---

ments are paid for straight through to a recipient or left at a port of entry, and in the rate charged, which is often different for a company and for its customers.

General Motors has one corporate office at headquarters at Detroit that oversees the logistics of all component operations reflecting a degree of centralization. Actual shipping operations, including implementation and documentation, are handled by two independent support companies—Burlington Air Express, which handles GM business in North America and Europe, and Air Express International, which covers South America and Asia. Until some time back, GM used to handle its own shipping, but turned to external contractors to maximize efficiency. The support companies do their own billing itemized for review by the logistics office at GM headquarters.

AT & T Microelectronics uses two AT & T primary distribution centers overseas—one in Singapore, the other in Frankfurt, both controlled by an office in Munich. Everything in the global supply chain of AT & T goes through one or both of these offices. Shipping costs are absorbed from a point of origin in the United States to the port of entry in the country of the recipient. Depending on the terms established, either AT & T or the customer picks up the tab between the port of entry in the recipient's country and the shipment's ultimate destination. Often, the forwarder acting as the middleman is required by AT & T to take the bills, invoice them to the United States, convert them to U.S. dollars, and bill AT & T in U.S. dollars.

At Dell Computer, the international logistics manager makes certain that the third-party logistics provider is state of the art and keeps them involved in Dell's strategic planning. Dell buys monitors finished and packaged, ready to deliver directly to the customer the world over. Since it does not add any value to the monitor itself, Dell tries to avoid any handling of the monitor preferring instead to have the logistic provider to warehouse it and to move it to Dell when the information system link with Dell drops an order into the warehouse computer. This saves Dell inventorying costs and gives it more operational flexibility.[14]

Many logistic companies are now moving to provide tailored logistic solutions in international markets for their clients. The Big Four freight forwarders—DHL, UPS, Federal Express, and TNT—operate separate divisions to offer custom made logistic solutions including warehousing, localization, inventory management, and order tracking and fulfillment. Novell, for example, has recently completed a pilot program with the logistic provider, R. R. Donnelley, which allows Novell to keep minimal inventory in Europe, with 75 percent of its products being drop-shipped from its warehouse in Santa Clara, California. In essence, these logistic providers are attempting to become one-stop logistic providers for firms and in the process are competing with other distribution companies around the world.

Circle International of Canada provides an excellent example. With 350 offices located worldwide, this Canadian company provides all logistical services including logistics information systems, global communications, air freight, ocean freight, inland transportation, customs brokerage, warehousing and distribution, and transportation insurance. For instance, a typical automobile manufacturer uses about 25 freight forwarders and vendors who share responsibility for exporting vehicles and parts to worldwide markets. Excess inventory and poor response time contribute to low return on assets and poor customer service. First, Circle develops a plan tailored to meet their needs to reduce inventory, shorten transit time, stream administration, and offer higher customer service. To accomplish these goals, this Canadian company establishes a central service center for all exports with its on-site staff that can reduce administrative costs by some 30 percent. Second, the company develops a logistics database to coordinate, track, and schedule material flows from the U.S. and other locations. This system enables employees to transmit data electronically to the client each day. Third, parts and vehicles are received at strategically located consolidation points where they are inspected, packed, assembled, and processed through the company's automated inventory system. This centralized approach to managing inventory allows for reduction of material handling and greater control over material. Fourth, the logistics company provides clients with customs brokerage services. Using its global information network, commercial invoice data are summarized and transmitted to the destination's customs operations. Finally, from the central service center, Circle coordinates material flow of goods, working directly with vendors and carriers around the world to ensure competitive shipping rates, accurate delivery time, and expedited distribution from origin to destination.[15] Since moving to one such logistic provider, Sun Microsystems reduced its year end inventory level in Europe from $62 million to $12 million.

For smaller firms, however, third-party logistics may not be a cost-effective alternative because of the relatively lower volumes over which the logistic provider can spread his volumes. Therefore, smaller firms will continue to have to manage at least some of the logistic functions in house. The logistics manager for such firms may then have to learn about existing and planned infrastructure at home and abroad and factor them into

---

[14]Silvia Ascarelli, "Dell Finds U.S. Strategy Works in Europe," *Wall Street Journal* (February 3, 1997), p. A8.

[15]Circle International Home Page, http://www.circleintl.com/index.htm, accessd June 20, 1997.

A major container port in Singapore used as a hub of global distribution.

his form's strategy. In some countries (for example, India), railroads may be an excellent transportation mode, far surpassing the performance of trucking—especially for movement of goods more than 150 miles into the interior from the seaports—while in others the use of railroads may be a highly uncertain mode of transport.

FREE TRADE ZONES

◆ ◆ ◆ ◆ ◆ ◆

A free trade zone (FTZ) is an area that is located within a nation (say, the United States), but is considered outside of the customs territory of the nation. Many countries have similar programs. In the United States, a free trade zone is officially called a Foreign Trade Zone. FTZs are licensed by the Foreign Trade Zone Board and operated under the supervision of the Customs Service. The number of approved FTZs and subzones increased from 75 in 1980 to over 370 in 1991 and was expected to cross 500 by 1995.[16] Subzones are adjuncts to the main zones when the main site

---

[16]"Updated Rules for Foreign Trade Zones Reflect Big Increase in Zone Activity," *Business America* (November 4, 1991), pp. 9–11.

EXHIBIT 16-2
BENEFITS OF USING A FREE TRADE ZONE (FTZ)

1. **Duty deferral and elimination:** Duty will be deferred until products are sold in the United States. If products are exported elsewhere, no import tariff will be imposed.

2. **Lower tariff rates:** Tariff rates are almost always lower for materials and components than for finished products. If materials and components are shipped to an FTZ for further processing and finished products are sold in the United States, a U.S. import tariff will be assessed on the value of the materials and components, rather than on the value of the finished products.

3. **Lower tariff incidence:** Imported materials and components that through storage or processing undergo a loss or shrinkage may benefit from FTZ status as tariff is assessed only on the value of materials and components that actually found their way into the product.

4. **Exchange rate hedging:** Currency fluctuations can be hedged against by requesting customs assessment at any time.

5. **Import quota not applicable:** Import quotas are not generally applicable to goods stored in an FTZ.

6. **"Made in U.S.A." designation:** If foreign components are substantially transformed within an FTZ located in the United States, the finished product may be designated as "Made in U.S.A."

cannot serve the purpose and are usually found at manufacturing plants. Legally, goods in the zone remain in international commerce as long as they are held within the zone or are exported. In other words, those goods (including materials, components, and finished products) shipped into an FTZ in the United States from abroad are legally considered *not* having landed in the customs territory of the United States and thus are not subject to U.S. import tariffs, as long as they are not sold outside the FTZ in the United States.

As summarized in Exhibit 16-2, an FTZ provides many cash flow and operating advantages to zone users. No duties, tariffs, or taxes are levied on any goods imported into an FTZ, until or unless they are brought into U.S. territory. Even when these goods enter the United States, customs duties can be levied on the lesser of the value of the finished product or its imported components.

Operationally, an FTZ provides an opportunity for every business engaged in international commerce to take advantage of a variety of efficiencies and economies in the manufacture and marketing of their products. Merchandise within the zone may be unpacked and repacked; sorted and relabeled; inspected and tested; repaired or discarded; reprocessed, fabricated, assembled, or otherwise manipulated. It may be combined with other imported or domestic materials; stored or exhibited; transported in bond to another FTZ; sold or exported. Foreign goods may be modified within the zone to meet U.S. import standards and processed using U.S. labor.

Aging of imported wine is an interesting way of taking advantage of an FTZ. A U.S. wine importer purchases what is essentially newly fermented grape juice from French vineyards and ships it to an FTZ in the United States for aging. After several years, the now-aged French wine can be shipped throughout the United States, when an appropriate U.S. import tariff will be assessed on the original value of the grape juice instead of on the market value of the aged wine. If tariff rates are sufficiently high, then cost savings from using an FTZ can be enormous.

Another effective use of an FTZ is illustrated by companies like Chrysler and Dell Computer. These companies rely heavily on imported components such as auto parts and computer chips, respectively. In such a case, the companies can get part of their manufacturing facilities designated as subzones of an FTZ. This way, they can use their facilities as ordinarily as they can, yet enjoy all the benefits accruing from an FTZ.

At the macro-level, all parties to the arrangement benefit from the operation of trade zones. The government maintaining the trade zone achieves increased investment and employment. The firm using the trade zone obtains a beachhead in the foreign market without incurring all the costs normally associated with such an activity. As a result, goods can be reassembled, and large shipments can be broken down into smaller units. Duties may be payable only on the imported materials and the component parts rather than on the labor that is used to finish the product.

In addition to free trade zones, various governments have also established export processing zones and special economic areas. As shown in Global Perspective 16-5, Japan, which has had a large trade surplus over the years, has developed a unique trade zone program specifically designed to increase imports rather than exports. The common dimensions for all these zones are that special rules apply to them, when compared with other regions of the country, and that the purpose of these rules is the desire of governments to stimulate the economy—especially the export side of international trade. Export processing zones usually provide tax- and duty-free treatment of production facilities whose output is destined abroad. The maquiladoras of Mexico are one example.

For the logistician, the decision of whether to use such zones is framed by the overall benefit for the logistics system. Clearly, transport and retransport are often required, warehousing facilities need to be constructed, and material handling frequency will increase. However, the costs may well be balanced by the preferential government treatment or by lower labor costs.

◆ ◆

GLOBAL PERSPECTIVE 16-5

JAPAN'S FOREIGN ACCESS ZONE TO INCREASE IMPORTS RATHER THAN EXPORTS

Japan has made some of its major trading partner countries turn protectionistic as it has run a huge trade surplus over the years. To increase imports into Japan rather than to encourage exports from Japan, the Japanese government announced "A Basic Plan for the Expansion of Imports" in 1993. It is a $20 billion program to create a national network of thirty-one import promotion areas scattered across the country, or as the Japanese call them "foreign access zones," where importers would get special tax breaks and other advantages. The foreign access zones could provide a major opportunity for American and other foreign businesses.

Operations based in the access zones would also get around most, if not all, of the existing impediments to foreign investment in Japan. The zones will provide inexpensive warehousing and storage, free or low-cost translation and marketing assistance, access to less expensive regional labor, and most important of all, local marketing opportunities that bypass the large trading companies and their traditional *keiretsu* distribution channels.

Source: Ronald A. Morse, "Foreign Access Zones: A Billion Dollar Opportunity with Japan," *Forum* (September 15, 1993), p. 5.

◆ ◆ ◆ ◆ ◆ ◆ MAQUILADORA OPERATION

The maquiladora industry, also known as the in-bond or twin-plant program, is essentially a special Mexican version of a free trade zone. Mexico allows duty-free imports of machinery and equipment for manufacturing as well as components for further processing and assembly, as long as at least 80 percent of the plant's output is exported. Mexico permits 100 percent foreign ownership of the maquiladora plants in the designated maquiladora zone.

Mexico's Border Industrialization Program developed in 1965 set the basis for maquiladora operations in Mexico. It was originally intended to attract foreign manufacturing investment and increase job opportunities in areas of Mexico suffering from chronic high unemployment. Most of them are located along the U.S.–Mexico border, such as Tijuana across from San Diego, Ciudad Juarez across from El Paso, and Nuevo Laredo across from Laredo. Over the years, however, Mexico has expanded the maquiladora programs to industrialized major cities such as Monterrey, Mexico City, and Guadalajara, where more skilled workers can be found.

Mexico has been an attractive location for labor-intensive assembly because, while hour wage rates in most developing countries have increased since 1980, in Mexico they have declined in dollar terms from $2.96 per hour in 1980 to $1.37 per hour in 1987, and to about $1.00 in 1995. This decline has resulted from a series of peso depreciations beginning in 1976, including the devastating depreciation that shook the Mexican economy in late 1994 and 1995. For example, workers in San Diego currently earn $310 a week, while in Tijuana, similar workers earn just $55 a week.[17] Employment in the maquiladora industry grew from 120,000 in 1980 to 300,000 in 1987, and has since more than doubled to 692,000 in 1996.[18] Automobile and electronics product assembly makes up the bulk of maquiladora industries.

In Tijuana, 24,600 people are employed by electronics manufacturers alone, including Samsung, Sony, Hitachi, and JVC. Together, they assemble more than 9 million television sets a year. In the United States, where more than ninety companies once built TV sets, television-manufacturing jobs—mostly production of picture tubes, receivers and cabinets—have fallen to 30,000 nationwide, according to the Electronics Industry Association. Mexican workers now have the ability to handle complex and sophisticated manufacturing processes. Now with trade barriers falling as a result of the North American Free Trade Agreement (NAFTA), it has become easier for multinational firms, particularly those from the United States, to make high-tech products in border towns like Tijuana and ship them worldwide.[19]

The competitive pressures of the world economy have forced many large manufacturing companies to abandon their assembly plants in the United States and move to Mexican maquiladoras. Furthermore, in order to meet local content requirements imposed by NAFTA, foreign firms, too, have been expanding their manufacturing

---

[17]"Border Booming, on Both Sides; U.S.–Mexico Belt Becoming Next Industrial Frontier," *Chicago Tribune* (May 19, 1996), Business 1.

[18]National Statistics Institute database, 1997.

[19]"Economics Lesson in a Border Town: Why That Asian TV Has a 'Made in Mexico' Label," *New York Times* (May 23, 1996), D1.

operations in the maquiladoras. Particularly, Asian companies, such as Sanyo, Sony, Samsung, and Daewoo, have invited some of their traditional components suppliers to join them in the maquiladoras to increase local procurement.

U.S. SPECIAL IMPORT TARIFF PROVISIONS

The dramatic growth of maquiladoras in Mexico is not entirely attributed to Mexico's Border Industrialization Program and inexpensive labor cost. Special U.S. tariff provisions have also encouraged U.S.-based companies[20] to export U.S.-made components and other in-process materials to foreign countries for further processing and/or assembly and subsequently to reimport finished products back into the United States. U.S. imports under these tariff provisions are officially called **U.S. imports under Items 9802.00.60 and 9802.00.80 of the U.S. Harmonized Tariff Schedule** (the 9802 tariff provisions for short).

The 9802 tariff provisions permit the duty-free importation by U.S.-based companies of their components previously sent abroad for further processing or assembly (i.e., tariffs are assessed only on the foreign value-added portion of the imported products). More specifically, item 9802.00.60 applies to reimportation for further processing in the United States of any metal initially processed or manufactured in the United States that was shipped abroad for processing. Item 9802.00.80 permits reimportation for sale in the United States of finished products assembled abroad in whole or in part made up of U.S.-made components.[21] Therefore, the higher the U.S. import tariff rates, the more beneficial it is for U.S.-based companies to be able to declare U.S. imports under the 9802 tariff provisions. Consequently, many U.S.-based companies have taken full advantage of both the 9802 tariff provisions of the United States and the maquiladora laws of Mexico in pursuit of cost competitiveness.

Under the provisions of NAFTA, however, U.S. import tariffs on products originating from Canada and Mexico continue to be reduced over the next decade or so. As a result, the tariff advantage for products reimported from Mexico into the United States under the 9802 tariff provisions will diminish over time. Nonetheless, the 9802 tariff provisions still benefit U.S.-based companies manufacturing outside of the NAFTA region as long as U.S.-made materials and components are used in production.

U.S. imports under the 9802 tariff provisions have increased at a much faster rate than the overall U.S. imports. In recent years, some 20 percent of total U.S. imports come under the 9802 tariff provisions. At a glance, this percentage figure does not appear significant. It is to be noted that about 40 percent of total U.S. manufactured imports are attributed to U.S. firms' foreign affiliates exporting back to the United States. This phenomenon is also called intra-firm sourcing or intra-firm trade. A good portion

---

[20]U.S.-based companies refer to both U.S. and foreign companies that are manufacturing in the United States.

[21]Masaaki Kotabe, "The Relationship between Offshore Sourcing and Innovativeness of U.S. Multinational Firms: An Empirical Investigation," *Journal of International Business Studies*, 21 (Fourth Quarter 1990), pp. 623–38.

of the provision 9802 imports is of intra-firm nature, thus representing a significant portion of intra-firm trade *managed* by U.S. multinational firms.[22]

◆ ◆ ◆ ◆ ◆ ◆ GLOBAL RETAILING

The face of distribution that consumers interact with is the retail store at which they shop. In developed parts of the world, retailing employs between 7 percent and 12 percent of the work force and wields enormous power over manufacturers and consumers. Retailers have grown into some of the world's largest companies, rivaling or exceeding manufacturers in terms of global reach. Wal-Mart, a discount chain, has grown to be the world's largest retailer with annual revenues of over $80 billion in 1996, which exceed many times over the annual revenues of some of its top suppliers. It is Procter & Gamble's single largest customer, buying as much as the household product giant sells to Japan. Each of Europe's top half-dozen food retailers has larger sales than any of the continent's food manufacturers except Nestlé and Unilever.

"Push" versus "Pull"

At the heart of this retailing revolution is the fundamental change in the way goods and services reach the consumer. Earlier, the distribution chain across the world was controlled by the manufacturer or the wholesaler. The retailer's main competitive advantage lay in merchandising—his or her skills in choosing the assortment of goods for sale in the store. The main use of a second advantage of the retailer—closeness to the customer—was to beat the rival retailer across the street. It was the manufacturer who decided what goods were available, and in most countries at what price they could be sold to the public.

That distribution system of earlier times has now been turned upside down. The traditional supply chain powered by the manufacturing *push* is becoming a demand chain driven by consumer *pull*—especially in the developed countries where the supply and variety of goods is far above base-level requirements of goods and services. In most industrialized countries, resale price maintenance—which allows the supplier to fix the price at which goods can be sold to the final customer—has either been abolished or bypassed. The shift in power in the distribution channel is fundamentally a product of the application of information technology to store management.

Now many multinational companies from industrialized countries are entering markets and developing their distribution channels in developing countries. A recent study by New York University's Tish Robinson shows that companies from Western countries seem to have difficulty competing with Japanese companies in fast-growing Southeast Asian markets and that it is attributed to different styles in managing distribution channels. In just three decades, the consumer electronics distribution systems in Malaysia and Thailand have come to be characterized by a striking presence

---

[22]Janet Y. Murray, Albert R. Wildt, and Masaaki Kotabe, "Locational and Ownership Aspects of Global Sourcing Strategy: A Study of Foreign Multinationals with Performance Implications," *Management International Review*, 35 (Fourth Quarter, 1995), pp. 307–24.

of exclusive dealerships with Japanese multinational manufacturers such as Matsushita, Sanyo, and Hitachi.

For example, Matsushita (a maker of Panasonics, National, and Technics brand names) practices a push strategy with 220 exclusive dealerships in Malaysia and 120 in Thailand. In Malaysia, these exclusive dealerships represent 65 percent of total Matsushita sales although their numbers represent only 30 percent of the retailers selling Matsushita products. On the other hand, General Electric and Philips use a pull strategy, relying on the multivendor distribution system without firm control of the distribution channel as practiced in Western countries. Competitors from the United States and Europe are feeling locked out of Japanese companies' tightly controlled distribution channels in Southeast Asia.[23] A push strategy appears to be more effective than a pull strategy in emerging markets.

On-Time Retail Information Management

Computer systems can now tell a retailer instantly what they are selling in hundreds of stores across the world, how much money they are making on each sale, and increasingly, who their customers are. This information technology has had two consequences.

Reduced Inventory. First, a well managed retailer no longer has to keep large amounts of inventory—the stock burden has been passed upstream to the manufacturer. The retailer has a lower chance of running out of items, as well. At Wal-Mart, more than half of its 5,000 vendors get point-of-sale data. The moment a 7–Eleven customer in Japan buys a soft drink or a can of beer, the information goes directly to the bottler or the brewery. It immediately becomes the production schedule and the delivery schedule, actually specifying the hour at which the new supply has to be delivered and to which of the 4,300 stores. In effect, therefore, Ito-Yokado Co. controls the product mix, the manufacturing schedule and the delivery schedule of major suppliers such as Coca-Cola or Kirin Breweries. The British retailer Sainsbury's supply chain is geared to provide inputs on demand from the stores with a scheduled truck service to its 350 stores. The stores' ordering cycle is also set to match the loading and arrival of the trucks, which almost run according to a bus schedule.

Market Information at the Retail Level. Second, it is the retailer who has real time knowledge of what items are selling and how fast they are selling. This knowledge is used to extract better terms from the manufacturers. This trend in the transfer of power to the retailer in the developed countries has coincided with the lowering of trade barriers around the world and the spread of free-market economies in Asia and Latin America. As a result, retailers such as America's Toys "Я" Us, Tower Records, and Wal-Mart; Britain's Mark & Spencer and J. Sainsbury; Holland's Mark; Sweden's IKEA; and France's Carrefour are being transformed into global businesses.

---

[23]Patricia Robinson, "A Case of Round Pegs in Round Holes?: Multinational Firms Transferring Practices from One Institutional Environment to Another," A working paper, New York University, 1997.

Strong logistics capabilities can be used as an offensive weapon to help a firm gain competitive advantage in the marketplace by improving customer service and consumer choice, and by lowering the cost of global sourcing and finished goods distribution.[24] These capabilities become increasingly important as the level of global integration increases, and as competitors move to supplement low-cost manufacturing strategies in distant markets with effective logistic management strategies. This point is well illustrated by Ito-Yokado's takeover in 1991 of the Southland Corporation that had introduced 7–Eleven's convenience store concept in the United States and subsequently around the world. Ito-Yokado of Japan licensed the 7–Eleven store concept from Southland in the 1970s and has invented just-in-time inventory management and revolutionized its physical distribution system in Japan. The key to Ito-Yokado's success with 7–Eleven Japan has been the use of its inventory and physical distribution management systems which result in lower on-hand inventory, faster inventory turnover, and most importantly, accurate information on customer buying habits. Ito-Yokado's 7–Eleven Japan now implements its just-in-time physical distribution system in 7–Eleven stores in the United States.[25]

Distribution is, thus, increasingly becoming concentrated; manufacturing, by contrast, is splintering. Thirty-five years ago, the Big Three automakers shared the U.S. auto market. Today the market is split among ten—Detroit's Big Three, five Japanese car makers, and two German car makers. Thirty-five years ago, 85 percent of all retail car sales were done in single-site dealerships; even three dealership chains were uncommon. Today, a fairly small number of large-chain dealers account for 40 percent of the retail sales of cars.

Given the increased bargaining power of distributors, monitoring their performance has become an important management issue for many multinational companies. Although information technology has improved immensely, monitoring channel members' performance still remains humanistic. In general, if companies are less experienced in international operations, they tend to invest more resources in monitoring their channel members' activities.[26] As they gain in experience, they may increasingly build trust relationships with their channel members and depend more on formal performance-based control.[27]

Retailing Differences across the World

The density of retail and wholesale establishments in different countries varies greatly. As a general rule, industrialized countries tend to have a lower distribution outlet density than the emerging markets. Part of the reason for this stems

---

[24]Roy D. Shapiro, "Get Leverage from Logistics," *Harvard Business Review*, 62 (May-June 1984), pp. 119–26.

[25]Masaaki Kotabe, "The Return of 7-Eleven . . . from Japan: The Vanguard Program," *Columbia Journal of World Business*, 30 (Winter 1995), pp. 70–81.

[26]Esra F. Gencturk and Preet S. Aulakh, "The Use of Process and Output Controls in Foreign Markets," *Journal of International Business Studies*, 26 (Fourth Quarter, 1995), pp. 755–86.

[27]Preet S. Aulakh, Masaaki Kotabe, and Arvind Sahay, "Trust and Performance in Cross Border Marketing Partnerships: A Behavioral Approach," *Journal of International Business Studies*, 27 (Special Issue 1996).

from the need in emerging markets for very small purchase lots and more frequent purchases due to low incomes and the lack of facilities in homes to refrigerate and preserve foods. At the same time, the advanced facilities available in the developed world allow a much higher square footage of retail space per resident, due to the large size of the retail outlets. The United States, for instance, has about 18.5 square feet of retail space per resident, compared to figures below 10 square feet for Western Europe.

The other prominent differential feature of distribution systems is the number of retailers and wholesalers per unit of population in a country. In 1988, there were 1.62 million retail stores in Japan (132 stores per 10,000 people) compared to 1.1 million retail

$\mathcal{G}$LOBAL PERSPECTIVE 16-6

FOREIGN RETAILERS FOLLOW TOYS "Я" US TO JAPAN

When U.S. President George Bush visited Japan in January 1992, Japan's retail distribution was a major issue between the United States and Japan. Toys "Я" Us had been trying to open its stores in Japan since 1989, but Japan's Large-Scale Retail Store Law and tight relationships among local toy manufacturers, retailers, and wholesalers thwarted the American toy retailer's entry to the Japanese market.

The Large-Scale Retail Store Law gave small retailers and wholesalers disproportionate influence over the Japanese market by requiring firms planning to open a large store to submit their business plan to the local business regulation council, the local chamber of commerce (made up of those small retailers and wholesalers to be affected), and the Ministry of International Trade and Industry. As a result of this "Catch-22" requirement, the process would take between one year and eighteen months, and was seen by foreign retailers as an almost insurmountable entry barrier.

Under U.S. government pressure, the Large-Scale Retail Store Law was relaxed in 1992. Toys "Я" Us exploited this opportunity and was ultimately successful in cracking the Japanese market. It boasted a total of thirty-seven stores in 1996, and plans to open an average of ten more per year across the country.

Following the success of Toys "Я" Us, other foreign-based retailers have begun to crack the Japanese market. Nearly a dozen other such foreign retailers have recently opened their stores in Japan. Foreign firms face more difficulties when opening a store for general merchandise than one for a niche product because the large Japanese general merchandise stores, such as Daiei, Ito-Yokado, and Seiyu, are well entrenched and already dominate the market. On the other hand, foreign niche retailers who face few competitors have been fairly successful.

For example, U.S.-based Tower Records, U.K.-based HMV, and Virgin Megastores have opened comparably large stores, selling both imported and domestic music tapes and CDs at competitive prices. Specialty retailers of outdoor goods and clothes are another brand of retailers to pour into the Japanese market recently. Among them, U.S.-based L.L. Bean and Eddie Bauer are the market leaders.

While Toys "Я" Us and Tower Records have a wholly owned subsidiary in Japan, L.L. Bean and Eddie Bauer team up with a well-known Japanese company. L.L. Bean Japan is a Japanese franchise 70 percent owned by Japan's largest retailing group, Seibu, and 30 percent by Matsushita Electric, a maker of Panasonics, Technics, JVC, and Quasar brands. Eddie Bauer Japan is a joint venture of Otto-Sumitomo, a Sumitomo Group mail-order retailer, and Eddie Bauer USA. The contrasting experiences of Toys "Я" Us, Tower Records, L.L. Bean, and Eddie Bauer raise an important question for future entrants to the Japanese market: whether to team up with a Japanese partner or open a wholly-owned Japanese subsidiary. In general, forming a joint venture or a franchise allows new entrants to start faster, although they might lose control of the company's operation in Japan. Future would-be entrants should bear in mind that Japan is not an easy place to do business because, in addition to regulations, land and labor costs are extremely high.

Source: Hayden Stewart, "Foreign Retailers Follow Toys "Я" Us Path to Success," *Journal of Japanese Trade and Industry*, 15 (3) (1996), pp. 52–54.

stores in the U.S. (45 stores per 10,000 people).[28] This is partially the result of retail laws that differ from country to country and tend to affect distribution internationally. For more than forty years after the Second World War, the Large-Scale Retail Store Law in Japan helped to protect and maintain small retail stores and, partly in consequence, a multilayered distribution system. Thus, where large manufacturers ship directly to cross-docking warehouses of retailers in the United States, manufacturers in Japan ship to the wholesaler, who ships to the sub-wholesaler, who ships to the retailer. This difference is partly an outcome of physical constraints. Unlike the United States, where shopping malls and discount stores developed along major highways, the structure of Japan's retail outlets was determined by the location of railway and subway stations. See Global Perspective 16-6 for international retailers cracking into the Japanese market.

In Germany, store hours are limited. Stores may not open on Sundays and should close on weekdays by 6 P.M. They may open one Saturday in a month until 2:30 P.M. The IFO Economic Research Institute in a German government commissioned report has recommended that stores be allowed to remain open from 6 A.M. to 10 P.M. on weekdays and until 6 P.M. on Saturdays; however, stores are still expected to be closed on Sundays.[29] Hence, while these laws are now being reviewed, even the situation after the proposed changes is still in contrast to the U.S., where retail stores may remain open seven days a week, twenty-four hours a day. Keeping stores open in this manner requires very strong logistics management on the part of retailers and the manufacturing firms supplying the retailers. The sending organization, the receiving organization, and the logistics provider (if applicable) have to work very closely together.

◆ ◆

NIGHTLY BUSINESS REPORT

VIDEOBOX

HYPERMARKETS IN JAPAN

Japan experienced six years of recession, characterized as the "Burst of the Bubble Economy," caused primarily by a decline in overinflated land prices, from 1990 to 1996. This long recession triggered price deflation across Japan. Furthermore, during the same time period, the Japanese yen appreciated drastically relative to the U.S. and other major currencies, making foreign imports cheaper in Japan.

Until recently, the Japanese distribution system was characterized as having stable relationships between manufacturers and their distributors. In a way, the channel was in large part controlled by large Japanese manufacturing companies such as Toyota, Panasonic, and Kao. The reduction in consumer demand and the rapid increase in less expensive imports from abroad made Japanese consumers very price-sensitive. Price discounters, such as large discount stores and hypermarkets, have suddenly become popular among the budget-weary Japanese consumers in recent years.

Procter & Gamble in Japan (P&G Japan), albeit an American company, manufactures almost all the products locally for the Japanese market, and has been affected by price deflation the same way Japanese companies have. What advice would you give P&G Japan in terms of its distribution and logistics strategy?

---

[28]Diane L. Manifold, "Accessing Japan's Distribution Channels," in Michael R. Czinkota and Masaaki Kotabe, eds., *The Japanese Distribution System* (Chicago: Probus Publishing Company, 1993), pp. 43–66.

[29]Marco Grühnhagen, Robert A. Mittelstaedt, and Ronald D. Hampton, "The Effect of the Relaxation of 'Blue Laws' on the Structure of the Retailing Industry in the Federal Republic of Germany," presented at 1997 AMA Summer Educators' Conference, August 2–5, 1997.

SUMMARY

Logistics and distribution have traditionally been a local issue and have had to do with getting goods to the final customer in a local market. However, while the intent of serving the customer remains, retailers have been transformed into global organizations who buy and sell products from and to many parts of the world. At the same time, with the increase in the globalization of manufacturing, many firms are optimizing their worldwide production by sourcing components and raw materials from around the world. Both these trends have increased the importance of global logistic management for firms.

The relevance of global logistics is likely to wax in the coming years because international distribution often accounts for between 10 percent and 25 percent of the total landed cost of an international order. The international logistics manager has to deal with multiple issues, including transport, warehousing, inventorying, and the connection of these activities to the corporate strategy of the firm. Not only are these logistics issues compounded by inflation, currency exchange, and tax rates that differ across national boundaries, but the international logistics manager can exploit those differences to their advantage—advantages not available to domestic firms.

Logistics management is closely linked to manufacturing activities, even though a new trend shows that logistics management can be outsourced from third-party logistics specialists. Many companies, particularly those in the European Union, are trying to develop a consolidated production location so that they can reduce the number of distribution centers and market their products from one or a few locations throughout Europe. Firms like Federal Express, Airborne Express, and TNT have evolved from document shippers to providing complete logistics functions—indeed, all these firms now sport a business logistics division whose function is to handle the outsourced logistics functions of corporate clients.

Various governments, including the United States, have developed free trade zones, export processing zones, and other special economic zones designed chiefly to increase domestic employment and exports from the zone. Various tax and other cost benefits available in the zones attract both domestic and foreign firms to set up warehousing and manufacturing operations. Many U.S.-based multinational firms, both domestic and foreign, take advantage of U.S. tariff provisions 9802.0060 and 9802.00.80 and many of Mexico's maquiladoras (a special Mexican version of free trade zones). Historically, cost advantage accruing from use of a combination of the U.S. tariff provisions and Mexico's maquiladoras has benefited many large multinational firms that could easily relocate labor-intensive assembly or processing operations there. As a result of NAFTA, however, maquiladoras have begun to attract increasingly high-tech industries as well.

Finally, retailing has long been considered a fairly localized activity subject to different customer needs and different national laws regulating domestic commerce. Nevertheless, some significant change is taking place in the retail sector. Information technology makes it increasingly possible for large retailers to know what they are selling in hundreds of stores around the world. Given this intimate knowledge of customers around the world, those retailers have begun to overtake the channel leadership role from manufacturers. The United States' Wal-Mart and Toys "R" Us, Japan's Ito-Yokado, and Britain's Mark & Spencer are some of the major global retailers changing the logistics of inventory and retail management on a global basis.

REVIEW QUESTIONS

1. Define the term *global logistics*. Enumerate and describe the various operations encompassed by it.

2. What factors contribute to the increased complexity and cost of global logistics as compared to domestic logistics?

3. What role do third-party logistics companies play in international trade? What are the advantages of using these companies over internalizing the logistics activities?

4. Describe the role of free trade zones (FTZs) in global logistics.

5. What are the reasons for the dramatic increase in cross-border trade between the U.S and Mexico?

6. How is information technology affecting global retailing?

7. The United States and Japan have similar income and purchasing power levels. Yet, there are significant differences in the retail structures between the two countries. Describe some reasons for these differences.

DISCUSSION QUESTIONS ◆

1. Some economists have brought attention to the importance of the role of geography in international trade. One example of this is the dramatic rise in trade between the United States and Mexico. This increase is attributed primarily to wage differences between the two countries and the proximity, with both countries sharing a joint border over 2,000 miles in length. Geographic proximity allows for the relative cheap movement of goods by train from the heart of Mexico to any corner of the United States within three to four days. On the other hand, advocates of globalization claim that the role of geography in international trade is limited and is reducing constantly. They contend that *direct* transportation costs as a percentage of the total value of the goods for most goods is low and is declining. Furthermore, it is not actual transportation costs, but the coordination of managerial resources and information that is the key to savings through global logistics. This reduces the role of geography in international trade to a minimal level. Comment on the two views.

2. Taking advantage of advancements in information technology and increased lowering of trade barriers, various catalog merchandisers have been increasing their global presence at a rapid rate. L.L. Bean is an example of one such success case. Its international sales in 1994 grew by more than 62 percent and now account for 13 percent of its total sales. However, problems of infrastructure, e.g., telephone and postal service in general, and the lack of international services such as 1-800 numbers in particular are significant barriers to the centralization of this business. These problems have led to 70 percent of L.L. Bean's international sales coming from one country (Japan).

   Assume that you are part of the top management team of a large retail chain that has a moderate presence in the domestic catalog business, but no presence in the international market. However, this company would like to enter the international catalog merchandising business and was willing to make long-term financial commitments for this endeavor. Given the constraints just mentioned, the relative nascent state of the business at a global level, and the significant advantages to be gained through coordination of global logistics, what would you recommend the company do in terms of choice of market, the centralization vs. decentralization of logistics activities, and the decision to outsource vs. internalize the logistic activities?

3. The world is moving closer to an era of free trade and global economic interdependence. The worldwide reduction in tariff and nontariff barriers and the increasing levels of world trade are testimony to this fact. These reductions in trade barriers will in the very near future make free trade zones an anachronistic concept. Hence, if you were making an investment decision, on behalf of your company, to establish a manufacturing facility in a developing country, placing too much emphasis on investing in free trade zones may be a short-term workable proposition, but a long-term mistake. Do you agree or disagree with this statement? Give reasons for your answer.

4. Reducing trade barriers and saturation of domestic markets are two forces in the 1990s that are encouraging large retail chains to move overseas. Large retail chains in the United States, Japan, and Europe are aggressively making forays into international markets, although there is a significant regional bias in these efforts. U.S. retail chains such as Wal-Mart have primarily focused on Canada and have now turned their focus to Mexico. Japanese retail chains such as JUSCO and Daimaru have made significant inroads into Southeast Asia, while Western European chains such as Julius Meinl (Austria), Promodes (France), Ahold (The Netherlands), and TESCO (U.K) are diversifying into Eastern Europe and other countries within Europe. Industry analysts point out that this internationalization of retail business will significantly alter the nature of competition. Significant rationalization through acquisitions of retail businesses is bound to take place. The verdict on the expected effects of this rationalization and increased competition on specialty chains is still unclear. What would you predict the retail business to look like ten

years from now? What would be the role of specialty stores and specialty chains?

5. The concept of "one-stop-shopping" for global logistics is fast catching on. There are now more than thirty large logistic companies, called "mega-carriers," who can provide truly global and integrated logistic services. What are the opportunities and threats that these trends offer to small and large transporters, freight-forwarders, and shippers (exporters)?

FURTHER READINGS ◆ ◆ ◆ ◆ ◆ ◆ ◆ ◆ ◆ ◆ ◆ ◆ ◆ ◆ ◆ ◆ ◆ ◆ ◆

Fawcett, Stanley E., Laura Birou, and Barbara Cofield Taylor. "Supporting Global Operations Through Logistics and Purchasing." *International Journal of Physical Distribution and Logistics Management*, 23(4) (1993): 3–11.

Johnson, Jay. "The Globetrotters: Retail's Multinationals." *Discount Merchandiser*, 35(9) (1995): 40–42.

Johnson, Jean L., John B. Cullen, and Tomoaki Sakano. "Opportunistic Tendencies in IJVs with the Japanese: The Effects of Culture, Shared Decision Making, and Relationship Age." *International Executive*, 38(1) (1996).

Rao, Kant, and Richard R. Young. "Global Supply Chains: Factors Influencing Outsourcing of Logistics Functions." *International Journal of Physical Distribution and Logistics Management*, 24(6) (1994): 11–19.

McGoldrick, Peter J., and Gary Davies (1995). *International Retailing: Trends and Structure.* London: Pitman Publishers, 1995.

Mueller, E. J. "Conquering the Global Market." *Distribution*, 92(10) (1993): 32–40.

Rapoport, Carla. "Retailers Go Global." *Fortune*, 131(3) (1995): 102–108.

Truett, Lila J., and Dale B., "Maquiladora Response to US and Asian Relative Wage Rate Changes." *Contemporary Economic Policy*, 11(1) (1993): 18–28.

Wood, Donald F. *International Logistics*, New York: Chapman & Hall, 1995.

EXPORT AND IMPORT MANAGEMENT

CHAPTER OVERVIEW

1. ORGANIZING FOR EXPORTS
2. INDIRECT CHANNELS OF DISTRIBUTION
3. DIRECT EXPORT MARKETING
4. LINKAGE BETWEEN FOREIGN DIRECT INVESTMENT AND EXPORTS
5. MECHANICS OF EXPORTING
6. ROLE OF THE GOVERNMENT IN PROMOTING EXPORTS
7. MANAGING IMPORTS—THE OTHER SIDE OF THE COIN
8. MECHANICS OF IMPORTING
9. GRAY MARKETS

An October 1994 survey by *Fortune* magazine of members of the National Association for Purchasing Management (NAPM) in the United States showed that 80 percent of the members were exporting—the highest percentage since NAPM began surveying export orders in 1988.[1] Smaller firms are also getting into exports in a major way. Export managers' favorable attitudes toward their value of exporting in the last ten years have increased their export involvement and performance.[2] A survey of almost 750 companies by Arthur Andersen & Co. and National Small Business United, a

---

[1]"The U.S. is Set to be the Winner from Worldwide Expansion," *Fortune* (November 28, 1994), pp. 22–23.

[2]Catherine N. Axinn, Ronald Savitt, James M. Sinkula, and Sharon V. Thach, "Export Intention, Beliefs, and Behaviors in Smaller Industrial Firms," *Journal of Business Research*, 32 (January 1995), pp. 49–55.

trade group, found that 20 percent of companies with fewer than 500 employees exported product and services in 1994.[3] That is up from 11 percent in 1992, the first year that the survey was conducted. With the rest of the world showing continued economic expansion through 2000, the demand for U.S. goods abroad will concomitantly increase, raising U.S. exports. Canada enjoyed a healthy 3 percent expansion in 1997 and Japan, after three years of little growth, began a gradual expansion in 1995 and has grown 4 percent in 1997. Although exports to Mexico were flat during 1995 due to the sharp devaluation of the peso, the stabilization of the peso means that the U.S. can expect to increase its exports to Mexico as well. Indeed, U.S. exports to Mexico grew more than 22 percent from $46.5 billion in 1993 to $56.8 billion in 1996.

Since 1945 world exports have expanded steadily ahead of the growth rate of the economic output. The World Trade Organization estimates that in 1995 world trade volume expanded by 8 percent (as compared to a growth in world output of goods, which was just 3 percent), on top of a 9.5 percent increase in 1995.[4] Another characteristic of merchandise exports is the trend toward increasing intermediate processing—that is, the process in which goods cross more than one national border in the course of processing and value addition before they reach the final buyer. This growth of intermediate processing was more concentrated in China and some other Asian countries.

Already the nature of world exports and imports has changed radically. The notion of developing countries as exporters of raw materials from which they earn revenue to pay for imports of manufactured goods is already hopelessly inappropriate. Manufactured goods accounted for almost 60 percent of the exports of developing countries, up from 5 percent in 1955.[5] Also, the effect of exports from the industrial countries to the developing nations on the economies of industrial nations is now considerable. From 1990 through 1993, U.S. exports to developing nations grew at an average annual rate of 12 percent, while those to other rich countries rose by only 2 percent a year. Over the same period, third-world countries increased their imports by 37 percent, while their exports grew at a more modest 22 percent. In other words, for the first time developing countries were acting as a *locomotive*, helping to pull the rich world out of its recession of the early 1990s. This said, as Exhibit 17-1 shows, the world's top six exporters still account for about 46 percent of total world exports.

At the same time, the importance of service exports is growing for the developed nations. The United States has been running a persistent deficit on the merchandise trade account and an equally persistent surplus (though smaller in magnitude) on the service trade account. Services accounted for about 28 percent of all exports in 1992, up from 17 percent in 1980.[6] About 60 percent of the surplus in services is generated by business and technical services such as engineering, accounting, computing, and legal services, and by entertainment and new technologies that earn royalties and licensing fees.

This chapter will look primarily at the export function; it will simultaneously attempt to understand the import function as the counterpart of the export function,

---

[3]"It's a Small (Business) World," *Business Week* (April 17, 1995), pp. 96–101.

[4]"Export Growth Slowed to 8% in '95, says WTO," *Wall Street Journal* (March 29, 1996), A9.

[5]"A Survey of the Global Economy," *Economist* (October 1, 1994).

[6]"U.S. Service Exports Are Growing Rapidly, But Almost Unnoticed," *Wall Street Journal* (April 21, 1993), pp. A1, A6.

EXHIBIT 17-1
SHARE OF WORLD EXPORTS (PERCENT) OF TOP SIX EXPORTERS

	1980–84	1985–89	1990	1991	1992	1993	1994
United States	11.6	11.2	11.5	12.3	12.2	12.8	12.3
Germany	9.3	11.1	11.9	11.7	11.7	10.5	10.2
Japan	7.7	9.3	8.3	9.2	9.3	10.0	9.5
France	5.4	5.8	6.3	6.3	6.4	5.8	5.7
United Kingdom	5.2	5.1	5.4	5.4	5.2	5.0	4.9
Canada	4.0	4.2	3.7	3.7	3.7	4.0	4.0

Source: "1995: The Year We Turned the Corner on Trade," *Business America* (Washington, D.C.: U.S. Department of Commerce, March 1996), pp. 9–13.

because for every export transaction there is, by definition, an import transaction as well. Aside from some differences between the procedure and rationale for exports and imports, both are largely the same the world over.

ORGANIZING FOR EXPORTS   ◆ ◆ ◆ ◆ ◆ ◆

Research for Exports

For a firm beginning exports for the first time, the first step is to use available secondary data to research potential markets. Increasingly international marketing information is available in the form of electronic databases, ranging from the latest news on product developments to new material in the academic and trade press. Well over 6,000 databases are available worldwide, with almost 5,000 available on-line. The United States is the largest participant in this database growth, producing and consuming more than 50 percent of these database services. It is to be noted, however, that export research for markets such as China and Russia and most of the former command economies must still be done largely in the field, because very little prior data exist and, even when available, they are often not reliable.[7] When entering a culturally and linguistically different part of the world, managers need to understand a completely new way of commercial thinking that is based on a different culture and works on a different set of premises.

The identification of an appropriate overseas market and an appropriate segment involves grouping by the following criteria:

1. Socioeconomic characteristics (e.g., demographic, economic, geographic, and climatic characteristics)
2. Political and legal characteristics
3. Consumer variables (e.g., lifestyle, preferences, culture, taste, purchase behavior, and purchase frequency)
4. Financial conditions

---

[7]Michael R. Czinkota and Ilka A. Ronkainen, "Market Research For Your Export Operations: Using Secondary Sources of Research," *International Trade Forum*, 3 (1994), pp. 22–34.

On the basis of these criteria an exporter can form an idea of the market segments in a foreign market.[8] First, regions within countries across the world are grouped by macroeconomic variables indicating the levels of industrial development, availability of skilled labor, and the purchasing power. For example, from an exporter's point of view the Bombay–Thane–Pune area in Western India has more in common with the Monterrey area and the Mexico City area in Mexico and the Shanghai–Wuxi area in China than with other areas in India. All these three areas already have a well-developed industrial base and purchasing power that is equal to that of the middle class in the developed nations. Such economically homogenous groups across the world are a result of the globalization of markets.[9] These apparently similar markets may, however, differ on political and legal dimensions. An exporter or importer has legal recourse in India if the importer or exporter violates terms and the court of adjudication is in India. Legal recourse is still largely wishful thinking in China. By tackling the consumer variables in addition to the macroeconomic ones, the exporter can successfully segment the international market into homogenous segments where similar elements of the marketing mix can be applied.

Data for grouping along macroeconomic criteria are available from international agencies such as the World Bank, which publishes the **World Development Report.** In addition, the United Nations produces a series of statistical abstracts on a yearly basis covering economic, demographic, political, and social characteristics that are very useful for grouping analysis. Data on international trade and finance are published quarterly and annually by the International Monetary Fund. Both the **Organization for Economic Cooperation and Development** (OECD—a group of advanced nations) and the **European Union** (EU) publish a variety of statistical reports and studies on their member countries.

Export Market Segments

As discussed in chapter 7, the grouping of countries and regions among countries enables the firm to link various geographical areas into one homogeneous market segment that the firm can cater to in meeting its export objectives. The next task is to develop a product strategy for the selected export markets. The export market clusters obtained by clustering regions within different nations would fall into various levels. At the country level would be countries with the same characteristics as the U.S. market. At a regional level within nations there would be geographical and psychographic segments in many different types of countries where the firm can export the same core product it sells in domestic markets without any significant changes. It is a form of market diversification in which the firm is selling a standardized, uniform product across countries and regions.[10] Mercedes automobiles and Rolex watches sell to the same consumer segment worldwide. Another example of a standardized product that sells worldwide is soft drinks. The Coca Cola Company markets essentially one Coke worldwide.

---

[8]For a comprehensive review of the export development process, see Leonidas C. Leonidou and Constantine S. Katsikeas, "The Export Development Process: An Integrative Review of Empirical Models," *Journal of International Business Studies*, 27 (Third Quarter 1996), pp. 517–51.

[9]Theodore Levitt, "The Globalization of Markets," *Harvard Business Review*, 61 (May/June 1983), pp. 92–102.

[10]Lloyd C. Russow, "Market Diversification: "Going International," *Review of Business*, 17 (Spring 1996), pp. 32–34.

Products that can be standardized may satisfy basic needs that do not vary with climate, economic conditions, or culture. A standardized product is the easiest to sell abroad logistically, since the firm incurs no additional manufacturing costs and is able to use the same promotional messages across different regions in different countries across the world. If those different regions have comparable logistics and infrastructural facilities, then the distribution requirements and expenses would also be similar.

Where it is not possible to sell standardized products, the firm may need to adapt its products for the overseas marketplace. In such instances, either the firm's product does not meet customer requirements or it does not satisfy the administrative requirements of foreign countries. Such markets may require modification of the product to succeed in the foreign market.[11] Brand names, for example, need to be changed before a product can be sold, because the brand name may mean something detrimental to the prospect of the product. Chevrolet Nova did not sell well in Latin America because Nova in Spanish means *no go*. A perfume named Mist probably will not sell in Germany because *mist* means manure in German slang. Sometimes, a new product has to be developed from a manufacturing viewpoint because the product as it is is not salable in the export market. Room air-conditioner units being exported to Egypt have to have special filters and coolers and have to be sturdy enough to handle the dust and heat of Egyptian summer.

INDIRECT CHANNELS OF DISTRIBUTION ◆ ◆ ◆ ◆ ◆ ◆ ◆

Indirect exporting involves the use of independent U.S. middlemen to market the firm's products overseas. These middlemen, known as export representatives, assume responsibility for marketing the firm's products through their network of foreign distributors and their own sales force. It is not uncommon for a U.S. producer who is new to exporting to begin export operation by selling through an export representative. Many Japanese firms have also relied on the giant general trading companies known as *Sogo Shoshas*. Use of middlemen is not uncommon when it is not cost-effective for an exporter to set up its own export department. Such a firm may initiate export operations through export representatives who know the market and have experience in selling to them. There are several types of export representatives in the United States. The most common are the combination export manager (CEM), the export merchant, the export broker, the export commission house, the trading company, and the piggyback exporter.

The **combination export manager** (CEM) acts as the export department to a small exporter or a large producer with small overseas sales. CEMs often use the letterhead of the company they represent and have extensive experience in selling abroad and in the mechanics of export shipments. CEMs operate on a commission basis and are usually most effective when they deal with clients who have businesses in related lines. Since credit plays an increasingly important role in export sales, CEMs have found it increasingly difficult to consummate export sales on behalf of clients without their credit support. As more and more firms begin exporting on a regular basis, CEMs

---

[11]S. Tamer Cavusgil and Shaoming Zou, "Marketing Strategy-Performance Relationship: An Investigation of the Empirical Link in Export Market Ventures," *Journal of Marketing*, 58 (January 1994), pp. 1–21.

Similar to a manufacturing firm that relies on an indirect export channel member for exporting, a service company may also work with a local agent for exporting services to (i.e., getting its business solicited in) a foreign country.

have become a vanishing breed, though a list of CEMs can be found in the *American Register of Exporters and Importers* and in the telephone yellow pages.

Export merchants, in contrast to the CEM, buy and sell on their own accounts and assume all the responsibilities of exporting a product. In this situation, the manufacturers do not control the sales activities of their products in export markets and are entirely dependent on the export merchant for the export of their products. This loss of control over the export marketing effort is a major drawback to using export merchants. The **export broker,** as the name implies, is someone who brings together an overseas buyer and a U.S. manufacturer for the purpose of an export sale and earns a commission for establishing a contact that results in a sale.

Foreign buyers of U.S. goods sometimes contract for the services of a U.S. representative to act on their behalf. This resident representative is usually an **export commission house,** which places orders on behalf of its foreign client with U.S. manufacturers and acts as a finder for its client to get the best buy. The export commission house acts on behalf of its clients and does not buy on its own behalf. **Trading companies** are large, foreign organizations engaged in exporting and importing. They buy on their

EXHIBIT 17-2

MAJOR TYPES OF TRADING COMPANIES AND THEIR COUNTRIES OF ORIGIN

Type	Rationale for Grouping	Some Examples by Country of Origin
General trading companies	Historical involvement in generalized imports/exports	Mitsui (Japan), East Asiatic (Denmark), SCOA (France), Jardine Matheson (Hong Kong)
Export trading companies	Specific mission to promote growth of exporters	Daewoo (Korea), Interbras (Brazil), Sears World Trade (US)
Federated export marketing groups	Loose collaboration among exporting companies supervised by a third party and usually market-specific	Fedec (UK), SBI Group (Norway), IEB Project Group (Morocco)
Trading arms of MNCs	Specific international trading operations in parent-company operations	General Motors (US), Volvo (Sweden)
Bank-based or affiliated trading groups	A bank at the center of a group extends commercial activities	Mitsubishi (Japan), Cobec (Brazil)
Commodity trading companies	Long-standing export trading in a specific market	Metallgesellschaft (Germany), Louis Dreyfus (France)

Source: Lyn Amine, "Toward a Conceptualization of Export Trading Companies in World Markets," in S. Tamer Cavusgil, ed., *Advances in International Marketing*, vol. 2 (Greenwich, Conn.: JAI Press, 1987), pp. 199–208.

own account in the United States and export the goods to their country of origin. Most of the well-known trading companies are Japanese or Western European in origin. Japanese trading companies such as Mitsui, Mitsubishi, and Sumitomo operate world-wide and handle a significant proportion of Japanese foreign trade. United Africa Company, a subsidiary of Unilever, operates extensively in Africa. Another European trading company is Jardine Matheson in Hong Kong, a major trading force in Southeast Asia. Exhibit 17-2 gives an idea of the major types of trading companies.

Piggyback exporting refers to the practice where U.S. firms that have an established export departments assume, under a cooperative agreement, the responsibility of exporting the products of other U.S. companies. The carrier buys the rider's products and markets them independently. The rider plays a peripheral role in the export marketing overseas. Piggybacking may be an option to enter an export market, but is normally avoided by firms who wish to be in exports over the long haul because of the loss of control over the foreign marketing operations.

DIRECT EXPORT MARKETING ◆ ◆ ◆ ◆ ◆ ◆

Direct export occurs when a manufacturer or exporter sells directly to an importer or buyer located in a foreign market. Direct exporting can manifest itself in various organizational forms, depending on the scale of operations and the number of years that a firm has been engaged in exporting. In its most simple form, a firm will have an export sales manager with some clerical help. The export manager is responsible for the actual selling and directing of activities associated with the export sales. Most of the other export marketing activities (advertising, logistics, and credit, for example) are performed by a regular department of the firm that also handles international trade transactions.

As export activities grow in scale and complexity, most firms create a separate **export department** that is largely self-contained and operates independently of domestic operations. An export department may be structured internally on the basis of function, geography, product, customer, or some other combination. Some firms prefer to have an **export sales subsidiary** instead of an export department in order to keep export operations separate from the rest of the firm. In terms of internal operations and specific operations performed, an export sales subsidiary differs very little from an export department. The major difference is that the subsidiary, being a separate legal entity, must purchase the products it sells in the overseas markets from its parent manufacturer. This means that the parent has to develop and administer a system of transfer pricing. A subsidiary has the advantage of being an independent profit center and is therefore easier to evaluate; it can also offer tax advantages, ease of financing, and greater closeness to the customer.

Instead of a foreign sales subsidiary, a firm also has the option of establishing a **foreign sales branch.** Unlike a subsidiary, a branch is not a separate legal entity. A foreign sales branch handles all of sales, distribution, and promotional work throughout a designated market area and sells primarily to wholesalers and dealers. Where used, a sales branch is the initial link in the marketing channel in the foreign market. Often there will be a storage and warehousing facility available so the branch can maintain an inventory of products, replacement parts, and maintenance supplies.

Indirect exporting and direct exporting are compared in Exhibit 17-3. Both have advantages and disadvantages, though over the long-term—for a firm desiring a permanent presence in international markets—direct exports tend to be more useful.

◆ ◆ ◆ ◆ ◆ ◆ LINKAGE BETWEEN FOREIGN DIRECT INVESTMENT AND EXPORTS

In March 1996, General Motors had a seventeen-day strike—the longest since 1970. Those fearing that the strike would severely affect the economy of the entire Midwest region in the U.S.-where most U.S. GM plants are based—forgot that over the previous ten years the entire region had developed a grass-roots base for exports that was substantially independent of the automobile infrastructure. Roughly two-thirds of Ohio's manufacturers, for instance, export about $21 billion in manufactures independent of the auto-

EXHIBIT 17-3
COMPARISON OF DIRECT AND INDIRECT EXPORTING

Indirect Exporting	*Direct Exporting*
Low set up costs	High set-up costs
Exporter tends not to gain good knowledge of export markets	Leads to better knowledge of export markets and international expertise due to direct contact
Credit risk lies mostly with the middlemen	Credit risks are higher, especially in the early years
Since it is not in the interest of the middlemen doing the exporting, customer loyalty rarely develops	Customer loyalty can be developed for the exporter's brands more easily

mobile value chain.[12] The export train from Ohio was led, in part, by Honda America, which is based in Marysville, Ohio. In Ohio, about 205,600 workers are employed by subsidiaries of foreign companies whose total investment in Ohio stood at $24.5 billion at the beginning of 1996. In 1995, Honda exported 100,000 vehicles from its American operations—the largest automobile exporter from the United States. Moreover, the presence of Honda attracts Japanese suppliers to meet the demands of a just-in-time manufacturing system. Ohio might not do well in exports solely on the basis of the auto industry, which appears to have peaked, but the state expects to do well on the export front on the basis of the large capital goods equipment and machine tools base that it has established partly as a result of foreign direct investment from other countries. On many occasions these subsidiaries export components or parts to their parent. Indeed, recent estimates suggest that up to 40 percent of international trade among nations in the Triad is between various enterprises of a multinational corporation.[13]

Many countries that have large potential markets for multinationals use that potential as a lure to multinationals to commit to exporting a percentage of their output as a precondition for being allowed to invest and operate in that country. For instance, Pepsi gained access to the Indian market in 1987 on the condition that it would export 25 percent of its total production value in any given year and that it would provide state-of-the-art food processing technology. More recently, McDonnell Douglas is setting up an aircraft servicing and aircraft component manufacturing plant in China with the understanding that components will be exported and the servicing facility will be used to earn hard currency. These trends suggest that foreign direct investment and exports are becoming interlinked and can no longer be thought of as discrete activities.

MECHANICS OF EXPORTING   ◆ ◆ ◆ ◆ ◆ ◆

To the uninitiated, the mechanics of exporting can seem to be cumbersome and full of meaningless, irrelevant paperwork. Form 7525-V, which is one of the many forms required to be filed by a prospective exporter (See Exhibit 17-4), gives a glimpse of the details that the government requires if you are in the exporting business. However, it is precisely a summarized, collated, and edited version of such data that was the basis of at least some of the secondary data that prospective exporters use in their research when exploring foreign markets. These data are also used to compile trade statistics, which are barometers of the health of an economy, the stock market, and foreign exchange rates.

Legality of Exports

Exporting starts with the search for a buyer abroad and the research that is required to locate a potential market and a buyer and the process of closing a sale. We covered the process of getting an order earlier in this chapter. Once an export contract has been signed, the wheels are set in motion for the process that results in the export contract. The *first* stage has to do with the legality of the transaction. The exporter has to check to see that the goods can be imported by the importing party—importing country licensing law can trip up a transaction unless looked at in advance.

---

[12]"The Outlook: Midwest Exports Blunt Some Effects of the Strike," *Wall Street Journal* (March 25, 1996), p. A1.

[13]*Survey of Current Business*, September 1995.

EXHIBIT 17-4
FORM 7525-V: INFORMATION TO BE REPORTED ON THE SHIPPER'S
EXPORT DECLARATION

1(a). **Exporter**—The name and address of the U.S. exporter—the principal party responsible for effecting export from the United States. The exporter as named on the validated export license. Report only the first five digits of the ZIP code.

1(b). **Exporter Identification Number**—The exporter's Internal Revenue Service Employer Identification Number (EIN) or Social Security Number (SSN), if no EIN has been assigned. Report the nine-digit numerical code as reported on your latest Employer's Quarterly Federal Tax Return, Treasury Form 941. The EIN is usually available from your accounting or payroll department.

1(c). **Related Party Transaction**—One between a U.S. exporter and foreign consignee, (e.g., parent company or sister company), where there is at least 10 percent ownership of each by the same U.S. or foreign person or business enterprise.

2. **Date of Exportation**—(Not required for vessel and postal shipments) The date of departure or date of clearance, if date of departure is not known.

3. **Bill of Lading or Air Waybill Number**—The exporting carrier's bill of lading or air waybill number.

4(a). **Ultimate Consignee**—The name and address of the party actually receiving the merchandise for the designated end-use, or the party so designated on the validated export license. For overland shipments to Mexico, also include the Mexican state in the address.

4(b). **Intermediate Consignee**—The name and address of the party in a foreign country who makes delivery of the merchandise to the ultimate consignee or the party so named on the export license.

5. **Agent of Exporter**—The name and address of the duly authorized forwarding agent.

6. **Point (State) of Origin or Foreign Trade Zone (FTZ) Number**
   (a) The two-digit U.S. Postal Service abbreviation of the state in which the merchandise actually starts its journey to the port of export, or
   (b) The state of the commodity of the greatest value, or
   (c) The state of consolidation, or
   (d) The Foreign Trade Zone Number for exports leaving an FTZ.

7. **Country of Ultimate Destination**—The country in which the merchandise is to be consumed, further processed, or manufactured; the final country of destination as known to the exporter at the time of shipment; or the country of ultimate destination as shown on the validated export license. Two-digit (alpha character) International Standards Organization (ISO) codes may also be used.

8. **Loading Pier**—(For vessel shipments only) The number or name of the pier at which the merchandise is laden aboard the exporting vessel.

9. **Method of Transportation**—The mode of transport by which the merchandise is exported. Specify by name, i.e., vessel, air, rail, truck, etc. Specify "own power" if applicable.

10. **Exporting Carrier**—The name of the carrier transporting the merchandise out of the United States. For vessel shipments, give the vessel's flag, also.

11. **U.S. Port of Export**
    (a) Overland—the U.S. Customs port at which the surface carrier crosses the border.
    (b) Vessel and Air—the U.S. Customs port where the merchandise is loaded on the carrier that is taking the merchandise out of the United States.
    (c) Postal—the U.S. Post Office where the merchandise is mailed.

EXHIBIT 17-4 (continued)

12. **Foreign Port of Unloading**—(For vessel and air shipments only) The foreign port and country at which the merchandise will be unladen from the exporting carrier.

13. **Containerized**—(For vessel shipments only) Cargo originally booked as containerized cargo and that placed in containers at the vessel operator's option.

14. **Commodity Description**—A sufficient description of the commodity to permit verification of the Schedule B Commodity Number or the description shown on the validated export license.

15. **Marks, Numbers, and Kinds of Packages**—Marks, numbers, or other identification shown on the packages and the numbers and kinds of packages (boxes, barrels, baskets, etc.).

16. **"D" (Domestic) or "F" (Foreign)**
    (a) Domestic exports—merchandise grown, produced, or manufactured in the United States (including imported merchandise which has been enhanced in value or changed from the form in which imported by further manufacture or processing in the United States).
    (b) Foreign exports—merchandise that has entered the United States and is being re-exported in the same condition as when imported.

17. **Schedule B Commodity Number**—The ten-digit commodity number as provided in Schedule B—Statistical Classification of Domestic and Foreign Commodities Exported From the United States. Check Digit (CD) is no longer required. See item 5 for a discussion of not repeating the same Schedule B numbers on the SED. See the Appendix showing a list of telephone numbers for assistance with Schedule B numbers.

18. **Net Quantity**—Report whole unit(s) as specified in Schedule B with the unit indicated. Report also the unit specified on the validated export license if the units differ. See the Appendix showing a list of telephone numbers for assistance with units of quantity.

19. **Gross Shipping Weight**—(For vessel and air shipments only) The gross shipping weight in kilograms for each Schedule B number, including the weight of containers but excluding carrier equipment. (Lbs. multiplied by 0.4536 = kilos. Report whole units.)

20. **Value**—Selling price or cost if not sold, including freight, insurance, and other charges to U.S. port of export, but excluding unconditional discounts and commissions (nearest whole dollar, omit cents). Report one value for each Schedule B number.

21. **Export License Number of General License Symbol**—Validated export license number and expiration date or general license symbol. See the Appendix showing a list of telephone numbers for assistance with licensing information.

22. **Export Control Classification Number**—(When required) ECCN number of commodities listed on the Commerce Control List in the Export Administration Regulations. See the Appendix showing telephone numbers for assistance with the ECCN.

23. **Designation of Agent**—Signature of exporter authorizing the named agent to effect the export when such agent does not have formal power of attorney.

24. **Signature/Title/Date**—Signature of exporter or authorized agent certifying the truth and accuracy of the information on the SED, title of exporter or authorized agent, and date of signature.

25. **Authentication**—For Customs use only.

Source: http://www.census.gov/ftp/pub/foreign-trade/www/corway1.txt, accessed August 22, 1997.

Standard specifications for products and services are especially important for Europe and Japan, as far as American exporters are concerned. As far as export transactions to third-world countries are concerned, the convertibility of the importing country's currency is something that needs to be checked even in this day of liberalization. If that country's currency is not convertible, then the importing party must have permission to remit hard currency. Finally, the exporter needs to make sure that there are no export restrictions on the goods proposed to be exported from the United States. Security concerns on encryption technology, for example, permit the exports of encryption technology that incorporate no more than 40 bits. All exports from the United States (except those to Canada and U.S. territories) require an **export license,** which may be a general export license or a validated export license. A **general license** permits exportation within certain limits without requiring that an application be filed or that a license document be issued. A **validated license** permits exportation within specific limitations; it is issued only on formal application. Most goods can move from the United States to the free world countries under a general license. A validated license is required to export certain kinds of strategic goods regardless of destination.[14] For most goods, the license is granted by the U.S. Department of Commerce's Office of Export Administration. For certain specific products, however, the license is granted by other U.S. government agencies, as shown in Exhibit 17-5.

Export Transactions

The logistics of the export transaction is the second pillar of an export transaction, which includes: (1) the terms of the sale, including f.o.b./c.i.f. payment mode and schedule, dispute settlement mechanism, and service requirements (if applicable); (2) monitoring the transportation and delivery of the goods to the assigned party—the assignee in the bill of lading and obtaining proof of delivery—the **customs receipt;** and (3) shipping and obtaining the bill of lading.

Once a company has a firm order for exports, it has to execute the order so as to deliver the product or service promised to the overseas customer. A **bill of lading** is a

EXHIBIT 17-5
U.S. EXPORT LICENSING AUTHORITIES FOR SPECIFIC COMMODITIES

Commodity	Licensing Authority
Arms, ammunition, and other war-related products	Department of State
Atomic energy material (including fissionable material and facilities for their manufacture)	Atomic Energy Commission
Gold and silver	Department of Treasury
Natural gas and electric energy	Federal Power Commission
Narcotic drugs	Department of Justice
Tobacco plants and seeds	Department of Agriculture
Endangered wildlife	Maritime Commission
Vessels	Maritime Commission

Source: U.S. Department of Commerce. The Export Administration Regulations, Washington, D.C., 1997.

---

[14]*The Financing of Exports and Imports 1980* (New York: Morgan Guaranty Trust Company of New York, 1980), p. 24.

contract between the exporter and the shipper indicating that the shipper has accepted responsibility for the goods and will provide transportation in return for payment. The bill of ownership can also be used as a receipt and to prove ownership of the merchandise, depending on the type of the bill of lading. A **straight bill of lading** is non-negotiable and is usually used in prepaid transactions. The goods are delivered to a specific individual or company. A **shipper's order bill of lading** is negotiable; it can be bought, sold, or traded while the goods are still in transit, (i.e., title of the goods can change hands). A shipper's order bill of lading is used for letter-of-credit transactions. The customer usually (depending on the terms of the export contract) needs the original or a copy of the bill of lading to take possession of the goods.[15]

A **commercial invoice** is a bill for the goods stating basic information about the transaction, including a description of the merchandise, total cost of the goods sold, addresses of the buyer and the seller, and delivery and payment. The buyer needs the invoice to prove ownership and to arrange payment terms. Commercial invoices are also used by some governments to assess customs duties. Other export documentation that may be required includes export licenses, certificates of origin, inspection certification, dock and/or warehouse receipts, destination control certificates (to inform shippers and other foreign parties that the goods may only be shipped to a particular country), shippers' export declaration (Form 7525-V provided in Exhibit 17-4 used to compile export trade statistics) and export packaging lists. To ensure that all required documentation is accurately completed and to minimize potential problems, firms entering the international market for the first time with an export order should consider using **freight forwarders**—who are specialists in handling export documentation.

Terms of Shipment and Sale

The responsibilities of the exporter, the importer, and the logistic provider should be spelled out in the export contract in terms of what is and what is not included in the price quotation and who owns title to the goods while in transit. **INCOTERMS,** which went into effect from July 1, 1990, and is an acronym for International Commercial Terms, are the internationally accepted standard definitions for the terms of sale by the International Chamber of Commerce.[16] The commonly used terms of shipment are summarized in Exhibit 17-6.

The terms of shipment used in the export transaction and their acceptance by the parties involved are important so that subsequent disputes will not occur. These terms of shipment also have siginincant implications on costing and pricing. The exporter should therefore learn what terms of shipment importers prefer in a particular market and what the specific transaction may require. A CIF quote by an exporter clearly shows the importer the cost to get the product to a port in a desired country. An inexperienced importer may be discouraged by an EXW quote because the importer may not have the knowledge of how much the EXW quote translates in terms of landed cost at home.

---

[15]*A Basic Guide to Exporting*, U.S. Department of Commerce, Washington, D.C., 1986.

[16]Ronald H. Ballou, *Business Logistics Management* (Englewood Cliffs, N.J.: Prentice-Hall, 1992).

EXHIBIT 17-6
TERMS OF SHIPMENT

Ex-works (EXW) at the point of origin	The exporter agrees to deliver the goods at the disposal of the buyer to the specified place on the specified date or within a fixed period. All other charges are borne by the buyer.
Free Alongside Ship (FAS) at a named port of export	The exporter quotes a price for the goods, including charges for delivery of the goods alongside a vessel at a port. The seller covers the costs of unloading and wharfage. Loading onto the ship, ocean transportation, insurance, unloading and wharfage at a port of destination and transport to the site required by the buyer are on the importer's account.
Free on Board (FOB) at a named port of export	In addition to FAS, the exporter undertakes to load the goods on the vessel to be used for ocean transportation and the price quoted by the exporter reflects this cost.
Cost and Freight (CFR) to a named overseas port of disembarkation	The exporter quotes a price for the goods, including the cost of transportation to a named overseas port of disembarkation. The cost of insurance and the choice of the insurer are left to the importer.
Cost, Insurance and Freight (CIF) to a named overseas port of disembarkation	The exporter quotes a price including insurance and all transportation and miscellaneous charges to the port of disembarkation from the ship or aircraft. CIF costs are influenced by port charges (unloading, wharfage, storage, heavy lift, demurrage), documentation charges (certification of invoice, certification of origin, weight certificate) and other miscellaneous charges (fees of freight forwarder, insurance premiums).
Delivery Duty Paid (DDP) to an overseas buyer's premises	The exporter delivers the goods with import duties paid, including inland transportation from the docks to the importer's premises.

Payment Terms

The financing and payments of an export transaction constitute the third set of things to do with regard to an export transaction. For example, is export credit available from an Exim Bank or a local agency supporting exports? What payment terms have been agreed on? Customary payment terms for noncapital goods transactions include cash with order, confirmed irrevocable letter of credit, irrevocable letter of credit, revocable letter of credit, sight draft—documents against payment (D/P), time draft—documents against acceptance (D/A), open account, and consignment basis payments. These terms are explained in Exhibit 17-7. The terms of payment between the exporter and the importer are a matter of negotiation and depend on a variety of factors. These factors include the buyer's credit standing, the amount of the sale transaction, the availability of foreign exchange in the buyer's country, the exchange control laws in the buyer's country, the risks associated with the type of merchandise to be shipped, the usual practice in the trade, and market conditions—i.e., a buyer's market or a seller's market and payment terms offered by competitors.

When negotiating payment terms with an importer, an exporter must be guided by the risks associated with the importer and the importer's country. **Credit risk** is the risk that the importer will not pay or will fail to pay on the agreed terms. The exporter has to consider this, along with foreign exchange fluctuation risks, transfer risks, and the political risks of the importer's country. **Exchange risk** exists when the sale is in the importer's currency and that currency depreciates in terms of the dollar,

EXHIBIT 17-7

TERMS OF PAYMENT IN AN EXPORT TRANSACTION

Cash with order	Cash payment when order is placed
Confirmed irrevocable letter of credit	A letter of credit issued by the importer's bank and confirmed by a bank, usually in the exporter's country. The obligation of the second bank is added to the obligation of the issuing bank to honor drafts presented in accordance with the terms of credit.
Unconfirmed irrevocable letter of credit	A letter of credit issued by the importer's bank. The issuing bank still has an obligation to pay.
Revocable letter of credit	A letter of credit that may be withdrawn from the beneficiary at any time without prior notice to the exporter. It does not carry a bank's obligation to pay.
Sight Draft	A draft so drawn as to be payable on presentation to the drawee (usually the buyer)
Time Draft	A draft maturing at a certain fixed time after presentation or acceptance
Open account	No draft drawn; transaction payable when specified on invoice
Consignment	A shipment that is held by the importer until the merchandise has been sold, at which time payment is made to the exporter

Source: John S. Gordon, *Profitable Exporting: A Complete Guide to Marketing Your Products Abroad, 2nd ed.* (New York: John Wiley & Sons, 1993) p. 141.

leaving the exporter with a lesser number of dollars. *Transfer risk* refers to the chances that payment will not be made due to the importer's inability to obtain U.S. dollars and transfer them to the exporter, while political risks refer to the risks associated with war, confiscation of the importer's business, and so on.

If an exporter sells for cash, there is virtually no risk. The possible nominal risk is associated with the timing of the order, as compared to the receipt of payment. A sale on a confirmed irrevocable letter of credit has slightly more risk. The confirmation places a U.S. bank or other known bank acceptable to you in front of the importer's bank—the payment risk assumed by the exporter devolves almost completely on this bank. If the sale is in a foreign currency, the exporter is still exposed to the risk of depreciation of the foreign currency relative to the dollar. An **unconfirmed** letter of credit exposes the exporter to the creditworthiness of the buyer's bank in the foreign country because a U.S. bank is no longer guaranteeing payment. The exporter thus faces the additional risk of a change in the value of the foreign currency (if the sale is not in U.S. dollars), the risk that the payment cannot be transferred to the United States, and the risk that the political conditions in the buyer's country will change to the exporter's detriment.

Exports on sight draft basis further increase the payment risk in an export transaction because there is no financial institution like a bank that has assumed the risk of payment. A time draft further escalates the risk because the buyer by "accepting the draft" will receive the title documents and can pick up the goods without payment. Finally, an open account sale has no evidence of debt (promissory note, draft, etc.) and the payment may be unenforceable. Usually, done on the basis of an invoice, an open account transaction is recommended only after the exporter and the importer have established trust in their relationship.

Associated with the payment and shipment terms is the marine insurance (applicable to all forms of shipping) of the goods being shipped. The exporter and the importer have to decide and mutually agree on the insurance terms as part of the contract. The exporter will be unable to enforce the provisions of an insurance coverage unless he or she holds an insurable interest in the transaction at the time of the loss. The exporter has such an interest if the cargo is lost, damaged, or destroyed and the exporter suffers a loss or fails to make an expected profit. Lack of clarity usually has a greater adverse impact on the exporter, as shown by the following example.

An exporter delivered goods to the docks to be loaded for export to a foreign buyer. The terms of sale were FOB (exporter's dock) and the seller received an on-board bill of lading (which means that the goods were supposed to be on board the ship). A fire engulfed the dock and the ship left the dock to save itself before the goods could actually be loaded. The buyer had insured the goods from the FOB point (on board the ship). The goods left on the dock perished in the fire. The seller's insurance company claims that it is not liable, as the shipper received the on-board bill of lading, and the buyer's insurance company claims that it is not liable, as the goods were never actually loaded.[17] The transaction continues to be in dispute by the concerned parties. In this case the dispute arose because of the unforeseen contingency of the goods not actually being on board the ship when they were legally supposed to be.

Currency Hedging

The fourth task of an exporter is to arrange a foreign exchange cover transaction with the banker or through the firm's treasury in case there is a foreign exchange risk in the export transaction. Such arrangements include reversing the forward currency transaction if required and hedging the foreign exchange risk using derivative instruments in the foreign exchange markets like currency options and futures. Where the U.S. exporter is receiving some currency other than the dollar, covering a trade transaction through forward sales, currency options and currency futures enables the exporter to lock in the dollar value of the export transaction up to a year in the future, thus enabling more certain cash flows and forecasting. Due care needs to be exercised in the uses of financial derivative instruments, because an unwary or uninformed firm can lose large amounts of money, as Procter & Gamble did in 1993 over derivative transactions.

◆ ◆ ◆ ◆ ◆ ◆ ROLE OF THE GOVERNMENT IN PROMOTING EXPORTS[18]

Export promotion activities generally comprise (1) *export service programs* (e.g., seminars for potential exporters, export counseling, how-to-export handbooks, and export financing) and (2) *market development programs* (e.g., dissemination of sales leads to local firms, participation in foreign trade shows, preparation of market analysis, and export news letters).[19] In addition, program efforts can be differentiated as to

---

[17]Gordon, p. 228.

[18]This section draws from Esra F. Gencturk and Masaaki Kotabe, "Performance Implications of Export Marketing Involvement and Export Promotion Assistance Usage," 1995 AMA Summer Educators' Conference, August 1995.

[19]William C. Lesch, Abdolreza Eshghi, and Golpira S. Eshghi, "A Review of Export Promotion Programs in the Ten Largest Industrial States," in S. Tamer Cavusgil and Michael R. Czinkota, eds. *International Perspectives on Trade Promotion and Assistance* (New York: Quorum Books, 1990), pp. 25–37.

whether the intent is to provide informational or experiential knowledge. Informational knowledge typically would be provided through "how-to" export assistance, workshops, and seminars, while experiential knowledge would be imparted through the arrangement of foreign buyers' or trade missions, trade and catalog shows, or participation in international market research.

Government expenditures on export promotion seem to make sense. One billion dollars' worth of exports creates, on average, 22,800 jobs. It has been estimated that $2 billion of GNP are generated per billion dollars of exports, together with $400 million in state and federal tax revenues.[20]

Although exports may be considered a major engine of economic growth in the U.S. economy, many U.S. firms do not export. Many firms, particularly small- to medium-sized ones, appear to have developed a fear of international market activities. Their management tends to see only the risks—informational gaps, unfamiliar conditions in markets, complicated domestic and foreign trade regulations, the absence of trained middle managers for exporting, and lack of financial resources— rather than the opportunities that the international market can present. Yet, these very same firms may well have unique competitive advantages to offer that may be highly useful in performing successfully in the international market.

For example, small- and medium-sized firms can offer their customers shorter response times. If some special situation should arise, there is no need to wait for the "home office" to respond. Responses can be immediate, direct, and predictable to the customer, therefore providing precisely those competitive ingredients that increase stability in a business relationship and reduce risk and costs. These firms often can also customize their operations more easily. Procedures can be adapted more easily to the special needs of the customer or to local requirements. One could argue that in a world turning away from mass marketing and toward niche marketing, these capabilities may well make smaller-sized firms the export champions of the future.

In 1993, in response to the need for the United States to step up its exports, President Clinton announced the **National Export Strategy**.[21] As part of this strategy, the U.S. Trade Promotion Coordinating Committee had set a goal of increasing the level of exports of goods and services from the $700 billion achieved in 1994 to $1 trillion by the year 2000.[22] In pursuit of this objective, the International Trade Administration of the U.S. Department of Commerce devotes a substantial amount of the tax dollars allocated to it to help U.S. firms export their goods and services. For instance, the Japan Export Information Center (JEIC), established in April 1991, is the primary contact point within the Department of Commerce for U.S. exporters seeking business counseling and commercial information necessary to succeed in the Japanese market. The JEIC's principal functions are to provide guidance on doing business in Japan, as well as information on market entry alternatives, market data and research, product standards and testing requirements, intellectual property protection, tariffs, and nontariff barriers.

---

[20]Masaaki Kotabe and Michael R. Czinkota, "State Government Promotion of Manufacturing Exports: A Gap Analysis," *Journal of International Business Studies*, 23 (Fourth Quarter 1992), pp. 637–58.

[21]"How the Commerce Department Helps U.S. Firms Export to Japan," *Business America* (November 1995), pp. 4–7.

[22]"Stocktaking: Implementing the National Export Strategy," *Business America* (October 1995), pp. 28–65.

The U.S. Department of Commerce also has industry specialists and country specialists in Washington, D.C. The industry specialists are available to give exporters information on the current state of the exporter's products overseas, comment on marketing and sales strategies, inform on trade shows and events and give other counsel. The country specialists are available to give information on the target country, current trade issues with the United States, customs and tariff information, insight on the business climate and culture, and any other information on a country required by the exporter.

Export–Import Bank

The **Exim Bank**—short for Export–Import Bank—plays a crucial role in promoting exports. The Exim Bank is a federally supported bank whose mission is to support exporters with the necessary credit. Increased emphasis by Exim Bank on project finance—which allows financing for ventures to go forward based on their earnings rather than relying on government funding or direct guarantees—is enabling more U.S. companies to successfully compete for the massive infrastructure projects that the big emerging markets will desire in the decade from 1995 to 2005. Annual spending on infrastructure projects like roads, railways, telecommunications, power generation and mining outside the U.S. is estimated to be in excess of $200 billion a year. The project finance division of the Exim Bank authorized $2.1 billion during 1995 in support of U.S. exports on project finance deals, up from only $350 million in 1994. This level is expected to rise as U.S. firms bid for more infrastructure projects in the emerging markets.

The Exim Bank is also combating the "trade distorting" loans of foreign governments through the aggressive use of its **Tied Aid Capital Projects Fund.** The idea is that the Exim Bank is willing to match foreign tied-aid offers that are commercially viable and pending, on a case-by-case basis, in order to be able to preemptively counter foreign tied-aid offer.

For instance, if a highway project in China gets a bid from a European or Japanese consortium of firms that offer to give concessional aid for the project but stipulate that in return for the aid the Chinese should buy machinery and materials from suppliers to be specified by the Europeans (or the Japanese), then a U.S. firm bidding for the same project can depend on being able to provide concessional financing through the resources of the Exim Bank. In addition, the U.S. government is no longer shy of representing American firms openly and of being powerful advocates on behalf of American businesses. Cabinet secretaries in the Clinton administration have led groups of top business executives to many emerging markets. Accompanying administration officials on foreign missions gives business executives a chance to get acquainted with decision makers in foreign governments—and many infrastructure projects are awarded by governments.[23] The U.S. government lobbied hard to obtain airplane orders for Boeing from Singapore Airlines, Cathay Pacific and Saudia, all of which were being lobbied hard by the French government to buy from Airbus–European consortium. As also shown in Global Perspective 17-1, various government agencies, backed by the Exim Bank's loan guarantee, are increasingly willing to help small U.S. firms successfully bid for major overseas contracts.

---

[23]"Why Executives Tour World With Politicians," *Wall Street Journal* (April 4, 1996), p. B1.

◆ ◆

$\mathcal{G}$LOBAL PERSPECTIVE 17-1

GOVERNMENT AGENCIES PROVIDE EXPORT ASSISTANCE AND COUNTER TIED AID

In 1995, Exim Bank, the Department of Commerce, the Department of Transportation, the U.S. Embassy, and the Trade and Development Agency (TDA)—all agencies of the government—teamed up to help a small Baltimore, Maryland company win a $15 million sale to Indonesia. Exim Bank approved a $22 million loan to Ellicott Machine Corp. International to sell five split barges, one tug boat and spare parts to P.T. Runkindo, Indonesia's state-owned dredging company. Support for Ellicott was also provided by the Department of Transportation, which in-

cluded a letter from the Transportation Secretary to the Indonesian Minister of Communications. TDA hosted a reverse trade mission so that Indonesian officials could familiarize themselves with American equipment, paving the way for the sale.

The government of Indonesia has been Ellicott's largest single customer of dredging equipment over the 110-year history of the company. Recently, Ellicott had lost market share in Indonesia to European competitors due to the "tied aid" soft loans. The help of the government agencies enabled Ellicott to retain a strong market presence in the dredging market in Indonesia. The TDA is also helping Ellicott obtain another order—this time from a South African company.

Source: "National Export Strategy," *Business America* (October 1995), pp. 28–65.

Critics may cavil at this active role of the U.S. government in promoting exports; however, if U.S. firms are to retain their position in existing markets and if they are to gain access to new markets, then they have to have the same facilities that are available to firms from other nations. It is for this reason that the policy of advocacy on behalf of U.S. firms fighting to enter new markets or to retain existing markets is a cornerstone of the National Export Policy.[24] As Exhibit 17-8 shows, U.S. government support of exports is among the lowest of the developed nations. Such advocacy is a relatively new phenomenon for the U.S. government. As a CEO of a major U.S.-based multinational commented, "For the first time in my 30-year career, the U.S. government and businesses are working together as a partnership to make American businesses competitive in the world."[25]

U.S. Tariff Concessions

Other areas in which the government plays a role in promoting exports include the establishment and maintenance of foreign trade zones (FTZs), foreign sales corporations (FSCs) and the Export Trading Company Act of 1982.

Foreign Trade Zone. As discussed in detail in chapter 16, foreign trade zones (free trade zones) let businesses store, process, assemble, and display goods from abroad without paying a tariff. Once these goods leave the zone and enter the United States they have to pay a tariff—but not on the cost of assembly or profits. If the product is re-exported, no duties or tariffs have to be paid. Thus, a U.S. firm can as-

---

[24]"Advocacy: Supporting U.S. Jobs in Global Competition," *Business America* (October 1995), pp. 66–89.

[25]Ibid.

EXHIBIT 17-8
FINANCIAL ASSISTANCE TO EXPORTERS, 1993

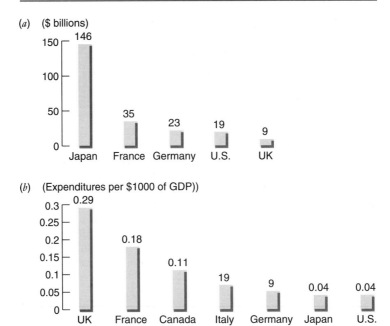

Source: OECD, Berne Country Reports, 1996.

semble foreign parts for a camera in a Florida FTZ and ship the finished cameras to Latin America without paying duty.

Foreign Sales Corporation. A foreign sales corporation (FSC) is a foreign corporation not located in a free trade zone that is allowed to earn some exempt and nontaxable income on its exports from the United States. In most cases this partial exemption can result in U.S. tax savings of up to 7.4 percent of the profit on export transactions for a manufacturer/exporter and up to 14.7 percent for a trading company/exporter.[26] The FSC is required to pay tax on the balance of its nonexempt income. To become an FSC, a corporation must be organized in a foreign country or a U.S. possession, must have no more than twenty-five shareholders, must have no preferred stock, and must have at least one nonresident on its board of directors.

American Export Trading Company. The Export Trading Company Act of 1982 encourages businesses to join together and form export trading companies. It provides antitrust protection for joint exporting, and permits banking institutions to own interests in these exporting ventures. This act makes it practical for small- and medium-size exporting firms to pool resources without the fear of antitrust persecution and inadequate capitalization. A bank may hold up to 100 percent stock in an export trading company and is exempted from the collateral requirements contained in the Federal Reserve Act for loans to its export trading company.

---

[26]Subhash C. Jain, *International Marketing Management, 4th ed.* (Belmont, Calif.: Wadsworth Publishing, 1993), p. 715.

Export Regulations

Although the U.S. government has become earnest in promoting exports it also has a hand in regulating exports. The Trade Act of 1974 bars the Exim Bank credit to most communist countries. The Foreign Corrupt Practices Act of 1977 (as amended in 1986) imposes jail terms and fines for overseas payoffs that seek to influence overseas government decisions—though payments to expedite events that are supposed to take place under local laws are no longer illegal. Many U.S. exporters, especially exporters of big ticket items, are of the opinion that the Foreign Corrupt Practices Act provides an unfair advantage to exporters from Europe and Japan who have been able to make such payments and get tax write-offs for the payments under export expenses. In 1996, under newly agreed provisions of WTO, firms from other countries will no longer be able to make such payments without incurring penalties—thus leveling the playing field somewhat for U.S. exporters. Regulatory mechanisms such as COCOM (Coordinating Committee on Exports) restrict what can be exported to former communist countries, though with the breakdown of the Soviet Union, COCOM has lost much of its relevance. Laws remain in place, however, that restrict exports of security-sensitive technology like encryption technology for computer software and hardware.

Antitrust laws prevent U.S. firms from bidding jointly on major foreign projects. Human rights legislation and nuclear nonproliferation policies require that the federal government has to recertify every year the Most Favored Nation status of major foreign trade partners like China. These are examples of the U.S. exporting its own rules to other nations under the aegis of WTO. To the extent that such actions result in the same rules for all nations engaging in international trade, such behavior benefits trade; however, such behavior can also be perceived as an infringement of national sovereignty by many nations.

Sometimes the actions of a foreign government can affect exports. These actions relate to tariffs and local laws relating to products standards and classification. For example, computer networking equipment exported from the United States to the European Union is charged a 3.9 percent tariff. A recent EU ruling decided that computer networking equipment like adopters, routers, and switches do not crunch data but transport data and so should be classified as telecommunication equipment. Telecommunication equipment, however, carries a higher tariff rate of 7.5 percent, increasing the landed price of these products in Europe.[27] Such actions by foreign governments are usually attempts to provide protection to local industry.

Finally, a government may tax exports with the purpose of satisfying domestic demand first or to take advantage of higher world prices. In April 1996, the European Union taxed flour exports for the first time in more than twenty years and also raised a tax on wheat exports, as world prices for the grain hit new records. Traders must pay a tax of 10 Ecus ($12.30) per ton on exports of wheat flour, while the tax on some EU wheat exports has been increased to 45 Ecus per ton ($55) from 35 Ecus ($43).[28] The goal of such measures is to curb exports and try to keep a lid on internal food industry costs as grain prices soar.

---

[27]"Europe's Computer Networking Tariffs May Lead to U.S. Complaint to WTO," *Wall Street Journal* (May 1, 1996), p. B7.

[28]clari.world.europe.union, April 25, 1996.

◆ ◆ ◆ ◆ ◆ ◆ MANAGING IMPORTS—THE OTHER SIDE OF THE COIN

So far the chapter has been devoted exclusively to exports, and we now turn to imports. For organizations in the United States importing is considerably easier than for most firms in the rest of the world. One of the primary reasons for this is the fact that unlike importers in most of the rest of the world, U.S. importers can pay the seller abroad in their own currency—the U.S. dollar—because the U.S. dollar is an internationally accepted denomination of exchange. Thus, unlike importers in Brazil or Indonesia who have to find U.S. dollars (or other hard currencies) to pay for imports, an importer in the United States can manage by shelling out U.S. dollars. About 60 percent of the world's trade is still denominated in U.S. dollars—the exporter wants dollars in return for the goods or services sold.

However, denomination of trade in dollars is changing, especially in Asia, where the Japanese yen is emerging as the currency in which trade is denominated. Most of the time, therefore, a U.S. importer does not have to bother with hedging foreign exchange transactions or with trying to accumulate foreign currency to pay for imports. On occasion a U.S. importer may not even need a confirmed letter of credit. This same advantage is available on a more limited geographical basis to Japan and Germany. Japan is now able to pay in Japanese yen for much of its imports from Southeast Asia, while Germany can pay in deutsche mark for its imports from much of Europe.

This is not to suggest that a firm can import anything for sale in the United States. There are restrictions on trade with countries like Iran, Libya, Iraq, and Cuba. Iran and Libya are thought to be supporters of state sponsored terrorism. Since the Gulf War, Iraq had been, until May 1996, under United Nations sanctions, which prevented it from exporting oil, while Cuba has been a pariah as far as the United States is concerned since 1959. Production and marketing considerations also limit what can be imported and sold profitably in the United States. For goods like soaps and cosmetics, the demand for imports is minimal. However, the United States is a surplus producer of many categories of goods including aircraft, defense equipment, medical electronics, and agricultural goods.

Importing any good is, thus, predicated upon the existence of a situation where the domestic production of the good in question is not sufficient to satisfy demand. For example, annual sales of cut flowers in the U.S. is close to $10 billion, but domestic production meets only about 30 percent of the demand, with Americans purchasing flowers not just for special occasions but also for sending messages, as a token of friendship, as a get-well wish, or just to convey "have a nice day" to someone. Imports of cut flowers are primarily from Columbia, Mexico, Costa Rica, Ecuador, Peru, Canada and Kenya.[29] The imported flowers must satisfy the selective U.S. consumer—in addition, the product must comply with the U.S. Plant Protection Quarantine Inspection Program and antidumping regulations. Since the product is highly perishable, air transportation and rapid transit through customs have to be ensured. Thus, the importer of flowers has to go through many hoops in terms of locating a

---

[29]Jerry Haar and Marta Ortiz-Buonafina, Import Marketing: *A Management Guide to Profitable Operations* (Lexington Books, 1989).

reliable seller and arranging the logistics. Importer behavior will, of course, depend on the category of goods being purchased abroad.

However, importer buyer behavior is a relatively under-researched area in the field of international trade—partly on account of most nations being more interested in maximizing exports rather than imports—and restricting imports is relatively simple, as compared to being a successful exporter. The most important of the organizational buying models is the BuyGrid model.[30] Besides elaborating on how the purchasing process evolves and highlighting the role of buyers' search in choice decisions, this framework was the first to categorize buy decisions as (1) straight buys, (2) modified rebuy, and (3) new tasks.

Although this framework was developed primarily for domestic purchases, it is applicable to import decisions as well. Applying the framework for an import decision and taking into account the increased uncertainty in international markets would translate into a procedure presented in Exhibit 17-9. This sequence of actions in an import situation appears logical, as in exports, but many international supplier relationships start with an "unsolicited export order," where importers place an order with a selected foreign vendor without any systematic vendor search and evaluation. The lack of a systematic approach to vendor identification and evaluation may stem

EXHIBIT 17-9
MODEL OF IMPORTER BUYER BEHAVIOR

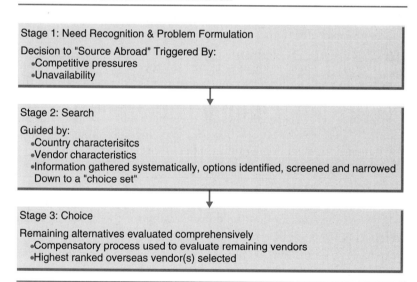

Source: Neng Liang and Rodney L. Stump, "Judgmental Heuristics in Overseas Vendor Search and Evaluation: A Proposed Model of Importer Buyer Behavior," *International Executive,* Copyright (November, 1996). Reprinted by permission of John Wiley & Sons, Inc.

---

[30]Patrick J. Robinson, Charles W. Faris and Yoram Wind, *Industrial Buying and Creative Marketing,* (Boston: Allyn and Bacon, 1967).

from a difficulty in accessing all relevant information and from the idea of *bounded rationality*—the notion that due to limited cognitive abilities, humans tend to satisfice and not optimize. Thus, given the information available, which cannot be complete, managers will not be able to make the *best* decision.[31]

◆ ◆ ◆ ◆ ◆ ◆ MECHANICS OF IMPORTING

An import transaction is like looking at an export transaction from the other end of the transaction. Instead of an exporter looking for a prospective buyer, an importer looks for an overseas firm that can supply it with the raw materials, components, or finished products that it needs for its business. Once an importer in the United States locates a suitable overseas exporter, it has to negotiate the terms of the sale with the exporter, including, but not restricted to:

- Finding a bank that either has branches in the exporter's country or has correspondent bank located in the exporter's country and establishing a line of credit with the bank if not already done so.

- Establishing a letter of credit with a bank with the terms of payment and how payment is to be made. This includes terms of clearing the goods from the docks/customs warehouse (sometimes with title for goods going temporarily to the bank), insurance coverage, terms of transfer of title, and so on.

- Deciding on the mode of transfer of goods from exporter to importer and transfer of funds. Transportation party provides proof of delivery to the exporter's bank or the exporter. Exporter (or his bank) presents the proof of delivery to the importer's bank (branch in importer's own country/correspondent bank). Importer's bank transfers funds to the exporter's bank and simultaneously debits the importer's account or presents a demand draft to the importer.

- Checking compliance with national laws of the importing country and the exporting country. Import restrictions into the U.S. include quotas on automobiles, textiles and steel and quarantine checks on food products. They also include a ban on imports from Cuba, North Korea, Libya, Iraq, and Iran.

- Making allowances for foreign exchange fluctuations through making covering transactions through the bank so that the dollar liability for the importer either remains fixed or gets lower.

- Fixing liability for payment of import duties and demurrage and warehousing in case the goods get delayed due to congestion at ports. These payments are normally the responsibility of the importer.

An examination of these mechanics of an import transaction reveals that the transaction is materially the same as an export transaction. The differences that are of interest to managers involved in the import of goods into the United States include

---

[31]Neng Liang and Rodney L. Stump, "Judgmental Heuristics in Overseas Vendor Search and Evaluation: A Proposed Model of Importer Buyer Behavior," *International Executive*, 38 (November/December 1996), pp. 779–806.

- a difference in risk profile. An exporter faces the risk of receiving no payment due to a variety of factors, whereas nonpayment is not an issue in imports. However, the quality of goods and services imported can be an issue for imports—this is not usually an issue in exports.

- the facility of being able to pay in its own currency (most of the time)—a facility not available to importers in almost any other country.

- everything else equal, it is easier for a U.S. firm to import than to export because of the primacy of the U.S. dollar. The strengthening of the U.S. dollar by more than 20 percent during 1997 can be expected to increase the propensity to import even further because this makes overseas goods cheaper.

Entry of Imports into the United States

Import Documents and Delivery. When a shipment reaches the United States, the consignee (normally the importer) will file entry documents with the port director at the port of entry. The bill of lading or the airway bill properly endorsed by the consignor in favor of the consignee serves as the evidence of the right to make entry. The entry documents also include an entry manifest, Customs Form 7533, Customs Form 3461, packing lists if appropriate, and the commercial invoice. The entry should be accompanied by evidence that a bond is posted with customs to cover any potential duties, taxes, and penalties that may accrue. A **bond** is a guarantee by someone that the duties and any potential penalties will be paid to the customs of the importing country. In the event that a custom broker is employed for the purpose of making entry, the broker may permit the use of the bond to provide the required coverage.

Entry may be for immediate delivery, for ordinary delivery, for a warehouse or may be unentered for a period of time. Merchandise arriving from Canada and Mexico, trade fair goods, perishable goods and shipments assigned to the U.S. government almost always utilize the **Special Permit for Immediate Delivery** on Customs Form 3461 prior to the arrival of the goods to enable fast release after arrival. An entry summary is then filed within ten days of the release of the goods. Imported goods coming in under ordinary delivery use normal channels including Form 7533. Under warehousing, goods are placed in a custom bonded warehouse if the entry of the imported goods is desired to be delayed. The goods may remain in a bonded warehouse for a period of five years. At any time during the period warehoused goods may be re-exported without payment of duty or they may be withdrawn for consumption upon the payment of duty. If there is a failure to enter the goods at the port of entry or the port of destination within five working days after arrival, the imported goods may be placed in the general warehouse at the risk and expense of the importer.

Import Duties. Import duties that have to be paid may be ad valorem, specific or compound. An **ad valorem duty,** which is the one most frequently applied, is a percentage of the value of the merchandise, such as 5 percent ad valorem. Thus, an auto shipment worth $100 million that has an ad valorem rate of 3.9 percent will pay $3.9 million as customs duty. A **specific duty** rate is a specified amount per unit of weight or other quantity, such as 5.1 cents per dozen, 20 cents per barrel or 90 cents per ton. A **compound duty** rate is a combination of an ad valorem rate and a specific rate, such as 0.7 cents per kilogram plus 10 percent as valorem. Duty rates in the U.S. are relatively low compared to many other countries. The average rate is estimated to be less than 5 percent.[32] The entry of imported merchandise into the United States is complete after the goods are cleared by the customs from the port of entry or the port of destination.

Antidumping import duties are assessed on imported merchandise sold to importers in the United States at a price that is less than the fair market value. The fair market value of merchandise is defined under articles of World Trade Organization as the price at which the good is normally sold in the manufacturer's home market. For some goods, **countervailing duties** are assessed to counter the effects of subsidies provided by foreign governments to goods that are exported to the United States, because without the countervailing duty the price of these imported goods in the U.S. market would be artificially low, causing economic injury to U.S. manufacturers. **Duty drawbacks** are a refund of 99 percent of all ordinary customs duties. Duty drawback may be a direct identification drawback or a substitution drawback. **Direct Identification Drawback** provides a refund of duties paid on imported merchandise that is partially or totally used within five years of the date of import in the manufacture of an article that is exported. **Substitution drawback** provides a refund of duties paid on designated imported merchandise upon exportation of articles manufactured or produced with the use of substituted domestic or imported merchandise that is of the same quality as the designated import merchandise.

As explained earlier, importing firms can also utilize foreign trade zones profitably. They can set up facilities in a FTZ to import finished goods, component parts, or raw materials for eventual domestic consumption or import merchandise that is frequently delayed by customs quota delays or import merchandise that must be processed, generating significant amounts of scrap. An important feature of foreign trade zones for foreign merchants entering the American market is that the goods may brought to the threshold of the market, making immediate delivery certain and avoiding the possible cancellation of orders due to shipping delays. Foreign sales corporations can be set up in the U.S. by the overseas subsidiaries of U.S. corporations to take advantage of the provisions governing foreign sales corporations.

◆ ◆ ◆ ◆ ◆ ◆   GRAY MARKETS

Gray market channels refer to the legal export/import transaction involving genuine products into a country by intermediaries other than the authorized distributors. From the importer's side, it is also known as **parallel imports.** Distributors, wholesalers, and retailers in a foreign market obtain the exporter's product from some other business entity. Thus, the exporter's legitimate distributor(s) and dealers face competition from others who sell the exporter's products at reduced prices in that foreign market. High-priced branded consumer goods like cameras, jewelry, perfumes, watches, and so on, where production lies principally in one country are particularly prone to gray market imports. Brand reputation is a critical element in gray market goods exports and the distribution is typically through exclusive wholesalers and distributors.

For example, if purchased on the gray market, a $54,000 Mercedes 500 SEL, which meets all the U.S. safety and pollution control requirements, can be purchased for about 20 percent less than the price charged by the local authorized dealer. Although gray market products look similar to their domestic counterparts, they may not be identical and may not carry full warranties. Nevertheless, the volume of gray market activities is signif-

---

[32]*A Basic Guide to Importing 1993*, 2nd ed. (Lincolnwood: Ill.: NTC Business Books, 1993).

icant. Industry sources estimate that 20 percent of Sharp Electronics' copiers and 22 percent of Mercedes cars sold in the United States were supplied by gray marketers.[33]

Why Gray Markets Develop[34]

Three conditions are necessary for gray markets to develop. First, the products must be available in other markets. In today's global markets, this condition is readily met. Second, trade barriers such as tariffs, transportation costs, and legal restrictions must be low enough for parallel importers to move the products from one market to another. Again, under the principle of GATT, now WTO, the trade barriers have been reduced so low that parallel importation has become feasible. Third, price differentials among various markets must be great enough to provide the basic motivation for gray marketers. Such price differences arise for various reasons, including currency exchange rate fluctuations, differences in demand, and segmentation strategies employed by international marketing managers.

Currency Fluctuations. The fluctuating currency exchange rates among countries often produce large differences in prices for products across national boundaries. Gray marketers can take advantage of changes in exchange rates by purchasing products in markets with weak currencies and selling them in markets with strong currencies.

Differences in Market Demand. Similarly, price differences may be caused by differences in market demand for a product in various markets. If the authorized channels of distribution cannot adjust the market supply to meet the market demand, a large enough price difference may develop for unauthorized dealers to engage in arbitrage process, that is, buying the product inexpensively in countries with weak demand and selling it profitably in countries with strong demand.

Segmentation Strategy. Although currency exchange rates and differences in market demand may be beyond the control of international marketing managers, segmentation strategy may result in planned price discrimination among various markets. Such price discrimination strategy is adopted for various reasons, including differences in product life cycle stage, customer purchase behavior, and price elasticity across different markets.

It is possible that the very conditions that foster global strategies also magnify the gray market opportunities.[35] As products sold across national boundaries with the same brand name become similar, the potential for gray market arbitrage grows. A key question for the exporter of branded products is whether a gray market will cause a global strategy to become less desirable. Closer control and monitoring of international marketing efforts can certainly reduce the threat of gray market goods to negligible levels. As presented in Exhibit 17-10, international marketers not only try to confront existing gray markets reactively, but also are increasingly developing more proactive approaches to gray market problems before they arise.

---

[33]S. Tamer Cavusgil and Ed Sikora, "How Multinationals Can Counter Gray Market Imports," *Columbia Journal of World Business*, 23 (Winter 1988), pp. 75–85.

[34]This section draws from Dale F. Duhan and Mary Jane Sheffet, "Gray Markets and the Legal Status of Parallel Importation," *Journal of Marketing*, 52 (July 1988), pp. 75–83; and Tunga Kiyak, "International Gray Markets: A Systematic Analysis and Research Propositions," A paper presented at 1997 AMA Summer Educators' Conference, August 2–5, 1997.

[35]Louis Bucklin, "The Gray Market Threat to International Marketing Strategies," Report # 90-116 (Cambridge, Mass.: Marketing Science Institute, 1990).

EXHIBIT 17-10
HOW TO COMBAT GRAY MARKET ACTIVITY

A. Reactive Strategies to Combat Gray Market Activity

Type of Strategy	Implemented by	Cost of Implementation	Difficulty of Implementation	Does It Curtail Gray Market Activity at Source?	Does It Provide Immediate Relief to Authorized Dealers?	Long-term Effectiveness	Legal Risks to Manufacturers or Dealers	Company Examples
Strategic confrontation	Dealer with manufacturer support	Moderate	Requires planning	No	Relief in the medium term	Effective	Low risk	Creative merchandising by Caterpillar and auto dealers
Participation	Dealer	Low	Not difficult	No	Immediate relief	Potentially damaging reputation of manufacturer	Low risk	Dealers wishing to remain anonymous
Price cutting	Jointly by manufacturer and dealer	Costly	Not difficult	No, if price cutting is temporary	Immediate relief	Effective	Moderate to high risk	Dealers and manufacturers remain anonymous
Supply interference	Either party can engage	Moderate at the wholesale level; high at the retail level	Moderately difficult	No	Immediate relief or slightly delayed	Somewhat effective if at wholesale level; not effective at retail level	Moderate risk at wholesale level; low risk at retail	IBM, Hewlett-Packard, Lotus Corp., Swatch Watch USA, Charles of the Ritz Group, Ltd., Leitz, Inc., NEC Electronics
Promotion of gray market product limitations	Jointly, with manufacturer leadership	Moderate	Not difficult	No	Slightly delayed	Somewhat effective	Low risk	Komatsu, Seiko, Rolex, Mercedes-Benz, IBM
Collaboration	Dealer	Low	Requires careful negotiations	No	Immediate relief	Somewhat effective	Very high risk	Dealers wishing to remain anonymous
Acquisition	Dealer	Very costly	Difficult	No	Immediate relief	Effective if other gray market brokers don't creep in	Moderate to high risk	No publicized cases

B. Proactive Strategies to Combat Gray Market Activity

Strategy								
Product/service differentiation and availability	Jointly, with manufacturer leadership	Moderate to high	Not difficult	Yes	No; impact felt in medium to long term	Very effective	Very low risk	General Motors, Ford, Porsche, Kodak
Strategic pricing	Manufacturer	Moderate to high	Complex; impact on overall profitability needs monitoring	Yes	Slightly delayed	Very effective	Low risk	Porsche
Dealer development	Jointly, with manufacturer leadership	Moderate to high	Not difficult; requires close dealer participation	No	No; impact felt the long term	Very effective	No risk	Caterpillar, Canon
Marketing information systems	Jointly, with manufacturer leadership	Moderate to high	Not difficult; requires dealer participation	No	No; impact felt in after implementation	Effective	No risk	IBM, Catepillar, Yamaha, Hitachi, Komatsu, Lotus Development, Insurance companies
Long-term image reinforcement	Jointly	Moderate	Not difficult	No	No; impact felt in the long term	Effective	No risk	Most manufacturers with strong dealer networks
Establishing legal precedence	Manufacturer	High	Difficult	Yes, if fruitful	No	Uncertain	Low risk	COPIAT, Coleco, Charles of the Ritz Group, Ltd.
Lobbying	Jointly	Moderate	Difficult	Yes, if fruitful	No	Uncertain	Low risk	COPIAT, Duracell, Porsche

Note: Company strategies include, but are not limited to, those mentioned here.

Source: S. Tamer Cavusgil and Ed Sikora, "How Multinationals Can Counter Gray Market Imports," *Columbia Journal of World Business*, 23 (Winter 1988), pp. 75–85.

SUMMARY ◆

The United States was the largest importer and exporter in the world in 1995. The low growth rates of economies in Western Europe and Japan will ensure that the United States will probably retain this position for some time. The U.S. government has a variety of programs to support exports, though many government policies—which are sometimes dictated by political compulsions—hinder exports from the U.S. export markets provide a unique opportunity for growth, but competition in these markets is fierce. With the rise of the big emerging markets like China, India, and Indonesia, competition is likely to intensify even more.

Procedurally, exporting requires locating customers, obtaining an export license from the federal government (a general or validated license); collecting export documents (such as the bill of lading, commercial invoice, export packing list, insurance certificate); packing and marketing; shipping abroad; and receiving payment—most of the time through a bank using a letter of credit. Conversely, imports require locating a seller, obtaining an import license, usually establishing a letter of credit, turning over import documents (like the bill of lading, etc.) to indicate receipt of goods, and making payment through the banking system. Methods of payment include cash in advance, open account, consignment sale, dollar draft, and a letter of credit. Of these, the last two are the most popular. Depending on the na-

ture of the payment terms and the currency of payment the exporter may need to make foreign exchange hedging transactions. The U.S. government is now taking a more active role in promoting exports of U.S. firms as they bid for big ticket items in the emerging markets.

Imports are the obverse of exports. A U.S. importer can make payments in U.S. dollars unlike an importer in many other countries. Any good coming in through a U.S. port has to pass through customs and pay the appropriate duty and be authorized by customs at the port of entry or the port of destination for entry. Unlike an exporter who faces a payment risk, the importer's risks are associated with delivery schedules and product quality. Foreign exchange risk is common to both imports and exports. Entry of some goods into the United States is restricted by bilateral and multilateral quotas as well as by political considerations.

Finally, globalization of markets has spawned gray marketing activities by unauthorized distributors taking advantage of price differences that exist among various countries due to currency exchange rate fluctuations, different market demand conditions, and price discrimination, among other factors. For companies marketing well known branded products, gray markets have become a serious issue to be confronted proactively as well as reactively.

REVIEW QUESTIONS ◆

1. How does a prospective exporter choose an export market?

2. What are the factors that influence the decision of the exporter to use a standardized product strategy across countries and regions?

3. What are the direct and indirect channels of distribution available to exporters? Under what conditions would the use of each be the most appropriate?

4. Terms of payment are an extremely important facet of export transactions. Describe the various terms of payments in increasing order of risk.

5. Describe the various terms of shipment and sale.

6. What is the role of government (home country) in export activities? Explain in the context of U.S. exporters.

7. Managing imports in the United States is by and large more easy and less risky than managing exports? Give reasons why this is true.

8. What are gray markets? What are the factors that lead to the development of gray markets?

DISCUSSION QUESTIONS ◆

1. A friend of yours, who owns a small firm manufacturing and selling CD-ROM–based computer games, would like to market the company's products abroad. Your friend seeks information from you on the following:
   a. Which markets should the firm target (what sources of information to tap)?
   b. How should it tap these markets (what are the steps you would advise)?
   c. What are the direct and indirect costs involved in exports?
   d. What kind of assistance can he get from governmental and nongovernmental agencies at any of the stages involved?
   What would your advice be?

2. General trading companies have played and continue to play a leading role in the exports and imports of products from and to Japan. The effectiveness of these companies is evident from the fact that in the recent *Fortune 500* list of the world's largest corporations, five of the top ten corporations (including the top three) are Japanese trading firms. Although there is little question about the effectiveness of these firms, various business executives, especially outside Japan, interpret the directing of exports and imports through such firms as adding to significant inefficiencies in terms of higher costs and lost opportunities. Do you agree with this contention? Why or why not? The top three trading houses, Mitsubishi, Mitsui, and Itochu, had profitability ratios (profits after taxes / total revenues) of 0.18 percent, 0.17 percent, and 0.07 percent, respectively. Would this information have any bearing on your answer?

3. You are the manager for international operations of a manufacturer of steel in the United States. You have received an offer at a very attractive price to purchase 5,000 metric tons of wires rods (used to draw wires for the manufacture of nails) from a large nail manufacturer located in a developing country X. What would you deem to be the most appropriate choice of export terms of payment and terms of shipment, given the following information (include any precautions that you would take to ensure the successful execution of the order):
   a. The prospective importer has its account at a local bank. Local government rules stipulate making payments only through this bank.
   b. The local bank does not have any international operations/branches.
   c. The currency of country X has been extremely unstable, with its value having depreciated by more than 20 percent recently.
   d. The interest rates are extremely high in this country.
   e. The legal system is weak in this country, but the firm that is willing to place the order has a good reputation based on past experience with other international manufacturers.
   f. Rain and summer heat can cause the product to deteriorate if kept for a time longer than necessary.
   g. This country exports a larger amount by the sea route than it imports. Hence, many ships have to go empty to get cargo from this country to the United States.

4. Nontariff barriers to international trade have significant implications, both for exporters as well as for importers. One of the most prevalent nontariff barriers used is antidumping duties or the threat of initiating antidumping investigations. The use of antidumping duties has recently received some criticisms as affecting certain high-growth industries adversely, while protecting some smaller inefficient (as claimed) industries. One typical example quoted is the manufacture of laptop computers. Antidumping duties were levied against Japanese manufacturers of flat-panel screens (used in the manufacture of laptop computers) at the behest of would-be flat-panel manufacturers in the United States. It was the contention of these U.S. producers that if the flat panels were not dumped by Japanese manufacturers, the U.S. producers would be able to raise capital to initiate production of this product. As a result of the duties levied, which would have added significant costs to the computers manufactured in the United States, most U.S. manufacturers (many of whom had plans to manufacture laptop computers within the United States) shifted to sites abroad. According to the computer manufacturers, the antidumping decision sacrificed the fastest-growing segment of the computer industry to a nonexistent domestic flat-panel industry. The proponents of antidumping legislation, however, contend that the threat of predatory practices is real and antidumping procedures take care of this threat. Whom would you side with, the proponents or the critics of antidumping actions?

5. You are part of the management team of a U.S. computer manufacturer. Recently, the Texas distributors of the company's products have been complaining of

significant gray imports taking place from Mexico that is adversely affecting their margins. The main reason for gray imports is attributed to the recent volatility of the Mexican peso, especially the downward pressures on its value. What steps would you suggest to take care of the current problem? What would be your advice to curb gray marketing in the future?

FURTHER READINGS ◆

Bello, Daniel C., and Ritu Lohtia. "Export Channel Design: The Use of Foreign Distributors and Agents." *Journal of Academy of Marketing Science*, 23(2) (1995): 83–93.

Cavusgil, S. Tamer, and Ed Sikora. "How Multinationals Can Counter Gray Market Imports." *Columbia Journal of World Business*, 23(4) (1988): 75–85.

Cespedes, Frank V., E. Raymond Cooey, and V. Kasturi Rangan. "Gray Markets: Causes and Curses." *Harvard Business Review*, 66(4) (1988): 75-82.

Goldsmith, Howard R. *Import/Export: A Guide to Growth, Profits and Market Share*. Englewood Cliffs, N.J.: Prentice Hall, 1988.

Leonidou, Leonidas C., and Constantine S. Katsikeas. "The Export Development Process: An Integrative Review of Empirical Models." *Journal of International Business Studies*, 27(3) (1996): 517–51.

Pollard, Pey. *Exportise*. Boston: The Small Business Foundation of America Inc., 1983.

Russow, Lloyd C., and Andrew Solocha. "A Review of the Screening Process within the Context of the Global Assessment Process." *Journal of Global Marketing*, 7(1) (1993): 65–85.

U.S. Customs Service. *Importing Into the U.S.*, Rocklin, Calif.: U.S. Department of the Treasury. 1987.

_____. *A Basic Guide to Importing*. Lincolnwood, Ill.: U.S. Department of the Treasury, 1996.

Wells, L. Fargo, and Karin B. Dulat. *Exporting: from Start to Finance*. New York: McGraw Hill, 1991.

ORGANIZING GLOBAL MARKETING EFFORTS

18

HAPTER OVERVIEW

1. KEY CRITERIA IN GLOBAL ORGANIZATIONAL DESIGN
2. ORGANIZATIONAL DESIGN OPTIONS
3. GLOBAL TEAMWORK
4. LIFE CYCLE OF ORGANIZATIONAL STRUCTURES
5. TO CENTRALIZE OR DECENTRALIZE?
6. CONTROLLING GLOBAL MARKETING EFFORTS

As a company's commitment to global marketing increases, it needs to come up with an organizational setup that enables it to successfully meet the threats and opportunities posed by the global marketing arena. This chapter centers around the organizational issues that the global marketer must confront, like: What is the proper communication and reporting structure? Who within our organization should bear responsibility for each of the functions that need to be carried out? How can we as an organization leverage the competencies and skill of our individual subsidiaries? Where should the decision-making authority belong for the various areas?

We will first consider the major factors that will influence the design of a global organizational structure. Mutinational companies (MNCs) can choose from a wide variety of organizational structures. In this chapter, we will expose you to the major alternative configurations. We will also highlight the central role played by country managers within the MNC's organization. More and more companies recognize the potential benefits of international teams in coordinating the global operations. We will show you what roles teams can play in this regard. Environments are dynamic. Change requires flexibility. This chapter will look into different ways that MNCs can handle environmental changes. MNCs must also decide where the decision-making locus belongs. The challenge is to come up with a structure that bridges the gap between two forces: being responsive to local conditions and integrating your global marketing efforts. The final section focuses on control mechanisms companies can utilize to achieve their strategic goals.

◆ ◆ ◆ ◆ ◆ ◆ ## KEY CRITERIA IN GLOBAL ORGANIZATIONAL DESIGN

As with most other global managerial issues, there is no magic formula that prescribes the "ideal" organizational setup under a given set of circumstances. Yet, there are some factors that companies should consider when engineering their global organizational structure. In the following discussion, we make a distinction between environmental and firm-specific factors. Let us start with a look at the major environmental factors.

Environmental Factors

Competitive Environment. Global competitive pressures force MNCs to implement structures that facilitate quick decision making and alertness. In industries where competition is highly localized, a decentralized structure where most of the decision making is made at the country level is often appropriate. Nevertheless, even in such situations, MNCs can often benefit substantially from mechanisms that allow the company to leverage its global knowledge base.

Rate of Environmental Change. Drastic environmental change is a way of life in scores of industries. New competitors or substitutes for your product emerge. Existing competitors form or disband strategic alliances. Consumer needs worldwide constantly change. Businesses that are subject to rapid change require an organizational design that facilitates continuous scanning of the firm's global environment and swift responsiveness to opportunities or threats posed by that environment.

Regional Trading Blocs. Companies that operate within a regional trading bloc (e.g., the European Union, NAFTA, MERCOSUR) usually integrate to some extent their marketing efforts across the affiliates within the block area. A case in point is the European Union. In light of the European integration, numerous MNCs decided to rationalize their organizational structure. Many of these companies still maintain their local subsidiaries, but the locus of most decision making now lies with the Pan-European headquarters. As other trading blocs, such as Asia's APEC and South America's Mercosur, evolve toward the European model, one can expect similar makeovers in other regions.

Nature of Customers. The company's customer base also has a great impact on the MNC's desired organizational setup. Companies such as DHL, IBM, and AT & T that have a "global" clientele need to develop structures that permit a global reach and at the same time allow the company to stay "close" to their customers.

These are the major external drivers. We now turn to the prime firm-specific determinants.

Firm-Specific Factors

Strategic Importance of International Business. Typically, when overseas sales account for a very small fraction of the company's overall sales revenues, simple organizational structures (e.g., an export department) can easily handle the firm's global activities. As international sales grow, the organizational structure will evolve to mirror the growing importance of the firm's global activities. For instance, companies may start with an international division when they test the international waters. Once their overseas activities expand, they are likely to adopt an area-type (country- and/or region-based) structure.

Product Diversity. The diversity of the company's foreign product line is another key factor in shaping the company's organization. Companies with substantial product diversity tend to go for a global product division configuration.

Company Heritage. Differences in organizational structures within the same industry can also be explained via corporate culture. Nestlé and Unilever, for example, have always been highly decentralized MNCs. A lot of the decision-making authority has always been made at the local level. When Unilever realized that its marketing efforts required a more Pan-European approach to compete with the likes of Procter & Gamble, the company transformed its organization and revised its performance measures to provide incentives for a European focus. One of Unilever's senior executives, however, noted that the changeover "comes hard to people who for years have been in an environment where total business power was delegated to them."[1] As long as a given formula works, there is little incentive for companies to tinker with it. Revamping an organization to make the structure more responsive to new environmental realities can be a daunting challenge.

Quality of Local Managerial Skills. Decentralization could become a problem when local managerial talents are missing. Granted, companies can bring in expatriates, but this is typically an extremely expensive remedy that does not always work out. For instance, expatriate managers may find it hard to accommodate to the local environment.

ORGANIZATIONAL DESIGN OPTIONS ◆ ◆ ◆ ◆ ◆ ◆

The principal designs that firms can adopt to organize their global activities are:

- **International division.** Under this design, the company basically has two entities: the domestic division, which is responsible for the firm's domestic activities, and the international division, which is in charge of the company's international operations.
- **Product-based structure.** With a product structure the company's global activities are organized along its various product divisions.

---

[1]"Unilever Adopts Clean Sheet Approach," *The Financial Times* (October 21, 1991).

- **Geographic structure.** This is a setup where the company configures its organization along geographic areas: countries, regions, or some combination of these two levels.
- **Matrix organization.** This is an option where the company integrates two approaches—for instance, the product and geographic dimensions—so, there is a dual chain of command.

We will now consider each of these options in greater detail. At the end of this section, we will also discuss the so-called **networked** organization model.

International Division Structure

Most companies that engage in global marketing will initially start off by establishing an export department. Once international sales reach a threshold, the company might set up a full-blown international division. The charter of the international division is to develop and coordinate the firm's global operations. The unit also scans market opportunities in the global marketplace. In most cases, the division has equal standing with the other divisions within the company.

This option is most suitable for companies whose product line is not too diverse and does not require a large amount of adaptation to local country needs. It is also a viable alternative for companies whose business is still primarily focused on the domestic market. Over time, as international marketing efforts become more important to the firm, most companies tend to switch to a more globally oriented organizational structure.

Global Product Division Structure

The second option centers around the different product lines or strategic business units (SBUs) of the company. Each product division, being a separate profit center, is responsible for managing worldwide the activities for its product line. This alternative is especially popular among high-tech companies with highly complex products or MNCs with a very diversified product portfolio. The approach is adopted by Ericsson, John Deere and Sun Microsystems (see Exhibit 18-1), for instance. Ford, the world's second largest car maker, recently shifted toward a product division setup. In 1994, Ford reorganized itself through five vehicle program centers, four in North America and one in Europe. Product development, manufacturing, purchasing, and marketing are planned to become fully integrated within the five centers. By integrating these efforts, Ford hopes to eliminate duplication.[2] Global Perspective 18-1 describes how Whirlpool implemented the global SBU approach for its microwave ovens and air treatment products.

There are several benefits associated with a global product structure. The product focus offers the company a large degree of flexibility in terms of cross-country resource allocation and strategic planning. For instance, market penetration efforts in recently entered markets can be cross-subsidized by profits generated in developed markets. In many companies, a global product structure goes in tandem with consolidated manufacturing and distribution operations. This approach is exemplified by Honeywell, the U.S. maker of control tools, which has set up centers of excellence

---

[2]"Tomorrow, the World," *The Financial Times* (April 22, 1994), p. 15.

EXHIBIT 18-1
THREE EXAMPLES OF A GLOBAL PRODUCT STRUCTURE

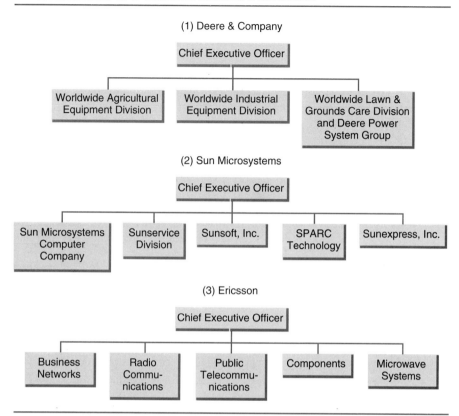

(1) Deere & Company

Chief Executive Officer

- Worldwide Agricultural Equipment Division
- Worldwide Industrial Equipment Division
- Worldwide Lawn & Grounds Care Division and Deere Power System Group

(2) Sun Microsystems

Chief Executive Officer

- Sun Microsystems Computer Company
- Sunservice Division
- Sunsoft, Inc.
- SPARC Technology
- Sunexpress, Inc.

(3) Ericsson

Chief Executive Officer

- Business Networks
- Radio Communications
- Public Telecommunications
- Components
- Microwave Systems

that span the globe.[3] That way, an MNC can achieve substantial scale economies in the area of production and logistics, thereby improving the firm's competitive cost position. Another appeal is that global product structures facilitate the development of a global strategic focus to cope with challenges posed by global players.[4]

The shortcomings of a product division are not insignificant. Lack of communication and coordination among the various product divisions could lead to needless duplication of tasks. A relentless product-driven orientation can distract the company from local market needs. The global product division system has also been criticized for scattering the global resources of the company.[5] Instead of sharing resources and creating a global know-how pool, international resources and expertise get fragmented. A too-narrow focus on the product area will lead to a climate where companies fail to grasp the synergies that might exist between global product divisions.

---

[3]Honeywell, 1995 *Annual Report.*

[4]W. H. Davidson and P. Haspeslagh, "Shaping a Global Product Organization," *Harvard Business Review* (July-August 1982), pp. 125–32.

[5]Ibid., p. 129.

WHIRLPOOL'S GLOBAL BUSINESS UNITS

Whirlpool has managed its worldwide operations principally through a regional business unit structure. Microwave ovens and air treatment products (e.g., room air conditioners, dehumidifiers) have become such global products that Whirlpool established two product-oriented business units. These units are responsible for product planning, development, manufacturing, and distribution on a global basis. The regional business units continue to be in charge of sales and marketing.

The Global Microwave Oven Business Unit was launched in mid-1994, based on a manufacturing facility in Norrköping, Sweden, and a joint venture in Shunde, China. The Shunde facility offers low-cost, large-scale production capability, while the Norrköping plant offers leading-edge technology. Swedish and Chinese engineers were rotated between the two facilities to integrate the two units and to address quality, logistics, and procurement issues.

The Global Air Treatment Business Unit was formed in fall 1995 after the creation of a Shenzen-based Chinese joint venture. Also for this SBU, Whirlpool exchanged staff between the Tennessee facility and the Chinese unit to foster global integration.

Source: Whirlpool Corporation, *1995 Annual Report.*

Geographic Structure

The third option is the geographic structure, where the MNC is organized along geographic units. The units might be individual countries or regions. In many cases, MNCs use a combination of country-based subsidiaries and regional headquarters. There are other variants. Coca-Cola, for instance, has five different regions, each one of them being further divided into subregions, as is shown in Exhibit 18-2. Area structures are especially appealing to companies that market closely related product lines with very similar end-users and applications around the world.

Country-Based Subsidiaries. Scores of MNCs set up subsidiaries on a country-by-country basis. To some degree, such an organization reflects the marketing concept. By setting up country affiliates, the MNC can stay in close touch with the local market conditions. The firm can thereby easily spot and swiftly respond to local market developments.

Country-focused organizations have several serious handicaps, though. They tend to be costly. Coordination with corporate headquarters and among subsidiaries can easily become extremely cumbersome. A country focus often leads to a not-invented-here mentality that hinders cross-fertilization. Some critics of the country model derisively refer to it as a mini-United Nations with a multitude of local fiefs run by scores of country managers.[6] Kenichi Ohmae sums up the weaknesses of the country structure as follows:

> One of the prime difficulties of organizing a company for global operations is the psychology of managers who are used to thinking by country-based line of authority rather than by line of opportunity. Lots of creative ideas for generating value are overlooked because such managers are captive to nation state-conditioned habits of mind. Once that

---

[6]Though some of the major MNCs operate in more countries than the number of UN member states.

EXHIBIT 18-2
THE COCA-COLA COMPANY: EXAMPLES OF A GEOGRAPHIC STRUCTURE

Operating Officers

Africa Group
President
    North Africa Division
    Southern Africa Division

Middle and Far East Group
President
    Middle East Division
    Southeast and West Asia Division
    South Pacific Division
    China Division
    North Pacific Division
    Philippines Division

Latin America Group
President
    Brazil Division
    Coca-Cola Interamerican
    River Plate Division
    North Latin America Division
    Central America and Caribbean Division
    Andean Division

Greater Europe Group
President
    Nordic and Northern Eurasia Division
    Northwest European Division
    East Central European Division
    Iberian Division
    Central Mediterranean Division
    German Division
    Coca-Cola G.m.b.H.

Coca-Cola Foods
President

North America Group
President
    Coca-Cola Operations
    Coca-Cola Fountain
    Coca-Cola Ltd., Canada

Source: The Coca-Cola Company, *1995 Annual Report.*

constraint is relaxed . . . a nearly infinite range of new opportunities comes into focus: building cross-border alliances, establishing virtual companies, arbitraging differential costs of labor or even services . . . . I strongly believe that, as head-to-head battles within established geographies yield less and less incremental value, changing the battle-ground from nation to cross-border region will be at the core of twenty-first century corporate strategy.[7]

New Role of Country Managers.

Corporate strategy gurus like Ohmae foresee the demise of the country manager. According to their opinion, the role of the country manager of the twenty-first century will be minimal.[8] Several forces are held responsible for this change of affairs.[9]

- The threats posed by global competitors who turn the global marketplace into a global chess-game
- The growing prominence of global customers who often develop their sourcing strategies and make their purchase decisions on a global (or pan-regional) basis

---

[7]Kenichi Ohmae, *The End of the Nation State. The Rise of Regional Economies* (New York: The Free Press, 1995), p. 112.

[8]Ibid., p. 115.

[9]John A. Quelch, "The New Country Managers," *The McKinsey Quarterly* (1992), pp. 155–165.

- The rise of regional trading blocs that facilitate the integration of manufacturing and logistics facilities but also open up arbitrage opportunities for gray marketers

At the same time, there are several developments that create a need for strong country managers.[10] Nurturing good links with local governments and other entities (e.g., the European Union) becomes increasingly crucial. Local customers are still the lion's share of most companies' clientele. Local competitors sometimes pose a far bigger threat than global rivals. In many emerging markets, strong local brands often have a much more loyal following than regional or global brands. Many winning new-product or communication ideas come from local markets rather than regional or corporate headquarters.

To strike the balance between these countervailing forces, country managers of the twenty-first century should fit any of the following five profiles, depending on the nature of the local market:[11]

- The **trader** who establishes a beachhead in a new market or heads a recently acquired local distributor. Traders should have an entrepreneurial spirit. Their roles include sales and marketing, scanning the environment for new ideas, gathering intelligence on the competition.
- The **builder** who develops local markets. Builders are entrepreneurs who are willing to be part of regional or global strategy teams.
- The **cabinet member** who is a team player with profit and loss responsibility for a small- to medium-sized country. Team-manship is key here, since marketing efforts may require a great deal of cross-border coordination, especially for global and pan-regional brands. Major strategic decisions are often made at the regional level rather than by the country subsidiary.
- The **ambassador** who is in charge of large and/or strategic markets. His responsibilities include handling government relations, integrating acquisitions and strategic alliances, coordinating activities across SBUs. Ideally a seasoned manager, the ambassador should be somebody who is able to manage a large staff. For instance, Asea Brown Boveri, a Swiss/Swedish consortium, views the tasks of its Asia-based country managers as "to exploit fully the synergies between our businesses in the countries, to develop customer-based strategies, to build and strengthen relationships with local customers, governments, and communities."[12]
- The **representative** in large, mature markets whose tasks include handling government relations and legal compliance.

Regional Structures. Many MNCs that do not feel entirely comfortable with a pure country-based organization opt for a region-based structure with regional headquarters. To some extent, a regional structure offers a compromise between a completely centralized organization and the country-focused organization. The intent

---

[10]John A. Quelch and Helen Bloom, "The Return of the Country Manager," *The McKinsey Quarterly* (1996), pp. 30–43.

[11]Ibid., pp. 38–39.

[12]Gordon Redding, "ABB—The Battle for the Pacific," *Long Range Planning*, 28 (1)(1995), pp. 92–94.

behind most region-based structures is to address two concerns: lack of responsiveness of HQ to local market conditions and parochialism among local country managers. In more and more industries, markets tend to cluster around regions rather than national boundaries. In some cases, the regions are formal trading blocs like the European Union or NAFTA that allow almost complete free movement of goods across borders. In other cases, the clusters tend to be more culture-driven.

A recent survey done in the Pacific region singles out five distinct roles for regional headquarters:[13]

- **Scouting.** The RHQ serves as a listening post to scan new opportunities and initiate new ventures.

- **Strategic stimulation.** The RHQ functions as a "switchboard" between the product divisions and the country managers. It helps the SBUs in understanding the regional environment.

- **Signaling commitment.** By establishing an RHQ, the MNC signals a commitment to the region that the company is serious about doing business in that region.

- **Coordination.** Often the most important role of the RHQ is to coordinate strategic and tactical decisions across the region. Areas of cohesion include developing pan-regional communication campaigns in regions with a lot of media overlap, price coordination in markets where parallel imports pose a threat, and consolidation of manufacturing and logistics operations.

- **Pooling resources.** Certain support and administrative tasks are often done more efficiently at the regional level instead of locally. RQH might fulfill support functions like after-sales services, product development, and market research.

Matrix Structure

Imposing a single-dimensional (product, country, or function-based) management structure on complex global issues is often a recipe for disaster. In the wake of the serious shortcomings of the geographic- or product-based structures, several MNCs have opted for a matrix organization. The matrix structure explicitly recognizes the multidimensional nature of global strategic decision making. With a matrix organization, two dimensions are integrated in the organization. For instance, the matrix might consist of geographic areas and business divisions. The geographic units are in charge for all product lines within their area. The product divisions have worldwide responsibility for their product line. So, there is a dual chain of command, with managers reporting to two superiors.

A typical example is Siemens AG, the German engineering conglomerate. Siemens uses a matrix that focuses on the business and geographic dimensions, as is illustrated in Exhibit 18-3. The Siemens group consists of around fourteen different business groups, each being a profit center of its own. The country organizations—the so-called LG's (*Landgesellschaft*)—also represent individual profit centers. The overall structure is overseen by a company board. Some operations such as finance are run at the corporate level.

---

[13]Philippe Lasserre, "Regional Headquarters: The Spearhead for Asia Pacific Markets," *Long Range Planning,* 29 (February 1996), pp. 30–37.

EXHIBIT 18-3
SIEMENS: EXAMPLE OF A MATRIX STRUCTURE

The Company

Groups				Managing Board	Corporate Departments	Corporate Offices

Managing Board

Groups				Corporate Departments	Corporate Offices
Power Generation (KWU)	Power Transmission and Distribution (EV)	Industrial and Building Systems (ANL)	Drives and Standard Products (ASI)	Finance (ZF)	Corporate Communications (UK)
Automation (AUT)	Public Communication Networks (ON)	Private Communications Systems (PN)	Defense Electronics (SI)	Research and Development (ZFE)	Economics and Corporate Relations (WPA)
Transportation Systems (VT)	Automotive Systems (AT)	Medical Engineering (Med)	Semiconductors (HL)	Human Resources (ZP)	Corporate Services Infrastructure Services (ID)
Passive Components and Electron Tubes (PR)	Electromechanical Components (EC)	Special Division Network Systems (VS)		Production and Logistics (ZPL)	Personnel Services (PD)
Separate legal units Siemens Nixdorf Informations systems AG, (SNI)	Osram GmbH			Planning and Development (ZU)	
Regional organization					

Source: Siemens, 1995 Annual Report.

Sometimes, the MNC might even set up a three-dimensional structure (geography, function, and business area). The various dimensions do not always carry equal weight. For instance, at Siemens the locus of control is shifting more and more toward the business areas.

There are two major advantages of the matrix structure.[14] Matrices reflect the growing complexities of the global market arena. In most industries MNCs face global *and* local competitors; global *and* local customers; global *and* local distributors. In that sense, the matrix structure facilitates the MNC's need to "think globally and act locally"—to be *glocal*—or, in Unilever's terminology, to be a *multi-local multinational*. The other appeal of the matrix organization is that, in principle at least, it fosters a team spirit and cooperation among business area managers, country managers and/or functional managers on a global basis.

In spite of these benefits, British Petroleum and Imperial Chemical Industries have disbanded their matrix structure. Others, such as IBM and Dow Chemical, have streamlined their matrix setup.[15] There are several reasons why matrix structures have lost their appeal among many MNCs. Dual (or triple) reporting and profit responsibilities frequently lead to conflicts or confusion. For instance, a product division might concentrate its resources and attention on a few major markets, thereby upsetting the country managers of the MNC's smaller markets. Another shortcoming of the matrix is bureaucratic bloat. Very often, the decision-making process gets bogged down, thereby discouraging swift responsiveness toward competitive attacks in the local markets. Overlap among divisions often triggers tensions, power clashes, and turf battles.[16]

The four organizational structures that we covered so far are the standard structures adopted by most MNCs. The simplicity of the one-dimensional structures and the shortcomings of the matrix model have led several companies to look for better solutions. Below, we discuss one of the more popular forms: the **networked organization.**

The Global Network Solution

Global networking is one solution that has been suggested to cope with the shortcomings associated with the classical hierarchical organization structures. The network model is an attempt to reconcile the tension between two opposing forces: the need for local responsiveness and the wish to be an integrated whole.[17] Strictly speaking, the network approach is not a formal structure but a mindset. That is, a company might still formally adopt, say, a *matrix* structure, but at the same time develop a global network. The networked global organization is sometimes also referred to as a **transnational.**[18]

---

[14]Thomas H. Naylor, "The International Strategy Matrix," *Columbia Journal of World Business* (Summer 1985), pp. 11–19.

[15]"End of a Corporate Era," *The Financial Times* (March 30, 1995), p. 15.

[16]Christopher A. Bartlett and Sumantra Ghoshal, "Matrix Management, Not a Structure, a Frame of Mind," *Harvard Business Review* (July-August 1990), pp. 138–45.

[17]Christopher A. Bartlett and Sumantra Ghoshal, "Organizing for Worldwide Effectiveness: The Transnational Solution," *California Management Review* (Fall 1988), pp. 54–74.

[18]Ibid.

EXHIBIT 18-4
A NEW ORGANIZATIONAL METAPHOR

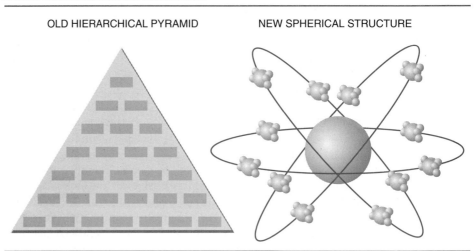

OLD HIERARCHICAL PYRAMID   NEW SPHERICAL STRUCTURE

Source: Raymond E. Miles and Charles C. Snow, "The New Network Firm: A Spherical Structure Built on a Human Investment Philosophy." Reprinted by permission of the publisher, from ORGANIZATIONAL DYNAMICS SPRING 1995 © 1995. American Management Organization, New York. All rights reserved.

According to advocates of the network model, MNCs should develop processes and linkages that allow each unit to tap into a global knowledge pool. A good metaphor for the global network is the atom (see Exhibit 18-4). At the center is a common knowledge base. Each national unit can be viewed as a source of ideas, skills, capabilities, and knowledge that can be harnessed for the benefit of the total organization.[19]

Ideally, the entire global organization functions as a "sphere." When one unit within the organization anywhere around the world faces a problem or an opportunity, the sphere rotates, thereby giving the unit immediate access to the company's global resource and expertise pool.[20]

Asea Brown Boveri (ABB), the Swiss-Swedish engineering consortium, is often touted as a prime example of a global networking.[21] Percy Barnevik, former CEO and one of the major forces behind ABB's reorganization, describes ABB's vision as follows:

> Our vision was to create a truly global company that knows no borders, has many home countries and offers opportunities for all nationalities. While we strived for size to benefit from economies of scale and scope, our vision was also to avoid the stigma of the big company with a large headquarters and stifling bureaucracy, countless volumes of instruc-

---

[19]Christopher A. Bartlett, "Building and Managing the Transnational: The New Organizational Challenge," in *Competition in Global Industries*, Michael E. Porter, ed. (Boston: Harvard Business School Press, 1986), pp. 367–401.

[20]Raymond E. Miles and Charles C. Snow, "The New Network Firm: A Spherical Structure Built on a Human Investment Philosophy," *Organizational Dynamics*, v. 23, n. 4 (Spring 1995) pp. 4–18.

[21]William Taylor, "The Logic of Global Business: An Interview with ABB's Percy Barnevik," *Harvard Business Review* (March-April 1991), pp. 91–105.

tions, turf defenders and people working far from their customers. With our thousands of profit centers close to customers we wanted to create a small company culture with its huge advantages of flexibility, speed and the power to free up the creative potential of each employee.[22]

There are several mechanisms to develop the required vision and cement the necessary linkages. One approach to which we will return shortly is the international teaming concept. The charter of the international management team might cover areas such as communicating the overall corporate vision ("missionary" work so to speak), new product development, technology transfer, strategy development, and so forth. ABB uses a company "bible" to tie together the different companies within its organization. ABB's bible describes the firm's mission and values, the long-term objectives, and guidelines on how to behave internally.[23] Heineken NV, the Dutch beer brewery, uses a set of *Rules and Guidelines* to cement the ties between its local operations. Rules for the Heineken brand cover the product formula, the use of its brand identity, its positioning, and procedures to maintain consistency in the brand's communication strategies. Less strict guidelines cover pricing, packaging, promotions, and so on.[24] Global Perspective 18-2 describes the efforts that 3M, the U.S. multinational, undertook in the early 1990s to revamp its European organization by setting up a network of "European Business Centers" (EBCs).

* *

ℊLOBAL PERSPECTIVE 18-2

3M'S EUROPEAN BUSINESS CENTERS

In 1993 3M, the U.S.-based multinational best known for its Post-it notes, revamped its European organization. The reorganization consisted of two major steps. First, to bolster cross-border effectiveness and speed up decision-making, 3M shifted most strategic and operational responsibilities from its local subsidiaries and brought them under the umbrella of nineteen product divisions. These units are known as "European Business Centers" (EBCs). The second move was to consolidate the remaining tasks (e.g., staff development, IT, finance, logistics) into ten European "regions." Three of these represent single markets, namely, France, Germany, and Italy. The remaining

seven encompass a cluster of countries (e.g., Iberian countries, Nordic countries).

The regional heads have equal rank to the EBC managing directors. Each country still has a full-time country manager to ensure 3M's local responsiveness. The EBCs are spread across five countries. Most of the EBCs were established in those countries with the biggest manufacturing site for a particular product area. For instance, chemicals went to Antwerp, computer disks went to France, and so on. Each EBC also has a core team with members of various nationalities. The teams' responsibilities are to visit customers and transfer product expertise across countries. In view of modern communications tools, 3M also decided to minimize the need for staff relocations. Therefore, most of the EBC team members remained stationed in their home country.

Source: "Here, There and Everywhere," *The Financial Times* (November 10, 1993), p. 11. Reprinted with permission.

[22]Asea Brown Boveri, 1995 *Annual Report*, p. 5.

[23]Manfred F.R. Kets de Vries, "Making a Giant Dance," *Across the Board* (October 1994), pp. 27–32.

[24]Karel Vuursteen, "Decision Making at Heineken," *Marketing and Research Today* (February 1996), pp. 42–45.

EXHIBIT 18-5
THE HUMAN INVESTMENT PHILOSOPHY

ASSUMPTIONS

1. Most people want to contribute to the organization and will act as partners in their own development. They also have the potential to continually develop their technical skills, their self-management competency, and their understanding of business matters.
2. Most people, both inside the network firm and across current and future partner firms, are trustworthy as well as trusting in their relationships. They can and will develop effective "relationship management" skills.

POLICIES:

1. Managers must view human capabilities from the perspective of an internal venture capitalist, building organization members' operational and entrepreneurial strengths by investing in their long-term education and competence.
2. Managers must act as a partner of individual employees and self-managing teams in locating opportunities to practice new skills and exercise new knowledge.
3. Managers must be prepared to make investments in technical and governance skills within other network-member firms.

EXPECTATIONS

1. Continuing, heavy investment in human capabilities builds adaptive capacity through the creation of widespread skill and knowledge reserves—a learning organization.
2. The more competent the manager's own organization, the more facile and effective are the network linkages it can make.

Source: Raymond E. Miles and Charles C. Snow, "The New Network Firm: A Spherical Structure Built on a Human Investment Philosophy." Reprinted by permission of the publisher, from ORGANIZATIONAL DYNAMICS SPRING 1995 © 1995. American Management Organization, New York. All rights reserved.

Miles and Snow suggest that global networking is typically coupled with a human investment philosophy that centers around three dimensions: a set of basic assumptions about people, managerial policies, and certain expectations.[25] These three pillars are described in Exhibit 18-5.

◆ ◆ ◆ ◆ ◆ ◆ GLOBAL TEAM-WORK

MNCs increasingly rely on international teamwork to coordinate their global or pan-regional strategies and operations. International teams often provide the "glue" for network organizations to function properly. Global Perspective 18-2 discusses how 3M set up core teams to implement its European Business Centers model. Kraft General Foods Europe (KGFE) set up eight "core teams" to foster cross-border collaboration. The teams cover KGFE's major product categories. Each team is headed by a coordinator based in Munich, Kraft's European headquarters, who identifies key issues, prepares research, and guides debates. Each core team meets three times per year. One of the principal goals of KGFE's core teams is to "get marketing people to focus on big new ideas and meaty projects, rather than on window dressing like minor line extensions."[26]

---

[25]Miles and Snow, pp. 10–15.

[26]"Cross-border Kraftsmen," *The Financial Times* (June 17, 1993).

EXHIBIT 18-6
A FOUR-STAGE TEAM-BUILDING PROCESS

Stage 1	**Forming the Team**
	• Company investment of HR department resources in team development
	• Senior management sponsorship
	• Use of diagnostic instruments to determine team resources
	• Understanding of business context and objectives
Stage 2	**Focusing the Team and Its Mission**
	• Team-building exercises
	• Development of team mission and norms
	• Clarification of objectives and performance measures
	• Cultural sensitivity intervention
Stage 3	**Maintaining the Team**
	• Group memory (visual record of agreements and action plans)
	• Transfer of facilitation skills to team members
	• Time spent practicing to become a better team
	• Continual update with sponsor
Stage 4	**Transfering Learning Throughout the Organization**
	• Celebrate, publicize, and reward success
	• Review group process with team and sponsor
	• Use of diagnostic instruments to determine team resources
	• Transfer learning to other teams and facilitators

Source: Charles C. Snow, Sue C. Davison, Scott A. Snell, and Donald C. Humbrick, "Use Transnational Teams to Globalize Your Company." Reprinted by permission of the publisher, from ORGANIZATIONAL DYNAMICS SPRING 1996 © 1996. American Management Organization, New York. All rights reserved.

The international team-building process can proceed through four stages, as shown in Exhibit 18-6. The first step is the launch of the international team. Each project is assigned a sponsor who will be the key channel with corporate headquarters. Ideally, the team should also have a facilitator. The second stage focuses on the team's mission statement. At this stage, the team also spells out each member's roles, team norms, and performance measures. The third stage, which takes place several years down the road, is the maintenance step. Team membership might change over the years. Hence, it is crucial that team skills and knowledge get transferred across team members. The fourth and final stage is to transfer learning throughout the organization, including other teams.[27]

MNCs create international teams for a multitude of reasons.[28] Teams are often formed to coordinate global strategy development and implementation efforts. International teams can also be effective in building up ties between headquarters (corporate or regional) and the local subsidiaries, thereby bridging the gap between the need for local responsiveness and global integration. The goal of the teams could

[27]Charles C. Snow, Sue C. Davison, Scott A. Snell, and Donald C. Hambrick, "Use Transnational Teams to Globalize Your Company," *Organizational Dynamics* (Spring 1996), pp. 50–67.

[28]Thomas Gross, Ernie Turner, and Lars Cederholm, "Building Teams for Global Operations," *Management Review* (June 1987), pp. 32–36.

EXHIBIT 18-7
LEADERSHIP ROLES AND TEAM DEVELOPMENT

Team Startup	**Advocacy Skills**
	• Building team legitimacy
	• Linking team mission and company strategy
	• Networking to obtain resources
	• "Bureaucracy busting"—eliminating old routines, facilitating experimentation, and knowledge dissemination
Team Evolution	**Catalytic Skills**
	• Working with external constituents
	• Differentiating individual roles and responsibilities
	• Building commitment
	• Rewarding members for valuable contributions
Team Maturity	**Integrative Skills**
	• Emphasizing excellence and accomplishment
	• Coordinating and problem solving
	• Measuring progress and results

Source: Charles C. Snow, Sue C. Davison, Scott A. Snell, and Donald C. Humbrick, "Use Transnational Teams to Globalize Your Company." Reprinted by permission of the publisher, from ORGANIZATIONAL DYNAMICS SPRING 1996 © 1996. American Management Organization, New York. All rights reserved.

simply be to establish communication channels between headquarters and the subsidiaries. The team's mandate might also include the transfer of technologies or skills in the various areas to the firm's subsidiaries. As shown in Exhibit 18-7, the team's roles will evolve depending on its life cycle.[29] Early on, **advocacy** skills (e.g., networking) matter most to defend the legitimacy of the team's charter and to define the strategic intent of the team. Once the team evolves, **catalytic** skills become useful, like encouraging team members to generate ideas. As the team matures, **integrative** skills are critical: coordinating activities, transferring knowledge, delegating tasks to the subsidiaries, and so on.

◆ ◆ ◆ ◆ ◆ ◆ **LIFE CYCLE OF ORGANIZATIONAL STRUCTURES**

A drastic change in the MNC's environment or internal circumstances sometimes requires a rethinking of the ideal way to organize the firm's global operations. In some cases companies have moved from one extreme to another before finding a suitable configuration. A case in point is Kraft General Foods Europe (KGFE).[30] In the early 1980s, KGFE tried to impose uniform marketing strategies across Europe. This attempt led to so much ill-will among KGFE's local units that Kraft soon abandoned its centralized system. It was replaced by a loose system where country managers developed their own marketing strategies for all Kraft brands, including the regional (e.g., Miracoli pasta) and global brands (e.g., Philadelphia cream cheese). Not surprisingly, this system created a great deal of inconsistency in the marketing strategies

---

[29]Snow et al., pp. 55–60.
[30]"Cross-border Kraftsmen."

used. More recently, in the early 1990s, KGFE introduced a system of core teams. With the new setup, KGFE hopes to be able to coordinate its marketing operations across Europe while still remaining alert to local market peculiarities. Global Perspective 18-3 reports the overhaul Royal Dutch Shell recently undertook to streamline its global operations.

Several management theorists have made an attempt to come up with the "right" fit between the MNC's environment (internal and external) and the organizational setup. One of the more popular schemas is the stages model shown in Exhibit 18-8 which was developed by Stopford and Wells.[31] The schema shows the relationship between the organizational structure, foreign product diversity, and the importance of foreign sales to the company (as a share of total sales). According to their model, when companies first explore the global marketplace they start off with an international division. As foreign sales expand without an increase in the firm's foreign product assortment diversity, the company will most likely switch to a geographic area structure. If instead the diversity of the firm's foreign product line substantially increases, it might organize itself along global product lines. Finally, when both product diversity and international sales grow significantly, MNCs tend to adopt a two-dimensional matrix structure.

Several scholars have criticized the Stopford–Wells staged model. First, the model is a purely descriptive representation of how MNCs develop over time based on an analysis of U.S.-based MNCs. So, it would be misleading to apply the frame-

◆ ◆

*G*LOBAL PERSPECTIVE 18-3

THE REVAMPING OF ROYAL DUTCH SHELL

Royal Dutch Shell, reportedly the world's largest oil company, drastically reorganized itself during 1995. Before Shell's reorganization the company used a three-dimensional matrix structure. Each country had its own unit and managers who reported back to the corporate headquarters. Shell was also split along its different activities (exploration, chemicals, refining, etc.). These operations were backed up by central companies that offered the various support services.

Under the new structure (see Exhibit 18-9 on p. 541), Shell is built around four business organizations—

Exploration and Production, Oil Products (covering refining, trading, shipping, and marketing), Chemicals, and Gas and Coal. These business organizations offer guidance, advice, and services to the operating (country) units. A "Committee of Managing Directors" makes the broad strategic and investment decisions. Tactical decisions, however, are still made by the local country managers. The corporate center, business organizations, and operating companies can draw on the expertise and advice of the service companies in areas such as finance, legal matters, and information technology.

The driving force behind these changes was a desire to adequately reflect the different kinds of decisions that need to be made. The heads of the operating companies need a lot of authority for decisions that affect their local markets. Strategic issues that have an impact on the group as a whole will be tackled by the business organizations.

Sources: "Barons Swept Out of Fiefdoms," *The Financial Times* (March 30, 1995), p. 15 and The "Shell" Transport and Trading Company, p.l.c., *Annual Report* 1995.

---

[31]John M. Stopford and Louis T. Wells, Jr., *Managing the Multinational Enterprise: Organization of the Firm and Ownership of the Subsidiary* (New York: Basic Books, 1972).

EXHIBIT 18-8
STOPFORD'S INTERNATIONAL STRUCTURAL STAGES MODEL

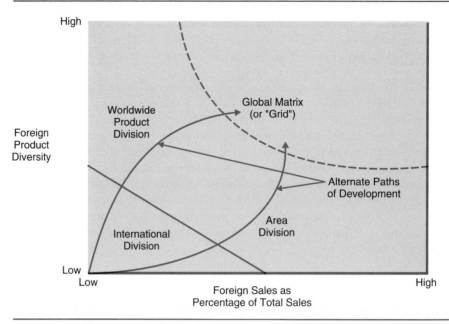

Source: Reprinted by permission of Harvard Business School Press. From: Christopher A. Bartlett, "Building and Managing the Transnational: The New Organizational Challenge," in *Competition in Global Industries*, M. E. Porter (Ed.). Boston, MA 1987, p. 368. Copyright © 1986 by the President and Fellows of Harvard College.

work in a prescriptive manner, as several people have done.[32] Second, the structure of the organization is only one aspect of a global organization. Other, equally important, components are the mindsets of the managers and managerial processes. The MNC's environment is dynamic; it changes all the time. Thus, fit between the environment and the MNC's organizational structure is not enough. Global organizations also need flexibility.[33]

An in-depth study of a sample of ten successful U.S.-based MNCs shows that the key challenge for MNCs is building and sustaining the right management process instead of looking for the proper organizational structure.[34] According to the study, the installation of such a process moves through three stages. The first step is to recognize the complexity of the MNC's environment. Country and regional managers must look at strategic issues from multiple perspectives—a **glocal mindset,** so to speak. During the second stage, the company introduces communication channels and decision-making platforms to facilitate more flexibility. In the final stage, the MNC develops a corporate culture that fosters collaborative thinking and decision

---

[32]Bartlett 1986, "pp. 367–401.

[33]Sumantra Ghoshal and Nitin Nohria, "Horses for Courses: Organizational Forms for Multinational Corporations," *Sloan Management Review* (Winter 1993), pp. 23–35.

[34]Christopher A. Bartlett, "MNCs: Get Off the Reorganization Merry-Go-Round," *Harvard Business Review* (March-April 1983), pp. 138–146.

Exhibit 18-9
SHELL'S NEW ORGANIZATIONAL STRUCTURE

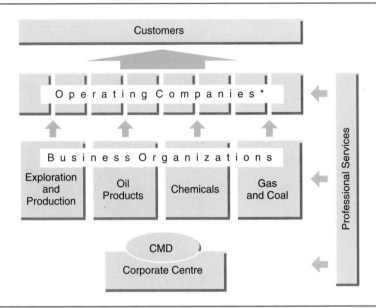

Source: The "Shell" Transport and Trading Company p.l.c., *1995 Annual Report.*

making. Such an agenda might include activities such as formulating common goals and values, developing reward systems, and evaluation criteria that encourage a cooperative spirit, providing role models.

To Centralize or Decentralize?

Power sharing between headquarters and local business units is a delicate but extremely important matter. Roughly speaking, companies can move into two opposite directions. With decentralized organizations the national operating companies are highly autonomous. Each one of the local units represents a profit center. Corporate headquarters may provide guidance and advice, but when push comes to shove, it is the local subsidiary that makes the decisions. Peter Brabeck-Letmathe, Nestlé's CEO, describes the decision-making process within his company as follows:

> We respond to what the local market says, and they may take another look and change their mind. But if they don't want something, we don't force them. We might send a couple of people to offer encouragement, but that's as far as it goes.[35]

Centralized organizations, on the other hand, consolidate most decision-making power at corporate headquarters. In practice, most MNCs are somewhere between these two extremes: certain tasks like finance and R & D are typically centralized, other tasks like pricing and advertising are the realm of the local subsidiaries. As is il-

---

[35]Andrew J. Parsons, "Nestlé: The Visions of Local Managers," *The McKinsey Quarterly,* no. 2 (1996), pp. 5–29.

EXHIBIT 18-10
NEW FORCES IMPACT ON INTEGRATION/DIFFERENTIATION

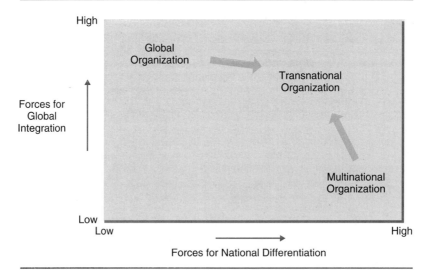

Reprinted by permission of Harvard Business School Press. From: Christopher A. Bartlett, "Building and Managing the Transnational: The New Organizational Challenge," in *Competition in Global Industries*, M. E. Porter (Ed.). Boston, MA 1987, p. 377. Copyright © 1986 by the President and Fellows of Harvard College.

lustrated in Exhibit 18-10, forces for global integration such as global brands, global customers, and scale economies push companies toward globalized decision making. Drivers toward local responsiveness favor a local autonomy approach. The two forces can jointly have a high impact. Under such conditions, a **transnational** solution is needed, where companies strike a delicate balance between centralization and decentralization.

Recently, several management theorists have offered **federalism** as a way to combine the autonomy of the local units with the benefits of coordination.[36] MNCs that follow this model share the following characteristics:[37]

- **Noncentralization.** Power is diffused. It belongs to the local units. Power cannot be taken away unilaterally by corporate headquarters. Charles Handy, a longtime preacher of federalism, notes that federal organizations are decentralized *and* centralized.[38]

- **Negotianalism.** Decisions are made via a bargaining process. Each local unit has a voice. Each local unit is listened to.

---

[36]See, for instance, Charles Handy, "Balancing Corporate Power: A New Federalist Paper," *Harvard Business Review* (November-December 1992), pp. 59–72.

[37]James O'Toole and Warren Bennis, "Our Federalist Future: The Leadership Imperative," *California Management Review* (Summer 1992), pp. 73–90.

[38]Barbara Ettorre, "A Conversation With Charles Handy. On the Future of Work and an End to the "Century of the Organization," *Organizational Dynamics* (Summer 1996), pp. 15–26.

- **Constitutionalism.** Another feature is that many of these companies often have a "constitution," like Asea Brown Boveri's company bible that we mentioned earlier.

- **Territoriality.** There are clear boundary markers based on geography or business areas.

- **Balance of power.** Federations seek balance of power between headquarters and units and among units.

- **Autonomy.** The units are self-governing. They can experiment with new ideas as long as they respect the principles spelled out in the company's constitution. As a result, a proper-working federal organization enables the company to gather the benefits of "big" and "small" companies.

What do companies do in practice? Exhibit 18-11 summarizes the results of a 1992 survey conducted in Europe on the different types of coordination that companies use. It shows that most companies provide a great deal of autonomy to their subsidiaries. However, MNCs increasingly set up steering committees to guide their strategic decisions. Some companies (like Mars, for instance) appoint Pan-European brand directors to manage their global or regional brands.

CONTROLLING GLOBAL MARKETING EFFORTS   ◆ ◆ ◆ ◆ ◆ ◆

To make global marketing strategies work, companies need to establish a control system. The main purpose of controls is to ensure that the behaviors of the various parties within the organization are in line with the company's strategic goals. We will first concentrate on formal control methods. We will then also turn to less formal means to implement control: establishing a corporate culture and management development.

Formal ("Bureaucratic") Control Systems

Any formal control system consists of basically three building blocks: (1) the establishment of performance standards, (2) the measurement and evaluation of performance against standards, and (3) the analysis and correction of deviations from standards.

EXHIBIT 18-11
TYPES OF COORDINATION USED IN THE
PAN-EUROPEAN MARKET

Little or no coordination:	4 percent
Some coordination:	45 percent
European Steering Committees:	31 percent
Lead Country:	6 percent
Pan-European Brand Directors:	13.5 percent

Source: Jean-Noël Kapferer, *Strategic Brand Management. New Approaches to Creating and Evaluating Brand Equity* (London: Kogan Page, 1992).

Establishing Standards.   The first step of the control process is to set standards. These standards should be driven by the company's corporate goals. There are essentially two types of standards: behavior and outcome-based. Examples of behavior-based standards include distribution coverage, amount of advertising spent, pricing policies, and R & D spending. Outcome standards focus on very specific outcome-oriented measures such as market share, sales, and customer satisfaction. For most companies, the two types of standards matter. Let us show you why with a simple illustration. Imagine headquarters wants country A to increase its market share by 3 percentage points over a one-year period. Country A could take different approaches to achieve this target. One path is to do a lot of promotional activities—couponing, price promotions, trade deals, and so on. Another route is to spend more on advertising. In both cases, the outcome might be achieved. However, with the first option—heavy dealing—the company risks cheapening the product's image and possibly even diluting the brand's equity. With the second option, the subsidiary would invest in brand equity. Thus, the same outcome can be realized through two totally different behaviors, one of which can ruin the long-term viability of the company's brand assets.

Ideally, standards are developed via a "bottom-up" and "top-down" planning process of listening, reflecting, dialoguing, and debating between headquarters and the local units. Standards should also strike a delicate balance between long- and short-term priorities.[39]

Evaluating Performance.   Formal control systems also need mechanisms to monitor and evaluate performance. The actual performance is compared against the established standards. In many instances, it is fairly straightforward to measure performance, especially when the standards are based on within-country results. To make global or pan-regional strategies work, MNCs also need to assess and reward individual managers' contributions to the "common good." For example, two-thirds of the bonuses payable to Unilever's senior executives in Europe are now driven by Unilever's performance in that region.[40] In practice, however, it is tremendously hard to gauge managers' contributions to the regional or global well-being of the firm.

Analyzing and Correcting Deviations.   The third element is to analyze deviations from the standards and, if necessary, make the necessary corrections. If actual performance does not meet the set standard, one needs to analyze the cause behind the divergence. If necessary, corrective measures will be taken. This part of the control system also involves devising the right incentive mechanisms—checks and balances—that make subsidiary managers "tick." Although proper reward systems are crucial to motivate subsidiary managers, a recent study has shown the key role played by the presence of **due process**.[41] Due process encompasses five features: (1) head office should be familiar with the subsidiaries' local situation; (2) there should be two-way communication in global strategy-making decision processes; (3) head office

---

[39]Guy R. Jillings, "Think Globally, Act Locally," *Executive Excellence* (October 1993), p. 15.

[40]"Unilever Adopts Clean Sheet Approach," *The Financial Times* (October 21, 1991).

[41]W. Chan Kim and Renée A. Mauborgne, "Making Global Strategies Work," *Sloan Management Review* (Spring 1993), pp. 11–24.

is relatively consistent in making decisions across local units; (4) local units can legitimately challenge headquarter's strategic views and decisions; and (5) subsidiary units get explanations for final strategic decisions.

Informal Control Methods

Aside from formal control mechanisms, most MNCs also establish informal control methods. We cover the two most common informal control tools, namely, corporate culture and human resource development.

Corporate Culture. For many MNCs with operations scattered all over the globe, shared cultural values are often a far more effective "glue" to incite subsidiaries than formal bureaucratic control tools. Corporate cultures can be **clan-based** or **market-based**.[42] **Clan cultures** have the following distinguishing features: they embody a long socialization process; strong, powerful norms; and a defined set of internalized controls. **Market cultures** are the opposite: norms are loose or absent; socialization processes are limited; control systems are purely based on performance measures. For most global organizations where integration is an overriding concern, a clanlike culture is instrumental in creating a shared vision.

Corporate values are more than slogans that embellish the company's annual report. To shape a shared vision, cultural values should have three properties:[43]

- **Clarity.** Meaning that the stated values should be simple, relevant, and concrete.
- **Continuity.** Values should be stable over time, long-term oriented, not flavor-of-the-month type values.
- **Consistency.** To avoid confusion, everyone within the organization should share the same vision. Everybody should speak the same language. Everyone should pursue the same agenda.

Exhibit 18-12 gives an overview of the cultural values defined by the Seagram Company, a leading beverage company. Seagram's values are simple and clear. They have also been fairly steady over the years.

Human Resource Development. The company's management development programs are another major informal control tool. Their role is critical in at least three regards.[44] First and foremost, training programs can help managers worldwide in understanding the MNC's mission and vision and their part in pursuing them. Second, such programs can speed up the transfer of new values when changes in the company's environment dictate a "new" corporate mentality. Finally, they can also prove fruitful in allowing managers from all over the world to share their best practices and success stories.

---

[42]David Lei, John W. Slocum, Jr., and Robert W. Slater, "Global Strategy and Reward Systems: The Key Roles of Management Development and Corporate Culture," *Organizational Dynamics* (Winter 1989), pp. 27–41.

[43]Bartlett and Ghoshal 1990, pp. 138–145.

[44]Lei, Slocum, and Slater, p. 39.

EXHIBIT 18-12
CORPORATE VISION OF THE SEAGRAM COMPANY LTD.

- The Mission of The Seagram Company Ltd. is to be the **best managed** beverage company in the world. To accomplish this goal, we will improve our financial performance and **competitive position,** build an organization that encourages individuals to contribute to our success, and create an environment in which all employees are **valued** and **motivated.**
- We will place authority and accountability as close to the **customer** as possible. We will encourage **innovation** and prudent risk taking. We will ensure that recognition and rewards are based on performance.
- We will achieve a long-term pattern of **earnings growth** and enhanced returns on our assets and sales in order to continue to provide superior returns to our **shareholders.**
- We will strengthen our portfolio of premium **brands** and focus on improving their **profitability** and competitive position.
- We will build on our sources of strength: our worldwide beverage distribution network; our **family** tradition; and the knowledge, skill and dedication of our **employees.**
- **Integrity** and the highest ethical standards will guide all our actions. We will foster a spirit of **teamwork** throughout the organization, and we remain committed to **equality of opportunity** and to the development of the full potential of our employees.

Source: The Seagram Company Ltd., *1995 Annual Report.*

SUMMARY ✦

In this chapter we discussed the structures and control mechanisms that MNCs can use to shape a global organization. Companies can pick from a variety of structures, ranging from a single international division to a global network operation. Formal and informal (culture, management development) control mechanisms are available to run global operations. However, the dynamics of the global marketing arena means that building a global organization is much more than just choosing the "right" organizational configuration and control systems. Global players constantly need to reflect on how to strike the balance between centralization *and* decentralization, local responsiveness *and* global integration, center *and* periphery. As with many other challenges in global marketing, there are no easy 1-2-3 solutions. In their search for the proper structure and strategic coherence, countless MNCs have come up with schemes that led to confusion, frustration, and ill-will among subsidiary managers. We can offer some pieces of advice, though:

- **Recognize the need for business asymmetry.** Due to relentless environmental changes, power sharing between the center and the periphery will vary over time, over business units, and even across activities (product development, advertising, pricing) within business units. Different SBUs within the organization have different needs for responsiveness and global coordination.[45] Especially widely diversified companies should recognize that each business unit needs a different format, depending on its particular circumstances and needs. For instance, Asea Brown Boveri has businesses that are *superlocal* (e.g., electrical installation) and *superglobal* (e.g., power plant projects). The principle of **business asymmetry** is illustrated in Exhibit 18-13 for Goodyear, the world's leading tire maker. Depending on the business area, units are structured on a regional or global basis.
- **Democracy is a must.** Getting the balance right also requires democracy. When building

[45]"Fashionable Federalism," *The Financial Times* (December 18, 1992).

EXHIBIT 18-13
GOODYEAR: EXAMPLE OF "BUSINESS ASYMMETRY"

Strategic Business Unit	Products and Markets	Geographic Markets Served
North American Tire	Original equipment, replacement tires for autos, trucks, farm, aircraft, construction	United States, Canada, Export
Kelly-Springfield	Replacement tires for autos, trucks, tractors	United States, Canada Export
Goodyear Europe	Original equipment, replacement tires for autos, trucks, farm, construction	Europe, Africa, Middle East, Export
Goodyear Latin America	Original equipment, replacement tires for autos, trucks, tractors	Central, South America, Export
Goodyear Asia	Original equipment, replacement tires for autos, trucks, farm, aircraft, construction	Southeast, Western Asia, North Pacific Rim, Export
Engineered Products	Auto belts, hose, body components, industrial products	Worldwide
Chemicals	Synthetic and natural rubber, chemicals for internal, external customers	Worldwide
Celeron	Crude oil transportation, related services	Operates only pipeline from U.S. West Coast to Texas
Goodyear Racing	Tires for all major motor racing series	Worldwide

Source: The Goodyear Tire & Rubber Company, *1994 Annual Report.*

up a global organization, make sure that every country subsidiary has a "voice." Subsidiaries of small countries should not be concerned about getting pushed over by their bigger counterparts. As we discussed earlier, global teamwork is one tool MNCs can resort to in order to establish a democratic forum.

- **Importance of a shared vision.** Getting the organizational structure right—the "arrows" and "boxes" so to speak—is important. Far more critical, though, is the organizational "psychology."[46] People are key in building an organization. Having a clear and consistent corporate vision is a major ingredient in getting people excited about the organization. To instill and communicate corporate values, companies should also have human resource development mechanisms in place that will facilitate the learning process.

- **Need for a good mix of specialists of three types—country; functional; business.** There is no such thing as a *transnational manager.*[47] Company should breed specialists of three different kinds: country, functional, and global business (SBU). Country managers in particular—once feared to become part of the endangered species list—play a key role. As we discussed earlier in this chapter, the country manager's skills and role will differ from country to country. Some subsidiaries need a "trader"; others need an "ambassador."

- **Moving unit headquarters abroad seldom solves the organization's problems.** In recent years, companies like IBM, Hewlett-Packard, and Siemens have moved business unit headquarters abroad. Several of these moves were done for very sensible reasons: getting closer to

---

[46]Bartlett and Ghoshal, 1990, pp. 138–145.

[47]"Global Executives Walk a Tightrope," *The Financial Times* (October 12, 1992).

the customer or supplier, being in the big guys' backyard, cutting costs. Unfortunately, in many cases the relocation typically turns out to be mere window dressing in a drive to become more global-oriented. Sometimes transfers can even be counter-productive. They may weaken your corporate identity when it is strongly linked to your firm's home country.

REVIEW QUESTIONS

1. How does a global networked organization differ from the matrix structure?
2. Describe how external environmental drivers influence the organizational design decision.
3. What are the pros and cons of a regional organization structure?
4. What mechanisms can companies use to foster a global corporate culture?
5. What does it take for an MNC to be a "multilocal multinational"?

DISCUSSION QUESTIONS

1. Ghoshal and Bartlett have noted in their writings that the key to successful MNCs is creating a matrix in managers' minds. The formal organizational structure is far less important. Comment.
2. Management theorists often argue that the most attractive approach to achieve a matrix in the managers' minds is via a "mingling of the different cultures." What would this mean in practice? Do you foresee potential roadblocks?

FURTHER READINGS

Bartlett, Christopher A. "Building and Managing the Transnational: The New Organizational Challenge." In *Competition in Global Industries*, M. E. Porter, ed. Boston: Harvard University Press, 1986: 367–401.

Bartlett, Christopher A., and Sumantra Ghoshal. "Organizing for Worldwide Effectiveness: The Transnational Solution." *California Management Review* (Fall 1988): 54–74.

Davidson, W. H., and P. Haspeslagh. "Shaping a Global Product Organization." *Harvard Business Review* (July-August 1982): 125–32.

Lasserre, Philippe. "Regional Headquarters: The Spearhead for Asia Pacific Markets." *Long Range Planning*, 29 (February 1996): 30–37.

Naylor, Thomas H. "The International Strategy Matrix" *Columbia Journal of World Business* (Summer 1985): 11–19.

Quelch, John A. "The New Country Managers." *The McKinsey Quarterly*, no. 4 (1992): 155–65.

Quelch, John A., and Helen Bloom. "The Return of the Country Manager." *The McKinsey Quarterly*, no. 2 (1996): 30–43.

Snow, Charles C., Sue C. Davison, Scott A. Snell, and Donald C. Hambrick. "Use Transnational Teams to Globalize Your Company." *Organizational Dynamics* (Spring 1996): 50–67.

APPENDIX
INFORMATION SOURCES FOR
GLOBAL MARKETING
MANAGEMENT

INTERNATIONAL INDUSTRY/PRODUCT INFORMATION/STATISTICAL SOURCES

United Nations. *Yearbook of Industrial Statistics.* HC59 .Y4. Annual.

United Nations. *Yearbook of International Trade Statistics.* HF91 .U473.

U.S. Bureau of the Census. *US Imports.* HF105 .C1372. Annual.

U.S. Bureau of the Census. *US Exports.* HF105 .C137166. Annual.

International Marketing Data & Statistics. HA42 .I56.
European Marketing Data & Statistics. REF HA1107 .E87.
Both publications give production/consumption figures for selected products by country.

Competitive Assessment of . . .
Assessment of US Competitiveness in . . .
Check online catalog under both titles for industries/products discussed in this series.
Done by the U.S. government to encourage exporting by US companies.

International Financial Statistics. Washington, D.C.: International Monetary Fund (monthly and annual). IIS fiche 3830-S2, 1983–. Covers most major statistics including GDP, interest rates, production, prices, exchange rates, government and national accounts. Many figures given in local currency.

Balance of Payments Statistics. Washington D.C.: International Monetary Fund (monthly and annual). IIS fiche 3840-S7, 1981–. Yearbook has two volumes. Volume 1 has aggregate and detailed figures by country, with stock data for some countries. Volume 2 has aggregates by category. All amounts for countries are given in SDRs.

Direction of Trade Statistics. Washington D.C.: International Monetary Fund (monthly and annual). IIS

fiche 3840-S1, 1983–. Distribution of total exports and imports for countries by trade partners. Regional tables and groupings such as Oil Exporting Countries. All amounts in U.S. dollars.

Main Economic Indicators. Paris: Organization for Economic Co-operation and Development (monthly). HC10.O68 An essential source of short-term statistics of OECD Member countries. Provides recent changes in the economies of the OECD countries and puts them in an international context.

Yearbook of Labour Statistics. Geneva: International Labour Office (annual). Labor force, employment, unemployment, hours of work, wages, labor cost, consumer prices, occupational injuries, strikes and lock-outs. Breakdowns by sex and industry.

World Development Report. New York: World Development Bank (annual). HC59.7.W659, 1978–, also IIS fiche 4530-S3, 1978–. Not just statistical, text focuses on the financial systems of developing countries. An excellent source of hard-to-find statistics such as income distribution, official development assistance, and total external debt. See also *Trends in Developing Economies*, Washington, D.C.: World Bank. (annual), HC59.69.T74, 1989–, also IIS fiche 4530-S45, 1989–., for brief country reports complementing *TIDE*.

World Economic and Social Survey. New York, United Nations, Department of Economic and Social Affairs. (annual). An analysis of world economic policies, trends and issues. Statistical tables in back include macroeconomic indicators, international trade and finance, and financial markets for developed market economies as well as economies in transition.

Big Emerging Markets. Lanham, MD: published by Bernan Press in conjunction with the NTIS, 1995. HF1379.B55 1995. Profiles of the 10 countries deemed to hold the most promise for U.S. exports and investment over the long term. Includes information on the major and potential market sectors, growth projections, market access, competition and more.

PlanEcon Report. Washington, D.C.: PlanEcon Inc. (approximately twice monthly). HC336.25.P424, 1987–. In depth reports on the developments in the economies of the former USSR and Eastern Europe. Each report focuses on a specific country with highlights of the political and economic situations, including monetary policies, debt markets, equity markets, foreign trade, balance of payments, exchange rates and statistical tables.

Statistical Yearbook for Latin America and the Caribbean. Santiago, Chile: Economic Commission for Latin American and the Caribbean, United Nations (annual). IIS microfiche 3230–S2.

Statistical Yearbook for Asia and the Pacific. Bangkok: Economic and Social Commission for Asia and the Pacific, United Nations (annual). IIS microfiche 3170-S10.

African Statistical Yearbook. Addis Ababa: Economic Commission for Africa, United Nations (annual). IIS microfiche 3190-S1.

Panorama of EU Industry. Luxembourg: Office for Official Publications of the European Communities. (annual). Provides a comprehensive review of the situation and outlook of the manufacturing and service industries in the European Union. Major developments in production, employment, trade and structural changes are covered.

Encyclopedia of Global Industries. Detroit, MI: Gale Research Inc. (biennial). HD2324.E539, 1996–. Chronicles the development, current status and history of 115 internatiopnal industries. Includes an overview of each industry, including current economic conditions, research and technology, industry leaders and more.

Manufacturing Worldwide. Detroit, MI: Gale Research Inc. (biennial). HD9720.4.M26, 1995–. Brief information on major manufacturing sectors, product categories and companies. Statistical profiles of 119 countries are given, including a listing of leading industries and summary data.

Economist Intelligence Unit Periodicals. EIU publishes a number of periodicals on major international industries. Some representative titles include: Motor Business International, HD9710.A1M65, 1985–. Motor Business Europe, B HD9710.A1E85, 1985–.

COUNTRY INFORMATION

United Nations. *Statistical Yearbook*. HA12.5 .U63. (annual). Updated by the *Monthly Bulletin of Statistics*, in PERIODICALS.

United Nations. *Compendium of Social Statistics*. HA12.5 .A1 U5. Economic/social conditions documented annually for member nations.

United Nations. *Yearbook of Industrial Statistics*. REF HC59 .Y4. (annual). Production figures by product classification by country.

International Yearbook & Statesmen's Who's Who. JA51 .I57. (annual). Includes many economic statistics for every country in the world.

Europa Yearbook. JN1 .E85. 2 v. (annual). Detailed political, economic and commercial information for *all* countries of the world, NOT just Europe.

Africa South of the Sahara. DT351 .A37. Detailed information on Africa countries.

OECD Economic Survey. HC241.2 .074. (annual). Detailed economic information for the 25 member countries of the Organization for Economic Cooperation and Development.

International Marketing Handbook. HF1009.5 .I537. Includes many economic statistics on 138 countries.

Country Studies. Ernst and Whitney. HG4538 .E754.

Doing Business in . . Price Waterhouse. HG4538 .P72. Information for U.S. business people relocating abroad.

Foreign Economic Trends & Their Implications for the U.S. HC10 .E416. U.S. government reports. Each country is reviewed twice yearly.

Overseas Business Reports. HF91 .U482. (annual). U.S. government reports to assist U.S. companies in their dealings abroad. Many reports are titled "Marketing in (name of country)."

Encylopedia of the Third World. HC59.7 .K87 1987. Data on the economic, political, social conditions in 126 countries.

Countries of the World and Their Leaders. G122 .C67. (annual). Overviews of every country.

Political Handbook of the World. JF37 .P6. (annual). Descriptions of the political situations in each country of the world.

Statesmen's Yearbook. JA51 .S7. (annual). Describes each country's government and lists officeholders.

Consult also such periodical indexes as *Infotrac's General Periodicals Index* and *National Newspaper Index, Business Periodicals Index, Public Affairs Information Service Bulletin (PAISI)*, under name of country.

United Nations. *Demographic Yearbook*. HA17 .D45 (annual).

United Nations. *Compendium of Social Statistics.* HA12.5 .A1 U5.

UNESCO *Statistical Yearbook.* AZ361 .U45. (annual).

United Nations. *Statistical Yearbook.* HA12.5 .U63. (annual).

Worldmark Encyclopedia of the Nations. G63 .W67 1988. 5 v. Best source of information on social conditions.

Encyclopedia of the Third World. HC59.7 .K87 1987. Economic, political, social conditions in 126 countries.

International Marketing Handbook. HF1009.5 .I537. 3 v. Covers 142 countries in some detail.

Consult also the online catalog for books, such as: *Canadian Encyclopedia, South American Handbook*, and the State Department's *Area Handbook* series. Books will be listed by country name, both by subject and by title keyword.

International Marketing Data & Statistics. HA42 .I46. (annual). Production/consumption of products data for non-European countries.

European Marketing Data & Statistics. HF1107 .E87. (annual). Data for consumer consumption of products, arranged by country.

Consumer Markets in Central & Eastern Africa. HF3909 .A45 C66 1987. Consumer consumption figures arranged by country and by product.

Consumer Europe. HD7022. C68 (annual). Detailed consumption figures for all European countries.

Country reports (quarterly), and *Country Profiles* (annual), London, U.K.: Economist Intelligence Unit, 1981 to date. Quarterly and annual overviews of the economic and politicial activity in over 180 countries. Quarterlies have an outlook and analysis of trends, while annuals provide a survey of background information.

Area Handbook Series. Washington, D.C.: Federal Research Division, Library of Congress. A good place to start for general background. Each volume covers a different country and includes chapters on history, politics, economics and national security issues. New volumes are published and updated as necessary.

Political Risk Yearbook. East Syracuse, N.Y.: Political Risk Services, 1987– (annual). Multi-volume set analyzing the political and economic situation and outlook for countries and the possible effects on business. 18 month and 5 year forecasts provided with possible scenarios for future government restrictions on trade and international investments.

OUTLOOKS AND PROJECTIONS

World Economic Outlook. Washington, D.C.: International Monetary Fund. HC59.W645, 1980–. Semiannual survey summarizing the current world economic situation and the short-term prospects. Charts, tables and a statistical appendix are included.

World Outlook. London: Economist Intelligence Unit. Economic and political forecasts for over 180 countries. Each country has a five year series of macroeconomic indicators. Numerical GDP forecasts are given for all OECD countries and selected others.

OECD Economic Outlook. Paris: Organization for Economic Cooperation and Development (biannual). HC10.O69, 1967–. An assessment of economic trends, prospects and policies in OECD countries. Each issue contains an overall analysis of the latest economic trends and short-term projections, and occasional special studies of timely issues. Historical tables provide percentage rates of change to illustrate the fluctuations of main economic variables over a 20-30 year period.

INTERNATIONAL ADVERTISING

Ulrich's International Periodicals Directory. Z6941 .U5. (annual). Periodicals listed by subject classification with an alphabetical title index. No arrangement by country.

Editor and Publisher International Yearbook. PN4700 .E4. (annual). Selective list of newspapers/periodicals by country, including circulation figures.

World Advertising Expenditures. HF5801 .A26. (annual). By country, by broad product group.

Croner. *Reference Book for World Traders.* HF1010 .R4. (annual updates). Information about various advertising media by country, with names and addresses.

Standard Directory of International Advertisers & Agencies. Wilmette Ill.: National Register Pub. Co. (annual). HF5804.S73, current only. Lists advertisers and agencies. Arranged alphabetically by company name. Includes geographic index by country and product index based on SIC codes.

Japan Marketing and Advertising Yearbook. Tokyo: Dentsu Inc. (annual). HF5415.12, J3D45, 1985/86–. Advertising expenditures and volume by industry, market research data, directories of newspapers and magazines with advertising costs, directories of advertising agencies, public relations and market research.

International Media Guides. Nashua, NH: IMG, Inc. Directories of foreign magazines and newspapers, with information on circulation and advertising rates. Three *Business/Professional* volumes cover Europe, Asia/Pacific, the Middle East/Africa and the Americas. Arranged by subject category, then by country, with a title index. Also, *Newspapers Worldwide* and *Consumer Magazines Worldwide*.

DIRECTORIES OF FOREIGN FIRMS

Dun and Bradstreet. *Principal International Businesses.* HF54 .U5 P4. Annual listing of foreign companies listed by country, SIC code, and alphabetically.

International Directory of Corporate Affiliations. HG4090 .Z5 I5. U.S. and foreign parent companies cross referenced with their national and international subsidiaries. Updated annually.

Directory of American Firms Operating in Foreign Countries. 3 v. HG4538 .A1 D5 1991. Companies listed by country.

Moody's International Manual. HG4009 .M66. Annual, weekly updates. The best source for financial information foreign companies.

Massachusetts Foreign Firm Directory. HF5065 .M38 M4 1985/86. Foreign companies operating in Massachusetts, arranged by country and by principal product.

Directory of Foreign Manufacturers in the United States. HG4057 .A76 1990.

International Consumers Yellow Pages. HF5429 .I547. Information about companies that sell/export to the U.S., arranged by product name. Products are consumer, not manufacturing, products.

Dun's Asia/Pacific Key Business Enterprises. Murray Hill, NJ: Dun and Bradstreet International (annual). HG4234.85Z65D86

Latin America 25,000. Bethlehem, PA: Dun and Bradstreet Information Services (annual). HG4091.5.A2.

D&B Europa. High Wycombe, England: D&B Europe, Ltd (annual). HG4132.25.D36.

D&B Central Europa. Praha, Czech Republic: Dun and Bradstreet (annual). HG3500.1.D18.

Major Companies of the Arab World. London: Graham & Trotman, Ltd. (annual). HF3866.M3.

Major Companies of the Far East and Australasia. London: Graham and Trotman (annual). HD2906.A1M3. Data on over 6,000 of the largest companies in the Asia-Pacific region. Includes executives, basic financial results, branch offices, principle business activities and number of employees.

European 5,000. London: Euromoney (annual). HG4132.E97. Data includes business summaries, officers, summary stock and financial information, as well as graphical representations for breakdown of sales and geographic area (domestic sales vs. other).

Europe's 15,000 Largest Companies. London: Europe's Largest Companies, Ltd. (annual). HD2356.EE9E93. The basis of this publication is a list of the top companies in Europe ranked by turnover, or in the case of banks, assets. Provides rankings by sales, profits, and number of employees.

The Times 1000. London: Times Books. (annual). HG4135.T54. Ranks the UK's top 1,000 companies by turnover and capital employed, and the top 25–100 companies in the USA, Japan, Canada, Australia, Hong Kong, Malaysia, Singapore, Thailand and South Korea by turnover.

Directory of Foreign Firms Operating in the United States. New York: Simon & Schuster. (irregular). HF54.U5A63. Foreign firms by country, and the American firm(s) owned by or affiliated with the foreign firm.

Directory of Japanese-Affiliated Companies in the USA and Canada. Tokyo: Japan External Trade Organization (biennial). HG4057.A18. Lists Japanese-affiliated companies operating in the U.S. and Canada. Any firm owned in whole or in part by a Japanese entity is treated as a Japanese-affiliated firm. Subsidiaries of Japanese firms, as well as subsidiaries of subsidiaries are also covered. Includes address, number of employees, type of busines, and year established.

Directory of Japanese-Affiliated Companies in Asia. Tokyo: Japan External Trade Organization (biennial). HG4244.6.Z65D62. Address, number of employees, type of business, and year established for Japanese companies operating outside Japan. Overseas companies are defined as those in which 10 percent or more of the ownership is held by one or more Japanese-based company.

Hoover's Handbook of World Business. Austin, TX: Reference Press (annual). HF5030.H662. Concise company descriptions with information on the company's strategy, history, executives and directors, products, services, brandnames, divisions, subsidiaries and more. Also included are key competitors and a 10 year table of financial data.

Japan Company Handbook. Tokyo: Toyo Keizai Shinposha (semiannual). HC461.J35. Financial information for companies listed on the Tokyo, Osaka, and Nagoya stock exchanges. Includes company description, short- and long-term outlooks, income data, sales breakdown, and basic pricing information.

Swiss Stock Guide. Zurich: Union Bank of Switzerland (annual). HG4226.S96. Covers the companies listed on the Swiss Stock Exchange, as well as basic stock and company information, including activities and prospects, summary balance sheets, market value and return.

INTERNATIONAL MARKETING AIDS/GUIDES TO DOING BUSINESS

Handbook of International Business. HD62.4 H36 1982. How-to's on all aspects of international marketing.

Croner's Reference Book for World Traders. HF1010 .R4. 3 v. Facts for international traders, arranged by country & updated.

Green Book: International Directory of Marketing Research Houses and Services. HF5415.2 .G69. Annual. Lists companies geographically.

Doing Business in the European Economic Community. HF1532.92 .D7 1983.

Worldwide Chamber of Commerce Directory. HF294 .W75. Annual. A listing of all U.S./foreign Chambers of Commerce plus all members of the diplomatic corps in the United States.

American Export Register. HF3010 .A6. Annual. U.S. corporate companies that export abroad, arranged by product/alphabetically.

Check also the on-line catalog under subjects such as "Marketing-Japan," and under the name of the country and/or product.

Economist Intelligence Business Newsletters. London: Economist Intelligence Unit. (monthly) CD ROM 1993–. This database provides the full text of eight specialized newsletters: *Business Africa, Business Asia, Business China, Business Eastern Europe, Business Europe, Business Latin America, Business Middle East,* and *Crossborder Monitor,* excellent sources for information on business and economic developments in both major and emerging markets. Use them to find changes in business regulations, information on industry trends, capital markets, financial management, trends in corporate organization, human resource management, market entry strategies, competitive approaches, global marketing and distribution, foreign trade, tax and investment developments, and recent government incentives.

Financing Foreign Operations. London: Economist Intelligence Unit (looseleaf with semiannual supplements). HG4538.B85. A multivolume set covering Europe, Asia, the Americas, and Africa/Middle East. Includes a business overview, currency outlook, foreign exchange regulations, the monetary system, capital incentives, financing and more. Includes a separate volume on cross-border sources of financing.

Investing, Licensing and Trading Conditions Abroad. London: Economist Intelligence Unit (looseleaf). HG4538.B87. A multivolume set covering Europe, Asia, the Americas, and Africa/Middle East. Includes a market watch and assessment, organizing an investment, incentives, licensing, competition and price policies, taxes, capital sources, human resources and foreign trade.

Country Commercial Guides. Washington, D.C.: National Trade Data Bank and Economic Bulletin Board, U.S. Department of Commerce (on-line). STAT-USA at http://www.STAT-USA/gov. Series of country reports with useful information for setting up a business or marketing in foreign countries. Overview of primary industries, trade regulations, distribution and sales channels, taxation, licensing and franchising, investment climate, project finance, economic trends and outlooks, leading sectors for U.S. imports and investments, and more.

Doing Business in . . . (name of country). New York: Price Waterhouse (irregular). Business guides to foreign countries covering investment climate, doing business, auditing and accounting, and taxation. Appendices give tax, and accounting and financial statement information.

Exporters Encyclopaedia. New York: Dun and Bradstreet International. (annual with biweekly updates). HF3011.E9, current only. The first stop for exporters. Arranged by country, with information on trade regulations, necessary documentation, taxes, tariffs, standards and ports. Also covers transportation and business travel.

Importers Manual USA. Edward C. Hinkelman et al. San Rafael, Calif.: World Trade Press (irregular). HF3035.I45. Encyclopedia for importing into the U.S. Broken out by products, providing such information as the key factors involved in the importation of the product, customs classifications, duties, entry and documentation, laws and regulations and more. Also included is a country index listing leading U.S. imports from the countries, opportunities, trade fairs, and bibliographics. Information on International Law, U.S. Customs Entry, and Packing, Shipping, and Insurance is also included.

Directory of United States Importers and *Directory of United States Exporters.* NYC: Journal of Commerce (annual). HF3010.U552. (importers) and HF3010.U553 (exporters) Lists importers and exporters alphabetically, by product and geographically by state. Provides U.S. Customs Service and other how-to-information, including banks and a directory of world ports.

A Basic Guide to Importing. Lincolnwood, Ill.: NTC Books. (Compiled by U.S. Customs Service) 1995. HF3035.B373 1995. A guide to basic importing procedures such as entry of goods, duty assessments, and special requirements.

A Basic Guide to Exporting. San Rafael, Calif.: World Trade Press. 1994. HF1416.5.B37 1994. A guide to basic exporting procedures and techniques such as export strategy, market research, distribution channels, making contacts, selling overseas and more.

Export/Import Procedures and Documentation. Thomas E. Johnson. New York: AMACOM. 1994. HF1416.5.J64 1994. Focuses on the procedures for exporting and importing and contains samples of many relevant documents used in foreign trade.

Exporting: From Start to Finish. L. Fargo Wells and Karin B. Dulat. New York: McGraw-Hill, 1996. HF1416.5.W45 1996. Practical information on exporting as well as options and means of financing, developing a successful export venture, and more.

COMPUTERIZED AIDS TO RESEARCH

The library offers, for a minimum fee of $10, a computerized research service that will produce a list of references to periodical/newspaper articles on any subject/company/industry specified. The resulting list of references allows the patron to locate the actual article either in this library or from other libraries through interlibrary loan. ILL is a free, convenient way to get articles, but it normally takes seven to fourteen days to get them. Listed below are some of the more useful databases available.

Foreign Trade & Economic Abstracts—references to world literature on foreign trade, including country-specific information on markets/industries.

Foreign Traders Index—lists companies in foreign countries, searchable by product, SIC code, country, firm size.

Hoppenstedt Directory of German Companies—lists most major companies in Germany, includes SIC codes, sales, subsidiaries.

ICC British Company Directory—lists most major companies in the United Kingdom, includes financial data.

PAIS International—indexes hundreds of English and foreign language documents on business and social policy. The paper version in this library lists only English language documents.

PTS Promt—indexes thousands of international and U.S. periodicals for articles about products, markets, countries, trade regulations.

PTS F&S Indexes—indexes large number of U.S. and international journals that deal with products, markets,

and companies in all countries. Paper versions for these indexes are available on the INDEX TABLES in Reference.

PTS Mars—Marketing and Advertising Reference Service. Indexes primarily U.S. journals with some international coverage, on the marketing/advertising industry and other topics of interest to them.

ABI/Inform. Ann Arbor, Mich.: Univeristy Microfilms International (quarterly). CD ROM. Provides indexing and abstracts for articles from over 800 business and trade journals. A good source for information on companies, industries, products and management policies. No full text.

Predicasts F&S U.S. and International. Cleveland, OH: Predicasts, Inc. (quarterly). CD ROM. Provides coverage on all manufacturing and service industries and a wide range of business and technology-related subjects. It is particularly useful for product and marketing information. Citations and informative abstracts from over 1,000 sources, including U.S. and international trade and industry journals, national and international newspapers, and business and economic publications are included.

EIU International Business Newletters. Norwood, MA: Economist Intelligence Unit; Silver Platter Information, Inc. (monthly). CD ROM. Provides the full text of eight specialized newsletters: *Business Africa, Business Asia, Business China, Business Eastern Europe, Business Europe, Business Latin America, Business Middle East* and *Crossborder Monitor.* Excellent sources for information on business and economic developments in both major and emerging markets. Use them to find changes in business regulations, information on industry trends, capital markets, financial management, trends in corporate organization, human resource management, market entry strategies, competitive approaches, global marketing and distribution, and more.

Wall Street Journal. Ann Arbor, Mich.: UMI (quarterly). CD ROM. Full text of the newspaper.

Dow Jones News Retrieval Service. Online. In addition to providing the latest business and financial data on U.S. companies, the full text of articles from many U.S. and international publications is accessible through the //TEXTM file, making it a valuable resource for information and news on international and U.S. companies and industries, and for all business topics.

Index to International Statistics. Washington, D.C.: Congressional Information Service. CD ROM or Print version. An indexing and abstracting service with an accompanying microfiche set to the statistical publications of approximately 100 international intergovernmental organizations. Representative organizations include the

UN system, the OECD, the European Community, development banks and others. An essential source to basic information on population, business and financial activities, education, health, demographics and more.

National Trade Data Bank (NTDB). Washington, D.C.: National Trade Data Bank and Economic Bulletin Board. U.S. Department of Commerce (monthly). Online. USA at http://www.STAT-USA.gov. The NTDB is a databank of more than 90,000 documents, tables, and periodicals that the U.S. Department of Commerce's Office of Business Analysis releases on a monthly basis. The sources included are trade promotion literature, how-to guides, market research, and international trade and economic statistics selected from more than fifteen federal agencies. It is particularly useful for international marketing and trade information and leads.

INTERNATIONAL BUSINESS AND MARKETING SITES ON THE WWW

The following Web sites are good sources for international business and marketing information. To find more, and new Web sites, use your browser. The WWW changes constantly!

Bobst Library International Business and Economics Homepage
http://www.nyu.edu/library/bobst/research/soc/bus-int/

International Business Resources on the Web
http://ciber.bus.msu.edu/busres.htm

International Business Resources Page
http://www.otginc.com/listing.html

Nijenrode Business Webserver
http://www.nijenrode.nl/nbr/

STAT-USA
http://www.STAT-USA.gov

VIBES: Virtual International Business and Economics Sources
http://www.unc.edu/lis/library/using/services/reference/intbus/vibehome.htm

MARKETING AND CONSUMER INFORMATION

International Marketing Data and Statistics. London: Euromonitor Publications (annual). HA42.I56. Marketing, demographic, and economic information, some with projections. "Marketing Geography" section has mini-profiles. Data on spending, by type of product; also data on retail sales, production, and export and import information.

European Marketing Data and Statistics. London: Euromonitor Publications (annual). HA1107.E87. Similar to *International Marketing Data and Statistics,* but pertaining to the European countries only.

Marketing in Europe. London: Corporate Intelligence on Retailing (monthly). HF5415.12.E8M37. Periodical providing marketing information for non-U.K. European Community countries. Products are divided into three major groups: (1) Food, Drink, Tobacco, (2) Clothing, Furniture, Leisure Goods, (3) Pharmaceuticals, Toiletries, Household Goods, Domestic Appliances, each covered four times per year. Index is in the back of each issue.

Market Research International. London: Euromonitor (monthly). HF5415.2.M23. Six different market reports in each issue on topics ranging from the Japanese noodle market, to Indonesian household cleaning products, to soft drinks in Brazil. An international view of a major consumer market, e.g., the world market for frozen food, is also covered in each issue.

Market Research Europe. London: Euromonitor Publications (monthly). HC240.A1E75. Each issue generally contains five or six reports, two covering the major and secondary European markets, while the remaining four reports each cover one product in one country. Each issue contains an index to the last five years.

Market Europe. East Syracuse, N.Y.: Political Risk Services (monthly). HC240.M265. Monthly newsletter covering product markets, market profiles and recent trends throughout Europe.

Eastern Europe Market Atlas. Hong Kong: Economist Intelligence Unit. HC244.E228. Uses pie charts, graphs, and maps to present market and country statistics, data on GDP and forecasts, budgets, foreign investment, imports, exports, and consumer data.

Consumer Europe. London: Euromonitor Publications (biennial). HD7022.C68. Statistical information on European consumption. Arranged by product groups, gives value and volume of consumption by country, providing six years' worth of data. Shows countries with major market shares. Covers Western Europe only.

Consumer Asia. London: Euromonitor (annual). HC411.C66. Covers major consumer products and markets in Asia, and provides product and consumption data by country.

Market Research Reports. Washington, D.C.: National Trade Data Bank and Economic Bulletin Board. U.S. Department of Commerce. (on-line). STAT-USA at http://www.STAT-USA.gov. Excellent sources of information on country consumer markets and products. Great for identifying key areas of import and export, and general business opportunities.

Retail Trade Review. London: Corporate Intelligence on Retailing (quarterly). (formerly *Retail Business* London: E.I.U., 1987–1993). HF5439.C7R482. Reviews of trends in U. K. retail sectors, plus summary company profiles.

Retail Business: Market Surveys. London: Corporate Intelligence on Retailing. (formerly *Retail Business: Market Report*, London: Economist Intelligence Unit, 1987–1993) (monthly). HF5349.G7R481. U.K. consumer products market surveys including key trends and future prospects.

European Policy Analyst (Formerly *European Trends*). London: Economist Intelligence Unit (quarterly). HC241.2.E87. Covers key issues and developments in the European Union and its market, including legislation, competitive policy, external relations, and environmental issues affecting the European business environment and how companies can best operate within that environment. Special features may include industry analyses and other issues of note.

CASES

1. STARBUCKS COFFEE: EXPANSION IN ASIA
2. GAP, INC.
3. SEGA: THE WAY THE WEST WAS WON
4. PROCTER & GAMBLE: FACELLE DIVISION FACIAL TISSUE
5. WASTE MANAGEMENT INTERNATIONAL PLC: STRATEGY FOR ASIA
6. BAXTER INTERNATIONAL—RENAL DIVISION: MARKET OPPORTUNITIES IN LATIN AMERICA
7. TILTING WINDMILLS: SANEX TRIES TO CONQUER EUROPE
8. CLUB MED: THE PARTY IS OVER
9. FORD MOTOR COMPANY AND DIE DEVELOPMENT
10. PHAMA SWEDE: GASTIRUP
11. ANHEUSER-BUSCH INTERNATIONAL, INC.: MAKING INROADS INTO BRAZIL AND MEXICO
12. TOYS "Я" US GOES TO JAPAN

❖ ❖

CASE 1

STARBUCKS COFFEE: EXPANSION IN ASIA

HISTORY

Starbucks Coffee Company was founded in 1971 by three coffee aficionados. Starbucks, named after the coffee-loving first mate in Moby Dick, opened its first store in Seattle's Pike Place Public Market. During this time, most coffee was purchased in a can directly from supermarket shelves. Starbucks' concept of selling fresh-roasted whole beans in a specialty store was a revolutionary idea.

In 1987, Howard Schultz, a former Starbucks employee, acquired the company. When Schultz first joined Starbucks in the early 1980s as director of retail operations, Starbucks was a local, highly respected roaster and retailer of whole bean and ground coffees. A business trip to Milan's famous coffee shops in 1983 opened Schultz's eyes to the rich tradition of the espresso beverage. Schultz recalls, "What I saw was the unique relationship that the Italian people had with the ubiquitous coffee bars around Italy. People used the local coffee bar as the third place from home and work. What I wanted to try and do was re-create that in North America."[1] Inspired by the Italian espresso bars, Schultz convinced executives to have Starbucks' stores serve coffee by the cup. And the rest is history!

Starbucks went public in 1993 and has done extremely well in turning an everyday beverage into a premium product. The green and white mermaid logo is widely recognized; the brand is defined by not only its products, but also by attitude. It is all about the Starbucks experience, the atmosphere and the place that is a refuge for most people to get away from everyday stresses. The average customer visits a Starbucks eighteen times in a month and about 10 percent of all customers visit twice a day. They have created an affinity with customers that is almost cult-like. Today, Starbucks is the leading roaster and retailer of specialty coffee in North America with more than 1,000 retail stores in 32 markets.

MISSION STATEMENT

Starbucks' corporate mission statement is as follows: "Establish Starbucks as the premier purveyor of the finest coffee in the world, while maintaining our uncompromising principles as we grow. The following guiding principles will help us measure the appropriateness of our decisions:

1. Provide a great work environment and treat each other with respect and dignity.
2. Apply the highest standards of excellence to the purchasing, roasting and fresh delivery of our coffee.
3. Develop enthusiastically satisfied customers all of the time.
4. Contribute positively to our communities and our environment.
5. Recognize that profitability is essential to our future success."

Starbucks' corporate objective to is become the most recognized and respected brand of coffee in the world. To achieve this goal, Starbucks plans to continue to expand its retail operations rapidly in two ways. First, to increase its market share in existing markets and secondly, to open stores in new markets. Starbucks' retail objective is to become a leading retailer and coffee brand in each of its target markets by selling the first quality coffees and related products. In addition, Starbucks provides a superior level of customer service, thereby building a high degree of customer loyalty.

This case was prepared by Valerie Darguste, Ana Su, Ai-Lin Tu, and Peggy Wei of New York University's Stern School of Business under the supervision of Masaaki Kotabe of The University of Texas at Austin for class discussion rather than to illustrate either effective or ineffective management of a situation described (May 1997).

EXHIBIT 1
NET EARNINGS
(IN MILLIONS)

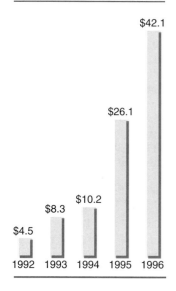

EXHIBIT 2
NET REVENUES
(IN MILLIONS)

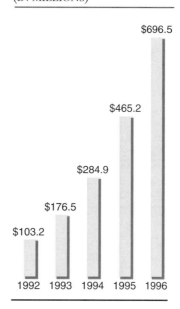

SALES & PROFITS

Starbucks' net earnings in 1996 were $42.1 million, which is a significant increase from the previous year's $26.1 million earnings (see Exhibit 1). Furthermore, its revenues grew by 575 percent from $103.2 million in 1992 to $696.5 million in 1996 (see Exhibit 2). The increase in revenues and sales was a direct result of the numerous new stores that were opened. During this period Starbucks stores grew 508 percent from 165 stores to 1,006 stores. But Starbucks has not stopped yet; it plans on opening 325 more stores in 1997.

COMMITMENT TO COFFEE

Starbucks is committed to selling only the finest whole bean coffees and coffee beverages. Starbucks roasts more than thirty varieties of the world's finest Arabica coffee beans, therefore the company goes to extreme lengths to buy the very finest Arabica coffee beans available on the world market, regardless of price. Arabica beans have a very refined flavor and contain about 1 percent caffeine by weight. These beans account for 75 percent of the world production, and are sought by specialty roasters.

 To ensure compliance with its rigorous standards, Starbucks is vertically integrated, controlling its coffee sourcing, roasting, and distribution through its company-operated retail stores. It purchases green coffee beans for its many blends and varieties from coffee-producing regions throughout the world and custom roasts them to its exacting standards. Currently, there are three roasting plants in the United States. Roasts that do not meet the company's rigorous specifications, or beans that remain in bins more than a week, are all donated to charity. Starbucks sells the fresh beans, along with rich-brewed coffees and Italian-style espresso beverages, primarily through its company-operated and licensed stores.

COMMITMENT TO THE COMMUNITY

Despite becoming extremely profitable, Starbucks has not lost sight of being socially responsible. Starbucks has contributed to CARE, a nonprofit charity organization for the needy in coffee-growing countries, since 1991. As North America's leading corporate sponsor, Starbucks has helped establish health and literacy programs in Guatemala, Indonesia, Kenya, and Ethiopia. This long-term charity program has helped improve living conditions in the coffee-producing countries that Starbucks buys from. It is the company's way of providing assistance to those developing nations with which it does business. In addition, in 1996, Starbucks established a Code of Conduct policy, which is the first step in a long-term commitment to improving social conditions in the world's coffee-growing nations.

CURRENT SITUATION

Coffee consumption in the U.S. has climbed to its highest level in nearly a decade. In 1989, there were only 200 specialty coffee stores in the U.S. Today, there are more than 5,000; the Specialty Coffee Association projects 10,000 stores by 1999. The entire coffee market is estimated to be a $30 billion industry.

In keeping with its corporate mission, Starbucks is expanding its retail outlets at an incredible rate. Most recently, Starbucks has entered several new markets including Toronto, Rhode Island, North Carolina, and Tokyo. In 1997, Starbucks is looking forward to enter Phoenix, Miami, Hawaii, and Singapore, and by the year 2000, Starbucks plans to have 2,000 locations throughout North America. Today, three million people a week visit Starbucks.

In addition to retail operations expansion, the company plans to selectively pursue other opportunities to leverage and grow the Starbucks brand through the introduction of new products and the development of new distribution channels (see Exhibit 3). Joint ventures with companies like Dreyer's Grand Ice Cream, Inc., Pepsi-Cola, and Capitol Records have enabled Starbucks to introduce new product lines into the market. In 1994, the company entered a joint venture agreement with Pepsi-Cola to develop ready-to-drink coffee products. By the spring of 1996, the company launched a new bottled coffee drink called Frappuccino™, a low-fat, creamy blend of Starbucks brewed coffee and milk. On October 31, 1995, a long-term joint venture with Dreyer's Grand Ice Cream was announced. The joint venture yielded a premium line of coffee ice creams distributed to leading grocery stores nationwide. This line has become the number-one selling super-premium coffee-flavored ice cream in the nation. Finally, joint ventures with record companies such as Capitol Records have enabled Starbucks to sell customized music CDs in its stores.

Starbucks specialty sales and marketing team has continued to develop new channels of distribution as the company is growing. Its plan to become a nationally known brand is being pushed forward by last year's deal with United Airlines, which gives Starbucks exclusive

EXHIBIT 3
STARBUCKS' BUSINESS VENTURES

March 1995	Released *Blue Note Blend* coffee and CD jointly with Capitol Records.
September 1995	First Starbucks retail store opened within an existing and newly opened state-of-the-art Star Markets.
October 1995	Signed an agreement with SAZABY Inc., a Japanese retailer and restaurateur, to form a joint venture partnership to develop Starbucks retail stores in Japan. The joint venture was called Starbucks Coffee Japan, Ltd. The first store opened in Tokyo in the summer of 1996 and marked Starbucks' first retail expansion outside of North America.
October 1995	A long-term joint venture with Dreyer's Grand Ice Cream was formed to market a premium line of coffee ice creams. Nationwide distribution to leading grocery stores occurred in the spring of 1996.
November 1995	Formed a strategic alliance with United Airlines to become the exclusive coffee supplier on every United flight.
January 1996	The North American Coffee Partnership was formed between Pepsi-Cola and Starbucks New Venture Company, a wholly-owned subsidiary of Starbucks. The partnership announced its plan to market a bottled version of Starbucks' Frappuccino™ beverage.
February 1996	Formed an agreement with Aramark Corp. to put licensed operations at various locations marked by Aramark. The first licensed location opened in the end of 1996.
September 1996	Introduced Double Black Stout™, a new dark roasted malt beer with the aromatic and flavorful addition of coffee with the Redhook Ale Brewery.
October 1996	Formed an agreement with U.S. Office Products Company, a nationwide office products supplier to corporate, commercial and industrial customers. The alliance will allow Starbucks to distribute its fresh-roasted coffee and related products to the workplace through U.S. Office Products' extensive North American channels.
1996	Formed a joint venture with Intel Corp. The venture will help push Starbucks into the market of cybercafes.

access to 75 million domestic and international travelers. However, the company's goal of expansion does not stop at airports. For two years, Starbucks has been the only coffee brand served in ITT Sheraton Corporate Hotels. In 1996, it also became the coffee of choice in Westin Hotels & Resorts. More recently it formed an alliance with U.S. Office Products to sell Starbucks coffee to offices throughout the U.S. This alliance is a tremendous opportunity for Starbucks to serve the workplace environment, and overall strengthen its customers' relationship with the Starbucks brand. Finally, Starbucks wants to grow its direct response and specialty sales operations. Starbucks' direct response group launched a new America Online Caffe Starbucks store to sell its products via Internet.

Though profits for Starbucks have increased significantly over the years, there is still cause for the company to be worried. Overall sales are still growing quickly, but the rate of growth is slowing at existing stores. Annual sales growth at stores has slid from 19 percent in 1993 to 7 percent in 1996. The biggest cause of sluggish sales growth is attributed to store cannibalization. Starbucks has been known to open stores within one block of each other in hopes of saturating the market. In addition, growth has also been hurt by poor merchandising efforts that has left many products—like mugs and coffee makers—on display for years.

INTERNATIONAL EXPANSION

With a stable business in North America, Starbucks plans on extensively expanding abroad. Starbucks' international strategy is to utilize two expansion strategies—licensing and joint-venture partnerships. The success of expanding into foreign markets is dependent on Starbucks' ability to find the right local partners to negotiate local regulations and other country-specific issues.

Currently, Starbucks exists in only two foreign countries—Japan and Singapore. The company felt that Asia offered more potential than Europe. According to one executive, "The region is full of emerging markets. Consumers' disposable income is increasing as their countries' economies grow, and most of all, people are open to Western lifestyles." Finally, coffee consumption growth rates in Southeast Asia are estimated to increase between 20 percent to 30 percent a year. With this in mind, Starbucks has plans to invest $10 million in developing its Asian operations and up to $20 million with its joint venture partners in Asia. The countries Starbucks is currently looking at include: Taiwan, South Korea, Hong Kong, Malaysia, and Indonesia.

Starbucks does not have a roasting plant in Asia as of yet. Instead, one shipment of coffee beans arrives in Asia every other week to supply the company's shops in Singapore and Japan.

JAPAN

On October 25, 1995, Starbucks Coffee International signed a joint venture agreement with SAZABY Inc., a Japanese retailer and restauranteur, to develop Starbucks retail stores in Japan. The joint venture partnership is called Starbucks Coffee Japan, Ltd. This alliance proves to be a strong one because it combines two major lifestyle companies that will provide the Japanese consumer a new and unique specialty coffee experience. Under this partnership, Starbucks opened its flagship Tokyo store in the upscale Ginza shopping district, its first retail store expansion outside of North America.

Japan is an essential part of Starbucks' international expansion plan because the nation is the third largest coffee consuming country in the world, behind the U.S. and Germany. Japan is also an ideal country because it has the largest economy in the Pacific Rim.

Starbucks currently has three stores in Tokyo and is expecting to open ten to twelve more stores by next September. The stores offer the same menu as it does in its U.S. stores, although portions are smaller. The names of items, such as 'tall' and and 'grande' are also the same as the ones used in the U.S. All of the stores will also feature the company's trademark decor and logo. In addition, Japanese customers are able to purchase Starbucks coffee beans, packaged food, coffee-making equipment as well as fresh pastries and sandwiches.

Currently Starbucks' Japanese sales are 25 percent above the originally expected sales figures. On opening day, the Japanese crowded into Starbucks and as many as 200 customers formed lines around the block to get a taste of Starbucks high quality coffee. Starbucks hopes to cultivate the same kind of coffee craze in Japan as the one it had created in North America. However, profits from the Japanese venture will not happen for several years. Operating costs, like rent and labor, in Japan are extremely high, and Starbucks will also have to pay for coffee shipment from its roasting facility in Kent to Japan. Retail space in downtown Tokyo is also more than double that of Seattle's rent.

Starbucks plans to eventually open a roasting plant in Japan to help keep costs down. However, this is contingent if the stores in Japan prove to be a success.

SINGAPORE

Economic Background

According to the 1990 U.S. Department of State, Singapore, otherwise known as the Lion State, has an annual growth rate (1998-in real terms) of 11 percent. The country's per capita income is $8,782, which is the third highest in Asia after Japan and Brunei. However, Singapore is a country that relies heavily on industry with the industrial sector (including food and beverages) making up about 17 percent of Singapore's real GDP. It imports about $44 billion in crude oil, machinery, manufactured goods and foodstuff from the U.S., European Community, Malaysia and Japan. In addition, Singapore is constantly looking for new products and new markets to drive its export-led economy. It is attempting to become a complete business center, offering multinationals, a manufacturing base, a developed financial infrastructure, and excellent communications to service region and world markets.

However, 1996 was not a very good year for Singapore. The economy grew by only 7 percent in 1996, which was down from the 8.8 percent in 1995. The main sector that was hurt by this slow growth was the manufacturing industry, which grew by 3.4 percent, down from 10 percent in 1995. In addition, the commerce sector grew by 6 percent, down from 9 percent in 1995. Analysts claim that weak economic growth, global competition, and a very slow tourist season made Singapore's retail industry very sluggish. The restaurants and hotels also recorded weak growth.

Despite slow economic growth, domestic demand grew by 12.5 percent compared to 7.2 percent in 1995. Total consumption expenditures grew by 10 percent, compared with 6 percent in 1995.

LIVING IN SINGAPORE

Singapore has one of the best living conditions in Asia. In 1995, its per capita GNP was U.S.$15,308.45. Furthermore, Singapore is known for its diversity. There are 3.01 million Singaporeans: ethnic Chinese, Malays and Indians make 77 percent, 14 percent, and 7 percent of the population, respectively. The most practiced religions are Buddhism/Taoism (53.9%), Islam (14.9%), Christianity (12.9%) and Hinduism (3.3%). The main languages are Malay, Chinese (Mandarin), Tamil and English. English is the language of administration, while Malay is the national language.

With a moderately high cost of living, Singaporeans are able to indulge in luxury goods. Much of Singapore's entertainment is influenced by Western culture. For instance, many theaters show Broadway musicals such as *Les Miserables* and pop concerts like Michael Jackson. Television programs are in English, Chinese, Malay, and Tamil. In 1992, pay TV channels such as CNN, Movievision, HBO, and Chinese Variety were introduced.

Singaporeans are known to indulge themselves with food. "So discriminating have the Singaporeans become on the subject of quality and price that eating has become a national obsession." Singapore has an array of restaurants, coffeehouses, fast-food outlets and food centers that are easily accessible and offer a variety of foods at affordable prices. Most of these food places are not air-conditioned except for those located in shopping complexes. However, eating in an air-conditioned restaurant, regardless of income level, is an affordable luxury. "The average lunch or high tea buffet spread offering a wide variety of dishes is available at many hotel coffee houses and restaurants, and it costs about $15 (Singaporean currency) or more per person. Most restaurants and coffeehouses impose a 10 percent service charge, but tipping is not encouraged."

SINGAPORE'S LOVE AFFAIR WITH COFFEE

According to Singaporean social commentator Francis Yim, "Coffeehouses are a sign that Singaporeans have achieved the status of a developed nation and we are breaking new ground in the area of becoming a cultured society." In the past during the construction of Singapore, Singaporeans did not have the time to enjoy their cup of Java. Regardless of their religion and beliefs, Singaporeans went to coffeehouses in the evenings for their meals and drank coffee in order to keep themselves awake. Now coffee is viewed as a beverage instead of a drink. People want to take the time to savor their coffee. It is not just a drink, but a personality altogether. The various flavors that coffeehouses offer reflect the different moods as well as taste.

The first Starbucks coffee outlet in Singapore opened on December 14, 1996, in Liat Towers, with the help of BonStar Pte. Ltd., a subsidiary of Bonvests Holding Ltd., a Singaporean company with food services and real estate interests. The store in Liat Towers is located in Singapore's main shopping district on Orchard Road, which is a very trendy shopping center where the French department store, Gallery Lafayette, and Planet Hollywood reside. There are plans to open ten to twelve more Starbucks in Singapore within the next year. The licensing agreement with Starbucks currently only covers Singapore, but Bonvests hopes to expand the franchises into other Asian markets. Starbucks' expansion into Singapore is its first expansion into Southeast Asia. Bonvests Holdings anticipates that the Starbucks retail stores will generate at least $40 million in sales over the next five to six years.

Bonvests is an ideal partner for several reasons. Bonvests has acquired expertise in running food businesses, like the local Burger King chain. They also know and understand the local consumer market, government regulations, and the local real estate market.

Starbucks chose Singapore for its entry in the Southeast Asian market because of the highly "westernized" ideas and lifestyles it had adopted. Some have described Starbucks as being another American icon, like McDonald's. Some even say that Starbucks has created an American coffee cult. Slowly, but surely, gourmet coffee bars have been penetrating into the food scene in Singapore. It is estimated that Singaporeans drink more than 10,000 gourmet cups a day. In addition, the market in Singapore has tremendous growth potential. According to Bruce Rolph, head of research at Saloman Brothers Singapore Pte. Ltd., "People should increasingly focus on Singapore not as a mature market with low earnings and growth potential, but as a uniquely positioned beachhead to get leverage over what's happening in Asia." Finally, the Singaporean market still has no clear leader in the specialty coffee industry. This means that Starbucks still has a good chance to become one of the top contenders in this market.

Despite the opportunities that exist for Starbucks in Singapore, there are still obstacles that Starbucks must overcome to be successful in Singapore. Competition is fierce with 14 players and 38 stores between them (see Exhibit 4). With Starbucks' entry into the Asian market, bigger retail stores, like Suntec Dome Holdings, are already gearing up for a coffee battle. However, smaller companies like Burke's Cafe and Spinelli are welcoming Star-

EXHIBIT 4
COMPETITOR PROFILES

SPINELLI

Spinelli Coffee Company, long-regarded by many as San Francisco's best coffee retailer, has been licensed by Equinox for expansion into Southeast Asia. Equinox is a joint venture between Golden Harvest, a Hong Kong film company, and Singapore Technologies Industrial Corp., a Singapore Conglomerate. Seven outlets are expected to be opened in Singapore's central business district by fall of 1997, with up to forty locations targeted for the region by the year 2000. In addition, Spinelli is also in the process of setting up roasting factories to supply the Asian Market. Spinelli brings to Asia years of experience in sourcing, producing and selling premium coffee drinks and whole bean coffee.

SUNTEC DOME HOLDINGS

Dome Café is a cafe modeled on European lines and was discovered by a Singaporean lawyer. It is best known for its distinctive sidewalk and atrium cafes, where the food menu is longer than the coffee list. They serve light snacks and full meals served all day, from sandwiches made with foccacia (a flat, Italian bread) to exotic entrees like duck and pumpkin risotto.

Suntec Dome Holdings was formed in 1996 when Suntec Investment, an investment vehicle for a group of Hong Kong tycoons, bought 51 percent stakes in the Dome Chain. Ronald Lee and Sebastian Ong, founders of Dome, imported the European-style Dome concept from Australia. They are expecting to increase the numbers of outlets from seven to seventeen within three years, an estimated $7 million is expected to be allocated for the expansion of outlets. Plans to build more roasting plants to distribute Dome's coffee in Asia are to follow, though roasting factories in Singapore and Australia exist already. Their growth strategy is to expand into several Asian countries, with six outlets within two years in Malaysia and plans for further expansion into Indonesia, Thailand, Hong Kong, and China are in the development stage.

COFFEE CLUB

Established coffee trading company Hiang Kie, now sixty years old, sniffed out the gourmet coffee trend and whipped up its first outlet in Holland Village in 1991. There are thirty-seven variations, from the humble Kopi Baba to the spicy, vintage tones of Aged Kalossi Coffee. The best attraction is the Iced Mocha Vanilla—Macciato coffee and milk topped with vanilla ice cream and a drizzle of chocolate syrup. In addition, they serve light meals of cakes, salads, sandwiches, and home-made ice cream.

COFFEE CONNECTION

Coffee Connection is the latest, trendier incarnation of Suzuki Coffee House, started in the 1980s by Sarika Coffee to showcase its Suzuki Coffee Powder. So far it is the mothership of coffee bars, with sixty-nine different drinks ranging from cool coffee jelly to Bleu Mountain Chaser. The best attraction is the Cappuccino Italiano—espresso infused with hot milk, topped with a frothy milk cap and dusted lightly with chocolate powder. They also serve ice cream, pasta, pizza, and foccacia sandwiches.

BURKE'S COFFEE

The origins of Burke's Coffee started from four Singaporean students who studied in Seattle, liked the espresso bars, and brought back the concept. Burke's Coffee is a Seattle-styled cafe, bringing the lifestyle of the Pacific Northwest to Singapore. Burke has made a name for itself as a friendly and inviting place in the midst of the hustle and bustle of downtown Singapore. The store has established a loyal customer base of young professionals who visit the store frequently. Burke's serve sandwiches, soups, and desserts. There are seven basic coffee drinks, plus twelve Italian syrups that you can add on request. The best attraction is the Mocha Freeze and Hazelnut Latte.

bucks' entry. Their strategy is to open an outlet right next to Starbucks to attract the customers that overflow from Starbucks.

One of Starbucks' biggest competitors, Suntec Dome Holdings, has already established itself in Singapore. Suntec Dome Holdings already has a good name recognition with Suntec Walk, Suntec City, Dome Cafe, and so on. Suntec is distinctive from the other retail coffee stores in that it is seen more as a restaurant than a coffee chain. It targets a broader market segment with a lower budget range. They are also backed by major supporters with the capital to counter Starbucks' expansion strategy. In addition to Singapore, Suntec Dome Holdings has plans to expand to other markets such as Malaysia, Indonesia, Thailand, Hong Kong, and China. Spinelli, a smaller competitor, also plans to expand into the region. With these plans of expansion to be completed by the year 2000, Spinelli will be potentially a major threat to Starbucks.

More well-known coffee spots to Singaporeans are Coffee Connection and Coffee Club, which are also direct competitors of Starbucks. The customers that go to Coffee Connection and Coffee Club like the atmosphere and the service they receive there. As reflected here, Singapore has seen a proliferation of gourmet coffee outlets in the past few years; therefore, the market is slowly becoming overcrowded.

Starbucks will need to turn some heads and create the brand equity they need to stay in competition with their competitors. However, they do have an advantage entering this market. Starbucks packages a coffee-drinking experience that the Singaporeans want, both trendy and American. As mentioned earlier, Singaporeans love American products and hopefully, that will translate into major dollars for Starbucks in Singapore.

Second, Starbucks faces a challenge in Singapore amid a prolonged and still-deepening crisis in the retail industry. Major retailers, like Kmart and France's Galeries Lafayette, have recently left Singapore after much failure.

CASE 2

GAP INC.

Since it started in 1969, Gap Inc. has been consistently growing and expanding. With more than 1,500 stores in the United States, Canada, the United Kingdom, France, and Australia, Gap Inc. is currently the second largest selling brand in the world and is ranked second among all U.S. retailers in sales. This case study begins with a brief history of Gap Inc., followed by details of its operating components, an analysis of its current and future foreign markets, and a conclusion.

A BRIEF HISTORY OF GAP INC.

Gap Inc. was established in August 1969 by Donald G. Fisher, a real estate developer educated at the University of California, Berkeley. Fisher conceived the idea when he went to a department store to exchange a pair of Levi's and was unable to because the jeans department was so disorganized. Backed by a $63,000 family investment and a $112,000 bank loan guaranteed by his father-in-law, Donald Fisher introduced the first Gap store in San Francisco. His original idea was to focus on the mid-teen market with three types of goods: records, cassette tapes, and

Source: This case was written by Masaaki Kotabe.

Levi's jeans. Unlike the local department stores, which stocked only a limited number of styles and sizes of Levi's jeans, the Gap store carried every size and style available. Furthermore, they were neatly arranged and easy to find. Donald Fisher and his wife had a discussion about the "generation gap" in 1969, and from that discussion came the name Gap Inc., under which the company was incorporated in California in July 1969. Gap Inc. was reincorporated in 1988 under the laws of Delaware.

Growth and Expansion

Although the original targeted customers were primarily young people, the convenience of a neatly organized jeans store with Levi's products attracted customers of all ages. In less than one year, Gap's business took off, and a second Gap was opened in San Jose. In less than two years, there were six Gap stores in California. By 1972, Gap Inc. had 25 stores in six states. In 1973, Gap Inc. ventured into the East Coast market, opening 12 stores in New York, New Jersey, and Pennsylvania. In 1974, Gap expanded into Washington, Minnesota, Missouri, Oklahoma, Maryland, Virginia, Georgia, Arizona, Texas, and Illinois, with a total of 90 stores. In 1976, Gap Inc. went public with its stocks selling at 75 cents a share. In 1979, Gap Inc. opened a modern distribution facility in Denver, Colorado. By 1981, Gap Inc. had opened 500 stores nationwide. In 1983, Gap Inc. purchased Banana Republic. By 1985, there were 613 Gap stores and 35 Banana Republics. The first GapKids store was introduced in 1987, then in 1988, the Old Navy Clothing Company was first introduced. In the same year, Gap opened two factory outlets selling merchandise at discount prices. In 1990, GapKids formed a separate department for baby clothing called BabyGap. In 1992, Gap stores also formed a separate department called Gap Shoes. As of January 1995, there are 892 Gaps, 369 GapKids, 188 Banana Republics, 58 Old Navy Clothing Companies, and a Gap Warehouse.

Selling Private Store Brand Product

Within three months of opening the Gap, Fisher realized that the real business was in selling Levi's jeans, so he dropped the records and cassette tapes from his inventory. Until the end of 1973, Gap advertised and carried only Levi's brand products. In 1974, Gap introduced its first private-label clothing into the merchandising mix. When price maintenance crumbled because of a Federal Trade Commission directive in 1976, Levi's products began to sell at discount, and Fisher was convinced that Gap's competitive advantage could not rely solely on the low prices of Levi's products. Since then, he has focused on reducing Gap's reliance on sales of Levi's products. As a result, Levi's products began to decrease as a percentage of Gap's total sales. By 1987, Levi's made up less than 50 percent of Gap's total sales. By 1985, Levi's sales dropped to 21 percent of Gap's total sales, then 14 percent in 1987. Finally, in 1990, Gap dropped Levi's altogether and started selling only private-labeled products.

GAP INC. OPERATING COMPONENTS

Gap Inc. is a specialty retailer that operates stores selling casual apparel, shoes, and other accessories for men, women, and children. It includes six registered trade names: Gap, GapKids, BabyGap, Gap Shoes, Banana Republic, and Old Navy Clothing Company.

Retail Divisions

Gap operates under five different divisions: Gap, Banana Republic, GapKids, Old Navy, and International Division. The first four operate domestically, and the last one operates all of the stores from the first four divisions that open overseas.

Gap Division. This division has by far the most stores—more than all of the other divisions combined—with 829 stores operating in the United States at the end of 1994. The Gap Shoes subdivision also operates under this division. All stores under the Gap division are called The Gap. The Gap stores are classified as clothing retail stores for men and women, with Standard Industrial Code 5651. In the United States, there are 145 domestic competitors for The Gap; and in 1994 The Gap ranked third in sales. In the beginning, products under this division consisted of an assortment of unisex basics; but recently they have evolved to become more gender specific.

Banana Republic Division. When purchased in February 1983, Banana Republic was already famous for its travel and safari wear, but only two Banana Republic stores existed in 1983 when Gap Inc. made the purchase. After the purchase was completed, the parent company created a new division to operate all Banana Republic stores. Gap Inc. also invested capital to create a product development and production team for Banana Republic, allowing it to introduce its own new private label fashions. In addition, there was rapid expansion into other parts of the country. Products under the Banana Republic division are more upscale, more tailored, and come in more refined fabrics than those in The Gap stores. Leather goods and jewelry goods have been introduced into the merchandise mix.

GapKids Division. After this division was formed in 1986, it became the fastest growing division of Gap Inc. All stores under this division are called GapKids stores. Products in this division are essentially miniature versions of The Gap products, but with more focus on color variations. These products have also switched from unisex to more gender specific. The formation of the BabyGap subdivision under GapKids is another reason for the rapid growth of this division. During the beginning of 1994, not all GapKids stores included a BabyGap section, but this was expected to change in 1995.

Old Navy Clothing Company Division. This division operates all Old Navy Stores and Gap Warehouse. There are now 58 Old Navy stores operating under this division since the first introduction in 1994. There is also a Gap Warehouse operating under this division. The formation of the Old Navy division came at a time when sales were down, and Gap Inc. needed new ways to attract customers. The strategy was to sell merchandise similar to Gap stores but at lower costs. This division is expected to surpass the GapKids division and become the fastest growing division of Gap Inc.

International Division. All stores located in foreign countries are under the control of International Division, which is led by President William S. Fisher. This division currently includes Gap stores, GapKids stores, and Banana Republic stores, but not Old Navy stores. The first overseas store was established in 1987 in London, thus gaining entry into the British apparel market. In 1988 the first store in Canada was established, and in 1993 the first in France was opened. As of 1994, the International Division operated 40 Gap and GapKids in England, 59 in Canada, and 3 in France. International Division also operates Banana Republic in Canada and Australia. International Division shows strong growth potential and continues to expand existing markets in Europe while preparing to gain first entry into two new markets: Germany and Japan.

Products and Customer Base

The Gap division sells mainly men's and women's casual and active wear. Clothing items including jeans, sweat suits, sweatshirts, denim wear, polo-style pocket T-shirts are marketed. The Gap division has also expanded its market to include handbags, shoes, and a higher fashion line of evening wear. In addition, during the 1990s the Gap division entered the bodycare products and cosmetics market, introducing soaps, body lotions, shower gels, shampoos, conditioners, aromatic candles, and other related items. In addition to selling travel and safari wear, the Banana Republic division sells men's and women's casual wear, made of finer fabrics and priced higher than can be found in Gap stores. Together, the Gap stores and the Banana Republic divisions target mainly customers 20 years or older. GapKids, which sells miniaturized versions of Gap store products, originally aimed at children aged 2 to 12, but with the introduction of BabyGap, it has been able to add even younger customers to its customer base. Old Navy Division, selling cheaper products, targets lower-income shoppers. International Division targets foreign customers in similar age groups mentioned earlier.

Sourcing

Gap purchases merchandise from some 700 sources located both in the United States and overseas. This procurement strategy is designed to reduce each supplier's importance, so that no single supplier can affect Gap's overall operations significantly. All suppliers account for no greater than 5 percent of the purchase. The suppliers manufacture the Gap's private-label merchandise according to the company's specifications. Gap purchases are comprised of 40 percent domestic-made merchandise and 60 percent foreign-made merchandise. Of the foreign sources, approximately 23 percent are from Hong Kong, and the remaining purchases are spread across 42 other countries. Hong Kong, Taiwan, South Korea, Singapore, and China constitute over 50 percent of Gap's foreign merchandise sources. Sudden political instability in any of these countries could quickly have an adverse effect on

Gap's sourcing operations, as would any imposition of import restrictions such as tariffs and quotas by the U.S. government on products made in these countries. Both the recent threat by the U.S. government to deny China most favored nation (MFN) status and China's impending takeover of Hong Kong in 1997 are causes for great concern for Gap's management.

Hong Kong is by far the most important foreign source of Gap's merchandise. Hong Kong has a total population of 6.019 million, of which 17.8 percent are engaged in manufacturing and 33.6 percent are in either retail trade or wholesale. Until recently, Hong Kong had an unemployment rate of only 2.2 percent, and the Hong Kong government has to import labor from abroad to counter a shortage in labor supply. Despite this labor shortage, the well-educated labor force in Hong Kong is relatively cheap to employ, and with the increased pressure of manufacturing companies moving across the border into China, even cheaper labor may result. U.S. retailers, including Gap Inc., have long been the target of criticism for selling goods imported from Hong Kong and other low-wage countries such as Taiwan and South Korea. In addition to its low wage rate, Hong Kong is a favored apparel source for many retailers because of the flexible manufacturing and quick response strategies introduced by the Hong Kong Productivity Council and adapted by many of Hong Kong's apparel producers. Both of these strategies reduce inventory costs for the retailers. Furthermore, the apparel industry in Hong Kong is now adapting to many new technologies and production methodologies, all aimed at reducing apparel production costs. Problems that might arise in the future include increased cost for apparel items from Hong Kong because of the strengthening of the Hong Kong dollar against the U.S. dollar, and the fear concerning Communist China's takeover in 1997. Despite the takeover, the leading spokespeople for Hong Kong's apparel industry are mostly optimistic that Hong Kong's apparel industry will remain strong.

Advertising

Gap Inc. advertises mainly through major newspaper publications, but it also advertises in fashion magazines and on mass transit posters, billboards, and exterior bus panels. All advertisements stress the central theme of American design, quality, and moderate pricing, although they are produced separately in each country to suit local tastes.

Distribution

All merchandise is shipped to distribution centers for distribution. These centers are located in California, Kentucky, Maryland, Canada, and the United Kingdom.

GAP'S EXISTING FOREIGN MARKETS

Gap's existing foreign markets include Canada, Britain, France, and Australia. Following is a detailed analysis of each market.

Canadian Market

As store openings increased across the United States during the 1980s, Gap Inc. began to realize the potential for expanding into the Canadian market.

General Economy. During the mid-1980s, prior to Gap Inc.'s Canadian involvement, Canada enjoyed a stable and slowly growing economy. This brief boom was followed by a recession in the late 1980s. While other Canadian companies suffered, Gap Inc. sought to gain first-mover advantages by riding a possible rebound in the economy and tried to become a dominant player in the Canadian apparel industry. The Canadian government imposes few restrictions on foreign direct investment. This was a major decision factor in Gap Inc.'s move to set up stores in Canada with the opening of eight stores in Vancouver in March 1989. The first of these was in Vancouver's Pacific Center.

Government Regulations. Since it is a good environment for apparel market penetration, Canada subscribes to the General Agreement on Tariffs and Trade. This greatly influenced Gap's later decisions to expand into other countries as well. Even though Gap Inc. conducts its sourcing mostly outside of the United States, it ships those goods back through the United States, so that they have to be imported into countries like Canada. In addition, Canada's goal of totally eliminating tariffs on goods of U.S. origin by 1998, which it has already begun implementing, provides Gap Inc. with an advantage on entering the Canadian apparel market. This trend has enabled American companies like Gap Inc. to lower their cost of doing business in Canada by making it cheaper to import their products from the United States. Canada even assists U.S. companies planning to enter the Canadian market through the United States and FCS Export Assistance Service. Along with fewer government restrictions, Gap Inc. did not encounter the traditional barriers of entry such as local content requirements, political turmoil, and import quotas.

Market Expansion. In 1992, Gap Inc. made a big expansion move further into the Canadian apparel market. In a joint venture with John Forsyth Company Inc., Gap Inc. began to compete on the same level as native Canadian apparel companies such as Hudson Bay Co. With the impending North American Free Trade Agreement, Canada's borders were now completely open to outside competition. This development paved the way for even more store openings for Gap Inc.

Now, Gap Inc. not only has to compete with Canadian apparel companies like Hudson Bay Co. for market share, but also with new U.S. companies in Canada such as The Limited. This increased competition has made Gap Inc. look at further Canadian expansion from a different perspective. According to Gap Inc.'s Ken Rapp, "The holdup is no longer a free trade issue, but a dearth of good retail space in Canada where there are fewer shopping malls per capita and lower vacancy rates."

With ever-increasing success, Gap Inc.'s Canadian stores began to branch out with Canadian versions of the U.S. GapKids and BabyGap in the early 1990s. This expansion was made possible in part by Canada's recovering economy and notable growth in the apparel industry. Turtleneck jerseys, a Gap staple, rose in sales 122 percent. Men's outerwear rose 17 percent after a three-year decline.

Growth Projections. Riding on the success of Gap and GapKids stores, Gap Inc. believes its Banana Republic division will not have a difficult time establishing stores in Canada. Banana Republic, a more upscale, higher-priced version of The Gap, opened stores in Eaton Center in Toronto and West Edmonton Mall in Alberta. Gap Inc. seeks to steal some market share from existing Canadian chain stores such as Roots, River Road, and Eddie Bauer by installing Banana Republic stores. As of February 1995, Gap Inc. had plans to open 30 mores Banana Republics within the next five years.

Market Characteristics. According to the International Trade Administration's Canadian Market Overview, the new trend in the Canadian apparel market is to economize by saving money on clothing. This is because of increases in housing costs and taxes. Female consumers are becoming more time-pressured, and as a result, they are spending half as much time per month shopping as they did ten years ago. In general, adult consumers are becoming more knowledgeable about the clothing they buy and are more careful in evaluating their purchases in terms of value.

United Kingdom Market

According to UK trade journals, American apparels are making a strong show in the British market and will continue to do so in the near future. Approximately 60 percent of men's apparel and 35 percent of women's apparel are sold through retail stores.

Market Size. According to the 1991 International Market Report, the British market for men's apparel is about $3.34 billion, and the women's apparel market is about $4.59 billion. Both are in decline because of recession.

Market Health. The UK market for apparels is currently in a recession. British retailers are hoping for "business as usual" once again in the not too distant future, but according to market analysts, recovery is still a long way off. There are occasional mini surges in consumer spending, and retailers have devised some strategies to capitalize on these surges. One strategy is to lower price while stressing quality. Another is to adopt the "one-stop-shopping" concept, that is, pairing men's and women's merchandise together in one store so both can be bought simultaneously. This strategy was in response to an observation that consumers now have a tendency to come in couples. Some retailers even place children's apparel items along with men's and women's apparel items, thus creating a true "one-stop-shop."

Market Trends. British consumers are highly receptive to U.S. designed and manufactured apparel items. Studies show that the average British consumer thinks of American designers as firm believers in making practical clothes for real people, as compared to European designers who make fashion show-style clothing that is unwearable. Outerwear sold by such retailers as Gap Inc. and Timber-land is very popular. Men's and women's apparel trends differ in that menswear tends to be more basic; the changes are usually in color and fabric, not style. Men are moving toward plainer pieces and away from heavily logoed styles. Women purchase with more focus on fashion designer labels.

Customer Base. The 15–25 year-old age group tends to make purchases in boutiques. Older consumers shop in stores that are well known for quality, durability, and good value. Most retailers now are focusing on customers who are over 25 years old. This is because of increasing youth unemployment and an aging population of baby boomers. A significant percentage of the customer base is made up of large-sized customers, particularly women.

Competitions. American-made apparels face competition from European designers, Asian-made apparels, and from each other. European designers from the European Union can ship their goods to the United Kingdom duty-free, and Asian-made items are usually produced by cheap labor.

Government Regulations and Market Access. There are few trade barriers for apparel. No special forms of documentation are required for apparel items going to the United Kingdom. No special standards are set. No import licenses are necessary. Textile raw materials enter the United Kingdom with up to 15 percent duty, while finished apparel items are charged with up to 14 percent duty and value-added tax of 17.5 percent. No duties have to be paid for goods imported temporarily to the United Kingdom or located in freeports (UK free-trade zones).

FRENCH MARKET

France is Gap's newest foreign market, and so far only three Gap stores operate in France. The following analysis of the French apparel market includes size of market, characteristics of growth, growth projection, industry structure, competitors and substitutes, and government regulations.

Size of Market. According to the U.S. Department of Commerce *World Apparel Market Research Report* published in 1993, France was the sixth largest market for apparel, with demand of $11.830 million. It was also the sixth largest market for apparel imports from the United States, with total demand of $152 million.

Market Characteristics and Current Growth. The French apparel market can be characterized as a mature, sophisticated, slow-growth market rather than an emerging market. It is experiencing 4 percent average annual growth and 2 percent annual growth in its market for U.S. imports. The United States does not have a large share of the French market at the moment. However, the French are becoming more receptive to U.S. fashion, especially U.S. sportswear. French women are just beginning to buy American-made apparel, and the natural "American look," especially Western-wear clothing, is becoming popular in France. The 15–25 year-old age group is very fashion conscious and strongly influenced by American styles, especially jeans and college or football team logo apparel.

Growth Projections. The industry has suffered from the worldwide economic slowdown since 1991, but analysts expected improvements in 1994 and 1995. Apparel sales are expected to grow at a rate of 2 percent. In spite of the low market share of U.S. firms, France is very promising for Gap Inc. The French have a high level of receptiveness to U.S. goods, and the market for U.S. imports is expected to continue to grow at 2 to 3 percent annually. Unfortunately, local and third-party competition is high, but market barriers in this area are negligible and do not pose a problem. According to the U.S. Department of Commerce International Trade Administration, the current two most promising subsectors in apparel for U.S. companies are sportswear and jeans.

Business Environment. The French commercial environment is very dynamic and sophisticated, and reflects consumer trends quickly. There is a strong market for high-quality consumer goods. Independent specialty stores are the main means of distribution in affluent cities.

Business Attitude Toward the United States and Exit/Entry Barriers. In general, the attitude toward American companies is favorable and the French are quite receptive to U.S. goods and services. However, strong interest groups have a lot of power in influencing business judgment and government action or inaction. These interest groups have been known to stage noisy demonstrations, but they usually are only a problem for companies that pose a major threat to French suppliers.

There are no major entry or exit barriers to doing business in France for most companies. Tariffs and duties on American products are discussed later.

Competitors and Substitutes. Local and third-party competition is rampant in the French market. It is particularly heavy in the consumer area where buyers are just beginning to look for "value" in their product choices, and most product lines that are available are mature. In this mature and sophisticated market, consumers are well served by suppliers around the world. Therefore, it is unlikely that any major business breakthroughs will occur, but opportunities can be created in niche markets.

There is a natural tendency now for the French to buy apparel from within the European Union because of the increasingly free flow of goods since the integration of Europe. Italy is and always has been a significant high-quality clothing competitor in France. However, Gap's main competitors are North African and Southeast Asian companies, which have a strong presence in France because of their low production costs. At the moment, Asian countries have 31.7 percent of the French market for women's clothing, and this number is expected to remain constant.

There has also been an increase in imports from Morocco, Tunisia, Portugal, and, recently, East Europe. Again, companies from these countries enjoy low production costs and close proximity to the French market. Morocco and Tunisia are actually the main suppliers of menswear imports to France, but the U.S. share of the menswear market has been increasing rapidly.

As far as substitutes, there has been a massive growth of supermarkets and hypermarkets (huge shopping stores with a wide variety of products) in France. This is not just in food but also in apparel. These stores could pose a threat to specialty stores such as The Gap if people begin doing all of their shopping at hypermarkets and stop going to the specialty stores.

Government Regulations and Controls. France has had a tradition of highly centralized administrative and governmental control of its essentially market economy. However, the apparel industry has little restrictions other than tariffs and duties on imported products.

As part of the European Union, the TARIC system applies duties to all imports from non-EU countries. This gives European companies a slight cost advantage over U.S. companies. However, this can be negated if production costs for U.S. companies can be lowered. Duties on manufactured goods from the United States are moderate, ranging from 5 to 17 percent; they are calculated as a percentage of the value of the imported good. Under the Lome Conventions, varying preferential tariff treatment is given to imports from developing countries in Africa, the Caribbean, and the Pacific, which gives companies an incentive to manufacture in these countries.

Australian Market

Following the lead of successful U.S. retailer Toys "Я" Us, Gap Inc. has been negotiating possible sites for another international outlet. Store location, product positioning, and marketing and advertising decisions depend heavily on how Gap executives assess the following conditions.

Economic Health. Consumption expenditures continue to increase in the face of high unemployment, which rose in 1992 by 2 percent, and by 7 percent in 1993. Analysts say that a reverse in this trend, which was expected in 1994 and 1995, is the key to a robust recovery. The average annual growth rate for the apparel market during this period is expected to be between 3 and 5 percent.

The downward push against inflation was one of the few positive effects of the recent recession. Lower inflation numbers are a positive sign to potential investors, many of whom have been discouraged by the sliding Australian dollar. A strong local currency is helpful for specialty retailers like the Gap on two levels. First, its products will become relatively more price competitive. Second, Gap would benefit from a strong Australian dollar through translation gains, as profits are repatriated.

Others are wary that the removal of quotas and tariffs will foster a fiscally unhealthy demand for imports. If past performance is any indication, economic expansion would most likely lead to a rise in the current account deficit. Officials cite that if the president's goal of 4 to 5 percent GDP growth is realized, the current account deficit will increase from 3.75 to 4.25 percent of GDP during the same period.

Market Barriers and Government Regulations. In the recent past, currency exchange-rate levels and hefty import duties made it difficult to sell U.S. apparel products in Australia. Thankfully, import duties are on the decline: currently 47 percent, as compared to 55 percent and 60 percent just two years ago. The Australian government promises that this figure will continue to fall, via the TCF tariff reduction program, by 3 percent annually until the year 2000. The tariff on textiles and apparel is then expected to level off at 25 percent. Add to this the abolition of import quotas in February 1993, and foreign apparel retailers and their products become increasingly attractive in the face of domestic competition. This despite the recent "Buy Australian" campaign, which Australian officials insist has successfully increased consumers' preferences for locally made products.

Gap Inc. executives must also consider the additional costs associated with the newest clothing standards to be adopted by Standards Australia, a national regulatory committee. The new standard rates clothing according to the protection it offers from the sun. If adopted, Gap must carefully consider which products should be introduced in Australia and possibly reconsider its own internal manufacturing standards.

Competitors and Competition. Competitors vying for the U.S.$1.3 billion in apparel revenues include traditional department stores, discount retailers, mail-order companies, home shopping clubs, and a growing contingent of specialty shops, including Gap. Industry sources estimate that 15 percent of the market is captured by traditional retailers, and 85 percent of the market is sold through other means. Experts also say that, of the expected 4 percent growth in the apparel market, an increasing proportion is expected to be captured by competitively priced imports. Competitors in Australia's apparel market break down as follows:

Department Stores: Department store leaders like Coles Myer, David Jones, and Georges sell to the middle of the market. These stores tend to sell higher-quality apparel goods, with various departments devoted to discount and specialty apparel. Coles Myer, for example, has a Myer's Bargain Basement department, and its rival Georges offers a floor devoted exclusively to international apparel. Gap will take business mainly from David Jones and Coles Myer.

Chain Stores and Boutiques: These stores generally sell according to the selective tastes of their target markets. Gap stores are somewhat different from these retailers in that they would sell Gap brand items exclusively. Sportsgirl, catering to female teenagers, and Portmans are the largest in this segment and would compete directly with the Gap.

Mail-Order Companies/Home Shopping Clubs: Through its subsidiary Myer's Direct, Coles Myer has broadened its attack on consumers on two fronts: mail-order catalogues and a new home shopping program. The initial response to the home shopping program was not very enthusiastic; however, its mail-order business, the largest in the country, has been more successful, averaging 50 to 60 percent growth since its inception in 1989.

Positioning. Gap Inc. should continue to take advantage of its niche appeal as a U.S./California-based apparel company. Although U.S. companies, in general, face heavy competition in Australia, single brand stand-alone stores like the Gap will always find opportunities in niche markets. Gap should avoid competing on the basis of price with imports from China and Hong Kong. Gap's greatest initial success will come from providing one of Australia's populous cities, such as Sydney or Melbourne, fashionable, high-quality "American" apparel products.

NEW MARKETS FOR GAP'S ENTRY

As of 1995, Gap Inc. had announced plans to expand into two new markets: Germany and Japan. Following is an analysis of the two markets.

The German Market

Although no contracts have been signed, Gap's financial director Robert Fisher has announced his company's intentions to open a store in Germany. Gap executives must consider the following challenges and opportunities that are unique to the German apparel market.

Market and Economic Health. In 1993, Germany was ranked at the top of the list of apparel importers at U.S. $26.7 billion. A closer look shows that the most promising subsectors were sports, leisure and casual wear (U.S.$6.1 billion), and jeans wear (U.S.$3.1 billion). Average annual growth for Germany's apparel industry through 1995 is estimated to be around 3 percent.

The German clothing industry fared well under the prevailing conditions of the late 1980s and early 1990s, which were a result of the ongoing reunification process. The opening of East Germany, with a population of 16 million, offers potentially large profits and a number of challenges for apparel managers seeking new markets. For the most part, apparel retailers are choosing to enter this market through joint ventures and partnerships, but others, like Levi Strauss, have chosen to establish their own branches. Still, progress in this region is painfully slow as the transition from a command economy to a market economy progresses.

Consumer Attitudes. Consumer spending is an integral part of economic growth in Germany and for Europe as a whole. Lately, however, German consumers have been unwilling to participate, and recovery in the region has stalled. Several factors have contributed to this cautious consumer attitude: rising unemployment, which was already 10 percent at the beginning of 1994, higher rents, which have increased by 6 percent in the west and by as much as 58 percent in the east, and high tax rates—currently 34.4 percent for the average worker. Even Germans from the east, who were hungry for consumer goods from the west, are becoming finicky shoppers. The bargain shopping attitude that is prevalent in the United States has found its way to East Germany. "They don't buy so many trendy articles—it's back to basics like T-shirts, jeans, blazers, and sweaters."

Competitors and Competition. Because of these recent changes in consumer attitudes, low-cost apparel imports now dominate the German market. Basic items from Eastern Europe, Turkey, and Asia can be found for one tenth of the price of comparable U.S. offerings. This is not to say that consumers in Germany are not willing to pay higher prices for U.S. goods. Items must not only be of good quality, but must also carry a well-known American trademark.

Leading competitors include Hugo Boss, a menswear manufacturer and retailer that is currently the most profitable in Germany. Boss's success is mostly a result of repositioning its product lines. It has recently included a lower-end product line under a different label, in addition to its traditional mid-priced and premium-priced offerings. Gap will be in direct competition with Hugo Boss for casual wear revenues. Adler, a discount fashion chain, has 54 stores in Germany, 7 of which were recently opened in East Germany. Gap should avoid competing head to head with Adler on a price per unit basis.

Positioning. Initially, Gap executives should expect to spend a considerable amount of capital in this market. A strong initial showing is important if Gap wants to become a recognizable American label. Germans have shown a willingness to pay a premium for highly recognizable American goods and have done so, paying between U.S.$80 and U.S.$100 for a pair of Levi's jeans. Strong, pervasive television and print advertising is the key to creating this image awareness.

The Japanese Market

With a total population of 75 million people, Japan would make an excellent market for Gap's products. Following is an overview of this market.

Size of Market. The U.S. Department of Commerce *World Apparel Market Research Report*, 1993 shows Japan as being the largest total market for apparel, with total demand of $69,360 million. It is the second largest market for apparel imports from the United States, with a demand of $573 million, but this statistic is slightly misleading. This is because the Dominican Republic, which tops Japan in this category, is merely a major assembly point for U.S. apparel and not a major market. The goods are assembled there in a low-cost environment but are transported abroad and sold in other countries. Thus, Japan is in reality the largest market for U.S.-made apparel products.

Market Characteristics and Current Growth. As a result of the economic recession in Japan over the last sev-

eral years, the average annual growth rate for apparel in Japan has only been 3 percent, but imports from the United States have been increasing at an annual rate of 11 percent. This large growth is due to the boom of "American casual fashion" in Japan.

In the past, European fashions, especially Italian fashions, were followed closely in Japan. However, today many Japanese prefer American fashions, in particular, casual apparel. Sports-related products such as T-shirts, sweat suits, and clothing with professional sports team logos are particularly popular, and so are jeans, outdoor wear, and any items with a casual, uniquely American look. Individuals in the 15–25 year-old age group follow U.S. fashion trends closely. However, women's wear and children's clothing wear in the United States are not gaining popularity quickly and are facing difficulties in the Japanese market.

Another trend in the Japanese market, and indeed in all sectors of business, is the growing tendency of consumers to demand "value." Consumers are noticing that their prices are much higher than those of comparable industrialized countries (Japanese consumer prices average 40 percent higher than those in the United States). Consumers still want high quality but are also demanding lower prices.

Growth Projections. According to the U.S. Department of Commerce International Trade Administration, apparel was the thirteenth best prospect industry sector in Japan for U.S. exporters in 1995. Analysts predict that the overall Japanese economy, which has been in recession until recently, will improve, but consumers are likely to be more cautious about spending money. This is in line with the growing trend toward "value." The apparel market is expected to continue growing at 3 percent, but import growth is expected to increase. Japan has a very high level of receptivity to U.S. goods, not much local and third country competition, and almost no market barriers to entry. For Gap Inc., this indicates a favorable environment. However, the distribution system in Japan is the main obstacle to market entry and may pose major problems. The most promising subsector in the apparel industry for 1995 is men's and women's wear.

Business Environment. The domestic market is very competitive, and consumers are highly brand conscious. Long-standing, close-knit relationships between individuals and firms are very important in business operations. Local business practices are very traditional and foreign company participation is not considered important. A long-term approach is essential for U.S. companies in Japan to develop the necessary business relationships and show a willingness to contribute to the local business community.

Business Attitude Toward the U.S. and Exit/Entry Barriers. Japan has a positive attitude toward U.S. suppliers, and many U.S. companies have established reputations in Japan for high quality, reasonably priced products. However, it is still proving difficult for some U.S. companies to overcome traditional Japanese attitudes toward foreigners as being "outsiders." In the past, Japanese laws and regulations prevented many U.S.-based companies from entering Japan after World War II. The result has been little interaction until recently, and Japanese companies are hesitant to trust American firms. Officially, Japanese government policy is to promote imports and international business interaction, but traditional business attitudes are making this difficult.

It is also difficult for many U.S. companies to be accepted as business partners by Japanese companies that are bound by *keiretsu* ties that prevent them from doing business with non-*keiretsu* companies. If a Japanese company that is part of the country's *keiretsu* is qualified in a particular business area, it will be chosen over a U.S. company. This is a significant barrier to market entry in Japan.

The most difficult obstacle for U.S. companies to overcome in Japan is the traditional distribution system. The *keiretsu* system controls many of these distribution networks and long distribution channels in which all participants must purchase from and sell to each other. This makes it very difficult for U.S. companies to get into a distribution system.

Competitors and Substitutes. Competition in the apparel industry comes mainly from low-cost Asian companies that also have the advantage of easy access to Japanese markets. However, U.S. brand image is very important and Asian products are considered low quality. European companies provide some competition, but this is mainly in the area of high-end brand name and designer clothing. Japanese companies' competitiveness is eroded by the high manufacturing costs resulting from the strong yen.

Substitutes in the form of low-price discount retailers are becoming increasingly prevalent in Japan. They could pose a threat to higher-priced apparel stores such as The Gap.

Government Regulation and Controls. There is an incredible amount of government regulation in the Japanese business environment. This is mainly in the form of licenses, permits, and approvals that are required to do business. These licenses often take a long time to process and are somewhat of a barrier to market entry. In addition, "administrative guidance" papers, which are informal edicts issued by government officials to companies, are used to control foreign companies and restrict market entry. Although the Japanese government has removed most of the legal and administrative restrictions on foreign business activities in Japan, anticompetitive and exclusionary business practices still exist at lower levels of government. However, the government is actively seeking ways to increase foreign investment and imports.

CONCLUSION

As Gap Inc. continues to expand into the foreign markets, it should consider several options to reduce costs and thereby increase profit. First, because Gap Inc. does not produce or procure merchandises in any of the foreign markets it is currently in, establishing free-trade zones in those countries might help increase profits by temporarily reducing duty and VAT costs, and no duties would be paid on extra merchandise. Second, attention should be paid to centralizing advertising to reduce cost. Third, the problems associated with sourcing from so many different regions should be considered and ways found to correct them. Finally, Gap Inc. should seek ways to take advantage of the many free-trade agreements that recently have been signed.

EXHIBIT 1
NET SALES COMPARISON (in US$)

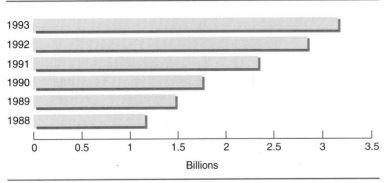

EXHIBIT 2
NET EARNINGS COMPARISON (in US$)

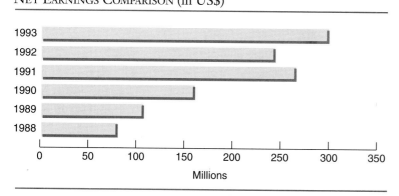

EXHIBIT 3
STOCK PERFORMANCE (in US$)

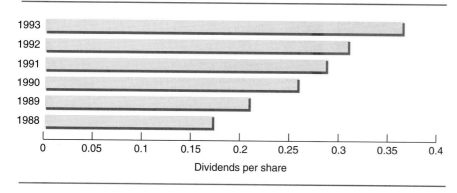

EXHIBIT 4
ANNUAL APPAREL IMPORTS FROM THE UNITED STATES (in US$ MILLIONS)

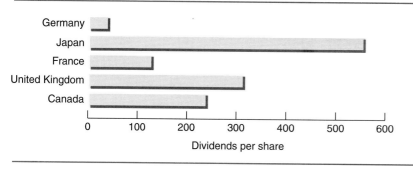

CASE 3

SEGA: THE WAY THE WEST WAS WON

HISTORY OF SEGA: OVERVIEW

Coming out of the Air Force after a tour of duty in Tokyo, David Rosen, a 20-year-old Brooklyn native, noticed that Japanese people needed lots of ID photographs, but the local photo studios were slow and expensive. To cater to this need, he established Rosen Enterprises and went into the instant photo booth business. In 1957, the Korean War ended and Japan's economy started to boom. To Rosen, this meant the time was right to get into the entertainment business. He imported used arcade games from Chicago and placed them in Japanese theaters and department stores. With his business prospering, he merged it with another American-owned business in Japan, Service Games, and formed SEGA Enterprises in 1965. In Japan, SEGA was involved in all aspects of the industry. This integrated approach included activities in operations, distribution, and manufacturing. Integration allowed considerable flexibility in the business, and as a reward for this flexibility, profits tended to be more considerably stable than SEGA's competitors, who were involved in only part of the industry. As a result of this integration, products manufactured by SEGA were not only sold to distributor/operators, but they were used in SEGA's own operations. SEGA was its own best customer.

Innovation was the key ingredient in SEGA's success. SEGA introduced the first generation of commercial video games to Japan in 1973 and marketed its first microprocessor-based game, *Rodeo*, in 1975. In 1979, SEGA introduced *Head On*, a game that incorporated SEGA's MultiPhase technology that allowed players to progress through increasingly difficult levels of the video game as their skills improved. The successful development and application of this feature essentially transformed the game into a learning machine. Introduced in 1980, *Astro Blaster* was the first commercial SEGA computer video game to combine MultiPhase programs with technology that enabled the game to "talk" to players. The combination of these advanced systems proved to be a magnet for computer video game enthusiasts and has made *Astro Blaster* a popular model at game centers around the country. SEGA's *Space Fury*, introduced in 1981, was the industry's first game to incorporate X-Y color systems. X-Y color technology produced graphic depth perception, color clarity, and graphic representations that were new benchmarks for the industry.

Source: This case was prepared by Masaaki Kotabe with his students' assistance.

OPERATIONS

Operations were the heart of the coin-operated amusement industry. It consisted of the actual installation, operation, maintenance, and coin-collection activities. This was where SEGA originally established itself to become Japan's number one company in the industry. The Operations Division was responsible for placing equipment on a revenue-sharing basis in restaurants, bowling centers, cocktail lounges, and other locations not primarily devoted to coin-operated amusement equipment. In addition, Operations sold equipment to privately owned businesses for use on their premises.

SEGA had close to 20,000 machines operating in approximately 7,000 locations throughout Japan in 1980. This operation was directed by approximately 75 district managers in the regional areas, who oversaw 330 service and maintenance personnel in the Operation. Because of the extensiveness of this operation, the company developed a sophisticated computer-aided system for monitoring, controlling, and directing the installation, service, and collection for this network. SEGA's experience in administering its operations in Japan had given it an expertise that was transferable to other markets in other countries around the world.

ARCADES

The Arcades Center Division directed the activities of SEGA arcades that operated the full line of SEGA products. In many cases, arcades were located in buildings housing one or more movie theaters. In addition to conventional arcades, the Arcades Division was also involved in managing amusement casinos. Patterned after Las Vegas casinos, these casinos contained slot machines, group games, and other nonskill machines that were played with tokens and operated for amusement only. There was no redemption for money or prizes.

DISTRIBUTION

SEGA's Sales Division distributed both products of its own manufacture and those imported by the company. SEGA imported into Japan a line of coin-operated phonograph machines for distribution and operation. For more than ten years, SEGA has held exclusive distribution rights in Japan for jukeboxes manufactured by Rock-Ola

Manufacturing Corporation, an American company. SEGA also imported, distributed, and operated pinball machines. These machines were imported under a distribution agreement with Williams Electronics, Inc., an entirely American-owned subsidiary of the Seeburg Corporation. SEGA had large facilities involved in the first-class reconditioning of used machines. Machines were returned from the Operations and Arcades Center Divisions for rebuilding and reconditioning and then sold to other operators or relocated on SEGA's routes.

MANUFACTURING

SEGA's main manufacturing facility is located near the Haneda Airport in Tokyo, Japan. It consists of approximately 135,000 square feet in three buildings and is devoted to assembly and reconditioning functions. SEGA designs and manufactures a broad line of coin-operated arcade games and casino-type machines. Because rapid product changes are necessary in the coin-operated amusement game industry, SEGA subcontracts most component production in order to concentrate mainly on assembly. SEGA's limited investment in plant and equipment allows it to have maximum flexibility to react quickly to competitive factors. Approximately 120 suppliers, some of which SEGA has welded into a vendor association, support SEGA's manufacturing effort.

For many years, SEGA has manufactured machines that have introduced new ideas and technology to the industry. SEGA machines have intentionally been overengineered to produce products with great durability and high resale value.

SEGA OF AMERICA

In 1984, SEGA Enterprise was bought by a partnership of SEGA Enterprises Japan management and CSK forming SEGA Enterprises Ltd., a Japan-based company. In 1986, SEGA Enterprises Ltd.'s stock was listed over the counter on the Tokyo Stock Exchange. Also, in 1986, SEGA of America Inc. was established to adapt and market video game products to a rapidly expanding American market. It was subsequently given the charter to develop software products specifically for the American market.

In the late 1980s, SEGA Enterprises introduced a line of extremely successful video game systems and software titles that propelled the company to international prominence, making it the world's second largest vendor of consumer video game products. In 1990, SEGA Enterprises Ltd.'s stock was listed on the first tier of the Tokyo Stock Exchange. In 1993, the stock was listed on the pink sheets of NASDAQ and available in ADR in the United States. SEGA's phenomenal growth over the last several years can be traced directly to growth in its largest divi-

sion, SEGA of America. From a staff of 35 in 1989, SEGA of America has shot up to its current strength of 700. In two years, SEGA of America had become the largest producer of video games in the world.

Today, SEGA Enterprises Ltd., which operates in Japan, is composed of SEGA Europe Ltd., SEGA of Canada Inc., SEGA of Mexico Inc., and SEGA of America Inc. The company is a $3.5 billion developer and worldwide marketer of video game entertainment systems and software and is known as the leader in interactive digital entertainment media, with operations on five continents.

THESIS

In the fantasy world of home video games, outsmarting opponents and zapping enemies has been a highly competitive business. Arcade companies survive vicariously through the fickle minds of the young video game junkies. Nintendo and SEGA have been in a constant race for the latest technology and best software. One reason for SEGA entering the U.S. market was that SEGA was better able to compete and thrive against Nintendo in the United States. SEGA has found the key to attaining market share through technological innovation, product quality and diversity, solid distribution, and an aggressive marketing strategy.

COMPETITORS AND PRODUCTS

The home video game business was once dominated by a single company. Nintendo, once the largest home video game firm, started in the market with its 8-bit system NES. Nintendo captured a huge market in Japan as well as in the United States. From being the first mover, Nintendo developed a strong brand name with the NES system. Not long after the introduction of the NES, SEGA started to formulate plans for a more advanced 16-bit system and the race was on. The programming acumen of SEGA's parent CSK, Japan's largest software house, helped SEGA beat Nintendo in the race for the 16-bit machine. Nintendo worked on a 16-bit machine of its own called the Super NES, which eventually arrived two years after SEGA's. By the time the Super NES hit the market, SEGA's software engineers had mastered all the 16-bit video tricks, and America's ever-fickle child consumers decided the rest. Another advantage SEGA had over Nintendo was the compatibility of its software. Patrons could use the same cartridges in 8-bit and 16-bit machines.

The next stretch of the race was the development of the 32-bit CD ROM system. The first company to market this system was 3DO. 3DO is a California-based company whose 32-bit RealMultiplayer came out in 1993. Due to the giants of Nintendo and SEGA, 3DO has only found limited success in attaining market share. SEGA also began the CD-ROM technology that brought Sony Corporation into the race. Sony offers a powerful compact disk-based system backed by its almost unmatched marketing power. Now Sony and SEGA both offer systems that play games on CDs, Sony's PlayStation and SEGA's Saturn. With their huge memory capacity and enhanced graphics, CDs enable software companies to create more complex and vivid games. SEGA also introduced a 38X power booster that enabled the 16-bit system to have the 32-bit experience. The compatibility of SEGA's software and hardware has been a reason for its success and customer satisfaction.

Nintendo has looked even further ahead and will try to fight back with the Ultra 64. The system is basically a robust 64-bit machine that plays games on traditional cartridges.

THE REAL MARKET

Software has become the problem and the solution to capturing the fast pace of the market and technological continuum. Hiroshi Imanishi, a senior executive at Nintendo games explains, "There are a lot of bad video games and too many of them are not selling." Nintendo is hoping that better games will boost the market. Terahisha Tokanaka of Sony Computer Corporation explains, "People are looking for something new, something totally different." Sony's PlayStation is being promoted in Japan by one of Sony's most lavish advertising campaigns ever. The goal, Tokanaka offers, is to expand the game market to older boys and women. The Japanese colossus Sony is betting on the CD-ROM because at $1 CDs are cheap to manufacture; both SEGA and Sony assert that the new CD games will be cheaper than the traditional cartridges, and this will be the key to growth in the game market. Lower costs should spur creativity as well. In the past, the expense of the cartridge games has made manufacturers wary of producing anything but absolute winners. With cheaper CDs, there is less risk and more willingness to experiment. The reality is that software drives the market, and everybody wants more sophisticated games.

THE FUTURE

With nearly $6 billion in sales, the U.S. video game business is bigger than the movie industry. After a decade of torrid growth the market, however, is slumping and all the major players are vulnerable. Kungoo Lee, an analyst with Dataquest Japan, offers a prediction on the winners and the losers, "Sony's machine is better than SEGA's, but SEGA will sell more systems because its games are better." Lee believes that Sony will acquire the number two position in the game market, followed by Nintendo.

Technology drives the business. SEGA superseded Nintendo on the strength of its superior 16-bit Genesis. Despite Atari's introduction of the 16-bit machine, the 32-bit CD-ROMS are the current craze. The 64-bit machines are bulky and expensive and use cartridge games. Already CD-ROM PCs have become very popular. In the future, game playing will probably not work on "dedicated machines." The PC could very well knock the traditional "platforms" out of the market. Nintendo and SEGA could fall to companies such as IBM. Further on the horizon lies the challenge from interactive television, offering the possibility of games being downloaded to home "entertainment." Through the digital ether, people can simply point, click, and rent any game they want. Nintendo has already made an interactive karaoke arcade that has been popular in the Japanese market.

MARKET SHARE

In the beginnings of the game industry, Nintendo's 8-bit machines held 90 percent of the U.S. market. Nintendo is carried in more stores and has a stronger brand name than SEGA. It also has 8-bit machines in over 28 million households. Since the introduction of the 16-bit machine, Nintendo's share price has dropped from a split adjusted high of $188 to $88. This valued Nintendo at 12.5 billion, 3.5 times its sales. In the 16-bit systems SEGA's market share in 1991 was 20 percent and has become dramatically higher. In 1993 the market began its slump. SEGA's earning dropped 64 percent and Nintendo reported a 41 percent drop. Since 1991, stock prices have dropped and there is no respite in sight. Currently SEGA holds over 50 percent of the consumer games market. Along with SEGA's advantage in software, part of its success was due to its introduction of hardware that upgrades current systems. An example of this is the 32X power booster, which enables the 16-bit machines to have the 32-bit experience.

STRATEGIC ALLIANCES

Despite technological innovations and good software, SEGA's success is attributed to their mastery of collaboration. Unlike Nintendo, SEGA has formed alliances with many huge corporations to take advantage of skills and information that they do not have. For communications, SEGA has formed an alliance with AT & T. SEGA uses Hitachi for the manufacturing of its computer chips. For excellent sound effects, SEGA formed a partnership with Yamaha. JVC also helps SEGA in the manufacturing of game machines. Currently the company has made agreements with 48 third-party titles with its 16-bit system. For its Game Gear system, SEGA has 17 third-party titles to develop software. For the SEGA CD multimedia system, SEGA has key licensing agreements with 38 third-party developers.

DISTRIBUTION

SEGA of America produces a high-quality product, which is a key to its success, but, without a good distribution channel, no one would be able to purchase it. By reviewing the history of SEGA Enterprise Ltd., one will recognize the importance that their distribution system played in the company's resurrection and boom in the U.S. consumer market.

David Rosen, an American living in Japan, established Rosen Enterprises in 1954 and immediately developed a good rapport with department stores and other retailers who carried his two-minute photo booths. Rosen began to import amusement games (i.e., pinball machines) from Chicago in 1956.

Rosen, with a solid distribution channel in place, decided to develop his own games. Therefore, in 1965 he purchased Services Games to acquire its factory and strengthen his distribution capabilities. Rosen decided to take on the Service Games logo stamped on boxes SEGA (SErvice GAmes). After general success in Japan, with its over 200 arcades, Rosen decided to sell his company to the American corporation Gulf and Western and expand to the United States. Rosen remained CEO of SEGA Enterprises, and he understood that to be more successful in Japan SEGA required greater distribution capabilities. In 1979, SEGA purchased a distribution company founded and owned by Hayao Makayama.

This strategic move proved crucial to the survival of SEGA, to its current business philosophy in America, and to its initial market-entry strategy. When the bottom fell out of the arcade market, Gulf and Western repurchased its stock and sold all of its U.S. and Japanese assets, while Nakayama, Rosen, and CKS (a Japanese software company) purchased the Japanese assets for $38 million. (SEGA today is worth about $3.5 billion.)

In 1986, SEGA Enterprises Ltd. established SEGA of America Inc. and reentered the U.S. market. SEGA of America immediately signed a distribution agreement with Tonka that provided SEGA with a strong foundation to its marketing and distribution programs throughout the United States and Canada.

Like its Japanese parent, SEGA of America understands the concept of reducing cost to lower prices. In anticipation of an increase in demand for SEGA products, SEGA of America built a distribution center in Hayward, California. It is able to handle the massive number of products imported and distributed throughout North America with an efficiency level of 99.9 percent. Radio frequency is one technique used in the Hayward distribution center to improve its efficiency. Workers scan bar codes on packages, and radio transmitters in their workbelts transmit a message to a central location. This allows better tracking of merchandise and eliminates wasted time.

With such an efficiency process, retailers receive their shipments on time, which means that customers do not have to leave their stores empty handed. One analyst credited some of SEGA's success during the late 1980s and early 1990s to the simple fact that customers became frustrated with the fact that Nintendo products were always out of stock. By planning ahead, SEGA of America made it easier for consumers to switch to SEGA hardware (e.g., 16-bit SEGA Genesis) because the software that people wanted would be in stock.

ADVERTISING

SEGA produces a high-quality product geared toward Americans, and stores are full of the products. But how does a Japanese company entice consumers to buy its products? At this point in time, the company had to adopt an American advertising strategy, and here is where Thomas Kalinske steps into the picture.

In 1990, Hayao Nakayama, CEO of SEGA Enterprises Ltd., hired Thomas Kalinske as CEO of SEGA of America. Kalinske's background is in marketing, not in a technical field like many of the top executives in the company. SEGA of America uses Japanese principles in regard to products and distribution. In marketing, they focus on the aggressive American style of advertising with a slight twist of Japanese influence. Almost immediately, Kalinske put the SEGA ad account up for grabs, and the young San Francisco advertising firm, Goodby, Berlin, and Silverstein won the account. G, B, & S launched an ad campaign trying to establish SEGA's products as the "coolest" on the market. Brash, fast-paced, eccentric ads bombard our televisions to this day, all ending with the signature SEGA scream *"SEGA!"* This strong association of company name and product is very Japanese. What is uncharacteristic are the direct comparisons made between SEGA products and those of its competitors. Nakayama was hesitant of direct comparison advertising, but he trusted Kalinske. This trust paid off in profits. G, B, & S ads have a dual function: first, to establish SEGA as the "coolest" for those between ages 10 and 14, and second, to widen the consumer range from 10–14 years old to 10–27 years old. The ads are designed to enthrall an older crowd, and they have succeeded. The ads have sported images of *"SEGA!"* from a giant Tyrannosaurus Rex, Sonic the Hedgehog, and an American icon, Joe Montana. With an advertising push like this, some say SEGA has become the system that you and your older brother could sit around and play.

Kalinske further expanded his marketing blitz on the 10–14 age group with SEGAVISION, a "gamers" magazine. The magazine offers tips to "gamers." Kalinske wants to seize all opportunities and now advertises through the Internet. Through the Internet, SEGA offers information on new products and tips for "gamers" between 14 and 27 years old. Marketers at SEGA did their homework and discovered that "gamers" spent a tremendous amount of time testing games before they bought them. As a result of this information, SEGA began building a strong relationship with video rental stores (i.e., Blockbuster). Video game rentals are now a mainstay for video stores across the United States, and they offer "gamers" the opportunity to test any game before they purchase it.

Thomas Kalinske has masterfully formed alliances with major corporations to promote SEGA's games and hardware. These collaborations open a myriad of possibilities, from 7-Eleven and Coca-Cola collaborating on Slurpee endorsements to Howard Johnson's, Blockbuster, and MTV promoting a slew of video game competitions. SEGA of America has become a part of American culture, and the SEGA scream is here to stay, *SEGA!*

CONCLUSIONS

Technology waits for no one in the video game business. Realizing this, SEGA has employed its skills and resources to optimum efficiency. The company produces a wide range of quality products including a factor of compatibility that gives its products an absolute advantage over its competitors. Through a staunch distribution system and an aggressive marketing system, SEGA has ensured that the hunger of the market will be sated. Effective collaboration has given SEGA strong alliances to ensure maximum efficiency in production and the best possible quality. By maintaining the Japanese style of operating, while acknowledging the qualities of the U.S. market, SEGA realizes that there is no second place in the technology race.

◆ ◆

CASE 4

PROCTER & GAMBLE: FACELLE DIVISION FACIAL TISSUE

Early in March 1992, Randall Beard was reviewing performance of the brands of facial tissue that Procter & Gamble had acquired in August 1991. "Now that we have had a few months to understand the tissue business in Canada," he thought, "it's time to build our plan for the future of the business. P&G hasn't spent $185 million in acquiring the Facelle division in order to stand still in the marketplace."

Although Procter & Gamble had global brands in some categories of paper products (e.g., Pampers, the leading disposable diaper), the Facelle acquisition was P&G's first step outside the U.S. in the tissue/towel business. For that reason, senior management would be closely watching the progress of the Facelle brands of fa-

cial tissue, paper towels, and bathroom tissue. In particular, the facial tissue market was especially challenging, as 1991 had seen more competitive product initiatives than the previous several years put together.

As Associate Advertising Manager for Tissue, Towel, and Facial Products, Randall Beard reported directly to Barbara Fraser, Vice President and General Manager of the Paper Products business in Canada. Together, the two would be responsible for several major decisions about tissue brands, including positioning, product formulations, and promotion. For his forthcoming meeting with Fraser, Beard wanted to have a set of definite recommendations on the future of the brands.

THE PROCTER & GAMBLE COMPANY

Procter & Gamble originated in 1837, when William Procter and James Gamble, two immigrant soap and candle makers, formed a partnership in Cincinnati, Ohio. The partnership rapidly flourished, gaining a name as a principled manufacturer of high quality consumer goods sold at competitive prices. The Procter & Gamble Company was incorporated in 1890, and in every decade since incorporation, sales more than doubled. By 1992, P&G was a multinational company with annual sales of almost $30 billion (U.S.), profits exceeding $1.8 billion (U.S.), and a long-standing reputation for quality products, high integrity, strong marketing, and conservative management.

As Procter & Gamble grew, it increasingly focused on international markets. In 1992, P&G's brands were sold in more than 140 countries around the world. Major areas and representative brands included laundry and cleaning products (e.g., Tide, Cheer, Mr. Clean), paper products (Pampers, Luvs, Always, Bounty, Charmin), health care (Pepto-Bismol, Metamucil), oral care (Crest, Scope), food and beverage (Jif, Crisco), bar soaps (Ivory, Zest) and cosmetics (Oil of Olay, Max Factor, Cover Girl). Many of these brands were leaders in their categories.

In Canada, P&G operated as Procter & Gamble Inc., with 1992 sales expected to exceed $1.7 billion, and earnings before taxes of over $100 million. P&G Inc. operated as four divisions, of which Paper Products was one, organized on a category basis within each division (e.g., Tissue/Towel/Facial within Paper Products).

Procter & Gamble in Paper Products

Procter & Gamble first entered the consumer paper markets in 1957 with its acquisition of Charmin Paper Company, a regional paper company with a strong presence in the north central U.S. In the early 1960s, P&G developed proprietary papermaking technologies which allowed it to deliver softness, strength and absorbency that were superior to conventionally manufactured products. This technology was used to strengthen the Charmin toilet tissue brand, leading to national expansion in the mid-sixties. Simultaneously, P&G launched Bounty towels, also employing the new technology, and subsequently expanded the brand to national distribution in 1972. Finally, P&G entered the facial tissue market in the early 1970s by launching the Puffs brand, which was initially sold as a regional brand, then expanded to the national market in 1990.

P&G built Charmin, Bounty and Puffs with similar strategies. First, proprietary technology was used to deliver products with superior performance at a competitive price. As well, consumers were offered "value-added" products which delivered additional benefits (e.g., Puffs Plus with lotion, Charmin Free with no inks, dyes or perfumes). Third, the brands were supported with successful advertising themes and consistently high media weights. Finally, P&G achieved competitive costs among premium brands by using Total Quality Methods to improve the papermaking process. Together, these strategies were extremely successful. Charmin and Bounty established clear market share leadership in their categories, with Puffs a close second (to Kimberly-Clark's Kleenex brand) in the facial tissue category.

The Facelle Acquisition

By 1991, P&G was sufficiently satisfied with its U.S. successes on Charmin, Bounty, and Puffs that it was ready to take its first step in expanding the business. Canada was the logical first choice for that step, given its proximity to the U.S., the advent of free trade between Canada and the U.S., and the attendant opportunities for North American supply sourcing. At the time, P&G had only one paper plant in Canada, which manufactured diapers in Belleville, Ontario.

Early in 1991, an attractive acquisition opportunity developed for P&G. Canadian Pacific Forest Product Company, a large diversified paper company, was prepared to sell Facelle Paper Products, its tissue division. Facelle was a medium-sized manufacturer and marketer of tissue, towel, and sanitary products, headquartered in Toronto. In 1990, Facelle reported an operating profit of $13.4 million on sales of $170.5 million. The deal was concluded in August 1991; for $185 million, P&G bought the Facelle Co., its plant in Toronto, and its franchise for facial tissue, paper towels and bathroom tissue, including the Royale, Florelle, Pronto, Dove, Facettes, and Festival brands.

THE CONSUMER PAPER BUSINESS IN CANADA

The Canadian consumer paper market in 1992 was about 25 million cases, where a case represented a shipping unit of approximately equivalent size for the three principal types of tissue. In the facial tissue category, a case contained the equivalent of 48 boxes of 150 two-ply tissues. Of the 25 million cases, bathroom tissue accounted for 13 million, paper towels seven million, and facial tissue five million. Tissue products were inexpensive (usually less than $2.00 per package), they were widely used (in more than 95% of Canadian households), and they were frequently purchased (on average, once every two weeks). Brand switching was high, as there were many acceptable substitutes and the risk associated with product failure was low. The challenge for manufacturers was to differentiate their products enough on performance to build loyalty.

Retailing

Not surprisingly, retailers viewed paper as a low-profit, low-loyalty category, and they used it primarily to draw consumers into their stores. Traditional food stores typically carried a full line of paper products and featured them frequently. In recent years, however, mass merchandiser and drug chains had expanded their paper business substantially, focusing almost exclusively on price deals to attract customers to their stores. Recently, "club stores," with their emphasis on everyday low pricing, further squeezed retail and manufacturer margins. The vigorous retail competition had led to heavy featuring, where some brand was on sale virtually every week of the year, with resultant low profit margins. The challenge for manufacturers was to convince retailers to use their brands as the key feature items while trying to find ways to help retailers build profit.

Manufacturing

The paper business in Canada had a few very large national manufacturers and a few smaller regional players. This structure was driven, in part, by the sizable scale efficiencies that had been achieved in papermaking. Therefore, the industry was characterized by high capital and fixed costs. A single paper machine cost at least $100 million (U.S.), and at capacity it could satisfy about 10% of the Canadian market.

This cost structure, combined with the consumer and retail customer behaviours described above, strongly encouraged paper manufacturers to run their machines near capacity to maximize their contribution. Thus, most manufacturers marketed broad product lines in an attempt to compete in all segments of the market and utilize as much capacity as possible. Also, they competed intensely for the product features which drove volume at the retail level. It was common in the industry for one manufacturer to market both premium and price brands in all three of the Tissue, Towel and Facial categories, to supply retailers with private label products in the same categories, and to sell the commercial and institutional markets as well. Further-

more, many retailers had moved to a "bidding" process that allocated featured promotions to the manufacturer with the most lucrative retail spending program.

The largest players in the Canadian consumer paper business were Scott Paper and Kimberly-Clark, both subsidiaries of successful large U.S. paper companies. In addition, there were several small regional players, of whom the largest was Irving Paper, operating in the Maritimes.

THE FACIAL TISSUE MARKET IN CANADA

A cost structure that Beard could envision for a national manufacturer competing aggressively in the facial tissue market is presented in Exhibit 1, based on the cost information presented above.

The size of the facial tissue market in 1991 was 4,894,000 cases shipped, up 7% over 1990 sales. Market shares of the major producers, indexed to 1990 shares, are presented in Exhibit 2. They will be discussed in the following paragraphs.

Brand Developments in 1991

Facelle Brands. Shipments of the Facelle brands of facial tissue in 1991 were only 587,000 cases, or 84% of the 1990 results. Two brands, Royale and Florelle, ac-

EXHIBIT 1
TYPICAL COST STRUCTURE: FACIAL TISSUE IN CANADA

		Cost Per Case of 48 Units
Net revenue		$54
Off-invoice allowance	$9[1]	
Co-op allowance	$10[2]	
Less: total discounts and allowance		19
Net sales		35
Less: variable manufacturing cost (including delivery)		16
Contribution		19
Manufacturing fixed cost	11	
Selling, research, & administration	3	
Marketing support[3]	1	
Less: total fixed costs		15
Profit		$ 4

[1]Average price reduction through the year, assuming feature price reductions of 25% were given on approximately 2/3 of the unit volume.

[2]Allowance for co-operative advertising and promotion. Some of these funds were actually used by retailers for this purpose, and the rest were retained by them.

[3]Advertising, couponing, sampling. For many of the existing brands, less than $1 per case was spent on advertising support.

EXHIBIT 2
FACIAL TISSUE MARKET SHARES—1981

Company/Brand	Percentage Share of 1991 Shipments	Total P&G Index vs. 1990 Shares
Royale	6.9	101[1]
Florelle[2]	5.8	67
Total P&G	12.7	84
Kimberly-Clark	39.5	107
Scott	23.0	88
Irving	4.2	n.a.
All others	20.6	98
	100.0	

[1]Index = (1991 share)/(1990 share) • 100. For example, the Royale index of 101 was calculated by dividing Royale's 1991 market share of 6.9% by their share of 6.8% in 1990.

[2]In data throughout the case. Florelle numbers will include the Facettes brand. Facettes was a minor price brand.

counted for most of Facelle's sales. Until recently, the Royale brand had been the only 3-ply tissue on the market, and it enjoyed a brand image as the traditional, strong, premium quality facial tissue. Its market share increased very slightly during 1991. Florelle was a 2-ply tissue that had received little promotional attention. Not surprisingly, it had low awareness, trial and image. It had lost about one-third of its market share in 1991, and was down to 5.8% at the beginning of 1992.

Kimberly-Clark. The Kleenex brand had enjoyed a very good year in 1991, gaining 2.5 share points to reach 39.5% of units shipped in the Canadian market. In fact, Kleenex's share reached 41.7% in the second half of the year. For several years in the late 1980s, Kimberly-Clark had made no significant changes in the Kleenex brand. However, there were several Kleenex product initiatives during 1991 which affected the brand's sales results. The new 300-tissue family size (2-ply) package, which had first been introduced in September 1989, had completed its national rollout in 1991; it achieved a share for the year of 8.2%, up from 3.1% in 1990. Also, the rollout of the 2-ply Kleenex 150, which replaced Kleenex 200s as the #1 stockkeeping unit (SKU) in the facial tissue category, was completed in 1991. Largely in support of this latter introduction, Kimberly-Clark increased merchandising support by 20% in food retailers and 13% in drug retailers. Finally, Kimberly-Clark introduced Kleenex Ultra, a 3-ply tissue which contained a silicone-based lotion, in the Ontario market in mid-1991.

Scott. Scott's major brand, Scotties, fell from a share of 18.9% in 1990 to 15.9% in 1991. The main reason for the decline was the loss of trade support relative to Kleenex 150s. Scott relaunched the brand in September 1991, positioning it as a product with high content of recycle material, and supporting it with heavy advertising. As well, a 300-tissue family size of Scotties was launched in December 1991. Early indications were that the brand was recovering. Scott's secondary brand, White Swan (sold only in 150s), maintained a 7.1% share in 1991. Increased merchandising in drug channels led to a share gain there, which compensated for the share loss in food channels in the face of Kleenex 150s with its stronger brand image.

Irving. Next to the aggressive developments in the Kleenex brand, the most significant competitive event in the facial tissue business in 1991 was the entry of Irving into the facial tissue market in the Maritime provinces and Quebec with its new Majesta brand. Majesta was packaged in an attractive format, and its feature pricing averaged 15–20% below Kleenex. It achieved a 4.2% national share in 1991.

All others. Overall, the other brands in the Canadian marketplace retained 95% of their cumulative market share in 1991. The group suffered some losses in the face of the merchandising support of Kleenex 150s, but these were balanced by gains in private label products in Western Canada.

Advertising

Advertising expenditures in the facial tissue category had historically been low, and quite inconsistent in "share of voice" and medium by manufacturer. Average industry annual expenditures were nearly $3.0 million over the last five years, with television accounting for 47% of spending, "out-of-home" (i.e., billboards, posters, and mass transit ads) 32%, consumer magazines 17% and daily newspapers 4%. Exhibit 3 summarizes copy and media strategy for the major brands in recent years, and share of advertising expenditures by brand.

Randall Beard believed that Kimberly-Clark had established a contemporary image for the Kleenex brand, but not a strong image for either softness or tissue strength. There had been no brand equity advertising on the softness theme for the Kleenex brand since 1979, although there had been introductory campaigns for the softness upgrades to the basic product in 1989 and 1991, and the launch of the lotion line extension Kleenex Ultra in 1991.

Until the past year, when all Scotties' advertising was focused on the recycled paper relaunch behind an environmentally friendly position, Scotties had consistently advertised softness. This was somewhat ironic, because, according to P&G's tests of softness, the Scotties product was inferior on that dimension.

Royale had historically focused on the superior cold care afforded by the softness and strength of the 3-ply tis-

EXHIBIT 3
ADVERTISING STRATEGY OF FACIAL TISSUE COMPETITORS

A. Copy Strategy

Brand	Years	Copy Strategy-Execution	Medium
Kleenex	1980–88	Heritage—family moments	TV, Print
		New Packaging—pack shot	Print
	1989–91	Improved softness	TV
		Lotion—demonstration	TV, Print, OOH[1]
Scotties	1967–89	Softest cold care—"Scotties soften the blow"	TV
	1990	Caring softness—"Softer than a kiss"	TV
	1991	Environmentally friendly	Print, OOH
Royale	1973–86	Superior cold care—3-ply softness and strength	TV
	1988–90	New packaging	OOH
	1991	"Kitteny soft"	TV
	1992	Superior cold care—3-ply demonstration	TV

B. Share of Advertising Expenditure

	Share of Advertising Spending			
Brand	1988	1989	1990	1991
Royale	25%	52%	49%	16%
Kleenex	2%	35%	15%	18%
Kleenex Ultra	—	—	—	21%
Scotties	50%	13%	25%	33%
White Swan	3%	—	10%	6%
Majesta	—	—	1%	6%
Other	20%	—	—	—
TOTAL	100%	100%	100%	100%

[1]OOH indicates advertising messages delivered Outside Of Home (e.g., through billboards or mass transit advertising).

sue. In 1991, ads for the product had emphasized softness, followed at year-end by the tactical cold season airing of an existing cold care execution.

By Procter & Gamble standards, advertising in the facial tissue category had not been strong. Not only were expenditures low, but only a small proportion of that spending was on brand equity. Furthermore, campaigns in the industry had tended to be of short duration, while P&G's extensive research on consumer advertising indicated that to be effective, advertising had to be sustained.

Consumer Promotion

Except for the Facelle brands, there was little consumer promotion activity in the category, relative to the norms

for other consumer packaged goods. In 1991, the three major facial tissue suppliers ran a total of 35 consumer promotions, with 21 of those for the Facelle brands (13 for Royale and 8 for Facelle, respectively). Of the 35 promotions, 19 were coupons, and the other 16 were a variety of sweepstakes, mail-in offers, samples, and cross-coupons. Altogether, P&G estimated, the 19 coupon promotions moved an incremental 42,000 cases of product for the three brands, or less than 1% of facial tissue shipments. In general, promotions did not pay for themselves because of the low absolute unit price of the product relative to the costs of the promotion. Therefore, promotions were likely to be used only as part of a more efficient group promotion, or as part of a strategy specifically directed at obtaining trial.

Pricing

While consumer promotions for facial tissues were relatively rare, price features were commonplace. There was always at least one brand on feature at any sizeable food or drug retailer. In fact, the vast majority of facial tissues sold at retail during 1991 were feature-priced. Typical prices for the major brands during 1991 are shown in Exhibit 4.

ISSUES FOR THE FACELLE BRANDS

In planning the future of Facelle brands, several problems had to be confronted. But first, Randall Beard reviewed a summary of the research which P&G had obtained in the seven months since acquiring the Facelle business.

The Royale Brand

Brand Image. Royale's long-term premium positioning, based upon its historically unique 3-ply product design and its softness claim, had built the leading brand image in the product category. In judgments by a brand's users, Royale received an overall score of 85 on a scale of 100, marginally superior to Kleenex (at an average score of 82) and Scotties (74), and considerably ahead of the store brands (averaging 69).

Exhibit 5 compares four leading brands on a number of specific attributes of image. Royale enjoyed an image advantage for strength and thickness versus all other competition, but an image weakness for package design. Furthermore, it was seen as less fashionable than Kleenex and Scotties. The

image data were particularly interesting to Beard and his product managers; despite low advertising spending in the category, historic campaigns appeared to have had a strong impact on brand image. For example, Scotties had a strong image for softness despite clearly inferior physical characteristics on that dimension relative to Royale and Kleenex. Almost ten years of advertising using the Little Softie character and the message "Scotties softens the blow" had evidently produced a strong image for the brand as a soft, gentle tissue that was good for sore nose care.

Although Royale enjoyed a very favourable overall brand image, knowledge about the brand was not as high as Beard would have expected. For instance, among those who had used it in the past three months, 47% thought that Royale was a 2-ply tissue, and only 48% correctly assessed it as 3-ply.

Product Usage

Although Royale enjoyed a very favorable overall brand image, that image did not translate to market share, as Exhibit 6 below demonstrates. Although half of households had used Royale sometime in the last year, only 13% claimed that it was their usual brand. Qualitative research indicated that Royale was used as a part-time brand that was bought on feature or specifically for cold care, but seldom for regular usage around the household. This pattern was confirmed by the image data which showed significantly less agreement with the statement "is inexpensive" for Royale (32%) than Kleenex (52%), Scotties (42%), or store brands (83%).

Furthermore, as Exhibit 7 shows, Royale usage was

EXHIBIT 4
TYPICAL PRICES—1991

Brand	-Ply	Count	Typical Shelf Price	Typical Feature Price
P&G				
Royale	3	100	1.19	.89
Florelle	2	200	1.09	.79
Kimberly-Clark				
Kleenex	2	150	.99	.79
Kleenex	2	300	1.99	1.59
Kleenex-Ultra	3	100	.99	.79
Scott				
Scotties	2	150	.99	.69
Scotties	2	300	1.99	1.49
White Swan	2	150	.89	.59
Irving				
Majesta	2	150	.89	.63
Private labels	2	150	.79	.49

EXHIBIT 5
BRAND IMAGES BY ATTRIBUTE[1]

| | Brand Rating | | | |
Attribute	Royale	Kleenex	Scotties	Store Brands
is soft	0	−	+	−
good for sore nose care	0	0	+	−
does not tear or fall apart when				
I blow my nose or sneeze	+	0	0	0
is absorbent	+	−	0	0
is thick	+	−	−	−
contains lotion	0	+	0	0
is 3-ply	+	−	−	0
design/colours on box are attractive	−	+	+	−
is caring	0	0	+	0
is fashionable	−	+	0	−
is contemporary	−	0	0	0
is inexpensive	−	−	−	+

[1]In this chart, 0 represents a score that was not different from the average rating for all brands, − a score that was lower than the average rating, and + a score that was higher.

heavily skewed to older consumers and smaller households.

Pricing vs. Kleenex

In the past, when the #1 SKU in the category was Kleenex 200s, feature price at retail on that product had been $0.99. Now, with the introduction of Kleenex 150s, feature price had dropped to $0.79, and sometimes lower in special promotions. In fact, in the past four months, average feature price for Kleenex had been $0.69, and for Royale $0.73. During this period, 80% of the Royale sold at retail had been on feature. In the longer term, P&G estimated that the typical feature price for Kleenex 150s would be likely to increase modestly, but not dramatically. Furthermore, data from recent comparisons of Royale share at different levels of price disparity with Kleenex indicated higher price elasticity for Royale when its price exceeded Kleenex's by more than $.20.

The Florelle Brand

In 1991, 80% of facial tissue units sold were standard 2-ply tissue, the segment in which Facelle was represented

EXHIBIT 6
TRIAL AND USAGE BY BRAND

| | Per Cent Usage by Brand | | | |
	Royale	Kleenex	Scotties	Store Brands
1991 Market share	6.9	39.5	15.9	20.6
Past 12 months used	51	91	52	29
Past 3 months used	34	79	33	22
Past 3 months usual brand	14	55	19	19
Loyalty: Used only this brand				
past 3 months	13	34	17	18
Share of total facial tissue				
usage past 12 months				
(among users of the brand)	14	45	36	80

EXHIBIT 7
DEMOGRAPHIC CHARACTERISTICS BY BRAND

	Usual Brand		
	Royale	Kleenex	Scotties
Age group	%	%	%
<24	3	5	2
25–50	48	68	63
>50	49	27	35
	100	100	100
Household size			
1	16	10	8
2	42	32	35
>2	42	58	57
	100	100	100

by the Florelle brand. Specialty sizes (e.g., pocket packs, man-size, and cube format) represented 8% of units, and 3-ply tissue about 12%.

Exhibit 8 presents data from a November 1991 panel study of 2215 households on their attitudes toward brands of facial tissue. Only 3% of those surveyed claimed that Florelle was their usual brand. Not surprisingly for a brand which had received no advertising or consumer promotion, ratings of Florelle were not high.

The obvious alternatives were to drop the Florelle brand, rejuvenate it with support, or continue it as an unsupported price brand.

The Softness Issue

A key success factor in the successful development of the Puffs brand in the United States was the effort that P&G invested in making the tissue softer. Softness is influenced by the process used in manufacturing the tissue, and the type of fibre employed. Longer fibres tend to make the resultant tissue stronger, but not as soft; shorter fibres, like eucalyptus, produce a softer tissue. A key issue in manufacturing facial tissue, therefore, is how the softness/strength tradeoff is managed.

Data from P&G's experience in the U.S. market indicated that consumer preference as a function of strength followed an S-curve, where additional strength above the functional level did not provide any additional consumer benefit. On the other hand, softness did not level off in terms of diminishing returns or customer perceptions—at least at the levels of softness which could currently be obtained.

Relative tissue strength depended upon the conditions of the test, especially whether the tissue was wet or

EXHIBIT 8
BRAND ATTITUDES

	All Users		Past 3 Months Brand Users	
Brand	Average Value Rating	Average Overall Rating	% Who Purchased In Past 3 Months	Average Overall Rating
Florelle	53	58	10	73
Royale	71	78	30	85
Kleenex	73	80	75	82
Scotties	68	81	29	81
White Swan	61	66	14	77
Majesta	49	55	8	75
Store brand	53	56	17	69

dry. A given brand of tissue, which had much higher dry strength than a second brand, would not necessarily have much higher wet strength. Procter & Gamble believed that dry strength (which affected ease of dispensing the tissue) was much less important than wet strength (which directly affected consumer's use of the product).

Exhibit 9 shows wet burst strength and softness for leading brands in the Canadian market. Softness was measured through tactile judgments of a panel of consumers, using Puffs as the standard zero-point on the scale.

Commenting on this data, Randall Beard said, "This just reinforces what I have been told about Facelle's strategy prior to the acquisition. They chose to maximize strength—particularly dry strength—but that approach cost them severely on the softness dimension."

A study of customer dissatisfaction asked participants whether, in the past three months, they had experienced a problem with tissue breaking. Only 1% of Royale users had experienced a problem, vs. 7% of Kleenex users.

In mid-1991, a blind paired comparison test was conducted with Royale and Kleenex Ultra. Attribute ratings on strength were the same for the two brands (8.5 on a 10-point scale), but Kleenex Ultra was rated significantly better on softness (9.1 vs. 7.4). When asked which brand they preferred overall, only 27% of participants chose Royale.

Beard was convinced that P&G needed to upgrade the softness of the Facelle products. By adding eucalyptus fibre and sacrificing some tissue strength, their softness could be significantly improved without the need for a major capital expenditure. In the long run, investments in process improvement could produce further softness enhancements, but the so-called "Eucalyptus Upgrade" could be done in a few months for a modest investment.

Accordingly, P&G carried out a pilot project to produce enough of the upgraded products for consumer acceptance testing. Early in 1992, "Single Product Blind Tests" (SPBT) were completed on the upgraded product, in both 2-ply and 3-ply form, as well as the current Royale, Florelle, Kleenex (Regular and Ultra), Scotties,

and White Swan. In a SPBT, a sample of facial tissue with no identifying features is sent to a participant, who then uses the product for several weeks and answers a questionnaire about it. Participants in Facelle's SPBT were female heads of households whose first language was English. There were eight groups of participants, one for each brand. Group sizes ranged from 259 to 280 individuals. Results of this study are presented in Exhibit 10.

Overall ratings of the brands were found to be a function of consumer impressions of a tissue's softness and its thickness. A multiple regression with these two independent variables explained more than 95% of the variation in overall rating scores. The resultant equation is presented below:

$$\text{Overall Rating} = 19.51 + (0.424° \text{ Softness Rating}) + (0.359° \text{ Thickness Rating})$$

One issue in introducing an upgraded tissue was its perception by current Royale and Kleenex users. Would a new 2-ply product cannibalize sales of 3-ply Royale, or would it take share from Kleenex? Would a new 3-ply product be seen as an improvement by users of the current Royale tissue? Exhibit 11 compares ratings of the upgraded products by users of Royale and Kleenex, respectively, with similar users' ratings of the existing Royale and Florelle products. It is noteworthy that current Royale users who received the 2-ply upgrade in the SPBT were less favourably impressed with it than a group who actually received Royale in the blind test. In other words, the improved softness of the upgrade did not offset the reduction from 3 plies to 2. The exhibit also enables a comparison of the group who received the 3-ply upgrade with one that received current Royale in the blind tests. In that situation, current Royale users rated the upgrade significantly higher on softness, slightly lower on strength and somewhat more favourably overall.

If the 2-ply upgrade were to be introduced, Randall Beard had to make a decision about what brand name would be used on it. Two apparent alternatives were Florelle (as an upgrade of the existing brand) and Royale (as a

EXHIBIT 9

SOFTNESS AND STRENGTH OF LEADING BRANDS OF FACIAL TISSUE

Brand	Softness[1]	Wet Burst Strength (g/sheet)
Royale	−2.5	69
Florelle	−2.1	32
Kleenex	−1.1	31
Kleenex Ultra	−0.5	76
Scotties	−2.0	57

[1]On this scale. Puffs tissues are rated at 0. Differences of 0.5 scale points or more are considered to be noticeable.

Exhibit 10
CONSUMER EVALUATIONS OF FACIAL TISSUES IN SPBT[1]

Brand	Overall[2]	Softness	Strength	Thickness	Absorbency
Facelle					
Royale:					
• current	82[3]	78	91	87	85
• 3-ply upgrade	88	93	90	87	85
Florelle:					
• current	73	70	74	68	70
• 2-ply upgrade	80	89	73	72	75
Kleenex					
Regular	75	82	68	65	71
Ultra	90	94	89	87	86
Scott					
Scotties	63	58	66	58	63
White Swan	62	50	74	63	65

[1]Ratings of English-speaking female heads of household, on a scale of 0–100 based on a single product blind test (SPBT) in home.

[2]Each respondent was asked: "Considering everything about the facial tissue sent to you, how would you rate it OVERALL?"

[3]For this sample size, differences of more than 5 scale points across groups (i.e., within a column in the table) are significant at the .05 level.

line extension). Furthermore, if the Royale name were chosen, a decision would have to be made about how to distinguish the 2-ply upgrade from the 3-ply upgrade of the traditional Royale brand. Another possibility would be to introduce the new product under the Puffs label that had been so successfully launched in the U.S. some twenty years earlier. Although Puffs had never been sold in Canada, there had been enough advertising spill-in from the U.S. that the brand was known to some Canadians. Exhibit 12 shows data on the image of Puffs among English and French Canadians.

CONCLUSION

Using the Puffs label in Canada would be a step toward making Puffs a North American brand, an alternative which would certainly have the blessing of the U.S. parent. However, the primary responsibility for the decision rested with Randall Beard and Barbara Fraser, and the choice had to be made soon if product, packaging and advertising and merchandising programs were to be ready for the fall cold season.

"This is the year that we have to begin our move to

Exhibit 11
SPBT[1] RATINGS OF CURRENT FACELLE PRODUCTS AND THE UPGRADES

Attribute Ratings	Users of Royale in Past 3 Months				Users of Kleenex in Past 3 Months			
	3-ply Upgrade	Current Royale	2-ply Upgrade	Current Florelle	3-ply Upgrade	Current Royale	2-ply Upgrade	Current Florelle
Overall	90	83	77	72	89	81	80	74
Softness	94	77	89	72	93	76	90	70
Strength	89	83	68	72	90	91	74	76
Thickness	90	88	68	63	88	86	72	69
Absorbency	87	85	74	69	86	84	75	71

[1]Single Product Blind Test ratings. Each column in the table represents ratings by a group who received the indicated product in a blind test. Differences across columns of 6 scale points or more are statistically significant at the .05 level.

EXHIBIT 12
CANADIAN CONSUMER EVALUATIONS OF THE PUFFS BRAND

	English HHs		French HHs	
	Royale	Puffs	Royale	Puffs
	%	%	%	%
Awareness	97	40	97	11
TV adv. awareness	36	18	33	3
Trial (past 12 mos.)	51	9	57	3
Overall rating	82	57	84	37
Judgment of value	66	48	72	39
Of those aware % agreeing that the brand is good for	42	77	30	33

make Facelle a major player in the market," said Randall Beard to himself, "and there are a number of issues we must face. Our long-term goal is a profitable leading share of the market, which is a long way from where we are now. To get there, it is essential that we establish a winning strategy for the Facelle Division brands." To do so, Beard felt, several interrelated questions had to be answered. What should be done about the Florelle brand? Should available technology from P&G be employed to increase the softness of Royale? What should be the position of the Facelle brand in the 2-ply segment? In fact, what brand should Facelle employ in that segment—a rejuvenated Florelle, a 2-ply Royale, the strong U.S. brand Puffs, or an altogether new brand?

◆ ◆

ASE 5

WASTE MANAGEMENT INTERNATIONAL PLC: STRATEGY FOR ASIA

Late in 1993, as Edwin G. Falkman considered the future, he had several questions on his mind. With the recession in Europe, he was wondering whether Waste Management International (WMI) should momentarily give up its expansion in this part of the world and focus its investments on faster growing regions. For a while now, Gregory Feutril, senior VP for Asia and the Pacific Rim, had claimed that, given the conditions in developed countries, "Asia was the perfect substitute." But, even though great successes such as the Hong Kong project could be achieved, Falkman also knew that developing business in this area was time-consuming and costly. Besides, since the needs differ from one country to another, he was doubtful about the possibility of setting up a global strategy.

Taking into account the fears expressed by his superior, Gregory Feutril started thinking about a strategic plan for Asia.

COMPANY BACKGROUND

WMX Technologies, Inc.

WMX Technologies, Inc. (formerly known as Waste Management) was founded in 1968. Since then, it has steadily grown into a $8.66 billion company (see Exhibits 1 and 2 for financial results). What is striking is that the company has maintained its profitability while growing at very high rates. This rapid pace of expansion resulted in significant changes in the activities of the company. On a technological basis, new skills have been developed. The traditional solid waste management now only accounts for

This case was prepared by Kristiaan Helsen, Professor of Marketing at the University of Chicago and Joseph Giblin, MBA student. It is intended as the basis for class discussion rather than to illustrate effective or ineffective handling of an administration. Certain industry and company data have been disguised. Copyright © 1994 by The University of Chicago, Chicago, IL. Not to be used or reproduced without permission.

Exhibit 1
Waste Management's Consolidated Balance Sheets 1991–1992 (in US$)

	1991	1992
Current Assets		
Cash	101,999	6,473
Short-term investments	120,149	61,599
Accounts receivable, less reserves	1,434,442	1,574,798
Employee receivable	12,691	16,396
Parts and supplies	114,522	126,594
Costs and estimated earnings in excess of billings on uncompleted contracts	111,541	379,841
Prepaid expenses	249,300	342,671
Total Current Assets	2,144,644	2,508,372
Property and Equipment, at cost		
Land, primarily disposal sites	2,478,758	3,048,834
Buildings	959,199	1,101,827
Vehicles and equipment	5,322,665	6,141,322
Leasehold improvements	86,081	90,692
Less—Accumulated depreciation	(2,147,228)	(2,624,472)
Total Property and Equipment, Net	6,699,475	7,758,203
Other Assets		
Intangible assets relating to acquired businesses, net	2,504,204	2,779,616
Funds held by trustees for acquisition or construction	196,610	153,803
Sundry, including other investments	1,030,377	914,186
Total Other Assets	3,728,191	3,847,605
Total Assets	12,572,310	14,114,180
Current Liabilities		
Portion of long-term debt payable within one year	512,126	597,674
Accounts payable	668,983	724,418
Accrued expenses	688,404	852,436
Unearned revenue	244,484	205,044
Total Current Liabilities	2,113,997	2,379,57
Deferred Items		
Income taxes	267,005	375,316
Investment credit	34,693	30,606
Other	1,361,845	1,417,643
Total Deferred Items	1,663,543	1,823,565
Long-Term Debt, less portion payable within one year	3,782,973	4,312,511
Minority Interest in Subsidiaries	878,697	1,278,887
Stockholders' Equity		
Common stock	493,621	496,203
Additional paid-in capital	722,351	708,296
Retained earnings	2,957,667	3,354,624
Less—Treasury stock	—	204,490
1988 Employee Stock Ownership Plan	40,539	34,988
Total Stockholders' Equity	4,133,100	4,319,645
Total Liabilities and Stockholders' Equity	12,572,310	14,114,180

EXHIBIT 2
WASTE MANAGEMENT'S CONSOLIDATED INCOME STATEMENTS 1990–1992 (IN US$)

	1990	1991	1992
Revenue	6,034,406	7,550,914	8,661,027
Operating Expenses	3,997,720	5,165,319	5,945,762
Special Charges	—	296,000	219,900
Selling and Administrative Expenses	821,202	910,935	1,048,047
Goodwill Amortization	47,460	61,682	77,144
Gains from Stock Transactions of Subsidiaries	12,755	(38,046)	(263,489)
Gains from Exchange of Exchangeable LYONs	(40,193)	(15,470)	(191)
Interest Expense	110,782	168,558	223,052
Interest Income	(45,775)	(55,800)	(57,693)
Minority Interest and Sundry (Income) Expense, Net	(17,209)	29,837	70,083
Income Before Income Taxes	1,173,174	1,027,899	1,398,412
Provision For Income Taxes	463,865	421,576	477,237
Income Before Extraordinary Item and Cumulative Effect of Accounting Changes	709,309	606,323	921,175
Extraordinary Item, Net of Income Taxes	(24,547)	—	—
Cumulative Effect of Accounting Changes, Net of Minority Interest in Portion: Relating to Subsidiaries			
Postretirement Benefits, Net of Tax	—	—	(36,579)
Income Taxes	—	—	(34,560)
Net Income	684,762	606,323	850,036
Average Shares and Equivalent Shares Outstanding	476,580	493,167	493,948
Earnings (Loss) per Common and Common Equivalent Share: Income Before Extraordinary Item and Cumulative Effect of Accounting Changes	1.49	1.23	1.86
Extraordinary Item	(.05)	—	—
Cumulative Effect of Accounting Changes			
Postretirement Benefits	—	—	(.07)
Income Taxes	—	—	(.07)
Net Income	1.44	1.23	1.72

half of the revenues whereas new services are growing quickly. In particular, energy, environmental and related services have grown by 256% between 1990 and 1992, because of the acquisition of a majority ownership in an American company, WTI, and account now for approximately 17% of total revenues. By pursuing a strategy of acquisitions, especially in Western Europe, international waste management services have grown by 78%. More strikingly, the profits provided by Waste Management International have doubled. The income from energy and environmental services has multiplied by five (see Exhibit 3).

From a geographic point of view, WMX Technologies, Inc. has diversified very quickly. In spite of this diversification, the United States still remains its major market in terms of assets. However, revenues and incomes have grown faster internationally. Thus, WMX has gradually become a global company. This was far from being obvious at WMX's inception, given the wide variety of services and technology involved and the diversity of the needs that had to be handled. Now, Dean L. Buntrock, CEO of WMX Technologies, Inc., is proud to say that his company is the "acknowledged worldwide leader in providing comprehensive environmental, waste management and related services of the highest quality to industry, government and customers using state-of-the-art systems responsive to customer need, sound environmental policy and the highest standards of corporate citizenship."

Nevertheless, the recession brought into sharp focus some identity and organizational problems. Among the

EXHIBIT 3
WASTE MANAGEMENT: EVOLUTION OF ACTIVITIES

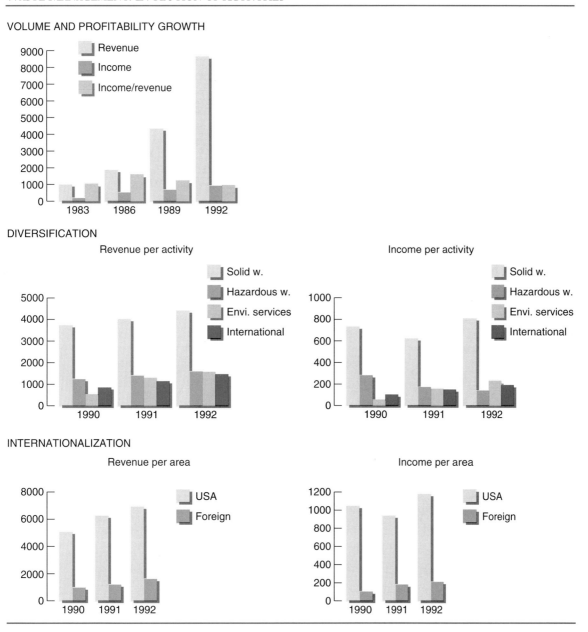

VOLUME AND PROFITABILITY GROWTH

DIVERSIFICATION

INTERNATIONALIZATION

most important responses was the decision to adopt the umbrella name WMX Technologies Inc. to identify the overall company. In the future, the name Waste Management Inc. will still characterize the traditional solid waste services business. However, the new name should convey to the customer the idea that a collection of technological and scientific resources unequaled in the industry is now available. The subsidiaries—Chemical Waste Management, Wheelabrator Technologies Inc., Waste Manage-

ment International and Rust International (see Exhibits 4, 5, and 6)—will keep their identity while benefiting technologically from the entire group.

Another major strategic decision was of the creation of Rust Inc. By combining the resources of environmental consulting, construction and engineering that were previously spread over several different subsidiaries, Rust became overnight a leader in its field with 13,900 employees. The whole Waste Management group will gain

EXHIBIT 4
WASTE MANAGEMENT INTERNATIONAL OWNERSHIP STRUCTURE

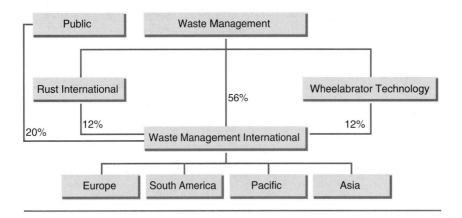

EXHIBIT 5
WMX'S FAMILY OF COMPANIES

Waste Management, Inc.
- Solid waste reduction
- Recycling
- Materials recovery
- Residential and commercial waste collection
- Processing
- Transfer
- Disposal
- Medical waste services
- Portable sanitation
- Relocatable office structures
- Special events services

Wheelabrator Technologies Inc.
- Trash-to-energy
- Cogeneration
- Water and wastewater treatment
- Biosolids management
- Composting
- Clean air technologies and services
- Industrial material design services

Rust International Inc.
- Environmental/infrastructure/process consulting
- Environmental/infrastructure/process engineering
- Marine/infrastructure/industrial construction
- Project management
- Demolition
- Hazardous/nuclear remediation
- On-site waste treatment technologies
- Industrial cleaning/maintenance
- Nuclear products/services
- Scaffolding

Chemical Waste Management, Inc.
- Hazardous waste reduction
- Recycling/recovery
- Collection
- Transportation
- Treatment
- Identification
- Thermal destruction
- Disposal
- Low-level radioactive waste services

Waste Management International plc
- Solid waste reduction
- Recycling
- Waste collection
- Waste transfer
- Trash-to-energy
- Comprehensive hazardous waste services
- City cleaning
- Special events services

Services	Customers									
	Residential	Construction	Commercial	Institutional	Agriculture	Government	Industrial	Utilities	Transportation	Waste Processing
Ash treatment and reuse		X	X			X	X			X
Biosolids management	X		X		X	X	X			X
City cleaning	X	X	X	X			X			
Clean air technologies and services		X	X	X		X	X	X	X	X
Cogeneration		X	X	X		X	X	X		X
Composting	X	X	X	X	X	X	X	X		X
Demolition		X	X	X		X	X	X		X
Disposal of solid, hazardous and special wastes	X	X	X	X	X	X	X	X	X	X
Environmental/infrastructure/ process consulting		X	X	X		X	X	X	X	X
Environmental/infrastructure/ process engineering		X	X	X		X	X	X	X	X
Hazardous/nuclear remediation	X	X	X		X	X	X	X	X	X
Hazardous waste identification	X	X	X	X	X	X	X	X	X	X
Hazardous waste reduction		X			X	X	X	X	X	
Hazardous waste services and treatment	X	X	X	X	X	X	X	X	X	X
Industrial cleaning	X	X	X	X		X	X	X	X	X
Marine/infrastructure/ industrial construction		X	X	X		X	X	X	X	X
Materials recovery/ hazardous and non-hazardous	X	X	X	X	X	X	X	X	X	X
Medical waste services			X	X	X	X	X	X	X	
Nuclear products/services			X			X	X	X	X	
On-site waste treatment technologies		X	X	X		X	X	X	X	X
Plant maintenance		X	X		X	X	X	X	X	
Portable sanitation	X	X	X	X	X	X	X	X	X	X

Continued

593

EXHIBIT 6 (continued)

Services	Residential	Construction	Commercial	Institutional	Agriculture	Government	Industrial	Utilities	Transportation	Waste Processing
Project management		X	X	X		X	X	X	X	X
Radioactive waste processing						X	X			
Recycling	X	X	X	X	X	X	X	X	X	X
Residential and commercial collection	X	X	X	X	X	X	X	X	X	X
Scaffolding		X	X			X	X	X		X
Solid waste reduction	X	X	X	X	X	X	X	X	X	X
Special event services	X	X	X	X	X	X	X	X	X	X
Specialty nuclear services						X	X	X		X
Street sweeping	X	X	X	X	X	X	X	X	X	X
Temporary fencing	X	X	X	X	X	X	X	X	X	X
Thermal destruction		X		X	X	X	X	X	X	X
Transfer	X	X	X	X	X	X	X	X	X	X
Transportation				X		X	X	X		
Trash-to-energy	X		X			X		X		X
Waste minimization	X	X	X	X	X	X	X	X	X	X
Water and wastewater treatment	X	X	X		X	X	X	X		X

EXHIBIT 7
ENVIRONMENTAL PRINCIPLES

1. Environmental protection and enhancement
2. Waste reduction, recycling, treatment and disposal
3. Biodiversity
4. Sustainable use of natural resources
5. Wise use of energy
6. Compliance with all legal requirements
7. Reduction of environmental, health and safety risk
8. Damage compensation
9. Research and development for integrated waste management
10. Public policy
11. Public education
12. Participation in environment organizations
13. Environmental policy assessment
14. Annual environmental report

synergy effects from this, for instance, by getting more efficient technical support.

To foster rapid growth, WMX Technology has introduced the Expanded Management System. This new program developed for management puts emphasis on the customer, the WMX people, the environment and the shareholders. This and the development of 14 environmental principles (see Exhibit 7) has increased the motivation of employees to comply with the Company's mission of providing remarkable services for a clean environment while making profit. In addition, a book entitled *Waste Management: A Corporate Success Story* was written about the Company.

Waste Management International

Waste Management International (WMI) is a leading provider of a range of solid and hazardous waste management services, including collection, recycling, transportation, storage, treatment, incineration, and disposal, as well as operating waste-to-energy facilities, and offering related services. The company currently operates in nine European countries (Britain, Denmark, Finland, France, Germany, Italy, The Netherlands, Spain and Sweden) as well as in Argentina, Venezuela, Australia, New Zealand, Hong Kong, Brunei and the Middle East.

In April 1992, WMX Technologies concluded a global public offering for Waste Management International plc and raised $700 million. It was among the most successful offerings of its kind. In less than 90 days after this offering, WMI has successfully achieved significant development in both existing and new international markets. In the first half of 1992, WMI plc's profit increased by 51 percent over the comparable period in 1991.

Europe. With a population of 400 million people, Western Europe had been the main focus of WMI's activities

in the past. A key factor in the company's growth in this region was the trend towards increasingly rigorous and harmonized environmental legislation and standards set by the European Union. Today, WMI's European operations serve over three million households through approximately 1,600 municipal contracts and provide hazardous waste management services to approximately 16,000 customers.

WMI has continued its growth following the acquisition of solid waste business in 1991. In May 1992, UK Waste Management also completed the acquisition of Marvin Ltd.—a storage, handling and chemical waste treatment facility in Great Yarmouth. This facility, which has a broad permit for storage, transfer and treatment of hazardous and industrial waste, will complement UK Waste Management's disposal capabilities in Risley. In France, the acquisition of SPAT gives WMI eight operating landfills in the Paris area. In Germany, WMI concluded a contract to construct and operate a waste-to-energy facility at Gütersloh. The facility is projected to start operations in 1997 and will be capable of converting a minimum of 180,000 tons of solid waste and 25,000 tons of sewage sludge a year to useful energy. Along with the company's other waste-to-energy facility in Hamm, Gütersloh will be the second privately owned facility of its kind in Germany.

WMI Sellbergs, the Swedish subsidiary, announced that it has signed a preliminary agreement with the Swedish Ministry for the Environment to acquire 90.1 percent of the government-owned SAKAB, the foremost hazardous waste treatment facility in Sweden which has an incineration capacity of 33,000 tons per year. WMI Sellbergs also acquired Servi Jatehuolto OY, the leading solid waste management company in Finland. "We are very excited by the number and range of opportunities that the company is currently pursuing throughout all our markets, some of which could be realized in the second half of this financial year," Said Falkman. The scope of these opportunities ranges from full-blown acquisitions to state-of-the-art treatment facilities.

Asia. WMI has been aware for a long time of Asian needs for environmental services. Nonetheless, current operations are limited to Brunei and Hong Kong, where the most sophisticated waste treatment plant of its kind has just been built. The company expects to start operating their US$304-million SENT landfill project in Hong Kong in late 1994.

In May 1993, WMI announced its joint venture with Bimantara, a leading Indonesian company, to develop a solid and hazardous waste business in that country. This is a significant development because WMI sees the Asian market as a major area for growth. Indonesia itself has the fourth largest population in the world and its government has expressed a commitment to safely managing its waste. WMI will be actively working with Bimantara to identify other projects involving waste water treatment, waste-to-energy systems, waste reduction, recycling and remediation activities, as well as the collection, treatment and disposal of municipal solid and chemical waste.

"The company's excellent reputation in our industry means we are a favored choice to benefit from increased governmental privatization projects, as shown by our success in Gütersloh and Indonesia," said one of the executive managers.

REASONS TO WORRY

In 1993, the financial results gave reason to worry. The situation had turned bad: pretax profit for the third quarter (ending September 30) slipped to £38.88 million ($58.32 million) from £40.08 million ($60.12 million). Consequently, on October 16, 1993, Waste Management International plc was obliged to announce a message of confidence in its earnings growth to calm its shareholders and stem the rumors on stock markets that were expecting better results.

Europe

Europe was the main cause of this deep distress. Because of the lack of economic recovery in Western Europe, the company had set up an extensive program of cost reduction and productivity improvement; however, the slowdown of the European economy hampered WMI's profitability. Besides, "the results were achieved in the face of difficult European trading and fewer acquisitions than anticipated," said WMI. Earnings growth and revenues were also hurt by delays in obtaining landfill permit extensions in Italy, which lowered turnover.

Asia

In contrast, WMI had made major progress in several Asian markets. It was bidding for several waste-to-energy products in Taiwan with its joint venture partner, Ret Ser, and was also exploring opportunities in other countries such as Thailand, Malaysia and Taiwan (see Exhibits 8a–8h).

Even though the company could maintain its earnings per share, investors knew that new opportunities had to be pursued. The company, which has grown steadily through acquisitions, remained on the lookout for more purchases.

THE ENVIRONMENTAL SITUATION

The International Situation

International concern about the environment has grown rapidly in recent years. The increased awareness of air, soil and water pollution by chemical plants, and of hazardous and solid waste has created new market opportunities. The worldwide industry for environmental technology, although still young, had developed into a US$200 billion market by 1992 (see Exhibit 9). Among the industry's most dynamic sectors were waste management, sewage treatment, air pollution control, and water purification and conservation.

In developed countries the focus increasingly shifted away from combating the damage caused by pollution and the disposal of industrial waste to the prevention of pollution during the production process. As a result, competition has become fiercer between firms making equipment to deal with pollution after the fact—so-called end-of-pipe-technologies. Until recently, these firms had dominated the industry.

Now, however, their significance was declining. In the last couple of years, the industry has seen a wave of takeovers and mergers as firms producing pollution control and energy-conservation equipment found their break-even sales level rapidly rising. Another factor that contributed to the increased concentration was the large amount of equity capital that is needed by companies in this industry in order to finance their major investments.

The Environmental Problem in Asia

Asian countries have experienced a boom in population growth over the last decades. Many countries suffer from overpopulation. This and the increasing trend towards rapid industrialization has led to more urbanization. This, in turn, has resulted in a sharp increase in household and industrial waste. As land becomes a scarce resource—especially in smaller countries, such as Hong Kong and Singapore—the harm done to the environment has become

EXHIBIT 8-a

INDIA

1. Environmental Situation and Needs

The environmental situation in India has continued to deteriorate due to rapid population, industrial and economic growth. The concern and commitment to environmental issues is growing, both in the government of India and in the Indian industry. The Indian market for industrial waste treatment equipment (US$ 100m in 1991) is estimated to expand to US$ 245m in 1995. The projected average annual real growth rate of the total market is estimated at 30% over the next 3 years.

2. Competition

Local companies in the environment business are numerous but small in size. They still lack the capabilities for more advanced waste treatments. Those techniques have to be imported from abroad. Here American companies have already established a strong foothold in the Indian market:

(US$ millions)	1990	1991	1992	Est. Avg. Annual Real Growth Next 3 Years
Import Market	27	30	29	20%
Local Production	70	78	75	
Exports	7	8	7	
Total Market	90	100	97	30%
Imports from US	7	8	10	20%

3. Legislation

The Indian government has recently established a number of new regulations to protect the environment. Main legal instruments in India for pollution control are the Water (Prevention and Control of Pollution) Act, 1974; the Air (Prevention and Control of Pollution) Act, 1981; the Environment Protection Act, 1986; the Hazardous Chemical Rules of 1989; and the Hazardous Wastes (Management and Handling) Rules. The Government's Central Pollution Control Board has established Minimum National Standards (known as MINAS) for various polluting industries.

In order to help companies to comply with these regulations, the Indian government is quite receptive to industry's pleas for various fiscal incentives for installation of pollution control equipment and waste disposal. Within the scope of the Asian Development Bank Operational Program for 1992–1994 US$ 600 thousand are provided for a river clean-up action plan to finance technical assistance.

4. Economic and Political Situation

The Indian government has recently restructured and liberalized the country's trade, investment and economic policies and the Government's rupee has become convertible. Thus, the business climate is more favorable now for foreign firms to enter the market.

Source: National Trade Data Bank

more and more visible. The situation is particularly harsh in major Asian cities where people stifle in the stench of garbage and breathe contaminated air.

Local governments have realized the problem and have become increasingly willing to change the current situation. They have started to enact tighter pollution controls and increase their political commitment to safeguard the environment. As Asian economies boom, their governments receive more tax revenues which enables them to invest in the environmental clean-up.

EXHIBIT 8-b

INDONESIA

1. Environmental Situation and Needs

One side-effect of Indonesia's growth has been a negative impact on the quality of Indonesia's environment. This has been most evident in cities with high population densities and/or regions with substantial production activities. Demand for pollution control has increased substantially since 1990. One reason for this increase is the implementation of the Clean River Program (PROKASIH) in eight provinces, including 17 rivers. This program is concentrating on decreasing pollution originating from industries known to contribute considerably to the decrease in river quality. It is estimated that the demand for water pollution equipment in 1991 was US$ 340 million, an increase of approximately 60% from the previous year. A new air pollution control program known as "Langit Biru" (blue sky), scheduled to begin in late 1993. This program involves a "crackdown" on pollution caused by private motor vehicles and industry sources. Total imports of such products increased from US$ 22.1 million in 1990 to US$ 44.6 million in 1991.

2. Competition

Local companies are already capable of providing approximately 60% of the equipment used in air and water pollution control. The remainder is covered by foreign suppliers:

(US$ millions)	1989	1990	1991	Est. Avg. Annual Real Growth Next 3 Years
Import Market	73.6	84.1	146.6	35%
Local Production	153.4	180.2	304.9	
Exports	0.4	0.6	0.8	
Total Market	226.6	263.7	450.7	30%
Imports from US	25.5	25.6	36.7	30%

Technology levels of local Indonesian manufacturers have increased considerably through technology transfer from the United States, Europe, Japan and other foreign partners. Some examples include PT Basuki with Keller Lufttechnik of Germany, and CV Lunto Prima with Farr of the United States. While technology levels of local companies are improving, they remain heavily dependent on engineering support from their foreign partners.

3. Legislation

Since 1982, the Indonesian government has issued various regulations to control the environment, or at least to achieve sustainable development. The most recent government regulation is the decree No. 03/MenKLH/II/1991 issued by the Minister of Population and the Environment, where the limits of pollution levels for the industrial sector are clearly defined. In June 1990, by virtue of Presidential Decree No. 23, the new Environmental Impact Management Agency (BAPEDAL) was formed as an implementation agency for pollution control. BAPEDAL assumed responsibility for the programs related to environmental pollution, environmental destruction, hazardous waste management and environmental impact assessment.

4. Economic and Political Situation

Indonesia is growing rapidly. In 1991, the country had a GDP of approximately US$ 115 billion and was expected to grow 5% in 1992. The government implementation of deregulation and debureaucratization reforms in 1987 is improving the environment for foreign business interests.

Source: National Trade Data Bank

Exhibit 8-c
Korea

1. Environmental Situation and Needs

89% of solid waste in Korea is landfilled, while only 2% is incinerated. Disposal of solid, municipal, industrial and hazardous waste is a major priority within the recently energized environmental field. The Korean Government considers that the construction of at least six additional hazardous solid waste treatment plants is required by 1996.

One need of which Korea is particularly aware is the retreatment of medical waste. The volume of medical refuse has grown exponentially in recent years due to the use of disposables to limit the spread of infectious diseases. There are 603 hospitals in Korea with 107,720 beds and 12,137 doctor's offices or clinics, producing 1,200 tons of medical waste monthly, large volumes of which have been illegally landfilled, stirring public concern.

2. Competition

US companies have an enormous competitive advantage in this country as it has been traditionally very close to the United States. One of the high officials of the Environmental Management Corporation (EMC) stated that they are eagerly seeking US technologies in various environment fields such as waste tire recycling, advanced treatment (the third treatment) of the industrial waste water as well as hazardous solid waste treatment in order to adopt the US advanced technologies. This would also decrease the chronic trade deficit with Japan.

Besides, in its effort to acquire US technologies, EMC is considering sending its engineers to the United States.

(US$ millions)	1990	1991	Est. Avg. Annual Real Growth Next 3 Years
Import Market	n.a.	n.a.	n.a.
Local Production	n.a.	n.a.	
Exports	n.a.	n.a.	
Total Market	n.a.	n.a.	n.a.
Imports from US	60.5	67.1	9%

3. Legislation

To monitor the environmental policy, the Government has set up the EMC which constructs and operates industrial waste water and hazardous solid waste treatment plants.

Nonetheless, the law is not yet enforcing firms to take their waste back. As for medical waste, the current Korean land use and management law still prohibits the construction of medical incineration plants. An amendment is about to be passed.

4. Economic and Political Situation

The economic expansion in Korea is among the most rapid in the world and its stable government encourages foreign firms to do business in Korea.

Source: National Trade Data Bank

Exhibit 8-d
Malaysia

1. Environmental Situation and Needs

As the Malaysian government tightens its enforcement of pollution control regulations, the market for related products and services will grow rapidly. Currently, pollution control equipment and services centers on air and water pollution as well as the disposal of solid and hazardous waste. The market for pollution control equipment and services in Malaysia is expanding quickly with the increased requirements for sophisticated products and higher levels of technology. The projected average annual real growth rate of the total market is estimated at 27% over the next 3 years.

2. Competition

There are many foreign suppliers in the pollution control industry and the competition is keen.

(US$ millions)	1990	1991	1992	Est. Avg. Annual Real Growth Next 3 Years
Import Market	27.8	42.4	61.5	30%
Local Production	0	0	0	
Exports	1.4	2.8	4	25%
Total Market	26.4	39.6	57.5	27%
Imports from US	8.9	10.9	12.8	17%

The largest foreign suppliers are from Singapore and Japan. Other suppliers are from Germany, Italy, Denmark, Switzerland, Canada, Belgium, Korea and France. Some are entering into joint ventures. For example, Biotem, a Belgium company, has entered into a joint venture on anaerobic digestion technology with a Malaysian Engineering firm.

3. Legislation

Since 1989, regulations to control the pollution have become stricter, especially with regard to water and air pollution. The government, however, has been criticized for not enforcing these regulations. Over the past ten years, the Department of Environment (DOE) has issued only an average of 40 citations a year. This is beginning to change. The government is coming under growing pressure from a better informed and more environmentally aware public for more uniform enforcement. As a result, the trend for the next three years will be toward tougher enforcement.

The government is investing large sums into pollution control. In 1991, local authorities spent about US$ 68 million on solid waste disposal, amounting to almost 80% of some local councils' operating revenue. In addition, the federal government has allocated more than US$ 10 million to conduct research on how to address the problem of solid waste disposal and to train local authorities. Beginning in 1992, the government will invest over US$ 180 million in sewerage projects.

4. Economic and Political Situation

Since becoming independent in 1957, Malaysia has become a role model of what developing countries can achieve. The high level of stability since independence has created an environment where economic forces have flourished. The next 5 year plan covering 1991 to 1996 calls for an annual growth rate of 7.5% to raise the nation's nominal output from US$ 42 billion to US$ 75 billion by 1996.

Source: National Trade Data Bank

EXHIBIT 8-e
PHILIPPINES

1. Environmental Situation and Needs

In the last few years, the Philippine Government has started turning serious attention to the environment. This is evidenced in the country's Medium Term Development Plan, 1987–92, which explicitly states government environmental policies, and the recent Philippine Strategy for Sustainable Development, which stresses the need to view economic growth and environmental protection as interdependent and mutually compatible.

2. Competition

There are many local companies involved in the environment but they remain small in size. The infrastructure is not present for the locals to build more sophisticated waste treatments. American companies already dominate the market:

(US$ millions)	1992	1993 (Estimated)	Est. Avg. Annual Real Growth Next 3 Years
Import Market	11.7	14.0	30%
Local Production	0	0	
Exports	0	0	
Total Market	11.7	14.0	20%
Imports from US	1.9	2.1	15%

3. Legislation

The responsibility for implementing the government's environmental strategies and policies rests with the Department of Environment and Natural Resources(DENR). The Environmental Management Bureau of DENR spearheads the government's efforts to protect the people and resources of the country from the growing menace of environmental degradation. Aside from DENR, the other government agencies concerned with environmental protection and management are Laguna Lake Development Authority, Department of Health, Philippine Coast Guard, Human Settlements Development Corp., and the National Water Resources Council.

Although there are a number of government agencies involved in environmental protection, the level of compliance with environmental regulations remains low. The poor level of compliance is attributable to government agencies' lack of technically qualified personnel, laboratory facilities and equipment to monitor pollution, and enforcement mechanisms. This deficiency has led to the rapid growth of non-governmental organizations (NGOs) concerned with the environment. These NGOs have been very active in bringing up environmental issues, leading protests against polluting firms and planned projects with polluting effects, and monitoring the environmental impact of projects. These developments augur well for purchases of pollution control equipment and services in the coming years.

4. Economic and Political Situation

Assuming daily power outages are reduced by third quarter 1993 as predicted, the Philippine economy may be on the verge of a modest turnaround after two years of stagnant growth. Philippine economic fundamentals have improved due to control of the fiscal deficit, reduction of inflation to single digit levels and moderation of interest rates. While President Ramos appears investor-friendly and reform-oriented, he has had difficulty getting support for his economic agenda in the Senate. Reconciliation efforts have helped reduce political unrest, but a still unsettled law and order situation, chronic power shortages, and inadequate infrastructure are restraining industrial expansion. These factors also remain key obstacles in attracting more foreign investment and achieving sustainable economic growth.

Source: National Trade Data Bank

EXHIBIT 8-f

SINGAPORE

1. Environmental Situation and Needs

Singapore's small land area, high population density and rapid industrialization brought environmental issues to the national consciousness. Although environmental awareness is prevalent in the market. Singapore is still at least five years behind the U.S. in the area of environmental technology.

The most promising subsectors with their estimated 1993 total market size (U.S.$ millions) are:

Filters	$25 million
Pollution Control Equipment	$50 million
Solid Waste Management Equipment	$40 million

2. Competition

Domestic production of industrial waste treatment equipment is relatively small. Presently, very few companies produce environmental equipment and the few that do are so small in size that their tabulation as a source of competition within the market is minimal at best. Total imports of the products increased about US$ 36 million from 1990 to 1991. There has been an increase of imports from the U.S. over the past two years. Singapore's private and public sectors are still actively seeking foreign partners to join forces with local firms to meet the region's needs for environmental controls, products and services. Local importers continue to look to the United States as their main supply source.

(US$ millions)	1990	1991	1992	Growth 91–93
Import Market	228	275	144	
Local Production	20	33	19	
Exports	87	113	61	
Total Market	161	195	102	
Imports from US	68	79	43	7%

There are a number of companies in Singapore that deal with industrial waste equipment. Usually, the equipment is imported by distributors who sell directly to factories or dealers. Obviously, the middleman can be eliminated and U.S. firms can sell directly to the various number of factories or regionally based MNC's or even set up their own distribution outlets.

3. Legislation

To combat the growing problem of pollution, the Singaporean Government established the Ministry of the Environment (ENV) in 1972. ENV acts as environmental authority, regulatory body, and the source of contract tenders for odor control, sludge treatment and incineration. Subsequent legislation for industrial waste soon followed with the Trade Effluent Regulations (1976), and more recently the Environmental Public Health Regulations (Toxic Industrial Waste) in 1988. According to the Ministry of the Environment Annual Report of 1990, factories discharging acid trade effluent are required to install continuous pH monitoring and recording systems. Singapore is a duty free port with only 4% of all goods imported being taxed. There are also no trade barriers, and the Singapore government does not interfere in the relationship between U.S. manufacturers and Singaporean agents and/or distributors. The Pollution Control Department must evaluate and approve new environmental control equipment. The PCD is also responsible for reviewing factory plans of new industries which might produce waste or pollution.

4. Economic and Political Situation

Strong and stable government.

EXHIBIT 8-g
THAILAND

1. Environmental Situation and Needs

Industrial output has been growing at double-digit rates in recent years and is expected to continue into the 21st century. Already, industry's share of the GDP is more than twice that of agriculture, and Thailand is on its way towards becoming a NIC. Traffic congestion, water shortages, solid waste, air, water and noise pollution problems have noticeably worsened during the last few years of rapid industrialization. The growth rate of industrial pollution follows the higher rate of industrial growth: 8% in the 1970s, 10% in the early 1980s and 13% in the late 1980s. The high profitability of much of the Thai industry suggests a degree of affordability of pollution-control expenditures without a significant loss of international competitiveness.

52% of the industries (76% in terms of GDP) are located in the Bangkok area. The concentration of industrial waste in a limited space destroys the environment's natural assimilative capacity through overloading. On the other hand, the concentration of industrial waste around Bangkok means economies of scale in pollution control and treatment.

Engineering Science Inc. (1989) has projected that the hazardous waste generated by the manufacturing sector will reach 1.9 million tons in 1991 and 5.7 million tons by 2010.

2. Competition

There are almost no environmental services provided so far in Thailand. Bangkok, a city the size of Los Angeles, does not even have a sewer system; household waste is being dumped at Soi Onnuch, where a waste mountain is growing bigger every day.

Only local companies have tried to set up businesses in waste management services. General Finance and Securities have spent 10m baht on two pilot projects to manage home waste in Chiang Mai and Phuket. So far, both projects have failed to be commercially viable because the company cannot get big enough concessions (the size of a province). Besides, public awareness of the issue must be created since no one is ready to pay for environmental services. These results dissuade foreign companies to intervene.

3. Legislation

Both environmental awareness and environmental legislation (setting of standards) have advanced considerably in recent years, but enforcement is lagging.

In choosing an appropriate pollution-control instrument, the government has given consideration to the type of industrial waste and the scale and geographic distribution of industry.

4. Economic and Political Situation

According to the US Embassy in Bangkok, US investors are highly positive about their operations and are generally reinvesting heavily. Besides, the Thai government implemented a number of reform measures (trade tariff reductions, reduction of the corporate tax). A possible obstacle to sustained rapid growth are infrastructural constraints (telecommunications, roadway, electricity generators). Another problem is the shortage of engineers and of skilled personnel.

Source: National Trade Data Bank

EXHIBIT 8-h
TAIWAN

1. Environmental Situation and Needs

Taiwan has one of the world's highest population densities (573 people per km²) and is becoming increasingly urbanized and industrialized. (Major cities: Taipei, Kaohsiung, Taichung and Tainan.) This evolution has resulted in a rapid increase in solid waste and the environmental damage to the island has become visible. According to estimates of the Environmental Protect Administration (EPA) municipal waste will increase by 6% p.a. from 7.6m metric tons (MTs) in 1992 to 9.7m MTs in 1996. The industrial waste is likely to grow at a rate of 3 to 5% p.a. over the same time period. At present, industrial waste amounts to 30m MTs a year of which 10% is hazardous. About 60% of the waste is disposed by regular means with 85% going to landfills, 4% to incinerators, 1% to composting sites and 10% to other forms of disposal. Due to the increased waste Taiwan is running out of available land to bury it. The EPA has developed a 5-year target plan (July 1992–Dec. 1996, Green Plan) under which 23 incinerators will be built, 722 collection and disposal vehicles will be purchased, 60 landfills will be constructed and 1 compost site will be developed. Areas with the strongest growth potential in waste include hospitals, the petrochemical industry and the pulp and paper industry.

2. Competition

There are some 370 firms in Taiwan engaged in pollution control equipment. Nevertheless, the bulk of the waste industry market is covered by foreign suppliers:

(US$ millions)	1989	1990	1991	Est. Avg. Annual Real Growth Next 3 Years
Import Market	36.0	49.5	88.4	25%
Local Production	2.1	4.5	11.1	
Exports	0.7	1.2	1.3	
Total Market	37.4	52.9	98.2	20–25%
Imports from US	10.7	15.7	47.9	23%

American firms dominate the public sector while Japanese equipment is preferred by private firms because of lower prices, their geographical proximity and better customer service. Major American firms that are active in the market include Westinghouse, Foster Wheeler, Agden Martin and American Ref-Suel. Principal Japanese firms are Mitsubishi, Takuma, Hitachi, Yamamoto and Toshiba. The Germans are represented by Fichtner, Schench and Katec.

3. Legislation

The EPA is currently completing a legislative framework with 19 laws and 53 regulations for the control of air, water, noise and soil pollution, toxic chemicals, vibration and waste disposal. Also, inspections and law enforcement are becoming more rigorous. A case in point is that the EPA has come up with a blacklist of 15,000 plants that are seen as air and water pollution offenders. If these factories do not install proper control facilities within the next 4 years, they will have to pay daily penalties of NTD 60,000. Government policy is to privatize the industrial waste treatment industry. To encourage private investments in pollution control, the authorities in Taiwan have provided attractive incentives and financial supports to polluting companies. These incentives comprise free import duties, investment tax reductions and low-interest loans.

4. Economic and Political Situation

Taiwan is politically stable and economically booming.

Source: National Trade Data Bank

EXHIBIT 9
WORLD MARKET FOR
ENVIRONMENTAL TECHNOLOGY

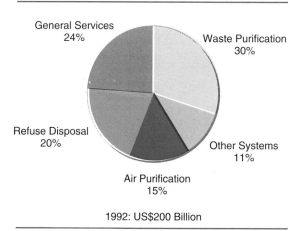

General Services 24%

Waste Purification 30%

Refuse Disposal 20%

Other Systems 11%

Air Purification 15%

1992: US$200 Billion

Asian countries also get support from several multi-national institutions. Besides the World Bank and the IMF, the United Nations Center on Transnational Corporation (UNCTC) currently investigates measures that will encourage and mobilize transnational development. Major areas of investigation are the protection of the atmosphere, land resources and the conservation of biological diversity. Environmental policies and programs are also raised to the same level of sophistication as those dealing with health and safety issues.

ASEAN in an alert report stressed the importance of the air quality in Asia. It recommended that the Pollutant Standards Index (PSI) developed by the United States Environmental Protection Agency be adopted by all member countries to standardize measurements within ASEAN.

The Asian Development Bank has established an operational ad hoc program for 1992–1994 to remedy damage that had been done to the environment. Support is provided in the form of loans, standby loans, technical assistance programs and for projects in the area of water pollution control, river cleaning, urban water supply and sewerage, as well as waste water treatment in South East Asian countries.

WASTE MANAGEMENT'S MARKET ENTRY STRATEGIES IN ASIA

After having established a strong foothold in Western Europe, WMI is now pursuing opportunities in Asian countries. In developed countries the company followed a strategy of acquiring well established players, while maintaining the names of the companies it bought and continuing to provide services under their logo. In the developing Asian countries, however, such companies basically do not currently exist. Although there are already some local competitors in place, they are small in size and offer very few environmental services. Therefore, WMI essentially had to start from scratch in Asia.

Key Issues

The focus on Asia is thereby purely motivated by the rapid growth in the region. Waste Management started its operations abroad in the 1970's in Saudi Arabia when a unique investment opportunity occurred. The highly positive cash flows that the project provided, helped finance acquisitions back in the United States. "Our strategy is not country specific, but region specific," said Gregory Feutril. "We are responding to opportunities with the highest profit potential."

Nevertheless, WMI considers itself as a conservative company that does not take chances. Despite alluring profit potentials, it only enters markets which fulfill certain criteria set by top management.

First of all, the project in question has to be large. This is because WMI is mainly in the public services business in Asia as governments are its principal customers. Vying for a new government contract requires a lot of time and money. It is only worth the effort if the expected return on investment is substantial.

Second, WMI must be able to find a suitable local partner. Local partners (often construction companies or influential members of the ruling family) normally do not have any knowledge or particular expertise in the field of waste management. But, they bring in valuable contacts with government authorities and potential industrial customers for WMI. They are also familiar with the way business is done in a particular country. In addition, the involvement of a local company is often required by Asian governments. WMI only aligns with a local partner if WMI is the majority owner and reaps the majority of the profits. It does so in order to compensate for the risk that is involved with their technology transfer. If oneof these requirements is not fulfilled, it stays out of the market.

Third, the regulatory environment that is in place in a specific country must be suitable. Waste Management has decided to go only to countries where environmental laws are established and strictly enforced. "If companies were not forced to take care of their waste, they would simply dump it into the next river or ocean," said Gregory Feutril.

Fourth, the environment for developing new business has to be attractive. WMI is therefore currently not looking into the Russian or the Eastern European markets. While Eastern Europe's pollution problem will make it an attractive market in the future, the region will hardly be in a position to support business development or come up with the finance necessary for environmental clean-up measures by itself.

Finally, the convertibility of the local currency is of primary importance. Restrictions on the repatriation of profits or high socio-economic risk of a country are unacceptable to WMI.

Getting the Contract

Once Waste Management decides to try to enter a new market, there are basically two ways to win contracts.

First, given WMI's international reputation, Asian governments may approach them and ask them to submit a bid for a particular project. But, as Asian authorities are not yet very experienced with environmental issues, their project requirements are often insufficient. Consequently, Waste Management spends a lot of time on counseling and giving advice to the various governments on how to improve their efforts to protect the environment. Similar activities are being undertaken by WMI's international competitors. The local governments then pick out issues from various proposals to form a new public offer and ask the companies involved to rebid.

This process alone usually takes 2 to 3 years. If the project is very sophisticated and only Waste Management has the expertise to provide all the required services, then WMI can set almost any price. If, however, the project can be done by a lot of other companies as well, competitive pricing becomes crucial for WMI. The actual bidding process in the latter case is thereby divided into two steps. Step 1 prequalifies interested companies and screens them based on whether their skills match the needed services. Step 2 then awards the project to the lowest bidder.

The other way to win a contract is to set up a local development office staffed with one or two people who establish contacts with government authorities and potential industrial customers directly. In order to foster the basis for an environmentally friendly legislation and behavior, WMI conducts a lot of education directed towards the governments of developing countries, major polluters and waste producers, and, the general public as well.

The idea is that a marketing person sets up contacts and when the opportunity for a new project arises, he or she calls in a team of management people to actually pull off the project. This is a time-consuming process. It often takes years until the team may get the project, and then another 5 to 7 years to build, for instance, a chemical waste plant. It is estimated that 80% of the public offers are eventually given to foreign companies, of which only approximately 50% are won by Waste Management. Nevertheless, the salespeople have to be paid and the costs for submitting various proposals are substantial, up to $8–10 million for the largest and most complicated projects.

Once the contract is won, WMI often has to train local people to make them familiar with the technology. This on the job training is expensive as it often has to be done in the United States. A frequent problem is thus, that when the people are finally highly qualified they get wooed away by other companies. To diminish this turnover, Waste Management established a lucrative incentive system. Furthermore, Waste Management has increasingly pursued a strategy of decentralization. It transfers the responsibilities to the local management in a specific country, who then are in charge of making their own decisions on whether and how to expand Waste Management's activities in the particular country or region.

The duration of a project, once the contract is won, varies depending on whether it is garbage collection, a chemical waste plant or a landfill. The number of years until a new bid is due to win an extension of the contract is also case specific.

Financing the Project

As these projects devour a lot of money, bank financing via loans is fairly difficult for Waste Management to obtain. Although Waste Management helps Third World countries to cope with their environment problems it receives no funding from the World Bank or the IMF. These projects are therefore financed either out of an existing cash flow or through public stock offers and bonds. In addition, local partners occasionally participate in the investments.

COMPETITION

The future East Asian market for environmental clean-up technology is estimated to be a 300-billion-dollar-plus market. With an opportunity of this magnitude many players are attempting to join in the game. At present, however, there are only a few dedicated environmental service companies that have the technology and resources to expand to Asia. On the other hand there are many firms involved in engineering, heavy industry, construction and power that have significant experience in similar large-scale undertakings and are trying to leverage on this experience in the waste management sector. Others are attempting to expand in their environmental niche they have developed elsewhere and bring it to Asia. Still others are aligning themselves with other companies to offer a more encompassing service. Local competitors are present also, but lack the technology to be a force in the market.

American companies are said to have a distinct advantage in the global arena because they have the most experience dealing with environmental regulation. But with the expansion of the environmental market in Mexico, and South and Central America, significant opportunities exist closer to home. European environmental firms have a tremendous amount of experience, but are battling a recession and are dealing with vast opportunities in Eastern Europe. Australian companies have the advantages of proximity to Asia and experience with environmental regulations, but are still in the midst of a deep recession in their country which started in 1988.

It is difficult to obtain specific numbers on waste management companies involved in Asia because the mar-

Exhibit 10

COMPETITIVE ENVIRONMENT

Country	Company	Activities
Australia	Cleanaway	• diverse waste management services • largest in Europe and Australia
Canada	Laidlaw	• diverse waste management services • one of the largest in North America • recent involvement in Asia
France	Bouygues	• civil engineering • experienced in waste water • established internationally • much Asian experience
	Generale	• very experienced in waste water • large presence in Asia
Germany	Edelhoff	• diverse waste management services • large European player • focus on former East Germany and Eastern Europe
	Otto	• diverse waste management services • large European player • focus on former East Germany and Eastern Europe
UK	Attwoods	• diverse waste management services • large in UK and Europe • recent involvement in Asia
USA	Bechtel	• environmental engineering • largest in the USA • presently involved in Asia
	Browning-Ferris	• diverse waste management services • one of the largest in North America • recent involvement in Asia
	WMX	• diverse waste management services • largest in the world • recent involvement in Asia

ket there is so new. The ones that are present are so concerned about maintaining and expanding their competitive advantage that they will only reveal information required by law. Furthermore, many organizations getting involved in waste management expertise are primarily subsidiaries of larger corporations (see Exhibit 10).

The following part describes a recent example of how WMI sets up a new project. This project in Hong Kong is the largest one of its kind that WMI has undertaken to date.

THE HONG KONG MODEL

Why Choose Hong Kong to Break into Asia?

"There are three criteria that a country must meet before Waste Management will enter their market: the economy must be strong, the government must be stable, and the currency must be freely convertible into hard currencies as well as being easily repatriated," emphatically stated Gregory Feutril. Economically, Hong Kong has sustained tremendous growth over the past 15 years. Its GDP has grown by 300% and its population has increased by 30%. In 1997, the territory will be unified with China. Politically, Hong Kong's situation was questionable back in 1989 with turmoil in Beijing and the union with China only 8 years away. But now China is committed to gradual reforms. So, the transition is likely to be smooth. Financially, the Hong Kong dollar is pegged at 7.78 to the US dollar and has fluctuated little since the inception of the linked rate policy in 1983. The Hong Kong dollar is freely convertible and there are no regulations that hamper inward or outward remittance of capital or profits.

High demand for environmental services is also evident. The territory's industrial and other wastes have increased by 500% over the past 15 years. Two industries

Hong Kong greatly relies upon, manufacturing and shipping, are two of the largest polluters of the environment. Up to this point, no government regulations exist to govern the disposal of hazardous waste. Companies dispose of chemical waste by dumping it into the sewers or directly into the sea. Consequently, Victoria Harbor which surrounds nearly all of Hong Kong has evolved into a toxic waste dumping ground.

Hong Kong also has geographic advantages. It is easily accessible and borders China. Being an international hub, the city also retains a high level of visibility. Because of its massive environmental problems and small size, it is thus a perfect place to showcase the many services of WMI.

How Should WMI Establish Itself in Hong Kong?

George Feutril explained: "The key to being a success in our business overseas is to take your time and choose the right local partner. The factors involved are that the partner must have the knowledge and experience of working with the local government." After over a year of searching, Waste Management decided on Citic Pacific and Kin Ching Besser of Hong Kong to be its partners. Citic Pacific, an arm of the Chinese government based in Hong Kong, acquired a 20% interest. Kin Ching Besser, a Hong Kong based group, took a 10% share. Waste Management renamed its Asian group Pacific Waste Management and retained a 70% interest.

Enviropace

"The group needed a name that could be easily translated into Cantonese and would convey its commitment to Hong Kong's environment," stated Gregory Feutril. This was a major concern to the directors of Waste Management because on a previous international project in Saudi Arabia it named its subsidiary, "Waste Management-Saudi Pritchard," which when translated into Arabic means, Saudi Pritchard the waste management company. Enviropace was the name chosen. In Cantonese and English, it conveys the environmental commitment.

How Should Enviropace Sell the Idea? Gregory Feutril noted: "Victoria Harbor surrounds the people of Hong Kong. The people and the government of Hong Kong must be made aware of the magnitude of this environmental problem. We must assist in making people aware of the dangers around them and how these dangers can be avoided." The first step involved pinpointing the magnitude of the problem and developing a solution to counter the environmental devastation. Next came the educational campaign. Pamphlets were distributed to government officials, companies creating hazardous waste and the general public of Hong Kong. Dialogue was established with

government officials. Partly as a result, the government drew up in 1989 an environmental plan designed to make sure that gross pollution would stop. Pollution control ordinances and regulations were enacted, and from that point on they would be enforced rigorously.

The new government focus can be best described by Chris Patten, Governor of Hong Kong. "By Hong Kong's normal standards of success, the environment is the one striking failure. We may have the tallest and finest buildings in Asia, but right next to them, we have a harbor into which we discharge 1.5 million cubic meters of untreated sewage and industrial waste every day. We may have some of the best natural parks in the world, but we dump 1,200 cubic meters of livestock waste into our rivers and streams each day. This daily discharge of filth has poisoned rivers and streams; almost extinguished marine life in the harbor; and become a serious hazard to public health. It has to stop."

The framework was established. Now Enviropace had to prove to the government that they possessed the savvy and the know-how to tackle this enormous challenges.

The Facility and Operation. "This will be the most comprehensive waste management facility in the world and it will be completed in the time frame of 2 years, January 1993," vice president, Greg Feutril explained. The plan called for the construction of a US$130 million integrated waste treatment plant on Tsing Yi island. The contract will run for 15 years and will span the transfer of Hong Kong from Britain to China. The facility breaks chemicals down by burning, separating and adding neutralizing agents. The plant has a purpose-built high temperature incinerator capable of destroying organic wastes such as spent polymers and solvents which cannot be recycled. Oily waste is treated in an oil-water separator, and the reclaimed oil used as fuel for the incinerator. Chemical and physical processes (lime dosing and filters) treat inorganic matter which accounts for about 70% of the waste. Whenever possible, materials are recycled and recovered. Prime candidates for recycling are copper etching solutions from printed circuit board factories and organic solvents from the electronics industry.

One of the greatest challenges facing Enviropace was the collection and transportation of the waste. Unlike the US and most European countries, where waste generally is produced by large facilities and transported on adequate road systems for disposal, waste producers in Hong Kong tend to be small companies located in cramped, congested areas. Enviropace developed a quasi just-in-time pick-up system. The company delivers empty containers only 20-200 liters in size to factories and picks them up a few days later. As for the collection of oily wastes generated by vessels in Victoria Harbor, Enviropace uses a purpose-built 650-ton barge to pick up oil-contaminated and chemical-contaminated water from container ships and delivers the waste directly to the facility.

The new plant initially cost approximately US$25 million a year to operate. Costs will increase as volumes increase. The waste center has been designed to evolve over the years as Hong Kong's industry changes. Enviropace is paid on an incentive basis: the company is paid by the government according to the hazardous material treated. The government estimates that on average it will pay the company US$25–65 million a year for the duration of the contract.

Avoiding the Fatal Flaw.
"If we want this technologically unique project to succeed we must do everything in our power to avoid the fatal flaw; this has been our philosophy during the entire project," said Gregory Feutril.

Some of the problems that endangered the whole Hong Kong project were:

> We had to take our time throughout; from choosing a partner to planning the facility. This is the only comprehensive hazardous waste management facility of its kind in the world. So, there could be no room for error in planning and all segments had to be completed on schedule.

The task sequencing system has worked remarkably well. As one group accomplished their unique mission, the other would join and perform their specialty and so on. The marketing team evaluated the problem, devised the solution and won the contract. The construction team built the facility to spec, on budget and on time.

> We had to ensure the government would create and enforce environmental regulations. What is the use of having the most technologically advanced facility in the world if no one uses it?

So far about 9,000 chemical waste producers have registered with the Environmental Protection Department as required by law. The maximum penalty for failing to register is a US$25,000 fine and six months in jail. The Enviropace consortium will be the first licensed waste collector/transporter.

> We needed qualified personnel to operate the facility.

Because this was the first facility of its kind in Asia, there were no individuals with the experience required to operate it. Enviropace sent all of its new management personnel to the United States for specific training. Once back in Hong Kong, these individuals were being lured away by other companies that realized the value of their training. Therefore, Enviropace constructed an incentive pay structure which stopped the defections.

Gregory Feutril now had to come to a conclusion. Where should Waste Management go from here? Asia sounded very promising. However, some questions still lingered:

> Which of the Asian countries should he choose? What do the various countries need?
>
> What is the competitive advantage of Waste Management that could make it successful in Asia?
>
> Are there any ways to pursue a global strategy?

◆ ◆

*C*ASE 6

BAXTER INTERNATIONAL—RENAL DIVISION: MARKET OPPORTUNITIES IN LATIN AMERICA

On February 14, 1994, Vernon R. Loucks, Chairman and Chief Executive Officer of Baxter International, announced to his shareholders that over the past year the company's earnings and stock price had not performed

This case was prepared by Vincent Chang, MBA student, and Kristiaan Helsen, Professor of Marketing at the University of Chicago. It is intended as the basis for class discussion rather than to illustrate effective or ineffective handling of an administrative situation. The authors gratefully acknowledge the assistance of Mr. William Hicks and Mr. Jim Austin, both at Baxter Healthcare. The development of the case was funded with a CIBER grant. Copyright © 1995 by The University of Chicago, Chicago, IL. Not to be used or reproduced without permission.

well. Loucks also presented strategic guidelines that would help Baxter to improve its performance in the future. These guidelines included restructuring the company's organization in 1994, holding operating and administrative expenses flat over the next two years, and making growth outside of the United States a higher priority. With regard to this last component Loucks stated: "In the developed nations, we are emphasizing technologies that serve advanced medical therapies. In less-developed nations, we are filling the demand for therapies such as peritoneal dialysis." Loucks talked about expansion opportunities for peritoneal dialysis in Latin America, specifically in Brazil, Colombia, Mexico and Venezuela.

COMPANY BACKGROUND

Don Baxter Intravenous Products Corporation was founded in 1931 by three partners: Dr. Donald Baxter, a West Coast physician, Dr. Ralph Falk, an Idaho surgeon, and Harry Falk, a venture capitalist. The new company was based on a recent medical innovation, intravenous (IV) therapy. Baxter manufactured intravenous therapeutic solutions and bottled them in vacuum-sealed containers.

In an attempt to provide its European customers with timely service and improved product availability, Baxter founded Baxter Laboratories of Belgium in 1954. In 1959, Baxter established an international division to market the company's products globally, marking the beginning of Baxter's worldwide strategy.

Baxter has always prided itself on innovation and advanced technology. Moving rapidly in research and development, Baxter developed the first artificial kidney in 1956, the VIAFLEX plastic container for its IV solutions in 1970, and the MINI-BAG plastic container in 1974. The latter innovation made use of pre-mixed doses of medication, giving pharmacists more control over IV therapy procedures and minimizing medication errors. Exhibit 1 shows Baxter's sales revenue growth over the last two decades.

CORPORATE STRATEGY AND INDUSTRY SEGMENTS

Baxter emphasizes a customized response to health care needs, leading it to establish a presence in most of the countries it serves. In addition to export offices in the U.S., Singapore and the United Kingdom, the company has sales offices in 29 countries. These local subsidiaries help Baxter to cope effectively with different government regulations as well as changes in economic and political conditions in each country. Baxter also strives to establish manufacturing and distribution facilities in those countries in which being closer to the customer provides efficiency gains.

The company operates in two industry segments: medical specialties and medical/laboratory products and distribution (refer to Exhibit 2). The medical specialties segment consists of biotherapy products, dialysis systems, medical products (outside the U.S.), and cardiovascular devices. The medical/laboratory products and distribution segment comprises medical/laboratory products, intravenous systems, and sales and distribution services. The medical specialties segment accounts for 36.6% of Baxter's total sales revenues, while the medical/laboratory products and distribution segment accounts for the remaining

EXHIBIT 1
BAXTER INTERNATIONAL, WORLDWIDE SALES DATA

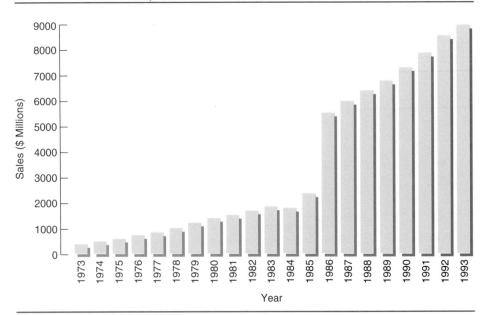

Source: Company Records

EXHIBIT 2
ORGANIZATION CHART

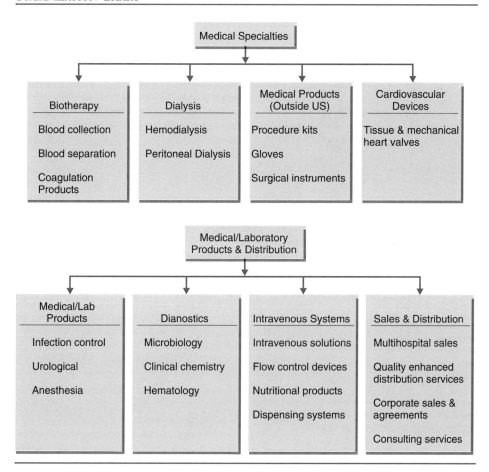

63.4%. Dialysis systems, which are used in the treatment of kidney disease, command the largest share of sales volume in the medical specialties segment.

BAXTER IN THE DIALYSIS MARKET

Baxter concentrates its R&D expenditures on potentially high growth, high return areas, which include therapies for treatment of end-stage renal (kidney) disease (ESRD). The company's R&D programs are directed at developing improved products for new and emerging markets as well as at making technological improvements in manufacturing processes. Self-manufactured products launched between 1988 and 1993 comprised approximately 35% of the company's total self-manufactured product sales for 1993.

The growth potential of renal therapy makes this field a priority for Baxter. As Donald Joseph, president of the Renal Division, put it: "Baxter is just beginning to scratch the surface" of the renal therapy market's potential. Baxter's research data confirms Joseph's point; for every treated kidney patient worldwide, there are five more untreated ones. Baxter prides itself on being the world leader in renal therapy, and it is aggressively positioning its capabilities to expand existing markets and tap into new ones.

Three types of treatments are used against kidney disease:[1] (1) hemodialysis (HD), (2) continuous ambulatory peritoneal dialysis (CAPD), and (3) kidney transplants. Hemodialysis (HD) is generally conducted at a hospital or clinic. Patients are connected to a machine

---

[1]See the Appendix for a more extensive overview of the various kidney treatment options.

EXHIBIT 3
SPS550 HEMODIALYSIS MACHINE

Baxter 550 Hemodialysis Machine

The Baxter 550: We Balanced Performance with Reliability to Create the Ideal Machine for Your Standard Dialysis Needs.

The Baxter 550 hemodialysis machine uses the ideal technology to achieve the best balance of performance and reliability. You expect performance *and* reliability, and that's what the Baxter 550 delivers.

Reliability...the Key to Economic Value.
- Superior reliability...continuous performance.
- One of the industry's lowest maintenance costs.
- Minimal service calls and downtime.

Easy to Use, Easy to Service.
- Rated number one by users in ease of use.
- All components easily accessible from front *and* back.
- Convenient service kits.
- Cost-effective on-site preventative maintenance.
- Easy to read logically-placed controls.

Performance...The Key to Effective Therapy Management.
- Advanced microprocessor technology.
- Volumetric Ultrafiltration System employs both Control *and* Monitor of fluid removal for patient safety.
- Ultrafiltration profiling to minimize hypotension.
- Variable sodium and bicarbonate...and much more.

Baxter 550...Balancing the Performance You Expect with the Reliability You Need.

Baxter 550 Standard Features
- Volumetric UF control and monitor accuracy at ± 50 ml/hr.
- UF Profiling.
- Computer interface (*"The Smart Connection"*) compatibility.
- Bicarbonate dialysis.
- Dialyzer clamp.
- I.V. pole.
- Concentrate cans.
- Fluid catchall.

Baxter 550 Optional Features
- Variable Sodium (non-variable sodium 550's are retrofittable with kit 5M5511).
- Automatic Disinfection Module.
- *"Smart Connection"* Treatment Data Management System.
- Blood Pressure Module.

Product Code	Description
5M5506	550
5M5516	550 with Variable Sodium
5M5507	550 with Auto Disinfect
5M5518	550 with Variable Sodium and Auto Disinfect
5M5540	Blood Pressure Monitor

that filters impurities from the blood (refer to Exhibit 3). HD is an effective method to remove waste from the blood. However, it is hard on patients and requires about four hours per treatment and three treatments per week. Patients are typically exhausted for a day or more after each treatment, at which point the next treatment is to be given. Baxter is considered to be a strong competitor in the global HD-market.

Baxter pioneered the second type of renal therapy, a revolutionary technology in continuous ambulatory peritoneal dialysis (CAPD), in 1979. A catheter is inserted into the patient's abdomen and across the peritoneum, the membrane lining the abdomen. Waste is filtered out of the body by a dialysis solution flushed into the abdominal cavity (refer to Exhibit 4). CAPD is generally performed by the patient himself, usually four times a day, and thus offers obvious lifestyle advantages over HD. CAPD provides increased mobility since it can be performed at home, in the car, or at the office. It is less traumatic to the patient's system and requires fewer dietary restrictions. CAPD is also less costly. Because it is self-administered,

no infrastructure (equipment, buildings, staff) is needed. Of all patients being treated with dialysis, 15% are using CAPD. This proportion is growing rapidly. Exhibit 5 gives an overview of CAPD usage worldwide.

Seventy percent of all CAPD patients say that they are extremely satisfied with their treatment, compared to only 30% of HD patients. Recognizing this trend, Baxter is currently directing its primary focus towards CAPD treatment. Baxter plans to bolster its position in the CAPD segment by pursuing a two-pronged strategy: (1) to improve its market penetration in developed countries, and (2) to expand rapidly in less developed nations, where CAPD is also fast becoming the treatment of choice.

Infection is a threat with CAPD. Baxter introduced a Twin Bag system that allows the patient to drain used fluid and infuse fresh solution within a closed-loop. This system remarkably lowered the infection rate to once every three years (versus once every four or five months a decade ago).

The third type of treatment, a kidney transplant, is preferred by almost all patients, but its use is limited by a shortage of donor organs.

Baxter is the overall market leader in renal therapy with a 25% market share. The company dominates the CAPD-segment, in which it has a whopping 80% global market share. Baxter holds strong positions in those countries in which CAPD is fully developed. The company is also attempting to further penetrate the HD market. It is negotiating a deal with a leading manufacturer of dialyzers. This action would challenge a Swedish competitor, Gambro, the leader in this segment.

Baxter's recent initiatives include promoting the Personal Cycler, a computerized solutions delivery/return system that enables physicians to tailor CAPD therapies to each patient. The dialysis is performed at night while the patient is sleeping. This product is expected to meet the needs of every major market in the world. It will be smaller, more reliable, and, less costly than the current alternatives.

COMPETITION IN THE DIALYSIS MARKET

Market experts predict an annual growth rate of 5% in the U.S. market for dialysis products and services through the year 2000, with a continual shift from HD to CAPD. Global markets are expected to grow by about 7% in sales revenues (See Exhibit 6). No major new competitors have entered the market since 1983 when governments started to cut budgets for renal diseases.

The world dialysis products market is dominated by ten large manufacturers located in the United States, Sweden, Germany and Japan. The remaining renal product manufacturers are about sixty small to medium-sized firms located mainly in the United States and Europe.

EXHIBIT 4
CAPD SYSTEM

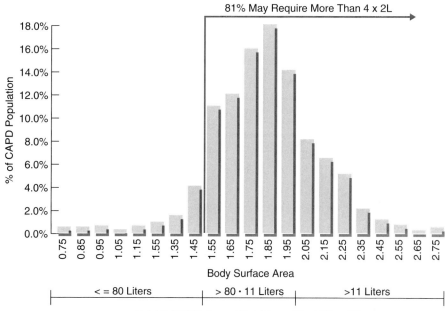

81% May Require More Than 4 x 2L

Body Surface Area

< = 80 Liters | > 80 · 11 Liters | >11 Liters

Total CAPD Delivered Vol. Mean 4 Hr. D/P = .67

A.

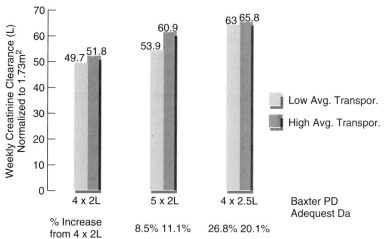

Low Avg. Transpor.

High Avg. Transpor.

Baxter PD
Adequest Da

% Increase
from 4 x 2L   8.5% 11.1%   26.8% 20.1%

B.   *Continued*

EXHIBIT 4 (continued)

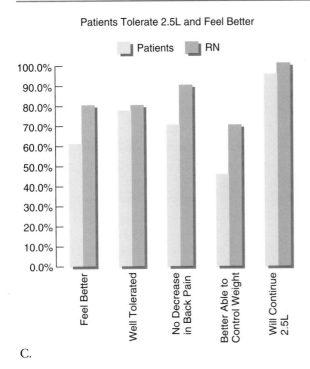

C.

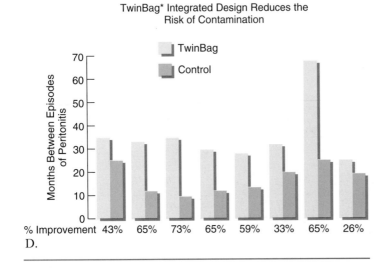

D.

EXHIBIT 5
PERITONEAL DIALYSIS WORLDWIDE

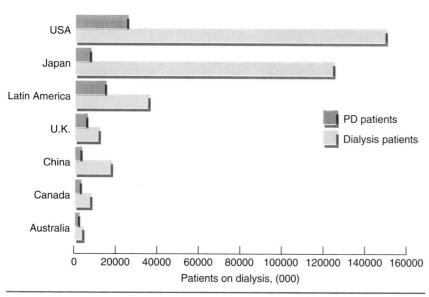

Source: Company Records

Exhibit 6 lists the major competitors in the dialysis industry and their respective market shares for 1991. Gambro is Baxter's leading competitor. While Baxter dominates the worldwide HD-market, Gambro, through its acquisitions of Hospal and Cobe, prevails in the HD-market. Both companies supply peritoneal dialysis systems. Baxter pioneered the use of this product and continues to remain the leader in this segment.

Other players in the dialysis market are Althin CD Medical, Fresenius AG, National Medical Care, and Renal Systems. Exhibit 7 gives profiles of these companies. In Japan, several smaller players (Terumo, Asahi, and Toray) concentrate on the domestic market, which is estimated to be large. Terumo is Japan's largest manufacturer of disposable medical devices and is considered to be an important alternative supplier of dialyzers and dialysis supplies to the U.S. market.

GLOBAL DIALYSIS MARKET TRENDS

The incidence rate of renal diseases is likely to remain high, especially in developed countries with an aging population. Baxter estimates that by 1995 more than 700,000 people worldwide will suffer from kidney failure. Moreover, it is expected that dialysis patient mortality rates will continue to improve due to earlier detection and treatment of ESRD and the use of new products that reduce the incidence of various other life-threatening conditions.

Although these preventive approaches may impact the rate of ESRD incidence, the effect is not likely to be seen in the 1990s.

In 1992, almost 14% of ESRD patients worldwide (around 65,000 patients) were maintained on CAPD. This represents an increase of 15,000 patients from 1990. Reliance on CAPD as a treatment of kidney diseases ranges from 5% in Japan up to 93% in Mexico. Data for other countries are given in Exhibit 8. The penetration of CAPD is to some extent driven by the mechanics of local reimbursement schemes. Jim Austin, Director of Global Strategy of the Renal Division, observes that in those countries where reimbursement of PD and HD therapies is economically neutral towards the doctor, PD penetration is in the 20–30% range. In Canada and the UK, where the governments push home-based therapies (such as PD) penetration is much higher (typically 30 to 40%). However, in countries like Japan, where the incentives favor HD, the spread of PD tends to be less than 10%.

Governments are trying to increase kidney transplants, as this method has significant cost advantages over continued dialysis and also improves quality of life for the patient. However, organ transplants, despite improvements, are not expected to outmode continued dialysis due to lack of organs. In 1984, the 3-year survival rate was estimated to be 78% for cadaver transplants and 91% for related donor transplants. Further, a major constraint on transplants is the availability of suitable kidneys; approxi-

EXHIBIT 6

RENAL DIALYSIS EQUIPMENT AND SUPPLIES, WORLDWIDE SALES, GROWTH RATE, AND MARKET SHARE ESTIMATES

	Sales (millions of current dollars at manufacturer's level)						
	1988	1992	1993	1994	1995	1996	2000
Equipment	$40	$48	$51	$53	$55	$56	$62
Supplies	$400	$544	$590	$635	$670	$705	$879
Total	$440	$592	$641	$688	$725	$761	$941

	Average Annual Growth Rate			
	1984–88	1988–92	1992–96	1996–2000
Equipment	5%	5%	4%	3%
Supplies	3%	8%	7%	6%
Growth rate of total	3%	8%	6%	5%

Company	Major Manufacturers and Estimated Market Share—1991	
	Equipment	Supplies
Althin/CD Medical (Drake Willock)	15–30%	5–15%
Baxter	30–50%	30–50%
CGH Medical (Cobe/Gambro/Hospal)	30–50%	30–50%
Fresenius	15–30%	5–15%
National Medical Care (W. R. Grace)		5–15%
Others		5–15%

Equipment—apparatus associated with hemodialysis and peritoneal dialysis including single and central delivery systems, blood pumps, heparin pumps, air bubble detectors, pressure monitors, and single needle systems.

Supplies—dialyzers, blood tubing, dialysate, needles, cannulae, and shunts for hemodialysis and peritoneal dialysis.

Source: Health Industries Handbook, SRI International, Menlo Park (CA), May 1992

mately 20,000 kidney donors die in the United States each year, but only 2,400 kidneys become available. Furthermore, 45% of patients receiving cadaver kidneys and 21% of patients receiving living donor kidneys still require some form of dialysis treatment.

Growth of the dialysis market is expected to be disproportionately large in the home-care, alternate site business due to the shifting demographics of an aging population and increased life expectancy. Government and private insurer pressure for cost-containment reinforces this trend. Worldwide, government reimbursement currently accounts for approximately 67% of payments for renal dialysis equipment and services, and this percentage is decreasing. Without government subsidies, demand for home-care will depend more heavily on the household's income.

In such a competitive environment, sustaining mar-

ket share will depend on the following pillars: competitive pricing, cost-effective manufacturing and distribution, development of new technology, and aggressive marketing. In particular, stronger support services for home users of dialysis products will be necessary to remain competitive. Operating margins for HD are around 10% as opposed to 20% for PD.

DISTRIBUTION STRATEGY

One of Baxter's key strategies has been decentralization of distribution. The company's subsidiaries and divisions, often with their own sales forces, carry out Baxter's sales efforts. Products are also sold to independent distributors, dealers and sales agents. Baxter distribution centers across the U.S. and throughout the world each serve several divisions.

EXHIBIT 7
COMPANY PROFILES

Althin CD Medical	• Major player in the hemodialysis delivery machine market • Maker of the new System 1000, touted to offer major savings over competitive models • Althin products are sold in 70 countries. It has sales and distribution offices mainly in Europe, Japan, Singapore, Australia, and Canada. • Regional distributors are used in Latin America and in the Asian Pacific region.
Baxter Healthcare Corporation Renal Division	• Dominant player in both hemodialysis and peritoneal dialysis markets • Introduced the first commercially developed dialyzer and first to market a portable kidney dialysis system known as CAPD in early 70's. • Over 80% of products are made by Baxter at its own manufacturing and assembly plants. • 75-member direct sales force based in the U.S. (dedicated to dialysis) and uses distributors overseas.
CGH Medical, Inc. Division of Cobe Renal Care (Gambro)	• Highly vertically integrated organization with position in manufacturing, sales and distribution, and dialysis services. • Active entering new markets and penetrating old ones through joint ventures and acquisitions. • The Gambro group has 90 subsidiaries in 23 countries and is represented in 90 countries. There are 23 production units in 10 countries. R&D is conducted in Sweden, Germany, France, Italy, Japan, and U.S. • Gambro, and its subsidiaries COBE Laboratories and Hospal, operate their own separate sales organizations overseas and display their own trademark in most markets. In U.S. sales organization is combined into one unit. • Main expansion efforts are in Central and Eastern Europe, China, and Asia Pacific markets. It expands mainly by joint ventures with local manufacturers. However, it is testing the market in Mexico: if successful this may open the doors of the rest of Latin America. • Owns dialysis centers in Sweden and Italy.
Fresenius AG (Germany)	• It acquired 1993 Abbott's renal dialysis business (laboratories in U.S., Australia, and New Zealand) and positioned itself as second largest provider of peritoneal dialysis products after Baxter. It also has a non-exclusive right to sell Abbott technology in the world except Canada, Mexico, Taiwan, and some Middle Eastern countries. • Is licensed by Baxter to produce some of its patented peritoneal dialysis products.

Continued

EXHIBIT 7 (continued)

	• Nationwide (U.S.) it has a 23-member direct sales force, organized on a regional basis with the entire dialysis product line (HD and PD). It sells to hospitals, clinics, and specialized treatment centers. Peritoneal dialysis products are delivered directly to the patients via trucks.
	• Currently becoming an international health care company. It is doing so by acquiring BASF Knoll's infusion and dialysis business and growing its dialysis business in the U.S. and Europe. BASF had operations in Germany, France, and the Netherlands.
	• In the U.S. most sales efforts go to direct calls. The firm markets extensively through direct mail and advertises in trade journals.
	• It has clinical support group, composed primarily of registered nurses, focused to train and assist company's customers.
	• Abbot is still main distributor for Fresenius product.
National Medical Care	• Leading manufacturer of dialysis supplies in the U.S. and its dialysis service unit is largest provider in the world. It has 440 dialysis clinics: 416 in the U.S., 20 in Portugal, 3 in Spain, and 1 in Czech Republic.
	• Sells direct and through distributors in 25 countries. In U.S., sales are made through Medical Products division and overseas sales are through Renacare unit (acquired in 1992) and the Riggers Medizintechnik GmbH unit (acquired in 1993).
	• Strategic plan is to grow health care business, specifically in the home infusion therapy segment of the alternate site health market.
	• Has plans for aggressive expansion in Eastern Europe.

Baxter maintains extensive distribution networks both in the hospital and clinical segment and in the home health care segment. The company employs a 75-member direct sales force in the United States. Baxter approaches HD and CAPD products as a single market despite the differences between them because patients constantly switch from one therapy to the other. In the U.S., free delivery of renal therapy products for home patients is provided as a value-added service. Baxter has over 100 trucks for this purpose. It also distributes products through Caremark Corp, the largest national home health care company.

Distribution is one of Baxter's strengths in the United States. Its distribution system stresses flexibility, meeting the needs of the smallest as well as the largest customers and allowing Baxter to contract with outside carriers when necessary to meet specialized customer needs. Baxter also views its distribution system as a strategic tool to control health care costs and manage the company's logistics costs.

EXHIBIT 8

CONTINUOUS AMBULATORY PERITONEAL DIALYSIS (AS PERCENTAGES OF ESRD PATIENT POPULATION)

Country	Percentage
Mexico	93%
United Kingdom	50%
Venezuela	47%
New Zealand	43%
Finland	38%
Canada	33%
United States	17%
France	<10%
Germany	<10%
Italy	<10%
Japan	5%

Source: "A look at CAPD Data Worldwide," *Nephrology News & Issues,* January 1994, p. 12

Baxter International has a sales and distribution presence in more than 100 countries, either on a direct basis or through independent local distributors. Baxter currently has customer service and distribution systems to provide products and services to patients in their homes in 23 countries. In Latin America, Baxter has manufacturing facilities in Brazil, Colombia, Costa Rica, the Dominican Republic and Mexico.

CUSTOMER SERVICE

Customer service is an integral part of Baxter's strategy for the renal division. The close bonds that Baxter nurtures with its CAPD patients have turned into a tremendous competitive advantage. Donald Joseph describes the role of customer service as follows:

> Our patients don't leave us. We retain 99% of our CAPD patients once they're with us. A patient is trained at the hospital by a nurse who was trained by us. The nurse introduces the patient to one of our home representatives. The two talk regularly. Next comes our home van driver. These are trained professionals who know and understand the requirements. They come to the home, establish and explain the inventory, open the boxes, rotate the stock, and place it anywhere the patient wants. For as long as the patient is on dialysis, s/he will probably see the same driver, and deal with the same home patient rep. The patient becomes connected to our people. When we promote one of the home patient reps, we often get a backlash from our patients . . . "What happened to Mary Jane? Why can't I talk with her anymore?" It's an unbelievable linkage. Our people provide not just service . . . it's almost friendship. So, I can talk about technology, technology, technology, but for many patients, it's "just make sure Harry comes to my house every month, and Mary Jane is there on the phone." Is good service important? It's a major part of our product.

PRICING STRATEGY

With its leadership position in the renal therapy market, Baxter, rather than offering marked-down or discount prices, focuses on continuously improving the quality of its products and services and maintaining leadership in pricing. However, the rapidly changing health care environment has led to increased competition among medical suppliers.

Baxter has launched an extensive restructuring plan to lower its costs so that it can meet the increased price competition. The program should enable Baxter to move into "best cost" positions in its markets while maintaining its profit margins. Improved manufacturing technology, increased economies of scale and efficient logistic processes are expected to enable Baxter to reduce costs drastically in the future.

COMMUNICATION STRATEGY

Baxter's promotional campaigns include the dissemination of educational materials to nephrologists and dialysis centers for their patients (refer to the Appendix for an example of these materials). Baxter strives to be seen as a support service for dialysis patients rather than simply as another product vendor. The promotional materials include a set of videotapes, one of which illustrates the different treatment options for end-stage renal disease patients, and another of which presents CAPD as an option. The videotapes do not specifically promote Baxter products.

As a leading supplier of health care products, Baxter has a strong reputation in the industry. Baxter's communication strategies foster the image of a high quality supplier offering products at a reasonable cost. This message is conveyed to present customers as well as prospective customers. Baxter does no media advertising.

Baxter also forms partnerships with clinics and laboratories worldwide to develop new technologies. The company's scientific track record and capital strength make it the first choice of many clinics looking for corporate research partners.

BAXTER'S EXPANSION IN LATIN AMERICA

Health Care in Latin America

In general, government expenditures for health care and demand for medical products in a given country are driven by a complex interplay among various economic, demographic, institutional and technological factors. Most importantly, however, spending patterns are determined by the incidence of various diseases, the availability of health care resources and facilities, and the ability to pay for the level of care desired or required.

Latin America's developing countries' lack of economic resources and rapid population growth have precluded development of a comprehensive health care delivery infrastructure capable of serving most segments of the population. The quality and availability of hospital and physician's services in Latin America often exceed those found in other third world regions. However, a large share of procedures and consultations are consumed by affluent members of the population and industrial workers covered by insurance plans. It is common for health care personnel to be clustered in urban areas, close to these affluent residents and industrial workers. Rural residents have access to limited, if any, health care. Private funding accounts for 44% of total health care spending in the region but covers only about 5% of the population. Some clinics in the more industrialized countries such as Brazil offer high health care standards Their services are not affordable to the vast majority of the population. Accordingly, the two major health-related challenges faced by

Latin American governments are (1) to improve access to professional medical care, and (2) to improve the quality and effectiveness of the available care.

In the last few years, Latin America has undergone an economic bounceback. After decades of protectionism and austere, inward-looking economic policies, much of the region is aggressively breaking down trade barriers and allowing the entry of foreign capital in a drive to industrialize and raise living standards. Even though most Latin American countries continue to rely primarily on agriculture and commodities, many of them are expected to surpass the world average GNP in the long term. Sustained growth will help these countries to overcome structural economic problems such as low per capita income, high unemployment and rampant inflation. Furthermore, increased income levels will allow governments to reduce debt, make more productive investments and boost health care expenditures.

Economic growth should serve as a catalyst for the improvement of the quality of health care delivery in the region. In 1987, the per capita outlay for health care in Latin America was $65.2 (compared to an average of $1,550 in developed countries). Governments are unable to fund universal health insurance. Local authorities also face a shortage of modern equipment, trained health care personnel, sophisticated pharmaceuticals, and state-of-the art diagnostic and therapeutic equipment.

Health care outlays are expected to grow by 11.2% per year through 1996 up to a total of $63 billion. Although it is expected that all health care segments in Latin America will expand, most growth will occur in the outpatient segment due to concerted government-sponsored efforts to broaden coverage in outlying areas. These efforts are evidenced by sharp increases in the employment of nurses dispatched to non-metropolitan and rural areas.

In line with the broader trends in health care spending, demand for medical products in Latin America is projected to increase by 10.8% per year through 1996 up to $16.5 billion. This increase will stem mainly from reusable goods and basic consumer first aid products. Disposable items cater more to the affluent customers who can afford them.

Analysis by Country

Below follows an overview of economic conditions and the health care industry in each of Baxter's targeted countries for expansion: Brazil, Colombia, Mexico and Venezuela (Refer to Exhibit 9 for a summary of comparative economic statistics).

Brazil. Of the Latin American countries targeted for expansion, Brazil is the largest in terms of population, geographic size and economic strength. The country's major industries include agriculture, mining and manufacturing, which developed only within the last two decades. The domestic economy stagnated in the late 1980s, and the country grappled with severe inflation. It was unable to meet foreign debt obligations and, thus, had few public resources available for expansion of the current health care system.

Health care spending as a percentage of GDP increased from 3.0% in 1985 to 3.5% in 1989, a fairly large increase by the standards of a developing country. However, the quality of health care is still limited by the lack of funding. Also, availability is hindered by the sheer size of the country and the wide dispersion of the population. Approximately 90% of those living in urban areas have access to medical services, as compared to only 15% of those living in rural areas. Rural residents represent one-third of Brazil's population. To compensate for the lack of quality and availability of health care, medical professionals tend to rely on prescribed medications instead of ongoing treatment and therapy.

The deficiency in ambulatory services in Brazil's health care system is offset to some extent by the large hospital sector. Brazil has one of the largest inpatient sectors in the world, boasting some 7,000 primary care facilities. The Social Security Ministry operates a health program which covers about 60% of the population for basic hospital and physician's services. The program is funded via payroll contributions and general tax revenues. The lack of public resources has provided an opportunity for private health programs to emerge. Private funding now accounts for nearly half of Brazil's total health expenditures.

Brazil is projected to be one of the few countries in the world in which increases in primary care facilities will outpace population growth, due in part to the current growth in outpatient treatment facilities. Also, it is believed that the increasing compensation levels for health care professionals will attract entry into these occupations and will stimulate the expansion of health care sector in Brazil.

Most of Brazil's health care equipment and pharmaceuticals are imported, although small domestic pharmaceutical manufacturers do exist. Apart from Baxter, Brazil has at least one other multinational pharmaceutical manufacturer, Akzo do Brazil, which produces contraceptives, hormonal drugs and other primary drugs.

Colombia. Colombia is the seventh largest industrialized economy in Latin America. Despite its relative economic strength, Colombia was plagued throughout the 1980s by a sluggish economy, low per capita income, little measurable improvement in the standard of living, and a deficient health care system.

The provision of most health services is restricted to wealthier, urban residents. Most rural inhabitants receive only infrequent examinations and vaccinations, performed by government-sponsored traveling medical teams. The public finances almost 70% of all health benefits through

EXHIBIT 9
HEALTH AND DEMOGRAPHIC STATISTICS BY COUNTRY—1989 ESTIMATES

	Latin American Countries	Brazil	Mexico	Venezuela	Colombia
Population (millions)	434.2	147.4	84.3	19.3	33.8
GDP/capita	$2,512	$2,918	$2,660	$4,453	$1,300
GDP (billions US$)	$1,090.6	$430.1	$224.2	$87.5	$43.9
Health Care Expenditures/capita	$86.5	$97.2	$98.2	$241.7	$50.0
Health Care Expenditures (% of GDP)	3.4%	3.3%	3.7%	5.3%	4.0%
Number of Deaths/capita (thousands)	7.0	6.6	5.8	5.8	6.0
Hospital Beds/capita (thousands)	3.0	4.6	0.9	2.6	1.5
Physicians' Visits/capita	1.2	1.1	1.1	1.5	0.9
Number of Nurses/capita	1.8	1.5	1.6	3.3	N/A
Total Health Expenditures (millions)	$37,560	$14,325	$8,275	$4,655	$1,604
By Source:					
Public	58.0%	50.9%	71.6%	47.3%	45.0%
Private	42.0%	49.1%	28.4%	52.7%	55.0%
By Type:					
Hospital Care	$15,718 / 41.8%	$7,204 / 50.3%	$2,343 / 28.3%	$1,965 / 42.2%	N/A
Outpatient Care	$9,817 / 26.1%	$2,488 / 17.4%	$3,403 / 41.1%	$1,519 / 32.6%	N/A
Drugs & Sundries	$9,265 / 24.7%	$3,543 / 24.7%	$1,904 / 23.0%	$850 / 18.3%	N/A
Other Expenditures	$2,760 / 7.3%	$1,090 / 7.6%	$625 / 7.6%	$321 / 6.9%	N/A
Medical Products Demand	$10,235	$3,888	$2,166	$1,057	N/A
Pharmaceuticals	$7,245 / 70.8%	$2,775 / 71.4%	$1,497 / 69.1%	$638 / 60.4%	N/A
Supplies & Devices	$2,330 / 22.8%	$865 / 22.2%	$520 / 24.0%	$330 / 31.2%	N/A
Equipment	$660 / 6.4%	$248 / 6.4%	$149 / 6.9%	$89 / 8.4%	N/A

payroll and employer taxes. However, private sector spending in health care is expected to increase in Colombia. This expected growth is due in part to the purchase of supplemental health insurance by the expanding middle class.

Growth is expected in the outpatient sector, since officials deem this sector to be a priority. Construction of primary care facilities, on the other hand, is not expected to increase significantly. Also, salary levels of health care professionals are expected to remain low, discouraging entry into medical occupations.

Because of the shortcomings of Colombia's health care services, great reliance is placed on pharmaceuticals, as a substitute for therapy. The primary medical imports are analgesics, antibiotics and bandages. Other pharmaceutical products and supplies are rare and expensive. All pharmaceuticals, medical supplies and equipment are imported. Entry of multinational health care manufacturers is anticipated in all medical segments in Colombia. No serious competition from any domestic producer is expected in the near future.

Mexico Mexico has experienced economic turmoil in the 1980s due to depressed world oil prices, high inflation and large foreign debt obligations. However, Mexico is expected to reap gains from large investments by foreign businesses in the domestic manufacturing sector. Also, economic agreements such as NAFTA and the free-trade agreement with Chile should bolster economic recovery. Increased economic activity might lead to prosperity, a higher standard of living and improvements in health care.

Health care spending in Mexico exceeds the Latin American average on a per capita basis and on a percentage-of-GDP basis. However, Mexico suffers from cost inefficiencies, inadequate infrastructure and poor administration. Despite the above-average spending, poor administration results in widespread shortages and a lack of availability. Many Mexicans have no access to health care. Further, Mexico ranks among the lowest of countries in the Western hemisphere in the number of facilities, beds, admissions and physician visits.

Health care in Mexico for such services as basic hospitalization, ambulatory services, some dental care and some pharmaceuticals is generally provided by the government. These services are offered to the elderly and the working population and are funded via payroll contributions and general tax revenues, with some patient contributions. More than 70% of Mexican health care expenditures is publicly funded.

To appreciably increase the quality of health care in Mexico, construction of primary and ambulatory care facilities must increase. Also, compensation levels should increase to attract needed talent into health care occupations. Outpatient expenditures are expected to be the largest growing segment of health care in Mexico.

Many of Mexico's pharmaceuticals are produced domestically, with some imports from the United States and Western Europe. Most health care equipment is imported from the United States.

Venezuela Venezuela's economy boomed in the 1970s when world oil prices reached their highest levels. Much of the resulting wealth was channeled into social programs, especially the health care system. Due in part to this economic expansion, Venezuela now boasts one of the highest per capita income levels in the region. Due to the collapse of world oil prices and economic mismanagement, economic conditions deteriorated in the late 80s and early 90s. Health care expenditures in Venezuela continue to be more than twice the Latin American average. As in the U.S. and Mexico, however, the system contains inefficiencies, as evidenced by statistics showing poor performance in health care relative to the number of dollars spent. In the 1980s, when oil prices dropped and remained low, the country experienced economic unrest, currency problems and a period of GDP decline. Nevertheless, due to market reforms introduced during the 1980s, Venezuela was rewarded with a strong economic recovery in the early 1990s.

The Venezuelan medical system includes both public and private elements. The Ministry of Health and Social Security provides government-sponsored health plans for the elderly and industrial and farm workers for basic hospital and ambulatory services. These programs are financed through payroll contributions and business and general tax revenue. Venezuela's population includes a fairly large affluent portion. An extensive network of technologically advanced medical facilities developed to serve this sector of the population. This wealthy sector has also contributed to the popularization of private care, which has grown to 53% of total Venezuelan health care outlays.

The least developed sector of the health care system in Venezuela is the inpatient sector. Construction of hospital facilities financed by oil profits was planned in the 1970s and 1980s, but development was derailed with the oil price collapse. Outpatient resources, on the other hand, are more abundant. Venezuela has more doctors per capita than most Latin American countries. There does exist a lack of physician specialists, but compensation increases should address this shortage.

Spending on supplies and medical devices is expected to experience the highest growth. In contrast, spending on expensive capital equipment is projected to be sluggish. The market for pharmaceuticals, a much-relied upon alternative to therapy, is expected to grow extensively over the next decade. Many multinational health care suppliers, including Abbott, Akzo, Ciba-Geigy, Glaxo and Johnson & Johnson, have a presence in Venezuela.

CAPD-Treatment in Brazil The number of CAPD-patients in Brazil has grown from less than 200 in 1984 to

2,274 in 1989 (see Exhibit 10). The number of HD-patients in 1989 was 10,450. Thus, CAPD is used in 21% of all dialysis cases in Brazil. No growth is expected in the number of HD patients for several reasons:

1. There are few dialysis units in Brazil. The number is not expected to increase.

2. HD equipment is subject to high import taxes, making it too costly for many health care facilities. (Under the General Agreement on Trade and Tariffs (GATT), tariffs are phased out for industrial countries only, effective July 1995; developing countries have an exemption period. A discussion on GATT follows this section.

3. The government has determined that HD treatment is not a cost-effective use of Brazil's public funds. Approximately 1.6% of the Social Security Ministry's budget is allocated to dialysis patients, which represent .008% of the population. A shift to CAPD as a low-cost alternative to HD and transplants is anticipated. At present, reimbursement economics actually favor HD. Reimbursement rates are $11,000/patient/year for PD and $15,000/patient/year/for HD.

CAPD-Treatment in Colombia, Mexico and Venezuela

- In Colombia, approximately 25% of dialysis patients are receiving CAPD treatment (250 out of 1,000 patients).

- The devastating earthquakes in Mexico in the late 1980s damaged or destroyed many dialysis centers. HD patients that relied on these centers switched to CAPD. Thus, a large percentage (93%) of the population receiving dialysis treatment currently uses CAPD (2,800 out of a total of 3,000 dialysis patients). In Mexico, only PD gets reimbursed.

- The Venezuelan government reimburses HD and CAPD treatments at the same rate. About half of the dialysis patients are being treated with CAPD.

CAPD has already received reimbursement approval as a dialysis treatment in each of the four countries. Approval is anticipated in other countries including Argentina. Argentina had about 4,000 dialysis patients receiving non-reimbursed treatment in 1989, making the pending approval a significant event.

Based on the average rate of treated patients in the U.S. and Japan, the estimated number of patients requiring dialysis treatment in the four targeted countries is approximately 272,000. Baxter patients (both HD and CAPD) account for only 18,000, or 6.6%, of this number. The remaining 93.4% either use a competing product or remain untreated (Refer to Exhibit 11).

General Agreement on Trade and Tariffs

Many issues in the health care and pharmaceutical arena were resolved during the Uruguay round of the General Agreement on Trade and Tariffs (GATT) negotiations. The three main areas of discussion were tariffs, subsidies and intellectual property rights.

Most tariffs on pharmaceutical products and medical equipment will be virtually phased out by July 1995 in all industrial and many developing nations. Subsidies are granted through joint ventures with the National Institutes of Health (NIH). Since the NIH is funded by the U.S. government, this arrangement could be construed as a "subsidy" to the U.S. pharmaceutical industry. Nevertheless, tricky negotiations resulted in GATT condoning such relationships. Thus, GATT successfully resolved the issues of tariffs and subsidies with respect to U.S. Health care manufacturers such as Baxter.

Complete success was not achieved in resolving intel-

EXHIBIT 10

PERCENTAGE OF PD PATIENTS IN LATIN AMERICA (APRIL 1989)

Country	Total Dialysis Patients	HD Patients	PD Patients	% of PD Patients
Brazil	12,724	10,450	2,274	18%
Colombia	1,000	750	250	25%
Mexico	3,000	700	2,300	77%
Venezuela	1,100	500	600	55%
Argentina	4,000	3,920	80	2%
Cuba	1,000	500	500	50%
Total	22,824	16,820	6,004	26%

Source: Status of Peritoneal Dialysis in Latin America, *Contributions to Nephrology*, Filho, J. C. Divino, 1991, vol 89, pp 11–15. Note that data presented to *Contributions to Nephrology* were obtained from Baxter-Brazil which was the only organized PD registry in Latin America at that time.

EXHIBIT 11

ESTIMATION OF LATIN AMERICAN MARKET
1993 DATA—POPULATION IN THOUSANDS

	Total Dialysis Patients	Projected Population	% of Pop Needing Dialysis
United States	200	258,162	0.077%
Japan	125	125,904	0.099%
Average	325	384,066	0.085%

POTENTIAL MARKET SIZE ASSUMES MARKET PENETRATION LEVELS EQUAL TO THE
US AND JAPAN AVERAGE 1993 DATA—POPULATION IN THOUSANDS

	% of Pop Needing Dialysis	Projected Population	Estimated Market	Patients On Baxter's Registry	Untreated or Non-Baxter Patients
Brazil	0.085%	165,083	140	13	127
Colombia	0.085%	36,182	31	1	30
Mexico	0.085%	97,967	83	3	80
Venezuela	0.085%	22,212	19	1	18
		321,444	272	18	254
			100%	6.6%	93.4%

Sources: 1993 Baxter Annual Report
Nephrology news & issues, January, 1994, p. 12
Maclay, Judith, State of Health Atlas, Simon and Schuster, New York, 1993
Health Industries Handbook, SRI International, Menlo Park (CA), May 1992

lectual property issues. Countries such as Brazil, Colombia and Venezuela fall into GATT's developing country classification and thus are not required to enforce patent protection for eleven and one half years (up to the year 2005). Patented Baxter products may therefore not be protected against infringement in these countries. Around 99% of Baxter's products are protected by patents, although licensing agreements are sometimes negotiated at the local level. Further, counterfeit drugs are proliferating in countries such as Brazil and Nigeria. GATT does not require the implementation of anti-counterfeiting statutes in developing countries for six and one half years (2000). In response, the U.S. government has exerted pressure on the developing countries to protect patents outside of the GATT framework. These problems are not an issue with Mexico since patents must be recognized and are protected under the NAFTA agreement.

ISSUES

The highest priority on Vernon Loucks' agenda is Baxter's global market expansion, with a special emphasis on developing countries. Furthermore, Loucks has stated that

CAPD will play a strategic role in Baxter's renal therapy business, in particular in the emerging markets of Latin America and Asia. Loucks wondered whether, and if so, how to implement Baxter's expansion in Latin America. Specifically, the following issues needed to be addressed:

• What opportunities do these countries offer?

• Are market conditions and industry trends in dialysis therapy favorable enough for a major expansion in Latin America? Will the developing health care systems in Latin America be able to support Baxter's expansion plans?

• How should Baxter allocate its resources across the targeted countries?

• Will CAPD's expected promise come to fruition in Latin America, or should Baxter focus on the more traditional treatment of HD?

• Will Baxter be able to duplicate its customer service support in that region?

• Under GATT, Baxter's patents are not protected in developing countries. How does this fact threaten Baxter's leadership position in this region?

CASE 7

TILTING WINDMILLS: SANEX TRIES TO CONQUER EUROPE

The message that rolled off the fax machine on August 3, 1993 in the office of Mr. Martin Muñoz, president of the Southern European division of the Household and Personal Care (HPC) business unit of the Dutch-based international company Sara Lee/DE was depressing: "The liquid soap you conceived and successfully commercialised in Spain seven years ago has failed to make any inroads in the UK market. Sorry." To his secretary's utter surprise and shock, Martin Muñoz simply smiled.

As he kept staring at the fax message, Martin's thoughts drifted to the heated conversation he had had a couple of years back with Roger,[1] the head of Nicholas Laboratories in the UK, the pharmaceutical company acquired by Sara Lee/DE in the late 1980s. Martin at the time had caught the attention of senior management in the company by engineering the successful launch and diffusion of a new Bath & Shower liquid soap called Sanex in the over-crowded and mature HPC market. Though initially the underdog in a market dominated by giants such as Henkel and Reckitt & Coleman, Sanex quickly outpaced the competition in Spain thanks to the clear positioning it mustered through its powerfully appealing concept: Healthy Skin. Impressed by this achievement, Sara Lee/DE headquarters had decided to roll out Sanex throughout Europe, and had asked Martin to act as the co-ordinator for this project. In one of the many meetings that ensued, Roger vehemently opposed introducing the product to English consumers under the Sanex brand name, which he felt had "sanitary" connotations and would be ill-received by English consumers. Roger further argued, and correctly so, that despite their proximity, European countries had vastly different histories and cultures: a strategy that might look appealing in one market might very well look appalling in another country. Martin strongly counter-argued that the success of Sanex in Spain was more due to rational reasons and had nothing to do with any idiosyncratic nature of the Spanish consumer. Martin did not want any of his proven marketing strategies to be disturbed irrespective of where the products were to be marketed. In his role as project co-ordinator, Martin realised that he lacked the formal authority to challenge the autonomy of a Sara Lee/DE subsidiary and force Roger to accept his line of thinking, although clearly, he felt Roger was wrong. Undeterred, Roger had gone ahead anyway and introduced Sanex in the UK under a different label and with different marketing strategies.

Martin's informal response to Roger's fax message from the UK was akin to saying: "I told you so" and was further confirmation of his faith in and opinion of the Sanex brand. Senior management at Sara Lee/DE headquarters, too, backed Martin. They completely believed in the Sanex concept and came to believe in the merit of having a consistent marketing strategy to support that concept, and they responded formally and immediately. The following week, the chairman of Sara Lee/DE summoned the presidents of the European countries in the HPC division to his office in Utrecht, the Netherlands, and made it clear that Sanex was to be rolled out across Europe just as it was. In essence, the chairman's decisive move gave Sanex a much needed shot in the arm, and Martin was given *carte blanche* to roll out the product across Europe.

On the flight back from Amsterdam to Spain, Martin's heart was light, although his newly assigned responsibility for making Sanex a Euro brand weighed heavily in his mind. He was convinced that the recent decision by Sara Lee/DE's chairman would make things much easier for him. The country managers would be more willing to listen to him and appreciate the necessity of maintaining the integrity of the Sanex concept through adopting the strategy he formulated and successfully implemented in Spain: same brand name, same advertising copy, same pricing policy, same level of advertising and distribution support, etc. As he started penning down the factors that had compelled him to believe in a pan-European marketing strategy for Sanex, he caught a glimpse of a huge windmill disappearing in the Dutch horizon. He suddenly felt a shiver running down his spine: "Am I a maverick ready to challenge all those management theories that talk about the importance of cultural differences across countries or simply another Don Quixote attacking windmills? Can I apply the knowledge I gained by making Sanex a winner against all odds in Spain and make it a Euro brand?"

SARA LEE/DE: HISTORY AND STRUCTURE

Sara Lee/DE, which is a part of Sara Lee Corporation, Chicago, USA, is a Dutch-based multinational manufacturer of high-quality branded consumer products with an-

---

This case was prepared by T. V. Krishnan and Chet Borucki of Nijenrode University, The Netherlands. Copyright 1996 by Nijenrode University, The Netherlands Business School.

[1]The name of this case character has been disguised for confidentiality reasons.

nual sales of around Dfl 6.5 billion and 15000 employees. The history of Sara Lee/DE can be traced back to 1753 to the founding of a family business—a small domestic grocery shop located in Joure in the north of the Netherlands that basically dealt in coffee, tea and tobacco. Many of its products were obtained from suppliers in the Far East. For seven generations, until 1976, the same family guided the development of the company, which was called Douwe Egberts.[2] In 1930 Douwe Egberts (DE) entered the export market, concentrating first on marketing tobacco products in Belgium and Germany. In the years following WWII, its export business really began to flourish. By 1960, DE accounted for more than half of Dutch tobacco and coffee exports and 39% of tea exports. The international growth of the company, in its true meaning, got its start in 1973 with the opening of its first coffee roasting plant in Brussels.

During the 1970s, the rich potential of DE captured the attention of senior management at Sara Lee Corporation, the Chicago-based consumer goods company, which at the time was trying to consolidate its businesses around a limited number of core product divisions. The history of Sara Lee Corporation, compared to that of DE, is rather short, but is more turbulent. Its roots go back to 1939 when Nathan Cummings took over a company in Baltimore that was trading in coffee, tea and sugar and was then operating under a different name. After the second world war, the company activities widened and it diversified through acquisitions primarily in the food business. In 1954, the company was renamed, aptly so, as Consolidated Foods Corporation (CFC). Soon thereafter, CFC moved its headquarters to Chicago. A notable turning point in the company's history occurred when Charles Lubin, who was managing a very successful and reputed bakery business in Chicago, merged his company with CFC. Lubin's leading product was a cheese cake named after his daughter, Sara Lee. From a reputational standpoint, Sara Lee cheese cake stood for consistent quality and had high brand equity. Initially, this merger had little impact on CFC as the growth of the company was almost totally fuelled by acquisitions of various sorts, including business units in non-food industry sectors. By the 1970s, CFC was a huge conglomerate comprised of 80 business units, many with successful brand names. But given the tremendous diversity of its businesses, the company lacked focus.

Things took a turn for the better when John Bryan became CFC's chairman in 1975. He undertook the massive task of refocusing the company around well-defined business units both within and outside of the food industry, and divested those units that did not fit that focus. He hated the name CFC which he felt connoted more an ag-

glomeration of diverse interests rather than a unified company. Though it took nearly a decade, Bryan was able to rename CFC the Sara Lee Corporation (SLC) which he believed sent an appropriate message to all stakeholders about the quality the company sought to ensure in its products. Bryan also did not hesitate to acquire other companies (such as Hanes and Nicholas Kiwi) that he felt would bolster SLC's core business units. He was always looking for products with powerful brand equity. It wasn't long before the Dutch company DE captured his attention due to its strong brand image (the "coffee lady" who first appeared in 1898 is the trademark that decorates its coffee packages today). He started investing in DE in 1975 in a bid to establish a strong international coffee and grocery business. What started as a minority investment by SLC in DE evolved into a complete merger when in 1989, the former assumed complete control of the latter. The name Douwe Egberts Koninklijke Tabaksfabriek-Koffiebranderijen-Theehandel nv was changed to Sara Lee/DE nv when SLC reached a 100% equity interest, 41% in the form of voting shares and 59% in the form of share certificates issued by the independent Stichting Administratiekantoor Douwe Egberts Sara Lee. Consequently, this independent Dutch trust office retained the majority of voting rights in Sara Lee/DE (SL/DE).

SLC focused on four major divisions: Packaged Meat and Bakery, Personal Products, Coffee and Grocery, and Household Personal Care. After it started acquiring DE in the late 1970s, SLC gradually turned over the management of its Coffee and Grocery business to SL/DE. With the support of SLC, the Dutch company immediately switched gears and consolidated its position around the globe, rapidly developing a stronghold in Europe. Like its parent, the Dutch company also pursued growth through acquisition. It acquired other European coffee and tobacco business units such as Maison de Cafe (France, 1977), Merrild (Denmark, 1979), Marcilla (Spain, 1980) and Van Nelle (The Netherlands, 1989). As a result, over the period between 1970 and 1990, sales grew from a mere Dfl 570 million to a mammoth Dfl 3.5 billion. As of 1990, the Coffee and Grocery division of SL/DE commanded the market leadership position in its home country the Netherlands (72%) and Belgium (55%) and had sizeable market share in Spain (21%), France (16%) and Denmark (30%), as well as in Norway, Hungary, and Australia, amongst others.

Even though it concentrates exclusively on two main businesses, SL/DE still consists of nearly 80 companies, of which a majority are active in Western Europe. For the most part, these companies operate autonomously and many have their own production, marketing and sales departments. Thus, unlike other multinationals such as Procter & Gamble and Philips, SL/DE operates under different names in different countries. As mentioned previously, SL/DE expanded geographically through the ac-

---

[2]Douwe Egberts was the son of the founder Egbert Douwes.

quisition of well-known name brands and companies in other countries.[3] When a firm was acquired, it was generally treated as a wholly-owned subsidiary: no changes were made in the name of the company and its brands. Characteristically, SL/DE seldom launched a new brand or company offshore from scratch.

The organisational structure of SL/DE is not the same for all operations and products. The retail coffee operations (Douwe Egberts, Merrild, Marcilla among others) are organised by country and are responsible for their own production, marketing and sales. These country organisations report directly to the board of management in the Netherlands. Douwe Egberts Beverage Systems, active in the out-of-home-consumption market, and Douwe Egberts Van Nelle Tobacco Company both have central production and marketing facilities in the Netherlands. In addition, both have their own sales organisations in a number of other countries. The HPC division largely consists of regional units (which are comprised of combinations of several countries) and product groups and reports per region to the board of management in the Netherlands.

SL/DE first entered the Household and Personal Care market in 1983 through an acquisition. That year, SLC started transferring control of its other business unit, Household and Personal Care (HPC) to SL/DE by selling off its interest in the Dutch company Intradal to SL/DE. Intradal was a household name in oral care (e.g., Prudent, Zendium) and toiletries in the Netherlands and Belgium. In 1984, SLC acquired the Australian company Nicholas

[3]In Appendix A, we reproduce from the 1991–92 Annual Report the various subsidiaries and the affiliated companies of SL/DE around the world.

Kiwi, which had operations all over the world with leading brands in the shoe care business. Later in 1988, control of this division also was transferred to SL/DE's HPC division. The activities of the HPC division were further widened with the acquisition of the consumer products division of the chemical giant Akzo in 1987. In summary, by the end of the 1980s, SLC wholly transferred control of the HPC division to SL/DE.

SL/DE managed the 'Coffee and Grocery' and 'Household and Personal Care' product divisions, and direct selling activities of its parent company Sara Lee Corporation from its headquarters in Utrecht, the Netherlands (see Figure 1). As of 1993, these two business units derived the greater percentage of their sales from Europe than the USA, whereas the sales from SLC's other two business units (Packaged Meat and Bakery, and Personal Products) came more from the USA than from Europe.

SL/DE's strategy of growth through acquisitions worked quite well. Table 1 illustrates the successful performance of the company from 1984 to 1992, with special focus on its HPC division.

The HPC division, which is comprised of several product groups such as detergents (Biotex, Blanc Nuclear, Dobbleman), cleaners (Ty-D-Bol, White King, Bloo, Tolett), shoe care (Kiwi shoe polish, spray and cream, Tuxan, Tana), insecticides (Catch, Bloom, Vapona), air-fresheners (Tolett, Ambi-Pur, Parry's), car care (Valma, Abel Auto, Kitten), body care (lotions, liquid soaps and deodorants under the names of Radox, Sanex, Amplex, Royal Ambree), oral care (Prudent, Zendium) and baby care (Zwitsal soap, cream and shampoo) had a turnover of 2.475 billion Dfl in 1992–93, approximately one-third of the total company turnover. Although there were many products in its portfolio, from its start, the HPC division came to be more widely known for its insecticide and shoe care busi-

FIGURE 1
SARA LEE AND SARA LEE/DE

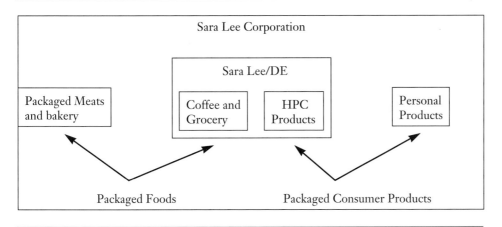

TABLE 1
SALES IN MILLIONS OF US $ OF THE TWO DIVISIONS OF SL/DE[4]

Year	1984	1985	1986	1987	1988	1989	1990	1991	1992
C&G	n.a.	1687	1626	1577	1663	1816	1834	1938	1919
HPC	643	812	943	983	1104	1281	1196	1319	1227

ness units than for its body care and baby care units. This is probably because the company was spending all of its efforts to maintain the image of the strong brands it acquired from other companies, such as Kiwi, and many of these well-known brands happened to fall in the shoe care and insecticide sectors.

THE SPANISH HPC MARKET AND MARTIN MUÑOZ

Cruz Verde-Legrain (CVL), SL/DE's 100%-owned subsidiary in Spain which was acquired in the early 1980s, was where the idea for Sanex originated. Up until the time it was acquired, CVL was primarily known for its insecticide products. The insecticide market periodically experienced erratic and often sizeable seasonal fluctuations as sales turnover was largely affected by varying weather conditions. To buffer CVL from these cyclical fluctuations, Martin Muñoz and the other members of the subsidiary's management team decided to research the possibility of adding other products to their limited portfolio. Martin and his management team agreed on two issues: first, the product should offer consumers some sort of "protection" like their insecticide products; secondly, the product should make use of the existing technical know-how within the company. With these two broad objectives in mind, CVL management went on a 'fishing expedition." They commissioned a firm to conduct semi-structured "focus group" interviews to surface new product ideas. During these interviews, focus group participants discussed several product categories, one of which was bath and shower gel. Unexpectedly, the interviewers noted that some of the participants complained bitterly about the irritating skin problems associated with the cosmetic-type liquid soaps available in supermarkets. When probed further, they also complained about the exorbitant prices of the medical-type liquid soaps carried by pharmacists. The "fishing expedition" had yielded promising results. Martin and his management team began to seriously think about the huge potential of a good liquid soap which could simultaneously offer "protection" to the skin and yet be readily available to the general public through

supermarket and other retail outlets. Pressing forward, CVL decided to exploit the vacant spot between the cosmetic-type liquid soap and the medical-type liquid soap. It entered the body care market through this "gap."

The Spanish body care market was totally dominated by Henkel (with its FA brand), Beiersdorf (with its Nivea brand), and Gillette (with its Magno brand). CVL was clearly a non-entity. Martin and his management team very well knew that any management guru would advise him against pursuing opportunities that did not fit well with his business's strength or core competency, and would advise him against entering a mature market such as HPC. But having made the decision to diversify from the volatile insecticide market, he chose to take the risk. In 1985, against all odds, he entered the market with Sanex,[5] a Bath & Shower liquid soap product. To the whole industry's surprise, the launching of Sanex was not only immensely successful, but also redefined the whole structure of the Spanish HPC market and was a milestone in CVL's and in Sara Lee/DE's history.

The HPC Market in Spain

The body care sector of the HPC market in Spain can be categorised into Bath & Shower Liquid Soap, Bar Soap, Hand Liquid Soap, Hair Shampoo, Deodorant and Body Colognes. The 1990 sales breakdown of this market by these six categories is provided in Table 2. Bath & Shower Liquid Soap leads the pack with annual sales totalling 51.7 million litres followed by Hair Shampoo with annual sales of 38 million litres.

The Bath and Shower Liquid Soap Market

The Bath & Shower liquid soap market experienced unprecedented growth in the 1980s thanks to Sanex. Table 3 illustrates the fantastic growth of this market in the ten year period from 1982 to 1991. From annual sales of 8.8 million litres in 1982, this market virtually exploded to annual sales of 57.4 million litres in 1991, registering a compounded annual growth of 20.7%.

---

[4]Toward the end of the 1980s and the early 1990s, the exchange rate between the US $ and the Dutch guilder fluctuated heavily, with Dfl more frequently appreciating against the dollar during this period.

[5]In reviewing the inventory of names CVL had registered that were available for use, Martin and members of his management team immediately chose Sanex due to its close association with the Spanish toast *Salud*, which means "to your health."

TABLE 2
1990 SALES BREAK-UP OF BODY CARE MARKET IN SPAIN

Category	1990 Sales in Million Litres	1990 Sales in Million US $
Bath & Shower	51.7	175
Bar Soap	8.7	51
Hand Liquid Soap	1.8	15
Hair Shampoo	38.0	154
Deodorants	34.0	103
Bath Colognes	13.6	54

Much, if not all, of the tremendous sales growth achieved by the Bath & Shower liquid soaps in Spain can be attributed to the successful launching of Sanex in 1985 and to the subsequent frenzy of competitive moves that took place thereafter. Sanex was able to make a big impact in the body care market by the invention of a new dimension in the liquid soap category. The introduction of Sanex gave a vital boost to liquid soap sales which otherwise were stagnant.

Positioning of Sanex

Prior to the introduction of Sanex in 1985, liquid soap was performing the usual and ubiquitous function of cleansing the body of its tough odours and dirt. Such a perception was reinforced by, for example, incorporating strong perfumes in liquid soaps and making them abrasive. Consumers using such liquid soaps came out of their bathrooms with a strong sense of having a dirt-free, odour-free, scented body. Under Martin's leadership, CVL first thought of viewing liquid soaps as more than a simple dirt and odour remover. CVL introduced properties that widened its scope. From being a mere body cleanser, liquid soap evolved into a dermo-protector (i.e., skin protector) in 1985 thanks to Sanex.

Table 4 identifies the main characteristics of the three key segments in the liquid soap, namely, cosmetics, dermo-protectors, and pharmaceuticals. It should be noted that this type of segmentation in liquid soap came into existence only with the introduction of Sanex. Thus, with Sanex, CVL could be considered a pioneer in inventing a new dimension (dermo-protection) in the liquid soap category.

The cosmetics-type liquid soaps address, true to their name, only the external effects on the skin, while the dermo-protector seeks to make the skin healthier and more hygienic. CVL differentiated Sanex from the existing cosmetics-type liquid soaps by carefully adopting several unique physical attributes.

While Martin and his management team tried to incorporate the health and hygiene factors into their liquid soap, they did not want Sanex to "degenerate" to the level of an absolute pharmaceutical product (such as Emopon and Multidermol) which would be a disaster in the mass consumer market. To achieve this goal, Sanex was produced in white colour (a non-cosmetic colour) to signal its hygienic properties and to differentiate it from the transparent nature of the pharmaceutical gels and the non-white colours of the cosmetics-type liquid soap. CVL made Sandex soft and slightly perfumed, while the cosmetics-type liquid soaps were clearly marked by their abrasive nature and strong perfumes and the pharmaceutical products were odourless. Sanex was also designed to produce foam lather which was to be more than that produced by a pharmaceutical product, but was to be less than that produced by a typical cosmetics-type liquid soap.

Thus, every effort was made to ensure that Sanex had the right combination of the pharmaceutical product and the cosmetic-type liquid soap, but was still well-differentiated from either of them. In this sense, CVL's management "discovered" a void between the cosmetics-type liquid soap which lacked medicinal properties and the pharmaceutical soaps which lacked mass appeal,[6] and cleverly filled it with

[6]By mentioning that CVL, under Martin's leadership, "discovered" the void, we implicitly assume that there always existed a need for such a product in the market. But one can argue that such a need never existed (i.e., the consumers did not have or know this need), and it was Martin who created this need with Sanex, very similar to what Kellogg did with corn flakes or Compaq did with its portable personal computer. In this sense, the need itself can be said to have been "invented" by Martin.

TABLE 3
LIQUID SOAP SALES GROWTH

Sales in	1982	1983	1984	1985	1986	1987	1988	1989	1990	1991
million litres	8.73	11.54	14.09	17.97	22.59	32.02	38.61	45.33	51.72	57.40

TABLE 4
THE THREE SEGMENTS OF LIQUID SOAP CATEGORY

Segment	Description	Sales in Million Litres	Stage of PLC
Dermo-protectors	Liquid, Low foaming, Slightly perfumed, White, Soft, Protection against bacteria	25.0	Growing
Cosmetics	Fluid, Foaming, Strongly perfumed, Coloured, Abrasive	23.5	Mature
Pharmaceutical	Non-perfumed, Liquid, Transparent, Low foaming, Protective	n.a.	Mature

Sanex. A detailed list of the two-way differentiating physical characteristics of Sanex is provided in Table 5.

Marketing Mix Elements of Sanex

In 1985, the body care sector of the HPC market in Spain was populated by about 107 brands managed by many different companies including corporate giants such as Beiersdorf (manufacturer of Nivea), Henkel, Johnson Wax and Revlon. The market was stagnant and very mature, and as such, the competition was severe. Cut-throat pricing was more the norm than the exception. No brand could muster more than a 7% market share. New products were being continually tested in the market since it was the only way a company could hope to increase its market share. As a result, the market was saturated with brands. And, it was in such a market Sara`Lee/DE (i.e., CVL), an almost non-entity, was trying to launch its new brand, Sanex.

Compared to other me-too new brands in the market, one thing that was different about Sanex was that it had clear and distinctively unique features contributing to healthy skin. What remained to be done was the right marketing of this unique selling point (USP) to the consumer. This was not an easy job by any standard because Sanex's USP had to be conveyed to the consumers with

[7]"Over" protective with respect to the dirt and odour accumulating in a day-to-day life of a typical consumer.

the right message and had to be "sold" to the consumer at the right price. Otherwise, it might not achieve its potential. When interviewed about his role in launching Sanex, Martin asserted: "If you are convinced about something, defend it with full force, since a half-hearted attempt would not reveal anything."

Advertising: As a first step, as CVL's senior manager, Martin made sure that Sanex maintained strong advertising support year after year, getting the highest share of voice (SOV) of all the liquid soaps (see Table 6).

However, high advertising expenditures were a necessary but insufficient condition. Martin decided that he had to handle the advertising of Sanex adroitly (to get the consumer's attention amidst the existing clatter of advertisement messages and make them *hear* what Sara Lee had to say about Sanex), and credibly (in order to make the consumer *listen* to CVL's claim on the usefulness of Sanex's USPs).

He handed over responsibility for copy-creativity to a very young advertising company called Casadevall & Pedreno and asked them to design the message with four specific objectives in mind:

- The message should get the attention of consumers.
- The communication had to be straightforward and clear, focusing on the product.
- The message had to be rational and not emotional.
- The message should concentrate on the main benefit of Sanex, namely, "Sanex for healthy skin."

TABLE 5
SANEX POSITIONING IN THE LIQUID SOAP MARKET

Cosmetics Type	Sanex	Pharmaceutical
Bright colours	White	Transparent
Thick gel	Liquid	Thin Fluid
Strongly perfumed	Slightly perfumed	Non perfumed
Foaming	Low foaming	Non foaming
Abrasive ingredients	PH balanced	Neutral
Nonprotective	Protective	(Over) protection[7]

TABLE 6
SHARE OF VOICE OF SANEX AND SOME OF ITS COMPETITORS

SOV of	1987	1988	1989	1990
Sanex	18%	29%	33%	37%
FA	7%	11%	9%	13%
NB	—	—	12%	14%
Lux	—	—	1%	10%

Casadevall & Pedreno came up with some brilliant advertisement copies. They minimised words (for example, typically the first 15 seconds of the advertising ran without any sound at all), and used no music for background, but maximised visual impact through slow motion and transition effects. All advertisement copies, however, were subject to the approval of CVL top management.

The initial advertisements that aired in early years clearly supported these objectives. Appendix B on page 645 which depicts the advertisement copies titled "Spot Salad" and "Spot Shower", directly addressed the issue of 'creating brand awareness' by seeking to educate the consumer about the new product and its benefits. The messages in these advertisements were loud, clear and to-the-point: using Sanex not only results in clean skin, but healthy skin. In the later years, however, as more and more competitive brands moved in, Martin authorised some seemingly unconventional advertising messages. For example, the advertisement titled "Spot Pregnant" was aimed to increase the awareness of healthy skin. To market Sanex deodorant, CVL aired the advertisement called "Spot Kiss" in which a woman was shown (in slow motion) kissing a man's armpit after he used Sanex. These "unconventional" messages were successful in *maintaining* the attention it had received from consumers. Table 7 provides further details on these three advertisements.

Whatever the advertisement message, efforts were undertaken to ensure that the message positioned the brand in the consumer's mind exactly as it was intended to be: the best combination of pharmaceutical and cosmetics-type liquid soaps. Whereas cosmetics-type liquid soaps focused on fantasy presentations and happy themes in their advertising messages and the pharmaceutical gels went for aseptic packaging and technical advertising, Sanex concentrated on informative and serious advertising. Although Sanex's later advertisements were somewhat less conventional, they nevertheless "hit the target" in terms of communicating Sanex's USP: *healthy skin.*

The advertisements were very successful not only for Sanex, but for Casadevall & Pedreno, the young advertising company, too. "The fact that their career success was tied to the success of Sanex," observes Martin, "possibly resulted in some fantastic advertisement copies for Sanex."

Pricing: Since Martin Believed that Sanex provided more benefits than an ordinary liquid soap, he thought it should be priced higher to signal the consumer that he or she was paying a premium to derive its extra utility. Pricing it at par with other liquid soaps and claiming better performance would prove to be an oxymoron. Hence Sanex was launched as a premium priced product and its 1985 shelf price was set at the level of market leader FA, which was at the top end of the market. Table 8 provides pricing information for Sanex and competing brands. Over the years, Sanex's price changed in line with general market trends.

Moreover, the high margin was found to be essential for providing support to the high expenses involved in advertisement and promotions. Of course, to minimise the potential downside of failure, CVL was very careful not to invest in huge manufacturing plants in the uncertain period following the launching of the brand. For the first

TABLE 7
ADVERTISING MESSAGES

Spot . . .	Year run	Expenditure $	SOV	Objective
Salad	1986–88	1, 2.2, 2.6	na, 18%, 29%	Consumer education, Product description, Brand awareness
Shower	1989–90	3.1, 4.5	30%, 37%	Brand awareness
Pregnant	1991	1.5	35%	Maintenance of awareness Notoriety

TABLE 8

PRICING OF SANEX

Price of . . . in Pesatas/Litre[9]	1986	1988	1990
Sanex	437	402	410
FA cosmetic	415	412	378
Nivea cosmetic	405	363	356
Neutrobalance	—	—	417
FA dermo	—	—	413
Nivea dermo	—	—	294

three or four years, though the formula was created by CVL Laboratories,[8] manufacturing was outsourced. As the product proved itself to be a success, manufacturing was gradually moved in-house. A greenfield plant was built that was dedicated solely to manufacturing current and future Sanex brand products. Thus at the start, CVL tried its best to spend as much as possible solely in marketing the concept.

The Evolution of the Liquid Soaps Market Segment

Soon after Sanex was launched in 1985, the market signals were very clear that it was likely to be a winner. And as imitation is the sincerest form of flattery, competitors rushed in: Tojadermao (of Nobel-Gillette) in 1986, Nelia Dermo (of Gal) and Shim Dermo (of Henkel) in 1987, Johnson's (of Johnson & Johnson) in 1991, to name a few. Table 9 provides the entry years of some of these followers in the dermo-type liquid soap market.

[8]CVL Laboratories was the name that CVL carefully chose to use in their Sanex packaging. The word Laboratories was added to signal to the potential buyers that the Sanex product shared only the "medicinal" attributes such as providing healthy skin with their core products (insecticides) and nothing else.

[9]Exchange rate: 1 US $ = 110 Pesetas

Almost all of the cosmetics-type liquid soaps extended their lines into the dermo-protective segment by 1991. In 1985, Sanex was the sole market entry in this category, but by 1990, more than 50 different dermo-type liquid soap brands had been introduced in the market place. However, by capitalising on its pioneering advantage as the first mover and through clever advertising, Sanex was able to maintain and even increase its market share lead over the years (see Table 10).

Partly because of the fact that consumers quickly accepted Sanex and partly because of the intense activity exhibited by all the players in the market place, the dermo segment of the liquid soap grew at an astonishing pace. Starting from virtually nowhere in 1985, within just six years this segment accounted for 50.5% of all the liquid soap sales, thus becoming its largest segment in 1991.

Extension of Sanex Concept to Other Categories

Without question, the success of Sanex created a storm in the highly intense HPC market, and this storm had started escalating beyond the Spanish borders to cross Europe and even the globe. This was because it was widely becoming known that Sanex was more of a concept than a product, and that this concept of *finding and exploiting a void between two extremes* would soon be applied by its competitors in other categories of the personal care market. Martin decided to move first and fast. Within two years of launching Sanex (rather a short time to come to any conclusion about a product's success), Sanex was launched in the "hand liquid soap" category in 1987. The same name was retained in order to quickly leverage the brand name.[10] The risk paid off. By 1991, Sandex became the second leading brand in the Hand Liquid Soap market, accounting for 25% of its sales.

[10]It may be that he already had the intention to make Sanex an umbrella brand and establish Sanex as the flagship-name of the company across Europe.

TABLE 9

ENTRY TIMINGS OF SANEX AND ITS FOLLOWERS

Company	Cosmetic Brands	Dermo Brands	Dermo Launched in
CVL	S3, Moussel	Sanex	1985
Henkel	FA, Shim	Fa dermo, Shim dermo	1989, 1987
Beiersdorf	Nivea gel	Nivea dermo	1990
Colgate-Palmolive	Palmolive	Palmolive dermo	1991
Nobel-Gillette	Tojapin, Magno	Tojadermo	1986
Reckitt & Colman	Nenuco	Nenuco dermo	1989
Johnson & Johnson	—	Johnson's	1991
Bayer	—	Delial	1989
Gal	Nelia	Nelia dermo	1987

TABLE 10

LEADERSHIP POSITION OF SANEX IN THE DERMO AND IN THE WHOLE LIQUID SOAP MARKET

Year	1986		1988		1990	
	Dermo	Liquid	Dermo	Liquid	Dermo	Liquid
Sales in million litres	2.281	22.58	12.585	38.61	25.034	51.72
Share of leader, Sanex	15%	8%	39.5%	12.9%	31.2%	15.1%
Share of first trailer	17.5%	8.6%	14.8%	7.4%	6.6%	7.0%
Share of second trailer	1.1%	4.4%	4.6%	4.2%	5.4%	5.3%

CVL continued to relentlessly capitalise on the success of the Sanex concept. It entered the deodorant category in 1988 (spray and stick types) and 1989 (roll-on type), in the body milk category in 1990, and in the bath cologne category in 1991 under the Sanex brand. It was a race against time. Nothing else mattered. Table 11 reveals the success story of these launches.

What was remarkable was not just the success of these extensions, but how success was achieved—by carrying over in all details the Sanex concept and the associated marketing philosophy from liquid soap to those categories. The Sanex brand name was used for the products in all of the categories. True to its name, it carried the same USP, too, in all the categories: *Sanex means Healthy Skin.* It was priced at the premium level and positioned similarly in all the categories, and it also had the similar packaging style (blue colour, contents conveying healthy skin message, etc.). In short, CVL, under Martin's leadership, made Sanex a concept that was simple, straightforward and could be applied with ease across all the body care products.

FROM SPAIN TO EUROPE

Sanex and SL/DE

For SL/DE, Sanex's performance in Spain was relatively minor compared to the brand equity enjoyed and the sales generated world-wide by its Douwe Egberts coffee and Kiwi shoe polish brands. However, Sanex was a break-

through for SL/DE in that it represented the first time that the company had launched *a brand new brand*, resulting in the following:

- Until 1983, SL/DE did not exist at all in the HPC market in Spain, a market that was populated with more than 104 brands, many of which were the likes of FA, Nelia and Nivea. However, thanks to Sanex, by 1990, SL/DE became a powerful force to reckon with in the Spanish HPC market.

- Until the late 1980s, SL/DE's body care products received less attention than the shoe care and insecticides products. Thanks to Sanex, the company started consolidating its position in the body care market by exerting extra effort to strengthen brands in the UK and by acquiring leading brands in Germany (Duschdas and Badedas) from SmithKline Beecham, and other brands such as Brylcream and Williams. The acquisition of these brands significantly strengthened the HPC division.

- Until 1990, the norm for SL/DE was that growth would be achieved primarily through acquiring already established brand names. After 1990, thanks to Sanex, it proved to itself, to its stakeholders and to its parent company SLC that it could build a good brand in-house from scratch.

- Until 1985, since SL/DE's growth for the most part was achieved through acquisitions, its marketing op-

TABLE 11

SANEX'S SUCCESS (AS OF 1990) IN EVERY PERSONAL CARE CATEGORY

Category	Sales in m. Litres	Sanex Entered in	Sanex Share	Sanex Position	Main Competing Brands
Liquid soap	51.7	1985	15%	1	FA, Nivea
Hand liquid soap	1.8	1987	25%	2	Tacto, Heno de pravia
Deodorants	34.0	1988/89	7%	3	FA, Rexona
Body milk	2.5	1990	6%	4	Natural honey, Nivea
Bath cologne	13.6	1991	—	—	S3, FA

erations were primarily geared towards maintaining and exploiting the acquired brand names. After 1990, thanks to Sanex, it could afford to allocate more resources to developing new brands at home.

The last statement is true not just for SL/DE but for the whole of SLC, because with the exception of the start-up brands Douwe Egberts and Sara Lee, most of the leading brands of SLC were acquisitions. This fact was reaffirmed when the tremendous success of brand names like Sanex[11] prompted a change in SLC's mission statement. Formerly, SLC's mission was "to be a premier, global branded consumer packaged goods company." Today Sara Lee Corporation's mission is "to BUILD consumer packaged goods brands world-wide." This change in the corporate mission statement was probably made to inform stakeholders of SLC's greater orientation toward brand building.

Hence it was no wonder that the management board of SL/DE at Utrecht, the Netherlands, was more than delighted to see an "invented here" brand making strong gains in unfamiliar territory. It also saw what Martin saw in Sanex: "Healthy skin" as a powerfully appealing concept and the tremendous potential to make it a global brand. And because building a global brand became an important corporate objective, SL/DE's chairman and Vice President of SLC asked Martin to launch Sanex throughout Europe. Martin willingly agreed and in 1988, put forth the following plan.

Martin's Plan to Make Sanex a Euro Brand

The objectives, the product policy, and the marketing policy of introducing Sanex were all identical for all the countries. The plan did not incorporate any modifications that would cater to any idiosyncratic characteristics of a country. What mattered was the integrity of the Sanex concept (whatever the contents, the look, the advertisement, or anything else). The plan was rather sharp (in content) and blunt (in appearance). It read as follows:

1. Global Objective:
   To have the same positioning, concept and product in all countries.
   To have a market share that places Sanex among the first 4 brands in each country.

2. Philosophy to be adopted:
   What is to be sold is not a product called Sanex, but a concept called Sanex, which simply implies "Healthy Skin."

[11]Another "brand new brand" was the Wonder-bra introduced by SLC in the USA in the early 1990s. Wonder-bra was a highly successful product and was appropriately recognised as such by *Fortune* Magazine in 1994.

3. Product Policy:
   Between cosmetic and pharmaceutical.
   Basically for the family.
   Common image for all the product categories.
   Formula is "keep skin healthy."

4. Marketing Policy:
   Premium price.
   Strong advertising that conveys the concept.
   Packaging (colour, message etc.) should be same, except, of course, the language.
   Launchings shouldn't be based on promotions, but on the possibility of getting to know the product.
   Massive distribution support to be ensured in a short time.
   Samples should be distributed only after a considerable level of awareness is reached.

5. Formula and specifications of the product to be controlled by R&D centralised in Spain.

6. Manufacturing to be centralised in Barcelona, Spain (IPC, International Production Centre).

7. Status report should go from each country to Spain (i.e., to Martin) every 2 months.

8. Monthly meeting initially, and quarterly meeting thereafter with the Sanex team in Spain.

9. Any change whatsoever, be it product formula, price, or advertising, to be approved by the IPC.

10. TV creativity in advertisement messages also to be directly managed by IPC.

11. Extensions into other categories:
    Everything remains the same except the pricing factor, which can be reduced if Sanex in that particular product category does not expect to bring any differential benefits to the consumers.

Initial Reaction from SL/DE Headquarters

The management board at SL/DE in the Netherlands, though new to the HPC market, had nonetheless been overseeing an international company for many years. The international structure of SL/DE, however, is different from that of other multinationals such as Procter & Gamble. SL/DE owns many companies offshore, but they all operate under different names. For the most part, these companies operate autonomously and many have their own production, marketing and sales departments. This is because SL/DE, like its parent, strongly believes in reinforcing and sustaining entrepreneurship qualities, and in fact, this has been one of the main objectives of the company right from the time of DE's merger with SLC.

Although the subsidiaries enjoyed full freedom, the management board in the Netherlands expected little opposition from them in launching Sanex throughout Europe. After all, who would say no to having a proven product with a successful track record like Sanex in his portfolio? Moreover, since SL/DE is new to the HPC market, it offered no equivalent brand in the HPC markets of most of these countries that would possibly be cannibalised by introducing Sanex. Hence the chairman of the board was very optimistic that Martin would easily obtain the necessary help to transfer Sanex to other European markets.

Thus, SL/DE headquarters completely agreed with Martin on the importance of maintaining the integrity of the Sanex concept, regardless of the country in which it was to be launched. Such integrity could only be maintained through adopting appropriate advertisement copies, packaging etc. that were consistent with the product image. And, since the set of marketing strategies adopted in Spain had already proven to be one such set of appropriate strategies, the chairman appointed Martin as the Manager of Sanex with the primary responsibility of co-ordinating the activities concerning the introduction of Sanex in other countries.

For Martin, too, the job seemed straightforward. He had a good product that had already proven its worth in a large country. In his opinion, Sanex helped the consumer satisfy a unique need, and that particular need would be more or less the same irrespective of the country in which the consumer resided. Hence, to introduce it in other European countries, he had to simply talk to his colleagues in these markets and educate them about key success factors, namely, the strategies concerning the positioning of the product and the supporting marketing mix elements, and the rest would take care of itself. However, he wanted to make sure that everything that figured in Sanex's success in Spain should be employed in other countries too without any change. With this idea in mind, the plan was proposed.

To the surprise of SL/DE's chairman and his senior management team at headquarters, the initial reactions from managers from other countries such as Denmark, the Netherlands, France, Belgium, UK, and Greece to the plan were quite unfavourable. Some of them were negative but accommodative, and some were absolutely negative.

Reaction from the Netherlands

The Netherlands was one country that offered considerable support for Sanex, though not initially nor directly. Ironically, the Netherlands was probably the only country that had every reason to abandon Sanex. Almost every member of Intradal, the SL/DE company in the Netherlands (the equivalent of CVL in Spain), had one objection or another to the brand name and product. Recalls Mr. Godert H. van Doornewaard, Product Manager of the company, "Some objected to its name, some objected to its packaging, some to its 'bad' perfume, . . ." Many op-

posed using the same name Sanex indicating that it implied the sanitary aspects of the product more than anything else. The packaging of Sanex (see Figure 5) in blue and white looked medicinal to many and signalled a product anything other than a bathroom product. "In fact, it is uniquely ugly with respect to the other bath products in the market such as Nivea" asserts Doornewaard. However, the marketing team understood very well that Sanex, which had been very successful in Spain, deserved more than off-the-cuff comments. In order to do a scientific analysis, the marketing team carried out detailed market research on Sanex in the "as is" condition, i.e., same name, same packaging, etc.

To everyone's relief in Intradal and to Martin's complete dismay, the market research showed that Sanex would be a disaster in the Dutch market. The survey respondents clearly hated the product. Intradal was not unfamiliar with market research studies, having carried out many in the past which had predicted actual outcomes remarkably well. In Sanex's case, Intradal would normally have abided by the marketing research results were it not for the assertiveness of its Marketing Director, Mr. Rien van der Veen.[12]

Luckily for Sanex, Rien happened to be an ex-CVL manager who had witnessed first-hand the introduction and growth of Sanex in Spain and who had personally experienced its success. During his stay at CVL, he had come to completely believe in the Sanex concept. As such, he placed less faith in the results of the Dutch market research studies. In the words of Rien, "it is very hard to design questionnaires for new products, especially for those that are radically new such as Sanex, since consumers hardly can tell anything about a new product." To him, it simply sounded foolish to ask the consumers about products that did not exist before. In an after-thought, Doornewaard completely agrees with him, noting the failures of market research studies carried out for New Coke and the Sony Walkman.[13]

Rien overruled the market research results and introduced Sanex in the Dutch market. He adopted the same name Sanex, adopted the same "ugly" packaging, same perfume, same market positioning, same pricing, same advertising, etc. He could not have been more correct. Sanex stormed into the Dutch market like a tornado. The product was so successful that SL/DE's competitors experienced formidable barriers to entering the market with

---

[12]The name of this case character has been disguised for confidentiality reasons.

[13]Coca Cola spent millions of dollars in marketing research in a bid to ensure that New Coke, the replacement for their historically successful 100 year-old mainstay soft drink product, would be very appealing to consumers, but on launch, the widely advertised New Coke failed miserably. On the other hand, market research predicted only a very small market for the Sony Walkman!

similar products. The few companies who managed to launch their own dermo-protector products did not get to see much daylight. Sanex virtually became a monopoly in the Dutch dermo-protector segment. It ended up receiving many accolades such as "Innovative product of 1991." Sanex Shower, a product extension, also got off to a very good start, capturing around 4% of the market within a year of its introduction.

And, the marketing research group at Intradal learned an important lesson.

"Of course we did manage to change one thing," confesses Doornewaard rather proudly. "The Spanish packaging indicates that the product is for both skin and hair, while the Dutch packaging stresses only skin and not hair." Mr. Van Bemmelen, the current President of Intradal, offers an interesting explanation to this: "In Spain, we have a cultural difference. It has become a custom not to treat hair differently from skin, but in the market such as ours, hair is looked at differently from skin." "For example," he continues, "shampoo, the hair-specific product, has never been as important in Spain as it is here."

Sanex was not only successful with its shower gel (liquid soap), but also was very successful with its deodorant and other product extensions. The runaway success of Sanex and its extensions in the Dutch market was partly due to the fact that the marketing team came up with many innovative promotional schemes. For example, door-to-door sampling was done for Sanex liquid soap in more than three waves; in 1991, the third year after Sanex liquid soap got off to a successful start, Sanex deodorant was introduced by giving away free samples to the purchasers of Sanex liquid soap. Thus, the Sanex user base was heavily inundated with product extensions, and before they knew it, had become strong and loyal consumers of Sanex products.

"It is not the Sanex soap or deodorant that our consumers buy," vociferously objects Van Bemmelen, "it is the Health factor that our consumers buy from us through purchasing our Sanex products." The marketing team saw to it that the "Health" concept, and not any specific product of Sanex, got projected in advertisements (they managed to maintain a 30 to 40% SOV in the first two years, which was very high in the Dutch market), packaging, etc. For example, they used the Spot Salad advertisement copy more than any other copy since it was only in that advertisement that the concept "Health," and only the concept "Health," came out. "What other connection could a consumer possibly make between a salad and a shower gel?" quips Van Bemmelen. This may have prompted the company to explore so many successful product extensions[14] around this "Health" concept, and

probably may not have happened if they had tried to build those extensions around, say, the Sanex liquid soap product.[15]

However, it became very clear to everyone at SL/DE that the key to Sanex's success in the Dutch market was purely due to its strong and clear positioning strategy and the absolute support it received from the President at Intradal. This victory was crucial for Sanex for many reasons: it was the first success outside Spain, the way success was achieved defied the prevailing rules of the game, and it hinged totally on top management support for the product and the winning Spanish theme.

Reaction from France

The initial reaction from France was similar to that from the Netherlands, but less negative. The management team of Kiwi France (the French subsidiary of SL/DE in the HPC sector) was appalled by the Sanex brand name and its packaging style. "To the French," asserts Mr. Corinne Oppenheim, the Sanex Product Manager of Kiwi France, "any word that ends with 'ex' sounds 'hard', and in our opinion, the name Sanex did not go well with the mildness (i.e., milder than pharmaceutical equivalent) property it portrayed." All such misgivings Corrine had were shared by everyone on his management team

Apparently not convinced by Sanex's success story in Spain, Kiwi France carried out a marketing research study on Sanex in the "as is" condition. The study revealed that the French consumers shared the beliefs held by the management team of Kiwi France. Though the results were not as disastrous as those that came out of the Dutch market research study, they did not show any positive support for the Sanex brand name and the packaging style.

However, the research results showed that Sanex could be a strong niche product. Corinne explains: "It addresses shower gel users who want to take care of their skin and all people who take showers and who are attracted by the convenience of gel but refuse existing gels because they are too aggressive and unnatural." The management team totally agreed on the fact that Sanex had a very clear USP in this segment:

Original & new: Not yet used in France.
Modern: Compared to present shower gels, the dermo-protector action is "up to date," credible and serious (the pharmaceutical aspects, i.e., the neutral Ph level, etc., are credible).

---

[14]Since brand extensions needed to be approved by the Sanex co-ordinating team in Spain, the Netherlands team sometimes had to fight with the board for good brand extensions.

[15]Mr. Van Bemmelen is rather proud that Intradal was able to successfully market the "Health" concept, which is much broader than the "Healthy Skin" concept marketed by his Spanish predecessor.

Attractive: For the shower gel users, Sanex is the gel that they have been waiting for that both washes and takes care of the skin, and for soap users, Sanex is attractive because it seems natural and less aggressive than other products.

Hence, the decision was taken to launch the product and Sanex appeared on the French retailers' shelves in January 1991. Kiwi France maintained the Spanish strategy in principle; they favoured the strong and distinctive positioning of Sanex and the pricing strategy (i.e., premium pricing), but were less in favour of the advertsing copies. Even in the positioning of the brand, Kiwi France made sure that Sanex addressed the needs of a good "shower" gel, and not the "shower & bath" product. "Addressing both bath and shower problems with a single product creates a misunderstanding since the French people use quite different products for bath (which is a leisurely affair) and shower (which is a quick affair)," explains Corrine. The French also prevented Sanex from targeting the hair-care sector, since in their opinion, it was not yet proven.

In the final analysis, Kiwi France maintained the same product, the same packaging (though the market research studies had showed that the French consumers wanted it to be a bit more attractive and lively), same price (i.e., premium price), and same advertising. "The main reason for adopting the same packaging and advertising in spite of lack of support from market research studies," confesses Corinne, "is the fact that they are 'distinct,' serious and clearly understandable, thus satisfying the vital functions of a good communicator." As a result, Sanex started off with a 1.2% share of the market (with sales 5.8 million FF) in 1991, and reached a market share of 2.2% (with sales of 18.6 million FF) the following year. The initial figures showed, in the words of Corinne, "Sanex looks successful in our country."

Reaction from Denmark

The initial reaction from Blumoller, Denmark, (the Danish subsidiary of SL/DE) was very similar to those from the Netherlands and France. It was very negative. The management team and its president, Mr. Vangt Sinius Clausen, both hated the name Sanex and its packaging style, but they were somewhat positive about the perfume. The Danish team also conducted marketing research to test the Sanex name, packaging style, etc. The results showed that the Sanex name would be a disaster in the market place and the packaging was found to be unattractive.

However, the fact that Sanex had been hugely successful in Spain and because SL/DE's chairman was interested in furthering its success made Vangt reconsider the issue. To the relief of both Martin and SL/DE senior management, he decided to give it a try. "In fact," Vangt reflected on a similar situation a few years back, "our initial market research about Zendium, our very successful toothpaste, was also equally very negative, but we went ahead with it anyway because we believed in its positioning." In Sanex's case, the management team in Denmark fully agreed that the brand had a fantastic positioning, so it was decided to ignore the market research results and launch Sanex. The initial results indicated that the decision was right. Sanex clearly showed the signs of a very successful launch. "I firmly believe," asserts Vangt, "that Sanex will eventually get a market share higher than it mustered in Spain in the same time span."

Reaction from the UK

Of all the negative reactions Martin received, probably those from the UK were the most severe. At the time, SL/DE did not have a full-fledged HPC division in the UK. It intended to use Nicholas Laboratories (acquired for some other purpose) for handling Sanex. The principal manager of the Laboratories was Roger. From the very start, Roger kept raising objections, in a very authoritative tone. He argued that Sanex would imply something similar to sanitary napkins to a typical UK consumer, and hence labelling the liquid soap package as Sanex would be disastrous. Martin, of course, was not pleased as his goal was to make Sanex a Euro brand, and later a highly recognised global brand, similar to brands such as Kiwi, Coca Cola, Douwe Egberts and Sara Lee. Though the name Sanex was derived from the Spanish word 'Sanos' which means "healthy," it had close links to similar sounding words in other languages which had somewhat similar meanings (Table 12). Martin further pointed out that all these different words in different languages were basically rooted in a Latin word which meant health.

"Sanex is not like Nova, the brand name the automobile giant General Motors tried to export to Mexico from the USA,"[16] Martin argued. However, Roger was not about to give up his fight. He countered, "Of course, all these words mean the same in the dictionary, but people in different communities perceive the same word with different implications depending upon the cultural and other influences in the surroundings."

Given SL/DE's policy of subsidiary autonomy, Roger won the battle with Martin. He changed the name Sanex to Sante, altered the marketing strategies accordingly in every aspect, and launched the product in the UK in 1991. But by 1993, the results showed that Roger had lost the war, and lost it heavily. The product failed miserably.

---

[16]It is rather well known that GM made a big mistake in carrying the car name Nova from the USA to Mexico, because the word Nova in Spanish implies "does not go."

TABLE 12
SANEX IN DIFFERENT LANGUAGES

Language	Closest word	Meaning
Spanish	Sanos	Healthy
French	Sanitair	Healthy, carrying a medical flavour
English	Sanitary	Healthy, carrying a medical flavour
Dutch	Sanitas	Healthy

The mistake could have been anywhere in the system: the product itself,[17] the new name Roger had adopted, the marketing plan, and/or simply the time of introduction. No one would know for sure what the reasons for failure were.

The Decisive Role of SL/DE Headquarters

"Without the unequivocal support granted by Headquarters," Martin recollects, "Sanex would have remained confined to Spain."

The board of management in the Netherlands was furious at the way things turned out in the UK. Members of the board had not initially intervened in the conversation between Martin and Roger, and in fact did not intervene in any of the countries' objections to Martin's plan and their marketing research. The board reasoned that the arguments would eventually result in a good plan for each country. That proved to be a mistake—a big and costly mistake.

SL/DE's CEO had a dilemma. Either he had to let things be as they were ("status quo," thus maintaining the subsidiaries' autonomy over the internationalisation plan), or he had to initiate changes in policies and procedures and let them be dictated as far as Sanex was concerned (thus restricting the autonomy of the subsidiaries to a certain extent). He was sure of one thing, however. In his view, the potential success of the Sanex concept throughout Europe was dependent on maintaining its integrity. Moreover, the initial positive signals he had been receiving from Denmark and France, and especially what he saw in the Netherlands where Sanex succeeded in the "as is" condition thanks to the unequivocal support from the President, greatly influenced his ultimate decision to award full authority to pursuing a pan-European strategy based on the original Spanish strategy. Further, he personally believed that an effective implementation of this strategy to make Sanex a Euro brand would need

- a strong strategic consensus among all the country managers,
- a greater centralisation of authority for setting policies and allocating resources, at least in the starting phase of Sanex, and
- outright support from the top management of SL/DE.

On the other hand, creating a new line of authority at the product level would certainly cause confusion and escalate organisational control problems. "Since SL/DE has so far been very successful thanks to the autonomy enjoyed by its subsidiaries," the board argued, "changing it for the sake of Sanex could prove to be a disaster."

After carefully weighing the pros and cons of these two options, the CEO and the board decided to retain Martin as project co-ordinator (i.e., a staff function and not a line function). However, they also took steps to ensure that all the country managers understood that the Sanex concept received the full support of top management. Thus, in the second week of August 1993, SL/DE's CEO called in all the country managers in the HPC division, and directly informed them of his decision: Sanex was to be introduced in every country, Martin was the co-ordinating manager for Sanex across Europe empowered with decision-making responsibility such that anything to do with Sanex was subject to his approval, and that Martin should expect full support from each country.

MARTIN'S RATIONALE FOR THE PAN-EUROPEAN STRATEGY

Martin was in good spirits on his return flight to Spain. He had already made up his mind that Sanex had to be introduced in other European countries in the same fashion as was done in Spain and he was pleased that the board and the CEO, in particular, supported his position on the matter. He reclined fully in his seat, and slowly went over the arguments he put forth the day before to the CEO:

1. Having a single product with the same name and a similar packaging for all countries would enable mass

---

[17]It is worth noting that SL/DE already had a brand called Radox in the UK body care market.

production in the International Production Centre at Barcelona for the whole European market.

Mass production ensures consistent image and quality across countries (which is an attractive feature in itself since people travel a lot these days, especially across Europe, and many of them look for—if not search for—the familiar brand wherever they travel). In addition, mass production results in huge economies of scale through centralised purchasing and logistics design, and it results in rapidly lowering operating costs thanks to a faster learning curve (the phenomenon of gradual reduction in the unit cost of production with experience). The cash saved from production could, if needed, be applied to improving the effectiveness of marketing, through ensuring that Sanex obtains the maximum SOV and distribution support in each country it is entering, which are very important for the brand's success in any overcrowded market.

2. Thanks to the policies adopted by the EU in the past four decades, the Western European countries tend to converge in terms of people's buying power, consumption patterns (for example, more out-of-home consumption), standard of living, general economy of the countries such as per capita income and inflation, consumers' attitude towards maintaining good health and environment, interest and involvement in sports and cultural activities, and their readiness to support products with good value (for example, private label products).

3. In the case of durable goods, where word-of-mouth plays a significant role, and in the case of groceries such as cereal or beverages, where the consumption pattern is affected by the particular upbringing in a family and a society, there is a valid reason to believe that differences in the societal behaviour between two countries might influence sales. However, in the case of Sanex, which appeals explicitly to the rational part of the consumers' purchasing process, it can hardly be expected that there will be any significant differences between consumers of two different countries.

4. Though Sanex addresses the whole market, it specifically appeals to those who care more about their health. These consumers tend to have similar lifestyle and purchasing behaviour patterns (as far as buying products like Sanex is concerned) regardless of the nation or culture they belong to, just like the Jazz lovers and Pizza lovers across the world.

5. The marketing conditions, such as the consumers' familiarity with various marketing tools and strategies, and their familiarity with brand proliferation and brand images do not look different from one country to another.

6. Retail and distribution sectors of all the key European countries look alike, with the result that consumers in various European countries are affected (in their purchasing intention and behaviour) in a more or less similar manner to the marketing mix activities such as end-aisle displays in the supermarkets, promotions, price discounts, and media advertising.

7. The market structure of the body care industry in terms of its key competitors and intracompetitive activities is not very different from one country to another.

8. Sanex is positioned in a global body care sector, whether we like it or not, and thus it faces competition mainly from other multinationals and not locals. Hence, a global strategy is needed to wage an international competition.

9. Last, but the most important of all the reasons, is the fact that the integrity of the Sanex concept should not be sacrificed for the sake of a country's idiosyncratic attributes. Moreover, its positioning is very strong and unique and cuts across all borders, whether national or cultural. And, we have a winning theme. Why disturb it?

Martin paused to reflect for a moment. However convincing his arguments were in favour of a concept-consistent pan-European strategy for Sanex, however strong the SL/DE board was in favour of it, and however convincing the success of Sanex in the Netherlands, Martin could not avoid thinking about the possibility of a failure of his strategy in one country or another. After all, the marketing research studies in the Dutch, the French and the Danish markets had initially rejected the product. "Moreover," he could not help continuing in that line of thinking, "though the results I have been receiving from these three markets signal that Sanex is currently performing well, still I cannot overlook the fact that these early sales are only signals, and perhaps unreliable ones at that."

As he adjusted his seat to the upright position in preparation for landing, his thoughts drifted back to the dancing shadows of the blades of the Dutch windmill which he noticed shortly after his plane departed from Schipol Airport a scant few hours ago. Immediately, the image of Cervantes' hero Don Quixote attempting to tilt windmills came to mind. The recognition of the similarity of his situation to this fictional Spanish *cabellero* initially made him laugh but then caused him to wonder: Was he not also a modern-day Don Quixote challenging dominant paradigms and market research? Was he seeing things clearly and were his instincts correct? Would his strategy to make Sanex a Euro brand succeed?

APPENDIX A:
SUBSIDIARIES AND AFFILIATED COMPANIES OF SL/DE AS OF 1992

In compliance with article 379, Book 2 of the Dutch Civil Code, the major consolidated companies are listed below.

SUBSIDIARIES

Unless otherwise stated the participation is 100%.

Australia
Harris/DE Pty. Ltd. (95%) — *Sydney, N.S.W.*

Austria
Temana GmbH — *Vienna*
Tuxan Schuhpflegemittel GmbH — *St. Leonhard*

Belgium
Chat Noir/Clé d'Or S.A. — *Brussels*
Decaf N.V. — *Tessenderlo*
Douwe Egberts N.V. — *Grimbergen*
Douwe Egberts Van Nelle Tobacco Belgium N.V. — *Brussels*
N.V. Korrman Intradal S.A. — *Brussels*
Intradal Produktie Belgium N.V. — *St. Truiden*
Jacqmotte S.A. (99.9%) — *Brussels*

Canada
Douwe Egberts Ltd. — *Burlington*
Douwe Egberts Coffee Systems Ltd. — *Toronto*
Tana Canada Inc. — *Montreal*

Czecho-Slovakia
Balirny Douwe Egberts AS — *Prague*

Denmark
A/S Blumoller — *Odense*
Merrild Kaffe A/S — *Kolding*

France
Abel Bonnex S.A. (98.7%) — *Rouen*
Bühler Fontaine S.A. (97.7%) — *Rouen*
Cafés de l'Eléphant Noir S.A. — *Le Blanc Mesnil*
Douwe Egberts France S.A. — *Le Blanc Mesnil*

Douwe Egberts Service Professionels S.A. — *Fontenay-sous-Bois*
Etablissements Lardenois S.A. — *Hermes*
Tana France S.A. — *Hermes*
Kiwi France S.A. — *Le Blanc Mesnil*
Union Française d'Industries et de Marques Alimentaires (UFIMA) S.A. (99.9%) — *Le Blanc Mesnil*

Germany
Coffenco International GmbH — *Mainz*
Douwe Egberts Agio GmbH (80%) — *Moers*
Douwe Egberts Getränke Service GmbH & Co. K.G. — *Mainz*
Eri Feine Schuhpflege Vertriebs GmbH — *Alsdorf/Hoengen*

Greece
Inco Hellas A.E. — *Athens*

Hungary
Compack Douwe Egberts R.T. (99%) — *Budapest*

Ireland
Douwe Egberts (Ireland) — *Mullingar*

Italy
Pessi Guttalin SpA (92%) — *Padua*

The Netherlands
Decaf B.V. — *Amsterdam*
Decem B.V. — *Joure*
Detrex B.V. — *Joure*
Douwe Egberts Coffee Systems International B.V. — *Joure*
Douwe Egberts Coffee & Tea International B.V. — *Joure*
Douwe Egberts Coffee Systems Nederland B.V. — *Joure*
Douwe Egberts Nederland B.V. — *Joure*
Douwe Egberts Van Nelle Diensten B.V. — *Rotterdam*

Douwe Egberts Van Nelle Operating
B.V.   *Utrecht*
Douwe Egberts Van Nelle
Tabaksmaatschappij B.V.   *Rotterdam*
Douwe Egberts Van Nelle Tabaks-
produktiemaatschappij B.V.   *Joure*
Duyvis B.V.   *Zaandam*
Grada B.V.   *Amersfoort*
Household & Personal Care
Research B.V.   *The Hague*
Intec B.V.   *Veenendaal*
Koffiebranderij en Theehandel Kanis
& Gunnink B.V.   *Kampen*
Koninklijke Douwe Egberts B.V.   *Joure*
Kortman Intradal B.V.   *Veenendaal*
Kortman Nederland B.V.   *Veenendaal*
Lassie N.V.   *Wormer*
Marander Assurantie Compagnie
B.V.   *Joure*
Tana B.V.   *Amersfoort*
Valma B.V.   *Amersfoort*
Van Nelle Foodservices Nederland
B.V.   *Rotterdam*
Van Nelle Produktie B.V.   *Rotterdam*

The Netherlands Antilles
Cofico N.V.   *St. Maarten*
Defico N.V.   *St. Maarten*

Norway
Tomten A/S   *Oslo*

Portugal
Cruz Verde Portugal Produtos de
Consumo Lda.   *Lisbon*

Spain
Cafés a la Crema J. Marcilla S.A.   *Barcelona*
Cruz Verde-Legrain S.A.   *Barcelona*
Marcilla Coffee Systems S.A.   *Barcelona*

Sweden
Merrild Coffee Systems AB   *Stockholm*
A.B. Fenom   *Göteborg*

Switzerland
Decotrade A.G.   *Zug*
Tana Schuhpflege A.G.   *Mellingen*
Temana Verkaufs A.G.   *Wädenswil*

United Kingdom
Ashe Ltd.   *Slough*
Douwe Egberts U.K. Ltd.   *London*
Douwe Egberts Coffee Systems Ltd.   *Borehamwood*
Temana International Ltd.   *Slough*

AFFILIATED COMPANIES

Unless otherwise stated the participation of Sara Lee
Corporation is 100%.

Australia
King Gee Clothing Pty. Ltd.   *Sydney, N.S.W.*
Kitchens of Sara Lee (Australia) Pty.
Ltd.   *Gosford, N.S.W.*
Kiwi Brands Pty. Ltd.   *Clayton, Vic.*
Sara Lee Holdings (Australia) Pty.
Ltd.   *Sydney, N.S.W.*
Sara Lee Personal Products Pty. Ltd.   *Melbourne, Vic.*
The Stubbies Clothing Company
Pty. Ltd.   *Brisbane, Qld.*

China
Fuijan Sara Lee Consumer Products
Pte. Ltd. (70%)   *Fuzhou*

Hong Kong
K.E.S. Trading Ltd.   *Kowloon*
Kiwi Hong Kong Ltd.   *Hong Kong*

Indonesia
P.T. Kiwi Indonesia (80%)   *Jakarta*
P.T. Prodenta Indonesia (80%)   *Jakarta*

Jamaica
Kiwi Brands Ltd. Jamaican Branch   *Kingston*

Japan
Nihon Kiwi K.K.   *Tokyo*

Kenya
Kiwi Brands Ltd.   *Nairobi*

Korea
Kiwi Korea Ltd.   *Seoul*

Malawi
Kiwi Brands Ltd.   *Blantyre*

Malaysia
Kiwi Brands (Malaysia) Sdn. Bhd.   *Kuala Lumpur*
Kiwi Products Sdn. Bhd.   *Johore Bahru*

Mexico
House of Fuller, S.A. de C.V.   *Mexico City*
Probemex S.A. de C.V.   *Mexico City*

The Netherlands
Kiwi European Holdings B.V.   *Bladel*

New Zealand
Hilton Bonds New Zealand (1991)
Ltd.   *Wellington*
Kiwi Brands (N.Z.) Ltd.   *Auckland*

Philippines
Kiwi Philippines Inc.   *Manilla*

Singapore
Kiwi International Pte. Ltd.   *Singapore*
Sara Lee/DE Asia Inc. Singapore
   Branch   *Singapore*
Kiwi Singapore Pte. Ltd.   *Singapore*

Taiwan
Kiwi United Taiwan Co. Ltd. (51%)   *Taipei*

Thailand
Kiwi (Thailand) Ltd.   *Bangkok*
Sara Lee Trading Ltd.   *Bangkok*

United Kingdom
Sara Lee Household & Personal Care
   U.K. Ltd.   *Slough*

United States
Kiwi Brands Inc.   *Douglassville, PA*
Superior Coffee and Foods   *Bensonville, IL*
McGarvey Coffee   *Minneapolis, MN*

Zambia
Kiwi Zambia Ltd.   *Ndola*

Zimbabwe
Kiwi Brands (Private) Ltd.   *Harare*

APPENDIX B:
T.V. Commercials (20″)
Gel (Salad)

To keep your body healthy you eat this.

You drink this.

You do this.

And now you can also shower with Sanex.
Our new skin care liquid soap keeps
your skin healthy because it does not irritate

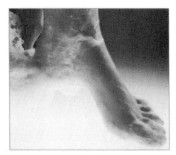

and prevents infections, too.

New Sanex liquid soap
for healthy skin.

APPENDIX C:
T.V. COMMERCIALS (20″)
GEL (APPLE)

Between an unprotected skin and

a protected skin, there's a lot of difference.

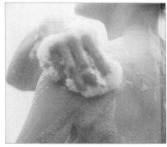

That's why now you have
New Sanex Dermoprotector gel.
Which protects your skin, not drying it out,

and helping to ward off bacteria.

New Sanex dermoprotector gel
Healthy Skin.

CASE 8

CLUB MED: THE PARTY IS OVER

Club Mediterranee, a corporation in the all-inclusive resort market, has found that is all-inclusive price is not as widely accepted as it has been in the past. The firm has found that consumers' preferences have changed. Vacationers are not willing to spend large amounts of money for vacations which include many activities that the vacationers are not using as much as they had been in the past. This change in preference poses a problem for the company because Club Med's competition has been able to customize travel packages for each consumer at prices that vacationers feel more comfortable with.

Though it appears easy for Club Med to also customize travel packages, the company is at a disadvantage compared to its competition. Most of the competitors are found in a small number of locations, while Club Med has resorts scattered all over the world. Currency devaluation and political boycotts are some of the situations that Club Med faces world-wide on an ongoing basis. These external factors are reducing the company's ability to increase sales and gain new customers.

BACKGROUND AND HISTORY

Club Mediterranee, otherwise known as "Club Med," was originally founded by a group of travelers, headed by Gerald Blitz, in 1950. However, through the years, as this group was increasing in size, it was becoming increasingly more difficult to manage. Blitz, therefore, took the opportunity to turn this "association" into a business, with the aid of Gilbert Trigano, in 1954. Trigano sought to establish this organization, and by 1985, Club Mediterranee S.A. was transformed into a publicly traded company on the Paris Stock Exchange. Club Med Inc. became the U.S.-based subsidiary of Club Mediterranee, headed by Trigano's son Serge. Today, Club Med encompasses over 114 villages, on six continents, and thirty three countries (see Exhibit 1). In addition, Club Med has two cruise ships.

This case was prepared by Karen Bartoletti, Alexandra Doiranlis, Steven Kustin, and Sharon Salamon of New York University's Stern School of Business under the supervision of Masaaki Kotabe of The University of Texas at Austin for class discussion rather than to illustrate either effective or ineffective management of a situation described (May 1997).

The Club Med style can be best described by the sense of closeness found among the managers. All managers are former village chiefs and are therefore knowledgeable of the company's everyday operations. This immediately reflects on the "friendly" relationships that the GO's (Club Med-speak for assistants) and GM's (Club Med-speak for guests) have with each other making every vacationer's experience a memorable one. A distinguishing feature of a Club Med resort is the living area, which is much simpler than that of a typical hotel chain. Rooms are sparsely decorated (i.e., no phones, televisions, etc.). This simpler approach has made Club Med very successful. Another key to success was Club Med's image as a place to go when you want to escape. Finally, unlike typical hotel chains, Club Med measures its capacity in each resort by the number of beds, not the number of rooms, since singles have roommates.

INDUSTRY STRUCTURE

Until 1986, Club Med had a very strong position in the all-inclusive resort market. The corporation's level of bargaining power with buyers, suppliers, and labor was high (see Exhibit 2). During that time period a client interested in duplicating "the Club Med experience" would have had to pay an additional 50 percent to 100 percent to have an identical experience at other resorts (see Exhibit 3). With regard to suppliers, companies that provided vacation-related services, such as airlines, were willing to give Club Med significant discounts in exchange for mass-bookings. Finding labor was not a problem for this resort chain because thousands of people were interested in working at such a pleasurable location.

COMPETITION

As of 1986, Club Med began facing competition. This company was no longer the only all-inclusive resort. Many of the firm's competitors were realizing similar success. In 1986, most of the all-inclusive competitors had adopted Club Med's style of recreational activities with staff members acting as directors of these organized games. By then, the only major difference that Club Med maintained was the fact that their price did not include drinks.

Exhibit 1
The Club Méditerranée Group Villages World Wide

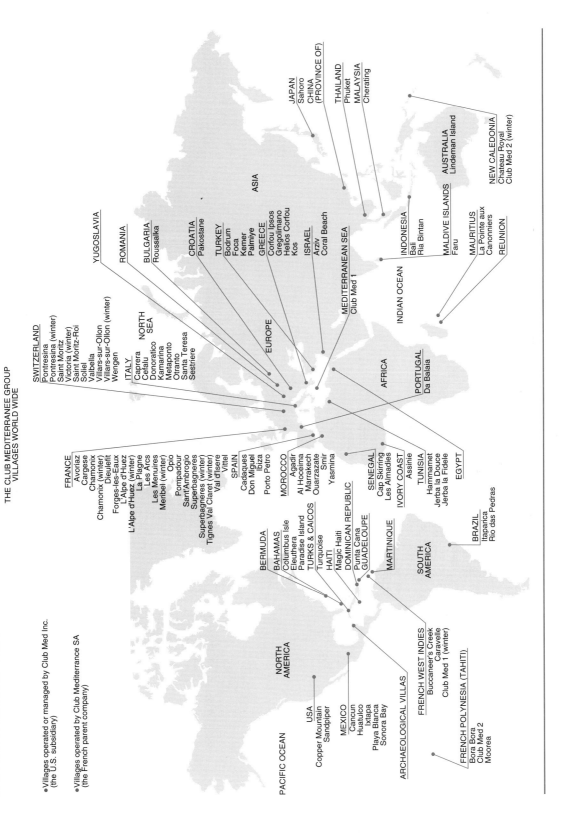

THE CLUB MEDITERRANEE GROUP
VILLAGES WORLD WIDE

• Villages operated or managed by Club Med Inc.
(the U.S. subsidiary)

• Villages operated by Club Mediterrance SA
(the French parent company)

SWITZERLAND
Pontresina
Pontresina (winter)
Saint Moritz
Victoria (winter)
Saint Moritz-Roi
Soliel
Valbella
Villars-sur-Ollon
Villars-sur-Ollon (winter)
Wengen

FRANCE
Avoriaz
Cargese
Chamonix
Chamonix (winter)
Dieulefit
Forges-les-Eaux
L'Alpe d'Huez
L'Alpe d'Huez (winter)
La Plagne
Les Arcs
Les Menuires
Meribel (winter)
Opio
Pompadour
Sant'Ambrogio
Superbagneres
Superbagneres (winter)
Tignes Val Claret (winter)
Val d'Isere
Vittel

ITALY
Caprera
Cefalu
Donoratico
Kamarina
Metaponto
Otranto
Santa Teresa
Sestriere

NORTH SEA

YUGOSLAVIA

ROMANIA

BULGARIA
Roussalka

CROATIA
Pakostane

TURKEY
Bodrum
Foca
Kemer
Palmiye

GREECE
Corfou Ipsos
Gregolimano
Helios Corfou
Kos

ISRAEL
Arziv
Coral Beach

EUROPE

ASIA

MEDITERRANEAN SEA
Club Med 1

AFRICA

PORTUGAL
Da Balaia

INDIAN OCEAN

SPAIN
Cadaques
Don Miguel
Ibiza
Porto Petro

MOROCCO
Agadir
Al Hoceima
Marrakech
Ouarzazate
Smir
Yasmina

SENEGAL
Cap Skirring
Les Almadies

IVORY COAST
Assinie

TUNISIA
Hammamet
Jerba la Douce
Jerba la Fidele

EGYPT

JAPAN
Sahoro

CHINA (PROVINCE OF)

THAILAND
Phuket

MALAYSIA
Cherating

AUSTRALIA
Lindeman Island

NEW CALEDONIA
Chateau Royal
Club Med 2 (winter)

INDONESIA
Bali
Ria Bintan

MALDIVE ISLANDS
Faru

MAURITIUS
La Pointe aux
Canonniers

REUNION

BERMUDA

BAHAMAS
Columbus Isle
Eleuthera
Paradise Island

TURKS & CAICOS
Turquoise

HAITI
Magic Haiti

DOMINICAN REPUBLIC
Punta Cana

GUADELOUPE

MARTINIQUE

SOUTH AMERICA

BRAZIL
Itaparica
Rio das Pedras

NORTH AMERICA

USA
Copper Mountain
Sandpiper

MEXICO
Cancun
Huatulco
Ixtapa
Playa Blanca
Sonora Bay

ARCHAEOLOGICAL VILLAS

FRENCH WEST INDIES
Buccaneer's Creek
Caravelle
Club Med 1 (winter)

FRENCH POLYNESIA (TAHITI)
Bora Bora
Club Med 2
Moorea

PACIFIC OCEAN

649

Exhibit 2
Forces Driving Industry Competition

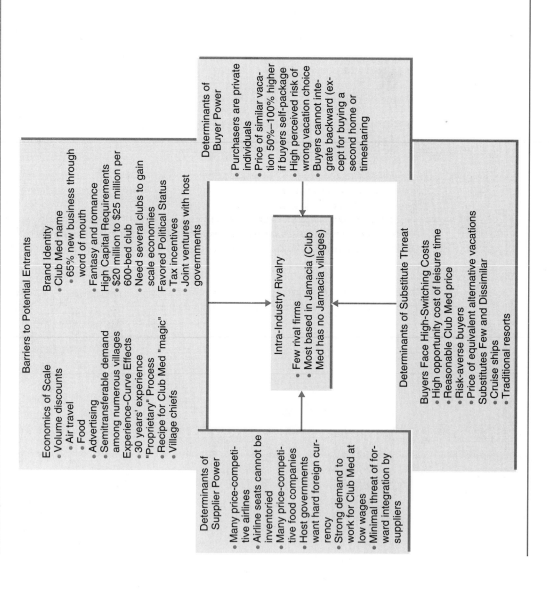

Barriers to Potential Entrants

Economics of Scale
- Volume discounts
  - Air travel
  - Food
  - Advertising
- Semitransferable demand among numerous villages
Experience-Curve Effects
- 30 years' experience
- "Proprietary" Process
- Recipe for Club Med "magic"
- Village chiefs

Brand Identity
- Club Med name
- 65% new business through word of mouth
- Fantasy and romance
High Capital Requirements
- $20 million to $25 million per 600-bed club
- Need several clubs to gain scale economies
Favored Political Status
- Tax incentives
- Joint ventures with host governments

Determinants of Buyer Power
- Purchasers are private individuals
- Price of similar vacation 50%—100% higher if buyers self-package
- High perceived risk of wrong vacation choice
- Buyers cannot integrate backward (except for buying a second home or timesharing

Determinants of Supplier Power
- Many price-competitive airlines
- Airline seats cannot be inventoried
- Many price-competitive food companies
- Host governments want hard foreign currency
- Strong demand to work for Club Med at low wages
- Minimal threat of forward integration by suppliers

Intra-Industry Rivalry
- Few rival firms
- Most based in Jamacia (Club Med has no Jamacia villages)

Determinants of Substitute Threat

Buyers Face High-Switching Costs
- High opportunity cost of leisure time
- Reasonable Club Med price
- Risk-averse buyers
- Price of equivalent alternative vacations
Substitutes Few and Dissimilar
- Cruise ships
- Traditional resorts

EXHIBIT 1
COST COMPARISON

Average costing of a 7-day holiday in Don Miguel	Normal Marbella prices	Typical Club Med holiday
Return airfare London/Malaga	£199	Included
Coach transfer to resort	£20	Included
UK Government departure taxes	£5	Included
Hotel (3 star equivalent) & breakfast	£300	Included
Seven three-course lunches (@ £15)	£105	Included
Wine with lunch & dinner (7 bottles @ £5)	£35	Included
Seven three course dinners (@ £17)	£119	Included
Cycling (6 days @ £5/hr)	£30	Included
Tennis lessons (6 days @ £8/hr)	£48	Included
Night Club entrance (6 X £5)	£30	Included
Tips to staff (7 X £2)	£14	Included
Child care facilities (6 X 4 hrs @ £5/hr)	£120	Included
TOTAL	£1,025	From £569

Other activities/facilities included in the price at Club Med Don Miguel:
Swimming Pool, Circus School, Archery, Weights Room, Keepfit Classes, Specialty Restaurant, Bridge, Evening Entertainment/Shows, Ping Pong, Jacuzzi, Sauna, Hamman.

Other on-site conveniences at Club Med:
Bank, Boutique, Medical Center, Bar(s)-(bar drinks extra cost), Car Rental, Laundry Service.

One competitor, Jack Tar Village, the Jamaica-based company, operates resorts located mostly in the Caribbean. Jack Tar positions the resorts as more glamorous and modern than those of Club Med. This can be seen in advertisements where the company implicitly criticizes the spartan rooms and methods of Club Med. Jack Tar's claim to fame in relation to Club Med is its open bar policy.

Another competitor that the firm must consider is the SuperClubs Organization, which operates four resorts in Jamaica. These resorts have reputations for being the most uninhibited and sexually-oriented resorts. SuperClubs also follow a system of having drinks included in their price, but the other distinction from Club Med is the vacation's packaging and distribution. Club Med bundles the ground transportation with the rest of their packages while air transportation was to be distributed directly to consumers or travel agencies. SuperClubs, on the other hand, bundled ground transportation packages to be sold through large tour wholesalers, who in turn grouped these packages to be sold to the travel agencies.

Activities that Club Med and their competition offer are similar, but the way they are offered is somewhat different. Club med's competitors offer the same activities but do not include them in the initial price of the vacation. A few of SuperClubs activities that were included were tennis, basketball, and exercise rooms, etc., but jet-skiing and parasailing were available for an additional fee. This allowed Club Med's competitors to offer lower prices and take away potential clients from Club Med. This concept has worked for the competition because consumers find that they are not using all the activities offered. Therefore, there is no reason to pay an all-inclusive price. Club Med, on the other hand, suffers from ecological, economical, and political constraints that prevent the firm from using this individual pricing method which could lead to customized packages for vacationers.

THE SERVICE CONCEPT

Club Med has a worldwide presence in the resort vacation business that has allowed the firm to grow and dominate this industry. The original mission statement includes the idea that the company's goal is to take a group of strangers away from their everyday lives and bring them together in a relaxing and fun atmosphere in different parts of the world. This feeling can be expected in any of the 114 re-

sorts. This mission is the key to Club Med's competitive advantage. Consumers anywhere in the world know they will get the same preferential treatment while they are in the Club Med villages.

The company's strategy of keeping members coming back, is carried out by having their guests join a club as members with an initiation fee as well as annual dues. With the membership, they receive newsletters, catalogs featuring their resorts, and discounts on future Club Med vacations. This makes people feel more like a part of the Club Med and creates strong brand loyalty. In fact, an average Club Med vacationer revisits four times after their initial stay at one of its resorts.

All Club Med villages are similar in their setup regardless of what part of the world they are in. The resort sites are carefully chosen by taking into consideration the natural beauty (i.e., scenic views, beachfront, woodland, no swampland, etc.), good weather, and recreational potential. Each resort has approximately 40 acres to accommodate all the planned activities: windsurfing, sailing, basketball, volleyball, tennis, etc. The resorts' secluded atmosphere is further exemplified by the lack of daily "conveniences" such as: TV, clocks, radios, even writing paper. This is done to separate individuals from civilization so they can relax as much as possible.

Club Med organizes everything in a manner that encourages social interaction between guests. The rooms are built around core facilities such as the pool. Meals are done buffet style and the tables seat six to eight people so guests can sit and meet with many different people at every meal.

All activities and meals are included in the fee paid before the vacation begins. The only exceptions are bar drinks and items purchased in the small shops; those items are put on a tab and paid for at the end of the vacation as guests check out. The goal behind this all inclusive price is to limit the amount of financial decisions made by the guests so, once again, they do not have to think of the pressures of the "real world."

Each day the guests have a choice of participating in a variety of activities. As evening sets in there are choices for after dinner activities like dancing and shows. All activities are designed to encourage guests to join in. Even the shows allow for audience participation.

PROBLEMS

Until recently, Club Mediterranee was predicted to have strong sales growth due to successful market penetration in other countries. Now, however, that same expansion which helped the firm become famous may be the cause of the firm's disadvantage in relation to its competitors. Club Med does not have as great of a sales increase as it had anticipated (see Exhibit 4). This is due to economic and ecological disasters in countries where Club Med resorts are located. This makes it difficult for Club Med to maintain its beautiful resorts in countries that suffer from such disasters.

With this knowledge taken into consideration, contracts are drawn up between Club Med and the government of the corresponding country. The key clause in these contracts states that if Club Med is allowed to enter the country, the firm will increase tourism in the area. In turn, the government will provide financial aid to help pay for the costs of maintaining the new resort facilities.

Joint ventures with host governments have proven to be not as profitable as expected. An example of such a disappointment is when the Mexican government agreed to maintain Club Med's facilities if the corporation would increase Mexico's tourism level. However, unexpected occurrences, such as depreciation in the country's currency, limited the amount of capital the Mexican government could allocate to maintain the resort's facilities. This put Club Med in a difficult situation when the firm had to suddenly maintain its facilities with less government funds than expected. Though Club Med's resorts are very profitable in Mexico, the devaluation of the peso has caused Club Med's maintenance costs to rise dramatically. This in turn prevents Club Med from reducing its prices and offering customized packages to its vacationers.

A second example of how international resorts reduce the firm's ability to compete effectively is Club Med's penetration into France. The resorts in the area had been doing well until March 1996. At that time, it became known that France had been conducting nuclear tests in the South Pacific. This caused Club Mediterranee to receive less bookings than expected in its Tahiti-based resorts. These resorts were avoided by tourists due to riots among residents concerned about the testing; this resulted in negative publicity in this part of the world. The riots, which occurred often in airports, deterred potential tourists from flying into this region.

The effects in one area where Club Med is based often indirectly affect other Club Med resorts as well. With a lower clientele in its Tahiti-based resorts, and in the surrounding territories, Club Med experiences lower revenues and, therefore, acquires less money to maintain these resorts. As a result, the firm compensates for such losses by using the profits from other resorts that have not suffered from similar disasters. Problems such as these prevent Club Med from reducing prices by

EXHIBIT 4
CLUB MÉDITERRANÉE S.A.

Club Mediterranee manages 140 resort villages in Mediterranean, snow, inland, and tropical locales in 35 countries. Its resorts do business under the Club Med, Valtur, Club Med Affaires (for business travelers), and Club Aquarius brand names. Club Mediterranee also operates tours and 2 cruise liners: *Club Med 1* cruises the Caribbean and the Mediterranean, and *Club Med 2* sails the Pacific. The company also arranges specialized sports facilities. Club Mediterranee's clientele is about 1/3 French, with the rest being mainly from North America and Japan.

Address:	Club Mediterranee S.A.
	11, rue de Cambrai
	Paris, NY 10019
Web Site:	http://www.clubmed.com
Phone:	+33-1-53-35-35-53
Fax:	+33-1-53-35-36-16
CEO:	Philippe Bourguignon
HR:	Franck Guegen
Ticker Symbol:	CLMDY
Exchange:	OTC
Fiscal Year End:	10/31
Sales Year:	1995
Sales (millions $):	1733.57
1-Yr. Sales Change:	1.73%

implementing a customized travel package, which would enable the firm to compete more effectively in the vacation resort market.

WHAT LIES AHEAD?

Club Med has been able to hold a large percentage of the all-inclusive resort market throughout the years. But with its continued growth in the number of its resorts and the amount of competition the firm faces, Club Med is now confronted with a marketing problem that it had not known in the past. The vast array of resorts that made Club Med famous have recently caused the firm to be subjected to a great amount of financial difficulty. In the past, Club Med has kept its all-inclusive pricing strategy throughout the years because it could afford to. Now, however, the organization must be willing to change with the times, because its competition can offer these similar services for a lower price.

Club Med currently has the advantage of being a well known company that provides a relaxing atmosphere time and time again. Now, however, the firm needs to move to the next level—instead of keeping sales steady, the managers must increase the level of their sales revenues. Merely maintaining the current sales levels will not increase profits. As of 1997, the company's sales are flat, which means that a decrease in sales is not far away. The managers of this firm must compensate for losses in one village with gains in another village. At the same time they need to develop a pricing strategy that attracts new clients while consistently keeping current clients coming back for the Club Med experience.

Former Club Med Sales president Jean Michel Landau is sure that Club Med is unique in what it has to offer and that there is a positive future for Club Med as a whole. "We are sure our concept is totally different from other all-inclusives. Many try to come close to our concept. They can improve on what we do with rooms and so on, but we have a real concept at Club Med. With our G.O, Gentils Organiseurs team, with the international aspects and the high quality, I think it will be a real battle. . . . We have to show the consumer we are different, that we have to be the best product and the best brand in the market."

◆ ◆

CASE 9

FORD MOTOR COMPANY AND DIE DEVELOPMENT

INTRODUCTION

Since the mid-1980s American companies have been altering their game to play Japanese-style. Major U.S. corporations started to revamp their corporate cultures recasting their investment practices to form cooperative links both vertically, down their supply lines, and horizontally, with universities, research labs, and their peers. By streamlining their lumbering corporate hierarchies, Corporate America has been emulating the Japanese by focusing on teamwork, quality and speed, and cost reduction. This new industrial pattern is called *American-style keiretsu*.

The automobile industry was no exception to this pattern, being deeply influenced by the Japanese approach. Along with the frustration of American manufacturers at being overtaken by Japanese auto manufacturers, the automobile industry in the U.S. received an additional source of inspiration for change. In a book called *The Machine that Changed the World*, based on the Massachusetts Institute of Technology (MIT) 5-million dollar, 5-year study on the future of the automobile industry in the late 1980s, researchers found that manufacturers of North America and Europe were relying on techniques that changed little since Henry Ford's mass-production system created in the 1920s. Given the state of the industry and the rapid gain in market share of Japanese companies, the MIT study concluded that American techniques were simply not competitive with a new set of ideas pioneered by the Japanese. Lean production, the Japanese approach, must supplant mass production in all areas of industrial endeavor to become the standard global production system of the twenty-first century.

One of the automobile manufacturers that represented a model of *keiretsu* was Toyota Motor Corp. of Japan, one of the 24 companies in the Mitsui Group. Toyota has been a tough competitor in the industry since its approach, mostly based on internal manufacturing capabilities built around its vertical *keiretsu*, known as the Toyota Group, has allowed the company to introduce its new

Professor Masaaki Kotabe of The University of Texas at Austin Graduate School of Business, Hiroshi Domoto of Mitsubishi Research Institute, Japan, and Marcelo F. Perez of New York University's Leonard N. Stern School of Business prepared this case as the basis for class discussion rather than to illustrate either effective or ineffective management of a situation described.

car designs into showrooms in four years as opposed to five to eight for US and European manufacturers. Along with *keiretsu*, the notion of target costing was a key concept implemented by most Japanese manufacturers like Toyota and Nissan Motor Company. Under this approach, manufacturers adjust costs to a target level in order to reduce prices and keep their current profit margin per unit. Under the markup approach (followed by U.S. manufacturers) any increase in costs would derive in higher prices, making American automobiles more expensive (see Exhibit 1).

RELATIONSHIP WITH SUPPLIERS

In the late 1980s **Ford Motor Company,** the manufacturer of automobiles, trucks and related parts and accessories, began to rearrange its supplier system to a pyramid structure, whose shape is similar to Japan's famed vertical *keiretsu* (see Exhibit 2 for Ford's financial statements). Bob May, vice president of corporate procurement, and Bill Cunningham, vice president of marketing operations, are in charge of managing the sourcing strategy for Ford.

In the past, Ford's relationship with suppliers was built under the same characteristics of the typical U.S. system, in which a large number of suppliers, most of them with few engineering capabilities, dealt directly with assembly makers on the basis of short-term contracts, with limited interaction, communication and information exchange. On the contrary, the Japanese supplier system built under a tiered structure emphasizes long-term relationships by encouraging the share of information about new procedures and products between assemblers and suppliers (see Appendix for differences between the U.S. and Japanese supplier system). Bob May and Bill Cunningham were aware of the differences.

In its *keiretsu* efforts, these executives at Ford reduced the number of its first-tier suppliers and positioned some of those suppliers as second- or third-tier suppliers, as Exhibit 3 shows. Thus, Ford can more easily control its first-tier suppliers and get them further involved in its operation.

THE DIE BUSINESS

For any car manufacturer, the development and setting of a die represents a major component in the whole process of designing and assembling an automobile. Although most car makers have in-house facilities to meet their die

EXHIBIT 1
HOW THE JAPANESE KEEP COSTS LOW

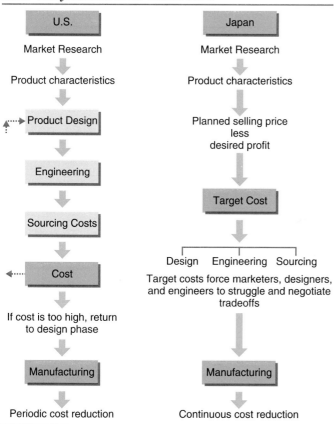

Source: Fortune, August 12, 1991.

set requirements, only a few independent suppliers can compete with these die shops in quality, development time, and cost.

Getting a particular die developer involved in product engineering is beneficial to auto assemblers. Die development for body panels, a complex sequence of information processing activities that extends from clay models and line drawings to stamping dies made of steel, is a major part of process engineering. The die development process is not just an exercise on paper; die engineers need to act on the information they receive and make commitments before product development work is officially complete. If an auto maker hopes to reduce lead time and to lower the cost of engineering changes on a project, a die maker with outstanding performance should be involved in the project.

As mentioned, the U.S. automakers have produced many parts in-house, in part due to union resistance to

shifting the work to external suppliers. But under pressure to hold down costs, the U.S. companies are buying more from outside suppliers. This has been a blessing to competitive die suppliers such as Ogihara Corporation.

Ogihara Corporation, a Japanese company, leads the die manufacturing business for the automotive market and is the largest die maker in the world. Ogihara is especially indispensable to those assemblers lacking capacities to develop the die set for large and complex body panel (e.g., a quarter panel or door) in a short period of time. Time-to-market is a crucial determinant of marketing success today.

Originally focused on supplying its die products only to Japanese car manufacturers, Ogihara started an international expansion in the mid-1970s. In 1984 Ogihara established a U.S. subsidiary, Ogihara American Corporation (OAC) in Howell, Michigan, extending its business from die development to stamping (see Exhibit 4).

EXHIBIT 2 FORD MOTOR COMPANY
FINANCIAL SUMMARY 1985–1995

	1985	1986	1987	1988	1989	1990	1991	1992	1993	1994	1995
Automotive											
Sales	52,915	62,868	71,797	82,193	82,879	81,844	72,051	84,407	91,588	107,137	110,496
Operating Income	2,902	4,142	6,256	6,612	4,252	316	(3,769)	(1,775)	1,432	5,826	3,281
Net Income	2,012	2,512	3,767	4,609	3,175	99	(3,186)	(8,628)	1,008	3,913	2,056
Financial Services											
Revenues	4,700	6,826	8,096	10,253	13,267	15,806	16,235	15,725	16,953	21,302	26,641
Net Income	504	773	858	691	660	761	928	1,243	1,521	1,395	2,083
Total Company Net Income	2,516	3,285	4,625	5,300	3,835	860	(2,258)	(7,385)	2,529	5,308	4,139
Total Assets	75,094	93,232	115,994	143,366	160,893	173,663	174,429	180,545	198,938	219,622	243,283
Long Term Debt	16,212	21,595	28,067	32,113	38,921	45,332	50,219	49,437	54,984	65,207	73,734
Stockholder's Equity	12,269	14,860	18,493	21,529	22,728	23,238	22,690	14,753	15,574	21,659	24,547
Vehicle Factory Sales (in thousands of units)											
Total Cars and Trucks in North America (1)	3,585	3,876	4,040	4,313	4,131	3,632	3,212	3,893	4,131	4,591	4,279
Total Cars and Trucks outside North America	1,966	2,075	2,131	2,349	2,477	2,391	2,411	2,047	2,053	2,262	2,327
Total Worldwide—cars and trucks	5,551	5,951	6,171	6,662	6,608	6,023	5,623	5,940	6,184	6,853	6,606
Total Worldwide—tractors	84	68	64	77	72	66	13	—	—	—	—
Total Worldwide—factory sales	5,635	6,019	6,235	6,739	6,680	6,089	5,636	5,940	6,184	6,853	6,606

Source: Ford Motor Company Annual Reports

(1) US, Canada and Mexico

EXHIBIT 3

FORD'S REARRANGEMENT OF SUPPLIERS

Assembly Maker:
Ford

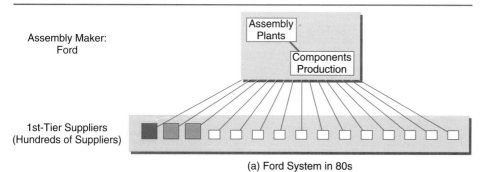

1st-Tier Suppliers
(Hundreds of Suppliers)

(a) Ford System in 80s

Assembly Maker:
Ford

1st-Tier Suppliers
(120 Suppliers)

2nd-Tier Suppliers

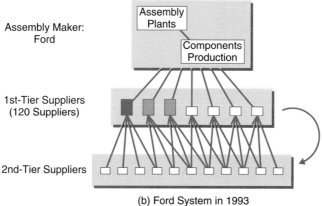

(b) Ford System in 1993

Assembly Maker:
Ford

1st-Tier Suppliers
(60 Suppliers)

2nd-Tier Suppliers

3rd-Tier and 4th-Tier
Suppliers

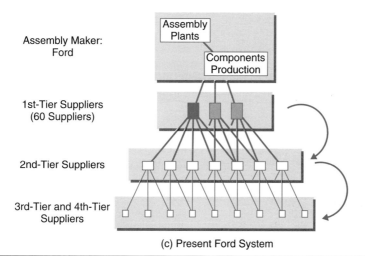

(c) Present Ford System

EXHIBIT 4
MAIN COMPANIES OF OGIHARA GROUP (IN 1994)

Name	Nation	Establishment	Capital (In Thousands)	Employee	Main Business Fields
Ogihara Corporation	Japan	1951	133,650 Yen	820	• Die Development • Jig Production
Ogihara Seiki Co., Ltd.	Japan	1965	10,140 Yen	170	• Die Development • Jig Production
Ogihara Kohki Co., Ltd.	Japan	1968	5,000 Yen	130	• Die Development
Ogihara Machining Service Co., Ltd.	Japan	1981	100,000 Yen	55	• Die Development
Ogihara Technical Center	Japan	1989	100,000 Yen	65	• Design Engineering
Japan Metal Co., Ltd.	Japan	1981	50,000 Yen	48	• Casting
Ogihara America Corporation	USA	1984	22,000 US $	458	• Stamping • Subassembly
Ogihara (Thailand) Company	Thailand	1989	186,000 Baht	190	• Die Development • Jig Production
China Ogihara Corporation	Taiwan	1990	347,000 NT Dollars	190	• Die Development • Stamping
Ogihara Europe Corporation	UK	1985	–	–	
Ogihara Beijing Office	China	1985	–	–	

Source: Ogihara Annual Report, 1994

The move proved to be successful. Based on its competitive strengths—the die expertise accumulated through experience bolstered by rapid market growth, the ability to cover all aspects of the die manufacturing process: starting the master model manufacture, die design, iron casting die construction, assembly of Body-in-White, construction of car body assembly lines and manufacture of pressings and subassemblies—Ogihara established trust and relationships with a large number of automobile manufacturers. Ford Motor Company was among them as well as European automakers. In fact, Mercedes-Benz, the German luxury carmaker, started building in North America its new four-wheel-drive sport-utility (the M-Series) with 100% of Ogihara's dies in 1997.

FORD'S RELATIONSHIP WITH OGIHARA

In 1986 Ford's Wixom Factory, the facility that produced the Lincoln model, awarded a large die stamping order to OAC, becoming the first independent stamping company with its corporate base in Japan to win a contract for major body stampings from any of the Big Four US automakers.

Ogihara Japan was able to provide Ford with a die set for the stamping of Ford Lincoln Continental at OAC's facility in Howell, Michigan. To do so, OAC completed Phase I installation in December 1986, setting up one tandem line and two transfer processes for stamping automotive body parts. Through these lines, OAC began produc-

tion of panels for Ford's Lincoln Continental in September of 1987. Then, OAC also started to stamp the panels for Mazda cars assembled in the United States.

These large orders were the lifeblood to improve productivity. To satisfy strict requirements, Ford encouraged OAC to be enthusiastically involved in the product development process and to make various proposals to improve productivity. As Ford gained OAC trust, OAC has relied more on Ford. As a result, Ford began to use OAC not only to produce panel stamping for other models, but also to assemble some auto body parts. Furthermore, Japanese staff often visits OAC, in order to maintain face-to-face contact and close communication in the die development process between Ogihara Japan and Ford.

In December 1988, OAC completed its Phase II expansion plan to produce Ford Lincoln Towncar panels and installed a new tandem line. In December 1991, OAC completed the Phase III expansion plan for the production of Ford Lincoln Mark VIII and added yet another tandem line. During this period, as Ford gradually shifted its panel orders to OAC from Budd, its German supplier, the Japanese company became one of the two or three largest independent suppliers of major steel body stampings to Ford in the U.S. in terms of parts numbers.

On December 14, 1994, Ford's Jaguar division sold a stamping factory in Telford, UK to Ogihara. It is very rare for an auto parts supplier to acquire a whole process in an auto manufacturer's plant. Ford intends to subcontract die development and panel stamping for Jaguar to Ogihara's plant in the UK.

By 1995 Ford depended on only three suppliers, Ogihara, Carmax (a Canadian supplier), and Budd, for its large-scale panel stamping. Virtually all body and structural stampings in the new sports sedans were purchased from die-stamping companies. Bob May was quite happy about this accomplishment as a corporate procurement executive.

DIE AND PRODUCT DEVELOPMENT

While many parts makers were removed from Ford's first-tier, Ogihara Japan and OAC succeeded in establishing a strong relationship with Ford.

Under the leadership of Bob May and Bill Cunningham, Ford has actively built closer reciprocal commitments with such a high-performing die developer group, Ogihara Japan and OAC, in order to improve the product development performance. Thanks to Bill Cunningham's involvement, customer inputs on product features and design were more effectively reflected in the product design process. It was not until Ogihara Japan and OAC were involved in Ford's product engineering that Ford was able to effectively reduce die lead time, which is the critical path in the product development process. Exhibit 5(a)–(c) summarize the pattern of engineering activities associated with development of die set for a large and complex body panels. Figure 3(a) shows the timing chart of a typical Japanese process. Japanese auto makers spend about 26 months in developing a die. Furthermore, most die sets for Japanese assemblers are manufactured in their in-house die facilities. In the case of a compact car produced by Subaru, the in-house rate of die set reaches about 80 percent. For comparison the timing chart of the past Ford Lincoln is illustrated in Figure 3(b).

On the previous development process, Ford had negotiated arm's length contracts with separate companies to carry out different manufacturing steps (e.g., molding suppliers for models, casting specialists for casting, machine shops for cutting and finishing, and jig suppliers for jigs). Such fragmentation made it difficult to conduct die making steps in parallel and thereby compress manufacturing lead time. Furthermore, managing many suppliers complicated Ford's engineering organization and made coordination within the company difficult.

Moreover, Ford lacked smooth communication flows between upstream and downstream operations (e.g., product engineering and die development). The product engineers in Ford were not encouraged to take manufacturability considerations into account, which imposes a greater problem-solving burden on downstream process. At Ford, upstream and downstream processes were serially conducted, and information flows were unilateral

from upstream to downstream; the designers of Ford had "throw-it-over-the-wall" mentality.

However, Ogihara Japan and OAC helped Ford create intensive communications between upstream and downstream. Since involved in product engineering, Ogihara Japan and OAC have frequently made counterproposals to Ford's product engineers. Ford has also accepted active and continuous flows of feedback information from the Ogihara Group. This pattern is typical of traditional auto development projects among Japanese firms. The early involvement is not just starting earlier; it is the exchange of information and insight to prevent problems before they become a die-development problem. The downstream (Ogihara) "front loads" information to the upstream (Ford) before it starts development. This helps Ford to "do it right the first time" and affords Ogihara earlier exposure to product designs and specifications, further reducing problem-solving lead.

As a result, Ogihara Japan and OAC, although geographically separated, have been able to offer Ford a vertical package from die-development, including planning and design, to stamping. What is even more important, the two companies' computers are linked permanently via satellite communications to exchange and design data and modifications.

This relationship between Ford and Ogihara has helped Ford reduce lead-time by integrating and overlapping some steps in the die development chart. To the extent that Ogihara accumulates expertise to develop a particular die set for the Lincoln models, Ford can benefit from better design quality and lower cost. This accumulation of engineering expertise becomes a competitive edge to Ford. Additionally, having one source for both die-development and stamping facilitates knowledge exchange between the two stages. Ogihara is able to detect potential production problems early on and thereby improve component quality.

Ford had spent ten more months in developing their die set than the average Japanese makers until getting Ogihara involved in its product engineering. As Ford has increased its reliance on Ogihara Japan and OAC, the time required to develop die set has gradually decreased. Ford has skillfully learned Japanese style die development process from Ogihara Japan and OAC, as well as successfully had Ogihara Japan and OAC participate in its product engineering. Therefore, as shown in Figure 3(c), Ford has been able to compress the development cycle by quickly constructing prototypes and dies, and by boldly overlapping product engineering and die construction.

However, Bob May, in particular, is aware of potential problems in this relationship. By increasing its dependence on Ogihara for its product design process, Ford may not only lose some bargaining power. While managing the long-term relationship with Ogihara, Ford must carefully control pricing for die set or stamping. But losing engineering expertise in die development also may make Ford

EXHIBIT 5(a)
TIMING CHART OF DIE DEVELOPMENT: A TYPICAL JAPANESE CASE

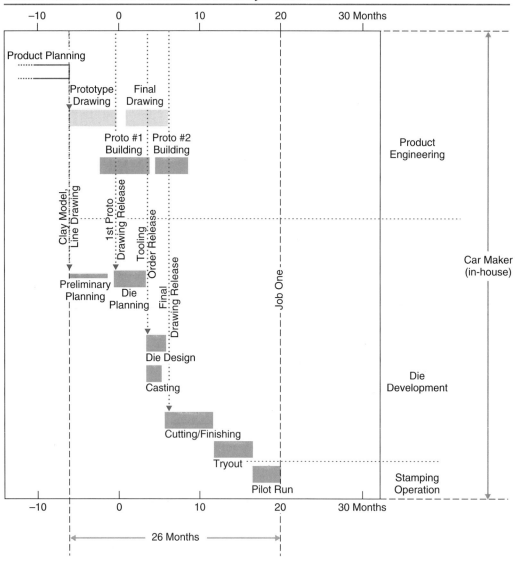

vulnerable in this key capability in the long term. Bill Cunningham does not agree with Bob May's concern.

CHALLENGE IN THE FUTURE

Along with the changes in its relationship with suppliers implemented since the late 1980s, Ford has renewed its effort to reduce costs and increase efficiency. In January 1995 the company announced the launching of a globalization project called Ford 2000, in which product divisions around the world were consolidated to share capa-

bilities and resources, with an estimated cost savings of $3 billion a year. Under this project, Ford wants to build a worldwide relationship with a smaller group of suppliers, reducing their number to only one-third of those currently used. The project is expected also to rationalize more than 200 different systems for parts numbering, purchasing and dealing with suppliers, so that the same rules apply in every division, factory or region.

In 1996 the relationship between Ford and Ogihara seemed to be at its highest point, increasing Ford's dependence on Ogihara Japan and OAC for its product development process each year. Ford awarded additional long-

Exhibit 5(b)
Timing Chart of Die Development: Ford Lincoln (Past)

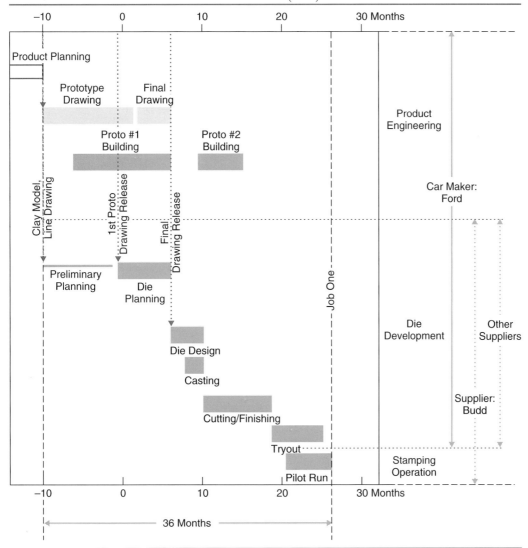

term contracts to Ogihara for its Lincoln division. At the same time, Ford provided Ogihara with its prospective engineering technologies in return for Ogihara's strong commitment to product engineering. Today, Ford allows Ogihara to join in certain R & D efforts and requires Ogihara to focus not on specific components, but on the total vehicle.

QUESTIONS

1. For Bill Cunningham, responsible for the planning and the implementation of global strategic actions,

how would the changes into a keiretsu-style relationship with suppliers in the industry as a whole, and in Ford in particular, have affected his task?

2. Given the current relationship between Ford and Ogihara, what are the main strategic implications for Ford in the short and long run? And why do Bill Cunningham and Bob May have different opinions?

3. Would you consider that Ford should keep the terms of its relationship with Ogihara as they are, or would you introduce some changes to it? If so, what are your specific recommendations?

Exhibit 5(c)
Timing Chart of Die Development: Ford Lincoln (Present)

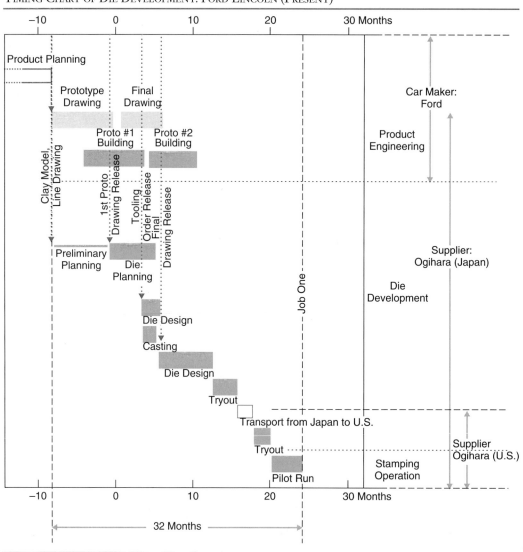

Appendix

Differences between the U.S. and Japanese Supplier Systems

In the 1980s, the U.S. and Japanese supplier systems used to stand in sharp contrast. The difference that is caused by the Japanese long-term business relationship enables more suppliers to hold engineering capability than the U.S. system.

The traditional U.S. system is characterized by a large number of suppliers that deal directly with assembly makers on the basis of short-term contracts. Except for a few highly capable firms, U.S. suppliers have little engineering capability, and because supplier-OEM relationships are treated as a zero-some game (i.e., you win, I lose), communication and interaction occur at arm's length and parties behave as adversaries. Information exchange is limited to prices and data on requirements and specifications. Suppliers are effectively treated as a source of manufacturing capacity; auto companies establish requirements and play suppliers off against one another in a contest for one-year contracts.

The Japanese supplier system has a tiered structure and emphasizes long-term relationships. The "first-tier" suppliers in the Japanese system are more deeply involved in the assemble makers' development-process and are provided with more information about the product and process than in the U.S. system. Therefore, suppliers can share much information about new product with the assemblers, as well as have an engineering capability.

Furthermore, the commitment and reciprocity between assemblers and suppliers in the Japanese system tend to enclose the first-tier suppliers in a particular *keiretsu* structure. Japanese assemblers are willing to give their suppliers information about a new product. However, the basic design and styling idea may leak to competitors through suppliers. Thus, they grant their suppliers long-term guarantees but request these suppliers to be affiliated with a single car maker system.

CASE 10

PHARMA SWEDE: GASTIRUP

Early in 1990, Bjorn Larsson, advisor to the president and the head of Product Pricing and Government Relations for Pharma Swede, in Stockholm, Sweden, was reviewing the expected consequences of "1992" on Gastirup in Italy. Gastirup was a drug for the treatment of ulcers. Since its introduction in Italy in 1984, this innovative product had achieved considerable success in its category of gastrointestinal drugs. However, the success had come as a result of pricing the drug at a significant discount below the prevailing prices for the same product in the rest of Europe. Higher prices would have disqualified Gastirup from the government reimbursement scheme, the system by which the state health insurance agency reimbursed patients for pharmaceutical expenditures. The government-negotiated prices for Gastirup in Italy were 46% below the average European price.

Bjorn Larsson was concerned that, with the anticipated removal of all trade barriers in Europe, Gastirup would fall victim to massive parallel trading from Italy to the higher-priced countries in the region. Furthermore, with the increased coordination among government health insurance agencies, also foreseen in the years following 1992, price differences among EEC countries were expected to narrow. This likely development highlighted the need for a consistent policy throughout Europe.

As head of Product Pricing and Government Relations, it was Bjorn Larsson's responsibility to recommend the actions that top corporate and local Italian management should take to avert potential annual losses for Gastirup, projected in the $20–$30 million range. Among alternatives being considered, the most extreme was to forego the large and growing Italian market altogether and concentrate the product's sales elsewhere in Europe. The Italian market for Gastirup had grown to $27 million in recent years and accounted for 22% of European sales. Another option was to remove Gastirup from the Italian government reimbursement scheme by raising the prices to levels close to those prevailing in the higher-priced

countries. This action would most likely reduce the drug's sales in Italy by as much as 80%. Still another alternative was to take legal action in the European Court of Justice against the Italian government's reimbursement scheme and the related price negotiations as barriers to free trade. Finally, the company could take a "wait and see" attitude, postponing any definitive action to a time when the impact of "1992" was better known.

COMPANY BACKGROUND

Pharma Swede was formed in 1948 in Stockholm, Sweden; it concentrated solely in pharmaceuticals. In 1989, the company employed over 2,000 people and earned $50 million on sales of $750 million, distributed among its three product lines: Hormones (20%), Gastrointestinal (50%), and Vitamins (30%). Gastirup belonged to the gastrointestinal product category and, as of 1989, accounted for roughly $120 million of Pharma Swede's sales. (see Exhibit 1 for a breakdown of Pharma Swede's sales.)

International Activities and Organization

As of December 1989, Pharma Swede had wholly-owned subsidiaries in 11 countries in Western Europe, where it generated 90% of its sales. The balance of sales came from small operations in the United States, Australia and Japan.

Due to high research and development costs as well as stringent quality controls, Pharma Swede centralized all R & D and production of active substances in Stockholm. Partly as a result of these headquarters functions, 60% of the company's expenditures were in Sweden, a country that represented only 15% of sales. However, the politics of national health care often required the company to

This case was prepared by Professor Kamran Kashani, with the assistance of Research Associate Robert C. Howard, as a basis for class discussion rather than to illustrate either effective or ineffective handling of a business situation. This case was developed with the cooperation of a company that wishes to remain anonymous. As a result, certain names, figures and facts have been modified. Copyright © 1991 by the International Institute for Management Development (IMD), Lausanne, Switzerland. Not to be used or reproduced without permission.

EXHIBIT 1
PHARMA SWEDE (SALES IN $ MILLIONS)

Product Line	1987	1988	1989
Hormones	90	130	150
Vitamins	175	205	225
Gastrointestinal	200	290	375
Total	465	625	750

have some local production. Consequently, a number of Pharma Swede's subsidiaries blended active substances produced in Sweden with additional compounds and packaged the finished product.

Pharma Swede had a product management organization for drugs on the market (refer to Exhibit 2). For newly developed drugs, product management did not begin until the second phase of clinical trials, when decisions were made as to where the new products would be introduced and how. (Refer to Exhibit 3 for the different phases of a new product's development.) Besides country selection, product management at headquarters examined different positioning and price scenarios, and determined drug dosages and forms. It had the final say on branding and pricing decisions, as well as basic drug information, including the package leaflet that described a drug's usage and possible side effects. As one product manager explained, the marketing department in Stockholm developed a drug's initial profile and estimated its potential market share worldwide. However, it was up to local management to adapt that profile to their own market.

As an example, in 1982 headquarters management positioned Gastirup against the leading anti-ulcer remedy, Tomidil, by emphasizing a better quality of life and 24-hour protection from a single tablet. To adapt the product to their market, the Italian management, with the approval of Stockholm, changed the name to Gastiros and developed a local campaign stressing the drug's advantages over Tomidil, the oral tablet which had to be taken two or three times a day.

As a rule, headquarters limited its involvement in local markets. It saw its role as one of providing technical or managerial assistance to country management who were responsible for profit and loss.

Product Pricing and Government Relations

The Product Pricing and Government Relations department located at the headquarters, was a recently established function within the company. It prepared guidelines for subsidiary management to use in negotiating drug pricing and patient reimbursement policies with local government agencies. The department was divided into Government Relations and Product Pricing. Those in Government Relations followed ongoing political events and prepared negotiating positions on such issues as employment creation through local production.

The role of Product Pricing, headed by Bjorn Larsson, was to determine the "optimum" price for new products. An optimum price, Bjorn explained, was not necessarily a high price, but a function of price-volume relationships in each market. An optimum price also reflected the cost of alternatives, including competitive products and alternative treatments like surgery, and the direct and indirect costs of non-treatment to society and the government. Each of these criteria helped to quantify a product's cost-effectiveness or, as government authorities saw it, its treatment value for money.

Using cost effectiveness data in price negotiations was a recent development in the pharmaceutical industry and corresponded to the increasing cost consciousness among public health authorities. Economic exercises which were initially performed in Stockholm to measure a drug's treatment and socioeconomic benefits were repeated with local authorities during negotiations. In Bjorn Larsson's opinion, the latest measure of "non-treatment cost" was becoming an important factor. He explained that a thorough understanding of the direct and indirect costs of an illness had come to play a key role in whether or not

EXHIBIT 2
PHARMA SWEDE PARTIAL ORGANIZATION CHART

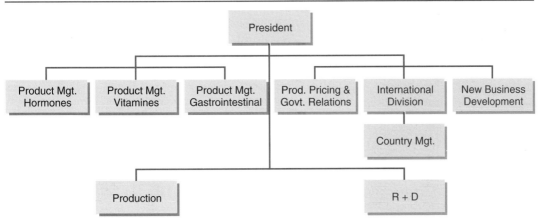

EXHIBIT 3
PHARMA SWEDE THE DEVELOPMENT OF A NEW DRUG

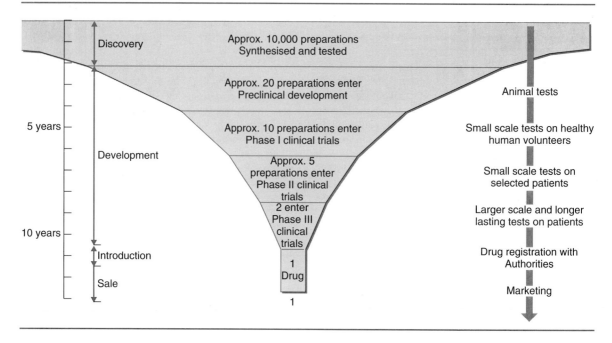

a government was willing to pay for a product by granting it reimbursement status, as well as the magnitude of that reimbursement. According to industry observers, the task of marketing to governmental agencies had become crucial in recent years as public agencies were scrutinizing drug prices more carefully. (Refer to Exhibit 4 for an overview and further description of Product Pricing and Government Relations.)

THE PHARMACEUTICAL INDUSTRY

As of 1989, approximately 10,000 companies worldwide competed in the $180 billion pharmaceutical industry. Industry sales were concentrated in North America, Western Europe and Japan, with the 100 largest companies in these areas accounting for nearly 80 percent of all revenues. Western Europe alone accounted for an estimated 25 percent of total volume.

The industry classified pharmaceutical products according to how they were sold and their therapeutic status. In the first instance, pharmaceutical sales were classified into two categories, ethical and over-the-counter (OTC). Ethical drugs, with four-fifths of all pharmaceutical sales worldwide and a 10% annual growth rate, could only be purchased with a doctor's prescription. These drugs were branded or were sold as a generic when original patents had expired. OTC drugs were purchased without a prescription; they included both branded and generic medi-

cines such as aspirin, cough syrups and antacids. At Pharma Swede, ethical drugs accounted for more than 90% of total sales.

Ethical drugs were also classified into therapeutic categories, of which gastrointestinal was the second largest, representing 15% of industry sales. Within the gastrointestinal category there were a number of smaller segments, such as anti-ulcer drugs, used to control and treat digestive tract ulcers, anti-diarrhoeas and laxatives. In 1989, the ethical anti-ulcer drug segment was valued at $7 billion worldwide and growing at 18 percent a year, faster than the total prescription market.

Trends in Europe

In parallel with worldwide trends, several factors were expected to play a role in shaping the future of the European pharmaceutical industry. Among these were an aging population, rising R & D and marketing costs, greater competition from generics, and government cost controls.

Aging Population. Europe's stagnating population was gradually aging. The segment of the population over 55 years old was forecast to grow and account for between 33 percent and 40 percent of the total by the year 2025—up from below 25 percent in the mid-1980s. During the same period, the segment below 30 years of age was forecast to drop from about 40 percent to 30 percent. The "graying

Exhibit 4
PHARMA SWEDE: PRODUCT PRICING AND GOVERNMENT RELATIONS

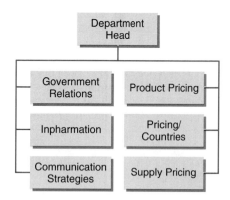

The Government Relations Group observed and recognized potential political problems for the division. When necessary, the group developed counterstrategies and oversaw their implementation.

Inpharmation gathered and managed all pharmapolitical information, on both a national and international basis.

The Communication Strategies group advised the division on product strategies and proposed communications programs.

During drug development, the Product Pricing group worked to secure drug registration, using economic and social data.

Pricing/Countries oversaw and helped build a favorable negotiating environment for pricing decisions.

Supply Pricing was responsible for administering prices and managing relationships with Pharma Swede's distributors.

Source: Company Records

of Europe" was expected to have two lasting effects on drug consumption. First, low growth was projected in the sales of drugs normally used by children or young adults. Second, drug companies marketing products for age-related diseases, such as cancer, hypertension and heart ailments, could expect growing demand.

Rising R & D and Marketing Costs. Research and development expenses included the cost of identifying a new molecule and all the tests required for bringing that molecule to the market.

Generally, for every 10,000 molecules synthesized and tested, only one made it through the clinical trials to appear in the market. Product development costs were estimated to average $120 million per drug, from preclinical research to market introduction. Industry estimates for research and development expenses averaged around 15 percent of sales in the late 1980s, with some companies spending as much as 20 percent of sales on new drugs. Research in more complex diseases like cancer, as well

as lengthy clinical trials and government registration processes, had raised these costs recently.

Marketing costs had also increased due to a general rise in the level of competition in the industry. In the early-1980s, pharmaceutical firms spent, on average, 31 percent of sales on marketing and administrative costs. By 1987, the ratio had increased to 35 percent and was still rising. Some companies were reported to have spent unprecedented sums of $50–60 million on marketing to introduce a new drug.

Growth of Generics. Generic drugs were exact copies of existing branded products for which the original patent had expired. *Generics*, as these drugs were known, were priced substantially lower than their originals, and were usually marketed by some other firm than the inventor. Price differences between the branded and generics could be as large as 10-to-1. Depending on the drug categories, generics represented between 5 percent and 25 percent of the value of the total prescription drug market in Europe,

and their share was expected to grow. For example, in the UK, sales of generic drugs had grown to represent an estimated 15 percent of the total National Health Budget and were forecast to reach 25 percent by 1995. In line with efforts to contain costs, governments in many parts of Europe were putting increased pressure on physicians to prescribe generics instead of the more expensive branded drugs.

Government Role. Governments were one of the strongest forces influencing the pharmaceutical industry in Europe where, in conjunction with public and private insurance agencies, they paid an average of two-thirds of health care costs. In Italy, for example, 64 percent of all ethical pharmaceutical expenditures were covered by the public health care system. In Germany, France and the UK, the respective shares were 57 percent, 65 percent, and 75 percent. These ratios had risen considerably throughout the 1960s and 1970s.

European governments were facing two opposing pressures: to maintain high levels of medical care while trying to reduce the heavy burden placed on the budget for such expenditures. Influence on pharmaceutical pricing, according to industry experts, had become an increasingly political as well as economic issue.

Not surprisingly, government agencies seeking to reduce health insurance costs increasingly encouraged the use of generics. In fact, before the advent of generics and official interventions, well-known branded drugs which had lost their patents in the 1970s, such as Librium or Valium, often maintained up to 80 percent of their sales for several years. In contrast, by the late 1980s, it was more likely that a drug would lose nearly 50 percent of its sales within two years after its patent expired.

GASTIRUP

Ulcers and Their Remedies

Under circumstances not completely understood, gastric juices—consisting of acid, pepsin and various forms of mucous—could irritate the membrane lining the stomach and small intestine, often producing acute ulcers. In serious cases, known as peptic ulcers, damage extended into the wall of the organ causing chronic inflammation and bleeding. Middle-aged men leading stressful lives were considered a high-risk group for ulcers.

Ulcers were treated by four types of remedies: antacids, H-2 inhibitors, anticholinergics, and surgery. Antacids, containing sodium bicarbonate or magnesium hydroxide, neutralized gastric acids and their associated discomfort. Some of the more common OTC antacid products were Rennie and Andursil. In contrast, H-2 inhibitors such as ranitidine reduced acid levels by blocking the action of the stomach's acid-secreting cells. Anti-

cholinergics, on the other hand, functioned by delaying the stomach's emptying, thereby diminishing acid secretion and reducing the frequency and severity of ulcer pain. Finally, surgery was used only in the most severe cases, where ulceration had produced holes in the stomach and where ulcers were unresponsive to drug treatment.

In 1989, the world market for non-surgical ulcer remedies was estimated at $8 billion, with most sales distributed in North America (30%), Europe (23%), and Japan (5%). Worldwide, H-2 inhibitors and OTC antacids held 61 percent and 12 percent of the market, respectively.

The Oral Osmotic Therapeutic System

Gastirup, introduced in 1982 as Pharma Swede's first product in the category of ulcer remedies, used ranitidine as its active ingredient. As of 1982, ranitidine was available as a generic compound, after having lost its patent protection in that year. The US-based Almont Corporation was the original producer of ranitidine and its former patent holder.

What distinguished Gastirup from other H-2 inhibitors, including ranitidine tablets produced by Almont and others, was not its active ingredient, but the method of administration called the oral osmotic therapeutic system (OROS). In contrast to tablets or liquids taken several times a day, the Oral Osmotic Therapeutic System was taken once a day. Its tablet-like membrane was specially designed to release a constant level of medicine over time via a fine laser-made opening. By varying the surface, thickness and pore size of the membrane, the rate of drug release could be modified and adapted to different treatment needs.

Furthermore, the release of the drug could be programmed to take place at a certain point in time after swallowing the tablet. Consequently, drug release could be timed to coincide with when the tablet was in the ulcerated region of the upper or lower stomach. (Refer to Exhibit 5 for a diagram and brief description of the OROS.)

Drugs supplied via OROS had certain advantages over the others. First, because of a steady release of the medicine, they prevented the "high" and "low" effects often observed with the usual tablets or liquids. Furthermore, the time-release feature also prevented over-functioning of the liver and kidneys. In addition, because drugs contained in an OROS had to be in the purest form, they were more stable and had a prolonged shelf life. Pharma Swede management believed that drugs administered by OROS could lead to fewer doctor calls, less hospitalization, and reduced health care costs for insurance agencies and governments.

Because OROS was not a drug per se but an alternative method of drug administration, it was sold in conjunction with a particular pharmaceutical substance. By

EXHIBIT 5
PHARMA SWEDE THE ORAL OSMOTIC DELIVERY SYSTEM

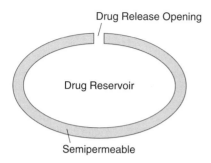

Drug Release Opening

Drug Reservoir

Semipermeable

Although OROS looked like a normal tablet, the system used osmotic pressure as a source of energy for the controlled release of active substance. Water, present throughout the body, passed through the semipermeable membrane as long as the reservoir contained undissolved substance. An increase in reservoir pressure, caused by the influx of water, was relieved by released drug solution through the opening. Up to 80% of the drug was released at a constant rate; the remainder at correspondingly declining rate. To guarantee the accuracy of the system, the opening had to comply with strict specifications. Hence, a laser was used to bore a hole through the membrane, in such as way that only membrane was removed, without damaging the reservoir.

Source: Company records

the end of 1989, Pharma Swede was marketing three drugs using OROS. Gastirup was the company's only OROS product in the gastrointestinal category; the other two were in the hormones category. The management of Pharma Swede characterized the use of OROS as an attempt to introduce product improvements which did not necessarily rely on new molecules but on new "software," leading to improved ease of use and patient comfort.

Ranitidine, the active ingredient in Gastirup, was not made by Pharma Swede, because of its complex manufacturing process and the fact that since 1982 it was available from a number of suppliers both inside and outside Sweden. Gastirup OROS tablets were manufactured by the company in Sweden; final packaging, including insertion of the drug information sheet, was done in a number of European countries including Italy.

Patent Protection

OROS was developed and patented by the Anza Corporation, a US company that specialized in drug delivery systems. In Europe, Anza had applied for patents on a country-by-country basis. Patent protection was twofold: OROS as a drug delivery system, and its use with specific drugs. The more general patent on OROS was due to expire in all EEC countries by 1991. The second, and more important patent for Gastirup, covered Oral Osmotic

Therapeutic Systems containing ranitidine. This latter patent, exclusively licensed to Pharma Swede for Europe, would expire everywhere on the Continent by the year 2000.

Although Pharma Swede sold more than one OROS product, it had an exclusive license from Anza for only the ranitidine-OROS combination. Over the years, a number of companies had tried to develop similar systems without much success. To design a system that did not violate Anza's patents required an expert knowledge of membrane technology which only a few companies had.

Competition

Broadly speaking, all ulcer remedies competed with one another. But, Gastirup's primary competition came from the H-2 inhibitors in general, and from ranitidine in particular. Since 1982, when ranitidine joined the ranks of generics, it was produced by a number of companies in Europe and the US. Despite increased competition, ranitidine's original producer, the US-based Almont Corporation, still held a significant market share worldwide.

Almont had first introduced its Tomidil brand in 1970 in the United States. After only two years, the product was being sold in ninety countries capturing shares ranging between 42 percent and 90 percent in every market. Tomidil's fast market acceptance, considered by many as the most successful for a new drug, was due to its high efficacy as an ulcer treatment and its few side effects. The drug had cut the need for surgery in an estimated two-thirds of cases. Pharma Swede attributed Tomidil's success also to centralized marketing planning and coordination worldwide, high marketing budgets and focused promotion on opinion leaders in each country. Although Almont was not previously known for its products in the ulcer market, and the company had little experience internationally, Tomidil's success helped the firm to grow into a major international firm in the field.

In the opinion of Pharma Swede management, Tomidil's pricing followed a "skimming" strategy. It was initially set on a daily treatment cost basis of five times the average prices of antacids on the market. Over time, however, prices were reduced to a level three times those of antacids. After 1982, the prices were cut further to about two times those of antacids. In 1990, competing tablets containing ranitidine were priced, on average, 20 percent below Tomidil for an equivalent dosage. In that year, Tomidil's European share of drugs containing ranitidine was 43 percent.

Pharma Swede management did not consider antacids and anticholinergics as direct competitors because the former category gave only temporary relief, and the latter had serious potential side effects.

Results

Gastirup's sales in Europe had reached $120 million by the end of 1989, or 7 percent of the ethical anti-ulcer market. (Refer to Exhibit 6 for a breakdown of sales and shares in major European markets.)

PRICING

Gastirup was premium priced. Its pricing followed the product's positioning as a preferred alternative to Tomidil and other ranitidine-containing tablets by improving the patient's quality of life and providing 24-hour protection in a single dosage. While competitive tablets had to be taken two or three times daily, the patient needed only one Gastirup tablet a day. The risk of forgetting to take the medicine was thus reduced as was the inconvenience of having to carry the drug around all the time. Because of these unique advantages, substantiated in a number of international clinical trials, management believed that using Gastirup ultimately resulted in faster treatment and reduced the need for surgery. Gastirup was priced to carry a significant premium over Tomidil prices in Europe. The margin over the generics was even higher. (Refer to Exhibit 7 for current retail prices of Gastirup and Tomidil across Europe.)

EXHIBIT 6
PHARMA SWEDE: SALES AND MARKET SHARES IN MAJOR EUROPEAN MARKETS*
(1989 SALES IN $ MILLION)

Countries	Total Market	Gastirup	Tomidil	Others**
	(100%)	(% Share)	(% Share)	(% Share)
Belgium	41	2	16	23
		(5%)	(39%)	(56%)
France	198	15	61	122
		(8%)	(31%)	(61%)
Germany	318	30	51	237
		(9%)	(16%)	(75%)
Italy	394	27	110	257
		(7%)	(28%)	(65%)
Netherlands	81	8	25	48
		(10%)	(31%)	(59%)
Spain	124	5	11	108
		(4%)	(9%)	(87%)
Sweden	34	10	5	19
		(29%)	(15%)	(56%)
United Kingdom	335	18	97	220
		(5%)	(29%)	(66%)
ALL EUROPE	**1,673**	**120**	**486**	**1,054**
		(7%)	**(29%)**	**(63%)**

*All ethical anti-ulcer remedies.

**Includes branded and generic drugs.

EXHIBIT 7

PHARMA SWEDE: RETAIL PRICES IN EUROPE
(1989: DAILY TREATMENT COST)

Countries	Gastirup	Tomidil	Gastirup % Tomidil
Belgium*	$3.86	$2.47	+56%
Denmark*	5.96	3.94	+51%
France*	3.69	2.12	+74%
Germany*	5.31	3.54	+50%
Greece*	3.43	2.36	+45%
Italy*	2.40	1.35	+78%
Netherlands*	5.66	3.11	+82%
Portugal*	3.13	2.24	+40%
Spain*	4.03	2.82	+43%
Sweden*	5.91	4.22	+40%
United Kingdom*	5.40	3.10	+74%

*Member of the EEC.

Pharmaceutical Pricing in the EEC

Drug pricing was a negotiated process in most of the EEC. Each of the twelve member states had its own agency to regulate pharmaceutical prices for public insurance reimbursement schemes. From a government perspective, pharmaceuticals were to be priced in accordance with the benefits they provided. Although the pricing criteria most frequently cited were efficacy, product quality, safety and patient comfort, European governments were putting increasing emphasis on "cost-effectiveness," or the relationship between price and therapeutic advantages. Among diverse criteria used by authorities, local production of a product was an important factor. As a result of individual country-specific pricing arrangements, there were inevitably widespread discrepancies in prices for the same product across Europe.

For new products, price negotiations with state agencies began after the drug was registered with the national health authorities. Negotiations could last for several years, eventually resulting in one of three outcomes: no price agreement, a partially-reimbursed price, or a fully-reimbursed price. In the event of no agreement, in most EEC countries the company was free to introduce the drug and set the price, but the patient's cost for the product would not be covered by health insurance. In many EEC countries, a drug that did not receive any reimbursement coverage was at a severe disadvantage. Partial or full reimbursement allowed the doctor to prescribe the drug without imposing the full cost on the patient. Any price adjustment for a product already on the market was subject to the same negotiation process.

Once agreement was reached on full or partial reimbursement, the product was put on a reimbursement scheme, also called a "positive list"—a list from which doctors could prescribe. Germany and the Netherlands were the two exceptions within the EEC employing a "negative list," a register containing only those drugs which the government would not reimburse. Drugs on the reimbursement list were often viewed by the medical profession as possibly better than non-reimbursed products. (Refer to Exhibit 8 for a summary of price setting and reimbursement practices within the EEC.)

Pricing Gastirup in Italy

Pharmaceutical pricing was particularly difficult in Italy. Health care costs represented 8 percent of the country's gross domestic product and one-third of the state budget for social expenditures. Government efforts to contain health care costs resulted in strict price controls and a tightly managed reimbursement scheme.

Italy was considered by Pharma Swede management as a "cost-plus environment" where pricing was closely tied to the production cost of a drug rather than its therapeutic value.

In May 1982, Pharma Swede Italy submitted its first application for reimbursement of Gastirup. The submitted retail price was $33 per pack of ten 400-milligram tablets. On a daily treatment cost basis, Gastirup's proposed price of $3.30 compared with Tomidil's $1.35. Although priced 25 percent lower than the average EEC price for Gastirup, Italian authorities denied the product admission to the positive list. They argued that Gastirup's therapeutic benefits, including its one-a-day feature, did not justify the large premium over the local price of Tomidil, which was already on the reimbursement scheme.

EXHIBIT 8
PHARMA SWEDE: PRICE SETTING AND REIMBURSEMENT IN THE EEC

Countries	Price Setting	Reimbursement
Ireland	No price control for new introductions	Positive list (prescription (recommended) Inclusion criteria: • efficacy/safety profile • cost-effectiveness profile
	Prices of prescription drugs are controlled through PPRS (Pharmaceutical Price Regulation Scheme). Control is exercised through regulation of profit levels.	Positive list for NHS prescriptions (National Health Service) Inclusion criteria: • therapeutic value • medical need
Belgium	Price control by the Ministry of Health on the basis of cost structure.	Positive list (Ministry of Health) Inclusion criteria: • therapeutic and social interest • duration of treatment • daily treatment costs • substitution possibilities • price comparison with similar drugs • Co-payment: 4 categories (100%, 75%, 50%, 40%)
Greece	Price control by the Ministry of Health based on cost structure (support of local industry appears to be of importance).	Positive list (IKA, Social Security Ministry).
Portugal	Price and reimbursement Negotiations with the Ministry of Health and Commerce based on: • local prices • lowest European prices • therapeutic value • cost-effectiveness	Positive list Inclusion criteria: • therapeutic value • international price comparison • cost-effectiveness
Spain	Price control based on cost structure.	Positive list (Social Security System) Inclusion criteria: • efficacy/safety profile • cost-effectiveness
France	No control for non-reimbursable products. Price negotiations with the Ministry of Health for reimbursed products.	Positive list (Transparence Commission and Directorate of Pharmacy and Pharmaceuticals, within the Ministry of Health) Inclusion criteria: • price • therapeutic value • potential market in France • (local R & D) Co-payment: 4 categories: • non-reimbursable • 40% of retail price • 70% of retail price • 100% of retail price.

EXHIBIT 8 (continued)

Countries	Price Setting	Reimbursement
Luxembourg	Price control by the Ministry of Health. Prices must not be higher than in the country of origin.	Positive list. Inclusion criteria: • therapeutic value • cost-effectiveness
Italy	Price control for reimbursed drugs by CIP (Interministerial Price Committee), following guidelines of CIPE (Interministerial Committee for Economic Planning) based on cost structure.	Positive list (Prontuario Terapeutico Nazionale) (National Health Council). Reimbursement criteria: • therapeutic efficacy and cost-effectiveness • innovation, risk-benefit ratio and local research also considered.
FR Germany	No direct price control by authorities.	Negative list. Reference price system since January 1989. Principles: • Drugs will only be reimbursed up to a reference price. • Patient pays the difference between the reference and retail prices. Co-payment: DM 3 per prescribed product (1992: 15% of drug bill).
Netherlands	No price control by authorities.	Negative list. Reference price system since January 1988.
Denmark	Price control based on: • cost structure • "reasonable" profits	Positive list: Inclusion criteria: • efficacy/safety profile • cost-effectiveness profile

Tomidil and another generic ranitidine-containing brand were produced locally, while Gastirup was to be manufactured in Sweden and only packed in Italy.

Despite the rejection by authorities, Pharma Swede chose to launch Gastirup in Italy without the reimbursement coverage. Management hoped to establish an early foothold in one of Europe's largest markets. Hence, early in 1983, Gastirup was introduced in Italy at a retail price of $37 for a pack of ten units, and under the brand name Gastiros. This price translated into a daily treatment cost of $3.70, or 16 percent below the EEC average retail price of Gastirup and nearly three times that of Tomidil in Italy.

The response of the Italian market to Gastiros was better than management had expected. Following an intensive promotional campaign aimed at the general practitioners, sales reached $500,000 a month, or 2 percent of the market. Meanwhile, the number of requests for reimbursement received by the Italian health care authorities from patients and doctors was growing daily. Management believed that these requests were putting increased

pressure on the authorities to admit the product to the positive list.

In a second round of negotiations, undertaken at the initiative of management nine months after the launch, Pharma Swede Italy reapplied for reimbursement status based on a price of $31 per pack of ten units. This price represented a daily treatment cost of $3.10 and was 30 percent below the EEC average. Once again the price was judged too high and the request was rejected. In November 1984, management initiated a third round of negotiations, and in April 1985 Gastiros was granted full reimbursement status at $24 per pack, a price that had not changed since.

Gastirup's Italian sales and market share among H-2 inhibitors grew substantially following its inclusion in the reimbursement scheme. By 1989, factory sales had reached $27 million, representing a dollar share of 7 percent of the market. Gastirup was Pharma Swede Italy's single most important product, accounting for nearly a quarter of its sales.

In Italy, as in other countries, Pharma Swede distributed its products through drug wholesalers to pharmacies. Typical trade margin on resale price for pharmacies was 30 percent. Gastiros' factory price to wholesalers of $15 per pack of ten tablets had a contribution margin of $3 for the Italian company, which paid its parent $1 for every 400-milligram tablet imported from Sweden. The transfer price was the same across Europe. In turn, the parent earned $0.70 in contribution for every tablet exported to its local operations. The variable cost of producing the tablets included raw materials and the licensing fees paid to Anza.

LIFTING THE TRADE BARRIERS

As 1992 drew closer, Pharma Swede management believed that two important issues affecting the European pharmaceutical industry would be manufacturing location and drug pricing. In the past, many of the cost-constraint measures taken by authorities had, by design or coincidence, an element of protectionism and represented national trade barriers. For example, local authorities might refuse a certain price or reimbursement level unless the sponsoring company agreed to manufacture locally. Under current EEC regulations, such actions were considered barriers to trade and illegal.

As a countermeasure to such barriers, companies could take legal action against local agencies at the European Court of Justice. With the support of the European Federation of Pharmaceutical Industries Associations (EFPIA), drug firms could sue the agencies for violating the EEC regulations. Although the EFPIA had won 12 cases over the preceding decade, litigation processes lasted sometimes up to seven years, and the results were often partial and temporary in value. Nonetheless, industry participants were relieved that, after 1992, the element of local production linked to price negotiation would disappear.

Since December 1988, under a new EEC regulation called the Transparency Directive, government pricing decisions were open to review by the pharmaceutical companies. The directive served to eliminate any interference with the free flow of pharmaceutical products within the community caused by price controls or reimbursement schemes. It required state agencies to explain how they set drug prices in general as well as in each case. If not satisfied, companies that believed they had been discriminated against could appeal a ruling on price, first to local courts, thereafter to the EC Commission and, ultimately, to the European Court of Justice.

In addition, the new law required that agencies act quickly when a new drug was approved for sale or when a company asked for a price adjustment. On average, it had taken Pharma Swede one year to reach agreement on a price for a new product. Price adjustments for old products, on the other hand, had taken as long as two years because of delays by local authorities.

Another development related to the creation of a single European market was the expected harmonization in pharmaceutical prices and registration systems among member states. Bjorn Larsson and others in the industry believed that, across Europe, pharmaceutical price differences would narrow in a two-stage process: Initially as a result of the transparency directive, and thereafter as part of a more comprehensive market harmonization. Bjorn thought that harmonization was a gradual process and that the completion of a single European market would occur at the earliest between 1995 and 2000.

Aside from narrowing of the differences in drug prices, possible outcomes for the post-1992 environment included a pan-European registration system and harmonized health insurance. Some observers predicted that a harmonized drug registration system would be put in place sometime between 1992 and 1995, although the exact form it might take remained open. Pharma Swede management believed it was unlikely that such a system would discriminate against non-EEC firms. Harmonization of national health insurance systems, a longer-term consequence of 1992, was not expected before 1995. Industry analysts believed that, in the interim, the states would continue to press for cost containment on a national basis. Private Pan-European insurance offerings, on the other hand, were expected to increase with deregulation and the completion of the internal market.

THE PROBLEM

Prior to 1992, Europe's parallel trade in pharmaceutical products had been limited to less than 5 percent of industry sales. Each country had local language packaging and registration requirements that tended to restrict or prohibit a product's acceptance and distribution in neighboring markets. Furthermore, according to some Pharma Swede managers, products produced in certain countries, such as Italy or France, suffered a poor quality image in other markets, such as Germany and England. National sentiments aside, distributors seeking to capitalize on parallel imports had to have approval from local authorities which often implied repackaging to meet local requirements.

Where parallel imports had been a minor problem in the past, they posed a serious challenge to drug firms, including Pharma Swede, in the post-1992 environment when such trade would be protected by law. Hans Sahlberg, the company's product manager for gastrointestinal drugs, explained that government insurance agencies were already examining price and reimbursement issues on a European-wide basis. For drugs already on the market, it was only a matter of time before authorities reimbursed on the basis of the lowest priced parallel import. As an example, this implied that Gastirup, priced at $2.40 per tablet in Italy and $5.40 in Germany, would be reimbursed in Germany at the lower price of imports from Italy. If this proved true, West German revenue losses from Gastirup alone could amount to $17 million on current sales. Furthermore, if a system should emerge after 1992 mandating a single EEC price, Pharma Swede would have to revamp its entire price setting policy.

Management Options

With the upcoming changes in Europe, Gastirup's pricing discrepancies had become a source of major management concern. If not carefully managed, Bjorn and his colleagues believed that the company could lose money, reputation or both. (Refer to Exhibit 9 for relative prices of Gastirup in Europe.)

In looking for options to recommend to top management at headquarters and at the Italian operation, Bjorn and his staff developed four alternatives. The first, and the most extreme option, was to completely remove Gastirup from the Italian market and concentrate sales elsewhere in Europe. This action would be in defence of prices in the more profitable markets. This alternative was not Bjorn's first choice as it implied sales revenue losses of $27 million. It also went counter to Pharma Swede's policy of marketing all of its products in every European country.

Bjorn feared that such a move would lead to heated discussions between headquarters and local management in Italy. It could even seriously damage the company's public reputation. "How," asked Bjorn, "could Pharma Swede, an ethical drug company, deal with public opinion aroused by the apparently unethical practice of denying Gastirup to the Italian market?"

As another alternative, Bjorn could suggest removing Gastirup from the reimbursement scheme by raising prices to levels closer to the EEC average. Such action would place Gastirup in the non-reimbursed drug status and lead to an estimated 80 percent loss in sales. Since the magnitude of this loss was nearly as great as in first option, headquarters did not believe the Italian management would be any more receptive. Moreover, if Gastirup were removed from the reimbursement scheme, both the product and the company might lose credibility with the medical profession in Italy. According to Bjorn, many doctors perceived the drugs on the reimbursement list as "economical" and "really needed."

Nonetheless, shifting the drug to non-reimbursement status would shift the financing burden from the government to the patient, thus coinciding with the Italian government's view that patients should assume a greater financial role in managing their health. With an increased emphasis on cost containment, such a proposal was liable to appeal to Italian authorities. Bjorn expected full support for this proposal from managers in high-priced markets whose revenues were jeopardized by low-priced countries such as Italy.

EXHIBIT 9
PHARMA SWEDE: RELATIVE RETAIL PRICES OF GASTIRUP

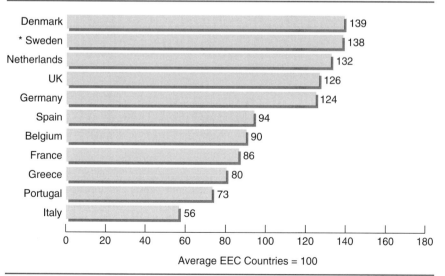

Average EEC Countries = 100

*Sweden not in EEC

There was, however, a possibility that changing the reimbursement status might backfire. Hans Sahlberg recalled a case in Denmark where, after removing a class of cough and cold drugs from reimbursement, Danish authorities came under pressure from a group of consumer advocates and were forced to reverse their decision. If Pharma Swede requested that Gastirup be removed from the Italian reimbursement scheme and the government were forced to reverse that position, the company's public image and its standing with local authorities might be damaged.

Still, a third option was to appeal to the European Commission and, if necessary, start legal action before the European Court of Justice. As Bjorn explained, the artificially-regulated low drug prices in Italy placed higher priced imported drugs at a disadvantage and, hence, acted as a barrier to the free movement of pharmaceutical products. Since the EFPIA had sued and won a similar case against Belgium, Bjorn believed that Pharma Swede might have a good case against the Italian government. But as much as Bjorn might want to pursue legal action, he recognized the risks inherent in using a legal mechanism with which Pharma Swede had no prior experience.

Headquarters management, on the other hand, looked favorably at this option as it provided the opportunity to settle "once and for all" the conflict with the Italian government over pharmaceutical pricing. Local management, however, feared that any legal action would create resentment and sour the atmosphere of future negotiations. At any rate, legal action could take several years and might even jeopardize Gastiros' status in Italy as a reimbursed drug.

A fourth option entailed taking a "wait and see" attitude until the full effects of "1992" became better known. Bjorn explained that for the next two to three years, governments would continue to concentrate on price controls. After 1992, pressure for harmonization would reduce differences in drug prices, though it was impossible to project the direction the prices might take. As an estimate, the Product Pricing and Government Relations staff had calculated that uniform pricing translated to an EEC-wide general decrease of 10 percent in drug prices, although prices in Italy would probably rise by about 15 percent. Thus, for the next few years, management at Pharma Swede could monitor the changes within the EEC and prepare as carefully as possible to minimize any long-term price erosion. Bjorn felt this option argued for vigilance and "having all your ammunition ready." But, he was not sure what specific preparatory actions were called for.

CONCLUSION

With the integration of Europe in sight, top management was deeply concerned about the impact that the changing regulatory environment might have on Pharma Swede's operations. Gastirup was the first product to feel the effects of harmonization, but it would not be the last. A decision on Gastirup could set the pace for the other products. In evaluating the alternative courses of action for Gastirup, Bjorn had to consider their likely impact on several stakeholders, including the country management in Italy, the management in high-priced countries and at headquarters, the Italian and EEC authorities, and the medical profession at large. Bjorn was not sure if any course of action could possibly satisfy all the parties concerned. He wondered what criteria should guide his proposal to the company president, who was expecting his recommendations soon.

CASE 11

ANHEUSER-BUSCH INTERNATIONAL, INC.: MAKING INROADS INTO BRAZIL AND MEXICO

HISTORY

In 1852 George Schneider started a small brewery in St. Louis. Five years later the brewery faced insolvency. Several St. Louis businessmen purchased the brewery, launching an expansion largely financed by a loan from Eberhard Anheuser. By 1860 the enterprise had run into

Source: This case was prepared by Masaaki Kotabe with his students' assistance.

trouble again. Anheuser, with money already earned from a successful soap-manufacturing business, bought up the interest of minority creditors and became a brewery owner. In 1864 he joined forces with his new son-in-law, Adolphus Busch, a brewery supplier, and eventually Busch became president of the company. Busch is credited with transforming it into a giant industry and is therefore considered the founder of the company.

Busch wanted to break the barriers of all local beers and breweries, so he created a network of railside ice-houses to cool cars of beer being shipped long distances. This moved the company that much closer to becoming one of the first national beers.

In the late 1870s, Busch launched the industry's first fleet of refrigerated cars, but they needed more to ensure the beer's freshness over long distances. In response, Busch pioneered the use of a new pasteurization process.

In 1876 Busch created Budweiser, and today they brew Bud the same way as in 1876. In 1896 the company introduced Michelob as their first premium beer. By 1879 annual sales rose to more than 105,000 barrels and in 1901 the company reached the one-million barrel mark.

In 1913, after his father's death, August A. Busch, Sr., took charge of the company, and with the new leadership came new problems: World War I, Prohibition, and the Great Depression. To keep the company running, Anheuser-Busch switched its emphasis to the production of corn products, baker's yeast, ice cream, soft drinks, commercial refrigeration units, and truck bodies. They stopped most of these activities when Prohibition ended. However, the yeast production was kept and even expanded to the point that Anheuser-Busch became the nation's leading producer of compressed baker's yeast through the encouragement of the company's new president in 1934, Adolphus Busch III.

August A. Busch, Jr., succeeded his brother as president in 1946 and served as the company's CEO until 1975. During this time eight branch breweries were constructed and annual sales increased from three million barrels in 1946 to more than 34 million in 1974. The company was extended to include family entertainment, real estate, can manufacturing, transportation, and major-league baseball.

August A. Busch III became president in 1974 and was named CEO in 1975. From that time to the present, the company opened three new breweries and acquired one. Other acquisitions included the nation's second-largest baking company and Sea World. The company also increased vertical integration capabilities with the addition of new can manufacturing and malt production facilities, container recovery, metalized label printing, snack foods, and international marketing and creative services.

CORPORATE MISSION STATEMENT

Anheuser-Busch's corporate mission statement provides the foundation for strategic planning for the company's businesses:

> The fundamental premise of the mission statement is that *beer is and always will be* Anheuser-Busch's core business. In the brewing industry, Anheuser-Busch's goals are to extend its position as the world's leading brewer of quality products; increase its share of the domestic beer market 50% by the late 1990s; and extend its presence in the international beer market. In non-beer areas, Anheuser-

Busch's existing food products, packaging, and entertainment will continue to be developed.

The mission statement also sets forth Anheuser-Busch's belief that the cornerstones of its success are a commitment to quality and maintaining the highest standards of honesty and integrity in its dealings with all stakeholders.

BEER AND BEER-RELATED OPERATIONS

Anheuser-Busch, which began operations in 1852 as the Bavarian Brewery, ranks as the world's largest brewer and has held the position of industry leader in the United States since 1957. More than four out of every ten beers sold in the United States are Anheuser-Busch products.

The company's principal product is beer, produced and distributed by its subsidiary, Anheuser-Busch, Inc. (ABI), in a variety of containers primarily under the brand names Budweiser, Bud Light, Bud Dry Draft, Michelob, Michelob Light, Michelob Dry, Michelob Golden Draft, Michelob Gold, Draft Light, Busch Light, Natural Light, and King Cobra, to name just a few. In 1993 Anheuser-Busch introduced a new brand, Ice Draft from Budweiser which is marketed in the United States and abroad as the preferred beer because it is lighter and less bitter than beer produced in foreign countries. Bud Draft from Budweiser was first introduced in the United States in late 1993 in 14 states, with a full national rollout in 1994 in the United States and abroad.

SALES

Anheuser-Busch achieved record sales during 1993. The increase in gross sales and net sales in 1993 as compared to 1992 was due to higher beer volume sales and higher sales by the company's entertainment subsidiaries. ABI, the company's brewing subsidiary and largest contributor to consolidated sales and profits, sold an industry record of 87.3 million barrels of beer in 1993, an increase of one-half of 1 percent compared to 1992 beer volume of 8.68 million barrels.

The gross sales for Anheuser-Busch Companies, Inc., during 1993 were $13.19 billion, an increase of $123 million over 1992 gross sales of $13.06 billion. Gross sales for 1992 were 3.4 percent higher than for 1991. Gross sales for 1991 were $12.63 billion, an increase of 8.8 percent over 1990.

Net sales for 1993 were also a record $11.51 billion, an increase of $111 million over 1992's net sales of $11.39 billion. Net sales for 1992 were 3.6 percent higher than 1991. Net sales during 1991 were $11.0 billion, an increase of 2.4 percent over 1990.

The company's principal product, beer, produced and distributed by its subsidiary, ABI, sold 87.3 million barrels in 1993 as compared with 86.8 million barrels in 1992 and

86.0 million barrels in 1991. Net sales for beer and beer related products in millions were $8,668.9 in 1993, $8,609.6 in 1992, and $8,323.5 in 1991.

ANHEUSER-BUSCH INTERNATIONAL, INC.

Anheuser-Busch International, Inc. (A-BII), was formed in 1981 to explore and develop the international beer market. A-BII is responsible for the company foreign beer operations and for exploring and developing beer markets outside the United States. Its activities include contract and license brewing, export sales, marketing and distribution of the company's beer in foreign markets, and equity partnerships with foreign brewers.

A-BII has a two-pronged strategy: (1) Build Budweiser into an international brand and (2) build an international business through equity investments or leading foreign brewers. In seeking growth, Anheuser-Busch International emphasizes part ownership in foreign brewers, joint ventures, and contract-brewing arrangements. These give the company opportunities to use its marketing expertise and its management practices in foreign markets. The success of these growth opportunities depends largely on finding the right partnerships that create a net gain for both companies. Other options for international expansion include license-brewing arrangements and exporting.

A-BII is currently pursuing the dual objectives of building Budweiser's worldwide presence and establishing a significant international business operation through joint ventures and equity investments in foreign brewers. Anheuser-Busch brands are exported to more than 60 countries and brewed under Anheuser-Busch's supervision in five countries. A-BII has experienced international growth in all operating regions with a 9 percent market share worldwide and has the largest export volume of any U.S. brewer. Anheuser-Busch had more than 45 percent of all U.S. beer exports and exported a record volume of more than 3.4 million barrels of beer in 1993.

MARKET SHARE

The top ten beer brands worldwide for 1993 in shipments and worldwide market share are as shown in the chart at the top of the next column.

Most recently, Anheuser-Busch has announced several agreements with other leading brewers around the world, including Modelo in Mexico and Antarctica in Brazil. These agreements are part of A-BII's two-pronged strategy of investing internationally through both brand and partnership development. Through partnerships A-BII will continue to identify, execute, and manage significant brewing acquisitions and joint ventures, partnering with the number-one or number-two

Brand	Company	Shipments (in millions)	Share of world beer market in 1993
Budweiser	ABI	44.2	4.4%
Miller Lite	Miller Brewing Co.	16.6	1.7
Kirin Lager	Kirin Brewery	16.5	1.7
Bud Light	ABI	15.4	1.5
Brahma Chopp	Companhia Cervejaria	13.7	1.4
Coors Light	Coors Brewing Co.	13.6	1.4
Heineken	Heineken NV	13.0	1.3
Antarctica	Antarctica Paulista	12.8	1.3
Polar	Cerveceria Polar SA	11.9	1.2
Asahi Super	Dry Asahi Breweries	11.5	1.2

brewers in growing markets. This strategy will allow A-BII to participate in beer industries around the world by investing in leading foreign brands, such as Corona in Mexico through Modelo. A-BII's goal is to share the best practices with its partners, allowing an open interchange of ideas that will benefit both partners.

LATIN AMERICA

The development of Budweiser in Latin America is one of the keys to long-term growth in the international beer business as it is one of the world's fastest growing beer markets and is a region with a growing consumer demand for beer. Anheuser-Busch products are sold in 11 Latin American countries—Argentina, Belize, Brazil, Chile, Ecuador, Mexico, Nicaragua, Panama, Paraguay, Uruguay, and Venezuela—with a total population of 346,892 million consumers.

Annual Beer Sales in 1995

Country	Sales (in millions)	Annual Growth
Venezuela	$1,015	52%
Chile	252	31
Colombia	898	25
Mexico	7,610	22
Argentina	1,096	19
Brazil	9,676	4

Brazil

Anheuser-Busch International recently made an initial investment of 10 percent in a new Antarctica subsidiary in Brazil that consolidates all of Antarctica's holdings in affiliated companies and controls 75 percent of Antarctica's operations. Anheuser-Busch will have an option to increase its investment to approximately 30 percent in the new company in the future. The amount of the initial investment was approximately $105 million. The investment has established partnership that gives Antarctica a seat on the board of Anheuser-Busch, Inc. and gives Anheuser-Busch International proportionate representation on the board of the new Antarctica subsidiary. The two brewers will also explore joint distribution opportunities in the fast-growing South American beer market.

According to Scott Bussen (South American representative for A-BII), A-BII is currently in the process of signing a deal that calls for an establishment of an Anheuser-Busch-controlled marketing and distribution agreement between the two brewers to support sales of Budweiser in Brazil.

The deal makes Anheuser-Busch the first American brewer to hold an equity stake in the Brazilian beer market, which is the largest in Latin America and the sixth-largest in the world. Last year the Brazilian beer market grew by more than 15 percent. Its potential for future growth markets is one of the most important global beer markets.

The second component of the partnership will be a licensing agreement in which Antarctica will brew Budweiser in Brazil. The joint venture will be 51 percent owned and controlled by Anheuser-Busch, 49 percent by Antarctica. Antarctica's production plants will produce Budweiser according to the brand's quality requirements. Local sourcing of Budweiser will allow more competitive pricing and increased sales of the brand in Brazil. The agreement is as expected to be signed sometime before the end of summer.

Antarctica, based in São Paulo, controls more than 34 percent of the Brazilian beer market. Its annual production in 1994 was 17 million barrels of beer. Antarctica has a network of close to 1,000 Brazilian wholesalers. Budweiser has already achieved a distribution foothold in the Brazilian beer market over the past four years in cooperation with its distributor, Arisco. Brazil has a population of 158,739 million people with per capita beer consumption in Brazil estimated to be 40 liters per year. With Brazil's population growing by 1.7 percent a year, reduced import duties, and free market reforms, Anheuser-Busch is expected to do well over the next decade in the Brazilian market.

The combined strengths of Anheuser-Busch and Antarctica in the booming Brazilian environment will lead to increased sales for both companies' products, resulting in a more competitive beer market, which benefits consumers, suppliers, and distribution in Brazil over the long term.

Mexico

In a further move to strengthen its international capabilities, Anheuser-Busch Companies purchased an 18 percent direct and indirect equity interest for $477 million in Grupo Modelo (located in Mexico City) and its subsidiaries, which thus far are privately held. Modelo is Mexico's largest brewer and the producer of Corona, that country's best-selling beer. The brewer has a 51 percent market share and exports to 56 countries.

In connection with the purchases, three Anheuser-Busch representatives have been elected to the Modelo board, and a Modelo representative has been elected to serve on the Anheuser-Busch board. The agreement gives Anheuser-Busch options to increase its investment in Modelo to approximately 35 percent, a minority position, and to acquire an additional minority interest in Modelo's subsidiaries. Anheuser-Busch has an option to acquire 43.9 percent of Modelo's voting rights by late 1997.

Additionally the agreement includes the planned implementation of a program for the exchange of executives and management personnel between Modelo and Anheuser-Busch in key areas, including accounting/auditing, marketing, operations, planning, and finance. Modelo will remain Mexico's exclusive importer and distributor of Budweiser and other Anheuser-Busch brands, which have achieved a leadership position in imported beers sold in Mexico. These brands will continue to be brewed exclusively by Anheuser-Busch breweries in the United States. Currently Anheuser-Busch brews beer for Mexico at their Houston and Los Angeles breweries, which are not very far away but add to the markup of ABI brands.

All of Modelo's brands will continue to be brewed exclusively in its seven existing Mexican breweries and a new brewery in North Central Mexico. U.S. distribution rights for the Modelo products are not involved in the arrangement. Corona and other Modelo brands will continue to be imported into the United States by Barton Beers and Gambrinus Company and distributed by those importers to beer wholesalers.

Modelo is the world's tenth-largest brewer and, through sales of Corona Modelo Especial, Pacifico, Negra Modelo and other regional brands, hold more than 51 percent of the Mexican beer market. Its beer exports to 56 countries in North and South America, Asia, Australia, Europe, and Africa account for more than 69 percent of Mexico's total beer exports.

Modelo is one of several companies that distribute Budweiser besides Antarctica in Brazil and other local import-export companies in other Latin American countries. Modelo is the exclusive importer and distributor of Anheuser-Busch beers in Mexico. The newest brand, Ice Draft, will be the fourth ABI brand distributed in Mexico by Modelo, joining Budweiser, Bud Light, and O'Douls.

The Modelo agreement is significant because beer consumption has grown 6.5 percent annually in Mexico in the past few years. Mexico's beer consumption is the eighth-largest in the world but still only half of U.S. consumption. The 1991 per capita beer consumption rate in Mexico was 44.3 liters, compared to 87.4 liters per person in the United States, which is high given that Mexico's per capita income is one-tenth that of the United States. The Mexican market is expected to grow 48 percent by 1997, based on 1992 statistics.

Anheuser-Busch does not have control over pricing. The local wholesalers and retailers set prices for Budweiser. A-BII also does not have plans to set up a full-scale production facility in Mexico at this time.

Right now Budweiser is imported, which makes it two to three times higher in price than local beers. So it is largely an upscale, niche market brand at this time. An equity arrangement in another brewery or an agreement with Modelo could lead to local production and make ABI brands more competitive with the local beer brands.

Besides the eleven Latin American countries mentioned, Anheuser-Busch announced in August 1994 that it has signed agreements with the largest brewers in Costa Rica, El Salvador, Guatemala, and Honduras to distribute and market Budweiser in their respective countries. Local breweries (Cervecerma Costa Rica in Costa Rica, La Constancia in El Salvador, Cervecerma Centroamericans in Guatemala, and Cervecerma Hondureqa in Honduras) will distribute Budweiser in the 12-ounce bottles and 12-ounce aluminum cans.

These distribution agreements will allow Budweiser to expand its distribution throughout the rest of Central America. These countries have an extensive national distribution network and, more important, have local market expertise to develop Budweiser throughout the region.

Under the agreements, the Central American brewers will import Budweiser from Anheuser-Busch plants in Houston, Texas, and Williamsburg, Virginia. Anheuser-Busch will share responsibility for Budweiser's marketing with each of its Central American partners, supported by nationwide advertising and promotional campaigns.

ADVERTISING

Event Sponsorship

Given Budweiser's advertising approach traditionally built around sports, the decision to hold the 1994 World Cup tournament in the United States gave A-BII a perfect venue to pitch Budweiser to Latin Americans. The company signed a multimillion-dollar sponsorship deal with the World Cup Organizing Committee, making Budweiser the only beer authorized to use the World Cup logo. "The World Cup has become a vehicle for us to reach Latin America," said Charlie Acevedo, director of Latin American marketing for Anheuser-Busch International.

For ten months, soccer fans in South America saw the Bud logo on everything from soccer balls to beer glasses. Soccer fans collected a World Cup bumper sticker when they purchased a 12-pack of Bud. When they watched the game on television, they saw Budweiser signs decorating the stadiums and a glimpse of the Bud blimp hovering overhead. According to Charlie Acevedo, the goal is to make Budweiser a global icon, like McDonald's golden arches or Coca-Cola.

Anheuser-Busch just signed its second two-year agreement with ESPN Latin America. "Being able to buy on a regional basis gives a consistent message that is very reasonable in terms of cost," said Steve Burrows, A-BII's executive vice president of marketing.

Latin America offers promise with its youthful population and rising personal income. Half of Mexico's population is under 21, and other Latin American countries have similar profiles, offering opportunities for advertisers to reach the region's 444.3 million population.

The biggest new advertising opportunities in the Latin American market are Fox Latin America, MTV Latino, Cinemax Ole (a premium channel venture with Caracas cable operator Omnivision Latin American Entertainment), USA Network, and Telemundo (a 24-hour Spanish-language news channel). Marketers will have yet another panregional advertising option. Hughes (the U.S. aerospace company) and three Latin American partners—Multivision in Mexico, Televisao Abril in Brazil, and the Cisneros Group in Venezuela—launched a $700 million satellite that will beam programs in Spanish and Portuguese into homes across the continent. The service is called DirectTV. Because of this satellite, Central and South America have added 24 new channels; with digital compression technology, its capability could reach 144 cable channels.

In the past Anheuser-Busch used CNN international as its only ad vehicle, but with all the new opportunities, "the company will begin adding a local media presence throughout Latin America," said Robert Gunthner, A-BII's vice president of the Americas region.

Anheuser-Busch will be using ads originally aimed at U.S. Hispanics, most of which were created by Carter Advertising of New York. A-BII will let the local agencies pick its messages, customize advertising, and do local media planning. In the past, there has been much criticism toward ABI's ethnocentric approach toward marketing Budweiser; however, because of the world obsession with American pop culture, they feel they don't need to tone down their American image. In Costa Rica, A-BII will use JBQ, San Jose; in El Salvador, Apex/BBDO, San Salvador; in Guatemala, Cerveceria's in-house media department; and in Honduras, McCann-Erickson Centroamericana, San Pedro.

Penetration of Paid Cable TV Channels

Location	TV households (in millions)	Paid subscribers	Penetration rate
Brazil	30.0	330,000	15%
Mexico	14.0	1,700,000	12
Argentina	9.0	4,300,000	47
Chile	3.4	200,000	6
Venezuela	3.3	90,000	3
Uruguay	0.7	35,000	5
Ecuador	0.5	25,000	5
Paraguay	0.5	45,000	9

Imported beers cost two or three times as much as locally brewed beers in South America, but thanks to cable television and product positioning in U.S. movies, Budweiser was already a well-known brand in South America when the company began exporting to the continent.

Strategy

According to Charlie Acevedo, Anheuser-Busch has seen double-digit increases in Latin American sales in the past five years. The gains came from both an increase in disposable income and increasingly favorable attitude toward U.S. products, especially in Argentina, Brazil, Chile, and Venezuela. Because Latin America has a very young population, Anheuser-Busch expects this market to grow at 4 percent annually. Furthermore, with NAFTA and a free trade zone, the company expects to see a significant rise in personal income in Latin American countries, which translates to great growth potential for Anheuser-Busch brands.

North American products and lifestyles are very much accepted in South America, but beer consumption still lags far behind U.S. levels. Argentines consume about 30 liters annually per capita. Brazilians 40 liters, Chileans 50 liters, and Venezuelans 65 liters, compared to 90 liters per person annually in the United States.

"The international focus will be almost completely on Budweiser because there is a worldwide trend toward less-heavy, less-bitter beers," and Jack Purnell, chair and chief executive officer of Anheuser-Busch International. They're counting on the American image to carry their beer, therefore opting for a universal campaign with American themes as opposed to tailoring Budweiser's image for local markets.

In the past ABI has tinkered with its formula and marketed Budweiser under different names to give a local flavor to their beer but had absolutely no success. Purnell said, "What the market does not need is an American brewery trying to make up from scratch, new European-style beers. Bud should be Bud wherever you get it."

OPPORTUNITIES

Mexico offers the U.S. exporter a variety of opportunities encompassing most product categories. Mexico is continuing to open its borders to imported products. Mexico's population of approximately 92 million is the eleventh-largest in the world and the third largest in Latin America (after Brazil and Argentina). Mexico is a young country, with 69 percent of its population under 30 years of age. In addition the Mexican government has adopted new privitization policies decreasing its involvement in the country's economy. As a result private resources, both local and foreign, are playing a greater role in all areas of the Mexican economy.

NAFTA, which aims to eliminate all tariffs on goods originating from Canada and the United States, is expected to create a massive market with more than 360 million people and $6 trillion in annual output.

DEMOGRAPHICS

Mexico's overall population in 1994 was estimated at 92.2 million people. Based on 1990 statistics, the age breakdown is as follows: under 15, 38.3 percent; 15–29, 29.4 percent; 30–44, 16.6 percent; 45–59, 8.9 percent; 60–74, 4.5 percent; 75 and over, 1.7 percent. In 1994 the average age of the Mexican population was 23.3 years.

Between 1970 and 1990 the ratio of the population living in localities with between 100,000 and 500,000 inhabitants grew from 12 to 22 percent. This was largely due to rural-urban migration. More than 71 percent of the population lives in urban areas of Mexico. In 1990, 22 percent of the national population lived in Mexico City and the State of Mexico.

The Mexican population is expected to rise to 102.9 million in the year 2000 and to 112.9 million in the year 2010.

Exhibit 1
Estimated Buying Power per Household (in US$)

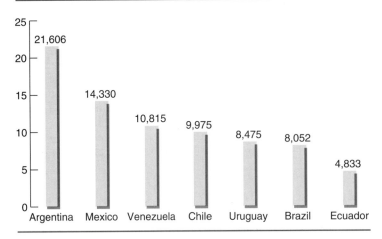

CASE 12

TOYS "Я" US GOES TO JAPAN

EXECUTIVE SUMMARY

Toys "Я" Us, the U.S. retail giant, became the first large-scale foreign retailer in Japan when it opened in suburban Tokyo in 1991. This expansion into the second largest toy market in the world came about only after overcoming tough opposition from both the Japanese toy industry and government. In spite of its record of successes in other foreign markets and a tremendous determination to enter Japan, Toys "Я" Us faced many difficulties in establishing its Japanese operation.

WHO IS TOYS "Я" US?

Toys "Я" Us is a 1000-store chain of large-scale toy outlets which dominates toy retailing in the United States. Toys "Я" Us stores offer large selection at low prices by applying a simple formula. The company buys toys in volume at a discount directly from manufacturers. Service is minimal and the stores themselves are essentially warehouses with no frills, with all available space used to stock inventory. These techniques are all designed to help keep cost, and thus prices, low. By applying this formula to the entire chain, Toys "Я" Us has shown remarkable sales and profit growth.[1] For example, while the toy retailing industry grew 37 percent from 1980 to 1984 Toys "Я" Us sales grew 185 percent.[2] The Paramus, New Jersey-based company reported 1991 sales of $5.7 billion worldwide in 1991, an 11.9 increase over 1990. In 1985, Toys "Я" Us claimed 14% of total toy retail sales in the United States.[3] Earnings grew steadily throughout the 1980's along with sales, and 1992 earnings were nearly $450 million. See Exhibits 1 and 2 (next page) for a graph of consolidated net sales and net earnings since 1983. Their success has allowed them to open an average of 100 new stores per year since 1987.[4] Exhibit 3 illustrates this store growth and the consolidated number of stores for Toys "Я" Us.

Brad Busby, I-Kong Fu, Edward Grulich, and Scott W. Snell, under the supervision of Professor Masaaki Kotabe, prepared this case as the basis for class discussion rather than to illustrate either effective or ineffective management of a situation described, 1995.

[1]Turn to *Appendix A* for an overview of the company's financial statements.

[2]Company Financial Statements.

[3]*Fortune*, October 28, 1985.

[4]Turn to *Appendix B* for a list of Toys "Я" Us store growth in the US by state.

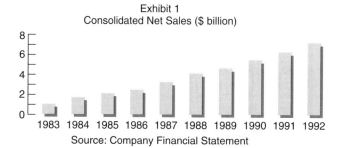

Exhibit 1
Consolidated Net Sales ($ billion)

Source: Company Financial Statement

Exhibit 2
Consolidated Net Earning ($ million)

Source: Company Financial Statements

Exhibit 3
Consolidated Number of Stores
(1993 Projected)

Source: Company Financial Statements

INTERNATIONAL EXPANSION

Toys "Я" Usfirst expanded to Germany in 1986, using the same strategy it employed in the United States. Robert Nakasone, vice chairman of Toys "Я" Us said: "Here, as earlier in the United States, conventional wisdom declared that the self-service concept and direct sourcing from manufacturers could not succeed in toy-retailing. However, we managed to succeed in Germany as we did in the States."[5]

This approach assures that costs can be held down and, combined with a philosophy of incorporating international as well as local perspectives in its operations abroad, it is the foundation of the company's international strategy. Exhibit 4 graphs the number of countries Toys "Я" Us has been operating in since 1984.[6]

[5]"Toys "Я" Us Comes Into Japan", *The Store News*, February 17, 1992.

[6]Turn to *Appendix C* for a list of Toys "Я" Us store growth internationally.

The company's greatest strength, however, is its ability to use local management to effectively market its stores to diverse regional tastes. This is the case because Toys "Я" Us' international units are run in the countries of operation, with only general guidance and assistance from the parent company in the United States. The international formula has worked so far, as is evident in Exhibit 5, which illustrates international net sales since 1984.

THE TOYS "Я" US JAPAN MANAGEMENT

Toys "Я" Us Japan is managed locally, like all overseas Toys "Я" Us operations. All functions are Japanese with the U.S. management still providing some support functions. Robert Nakasone, vice-chairman of Toys "Я" Us is the top international manager. Below him is Larry Bouts, the president of Toys "Я" Us International Division. The vice-president and chief financial officer of the International Division is Lawrence H. Meyer. These three men were responsible for most of the top-level decision making that would bring Toys "Я" Us into Japan. McDonald's

Exhibit 4
Consolidated Number of Stores
(1993 Projected)

Source: Company Financial Statements

Exhibit 5
Net Sales – International Division ($ million)

Source: Company Financial Statements

Japan bought 20 percent of Toys "Я" Us Japan and Den Fujita, the chairman of McDonalds Japan, received a seat on the board of directors. Mr. Fujita is one of Japan's most knowledgeable men in real estate development and his addition gave Toys "Я" Us Japan instant credibility with the business community.

The management of Toys "Я" Us Japan is structured with four executive vice-presidents overseeing merchandising, finance, real estate, and logistics.[7] They report to the president of Toys "Я" Us Japan. The president, who is Japanese, in turn reports to Larry Bouts back in the United States. The goal for Toys "Я" Us Japan is that eventually the operation will be self-functioning and top U.S. management will have to do no more than make semiannual trips over to observe and offer advice.

THE JAPANESE ECONOMY TO 1991[8]

The Japanese economy, almost entirely rebuilt from the ruins of the Second World War, was the world's second largest by 1990.[9] Rapid economic expansion since late

---

[7]Turn to Appendix D for a list of Toys "Я" Us International management and simplified organizational chart of Toys "Я" Us Japan.

[8]The following section borrows from: Bank of America, World Information Services "Country Outlooks—Japan", 1989–1990.

[9]See Appendix E for Japan Fact Sheet which provides an overview of the economy in the late 1980s.

1986 enabled Japan to record the fastest rate of growth among the major industrial countries. Japanese industry adjusted with relative ease to the yen's more than 50 percent appreciation from 1985 to 1990 by spending heavily on new capital equipment to improve productivity and boost capacity. Investment spending remained high during this time despite a slight tightening of monetary policy to dampen inflation and defend the yen against a weak dollar.

Consumer spending also contributed strongly to the expansion, despite a brief spending slump following the imposition of a new sales tax April 1989. The combination of strong business investment and robust consumer spending helped keep domestic demand growing at a rate faster than the overall economy, offsetting the effects of a restrictive fiscal policy.

Japan's economy benefited from strong business and consumer spending and the effects of income gains from rising asset values. The economy grew by 4.5 percent in 1989, with domestic demand growing by 5 percent. Strains evident earlier in 1989 in consumer spending vanished by 1990, as spending was pushed by rising real wages and demand for higher-value consumer goods. Japanese businesses overcame the effects of yen appreciation with cost-cutting measures and new investment.

With Japan's growth no longer quite so dependent on outside demand and more and more wealth being generated internally, Japan's economic prospects looked bright in comparison with other industrialized countries. Higher pay bonuses and greater access to foreign goods were expected to support further growth in consumer spending. This would bring additional business investment, as inventory levels and excess capacity in many industries remained low. Flush with rapidly rising profits and gains from sales of real assets, the cost of capital was expected to remain quite low, despite tighter monetary policy. In the longer term, domestic demand was supposed to weaken slightly because of continuing fiscal drag from the government sector and weaker foreign demand and economic growth would slow accordingly.

Japan's most obvious constraint to growth was the increasing shortage of skilled workers. Unemployment fell to 2.2 percent, while the ratio of job vacancies to job applicants rose to above 1.3, nearly twice the average ratio in 1985–87. Given the slow rate of growth in Japan's labor force, just 1.3 percent in 1987 and 1988, any gains in economic growth had to come from improvements in industrial efficiency. Japan's rapid expansion in capital spending relieved the labor constraint on production, but there was continuous upward pressure on wage rates and employee compensation.

The consistent, long-term success of the Japanese economy was a major factor in attracting Toys "Я" Us to Japan. The high per-capita income and upward trends in consumer spending were extremely encouraging. Capital was readily available at reasonable rates and inflation was steady. The economic environment seemed ideal.

BUSINESS CONDITIONS IN 1991[10]

Despite rapid economic growth, in the early 1990s Japan remained a very difficult market for foreign exporters to penetrate.[11] A high percentage of the recent increase in Japanese imports reflected growing intra-company trade by Japanese multinationals. Nonetheless, gradual steps were being taken to open Japanese goods markets to foreign suppliers and to unclog Japan's complex distribution system. Reforming Japan's distribution system was, and still is, the subject of high level negotiations within the Japanese government and between Japan and the United States.

At the same time, new tax incentives were being considered to promote imports, and there was talk of permitting direct importing by 1992. Direct importing would allow large retailers and consumers to bypass Japan's wholesale distribution system and buy goods directly from foreign distributors. Foreign exporters experienced some benefits from Japan's robust economic growth and consumer spending binge. Consumer acceptance of foreign goods has become more widespread as Japanese consumers have increased their travels abroad. They have also become more price sensitive and demand greater access to lower-priced foreign goods. Fueling this spending spree is Japan's per capita income, the world's highest (see *Appendix E*), and a growing demand for leisure goods and services like entertainment and dining out. Spending on durables is limited because of residential space constraints. The requirements of Japanese industry, outside of raw materials, are largely met by local suppliers, though capital goods imports have been on the rise lately.

Japanese businesses recorded strong income gains in the late 1980s and into 1990. Japanese corporate profits rose by 15 percent in 1989 on sales growth of 13 percent, following a 22 percent gain in 1988. Profit margins did begin to fall in 1991 as wage and capital costs rose and sales growth weakened. Shortages of skilled and unskilled labor pushed wages up by 6 percent to 7 percent in 1990, compared with a 5.1 percent gain in 1989. Interest rates on working capital loans also rose above 6 percent, which slowed growth. Real estate and office rents have continued to climb, although not as rapidly as in the recent past. Office space, as of 1990, was renting for an average of $2,200 a square meter in Tokyo, giving the city the highest rental costs in the world.

Japanese subsidiaries of foreign multinationals also saw new revisions in Japan's business tax environment. The unpopularity of Japan's 3 percent sales tax resulted in the tax being scaled back and the lost revenue made up with new business taxes. Despite the high costs, Toys "Я" Us felt that the overall business environment in Japan was positive, especially for retailing, and achieving profitability would be merely a matter of time.

THE JAPANESE TOY INDUSTRY

The typical Japanese toy store is a "mom and pop" operation that stocks about 2,000 items. These stores cannot compete with Toys "Я" Us in terms of selection, since inventory at one Toys "Я" Us can be many times larger.[12] These mom-and-pop toy stores are subject to the *tatene* system of manufacturer-suggested pricing and the usual complex web of distributors in Japan.[13]

The mom-and-pop stores have limited selection because of their sizes, but offer personalized service. Some toy stores even employ knowledgeable sales staffs that can explain how the various products work and help customers choose appropriate toys. The high overhead costs associated with this type of operation and the costs imposed by the Japanese distribution system force these stores to charge premium prices.

---

[10]Information taken from: Bank of America, World Information Services "Country Outlooks—Japan", 1989–1990.

[11]See, for example, the section below on the Strategic Impediments Initiative.

[12]Teresa Watanabe, "Selling American to the Japanese," *Business Week*, January 13, 1992, p. D1.

[13]Specifics on the Japanese distribution system are given below in the "Distribution, Marketing, and Finance" section.

JAPANESE TOY CONSUMERS

Japanese are prodigious gift-givers. Exchanging gifts is an important part of holidays, celebrations, and even visits to friends' homes. Japanese are also very fond of their children and with families today having fewer children, more attention is paid to the one or two children most couples have. This family-oriented environment where gifts play a large role in social activities is an ideal market for a toy retailer.

Although Japanese consumers have traditionally favored brand-name products at premium prices, they are beginning to change this view. One Japanese entrepreneur, Genichiro Nishimura, inspired by a trip to the United States twenty years ago, noted that the Japanese consumer has become more educated and able to make purchasing decisions "without blindly following a brand." Furthermore, notes Nishimura, Japanese consumers have begun to view many products almost as commodities with no outstanding differences between brands.[14]

Japanese consumers are also beginning to adopt the U.S. view that trade barriers make products more expensive. They are frustrated with their living standards, which do not reflect the amount of wealth generated by corporate successes. Japan's normally apathetic voters are increasingly angry that politicians don't push consumer issues harder. The leadership is perceived as moving against entrenched interests only under pressure from Washington.[15]

These consumers have traditionally been nurtured to support the status quo by Japanese firms' excellent service and seller-customer relations. However, as they begin to realize how much more they are paying for goods, compared to consumers in other advanced industrial economies, Japanese consumers are beginning to look for bargains. Discounting is slowly gaining in popularity as a result. At the time of Toys "Я" Us' entry, some Japanese companies that were large enough to do so were beginning to circumvent the traditional distribution system and attract consumers by offering lower prices.

THE DECISION TO GO TO JAPAN

The attractiveness of the Japanese market and the obstacles to entering the market were major factors influencing whether Toys "Я" Us would go to Japan. The attractions of the market were clear. Japan has the world's second largest toy market after the U.S., totaling over $6 billion in annual sales.[16] After Toys "Я" Us went international in 1984, expanding into Canada, Europe, Hong Kong and Singapore, they began to consider expanding into Japan. However, the major obstacles of local opposition, the Large-Scale Retail Store Law and real estate problems stood in the way.

LOCAL OPPOSITION

The initial reaction of small retailers to the proposed opening of Toys "Я" Us stores in Japan was one of opposition. The small toy store owners feared that competition with the discounting giant would drive them out of business. One small store owner compared competing with Toys "Я" Us to "trying to fend off a B-29 with bamboo spears—impossible."[17] The store owners' most powerful weapon, one they did not hesitate to use, was the Large-Scale Retail Store Law.

Large-Scale Retail Store Law

The most significant obstacle to Toys "Я" Us entering Japan was the existence of the Large-Scale Retail Store Law (LSRS). Originating from the pressure of small business in the 1960s, the LSRS was passed in 1973 and strengthened in 1978. The goal of the law was to contain expansion of large retail stores, protecting small stores from superstores. The effects of the law were significant. From the time of its passage until the revision of the law in 1990, market share of large retailers remained around 22%. During this same time period, no foreign-owned retail stores opened under the LSRS.

The LSRS divided stores into two classes. Class one stores, larger than 1500 square meters (3000 meters in large cities), were under the jurisdiction of MITI. Class two stores, between 500 and 1500 square meters (between 500 and 3000 in large cities), were under the jurisdiction of local governments.[18] Retailers planning to open a store exceeding these limits had to notify the authorities. MITI, in consultation with the local government, then examined the impact of the store on local business. The authorities could then determine the store's opening date and place restrictions on its size, business hours, and number of days open each year. On paper, the implementation of this process should have taken about two years. However, in many cases it often dragged on for over a decade. As a result, small stores were either able to veto the opening of large retail stores or extract many concessions.

[14]Gale Eisenstodt, "Bull in the Japan Shop", *Forbes*, January 31, 1994, p. 41.

[15]*Business Week*, April 23, 1990, p. 52.

[16]"Guess Who's Selling Barbies in Japan Now?," *Business Week*, December 9, 1991, p. 60.

[17]"Selling American to the Japanese," *Los Angeles Times*, January 13, 1992, p. D1.

[18]"Phase I: Japan's Distribution System and Options for Improving US Access," *Report to House Committee on Ways and Means, United States International Trade Commission Publication 2291*, June 1990, p. 42.

Toward the end of the 1980s, several groups began to argue in favor of amending or abolishing the LSRL. Opposing this trend was the Japan Chamber of Commerce and Industry who stated: "In view of the large number of small and medium-sized retailers densely packed into the Japanese retail structure, allowing large-scale retailers to open stores freely would cause friction and confusion in the local committees. For this reason, it is more appropriate to leave the framework of the LSRL as is, and to plan on improving its practical application."[19]

Critics of the law, such as large retailers, argued that the law resulted in higher costs for the consumer by preventing possibly more efficient large stores from doing business. The U.S. government was also critical of the law. Under the Structural Impediments Initiative (SII), initiated in 1989, the United States pressed Japan for changes in the law. Since a fairly clear connection could be made between LRSL and higher prices in Japan, a change in the law was perceived by many Japanese to be beneficial. Thus, Japan agreed to the changes suggested by the U.S. government. A U.S. negotiator said, "Our interests dove-tailed with those of the business community, retailers (particularly supermarkets), and consumers."[20] Of course, without support for these changes from within the Japanese bureaucracy, change would not have occurred. Many in the Japanese government who favored change saw some benefits from the SII talks. One MITI official remarked: "Before, we had a proposal for these changes, but without a timetable. SII gave us a timetable. Because we already discussed this at length, we had a good idea of what we wanted to do."[21]

Toys "Я" Us executives also were positive about U.S. government involvement in the LRSL issue. Larry Bouts, president of the international division of Toys "Я" Us said that the backing of U.S. Trade Representative Carla Hills was critical in getting MITI to change the LRSL.

As a result of the support of various groups in Japan favoring reforms, encouraged by U.S. government pressure, the Large-Scale Retail Store Law was revised in 1990.[22] Under these revisions, the maximum time frame required for approval of an application was reduced to eighteen months, thus doing away with the possibility that the application process could drag on for over a decade. While this revision opened the door for large retailers like Toys "Я" Us, some roadblocks still existed. The revision also created a local council to represent the interests of the area in which the large retailer is seeking approval to build a store. This council, while lacking the power to indefinitely delay the application, does have the power to recommend reduced store size, reduced business hours and reduced number of days open per year. These recommendations can be appealed to MITI by the retailer, but applications for revision have traditionally been rare.

Real Estate

In deciding whether to enter Japan, the exorbitant prices of real estate and the reluctance of some landlords to lease lands to Toys "Я" Us because of strong opposition to the large retailer from small retailers were key factors to be considered. Land prices in Tokyo rose by 23.8 percent in 1987 and 65.3 percent in 1988. In addition, although the United States is 25 times the size of Japan, by 1990 Japan's real estate assets were four times the value of U.S. real estate. Such extremely high land prices were becoming a trade issue, as U.S. companies argued that the high prices made doing business in Japan prohibitively expensive. Toys "Я" Us discovered that the major expense they faced going into Japan would be real estate and the cost of building their stores. Large stores in Japan, other than department stores, commonly deal with real estate costs by locating in the suburbs of major cities where land costs are lower. Because of their stock of thousands of items, Toys "Я" Us Japan chose to follow this pattern and selected Arakawa-Oki outside of Tokyo as the location for its first store.

DISTRIBUTION, ADVERTISING, AND FINANCE

Distribution

When doing business in Japan, one of the greatest challenges for any foreign firm is dealing with the Japanese distribution system. In Japan, the distribution system is very different from the system in the United States, in two respects.

The first is that in Japan, the majority of retail outlets are fairly small when compared to those in the United States. U.S. retail stores have over twice as many employees on average as do Japanese retail stores (8.1 vs. 3.7) and more than twice the average sales per store.[23] These small

[19]"Phase I: Japan's Distribution System and Options for Improving US Access," *Report to House Committee on Ways and Means, United States International Trade Commission Publication 2291,* June 1990, p. 71.

[20]"Japan's Distribution System and Options for Improving US Access," *Report to House Committee on Ways and Means, United States International Trade Commission Publication 2327,* October 1990, p. 123.

[21]Stern, James, "Toys "Я" Us Opens Doors in Japan," New York Times, Dec. 21, 1991, Section 1, p 33.

[22]"Japan's Distribution System and Options for Improving US Access," *Report to House Committee on Ways and Means, United States International Trade Commission Publication 2327,* October 1990, p. 67.

[23]Michael Czinkota and Masaaki Kotabe (ed). "The Japanese Distribution System: Opportunities and Obstacles, Structures and Practices", p. 25.

stores tend to be local and independently operated. It is largely to serve these small outlets that a large distribution system has evolved. This can be demonstrated by the fact that the ratio of wholesalers to retailers is about the same in Japan as it is in the United States.[24] This close relationship between the structures of the retailing and wholesaling industries in Japan means that the distribution system is designed primarily to serve small retailers and may be a source of difficulty for large-scale stores.

The distribution channels in Japan also tend to be multi-layered, meaning goods are handled by many wholesalers before they get to the retailer. This is shown by the high ratio of sales from wholesalers to other wholesalers. In Japan in 1982, 41.9% of wholesalers' sales were of this nature whereas in the United States they only accounted for 24.8% of wholesalers' business.[25]

Another aspect of Japanese distribution is the *tatene* system. This allows the manufacturer to set the prices on every level of distribution all the way up to the retailer. In return, the manufacturers agree to buy back all unsold inventory at the price the retailer paid for it. This multi-layered, inflexible system adds costs to the goods, which are passed on to the consumer in the form of uniformly high prices. Retailers who disagree with this system of pricing or try to place too many imported items on their shelves may face boycotts from the manufacturers they depend upon.[26]

When making the decision to enter Japan, Toys "Я" Us management had to decide how to deal both with the distribution system itself and the reluctance of manufacturers to deviate from the system, a system which had made them rich. They concluded that they would attempt to implement a U.S.-style direct-from-the-manufacturer system just as they had done in other foreign markets. Robert Nakasone, the president of Toys "Я" Us International, said, "Since the company was founded, we have never changed our basic operating approach, that is self-service and buying directly from the manufacturers and we are not about to change that."[27]

Advertising

Advertising in Japan is just as important a factor in retail success as it is in the United States. Most Japanese watch a great deal of television and regularly read daily newspapers. However, even successful advertisements from America often do not work very well in Japan. Japanese advertisements do not show their products or services

competing head-to-head. Rather, they must win over consumers by demonstrating the strengths and merits of products.

Toys "Я" Us relies heavily on advertising to attract customers in all of its markets. The Geoffrey Giraffe character is very well known in these markets, as is the "World's Largest Toy Store" slogan. Both television and print ads are heavily used to reach potential customers. Because of its success in so many markets, Toys "Я" Us does not want to alter advertising greatly from one country to another. A Japanese advertising agency was hired to help adapt the ad campaign to local tastes. They decided to use the same advertising messages in Japan as Toys "Я" Us did elsewhere, with the ads in Japan featuring the "Geoffrey and Family" characters, who were expected go over well with Japanese consumers. The campaigns were similar to that used in other countries with adjustments made for language and cultural differences.[28]

In normal times, Toys "Я" Us relies on a standard mix of television and print advertising in its various markets. Print ads are less expensive and for Toys "Я" Us television advertising is an issue of scale. This meant that most advertising would be done via pamphlets and newspapers with television advertising to wait until more stores had been built.

Toys "Я" Us also attracted a great deal of free advertising when it entered Japan. The Japanese press covered the Toys "Я" Us entry as a major story. This blanket coverage provided exposure the company could not normally have afforded and made a large percentage of Japanese consumers aware of Toys "Я" Us. It was hoped this would allow Toys "Я" Us to gain sales volume quickly.

Finance

Financing was to be a combination of long and short-term debt. Toys "Я" Us did not intend to get a listing on the Tokyo Stock exchange since it decided against using equity financing. Most debt was accrued through twenty-year bond issues, although shorter issues were also used. All borrowing was yen based. While this did expose the company to local currency fluctuations, it had advantages in terms of securing local financing.[29]

THE GRAND OPENING

Toys "Я" Us faced many concerns as the grand opening neared. There was concern about how willing Japanese toy buyers would be to sacrifice the service they had come

---

[24]Czinkota and Kotabe, p. 26

[25]Ibid, p. 28.

[26]Kathleen Morris, "Adam Smith in Tokyo," *Financial Times,* January 4, 1994, p. 22.

[27]"Toys "Я" Us Comes Into Japan," *Discount Store News,* February 17, 1992.

[28]Personal Interview with Lawrence H. Meyer, CFO, Toys "Я" Us International Division, April 22, 1994.

[29]Personal Interview with Lawrence H. Meyer, April 22, 1994.

to expect in return for more selection and lower prices. There was also the question of how many people would be willing to go out of their way, perhaps traveling two or three hours, to go shop at Toys "Я" Us.

The heavy exposure Toys "Я" Us Japan received prior to opening proved to be a huge boon and the attraction of huge selection at low prices attracted the toy-buying public. The result was that 60,000 customers went through the doors of the Ibaraki store in the first three days of operation.[30] Toys "Я" Us Japan was off to a roaring start.

INTRODUCTION

Toys "Я" Us Japan had a hugely successful launch after overcoming a series of difficulties including the Large-Scale Retail Store Law, finding distribution sources, and financing the very high costs associated with retailing in Japan. The problems did not end on December 20, 1991, however. There are many issues that Toys "Я" Us Japan continues to deal with since the opening of its first store.

CURRENT ECONOMIC SITUATION

The Japanese economy since Toys "Я" Us opened its first store in late 1991 has been in recession. During the early part of 1991 the Japanese economy bid farewell to the "Heisei Boom," a period of sustained expansion that fueled growth in almost every sector for more than four years. The end of the boom marked the beginning of a profit crunch for all businesses operating in Japan, including those set up with foreign capital (*gaishi*). The increasing value of the yen has made exported Japanese products more expensive, although Japan still has a strong trade surplus. Real estate prices have fallen and the stock market has slid down since the highs of the early 1990's. This has made capital less readily available for expansion and investment.[31]

A slowdown in consumer spending has also contributed to the recession. Consumers faced with high interest rates and a relatively unstable economic situation have been reluctant to buy at the pace they did through the 1980s. Many businesses are feeling the pinch from all sides. The American recession added to Japanese companies' woes, as U.S. consumers were not buying enough to help Japanese manufacturers ride out the domestic downturn.

This recession has affected Toys "Я" Us Japan. The company's long-term objective is to open eight to ten stores

a year until they have at least 100 stores in Japan. Lawrence Meyer discussed the effects. "We have had a downturn and overall performance has been hurt," he said.[32]

TOYS "Я" US JAPAN'S EFFECTS ON THE TOY INDUSTRY

Toys "Я" Us was the first large-scale retailer of its kind in Japan. It was seen by the Japanese retailers as the retail equivalent of Admiral Perry's "Black Ships" that opened an unwilling Japan in 1863.[33] Toys "Я" Us has definitely changed the retail toy industry in Japan. By flexing its economic muscle, Toys "Я" Us has thus both spawned imitators and incurred the wrath of small retailers.

Even the snobbish department stores have begun to offer discounts. Especially because of the current recession, some retailers are struggling to change the existing price structure thus offering consumers better prices.

REACTIONS FROM THE CONSUMER

To maintain the business that it initially attracted, Toys "Я" Us has to provide overall value to the Japanese customer. In Japan, consumers are very fussy and expect a lot for their money. Generally, for a retailer, providing value involves the quality of the products sold and the service that comes with them. Price, and to some degree selection, do not weigh in as much as they do in the United States or other markets. This is because the small size of most retail outlets limits selection and high overhead cost keeps prices high. Recognizing this, the Japanese consumer, usually the housewife, demands that she get what she pays for.

As a discount store, Toys "Я" Us works on the exact opposite basis of its Japanese competition. Toys "Я" Us Japan's stores are huge by Japanese standards and can thus offer a wider range of products, up to 15,000, several times more than any of its competitors. By virtue of buying huge quantities directly from manufacturers, Toys "Я" Us is able to price its toys 30 percent below the prices found in Japanese stores while still offering far more choices. Because Japanese consumers have traditionally not been given so large a selection and are not used to stores of Toys "Я" Us proportions, some shoppers are a little overwhelmed. They are, however, showing a willingness to drive further to find better selection at lower prices.[34] (See Exhibit 6, next page, for a price comparison)

---

[30]Betsy Pisik, "Japanese Proving Toys Я Them, Too", *The Washington Times*, January 7, 1992.

[31]Uda, Hiroyuki & Nozu, Shigeru. "Foreign Business at a Turning Point," *Tokyo Business Today* August 1992.

[32]Personal Interview with Lawrence H. Meyer, April 22, 1994.

[33]"Toys "Я" Us Comes Into Japan," *Discount Store News*, February 17, 1992.

[34]James Sterngold, "Toys "Я" Us Opens Doors in Japan," *The New York Times*, December 21, 1991, Section 1, p. 33.

EXHIBIT 6
PRICE COMPARISON

Toy	Price in Japan[35]	Price in U.S.
Nintendo Game Boy	71.38	89.99
Crayola 72-crayon set	6.25	9.99
Monopoly	15.44	9.99
My First Barbie	12.19	9.99
Mattel Hotwheels Cars	1.21	.99
Lego Basic tote pack 525	13.41	9.99

Source: Prices Checked by Associated Press at the Toys "Я" Us store visited by President Bush (January, 1992)

The product mix in Japan is slightly different from the mix in the United States, with more emphasis on video and electronic games and locally known toys replacing similar toys that would be found in an American store, but the selection is basically the same.[36] Likewise, knowing how selective Japanese consumers are, Toys "Я" Us is careful to offer toys that meet its customers' demands for quality by offering well-known brands such as Nintendo and Fisher-Price, just as it would do in the United States.

In return for the wide selection and low prices, service at Toys "Я" Us is limited, especially by Japanese standards. At small Japanese toy stores, the employees help the customers decide what purchases to make. By working with a minimal number of employees, whose jobs are primarily inventory restocking and working at the checkout counters, Toys "Я" Us keeps prices low but cannot offer much personal attention.

Toys "Я" Us is also benefiting from changes in the behavior of Japanese families. Younger fathers these days are less likely to be workaholics and spend more time with their families. A new form of leisure activity is going browsing on Sundays at stores such as Toys "Я" Us. Says Yoshikazu Hashimoto, president of Japan's Toys Magazine: "Toys "Я" Us has made (toy) shopping into a form of leisure in Japan."[37]

The overall initial reaction from Japanese consumers has been generally very positive. One consumer, who drove three hours to shop at Toys "Я" Us, found Legos there for $48 that were $75 at a Tokyo department store. "We think it's great" she said. "Toys are so expensive in Japan . . . They should have many more stores like this."[38]

LARGE-SCALE RETAIL STORE LAW AFTER 1991

While the revisions of the LSRL made it possible for Toys "Я" Us to enter the Japanese market, the process that large retailers still must go through in order to get approval can result in several types of restrictions on the stores. For example, in order to open a store in the Tokyo suburb of Sagamihara in July 1990, Toys "Я" Us had to submit applications to MITI, Kanagawa Prefecture, Sagamihara City and the Chamber of Commerce. Next, the approval of Sagamihara's Commercial Activities Council was required. By June 1991, approval was granted. However, Toys "Я" Us was required to close by 8 P.M. every day and close the store thirty days each year. Similarly, one of the stricter local council decisions has recently come from the council in Hokkaido which reduced the proposed size of the store by nearly one-fourth, reduced business hours, and did not approve plans to stay open 365 days a year.

Another example of local opposition occurred when Toys "Я" Us applied to open a store in Niigata in 1990. Negative reaction was strong and very vocal, making international headlines. The extent of the opposition was sufficient to delay the opening of the store until 1993.

More changes were made to the Large-Scale Retail Store Law in 1992. The eighteen-month waiting period was reduced to twelve months. Class one stores[39] were expanded in size from at least 1,500 square meters (or 3,000 square meters in large cities) to at least 6,000 square meters. Class two stores were then redefined to be between 500 and 6000 square meters.[40]

Even as these new reforms were implemented, however, the reaction Toys "Я" Us drew in Niigata was not repeated anywhere on the same scale and local opposition in some areas seems to be declining. One small toy store owner even said, "An integrated store for children is a good thing . . . my wife can't wait to go shopping there for our kids."[41] The owner hopes to compete with Toys "Я" Us by finding a productive niche, perhaps taking advantage of the negative reaction of some consumers to the self-service nature of Toys "Я" Us stores.

REAL ESTATE

As part of expansion plans, Den Fujita has advocated the idea of locating McDonalds, Toys "Я" Us, and Blockbuster Video stores together in suburban shopping areas,

---

[35]Japanese prices, in yen, have been converted to dollars.

[36]Personal Interview with Lawrence H. Meyer, April 20, 1994.

[37]Gale Eisenstodt, "Bull in the Japan Shop," January 31, 1994, p. 41.

[38]Teresa Watanabe "Selling American to the Japanese," *Los Angeles Times,* January, 13, 1992.

[39]See Case A for a discussion of Class one and Class two definitions.

[40]"Japan Enacts Amended Large Store Law Reducing Waiting Period for Applications," *International Trade Reporter,* February 5, 1992, Volume 9, Number 6, p. 228.

[41]"Guess Who's Selling Barbies in Japan Now?," *Business Week,* December 9, 1991, p. 60.

creating a family shopping center. This would help to overcome the barrier of extremely high land prices by having the three stores build together, thus lowering land costs. This plan, called MTB Rengo, is referred to by Fujita as "the Meiji Ishin of distribution."[42] The second difficulty, the reluctance of landlords to lease land, has been overcome. Since Toys "Я" Us drew such huge crowds upon entering the market, landlords have become less reluctant, seeing the number of consumers that Toys "Я" Us scan attract to their areas. One beneficial side effect of the recession is that land prices have gone down significantly, making it easier for Toys "Я" Us Japan to obtain the land it needs.

DISTRIBUTION

According to Lawrence H. Meyer, chief financial officer and vice-president of Toys "Я" Us International, establishing the type of distribution system that Toys "Я" Us uses has been perhaps the largest challenge the company has faced. When Toys "Я" Us entered Japan it had to deal with a distribution system different from what it had known in any other countries. Toys "Я" Us is one of the premier large-scale retail outlets in the United States, a country accustomed to large retailers, and it relied on direct sourcing from manufacturers. This allowed them to sell the toys at discount prices while still maintaining reasonable margins. With its direct sourcing, store size, and discount strategy, Toys "Я" Us ran counter to everything on which Japanese distribution and retailing was based.

The media focused on how different the sourcing methods of Toys "Я" Us are. The company had applied the same distribution methods to its international operations in Germany and Spain, but it was even more controversial in Japan.

Today, Toys "Я" Us does source most of their products directly from Japanese manufacturers, but this was accomplished despite great reluctance. Mr. Meyer said it was difficult to convince the manufacturers to go outside their normal distribution channels and that the company must still work to maintain the system they have put in place. He believes, however, that success with consumers will drive the manufacturers to work closely with Toys "Я" Us. Does the Toys "Я" Uss strategy upset some distributors? Yes, says Mr. Meyer, but that is how business works. "If I bring a product to consumers that they want, then I am doing my job. Why are other toy stores' prices so high?"[43]

The strategy appears to be working. At the time that Toys "Я" Us opened its first Japanese store in December of 1991, they had reached agreements with twenty Japanese manufacturers and 50 percent of the merchandise was imported.[44] Today, 75 percent of Toys "Я" Us Japan's products are bought locally. This is in large part due to the rapid success of Toys "Я" Us. As Toys "Я" Us continues to grow, manufacturers become convinced of the company's long-term commitment to the Japanese market and are more willing to deal with the company.[45] The most significant watershed occurred when the company secured an agreement to buy directly from Nintendo rather than go through the usual distribution channels. Other manufacturers are also starting to make similar deals.

Toys "Я" Us' success is hitting Japanese retailers where it hurts: in the pocketbook. According to Yujiro Eguchi, dean of the business school at Soka University in Tokyo, Toys "Я" Us has grabbed a substantial share of the market and this is affecting other toy retailers. "His Christmas (1993) was different because of Toys "Я" Us," he said. "The toys were cheaper" and shops for Japanese made toys "did poorly."[46]

TOYS "Я" US JAPAN'S ADVERTISING STRATEGY

With only a few stores, the returns on television advertising in Japan would be relatively small, since the vast majority of Japanese still do not have a Toys "Я" Us nearby. As Toys "Я" Us expands at the rate of eight to ten stores a year toward its goal of 100 or more stores, television will soon become more feasible as an ad medium. While it does use a few television advertisements, even after two years in Japan, Toys "Я" Us is still relying on printed advertising such as newspaper ads, flyers, and direct mail, as well as word of mouth.

CURRENT SITUATION AND PROBLEMS

Toys "Я" Us management is optimistic despite the recent economic downturn. "We have not slowed down in terms of store-building (despite the recession)," says Lawrence Meyer. "We have stores all over Japan, from Sapporo to Fukuoka." The company currently has sixteen stores in Japan and expects to maintain the pace it has set until its goal of 100 stores is reached.

---

[42]Japan-US Franchises' Distribution Patterns," *National Trade Data Bank, Market Reports*, August 22, 1991.

[43]Personal Interview with Lawrence H. Meyer, April 22, 1994.

[44]"Toys "Я" Us Comes Into Japan," *Discount Store News*, February 17, 1992.

[45]Personal Interview with Lawrence H. Meyer, April 20, 1994.

[46]Charles A Radin, "Discount Stores Shake Up Japanese Retailing," *The Toronto Star*, Jan. 2, 1994, B5

In terms of profitability, Toys "Я" Us Japan has still not reached the level of its U.S. parent. While no specific estimate on when Toys "Я" Us Japan will be in the black is available, profit margins are starting to approach that of the U.S. stores. Currently Toys "Я" Us outlets in the United States have the best margins with an average of 10 percent. International stores see margins of 6.5 percent and Japanese stores are slightly behind other international stores. This low margin is primarily due to the high cost of ongoing investment, but management expects returns to grow as more stores are built.[47]

Profitability is based on sustained customer loyalty. Some believe, however, that after the novelty wears off fewer customers will make the longer trip to Toys "Я" Us and sacrifice the service they can get nearer home just to save some money.[48] Others disagree. Mike Allen, the retailing analyst at Barclays Securities in Tokyo, said "People have already shown that when they are given a choice, they are willing to drive or whatever to get discounts. The problem before was not tradition or culture, but that they had no choice."[49]

[47]Personal Interview with Lawrence H. Meyer, April 20, 1994.
[48]Teresa Watanabe, January 13, 1992.
[49]James Sterngold, "Toys "Я" Us Opens Doors in Japan," December 21, 1991.

POTENTIAL FUTURE PROBLEMS

Toys "Я" Us is not assured of long-term success in Japan. Even after the current recession ends, it is uncertain how the Japanese public's spending will have been altered. Toys "Я" Us has the advantage of being a discount chain, but because its products are strictly discretionary, it may be affected if consumers become unwilling to spend heavily on luxury items. The company may also be a victim of its own success in the sense that more and more discount stores are being established in Japan. This trend will eventually reduce Toys "Я" Us' currently significant price advantage. If more conveniently located stores can compete on price, Toys "Я" Us will have to work much harder to maintain its position as the top discount toy retailer in Japan.

CONCLUSION

Toys "Я" Us sees Japan as an indispensable market. The company has demonstrated its willingness to persevere in the face of difficulties and it has succeeded as a result. Most significantly, Toys "Я" Us represents the first generation of a new kind of retailing in Japan. Toys "Я" Us' decision to deal directly with manufacturers and thus circumvent the traditional distribution system is one that will have repercussions beyond its own success. By sticking to a formula that has served it well throughout the world, the company has helped to change the way the Japanese people shop and the way the retail industry works in Japan.

APPENDIX A
Toys "Я" Us
CONSOLIDATED STATEMENTS OF EARNINGS
(IN THOUSANDS EXCEPT SHARE INFORMATION)

	1/30/93	2/1/92	2/2/91	1/28/90	1/29/89
Net Sales	$7,169,290	$6,124,209	$5,510,001	$4,787,830	$4,000,192
Costs and expenses:					
Cost of sales	$4,968,555	$4,286,639	$3,820,840	$3,309,653	$2,766,543
Selling, advertising and administrative	$1,342,262	$1,153,576	$1,024,809	$866,399	$736,329
Depreciation and amortization	$119,034	$100,701	$79,093	$65,839	$54,564
Interest expense	$69,134	$57,885	$73,304	$44,309	$25,812
Interest and other income	($18,719)	($13,521)	($11,233)	($12,050)	($11,880)
	$6,480,266	$5,585,280	$4,986,813	$4,274,150	$3,571,368
Earnings before taxes on income	$689,024	$538,929	$523,188	$513,680	$428,824
Taxes on income	$251,500	$199,400	$197,200	$192,600	$160,800
Net earnings	**$437,524**	**$339,529**	**$325,988**	**$321,080**	**$268,024**
Net earnings per share	$1.47	$1.15	$1.11	$1.09	$0.91

Source: Company Financial Statements

APPENDIX A (continued)
TOYS "Я" US
CONSOLIDATED BALANCE SHEET
(IN THOUSANDS EXCEPT SHARE INFORMATION)

	1/30/93	2/1/92	2/2/91	1/28/90
ASSETS				
Current Assets:				
Cost and cash equivalents	$763,721	$444,593	$35,005	$40,895
Accounts and other receivable	$69,385	$64,078	$73,170	$53,098
Merchandise inventories	$1,498,671	$1,390,605	$1,275,169	$1,230,394
Prepaid expenses and other	$52,731	$35,377	$20,981	$13,965
Total Current Assets	**$2,384,508**	**$1,934,653**	**$1,404,325**	**$1,338,352**
Property and equipment:				
Real estate, net	$1,876,835	$1,751,229	$1,433,489	$1,141,690
Other, net	$920,894	$800,276	$700,481	$553,104
Leased property under capital leases, net	$5,821	$6,582	$7,371	$8,180
Total Property and Equipment	$2,803,550	$2,558,087	$2,141,341	$1,702,974
Other Assets	$134,794	$89,868	$36,777	$33,362
Total Assets	**$5,322,852**	**$4,582,608**	**$3,582,443**	**$3,074,688**
LIABILITIES AND STOCKHOLDERS' EQUITY				
Current Liabilities:				
Short-term borrowings	$120,772	$291,659	$386,470	$205,513
Accounts payable	$941,375	$858,777	$483,948	$517,903
Accrued expenses and other current liabilities	$361,661	$332,185	$275,579	$280,517
Income taxes payable	$163,841	$123,750	$81,591	$96,033
Total Current Liabilities	**$1,587,649**	**$1,606,371**	**$1,227,588**	**$1,099,966**
Deferred Income Taxes	$175,430	$158,871	$113,405	$96,391
Long-Term Debt	$660,488	$379,880	$182,695	$159,518
Obligations Under Capital Leases	$10,264	$11,418	$12,462	$13,467
Stockholders' Equity:				
Common Stock	$29,794	$29,794	$29,794	$19,797
Additional paid-in-capital	$465,494	$384,803	$353,924	$324,616
Retained earnings	$2,529,853	$2,092,329	$1,752,800	$1,436,855
Foreign currency translation adjustments	$14,317	$47,967	$40,428	$23,010
Treasury shares, at cost	($150,437)	($127,717)	($129,340)	($96,973)
Receivable from exercise of stock options		($1,108)	($1,313)	($1,959)
	$2,889,021	**$2,426,068**	**$2,046,293**	**$1,705,346**
Total Liabilities and Stockholders' Equity	**$5,322,852**	**$4,582,608**	**$3,582,443**	**$3,074,688**

Source: Company Financial Statements

APPENDIX A (continued)
Toys "Я" Us
CONSOLIDATED STATEMENTS OF CASH FLOWS
(IN THOUSANDS EXCEPT SHARE INFORMATION)

	1/30/93	2/1/92	2/2/91	1/28/90	1/29/89
CASH FLOWS FROM OPERATING ACTIVITIES					
Net earnings	**$437,524**	**$339,529**	**$325,988**	**$321,080**	**$268,024**
Adjustments to reconcile net earnings to net cash provided by operating activities:					
Depreciation and amortization	$119,034	$100,701	$79,093	$65,839	$54,564
Deferred income taxes	$13,998	$15,817	$14,039	$17,572	$25,463
Changes in operating assets and liabilities:					
Accounts and other receivable	($5,307)	$9,092	($20,072)	$14,932	($5,886)
Merchandise inventories	($108,066)	($115,436)	($44,775)	($299,274)	($158,287)
Prepaid expenses and other operating assets	($36,249)	($16,176)	($9,043)	($11,391)	($14,366)
Accounts payable, accrued expenses and other	$112,232	$462,152	($40,130)	$92,316	$158,802
Income taxes payable	$40,091	$7,071	($10,424)	—	—
Total Adjustments	$135,733	$463,221	($31,312)	($120,006)	$60,290
Net Cash provided by operating activities	**$573,257**	**$802,750**	**$294,676**	**$201,074**	**$328,314**
CASH FLOWS FROM INVESTING ACTIVITIES					
Capital expenditures, net	($421,564)	($548,538)	($485,269)	($371,851)	($327,010)
Other assets	($22,175)	($17,110)		($5,114)	$4,463
Net cash used in investing activities	**($443,739)**	**($565,648)**	**($485,269)**	**($376,965)**	**($322,547)**
CASH FLOWS FROM FINANCING ACTIVITIES					
Short-term borrowing, net	($170,887)	($94,811)	$180,957	$129,380	$58,476
Long-term borrowing, net	$318,035	$197,802	$33,152	—	$693
Long-term debt repayments	($7,926)	($1,590)	($10,864)	($1,199)	($3,899)
Exercise of stock options	$86,323	$32,707	$30,344	$19,861	$52,429
Share repurchase program	($27,244)		($32,692)	($54,168)	$36,550
Net cash provided to financing activities	**$198,301**	**$134,108**	**$200,897**	**$93,874**	**$71,149**
Effect of exchange rate changes on cash and cash equivalents	($8,691)	$38,378	($16,194)	—	—
CASH AND CASH EQUIVALENTS					
Increase (decrease) during year	$319,128	$409,588	($5,890)	($82,017)	$76,916
Beginning of year	$444,593	$35,005	$40,895	$122,912	$45,996
End of year	$763,721	$444,593	$35,005	$40,895	$122,912

Source: Company Financial Statements

APPENDIX B
TOYS "Я" US UNITED STATES LOCATIONS

	1993	% change	1992	% change	1991
Total	540	8.65%	497	10.20%	451
Alabama	6	0.00%	6	20.00%	5
Arizona	10	11.11%	9	50.00%	6
Arkansas	2	0.00%	2	0.00%	2
California	69	9.52%	63	10.53%	57
Colorado	9	12.50%	8	33.33%	6
Connecticut	7	16.67%	6	0.00%	6
Delaware	1	0.00%	1	0.00%	1
Florida	33	3.13%	32	3.23%	31
Georgia	12	9.09%	11	0.00%	11
Hawaii	1	0.00%	1	0.00%	1
Idaho	1	0.00%	1	0.00%	1
Illinois	31	6.90%	29	7.41%	27
Indiana	11	0.00%	11	0.00%	11
Iowa	5	25.00%	4	33.33%	3
Kansas	4	0.00%	4	0.00%	4
Kentucky	7	16.67%	6	0.00%	6
Louisiana	8	14.29%	7	16.67%	6
Maine	2	0.00%	2	0.00%	2
Maryland	15	7.14%	14	7.69%	13
Massachusetts	14	27.27%	11	22.22%	9
Michigan	21	10.53%	19	0.00%	19
Minnesota	9	12.50%	8	33.33%	6
Mississippi	3	0.00%	3	0.00%	3
Missouri	11	22.22%	9	28.57%	7
Montana	1		0		0
Nebraska	1	0.00%	1	0.00%	1
Nevada	3	0.00%	3	0.00%	3
New Hampshire	5	25.00%	4	33.33%	3
New Jersey	21	16.67%	18	0.00%	18
New Mexico	3	200.00%	1	0.00%	1
New York	34	6.25%	32	3.23%	31
North Carolina	14	0.00%	14	40.00%	10
Ohio	26	0.00%	26	4.00%	25
Oklahoma	4	0.00%	4	33.33%	3
Oregon	5	0.00%	5	0.00%	5
Pennsylvania	25	8.70%	23	0.00%	23
Rhode Island	1	0.00%	1	0.00%	1
South Carolina	8	0.00%	8	0.00%	8
Tennessee	11	22.22%	9	28.57%	7
Texas	41	5.13%	39	14.71%	34
Utah	5	0.00%	5	66.67%	3
Virginia	14	0.00%	14	16.67%	12
Washington	9	0.00%	9	0.00%	9
West Virginia	3	50.00%	2	0.00%	2
Wisconsin	11	10.00%	10	42.86%	7
Puerto Rico	3	60.00%	2	0.00%	2

APPENDIX C
TOYS "Я" US INTERNATIONAL LOCATIONS

	1994	% change	1993	% change	1992	% change	1991
Total			167	32.54%	126	29.90%	97
Austria			5	—	—	—	—
Canada			44	15.79%	38	18.75%	32
France			17	54.55%	11	10.00%	10
Germany			32	33.33%	24	33.33%	18
Hong Kong			4	33.33%	3	0.00%	3
Japan	**16**	**166.67%**	6	200.00%	2	—	—
Malaysia			2	0.00%	2	0.00%	2
Singapore			3	50.00%	2	0.00%	2
Spain			12	50.00%	8	—	—
Taiwan			3	0.00%	3	50.00%	2
United Kingdom			39	18.18%	33	17.86%	28

APPENDIX D
TOYS "Я" US INTERNATIONAL—OFFICERS AND COUNTRY MANAGEMENT

Larry D. Bouts President	**Lawrence H. Meyer** Vice President Chief Financial Officer	**Joseph Giarnelli** Vice President Information Systems
Gregory R. Staley Senior Vice President General Merchandise Manager	**Philip Bloom** Vice President General Merchandise Manager	**Adam Szopinski** Vice President Operations
Keith Van Beek Vice President Development		

COUNTRY MANAGEMENT—JAPAN

Manubu Tazaki
President
Toys "Я" Us Japan, Ltd.

4 Executive VPs

Merchandising   *Finance*   *Real Estate*   *Logistics*

APPENDIX E
(JAPAN COUNTRY FACT SHEET)[1]

Profile: 1990

A. Population: 123.61 million
B. Religious: Shintoism, Buddhism, Christianity (1%)
C. Government: Type: Parliamentary Democracy
                 Head of Government: Prime Minister
D. Language: Japanese

Economy:	1988	1989	1990
A. GNP (, Nominal)	2,916	2,890	2,964
B. GNP Growth Rate (real, 1985 base)	6.2	4.7	5.6
C. GNP per capita (in dollars)	23,750	23,448	23,971
D. Gov't spending as a % of GNP	15.8	15.6	15.4
E. Inflation (CPI, 1985 base, %)	0.7	2.3	3.1
F. Unemployment (%)	2.5	2.3	2.1
G. Foreign Exchange Reserves	97.7	84.9	77.1
H. Average Exchange Rate ($1=)	128.15	137.96	144.79
I. U.S. Economic Assistance	0	0	0
J. Output/hour manufacturing (1985 = 100)	90.7	92.8	94.6
K. Domestic Demand (% growth)	7.6	5.9	5.8
L. Household Savings Rate (%)	14.3	14.1	13.8

Trade:	1988	1989	1990
A. Total Japanese Exports $ M)	265,917	275,175	286,948
B. Total Japanese Imports ($ M)	187,354	210,847	234,799
C. Total U.S. Exports (FAS value, $ M)	322,426	363,812	393,893
D. Total U.S. Imports (customs val. $ M)	440,952	473,211	494,903
E. U.S. Exports to Japan (FAS, $ M)	37,725	44,494	48,585
F. U.S. Imports fm Jpn (customs val. $ M)	89,519	93,553	89,655

Principal U.S. Exports: automatic data processing machines and office equipment; wood, in the rough or roughly squared; aircraft, spacecraft, and associated equipment; seafood products; semiconductors and other electronic components

Principal U.S. Imports: motor cars and other motor vehicles, automatic data processing machines and office equipment, parts and accessories of motor vehicles, scientific optical equipment, and semiconductors and other electronic components

Foreign Supplier Share of Japanese Imports in 1990:

1. S.E. Asia:	23.3%		4. Middle East:	13.2%	
2. U.S.:	22.4%		5. Indonesia:	5.4%	
3. E.C.:	14.9%		6. Australia:	5.3%	

BOP Current Account Balance:

1989: $57.16 billion
1990: $35.79 billion

Trade Balances with Leading Partners	1990 ($ B):
1. U.S.:	41.07
2. S.E. Asia:	28.12
3. E.C. (including the Federal Republic of Germany):	18.49
4. Federal Republic of Germany:	6.30
5. Republic of Korea:	5.75
6. Middle East:	−21.46

[1]US Department of Commerce, International Trade Administration, December 1991.

AUTHOR INDEX

SUBJECT INDEX

PHOTO CREDITS

CHAPTER 17
Page 496: Courtesy of Pharmaco. Reproduced with permission.

CASE 6
Page 612: Courtesy Baxter International.

CASE 7
Pages 645 and *647:* Courtesy Kortman Intradal, een maatschappij van Sara Lee/DE.